Also by Robert A. Caro

The Years of Lyndon Johnson:

The Path to Power

(1982)

Means of Ascent

(1990)

The Power Broker:

Robert Moses and the Fall of New York

(1974)

MASTER
OF THE SENATE

THE YEARS OF
LYNDON
JOHNSON

★ ★ ★

MASTER

OF THE

SENATE

Robert A. Caro

JONATHAN CAPE LONDON

Published by Jonathan Cape 2002

2 4 6 8 10 9 7 5 3 1

Copyright © 2002 by Robert A. Caro, Inc.

Robert A. Caro has asserted his right under the Copyright, Designs and
Patents Act 1988 to be identified as the author of this work

Portions of this work were previously published in *The New Yorker*

First published in Great Britain in 2002 by Jonathan Cape
Random House, 20 Vauxhall Bridge Road, London SW1V 2SA

Random House Australia (Pty) Limited
20 Alfred Street, Milsons Point, Sydney, New South Wales 2061, Australia

Random House New Zealand Limited
18 Poland Road, Glenfield, Auckland 10, New Zealand

Random House South Africa (Pty) Limited
Endulini, 5A Jubilee Road, Parktown 2193, South Africa

The Random House Group Limited Reg. No. 954009
www.randomhouse.co.uk

A CIP catalogue record for this book is available from the British Library

ISBN 0–224–06287-5

Papers used by The Random House Group Limited are natural, recyclable
products made from wood grown in sustainable forests; the manufacturing processes
conform to the environmental regulations of the country of origin

Printed and bound in the United States of America

Front endpapers: The Chamber of the United States Senate
Back endpapers: The Senate Chamber, 1810–1859

For Ina, always

and

For Bob Gottlieb

Thirty years. Four books. Thanks.

I do understand power, whatever else may be said about me. I know where to look for it, and how to use it.

—LYNDON BAINES JOHNSON

Contents

PHOTOGRAPHS   *follow pages 196 and 612*

INTRODUCTION

The Presence of Fire

When you come into the presence of a leader of men, you know you have come into the presence of fire; that it is best not incautiously to touch that man; that there is something that makes it dangerous to cross him.

— WOODROW WILSON

THE ROOM on the first floor of the Barbour County Courthouse in the little town of Eufaula, Alabama, was normally the County Clerk's Office, but after it had closed for the day on August 2, 1957, it was being used by the county's Board of Registrars, the body that registered citizens so they could vote in elections—not that the Board was going to register any of the three persons who were applying that day, for the skin of these applicants was black.

It was not a large room, and it was furnished very plainly. Its walls, white and in need of a fresh coat of paint, were adorned only by black-and-white photographs of former county officials. Against the rear wall stood a row of battered old filing cabinets that contained records of deeds and mortgages and applications for driver's licenses, and in front of the cabinets were six small, utilitarian gray metal office desks, each with a small, worn chair. Then there was a waist-high wooden counter at which people doing business with the County Clerk's Office usually stood. Today, the three registrars were standing behind the counter, and the applicants were standing in the bare space in front of it. No one offered them a chair, and the registrars didn't bother to pull up chairs for themselves, because the hearing wasn't going to take very long.

Trying to register to vote took courage for black people in Alabama in 1957, even when physical intimidation or violence wasn't employed to discourage them—as it often was. Everyone knew about black men who had registered and who shortly thereafter had been told by their employers that they no longer had a job, or about black farmers who, the following spring, went to the bank as usual for their annual "crop loan"—the advance they needed to buy the seed for the crop they were planning to plant that year—only to be informed that this year there would be no loan, and who had therefore lost their farms, and had had to load their wives and children into their rundown cars and drive away, sometimes with no place to go. Indeed, David Frost, the husband of Margaret Frost, one of the three applicants that August day, would never forget how, after he himself had registered some years before, a white man had told him that "the white folks are the nigger's friend as long as the nigger stays in his place," but that "I had got out of my place if I was going to vote along with the white man," and how, for months thereafter, instead of calling him "David" or "Boy" as they usually did, white people called him by the word he "just hated, hated": "Nigger"—pronounced in Alabama dialect, "Nigra"—and how, when they learned he was planning to actually vote, a car filled with men had stopped in front of his house one night and shot out the porch lights, and how, cowering inside, he had thought of calling the police, until, as the car drove away, he saw it was a police car.

And of course there was the humiliation of the registration hearings themselves. Many county Boards of Registrars required black applicants to pass an oral test before they would be given the certificate of registration that would make them eligible to vote, and the questions were often on the hard side—name all of Alabama's sixty-seven county judges; what was the date Oklahoma was admitted to the Union?—and sometimes very hard indeed: How many bubbles in a bar of soap?

The Barbour County registrars used a less sophisticated technique. They asked more reasonable questions—the names of local, state, and national officials—but if an applicant missed even one question, he would not be given the application that had to be filled out before he could receive a certificate, and somehow, even if a black applicant felt sure he had answered every question correctly, often the registrars would say there was one he had missed, although they would refuse to tell him which it was. Margaret Frost had already experienced this technique, for she had tried to register before—in January of 1957—and forty years later, when she was an elderly woman, she could still remember how, after she had answered several questions, the Board's chairman, William (Beel) Stokes, had told her she had missed one, adding, "You all go home and study a little more," and she could still remember how carefully blank the faces of Stokes and his two colleagues had been, the amusement showing only in their eyes.

Nonetheless, despite the humiliation of her earlier hearing in the County Clerk's Office, Mrs. Frost—a soft-spoken woman of thirty-eight—had returned to that dingy room to stand in front of that counter again. "I was scared I would do something wrong," she recalls. "I was nervous. Shaky. Scared that the white people would do something to me." But, she says, "I wanted to be a citizen," truly a part of her country, and she felt that voting was part of being a citizen. "I figure all citizens, you know, should be able to vote." In the months since January, she had, with her husband asking her questions, studied, over and over, all the questions she felt the Board might ask, until she thought she would be able to answer every one. And on August 2, she put on her best clothes and went down to the courthouse again.

As it turned out, however, the diligence with which Margaret Frost had studied turned out to be irrelevant, because the Board examined her and the two other applicants as a group, and one of them wasn't as well prepared as she.

When she asked Stokes for an application, he said, "There's twelve questions you have to answer before we give you an application." He asked just two. Mrs. Frost answered them both correctly, as did one of the other applicants. But the third applicant answered the second question incorrectly, and Stokes told them that therefore they had all failed. "You all go home and study a little more," he said.

MARGARET FROST left the room quietly, and she never sued or took any other legal action to try to force the Board to register her. Doing so, however, would almost certainly not have helped. In August, 1957, black Americans in the South who were denied the right to vote, and who asked a lawyer (if they could find a lawyer who would take their case) what law would assist them to do so, were informed that there was no such law—and that information was accurate. Summarizing the situation, a study made that same year by the United States Department of Justice concluded that "There is no adequate legal remedy" for a person who had been denied a registration certificate by a county Board of Registrars.

The scene that had occurred in the Eufaula courthouse was not an unusual one in the American South in 1957. After the Civil War almost a century before, there had been an attempt to make black Americans more a part of their country, to give them the basic rights of citizens—which included, of course, a citizen's right to vote—and in 1870, the Fifteenth Amendment to the Constitution had supposedly guaranteed that right, forbidding any state to "deny or abridge" the "right of citizens . . . to vote" because of their race or color. But the amendment proved to be an insufficient guarantee in the eleven southern states that had seceded from the Union and formed the rebel Confederacy; specific laws to give the amendment force and make it meaningful—federal laws, since there was no realistic possibility that any southern state would pass an effective statute—were going to be necessary. During the eighty-seven years since the Fifteenth Amendment had been ratified, scores, indeed hundreds, of proposed federal laws had been introduced in the Congress of the United States to ensure that black Americans would have in fact as well as theory the right to vote. Not one of these bills had passed. And in Barbour County, in which there were approximately equal numbers of black Americans and white Americans, out of 7,158 blacks of voting age in 1957, exactly 200—one out of thirty-five—

had the right to vote, while 6,521 whites had that right. In Alabama as a whole, out of 516,336 blacks who were eligible to vote, only 52,336—little more than one out of ten—had managed to register. For the eleven southern states as a whole, out of more than six million blacks eligible to vote, only 1,200,000— one out of five—had registered. And of course, even those blacks who *had* registered to vote often didn't dare go to the polls to cast ballots, because of fear of violence or economic retaliation. In 1957, there were scores of counties in the South which had tens of thousands of black residents, but in which, in some elections, not a single vote had been cast by a black.

THE ROOM in another city eight hundred miles to the northeast—in Washington, D.C.—was hardly more impressive than the Eufaula County Clerk's Office. It was L-shaped, and the short leg of the L was lined with telephone booths only slightly larger than conventional booths and distinguished from them only by a small light bulb above each one that was lit when the booth was in use. The other leg—the main part of the room—was narrow and drab, its two long walls a pale tan in color and undecorated except for a few black-and-white lithographs and dull green draperies. Aside from a rickety little desk and a small fireplace on the right wall and a pair of swinging doors on the left, both walls were lined with couches and armchairs covered in cracked brown leather, and they were set so close together that their arms almost touched. On the room's far wall, however, was a feature that didn't fit in with the rest of the furnishings: a huge mirror. Twice as tall as a man and wide enough to fill almost the entire wall, bordered in a broad frame of heavy gold leaf, it was a mirror out of another age, a mirror large enough for a man to watch as he swirled a cloak around himself and to check the way it sat on his shoulders—or, having removed the cloak and handed it to a waiting pageboy, to check every detail of his appearance before he pushed open those swinging doors. And when those doors swung open, suddenly, framed between them in the instant before they swung shut again, were long arcs of darkly glowing mahogany, semi-circles of desks whose deep reddish-brown surfaces had been burnished so highly that they gleamed richly with the reflection of lights in the ceiling high above them. There were ninety-six desks. The narrow room, drab though it was, was one of the cloakrooms, the Democratic cloakroom, of the United States Senate.

The cloakroom was generally rather empty, a comfortable, comradely place whose manners as well as furniture resembled those of a men's club (the only woman among the ninety-six senators was a Republican), a place of handshaking and backslapping and bluff camaraderie; a sleepy place—literally sleepy, since among the dozen or so senators present on a typical afternoon, several elderly men might be taking naps in the armchairs. In that August of 1957, however, the cloakroom was often crowded, with senators talking earnestly on sofas and standing in animated little groups, and sometimes the glances between various groups were not comradely at all—sometimes, in fact, they glinted with a barely concealed hostility, and the narrow room simmered with tension, for the main issue before the Senate that summer was civil rights, a proposed law intended to make voting easier for millions of black Americans like Margaret Frost, and the liberals among the Democratic senators were grimly determined to pass that law, and the southerners among the Democrats were grimly determined that it should not be passed.

The liberals in the Democratic cloakroom—the majority cloakroom; there were forty-nine Democratic senators in 1957 and forty-seven Republicans—included some of the great figures of the fight for social justice in America in the middle of the twentieth century. Among them was Hubert Horatio Humphrey of Minnesota, who as a crusading young mayor had courageously fought not only underworld gambling interests but the racial and religious bias that had made Minneapolis "the anti-Semitism capital of America"—one of the mightiest orators of his generation, he had, in the face of warnings that he was fatally damaging his career, delivered one of the most memorable convention addresses in the nation's history, a speech that roused the 1948 Democratic National Convention to defy the wishes of its leaders and adopt a tough civil rights plank. Among the other liberals in the cloakroom were white-maned Paul Douglas of Illinois, war hero and renowned professor of economics, who had battled for rights for black Americans on a dozen fronts with the same unwavering independence with which he had taken on Chicago's rapacious public utilities and corrupt political machine, and Estes Kefauver, who had won his Senate seat by defeating Tennessee's notorious, venal—and racist—Crump Machine. Among them, too, was a younger senator who would become a great figure: John Fitzgerald Kennedy of Massachusetts.

With the exception of Kennedy, the names of these senators, and of others, too—Wayne Morse of Oregon, Stuart Symington of Missouri, Frank Church of Idaho, Henry (Scoop) Jackson of Washington—would be all but forgotten forty years later, when this book was being written, so exclusively had the history of America come to be thought of in terms of America's Presidents, but in 1957, these men were icons of the liberal cause. In their ranks were eloquent orators, profound believers in social justice, senators of principles and ideals. Their ranks included senators who had long stood staunchly for the rights of man. And now, in 1957, these heroes of liberalism were united behind the latest civil rights bill, all of them determined that this year, at last, a civil rights bill would be passed.

Yet, eloquent though they were, courageous and determined though they were, honorable as their motives may have been, these men had been eloquent, courageous, determined and honorable in many previous fights for civil rights legislation, and each time they had lost. If, for eighty-seven years, every attempt to enact federal voting rights legislation had been blocked in Congress, most of the more significant of these bills had been blocked in the Senate, for it was in the Senate that the power of what had come to be called the "Southern Bloc"—the congressional delegations from the eleven former Confederate states—was strongest. And the situation was virtually the same with the Fourteenth Amendment, which had been passed two years before the Fifteenth—in 1868—supposedly to guarantee black Americans "the equal protection of the law" in areas of life outside the voting booth. During the intervening decades, generations of senators committed to the rights of black Americans—Progressives, reformers, liberals; from Charles Sumner of the mid-nineteenth century to Herbert Lehman of the mid-twentieth—had attempted to pass laws that would make that amendment effective. Hundreds of pieces of legislation had been proposed—bills to give black Americans equality in education, in employment, in housing, in transportation, in public accommodations, as well as to protect them against being beaten, and burned, and mutilated—against the mob violence called "lynching." Exactly one of those bills had passed—in 1875—and that lone statute had later been declared unconstitutional. It was not, therefore, only in the area of voting rights that black Americans had been denied the help of the law. No civil rights legislation of any type had been written permanently into the statute books of the United States since the ratification of the Fifteen Amendment. And, despite the determination that this latest generation of liberal senators had displayed in the civil rights battles they had waged in recent years, not only had they been unable to reach their goal, they were not getting closer to it; rather, it was receding from them. In the last battle—in the previous year, 1956—not only had a civil rights bill been crushed in the Senate, it had been crushed by a margin greater than ever before.

In this summer of 1957, it seemed all but certain that the liberals—and the black Americans like Margaret Frost for whom they were fighting—were going to lose again. Among Democratic senators, it was not the liberals who held the power in the Senate; it was the senators who stood in their own, separate groups: the southerners. Of the eight most powerful Senate committees, the southerners held the chairmanships of five; another was held by a dependable ally of the South. And the southerners were led by a senator, Richard Brevard Russell of Georgia, who during a quarter of a century in the Senate had never lost a civil rights fight, a legislative strategist so masterful that he had, in long years of uninterrupted victory, been called the South's greatest general since Robert E. Lee. Russell was a senator whose name is also all but lost to history, so that most Americans touring Washington today hardly know for whom the "Russell Senate Office Building" is named, but during his years in the Senate he was a figure so towering that an admiring journalist would recall years later, "Back then, when the U.S. got into trouble and Truman or Ike or Kennedy asked for help, Russell would gather up his six-foot frame, stick a forefinger into his somber vest and amble down those dim corridors to see if he could help his country. Everybody watching felt better when he arrived."

· · ·

IN THE CLOAKROOM AS WELL, however, standing near its center, the focus of activity in it, was another senator, the Democratic Leader and hence the Senate's Majority Leader, Lyndon Baines Johnson.

He was not a member of the liberal faction, far from it. His state, Texas, had been one of the eleven Confederate states, and his accent was often (not always, for his accent changed depending on whom he was talking to) the same syrupy southern drawl as that of the Barbour County registrar, and he used many of the same words and phrases—including the word that David Frost hated; Lyndon Johnson was, in fact, using that word a lot in the Democratic cloakroom that Summer. "Be ready to take up the goddamned nigra bill again," he told one of the southern senators, Sam Ervin of North Carolina. Walking over to a group of southerners, he told them there was no choice but to take it up, and to pass at least part of it. "I'm on your side, not theirs," he told them. "But be practical. We've got to give the goddamned niggers *something*." "Listen," he told James Eastland of Mississippi, who was anxious to adjourn for the year, "we might as well face it. We're not gonna be able to get out of here until we've got *some* kind of nigger bill."

Johnson's voting record—a record twenty years long, dating back to his arrival in the House of Representatives in 1937 and continuing up to that very day—was consistent with the accent and the word. During those twenty years, he had never supported civil rights legislation—any civil rights legislation. In Senate and House alike, his record was an unbroken one of votes against every civil rights bill that had ever come to a vote: against voting rights bills; against bills that would have struck at job discrimination and at segregation in other areas of American life; even against bills that would have protected blacks from lynching. His first speech in the Senate—a ringing defense of the filibuster that was a key southern tactic—had opened with the words "We of the South," and thereafter, as this book will demonstrate, he had been not merely a member of the Senate's southern anti–civil rights bloc, but an active member; not merely one of the senatorial "sentries" whom Richard Russell deployed on the floor to make sure that the liberals could not sneak a bill through (although he was a vigilant sentry), but one of the South's strategists. He had been raised to power by the Southern Bloc, had been elected Democratic Leader through its support. He was, in fact, the protégé, the anointed successor, of the bloc's great general, the senator Richard Russell had chosen to carry its banner when he himself should one day be forced to lay it down.

Johnson's methods, moreover, were different from the methods of the liberals, not a few of whom disliked and deeply distrusted him. They spoke of principles and ideals—the traumas of his youth had made him despise men who spoke in such abstractions; calling them "crazies" and "bomb-throwers," he cut off their attempts to move conversations to high ground by saying, "It's not the job of a politician to go around saying principled things." While they spoke of kindness, compassion, decency, he had already displayed a pragmatism and ruthlessness striking even to Washington insiders who had thought themselves calloused to the pragmatism of politics. While the Douglases and Humphreys spoke of truth and honor, he was deceitful, and proud of it: at that moment, in the Democratic cloakroom, as he talked first to a liberal, then to a conservative, walked over first to a southern group and then to a northern, he was telling liberals one thing, conservatives the opposite, and asserting both positions with equal, and seemingly total, conviction. Tough politicians though some of the liberals were, they felt themselves bound, to one degree or another, by at least some fundamental rules of conduct; he seemed to feel himself bound by nothing; he had to win every fight in which he became involved, said men and women who had known him for a long time—"*had* to win, *had to!*"—and to win he sometimes committed acts of great cruelty.

But he was about to become—beginning in that summer of 1957—the greatest champion that the liberal senators, and Margaret Frost and the millions of other black Americans, had had since, almost a century before, there had been a President named Lincoln.

THIS BOOK is in part the story of that man, Lyndon Baines Johnson. He is not yet the thirty-sixth President of the United States, but a senator—at the beginning of the book, in 1949, the newly elected junior senator from Texas; then the Democratic Party's Assistant Leader, then its Leader, and finally, in 1955, when the Democrats became the majority party in the Senate, the Senate's Majority Leader. And the Lyndon Johnson of this book is very different from the man Americans would later come to know as President.

His physical appearance was strikingly different. He was a tall man—a shade under six feet four inches tall—with long arms, and heavily mottled hands so huge that they seemed to swallow the hands of other men, and a massive, powerful head; the back of his skull rose almost straight out of his neck with only a slight softening curve. His features were boldly dramatic: his face, framed by large ears with very long lobes, was a portrait in aggressiveness with its downward-hooking nose that jutted far out of it, its big, sharply pointed jaw that jutted out almost as far, and, under heavy black eyebrows, piercing eyes. But during his Senate years, he was much thinner than he would be as President. Because of his gargantuan appetite, and his repeated attempts at dieting, his weight was constantly rising and falling, but as a senator, he usually weighed scores of pounds less than he would as President. Although his presidential weight was, as one aide puts it, "as closely guarded as a state secret" and he tried to conceal his girth with a heavy girdle, it was sometimes more than 240 pounds; in the Senate, it was generally far less—at the time of the 1957 civil rights fight, for example, he weighed about 180. And during his Senate years, not only did his body seem, in contrast with his presidential years, lean, hard, powerful, vibrant beneath his richly tailored suits, but, with nothing to blur their edges and soften them, the nose and jaw and eyes were even more prominent than they would be later. During the Senate years, furthermore, the furrows that care and time would later gouge cruelly deep into his cheeks and, in layer above layer, into his forehead were only beginning to appear. By the end of his presidency, the face of Lyndon Johnson, sixty years old when he left office, would be the face of a man harried, grim, beleaguered, and sometimes looking considerably older than his age; the face of Senate Leader Lyndon Johnson, in his forties for most of his senatorial years, was the face of a man confident, cocky, tough, the face of a man in the full flush of power.

It was, however, not in his appearance but in his manner that the contrast between President Johnson and Senator Johnson was most dramatic.

As President, conscious always of television, he tried to be what he conceived of as "presidential," composed his face into a "dignified" (expressionless, immobile, carefully still) mask, spoke in deliberate cadences that he believed were "statesmanlike," so that on television, which is where most Americans got to know him, he was stiff, stilted, colorless, unconvincing.

As Senator, he was the opposite.

Still was the last thing his face was then. The bold visage was as mobile as the face of a great actor; expressions—whimsical, quizzical, beseeching, demanding, pleading, threatening, cajoling—chased themselves across it as rapidly and vividly as if some master painter were painting new expressions on it; a "canvas face," one journalist called it. It was a face that could be, one moment, suffused with a rage that made it a "thundercloud," his mouth twisted into a snarl, his eyes narrowed into icy slits, and the next moment it could be covered with a sunny grin, the eyes crinkled up in companionable warmth. (Although there was, even in these moments, a wariness in those eyes.) He grinned a lot more often then, and he laughed a lot more often, and when he laughed, he roared, his mouth wide in a roar of laughter, the whole face a mask of mirth. And he was, when he needed to be, irresistibly charming, a storyteller with an extraordinary narrative gift, who could bring to dramatic life the drunks and hellfire preachers and lonely elderly farm wives of his native Texas Hill Country, and, because he was a remarkable mimic, the legendary figures of Washington as well: when he imitated Franklin Roosevelt, a fellow senator says, "you *saw* Roosevelt"; when he imitated Huey Long filibustering on the Senate floor, there was Huey in the flesh. He was a teller of tales that not only amused his listeners but convinced them, for when a point needed to be made, he often made it with a story—he had what a journalist calls "a genius for analogy"—made the point unforgettably, in dialect, in the rhythmic cadences of a great storyteller.

Still was the last thing his hands were. When, as President, he addressed the nation, they were often clasped and folded on the desk before him as if to emphasize the calmness and dignity he considered appropriately "presidential." During his years as a senator, they were moving—always moving—in gestures as expressive as the face: extended, open and palms up, in entreaty, or closed in fists of rage, or—a long forefinger extended—jabbing out to make a point. Or they were making some gesture that brought a story vividly to life; Hubert Humphrey, recalling years later Lyndon Johnson explaining that "If you're going to kill a snake with a hoe, you have to get it with one blow at the head," said he would never forget "those hands that were just like a couple of great big shovels coming down."

And, not on television but in person, he was, in the force of his personality, overwhelming. In the Senate's cloakroom or its corridors or on the Senate floor, one thick arm would be around a fellow senator's shoulders, pulling him close, and the other hand would be grabbing his colleague's lapel, or straightening his tie, and then the forefinger of that hand would be poking his points forcefully into the senator's chest. His face would be very close to the senator's face, looming above it and forcing the other man's head back, or, in a peculiar cocking gesture, turning sideways, and coming up under his colleague's face. And all the time he would be talking, arguing, persuading, with emotion, belief, conviction that seemed to well up inside him and pour out of him—even if it poured out with equal conviction on opposite sides of the same issue; if Lyndon Johnson seemed even bigger than he was—"larger than life," in the phrase so often used about him—it was not only because of the size of his huge body or his huge hands but because of his passions: burning, monumental. His magnetism drew men toward him, drew them along with him, made them follow where he led.

AND WHEN, on the floor, Lyndon Johnson was running the Senate, he put on a show so riveting that Capitol Hill had never seen anything like it during the previous century and a half of the Republic's existence—as it has never seen anything like it since.

Tall and confident, with a gangling, awkward, but long and swinging stride, "the Western movie barging into the room," in the words of one journalist—he would prowl the big chamber restlessly, moving up and down the aisles, back and forth along the rows of desks. Throwing himself down beside a senator who was sitting on one of the couches in the rear of the Chamber, he would talk to him out of the side of his mouth. Another colleague would enter. Jumping up, Johnson would hug him, joking with him or whispering earnestly in his ear. Moving over to a senator seated at a desk, and then to another, he would sit down beside a man or bend over him, sometimes with both his arms planted firmly on the target's desk, so that he could not rise and get away. Taking another man by the arm, he would lead him off to one side of the Chamber, drape his arm around his shoulders, and begin whispering urgently. And when Lyndon Johnson was talking to one of his colleagues, his hands seemed never to stop moving, patting a senatorial shoulder, grasping a senatorial lapel, jabbing a senatorial chest—jabbing it harder and harder if the point was still not being taken—and then hugging the senator when it was. Or, if it wasn't, the reporters in the Press Gallery above would see Johnson bending closer and talking in a very low voice—and they would see the other senator's face change, as the threat was pounded in, along with Johnson's determination to carry it out.

And then, at the climactic moments—the moments when the clerk called for the yeas and nays, and the Senate of the United States made its decision on whether to transform a bill into the law of the land—the power of Lyndon Johnson as Majority Leader was fully revealed, in a manner that veteran Senate watchers, accustomed, some of them over decades, to the body's traditionally slow-paced, drowsy atmosphere and to the previous courtliness and decorum of its rituals, at first found all but incredible.

When after days of maneuvering, with votes changing back and forth and back again, Johnson suddenly had enough votes in hand for victory, so long as none of the votes changed again, he wanted the vote taken—immediately. His front-row center desk at the edge of the well below the dais was a step up from the well, and he was so tall that when he stood at his desk, his eyes were almost at a level with those of the presiding senator across the well. "Call the question!" Johnson would say—and if the senator did not respond fast enough, he would snarl at him, in a voice clearly audible in the gallery, "*CALL THE QUESTION!*"

And when the vote was taken, it was taken at the precise pace Lyndon Johnson wanted. Sometimes he had all his men there at the moment of the vote, and his opponents didn't; sometimes he didn't have all his men there—stragglers were still being rounded up, sometimes they hadn't been found—so sometimes he wanted the roll call fast, and sometimes he wanted it slow. And he set the tempo accordingly. Standing at his desk, directly in front of the clerk calling the roll, Lyndon Johnson would raise his big right hand, and with the pen in his hand, or simply with a long forefinger, would make circles in the air, "like an airport mechanic signaling a pilot to rev up the motors," as *Time* magazine put it. This signal to the clerk meant, as Johnson's aide George Reedy would say, "hurry up—he had the votes and wanted them recorded" before the situation changed. Or he would make a downward shoving motion with his open hands, meaning "slow down"—"he didn't have the votes but would get them if only he had a little more time." Senators would be hurrying into the Chamber, crowding into the well. Lyndon Johnson would stand at the edge of the well—looking, because he was a step above the men in it, even bigger than he was, towering over the men before him—a long arm raised over them, making big circles, "for all the world," as *Time* said, like "an orchestra conductor" leading the Senate the way a conductor led an obedient orchestra.

The journalists above marveled at what they were seeing. "It was a splendid sight," Hugh Sidey would say. "This tall man with the canvas face, his mind attuned to every sight and sound and parliamentary nuance. . . . He signaled the roll calls faster or slower. He'd give a signal, and the door would open, and two more guys would run in. My God—running the world!"

THIS BOOK is also an examination of the particular type of power that Lyndon Johnson wielded in the Senate.

In an America that has been focused for most of the two centuries of its existence on executive, or presidential, power, legislative power, very different, is very little understood. But the life of Lyndon Johnson is a uniquely effective prism through which to examine that kind of power. When he arrived in the Senate, that institution had for decades been almost a joke—an object of ridicule to cartoonists and comedians, of frustration and despair to historians and political scientists. Hamstrung by archaic rules and customs which it was determined to keep unchanged, it seemed hopelessly unable to adapt to the new needs of a modern, more complex world, and its rigid adherence to a seniority system thoroughly drained it of energy and vitality and initiative while keeping in some of its most influential positions men so elderly that wags called it the "senility system."

Among the main causes of senatorial inertia and impotence was the fact that its so-called "Leaders" had had no power over their colleagues: "I have nothing to promise them," one of Johnson's immediate predecessors as Majority Leader complained. "I have nothing to threaten them with." But these Leaders were not Lyndon Johnson. "I do understand power, whatever else may be said about me," he was to tell an assistant. "I know where to look for it, and how to use it." That self-assessment was accurate. He looked for power in places where no previous Leader had thought to look for it—and he found it. And he created new powers, employing a startling ingenuity and imagination to transform parliamentary techniques and mechanisms of party control which had existed in rudimentary form, transforming them so completely that they became in effect new techniques and mechanisms. And he used these powers without restraint—as he did powers that had been used by Leaders before him, but that had seemed inconsequential because in their hands they *had* been used with restraint. Lyndon Johnson used all these powers with a pragmatism and ruthlessness that made them even more effective. Scoop Jackson would say that when Jack Kennedy, as President, urgently needed a senator's vote, he would summon him to the Oval Office and "would explain precisely why the bill was so important and how much he needed the senator's support." If, however, the senator said his constituency would not permit him to give that support, that if he gave Kennedy the vote he needed, the vote might cost him his seat in the Senate, "Kennedy would finally say he was sorry they couldn't agree, but he understood." Lyndon Johnson, Jackson would say—and Jackson worked closely with Johnson as Representative and Senator for twenty-five years— Lyndon Johnson wouldn't understand, would refuse to understand. He would "charm you or knock your block off, or bribe you or threaten you, anything to get your vote," Jackson would say. He would do anything he had to, to get that vote. "And he'd get it. That was the difference." Lyndon Johnson once told a friend: "I'm just like a fox. I can see the jugular in any man and go for it, but I always keep myself in rein. I keep myself on a leash, just like you would an animal." That self-assessment is only half true. Power corrupts—that has been said and written so often that it has become a cliché. But what is never said, but is just as true, is that power *reveals*. When a man is climbing, trying to persuade others to give him power, he must conceal those traits that might make others reluctant to give it to him, that might even make them refuse to give it to him. Once the man has power, it is no longer necessary for him to hide those traits. In his use of power during his Senate years, Lyndon Johnson sometimes reined himself in—and sometimes he didn't. He used the powers he found and the powers he created with a raw, elemental brutality. Studying something in its rawest and most elemental form makes its fundamental nature come clear, so an examination of these sources of power that Johnson discovered or created, and of his use of them, should furnish insights into the true nature of legislative power, and into its potentialities.

But it is not only depths that power reveals. Throughout Lyndon Johnson's life, there had been hints of what he might do with great power, should he ever succeed in attaining it—bright threads gleaming in a dark tapestry: hints of compassion for the downtrodden, and of a passion to raise them up; hints that he might use power not only to manipulate others but to help others—to help, moreover, those who most needed help. No teacher in the "Mexican school" on the wrong side of the tracks in the desolate South Texas town of Cotulla had ever really cared if the Mexican children learned or not. Twenty-year-old Lyndon Johnson cared—cared, and helped. And the compassion had at least once been combined with a rare capacity to make compassion meaningful, a startling ability to mobilize the forces of government to fulfill what his father, an idealistic Populist legislator, had said was government's most important function: to help people "caught in the tentacles of circumstance," to help them fight forces too big for them to fight alone. As a twenty-eight-year-old congressman, Lyndon Johnson had seen what his two hundred thousand constituents, scattered on lonely farms and ranches, needed most: electricity to ease the terrible drudgery that was their lot because, without electricity, they had to do all farm chores by hand. And, against seemingly impossible odds, he had used federal agencies to "bring the lights" to the Texas Hill Country. So long as he was still seeking power, however, that passion had been subordinated to the passion for power—subordinated almost totally. Now, once he had acquired power in the Senate, the compassion, and the ability to make compassion meaningful, would shine forth at last.

· · ·

THIS BOOK must try to be an examination not only of legislative power, but of legislative genius. This type of political genius is very different—indeed, in some aspects, diametrically opposite to—presidential genius, and is also, in America, little understood. But in his creation of and use of legislative power, Lyndon Johnson proved himself to be possessed of a talent that was beyond talent—a rare, instinctive gift. Part of the nature of genius is to do something new and remarkable, something unique. That is what Lyndon Johnson did. At the time he arrived in the Senate, seniority governed all its workings. New members were not supposed to speak much, or at all, on the floor during their first year or two, and during the remainder of their first six-year term to speak only infrequently, and to participate in other Senate activities in a largely apprentice role. After *his* first two years in the Senate, Lyndon Johnson was Assistant Leader of his party. In another two years, while he was still in his first term, he became his party's leader, the Democratic Leader of the Senate. Since the Democrats were in the minority, he was therefore Minority Leader. When, two years later, the Democrats became the majority, he became Majority Leader, the most powerful man in the Senate after just a single term there, the youngest Leader in history—after a rise unprecedented in its rapidity.

And it was not merely the velocity of his rise within the institution that was unique. He made the Senate work. It had worked—fulfilled the functions the Founding Fathers had designed it for— during the Republic's early days, in the decades between its founding and its Civil War, when the "Great Triumvirate"—Daniel Webster, Henry Clay, and John C. Calhoun, none of them a party leader (the institution of Senate "Leaders" had not yet been created) but all three among the most celebrated Americans of their time—had strode the Senate floor together. But that had been a century earlier. Despite a few significant leaders—most notably, perhaps, the Republican Nelson Aldrich at the turn of the century and the Democrat Joseph Robinson in the 1930s (but even their power had been in the last analysis no more than the power of a first among equals)—the Senate hadn't really worked since, falling more and more out of step with a constantly changing world. Lyndon Johnson transformed the Senate, pulled a nineteenth-century—indeed, in many respects an eighteenth-century—body into the twentieth century. It was not only men he bent to his will but an entire institution, one that had seemed, during its previous century and three-quarters of existence, stubbornly unbendable. Johnson accomplished this transformation not by the pronouncement or fiat or order that is the method of executive initiative, but out of the very nature and fabric of the legislative process itself. He was not only the youngest but the greatest Senate Leader in America's history. His colleagues called him *Leader.* "Good morning, Leader," they would say. "Could I have a minute of your time, Leader?" they would say. "Great job there, Mr. Leader." "Mr. Leader, I never thought you could pull that one off." And a Leader he was. He was master of the Senate—master of an institution that had never before had a master, and that at the time, almost half a century later, when this book is being written, has not had one since.

. . .

PERHAPS THE CLEAREST illustration of this mastery was the struggle in which this entwining of personality and power was most vividly played out: the collision in 1957 between the seemingly irresistible political force that was Lyndon Baines Johnson and the seemingly immovable political object that was the United States Senate—the struggle in which Johnson used all his cunning, and all the power he had amassed, to accomplish what had seemed impossible to accomplish, the passage by the Senate of a civil rights bill.

For decade after decade, the Senate had been not only a joke, but a cruel joke. For almost a century, it had not merely embodied but had empowered, with an immense power, the forces of conservatism and reaction in America, had stood as an impregnable stronghold against which, decade after decade, successive waves of demand for social change, for governmental action to promote justice and to ease the burdens of impoverished and disadvantaged Americans, had dashed themselves in vain. At the beginning of 1957, the Senate still stood—as it had stood, with rare exceptions, since the founding of the Republic—as a defiant fortress barring the road to social justice. It stood, more particularly, as the stronghold of the South, of the cause that had been lost in the Civil War—and then, over the intervening decades since the war, had been won in the Senate. The Senate, William S. White, the body's most prominent chronicler, wrote in 1956, is "the South's unending revenge upon the North for Gettysburg." Not just revenge, *unending* revenge. When the Senate convened in 1957, the gavels of its great standing committees were still overwhelmingly in the hands of the South, and no end to that revenge seemed in sight. And after the crushing of the 1956 civil rights bill by the largest margin in Senate history—a result in which Majority Leader Lyndon Johnson played a leading role—southern control of the Senate seemed firmer than ever; the 1956 defeat seemed to foreclose any chance of meaningful progress for black Americans for years to come. Never had the hope that blacks like Margaret Frost would be able to vote seemed further from any possibility of realization. In the Summer of 1957, however, Lyndon Johnson, in an abrupt and total reversal of his twenty-year record on civil rights, would push a civil rights bill, primarily a voting rights bill, through the Senate—would create the bill, really, so completely did he transform a confused and contradictory Administration measure that had no realistic chance of passage; would create it and then, in one of the most notable legislative feats in American history, would cajole and plead and threaten and lie, would use all his power and all his guile, all the awe in which his colleagues held him, and all the fear, to ram the bill through the Senate. It was, thanks to him, a bill that the House could also pass, and that the President could sign—the first civil rights legislation to be added to the statute books of the United States since 1870. The Civil Rights Act of 1957 made only a meagre advance toward social justice, and it is all but forgotten today, partly because it was dwarfed by the advances made under President Lyndon Johnson's Civil

Rights Acts of 1964 and 1965. But it paved the way—its passage was neces-sary—for all that was to come. As its Leader, he made the Senate not only work, but work toward a noble end.

Icons of the fight for social justice—the Humphreys and Douglases and Lehmans and the generations of liberal senators before them, eloquent, coura-geous senators, men of principles and ideals—had been trying for decades to pass a civil rights bill, with absolutely no success. It was not until Lyndon Johnson, who had never before fought in their cause, picked up the banner of civil rights that it was carried at last nearer to its goal. It took a Lyndon John-son, with his threats and deceits, with the relentlessness with which he insisted on victory and the savagery with which he fought for it, to ram that legislation through. As I wrote in the second volume of this work, "Abraham Lincoln struck off the chains of black Americans, but it was Lyndon Johnson who led them into voting booths, closed democracy's sacred curtain behind them, placed their hands upon the lever that gave them a hold on their own destiny, made them, at last and forever, a true part of American political life." His great voting rights legislation, the supreme accomplishment of his life and his career, would be passed during his presidency, of course; it was then that he most firmly took the hands of black Americans. But he first reached for their hands not as President, but in the Senate.

So, FINALLY, this book is a study of—the story of—America's Senate itself. For of all the remarkable aspects of the passage of the Civil Rights Act of 1957, none is more remarkable than the fact that it was in the Senate that it was ham-mered into shape and passed.

Part I

THE DAM

1

The Desks
of the Senate

THE CHAMBER of the United States Senate was a long, cavernous space—over a hundred feet long. From its upper portion, from the galleries for citizens and journalists which rimmed it, it seemed even longer than it was, in part because it was so gloomy and dim—so dim in 1949, when lights had not yet been added for television and the only illumination came from the ceiling almost forty feet above the floor, that its far end faded away in shadows—and in part because it was so pallid and bare. Its drab tan damask walls, divided into panels by tall columns and pilasters and by seven sets of double doors, were unrelieved by even a single touch of color—no painting, no mural—or, seemingly, by any other ornament. Above those walls, in the galleries, were rows of seats as utilitarian as those of a theater and covered in a dingy gray, and the features of the twenty white marble busts of the country's first twenty vice presidents, set into niches above the galleries, were shadowy and blurred. The marble of the pilasters and columns was a dull reddish gray in the gloom. The only spots of brightness in the Chamber were the few tangled red and white stripes on the flag that hung limply from a pole on the presiding officer's dais, and the reflection of the ceiling lights on the tops of the ninety-six mahogany desks arranged in four long half circles around the well below the dais. From the galleries the low red-gray marble dais was plain and unimposing, apparently without decoration. The desks themselves, small and spindly, seemed more like schoolchildren's desks than the desks of senators of the United States, mightiest of republics.

When a person stood on the floor of the Senate Chamber, however—in the well below the dais—the dais was, suddenly, not plain at all. Up close, its marble was a deep, dark red lushly veined with grays and greens, and set into it, almost invisible from the galleries, but, up close, richly glinting, were two bronze laurel wreaths, like the wreaths that the Senate of Rome bestowed on generals with whom it was pleased, when Rome ruled the known world—and the Senate ruled Rome. From the well, the columns and pilasters behind the dais were, suddenly, tall and stately and topped with scrolls, like the columns of the Roman Senate's chamber, the columns before which Cato spoke and Caesar fell, and above the columns, carved in cream-colored marble, were eagles, for Rome's legions marched behind eagles. From the well, there was, embroidered onto each pale damask panel, an ornament in the same pale color and all but invisible from above—a shield—and there were cream-colored marble shields, and swords and arrows, above the doors. And the doors—those seven pairs of double doors, each flanked by its tall columns and pilasters—were tall, too, and their grillwork, hardly noticeable from above, was intricate and made of beaten bronze, and it was framed by heavy, squared bronze coils. The vice presidential busts were, all at once, very high above you; set into deep, arched niches, flanked by massive bronze sconces, their marble faces, thoughtful, stern, encircled the Chamber like a somber evocation of the Republic's glorious past. And, rising from the well, there were the desks.

The desks of the Senate rise in four shallow tiers, one above the other, in a deep half circle. Small and spindly individually, from the well they blend together so that with their smooth, burnished mahogany tops reflecting even the dim lights in the ceiling so far above them, they form four sweeping, glowing arcs. To stand in the well of the Senate is to stand among these four long arcs that rise around and above you, that stretch away from you, gleaming richly in the gloom: powerful, majestic. To someone standing in the well, the Chamber, in all its cavernous drabness, is only a setting for those desks—for those desks, and for the history that was made at them.

The first forty-eight of those desks—they are of a simple, federal design—were carved in 1819 to replace the desks the British had burned five years before. When, in 1859, the Senate moved into this Chamber, those desks moved with them, and when, as the Union grew, more desks were added, they were carved to the same design. And for decades—for most of the first century of the Republic's existence, in fact; for the century in which it was transformed from a collection of ragged colonies into an empire—much of its history was hammered out among those desks.

Daniel Webster's hand rested on one of those desks when, on January 26, 1830, he rose to reply again to Robert Hayne.

Every desk in the domed, colonnaded room that was then the Senate's Chamber was filled that day—some not with senators but with spectators, for so many visitors, not only from Washington but from Baltimore and New York, had crowded into the Chamber, overflowing the galleries, that some senators had surrendered their seats and were standing against the walls or even among the desks—for the fate of the young nation might hang on that reply. In the South, chafing under the domination of the North and East, there was a new word abroad—*secession*—and the South's leading spokesman, John C. Calhoun of South Carolina, had, although he was Vice President of the United States, proposed a step that would go a long way toward shattering the Union: that any state unwilling to abide by a law enacted by the national government could nullify it within its borders. In an earlier Senate speech that January of 1830, the South, through the South Carolina Senator Robert Y. Hayne, had proposed that the West should join the South in an alliance that could have the most serious implications for the future of the Union. The specific issue Hayne raised was the price of public lands in the West: the West wanted the price kept low to attract settlers from the East and encourage development; the East wanted the price kept high so its people would stay home, and continue to provide cheap labor for northern factories. The East, whose policies had so long ground down the South, was now, Hayne said, trying to do the same thing to the West, and the West should unite with the South against it. And the Senator raised broader issues as well. Why should one section be taxed to construct a public improvement in another? "What interest has South Carolina in a canal in Ohio?" And what if Ohio didn't want it? Why should the national government decide such issues? The sovereignty of the individual states—their rights, their freedom—was being trampled. The reaction of many western senators to Hayne's proposal of an alliance had been ominously favorable; Missouri's Thomas Hart Benton asked the South to "stretch forth" a "protecting arm" against the East. And to Webster's first speech in response, Hayne—slight, slender, and aristocratic in bearing although dressed in a "coarse homespun suit that he had substituted for the hated broadcloth manufactured in the North"— had passionately attacked the North's "meddling statesmen" and abolitionists, and had defended slavery, states' rights, and nullification in arguments that were considered so unanswerable that the "white, triumphant face" of a smiling Calhoun, presiding over the Senate as Vice President, and the toasts in Washington taverns to Hayne, to the South, and to nullification reflected the general feeling that the South had won. And then two days later, on the 26th, Senator Webster of Massachusetts, with his dark, craggy face, jet-black hair, and jutting black eyebrows—"Black Dan" Webster, with his deep booming voice that "could shake the world," Webster, Emerson's "great cannon loaded to the lips"—rose, in blue coat with bright brass buttons, buff waistcoat, and white cravat, rose to answer, and, as he spoke, the smile faded from Calhoun's face.

He stood erect as he spoke, his left hand resting on his desk, his voice filling the Chamber, and, one by one, he examined and demolished Hayne's arguments. The claim that a state could decide constitutional questions? The Constitution, Webster said, is the fundamental law of a people—of *one* people—not of states. "We the People of the United States made this Constitution. . . . This government came from the people, and is responsible to them." "He asks me, 'What interest has South Carolina in a canal to the Ohio?' The answer to that question expounds the whole diversity of sentiment between that gentleman and me. . . . According to *his* doctrine, she has no interest in it. According to his doctrine, Ohio is one country, and South Carolina is another country. . . . I, sir, take a different view of the whole matter. I look upon Ohio and South Carolina to be parts of one whole—parts of the same country—and that country is my country. . . . I come here not to consider that I will do this for one distinct part of it, and that for another, but . . . to legislate for the whole." And finally Webster turned to a higher idea: the idea—in and of itself—of *Union,* permanent and enduring. The concept was, as one historian would note, "still something of a novelty in 1830. . . . Liberty was supposed to depend more on the rights of states than on the powers of the general government." But to Webster, the ideas were not two ideas but one.

> When my eyes shall be turned for the last time on the meridian sun, I hope I may see him shining brightly upon my united, free and happy Country. I hope I shall not live to see his beams falling upon the dispersed fragments of the structure of this once glorious Union. I hope that I may not see the flag of my Country, with its stars separated or obliterated, torn by commotion, smoking with the blood of civil war. I hope I may not see the standard raised of separate State rights, star against star, and stripe against stripe; but that the flag of the Union may keep its stars and its stripes corded and bound together in indissoluble ties. I hope I shall not see written, as its motto, *first* Liberty, and *then* Union. I hope I shall see no such delusion and deluded motto on the flag of that Country. I hope to see spread all over it, blazoned in letters of light, and proudly floating over Land and Sea that other sentiment, dear to my heart, "Union *and* Liberty, now and forever, one and inseparable!"

Tears in the crowded Senate gallery; tears on the crowded Senate floor. "Even Calhoun," it was said, "revealed the emotions he tried so hard to conceal. Love and pride of country—these were things he could understand, too." Men and women were weeping openly as Daniel Webster finished. Among those men were western senators, ardent nationalists, who had "thrilled to the patriotic fervor of Webster's final words." Those words crushed the southern hope for an alliance with the West. They did more. Webster revised the speech before it was published in pamphlet form, trying to convert the spoken words, "embellished as they had been by gestures, modulations of voice, and changes of expression, into words that would be read without these accompaniments but would leave the reader as thrilled and awed as the listening audience had been." He succeeded. Edition followed edition, and when copies ran out, men and women passed copies from hand to hand; in Tennessee, it was said, each copy "has probably been read by as many as fifty different" persons. "No speech in the English language, perhaps no speech in modern times, had ever been as widely diffused and widely read as Webster's Second Reply to Hayne," an historian of the period was to write. That speech "raised the idea of Union above contract or expediency and enshrined it in the American heart." It made the Union, as Ralph Waldo Emerson would put it, "part of the religion of this people." And as for the last nine of those words—that ringing final sentence—the only change Webster made in them was to reverse "Union" and "Liberty," so that the sentence read: "Liberty *and* Union, now and forever, one and inseparable!" Those words would be memorized by generations of schoolchildren, they would be chiseled in marble on walls and monuments—those words, spoken among those desks, in the Senate.

THE LONG STRUGGLE of the colonies that were now become states against a King and the King's representatives—the royal governors and proprietary officials in each colony—had made the colonists distrust and fear the possibilities for tyranny inherent in executive authority. And so, in creating the new nation, its Founding Fathers, the Framers of its Constitution, gave its legislature or Congress not only its own powers, specified and sweeping, powers of the purse ("To lay and collect Taxes . . . To borrow Money on the credit of the United States . . . To coin Money") and powers of the sword ("To declare War, grant Letters of Marque and Reprisal . . . To raise and support Armies . . . To provide and maintain a Navy . . .") but also powers designed to make the Congress independent of the President and to restrain and act as a check on his authority: power to approve his appointments, even the appointments he made within his own Administration, even appointments he made to his own Cabinet; power to remove his appointees through impeachment—to remove *him* through impeachment, should it prove necessary; power to override his vetoes of their Acts. And the most potent of these restraining powers the Framers gave to the Senate. While the House of Representatives was given the "sole power of Impeachment," the Senate was given the "sole power to try all Impeachments" ("And no person shall be convicted without the Concurrence of Two Thirds of the Members present"). The House could accuse; only the Senate could judge, only the Senate convict. The power to approve presidential appointments was given to the Senate alone; a President could nominate and appoint ambassadors, Supreme Court justices, and all other officers of the United States, but only "by and with the Advice and Consent of the Senate." Determined to deny the President the prerogative most European monarchs enjoyed of declaring war, the Framers gave that power to Congress as a whole, to House as well as Senate, but the legislative portion of the power of ending war by treaties, of preventing war by treaties—the power to do everything that can be done by treaties between nations—was vested in the Senate alone; while most European rulers could enter into a treaty on their own authority, an American President could make one only "by and with the Advice and Consent of the Senate, provided two thirds of the Senators present concur." As Arthur Schlesinger Jr. was to write:

> The Founding Fathers appear to have envisaged the treaty-making process as a genuine exercise in concurrent authority, in which the President and Senate would collaborate at all stages. . . .

One third plus one of the senators . . . retained the power of life and
death over the treaties.

Nor was it only the power of the executive of which the Framers were
wary. These creators of a government of the people feared not only the people's
rulers but the people themselves, the people in their numbers, the people in
their passions, what the Founding Father Edmund Randolph called "the turbulence and follies of democracy."

The Framers of the Constitution feared the people's power because they
were, many of them, members of what in America constituted an aristocracy,
an aristocracy of the educated, the well-born, and the well-to-do, and they mis-
trusted those who were not educated or well-born or well-to-do. More specifically, they feared the people's power because, possessing, and esteeming,
property, they wanted the rights of property protected against those who did not
possess it. In the notes he made for a speech in the Constitutional Convention,
James Madison wrote of the "real or supposed difference of interests" between
"the rich and poor"—"those who will labor under all the hardships of life, and
secretly sigh for a more equal distribution of its blessings"—and of the fact that
over the ages to come the latter would come to outnumber the former. "According to the equal laws of suffrage, the power will slide into the hands of the latter," he noted. "Symptoms, of a leveling spirit, as we have understood, have
sufficiently appeared in certain quarters to give notice of the future danger."
But the Framers feared the people's power also because they hated tyranny, and
they knew there could be a tyranny of the people as well as the tyranny of a
King, particularly in a system designed so that, in many ways, the majority
ruled. "Liberty may be endangered by the abuses of liberty as well as by the
abuses of power," Madison wrote. These abuses were more likely because the
emotions of men in the mass ran high and fast, they were "liable to err . . . from
fickleness and passion," and "the major interest might under sudden impulses
be tempted to commit injustice on the minority."

So the Framers wanted to check and restrain not only the people's rulers,
but the people; they wanted to erect what Madison called "a necessary fence"
against the majority will. To create such a fence, they decided that the Congress
would have not one house but two, and that while the lower house would be
designed to reflect the popular will, that would not be the purpose of the upper
house. How, Madison asked, is "the future danger"—the danger of "a leveling
spirit"—"to be guarded against on republican principles? How is the danger in
all cases of interested coalitions to oppress the minority to be guarded against?
Among other means by the establishment of a body in the government sufficiently respectable for its wisdom and virtue, to aid on such emergencies, the
preponderance of justice by throwing its weight into that scale." This body,
Madison said, was to be the Senate. Summarizing in the Constitutional Convention the ends that would be served by this proposed upper house of Con-

gress, Madison said they were "first to protect the people against their rulers; secondly to protect the people against the transient impressions into which they themselves might be led."

"The use of the Senate," Madison said, "is to consist in its proceeding with more coolness, with more system, and with more wisdom, than the popular branch." It should, he said, be "an anchor against popular fluctuations." He drew for parallels on classical history, which, he said, "informs us of no long-lived republic which had not a Senate." In two of the three "long-lived" republics of antiquity, Sparta and Rome, and probably in the third—Carthage (about whose governmental institutions less was known)—senators served for life. "These examples . . . when compared with the fugitive and turbulent existence of other ancient republics, [are] very instructive proofs of the necessity of some institution that will blend stability with liberty." Thomas Jefferson had been in Paris during the Convention, serving as minister to France. When he returned, he asked George Washington over breakfast why the President had agreed to a two-house Congress. According to a story that may be apocryphal, Washington replied with his own question: "Why did you pour your tea into that saucer?" And when Jefferson answered, "To cool it," Washington said, "Just so. We pour House legislation into the senatorial saucer to cool it." The resolution providing for a two-house Congress was agreed to by the Constitutional Convention with almost no debate or dissent.

And to ensure that the Senate could protect the people against themselves, the Framers armored the Senate against the people.

One layer of armor was bolted on to allay the fears of the states with fewer people, that the more populous states would combine to gain a commercial advantage or to control presidential appointments and national policies; the small states were determined that all states should have an equal voice in the Congress, so, in what became known as the "Great Compromise," it was agreed that while representation in the House would be by population, in the Senate it would be by states; as a result of that provision, a majority of the people could not pass a law; a majority of the states was required as well. But there were other, even stronger, layers. One was size. "Numerous assemblies," Madison explained, have a propensity "to yield to the impulse of sudden and violent passions, and to be seduced by factious leaders into intemperate and pernicious resolutions." So the Senate would, in Madison's phrase, be "less numerous." Each state, the Framers decided, would be represented by only two senators; the first Senate of the United States consisted of just twenty-six men. Another was the method by which senators would be elected. When one of the Framers, James Wilson of Pennsylvania, suggested that they be elected by the people, not a single member of the Convention rose to support him. "The people should have as little to do as may be about the government," Roger Sherman declared. "They lack information and are constantly liable to be misled." After Elbridge Gerry said that "The evils we experience flow from an excess of democracy," the Framers took steps to guard against such an excess. There would, they decided, be a "filtration" or "refinement" of the people's will before it reached the Senate: senators would be elected not by the people but by the legislatures of their respective states—a drastic filtration since in 1787 the franchise was so narrow that the legislatures themselves were elected by only a small percentage of the citizenry.

Senators would also be armored against the popular will by the length of their terms, the Framers decided. Frequent elections mean frequent changes in the membership of a body, and, Madison said, from a "change of men must proceed a change of opinions; and from a change of opinions, a change of measures. But a continual change even of good measures is inconsistent with every rule of prudence and every prospect of success." What good is the rule of law if "no man . . . can guess what the [law] will be tomorrow?" Guarding against "mutable policy," he pointed out, requires "the necessity of some stable institution in the government." Edmund Randolph, as usual, was more blunt. "The object of this second branch is to control the democratic branch," he said. "If it not be a firm body, the other branch being more numerous and coming immediately from the people, will overwhelm it." Senators, he said, should "hold their offices for a term sufficient to insure their independency." The term sufficient, the Framers decided, would be six years. Senators would hold office three times as long as the members of the "democratic branch." They would hold office longer than the President held office. And around the Senate as a whole there would be an additional, even stronger, layer of armor. Elections for senators would be held every two years, but only for a third of the senators. The other two-thirds would not be required to submit their record to the voters (or, to be more accurate, to their legislatures) at that time. This last piece of armor made the Senate a "stable institution" indeed. As a chronicler of the Senate was to write almost two centuries after its creation: "It was so arranged that while the House of Representatives would be subject to total overturn every two years, and the Presidency every four, the Senate, as a Senate, could *never* be repudiated. It was fixed, through the staggered-term principle, so that only a third of the total membership would be up for re-election every two years. It is therefore literally not possible for the voters ever to get at anything approaching a majority of the members of the Institution at any one time." Randolph's *desiderata*—"firmness" and "independency"—are picked up repeatedly in the convention's deliberations; over and over again it is emphasized that the Senate must be firm and independent. And the firmness about which the delegates were talking was firmness and independence against public opinion. That, for example, was Alexander Hamilton's rationale for vesting in the Senate the power to try impeachments:

Where else than in the Senate could have been found a tribunal sufficiently dignified, or sufficiently independent? What other body

would be likely to feel confidence enough in its own situation to preserve, unawed and uninfluenced, the necessary impartiality between
an individual accused and the *representatives of the people, his
accusers*? [italics added]

Additional armor was bolted into place. Some of it was to emphasize the
difference between members of the Senate and members of the House;
because, as Madison explained, "the senatorial trust . . . requiring greater extent
of information and stability of character, required at the same time that the
senator should have reached a period of life most likely to supply those advantages." A man could become a member of the House of Representatives at the
age of twenty-five; he could not become a senator until he was at least thirty—
and, "as the Senate is to have the power of making treaties and managing our
foreign affairs," and consequently "there is peculiar danger and impropriety in
opening it to those who have foreign attachments," a senator was required to
have been a citizen for longer—nine years instead of seven. The coat of constitutional mail bolted around the Senate was sturdy indeed—by design. Under
the new Constitution, the power of the executive and the power of the people
would be very strong. So to enable the Senate to stand against these powers—
to stand against them for centuries to come—the framers of the Constitution
made the Senate very strong. Wanting it to protect not only the people against
their rulers but the people against themselves, they bolted around it armor so
thick they hoped nothing could ever pierce it.

AND FOR MANY YEARS the Senate made use of its great powers. It created
much of the federal Judiciary—the Constitution established only the Supreme
Court; it was left to Congress to "constitute tribunals inferior," and it was a
three-man Senate committee that wrote the Judiciary Act of 1789, an Act that
has been called "almost an appendage to the Constitution." The Judiciary Act
established the system of federal and district courts, and the jurisdictional lines
between them, that endure to this day, and established as well the principle, not
mentioned in the Constitution, that state laws were subject to review by federal
courts. And when, sixteen years later, this new creation was threatened by a
concatenation of the very forces the Framers had feared—presidential power
and public opinion—the Senate saved the Judiciary.

The desks (there were thirty-four of them by 1805) had been removed for
this occasion, and the Old Senate Chamber had been arranged as if it were a tribunal. In the center of one wall stood the chair of the presiding officer, Vice
President Aaron Burr, as if he were the chief judge, and extending on his right
and left were high-backed, crimson-covered benches, on which the senators
sat, in a long row, judges in a court from which there was no appeal.

Before them, flanked by his lawyers, sat the accused—a tall, bulky, white-haired man with a face so ruddy that he was called "Old Bacon Face," but with a mind and tongue so keen that he was also called "the Demosthenes of Maryland." He was Samuel Chase, a justice of the Supreme Court of the United States, on trial for his opinions.

A President, maneuvering through his allies in the House of Representatives, had brought him there—a President at the zenith of his popularity. In November, 1804, Thomas Jefferson had won re-election by a landslide, taking 162 of 176 electoral votes and leading his Republican Party to overwhelming majorities in both House and Senate. "Rarely was a Presidential election better calculated to turn the head of a President, and never was a President elected who felt more keenly the pleasure of his personal triumph," wrote Henry Adams, who was of course no admirer. "Such success might have turned the head of any philosopher that ever sat on a throne." Whether or not Jefferson's head was indeed turned, the President now focused his attention on the lone branch of government still dominated by the Federalists, resorting, in Schlesinger's words, "to impeachment as a way of ridding the federal bench of judges whom he considered dangerous to his views." The Republicans succeeded in removing an alcoholic federal district judge in New Hampshire, and on the same day the New Hampshire verdict was handed down, the Republicans turned to a bigger target—Chase. And if Jefferson hit this target, it was widely believed, he would move to a bigger target yet: Chief Justice John Marshall, whose decisions had been angering the President.

As a young man, Chase had been a fiery leader of the Sons of Liberty, a signer of the Declaration of Independence, a member of the Continental Congress. He was a fierce and outspoken Federalist, whose handling of some cases since his appointment to the Supreme Court by George Washington has been called "outrageously high-handed," but, as the historian Dumas Malone has written, "he towered in the Supreme Court, both physically and intellectually." He had undoubtedly committed judicial excesses, but these were not the real issue, as was clearly revealed by Jefferson's key senatorial representative, William Giles of Virginia. Impeachment, Giles contended, was "nothing more than enquiry, by the two Houses of Congress, whether the office of any public man might not be better filled by another"; a conviction for impeachment, Giles said, need imply neither criminality nor corruption but only "a declaration by Congress to this effect: you hold dangerous opinions, and if you are suffered to carry them into effect you will work the destruction of the nation." Mere error in a judge, he was saying, was sufficient grounds for removal from office. Chase's conviction would have established a precedent that would have undermined the independence of the courts, and thereby endangered justice itself. Yet few doubted that Chase would indeed be convicted. The move to purge judges possessed of "dangerous opinions" was gathering momentum— in Pennsylvania, for example, the Jeffersonian-dominated lower house of the state legislature had recently impeached three justices of the state's Supreme Court whose views were too Federalist for the legislature's taste. And in

Congress, the discipline of the Republican majority appeared ironclad—as was demonstrated in the House vote to send the articles for Chase's impeachment on eight counts to the Senate; the resolution was presented as a strictly party measure, and, in the 73–32 vote, not a Republican voted against it. Two-thirds—twenty-three votes—of the thirty-four in the Senate were necessary for conviction, and twenty-five of the senators were Republicans; even if no Federalist voted against Chase, there would be enough votes to give Jefferson his conviction. A tide of public opinion, backed by presidential power, was sweeping the country.

And then, in the trial of Samuel Chase, that tide reached the Senate.

During the week-long trial, attended by foreign ambassadors and high federal officials while, before the row of thirty-four senators, Chase and his attorneys, among the most distinguished in the nation, sat in one box, the impeachment's "managers" from the House in another, a lot of words were spoken—the testimony filled over six hundred pages in the *Annals of Congress,* forerunner of the *Congressional Record*—and some went to the point. One of Chase's attorneys, Robert Goodloe Harper, appealed for sympathy for the "aged patriot" who after years of service to his country "is arraigned as an offender. . . . Placed at the bar of the court, after having sat with honor for six-teen years on the bench, he is doomed to hear the most opprobrious epithets applied to his name, by those whose predecessors were accustomed to look up at him with admiration and respect. . . . His footsteps are hunted from place to place, to find indiscretions, which may be exaggerated into crimes." But Harper also appealed to principle, telling the senators that impeachment should not be employed against a judge, or any official, just because he held opinions contrary to those of the party in power. "Justice, 'tho it may be an inconvenient restraint on our power, while we are strong, is the only rampart behind which we can find protection when we become weak," he said. That principle was of course the one that had been so prominent in motivating the Founding Fathers to create a Senate—that the rights of a minority must be protected against the tyranny of the majority—and that principle was reaffirmed, not just by Federalist senators but by Republican senators, and not by just a handful of Republican senators, either. One Federalist, Uriah Tracy of Connecticut, ill with pneumonia, left his bed and was carried to his seat because Chase's supporters believed that every vote would be needed. They were wrong—as was shown by the very first vote cast by a Republican senator on the first article of impeachment. The vote, by Stephen Bradley of Vermont, was "Not guilty." So were the votes of ten other Republicans; the final tally on the first article was 18 to 16 against conviction. For two hours each article of impeachment was read separately, and each senator then voted, and on each count enough Republicans voted "not guilty" to prevent a conviction. Despite the power of a President (all during the trial, senators had filed into the White House for dinner and private conversation), and despite the pressure of a party, and the roar of public opinion (and their own anger at Chase's partisan words, drummed into their ears over and over that week by the House prosecutors), on not one of the counts were the Republicans able to muster the necessary twenty-three votes.

The man who presided over the trial understood the historic significance of the scene that had been acted out before him. At the time he was presiding, Vice President Burr was under indictment for fatally wounding Alexander Hamilton, and three days after the trial, he would leave Washington for the Southwest, where he would shortly become embroiled in the shadowy intrigues that would becloud his memory. But the Senate seemed to bring out the best in him; attempting before the trial to ensure Burr's loyalty to the Republican cause, President Jefferson, who had once called him "a crooked gun, or other perverted machine," offered two of Burr's relatives and one of his intimate friends choice governmental posts, but even Federalist senators acknowledged the dignity and impartiality with which the Vice President conducted the trial; because of his fairness, one Federalist said, "I could almost forgive Burr for any less crime than the blood of Hamilton." And Burr ended his time in the Senate with a speech that restated the great ideal on which the body had been founded. The assault on the independence of the judiciary by a powerful President backed by the power of public opinion—and the refusal of the Senate to bow to those powers—were "fresh in his mind" when he spoke (amid, as an historian of Congress has written, "a stillness among both friend and foe"). "This House," Aaron Burr said, "is a sanctuary; a citadel of law, of order, and of liberty; and it is here—it is here, in this exalted refuge; here if anywhere, will resistance be made to the storms of political phrensy and the silent arts of corruption. . . ." A senator who served almost two centuries later—Robert Byrd of West Virginia, who loved the Senate so much that he wrote a four-volume history of it—would invoke the trial of Samuel Chase as an example of all that the Senate could be, saying that "The Senate exercised in that fine moment of drama the kind of independence, impartiality, fairness and courage that, from time to time over the years, it has brought to bear on the great issues of the country." In the trial of Samuel Chase, the principle had been proven. The Senate had been created to be independent, to stand against the tyranny of presidential power and the tides of public opinion.

It had stood.

THE SENATE CHAMBER gutted by British troops was restored in 1819. Located in the Capitol's central section, it was a rather small, semi-circular room. Slender, fluted, gilded columns formed a loggia along the curved wall and supported a narrow gallery, like a theater balcony, with a delicate gilt balustrade. Walls unbroken by recesses and a low-vaulted, domed ceiling made the acoustics excellent, so the Chamber was, as an historian of Congress has written, "ideal for the ringing voices of eloquent men." And the deep, rich crimson and gold of its carpet and draperies, and of the sweeping canopy, surmounted by a great golden shield of the Republic and a broad-winged gilded eagle, above the presiding officer's dais, made it an ornate, dramatic background for the forty-eight new mahogany desks—each with its silver-mounted inkwell and small bottle of blotting sand, each with a low-backed mahogany and red leather armchair—that were arranged in four rising arcs.

And for forty years after 1819, among those desks (at which senators studied reports and wrote speeches and letters, since most senators did not have offices of their own), the senators of the United States grappled—as, once, the senators of ancient Rome had grappled—with the concerns of expanding empire: should the borders of the young republic be extended west of the Mississippi, and if so how far west—to the Great Plains, or even further, to the mighty mountain chain of the West and the shore of the great ocean beyond? (Many senators considered this last suggestion ridiculous. When, in 1824, there was a proposal for the erection of a fort on the Pacific shore of the Oregon Territory, Mahlon Dickerson of New Jersey said there was no realistic possibility that Oregon, separated from the United States by virtually impassable deserts and mountains, could ever become a state; even if its congressmen managed to cover twenty miles a day, he pointed out, they would need 350 days to get to Washington and back. Benton of Missouri rose at his desk to reply angrily that "Within a century from this day, population, greater than that of the present United States, will exist on the West side of the Rocky Mountains," but the proposal was defeated.) Among those desks was debated peace and war: whether, once it was decided twenty-five years after the Columbia River Fort was debated that Oregon was worth settling after all, to go to war with England over it ("54-40 or fight!"); whether to march against Mexico or instead negotiate for sovereignty over California and Texas and the vast arid stretches of the Southwest. It was at one of those desks that the first senator from newly annexed Texas, Sam Houston, who usually sat silently, dressed in sombrero and a waistcoat of panther hide with its hair still on, whittling away at small pine sticks, finally rose during a debate on the legal technicalities of the issue to tell the Senate bluntly that Texas was already at war with Mexico and that the United States, in annexing Texas, had inherited that war. Among those desks was debated the great questions involved in the settlement of the vast new territories of the West: would their land go to speculators or to brave and enterprising individual families?—it was in the Senate that Benton proposed the Homestead Act that made him "the father of the cheap land system"; would it be the federal government or the new states and territories who would pay for the roads and canals that would knit them together? And, of course, it was among those desks that, for these forty years, was debated the great problem that overshadowed all questions about the new territories and states: whether they should be slave or free? It was not only Webster's reply to Hayne that preserved the Union; among those desks, the desks of the Senate, men fought to save it for forty years.

The forty years—1819 to 1859—after the Senate moved back into its elegant domed Chamber would be called the Senate's "Golden Age."

In part, the phrase was inspired by the hue of the Chamber itself, by the immense gold eagle atop the dais, by the radiance of the great chandelier, by the gallery's gilt columns and balustrade. In part, it was inspired by the debates that took place in that Chamber, by oratory as brilliant as the surroundings, and by the men who participated in those debates, particularly the shining figures of Webster, Clay, and Calhoun—the "Great Triumvirate." And in part those four decades were the Senate's Golden Age because it was the period in which the Senate came closest to living up to the greatness that the Framers had envisioned for it. During those forty years the Senate held center stage in the great arena of American history, becoming the focus and balance wheel of government—while, true to the principles on which it had been founded and which Washington so pithily summarized to Jefferson, it "cooled" passions, tried to reconcile the unreconcilable. For some decades after the founding of the Republic, the House of Representatives had overshadowed the Senate; Webster and Clay had been members of the lower house then. But now, as the population of the new nation expanded, the House expanded with it—by 1820, it had 213 members and its membership grew faster and faster with each census—and became too unwieldy: rules had to be adopted that inhibited the role of debate, and sheer size worked against calm consideration of delicate issues. And, beginning in 1819, when the Senate twice stood fast against inflammatory House measures and then, in 1820, forged the territorial division known as the Missouri Compromise, it was in the Senate, now the true deliberative body that the Framers had envisioned, that were enacted the great compromises that, for forty years, pulled the Union back from the edge of abyss.

It was at one of those desks that Calhoun sat in 1833 after his return to Washington—a Washington buzzing with whispers that President Andrew Jackson had sworn to hang him if he returned. When Hayne had debated Webster in 1830, he had been speaking for Calhoun, then Vice President, and, as presiding officer of the Senate, not permitted to speak there; Hayne was defending Calhoun's doctrine of the ultimate sovereignty of the individual states, of a state's right to nullify a federal law if it felt the law exceeded the power granted to the federal government by the Constitution; and if the government insisted on enforcing the law, to secede. Now, in 1833, Calhoun was a senator, and spoke for himself. Jackson was still proposing a tariff bill the South considered onerous and unconstitutional, and was sending to the Senate a Force bill, authorizing enforcement of the tariff by military force. The South Carolina Legislature authorized the use of the militia to resist; Calhoun continued to publish papers reaffirming the constitutionality of nullification; and Jackson warned that "Disunion by armed force is treason." "Within three weeks, sir," the enraged President told a South Carolina delegation—within three weeks after the first blow is struck—"I will place fifty thousand troops in your state." Calhoun had resigned the vice presidency, and Hayne had resigned his Senate seat, so that Calhoun, named by the South Carolina Legislature to succeed him, could present the South's case himself, and the South's greatest orator was seated at his desk, grimly taking notes, as Jackson's message requesting passage of the Force bill was read.

On the day Calhoun was to deliver his major speech against the measure, there was a heavy snowfall, but carriages jammed the Capitol plaza, carrying people who had come to hear John C. Calhoun speak. While the verbiage of other leading orators of the day was flowery, Calhoun's was "stripped bare"— down to the bones of a remorseless logic. His sentences were often long and involved, as was the intricate process of his reasoning, and he spoke so fast that journalists considered him the most difficult man to report in the Congress. But, he was a gaunt, unforgettable figure, his eyes burning in a pale face, his great mass of hair rising like a lion's mane, his voice ringing metallically in every corner of the Chamber. "The commanding eye, the grim earnestness of manner, the utter integrity of sentiment held the galleries in anxious attention," as one historian wrote. "His voice was harsh, his gestures stiff, like the motions of a pump handle. There was no ease, flexibility, grace or charm in his manner; yet there was something that riveted your attention as with hooks of steel." As he rose now, the galleries could see how much the fifty-year-old South Carolinian had aged in a few months as he saw his beloved South being forced to the brink. The blazing eyes were sunk deep in his head, the furrows in his cheeks had become gashes, the lion's mane was gray now. To his opponents, the gaunt figure looked like "the arch traitor . . . like Satan in Paradise." To others, he was "a great patriot with his back against the wall, battling fiercely in defense of violated liberties." Consumed with his feelings, he paced back and forth between the desks "like a caged lion." The Force bill, he said, exhibited "the impious spectacle of this Government, the creature of the States, making war against the power to which it owes its existence. . . . We made no such government. South Carolina sanctioned no such government." The Force bill, he said, "enables him [Jackson] to subject every man in the United States . . . to martial law . . . and under the penalty of court-martial to compel him to imbrue his hand in his brother's blood."

The Senator from South Carolina paced as he spoke. The Senator from Massachusetts stood immobile beside his desk—as he had done three years before, again wearing his blue coat with the brass buttons and his stiff cravat— as again, in another great speech, he defended the Constitution as the overriding law. The Senator from Kentucky strolled among the desks—as casually as if they had been props in a theater.

When he was a lawyer in Kentucky, it had been said of Henry Clay that he could "hypnotize a jury"; as a national spokesman for the Whig Party, he had attracted crowds so large on a speaking tour that it was said that he "depopulated the fields and forests of the West"; as a dinner party guest he was so charming that "the white gloves kissed by Clay became treasured mementoes." He charmed the Senate as well. "No lover was ever more ardent, more vehement, more impassioned, or more successful in his appeal than Henry Clay" when he was courting the Senate, an observer wrote, watching him "stepping gracefully, backward and forward and from side to side, flourishing a silk hand-kerchief," an actor born to center stage. From time to time, Henry Clay returned to his desk to pick up his snuffbox, and carried it with him for a while, taking a pinch to punctuate an anecdote, tapping it with a forefinger to empha-size a point. Tall, slender, and graceful in a black dress coat and a high white stock, his face was bright, playful, and grinning as he told his wonderful sto-ries, his voice "so penetrating that even in a lower key" it rang through the Chamber "as inspiring as a trumpet." And when he turned serious, the stamp of his foot and the raising of a tight-clenched fist "made the emotion visible as well as audible," an historian wrote. "Harry of the West," "Brave Prince Hal," "the Gallant Star"—Henry Clay, who had been elected Speaker of the House of Representatives the day he arrived in it, leader of the War Hawks in 1812, Henry Clay whose previous triumphs had already earned him the nickname of "the Great Compromiser"—now, in 1833, with North and South on the very brink of civil war, he proposed a compromise tariff bill that he said was not an ordinary piece of legislation but "a treaty of peace and amity"—a true compro-mise in which each side would sacrifice something for the sake of unity.

The North—President Jackson—"would, in the enforcement act, send forth alone a flaming sword," Clay said. "We would send that also, but along with it the olive branch, as a messenger of peace. They cry out, 'The Law! the law! the law! Power! Power! Power!' . . . They would hazard a civil commo-tion, beginning in South Carolina and ending, God only knows where. . . . We want no war, above all no civil war, no family strife. We want no sacked cities, no desolated fields, no smoking ruins, no streams of American blood by Ameri-can arms!"

Calhoun rose to respond in a great silence, for spectators and senators alike knew how much hung on his next words, as so much had hung on Web-ster's words three years before. When he agreed to Clay's proposal, "such was the clapping and thundering applause that . . . the sensation was indescribable," an observer wrote. As Jackson's Force bill moved through the Senate and House, Clay's compromise tariff bill moved in tandem with it. And the moment the tariff bill passed, Calhoun was on the road to South Carolina. He traveled, as the historian Merrill Peterson has written, "day and night over snow-covered and rain-soaked roads, sometimes in open mail carts," in order to stop a state convention from taking rash action. When he persuaded the convention to repeal the nullification ordinance, the crisis was over. And "the Compromise Act of 1833," that Act created among the desks of the Senate, "would generally be celebrated as an act of deliverance."

Webster, Clay, and Calhoun, three men who each longed for the presi-dency, and never attained it. The mark they made was in the Senate. But it was quite a mark. The battles they fought—sometimes, in opposition to Andrew Jackson, united; often opposed to each other (increasingly, Calhoun isolated from the other two and from most of the Senate)—were battles over the most momentous issues of the age, and the Senate was often the dominant arena in which those issues were decided, for it was not the White House but Capitol Hill that was the epicenter of government then, and the Senate was the dominant house of Congress. As Peterson has written,

> Webster, Clay and Calhoun . . . were the ornaments of American statesmanship in the era between the founding and the Civil War. At home and abroad, making exception for their common enemy, they were the most celebrated Americans of the time; . . . All across the country their speeches were read as if the fate of the nation hung on them. . . .

Sixteen years later, in 1849, it was again in the Senate that Clay, seventy-two years old now, rose to again urge compromise. He had always been thin, but now he was too thin, and frail—he had had to be helped up the stairs in front of the Capitol—and racked by the cough that his friends suspected was consumption although no one dared even to whisper the dreaded word. He didn't stroll through the desks this time, didn't move about much at all, in fact, as if he was trying to conserve his strength during the two days he spoke, standing for the most part at his back-row desk in a far corner of the Chamber, but "he spoke with the musical voice of old, with the same passionate intensity"—and, at crucial points, he still tapped the snuffbox. The spectre of sacked cities and desolated fields was very near now, but he was still fighting against it. Victory in the war with Mexico had brought the United States vast new territories—Texas, Arizona, New Mexico, California—and the explosive issue of whether these territories should be slave or free was splitting the nation apart, and the dispute was being played out on the floor of the Senate, where for years Calhoun and his followers had successfully blocked admission of the territories as free states, had blocked admission while talk grew of secession, and of civil war. "If any solution to the [problem] . . . was to be found, it would be up to the Senate to take the lead"—up to the Senate, and to its "Great Compromiser." For three weeks, Clay had worked and reworked alternate plans, and then, having finally settled on a complicated package of eight separate resolutions, one rainy January evening, haggard and coughing constantly, he had impulsively climbed into a carriage and visited Daniel Webster at Webster's boardinghouse, and outlined his plan—to which Webster consented. And now, as his biographer wrote, Brave Prince Hal "rose in the Senate chamber and began his last great struggle to save the Union that he loved."

From his position in the far corner, the long semi-circle of desks stretched below and away from him, and his gaze traveled along the upturned faces of the men sitting at them as he said: "I implore Senators—I entreat them, by all that they expect hereafter, and by all that is dear to them here below, to repress the ardor of these passions, to look at their country in this crisis—to listen to the voice of reason." Sometimes the physical effort seemed too much for him, and he faltered, but he always went on, for two long days, and one observer wrote, "when in moments of excitement, he stands so firm and proud, with his eyes all agleam, while his voice rings out clear and strong, it almost seems that . . . the hot blood of youth was still coursing through his veins. . . . The wonderful old man!" In a stroke, as Peterson puts it, he "seized the initiative from the President, centered it in the Senate. . . . and set the legislative agenda for the country." "What a singular spectacle!" wrote the editor of the *New York Herald*—a newspaper long hostile to Clay. "Of all the leaders of the old parties, of all the aspiring spirits of the new ones, including [the President] and the whole of his cabinet, from head to tail, not a single soul, not a single mind has dared to exhibit the moral courage to come out with any plan for settling the whole except it is Henry Clay . . . solitary and alone."

One of the desks below Clay's had been vacant while he spoke. It was a desk near the center of the Chamber, third from the aisle in the second row on the right—Calhoun's desk. Calhoun's boardinghouse was just across from the Capitol, but Calhoun was too ill to attend. When he read Clay's speech in the newspapers, though, he determined to reply, and his supporters said he would be present on March 4. The galleries again were packed, the walls were lined with spectators, and shortly after noon Calhoun came. "He was emaciated and feeble," one of his biographers has recounted, "his sallow cheeks sunken, his long hair now almost white, his step short." He had hoped to deliver his own speech, but he didn't have the strength. While Senator James Mason of Virginia, standing at his shoulder, read the words Calhoun had written, Calhoun sat at his desk, with a great black coat drawn around him, and a journalist described "his eyes glowing . . . as he glanced at Senators upon whom he desired to have certain passages make an impression." And the speech was as defiant as ever. It was on a great theme—"the greatest and gravest question that can ever come under your consideration: How can the union be preserved?"—and he said the question had a simple answer: Only by adopting measures to assure the southern states that they could remain in the Union "consistently with their honor and safety." The speech rallied the South—against the compromise—and when, on March 7, 1849, Webster stood to reply to Calhoun, at his desk also near the center of the Chamber, "not since the Reply to Hayne did the fate of the nation seem to hang so fatefully on the wisdom, eloquence and power of one man." Standing in the same Chamber, on almost the same spot, twenty years before, Black Dan Webster had given a speech that would live in history. Now he began another such speech: "Mr. President, I wish to speak today, not as a Massachusetts man, nor as a northern man, but as an American, and a member of the Senate of the United States. It is fortunate that there is a Senate of the United States; a body . . . to which the country looks with confidence, for wise, moderate, patriotic and healing counsels." Webster, too, was old, but his voice still pealed through that Chamber like an organ, rolling across the long arc of desks and the crowded galleries as he continued: "I speak today for the preservation of the Union. Hear me for my cause."

Calhoun had had to be helped from the Chamber after his speech was read; it was expected that he would never return. But he had returned for Webster's speech. Not seeing his old foe at first, Webster said he regretted his absence. Then another senator shouted: "He is here." And near the conclusion of Webster's speech, Calhoun engaged him in a brief, harsh exchange, at the end of which there was an exchange that was less harsh, as if Webster had suddenly realized that it might be the last they would ever have. The "honorable member" had as always refused to cloak his opinions in gentle phrases, Webster said. "He did avow his purpose openly, boldly and manfully; he did not disguise his conduct or his motives."

MR. CALHOUN.   Never, never.
MR. WEBSTER.   What he means he is very apt to say.
MR. CALHOUN.   Always, always.
MR. WEBSTER.   And I honor him for it.

Those were indeed the last words they ever exchanged. Calhoun's health deteriorated rapidly. In his boardinghouse room, he said, "If I could have but one hour to speak in the Senate. . . ." He died on March 31; his funeral was held in the Senate, of course.

The great debate was to roll on among those desks all that year and the next: the great speeches coming one after another—Clay fighting for his compromise (despite his poor health he spoke seventy times during the debate), northerners opposing it because, as William Seward put it, slavery was forbidden by "a higher law than the Constitution." Once Clay's clashes with Benton grew so fierce that the Senate adjourned to give the tempers of the two old men time to cool. And there was at least one moment of greater drama still, when an enraged Benton left his desk and advanced on diminutive southern Senator Henry S. Foote of Mississippi during an especially angry exchange, and Foote drew a pistol; the old frontier brawler did not pause but continued striding toward him, shouting, "I have no pistols. Let him fire! Stand out of the way, and let the assassin fire!" until finally Senator Dickerson of New Jersey took the pistol out of Foote's hand. When, after months of debate in the sweltering summer months, most of Clay's plan was passed, the Union was preserved by what Peterson calls "a truly monumental legislative achievement."

Within two years of the Compromise of 1850, all of the Great Triumvirate would be dead; when, in 1859 the Senate, grown too numerous for its beautiful Chamber, moved to larger, but drab, quarters in the Capitol's new north wing, Vice President John C. Breckinridge, in a final address in the Old Chamber, summed up its spirit by evoking "the mighty three, whose names and fame, associated in life, death has not been able to sever"—and by pointing to their desks: "There sat Calhoun, *the* Senator, inflexible, austere, oppressed. . . . This was Webster's seat. His great efforts are associated with this Chamber, whose very air seems yet to vibrate beneath the strokes of his deep tones and mighty words. On the outer circle sat Clay. . . ."

In the end, of course, the triumvirate could be said to have failed. The Civil War came. Ironically, it was in the Senate, scene of the great—and for decades successful—efforts to preserve the Union, that the fuse was lit that did so much to blow it apart. In 1854, Senator Stephen A. Douglas, to get a railroad built that would benefit his Illinois constituents, persuaded his Senate Committee on Territories to report out a southern-supported bill—the Kansas-Nebraska Act—that would in effect repeal not only the Compromise of 1850 but the Missouri Compromise as well by allowing the creation of a state—Kansas—under conditions that virtually guaranteed that it would be a slave state. Abolitionists assailed the measure; Douglas was to remark that he could travel all the way from Chicago to Washington by the light of his burning effigy. But southern senators saw the chance to force the nation to accept slavery on their terms or break up the Union; for forty years the Senate had been the center of compromise; now it was the center of conflict; "as was so often the case during those great nineteenth-century debates, it seemed as if the whole population of Washington sought admittance to the Senate galleries," an historian was to write. It was from one of the Senate desks that Charles Sumner of Massachusetts, an uncompromising foe of slavery, struggled to rise when, two days after he passionately denounced the "Crime Against Kansas," a South Carolina congressman entered the Chamber, came up behind him and struck him again and again on his head with a heavy cane, while another South Carolinian, with another cane, faced the other senators to keep them from intervening. It was under his desk that Sumner's leg became so entangled that he could not rise as the blows rained on his head and blood began pouring from his wounds; after he finally wrenched himself free, it was among the desks that he reeled, "backwards and forwards," until he fell. (Whereupon southern senators congratulated the assailant.) By the time, three years later, that Sumner was able to return to the Senate, attempts at compromise had ended, and the smoking ruins and the streams of American blood were almost at hand. But did the triumvirate really fail? The compromises fashioned by Webster, Clay, and Calhoun (and by other senators, too, Benton notable among them) might be said to have merely postponed the settlement of the slavery issue, merely postponed the terrible war. But another view is that perhaps nothing could have stopped that war from coming. And if that is the case, then the Senate's compromises had bought the time that America needed. An infant Union was crumbling; the Senate's compromises had held it together year after year, decade after decade, had held it together long enough—as if those compromises had been a great delaying action to give the infant time to grow strong enough to win the war and to endure. Writing of the last of the compromises—the Compromise of 1850—

and of the senators who had created it, Senator Byrd was to say, "Perhaps the greatest credit we can give them is to note that the Civil War began in 1861 rather than in 1851; for, if the war had broken out during the 1850's, when . . . public opinion in the North was still divided over the slavery issue, we might today be two nations rather than one." During a period of about four decades—a period roughly coinciding with the years, 1819 to 1859, during which the Senate occupied its ideal stage—it played magnificently the role the Founding Fathers had written for it. Its compromises cooled seemingly uncoolable passions, and its resistance to "King Andrew" in the Bank War and James Polk in the Mexican—and in the Oregon dispute—made it the republican tribunate against aggressive executive power, the great bulwark of liberty and self-government against the possibility of executive tyranny, that the Founding Fathers had hoped it would be. And the Senate was more. As Peterson says,

> Beginning in comparative seclusion, with a vaguely patrician character, like the Senate in ancient Rome, . . . its debates at first secret and then for many years barely reported, the Senate had emerged from the shadow of the House of Representatives as the first place of legislative deliberation and leadership. . . . Whatever the cause of its rising prestige—the triumvirs who graced it, its smallness (only forty-eight members until 1836), its indirect election (which some thought ensured superior wisdom and made the Senate what it ought to be, a congress of ambassadors from sovereign states), perhaps even its superb acoustics under a low-vaulted dome . . . the Senate fulfilled the . . . ideal of a great deliberative body, at once solid and brilliant. . . .

Contrasting the Senate with the "vulgar demeanor" of the House of Representatives, de Tocqueville, after his tour of the United States in 1831, was to comment that "The Senate contains within a small space a large proportion of the celebrated men of America. Scarcely an individual is to be seen in it who has not had an active and illustrious career: the Senate is composed of eloquent advocates, distinguished generals, wise magistrates, and statesmen of note, whose arguments would do honor to the most remarkable parliamentary debates of Europe." De Tocqueville was not the only foreign observer deeply impressed. The Victorian historian Sir Henry Maine said that the Senate was "the only thoroughly successful institution which has been established since the tide of modern democracy began to run." Prime Minister William Gladstone called it "the most remarkable of all the inventions of modern politics."

ON JANUARY 21, 1861, Mississippi's Jefferson Davis rose at his desk to end the forty-year Senate effort to preserve the Union by telling his northern colleagues, "It only remains for me to bid you a final adieu." Then he and four other southerners strode out of the Chamber. In the next weeks all but one of the twenty-two southern senators followed suit, leaving the Senate as their states were leaving the Union. (Only Andrew Johnson of Tennessee elected to remain loyal.) Three months later, with a Confederate force on the south side of the Potomac menacing Washington and breastworks of iron plates braced on the Capitol's porticoes, rifles were propped among the desks and soldiers sprawled in the red leather armchairs; the Sixth Massachusetts Regiment, hurriedly summoned by the newly elected President Lincoln to defend Washington (thirty-one of the regiment had been wounded in a battle en route), was quartered in the Senate Chamber; one soldier angrily hacked at Jefferson Davis' desk with his bayonet.

Lincoln had insisted that construction on the Capitol go forward ("If people see the Capitol going on, it is a sign we intend the Union shall go on"), and all through the war the great dome continued to rise above Washington as if to symbolize the growth of a great new nation—and all through that war, in its new Chamber, a Senate freed at last by the departure of the southerners enacted laws that knit together a mighty continent, filled it with people, and educated those people—Acts that spurred the creation of a transcontinental railroad that bound at last the continent's far Pacific shore to its Atlantic and made possible the development of its Great Plains; that encouraged its settlement by promising a family 160 acres of the public domain for its enterprise and courage in settling it; and that provided for the sale of public lands to fund the creation of colleges. The Pacific Railway Act of 1862; the Homestead Act of 1862; the Land Grant College Act of 1862—it became very clear as these passed the Senate how the South had for so long shackled the Union.

AFTER THE WAR, among those desks in the new Senate Chamber, there was another moment of glory—as phrases in the Constitution ("When the President of the United States is tried, the Chief Justice shall preside . . .") came to life. Four years of struggle between a Congress dominated by Radical Republicans determined to solidify the equality of races and humble the Confederacy and a President more interested in reconciliation than in revenge—four years in which legislation, of doubtful constitutionality, was passed (over Andrew Johnson's vetoes) forbidding the President to remove federal officials, or to interfere with General Ulysses S. Grant's command of the army without the Senate's consent—was ended when the House, under the leadership of Representative Thaddeus Stevens ("Andrew Johnson must learn . . . that as Congress shall order he must obey"), voted by an overwhelming margin to impeach the President, and send the articles of impeachment to the Senate for trial.

On that trial hung great issues. "Johnson's opponents wanted to save a Reconstruction based on racial justice," an historian says. "But his supporters had an honorable motive too. They wanted to save the presidency." At first, conviction seemed all but certain, so overwhelmingly did public opinion in the

North demand it. As one observer wrote on the eve of the trial, "The condition of the public mind was not unlike that preceding a great battle. The dominant part of the nation seemed to occupy the position of public prosecutor, and it was scarcely in the mood to brook delay for trial or to hear defense. Washington . . . swarmed with representatives of every state of the Union, demanding in a practically united voice the deposition of the President." Representative Stevens had coldly warned both houses: "Let me see the recreant who would vote to let such a criminal escape. Point me to one who will do it and I will show you one who will dare the infamy of posterity." And the House of Representatives had taken the warning: every Republican had voted for impeachment. In the Senate, with the eleven Confederate states still excluded, there were only fifty-four senators. Thirty-six votes were therefore required for conviction—and forty-two senators were Republicans. As the trial opened with Chief Justice Salmon P. Chase presiding and administering to each senator, as he rose at his desk, an oath "to do impartial justice," Benjamin Wade, president *pro tempore* of the Senate and therefore next in line for the Presidency, was confident that he would soon be in the White House.

One of the Republicans, however, was Lyman Trumbull of Illinois. Trumbull hated Johnson, and hated Johnson's stand on Reconstruction; he was, in fact, the author of much of the Reconstruction legislation that the President had vetoed. But now Trumbull said:

> The question to be decided is not whether Andrew Johnson is a proper person to fill the Presidential Office, nor whether it is fit that he should remain in it. . . . Once set, the example of impeaching a President for what, when the excitement of the hour having subsided, will be regarded as insufficient cause, no future President will be safe. . . . What then becomes of the checks and balances of the Constitution? . . . I cannot be an instrument to produce such a result.

Another Republican was William Pitt Fessenden of Maine, known for his "reverence" for the Constitution, and for his independence. "His level gaze, high-bridged nose, and firm lips and chin identified a man who would be intimidated by none," an historian wrote. Like Trumbull, Fessenden despised Johnson—not long before, he had said of the President: "He has broken the faith, betrayed his trust and must sink from detestation to contempt"—but none of those crimes were among those enumerated in the Constitution to justify impeachment, and now Fessenden wrote a friend that while "The country has so bad an opinion of the President, which he fully deserves, that it expects his condemnation. . . . I will not decide the question against my own judgment. . . . Make up your mind, if need be, to hear me denounced a traitor and perhaps hanged in effigy. The public, when roused and excited by passions and prejudices, is little better than a wild beast."

When it became known that seven Republican senators might be planning

to vote against impeachment—the exact number necessary to prevent conviction of the President—the GOP was convulsed by rage. The seven were del-
uged by what the *Philadelphia Press* called "a fearful avalanche of telegrams
from every section of the country," representing "a great surge of public opinion." In Illinois, where for decades Trumbull had been a revered public figure,
a Republican convention resolved that "any senator elected by . . . Republicans,
who at this time blenches and betrays, is infamous and should be dishonored
and execrated." James W. Grimes of Iowa was also refusing to go along with
impeachment. So vicious were the abuse he was exposed to and the physical
threats against him that they were blamed for a stroke he suffered two days
before the vote was to be taken on the first article of impeachment. It was
expected that he would not be able to attend the vote—or, as one chronicler
sneered, "would plead that his illness prevented him from attending to cast the
vote that would end his career"—and that the absence of his vote might give
victory to the impeachers. On the day of the vote, however, the doors in the rear
of the Chamber opened, and four men appeared, carrying Grimes to his seat.
(Fessenden grasped his hand and gave him a smile.) Although senators stood to
cast their impeachment votes, the Chief Justice said Grimes could vote while
sitting, but when his name was reached in the balloting, he struggled to his feet,
to say "Not guilty." The Chief Justice asked each senator individually, "Mr.
Senator, how say you?" and seven Republicans voted not guilty, making the
vote 35 to 19, one vote short of the necessary two-thirds. Immense pressure
was then put on every Republican to vote guilty on the other ten articles. But on
each vote, at least seven rose among the desks of the Senate and said "Not
guilty." Sixty-four years before, in the trial of Samuel Chase, the Senate had
saved the judiciary. Now it saved the presidency.

In political terms, their "not guilty" votes cost the seven senators dearly.
The fate Fessenden had foreseen for himself came true for all of them. All were
denounced as traitors, not merely to their party but to their country ("We have
had Benedict Arnold, Jefferson Davis, and now we have James W. Grimes,"
Horace Greeley sneered in the *New York Tribune*), all were hung in effigy, and
all were renounced by the party organizations of their respective states; not one
of them was re-elected. But there were other terms. Shortly before he died,
Grimes told a friend, "I shall ever thank God that in that troubled hour of trial,
when many privately confessed that they had sacrificed their judgment and
their conscience at the behests of party newspapers and party hate, I had the
courage to be true to my oath and my conscience." And he remembered Fessenden's smile. "I would not today exchange that recollection for the highest
distinction of life." And in broader terms, the votes of those seven senators preserved the constitutional principle of the separation of powers. The removal of
a President by Congress solely because of a dispute over policy could have
transformed the entire American political system.

The "excitement of the hour"—the "great surge of public opinion"—had demanded a President's head. But only one house of Congress had bowed to that demand. The other had not. The Founding Fathers had created the Senate to stand against the "excitement of the hour."

Once again, the Senate had stood.

BUT THAT MOMENT of glory was only a moment. After the Civil War, the Senate's Golden Age was over, and the institution began to turn into the Senate that Lyndon Johnson was to find when he arrived in it more than three quarters of a century later.

The Senate's power wasn't over—far from it. Reconstruction was crafted not in the White House but on Capitol Hill. The Civil Rights Act of 1866 became law and the Freedmen's Bureau a fact over presidential vetoes. It was Congress, not the President, that divided the South into military districts as if it had been conquered Gaul and placed over each district a commander with powers as broad as those of a Roman proconsul. And although Reconstruction policy was created by the Senate in tandem with the House of Representatives, and on the Joint House-Senate Committee the dominant figure was Representative Stevens, during the period after Reconstruction, beginning with the inauguration of Ulysses S. Grant as President in March, 1869, the power of the House declined, and the power of the Senate grew, and grew again.

The expansion of senatorial power was to some extent a coefficient of the House's weakness. There were 293 representatives in 1870, 332 in 1880—and the House, without strong leaders after Stevens' death in 1868, became the place of din and confusion that was to be described as "one of the most disorderly and inefficient legislative bodies in the world." With the majority switching back and forth between Democrats and Republicans virtually every two years, it seemed to be in a continuous state of reorganization, symbolized by the bitter, time-consuming biennial battles over selection of the Speaker and committee chairmen and members. In the Senate, however, the two parties had agreed in December, 1845, on a new procedure for choosing committee chairmen and members. No longer would they be elected by secret ballot of the whole Senate—a method which had given senators considerable independence from party control. Henceforth, they would be nominated in party conferences, or caucuses; the Senate as a whole would vote on the nominees, and since the vote would almost always follow party lines, it would simply ratify the majority party's selections. This gave party leadership new power, enabling it to impose a degree of party discipline, and discipline was also increased—and Senate proceedings made more efficient—because party "steering committees" were given more power over the flow of legislation to the floor. In addition, the Senate was armored against the shifts in public opinion that led to continual transfers of power in the House, and senators were still chosen by state legislatures often dominated by Republicans; the GOP controlled the Senate in fourteen of the sixteen Congresses between 1869 and 1901. Senate committee chairmen stayed in their posts—building up, year after year, power that made them figures to be reckoned with in Washington. Also increasing the Senate's power in relation to the House was another development: the hardening of the custom under which the Senate would not consent to a presidential nomination if either senator from the nominee's home state objected. This "senatorial courtesy" gave a senator almost a veto power over patronage.

The expansion of the Senate's power was a coefficient also of the weakness of Presidents. The three decades between 1869 and the end of the century were a Republican era in the White House as well as in the Senate. Grant, Hayes, Garfield, Arthur, Harrison—all were Republicans. The Republican philosophy—that Congress should be stronger than the President, and the Senate stronger than the House—ruled. The Presidents were almost all weak, and, as congressional historian Alvin Josephy puts it, "after its experience with Johnson, the Congress by and large kept them weak." When, immediately after his inauguration, the war hero Grant, a political *naif*, began filling Cabinet posts without consultation with the Senate, the Senate taught him a lesson. Blocking one Cabinet appointment, it forced the President to nominate the man *it* chose; it let other Grant nominees know that the same fate was in store for them, and several withdrew. Having refused to consent, the Senate now advised; traveling by coach the two miles of Pennsylvania Avenue to the White House, a senatorial delegation laid down the law; when Grant "agreed to 'harmony,' " says Josephy, "by his capitulation [he] confirmed, in his first month in office, control by the Senate Republicans over patronage and the government"—control that would last, with rare exceptions, for the rest of the nineteenth century.

But mostly the power of the Senate grew because of the changes in America. At the close of the Civil War, the nation that sent senators to Washington was still primarily an agricultural country, its young manufacturing and industrial plant a child alongside that of a Great Britain or a Germany. But although the soldiers of the Blue and Gray went back to the farm when they laid down their rifles, many of them would later move to the city, or their children would move to the city—to old cities into which, at the same time, European immigrants were flooding by the hundreds of thousands, by the millions, or to the new cities that were springing up across the continent. Railroads were knitting that continent together; its gold and silver and iron ore was being hauled out of the earth in the West, its black gold was being pumped out of the earth in Pennsylvania and Texas—America was in the midst of a gigantic industrial expansion; by the end of the century, from a child among nations of the earth it had become a colossus.

The great industrialists of the post–Civil War era—the robber barons of these "Middle Ages of American industry"—needed government, needed it for franchises and land grants for their railroads, for legislative sanctions that would allow them to loot the new nation's oil and iron, for subsidies for the monopolies they were creating. So they moved into government, pouring money into political campaigns—and into politicians; the Standard Oil Company, it was said, did everything possible to the Pennsylvania State Legislature except refine it—with unhappily predictable results: by 1920, America's elected representatives had turned over to the railroad barons as much land as the states of Illinois, Indiana, Michigan, Ohio, and Wisconsin combined. At the same time that business was going into politics, politics was becoming more businesslike. State political machines, fueled by businessmen's contributions, grew stronger, better organized. And with government necessarily taking on more functions in a steadily more complex society, tens of thousands of new federal jobs were being created, and control over this burgeoning patronage was solidified in the state machines, whose leaders became great political bosses. Finding that they had an identity of interest, barons and bosses forged what Josephy calls an "unspoken alliance"—

> In return for their contributions to the machines and favors to the leaders, the railroad builders, oil and steel men, pork packers, mining and timber interests and scores of other corporate groups got public lands, rights of way, charters, subsidies, franchises and other legislative advantages.

And the stronghold of that alliance was the Senate. Some of the captains of finance and industry who ruled this era—Leland Stanford, founder of the Central Pacific Railroad; James G. (Bonanza) Fair of Nevada, who extracted $30 million from the Comstock Lode; Philetus Sawyer of Wisconsin, a onetime lumberjack who made a fortune in timber, and who was so illiterate that he could not spell his first name but so powerful that he bought men "as he bought saw logs"—decided to go to Capitol Hill, and of course it was to the Senate, elected by the legislatures, that they went, rather than the House, since why would men who controlled legislatures submit their fate to the people? During this era, the Senate numbered men rich not only in cash but in political currency as well. Gaunt, horse-faced Zach Chandler dispensed thousands of state and federal jobs in Michigan while he entertained like a king in his Washington mansion. Golden-bearded Roscoe Conkling of New York, "the chief ornament of a gaudy era's public life," swaggered among the Senate desks, conspicuous among his soberly clad colleagues in a costume that might consist of green trousers, a scarlet coat with gold lace, and yellow shoes. His vast army of ward heelers included the thousand employees of the notorious New York Customs House. During these thirty years, the Senate was the "fount of political power" not only within the national Republican Party, which, as Josephy puts it, "was more like an organized confederacy of many individual senator-bosses," but within the government. An historian calls these decades the era of the "Senate Supreme."

But supremacy did not mean glory. Mark Twain's bitter name for the era was the "Gilded Age"—gilt atop brass; dazzling on the surface, base metal below; brazen and tawdry, as the frantic rush to wealth, coupled with a morality suddenly loosened after the tension of war, spawned corruption in business and in all levels of government: the historian Vernon L. Parrington called the era the "Great Barbecue," because the rush for a share of the national pie reminded him of hungry picnickers crowding around a savory roast. And sometimes it seemed as if the Senate was leading the rush.

It was the age of "Crédit Mobilier," the scheme in which millions in bribes were distributed in Washington by the promoters of the Union Pacific Railroad. The House of Representatives at least made a gesture at censuring its members who were involved; the Senate would not deign to make even a gesture. Crédit Mobilier came to light in 1872; it was only a harbinger of the scandals to come, of graft and plunder "unequaled before or since in the history of the country," and in these scandals senators were often leading figures. In his novel *Democracy,* published in 1880, Henry Adams called the United States "a government of the people, by the people, for the benefit of Senators."

THERE WERE STILL MOMENTS in which the Senate grappled, as the Founders had intended it to grapple, with the fundamental issues facing the nation.

Outside government, concern about new problems was rising. As industry became concentrated in fewer and fewer hands, the old *laissez-faire* belief faded before fears that the huge new industrial combinations were destroying America's cherished freedom of opportunity, making it harder for men to rise through their own efforts; that the country's natural resources were being cornered and squandered by the few; that city slums were growing and farmers becoming a forgotten class.

Americans confronting forces too big for them to fight alone asked for help in fighting them, from the only force big enough to fight them: the government—their government. It seemed logical to them that government should help. Government was, after all, a basic cause of the problems. It was government that, through its mineral concessions and subsidies, had made the mine owners powerful, so that the men who worked in mines worked their cruelly long hours in danger, and lived as near serfs in company towns. Should not now government protect the miners, or at least make it possible for them to organize, so that they could protect themselves? It was government whose unconscionable subsidies of land had made the railroads powerful, and it was railroads whose freighting charges were strangling the farmer; should now government not stretch forth its hand to farmers by regulating railroads? It was government whose high tariffs had shielded manufacturers—at the expense of the poor and of the farmers, keeping the prices of shoes high while forcing low the price of steer hides that farmers sold to shoe manufacturers. Should not government now revise the tariff system? It was government whose policies had nurtured the growth of the giant corporations that kept wages low and hours long, and made women and children work in sweatshops and live in slums; should not government now intercede on behalf of women and children?

At times during these gilt decades government did help, or at least try to: the Interstate Commerce Act of 1887 established the first regulatory commission with power over a segment of industry; the Sherman Anti-Trust Act of 1890, named for Senator John Sherman, "the Ohio Icicle," made a gesture at restoring competition to American business life. But such moments were rare.

The Senate's leaders during these decades—Republicans all—were men like spade-bearded William Allison of Iowa, trusted friend of the railroads and the banks, who sat in the Senate for thirty-five years, and Nelson Aldrich of Rhode Island, the son of an impoverished farmer, who made one fortune in business, married another, sat in the Senate for thirty years, and thought of "sugar" or "steel" as "a social and political entity" as deserving of representation in Congress as any state or group of citizens.

Allison and Aldrich were members of the "Philosophy Club," a group of wealthy senators who met regularly for dinner and poker. Their doctrine was the survival of the fittest—not surprisingly, since, as Senator George Hearst of California assured his colleagues, "The members of the Senate *are* the survival of the fittest." These robber-baron senators felt that "the best government was the least government—unless they could mold it as a weapon and tool to help the strongest have their way over the weak." The response of the Senate—and of the House, too—to public concern was, in Josephy's words, "to keep hands off of—or to help—the [industrial] development, but certainly not to get in its way."

Before the Civil War, the Senate had been the forum for great debates, for thoughtful deliberation on the floor, that the Founding Fathers had designed it to be. During the decades after the war—the decades of the Gilded Age—it was, as the historian Matthew Josephson reported, "behind closed doors that the real work of Congress is done. Moving noiselessly through committee rooms, parliamentary leaders perfected the process . . . known as 'invisible government.' " Aldrich, it was said, had "but to whisper in the committee rooms" to pass or kill a bill. Since debate mattered less and less, senators spent less and less time on the Senate floor.

The Philosophy Club ran the Senate as if it were a club, too. For more than thirty years, except for a two-year Democratic interlude, one or both of the key Appropriations and Finance Committees was chaired by Allison and Aldrich, as was the Republican caucus, whose decisions now became binding, and the party's Committee on Committees, which determined Republican committee assignments. The initial assignments of newly elected senators to committees had become the entrée to power. Not long after the agreement in 1845 to allow parties to select committee members and chairmen, there had been an additional development. Since the agreement's aim was to reduce intra-party squabbling, it seemed only logical that the assignment of senators to committees and, within committees, their elevation to the chairmanship should no longer be a matter of discussion but rather should be subject to some arbitrary, objective principle—and what principle more objective than simple length of service? The seniority system had thus been introduced in the Senate, and during the intervening decades, the unwritten "seniority rule" had acquired almost the force of law: with rare exceptions, once a man was on a committee, he stayed on it. The effect of this had been to negate the original aim of establishing the system, which was to increase party discipline and loyalty. Since, once a senator was on a committee, he couldn't be removed from it by his party except in the most extraordinary circumstances—in three quarters of a century only three senators were removed—the party lost control of him. So great care was taken in making those initial assignments. The most coveted committee seats went to men whom Aldrich and Allison regarded as "safe." "Dissidents," as Byrd says, were ruthlessly "excluded from influence." (Even before the Civil War, some of seniority's implications had become apparent; since the system made length of incumbency rather than ability the crucial determinant for advancement within a committee, the senators who advanced would in general be senators from "safe" states—states in which voters routinely re-elected incumbents. The safest of states, of course, were "one-party" states, and during the decade before Fort Sumter the South had become more and more one-party—Democratic—so the system had worked to give a disproportionate share of power to that single section of the country. By 1859, a northern senator was complaining that the seniority system had "operated to give to senators from slaveholding states the chairmanship of every single committee that controls the public business of this government. There is not one exception.")

BY CONTROLLING THE SENATE, the Senate "philosophers" were, of course, not merely exercising the Senate's power, but were enjoying as well the protection of the armor that the Founding Fathers had bolted around that institution with so much care—the armor that insulated the Senate against the power of the people.

That armor was as strong as ever. The Coinage Act of 1873 pleased bondholders and bankers, the well-to-do, by making gold the monetary standard, completely eliminating silver as a standard. But farmers and working people, debtors of all types—"those who labor under all the hardships of life," in Madison's words—were infuriated by the "Crime of '73," and this was a majority that in a democracy theoretically exercised political power. In 1874, public feeling did indeed sweep over one wing of the Capitol: the Republicans were removed from power in the House of Representatives for the first time since before the Civil War. But only one-third of the Senate was subject to public feeling; there the Republicans remained, by far, in the majority. The Coinage Act was a major element in plunging the nation into one of the longest depressions in American history, and for the next quarter of a century there would be debate after debate over easing the gold standard. Occasionally, a President would make a move—or the House pass legislation—in that direction. Not the Senate. The same pattern prevailed on the tariff. In 1890, the Democratic President Grover Cleveland proposed tariff reform, and the House, with an eye to the imminent November elections, passed it. The Senate didn't. Year after year, all through the Gilded Age, its power kept the tariff in place.

That pattern prevailed on other major issues. House procedures gradually became more orderly after the election of "Czar" Thomas Reed as Speaker, but senators—particularly those committee chairmen who had held their positions for years—were still the balance wheel of the federal government. A law to authorize federal action against the renewed disenfranchisement of black voters in the South was passed in the House but blocked in the Senate. So was a law that would have banned violence against strikers by private police forces. The Gilded Age, as Josephy says, "was not a day for the weak, the unorganized or the powerless"; the legislative pages of that age are sparse indeed if one searches them for laws that would help farmers, labor, minorities, consumers, or the crowded poor in the wretched slums of the great new cities. All during this time, Americans asked their government for help, but, except for scattered moments like the Sherman Act, help was not forthcoming. Congress, summed up one observer, "does not solve the problems, the solutions of which is demanded by the life of the nation." And for this the Senate must bear a large part of the blame. To a degree perhaps unequaled in any other period of American history, the Gilded Age was the era in which the Senate was the preeminent force in the government of the United States—the "Senate Supreme" indeed. And it was during this era that the government was, as the historian John Garraty puts it, "singularly divorced from what now seem the meaningful issues of the day"—divorced to a degree perhaps unequaled in any other period of American history. Between 1874, when Charles Sumner died, and 1900, not a single figure comparable to Clay, Calhoun, or Webster—or to Benton, or to Seward or to Douglas or to any of a score of other senators of the Senate's Golden Age—sat in that tiered semi-circle of desks. In creating a Senate for the new nation, its Founding Fathers had tried to create within the government an institution that would speak for the educated, the well-born, the well-to-do, that would protect the rights of property, that would not function as an embodiment of the people's will but would rather stand—"firmly"—as a great bulwark against that will.

They had succeeded.

DURING THE GILDED AGE—the era of its greatest power—the Senate sunk from the heights of public esteem to the depths. Its inertia was a subject of public ridicule—"The Senate does about as much in a week as a set of men in business would do in half an hour," one newspaper correspondent wrote—as was the corruption that infected it. And it was the subject of public anger.

Once, Senate and senators had been immortalized in paintings, in a classi-

cal, heroic style that became famous—George Healy's glowing *Webster Replying to Hayne;* Peter Rothermel's majestic *The United States Senate, A.D. 1850;*
Henry F. Darby's *Henry Clay;* Rembrandt Peale's *John C. Calhoun;* Francis
Alexander's "Black Dan" portrait of Webster. Now, it was not classicism but
caricature with which the Senate was depicted. It was chronicled in cartoons—
cartoons so savage and telling that *they* became famous. One of a hundred brilliant depictions of the Senate that appeared in the pictorial weekly *Puck,*
founded in 1877, was Joseph Keppler's "The Bosses of the Senate." The cartoon shows the desks of the Senate, and the senators sitting at them, men drawn
small. Behind the desks, looming menacingly over the little senators, stands a
row of huge, pot-bellied, top-hatted, arrogant "bosses" labeled "Copper Trust,"
"Standard Oil Trust," "Sugar Trust," "Tin Trust." Behind these figures is a sign:
"This Is A Senate of the Monopolists, By the Monopolists, and For the Monopolists." Above, in the gallery, is a "People's Entrance," barred with a padlock
and marked "Closed." Once foreign observers had marveled at the Senate as
"the most remarkable of all the inventions of modern politics." Now their tone
had changed. Writing in 1902, the Russian-born, French-educated political scientist Moisei Ostrogorski would say,

> The Senate of the United States no longer has any resemblance to
> that August assembly which provoked the admiration of the Tocque-
> villes. It would be no use looking for the foremost men of the nation
> there; neither statesmen nor orators are to be found in it. [The body is
> filled] with men of mediocre or no political intelligence, some of
> whom, extremely wealthy, multi-millionaires, look on the senatorial
> dignity as a title for ennobling their well or ill gotten riches, [and
> with] crack wirepullers [and] state bosses [who] find the Senate a
> convenient base of operations for their intrigues and their designs on
> the public interest. . . .

DURING THE GILDED AGE, the Senate's power reached its peak not only in
domestic affairs but in foreign. One-third plus one of the Senate had of course
been given power to reject treaties by the Constitution, and in 1868 the Senate
was given additional power by itself: it revised its standing rules so that treaties
could be *amended*—their text changed—by a simple majority. And throughout
three decades, as Schlesinger notes, "the Senate exercised its power in this
realm with relish, freely rewriting, amending and rejecting treaties negotiated
by the executive." Rejecting was the operative term: between 1871 and 1898
the Senate did not ratify a single significant treaty. Writing in 1885, Professor
Woodrow Wilson said that since a President was forced to deal with the Senate
on treaties "as a servant conferring with a master," its power was unbalancing
the whole system of checks and balances. During this era, senators made policy

in another way as well: as had in fact been the case during the entire nineteenth century, most secretaries of state were former senators.

Nor did the Senate confine its foreign policy role to treaties. Together with the House (and the yellow press), it pushed a cautious President ("I have been through one war," McKinley told a friend. "I have seen the dead piled up, and I do not want to see another") into war with Spain. Only with reluctance was the President finally induced to send the *Maine* to Havana. After it blew up, McKinley still resisted intervention, but a delegation of senators went to Cuba to make their own investigation, and when, upon their return, they told on the Senate floor of Spanish brutality and mass starvation in the *reconcen-trado* camps, the journalistic clamor was suddenly clothed with authority. The Allison-Aldrich clique came down for war; three days later, McKinley issued an ultimatum to Spain; on April 25, 1898, it was war—war on both sides of the world as the young nation's cruisers steamed aline into Manila Bay to destroy the fleet of the old.

And when the war ended, after just four months, and the country suddenly had to confront a great decision, it was among the desks of the Senate that that decision was made. As once, three quarters of a century before, the Senate had debated the wisdom of building a fort on the shore of the far-off Pacific, now the Senate debated the question of whether America's expansion should stop at that shore—or go beyond it; of whether a young nation which had so quickly become a giant power would confine its power to its own continent—or extend it throughout the world; of whether it would still be merely a nation—or an empire. In December, 1898, under a peace treaty hammered out in Paris, Spain relinquished Cuba, and ceded to the United States Puerto Rico, Guam, and, for a token $20 million, the Philippines, an island archipelago seven thousand miles west of the United States.

Subject, of course, to the advice and consent of the American Senate.

The debate in the Senate over ratification of the treaty ending the Spanish-American War was a national soul-searching. It was among the Senate desks—eighty-four of them now—that the imperatives of imperialism confronted other imperatives, imperatives dramatized because even as the debate raged, Filipino nationalists rose in rebellion against American troops, and the debate was conducted against a backdrop of atrocities committed by both sides in a brutal guerrilla war that would last three years and require the commitment of seventy thousand American troops before the independence movement was crushed. Rising for the first time among those desks, thirty-seven-year-old Albert Beveridge of Indiana proved that a single speech in the Senate could still catapult a newly elected senator to national fame. "The Philippines are ours forever," Beveridge said,

> And just beyond the Philippines are China's illimitable markets. We will not retreat from either. . . . We will not renounce our part in the

mission of our race, trustees under God, of the civilization of the world. . . . God has marked us as his chosen people, henceforth to lead in the regeneration of the world. . . . He has made us adept in government that we administer government among savages and senile people.

And it was among those desks that seventy-two-year-old George Hoar of Massachusetts rose to reply—in a voice trembling with anger.

I have listened, delighted, as have, I suppose, all the members of the Senate, to the eloquence of my honorable friend from Indiana. . . . Yet, Mr. President, as I heard his eloquent description of wealth and commerce and trade, I listened in vain for those words which the American people have been wont to take upon their lips in every crisis. . . . The words Right, Justice, Duty, Freedom were absent, my friend must permit me to say, from that eloquent speech.

Anti-imperialists said governing a foreign country without its consent was a violation of the spirit of the Declaration of Independence; the United States was "trampling on our own great Charter" in the Philippines, Hoar declared. Henry Cabot Lodge responded that that was not the point, since "the Philippines mean a vast future trade and wealth and power."

The vote on the treaty was very close. Fifty-six of the eighty-four votes would be necessary for ratification, and the vote, taken in February, 1899, was 57 to 27. That was the vote—a vote in the Senate—that set the stage for the American Century.

As the nineteenth century drew to a close, the Senate had been the dominant entity in the American government for perhaps three quarters of that century. If its glory was gone, its Golden Age vanished long before, its power seemed as great as ever.

BUT THEN CAME the twentieth century.

Suddenly, with that treaty, the United States was no longer merely a nation but an empire—an empire with colonies stretching from the Caribbean to the China Sea. The oceans were no longer broad moats that protected and insulated an infant republic and let it grow strong, but lakes over whose surface sped the Republic's powerful fleets, lakes on the far side of which were the Republic's colonies and coaling stations, sources of its raw materials, markets for its industries, lakes dotted with islands—Puerto Rico, Cuba, Hawaii, the Philippines, Guam, Samoa, other, smaller Pacific islands—vital to American interests, in some cases garrisoned by American troops. And with the acquisition of colonies came, all at once, new needs—a navy powerful enough to keep open the sea lanes to the colonies, an Isthmian canal so the navy's squadrons could be shifted rapidly between ocean and ocean, protection for the canal's Caribbean approaches. Indeed, the acquisition of colonies created problems beyond the immediately obvious: had not America brought peace and stability to Cuba?—was it not only logical then, "for economic, strategic and humanitarian reasons," to bring peace and stability to the entire region, to supervise much of the Caribbean and Central America? And, as Americans were to discover in the very first years of the "American Century"—in that "revolt" (or "War for Independence") in the faraway Philippines—conquering a country was easier than governing it. All at once, with American citizens, property, and commercial interests scattered all over the globe, there were decisions to be made: whether or not to send troops to protect them from imminent menace; decisions on how far to go in countering Russian expansion in Manchuria; on how to deal with Santo Domingo's default on debts to European nations—a default that led France and Italy to threaten immediate intervention in the Western Hemisphere. And these were decisions that couldn't wait for Senate deliberations; there were threats and maneuvers that might come when the Senate was not in session, and that had to be met immediately.

And suddenly there was a President who was confident that he could make these decisions by himself. Senatorial power had been a coefficient of presidential weakness, and for thirty years, Presidents had been either inexperienced like Grant, or indecisive, or simply cowed by the mighty Senate. But with the crack of the assassin's gunshot that struck down McKinley, and, to the rage of Senator Mark Hanna, put "that damned cowboy" Theodore Roosevelt in the White House, the era of weak Presidents was over.

The executive agreement—the international covenant devised by the President acting alone—had had its origin almost a century before in certain murky phrases in the Constitution. "Gradually, in a way that neither historians nor legal scholars have made altogether clear"—but largely, it appears, because in the early nineteenth century the Senate accepted the device to spare itself the task of considering a multitude of technical agreements—it obtained the color of usage, but almost entirely for minor matters. But when, in 1901, Roosevelt became President, the executive agreement became almost the order of the day.

When the Senate moved too slowly for Roosevelt's taste in ratifying a treaty with Santo Domingo to forestall European intervention, Roosevelt, as he himself described it, "put the agreement into effect, and I continued its execution for two years before the Senate acted; and I would have continued it until the end of my term, if necessary, without any action by Congress." In another executive agreement—one kept so secret that historians would not discover its existence for two decades—Roosevelt agreed to Japan's imposition of a military protectorate on Korea.

Coupled with the rise of the executive agreement was what Arthur Schlesinger calls a "new presidential exuberance" about the use of armed force "on the pretexts of protecting American citizens and property." Roosevelt, often without congressional permission, dispatched American regiments to Caribbean countries and installed provisional governments.

What would have been the result had the Senate resisted TR's expansion of executive authority in foreign affairs cannot be known—because the Senate did not resist. It refused to assert the powers in foreign affairs that the Framers had given it. Time after time, when a senator proposed an amendment limiting the new executive authority—denying appropriations for military forces sent to foreign countries without congressional consent, for example—the Senate's GOP rulers saw to it that the amendment was voted down. "I say there is no law, and I do not believe there ever was a law to prevent the Commander-in-Chief of . . . the United States from . . . giving [American citizens] the protection required by self-respect," Senator Elihu Root declared. A President's authority as Commander-in-Chief therefore allowed him to send troops "unless it be for the purpose of making war, which of course he cannot do." As the trend toward executive action continued during the Taft Administration, protests in the Senate grew louder. But, as Schlesinger summarizes, "whatever the nuances of arguments, limitations were evaporating. The executive was becoming habituated to the unconstrained deployment of American forces around the world, and Congress chose not to say him nay." As Roosevelt himself was to say, "The biggest matters, such as the Portsmouth peace, the acquisition of Panama, and sending the fleet around the world, I managed without consultation with anyone. . . ." To a considerable extent, TR was only telling the truth. Furthermore, precedents had now been established. Following bloodshed in Tampico in 1914, Woodrow Wilson asked congressional sanction to send troops to protect American citizens in Mexico. There was doubt among senators over whether the provocation justified Wilson's reaction, but, trapped by what Hamilton had called the "antecedent state of things," they approved the move. No President—and perhaps no outside force of any type—could have so drastically weakened the Senate's power in foreign affairs. The Founding Fathers had given the Senate armor that should have prevented that. But the Senate could weaken itself—and it had done so, stripping away much of its own authority over foreign affairs.

BUT NOT ALL OF IT—as, in 1919, Woodrow Wilson discovered.

When the President sailed for Europe to personally represent the United States at the peace conference convening in Paris, warships in New York Harbor fired salutes, a huge throng filled Battery Park to cheer him off on his historic journey, and as his liner passed through the Narrows, his fellow passengers saw, all along the Brooklyn and Staten Island shorelines, children waving flags. When the ship pulled into Brest, posters on the walls of the old slate-roofed stone houses called on all Frenchmen to praise this world hero

who had come "to found a new order on the rights of peoples, and to stop forever the return of atrocious war." The American President's idealistic aims had
captured the imagination of a war-weary world. In isolated villages in Italy,
peasants burned candles before his portrait. All over Europe, crowds cheered
him as he paraded through the streets, a reception which, as one historian puts
it delicately, "tended to increase his sense of mission." And not only was the
peace treaty signed at Versailles in May, 1919, the remarkably moderate treaty
that Wilson wanted, but incorporated within the body of the treaty was a
Covenant, or Constitution, for a world organization for peace, a "League of
Nations," which he had determined to bring into being, so that the treaty would
be "definitely a guarantee of peace." And the American people were, by a substantial majority, in favor of the proposed League in principle, and newspapers
supported it by a margin of four to one.

But it was not the people of the United States who would determine the
fate of the League of Nations but the Senate of the United States—and the
Majority Leader of the Senate, who commanded from Daniel Webster's desk,
was Henry Cabot Lodge.

Dr. Lodge (Ph.D., Harvard), historian and author, had been known as "the
Scholar in Politics" before the advent on the political scene of Dr. Woodrow
Wilson (Ph.D., Johns Hopkins), historian and author, who promptly was
awarded that title as if Lodge had never held it. The Senator loathed the President. "I never expected to hate anyone in politics with the hatred I feel toward
Wilson," he had written a friend some years before; he told other friends that
the President was "shifty," "the most sinister figure that ever crossed the country's path." The feeling was reciprocated. The Republican senators, particularly
Lodge, were "pygmy-minded—narrow . . . selfish . . . poor little minds that
never get anywhere but run around in a circle and think they are going somewhere," Wilson said. So strained were relations between the two men that at
one ceremony Wilson refused to sit on the same platform with the Senator.

Piled atop the personal considerations were the political. In a wartime
truce on politics, Republicans had in many instances supported Wilson's war
program more loyally than Democrats, but just before the 1918 congressional
elections, Wilson had suddenly appealed to voters to return Democratic majorities to both houses. Furious Republicans considered the appeal a betrayal, and
some of them—none more so than Lodge—saw it as confirmation of what they
had long suspected was the President's unbridled lust for power; Lodge
believed that Wilson was planning to run for a third term, in 1920, and, that the
President, anxious to be acclaimed as the peacemaker to boost his re-election
prospects, was sacrificing the independence of the United States to the League.
And when Wilson's appeal backfired—the Republicans took control of both
houses, although by a mere two-vote margin in the Senate—the President's
most bitter enemy was elevated not only to the Senate's majority leadership but
to the chairmanship of its Foreign Relations Committee.

For Lodge, moreover, the personal and political considerations were reinforced by the philosophical. His twenty-six years in the Senate had been
twenty-six years of uncompromising advocacy of an assertive, unilateralist foreign policy backed by strong armed forces. He wanted a peace that would
strengthen America's position relative to the European powers. "The thing to
do," he had said during the war, "is to lick Germany and tell her what arrangements we are going to make." Above all, he believed in the sovereignty and
independence of the United States; the international cooperation that was the
centerpiece of Wilson's League he viewed as a menace to America's need to
preserve absolute freedom of action to pursue and protect its own interests.

And he believed in the sovereignty and independence of the Senate of the
United States. He revered the Senate, with a reverence grounded in the same
philosophy that had inspired the Founding Fathers to create it. As he was to
write in 1921,

> [it] has never been, legally speaking, reorganized. It has been in con-
> tinuous and organized existence for 132 years, because two-thirds of
> the Senate being always in office, there has never been such a thing
> as the Senate requiring reorganization as is the case with each newly
> elected House. . . . There may be no House of Representatives, but
> merely an unorganized body of members elect; there may be no
> President duly installed in office. But there is always the organized
> Senate of the United States.

Never, he felt, had the threat to senatorial sovereignty been greater. A
series of strong Presidents had chipped away at it, aiming "at weakening if not
breaking down the government as nearly as possible to one which consists of
the executive and the voters, the simplest and most rudimentary form of human
government which history can show," he said. And now Wilson was trying to
destroy it entirely.

The very symbol and heart of that sovereignty was, to Lodge, the Senate's
power over treaties. "War can be declared without the assent of the Executive,
and peace can be made without the assent of the House," he had once pointed
out. "But neither war nor peace can be made without the assent of the Senate."
A treaty, he emphasized, is not a treaty just because a President has entered into
it. A treaty is "still inchoate, a mere project for a treaty, until the consent of the
Senate has been given to it." Therefore, he said, "The responsibility of a Senator in dealing with any question of peace is as great in his sphere as that of the
President in his." Personal malice toward Wilson, political scheming—these
were elements in Lodge's motivation. But, as James MacGregor Burns has
written, "at the core of the hostility . . . lay genuine differences of outlook and
principle."

Woodrow Wilson's "faith in representative democracy, in majority rule, in
the ultimate wisdom of the people, went," as Burns put it, "to the very core of

his being"—as did his belief in the superiority of his mental processes to those of "pygmy-minded" senators. This feeling was evident in the makeup of the five-member delegation he selected to accompany him to Paris. While President McKinley had included three senators on the five-member delegation negotiating the treaty ending the Spanish-American War, Wilson took no senators with him; he apparently was resolved to have no opposition in his delegation. His announcement that his chief adviser would be his little-known personal confidant, Colonel Edward M. House, caused distress even on the Democratic side of the Senate. "Who is this Colonel House?" Arizona's Henry Ashurst demanded. "Whence did he come, what has he accomplished, and where is he headed?" Wilson was unmoved. Returning to the United States for necessary bill-signing work in March, he reported that the treaty and the Covenant were linked—and then sailed again for France. When Lodge fired a warning shot across his bow—rising at his desk to read to the Senate just before it adjourned at midnight, March 3, 1919, a "Round Robin" declaring that the League "in the form now proposed" was unacceptable to the United States, a Round Robin bearing the signatures of thirty-seven Republican senators and senators-elect—Wilson reacted with contempt. "Anyone who opposes me . . . I'll crush!" he told the French ambassador. "I shall consent to nothing. *The Senate must take its medicine.*" He had outsmarted the Senate, he felt. He boasted to the world that when the treaty was brought back, "the gentlemen on this side will find the Covenant not only tied into it, but so many threads on the treaty tied to the Covenant that you cannot dissect the Covenant from the treaty without destroying the whole vital structure." He assumed, in the words of one historian, that "The Senate would not dare to kill the peace treaty outright." It would have no choice but to consent.

Which showed that the onetime constitutional scholar had forgotten some of his lessons. Thirty-seven Republicans, more than the thirty-one necessary to block a treaty, had already declared this treaty unacceptable. Even if every Democrat voted to ratify it (and several Democrats had their own reservations about it), it would not be ratified so long as the Republicans remained united.

And the leader of the Republicans knew how to keep them united; Lodge had, after all, served his apprenticeship under Aldrich and Allison. Now, in 1919, "No one knew better than he the various devices and methods by which a treaty could be killed, nor had anyone more practice in the use of them," commented the historian W. Stull Holt. More than a dozen Republicans, led by the rigid isolationists Robert La Follette, William E. Borah, and Hiram Johnson, felt even more strongly about the treaty than did Lodge, so strongly that they were dubbed the "irreconcilables." About a dozen "mild reservationists" approved the League in principle but wanted minor alterations. And a middle bloc of Republicans—"strong reservationists"—were willing to go along with the League only if American sovereignty was guaranteed. In a series of compromises, Lodge bound the three groups together in a solid front behind a series of fourteen reservations (fourteen to match Wilson's Fourteen Points;

newspapermen would dub them the "Lodge Reservations") so that the Treaty of Versailles could be ratified only if these reservations—which would protect America's sovereignty and freedom of action (but which would also have made the League a substantially weaker organization than the one Wilson had envisioned)—were added to the treaty. At the height of public enthusiasm for the treaty, Lodge had calmly reassured an ally, "The only people who have votes on the treaty are here in the Senate." And he, not the President, had the votes.

Moreover, he had the Senate's inviolable rules under which a proposed treaty had to be considered by the Foreign Relations Committee before it could be considered by the Senate as a whole—and on the committee, he had a solid majority, for its Republican members were either "irreconcilables" or less ideological skeptics like Warren G. Harding of Ohio. By the time the President of the United States returned from Versailles in his glory, the Senate of the United States was arrayed against him in its might. On July 10, 1919, the day following his return, Woodrow Wilson entered the Senate Chamber with a bulky copy of the treaty under his arm and presented it to the Senate in a speech that enunciated the noble ideals behind it—"Dare we reject it and break the heart of the world? . . . We cannot turn back. We can only go forward, with lifted eyes and freshened spirit, to follow the vision. . . . America shall in truth show the way. . . ." But hardly had the President finished and left the Chamber when Senator Lodge rose at his desk to utter a single quiet sentence that had as much significance as all Wilson's eloquence. He wished to move, the Senator said, to refer the treaty to the Foreign Relations Committee.

Woodrow Wilson was now to be reminded of the power of the Senate. The President's eloquence, as Burns puts it, "reverberated through press and public," a press and public favorable to the idea of a League of Nations. But Lodge and other opponents of the League believed that if the public was educated to the possible sacrifices of American sovereignty to an international body, public opinion would change. Ample funding from Republican bankers was available to finance this education—a massive public relations campaign—but time was needed for the campaign to accomplish its purpose. And the Founding Fathers had created the Senate to provide such time, to be the "cooler" for public opinion, to "refine and enlarge the public views" and produce "the cool and deliberated sense of the community."

The proposed treaty was 268 pages long. Lodge began the Foreign Relations Committee hearings by reading the treaty aloud—every page—in a committee room empty except for a single clerk, who took down what he said. That took two weeks. Then the committee called witnesses, scores of witnesses, to testify against the treaty. And while Lodge was thus playing for time, his allies were flooding the country with anti-League advertising and holding anti-League rallies in major cities, rallies at which the speakers were often senators.

The battle was a throwback to the great senatorial debates of the previous century in which long, closely reasoned Senate speeches had been reported fully in the press and discussed, in town meetings and on street corners, across the country. One speech—two hours long, delivered in August in a steaming hot Chamber by Lodge himself—is all but forgotten today, but whatever the validity of its reasoning, it nonetheless expressed that reasoning with the eloquence and power of that earlier age.

> You may call me selfish, if you will, conservative or reactionary, or use any other harsh adjective you see fit to apply, but an American I was born, an American I have remained all my life. I can never be anything else but an American, and I must think of the United States first in an arrangement like this. I am thinking of what is best for the world, for if the United States fails the best hopes of mankind fail with it. I have never had but one allegiance—I cannot divide it now. I have loved but one flag and I cannot share that devotion and give affection to the mongrel banner invented for a League.

For many of the speeches, the galleries were as packed and attentive as they had been for Webster, Clay, and Calhoun. As one historian has written, if Lodge "had wondered whether the campaign to convert the American people to his views was working, on the day he spoke he received ample and gratifying proof from the galleries"—which were packed, not only with representatives of women's organizations but with a contingent of Marines who had fought at Château-Thierry, and who had, in fact, come to the Senate Chamber directly from a parade in which they had passed in review before President Wilson. When Lodge finished, mothers and Marines stood and cheered him before the ushers could quiet them down. And there was another reminder of the Great Triumvirate: hundreds of thousands of copies of Lodge's speech were printed and distributed across the country.

Although Wilson fumed at the slow pace of Lodge's hearings, the President couldn't persuade the senators to speed up. "Mustering," in Burns' words, "all his presidential and personal influence," he used face-to-face persuasion, "talking to senators individually and in small groups," writing "private letters" to wavering Republicans. But the Founding Fathers, fearing executive power, had armored the Senate against it. The power of the President may have swept across the country, and indeed across part of Capitol Hill. It came to a halt at the door to the Senate Chamber.

When Wilson summoned Senator James Watson of Indiana to the White House and asked him, "Where am I on this fight?" Watson replied, "Mr. President, you are licked. There is only one way you can take the United States into the League of Nations." "Which way is that?" "Accept it with the Lodge reservations." "*Lodge* reservations? Never! I'll never consent to any policy with which that impossible name is so prominently identified." The President decided to rally public opinion behind the League by going on a cross-country speaking tour, to, he said, "appeal to Caesar"—the people. But Wilson had evidently forgotten what happened to Caesar—and who did it.

Wilson's tour of the country was an epic of eloquence. "I have it in my heart that if we do not do this great thing now, every woman ought to weep because of the child in her arms," he prophesied. "If she has a boy at her breast, she may be sure that when he comes to manhood this terrible task will have to be done once more." It was an epic of courage and will, as the President fought against mind-numbing headaches that seemed to grow steadily worse until finally he was struck by a premonitory stroke—and even then he tried to fight against returning to Washington, where, after another stroke, he hovered paralyzed and nearly blind for weeks on the edge of death. But eloquence, and the public opinion aroused by it, couldn't make even a dent in the Senate armor. As Burns summarizes: "By crusading for the League, Wilson had indeed nearly thrown his own life away—yet he had not succeeded in changing a single vote in the Senate."

Refusing to compromise, the President instructed the Democrats to vote against Lodge's fourteen amendments, and they were defeated. But Wilson's proposed treaty was defeated, too. "For decades," as Burns puts it, "scholars have asked why Wilson allowed the treaty to go down in defeat, why he did not just swallow hard and accept the Lodge reservations as one more necessary concession." Many have speculated that the reason was physical, that Wilson's judgment was clouded, his stubbornness increased, by his stroke. But there was a political reason, too—a definitive one in political terms. There was no necessity for the Republican moderates to compromise. Two-thirds plus one of the Senate was required for passage of a treaty, and Wilson didn't have two-thirds. Wilson's last hope—his attempt in 1920 to make the upcoming presidential election "a great and solemn referendum" on the issue of the League—was snuffed out by the election of Senator Harding, who declared in his inaugural address that "We seek no part in directing the destinies of the world."

The Senate's victory over the Treaty of Versailles proved again that the powers given that body by the Founding Fathers were strong enough to stand against the power of the executive and the power of public opinion—strong enough to stand, if necessary, against both at once. "Ultimately," as Burns has written, "Wilson's League was not killed by him, by the Senate Democrats who voted as Wilson instructed them, by the irreconcilables, or even by Lodge. It was thwarted by a political system. . . . Lodge, it is true, manipulated that system brilliantly, but he had only inherited it. In the struggle over the Treaty of Versailles, the American system of checks and balances worked as the Founding Fathers intended that it should." Woodrow Wilson was defeated by a body he considered both unrepresentative and oligarchical. He was right. The Senate was unrepresentative and oligarchical. But it had the power.

. . .

BUT WHAT had the Senate done with that power? "If we do not do this great thing now . . . the terrible task will have to be done once more," Woodrow Wilson had warned. Was his analysis correct? Would another world war have come—as it came only twenty years later—if the Senate of the United States had ratified the Treaty of Versailles, and the Covenant of Nations?

No one can be certain of the answer. Even if the United States had joined the League, would the country, with an isolationist spirit still heavy on the land, have been willing, when called upon, to meet its obligations? Would the other great powers have been willing? In the event, of course, when they were challenged by aggressor nations, they proved, despite many pledges, to be unwilling. But there is at least a possibility that America's participation in the League might have heartened the Western democracies when Hitler and Mussolini began to test their will. There is at least a possibility that if *all* the democracies had been united, history might have been different. The Senate, which in the previous century, during its Golden Age, had kept alive for forty years—forty vital years—the possibility of peace for the Union, in the twentieth century had struck a great, perhaps mortal, blow at the possibility of peace for the world. In the nineteenth century, the Senate had played a significant—for a considerable portion of that century, a dominant—role in America's foreign policy. In the first two decades of the twentieth century, it had played a much more minor role in foreign affairs. It had made a single significant decision—and that decision had been a tragedy.

AND IN DOMESTIC AFFAIRS, the record was—if possible—worse.

With the dawn of the new century, the public's demand for an end to trusts and to the high protective tariff that was "the mother of trusts," the tariff that robbed farmers and gouged consumers, and that had now been in place for almost fifty years—the demand, for legislation to ameliorate the injustices of the Industrial Revolution, that had begun to rise during the Gilded Age, only to be thwarted in part by the Senate—began to rise faster, fed by the books of Jacob Riis and Lincoln Steffens and Theodore Dreiser and a hundred other authors; by the new mass-circulation magazines, which, in the very first years of the twentieth century, educated America about the manipulations of Standard Oil and stirred its conscience to the horrors of sweatshops and child labor (in 1900, almost two million boys and girls were working, often alongside their mothers, all the daylight hours seven days a week in rooms in which there might not be a single window); and by the Populist and Grange movements, which gave farmers insight into the power that railroads and banks had over their lives, and into their helplessness against them. These feelings now crested in a great wave of humanitarian concern, an outraged, impassioned demand for social justice, that became known as the Progressive Movement. That wave swept over city halls. Long-entrenched boss rule was swept aside by reform mayors in a hundred cities. It swept over statehouses; reform governors pushed through child labor laws and laws increasing protection from, and compensation for, on-the-job injuries. And with McKinley's assassination, there was suddenly, in Theodore Roosevelt, a President who reformers felt was one of their own—their moral leader, in fact: the very embodiment of the popular will, of the spirit of reform, of Progressivism, was in the White House.

At the other end of Pennsylvania Avenue were the Supreme Court, the House, and the Senate. All were far more conservative than the spirit of the age, but the Court could act only in areas in which it was asked to rule, and while the House was a force against Progressivism during a relatively brief period in which Joseph Cannon reigned as Speaker, the rest of the time that still-growing body—it would reach 435 members in 1910—was in its customary disarray, a force against, or for, nothing.

The Senate was not in disarray. As the Foreign Relations Committee had been its stronghold against the League, against Progressivism the stronghold was the Finance Committee, still dominated by Allison, Aldrich, John Spooner of Wisconsin, and Thomas Platt of New York. The "Senate Four" or the "Big Four," as they were known, still met in summer at Aldrich's great castle in Narragansett, near Newport—four aging men in stiff high white collars and dark suits (Aldrich, being at home, might occasionally unbend to wear a blazer) even on the hottest days, sitting on a colonnaded porch in rockers and wicker chairs deciding Republican policy—a policy that was still based on an unshaken belief in *laissez-faire* and the protective tariff. And, as the *New York Times* reported: "The four bosses of the Senate can and do control that body. This means that these four men can block and defeat anything the president or the House may desire." Aware of this power, the new President was aware too that senators would play a key role in disposing of the presidential renomination he coveted. And while in certain areas he moved against the "trusts" with unprecedented vigor, ordering his Attorney General to initiate suits to protect miners from the strike-breaking tactics of the big coal operators, and although he continually proclaimed the need for "Government" supervision "over business," the supervision turned out, during his first term, to be limited to "executive actions" he could take on his own authority, without the need for legislation from Congress. When he ventured toward broader moves he always took the Senate into account. His rhetoric was as dramatic as even the most passionate Progressive could have hoped, but in August, 1902, the Big Four, along with several other senatorial elders, including Mark Hanna, the man who made McKinley, traveled to Roosevelt's home on Long Island for an all-day conference. A month later, there was another conference—and this time it was the President who came to the senators, sailing across Long Island Sound to Narragansett, where the senators were waiting for him at Aldrich's castle. And thereafter TR's speeches on the tariff and the monetary system were first submitted to Aldrich for approval; on one occasion, the President wrote the Senator that "I want to be sure to get what I say on these two subjects along lines upon which all of us can agree." Dynamic in delivery though the speeches continued to be, they were somewhat less so in content; abrupt changes in the tariff would be dangerous, he said; any changes that were made should be managed by experts, working "primarily from the standpoint of business interests." ("Sound and wise" words, Allison and Spooner said.)

In 1904, the American people's demand for social justice—a demand now in its fourth decade—carried Roosevelt to election in his own right. "The current he rode was . . . public opinion," Josephson says. "In 1904 it ran more swiftly, stronger than ever in the direction of popular reform." Encouraged, the President turned to what he called the "paramount issue": the regulation of railroads for which farmers had pleaded for thirty years, while for thirty years, discriminatory freighting charges had kept rising. The country rallied behind TR when he called on Congress to give the Interstate Commerce Commission authority over rates and regulations, and the House, by a majority of 346 to 7, passed a strong bill.

At first glance, prospects in the Senate seemed unprecedentedly favorable. Platt was dying, Allison and Spooner were in their last terms; 1905 marked the arrival in the Senate of a group of independent Republicans such as Borah of Idaho, who took their cue from Wisconsin's "Little Giant," the reformer Robert La Follette. Progressives felt their time had come.

Dying though the Old Guard may have been, however, it wasn't surrendering. When Beveridge spoke for railroad regulation, Aldrich, his suave façade cracking for once, snarled at the young senator, "We'll get you for this." When La Follette, fresh from his triumphs in the provinces, rose in the Senate to give his maiden speech, a plea for regulation, one by one the Republican elders stood up at their desks and stalked out of the Chamber. By the time the railroad bill finally emerged from the Senate, and then from a Senate-House conference committee, the strong House measure had been drastically watered down.

Theodore Roosevelt's subsequent victories in the Progressive cause—protection of the nation's forests, for example, and regulation of the food and drug industries—were generally victories that did not require Senate concurrence (or, after 1905, when Speaker Joseph Cannon solidified his control of the House, the concurrence of that body). Denouncing "malefactors of great wealth," the President came out for federal income and inheritance taxes that would begin a leveling of wealth, for broader regulation of corporations, and for reforms in factory working conditions. The Senate's Old Guard (and the House's Cannon) decided that reform had gone far enough—and that was as far as reform went. Although as the champion of the American people, TR had campaigned for almost eight years against economic injustice, his victories—at

least his domestic victories—were generally achieved by the exercise of his
executive authority. He had managed to broaden that authority, but only to the
point at which it conflicted with legislative power. When he left office there
was still no federal child labor law, no effective federal workmen's compensation law. The problems posed by trusts and tariffs had not been resolved. And
the Senate was the principal reason.

AND WHEN, IN 1909, there was a new President, there was still the Old
Guard—as was demonstrated in their first encounter. William Howard Taft had
been advocating tariff reduction—a reduction desired by the overwhelming
majority of the American people—since he was a young man. The Republican
Party platform of 1908 had contained an "unequivocal" pledge for tariff revision, and Taft quickly summoned Congress into special session to pass a tariff
bill "drawn in good faith with the [platform's] promises." The House of Representatives passed one—a measure that would substantially reduce many
duties—but its bill was then sent to the Senate Finance Committee. Allison,
Platt, and Spooner were gone, but their places around the green baize committee table were filled by other Old Guard stalwarts, and the committee's gavel
was still in the hand of Nelson Aldrich. Hearings were held behind closed
doors, and the bill that was reported out was no longer a bill for tariff reduction
but for tariff increases: of 847 amendments on individual items, 600 raised
existing rates.

As a "prairie fire" of indignation spread across an outraged nation, editorials denounced Aldrich as "dictator," "despot," "tyrant," but the Founding
Fathers had armored the Senate against indignation, and Aldrich did not even
attempt to conceal his contempt for the people. His only response was a sneer
on the Senate floor. Certainly, the Republican platform had promised tariff
"revision," he said, but "where did we ever make the statement that we would
revise the tariff *downward*?"

Taft gave in, but ten Progressive Republicans, led by La Follette, decided
to fight. Among them were some of the era's greatest orators, and the battle
they made on the Senate floor day after day, all through a long, hot, Washington
summer, in a debate out of the Senate's long-gone Golden Age—a battle
against not only a President of their own party but against the mighty Aldrich as
well—was the great topic of the hour; reporters crowded the Press Gallery
above the presiding officer's dais; teletypes clattered with news; on the
summer-baked streets of cities and towns all across America men and women
discussed the arguments made on the floor of America's Senate, among those
four curved rows of mahogany and red leather. And all during that summer of
1909 public outrage against Aldrich and the Old Guard rose.

But the Senate had been created to stand against public opinion. Aldrich's
bill passed easily, and so did the "compromise" Act that emerged from a

stacked conference committee—an Act that La Follette branded "the consummation of privilege more reprehensible than had ever found a place in the statutes of the country." It was quickly signed into law by Taft. When Aldrich had first reported his bill out of committee, and the "prairie fire" had been raging against it, the Senator had predicted calmly that the bill would pass substantially as he had written it. The prediction had proven correct.

DURING THE remaining years of Taft's presidency, there would be a few victories for reformers to celebrate, but only a few. By March, 1910, Cannon had been ousted as Speaker, and in the elections that November, public indignation removed the GOP from control of the House. But in the Senate, that indignation echoed only faintly, and when, in 1911, Aldrich retired, the Old Guard's ranks simply closed around the gap, as solidly as ever. And Taft continued to "compromise" with—more accurately, to surrender to—the Senate's power. At the end of the Taft Administration in 1913, as at the end of the Roosevelt Administration in 1909, a supposedly representative republic had not come to grips with concentrated economic power, or with the impact of that power on the human condition. A tide of concern about the impact of industrial concentration on America had begun rising during the Gilded Age—had begun rising soon after the end of the Civil War in 1865, in fact. At first, the tide had risen slowly, but by the 1880s and '90s, it was rising fast. But all through the Gilded Age, the Senate had stood against the tide.

At the turn of the century, with the onset of the Progressive Era, the tide became a wave—a great wave of conscience, of anger over injustice, of demand for a cleansing of government and for a mobilization of government to meet the needs of its people. The wave of Progressivism and reform washed across America, through statehouses and city halls, even through the White House. When the wave crashed against the Senate, it broke on the Senate, the waters falling away from it as they had been falling away for half a century. The Senate stood as it had been standing for so long—a mighty dam standing athwart, and stemming, the tides of social justice.

2

"Great Things Are Underway!"

IN 1913, Woodrow Wilson, who had been swept into the White House by the wave, was inaugurated—and the gates of the dam swung open at last.

In his inaugural address, Wilson said that "We have not hitherto stopped thoughtfully enough to count the human cost . . . of our industrial achievements. . . . The great Government we loved has too often been made use of for private and selfish purposes, and those who used it had forgotten the people." And he knew the cure: presidential leadership; the President, who had the people behind him, must, to meet "conditions that menace our civilization," formulate a comprehensive legislative program and push it through to passage.

For a century—ever since Thomas Jefferson, to emphasize the separation between executive and legislative branches, had ended the practice—no President had appeared in person before Congress. But in April, 1913, Wilson did so, announcing to a joint session the first bill he wanted Congress to take up: a new tariff reduction measure. (The revenue lost was to be made up by instituting a graduated income tax.) For the first time in a quarter of a century, there were Democratic majorities in both houses of Congress, and many of the new Democrats in the Senate shared Wilson's philosophy, and were willing, at least during the first year of his Administration, to accept his direction, as was the Leader they selected, John Worth Kern of Indiana, who had been in the Senate only two years. The Republican ranks had been broken at last—by death and retirement and new additions to La Follette's insurgent Republican bloc. And Wilson kept attacking. The day after his address, he was in the Capitol again, meeting privately with Democratic leaders.

A tariff reduction bill passed the House, but the House had passed such bills before, and always the reductions had become increases in the Senate, or had died there, and reformers who had cursed the protective tariff for decades had come to believe that tariff reform would always die in the Senate. But this time, Wilson went to the people with a dramatic appeal against the lobbyists' power, saying that "only public opinion can check and destroy it." And the Senate bill, passed 44 to 37, contained rates even lower than those the House had approved, as well as the momentous income tax that marked the beginning of the democratization of the federal financial structure. "Think of it—a tariff reduction downwards after all," wrote Agriculture Secretary David Houston. "Lower in the Senate than in the House! . . . A progressive income tax! I did not much think we should live to see these things."

Even while Congress was still debating the tariff bill, Wilson had summoned it into a second joint session, at which he called for the creation of a system of regional banks controlled by a Federal Reserve Board (its seven members would be appointed by the President with the advice and consent of the Senate) that would end Wall Street's control of money and credit. His private sessions on Capitol Hill were also continuing; sitting in the ornate President's Room just off the Senate Chamber, he conferred with—and brought the powers of the presidency to bear upon—individual senators. He installed a private telephone line between the White House and the Capitol. So successful were Wilson's methods that not a single Democratic senator voted against the Federal Reserve Act. And as soon as it passed, Wilson was back, again appearing before Congress to ask for laws—the Federal Trade Commission Act and the Clayton Anti-Trust Act—to investigate and police trusts and monopolies (and to protect organized labor from injunctions). And these passed, too. The President held Congress in session for a year and a half, the longest session in history, and during it transformed the balance of power between executive and legislature in America's government, pushing through Congress social laws that Progressives had all but given up hope of seeing passed in their lifetime.

The Senate's "Golden Age" had begun in 1819, and although those days of Senate glory had lasted only about forty years, the days of Senate power had lasted another fifty and more. At the end of the nineteenth century, the Senate had still been the "Senate Supreme." And while, during the Theodore Roosevelt and Taft presidencies at the beginning of the twentieth century, senatorial power had diminished in foreign affairs, it had remained intact—if anything, it had increased—in domestic affairs. For better and for worse, the institution had stood firm against both executive and popular tyranny for almost a century. The year 1913 (a year which also saw the ratification of the Seventeenth Amendment, which mandated the popular election of senators that reformers had long believed would make the Senate more responsive to the will of the people) marked the first substantial break in that power.

And then the gates of the dam swung shut again.

By the summer of 1914, in fact, the first signs of reaction were already perceptible. And that was the year of the guns of August, and thereafter Woodrow Wilson's energies were increasingly focused on international affairs, and over his relationship with the Senate there crept, year by year, deeper and deeper shadows. The tariff reduction bill was the signpost of the beginning of Wilson's relationship with the Senate; the signpost at the end was the Treaty of Versailles.

AND AFTER WILSON came the "return to normalcy." Most of the men puffing the big cigars in the legendary smoke-filled room at the 1920 Republican convention were senators—someone remarked that the room looked like a Senate in miniature with Henry Cabot Lodge biting off brief comments while the others ruffled through possible presidential candidates "like a deck of soiled cards"—and, determined to reassert the Senate's authority, they wanted a pliable President who, in Lodge's job description, "will not try to be an autocrat but will do his best to carry on the Government in the old and accepted Constitutional ways." Who better than one of their own to fill this role?—and the Old Guard's Warren G. Harding was elevated directly from his Senate desk to the White House, in his ears his colleagues' admonition to "sign whatever bills the Senate sent him and not send bills for the Senate to pass." Under Harding and Coolidge and Hoover, this "normalcy" was to last for almost a decade—a decade during which, slowly but steadily, the tariff began to rise again, and federal spending to fall; federal regulations on business were relaxed; and the tax burden was shifted from the rich to the middle class and the poor. The Twenties were, of course, a decade in which a prosperous America was content to rely on big business rather than government for leadership, and little of that commodity came from the White House, or from either of the two chambers on Capitol Hill. The Senate's philosophy was a philosophy that favored free enterprise over social reform. Tighter Republican control of the House enabled it to rise to equality with the Senate—but that only meant that the two bodies, squabbling continually over details, spent the decade "bouncing bills back and forth."

And when, on Black Friday, 1929, normalcy abruptly ended, the Senate had little to contribute to solving the crisis. While it had once been the deliberative body the Framers had envisioned—one among whose desks fundamental policies had been debated, in debates that educated a nation—that educative function had atrophied during decades of making decisions behind closed doors. Once it had been a place of leaders, men who conceived daring solutions to daunting problems, and then persuaded public and colleagues to support those solutions. Decades of the seniority rule had conferred influence in the Senate not on men who broke new ground but on men who were careful not to. So that when in 1929 crisis came, and with the last of those passive presidents still in office, leadership was so desperately needed, the Senate had as little to offer as the House.

The President and the leadership of Congress—that leadership that was still staunchly conservative in both houses—clung to their belief that the best cure for the business crisis was business as usual. Business as usual meant raising the tariff, and, during the months following the Crash, that was the priority on Capitol Hill. The bill drawn by ardent protectionists Senator Reed Smoot of Utah and Congressman Willis C. Hawley of Oregon raised duties to prohibitive levels. Senator La Follette called the bill "the product of a series of deals, conceived in secret, but executed in public with a brazen effrontery that is without parallels in the annals of the Senate" (a remark that revealed his ignorance of Senate annals). When, in June, 1930, President Hoover signed the Smoot-Hawley Tariff Act, using six solid gold pens, one historian wrote that Nelson Aldrich's ghost "no doubt smiled down in approval."

National concern over the deepening Depression gave the Democrats control of the House of Representatives in 1930 for the first time since 1919, and while the GOP clung to a 48–47 plurality in the Senate, the margin was meaningless, since La Follette's insurgent Republicans were not inclined to follow President Hoover's policies. And when Congress convened in December, 1931, the month in which twenty-three-year-old Lyndon Johnson arrived in Washington as secretary to one of the newly elected Democratic congressmen, it did so in the midst of a nationwide demand for action. The mail sacks that the staffs of senators and representatives opened each morning were filled with desperation now, as a nation's people begged their government for help.

But little help came from the White House. President Hoover's solution to the Depression was still largely to maintain that it was over, and that proposals for direct federal aid for relief, or for increased spending on public works, were as unnecessary as debt relief for farmers—although thousands of American families were losing their farms, relief funds had run out for states and municipalities, and every day the soup kitchen lines grew longer.

And little help came from Capitol Hill. The House was even more confused and disorganized than usual; a columnist called it "the Monkey House," and his sentiment was echoed by some of the congressmen themselves; declared John McDuffie of Alabama: "Representative government is dead." In the other wing of the Capitol, some senators—the younger La Follette, New York's Robert F. Wagner, George W. Norris of Nebraska, Hugo Black of Alabama—sought to rise to the crisis, with proposals for a federal public works program, a federal system of unemployment insurance, direct federal relief. But there was little agreement among these senators, and little leadership. Many senators seemed to doubt whether Congress could do anything in the crisis. Senator Thomas Gore of Oklahoma was probably expressing the general sentiment when he said dourly that you could no more relieve the Depression by legislation "than you can pass a resolution to prevent disease." When, after months of wrangling over details, a relief and public works bill finally passed Congress, Hoover vetoed it, and there was never a realistic chance that the Senate would override the veto. And that was the high point of congressional action to fight the Depression; in the midst of one of the nation's gravest crises, Congress failed to meet for nine months—adjourning in March, 1931, it did not reconvene until January, 1932.

By the time it reconvened, there were between 15 million and 17 million unemployed men in America, many of whom represented an entire family in want. Reminders of the nation's desperation were all over Washington— "Bonus Marchers," twenty-five thousand penniless World War veterans, paraded up Pennsylvania Avenue in May and then pitched tents in parks, so that "Washington, D.C., resembled the besieged capital of an obscure European state." But for Congress, 1932 was seven months of wrangling and delay, and the measures it passed were so inadequate as to be all but meaningless; under its relief bill, passed after months of haggling, the average stipend for a family of four was fifty cents per day. When vital tax and tariff reforms were introduced, special interest groups and states traded tariff proposals back and forth until, in May, one senator shouted, "Have we gone mad? Have we no idea that if we carry this period of unrest from one week to another, a panic will break loose, which all the tariffs under heaven will not stem? Yet we sit here to take care of some little interest in this state or that. . . . 'My state! My state!' My God! Let's hear 'My country!' What good is your state if your country sinks into the quagmire of ruin!" For months, *Forum* magazine said, "the country [has] been looking on, with something like anguish, at the spectacle of the inability of the national legislature for dealing with the crucial problem of national finance."

Congress adjourned in July, 1932. By the time it reconvened in December, 158 of its members had been defeated in the election, as had President Hoover. But the congressmen—and Hoover—were still going to be in office until March.

The winter ahead was a winter of despair. When the lame-duck Congress convened, crowded around the Capitol steps were more than twenty-five hundred men, women, and children chanting, "Feed the hungry! Tax the rich!" Heavily armed police herded the "hunger marchers" into a "detention camp" on New York Avenue, where, denied food or water, they spent a freezing night sleeping on the pavement, taunted by their guards. Thereafter, when Congress was in session a double line of rifle-carrying police blocked the Capitol steps. And behind these bodyguards, Congress spent yet more months posturing and procrastinating, angrily deadlocking over conflicting relief bills, while arguing interminably over whether to legalize beer. As for the "President-reject," as *Time* called him, he spent those months trying to commit his successor to a continuation of his discredited policies. As, that winter, farmers began to march in what might have been the prelude to revolution, as the nation's great banks began to close, Washington still did nothing substantive. A great nation was collapsing, and its government, of which the Senate had once been a pillar, seemed paralyzed, utterly unable to prevent the collapse. Senators came to the Chamber wearing money belts as the safest place to keep their cash. The institution which had once excited the admiration of great statesmen now aroused only contempt.

·   ·   ·

THEN, AT HIS INAUGURATION on March 4, 1933, the new President, Franklin Delano Roosevelt, declaring that "This nation asks for action, and action now," summoned Congress into special session. If there was a single moment in America's history in which the slow slide of power—now in its fourth decade—from Capitol Hill to the White House suddenly became an avalanche, so that, for decades thereafter, governmental initiative came overwhelmingly from the Executive Branch, with the legislature only reacting to that initiative, it was that session—the session that lasted a hundred days, and was so significant a landmark in the nation's history that it became enshrined as *the* Hundred Days, the session in which a President proposed, and proposed, and proposed again, in which he proposed the most far-reaching of measures—a session in which Congress scampered in panic to approve those proposals as fast as it could.

Should Congress fail to provide immediate action, the second Roosevelt said, "I shall not evade the clear course of duty that will then confront me. I shall ask the Congress for the one remaining instrument to meet the crisis—broad executive power to wage war against the emergency." When Congress convened on March 9, he had waiting for it an Emergency Banking Relief Act that included sweeping presidential authority over the Federal Reserve System. The bill had not yet been printed—only one typed copy was available—and it was read to the House, which limited debate to forty minutes; even before that time expired, representatives were shouting, "Vote! Vote!" and the vote was by a unanimous shout. The Senate was in a similar rush. When Huey Long of Louisiana proposed an amendment, he was shouted down, and the bill—a bill few senators had even seen—was passed, 73 to 7. Roosevelt signed the legislation into law on the same day, less than eight hours after he had sent it to Capitol Hill. An hour later, he was outlining to congressional leaders—long habituated to deference to the powerful veterans' lobby—an economy program that included a reduction of veterans' pensions, to be accomplished through delegation of sweeping authority to the President. Four days later, the House having passed the bill, the Senate voted for it, 62 to 13, and on the same day voted to amend the Volstead Act to allow the sale of beer and light wine, thereby defying the Prohibitionist lobby, as powerful as the veterans.

"COME AT ONCE TO WASHINGTON," the second La Follette telegraphed Donald Richberg, an old Theodore Roosevelt Progressive. "GREAT THINGS ARE UNDERWAY!" Said Will Rogers: "They know they got a man in there who is wise to Congress, wise to our so-called big men. The whole country is with him, just so he does something. If he burned down the capitol, we would cheer and say, 'Well, we at least got a fire started anyhow.' " Even conservatives cheered. And before Congress adjourned on June 15, Roosevelt had sent a total of fifteen measures to Capitol Hill, fifteen measures that resulted in fifteen major legislative Acts that would transform forever the relationship between America's government and its people—that would extend at last to that people, battered by forces too big for them to fight alone, the helping hand of government for which they had been asking not only during the three years of the Depression but for many decades before. These Acts embodied concepts expounded by Theodore Roosevelt and Woodrow Wilson, concepts that had headed the Progressive agenda for decades but that for decades had perished on Capitol Hill, so often among the desks of the Senate. During the Hundred Days, the chairmanships of many major Senate committees were, thanks to seniority, in the hands of conservative southern Democrats. But the Senate— like the House—passed the fifteen bills with so little debate that one might have thought there had never been any resistance to the philosophy behind them. Congressmen and senators often had little idea of what they were voting on, or how it would affect America, but the new bills were enthusiastically rushed to passage.

Following adjournment, when Capitol Hill had time to reflect, some of the enthusiasm faded. "Roosevelt had gone far beyond any other President in asserting executive authority, not only asking for legislation but sending over a brief message and a detailed draft of each bill he had wanted passed, and many Congressmen resented the feeling of being 'lackeys' or 'rubber stamps' of a chief executive who had taken over the legislative function," Alvin Josephy says. "A number of southerners, particularly, were concerned about the exten-sion of federal power at the expense of the states." Enthusiasm faded in both House and Senate, but some senators were uncomfortably aware that the Sen-ate was supposed to be the principal bulwark against executive authority; after a century and a half of fulfilling that responsibility, during the Hundred Days the Senate had abdicated it. Nonetheless, there were heavy House and Senate majorities behind the New Deal in 1934 and 1935, years which saw passage of a Social Security Act which set up a national system of old-age insurance, and of laws to break the power of private utilities and make possible the electrifica-tion of rural America, and to raise the taxes of the wealthy. And the New Deal was ratified by the Democratic landslide of 1934. In 1936, Roosevelt declared, "I should like to have it said of my first administration that in it the forces of selfishness and lust for power met their match. I should like to have it said of my second administration that in it these forces met their master." And the ensuing Roosevelt landslide gave his party unprecedented majorities on Capi-tol Hill; when Congress reconvened in January, 1937, there would be only eighty-nine Republicans left in the House, and in the Senate there were so many Democrats—seventy-six—that they could not all be seated on the right side of the Chamber, as was traditional; twelve freshmen Democrats, along with four minority-party senators, were placed in the last row on the left side, behind the sixteen Republicans, all that was left of the once-invincible GOP majority.

DURING THE NEW DEAL, there were isolated reminders of what individual senators could still accomplish. The Tennessee Valley Authority is generally

listed by historians as a creation of the Roosevelt Administration, and indeed
Roosevelt saw the need and the promise in a plan to revitalize the impoverished
Tennessee River Basin by using the huge Woodrow Wilson Dam at Muscle
Shoals, idle since the First World War, and constructing a network of other
dams, in a vast program of flood control, soil conservation, rural electrification,
and diversification of industry. And Roosevelt pushed that plan to reality in
1933. But on the day FDR decided to push it, he said to a man standing looking
down at Muscle Shoals with him, "This should be a happy day for you,
George," and Senator George Norris of Nebraska replied, "It is, Mr. President.
I see my dreams come true." All through the 1920s, businessmen had lobbied
Congress to turn the dam over to them and let them operate it strictly for profit,
and all through the Twenties, in the face of that decade's pro–private business
attitude, and of the determination of Harding, Coolidge, and Hoover to priva-
tize the dam, Norris had fought to keep it under government ownership. His
power as chairman of the Senate Agriculture Committee had enabled him to do
so. If a single senator had not, through the administrations of three antagonistic
Presidents, succeeded in preserving from private hands the power generated by
the river's waters, that power would not still have been available for public
development when a friendly President arrived on the scene. Similarly, the
great National Labor Relations Act of 1935, the "Magna Carta for Labor,"
which at last placed between the power of mighty corporations and the masses
of their workers the shield of government protection, was the creation of Senator Robert F. Wagner of New York, who pushed it through the Senate after
Roosevelt had promised southern Democrats, adamantly opposed to the measure, to remain neutral. Roosevelt "never lifted a finger" in its behalf, Secretary
of Labor Frances Perkins was to say. The TVA, the National Labor Relations
Board, and other accomplishments of the 1930s often lumped together with
accomplishments of the Roosevelt Administration, are actually monuments to
senators. And when, in a single vivid historical moment, the need for the powers bestowed on the Senate by the Founding Fathers was suddenly made blind-
ingly clear, the Senate as a whole demonstrated that it still possessed those
powers—and could use them.

Not only had the 1936 Roosevelt landslide given his party overwhelming
legislative majorities, the leaders of those majorities—House Speaker John
Bankhead and Senate Majority Leader Joseph Robinson—had, as one account
put it, demonstrated "an all but unblemished record of perfect subservience to
the White House." FDR's control of two branches of the American government
seemed as firm as Thomas Jefferson's had seemed after *his* landslide victory in
1804.

About the 1804 election Henry Adams had commented that "the sunshine
of popularity and power" had "turned the head of a President." After the 1936
election, perceptive observers had the same concern. Watching FDR's triumphant return to Washington after the election, "the smiling President in his
open car," the cheering mobs who "turned out in tens of thousands to receive

him as a conquering hero," Joseph Alsop and Turner Catledge were reminded
of a Roman triumph and wondered "whether the President possessed an inner
censor, to take the place of the ribald slave who stood in each triumphing general's chariot to remind him that, after all, he was no more than mortal." Their
concern would soon prove justified. After his landslide, Jefferson, in control of
two branches of government, had turned his attention to the lone branch still
dominated by the other party—the judiciary—moving, in the impeachment of
Samuel Chase, to curb its independence. Now Roosevelt, too, moved against
the judiciary's independence. The Supreme Court had declared crucial New
Deal measures unconstitutional. The President drafted a plan to enlarge the
Court by appointing as many as six new justices whose philosophy agreed with
his. And he made his move, as Alsop and Catledge were to write in *The 168
Days,* their colorful study of the Court-packing fight, in a way that showed that
his triumph at the polls had filled him with "such an overconfidence as must
come to any man after four years of glittering, uninterrupted success in great
matters."

Having had the Court plan prepared in strict secrecy, he didn't bother to
discuss it with his party's congressional leaders, as if such discussion was no
longer necessary. When he summoned them to the White House on February 5,
1937, they had not the slightest inkling of what the meeting would be about.
When they arrived, headed by the white-haired, ruddy-faced Vice President
Garner, a conservative Texan who, beloved and respected on Capitol Hill, not
only presided over the Senate but wielded almost as much influence in it as
Robinson (but who had also been kept completely in the dark), and had all been
seated in the Cabinet Room, a secretary came in with mimeographed copies of
the bill, already drawn up in final form, and of the President's accompanying
message, and distributed them around the table. As they began reading these
documents, the President summarized their contents—cursorily. He had very
little time, he explained; he was holding a press conference to announce the
Court plan in a few minutes. And with that, he wheeled himself out of the
room.

The congressional leaders' first reaction was a stunned silence. Then, in
the car driving them back to the Capitol, Hatton Sumners of Texas, chairman of
the House Judiciary Committee, said, "Boys, here's where I cash in my chips."
And when, in the long lobby behind the Senate Chamber, senators clustered
around Garner asking his opinion of the President's bill, the Vice President told
them—in pantomime: holding his nose with one hand, with the other, he made
a Roman thumbs-down gesture. But Roosevelt was unconcerned. When, a few
days later, the congressional leaders returned to the White House to discuss
compromise, Roosevelt made clear that compromise would not be necessary.
Congress would approve the bill as he had dictated it, he said. "The people are
with me." And Roosevelt's confidence was understandable. Who could stand
before such a President, at the very zenith of his popularity and power?

But America's Founding Fathers had created the Senate to stand against just such a President—to stand against the President and the people, to protect the minority from the tyranny of the majority. In 1805, in a battle to preserve the independence of the judiciary, it had stood firm. And now, in 1937, in another such battle, it was, all at once, standing firm again. Roosevelt wanted his bill to be taken up first in the House, "because," as the journalist Leonard Baker explains in a study of the Court-packing fight, "all House members run for reelection every two years" and the Administration therefore "believed that FDR's political coattails had most impact on that side of the Capitol"; the bill, having passed the House, would then arrive in the Senate with momentum behind it. But Sumners, equally aware of those considerations, refused to call the measure up in his House Judiciary Committee so that the Senate would take up the measure first. And suddenly, as Alsop and Catledge wrote, "the shabby comedy of national politics, with its all-pervading motive, self-interest, its dreary dialogue of public oratory and its depressing scenery of patronage and projects, was elevated to a grand, even a tragic plane."

The President fought with a President's weapons—with eloquence, matchless eloquence. In a March 4 speech at a triumphal victory dinner of his party—to thirteen hundred of the top Democratic federal jobholders at the Mayflower Hotel—he reminded them of why they held their jobs: because their party, in its New Deal, embodied the majority desires for meaningful social legislation. He reminded them of how the Supreme Court had "vetoed" New Deal legislation. And he warned them that if the party permitted the Supreme Court to thwart the people's will, the people would turn away from the party. "Here is one-third of a nation ill-nourished, ill-clad, ill-housed—now! Here are thousands upon thousands of farmers wondering whether next year's prices will meet their mortgage interest—now! Here are thousands upon thousands of men and women laboring for long hours in factories for inadequate pay—now! If we would keep faith with these who had faith in us, if we would make Democracy succeed, I say we must act—now!" Five days after the speech came an even more effective weapon: the chat. Out of ten million radios on March 9 came the warm, rich voice, simply asking his followers to trust him:

> You who know me can have no fear that I would tolerate the destruction by any branch of the government of any part of our heritage of freedom. . . . You who know me will accept my solemn assurance that in a world in which democracy is under attack I seek to make American democracy work. . . .

And he fought with a President's private weapons—which he likewise wielded with matchless skill. As it became apparent that opposition to judiciary "reform" was more widespread than he had anticipated, presidential aides began to sound out individual senators more carefully, and there were surprises.

One senator of whose vote the White House had been certain—regardless of his views on the particular issue—was Joseph C. O'Mahoney of Wyoming. Not only had he been a loyal assistant to Postmaster General James A. Farley, Roosevelt's political major domo, but, as the representative of a beet-sugar state, he "was also heavily obligated to the administration on sugar bills, and would need more help in the future." Now it was reported that O'Mahoney was calling the bill "undemocratic," and Farley contacted him—and thereafter assured Roosevelt that O'Mahoney was "on board." The Man in the White House was a master at pulling levers attached to senators. "Kentucky's Democratic Senator Marvel M. Logan had been recalcitrant about the Court plan," Leonard Baker reports, but Kentucky needed flood control projects. "Senator Logan became a supporter of the plan. Kentucky got its flood control projects." Routine judicial and patronage appointments in many states were suddenly held up because "Mr. Farley is working on them." And the Senate was a New Deal Senate, after all. Democratic Leader Robinson counted the votes now, and assured Roosevelt of a majority.

And indeed if the vote had been taken then, not long after the proposal was made, the President would probably have had his majority.

But the vote wasn't going to be taken then, for the Senate, thanks to the Founding Fathers, also had weapons, most crucially its rule allowing "unlimited" debate. Deliberation requires time—and the Senate was going to get time. Roosevelt and Robinson summoned the chairman of the Senate Judiciary Committee, Ashurst of Arizona, to the Oval Office. Ashurst was usually soft-spoken and complaisant, but he was, as they may have forgotten, the same Senator Ashurst who eighteen years before had demanded, "Who is this Colonel House?" Roosevelt and Robinson attempted to persuade him to place a limit—perhaps two weeks apiece—on the length of time each side would have to present witnesses before his committee, but Ashurst felt that the Court-packing proposal was "the prelude to tyranny," and, thanks to the Founders, he had a weapon to fight "tyranny." "I replied that I would avoid haste, would go slowly and give the opponents of his bill ample time and opportunity to explore all its implications," he told the President. There would, he said, be no time limit at all.

The President, Ashurst was to recall, "received this statement with disrelish." But there was nothing the President could do about it. Judiciary Committee hearings in the Senate Caucus Room went on for more than two months, and during that time there were many speeches on the Senate floor, and the passage of time did just what the Founders had intended. As Alsop and Catledge wrote:

> It is easy to make fun of such public speaking as the country was treated to during the court fight. Turgid, repetitious, crammed with non-sequiturs, richly ornamented with appeals to prejudice and self-

interest, couched in an English which would have made Edmund Burke weep for very horror at the fate of the language—most of it was all these things. But it gave the country a chance to think the issue over. By sheer force of its repetitions it dinned the arguments for and against into the ears of the electorate.

In 1937, as in 1919, there were "the great stump-speaking tours across the country, which senators resorted to as they never had before except in the League of Nations fight." Their speeches were reported in depth in newspapers, and heard on the radio; the airwaves were filled each night with the oratory of both sides in a remarkable public debate. And as America heard the arguments, America's initial enthusiasm for the President's proposal began to diminish.

And the delay, moreover, was affording not only America's people but America's senators "a chance to think the issue over." Every time a Roosevelt supporter who had given a hint of wavering appeared in the cloakroom or in a Capitol corridor, a reporter wrote, "you were certain to see one or two opposition senators pleading, persuading, exhorting or shaming the worried man into independence." More and more senators began to feel that the issue was too big for them to be influenced by customary political considerations. Summoned to the Oval Office along with a prominent liberal professor from Harvard, Wyoming's O'Mahoney found himself the recipient of a lecture on the need for "co-operation" between the executive and the judiciary. The lecture was delivered with the full measure of presidential charm, and, Alsop and Catledge wrote, beet sugar "may not have been completely absent from O'Mahoney's mind." But, they wrote, the concept of the American constitutional structure held by the Senator and the professor was "rather more conventional than the President's. As they listened to the President calmly explaining what he wanted, they could not forget the doctrine of separate powers." Not long thereafter, O'Mahoney unexpectedly appeared at a meeting of senators opposed to the bill. He wanted to join them, he said; he would oppose the bill to the end, no matter what the political cost.

Similar evolution was taking place in the attitude of other senators, as day by day, the great issues involved were examined and re-examined. Burton K. Wheeler of Montana, long a leader in Senate fights for liberal causes, was coming to see that the Court plan implied an alteration in the whole balance of governmental power in favor of the White House. What, he wondered, would come next? He refused to fight for this cause. Wheeler was a senator other senators followed. Roosevelt sent his aide Thomas G. Corcoran to him with an offer. Its details would be a matter of dispute; at the very minimum, Wheeler would be allowed to give "advice" on the nominations of two of the six justices. Wheeler had accepted other offers from Corcoran before, but he refused to do so on the Court-packing plan. "I'm going to fight it with everything I've got," he told Corcoran. The President hurriedly invited his old friend Burt to dine at the

White House that evening; the Senator replied that the President had better "save the plate for someone who persuaded more easily." George Norris, "the great old man of liberalism," asked himself the question, how would he have stood "if Harding had offered this bill." And then he gave his answer: he would have opposed the bill had Harding offered it—and he would oppose it though Roosevelt offered it.

And while much of the repetition of arguments was boring and banal, some was not—particularly when, the Judiciary Committee having reported it out unfavorably by a 10–8 vote, with the formal recommendation that it not pass, debate on it began on the floor.

As Majority Leader Robinson rose at his desk, in "the high, wide chamber, so meaninglessly decorated with square yards of tan and gray and faded yellow, [so] colorlessly illuminated by its huge sky-light," the galleries were jammed, Alsop and Catledge were to relate. "There were senators' wives, diplomats, connoisseurs of the Washington scene, hundreds upon hundreds of sight-seers. . . . The overwhelming impression was that the plain people of America had come to see their government in action. In the pitlike space which the galleries enclose was the government they had come to see, scores of rather elderly, remarkably ordinary-looking men."

As Robinson roared threats, and defended the President, opposition senators bombarded him with questions that emphasized loyalty not to a President but to a Constitution. As senators dueled with words, the rage on both sides often boiled over; on one such occasion, "Robinson and his followers and the leaders of the opposition were all on their feet, all bellowing at once. Order was gone; the fascinated galleries buzzed with excitement; and on the floor such a scene of bitterness and hatred, fury and suspicion was enacted as the Senate had not witnessed in a quarter century."

There were moments when the debate served the purpose that the Founding Fathers had intended—as, for example, when the speaker was Senator Josiah Bailey of North Carolina. Bailey was usually ponderous, given to pounding on his desk and shouting out the points he wanted to stress. But the independence of the judiciary was sacred to him, and he had been preparing this speech for weeks—and he delivered it with pounding and shouting, but also with what Alsop and Catledge call "all the force of absolute conviction." Listening senators rose, walked hastily to the cloakrooms and brought colleagues to the floor to hear, or sent pages to fetch others from their offices. Soon "every desk for rows around the speaker was filled—a sure sign of interest—and the chamber was perfectly still. That rare thing, a successful and convincing argument, was being made on the floor." Leaving the Chamber, Robinson telephoned his White House liaison. "Bailey's in there and he's making a great speech," he said. "He's impressing a lot of people. . . ." In the back, on "freshman row," where the new Democrats were seated behind the Republicans, were three senators of whose votes Robinson had been confident. Now,

they changed their minds and went (along with a fourth freshman who had earlier decided to oppose the bill) to inform Roosevelt to his face of their decision.
Thus confronting a popular President would have posed immediate political
danger for a member of the House of Representatives, up for re-election in
another year, but these senators were safe in their seats for another five years;
Roosevelt might not even *be* President when they stood for re-election.

After two weeks of debate, Robinson suffered a heart attack in his apartment, where a maid found him dead. Following a state funeral in the Senate
Chamber, thirty-eight senators accompanied the Majority Leader's body home
to Arkansas, aboard a train on which the debate raged as bitterly as ever. Vice
President Garner, who had come up from Texas to travel with the senators,
arrived—the senators greeted him "like a long-lost father"—counted votes, and
on the return to Washington, went directly to the White House and asked the
President, "Do you want it with the bark on or the bark off?" and when the
President opted for the latter, told him flatly he was licked, and with his permission, arranged a "compromise" that left the Supreme Court untouched.
Attempts were made to couch the result in terms that would save the President's face, but old, sick Hiram Johnson of California stumbled heavily to his
feet and asked, "The Supreme Court is out of the way?" And when Senator
Logan replied solemnly, "The Supreme Court is out of the way," Johnson said:
"Glory be to God!" The old senator had spoken the words half to himself, but
the galleries heard them. For a moment, the Chamber of the Senate of the
United States was silent and frozen—the red-faced, white-haired little man on
the dais, the men sitting at the quadruple arc of mahogany desks who had
beaten the unbeatable President, the crowd in the galleries above. And then
there was a burst of wild cheering. Garner still held his gavel, waiting to call for
the yeas and nays. But before he did so, he let the people cheer their fill.

THE BATTLE OVER THE SUPREME COURT, like the battle over the Treaty of
Versailles, ended in victory for the Senate—and the victory reverberated far
beyond the issue itself. Franklin Roosevelt, who by his political genius and his
popularity had stripped the Senate of its power, now had inadvertently, by his
arrogance and miscalculation, handed that power back, uniting the opposition
senators against him, as an historian of the Senate puts it, "in a way they would
have been completely incapable of achieving on their own." Uneasy though
they were over the New Deal's heavy spending, its support of labor and blacks,
its whole liberal agenda of social reform, conservative Democratic senators,
particularly from southern and border states, had been cowed by FDR's seemingly invulnerable popularity. They were cowed no longer. Moreover, in opposing the Court-packing bill, they had worked with Republican senators—and
had realized the similarity of the Republicans' philosophy to their own.

The bipartisan conservative coalition that formed in both houses of Con-

gress demonstrated its strength within the year. With the number of unemployed creeping ominously upward again, in November, 1937, with the Court
fight over, the President, in an attempt to end this "Roosevelt recession," summoned Congress into special session and presented it with an ambitious package of "must" bills. Not one passed.

A President—even Roosevelt—was all but helpless to break this power.
When in 1938 he attempted to "purge" Senate Democrats Walter George of
Georgia, Millard Tydings of Maryland, and Ellison (Cotton Ed) Smith of South
Carolina, going into their own states to campaign against them, the resentment
of southern voters to presidential intervention in their states' internal politics
was summarized in newspaper headlines—in Maryland denouncing Roosevelt's "invasion," in Georgia likening his campaign to General Sherman's pil-
laging of the state during the Civil War. And the intervention gave Roosevelt
not a single victory. In George, Tydings, and Smith, moreover, Roosevelt had
selected incumbents he had felt could be defeated. He never even tried to take
on other, more solidly entrenched conservative senators running in 1938, such
as Nevada's Patrick McCarran and Colorado's Alva Adams. Exasperated by
"the sense that Congress did not reflect the sentiments of the country," the New
Dealers had, as the historian John Garraty puts it, "attempted to nationalize the
[Democratic] party institution, to transform a decentralized party, responsible
only to local electorates, into an organization responsive to the will of the
national party leader and the interests of a national electorate." But the Senate
had been armored against the will of a national leader or a national electorate.
It had been designed not to respond to but, should it wish to do so, to resist the
"sentiments of the country." Even if the President had succeeded in ousting
George, Tydings, and Smith; even if he had fought, and defeated, McCarran
and Adams; even if he had campaigned against, and defeated, every incumbent
senator, of any persuasion, running in 1938, he would have changed the membership of only one-third of the Senate. Two-thirds of the Senate would still
have been untouched.

The conservative Democrat-Republican coalition was formidable in both
houses of Congress—in the House of Representatives its heart was the Rules
Committee headed by Howard Smith of Virginia—but most of the coalition's
key figures were senators: southerners like Bailey, Tom Connally of Texas, and
Carter Glass and Harry Byrd of Virginia; border-staters like Tydings; Republicans like Arthur Vandenberg and, after 1939, Robert Taft of Ohio. And year by
year its strength grew. The Court fight, as Garraty says, "marked the beginning
of the end of the New Deal." During the remaining seven years of Roosevelt's
Administration, Congress blocked every major new domestic law he proposed.
One by one, the older Supreme Court justices resigned, and as Roosevelt filled
their places, the Court moved steadily to the left. The lower levels of the federal
judiciary also moved left, as the effect of presidential appointments accumulated. Congress moved nowhere. The Senate moved nowhere. In domestic

affairs, the Senate was again what it had been with brief exceptions during the four generations since the Civil War: the stronghold of the *status quo,* the dam against which the waves of social reform dashed themselves in vain—the chief obstructive force in the federal government.

The Constitution's Framers had given the Senate power to block legislation, to stand as the rampart against the exercise of popular and presidential will. This power was only a negative power, a naysaying power, the power to obstruct and to thwart. But it was an immense power—and the Framers had built the rampart solid enough so that it was standing, thick and strong, in the twentieth century as it had stood in the nineteenth century.

BUT THE FRAMERS had intended the Senate—had intended Congress as a whole—to have other, more constructive, powers. In the nineteenth century, the Senate had exercised these powers. In the twentieth century it didn't.

In part the explanation lay in changes in the world outside the Senate, in the enormous growth and complexity of government which demanded a dispatch and a body of expertise possessed more by the executive than the legislature; in the activist presidents who attracted the attention of press and public at the expense of Congress.

But in part the explanation lay in the Senate itself.

"Congressional procedure," *Life* magazine was to note in 1945, is largely "the same as it was in 1789." As for the Senate's basic committee and staff structure, that had been established in 1890. During the intervening decades, government had grown enormously—in 1946 the national budget was three hundred times the size it had been in 1890—but the staffs of Senate committees had grown hardly at all. To oversee that budget, the Senate Appropriations Committee staff consisted of eight persons, exactly one more than had been on that staff decades earlier. Not only were they ridiculously small, the staffs of Senate committees had little of the technical expertise necessary to understand a government which had become infinitely more complicated and technical. The salaries of congressional staff members were so low that Capitol Hill could not attract men and women of the caliber that were flocking to the executive branch. A study done in 1942 concluded that only four of the seventy-six congressional committees had "expert staffs prepared professionally even to cross-examine experts of the executive branch." As for senators' personal staff, as late as 1941, a senator would be entitled to hire only six employees, and only one at a salary—$3,000—which might attract someone with qualifications above those of a clerk. So little importance was attached to staff that many senators didn't hire even the six to which they were entitled, and an astonishingly high proportion of the approximately 500 employees on senators' personal staffs and the 144 on the staff of Senate committees were senators' relatives. The Founding Fathers had envisioned Congress as a check on the executive. Congress couldn't make even a pretense of analyzing the measures the executive submitted for its approval. During the decades since 1890, when the Senate had authorized a staff of three persons for its Foreign Relations Committee, the United States had become a global power, with interests in a hundred foreign countries. In 1939, the staff of the Senate Foreign Relations Committee was still three: one full-time clerk who took dictation, typed, and ran the stenotype machine, and two part-time clerks. As one observer put it, "There could be no adversary relationship between the two branches of government [in foreign relations] because most of the professional work had to be done in the Department of State." Anyone seeking an explanation of the Senate's willingness to allow the rise of the executive agreement, which freed it from the details of foreign policy, need look no further: the Senate simply had no staff adequate to handle the details of foreign policy. The adversary relationship—the relationship that had lain at the heart of the Framers' concept of the American government they thought they were creating—had become impossible in virtually all areas; even Senate Parliamentarian Floyd Riddick had to admit that "with occasional exceptions, Congress did little more than look into, slightly amend or block the bills upon which it was called to act."

Unable to analyze legislation, Congress was equally unable to create it.

This was perhaps the most significant alteration in the power of the House and the Senate. The Framers of the Constitution had given Congress great power to make laws, vesting in it "all legislative powers," and during the early, simpler days of the Republic, Congress had jealously guarded that power; as late as 1908, the Senate had erupted in anger when the Secretary of the Interior presumed to send it a bill already drafted in final form. But by the 1930s, with government so much more complicated, bill-drafting had become a science. Knowledge of that science was in extremely short supply on Capitol Hill. There were plenty of legislative technicians with the necessary expertise at the great law firms in New York. There were plenty at the White House, and in the executive departments—the legislative section of the Agriculture Department alone had six hundred employees. In 1939, the Legislative Drafting Service that helped both houses of Congress consisted of eight employees. And of all the scores of major statutes passed during the New Deal, approximately two per year were created by Congress—because, as Tommy Corcoran explained, Congress simply lacked the "technical equipment to draft a big, modern statute."

To draft one—or even to explain one and defend it in detail, as was often required when major new legislation was being presented to the Senate. The Senate was going through the same rituals it had gone through in the nineteenth century, but frequently now they were rituals without meaning—as was known by those Senate insiders who understood the significance of the fact that often the new Majority Leader, Alben Barkley of Kentucky, rising to speak, would signal a page to place a small portable lectern atop his desk. His intimates knew that Barkley, a gifted extemporaneous orator, needed a lectern only when he was reading a speech written by someone else—and that often the someone else was a White House official. Barkley was not alone. Senatorial floor managers of major legislation were relying more and more often on explanatory speeches written by White House aides. The legislative power was in effect being exercised increasingly by the executive. The Framers had vested in the Congress the power to make laws, but Congress itself had made it all but impossible for it to exercise that power. And the explanation for the lack of adequate Senate staff was as significant as the lack itself. For the fundamental explanation was that the Senate didn't want the staff it needed. Repeated proposals to add an expert permanent staff to committees—House and Senate—were applauded in principle, and died away without action being taken.

The reason for this rested partly on philosophic considerations, extremely shortsighted ones. Describing the senatorial attitude, *Time* magazine's long-time congressional correspondent Neil MacNeil says, "The damned staff cost money," and conservative senators believed in reducing government spending, not increasing it. Senators who did not spend even the meager allocation for personal staff boasted when, at the end of the year, they turned the money back to the government. For many senators, large, bustling staffs fit in neither with their concept of their beloved institution—"It was a quiet, sleepy place, and they wanted to keep it that way," MacNeil says, "and besides, they didn't want the institution to change, and they never had *had* staff"—nor with their concept of themselves: "They were *senators,* senators of the United States, not corporation executives supervising staffs." A senator, MacNeil says, "would go back to his office, and put his feet up on his desk, and think about what was going on in the world, and after a few weeks, he'd make a speech. He'd sit there and *think,* and come up with ideas and theories. And that didn't work with a staff." Most senators seemed to have no concept of what a staff could do. When the Librarian of Congress, Archibald MacLeish, proposed augmenting the tiny Legislative Reference Service so that congressional committees would have "scholarly research and counsel . . . at least equal to that of" the witnesses from the executive branch and private industry who testified before them, Congress rejected the proposal.

There were more pragmatic considerations as well. The staff of senatorial committees was controlled by the committee chairmen; giving individual senators more staff would therefore dilute the chairmen's power, and the chairmen were not eager to have it diluted. The press referred to the proposed administrative assistants as "assistant senators," reinforcing senators' apprehensions at establishing "a cadre of political assistants who would eventually be in a position to compete for their jobs." Senior senators, entrenched in power under the old system, had, as one would put it, a "suspicion . . . that they had little to gain and much to lose from a change in the *status quo*." Richard Strout of *The New Republic* was to say that "Congress has a deep, vested interest in its own inefficiency." It wasn't outside forces that kept the Senate inefficient—fifty years out of date. It was the Senate itself, for its own reasons.

The same was true of the other reasons for the Senate's increasing inability to perform the function for which it had been created: the autocratic, paralyzing power of the committee chairmen, their selection not by ability but by seniority alone—these practices were not changed because the Senate did not want them changed, and in fact had incentives not to change them. And the Senate did not have to change them. It was increasingly unable to respond to the demands of a changing world, but, because of the armor that the Framers of the Constitution had bolted around it, that world couldn't touch the Senate. The Framers had sought to insulate the Senate against the executive and the people, against outside forces, and they had done the job too well. No one could take away the Senate's power to play the role the Framers had envisioned for it; the Senate had, without consequence to itself, given that power away.

AND WHEN, in foreign affairs at least, it attempted to play that role, the attempt resulted in a tragedy that vividly illuminated the full potential for disaster that could be caused by the Senate's unshakable power—and that illuminated as well the Senate's utter inability to respond to the modern world.

After the First World War, an America sickened by the war's horrors, disillusioned by its apparent senselessness, and cynical and distrustful of the political maneuvering of foreign powers turned its back on the world, refusing to accept responsibility for maintaining the peace; insisting rigidly on the repayment of the colossal war debts it was owed by its struggling Allies, while raising tariff walls against them and thereby exacerbating international tensions. While totalitarian regimes in Italy, Germany, and Japan were building huge military machines, America scrapped its navy, reduced its army, tried to lull itself into a belief that trouble could best be avoided by ignoring it, and refused to participate in attempts to create a collective security and an international rule of law. The Twenties and Thirties were decades of a tragic national self-delusion, of shortsighted diplomacy, of a refusal to understand the terrible new forces arising in the world, of a belief that America could simply isolate herself from them. And the Senate was the stronghold of isolationism.

Many of the most influential senators—Wheeler, Norris, both La Follettes, Vandenberg, Taft, Key Pittman, Hiram Johnson—were isolationists, as was Henry Cabot Lodge's successor as Chairman of the Senate Foreign Relations Committee, William E. Borah of Idaho.

In a Chamber filled with renowned orators, Borah, a former Shakespearean actor, was the orator without peer. Whenever during his thirty-three-year senatorial career word spread through the Capitol that "Borah's up," spectators would pour into the galleries, and senators would hurry onto the floor to hear him speak. "The Lion of Idaho" possessed, as well, a gift for

attracting the journalistic spotlight. At his daily three o'clock press conferences, journalists crowded into his office, leading a disgruntled President
Coolidge to comment that "Senator Borah is always in session." For decades, a
historian says, "it seemed impossible to pick up a newspaper without reading a
Borah pronouncement." And while Borah, a liberal Republican on domestic
issues, often employed his eloquence on behalf of the farmer or the factory
worker, its impact was greatest on foreign policy.

In rejecting the Treaty of Versailles in 1919, the Senate had undermined
the possibility of peace in the world. For more than twenty years thereafter, it
carried on that work. In 1923, President Coolidge proposed that the United
States become a member of the World Court. Since this tribunal could settle
disputes only when every member agreed, its threat to America's sovereignty
was minimal, and not only the President but both political parties, in their platforms of 1924, and the House of Representatives, by an overwhelming vote of
303 to 28, and in polls, a majority of the American people, endorsed the World
Court treaty. But treaties require Senate ratification, and the Senate, following
Borah's lead, made ratification contingent on five conditions. The Court's
twenty-one member nations accepted four of them, and expressed a willingness
to negotiate on the fifth, but the Senate made clear that its resolution was non-
negotiable—and America's failure to become a member made the Court ineffective. In 1931, the Japanese invaded Chinese Manchuria, and quickly began
turning it into a puppet state. Amid warnings that failure to force Japan to dis-
gorge its new territory acquired by naked aggression would encourage not only
the Japanese but other potential aggressors, the League of Nations met to consider action, and American representatives sat in on the discussions. But the
discussions were shadowed by the old concern: even if the League members
agreed on some course of action, what would the American Senate do? And
nothing—at least nothing effective—was done. In 1933, President Roosevelt
asked for congressional authority to block arms shipments to aggressor countries. The House gave it to him. The Senate didn't. In fact, it amended the
House resolution to force the President to embargo shipments to *every* country
involved in a war—an amendment which, as Arthur Schlesinger puts it,
"destroyed the original purpose of the resolution, which was precisely to discriminate against aggressors," and which would actually have an effect opposite to what Roosevelt had wanted, "by strengthening nations that had arms
already" at the expense of those who didn't.

For almost two years beginning in September, 1934, the high-ceilinged,
marble-columned Senate Caucus Room was the chief rallying point for isolationist sentiment in the United States, as a special Senate committee, chaired
by the ardent isolationist Gerald P. Nye of North Dakota, held ninety-three
hearings, staged with great public fanfare, to "prove" that America had been
lured into the Great War to boost arms makers' profits. In 1935, with Hitler rapidly rearming, the danger of a worldwide conflagration increased as Mussolini

massed troops on the borders of the primitive kingdom of Ethiopia. When Roosevelt asked for authority to impose an arms embargo, the Senate's response was to pass, in twenty-five minutes, the Neutrality Act of 1935, which tied the President's hands by making it impossible for him to exert effective influence against Italy by forbidding the export of munitions to *all* belligerents. While noting that the bill penalized not Italy but Ethiopia, Roosevelt, afraid of exacerbating isolationist passions, felt he had no choice but to sign it. That same year, the President urged the Senate—as, twelve years before, President Coolidge had urged the Senate—to allow America to join the World Court. From the Senate floor came the response. "We are being rushed pell-mell to get into this World Court so that Señor Ab Jap or some other something from Japan can pass upon our controversies," Huey Long shouted. "To hell with Europe and the rest of those nations," Minnesota's Thomas Schall cried. Although there were seventy-two Democrats in the Senate, the proposal could garner only fifty-two votes, a majority but short of the two-thirds needed for passage. At the very height of Roosevelt's popularity, twenty Democratic senators had deserted him. "Thank God!" Borah said. That same year, the Senate passed legislation, drafted by Borah, strictly limiting expenditures for warships or for any other form of national defense. Nineteen thirty-six brought a further escalation in international tensions, so the Senate passed that year's Neutrality Act, which restricted even more tightly America's ability to deter aggressors by adding to the earlier restrictions on arms aid to all belligerents restrictions on financial aid as well. By the time Congress convened in 1937, Francisco Franco's fascists, armed and aided by Hitler, had launched a campaign against Spain's Republican government. This was a civil war, and the Neutrality Acts of 1935 and 1936 did not apply to civil wars. So Congress passed the Neutrality Act of 1937, which broadened the embargo so that it *would* apply to civil wars. "While German planes and cannon were turning the tide in Spain, the United States was denying the hard-pressed Spanish loyalists even a case of cartridges," Garraty observes.

"With every surrender the prospects of European war grow darker," Roosevelt was warned by his ambassador to Spain, but it was not the President but Capitol Hill's isolationists who were shaping American foreign policy. The Senate vote for the Neutrality Act of 1937 was an overwhelming 63 to 6. In October, 1937, with Japanese troops now pushing into North China, with the fascists winning in Spain, with Germany having reoccupied the Rhineland in violation of the Versailles treaty and with Germany, Italy, and Japan having formed a military alliance, Roosevelt warned that if totalitarianism rolled over one country after another, America's turn would eventually come. Predicting that there would be "no escape through mere isolation or neutrality," he called for a "quarantine" of aggressor nations. Nye and Borah accused the President of trying to police the world and plunge America into another "European war." In December, 1937, Japanese warplanes sunk the United States gunboat *Panay* (foreshadowing another surprise attack on a December Sunday morning) as it lay in a Chinese river. Borah reminded the reporters crowded into his office that America had "the Atlantic on one side and the Pacific on the other," and was therefore safe from invasion. "The United States is getting worked up over the prospect of war. I'm not," he said.

Forced to abandon his hopes for collective security, Roosevelt began concentrating on America's own military preparedness, calling for huge defense appropriations. To these Congress agreed, particularly after Nazi tanks rolled into Austria in May, 1938. But when, in September, with Hitler now menacing Czechoslovakia, the President asked also for a modification of the Neutrality Acts that would allow him at last to discriminate, in supplying arms, between aggressors and their victims, the isolationists on the Senate Foreign Relations Committee flatly refused to report out any modifications at all; they, not the President, were the best judges of the international situation, they made clear. When Roosevelt predicted that war in Europe was imminent, Borah replied confidently: "We are not going to have a war. Germany isn't ready for it. . . . I have my own sources of information." In March, 1939, in violation of his promises at Munich, Hitler invaded Czechoslovakia. Borah had a reaction: admiration. "Gad, what a chance Hitler has!" the Senator said. "If he only moderates his religious and racial intolerance, he would take his place beside Charlemagne. He has taken Europe without firing a shot." The Senator's sources of information were evidently still operative. "I know it to be a fact as much as I ever will know anything . . . that Britain is behind Hitler," he said at this time. Roosevelt again appealed to the Senate to repeal the arms embargo, but on July 11, 1939, in a showdown vote, the Foreign Relations Committee decided, 12 to 11, to defer consideration of the matter until the next session of Congress. In August, Hitler and Stalin signed a non-aggression pact. In desperation, Roosevelt called the committee members to the White House and, urging them to reconsider, came as close as Franklin Roosevelt ever came to begging. The world was on the verge of a catastrophe, he told them, and he needed all the power he could muster to avert it. "I've fired my last shot," he said. "I think I ought to have another round in my belt." The senators sat there coldfaced. Vice President Garner, their leader in 1939 as he had been in the courtpacking fight, showed Roosevelt who was boss. After polling the senators one by one in front of the President, he turned to him, and said: "Well, Captain, we may as well face the facts. You haven't got the votes, and that's all there is to it." (Not until Germany invaded Poland in September, and World War II was actually under way, was the arms embargo finally repealed. And even then—and even after a poll that showed that 84 percent of the American people wanted an Allied victory—it was repealed only after six weeks of acrimonious Senate debate, during which Borah, still adamantly insisting that America need not be involved in war, made his last impassioned radio address to the American people.)

In April, 1940, the full force of the Nazi blitzkrieg struck Europe. Denmark fell, and Norway, and Holland and Belgium and then France. And month after month the Nazis rained bombs on London as a prelude to a planned invasion of the last country to stand between America and Hitler's military machine. Americans were suddenly forced to confront some facts about Senator Borah's invincible oceans. Fleets could sail over them, and Britain's might soon be flying the swastika. And planes, as Roosevelt pointed out, could leave West Africa with their bomb bays crammed with bombs and re-emerge over Omaha. As the national mood changed with dramatic swiftness, Senate and House acted with unaccustomed speed in approving Roosevelt's requests for vast new sums for the Army and Navy.

But when Britain, alone, beleaguered, asked for help to keep fighting— fifty or sixty overage World War I destroyers to combat Nazi submarines— Roosevelt feared the Senate mood hadn't changed, at least not enough. "A step of that kind could not be taken except with the specific authorization of Congress, and I am not certain that it would be wise for that suggestion to be made to the Congress at this moment," he told Churchill. The accuracy of the President's assessment was demonstrated that summer, when the Senate amended the Naval Appropriations Bill to stipulate that military equipment could be released for sale only if the Navy certified it was useless for defense. A nation may have been jolted awake; its Senate hadn't. Roosevelt, fearing that if he went to Congress, the isolationists might very well block the proposals, at last determined to bypass Congress and trade the destroyers for the lease of a number of British naval bases through an executive agreement that did not require its approval. The help given England in its darkest hour was given in spite of the United States Senate.

Following his re-election in November, 1940, Roosevelt, with Britain running out of funds to purchase military equipment, hit upon the idea of lending or leasing arms and supplies. First he took his case to the American people in momentous fireside chats, and then he took it to Congress.

Borah had died in January, 1940. His death spared him from seeing the consequences of the policies in which his eloquence had been enlisted. But the Senate's other isolationists were not to be so lucky, not that some of them understood, even yet. Their statements against the Lend-Lease Bill were as harshly uncompromising as ever. It was at a desk in the Senate—Burton K. Wheeler's desk—that the Lend-Lease Bill was called "the new Triple A Bill" because "it would plow under every fourth American boy." ("Quote me on that. That's the rottenest thing that has been said in public life in my generation," Roosevelt replied.) Once again, a Senate Foreign Relations Committee heard witnesses ("The chair calls Colonel Charles A. Lindbergh") in the Caucus Room in which the League of Nations had been destroyed, and the World Court, and the arms embargoes, and so many other initiatives to preserve peace through international cooperation. The Foreign Relations gavel was held now not by Lodge or Borah but by Walter George, whom Roosevelt had once tried to purge but who now supported Roosevelt's foreign policy, and Lend-Lease passed the Senate ("I had the feeling . . . that I was witnessing the suicide of the Republic," Arthur Vandenberg mourned). The Senate isolationists still fought on. All through 1941—at least through the first eleven months and six days of 1941—the America First Committee continued its attempts to rally the country against interventionism, and to insist that America was not going to have to go to war, and Nye and Wheeler and other senators argued for this proposition in nationwide speaking tours reminiscent of those the Senate irreconcilables had made in 1919.

The first reports on December 7 discredited them—and the Senate. Nye was speaking before twenty-five hundred people at an America First rally in Pittsburgh when the note was laid on the podium before him. Doubting its veracity, the Senator completed his address before announcing that there were rumors that Japanese planes had bombed the American naval base at Pearl Harbor. It was appropriate that a senator was speaking at the moment the news came. Senators had been assuring the American people for more than twenty years that America could stay neutral in a world at war. Now, as an historian of the Senate wrote, "Twenty years of political debate ended in a beautiful Hawaiian harbor, marred by the burning hulls of a fleet of American warships." That evening Roosevelt summoned congressional leaders, including members of the Senate Foreign Relations Committee, to the White House. As the isolationists walked past the crowd of reporters outside, some of them, for once, had nothing to say.

IN A SINGLE FLASH, the flash of bombs, the policy of the Senate of the United States was exposed as a gigantic mistake. The failure of the world's most powerful nation to lead—or in general even to cooperate—in efforts, twenty years of efforts, to avert a second world war must be laid largely at the door of its Congress, and particularly at the door of its Senate. That has been the verdict of history. Walter Lippmann was to write that it was with the actions of the Senate Foreign Relations Committee during the late 1930s "that the emasculation of American foreign policy reached its extreme limit—the limit of total absurdity and total bankruptcy." That was the verdict of the President, who had pleaded in vain with the senators for "another round in my belt." Returning during the war from the Yalta Conference, Roosevelt startled his young assistant Charles Bohlen by the bitterness with which he denounced the Senate "as a bunch of incompetent obstructionists." "[He] indicated that that the only way to do anything in the American government was to bypass the Senate," Bohlen was to say. That was the verdict of the President's most respected opponent: Wendell Willkie, the Republican candidate in 1940, was to speak of devoting the rest of his life "to saving America from the Senate."

And that was the verdict of the Senate itself (and of the House). Schlesinger was to write of Congress that "many of its more thoughtful members now confessed to a sense of institutional inferiority if not institutional guilt. . . . No one for a long time after [Pearl Harbor] would trust Congress with basic foreign policy. Congress did not even trust itself."

BEFORE THE WAR, Roosevelt's New Deal had been constructed on the basis of specific authorization granted by Congress, but wartime urgencies required broader, less specific, authority. Congress quickly gave it to him—in two War Powers Acts granting the President enormous discretionary authority—and he quickly used it, and, in his role as wartime Commander-in-Chief, went beyond it. Not congressional legislation but an executive order created an Office of Emergency Management—under which, in turn, were created twenty-nine separate war agencies. Most of the immense agencies under which America was mobilized were similarly established by some form of presidential decree. And in general Congress, despite occasional champing at the bit of presidential authority, and constant bridling at the new agencies' bureaucrats, acquiesced in their establishment in response to wartime necessity. When faced with requests for huge appropriations, Senator George admitted, "All we can do is ask, 'Do you really need all that?' Then we grant the funds."

As for the direction of the war overseas, Roosevelt's undisputed authority over military strategy as Commander-in-Chief, the world-shaping diplomatic pronouncements that emerged from wartime summit conferences—all these made the war a war directed almost entirely by the President, and Congress acquiesced in that arrangement, too. Congress was an irrelevancy, a fact more striking in the case of the Senate than of the House because it was the Senate that the Constitution had entrusted with the primary congressional power in foreign affairs. In the greatest crisis to face America in the twentieth century, America's once-mighty Senate played an insignificant role.

For a time, Congress seemed similarly cowed on the home front. When, in 1942, for example, Roosevelt's proposed farm price support legislation met congressional resistance, the President set a deadline: three weeks. "In the event that Congress should fail to act [within that time], and act adequately, I shall accept the responsibility, and I shall act," he said. (Congress rushed through the legislation in time to meet the deadline.) Then bitterness began to mount on Capitol Hill—against the President, whom not a few conservative congressmen viewed as a would-be dictator; against his "ass-kissing New Dealers"; against the administrative agencies which conservatives felt were misusing the powers granted by Congress to extend the New Deal under the cloak of wartime necessity; against the new agencies' regulations that conservatives felt were creating a vast, unconstitutional body of "administrative law." With what one commentator described as "a real, deep and ugly hatred" escalating "between the Hill and the White House," Congress began attempting to reassert its status as a coequal branch of government.

Undermining the attempt, however, was the performance. Returning from the Army at the end of 1943 to cover the Senate for the United Press, Allen

Drury, who would later write perceptive novels about Washington, began keeping a perceptive personal journal on the Senate's activities. Noting in it shortly after his return that senators "have been worrying for years because they let so much power slip out of their hands," he at first predicted that the moment "the war ends, Congress will begin stripping the Presidency of one power after another." But then Drury began scrutinizing the Senate in action.

> The Senate met for 13 minutes. . . . The Senate met again today—nine minutes this time. . . . The Senate met today for an hour or two while [James] Tunnell talked about the poultry situation in Delaware, and then went over until tomorrow, when it will again go over to Friday. . . .

He watched the Senate "debating" a major bill.

> Debate was desultory and interest slack. Thirteen Senators were on the floor at one point when it seemed the bill might pass. When it turned out it wouldn't, five of them left. . . . In a day or two, after more half-hearted discussion, it will rather absent-mindedly pass one of the most important pieces of legislation to come before it in this era, and out of which there will subsequently grow many bitter and indignant attacks upon the Administration as it reads into the loose language of the law things which it was *never* the intent of Congress to authorize. The answer to that one lies in 13 Senators, who subsequently became 8.

At first Drury was reassured when old Senate hands told him that there were few senators on the floor only because most were hard at work in committee meetings. But then Drury started attending committee meetings.

> The hearings drag on and on. The routine is unvarying. Each morning the committee is scheduled to meet at 10:30. . . . At 10:35 Bob [Senator Robert] Wagner comes in, looks around at the press table with an invariable chuckle and, "Well, the press is here anyway." By 10:40 he had requested the committee secretary to call the other members on the phone and find out if they will be there. . . . After they finally arrived, everybody then settles down for a session that usually lasts until 1 PM when Wagner breaks in apologetically on the witness and asks if he would mind coming back after lunch. . . . Wagner adjourns the hearing until 2:30. . . . At 2:35, with a wisecrack for the press, Wagner enters. . . .

Drury was privy to senators' true feelings about a proposed reorganization of Congress's archaic procedures and maze of overlapping committees, and about proposals to add staff adequate for the modern era. "You can overdo this streamlining business," one senator told him. And he saw how the Senate dealt with the great problems that were urgently confronting it: the planning of postwar demobilization and the reconversion of a wartime to a peacetime economy to avoid massive dislocations and hardships to the millions of men and women who were serving their country in war. Not even the urgency of these issues could interfere with the inviolability of congressional vacations. "Everybody is ready to go home on March 31 and not come back until April 17," Drury wrote in 1944. "Why, nobody knows—except that there is an 'agreement.' . . . It is inexcusable. Reconversion is hanging fire and a terrific rumpus has been raised because 'Congress was being bypassed,' yet here goes Congress off home. . . ." There was another vacation—five weeks long—in July, and Drury knew that after the Senate returned, "the first week or so is going to be a mere formality anyway. [Senator] Jim Murray [of Montana] is on the coast holding hearings. . . . Nothing can be done to bring his conversion bill out of committee until he returns. . . ." When his mind turned to the men and women fighting on Pacific islands and in the hedgerows of Normandy, Drury wrote,

> a kind of desperation sometimes rests upon the heart. No one here is
> talking their language, no one here is inspiring them or giving them
> purpose. Nothing is planned to help bring forth tomorrow's world, or
> if it is it will be referred to committee and hearings will be held and
> someday if it is really lucky, it will appear upon the floor and become
> the center of a bitterly partisan fight that will presently rob it of all its
> heart and spirit.

Capitol Hill, he concluded, has a "subtle influence," a "certain indefinable inertia, the scarcely noticeable desiccation of ambition, force and will." Senators fall all too easily under this influence, are beaten "just by the sheer ponderous weight of an institution moving too slowly towards goals too petty and diverse."

As the war churned toward its conclusion, he noted with interest "the way in which, all over the Hill, thoughts are beginning to turn to the Senate and the coming peace debate." But, he also noted, the thoughts were not sanguine. "Deep down underneath," he wrote, "all of us are afraid of what the Senate will do. The press is afraid, the Senate is afraid. The responsibility is so great, and no one can be sure that the strength will be found to meet it. . . ." During his early days in the Press Gallery, Drury had longed for the men on the Senate floor below to assert their power. Now, having spent more time observing them, he was no longer sure he wanted them to assert it. "There are times when you sit in the gallery and watch the Senate as though you were observing some fearful force," he wrote. "You can't help a certain amount of foreboding. In spite of all the ridicule that comes their way, and in spite of all the derogation they receive, they are still terribly important and terribly powerful people." What would they do with a peace treaty? Would they do again what they did with the Treaty of Versailles?

DRURY'S UNEASINESS WAS SHARED by the country at large. During the war, public regard for congressmen, already low, sank still lower. During the war's very first months, while an unprepared America—an America unprepared largely because of Congress—was reeling from defeat after defeat, a bill arrived on Capitol Hill providing for pensions for civil service employees. House and Senate amended the bill so that their members would be included in it, and rushed it to passage—before, it was hoped, the public would notice. But the public *did* notice: the National Junior Chamber of Commerce announced a nationwide Bundles for Congress program to collect old clothes and discarded shoes for the destitute legislators. Strict gasoline rationing was being imposed on the country; congressmen and senators passed a bill allowing themselves unlimited gas. The outrage over the pension and gasoline "grabs" was hardly blunted by a hasty congressional reversal on both issues. Quips about Congress became a cottage industry among comedians: "I never lack material for my humor column when Congress is in session," Will Rogers said. The House and the Senate—the Senate of Webster, Clay, and Calhoun, the Senate that had once been the "Senate Supreme," the preeminent entity of American government—had sunk in public estimation to a point at which it was little more than a joke.

3

Seniority
and the South

AFTER THE WAR, the institutional inertia seemed to grow worse, in part because with the war's end the rationale for executive dominance lost some of its force, in part because the war's end allowed journalists to focus on the inertia more intensely—and in part because with the passage of time one cause of the inertia was indeed growing worse, since its root cause *was* the passage of time, and its effect on men.

Seniority—not even mentioned in the original Senate rules, much less in the Framers' deliberations; not even a consideration during the first half century and more of the Senate's existence—was in a way a child of slavery. That issue came to overshadow all others, so political parties had to be able to count on loyalty from senators who sat on or chaired the committees that dealt with its various aspects. In December, 1845, party caucuses took over the power of committee appointments within the Senate, passing resolutions that committees would be chaired by members of the majority party, that members of committees be carried over from Congress to Congress, that rank within each committee be determined by length of service in the Senate, and that the most senior member of the majority party would automatically become chairman.* Thereafter, party caucuses drew up lists of committee appointments; the Senate as a whole simply accepted them. A senator's rank on a committee was therefore determined by one qualification, and one alone: how long he had sat on it. And, as a student of the Senate noted, "once appointed to a committee," he could sit on it "as long as he desires." In his 1956 book on the Senate, *Citadel,* William S. White wrote that chairmanships "are not awarded by any party leader or group of hierarchs but, in nearly every instance, simply go to that man

---

*After a revision of the Senate rules in 1921, the seniority that determined rank within a committee was seniority within that committee, not in the Senate as a whole.

of the dominant party who has been longest on the committee," and "once a chairmanship is attained it is not in practice lost by any man" except when his party loses its majority in the Senate, and when his party regains the majority, he regains his chairmanship. "The perquisite . . . may be considered to be for the political life of the holder; it is in this sense hardly less than an old-fashioned kingship."

By the beginning of the Gilded Age, the "seniority rule" had hardened into unwritten law; it was because not even the Senate Four would contravene it, not even when a member's views turned out to offend them, that the Four were careful in assigning new senators to committees. "The committee assignments of one year would affect chairmanships ten years later," a Senate historian notes. Although other factors contributed, the Senate's decline during the Gilded Age paralleled this hardening.

By the mid-twentieth century, when Lyndon Johnson arrived in the Senate, seniority had been what White called "an ineluctable and irresistible force" for decades. It governed every aspect of formal Senate business, determining not just where senators sat at the long committee tables (ranking down from the chairman to the newest members at the far end; when the most junior member came to his first committee meeting, he found his name plaque at the table's foot), but the order in which they could question witnesses: questioning, as White wrote, "proceeds in the immemorial way—by seniority—first from the top man on the majority side, then to the top man on the minority side, back again to the majority side, and so forth." It determined not only committee but also subcommittee chairmanships: when a subcommittee (whose members had been appointed by the chairman of the parent committee) met for the first time, the chair was taken automatically by the senator from the majority party who had been on the parent committee longest.

Seniority also governed the Senate in ways that were seldom written about, but that were decisive in the body's impact on national life. Little journalistic attention was paid, for example, to the "conference committees," composed of delegations from each house which were appointed ostensibly only to resolve differences between the Senate and House versions of a bill (but in the case of the Senate, its conferees were authorized to insert new material) and to report back to each house an agreed-upon "compromise" version for final ratification. But after the more dramatic floor debates and votes were over, these committees met behind closed doors, generally in the Senate wing of the Capitol, and these secret meetings were often decisive in determining a bill's final form, since the version reported back to the two houses was generally accepted; as George H. Haynes, author of the most authoritative work on the Senate's first 150 years, the two-volume *The Senate of the United States,* asked: "What chance is there, especially in the hectic closing hours of Congress, for members to decide whether they ought to agree to concessions that have been made?"—particularly since reopening the subject would mean reopening debate on the entire bill, thus effectively killing it. And since the members of conference committees were almost invariably the most senior members of the committees that had reported out the bill in the first place, the reliance on these "conferences" led, in Haynes' words, to the assigning of "tremendous powers over legislation to a small group of senior senators" more conservative than the Senate as a whole. As the liberal Hubert Humphrey, who also came to the Senate in 1949, was to discover,

> Too often, particularly in areas of concern to liberals, [the] senior members . . . had voted against the bill in question or against important amendments which had been added as the result of floor debate. It was not unusual, therefore, for legislation to come back in final form without important parts that already passed the Senate. It was a take-it-or-leave-it situation then and the ultimate weapon for conservatives who might have been beaten earlier.

Seniority governed not only formal but informal Senate business. A newly elected senator encountered it on his first day on Capitol Hill, when he applied to the Rules Committee for one of the ninety-six office suites—and was informed that he had his choice only of those that had not already been chosen by senior members, and that even after he had chosen a suite, and moved in, should a more senior member change his mind and ask for it, it would be reassigned to him. Seniority governed the assignment not only of offices but of desks on the Senate floor, and of parking spaces in the Senate garage. It determined a junior senator's place at official dinners—far below the salt. So vital was the exact degree of his seniority in a senator's career that elaborate—and rigid—formulas had been devised to determine it. Senators sworn in on the same day, for example, were ranked according to previous service in the Senate, followed by service in the House, and then within the Cabinet. If necessary, the holding of a governorship was factored in. And if it was still impossible to differentiate between two senators, White says, "one may be declared senior to the other simply because his state was the earlier of the two involved to enter the Union. . . ."

Only what White calls "the passage of time" could make it appropriate for a freshman senator to rise on the floor. A new member of almost any legislative body is well advised to remain silent for a time, but in the Senate that time was supposed to last longer—until, in fact, the elders let him know it was time for him to speak. A young senator was to recall that for months after he had been sworn in, he "did not rise once." Then, "one day, a matter came up with which I had had considerable experience." An older senator "leaned over to me and said, 'Are you going to speak on this?' I said, 'No.' . . . 'I think you should speak,' he replied." And when the freshman remained reluctant, the older senator said, " 'Look, I am going to get up on the floor and ask you a question about this bill. Then you will have to speak!' And that's how I made my first speech in the Senate." Waiting for such permission was wise. "Any fledgling who dared to so much as open his mouth on the floor" without it, one observer wrote, might suddenly realize that the senior senators seated at their desks were staring at him with expressions he could hardly consider approving. And as word of what he was doing circulated, other senior senators would come to the Chamber and sit at their desks, so that they, too, could join in the cold stares.

The feelings about premature speech were very strong. Once, a freshman finished a speech on the floor and sat down next to the great Walter George. When no compliment on his oration was forthcoming, the freshman, trying to make conversation, asked George how the Senate had changed since his own early days in it. "Freshmen didn't use to talk so much," George replied. An elderly senator loved to recall the birthday of the revered Senator Borah years before. "A number of the older men got up and offered brief, laudatory speeches about it. Borah was pleased. Then a freshman senator—one who had been in the Chamber three or four months—got to his feet" to join in the chorus of praise. "That son of a bitch," Borah whispered loudly. "That son of a bitch." Borah "didn't dislike the speaker," the elderly senator would explain. "He just didn't feel that he should speak up so soon."

The more impressive a new senator's pre-Senate accomplishments might be, the more determined were the Senate elders to teach him that those accomplishments meant nothing *here*.

"We are skeptical of men who come to the Senate with big reputations," one "old-timer" said during the 1950s. Former governors were the worst; they seemed to think that they deserved more respect than the average freshman. They were quickly disabused of this notion. As one former governor related, "Back home everything revolved, or seemed to revolve, around the Governor. I had a part in practically everything that happened. There was administration. There was policy making. But [in the Senate] there was just a seat at the end of the table." Senators who had previously "reached national fame . . . have found four years and more not to be long enough to feel free to speak up loudly in the Institution," White wrote.

THE PASSAGE OF TIME had another, darker side, of course.

Because senators' terms were so long, and because many of them served so many terms (in 1949, when Lyndon Johnson came to the Senate, ten senators were in their fourth or fifth term, which meant they were nearing, or had passed, a quarter of a century in the Senate), the body's membership changed little from decade to decade—which meant that the membership was growing steadily older. In the nineteenth century, the average age of senators had been forty-five: by 1900, it had passed fifty. By 1940, it was sixty, and thirteen senators were in their seventies or eighties (in an era in which the average life span was far shorter than it would become later), and there were increasing references to Capitol Hill's "senility system," a phrase which seemed funny only until Hiram Johnson, born in 1866, shuffled slowly into the Foreign Relations Committee room, in which he had once been a towering figure, leaning heavily on a cane and supported by his wife, to sit through hearings, usually silent but occasionally straining to address a question in a barely audible voice with long, painful pauses between words: "Is—it—not—true—that . . ." (When reporters asked Johnson if he planned to run again in 1946, when he would be eighty years old, he said he did—and probably would have, had he not died in 1945.) One day in 1945, seventy-seven-year-old Kenneth McKellar of Tennessee fainted during a speech. His ailment proved to be only indigestion, but Allen Drury, observing from the Press Gallery the anxiety on other senators' faces as they huddled in little groups below him, realized that "the ghost of Death" is "never far from the mind of the Senate." Rome's Senate had, of course, been conceived as an assembly of elderly men, and of all the Roman concepts that had been realized in America's Senate, none had been realized more fully. It was a place of old men, old men in a young nation; not a few of them had been born before their states had even *been* states.

Since chairmanships were awarded by seniority, the seniority rule's most significant impact on America's Senate—and on America—therefore came through the chairmanships of the Senate's fifteen great standing committees, those committees whose decisions were almost never overruled. The chairmen were the real powers in the Senate; a committee could not even meet except at its chairman's call. He and he alone set his committee's agenda, he alone appointed its staff, decided the number of subcommittees that would be established, and what bills would be referred to them. A party leader—a Majority or Minority Leader—was only a mere *primus inter pares* (and not all that *primus* either) among fiercely independent senatorial barons, unassailable in the committee rooms that were their strongholds. The removal of a chairman was all but unthinkable; no chairman had been removed for more than a quarter of a century. "The 'Old Bulls'—the committee chairmen—ran the Senate," one observer recalls. And a gavel in one's hand was no defense against the infirmities of age. In 1940, when seventy-five-year-old Arthur Capper of Kansas became ranking Republican member of the Agriculture Committee, he was already deaf, an old man so frail that one reporter called him "a living shadow, one hand cupped behind his ear and a strained expression on his face" as he tried to hear witnesses' testimony, "breaking in from time to time with some hurrying querulous question." But in 1946 the Republicans became the majority party in the Senate, and seniority elevated Capper, now eighty-one, to Agriculture's chairmanship, although by that time, as another reporter noted, "he could neither make himself understood, nor understand others." Democrat Carter Glass of Virginia had ascended to the chairmanship of the Appropriations Committee in 1932, when he was seventy-four. During the 1940s, Glass was very ill—had been very ill for years, sequestered in a suite in the

Mayflower Hotel that always had a guard at the door. He had not even appeared on Capitol Hill since 1942. By 1945, there were even suggestions that perhaps Glass, then eighty-seven, should resign. But, as Drury reported, "from the guarded suite . . . through whose doors no outsider has passed in many months to see what lies within, has come the usual answer. Mrs. Glass has replied for the Senator. The suggestion will not be considered." In Glass' temporary absence, the seventy-seven-year-old McKellar presided over Appropriations. "In his day," Allen Drury wrote, "Old Mack from Tennessee" had been "the most powerful and the most ruthless man in the Senate," but that day was drawing to a close. More and more frequently during the 1940s, after he had been presiding over a committee hearing for some hours, he would pound the gavel to signal the session to begin. (McKellar was sensitive about his age. Once he was politely asked in a Senate corridor, "How are you today, Senator?" As the journalist Russell Baker relates, "In reply, the old man, interpreting the words as a reflection on his failing health, raised his cane, thwacked it angrily across the fellow's collarbone, and passed on without a word.") When Lyndon Johnson arrived in the Senate in 1949, McKellar, now eighty-one, was still Chairman of Appropriations; five other committee chairmen were in their seventies.

As disgust with the Senate's ineptitude intensified after the war, a hundred critics focused on the seniority system as a major culprit. Columnist Ernest K. Lindley wrote in 1949 that "it has been condemned in recent years by almost every authority or impartial observer of Congress." Pointing out that under that system, ability counted for nothing, energy counted for nothing—intelligence, passion, will, principles, all counted for nothing—they noted that, in the words of Roland Young, secretary of the Senate Foreign Relations Committee, the seniority rule makes impossible "the utilization of the best material for the most important offices. Tenure and ability are not the same thing." The *Washington Post,* referring to Congress as a "gerontocracy," said that "to consider nothing but length of service in the choice of chairmen is to put Congress under a crippling handicap." And there was another point. Since chairmen owed their places not to their party's leader in the Senate or to their national political party but solely to what the political scientist George B. Galloway called "the accident of tenure," they were therefore independent not only of the senatorial leader but indeed of their party, and of its platforms, promises, and philosophy—of party responsibility in the largest sense. The system "flaunts established political principles: that of party government; of a legislature responsible to the electoral mandate," Young said. Furthermore, since, particularly in the Democratic Party, "the seniority line," as the political scientist E. L. Oliver put it, "is also the line of cleavage between progressives and conservatives," reliance on seniority put effective control of the Senate (and of the House) "into the hands of men wholly out of sympathy with the party platform, with the national administration, and with the clear majority of Congressmen elected upon the party ticket." "Adherence to blind choice under the seniority rule . . . makes a farce out of the democratic principle," the *Washington Post* said. Such arguments ignored the fact that it was not that principle but rather independence (including independence of the "electoral mandate") that was the Founding Fathers' most cherished *desideratum* for senators—that the seniority rule was, as one Senate historian did in fact note, "a protection against boss rule of the Senate." But it was also true that parties had not been a major factor in government when the Fathers had been drafting the Constitution, and that independence of party, when parties had become so integral a part of the governmental process, had skewed the Senate's relationship to that process. Seniority therefore added, in George Goodwin's words, "a new non-constitutional dimension . . . to our constitutional system of separation of powers." Feeling that the will of the people would be thwarted as long as the rule stood, the critics demanded that it be abolished. "If either of the two major parties is to serve as a vehicle for social action," Oliver wrote, this "archaic procedure . . . will have to be scrapped. . . . Unless such a change is made, the expressed attitudes of the people will not be embodied in legislation."

ADVOCATES OF THE SENIORITY SYSTEM, however, pointed out that its rigidity eliminated the bitter, time-consuming fights and political logrolling that would otherwise accompany the selection of committee chairmen at the beginning of each new session of Congress. "Nobody has ever produced a really workable alternative," William White says. And harshly though that system might be assailed, it was protected by a very powerful force: itself. Junior senators might sneer at it, but senators are human, and as, with the passage of years, they accumulated the power and perquisites which were based on that system, the logic behind it, its fairness and justice, became increasingly clear to them. It was, in many cases, the rock on which they based their campaigns for re-election, since their more sophisticated constituents—the ones most deeply concerned about the outcome of that campaign—were well aware of the benefits the incumbent's seniority gave to his state, gave, to a disproportionate extent, to them. "The longer I stay in Washington, the more sympathetic to [the seniority rule] I become," Senator Leverett Saltonstall of Massachusetts said. The chairmanships that senior senators held because of that rule—had become, as one observer was to put it, a part of their identity, "a part of their being . . . almost of life itself." There seemed no realistic possibility of persuading them that the rule should be changed. And since these were the senators who held the power—all the power—in the Senate, there was no realistic possibility that the rule would be changed. William White said flatly that "The Senate would no more abandon it than it would its name."

NOTHING ABOUT THE SENATE would be changed, it seemed. The Senate's world was made up not only of the Capitol's north wing but of another building, which pointed at that wing from across broad Constitution Avenue. This building was known simply as the "Senate Office Building" (there was only one Senate office building then; new senators were warned to spell out its name in full when giving a constituent their address; as one senator observed, "If you give him the abbreviation—S.O.B.—he will not know whether you are calling him one, or expect him to call you one"), and it indeed contained only offices and committee rooms, but these were the offices of *senators* and *Senate* committee rooms, and the building was the *Senate* office building; "Never in the history of the world was there such an office building," the *New York Times* marveled when it opened in 1909.

In authorizing its construction, the Senate had made clear that it should embody senatorial philosophy—the same philosophy of restraint and dignity that had motivated the body to decree that its Chamber should be unadorned. The man directing the search for an architect said he was looking for one "of mature years . . . and it would not scare me off to hear his colleagues say that 'He is a little old-fashioned . . . ! That is what we need now: a little of the old-fashioned but correct architecture." And the architects selected—Carrère & Hastings of New York—had captured that philosophy perfectly.

It was a vast structure—low (only three stories high on the side facing the Capitol, five stories on the far side, so steeply did Capitol Hill fall away) but long, so long that from its majestic entrance pavilion, modeled on the pavilions of the Louvre, stretched away a colonnade of thirty-four thirty-foot-high columns, columns fluted for beauty and paired for strength, a towering colonnade that was in itself longer than a football field and that angled away from the Capitol in a diagonal that seemed to go on endlessly—except that there was, far down Constitution Avenue, an end: another, matching, if slightly smaller, entrance pavilion. In this building, the *Times* said, "a thousand men would feel lonesome"; it covered "what in New York would be a space of several city blocks." The building's exterior was a white Vermont marble selected for its unusual purity and hardness. The trees in front of that colonnade were still small enough in 1949 so that their leaves did not yet blur the façade or soften it, and from the Capitol's Senate wing the long line of tall columns and the majestic pavilions that flanked them gleamed at you across the Capitol's lawns, brilliant and dazzling in the late-afternoon sun, or loomed majestically through rain on a gray day.

But like the House Office Building on the other side of Capitol Hill, also by Carrère & Hastings, the Senate Building was designed so that it would not compete with but complement the Capitol, toward which both buildings were canted in such a way that they were in effect pointing at it.* The building's roof

---

*Although the House and Senate Office Buildings were originally quite similar in design, a fourth story was added to the House Building in 1908. (To ease overcrowding, a second House Office Building was built in 1933.) Trying to economize, the House used imitation marble and limestone in the interior; the Senate insisted on the finest marble throughout the interior, at an additional cost of about a million and a half dollars. The contrast in the cornerstone-laying of the two buildings displayed the difference in philosophies. The cornerstone-laying for the

would be ornamented only by a simple balustrade, the architects said, not by prominent decorative elements which might "detract from the effect of the Capitol building." And while the Capitol's exterior was lavishly ornamented, it was decided that that would not be the case with the façade of the Senate and House Office Buildings.

The ground level of the Senate Building, the base of the long row of columns, was of the simplest design: Concord granite rusticated but otherwise unadorned so that except for small arched windows, the long lines of that hard stone stretch unbroken down Constitution Avenue. The capitals of those formidably paired columns are very simple, and the long entablature, a football-field-length entablature, that the columns support is very different from the Capitol's entablatures, crammed as are the Capitol's with reliefs of heroic figures. The entablature of the Senate Building is unbroken by a single decoration: on its entire length there is not a single carving of a leaf or an acorn or a bird—stretching down Constitution is nothing but a long, broad band of gleaming white marble, with, above it, only the simplest narrow classic egg and dart molding, and that simple balustrade. Architectural historians noted that the Senate Building was "more conservative" than other government buildings of the time. If the exterior was stately, even majestic, the stateliness and majesty were restrained, dignified, severe, uncompromisingly austere—testimony in granite and marble, that very hard marble, to the Senate's grandeur and power, and to its philosophy.

THE BUILDING'S INTERIOR was testimony to other aspects of that philosophy. Inside its main entrance across from the Capitol was a circular arcade of piers (modeled on the piers of the Royal Chapel at Versailles) out of which rose arches supporting a circle of eighteen columns that in turn supported a coffered dome that soared up to a circular skylight sixty-eight feet above the floor. But the grandeur of this spacious rotunda was a grandeur of utter simplicity, of what one critic described as an "elegance" that was "almost stoic" in its "exceptional restraint." Suggestions had been made that colored marbles be used on the columns, but this was the home of the body that had kept its Chamber untainted by a single painting; "Color would take away from the dignity and monumental character of the design," John Carrère replied. He allowed gray marble circles to be set into the rotunda's shining white marble floor.* Otherwise, the white marble of the entire grand entrance to the Senate

---

House Office Building, in 1905, was carried out with pageantry and speeches, including one by President Theodore Roosevelt: his celebrated "muckraking" speech. The Senate instructed the Capitol architect to "omit everything that would give the laying of the stone any prominence." There were no speeches at all; as the *Washington Post* reported, "workmen went about the job as if it were an ordinary piece of stone." Only a few spectators—and, so far as can be determined, no senators—were present.

*The coffered panels in the ceiling would, decades later, be painted crimson and outlined with gold leaf.

Office Building—piers, arches, columns, dome—was unrelieved by any color except for the marble's grayish veins. Opposite the doorway, beyond the circle of piers, was a palatial double stairway, in the same white marble and in the style of the Italian Renaissance, and at the top was the Senate's "Conference Chamber," a room (later known as the "Senate Caucus Room") worthy of the Senate: spacious (it would seat three hundred spectators comfortably), high-ceilinged, its marble walls ranged by twelve massive Corinthian columns. And out from the rotunda stretched the corridors lined with other, smaller marble chambers for public investigations and hearings, and with the individual office suites of the senators themselves.

These were senatorial corridors.

They were long—four hundred feet long, some of them; there were more than three miles of corridors in the Senate Office Building—and their ceilings were so high that, broad though they were, they appeared narrow. And they were dim and somber. A row of old-fashioned lighting globes dotted the ceilings, and their lights were reflected down the center of the white marble floors in a line as rigid as if it were an element set into the marble. But the globes were too high and spaced too far apart to cast much light, and the corridors were so long that even on sunny days the light from the window at their far end penetrated only a little way down them, and some corridors had no windows at the end. And along each side of a corridor was a row of very tall, dark mahogany doors, towering over anyone walking past them and stretching down each side of the dim corridor like a long line of forbidding sentinels guarding the dignity of the men within.

The corridors were empty—empty not only of ornament (there were no flags, national or state, in the hallways of the Senate Office Building then, no state seals on the doors; "it was considered beneath the dignity of a senator to put out a flag or a seal," one reporter who spent a lot of time in that building recalls; "the only thing you would see in the halls was umbrellas on rainy days") but of people. There were relatively few visitors—the influx of constituents dropping by their senators' offices in 1949 was only a trickle compared to what it would later become in the era of mass air travel—and so vast was the building that visitors were swallowed up by it. And so were the approximately eleven hundred people—ninety-six senators, their staff and Senate maintenance people—who worked in the building in 1949, particularly because there was very little visiting between offices then. The building's mores were as rigidly formal as its architecture. In his thirty-fifth year in the Senate, John L. McClellan of Arkansas was to boast that during those thirty-five years he had never once been inside another senator's office. Robert C. Albright, who covered the Senate for the *Washington Post,* wrote in 1949 that "You can tread marble miles of Senate Office Building corridors without ever seeing an open door." When a door was opened, furthermore, the face of the receptionist inside was not always all that welcoming; "dropping in was not encouraged," a secretary recalls. About ten in the morning, many staffers congregated in the "cafeteria" (a cafeteria lined with fluted pilasters) on the second floor for coffee, and to socialize with their counterparts on other staffs; the rest of the time there was little socializing—and little traffic in the halls. Sometimes when you turned into one of those corridors, there would be a little knot of reporters waiting outside a closed door or questioning a senator who had just come out; a remarkably large proportion of committee sessions then were executive, or closed, sessions. Sometimes a figure—black against the light from the window behind him, his face all but unrecognizable in the gloom even if he was a senator—would be walking toward you. But quite often, it seemed, when you turned into a corridor there would be, in that long, long space, no one at all.

The corridors were silent. Voices seemed to be swallowed up by their length and their height. And of course so empty were they that often there was no voice to be heard, and you would be walking down a corridor in a silence broken only by the click of your heels on the marble floor and the distant pings of elevator bells, walking in silence between the rows of tightly closed doors that towered over you in the gloom.

And the building, grand though it was, was merely a setting for the men for whom it had been built—those ninety-six human institutions known as "senators."

The senators were very conscious of their prerogatives. Carl Hayden of Arizona was outwardly polite and courtly to the members of his staff, and to anyone who greeted him in the halls, but when he had lunch, or a cup of coffee, in the cafeteria, he would lay his cane on the table at which he had decided to sit, even if there were already staffers sitting at it, and, recalls one, "when he got to the head of the line and came back, you'd better be gone."

And more than a few senators were not friendly and polite at all—except to their fellow senators. Staff was staff, and that meant they were so far below the level of senators that even the most ordinary courtesies would be wasted on them. There were senators who would not even return the greeting of a staff member if they met him in a corridor of the Senate Office Building. Some senators—Taft was a prime example—seemed to make a point of not returning a greeting. "If you saw Senator Taft coming down the hall, you wouldn't say hello to him," one staff member says. "He just wasn't a man you would say hello to. He was always deep in thought."

They knew how to deal with violations of their prerogatives. A senator wanting to use an elevator pushed the buzzer three times. The elevator operator was supposed to ignore all other buzzes and proceed immediately to pick the senator up. In fact, even if there were passengers already in the elevator, with the elevator going in the opposite direction, the operator's instructions were to immediately reverse direction and proceed to the senator's floor, bringing his passengers along. These instructions were ignored at an operator's peril. If he was not on the alert and did not immediately respond to the magical three buzzes, some senators were understanding, but others were not. Hearing an elevator car continue to move away from him after he had rung, Senator William Jenner of Indiana would, in an instantaneous burst of rage, smack his palm repeatedly against the bronze elevator door. And everyone in the building knew what had happened when, one day, Pat McCarran of Nevada "got passed by" after he had rung. "He just turned on his heel and went back to his office and called the Sergeant-at-Arms and the kid was fired on the spot," recalls an aide.

Senators were deeply conscious of what they called their "dignity." One of them, forced by defeat to leave the Senate, lamented what he had lost. "Where else in our land can be found perquisites so plentiful, traditions so rich, individual respect so deep . . . dignity and honor so complete?" he asked. There were occasional angry outbursts and individual feuds that lasted for years, and it had become noticeable during the 1940s that some of the new senators were a little more informal than their frock-coated predecessors. But the older senators—and these were, of course, the ones who ran the Senate and set its tone: most of the twenty-two southerners, of course, and the New England Brahmins like Lodge and Saltonstall, and Republican leaders like Taft and Eugene Millikin, and, naturally, Chairman Hayden of the Rules Committee—were, in dealing with each other, models of senatorial formality. They talked to each other in private, in fact, as they talked to each other in public, addressing each other not by name but by title, and duplicating the elaborate formality of the Senate floor even behind the closed doors of executive sessions. During one such Rules Committee session, for example, Chairman Hayden began a statement by saying: "My distinguished colleague, the Senator from New Hampshire, Mr. Bridges, advised the chairman of this committee that . . ." Another member of the Rules Committee then said: "I think that is right. The wise chairman of this committee, as usual, has made a very valuable statement." The closed doors of their offices were a symbol of the fact that informality was not encouraged. Personal relationships were governed by ceremony and ritual. When one senator wanted to visit another in his office, he would telephone to ask when it would be convenient for him to drop by and, when he arrived, would never walk into the senator's private office until the receptionist had telephoned to announce him. And on such visits, the business talk was invariably preceded by a long ritual of senatorial friendship. "You just didn't barge in and start talking business," one administrative aide recalls. "It just wasn't done." The Senate Office Building was, in January, 1949, a place of courtesy, of courtliness, of dignity, of restraint, of refinement and of uncompromising austerity and rigidity. Its corridors were corridors of power—of the Senate brand of power, cold and hard.

As SENIORITY'S GRIP had tightened on the Senate, so had the grip of the South. The correlation between the two had, of course, been apparent even before the Civil War; seniority had, after all, given "the chairmanship of every

single committee" to the "slaveholding states" by 1859. Republican opposition
to slavery had made the South so solidly Democratic that it was the most
rigidly one-party section of the United States. Its senators were sent back to
Washington term after term, long-running stars ("Human institutions with
southern accents," one journalist called them) on a capital stage on which the
rest of the cast seemed to be constantly changing. (A notable exception were
the southern members of the House of Representatives.) And although the
eleven states of the Old Confederacy held only twenty-two of the ninety-six
seats on the Senate floor, they held a far larger proportion of the gavels in the
Senate committee rooms—particularly the gavels that represented the greatest
power. In 1949, when Lyndon Johnson came to the Senate, the three most
powerful Senate committees, by most rankings, were Appropriations, Foreign
Relations, and Finance. Southerners were chairmen of all three. And southern
dominance extended further down the list of the fifteen Standing Committees.
Only two of the fifteen—District of Columbia, which administered the capital
city, and Rules, which handled "the housekeeping administration of the
Senate"—were, White was to say, "not especially relevant to great public
issues." Of the other thirteen committees, exactly one was not chaired by either
a southerner or by a senator who was a firm ally of the South. Nor was the dominance limited to the chairmanships of those committees. The more powerful
the committee, it seemed, the more its membership was stacked in depth by
southerners. If there was one committee which in 1949 was considered the
most powerful of all, it was Appropriations, because of its control of funding
for the departments and agencies of the federal government; "No matter how
much you legislate, the main ingredient is money and whatever type of program you have, its success is dependent on adequate financing," a senator was
to say. Successful though a senator might be in winning authorization from one
of the legislative committees for a project vital to his state, the money for the
project still had to be appropriated. Of the thirteen Democrats on Appropriations, seven were southerners. And decisions on appropriations requests were
made first—and very seldom overruled—by one of Appropriations' subcommittees, each of which was given, as a student of the process noted, such great
"latitude" in its field that decisions went "largely unchallenged" by the full
committee. In 1949, Appropriations had ten subcommittees. Southerners were
chairmen of six. Nor was the dominance of subcommittees—of Appropriations or other committees—limited to *their* chairmen. One senator—not a
southerner—was to describe "an interlocking directorate of southerners who
are on every subcommittee in depth. If you get rid of one, you still have another
southerner."

The power thus conferred on the South was reinforced by other factors.
One was ability. Unlike senators from other sections, southern senators, White
wrote, "had no chance of getting a serious nomination for the Presidency, and
they knew it." And because in the South *United States Senator* was therefore the

highest title at which political men could realistically aim, that title attracted men of a very high caliber, so that many southern senators were exceptional individuals, of great personal force and talent.

Another factor was a particular use to which abilities were put. When southerners came to the Senate, they came to stay; they studied the Senate's rules and precedents with the concentration of men who knew they would be living by them for the rest of their lives. Forty "Standing Rules" had been adopted by the Senate in 1884, and amended and re-amended over the ensuing decades, and there were hundreds of pages of precedents establishing the rules' meaning. Many of the southern senators did a lot of reading in those rules and precedents. They gave themselves individual seminars in them: in the 1920s, Vice President Charles G. Dawes, presiding over the Senate, realized that on the lower dais before him was "a modest young man who knew all the rules"; in 1935, Charles L. Watkins of Arkansas, a lowly clerk who had been helping to keep the Senate *Journal,* or minutes, was appointed the Senate's Parliamentarian, and southern senators would drop in to his office just off the Senate floor and sit for long, leisurely conversations about rules and precedents, and about the theory and logic behind them. As a result, they knew what they covered, and what they didn't cover; knew how to use them—and how to get around them. "Because of his instinctive sympathy with the Institution and all that is in it, the southern senator is like a man who can put his hand instantly to any book in a cherished library," White wrote. "In consequence he is a past master of the precedents, the practices, and even the moods of the Senate and as a parliamentarian formidable in any debate or maneuver." With a frequency that would be almost unimaginable at the end of the century, there would be detailed discussions on the Senate floor about parliamentary procedures. In skirmishes and pitched battles in any parliamentary body, of course, rules and precedents play an important role, and the degree to which the southerners had mastered them more fully than their opponents was repeatedly apparent: it was striking, for example, how often, in such fights, after the South's opponents had launched a maneuver, a southern senator would rise to beg to point out, courteously but firmly, that the maneuver was, under one precedent or another from some long-past decade, simply out of order, and how often, when the presiding officer looked up the precedent, he had regretfully to rule that that was indeed the case. Once, in a Democratic caucus, one of the Senate elders was saying that he had made a practice, at the beginning of each new Congress, of reading through the volume of *Senate Procedures,* hundreds of pages long, underlining passages as he went. "I recommend that every senator read that book frequently," he said. Turning to a colleague, a non-southern senator whispered sneeringly, "This is one senator who has no intention of *ever* reading that book." The senator who was not from the South thought he was demonstrating his sophistication, or perhaps his sense of humor. What he was really demonstrating was why, when liberals tried to fight on the Senate floor, they were like children in the southerners' hands.

And the South's power in the Senate rested on another keystone that was as solid as the chairmanships and the seniority rule, although it was not a rule, not even an informal one, but rather a rule's absence. This missing rule was one that would force senators to stop talking about a bill, and vote on it.

A provision to make possible this most fundamental of legislative functions—a provision for "moving" the "previous question," for a senator to make a motion demanding that a measure be brought to a vote without further debate or amendment—had been adopted by the British Parliament in 1604. America's House of Representatives had adopted it in 1789, later—because it had so many members—coupling it with a provision that the maximum time a member could hold the floor was one hour. By 1948, some version of this motion had been incorporated into the functioning of forty-five of America's forty-eight state legislatures, and of most of the legislative bodies in the world's other countries as well. Indeed, the so-called "previous question" motion had been one of the first rules adopted by the Senate itself in 1789, but when the rules were modified, in 1806, it was omitted, as was perhaps understandable in a body created as insurance against the will of a majority of states being imposed over the wishes of a minority of states, since what better insurance could there be than to make sure that a measure embodying the majority will would never come to a vote so long as a small group of states, or for that matter one state (or for that matter one senator), didn't want it to? For many years after 1806—for 111 years, to be precise—the only way a senator could be made to stop talking so that a vote could be taken on a proposed measure was if there was unanimous consent that he do so, an obvious impossibility. And there took place therefore so many "extended discussions" of measures to keep them from coming to a vote that the device got a name, "filibuster," from the Dutch word *vrijbuiter,* which means "freebooter" or "pirate," and which passed into the Spanish as *filibustero,* because the sleek, swift ship used by Caribbean pirates was called a *filibote,* and into legislative parlance because the device was, after all, a pirating, or hijacking, of the very heart of the legislative process.

Like seniority, filibustering became a tool of the South early on. The first senatorial *filibustero,* in fact, was Randolph of Virginia, who in 1825 talked day after day to prevent a vote on a series of measures, proposed by President John Quincy Adams, that Randolph felt would give industrial New England an advantage over the agrarian South. During the decades after the Civil War, the filibuster would be used by senators of other sections or persuasions to block votes on a variety of subjects—the elder La Follette was one of the most aggressive filibusterers—but most frequently by southerners, and in 1872, at southern instigation, the device was strengthened by a precedent that held that, in the absence of any rule to the contrary, a senator could not be called to order for irrelevancy in a debate, that he could therefore prevent a vote on any bill by talking about any subject he chose.

A curb on the practice was enacted in 1917, after President Wilson had added a phrase to the American political lexicon by denouncing "a little group of willful men" (actually eleven senators, including La Follette and his fellow liberal George Norris) who had talked to death Wilson's proposal to arm American merchantmen against German submarine attack. The Senate, at Wilson's goading, passed a rule, Rule 22, permitting debate upon a "pending" measure to be closed off when, after a petition for such "cloture" was presented by sixteen senators, it was approved by two-thirds of the senators present and voting. (After a cloture motion was passed, each senator was allowed to speak for one hour before the vote was taken.)

The rule was drafted by a bipartisan committee, "whose stated purpose was to terminate successful filibustering," Galloway says, but the committee had made a mistake, one of omission, leaving a loophole, and you couldn't make mistakes against the South. While Rule 22 made cloture possible on any pending measure—any bill that had been brought to the floor to be dealt with next— other Senate rules required a motion, and vote, to *make* a measure pending, and the 1917 rule neglected to mention such a vote. A senator or group of senators could therefore begin talking as soon as a motion was made to bring to the floor a bill they didn't like—and there was still no procedure to impose "cloture" and stop them from talking, and therefore a vote on that motion could never be taken, and the bill would never get to the floor, thus never reaching the stage at which cloture could be applied. Nor was this the only loophole. The other, also discovered by a southern senator, was created by an apparently unrelated clause in Rule 3, which said that each day's session should be begun by reading the previous day's *Journal,* or minutes. This reading was normally simply waived, or "suspended," but, Rule 3 said, "the reading of the *Journal* shall not be suspended unless by unanimous consent; and when any motion shall be made to read or correct the same, it shall be deemed a privileged question, and proceeded with until disposed of." One day in 1922, the Senate was about to take up a bill designed to stop the practice of lynching. Tall, courtly Pat Harrison of Mississippi sauntered up to the dais, and asked Parliamentarian Watkins if that meant that so long as he was discussing the *Journal* on the floor, cloture could not be imposed on him. Watkins told Harrison that was indeed the case, and Harrison and other southerners thereupon discussed the *Journal,* keeping from the Senate floor not only the anti-lynching bill but any other bill, until the bill's sponsors gave up and withdrew it.

Like the seniority system, the filibuster was protected by a very powerful force: itself. Since the loophole in Rule 22 allowed any motion to bring a bill to the floor to be filibustered, bringing a civil rights bill to the floor would require a change in Rule 22. And changing Rule 22 would require a motion to change it— which could be filibustered. This was perhaps the ultimate legislative Catch-22: any attempt to close the loophole allowed the loophole to be used to keep it from being closed. And because of it there was no realistic possibility that the filibuster would be changed. The filibuster was not a device employed in normal

Senate activities as the chairmanships were, since it was used mainly in cases of exceptional threat to the South. But the threat of the filibuster was always there—hanging over, and influencing, every attempt by the body to deal with matters dear to the South. The Senate's tradition of unlimited debate was perhaps even more important to the South than the seniority system, as was demonstrated by the fact that while the South held a disproportionate share of committee chairmanships in the House as well as the Senate, there was no filibuster in the House, and that body therefore not infrequently passed civil rights legislation—which then died in the Senate.

The Senate, White summed up, "is, to most peculiar degree, a *Southern* Institution . . . growing at the heart of this ostensibly national assembly." To a southern senator, White wrote, the Senate was "his great home." And because of the southerners' "entrenched position of minority" within the Democratic Party in the Senate, the home rested on a deep bedrock of power. "In the final decisions of the Senate it is nearly always the Southerners whose influence is most pervasive and persuasive." Not only was the Senate "the South's unending revenge . . . for Gettysburg," he said, it was "the only place in the country where the South did not lose the war. . . . While his party has in general maintained a liberal and forward-looking outlook," for generations the southern senator has "kept unchanged his dream of the past." And, White said, as long as the South held the Senate—its great stronghold—that dream would continue unchanged.

THIS REALITY WAS in a way softened in the public consciousness by the trappings, and the values, of the Senate, as if their identity with the values of the South were what mattered. Courtesy and courtliness were characteristics of the southern aristocracy—and of the Senate, where these traits were not only esteemed but were reinforced by the body's rules. The rules imposed a verbal impersonality on debate to ensure civility and formality. All remarks made on the floor were required to be addressed not directly to another senator but to "Mr. President" (the presiding officer at the time)—a device that functioned as a psychological barrier between antagonists. Senators speaking on the floor were also required to refer to each other only by title, a device which placed the emphasis on the office rather than the individual ("If I may venture to offer a reply to the distinguished senior Senator from North Dakota") and was therefore, as a Senate historian notes, "a safeguard against asperities in debate and personalities of all kinds." Referring to another senator by name—or by any form of the second person—was forbidden. "There is but one 'You' in the Chamber, and that is the Presiding Officer," Senator George Hoar had said in 1909. " 'You' can never under any circumstances be applied to an individual senator." During the 1940s, as a Senate observer wrote, addressing a fellow senator in the second person was still "almost an unforgivable sin. It must always be in the third person." Using exaggeration to make his point, Alben Barkley of Kentucky advised a freshman, "If you think a colleague is stupid, refer to him as 'the able, learned and distinguished senator,' but if you know he is stupid, refer to him as 'the *very* able, learned and distinguished senator." The Senate rule—Rule 19—against "asperities" applied not only to individuals ("No Senator in debate shall directly or indirectly, by any form of words, impute to another Senator or to other Senators any conduct or motive unworthy or unbecoming a Senator") but to states ("No Senator in debate shall refer offensively to any State of the Union"). It was out of order not only for a senator to attack a colleague, but even to read on the floor an attack by someone else—a newspaper article or letter, for example; "when such matter by inadvertence has been read, by direction of the Senate, it has been expunged from the record," says the Senate historian. And should a senator violate that edict, not only the senator attacked but any other senator, or the presiding officer, could call him to order, and "when a Senator shall be called to order" under Rule 19, "he shall sit down"—at once, without another word—"and not proceed without leave of the Senate," leave which could only be granted by formal motion. And, says another historian, "To be called to order under Rule 19 was considered a disgrace then [during the 1940s and '50s]. Your colleagues wouldn't meet your eyes. You were *in disgrace.*" The decorum that characterized the floor of the United States Senate at mid-century was difficult even to imagine at the century's end. So thoroughly had southern influence brought to the Senate floor the flavor—the graciousness, the formality, the civility (right down to a gift for "gracefully waving away mere political differences with an opponent")—of the Southland that, in the words of Russell Baker, writing in 1961, the Senate's manner was "as elaborately courteous as a Savannah lawyer's."

The South was a land of oratory, and many of the great moments in the Senate's history, even during the dark postwar years, were, as White relates, moments when one of the "archaically eloquent" southern orators rose to make a full-dress speech.

> He will begin softly, with wry self-deprecation, almost with an embarrassment of humility. . . .
> He will find to have been very sound, indeed, nearly all that has been said before, by foe and friend. And then, as he goes along and the clock hands slip by, the tone, at first imperceptibly, will change. The voice toward which men had been leaning more or less intently, so low and calm was it, will begin to rise in volume and to fall in tone. And at the end it has become a commanding pipe organ, rolling and thundering out before the wicked, the foolish and the insensitive.

The very philosophy on which the Senate had been founded "was peculiarly Southern both in flavor and structure," White noted. The "most influential" of the Senate's founders—Madison, Charles Pinckney and others—"were themselves men of Southern trait and Southern view," he pointed out. They embodied in its very conception "a quite unhidden concept not only that the Institution should *not* be popular but that its personnel should be aristocratic." One of the keystones of the philosophy on which they constructed it—"that providing for the equal voice of each state in the new Institution"—was of course the philosophy that has been cherished by the Senate, and the South, to this day. Another was continuity. "The breath of life of the Senate is, of course, continuity," White wrote. "And . . . continuity of service is" the southerners' "special property."

So dominant was the southern senator within the Senate, in fact, that the public saw that institution in his image, an image of a senator with a flowing mane of gray hair, a cutaway coat, string tie, and an organ-like, melodic, mellifluous voice. The image had been embodied in the famous radio cartoon character, Senator Claghorne, whose unctuous drawl delighted America on the Fred Allen comedy show every Sunday night; Claghorne was the dominant image in the public mind of the American senator, part of the joke that the Senate had become.

BUT IT WAS a cruel joke.

The enormous power held by each of the southern committee chairmen individually was multiplied by their unity, by what White called a "oneness found nowhere else in politics." The symbol was the legendary "Southern Caucus," the meetings of the twenty-two southern senators which were held in the office of their leader, Richard Brevard Russell of Georgia, whenever crisis threatened—meetings that were, White said, "for all the world like reunions of a large and highly individualistic family whose members are nevertheless bound by one bond." In those meetings, the southern position was agreed upon, its tactics mapped, its front made solid. Sometimes, leaving that office, its members would walk as a body to the Senate Chamber and enter together, in an unspoken show of unity. The tall double doors in the center of the Chamber's rear wall would swing open, and there they would be: George of Georgia, Byrd of the Byrds of Virginia, Old Mack from Tennessee, Cotton Ed, and, in cutaways, string ties and flowing gray manes, Clyde Roark Hoey of North Carolina, who still wore a high wing collar, and Marse Tom Connally of Texas. Up in the Press Gallery, a reporter would whisper to his fellows, "The South has arrived."

And of course the South had allies, and not alone from the border states of Kentucky, Missouri, Maryland, and West Virginia—states in which, during the Civil War, Confederate sympathies had run high. Its allies also included Republican conservatives who had been driven into their arms during the 1937 Court-packing fight, and had remained there ever since. And since these

Republicans were from the safest Republican states, the essentially one-party bastions of conservatism in the Midwest and New England that also returned senators term after term, they, too, had long tenure—and the power that goes with it. So even during the rare Congresses in which the Democrats were in the minority, this conservative coalition, its power cemented into place by a firm admixture of seniority, still ruled the Senate, and the South still held its power there. Southerners helped GOP conservatives defeat liberal economic legislation, and in return these conservatives, most of them from states without enough black voters to punish them, tacitly refrained from supporting the civil rights legislation anathema to the South, and from breaking southern filibusters.

The coalition was, in fact, growing steadily stronger, as was shown by the fate of the major domestic bills that Roosevelt sent to Capitol Hill after 1937. Although he had won re-election in 1940 and 1944, two victories which might be considered an endorsement of the New Deal and a mandate to extend its liberal domestic policies, to pass new social legislation for the third of a nation still ill-clothed, ill-housed, ill-fed, not one of those bills had passed. A Congress dominated by southern conservatives may have given the President a free hand in running the war; on the domestic front, Roosevelt never got a single major domestic bill through Congress after the Court-packing fight.

OF ALL THE AREAS in which the Senate failed America, it failed most memorably on the issue that was the single most important issue of the time: race.

So strong was the South, with its conservative allies, in that body that sometimes it disdained to use the two loopholes that allowed filibusters to keep civil rights bills from coming to the floor. It let the bills come to the floor—and filibustered them there, confident that civil rights proponents could not muster the two-thirds vote necessary to impose cloture. Nor was this confidence misplaced. In January, and again in February, 1938, after an outbreak of horrifying lynchings in the South, anti-lynching bills had been introduced in the Senate. Southern filibusters were begun, cloture petitions were filed, and in neither case could even a simple majority, much less the needed two-thirds, be obtained.

Liberals had hoped that because of the contradiction between fighting for democracy abroad while denying it to some citizens at home, the war might shame Congress into allowing the passage of the most modest of civil rights proposals: to outlaw the poll tax, or to make permanent the Fair Employment Practices Commission or FEPC. While shame could move the House, however, it couldn't budge the Senate. The House passed Roosevelt's poll tax bill in 1942, and sent it to the Senate, where a filibuster led by Theodore Bilbo of Mississippi killed it. The Administration tried again in 1944. The House passed the bill again, and civil rights advocates mounted an all-out effort to persuade the

Senate to act this time. Looking out over the packed visitors' galleries, Drury saw some—not many, but some—black faces. "We seldom seem to have these visitors except when the poll tax or the FEPC is under discussion," he wrote in his *Senate Journal*. "It is as though somebody had the idea that their presence might be a silent reproach. . . ." The committee room was packed, too, "with hopeful Negroes who applaud the witnesses eagerly and from time to time stand in silent prayer that the bill will pass." But, sitting in the Press Gallery, Drury also saw the double doors swing open, and "the poll-taxers suddenly trooped in, obviously just done with a conference." And the reproach, he saw, was "utterly wasted on the southerners."

So long as they felt threatened, felt that there was a significant danger that a filibuster might be cut off by a cloture vote, and that they therefore might need the support of at least a few moderate senators, the southerners veiled their arguments in principles palatable to moderates: in the sacredness of the Constitution and the sovereignty of the states. But as soon as they began to feel that they had enough support to win, the veil dropped away in private conversations to reveal what lay beneath. "Hell," a young southern spokesman calmly told Drury in confidence one day in 1944, "this wouldn't put niggers on the voting lists even if it did go through. Niggers don't vote in my state and niggers aren't going to vote in my state." That, he said with a grin, was that. And, Drury noted, when the southerners felt totally secure, the veils were let fall on the Senate floor itself, as the southern senators, "leaving the realms of practical constitutionality where they had the company of sound men . . . repaired instead to the ancient bloody ground on which whites and 'Nigras' contend." Senator Bankhead of Alabama (son of Senator Bankhead of Alabama) began the trend,

> warning direly of a reviving Ku Klux Klan "if you force this on us."
> Smacking his lips and managing to look dour, kindly and upset all at once, he remarked with the most exasperating yet the most innocently patronizing air that if you "treat the Nigras right, treat them good, give them justice, they'll stand by you. . . . But when you threaten white supremacy, that's something else. Our women, our children, our institutions" are in danger. The K.K.K., if need be, will ride again.

("Dotted here and there through the galleries, Negroes, many in uniform, sat silent and impassively listening," Drury wrote in his *Journal*. "Of the hopeless despair that must have been in some of their hearts they gave no sign.") Burnet Rhett Maybank of South Carolina added that "Regardless of what decisions the Supreme Court may make and regardless of what laws Congress may pass," the South would handle black Americans as it saw fit. "Mark my words," a southerner told Drury, Maybank "*is not joking;* the South isn't joking any more." Things were coming "to a boil. . . . Back them [the southern senators] into the corner a little further and see what they do." Drury felt that he had not even begun to comprehend the depth of southern rage and resentment over the proposed federal interference in its affairs. "As far as the eye can see there is discontent and bitterness, faint intimations of a coming storm like a rising wind moving through tall grass. . . ." And at the climax of the 1944 debate, when the vote came—the vote on cloture for which a two-thirds vote was required—not only was there once again not two-thirds, there was, once again, not even a majority; thirty-six senators voted for cloture, forty-four voted against.

THEN, IN 1945, there was a new President, who had been one of them—a senator popular with his colleagues—until just four months before, and, as David McCullough writes, conservative senators of both parties were "happily claiming that the New Deal was as good as dead, the 'Roosevelt nonsense' was over, because they 'knew Harry Truman.' "

Truman's first address to Congress was what McCullough calls "a rude awakening" to his former colleagues: a call not merely to continue the New Deal but to extend it, to "widen our horizon further." With Japan's surrender soon thereafter, the need for new initiatives became more compelling. The war had brought homebuilding virtually to a halt; the families of hundreds of thousands of returning veterans were living in inadequate housing; the new President proposed a broad federal program to construct a million new housing units, as well as to provide rent supplements to enable lower-income families to live in them; and to make at least a start on clearing the nation's slums. Social Security had spread a safety net between millions of the nation's families and the bottomless abyss of old age in an industrialized society, but tens of millions were still unprotected; Truman called for coverage for an additional three million workers, as well as for an increase in benefits eroded by inflation. He asked for a higher minimum wage for workers on the low end of the industrial totem pole, who in 1945 were still working for sixty cents an hour, and for broad new assistance for the unemployed.

Those were only the first of Harry Truman's demands on Congress. In succeeding messages, he proposed a federal education program of broader dimensions, and of a new focus: on poorer states. He proposed tax reforms to shift the burden off "the little man" onto the corporations which had reaped huge profits from the war. Health insurance that would make the miracles of modern medical care available to all citizens without regard to their ability to pay had been a dream of liberals for decades; now Truman proposed a system of national health insurance. And the new President went further on race than his great predecessor had dared. Injustice fell most heavily on the twelve million Americans whose skins were black—no meaningful progress against social and economic racial discrimination had been made since the Civil War.

Truman not only resubmitted Roosevelt's FEPC and poll tax legislation but also proposed what Roosevelt had not: bans on racial discrimination in schools, hotels, restaurants, and theaters, and, to enforce these laws, the creation of a new Civil Rights Commission and of a new civil rights enforcement arm within the Department of Justice. Thirty-one black Americans were known to have died at the hands of lynch mobs—mobs that went unpunished by local officials and juries—since 1940; Truman proposed making lynching a crime under federal law.

Congress knew how to deal with such presidential presumption. Truman's major domestic proposals were presented in September, 1945. One of them—to outlaw the poll tax—was passed by the House; it was filibustered—and killed—in the Senate. As for the others, when December came, every one had been blocked or ignored. And December, of course, brought other priorities. "Congressmen, who habitually put off thoughts of legislation with the first glimpse of holly, were scrambling again to get home for the holidays—no matter what kind of a mess they might be leaving," *Time* reported. "And a mess it was."

The mess continued through the congressional session of 1946. November of that year brought a change in party control of Congress—the Republicans won both houses for the first time in eighteen years—but not in philosophic control; in 1947 and 1948, the conservative coalition, now headed not by a Democrat but by Ohio's coldly aristocratic Senator Robert Taft, still ruled; it was, as *U.S. News & World Report* noted, "rewriting the Truman legislative program, line by line." Tax relief was indeed given—but mostly to corporations and to upper-income taxpayers. The minimum wage was left unchanged. Three years after the President had proposed a low-cost homebuilding program to meet a desperate national need, there was no homebuilding legislation. Three years after he had proposed a massive program to improve education, there was no education legislation. The major domestic accomplishment of the Eightieth Congress was a Labor-Management Relations Act, the "Taft-Hartley Law," which union leaders called the "slave labor law." On some issues during these years, the House, despite the dominance of conservative committee chairmen, had given in to the public eagerness for change. But when it did, the Senate stood firm. In May, 1946, with the nation paralyzed by a railroad strike and editorial writers hysterical, Truman appeared before a joint session of Congress to ask for legislation that would allow him to assume government control of vital industries hit by strikes, to punish defiant union leaders, and to draft strikers into the military. One house of Congress—the lower house—rushed to comply, by a 306–13 margin. The other house didn't. Confronted by the spectre of federal intervention in business, the Senate, refusing to bow to the hysteria of the moment, voted against the bill, 70 to 13.

.   .   .

OCCASIONALLY THE HOUSE seemed swayed—almost despite itself—by cries for justice. On the thorniest issue, the issue on which the House's defenses had crumbled more than once, the Senate stood like a rock.

"My very stomach turned over when I learned that Negro soldiers, just back from overseas, were being dumped out of army trucks in Mississippi and beaten," Harry Truman wrote in a letter at this time. "When the mob gangs can take . . . people out and shoot them in the back, and everybody in the surrounding country is acquainted with who did the shooting and nothing is done about it, that country is in a pretty bad fix from the law enforcement standpoint." In a special message to Congress in 1948, the President repeated his pleas for more effective laws to ban the poll tax and to protect the right to vote, to strengthen and make permanent the FEPC, to end discrimination in interstate travel by train, bus, and airplane—and he called for a federal law against "the crime of lynching, against which I cannot speak too strongly." Tom Connally denounced Truman's message as "a lynching of the Constitution." The actions of other southern senators, as David McCullough writes, spoke as loudly as their words. Much as he usually enjoyed attending the Democrats' annual Jefferson-Jackson Dinner in Washington, Senator Olin Johnston of South Carolina said he would boycott it this year because Truman would be the guest of honor, and "because, as he explained to reporters, he and his wife might be seated beside a 'Nigra.' " (He needn't have worried. The three black Americans among the eleven hundred guests were seated at a table in the rear.) And of course in 1948—as in the previous three years of Truman's presidency—no civil rights legislation was passed. During the thirty-one years since the passage of the cloture bill "to terminate successful filibustering," cloture had been invoked nineteen times—and passed four times, the last time in 1927. And none of these cloture petitions had concerned civil rights legislation. The Senate had never—not once—overridden a filibuster on civil rights.

Public contempt for Congress was growing steadily. Journalists discussed the institution in clichés: "The inefficiency of Congress is a national scandal," Richard Strout wrote. Academics placed its inefficiency in broader context. Yale Professor Wallace Hamilton said that because of congressional ineptitude, "the life of representative government is at stake." Commentators made jokes about it. "The Senate's rules provide that the Senate may not perform its duties," Russell Baker was to say. There was, in a way, a national consensus on the issue. "For generations," *Fortune* was to say, "Americans swore that there was no better government in the world or in history. . . . Is it the truth? It no longer is. Now [there is] a situation that admits of no national complacency: the legislative machinery, which is the heart of democracy, is breaking down." Even many congressmen agreed; as one said, "The people think we are a bunch of clowns." And in particular the Senate, whose incompetence had been thrown into dramatically sharp relief by the flames of Pearl Harbor, and, since the war, by its use of the colorful filibuster, was viewed—with anger—as the principal obstruction to America's majority will. As Russell Baker was to write, "For years the House diligently passed comprehensive civil rights legislation and the Southern minority in the Senate just as regularly killed it." The Senate had been an object of ridicule for almost a century; "never," one of its historians was to write, had Americans been "more critical of the United States Senate than in the years which followed World War II." "I've never seen such chaos," Alben Barkley said.

In 1948, President Truman ran against the "Do-Nothing Eightieth Congress"—how deep a chord he hit when on his come-from-behind cross-country whistlestop tour he said it was "run by a bunch of old mossbacks still living back in the 1890s" was demonstrated by the election results (and by the roars of approval when he told audiences, "After a new Congress is chosen, maybe we'll get one that will work in the interests of the people and not the interests of the men who have all the money"). When, before the election, in a political masterstroke, he called Congress into special session, demanding that it pass some of the legislation he had advocated (and that the Republican platform had advocated, too), GOP national campaign manager Herbert Brownell told congressional Republicans that it might be a good idea to make at least a gesture at passing some of that legislation, particularly some relating to civil rights, since the black vote was becoming an important factor in presidential elections.

But when Truman entered the House to deliver his speech opening the special session, some senators and representatives did not even rise from their seats. "No, we're not going to give that fellow anything," Senator Taft said. What did the Senate care about public opinion? Its opinion about majority rule had boiled over repeatedly during the Truman Administration, an opinion held not only by Senate demagogues like Bilbo (who had taken the floor to say that "a mob is a majority; without the filibuster the minority would be at the mercy of the majority") but by Senate grandees like Tydings, who, asked on the Senate floor whether democracy was not "predicated on the rule of majority," replied, shouting in anger: "The rule of the majority. The rule of votes. Majority to Hades! The rule of the majority! The rule that has brought more bloodshed and turmoil and cruelty on this earth than any other thing I know of!" Liberals, and, most infuriatingly, that liberal Washington press corps, might criticize the filibuster, but the southern senators worshiped it: it was their defense against that despised majority. Any threat to the filibuster they regarded as a threat to the rights of man. To a request to impose cloture, the stately Walter George solemnly intoned: "We are called upon to go Nazi." "It was cloture that crucified Christ on the cross," Tydings cried.

When emotions rose, the southern senators couldn't even be bothered to conceal the fact that it was not "Nigras" alone whom they despised. Mississippi's Bilbo addressed a letter to a New York woman of Italian descent, "Dear Dago." The Magnolia State's other senator, James O. Eastland (who would some years later stare coldly down a committee table at Senator Jacob Javits of New York, a Jew, and say, "I don't like you—or your kind"), now said that if the FEPC bill was constitutional "ten thousand Jewish drygoods merchants represent a discrimination against the Anglo-Saxon branch of the white race" and Congress should therefore "limit the number of Jews in interstate business." It wasn't only Italians and Jews whom the southerners wanted kept in their places. While Jim Dombrowski of the Southern Conference for Human Welfare was testifying before the Senate Judiciary Committee, Eastland repeatedly sneered at his "typically old Southern name." And of course there were always the Native Americans. Defending American businessmen who did not want to employ them, Senator Bankhead explained that "There is something peculiar about an Indian which causes the white American not to want to be too closely associated with him."

"This is the spectacle presented by the United States in the wake of a war against fascism and racism," I. F. Stone wrote caustically in *The Nation* in 1948. A majority of the American people might endorse Truman's proposals, not merely on civil rights but on a dozen other issues, and in towns and cities across the United States audiences might cheer the President's assault on the Capitol Hill "Do-Nothings"—the Senate didn't care. To many senators the New Deal was nothing more or less than "socialism," and in opposing it, they were simply doing their duty. The majority might call for change—social change, economic change; these senators knew what a majority was: the majority was "the mob." They had been elected to protect America against the mob. Against long odds, a President had just swept all before him. What was a President to them, to these senators who said, "We were here before he came, and we'll be here after he's gone"?

And, of course, the Senate—particularly these southern senators who dominated it—didn't have to care. The six-year terms and the staggering of those terms decreed by the Founding Fathers had armored the Senate as a whole against public opinion in the nation as a whole; the majority will of the United States could reach the Senate of the United States only in very diluted form—"the Senate, as a Senate," could indeed "*never* be repudiated." And by decreeing that in the Senate each state would have the same two votes regardless of population, the Fathers had further ensured that within the Senate, population wouldn't matter—that the majority wouldn't matter. The right of unlimited debate—a logical outgrowth of the Founders' insistence on protecting minority rights—had bolted around the small states yet another layer of armor against the majority will. Nor could national public opinion touch an individual senator. Each senator was answerable only to the will of the majority of voters in his own state, and of course the stands the southern senators were taking did not hurt but helped them with those voters. And thanks to the seniority rule, once these senators were re-elected, the only thing that mattered was that they *had* been re-elected: their inexorable progress to the committee chairmanships would continue. The Senate decided who would hold its posts of power—and the Senate decided alone.

The 1948 elections proved the point. Infuriated by the liberalism of their party's President and their party's platform, which actually included a fairly strong civil rights plank, a States Rights Party was formed, with its own presidential candidate, Strom Thurmond of South Carolina, who denounced the FEPC as "Communistic," Truman's proposed integration of the armed services as "un-American," and said, "There's not enough troops in the Army to force the southern people to admit the Negro race into our theaters, into our swimming pools, into our churches." But despite all the furor engendered by the new party, it carried a mere four states. Not only had President Truman won, he had won by turning the election into a referendum on Congress. In terms of majority rule, the South had been thoroughly repudiated. Although Truman had won, however, the southern senators hadn't lost. A liberal tide had washed over the rest of the country, as it had washed over the country in 1904 and 1912 and 1936. But while it had swept a liberal majority into the Senate, not a single southerner standing for re-election had been defeated. The majority party—in both houses of Congress—would be Democratic, not Republican. But in both House and Senate, the committee chairmanships would again be held by southerners. If anything, southern power on Capitol Hill would be stronger, not weaker; the attribute which in the Senate meant power was seniority, and seniority was inexorable and cumulative; the senators who would return in January would return with more—not less—of that asset. The South's point of view might have been repudiated; its "position of entrenched minority" in the Senate was untouched.

Although Truman had won on the basis of his "Fair Deal" program, that program's fate would still be controlled by anti–Fair Deal southerners. And in the unlikely event that Truman's proposals somehow emerged from committee, there was still the filibuster in the Senate. What was the legislation that had been defeated in the Senate in 1948? Legislation for civil rights, for aid to education, for aid to housing, for a fairer minimum wage, for better health care. An entire agenda of social justice—to a considerable extent endorsed by the nation—had been blocked in the Senate. Similar legislation had been blocked in the Senate for a decade and more. There was no reason, despite Truman's victory, to think it would pass now.

The Senate's Golden Age had ended almost a century before. During the ensuing decades, the institution had been subtly altered, decade by decade, into something significantly different from the body that had been envisioned by the Founding Fathers. They had wanted it to be independent, a place of wisdom and deliberation armored against outside forces. But the rise inside the Senate itself of forces they had not sufficiently foreseen—the rise of parties and party caucuses, and of party discipline; the transformation of America's infant industries into gigantic economic entities which had representatives sitting in the

Senate itself—had undermined the Senate's independence from within, and the impact of these new forces on the Senate had been heightened because the armor against outside forces remained in place. Still protected against the people and the President, both of which wanted social progress, the Senate was unprotected against internal forces that opposed social progress, and that were indeed making it much less a place of wisdom and deliberation. Other internal developments—most importantly, seniority and the filibuster—had further distorted the Founders' dream. They had envisioned the Senate as the moderating force in government, as the cooler of the popular will; cool had become cold, had become ice, ice in which, for decades, with only a few brief exceptions, the popular desire for social change had become frozen. Designed as the deliberative power, the Senate had become instead the negative power, the selfish power. The "necessary fence" against executive and popular tyranny had been transformed, by party rule and by the seniority rule, into something thicker and higher—into an impenetrable wall against the democratic impulses it had originally been supposed only to "refine" and "filter," into a dam against which waves of social reform, attempts to ameliorate the human condition, dashed themselves in vain. Except for brief moments—the beginning of Wilson's presidency, for example, and the Hundred Days of Roosevelt's—when the floodgates in the dam suddenly swung wide and the tides swept through, cleansing the great Republic, the Founders' armor had resisted every attempt by others to force them open; the Senate had been designed as the "firm" body; it had become too firm—too firm to allow the reforms the Republic needed.

Never had the dam been more firm than during the last decade, the decade since the conservative coalition had learned its strength. During that decade, despite the mandate of three presidential elections, it had stood across and blocked the rising demand for social justice, had stood so solidly that it seemed too strong ever to be breached.

In January, 1949, when Lyndon Johnson arrived in it, it was still standing.

Part II

LEARNING

4

A Hard Path

NEWLY ELECTED SENATORS of the United States are sworn in in groups of four. They stand in the rear of the high-ceilinged Senate Chamber, their "sponsors" (generally their state's senior senator) at their side, and when each new senator's turn comes, his sponsor takes his arm and escorts him ceremoniously down the broad, shallow steps of the center aisle, between the rows of mahogany desks at which Webster sat, and Clay and Calhoun, and Borah and Norris and the La Follettes, father and son, down to the well, where, on the dais, above it, the Senate's President is waiting, framed by marble columns. When, on January 3, 1949, the Secretary of the Senate called Lyndon Johnson's name, old Tom Connally, a hero in Texas since Johnson had been a boy, took his arm in a firm grip, and they walked together down to the dais where the legendary Arthur Vandenberg was standing, stiffly erect, right hand already raised for the oath. "Do you solemnly swear that you will support and defend the Constitution of the United States?" Vandenberg asked, and Lyndon Johnson said "I do."

He had traveled a hard path to get to the Senate—from a hard place: the remote, barren Texas Hill Country, a land of loneliness and poverty, and for the young Lyndon Johnson, born on August 27, 1908, son of failed and ridiculed parents, a land of humiliation and fear, even the fear of having his home taken away by the bank.

For a while he had come along that path fast—remarkably fast.

At twenty-one, while still an undergraduate at a little teachers college known as a "poor boys' school," he was running two campaigns, one for a state legislator, the other for a candidate for lieutenant governor, in a block of Hill Country counties, and politicians all over Texas began hearing about "this wonder kid" who "knew more about politics than anyone else in the area." By the time he was twenty-three, a congressman's aide who had only recently arrived in Washington with a cardboard suitcase and no clothes warm enough for a northern winter (and who for months didn't have enough money to buy any), he

was the "Boss of the Little Congress," a club of congressional aides that he had
made influential on Capitol Hill. By twenty-six, he had been appointed the
National Youth Administration's director for the State of Texas, thereby becoming perhaps the youngest person the New Deal ever put in charge of a
statewide program. At twenty-eight he was elected to Congress, after a campaign against seven better-known opponents. Within four years, using money
from Texas contractors and oilmen, he injected new energy into a stagnant
Democratic Congressional Campaign Committee, gained influence over other
congressmen, and a toehold on national power. And when, in April, 1941, one
of his state's senators died, and a special election was called to fill the vacancy,
Franklin Roosevelt allowed him to announce his candidacy from the White
House steps, and the belief in Washington was that Lyndon Johnson, still only
thirty-two years old, would become America's youngest senator. During that
campaign, polls showed him pulling steadily away from his principal opponent, Texas Governor W. Lee (Pappy) O'Daniel, and that belief seemed
justified.

And then, in an instant, with one slip, he was stopped.

He hadn't made many slips. He was always telling his aides, "If you do
everything, you'll win," and during his decade-long ascent of the political ladder, he had done *"everything,"* had worked so hard that a tough Texas political
boss said "I never thought it was *possible* for anyone to work that hard," had
worked with a feverish, almost frantic intensity that journalists would describe
as "energy" when it was really desperation and fear, the fear of a man fleeing
from something terrible. Throughout all that decade, moreover, he had planned
and intrigued, trying to think of everything, unceasingly careful and wary. But
at the very end of that 1941 race—on Election Day itself—he had relaxed. In
his euphoria over apparent victory, he violated an old adage of Texas politics
by reporting too early in the day the vote totals from the corrupt counties he
controlled, thereby letting O'Daniel know how many votes were needed from
the corrupt counties *he* controlled, and giving him the opening necessary
to win.

And with that defeat, the years of triumph ended—to be followed by very
different years. He had expected that another chance at a Senate seat would
come almost immediately, with the election in 1942 for the full term, but the
Second World War deprived him of that chance—and he was not to get another
for seven years.

THOSE YEARS—1941 to 1948—were Lyndon Johnson's years in the wilderness. He had been lured always by the gleam from a single goal. As a youth,
working on a road gang with the reins of a mule-drawn "fresno" scoop shovel
looped around his back so that he was in effect in harness with the mules, his
hands blistered and bleeding from the fresno's handles, his face seared in

Summer by the fierce Hill Country sun and in Winter by the fierce Hill Country wind, the tall, skinny, awkward youth had told his fellow workers, "I'm going to be President of the United States one day." Once he was on the path he had mapped out to that goal, mapped out with a sophistication and pragmatism striking in one so young, he almost never spoke of it, but despite his silence those who knew him best understood his ambition. James H. Rowe Jr., who spent more time with Johnson than any of the other rising young New Dealers, says, in words echoed by other members of their Washington circle, "From the day he got here, he wanted to be President." Johnson was later to tell journalists that his two daughters had been given the same initials as he because "this way we can use the same luggage," but during his House years he would be more frank with his aide Horace Busby. Telling Busby to refer to him in press releases as "LBJ," the young congressman said: "FDR–LBJ, FDR–LBJ—do you get it? What I want is for them to start thinking of me in terms of initials." It was only presidents whom headline writers and the American public referred to by their initials; "he was just so determined that someday he would be known as LBJ," Busby says. And sometimes, as if he could not endure the frustration of his hopes, what he really wanted burst out of him, as it did one evening when he was alone with his old friend Welly Hopkins: "By *God*, I'll be President someday!" So long as the path to that goal lay open before him, nothing could make him turn off it. It ran only through Washington—national power, not state power, was the key. He refused to run for the governorship of Texas; to aides who assured him he would win the governorship, he explained that he didn't want to—that that job could never be more than a "detour" on his "route," a detour that might turn into a "dead end."

So long as the path lay open, not even the chance for financial security could turn him from it. Tormented during his prewar House years by his lack of money, continually complaining that he had "nothing" (not a thousand dollars in the bank, he said), he spoke constantly of ending up like his father, who had died penniless, and pleaded with the Texas tycoons who had bankrolled his career, to bankroll *him;* to put him in the way of making "a little money." But when, in 1940, they offered him a lot of money—a partnership in an oil company, offered on terms that made it virtually a gift, worth perhaps three quarters of a million dollars—he turned the offer down because, he explained, "I can't be an oil man"; if the public knew he had oil interests, "it would kill me politically." In discussing his political ambitions, Johnson had previously spoken to these men only of the House and Senate—he had said over and over that, as one of them recalls, "he wanted to remain in Congress until a Senate seat opened up, and then run for that seat, that the Senate was his ultimate goal in politics"—and had never mentioned any other office. But Johnson's congressional district was safe—being an oilman couldn't hurt him there. And it certainly couldn't hurt him if he ran for the Senate in oil-dominated Texas. Then these supporters realized that there was another office for which, indeed, a candidate

would be "killed" by being an "oilman"—and they realized at last what Lyndon
Johnson really wanted, and how much he wanted it.

But now, after 1941, the path was closed. For the next seven years, Lyndon
Johnson remained stuck in the House of Representatives. Men and women who
knew him in Washington describe him in words that echo words used to
describe him by men and women who knew him in Johnson City—words
which, in fact, he had, in his youth, used about himself. "He had to *be somebody*," they would say, "just *had to*," could not stand, in the words of one of
them, "to be one of a crowd—just could not *stand* it." But in the House, with its
435 members who jammed its cloakrooms and jostled in the aisles of its chamber, its 435 members of whom only a few handfuls—members who had been
there for decades—had significant authority, he couldn't, as a junior congressman, be anything *but* one of a crowd.

His lack of interest in the body's general legislative work had always been
noticeable, and it remained so, particularly after a 1943 fiasco in which he tried
to push himself into national prominence by introducing a bill that would have
usurped the jurisdiction of a committee of which he was not a member. During
the more than eleven years that Lyndon Johnson would eventually serve in the
House, he would introduce only four bills that would have had an effect beyond
the borders of his own congressional district. In fact, he introduced only three
intra-district bills: a total in eleven years of only seven bills, less than the number introduced by any of the twenty other representatives who entered Congress in the same year he did. (Only two of his bills—two minor measures that
affected only his own district—were enacted into law.) He made almost as few
formal speeches as laws, and seldom participated in informal discussions and
debates, the daily give-and-take of legislative business. Entire years passed in
which he did not rise even once to make a point of order, or any other point; to
ask or answer a question; to support or attack a bill under discussion; to participate, by so much as a single word, in an entire year's worth of floor proceedings. Although Johnson adherents would contend in later years that he was
active in the House in other ways—by quietly lobbying his colleagues in the
cloakrooms on behalf of liberal causes, for instance—this picture could hardly
be contradicted more strongly by the men who knew: the men he had supposedly lobbied. As one of his fellow congressmen says: "He just simply was not
especially interested in general legislation that came to the floor. Some of us
were on the floor all the time, fighting for liberal causes. But he stayed away
from the floor, and while he was there, he was very, very silent." Liberal colleagues believed him to be liberal at heart; conservative colleagues believed
him to be conservative. Says one extremely conservative Republican congressman, "Politically, if we disagreed, it wasn't apparent to me. Not at all." In fact,
no one really knew his heart because he seldom fought for an issue or even
expressed a definite opinion about it.

His insistence on being the center of attention, of dominating any room in
which he found himself, had never slackened. At Washington dinner parties, he

wanted to do the talking, and if someone else held the floor for any length of time, he would go to sleep at the table—or pretend to, his eyes closing, his head nodding forward. When he woke up, friends say, "he woke up talking," and if he was still not allowed to hold the floor, his eyes would close again. But in Washington, people's willingness to listen is a coefficient of the power of the person talking. Lyndon Johnson didn't have much power, and as it became more and more apparent that he wasn't *going* to have much, at least in any foreseeable future, it became harder for him to hold the stage. And on Capitol Hill, Johnson was constantly trying to "domineer" over his fellow congressmen, to lecture them on politics in a dogmatic, overbearing tone, to act as if they owed him favors, and these efforts were arousing more and more resentment. Frequently, when he indulged in a characteristic habit of putting one arm around a colleague's shoulders and grasping the colleague's lapel with his other hand, the colleague would draw back from the hand; at least once, a colleague angrily knocked it away. All too frequently, colleagues with whom he had served for years would come into the House Dining Room and pointedly ignore him as they walked past his table. Lyndon Johnson hated his years in the House, the House in which—this man who could not stand being only "one of a crowd"— he was only one of the hundreds of congressmen who had no power or ability to accomplish anything, whose days were punctuated with reminders of his lack of status. He started avoiding the Democratic cloakroom and the floor; "He couldn't work up the enthusiasm anymore," a colleague says. The seven years from 1941 to 1948 were years of hopelessness and despair, seven years in what was for Lyndon Johnson the bleakest possible wilderness: a life without any political power that he considered meaningful.

DEEPENING THE DESPAIR was another consideration—one that sometimes seemed to prey upon Lyndon Johnson's mind more than any other. Power in the House of Representatives could come only through seniority—through waiting; waiting for many years—and Lyndon Johnson was convinced that he didn't *have* many years. Throughout his boyhood, he had heard relatives repeating a piece of family lore: that all Johnson men had weak hearts and died young. Then, while he was still in college and his father was barely fifty years old, his father's heart had begun to fail; Sam Ealy Johnson died, after years of heart trouble, in 1937, twelve days after his sixtieth birthday. One of Sam's two younger brothers—Lyndon's uncles—died of a massive heart attack in 1939, at the age of fifty-seven. The other suffered one heart attack in 1946, at the age of sixty-five, and a second in 1947, and was to live his last years as a near-invalid. Lyndon was always deeply conscious of his marked physical resemblance to his tall, gawky, big-eared, big-nosed father; his shoulder-hugging and lapel-grasping was an inherited mannerism. Wright Patman, who served in Congress with Lyndon Johnson and in the Texas Legislature with his father, says "Lyndon clutched you like his daddy did when he talked to you. They looked alike, they walked the same, had the same nervous mannerisms. He was so much like his father that it was humorous to watch." Lyndon was convinced, to what one of his secretaries calls "the point of obsession," that he had inherited the family legacy. "I'm not gonna live to be but sixty," he would say. "My daddy died at sixty. My uncle . . ." Now, as he grew older, whenever it was suggested that he might make his career in the House of Representatives, he would reply, in a low voice, "Too slow. Too slow." The long, slow path to power in the House might be the only one open to him, but he felt it was not a path feasible for him to follow.

CONSTANT AS WAS HIS ULTIMATE AMBITION, during those seven years there sometimes seemed no possibility of its realization, and without that possibility—or at least the chance for some form of increased power—the complexity of Lyndon Johnson's motivations became clear.

Despite repeated campaign promises to "serve in the trenches" if war came, for months after Pearl Harbor he maneuvered to stay out of any combat zone, and finally, forced into one, flew on a single bombing mission as an observer and then hurried back to Washington. There he tried to obtain high civilian rank—he campaigned vigorously for an appointment as Secretary of the Navy which would have made him one of the youngest Cabinet officers in history—but when he didn't get the job, his interest in the war faded, so markedly that to an aide it was obvious that if he couldn't have real authority in it, "he regarded it as an interference with his agenda"; he attempted to dissuade his young assistants from enlisting, or, if they were drafted, often tried to have their draft notices rescinded so that they could continue serving him rather than their country.

During his prewar years as a congressman, he had, in a monumental feat of ingenuity and resolve, brought electricity to his isolated district, in a single stroke bringing the farmers and ranchers of the Hill Country into the twentieth century. And he had maximized the effect within it of so many New Deal programs that he had been called "the best congressman for a district there ever was." During these next seven years, with his programs in place and being carried forward by an efficient staff, his interest in his district steadily waned. In a state which routinely re-elected incumbent congressmen, there was no realistic chance he would lose his seat, but he was increasingly less involved with his job. He had been interested, deeply involved, in working for his constituents so long as that work held out the prospect—the imminent prospect—of leading to something more, but so dramatically did his interest wane the moment it appeared that his work for his district might have to be an end in itself, that helping people seemed to mean as little to him as helping the war effort. Without the prospect of new, greater power, the power he possessed was meaningless to him.

So long as the path to power lay open before him, he had been willing to defer, even to sacrifice, his need for financial security. Now, with that path closed—perhaps forever—the deferring was over. During the seven years following his defeat in the 1941 Texas senatorial election, Lyndon Johnson grabbed for money as greedily as he had grabbed for power, using his political influence to do so, and using it so successfully that by 1948 he was boasting that instead of a thousand dollars he had a million, a small fortune at that time.

In 1948, he decided to take one last desperate gamble, entering a race for the Senate although he would be running against Coke Robert Stevenson, the only man in the state's history to hold all three of its top governmental posts—Speaker, Lieutenant Governor, Governor—and a public figure so beloved in Texas that in the last Democratic primary he had entered, the crucial election in a one-party state, he had carried every one of the state's 254 counties, the only candidate for Governor or Senator who had ever done so. "The Cowboy Governor," as he was known, was considered invincible.

The stakes of the gamble were all the higher because under Texas law Johnson could not run for the Senate without relinquishing his House seat and his eleven years of seniority. One of Johnson's key advisers was not exaggerating when he says of the 1948 race, "That was *it*! All or nothing." Johnson himself recoiled from the risk. "At first," he was to say, "I just could not bear the thought of losing everything." But he took the gamble—because the imperatives of his character gave him no choice: another congressman might have decided not to take such a risk, because losing would mean he might have to leave Washington, with its excitement and glamour. But for Lyndon Johnson, not excitement or glamour but power was the basic need; to stay on in Washington without it was intolerable to him. If he lost, he said, he would leave politics forever, and go into business; he may have been born to politics, may have been a master of the political game, but without power he didn't want to remain in it.

EVERY STAGE of Lyndon Johnson's career had been marked not only by pragmatism but by what is, in a democracy in which power is conferred by elections, the ultimate pragmatism: the stealing of elections. Even at little Southwest Texas State Teachers College in San Marcos, where campus politics had previously been little more than a joke and elections the most casual of affairs, Johnson stole elections. On Capitol Hill, the pattern was repeated. Lyndon Johnson cheated not only in the election in which he won the presidency of the Little Congress, but in succeeding elections in which his allies won; "Everyone said it: 'In that last election, that damn Lyndon Johnson stole some votes again,' " and on the one occasion on which a Little Congress ballot box was actually opened, the accusations proved to be true. He had stolen thousands of votes in his first campaign for the Senate. When that number proved insufficient (because, thanks to his mistake, his opponent was able to steal even more), his reaction was to try to steal still more—by trying to persuade the corrupt border county dictator George Parr to go further than Parr had ever gone before. But even the notorious Parr would not go to the lengths that Johnson wanted. "Lyndon, I've been to the federal penitentiary, and I'm not going back for you," he said. At every stage of Johnson's political career, he had stretched the rules of the game to their breaking point, and then had broken them, pushing deeper into the ethical and legal no-man's-land beyond them than others were willing to go. In this 1948 campaign—in this "all or nothing" campaign, his last chance—the pattern became even clearer. He stole not thousands but tens of thousands of votes, and when they weren't sufficient to defeat Stevenson (asked about the attempt made decades later to portray Stevenson aides as also stealing votes, Edward A. Clark, the longtime "Secret Boss of Texas," would laugh, "They didn't know how, and Governor Stevenson didn't know how"), he stole still more, and in this later theft, which culminated in the finding of the decisive "votes" (supposedly cast by 202 voters who voted in alphabetical order) six days after the polls closed, he went further than anyone had gone before, violating even the notably loose boundaries of Texas politics. Even in terms of a most elastic political morality—the political morality of 1940s Texas—his methods were immoral.

An investigation into the theft was halted, largely through the legal ingenuity of Johnson's brilliant attorney Abe Fortas, at the very moment at which testimony was coming to a climax before a federal Master in Chancery appointed by a United States District Court judge. Asked later what his report would have concluded had the proceeding been allowed to continue, this official said flatly: "I think Lyndon was put in the United States Senate with a stolen election."

No matter how he was put there, however, he was there. "Do you solemnly swear?" Vandenberg asked, and when Lyndon Johnson replied, "I do," his years in the wilderness were over.

5

The Path Ahead

AT FIRST GLANCE, the place he had worked so hard to reach seemed peculiarly unsuited to him—unsuited both to his nature and to his ambition.

Austere, restrained, dignified, courtly, refined—these were not the adjectives that, in January, 1949, sprang first to mind in describing Lyndon Johnson. Big as he was, he seemed even bigger. In part, the reasons were physical. Everything about him was outsize, dramatic. His arms were long even for a man of his height, and his hands, those huge, mottled hands, were big even for those arms, and then there was his great head, with the big, jutting nose, the big, jutting jaw, those immense ears, the powerful shape of the massive skull emphasized because his thinning hair was slicked down flat against it with "Sta-comb" hair tonic. And, most of all, there were his eyes, under long, heavy black eyebrows. People in the Texas Hill Country believed that the key to understanding Lyndon Johnson was to remember that he was a descendant of a clan, legendary in the Hill Country, named Bunton. Generations of Bunton men had possessed not only great ambition and a "commanding presence" that enabled them to realize it (they were elected to public office—to the Congress of Texas when it was an independent republic, to the Texas Legislature after it became a state—in their twenties, as Lyndon Johnson had been elected to public office in his twenties), but they were also tall like Lyndon—always over six feet—and had features strikingly similar to his, including the big ears, jaw and nose, the heavy black eyebrows and, in particular, what the Hill Country called "the Bunton eye." Generations of Buntons had eyes so dark a brown that they seemed black, so bright that they glittered, so piercing that their glare was memorably intimidating. "If you talked to a Bunton," said Lyndon's cousin Ava Johnson Cox, "you never had to wonder if the answer was yes or no. Those eyes told you. Those eyes talked. They spit fire." From the time he was a baby, all through his youth and young manhood, Lyndon Johnson, the Hill Country agreed, had the Bunton eye. And in Washington, where no one had ever heard of the Buntons, people were also struck by Lyndon Johnson's eyes. Years later, a British journalist would leave his first audience with the President to write, "Afterward, you chiefly remember the eyes, steady and unrelenting under half-lowered lids." (The journalist would also write that those eyes showed an "exceptional wariness," and he was correct about that, as correct as he would have been had he been writing in 1949. Johnson's assistants, who often said among themselves that their boss never trusted anyone, were joking that January that he didn't even trust Santa Claus. On the day before Christmas, 1948, walking with several of them along a Washington street, he had come across a costumed Santa Claus—a friendly-faced elderly man—soliciting contributions for the Salvation Army. Johnson had asked the man if he could hire him to entertain the children at a Christmas party in his home that evening, and when the man agreed, had handed him two twenty-dollar bills as a down payment. As he was walking away, however, he whirled around, came back, and demanded the bills. When the Santa Claus returned them, he tore them in half, and gave one half back to the man. "Here," he said, "you get the other half if you show up.")

Johnson's size was also emphasized by his awkwardness, by his long, lunging strides, by the vigorous, sweeping gestures of his arms to make a point. When he burst through a door, with those long strides and that commanding air, "he just filled up a room," as one acquaintance put it. His clothes were dramatic, too. Although he owned blue suits, most of them didn't look like those worn by other senators; so rich and shimmering was their fabric that friends joked about Lyndon's "silver suits," and even with his conservative blue suit, and even when he was wearing it with a starched white shirt, he often didn't wear one of his many understated Countess Mara neckties but rather one of the style known in Texas as a "Fat Max" tie: short, very wide, and garishly hand-painted, some with placidly grazing horses, some with bucking broncos—one favorite had shapely cowgirls astride—some with oil field derricks. Gold glinted from his wrists—the cuffs of his shirts were fastened by notably large solid gold cuff links in the shape of Texas, with a diamond in the center to show the location of Austin; his gold watch was so heavy that when he went to a doctor, he was careful to remove it before he stepped on the scale—and it glinted from his waist, where his belt buckle was also large and solid gold. His initials seemed to be everywhere: his belt buckle was monogrammed, as were his shirts (not only on the breast pocket but on at least one cuff) and his pocket handkerchief, and when he wasn't wearing the Texas cuff links, he was wearing links that proclaimed, in solid gold, "LBJ" from each wrist. And the shirts he preferred weren't white—he often wore shirts and ties which were both cut from the same bolt of checked or polka-dotted cloth—and the suits he preferred weren't blue. When he wore one of his favorite outfits, of which every element—trousers, vest, jacket, tie—was a monochromatic pale brown, Lyndon Johnson was, one journalist recalls, "a mountain of tan."

Beyond all this, the suits were outsize. Wanting them to conceal his weight—a disproportionate amount of which was in his stomach; he would shortly begin wearing a girdle in an attempt to conceal what was sometimes an enormous paunch—he had them cut extremely full and long, with wide lapels, and there was therefore a lot of that rich, glossy fabric on display; so generous was the cut that even when his weight was at its upper limits (not the 240 of his presidential years but about 220 or 225), the unbuttoned jackets of his suits flared out around his hips when he walked fast or whirled around, and when he was thinner, his jackets not only flared open but flapped around him. And his trousers were cut extremely long and full, to the despair of his tailor, who complained that Johnson always looked as if he was stepping on the cuffs, and they flapped around his ankles as he rushed down a corridor or up a flight of stairs. Even when he wore a fedora or other conventional eastern hat, it was usually tilted all the way back on his head, in the casual manner of the Southwest, and he often wore a big, gray, broad-brimmed Texas Stetson instead. And while he might be wearing black shoes, at other times he wore cowboy boots, richly embroidered and polished to a high gloss; "You could see him bend down a dozen times a day to buff them up with a handkerchief," a colleague recalls. Hurrying down the crowded corridors of the House Office Building—and he seemed always to be hurrying, always to be rushing, rudely elbowing people— he had seemed, with his Texas stride and his Texas boots and his Texas hat and his Texas tie, very much the representative of the great, raw province in the Southwest, swaggering through the halls of state. How would he fit in at the Senate Office Building?

And he seemed even bigger than he was for reasons that went deeper than the physical.

He could dominate a room with his charm. In his circle of young New Dealers in Washington, he was the life of every party with his practical jokes, his quick wit, his wonderful "Texas stories" about the hellfire preachers and tough old sheriffs of the Hill Country, his vivid imitations of Washington figures, and his exuberance; jumping up on a table in a Spanish restaurant, he pulled little Welly Hopkins up with him to dance a flamenco. "At parties, he was *fun*," Elizabeth Rowe says. "That's what no one understands about Lyndon Johnson—that he was *fun*." Said Abe Fortas: "There was never a dull moment around him. The moment he walked in the door, [a party] would take fire. Maybe in a different way than the party had been going when he came in, but it would take fire." And he wanted to dominate every room he was in. If he couldn't lead, he didn't want to play—*wouldn't* play. That had been true in Johnson City, the isolated, impoverished little huddle of houses deep in the Hill Country vastnesses, where as a teenager who owned the only regulation baseball in town, he had brought a saying to life; "Lyndon was a terrible pitcher," one Johnson City boy remembers, "but if we didn't let him pitch, he'd take his ball and go home." It had been true at the Georgetown parties at which he would go to sleep at the dinner table. He had to win every argument—"just *had to*." That was what had been said about him by the Johnson City boys and girls among whom he had grown up. That was what had been said about him by his college classmates. That was what had been said about him by his colleagues in the House of Representatives. And in every setting, his demeanor in disputation had been the same. One of those Johnson City companions was to recall about young Lyndon that "if he'd differ with you, he'd hover right up against you, breathing right in your face, arguing your point. . . . I got disgusted with him. Sometimes, I'd try to walk away, but . . . he just wouldn't stop until you gave in." And, of course, in the House of Representatives as in the Legislature in Austin which he visited with his father, he had "clutched you like his daddy did when he talked to you."

Imbuing his arguments with special force was a theory that he held very strongly—according to his brother, had held ever since, as a boy, he had heard a salesman say, one day in the Johnson City barbershop, "You've got to believe in what you're selling." The remark made such an impression on Lyndon that during his boyhood, Sam Houston Johnson says, "he was always repeating that." Decades later, in retirement at his ranch near Johnson City, Lyndon Johnson would still be repeating it, in expanded form, telling Doris Kearns Goodwin: "What convinces is conviction. You simply *have* to believe in the argument you are advancing: if you don't, you're as good as dead. The other person will sense that something isn't there, and no chain of reasoning, no matter how logical or elegant or brilliant, will win your case for you."

He made himself believe in his arguments—believe with absolute conviction—through a process that was characteristically intense. Having observed the process repeatedly, longtime associates had been so impressed with it that they coined phrases to describe it: the "revving up," they called it, or the "working up." Ed Clark, who had known Johnson since his NYA days, and who for almost twenty years would be his principal attorney and principal operative in Texas, would say that "He [Johnson] was an emotional man, and he could start talking about something and convince himself it was right, and get all worked up, all worked up and emotional, and work all day and all night, and sacrifice, and say, 'Follow me for the cause!'—'Let's do this because it's *right*!' " The process was all-consuming. In describing Lyndon Johnson talking about a cause in which he believed, his Washington and Texas circles use words like "vibrancy," "intensity," "energy," "passion"—and "spellbinding." It was not just the big body but the passions and emotions boiling up within it that made him seem so big. "He was big all right," says one acquaintance, "but he got bigger as he talked to you."

Using his own phrase to describe the process, Johnson would tell his young assistants that in order to carry a point, it was necessary to "fill yourself up" with the arguments in its favor. "You just have to get full of your subject and let it fly," he was to say. And he accomplished this so thoroughly that he filled himself to overflowing, as if the body, big as it was, could not contain the emotions, and they blazed out of his eyes, made one of his arms grab his listener's lapel to hold the man close while he tried to persuade him, made a forefinger jab into the man's chest, made his face push into his auditor's, forcing the other man's head back, as if to physically insert the arguments into it—getting closer also to better ascertain if the arguments were working. "I want to see 'em, feel 'em, smell 'em," he said—he wanted his hands on them as he spoke to them. This was not a style of discourse which had endeared itself to colleagues in the House of Representatives, and it hardly seemed likely to do so with the new colleagues he was going to have now.

The physicality of Lyndon Johnson extended into areas besides that of argument. During the 1940s, Capitol Hill was, of course, very much a man's world, in which locker-room humor and morals were common; besides, almost half the members of the House, having been raised on farms, were accustomed to earthiness. But even some of these men were startled at Lyndon Johnson's earthiness. "He would piss in the parking lot of the House Office Building," says Wingate Lucas, a farm boy who represented Fort Worth. "Well, a lot of fellows did that. *I* did it. But the rest of us would try to hide behind a car or something. Lyndon wouldn't. He just didn't care if someone noticed him." In fact, Lucas says, he seemed to want to be noticed. "I remember once, we were walking across the lot and some [female] secretaries were behind us, and he just stopped and began to take a piss right in front of them."

He would also urinate in front of his own secretaries—and since some of them were attractive young women, this, too, was startling to those who witnessed it. During the years in the House, he had a one-room hideaway office on the top floor of the House Office Building—without a toilet, but with a washbasin in the corner of the room, concealed behind a wood and green-burlap screen. While entertaining guests in the hideaway, or dictating to a secretary, he would pull the screen aside and urinate in the basin. Sometimes he would put the screen back before he did so—and sometimes he wouldn't.

He had always displayed great pride in his sexual apparatus. Even at college, where sexual boastfulness is a staple of campus existence, Lyndon Johnson's boastfulness—and exhibitionism about his sexual prowess—had been striking to his fellows. Exhibiting his penis to his roommates, Johnson called it "Jumbo"; returning to his room after a date, he would say, "Jumbo had a real workout tonight," while relating physical details of the evening, including details of his companion's most intimate anatomy. And if he was urinating in a bathroom of the House Office Building and a colleague came in, Johnson, finishing, would sometimes turn to him with his penis in his hand. Without putting it back in his pants, he would begin a conversation, still holding it, "and shaking it, as if he was showing off," says one man with whom he did this. He asked another man, "Have you ever seen anything as big as this?"

None of the body parts customarily referred to as "private" were private when the parts were Lyndon Johnson's. Nervous and restless, he couldn't seem in public to stop moving, and among the movements was an inordinate amount of scratching: of his chest, of his stomach—and of areas not generally scratched in public. He was constantly pulling his trousers lower, either in front or back, while complaining about his tailor's failure to provide him with sufficient "ball room," and he was continually, openly and at length, scratching his rear end—quite deeply into his rear end sometimes. He would plunge a hand into a side pocket of his trousers and scratch his groin. "Crude," says Representative Richard Bolling of Missouri. "Crude. Barnyard. Always scratching his crotch and picking his nose in mixed company. I'll never forget—one time he had some injury—hernia or something—and even with the girls present in his office he pulled his pants down to show it. And he'd sit at his desk, and it wouldn't matter if there was a woman there—he'd pull up his scrotum while talking. We men used to be a bit embarrassed."

There was, in fact, a purpose to at least some of his crudeness. Years before, while he was still only an assistant to a congressman, Lyndon Johnson himself had had two assistants, two teenage young men who had been his students when he was a high school teacher back in Texas. One, Gene Latimer, gave Johnson the unquestioning deference Johnson wanted; he would work for him for thirty-five years as "his slave—his totally willing slave." The other, Luther E. Jones, would not; ambitious and independent, he was afraid that "you lose your individuality if you allow someone to be too demanding for too long," and if he disagreed with Johnson about something, he would voice his disagreement. Jones, a neat young man who was invariably well scrubbed, with his hair carefully slicked down, was reserved, almost prim, in physical matters; "Any kind of coarseness or crudeness just disgusted him," a friend says. Johnson began summoning Jones to take dictation from him while he was sitting on the toilet. "At first," Latimer says, "L.E. attempted to stand away from the door, but Johnson insisted he stand right over him. L.E. would stand with his head averted, and take dictation." As both Latimer and Jones understood, the tactic was a "method of control"—employed to humiliate Jones, and make him acknowledge who was boss. Years later, Richard Goodwin, a speechwriter who had just begun working for Johnson, was summoned to the President's bathroom in the White House. Watching Johnson, "apparently in the midst of defecation," staring at him "intently, looking for any sign of embarrassment," and "lowering his tone, forcing me to approach more closely," while "calculating my reaction," Goodwin realized that he was being given a kind of "test." Goodwin passed—and so had many of the staff members to whom Johnson had given the same test during his years in the House of Representatives.

For other aspects of Lyndon Johnson's personal style as well, adjectives like "restrained" or "dignified" seemed inappropriate. Among his chronic health problems were a severe eczema-like rash on his hands, and a bronchial condition, and the prescribed remedies were employed with a notable openness. He often kept a large bowl of a purple-colored salve called "Lubriderm" on his desk, and would, even with visitors present, plunge his hands into the bowl, and assiduously rub gobs of ointment into his hands. To combat the nasal congestion produced by the bronchitis, doctors had recommended the use of a nasal inhaler, and the use was frequent—not only in his House office but even on the House floor. Throwing his head all the way back, he would stick the inhaler into one nostril and inhale, with a slurping sound so loud it could be heard clearly in the Press Gallery above. Few settings seemed less appropriate for such behavior than the Senate Office Building, or the Senate Chamber.

THE PLACE to which Lyndon Johnson had come seemed peculiarly unsuited to him, in addition, for reasons more serious than personal style. Because it was ruled by seniority, ability couldn't move him along the long tables in the committee rooms toward those gavels at the end that conferred power in the Senate. Energy couldn't move him along. Only the passage of time could do that. There was, it was universally agreed, only one way to become one of the Senate's rulers: to wait.

Lyndon Johnson had already had a lesson—a terribly harsh lesson—in how long seniority might make him wait. Upon his arrival in the House of Representatives, in 1937, he had been assigned to its Naval Affairs Committee, whose chairman was Carl Vinson, "the Georgia Swamp Fox," then in his twenty-third year in Congress but still only fifty-three years old, and, as a southern Democrat, virtually guaranteed his seat as long as he wanted it. And of course even Vinson's death or retirement would not make Johnson chairman. Some of the committee's Democrats who sat between him and Vinson would lose their seats, some would die, some would become senators—but some would remain on the committee. He would have to survive the chairmanships of these remaining Democrats, the chairmanships laid end to end, before he could become chairman. That prospect was bleak enough, but then, in 1946, Johnson had received a brutal reminder that, because so many years were involved, no one could predict what might happen—so that even waiting was no guarantee. In that year, an unusual concatenation of deaths and defeats among the Democrats on Naval Affairs had left him as the committee's third-ranking Democrat. Only a single member of his party sat between him and Vinson; the chairmanship had begun to seem within his reach. (Only, of course, because Johnson could not foresee Vinson's longevity; the Swamp Fox would not retire until 1965, at the age of eighty-one; had Johnson remained on the House Naval Affairs Committee, he would actually have had to wait twenty-eight years before he became chairman.) But it was in 1946 that the House adopted the recommendations of a bipartisan Joint Committee on the Reorganization of Congress, and one of those recommendations was for merging the Naval Affairs and Military Affairs Committees into a single new House Armed Services Committee. Six Democratic members of Military Affairs possessed greater seniority in the House than he did. His old committee had suddenly disappeared; on his new one, he was not the third-ranking Democrat but the ninth. Nor was that the end of the lesson. In November, 1946, the GOP won control of the House: a vivid reminder of the fact that even outwaiting or outliving all the Democrats ahead of him would not make him chairman if, when his turn in the Democratic line finally arrived, the Democrats were not the body's majority party.

Lyndon Johnson had fought and twisted in the House to try to break free of the seniority trap. When the traditional "Texas seat" on the powerful Appropriations Committee became vacant, he planted newspaper stories hinting that President Roosevelt wanted him to have it, and half persuaded Speaker Rayburn that if no one else demanded it, he could have it. But someone else did demand it: Texas congressman George Mahon, who had more seniority. "Rayburn followed the rules," Mahon was to recall; regardless of the Speaker's fondness for Johnson, "If you were in line for it, you got it—that was the way the unvarying rule was."* Rayburn himself had, long before, learned the lesson the hard way. His patron John Nance (Cactus Jack) Garner had said, "The only way to get anywhere in Congress is to stay there and let seniority take its course." Rayburn had not wanted to believe that, but as the years passed, he had realized he had no choice. He had come to Congress in 1912, at the age of thirty; he did not get his first real power—the chairmanship of the House Interstate Commerce Committee—until 1931, when he was forty-nine; he would eventually become Speaker, all right, but not until 1940, when he was fifty-eight. Lyndon Johnson had studied Rayburn's career, and had known it wouldn't do for him. *"Too slow. Too slow."* The House had been too slow for Lyndon Johnson. What would the Senate be?

AND THE SENATE was ruled by the South, by that mighty Southern Caucus whose unity—that "oneness found nowhere else in politics"—was rooted in its members' allegiance to a cause almost holy to them. Rising to power in the Senate—to a position within the Senate from which a senator could run for President—depended on the support of southern senators, support which would be forthcoming only after they had been thoroughly convinced that their colleague's allegiance to that cause was firm.

But that allegiance, essential for success within the Senate, would be fatal to success beyond it—would be fatal in pursuing the goal of which Lyndon Johnson had so long dreamed. There were only eleven southern states, and in

---

*In an attempt to help Johnson advance outside the traditional House structure, near the end of World War II Rayburn appointed him to two prestigious new "Select" postwar planning committees whose other members were senior members of the House. But Johnson's attempt to take a leading role on the Select committees earned him the seniors' displeasure, and the attempt was abandoned.

many of the other thirty-seven, sympathy for that Lost Cause was not a recommendation. In the eight most populous states, all of which were in the North or the West, it was, in fact, a taint. In the Senate, these eight states cast only sixteen of ninety-six votes, but in a presidential election, they accounted for more than 40 percent of the electoral vote. "No Democrat could win without us," Illinois' Paul Douglas was to say. No Democrat could become president without the North's support—support not available to an advocate of segregation.

It was, therefore, an article of faith in Washington that no southerner could ever become President of the United States. This belief was stated over and over—without qualification, since no qualification was thought necessary—in conversation, and in articles and columns and editorials. When Lyndon Johnson rode in Speaker Rayburn's chauffeured limousine, staring at him was a plaque that the Speaker's Democratic colleagues had had affixed to the back of the front seat: "To our Beloved Sam Rayburn—Who would have been President if he had come from any place but the South."

Lyndon Johnson was from Texas, one of the eleven states of the Confederacy. The taint of the South was on him. For him to realize his great ambition, that taint would have to be removed. But he could rise to a position from which he could run for President only with the South's enthusiastic, unqualified support. He had trod a very rocky, narrow path to power before. Was this path—the Senate path—to prove too rocky and narrow even for him?

IN ADDITION, he had a problem with his staff—an old problem.

Working for Lyndon Johnson was, in a way, very exciting, for he filled his office with a sense of drama and a sense of fun. Horace Busby had received a full dose of both on the day in 1948 on which he arrived there—a short, curly-haired young man whose editorials in the University of Texas student newspaper had caught Johnson's eye, and who had been brought to Washington, a few days after his twenty-fourth birthday, to be the congressman's "idea man" and speechwriter. Busby idolized Franklin Roosevelt, and Johnson had been told that, and when the young man was shown into Johnson's office to meet him, there, sitting behind the desk, was Franklin Roosevelt, complete to pince-nez glasses, long cigarette holder, and uptilted, outthrust jaw. "Come in, young man, come in," the figure behind the desk said, in a perfect imitation of Roosevelt's patrician voice, and, wheeling his big swivel chair around the desk since of course he was paralyzed and couldn't walk, he took the astonished young man's hand and said graciously, "Sit down, sit down." Then, with obvious difficulty, he wheeled himself slowly and painfully back behind the desk, and looked Busby directly in the eye. The big jaw thrust even farther out and up. "We have nothing to fear but fear itself," Franklin Roosevelt said. There followed one of Roosevelt's fireside chats—"about ten minutes of it," in Busby's recollection; "I looked it up later, and it was practically word for word." And that was the end of the drama, and time for the joke. Summoning his assistant Walter Jenkins, Johnson reverted to his role as congressman, and, in his own voice, began a serious discussion with him—in the midst of which the cigarette, without warning, suddenly flew out of the holder, and, sailing across the desk, landed smack in an ashtray right in front of the astonished Busby. Johnson's cigarette holder, he would learn, was equipped with a spring that ejected cigarettes, and Johnson could aim it with accuracy, thanks to hours of practice.

There had been many such scenes in Lyndon Johnson's suite in the House Office Building, for, says his chief aide, John Connally, "Johnson created his own theater," staging real-life dramas which he claimed to have witnessed, using members of the staff in supporting roles. A favorite was the scene in Sam Rayburn's Capitol hideaway the day Roosevelt died, and the White House had telephoned to summon Vice President Truman, who was having a drink in the hideaway, to take the oath. "Johnson acted the whole thing out," Busby would recall. "He placed the chairs—'This is how close [to Truman] I was.' He played Rayburn and Truman. He moved over to where Rayburn would have been sitting, and put on Rayburn's grim scowl. 'Harry, the White House is on the line.' Then he showed us Truman walking banty-style across the room," and spoke with thin lips hardly moving, as Truman sometimes spoke. " 'They want me at the White House, Sam.' " Then Johnson played himself for a moment; not knowing what had happened, he said, he started to ask Rayburn a question, and told Busby to give Rayburn's response. "Say, 'No, no, Lyndon, not now.' " So Busby said, "No, no, Lyndon, not now," trying to scowl grimly as he did so. It detracted nothing from the drama, in Busby's eyes, when he learned later that, despite what Johnson said, he had not, in fact, been present at this historic occasion, but had only heard about it later from other men who had been.

Johnson inspired his staff, too, giving each of them whatever would inspire him and cement his allegiance—making some of them, who wanted to make their mark on the world, to be a part of history, feel that if they stuck with him, they would be; as one put it, "You felt that the world was moving, and Lyndon was going to be one of the movers, and if you worked for him, *you'd* be one of the movers"; making others, who wanted less to make a mark than to advance in life, believe that sticking with him was the way to do that, too; as J. J. (Jake) Pickle, one of his men in Texas, put it, "that Mr. Johnson had the prospects of being a . . . national figure, and he'd take you along with him. . . . It was the best way to get ahead."

But drama and fun and inspiration weren't all he filled his office with. Entering his office in the morning, he would stride from desk to desk. If an assistant's desk was cluttered with papers, he might say, with a snarl in his voice, "Clean up your fucking desk." If an assistant's desk was clean, he might say, with a snarl in his voice, "I hope your mind isn't as empty as that desk." Moving from desk to desk, he would pick up or yank out of a typewriter whatever paper an aide was working on, and, one says, "look to see if anything was wrong with it—and God help you if he found something. Jesus, he could rip a man up and down." "God, you're stupid," he would yell at one assistant. "You couldn't find your ass if you were using both hands!" To another he would shout, "You couldn't pour piss out of a boot if the instructions were printed on the heel." Or a letter might remind him of a phone call he had been intending to make; he would reach out and grab the nearest phone—even if at that moment a secretary was talking to someone on it. Ripping the phone out of her hands as she was in the middle of a sentence, he would cut off the call and dial the number he wanted. As for incoming calls, they had to be answered on the first ring—or else. "If you were on the phone with someone and someone else called, you had to put that [first] person on hold *immediately,* so you could pick up the second [person] on the first ring," says Ashton Gonella, who would come to work for Johnson several years later. After several tongue-lashings when she violated that rule, Ms. Gonella devised the strategy of keeping her phone off the hook, so that when it rang she could answer it by simply pressing the button that lit up on her six-line telephone console. Opening the top drawer of Jenkins' desk, Johnson would take out the sheet Jenkins had to fill out each evening showing how many constituent letters each member of the staff had answered the previous day. The daily quota was a hundred letters per person; if a box on the sheet contained the number "fifty-five," he would shout, "That's forty-five good Texans who didn't get the service they deserved yesterday"— and that was only the first shout. "His rages were terrible," says Congressman Richard Bolling, who witnessed some. "I mean almost literally—if he'd had a whip in his hand, I'm sure he would have given them a couple of lashes with it." Once, Gene Latimer felt it would make sense to draw a large map of Texas, with each of the state's 254 counties and the name of its county chairman, and pin it up in the office so that his fellow aides could see which chairman to notify about a constituent's problem. Because it took all day for him to do that, however, the next morning the box by the name "Latimer" had a zero in it. Johnson turned that stare—"that terrible stare"—on the little man who adored him so and was so psychologically dependent on him. When Latimer explained what he had done, Lyndon Johnson asked, "I don't pay you to make maps, do I?" Latimer said he didn't. "The next time you do something like that, I'll rip the fucking thing right off the wall," Johnson said. On another occasion, when he had buzzed out from his inner office for a Scotch, a secretary made a mistake and poured sherry instead. Yelling "You've poisoned me!" Johnson hurled the glass against a wall so hard that it shattered. And then he sat at his desk, not saying a word, just staring at the secretary, through the long minutes during which, using paper towels from the bathroom, she knelt on the floor blotting up the sherry and picking up the pieces of glass. On another occasion, when, as Nellie Brill Connally, John's wife, who worked for Johnson for four years, recalls, "I didn't get a telephone number fast enough for Mr. Johnson, he threw a book at me. I was a little afraid of him after that."

The general abuse he would direct at offenders was, aides say, "not so bad" no matter how loud it was shouted at you in front of your fellow workers, not compared to the personal remarks Lyndon Johnson made, for he possessed not only a lash for a tongue but a talent for using it to find a victim's most sensitive spot. When he would buzz for coffee, "it had to be hot," recalls one secretary, who was recently divorced and very sensitive about that fact. One morning it wasn't hot enough: "No wonder you couldn't keep your husband," Johnson said to her. "You can't even make coffee."

He insisted on ordering every aspect of his staff members' lives—the way they dressed down to the knots in his men's neckties; or his women's weight, hairdo, and makeup. "Well, I see we're putting on a few pounds, aren't we?" he would say to a secretary. ("Which meant that you'd better go on a diet," says Yolanda Boozer, one of his secretaries.) "Or if you hadn't had your hair done, he would come into the office and say, 'Well, it's getting a little windy out there, isn't it?' " If such hints did not produce the desired result, he would be more direct. To one secretary—with whose appearance he was still dissatisfied—he said, "Why don't you put on some lipstick, and then I'd like you to send a letter." "He was adamant about your not having a run in your stocking. He could see it a mile away. I'd be so nervous every time I'd start to walk away from him. I knew I would get the complete up-and-down look. I mean *scrutiny*. And if you had even a little bit of a run, you'd better change those stockings. It was best always to have an extra pair in your drawer." He explained his concern about weight to Busby, telling him, "I don't see the front of my secretaries, I don't see them until they've put something down on my desk and are walking away. I don't want to look at an Aunt Minnie. I want to look at a good, trim back end." And Ashton Gonella understood his insistence on other aspects of appearance. "Everybody had to be perfect, so appearance was all-important to him. When I came to work for him, I had long hair, which was the style at the time. One morning, he said, 'You're going to the beauty shop today, and you're going to have ten pounds cut off that.' "

The members of his staff knew that they would have to work in the Senate Office Building the same hours they had worked in the House Office Building—hours which had astonished people who learned about them. All members of that staff worked six days a week, and sometimes seven; the men who handled the mail had to work alternate Sundays. And these were very long days. Some of the staff—those who unloaded the mail each morning from the big gray mailbags—had to be waiting at the office when the bags arrived at seven o'clock. Others started the day at either eight or eight-thirty. And no matter when they started in the morning, they usually had to work into the evening—sometimes quite late into the evening. Nadine Brammer, who would come to work for him in 1955, wrote a friend that she arrived early in the morning, "and sometimes I don't see daylight again until the next morning. Usually, we have a sandwich at our desks for lunch, and it's dark, most evenings, when we leave." Nor did the workday end when they went home. If Johnson had a thought during the night that he wanted to communicate to a member of his staff, he simply picked up the telephone and called him or her at home, no matter what the hour. "There wasn't even a hello, or a 'This is Congressman Johnson,' " one says. "You were woken up at two or three A.M. and there was a voice in your ear giving an order." The men on the staff were worked to exhaustion. One congressman was having a drink with Lyndon Johnson late one evening in his House hideaway office, and Johnson buzzed for Walter Jenkins. "The door opened, and there was this guy—shirt rumpled, tie askew, face pale, standing in the door holding a yellow legal pad waiting for orders—like a slave." A friend of Jenkins who would visit him in Washington and board with him for a few nights recalls him returning to his home so tired that he fell asleep in the bathtub. "Johnson was working him like a nigger slave," he says. And always Johnson was reminding the staff that the indispensable quality he required in them was "loyalty"—and he defined what he meant by that: "I want *real* loyalty. I want someone who will kiss my ass in Macy's window and stand up and say, 'Boy, wasn't that sweet!' "

Because his treatment of his staff had become known on Capitol Hill, Johnson had been stymied for years in the House in attempts to recruit talented individuals to work for him—with a single exception, his administrative aide John Connally. The remarkable abilities of this future Governor of Texas (which impressed everyone who came into contact with him: John Kennedy would make Connally his Secretary of the Navy, Richard Nixon his Secretary of the Treasury—and Nixon called him the man best qualified to succeed him as President) had camouflaged the lack of other top-flight talent on Johnson's congressional staff. The Congressman himself felt Connally possessed an abundance of the indispensable attribute. "I can call John Connally at midnight, and if I told him to come over and shine my shoes, he'd come running," Johnson would say. "*That's* loyalty!" But now Connally had evidently decided that ten years of doing it in Macy's window was enough. Not long after the election that sent Johnson to the Senate, Connally flatly refused to return to Washington with him, and accepted a job with the Austin law firm of Alvin J. Wirtz, the former state senator and canny political string-puller who was the single most powerful figure in Johnson's congressional district and a key figure in Johnson's career.

Johnson had several replacements in mind, men of outstanding qualifications and Washington expertise, but, having observed how he treated his staff, they declined to join it. Trying to tempt Bryce Harlow, who would later serve as a high-level assistant to Presidents Eisenhower and Nixon, and who was already a highly respected congressional aide, Johnson offered him not only a salary but stock in his radio station. And Johnson's proposition was reinforced by Connally, who was friendly with Harlow and came to his office to plead with him to take his job, saying, "For God's sake, I can't go on like this." But

there was a problem of ethics; pragmatic though Harlow might be about politics, he knew he would have a problem with Lyndon Johnson's brand of pragmatism. "I went and spoke to Vinson about it. This was a man whom Lyndon
was close to. The old man sat there and looked at me very penetratingly. Then
he wheeled around and looked out the window. Dead silence. Wheeled back
around: 'Bryce, it won't work. You wouldn't last six months. Lyndon cuts his
corners too close.' And I knew he was right. I knew somewhere along the line
he would take some action I could not go along with, and I'd have to say, 'I
can't do that, Senator.' " And there was a personal problem. "Lyndon would
maneuver people into positions of dependency and vulnerability so he could do
what he wanted with them. I had watched what he did with Walter Jenkins. He
broke Jenkins. To work for Lyndon Johnson, you had to be willing to accept the
blacksnake [whip], and not even scream." Harlow determined that, no matter
what Johnson offered him, he would never work for him. Then Johnson offered
the job to Jim Rowe, a successful lawyer and one of Washington's most
respected political insiders. But Rowe says, "It was all right to deal with Johnson as long as you had a little independence. But if you were on his payroll—
well, I had seen how he treated people who were on his payroll." And the effect
of Connally's absence was going to be exacerbated by the fact that Johnson was
in the Senate now—as became apparent to Johnson with the first assignment he
gave one of Connally's assistants, Warren Woodward.

"Woody" was one of the young men deeply dependent psychologically on
Lyndon Johnson. Handsome and courageous—during World War II, he had
flown thirty-five missions over Europe—he was keenly aware of his limitations. Asked years later about his role in Johnson's organization, he would say,
"Well, I wasn't in on strategy. I carried his socks and underwear. That's what
I could do for him, and I was proud to do it." And, knowing he was going to
have to take over some of Connally's duties, he was nervous. "There was a
feeling in the office when we moved to the Senate that we had to step up our
game to a new level—that the Senate was the Big Leagues," he would say. And
with his first assignment, he—and his boss—found out that the nervousness
was justified.

The assignment—in early December, before Johnson had even been
sworn in as a senator—was to obtain enough extra tickets to President Truman's Inaugural Ball so that Johnson could accommodate all his financial
backers who wanted to attend.

"I was just as green as a gourd," Woody would recall. The official he saw
first at Inaugural headquarters was unable to satisfy his request, and sent him to
see a woman whose name Woody caught as "Miss Masters."

"I went in and poured out my story" to the lady, Woody said, and when she
agreed to help, decided to do her a great favor in return: with the air of someone
giving a thrill to a functionary who would be honored to dance with a senator,

he said, "I know Senator Johnson will be very grateful, and I wouldn't be surprised if he wants to have a dance with you."

When he related the story to Johnson, Johnson was puzzled as to the identity of "Miss Masters"—until the light dawned. "Her name wouldn't be Mesta, would it?" he said. "You were talking to Perle Mesta!" His assistant had told Washington's most famous hostess that he would, as a favor, have his boss give her a dance. "Well, that was how green we all were, without John there with his sophistication," Woody says. Not long after this (and after Harlow and Rowe—and several others—had refused to fill Connally's place), Johnson began telephoning Connally at Wirtz's law firm, cajoling and pleading with him to return. "You got to come, John. You got to hire my staff. You got to help me. I'm going to be new. I need help, John." And when the pleading and cajoling failed, the big hand tightened on the telephone and the voice became low and threatening—"Now, you listen to *me*! By God, you either come back and reorganize my staff, or find me someone who can!"—and then he slammed the receiver down so hard that the base shook. And a moment later, he picked the up receiver again—to telephone Connally's new boss. And a few minutes later, Connally would recall, "Senator Wirtz called me in. He said, 'John, I know you don't want to go to Washington. I don't blame you. But, you know, I just don't really think we have any choice.' " Connally told Johnson, however, that, choice or not, he would stay for only a single Senate session, and his unhappiness in the job was so evident that, at the end of the session, Johnson allowed him to leave for fear he would infect the rest of the staff.

6

"The Right Size"

HIS FIRST STEPS along the Senate path showed how rocky it might be for him.

All Lyndon Johnson's life he had been grabbing—for more than his share of boardinghouse food, for more than his share of radio advertising, for House committee seats to which he was not entitled. And now he tried to grab for the first two things he wanted in the Senate: committee seats and office space.

He made his moves fast. The three most desirable committees were Appropriations, Finance, and Foreign Relations, and luckily, or so Johnson thought, the senior senator from his own state, Tom Connally, was not only a power on two of them—chairman of Foreign Relations and ranking member of Finance—but was also, thanks to the Senate's long Christmas recess, ready to hand. And hardly had Connally arrived back in his hometown of Marlin in early November when Johnson flew up to see him, accompanied by John Connally (no relation to the Senator). They were met at Waco, the nearest airport, by Frank C. (Posh) Oltorf, then a second-term member of the Texas Legislature, who drove them to Marlin and went up with them to Connally's suite in the Falls Hotel, where the two younger men sat on a sofa as the old senator and the new one chatted.

"After a while," Oltorf recalls, "Lyndon said he'd like to discuss committee assignments, and he'd like to be on Foreign Relations and of course he'd like to be on Finance."

Senator Connally, Oltorf recalls, took out of his breast pocket a little book with the list of Senate committees, and pulled his glasses down on his nose to leaf through it. He took a long, leisurely puff on his big cigar. Then, looking at Johnson over his glasses, he said, "Well, now, Lyndon, let's see. Oh, now, here's the Agriculture Committee. You could get on that, and you could help the farmers. You're for the farmers, ain't you, Lyndon?"

Johnson said he was. "I thought I heard you say something about it during the campaign," Senator Connally said. Connally's "eyes were just twinkling," Oltorf recalls, and he paused to savor the moment. "And you can get on the

Armed Services Committee," Connally said, "and then you could help A&M [the Agricultural & Mechanical College of Texas, which depended on federal grants for military research and Officers Training Corps programs]. You're for A&M, ain't you, Lyndon?" Oltorf does not recall whether or not Johnson made any reply to this question. "By this time he was sitting there with his arms crossed; he never cracked a smile. Johnson didn't like to get worked over."

Connally looked at him again over his glasses. "And then, Lyndon, after you've been in the Senate for a while, then you can get on the Foreign Relations Committee or the Finance Committee, and render a *real* public service."

Speed was of no more assistance on office space. Within days of his election, Johnson was telephoning Carl Hayden, whose Rules Committee assigned offices. Of course, he said, he understood that offices were generally allocated according to seniority, but he hoped that an exception could be made in his case, since under seniority he would be entitled only to a three-room office, not one of the more desirable four-room suites, and his circumstances were exceptional, since Texas was the largest state in area and sixth-largest in population, and he would need a large staff to serve his constituency. Hayden gave him a noncommittal reply on the phone, and then sent a letter, saying simply that as a result of retirement or defeat, six four-room suites were to be vacated, and they would be "tendered to the six senior senators now occupying three-room suites."

These rebuffs only made Johnson intensify his efforts, using the lever which could move so much in Washington. Aware that both Hayden and former Majority Leader Alben Barkley, who was leaving the Senate to become Vice President but was still immensely popular on Capitol Hill, were old friends of Rayburn, he asked the Speaker to intercede with them, and Rayburn did. And Johnson had his own coterie of friends within the Truman Administration, most notably his fellow Texan, Attorney General Tom Clark, who assured him that he could persuade the President to "put in a good word with" Barkley, and he asked these friends to make some calls, and they did. He wrote more letters. Giving up on Foreign Relations and Finance (since without Connally's support, appointment to either one would be highly unlikely), he switched his attention, writing to Appropriations Chairman Kenneth McKellar that "I want very much to . . . have you as my chairman," and to Barkley and the influential Walter George that "Since Texas joined the Union in 1845, only *one* Texas Senator has served" on Appropriations, "and this was more than twenty-five years ago," and that this inequity was all the more glaring because Texas was currently receiving more federal appropriations than all but three other states. And in mid-December, Johnson went up to Washington to make his mark on the Senate in person.

His first encounter was with a young Capitol policeman who was stationed outside the Senate Office Building entrance to ensure that no one but senators parked near that door—he was one of the young men who had been told, about senators, "Whatever they want you to do, you do it." There were no assigned parking spaces, but as could be expected the more junior senators left the three or four spaces nearest the entrance for their seniors.

Pulling around the corner from Massachusetts Avenue, Johnson drove his Cadillac onto Delaware and pulled into the parking space nearest the door. Since Johnson had not yet been given a District of Columbia license plate with a senatorially low number, the young policeman did not know he was a senator, and came up to the car to protest. Johnson simply ignored him, and went inside; the young man, having ascertained his identity, didn't say anything when he returned. Arriving earlier than any other senator for the next few mornings, Johnson parked in the same space, but one day he found another car already in it. Although there were other empty spots along the curb immediately behind it, Johnson's fury led the policeman to secure a "Reserved" stanchion and put it in that spot the next day to ensure that it would be available for Johnson. Nonetheless, not long thereafter there was again another car in that spot when Johnson pulled up. Telephoning the Capitol Police Chief, Olin Cavness, Johnson told him to "Get that goddamned car out of there!" Calling Johnson back a few minutes later, Cavness said that he had checked with the policeman, and the car belonged to a senior senator. Cavness evidently felt that that explanation would end the matter, but it didn't. "Well," Johnson said, "while I'm getting some more seniority, you put a cop there every morning to guard my space until I get there!" Cavness told the policeman to put not one but two "Reserved" signs in that space. That device worked because no one cared to inquire about the signs, and they would remain until Johnson's car would turn onto Delaware, and the officer, who had been watching for him, would hastily roll them up out of the space so Johnson could park there.

But that was his only victory on the mid-December trip; he may have been able to win in a conflict with a young "policeman"; he had less luck with senators.

For two or three days he did what he had done during his days in the House, striding around the Senate Office Building corridors to various offices, bounding in the door with a big smile, saying, "Hi! I'm Lyndon Johnson from Texas, How's everyone from Pennsylvania today?" saying it so winningly that he would draw smiles even from the traditionally dour Senate receptionists, asking, "Is the Senator in?" "Is he alone?" and, if the answers were affirmative, walking over to the door to the private office, knocking on it, opening it, and asking if he could come in and chat for a few minutes.

He got the chats—the invariably courteous Hayden, for example, "never refused to see anyone," and of course he would never be too busy to see a friend of Mr. Sam's—but the chats (and *pro forma* promises to "do everything I can to help") were all he got. The levers Johnson had tried to use were levers outside the Senate, and the Senate reacted to their use as the Senate always reacted to outside pressures. Barkley brushed him off with a letter so cold that Rayburn, to whom Johnson showed it, tried to console him by saying that "of course" it must have been "written and signed by one of his secretaries." Walter George was courtesy itself at first as he let Johnson know that it was "inappropriate" for a new senator to try to bypass the seniority system, but when Johnson persisted in his arguments, he all but showed him out of his office. He tried writing Barkley again; this time the former Majority Leader *did* in fact let his secretary reply to "your letter with further reference to your desire to be assigned to Appropriations," in a missive even colder than the first. After all the letters he had written and the phone calls he had made to try to force his way onto Foreign Relations or Finance or Appropriations, he was no closer to a place on these committees than if he had written no letters or made no phone calls at all. As for office space, Hayden told Johnson that while he had more seniority than four of the House members who had "come over" with him, and, of course, more than the eight newly elected senators who had no House service, he had less seniority than the eighty-three other senators, and he wouldn't be assigned an office suite until all eighty-three had chosen theirs. It appeared to him, Hayden said, that the most desirable three-room suite available for Senator Johnson might be Number 231, which would be appropriate since it was the suite that had been occupied by his two predecessors from Texas, Senators Morris Sheppard and Pappy O'Daniel. Perturbed not only by 231's size but by its location—next to a snack bar and, in the northwest corner of the building, inconveniently distant from the "subway" to the Capitol—and possibly misled by the softness of Hayden's tone, Johnson may have pressed him too hard to alter this line of reasoning; Hayden finally ended the discussion with a remark which, for Hayden, was unusually sharp: "The trouble with you, Senator, is that you don't have the seniority of a jackrabbit." And not long thereafter another letter from Hayden arrived: "I am pleased to inform you that the three-room suite 231, Senate Office Building, now occupied by Senator O'Daniel, has been assigned to you for your office." And when Johnson said he assumed that, in that case, he would also be assigned the extra little room in the basement—102-B—that O'Daniel had had the use of, Hayden replied that unfortunately Senator Forrest Donnell of Missouri had requested that extra room. Senator Donnell had more seniority than Senator Johnson. That room would be assigned to Senator Donnell. Lyndon Johnson's trip got him nothing that he had gone to Washington to obtain.

UNPRODUCTIVE THOUGH THAT TRIP to Washington may have been, however, Lyndon Johnson did not return from it unhappy. For the Senate Office Building had not been the only place he had visited on that trip. He had also gone over to the Capitol—and had looked, for the first time as a senator, at the Senate Chamber.

Walter Jenkins, who was with him at the time—they had entered the Chamber by the side door near the Senate Reception Room, he would recall years later—would never forget that moment. With the Senate not in session, only a single row of lights was turned on in the ceiling high above, and the Chamber was shadowy and dim, but those lights reflected off the polished tops of the ninety-six senators' desks as the long arcs stretched away in the gloom.

Lyndon Johnson stood just inside the doorway, silently staring out over the Chamber, for what Jenkins would remember as "quite a long time." And then he muttered something, speaking in such a low voice that Jenkins felt he was "speaking to himself." And if Jenkins would not recall Lyndon Johnson's exact words, he did recall the gist of what he said—that the Senate was "the right size."

Jenkins felt he understood what Johnson meant by that, as did Horace Busby, to whom Jenkins repeated the words not long thereafter.

While Lyndon Johnson was not, as his two assistants knew, a reader of books, he was, they knew, a reader of men—a great reader of men. He had a genius for studying a man and learning his strengths and weaknesses and hopes and fears, his deepest strengths and weaknesses: what it was that the man wanted—not what he said he wanted but what he *really* wanted—and what it was that the man feared, *really* feared.

He tried to teach his young assistants to read men—"Watch their hands, watch their eyes," he told them. "Read eyes. No matter what a man is saying to you, it's not as important as what you can read in his eyes"—and to read between the lines: more interested in men's weaknesses than in their strengths because it was weakness that could be exploited, he tried to teach his assistants how to learn a man's weakness. "The most important thing a man has to tell you is what he's not telling you," he said. "The most important thing he has to say is what he's trying not to say." For that reason, he told them, it was important to keep the man talking; the longer he talked, the more likely he was to let slip a hint of that vulnerability he was so anxious to conceal. "That's why he wouldn't let a conversation end," Busby explains. "If he saw the other fellow was trying not to say something, he wouldn't let it [the conversation] end until he got it out of him." And Lyndon Johnson himself read with a genius that couldn't be taught, with a gift that was so instinctive that a close observer of his reading habits, Robert G. (Bobby) Baker, calls it a "sense"; "He seemed to *sense* each man's individual price and the commodity he preferred as coin." He read with a novelist's sensitivity, with an insight that was unerring, with an ability, shocking in the depth of its penetration and perception, to look into a man's heart and know his innermost worries and desires.

Such reading is a pursuit best carried out in private—Lyndon Johnson alone with a man, getting to know him one on one. And Johnson's gift was not only for reading men but also for using what he read—for using what a man wanted, to get from him what *he* wanted, to sell the man on his point of view, or on himself. And this, too, as Jenkins and Busby knew—as indeed everyone who had spent much time with Lyndon Johnson knew—was a talent that operated best in private. "Lyndon was the greatest salesman one on one who ever lived," George R. Brown said of him, and in that sentence "one on one" was the operative phrase. The essence of his persuasiveness was his ability, once he had found out a man's hopes and fears, his political philosophy and his personal prejudices, to persuade the man that he shared that philosophy and those prejudices—no matter what they happened to be. In words that are echoed by Busby and Jenkins, and by many others who had an opportunity to observe Lyndon Johnson at length, Brown was to say that "Johnson had the knack of always appealing to someone about someone [that person] didn't like. If he was talking to Joe, and Joe didn't like Jim, he'd say he didn't like Jim, too—that was his leadership, that was his knack." But such a technique worked, of course, only if Jim wasn't around—and only if there was also no one around who might one day happen to mention to Jim what Johnson had said about him. It worked best if *no one* was around, if the conversation was strictly "one on one." Moreover, since Johnson used the technique not only about personalities but also about philosophies—liberals thought he was a liberal, conservatives that he was a conservative—it worked best if there was no one present from the other side. He "operated best in small groups, the smaller the better," Jenkins said.

For eleven years, however, Lyndon Johnson had been trapped in a body so large that he couldn't work in small groups, much less one on one. Everything in the House of Representatives was done en masse, from the swearing-in by the Speaker at the opening of each Congress—where all 435 members, crowded together on the long benches in the House Chamber, stood up together, raised their hands and repeated the words of the oath in unison, as if they were a group of draftees being inducted into the Army—to committee meetings: each House committee was a substantial body in itself; on the House Armed Services Committee Johnson had been one of thirty-six members, so many that at meetings they had to sit on a long dais in two tiers. With its hundreds of members, its crowded, noisy corridors and cloakrooms, with its strict formal rules and leadership structure made necessary by its size, the House was an environment in which, as one observer put it, members "could be dealt with only in bodies and droves."

The Senate was very different. With fewer than a hundred members, it was less than a quarter of the size of the House, a much more personal, more intimate, body, one in which, as a commentator puts it, "most interactions were face to face." The great reader of men would have to read only a relatively small number of texts. Furthermore, because of the longer senatorial terms, those texts would not be constantly changing as they were in the House. They could be perused at length, pored over; studied and restudied. What text could, under such favorable circumstances, remain impenetrable to Lyndon Johnson's eyes? He would have ample opportunity not only to read his men, but to make use of what he read—in ideal conditions. In subdivisions of the Senate, the contrast with the House became even more dramatic. Most Senate committees had only thirteen members, so that a committee meeting was a small group of men sitting relaxed around a table. Each Senate committee had subcommittees to handle specific areas of the committee's business, and most Senate subcommittees had only five, or perhaps seven, members; not a few had only three. A member of a three-man subcommittee needed to sell only one other senator to carry his point. And Lyndon Johnson was "the greatest salesman one on one who ever lived."

And, Jenkins would say, Johnson appears to have felt all this—to have felt the implications of the Senate's smallness for his particular talents—in that moment in the doorway of the Senate Chamber, in that moment when he stood staring out at those ninety-six individual desks. "From the first day on," Jenkins says, and Jenkins explains that he means from that day when Johnson stood in the doorway, "from the first day on, he knew he could be effective there, make his influence felt. It *was* the right size—just the right size. It was *his* place. He was at his best with small groups, and he was one of only ninety-six senators. With only ninety-five others—he *knew* he could manage that."

THE DIFFERENCE—and the implications—must have been dramatized to Johnson even more vividly by the swearing-in ritual for the thirty-two newly elected or re-elected senators at the opening ceremonies of the Eighty-first Congress. He was in the fifth group of four senators to be sworn in, and it was a distinguished group. Behind Johnson as he walked down the aisle, escorted by old Tom Connally, Chairman of the mighty Foreign Relations Committee, was the young Tennessean, Estes Kefauver, his arm held by the old Tennessean McKellar, Chairman of Appropriations, and then Robert S. Kerr of Oklahoma, escorted by old Elmer Thomas of Oklahoma, Chairman of Agriculture, and South Carolinian Olin Johnston, escorted by the Charleston aristocrat Burnet Rhett Maybank, Chairman of Banking and Currency. They walked down the aisle slowly—McKellar hobbling on his cane, Thomas, his eyesight almost gone, shuffling, feeling for each of the four steps with his feet—but with dignity, and the face of Vandenberg above them as they approached was the face of "the Lion of the Senate" familiar from a score of magazine covers. All four of the just-elected senators were over six feet tall; they stood very straight as, their right hands raised, they took the oath with the older men beside them. And after they had answered, "I do," a clerk pushed the Senate Register ("a well-bound book kept for that purpose") toward them, and Lyndon Johnson signed, at nine minutes past noon, and went not to a crowded bench but to a desk, his own desk.

LATER, he took the little subway beneath the Senate to the office he hadn't wanted. And though Suite SOB 231 may have had only three rooms instead of four, they were senatorial rooms—high-ceilinged, spacious. On one wall of his private office, adjacent to his private bathroom, was a delicate marble fireplace, the hearth flanked by two slender marble columns. Above the fireplace was a tall gilt-framed mirror. And behind his desk was a high, wide, arched window, recessed and framed in mahogany. It looked out over the green parks of the Capitol Plaza, and beyond the plaza was the long Mall, and the great pillar of the Washington Monument. Margaret Mayer of the *Austin American-Statesman,* who had known him for many years in Texas and who had covered the 1948 campaign, went to interview him there. Referring to the hard campaign—and perhaps, since Ms. Mayer was a perceptive reporter, to his hard life—she asked him if it had all been worth it to be seated at last in that office. Lyndon Johnson winked at her, and nodded—and grinned.

HIS PATH IN THE SENATE was also made smoother by other gifts that he possessed—talents that he had been demonstrating all his life, and that he now demonstrated again, vividly, during his first year in the Senate.

One was an ability to transform his outward personality, his demeanor and mannerisms—not to change his nature, but to conceal it—an ability that had always been one of Lyndon Johnson's most striking characteristics, as had a strength of will that enabled him to make a transformation remarkably thorough.

The most recent of these changes had occurred during the very election that had won him this Senate seat. The campaign's first months, when he had been confident of success, had been filled with the familiar explosions at his subordinates: vicious tirades, laced with obscenities and with insults designed to find his target's most vulnerable point, that made both women and men weep. He had refused to control himself—had seemingly found it impossible, so sudden and violent were the rages, to control himself—even in public, even in places where the tirades would be witnessed by the voters he was trying to court. Arriving at one Rotary Club meeting where he had expected to give only brief remarks, he was told that a longer talk would be desirable; wheeling on his hapless advance man, he screamed, as the club members gaped, "I thought it was just gonna be coffee, doughnuts and bullshit!" Armored against critical newspaper articles by his friendships, crucially important in Texas journalism, with publishers, he refused to control himself even in front of reporters, not only shocking them with his treatment of secretaries (unable to bear watching him shout "unbelievable" obscenities at the sweet-faced, soft-voiced Mary Rather, who was standing head bowed and crying in front of him, Felix Mc-Knight of the *Dallas News* suddenly found himself jumping in front of her, yelling "You can't talk to her like that! Apologize to her!"), but giving them a taste of the treatment themselves ("C'mon," he shouted to stubby Dave Cheavens of the Associated Press, who was sensitive about his weight, "Won't those fat little legs of yours carry you any faster than that?").

His treatment of people not connected with the campaign who were similarly unable to defend themselves—waiters and bellhops, desk clerks and cooks—was the same. Storming into a hotel kitchen, a towering figure holding a large steak in one hand and waving it in a cook's face, he raged: "Who ever told you you were a cook? Didn't you ever hear of cutting the fat off? I've never seen so much fat on a steak in my life." And he seemed to feel he didn't have to control himself; "Lyndon just seemed to think he was entitled to talk to people that way," one reporter says.

But in the latter stages of the campaign—when he had suddenly realized, with only a month to go, that he was almost hopelessly behind and could not afford to antagonize voters—the tantrums ended, instantly and completely. Busby, who had been assigned to accompany him on the next trip, was dreading the experience ("I had learned one thing—when he got angry, *hide!*"). Now he watched in astonishment as Johnson greeted the first desk clerk he encountered with a gracious smile, and gracious words, saying, "You have a very fine hotel here. I stayed in it before and I'm looking forward to this visit." He told the bellhop who carried his baggage to his room, "I'd like to shake hands with you if your hands weren't so busy." After the bellhop had put down the bags and had had the handshake, Busby started to give him a tip. "Son, he's a cheap tipper; I don't want him tipping you," Johnson told the bellhop, giving him a five-dollar bill. And the next morning, Busby awoke to find Lyndon Johnson sitting beside his bed. He wasn't there to give Buzz orders. He was holding something in his hands. "Here, Buzz," he said, "I went down and got a coffee and doughnut for you." And he didn't simply hand the two items to Busby. He would hand the sleepy-eyed young man the coffee, wait until he had taken a sip, and take the coffee back—and only then would hand him the doughnut. After Buzz had taken a bite, Johnson would take the doughnut back, and then hand him the coffee again—sitting beside the bed holding one of the two items himself, so that his assistant wouldn't have to hold two things at once. During that entire month, that "all or nothing" month, no matter how high the tension rose, Lyndon Johnson was, in Busby's phrase, "a changed man." He never lost control of himself—not once.

Now, after the campaign, safely in the Senate, he changed back—but only in some areas of his life.

He was the old Lyndon Johnson driving to work in the morning from his home, a two-story, white-painted brick colonial at 4921 Thirtieth Place in a quiet residential area in northwest Washington—driving down Connecticut Avenue with one hand on the wheel, the other frenziedly twisting the dial on the car's radio back and forth from one station to another searching for news broadcasts, shouting obscenities at broadcasters who said something with which he didn't agree. He was constantly sounding his horn to get other drivers out of his way—if they didn't move aside quickly enough, he would lean out the window and curse them; passing them on their right, he would bang his big left hand down on the outside of his car door to startle them.

His arrival on Capitol Hill was still as ostentatiously attention-getting as possible. His long affair with Alice Glass, the tall, spectacularly beautiful small-town girl from Marlin who had become the elegant hostess of a manor house in the Virginia hunt country, had faded out during the war. That affair, the most serious of Lyndon Johnson's life, had been kept very secret, in part because Alice was the mistress—she would later be the wife—of a man very important to Johnson, Charles Marsh, publisher of the *Austin American-Statesman;* in part perhaps because of Johnson's feelings for her, which men and women privy to the affair believed were so intense that they felt Johnson might divorce Lady Bird and marry her. During his last years in the House, after that relationship ended, Johnson began arriving on Capitol Hill in the morning in the company of another tall, beautiful woman—one who was famous as well. And now that he was in the Senate, he sometimes still got out of his car with her, and they walked to his office openly holding hands.

When Helen Gahagan Douglas was named one of "the twelve most beautiful women in America," the critic Heywood Broun begged to disagree. "Helen Gahagan Douglas is ten of the twelve most beautiful women in America," he wrote. At the age of twenty-two, the tall, blond Barnard College student with a long, athletic stride became an overnight sensation in the Broadway hit *Dreams for Sale,* and she was to star in a succession of hit shows, marrying one of her leading men, Melvyn Douglas. Deciding to study voice, she made her debut in the title role of *Tosca* in Prague, and toured Europe in operas and concerts for two years, before returning to more Broadway starring roles and radio appearances. On screen, she played the cruel, sensual Empress of Kor in the film version of H. Rider Haggard's novel *She.* By 1936, the *New York Herald Tribune* noted that "Helen Gahagan Douglas has made her name in four branches of the arts—theatre, opera, motion pictures, and radio."

Driving across country with Douglas after their marriage, Helen had been touched by the plight of Okies trekking west, and plunged into a new field—politics—with her usual success. She became Democratic national committeewoman from California, and in 1944, at the age of forty-three, ran for Congress from a Los Angeles district, and won, becoming one of nine women members of the House of Representatives. Washington, one journalist wrote, "had prepared for her tall, stately and gracious beauty, but they weren't prepared for her brilliance, in short, her brains." A friend of Eleanor Roosevelt's (whose husband, Helen said, was "the greatest man in the world"), she was a frequent guest at the White House, while Melvyn remained back in Hollywood making movies. On the House floor she was a striking figure, generally "surrounded," as one account noted, "by attentive male colleagues," and she was a riveting, charismatic speaker in her advocacy of liberal causes, particularly civil rights. Declaring that "she stood by the Negro people when they needed a sentinel on the wall," Mary McLeod Bethune called her "the voice of American democracy." She won re-election in 1946, and again in 1948, and was one of the most sought-after speakers for liberal rallies across the country. And in an era in

which age supposedly dimmed a woman's charms, hers seemed as bright as
ever. A profile in the *New York Post* in 1949 commented that during her years in
Congress "her waistline has grown even slimmer, her face leaner." In her
speech at the Democratic National Convention in Philadelphia the previous
year, the *Post* said, "she boosted her stock still higher by turning out to be gor-
geous on television." The *New York Daily News* called her the "Number One
glamour girl of the Democratic Party." It was widely expected that she would
run for the Senate from California in 1950, and would win.

SHE HAD FIRST MET LYNDON JOHNSON in 1945 when, shortly after she
arrived in Congress, he dropped around to her office, "draped his long frame in
one of my easy chairs," and asked how things were going. When she said that
she was having trouble organizing her office, he said, "Well, come up and see
how my office is run." She found his office "very impressive. It worked. If he
wanted something, it came within a half second." There were "other industri-
ous offices," she was to recall, "but the efficiency of this office and the extent
that they went to reach . . . the lives of his constituents in an intimate way was
something that utterly fascinated me." She was impressed as well by qualities
which she discerned, with a very penetrating eye, in his character: by his
instinct for power ("He never got very far away from Rayburn"); by his ambition (he was "in a hurry—in a great, great hurry" and "He was willing to make
the compromises necessary, I believe, to stay in Congress"); and by the method
by which he concealed views that might stand in the way of the realization of
that ambition—a method that, she felt, required great strength. Lyndon Johnson talked so much, she saw, but he never said anything that could be "quoted
back against him later." "Was it just caution?" she was to say. "Just that he
didn't want to have a lot of his words come back at him? . . . He was witty, he
would tell stories, he was humorous. But he was always aware that what he said
might be repeated or remembered—even years later. And he didn't want someone to come back years later, and say, 'I remember when you said . . .' " She
began to realize, she says, that Lyndon Johnson was very "strong." In Washington, she was to say, "everyone tried to find out where you stood. But he had
great inner control. He could talk so much—and no one ever knew exactly
where he stood." This tall, lanky, charming man was actually "one of the most
close-mouthed men I ever knew." When, years later, "John Kennedy was
killed," and she realized that Lyndon Johnson would be President, "I remember
thinking that one thing was sure, we had heard the last frank response to a question from the press." And, she felt, she knew where Johnson really stood: she
was sure he was a New Dealer like her. "He cared about people; was never callous, never indifferent to suffering. . . . There was a warmth about the man."
That was why, she says, that "despite some of his votes, the liberals whom he
always scoffed at . . . nevertheless forgave him when they wouldn't forgive

someone else." While his attempt to portray himself as an insider offended some of his House colleagues, it didn't offend her. "He knew what was going to happen. . . . The friendship of Sam Rayburn . . . had much to do with it, but there was also Lyndon's own presence, which exuded the unmistakable air of the keeper of the keys." They shared the same feelings for Roosevelt, she was to say, and "on the day of his funeral" in April, 1945, "we were both very depressed." Lyndon invited her to come to his fifth-floor hideaway, and "we sat very quietly during the time of the funeral, reminiscing about our President. In this way we became friends. Mutual admiration of Franklin Roosevelt."

Soon Johnson was coming to the House floor more often than formerly, to sit beside her when she was there—although he didn't stay long. On the floor, "he looked the picture of boredom, slumped in his chair with his eyes half-closed," she recalls. "Then, suddenly, he'd jump up to his feet nervous . . . restless, as if he couldn't bear it another minute." And he would leave, "loping off the floor with that great stride of his as though he was on some Texas plain."

On one occasion on the floor, however, he came to her rescue—or to be more precise brought Rayburn to her rescue.

John Rankin of Mississippi was speaking when he suddenly pointed to a group of liberal representatives who were sitting together and referred to them as "these communists." The other liberals sat silent, afraid to challenge the Mississippi demagogue—all except Helen Douglas. Standing to make a point of order, she said, "I demand to know if the gentleman from Mississippi is addressing me!"

"Rankin looked at me—oh, what a look—and went right on talking," she was to recall. Most congressmen had learned not to confront him, and Helen Douglas had herself once been warned by Majority Leader John McCormack, "Remember, Rankin is a killer." But she didn't sit down. Instead, in her ringing, melodic voice, she said again, "I demand to know if the gentleman from Mississippi is addressing me!" and went on standing—a tall blond figure on the House floor.

Since the Speaker had to be in the chair for a point of order, Rayburn entered the Chamber and took the podium, saying, "The gentleman from Mississippi will have to answer the congresswoman," but Rankin, acting as if he had not heard Rayburn, went on talking; as Ms. Douglas recalls, he "was such a fearsome man, he appeared to believe himself untouchable." Rayburn, not quite sure what the fuss was about, was letting him do so, when Johnson hurriedly approached the podium, Ms. Douglas says. He "had been in the House coffee shop when someone ran in and told him, 'Helen is taking on Rankin!' I was told later that he had bounded up the stairs to the Chamber three at a time." As always he knew the right words to persuade someone to do something. "Who runs this House, you or Rankin?" he whispered up to the Speaker. "Sam scowled and banged his gavel again," Helen Douglas recalls. "This time his voice was fierce with warning as he again ordered Rankin to answer me."

Rankin "measured Rayburn," she was to recall. The Speaker did not say
another word, but simply stared at Rankin, his face set in the stern mask that
men feared. "With obvious pain," as Helen Douglas recalls, Rankin said, "I am
not addressing the gentlewoman from California."

MORE AND MORE FREQUENTLY, Lyndon and Helen began arriving on Capitol
Hill in the mornings in the same car—sometimes hers, more often his. They
would park on New Jersey Avenue, about a block and a half from the House
Office Building, and walk to it together, holding hands: a conspicuous couple,
both tall, both with dramatic features, walking with long strides as they came
up Capitol Hill. Often, at the end of the day, they would drive, together or in
separate cars, to Helen's home on Thirty-first Street, where they would have
dinner together. They went to parties together. (During the first six months
Helen was in Washington, Melvyn was in India, and when he returned, his relationship with Helen proved difficult; "over the next several years," her biographer Ingrid Winther Scobie was to write, "[their] relationship continued to
deteriorate." He returned to California. In May, 1946, their two children went
to California for the Summer, and in September were enrolled in a boarding
school near Los Angeles.)

Whatever the considerations that had deterred Lyndon Johnson from
advertising his relationship with Alice Glass, they evidently didn't apply to
Helen Douglas. He made sure that people believed he was having a physical
relationship with her. Not only would they be holding hands when they arrived
together in the morning, they sometimes strolled through the Capitol together,
with tourists coming up to the former actress to tell her they had enjoyed one of
her performances, and they held hands during those strolls. "They were a handsome couple," one of Helen's friends, United Nations bureaucrat Charles
Hogan, was to recall. "A strikingly handsome couple together. She's so much
better looking than poor Lady Bird."

In particular, it seems, he wanted Alice Glass to believe it. When he
parked on New Jersey Avenue, he usually parked in front of Number 317, a
small building in which Alice's sister, Mary Louise, who was then working on
the staff of a Pennsylvania congressman, had an apartment. "Helen Douglas'
affair with Lyndon started just after she got to Washington," Mary Louise says.
"I know because I used to see them going to work in the mornings holding
hands." And, Mary Louise says, she knew because Johnson wanted her to
know. "They would park on the street in front of my house," even if there were
spaces available on New Jersey Avenue closer to the House Office Building,
she says, and she felt he parked there so that she would see the hand-holding,
and tell Alice about it. If she happened to be coming out of her building while
they were parking, Johnson and Helen would walk to work with her; "we'd all
go in together." In fact, she says, Lyndon himself told her sister about his new

affair. Before the war, Alice and Charles Marsh had attended the annual Music Festival in Salzburg, Austria, and Helen Gahagan Douglas had sung several concerts there. "Well, I've got another girl who spent the summer at Salzburg," Lyndon told Alice, in a remark that hurt her, and angered Mary Louise. "Just bragging—kissing and telling," she says.

Some of Johnson's staff believed the affair was still going on after Johnson was in the Senate. When Horace Busby arrived in 1948, he was told about it by other staff members, and then he saw the hand-holding for himself. "It started not long after she came to the House in 1944, and continued on and off for years," Busby was to say. Johnson and Douglas would come back to Suite 231 in the Senate Office Building together, enter Johnson's private office through the door from the corridor, and stay inside "for quite a long time." Others believed it, too. "Lyndon would park his car in front of the [Douglas] house night after night after night," says Creekmore Fath, an attorney from Austin who was a Department of Interior official living in Washington at the time. "It was an open scandal in Washington." More than one friend of the two principals urged Helen to break it off, telling her, "You've got to stop Lyndon from doing this."

This intense phase of the relationship would end in August, 1949, when Helen Douglas returned to California to run for the Senate the following year, in the infamous campaign in which she was defeated by Richard Nixon after his staff published a pamphlet, printed on pink paper, to "prove" she was "soft on Communism," and launched a whispering campaign harping on the fact that her husband was Jewish. (Lyndon Johnson helped her with advice—it was at his suggestion that she campaigned by helicopter as he had done in Texas in 1948—and with campaign contributions from his Texas financial backers.) She never ran for public office again. According to her biographer, Scobie, she decided her family had "suffered enough" from the demands of her career and tried to repair the damage, but with only limited success. Her attempts to resurrect her stage and singing career met with the same result. She did not again live in Washington. Yet while Johnson was Vice President, he telephoned Busby one weekend—a weekend when Lady Bird was in New York—and told him to come to his house. When he arrived, he found Johnson and Helen Douglas lounging by the swimming pool in the back yard. They held hands throughout the conversation and Busby was struck by the "real and deep feelings" between them.

ENTERING THE SENATE OFFICE BUILDING each morning—through the main entrance if he had dropped off Congresswoman Douglas first; otherwise, having parked in that space reserved for him on Delaware Avenue, through the Delaware entrance—he was the same Lyndon Johnson. The Delaware entrance was a back door, but the door was bronze, tall and heavy, and the walls inside

were marble—highly polished marble adorned with fluted pilasters and ornate
bronze sconces. Then there were columns, and, beyond them, across a circular
vestibule, a bank of three elevators—set within tall arches, whose heavily ornamented bronze doors shone like gold. He would press the buttons on all three
elevators—and, in a fever of impatience, press them again. And if an elevator
did not then instantly arrive, he would whirl, his jacket flaring out around him,
and run up a long, curving flight of stairs—a hulking, hurrying, forward-lean-
ing figure in a flapping suit and wide, garish, hand-painted necktie, taking
stairs two at a time in that setting of marble and bronze. As a young congressional assistant almost twenty years before, coming up Capitol Hill in the
morning from the modest hotel where he lived in a basement room, he had had
to pass the Senate Building and the Capitol to reach his office in the House
Office Building, and he had run past them in his haste to get to work. He had a
shorter way to go to reach his office now, as he had a shorter way to go to reach
his great goal, but he was still running. At the top of the stairs his loping steps
would carry him between a pair of tall columns, into that long, high-ceilinged
corridor with its marble floor reflecting the ceiling lights, and its row of tall
mahogany doors—to the second one on the right, the door to the reception
room of his office.

When he pushed open that door, he was, in dealing with his staff, the same
Lyndon Johnson. With the exception of Connally, the staff was composed of
the kind of men and women Lyndon Johnson wanted—men and women who
had demonstrated an unusual willingness to absorb personal abuse: Woody;
Mary Rather, who stood head bowed while obscenities swept over her; Glynn
Stegall, whose hands would shake as Lyndon Johnson humiliated him in front
of his wife; Walter Jenkins, whom Johnson worked "like a nigger slave"—two
roomfuls of men and women willing to let him use the blacksnake.

And he used it. When he arrived at 231 each morning, after screeching
into that parking space in front of the SOB as the young policeman hurriedly
pushed the "Reserved" stanchions out of his way, "the door would," in the
words of one man, "blow open and Johnson—Jesus God, he filled up the whole
room the minute he came in, and if he was really in a bad mood, he would be so
excruciatingly rude I would gasp."

"First thing every morning, he would make the rounds, stopping at every
desk, and beating up on them," Horace Busby recalls. Then, with a parting
bellow—"C'mon, let's function! let's function!!"—he would vanish through
the door to his private office, leaving behind two rooms in which, frequently, at
least one woman would have been reduced to tears, and men would be sitting
stunned by their boss's fury. And even then he might reappear. "If a phone rang
a second time, you could be sure that that door would open, and . . ."

And there was in all his abuse and inspections and orders an element of
crudity—of that "barnyard" talk that made men "a bit embarrassed" when it
poured out in front of female members of the staff. While Johnson was making
his round of the desks one morning, John Connally was talking on the phone to

Jake Pickle, who worked for Johnson in Texas, and told Johnson, calling across the room, that one of Pickle's assignments had not yet been completed. "Tell Jake to get his finger out of his ass," Johnson yelled back. On another occasion, Jenkins told him about a lack of cooperation from some agency bureaucrat. "What does he want?—me to kiss his ass?" Johnson shouted. "Tell him I'll kiss him on both cheeks. I'll kiss him in the middle, too, if he wants it." His office conversation was permeated by sexual imagery. "Take that tie off," he would tell one of his male staffers. "That knot looks like a limp prick." Standing in the middle of the outer-office desks, he retied the tie in the Windsor knot, wider and more shaped than the traditional four-in-hand, which was becoming fashionable in 1949, and then stepped back to admire his handiwork. "Look at that!" he said. "He's got a man's knot now, not a limp one." And assignments to his staff were sometimes made in the same tone. When, during his presidency, a woman reporter wrote critical articles about him, he would tell White House counsel Harry McPherson, "What that woman needs is you. Take her out. Give her a good dinner and a good fuck." And, McPherson would learn, the President wasn't kidding. Joseph A. Califano Jr., to whom McPherson related the incident, writes that "Periodically the President would ask McPherson if he'd taken care of the reporter. Every time she took even the slightest shot at the President, he'd call Harry and tell him to go to work on her." Lyndon Johnson was never kidding when he gave such instructions. He had been doing it at college, even if his language had been more circumspect, in keeping with that earlier time; says Wilton Woods, one of the "White Stars," the San Marcos social group that Johnson turned into a political organization: "Lyndon's idea was to get a real nice-looking girl and see if you could control her. Date her and see how she comes out. . . ." Sometimes, during his presidency, the instructions were more specific, as befitted the sexually more explicit Sixties. Califano writes that "LBJ made a similar suggestion [similar to the one he made to McPherson] when I advised him of the problems James Gaither, an aide on my staff, was having with Edith Green, the irascible Democratic congresswoman from Oregon. . . . Johnson became irritated with our inability to deal with her. In exasperation one evening he said to me, 'Goddamn it! You've been trying to drag me into this thing when I've got a hundred other problems. Well, I'm going to tell you how to get our bill. There's no point in my calling that woman. Gaither is a good-looking boy. You tell him to call up Edith and ask her to brunch this Sunday. Then he can take her out, give her a couple of Bloody Marys, and go back to her apartment with her. Then you know what he does? Tell him to spend the afternoon in bed with her and she'll support any Goddamn bill he wants." During Johnson's Senate years—the still relatively discreet Fifties—his instructions in this area were generally couched more circumspectly: suggesting that a "handsome young staff member" date a woman whose support he needed, he simply said, "Let nature take its course"—but they were nevertheless clear.

But if that was still Lyndon Johnson's manner inside his office, it was no longer his manner outside. As Paul F. Healy wrote in the *Saturday Evening Post,* "when he barks commands, his underlings jump like marionettes," but "away from the [office], his tone is casual and conciliatory." Behind the closed doors of 231, he may have been the old Lyndon Johnson, but as soon as he stepped out of his office, he was a new Lyndon Johnson—a senatorial Lyndon Johnson.

"The other senators weren't coming to him," Warren Woodward recalls. "He had to go to them." And as he went, usually leaving 231 by the door to his private office, and heading down the dim corridors, his very stride changed, into a slower, calmer, more dignified pace. And when he reached the office to which he was heading, his demeanor in January could hardly have been more different from his demeanor the month before. The aggressiveness was replaced by the most elaborate courtesy. Not only did he no longer barge into senators' private offices, he took steps to emphasize that he wouldn't even think of barging in. Even if he had already telephoned for an appointment, he would, entering the senator's outer office, ask the receptionist if the senator was free, and even if he was told that the senator was free—even if he was told that the senator was expecting him, and he could go right in—he wouldn't go in until the assistant had sent in a note saying that Senator Johnson was in the outer office and would like to see him. And in the case of the most formal senator of all, he went even further. Recalls Harry Byrd's administrative assistant, John (Jake) Carlton: "He [Johnson] would come in and sit on my desk, and he would say, 'Hi, Jake,' and chat with me. After a while, he would say, 'Oh, by the way, Jake, is the Senator in?' 'Yes, would you like to see him?' Johnson would say, 'I'd like to if you don't mind,' but he wouldn't walk right in even if I motioned to him that he could. He would wait until I got up and opened the door—so the Senator [Byrd] would know that he was going in only after I had opened the door."

When he was in a senator's private office, furthermore, Johnson no longer launched straight into the business about which he had come. "He wouldn't say, 'Senator, I've got to talk to you about . . .' " He would ask about the senator's health, about his wife's health, would solicit his advice, his opinions, inquire about the manner in which some national issue was playing with voters in his home state, get him talking about things he wanted to talk about. And, while the senator talked, Lyndon Johnson listened—listened with an obsequiousness, a deference "that you wouldn't believe."

The deference was unvarying not merely in private but in public—on the little stage that was the Democratic cloakroom.

The senator who was a fixture there seemed as much out of another, earlier, age as the room itself. Directly opposite the pair of swinging doors opening into the Senate Chamber were two deep leather armchairs. In the afternoons, the distinguished Walter George was given to sitting in one of them, telling stories of old Senate battles. Often now, as the revered George of Georgia held forth, squinting a bit through his thick-lensed glasses, patting his white hair into place, Lyndon Johnson would be sitting in the chair next to him. He would not be sitting on the floor—he was a senator now, not a student—but in the adjacent armchair, yet his posture and demeanor would have been familiar to his San Marcos classmates. His long legs would not be stretched out but tucked back against the chair, and he would be sitting erect and attentive, his chin resting on one hand, his face, tilted back so he could look full into George's face as the older man sat beside him, wearing an expression of the deepest interest, his eyes almost shining in admiration as he listened to one anecdote, and then asked George to tell him another. Day after day Walter George held court—with, day after day, the same admiring courtier in attendance. Recalling Lyndon Johnson in his early months in the Senate, Warren Woodward says, "He took his time to maybe ingratiate himself with his fellow senators. Once he got settled down, he saw that [was necessary]. He saw he needed to take his time." Lyndon Johnson had been running all his life. It was very hard for him to stop running. But he stopped.

THE DEFERENCE was particularly appealing to the senators because it was cloaked in the broad senatorial badinage with which they were comfortable. Johnson had picked this up very quickly, too. He was, in fact, proficient in this aspect of senatorial style by the swearing-in ceremony, when, immediately after the new senators were sworn, the Senate voted for its president *pro tempore,* and Vandenberg, being a Republican and therefore now in the minority, was voted out in favor of Kenneth McKellar. Johnson had of course voted with the Democrats, and after the ceremony he went up to Vandenberg. I want to apologize, he said jokingly, referring to the fact that Vandenberg had sworn him in, for voting against "the man who made me a senator." He gave the old statesman a warm smile. Vandenberg, usually so reserved with junior senators, instantly responded, "Well, you shouldn't bite the hand that feeds you," and then he gave Johnson a warm smile back.

When, on February 2, the twelve new Democratic senators met in the office of Secretary of the Senate Leslie L. Biffle to draw lots for their permanent desk assignments—the last of their seniors having finally made his selection—Johnson began bemoaning the fact that he never had any luck at drawings. Clinton Anderson said he'd bet him a nickel over who would get the better seat, "Well, Ah don't know, Clint, Ah just don't know," he responded. Finally, he agreed to bet a nickel. Anderson drew Desk Number 95, a rear seat, and Johnson and Bob Kerr fell into a joking debate over who would draw last, since Kerr felt the last draw was best. "You were in Congress before me," Kerr said in a jokingly bullying manner. "Go ahead and draw." "But you were Governor of a state," Johnson replied. "That's higher than a Congressman. You draw first." Finally they decided they would both draw at the same time. They stuck their hands into Biffle's fedora together, and despite their bad luck—the desks they selected were two of the worst in the Chamber, Kerr's Number 19 being the very last one on the far end of the lowest arc on the Democratic side, Johnson's Number 18, the desk next to it—when they saw that they had drawn adjoining desks, they grinned at each other, Kerr with a friendliness in his eyes quite unusual for him. (Poor though Desk 18's location may have been, its provenance could hardly have been better. When Johnson opened its drawer, among the names of its former occupants carved inside was *Harry S Truman.*)

Encountering a senator in an SOB corridor, Johnson wouldn't approach him in a businesslike way but in a comradely, good-humored fashion. "Say, Ah saw one of your constituents the other day," he might say. "Ah bragged on you. Ah surely did. Ah tell you—by the time Ah got through, he didn't even recognize you." Or, Warren Woodward says, "He'd tell a story, and get the other senator laughing. It's human nature to like that. He ingratiated himself in a way by being fun to be with. He was a great mimic, a great storyteller, and he always had a story ready. But it was always a light-hearted approach. He wouldn't approach them in a serious way. He stopped saying 'Senator, I need to talk to you about . . .' "

And at the first Democratic caucus, there was no grabbing of lapels, no leaning into the faces of his colleagues, not a trace of the former pomposity or aggressiveness. What there was was the friendliness and politeness of "the junior to the senior," and when he introduced himself, he did so with a deprecatory nickname that referred to his narrow, last-gasp victory in the recent election. Coupled with a grin, it was very charming. "Howdy," he said to old senators and new, southern senators and northern. "Howdy, I'm Landslide Lyndon."

The transformation was very thorough. At the caucus, he was standing to one side chatting with Kerr and Anderson—he had struck up a friendship very quickly with these two fellow newcomers, the former Governor of Oklahoma and the former Secretary of Agriculture, so much so that the three tall southwesterners were already a small "in group" within the Class of '48—when an Associated Press photographer asked them to pose. Kerr held up a forefinger, as if making a point, as if he were the leader of the threesome. Anderson allowed him to do so, smiling at Kerr for the cameras. And so did Lyndon Johnson. One aspect of his behavior that had annoyed his colleagues in the House of Representatives was his constant subtle—and sometimes not so subtle—maneuvering to get into the center of photographs and to make gestures, such as holding up a commanding finger, that made him the photographs' focal point. But now he simply smiled at Kerr in the friendliest way, as Kerr held up a finger in his face.

Nothing—not even an insult—could shatter the new façade. The most insulting of senators was Robert Taft, who could cut and hurt. At a party at the home of Philip and Katharine Graham, another guest watched as Taft was "rude and insulting" to Johnson—and the guest noted that Johnson "passed the matter off . . . in such a gentlemanly manner."

The greatest potential for conflict was with the other senator from his own state, and Johnson had, on that trip to Marlin, gotten off on the wrong foot with crusty, irritable Marse Tom Connally. But he did everything possible to change the footing. Hardly had John Connally and Walter Jenkins settled into their desks in 231 when tension arose between them and Senator Connally's assistants over who was going to issue the press releases—and thus obtain the lion's share of the credit—for public works projects and other federal benefits for Texas. The issue, a long-festering source of conflict between Connally and Pappy O'Daniel, seemed likely to become one with 231's new occupant, particularly since, as Connally and Jenkins well knew, Representative Johnson had fought unceasingly to get the credit even for projects in other congressmen's districts—even for projects with which he had absolutely no connection. But, they found out, Senator Johnson had a different view. He gave Busby instructions, which Buzz relayed to Connally and Jenkins in a memo, and the operative order was to "avoid a clash of any variety with the Senator [Connally]." For one thing, Johnson let his aides know, senators were notified before representatives, and there were enough federal projects so that he would get his share of the credit. And, Johnson made clear, a share was enough. Lyndon Johnson had, throughout his life, grabbed for more than his share.

He wasn't grabbing now.

In the afternoons now, Lyndon Johnson would sometimes leave 231, without telling his staff where he was going, and would be gone for hours. For a while, no one in the office knew where he was spending those hours—until one day a Senate page telephoned with a message for Horace Busby. Senator Johnson wanted him to come over to the Capitol and join him on the Senate floor.

After that, Busby would be summoned frequently, either by telephone or by a page who would come to 231 in person and escort him to a side door of the Senate Chamber. Seeing his curly-haired young aide, Johnson would motion him over to his desk, and the page would bring a folding chair and place it next to Johnson's.

Sometimes the reason for the summons was apparent: a speech was being given that Johnson wanted Busby to hear. Busby understood that Johnson wanted his speeches to sound senatorial, so he wanted his speechwriter to hear what senators sounded like. "He paid particular attention to Senator George," Busby says, but he also wanted Busby to hear senators who were not regarded as particularly outstanding orators, but who sounded senatorial. "He always wanted me to hear [Leverett] Saltonstall. And he was kind of taken with Henry Cabot Lodge."

Often, however, Busby would be called to the floor when no major speech was being given, and the Senate was merely transacting routine, monotonous, business. He would sit down next to Johnson as a desultory discussion or slightly more interesting debate ensued, or as a quorum call droned on. Sometimes Johnson would whisper to him behind a cupped hand. "Somebody would be making a motion, and he'd be very attentive to that. He hadn't had to do that in the House—he wasn't part of the action over there, and the Speaker or whoever was in the Chair had all the authority over there. There would be some maneuver, and he'd talk to me behind his hand: 'You think he's going to succeed at that?' " But often Johnson wouldn't say anything at all—for quite a long time.

"Usually, there weren't many senators around," Busby recalls. Two or three senators interested in a particular bill would come onto the floor, and, the bill disposed of, would leave, to be replaced by two or three others. Individual senators would wander in and out. Stars and spear carriers changed: the majority and minority leaders wandered in and out; the Senate reporters who recorded every word spoken on the floor changed regularly, every thirty minutes; clerks would come and go on the lower level of the dais. But Lyndon Johnson would remain, sitting at his desk, intent and still, a long, motionless figure slouched down deep in his chair, his head resting on a big hand, among the long, empty arcs of desks. "He was just sitting there watching the Senate," Busby recalls.

Busby soon came to understand that he had really been summoned because Johnson was going to be there for many hours, and wanted company. "It was like part of him was a spectator, and he liked to have someone sitting there with him," Busby says. But for a long while he couldn't understand why Johnson was there for so many hours. "It was obvious that the reason was very important to him, but I didn't know what it was," he says. "I didn't know what he was doing there," sitting hour after hour on the almost-deserted Chamber floor as the afternoon oozed away in quorum calls and the dull staccato chant of the Calendar Call. And then Busby did understand. "He was learning, studying."

In part, he was studying senatorial procedure, those arcane Senate rules, although, Busby noticed, after Johnson observed that on thorny parliamentary points the party leaders or the senator in the chair usually consulted the Senate Parliamentarian, Charles L. Watkins, instead of relying on their own knowledge, he became less interested in procedure; he, too, would be able to refer questions to Watkins. In part, he was studying senatorial demeanor—the manners of senators of the United States.

Woodward says, "He [Johnson] had a general feeling that when you moved to the Senate you had to be more statesmanlike, more senatorial." Saltonstall and Lodge and Alabama's Lister Hill were being studied not merely because they spoke in a senatorial manner, but because they acted "senatorial": formal, dignified, courtly in the best sense of those words. Saltonstall and Lodge, Busby says, "were gentlemen, real New England gentlemen, the kind of person you didn't find in Texas." Hill was a gentleman, too, if of the southern mode. What Johnson was trying to learn from them was not merely speech-making but a mode of senatorial discourse, the manner in which they introduced motions and bills, and spoke in debate.

And in part, Johnson was studying men, not their demeanor but what lay underneath.

The Senate Chamber, was, after all, a good place to observe his new colleagues. Most of the time, senators were in their offices or in the hearing rooms of their committees; you might get to know the senators who served on the same committees as you yet see other senators seldom—unless you saw them on the floor. In the Chamber, Johnson could study all the senators—could *read* them.

From his desk at the far end of the lowest arc, Lyndon Johnson watched the figures moving among the desks, coming up and down the center aisle, chatting together in the well. He watched which senators went over to other senators to chat with them—and which senators sat at their desks and let other senators come to *them*. He watched two senators talk, and watched if they talked as equals. He watched groups of senators talk, and watched which one the others listened to. And he watched with eyes that missed nothing. Woody understood. Other observers thought the "Big Bulls" were simply the committee chairmen, that being a chairman automatically made you a "Big Bull." Lyndon Johnson knew better; the reader of men was doing a lot of reading sitting there in the Chamber. Lyndon Johnson was studying which senators had the respect of their fellows—and why they had that respect.

Studying men—and making friends with them. "Just because he was there," Busby explains, some of the other senators would "come by and say something to him." The senators who wandered over to say a word would not be Taft or Kenneth Wherry: Johnson was too junior for the Republican Leaders to cross the aisle to talk to him. "But occasionally" his own Leader, Scott Lucas, "might come over and say something."

These studies took a lot of time. The session would go on for hours, and hour after hour Lyndon Johnson would sit slouched down in his chair, head on hand, all but unmoving. All his previous life had been marked by burning impatience—by a restlessness terrible in its urgency, by an unwillingness to wait, by a feeling that he *couldn't* wait. But in the Senate, he had seen at once, waiting—patience—was necessary. So there would be patience.

FINALLY SCOTT LUCAS would move that the Senate adjourn for the day. Standing and stretching, Lyndon Johnson would say, "C'mon, Buzz," leave the Chamber, and walk down to the subway to the Senate Office Building. Entering 231, he would often throw a violent tantrum, bellowing at his staff. After he went into his private office, slamming the heavy door behind him, one of the four buttons on Jenkins' telephone would light up with the pale yellow light that meant it was in use; Walter and John and Buzz and Woody would know the Chief was on the telephone. But often the person he had called was another senator, and if that was the case, the Chief wouldn't be doing much talking. Recalls John Connally: "Time and again, I'd go in there, and I would see him leaning back in his chair, just listening"—saying hardly a word.

The big leather chair was in front of the wide, high, arched window, which faced west so that the late-afternoon sun came through the Venetian blinds in bright bars. As Lyndon Johnson leaned back in the chair, or slouched down into it on the base of his spine, his big, brightly polished black shoes resting on the desk, one hand holding a telephone to his ear, the other hand would almost invariably be holding a cigarette, and another cigarette or two would be dying in an ashtray on the desk, and the smoke from the cigarettes would curl lazily up through those bars of light. And often those curls of smoke would be the only things moving in that end of the room, so intently was Lyndon Johnson concentrating on what he was hearing. The big head that loomed dark, almost black, in front of those bright bars was very still. Woodward, in whose mind the face of Lyndon Johnson was never still, could hardly believe what he was seeing. He knew—after years of traveling with Johnson, no one knew better—how hard it was for Lyndon Johnson to listen. But after listening on the Senate floor all afternoon, now, in the evening, Lyndon Johnson was listening still.

How complete was the transformation in Lyndon Johnson? How successfully did he change his outward character? When, in 1950, the first major article appeared about him in a national magazine, it described him as "mild-mannered." The first cover story about him, in *Newsweek* in 1951, said, "His manner is quiet and gentle, and everything he does, he does with great deliberation and care." And perhaps the definitive word came from that epitome of senatorial civility, Majority Leader Lucas. Asked about Lyndon Johnson, Lucas said, "I found him at all times what I would term a gentleman of the old school."

AND LYNDON JOHNSON had other gifts which made the Senate, at first glance so unsuited to him, very well suited indeed.

For one thing, it was a place ruled by old men; the most powerful senators, the Big Bulls who could help him along his path, were almost all old. And Lyndon Johnson had always had a gift with old men who could help him. As with all his talents, he had analyzed it himself. "I always liked to spend time with older people," he would tell Doris Kearns Goodwin, and, besides, spending this time had a purpose, even when he had been a boy. "When I was a boy, I would talk for hours with the mothers of my friends, telling them what I had done during the day, asking what they had done, requesting advice. Soon they began to feel as if I, too, was their son and that meant that whenever we all wanted to do something, it was okay by the parents as long as I was there."

It was a remarkable gift. At college, his deference, humility, obsequiousness with older men and women who possessed the academic world's version of power—college administrators and professors—had been carried to such extremes that his awed classmates say that if they described it fully, "no one would believe it." It included the posture he adopted with his professors. "Literally sitting at [their] feet," a classmate would recall; if a professor or dean was holding an informal bull session on a lawn on College Hill, sitting on a bench, other students might be sitting next to him or listening while standing up; Lyndon Johnson would almost invariably be sitting on the ground, his face turned up to the professor, his expression one of deep interest and respect. He would, another classmate says, "never disagree with anything a faculty member" said, and he would go further: "he would make a statement that he knew the faculty member would agree with"—make it with the deepest enthusiasm, although, not long before, the same classmate had heard him, with a professor of opposite views, espousing *those* views with the deepest enthusiasm. It included flattery not only oral but written, written privately in notes to his teachers strategically placed at the end of his examination papers (such as one to an English professor who was a devout Baptist thanking her for "strengthening" his religious faith), and publicly: during his editorship of the *College Star,* the traditional sly digs at college administrators of earlier years were replaced with editorials full of extravagant praise—flattery from a young man gifted not only in reading men but in using what he read. Instead of ignoring a trait embarrassing to his subject, Johnson's editorial would focus on that trait, praising it, as if, only twenty years old though he was, he possessed an instinctive, untaught understanding that his subject must be aware of his weak point, so that a word of reassurance about it would be the word that would mean the most: describing a speech by a professor whose pedantic dullness made students snicker, Johnson wrote that "he made his talk bristle with interesting facts"; writing about a stern Dean of Women so rigid about campus morals that she had once expelled a boy for giving a coed a lift in an automobile, Johnson said that "the boys think [Dean Brogden] is one of the best sports on the Hill." And much of the flattery had a particular—and very cunningly calculated—objective: to make the subject feel for Lyndon Johnson that particularly strong form of fondness, maternal or paternal affection. After telling a female administrator how much he loved and respected his mother, he would tell her that *she* reminded him of his mother. He would ask her advice about some problem, and when she gave it, would say, as one administrator recalls, that "what I had said was like what his mother had said. . . . I was sort of flattered." He would tell a male professor how much he loved and respected his father. He would tell the professor that he so much appreciated his help. "If you were my own father, you couldn't have done more for me," he said to one.

In Washington, as secretary to Congressman Richard Kleberg of Corpus Christi, the techniques were the same—right down to the posture and the particular form of flattery. Kleberg's office was the site of a late-afternoon drinking group of powerful reactionaries, including the Red-baiting Congressman Martin Dies and the legendarily powerful lobbyist and financier of Red-baiting causes, Roy Miller of Corpus Christi, any one of them so anti-Roosevelt that he might have posed for Peter Arno's *New Yorker* cartoon of wealthy businessmen ranting and raving against That Man in the White House. Through an open door in Kleberg's office suite, the Congressman's two other young assistants could see Johnson, even when there was a vacant chair, sitting on the floor, face worshipfully tilted up toward whoever was speaking, in L. E. Jones' words, "very much the young man, very starry-eyed, very boyish, very much the junior to the senior. 'Yes, sir.' 'No, sir.' " And when only one of the older men was with him, he again played the paternal card, telling one powerful lobbyist, "You've been like a Daddy to me."

These techniques aroused contempt from Johnson's contemporaries on both College and Capitol Hills. In talking with the author, both a classmate and a fellow congressional aide used the same term—"a professional son"—to describe him. The college yearbook chronicled his "sucking up" in print ("Believe It Or Not—Bull Johnson has never taken a course in suction"), and his classmate Mylton Kennedy says, "Words won't come to describe how Lyndon acted toward the faculty—how kowtowing he was, how suck-assing he was, how brown-nosing he was." Hearing Johnson "talking conservative" with the ultra-reactionary Dies, and, a few minutes later, "talking liberal" with liberal Congressman Wright Patman—and espousing diametrically opposite points of view with equal passion—many of his fellow congressional assistants felt that, as one says, "There's nothing wrong with being pragmatic. Hell, a lot of us were pragmatic. But you have to believe in *something*. Lyndon Johnson believed in *nothing,* nothing but his own ambition." They sneered as they watched Johnson ignore the young, single women at the monthly Texas State Society dances in order to dance almost exclusively with the elderly wives of congressmen and Cabinet officers so that "the wives would introduce him to their husbands." And on both hills the contempt was tinged with anger because Johnson was as overbearing to those beneath him, or on the same level as he, as he was obsequious to those above him; so much, in rapid alternation, the bully and the bootlicker that Charles Marsh's daughter, who had a ringside seat as Lyndon fawned humbly over her father while, behind his back, sleeping with her mother (and who was a devotee of Charles Dickens), was reminded "every time I saw Lyndon" of "a Uriah Heep from Texas."

But on both Hills, the reaction of Johnson's targets was proof of the adage that where flattery is concerned, no excess is possible. "Boy," one classmate says of the San Marcos faculty, "you could see they loved it." And it was the faculty's patronage that gave Johnson the rewards he wanted at college. In Washington, his techniques were observed by men capable of analyzing—and of appreciating—the talent, and these men say that "deference" and "flattery" are inadequate to describe it. Watching Lyndon Johnson "play" older men, Tommy Corcoran, a prince of flatterers himself, knew he was watching a king. "He [Johnson] was smiling and deferential, but, hell, lots of guys can be smiling and deferential. Lyndon had one of the most incredible capacities for dealing with older men. He could follow someone's mind around, and get where it was going before the other fellow knew where it was going. Lyndon was there ahead of him, and saying what he wanted to hear before he knew what he wanted to hear." The very keen-eyed Ed Clark says, "I never saw anything like it. He would listen *at them* . . . and in five minutes he could get a man to think, 'I like you, young fellow. I'm going to help you.' "

The man on whom his talents had been employed most intensively was Sam Rayburn.

Although adults backed away from the hard-faced, frowning Speaker, who was as powerful—awesome—in personality and in physical strength, with his short, massive body, as he was in position, children took to "Mr. Sam" instinctively, crawling all over him and rubbing their hands over his great bald head. Talking to a little boy or girl, he could sit for hours with that grim face transformed by a broad, gentle smile. But Rayburn had no children. Terribly shy and insecure with women—as, indeed, he was shy in any social situation— he had married once, but the marriage had lasted only three weeks; no one ever knew why. He dreaded loneliness. "Loneliness breaks the heart," he said once. "Loneliness consumes people." But, a man with so much power and so fierce a temper that some congressmen were "literally afraid to start talking to him," he had to live—all his life—with what he dreaded. While the House was in session, of course, men crowded around him, clamoring for his attention, hanging on his every word, but in the evenings and on weekends, when the House wasn't in session and other congressmen went home to their families, the Speaker went home to a small apartment near Dupont Circle. Convinced that he couldn't make small talk, that he made a fool of himself whenever he tried, he seldom went to parties. Too proud to let anyone know he was lonely, he rejected dinner invitations from his assistants. On Sundays, he would walk for hours around the empty streets of downtown Washington, his face set in a stern mask as if he wanted to be alone, as if he didn't want anyone to talk to him. Sometimes, unable to bear the loneliness, he would telephone an assistant and ask him to come to his office on a weekend, as if he had some urgent task for him. But these young men, watching him opening all the drawers of his desk and taking out every paper, "looking for something to do," knew the truth—and pitied him. Once, he wrote to a friend, "God, what I would give for a tow-headed boy to take fishing."

From his arrival in Washington in 1931, congressional secretary Johnson sought to cultivate the Speaker, using as entrée the fact that his father had served in the Texas Legislature with Rayburn, but the attempt did not take root until he married Lady Bird in 1934. Rayburn's heart went out to this young woman who he saw was as shy as he. Growing paternally fond and immensely protective of her, he began coming to the Johnsons' small apartment for dinners, at which Lady Bird cooked "Mr. Sam's" favorite Texas foods, and he accepted invitations regularly for breakfasts on Sundays, the Sundays on which he had nothing to do. The "professional son" had ample opportunity to employ his talents. Sometimes, to the amazement of all who witnessed it, Lyndon would lean over and kiss the feared Speaker on his bald head.

Once, with Lady Bird back in Texas, Lyndon, alone in Washington, developed pneumonia. Rayburn sat beside him all night in the hospital, so afraid of waking the young man that he wouldn't stand up even to brush away the ashes from the cigarettes he chain-smoked during the night. In the morning, his vest was covered with ashes. Not long thereafter Rayburn placed Lyndon Johnson on the first rung of the ladder he wanted to climb. Known never to ask anyone— not even a friend—for a favor, for Johnson he begged a favor of a man with whom he had never been friendly, asking Senator Tom Connally to obtain the Texas state directorship of the newly formed National Youth Administration for a twenty-six-year-old congressional secretary without a shred of administrative experience, refusing to leave Connally's office until the senator agreed. When, two years later, Johnson returned to Washington as a congressman, Rayburn made him a "regular" at the famed "Board of Education" sessions he conducted every afternoon in a House hideaway. There would be a break in their relationship early in 1939, when, for the first time, Rayburn was in the way of Johnson's ambition. Because Rayburn was the logical choice to succeed John Garner as Roosevelt's key man in Texas—chief dispenser of New Deal patronage in the state—and Johnson wanted the job himself, he betrayed Rayburn, poisoning Roosevelt's mind against him. For almost three years thereafter, Rayburn rebuffed Johnson's attempts to resume relations. But when, after Pearl Harbor, Johnson enlisted and left Washington—for a war zone, Rayburn assumed—Rayburn's heart melted toward Lyndon as the coldness of a father toward an estranged son melts in a moment when the boy is in danger.

During the rest of Rayburn's life, Johnson would sometimes blurt out remarks like the one he once made in Texas: "Goddammit, I have to kiss his ass all the time. . . ." But in Rayburn's presence, Johnson would play on the Speaker's paternal feelings, repeatedly telling others, in Rayburn's presence, that he was "just like a Daddy to me." At one banquet, Senator Ralph Yarborough was to recall, "Lyndon was telling how 'he's been like a father to me.' I saw tears come out of Rayburn's eyes and roll down his cheeks."

A note Johnson received from another elderly, lonely House power during his first weeks as a senator demonstrated the effectiveness of his techniques. Carl Vinson may have seen Johnson's flaws clearly, as his advice to Bryce Harlow shows, but that didn't stop him from missing him. Most junior members of Vinson's Armed Services Committee tried to stay out of the way of the cigar-chewing, tobacco-juice-spitting little dictator known as "the Admiral." Johnson had put himself in Vinson's way—and had stayed there, despite many early rude rebuffs, dropping around, week after week, year after year, to the apartment in which Vinson lived with his invalid wife to tell him the ribald stories and the latest congressional gossip he loved. And now, in 1949, the note Johnson received was in the pleading tone of an elderly man who misses, very much, a young one. "Don't forget your old friend during this session of Congress," Carl Vinson wrote. "Keep in touch with me."

Now LYNDON JOHNSON was in the Senate. He had learned who the Senate's "Big Bulls" were—and almost without exception, these bulls were Old Bulls. So, Doris Kearns Goodwin wrote, "he could see at once what was required." After her conversations with Johnson, Ms. Goodwin was to write that he recognized "that the older men in the Senate were often troubled by a half-conscious sense that their performance was deteriorating with age." Johnson told her—these are his words: "Now they feared humiliation, they craved attention. And when they found it, it was like a spring in the desert; their gratitude couldn't adequately express itself with anything less than total support and dependence on me."

The attention was tailored to the man—by a master tailor. James E. Murray of Montana, ranking Democratic member of the Senate Labor Committee in 1949, and, after 1951, chairman, was a liberal hero, and deservedly so. "He is a classic prototype of the New Deal," a writer was to say, "as nearly pro-labor on all questions as it is possible to be. . . . To hear Senator Murray's response when his name is reached on a roll-call is to know at once what the New Deal–Fair Deal position on an issue is." But in 1949, Senator Murray was seventy-three years old. Once a broad-chested man, bursting with vitality, his stride was now slower, even at times a bit uncertain. And while he was not senile, his mind was not what it had been, and it preferred to dwell in the past, in the days of labor's triumphs, in the days when it had found, in Franklin Roosevelt, its great champion. Sometimes—increasingly, to one who observed closely—when Murray was dealing with current issues, with current Senate maneuvers and stratagems, the Senator seemed a little tense, a little uncertain. Lyndon Johnson, who had been close to Roosevelt, close to Corcoran and Benjamin V. Cohen and the other young New Dealers with whom Murray had worked in the great days of the New Deal, would, in talking to Murray, turn the conversation to those days—and keep it there. It was noticeable how Murray, once he realized that it was to be kept there, relaxed and became his old charming self. It was noticeable how Murray's face lit up when, entering the Senate cloakroom, he saw Lyndon Johnson there.

The question of deteriorating performance was handled, too. Reports were a constant of Senate life, and many senators did not have assistants capable of writing reports of which they would not be ashamed. Johnson did, and in the most delicate of terms, he would sometimes offer an older senator the services of such an aide.

Old men crave not only attention but affection, and Johnson did not forget that, instructing aides drafting letters to them for his signature to make the letters "real sweet." Old men want to feel that the experience which has come with their years is valuable, that their advice is valuable, that they possess a sagacity that could be obtained only through experience—a sagacity that could be of use to young men if only young men would ask. Lyndon Johnson asked. "I want your counsel on something," he would say to one of the Old Bulls. "I *need* your counsel." And when the counsel was given—and of course it was given: who could resist so earnest an entreaty?—it was appreciated, with a gratitude rare in its intensity. He would pay another visit to the senator's office to tell him how he had followed his advice, and how well it had worked. "Thank you for your counsel," he would say to one senator. "I *needed* that counsel." "Thank you for giving me just a little of your wisdom," he would say to another senator. "I just don't know what I would have done without it." When one of the Old Bulls, asked for his advice, told Johnson that he didn't know enough about the matter, Johnson would say, "Oh, I'll rely on your judgment any time. Your judgment's always *been* good." And the earnestness—the outward sincerity—of his words, the obvious depth of his gratitude, made the words words that an old man might treasure.

In Senate as college, he proved the adage that no excess was possible. He gave gruff Edwin C. (Big Ed) Johnson of Colorado a nickname: "Mr. Wisdom," and used it not only orally but in writing; once, when Big Ed was back in Colorado, Lyndon wrote him: "I certainly do miss the able counsel of Mr. Wisdom." He used it not only in private but in public. "Boy, whenever you're in trouble, the thing to do is go to Mr. Wisdom," he would say, in Ed Johnson's presence, to whoever else happened to be present. And beyond the specific flatteries and sweetnesses was Lyndon Johnson's overall demeanor with the Old Bulls: a deference, an obsequiousness, a "fawning" and "bootlicking" so profound that more than one Senate staffer likened him to the same Dickens character. "During Lyndon Johnson's early days in the Senate, he was a real Uriah Heap," says Paul Douglas' administrative assistant, Howard Shuman.

"The very frequency of his statements that an older politician was 'like a Daddy to me' tends to cast doubt on the profundity of some of these relationships," an academic was to write after interviewing many senators; the doubts would have been confirmed had he been walking beside Lyndon Johnson and John Connally just after they left the office of an elderly senator to whom Johnson had just been, for quite a few minutes, elaborately and fawningly grateful for a piece of advice. "Christ, I've been kissing asses all my life," Lyndon Johnson said, with what Connally recalls as a "snarl." But the technique was as effective as it had always been. "Johnson thought, in those days at least, that that kind of technique was effective with anybody," says Booth Mooney, one of his Senate aides, and the belief was borne out by the results, the results even with Rules Committee Chairman Hayden. In December, Hayden had refused to give Johnson that extra room in the basement that he had asked for; in February

Hayden found that an extra room was, indeed, available. Soon it had become apparent that most of the Senate's Old Bulls were looking fondly on Lyndon Johnson. And their feelings contributed to a change in Johnson's behavior that was noticeable to the assistants who had worked for him in his pre-Senate days. Busby, struck by Johnson's calm during their learning sessions on the Chamber floor, now began to notice the calmness spreading to activities outside the office. "When he got to the Senate," Busby says, "all of a sudden, he didn't act so driven any more." John Connally says that "After a month or two, he seemed to be—outside the office, I mean—so much more at ease than he had ever been before." And Walter Jenkins uses a somewhat different, and very telling, image. "Mr. Johnson took to the Senate as if he had been born there," he says. "It was obvious it was *his* place."

His place. All at once, in the Senate—in this place that was so different from any other place he had ever been—Lyndon Johnson seems to have felt, within a very few weeks of his arrival in it, at home.

AND THERE WAS ANOTHER ASPECT of the Senate that was especially well suited to Lyndon Johnson, and was particularly helpful to his advancement within it. While the Senate may have been ruled by its southerners, the southerners were ruled by one man—and he was lonely.

Johnson had learned this, too, that December—had learned it at least partly in a conversation in his old House office near the end of the month.

The conversation was with a young man named Bobby Baker. Baker was only a twenty-year-old Senate page, but he already possessed a reputation that distinguished him from the other pages—a reputation to which Johnson referred when, on that December trip, he telephoned him and said, "Mr. Baker, I understand you know where the bodies are buried in the Senate. I'd appreciate it if you'd come by my office and talk to me."

Baker knew little about Johnson, he was to recall. "He was just another incoming freshman to me." But by the end of the talk, he knew a lot more. Johnson, he was to recall, "came directly to the point. 'I want to know who's the power over there, how you get things done, the best committees, the works.' For two hours, he peppered me with keen questions. I was impressed. No senator ever had approached me with such a display of determination to learn, to achieve, to attain, to belong, to get ahead. He was coming into the Senate with his neck bowed, running full tilt, impatient to reach some distant goal I then could not even imagine." A waiter from the Senate Dining Room who brought sandwiches and coffee to the two men saw a rapport forming; Baker "leaned across the table as if drawn to LBJ by some invisible magnet." And if Johnson wanted to know where true power lay in the Senate, Baker knew the answer. "Dick Russell was *the* power," he was to say. And, he was to say, Johnson immediately "recognized" something about Russell: "that Russell, who was no longer so young, was a bachelor and lonely."

That was perhaps the single most important piece of information that Lyndon Johnson acquired that December. At each stage of his life, his remarkable gift for cultivating and manipulating older men who could help him had been focused at its greatest intensity on one man: the one who could, in each setting, help him the most. This focus, too, was deliberate; while he was still in college, Lyndon Johnson told his roommate Alfred (Boody) Johnson: "The way to get ahead is to get close to the one man at the top."

In Texas, the older men most responsible for Lyndon Johnson's earliest success were the college's president, Cecil Evans, and the canny—and feared—Alvin Wirtz. Each of these men had a daughter. Neither had a son.

Crusty, aloof "Prexy" Evans seemed to other students to be surrounded by an "invisible wall." But Lyndon Johnson, refusing to be rebuffed, babbling boyishly away while gazing at him with adoration, flattering him in editorials ("Great as an educator and as an executive, Dr. Evans is greatest as a man"), telling him he looked on him as a father, had breached the wall, and Evans treated Johnson with more affection than he had ever shown a student—a notably paternal affection.

In Austin, Johnson would tell Wirtz's associates—men he knew would repeat the remark to Wirtz—"Senator Wirtz has been like a father to me." And when Johnson entered Wirtz's office, that studiously calm, reserved, and ruthless political string-puller would jump up and hug him, saying, "Here's m'boy, Lyndon. Hello Lyndon, m'boy." Johnson's success in making Wirtz as well as Evans feel that Lyndon looked upon him almost as a father, in making Wirtz, like Evans, feel that Lyndon was the son he had never had, is attested to by Wirtz's inscription on a photograph of himself: "To Lyndon Johnson, whom I admire and love with the same affection as if he were in fact my own son."

IN WASHINGTON, the pattern had been repeated with two men. One was Sam Rayburn, and the other's last name also began with the letter *R*.

Franklin Delano Roosevelt had sons, four of them, but he was so distant from them, and, indeed, to some extent, from his wife, that in a way he was lonely, too.

The instant rapport that had been kindled between Roosevelt and Johnson at their very first meeting—the rapport that had led the President to tell Tommy Corcoran, "I've just met the most remarkable young man," and to order Corcoran to "help him with anything you can" (and to arrange Johnson's appointment to the House Naval Affairs Committee because he, Roosevelt, had been active in naval affairs when *he* was a young man)—had lasted and deepened with time. The President would tell Secretary of the Interior Harold Ickes that Johnson was "the kind of uninhibited young pro he would have liked to have been as a young man"—and might have been "if I hadn't gone to Harvard." The President offered to appoint Johnson Administrator of the Rural Electrification Administration, put him in charge of the Democratic Congressional Campaign

Committee—intervened in Johnson's 1941 race for the Senate to an extent he had never done in any congressional race since his disastrous attempt to intervene in 1938 Senate races, and that he had vowed he would never do again. His feeling for Johnson, says Jim Rowe, the Roosevelt aide in the best position to observe the interplay between the two men, was a "special feeling."

About the basis of this feeling relatively little is known, because the meetings between Johnson and Roosevelt took place in the privacy of the White House living quarters. Describing the President as a lonely man whose wife was often traveling, Johnson was to say that "He'd call me up" and "I used to go down sometimes and have a meal with him"—breakfast alone with the President in Roosevelt's spartan bedroom, the President sitting up in bed, or in the President's private study, with the two men dining off a bridge table. And the President and the young congressman would talk together not only in the upstairs, private quarters of the White House but in the Oval Office as well. The frequency of these meetings is unknown, as is the nature of the conversations at them. When Roosevelt died, Johnson told a friendly reporter, "He was just like a Daddy to me; he always talked to me just that way." But it is not known whether he used the Daddy image—or other fatherly images—when he was talking to FDR, nor to what extent he was with the President the "professional son." There were certainly other reasons for the rapport between the older man and the younger, among them, as Rowe notes, Roosevelt's confidence in Johnson's complete loyalty to the New Deal (a confidence that would prove unfounded almost as soon as Roosevelt died, when Johnson began publicly disassociating himself from the New Deal), and in Johnson's ability: "Johnson was in many ways just more capable than most of the people Roosevelt saw. . . . You've got to remember that they were two great political geniuses." But, Rowe feels, as do other presidential aides, that there was also a "father-son" element to the relationship, and there are moments, such as Roosevelt's determination to cheer "Lyndon" up following his 1941 defeat, that are difficult to attribute to solely political considerations. And the aides agree that whatever the reason for the "special feeling," special the feeling certainly was. Men like Corcoran and Cohen conjecture that with Roosevelt, as with Rayburn, Lyndon Johnson read the older man, studied him, learned him—and used what he learned. And whatever the reasons, Roosevelt indisputably put his power behind Johnson's career to an extent he did for few, if any, other congressmen.

NOW JOHNSON HAD BEEN TOLD that *the* power in the Senate was Russell, Russell who, like Johnson's two great Washington patrons, had a lonely personal life—Russell who, like Rayburn, had no one. Schoolchildren in midcentury America learned their so-called "three *R*s"—readin', 'ritin' and 'rithmetic. Lyndon Johnson, who had already learned two *R*s so well, set out now to learn his third.

7

A Russell of the
Russells of Georgia

WHEN RICHARD BREVARD RUSSELL JR. was a boy growing up just after the start of the century barefoot and in overalls in a sleepy Georgia farm town, he would often play alone for hours in a big field near his home, carrying a long stick that had been carved to resemble a rifle. Sometimes he would run headlong across the field brandishing the rifle, fall as if wounded, then leap to his feet, pick up the rifle, wave to rally his troops back to the charge, and run forward again. Sometimes he would station himself inside a little circle of wooden planks set atop a low mound of dirt he had piled in the middle of the field, and aim the rifle out as if he was defending a fort.

To friends curious about the long hours Richard spent at the game, Richard's family explained that the boy loved to play at war, but although there was a war in newspaper headlines at the time—the Russo-Japanese War—that was not the war he was fighting, nor was it war in general but a single war in which he was interested. The charges he was re-enacting were the screaming rush of Longstreet's brigades at the Second Manassas and Pickett's last forlorn charge at Gettysburg. The fort he had built he had named Fort Lee. The cause for which he fought was the Lost Cause.

Richard Russell's boyhood imagination was bound up in that cause—and so was his entire life.

His roots were bound up in it—in the lost dream of the Old South that was crushed at Gettysburg and at Antietam and Vicksburg and Appomattox. His ancestors were part of the upper reaches of the slave-owning patrician aristocracy that dominated the South's plantation culture and embodied its social graces. The Russells, of English background, had owned plantations in Georgia and South Carolina since Colonial times; Richard's grandfather established a successful cotton mill near Marietta, Georgia, and married a Brevard, one of the North Carolina Brevards.

But, like so much of that aristocracy, Richard's family was ruined by the War Between the States: the mill lay in Sherman's path and was burned down to its brick chimney and floor, while the Russell slaves were freed by Sherman's troops; Richard's grandmother fled in a carriage driven by a slave named Monday Russell (for the day of the week on which he was born), who during Reconstruction became a member of the State Legislature; and the family was plunged into poverty. Like so much of that aristocracy, Richard's family never recovered. It was still an impoverished family when his father, who was descended, as *Eminent Georgians* noted, "from the oldest and choicest American stock," was born.

Richard Brevard Russell Sr. yearned to restore the family's name and fortune, and for a time it seemed he would do so. Tall and handsome, a brilliant student at the University of Georgia, from which he graduated at eighteen with a command of five languages, including Latin and Greek, he graduated from law school at nineteen, almost immediately won a reputation as a young lawyer of "remarkable ability," and was elected to the Georgia House of Representatives at twenty-one as its youngest member. There he quickly established himself as what one writer called "the champion of Georgia's institutions of higher learning," leading legislative efforts to establish the state's first technological college and first women's college.

Leaving the Legislature at twenty-seven, he was elected solicitor general, or prosecuting attorney, for a seven-county judicial circuit, and would later be elected judge of a succession of Georgia courts, including its Supreme Court—of which he was Chief Justice for sixteen years. He was highly respected as a judge both for "the brilliance of his mind" and for his diligence ("On more than one occasion," an admirer wrote, "the Chief Justice was known to have worked and labored all night long"); indeed, some of his judicial opinions were called "gems of legal literature."

But he was not satisfied to be a judge; "always looking," as one writer put it, "for larger fields to conquer," he wanted to be Governor or United States Senator—"the Senate post was the one he wanted most." Richard Russell Sr. could not be politic, however. As a prosecutor his "fearless" disregard of political considerations had angered local politicians. A booming, eloquent stump speaker, he would never deign to moderate his views, "speaking his mind bluntly no matter whom he angered." Some of his positions were regarded in Georgia as "radical" or even "socialist," including his insistence that all qualified students (white students, of course) be able to attend the University of Georgia regardless of ability to pay; "the poorest students" should "have an equal chance with the richest," he said. His bluntness and independence alienated the three or four powerful factions that dominated Georgia politics, so his dreams of higher office were unrealistic. But he pursued them anyway, with a fervor that, as a biographer says, "got in the way of practical considerations, and even of common sense." He ran for Governor twice, for Senator once, as well as for Congress twice, and lost each time—usually by humiliatingly large margins.

For these ambitions, it was not he alone who sacrificed. Shortly after he married Ina Dillard, a schoolteacher from Athens, Georgia, who loved the intellectual life of the University of Georgia community, he informed her that they were moving to the tiny farm hamlet of Winder in Barrow County, twenty miles out in the country, because residence there "would be politically advantageous . . . or so he believed." Ina, recounts Russell's biographer Gilbert C. Fite, was "distraught" over the move, but a few years later, the Russells moved even further into the country, into a larger, rambling white frame house about a mile and a half outside the town. The second move was made necessary by the number of Russell children; Ina was to spend much of the first twenty years of her marriage pregnant; she would eventually give birth to fifteen children, thirteen of whom grew to maturity. Attempting to curry political favor with some newly formed county, the Judge would temporarily name his latest child after it.

The lives of the thirteen Russell children—seven boys and six girls—were filled with their father's dreams and defeats. "I was brought up hearing about his political campaigns, or observing them," Richard Jr. was to recall. It was a boyhood decorated with the trappings of privilege; the Russell children were taught by a governess in their own "private school"; the Legislature incorporated the area around the new house as the town of Russell; the Seaboard Railroad established a tiny station there, not far from the house—on mornings on which the Judge had to travel to court in Atlanta, one of the children would station himself at a curve about half a mile away to wave his handkerchief to flag the train down. Catching a glimpse of the train, he would shout, "Round the curve! Round the curve!" The word would be relayed by another child to the house, where Judge Russell sat regally at his table, refusing to be rushed through his breakfast, and then, at the very last moment, the Judge, a lordly figure—still tall and erect, with a flowing mustache and a full head of black hair—would stride out to the station, still holding his coffee cup. Often he would not get there quite in time, and the train would be passing the station, but he would wave at the engineer, who would put on his brakes and then back the train up so that the Judge could board, taking a last sip as he stepped aboard and handed the cup down to one of his children.

But the trappings were threadbare. The Russells lived in near poverty. In an attempt to augment his meagre judicial salary, the Judge purchased land, and moved in six black sharecroppers, and operated a tiny "commissary" to sell them goods. The firmest of believers in the Old South, his attitude toward these black families is perhaps summed up in the remark made—admiringly—by one of his daughters that "he might have been a typical plantation owner if he had been born a generation or two earlier." But he seemed never to finish the year with a profit. Intermittently, mired in debts, he had to resign from the bench to pay them off; so highly prized were his skills as an attorney that he was always able to do so, but invariably, as soon as he did, he returned to the bench, and to his unsuccessful attempts to win some other, higher, office. The Russells had few servants, and with Judge Russell usually away in Atlanta, the burden of raising thirteen children fell on their mother. Unable to afford clothing for them, she made most of it herself, sewing late into the night by the light of an oil lamp; recalling his mother's endless drudgery, Richard Jr. was to say that he was ten years old before he saw his mother asleep; previously, he had "thought that mothers never had to sleep." "My mother," he was to say, "was the greatest woman I've ever known."

The relationship between father and mother was warm and loving. Ina believed that her husband's abilities justified his ambition, and that surely he would become Governor or Senator and have a chance to prove his greatness. And she shared as well his determination to restore the family to its rightful place in Georgia. Richard Russell adored his wife. After they had been married for almost forty years, he sent her a note saying, "With a sense of love and gratitude that is overpowering, I can only say God bless you, idol of my heart."

The family as a whole was unusually close. The big white frame house seemed always to be filled with the children's friends and numerous cousins. And the children idolized their gruff father for his independence and adherence to principle; they remembered with pride the night a gang of men, angered by one of his political positions and unaware that he was away in Atlanta, drove around in circles in front of the house shouting threats and singing "Hang Dick Russell from a sour apple tree" while young Dick and his brothers lay on the roof with shotguns ready to defend their house. The Judge was usually in Atlanta all week, but when the train squealed to a stop on Friday evenings, and he stepped off, there would be parties in the front parlor, with the Judge doing clog dances and singing what one daughter remembers as "those funny songs" while his wife played the piano and the children sang along. No child could go to bed without a big kiss good night, "although," as another daughter recalls, "they squirmed as his huge coffee-and-tobacco-stained mustache scratched them."

Within this large circle of love and warmth, there was one very special relationship: between the father and his eldest son. The birth—on November 2, 1897—of a male heir was a great event to a father with a strong sense of family. His first three children had been girls, and he had vowed that if necessary he would populate Georgia with girls until he sired a son; when his fourth child was a boy, he thought, "My own R. B. Russell, Jr.—I was crazy with happiness." He said then what he was to repeat many times: "That is me living all over again."

He early began taking the boy on trips: to Savannah, to see the Civil War forts and cannon emplacements, and to sites of particular meaning to the Russell family: to "where Grandpa's slaves are buried," as the boy put it; to the mill that had been destroyed—and with it the Russells' patrimony. Quiet and serious, the boy loved reading ("I read all morning," he wrote at the age of nine in the diary he kept in a school composition notebook), particularly history ("I like to read histories of all countries") and more particularly still Civil War history; he seemed never to tire of listening to the stories told by the Confederate veterans who stationed themselves every day in front of the Winder general store. His father would sit with him on the broad front porch of the Russell home discussing history and the Lost Cause for hours on end. And, early also, he made the boy aware of his special role—as heir to his name—in his shining dream of restoring the Russells to their rightful place.

From the time he was sent away to boarding school at the age of thirteen, Richard Brevard Russell Jr. was reminded of his responsibility in a steady stream of letters. "You are my oldest son and you carry my full name," the Judge wrote once. "You can have—and *you must have*—a future of usefulness and distinction in Georgia or it will break my heart. . . . My son—my namesake—*never* let this thought leave your mind and may it influence your every act." On Richard Jr.'s fifteenth birthday, his father wrote: "Son I swear you to carry on my work and fulfill what I leave undone." You "can make the name of R. B. Russell live long after I die and thus you will help to keep me alive." The theme was echoed by the youth's mother, who wrote him, "I'm always expecting my R. B. Russell, Jr., never to fail in anything." ("She wrote letters that would make you feel ashamed," Richard would recall when he was an old man. " 'You're Richard Russell, and you can do anything. If you don't do it, it's just your own fault.' She had so much confidence in me, and predicted such great things for me that in a way it was a challenge to me"), and the theme was echoed by his brothers and sisters, who urged their sibling not to do anything at school that might sully the family name. One sister wrote that she hoped he was behaving himself "becomingly"; she herself, she said, could never do anything "unbecoming" if she just paused "long enough to think whose child I am."

As defeat followed defeat for the father—after one, Ina wrote to Richard Jr., "Oh, how it hurt"—he shifted more and more of the burden of the family's dreams to his namesake. "You bear my name," he wrote his son after one gubernatorial defeat, "and I want you to carry it higher than I have ever done or can do in my few remaining days."

The quiet youth admired—revered—the imposing, elegant figure whom he had, on visits to Atlanta, watched dispensing justice from the bench. When Richard Jr. was old, having sat in the United States Senate for thirty-eight years listening to great Senate orators, he would say that "the finest speech I ever heard" was an extemporaneous talk his father had once given to the Georgia Bar Association. And he accepted, without reservation, his responsibility in the father's dream. Among the diary entries of his ninth year, the year in which his father lost his first race for Governor, is: "I expect to be Governor some day." When he was fourteen, and his father wrote him in despair after his second gubernatorial defeat, the youth wrote him back to tell him to be of good cheer: "It is too bad we got beat but we will try again." "He seemed," says Gilbert Fite, "to take it for granted that he would achieve the greatness that his father hoped for him." After graduating from the University of Georgia, and its law school, he rejected invitations to join the big Atlanta law firms and entered law practice with his father—"Russell & Russell" was painted on a second-floor window in the People's Bank Building in Winder—moving back into the big white Russell house ("almost as if he had never been gone"). At the first opportunity, in 1921, when he was twenty-three, "young Dick," as he now was called, ran for state representative, and won. And as soon as he reached the Legislature, he revealed that he possessed not only the willingness to pick up his father's banner, but the ability as well.

HIS RISE TO LEADERSHIP in the Legislature was remarkably rapid—in part, perhaps, because, much as he loved and admired his father, he had absorbed lessons from his father's failed career.

Richard Russell Jr. was just over six feet tall, slender, but with broad shoulders, and, like his father, he held himself very straight. His face was the face of a young aristocrat: long, and appearing even longer because his hairline was already receding, with a large, hawked nose of the type known as "Roman," and a mouth that always smiled pleasantly, if seldom broadly or enthusiastically. And the aristocratic aura was intensified by his habit of tilting his head slightly back, as if he was looking down that large nose. When he spoke in the Legislature, he stood even more stiffly erect than usual, with the extended fingers of one hand resting firmly on the top of the desk before him. And he spoke in a resonant, ringing voice.

He could be as memorable an orator as his father, particularly when he was speaking on that topic that had captured his imagination; describing one of his speeches, a newspaper said, "His tribute to noble women of the Lost Cause was great, while he did not forget the private soldier who on the bloody fields of the South so nobly illustrated the courage and chivalry of these great people." While he possessed his father's eloquence, however, he was much more sparing in its use. His speeches were rare. And also in contrast to the mustachioed old campaigner, whose blunt and controversial stands had aroused so much antagonism, Russell, as Fite puts it, "was careful not to jump out in front" on issues, since "the point man always . . . made enemies." It was not on the floor of the Legislature but in the Atlanta hotel rooms in which the legislators sat around and chatted in the evenings that he began to make a mark.

In those hotel rooms, his voice was a soft, friendly, musical southern drawl. Yet the friendliness did not often—if ever—lead to familiarity. Already, at twenty-three, there was a dignity and reserve about Dick Russell that set him off from other men. When arguments arose, he would listen to both sides with grave, thoughtful attention. He never volunteered an opinion; if asked for one, he would give it with a quiet objectivity striking to those who knew his fiery, impulsive father. Although he was one of the youngest of forty so-called Young Turks—many of them World War I veterans, most of them college-educated and embarrassed by Georgia's "redneck" image—who had arrived in the Legislature in 1921, they began coming to him to settle disputes. The judiciousness and fairness with which he analyzed both sides and calmly delivered an opinion won him his peers' respect, and he was soon their acknowledged leader.

In 1922, his sixty-one-year-old father ran for Chief Justice of the Georgia Supreme Court, a post for which he had been defeated years before. This time, however, he had an asset he had not possessed in his first attempt: the legislators all over the state who were his son's friends. Richard Jr. worked very hard in this campaign, and his father won. But in 1926, Fite says, "Dick had to undergo the embarrassment and sadness of his father making another unsuccessful, some said foolish, campaign." Without resigning as Chief Justice, Richard Russell Sr. ran for the job he had always most wanted: United States Senator. He was running against the beloved and redoubtable Walter George, and even his son's network of friends could not help him. And the Judge was making one campaign too many: newspapers ridiculed him as "an old stager and stump artist," "a tragedy" who "had been feeding at the public trough all his life."

Aware though Dick was of the futility of the effort, no son could have tried harder for a father, managing the campaign and speaking all over the state; his youngest brother would never forget "a great bit of courage" when, at a big rally near Kirkwood, hired thugs threatened to storm the platform on which Dick was speaking, and with clenched fists Dick dared them to come up and fight. But his father polled only 61,000 votes to George's 128,000.

The next year, Dick, at the age of twenty-nine, was nominated for Speaker of the Georgia House by a colleague who said, "Though young in years, his demeanor has shown him to be a leader." No one ran against him. A year after the father's hopes had been crushed in a final humiliation, his son had become a leading figure in the state.

WHEN HE WAS SPEAKER, other traits became apparent. One was an integrity and independence that became a byword in Atlanta. Powerful lobbying groups had become accustomed to dictating the membership of key House committees, and one "prominent citizen" now approached Russell and held out a list of names, saying, "These are the persons we would like to see appointed to committees." Russell did not extend his hand to take the list. He told the lobbyist that he would be better advised not to give it to him: any man whose name was on it, he said in that quiet voice, would never be appointed to a committee, even if Russell himself had previously been planning to appoint him. "Dick Russell is the closest thing I've seen to an honest politician," a Georgia legislator said. Not only would he "tell you if it's impossible to get what you want," he would "tell you if he doesn't think you should be asking for what you want."

He also had the ability, so lacking in his father, to persuade men to cooperate and unite behind his aims. Georgia's decades-long governmental disorganization had reached a level of chaos that seemed to defy solution, with no fewer than 102 departments, boards, bureaus and commissions, each capable of mobilizing a constituency to resist change, with duplicating functions and salaries, and no semblance of central budgetary controls or of control over expenditures, which annually exceeded revenues by so much that for three years the state had been unable to pay many of its bills. Not only was the public school system inadequate, many students could not even afford to buy textbooks, so high were prices kept by a legislatively sanctioned "schoolbook trust." And a "bond crew" whose hold over the Legislature was well-known in Georgia saw to it that the state repeatedly passed huge bond issues, which drained its revenues to make highway contractors and politicians rich while the state's highway system became more and more outdated. Russell proposed paying for new highways not by bonds but by a gasoline tax, which could provide money also for the schools. But he didn't make the proposals publicly. He "liked to work things out in private." He let others make suggestions, and supported them, and let them think the ideas came from them. When there were differences of opinion, he mediated between them, and a solid front was maintained. The supposedly unstoppable bond issue was stopped—and replaced with a gasoline tax, the revenues earmarked for education. Russell, a legislator said, was the type of "leader who leads without one's consciousness of his leadership." He always gave credit to others. And his colleagues, as this legislator said, had come to "love him and trust him." In 1930, at the age of thirty-two, Russell entered the race for Governor.

THREE OF THE STATE'S most prominent politicians, each with a well-financed statewide organization headquartered in Atlanta, were already running for the post. Russell had neither organization nor money; his campaign, run out of a small store in Winder, was financed mainly with a thousand dollars he borrowed on a life insurance policy. He was mocked by his opponents as "the schoolboy candidate" because of his age, or as "the Boy Scout candidate" because of his emphasis on honesty in government, and by the press, which called his campaign "small-town" because it did not have an Atlanta office. In fact, his candidacy was not taken seriously at first, with political observers and press concurring that he had entered the race only "to get his name before the people" in preparation for a later, more serious, campaign. But to reports that he was trailing so badly that he would drop out of the campaign, he replied that "nothing save death" would make him drop out. Though he didn't have a for-

mal campaign organization, he had his family. There may have been newspapers, and politicians, in Georgia who ridiculed his father, but there were also
people throughout the state who remembered the old Judge, and respected him,
and who wanted to help his son—so many of them that there was almost an
informal statewide network of support. The Winder campaign headquarters
was a family operation. Dick's younger brother Robert E. Lee Russell was the
campaign's public relations man; Dick's other brothers and sisters typed letters
and manned the phones. They worked very hard; they all knew, as Dick knew,
that he wasn't running only for himself. And he had friends: while in many of
the state's counties he knew few voters, in each county there was at least one
person who knew *him*—the county's legislator. Of the politicians who knew
Richard Russell best—the state's legislators—fully ninety percent were supporting him.

And he had himself. Forty years later, sitting on the porch in Winder and
reminiscing about that gubernatorial race, he would say, "No man has ever
worked as I did," traveling from one dusty Georgia town to another in a battered old Oldsmobile coupe, giving twelve, fifteen speeches a day, sleeping in
the car's back seat or in friends' houses because he couldn't afford hotels.

In other ways, too, he was an untraditional candidate. In Georgia, it was
said, "the rustics rule," and the typical candidate therefore tried to make
the farmers—"the woolhat boys," "the one-gallus boys," "the red-suspender
boys"—believe he was one of them. Richard Brevard Russell Jr. was not one of
them, and he would not pretend that he was. He was a Russell of the Russells of
Georgia, and he wore a white shirt, and a necktie, and a suit, and, except on the
hottest days, he would not remove his jacket when talking to a crowd of farmers. And while he joked with the farmers, in a wonderfully friendly way, in the
words of one observer he "never used poor English or engaged in emotional
tirades against far-off interests who were oppressing the farmer," and he would
not tone down his classical or biblical allusions; asked about one opponent,
Russell said he "made Ananias look like a man of great integrity."

And somehow the farmers didn't seem to mind that he hadn't undone his
tie or taken off his jacket. "Russell sincerely believed that farming was a superior way of life," as his biographer Fite puts it. "A true Jeffersonian, he emphasized that the nation's purity and stability, and its economic strength, depended
on its farmers." And, Fite writes, "farmers seemed to appreciate his direct, honest approach to their problems. . . . He did not promise to do things for them
that were impossible. . . . He refused to make unrealistic promises. Farmers
responded to his friendly but somewhat reserved manner, his realism, and his
integrity."

And so did the state as a whole, which was coming to understand the
affection and respect with which his colleagues regarded the clean-cut, earnest
young politician. As "Russell met more and more people, his personality began
to play a vital role in his growing strength," Fite says. "People just liked Dick

Russell." In the first primary, he received more votes than any of the three veteran politicians, and in the runoff against one of them (whose campaign, Russell said dryly, should be referred to with reverence "as one should do in speaking of the dead"), he won by the largest majority recorded by any gubernatorial candidate in the state's history.

When he was sworn in, in front of the State Capitol in Atlanta, on June 27, 1931, Richard Brevard Russell Jr. became, at thirty-three, the youngest Governor in the history of Georgia. His left hand rested on the family Bible, which was held by the Chief Justice of the Georgia Supreme Court, a tall, white-haired and white-mustached old man in an old-fashioned wing collar. As the Judge recited the oath—the oath he had wanted so desperately, for so long, to take himself—the new Governor stood opposite him, at rigid attention, staring into his father's eyes. His right hand, upraised to take the oath, was held so high it might almost have been a salute.

RUSSELL WAS AN UNCONVENTIONAL GOVERNOR. He conducted gubernatorial business only until about four o'clock in the afternoon, and then, closing the door to his private office, began what, in his biographer's words, "he considered his real work." Part of that work was answering mail. Routine correspondence was disposed of by his assistants, but if a letter, whether from a prominent figure or a farmer, dealt in any depth with a governmental issue, Russell insisted on answering it—in detail—himself. And part of the work was reading: novels (Borodino was almost as real to him as Gettysburg, so many times had he reread *War and Peace:* decades later, during a tour of Russia, he would be guided around that battlefield by an expert on the battle, who realized, as he was talking with this American, that he was talking to another expert), biographies, works of history: Roman historians and Greek historians, and English—Livy and Thucydides and Macaulay—works that described how kings and emperors and prime ministers had handled issues. And of course anything at all—anything and everything—that was written on the War Between the States. This work went on for hours. Russell dated women frequently, although, as had been the case during his legislative days (and, in fact, during his college and law school days), whenever one of the romances threatened to become serious, he broke it off. But on many evenings, he did not go out at all. "The lights glow at midnight through the windows of the Governor's office," a reporter wrote—glowed as they had once glowed in the office of the Governor's father.

The governorship of Richard Russell became one of the most significant periods in Georgia's history. Taking office with the state broke, and with tax revenues so eroded by the Depression that it was unable to meet its obligations to public schools and public institutions or to pay the pensions it owed its veterans, he almost immediately secured passage of the Russell Reorganization

Act, which reduced the number of agencies from 102 to 18, and imposed on the eighteen department heads budget controls so strict (while simultaneously creating the state's first central purchasing agency, and requiring that no purchase be made except on the basis of sealed bids) that within eighteen months the state had not only paid its obligations to schools, institutions, and veterans, but had also reduced its total debt by more than a third. He launched the construction of major highways and broke the power of the schoolbook trust. And, convinced that the impoverished state must cease relying so heavily on its cotton crop, the new Governor somehow found funds for agricultural research— establishing laboratories, for example, to develop a tomato-plant industry, and to find new uses for Georgia's extensive pine forests—that would improve the state's economy for generations to come.

These achievements were based on the same techniques he had employed as House Speaker. He neither publicized his ideas nor pressed them on legislative committees; he would, he promised one committee chairman, "get squarely behind the plan of reorganization that you finally decide on." This was a tough job, he wrote the chairman, "but you are equal to it and when it is completed you will have rendered a real service to the state." He would "flatter, cajole, encourage and support others to get out in front to achieve a desired goal," Fite explains. "Russell had a knack for making other people feel important," for giving credit to others; "he led without people realizing that the action was his rather than their own." Within eighteen months, many of his goals had been achieved. The opinion of the *Atlanta Constitution*—"A new day for Georgia"—was a reflection of the attitude throughout the state toward its youthful Governor.

Yet eighteen months was to be his total term as Governor. In 1932, the state's senior United States Senator, William J. Harris, suddenly died of a heart attack. Russell called a special election for September, and announced he would be running in it—for the post his father had "wanted most." His opponent was United States Representative Charles Crisp, Dean of Georgia's congressional delegation, acting Chairman of the House Ways and Means Committee, and member of one of Georgia's most powerful political families. "He'll be the worst defeated man you ever saw," Richard Russell told reporters.

In this campaign, Russell showed his courage (he was hurled through the windshield of his car in an automobile accident, and his upper lip was torn open from one end to the other and four of his teeth knocked out; putting the teeth in his pocket, and fastening his lip down with adhesive tape, he continued campaigning without canceling a single speech). And he showed as well his skill as a campaigner. To dramatize Crisp's close links with the "Power Trust," which was driving up electric bills, Russell gave him a nickname that destroyed his campaign: "Kilowatt Charlie." After a stunningly one-sided victory, the "boy wonder of Georgia politics," the man who had been the youngest Governor in the history of Georgia, became, at thirty-five, the youngest Senator of the

United States, after he was escorted down the Senate's center aisle for his swearing-in by the state's senior Senator, Walter George, who had, not so long before, humiliated his father.

RICHARD RUSSELL ROSE AS RAPIDLY in the nation's Senate as he had in his state's legislature, in part because he displayed the same quiet, polite but unbending independence in Washington as he had in Atlanta, and in part because a rare concatenation of coincidences turned that independence into an asset instead of a liability.

The moment at which Russell was sworn in to the Senate—January 12, 1933—was the moment of the greatest upheaval in its membership in modern Senate history. The Democrats had been out of power since the elections of 1918; now, thanks to the massive Depression-induced repudiation of the GOP, they were back in the majority, and sixteen of them were newly elected like Russell, the largest number of new members of one party ever to come to the Senate in a single year. So sweeping had been the ouster of incumbents that there was an unprecedented number of vacancies on major committees, so many that senior Democrats, moving at last into the chairmanships and other prominent posts they had coveted so long, were willing to forgo their right to some of these other seats. When, immediately upon Russell's arrival, Majority Leader Joseph Robinson asked him for a list of his committee preferences, Russell replied that he had only one: Appropriations. And when Robinson explained with a patronizing smile that the seniority system made a freshman's appointment to the Senate's most powerful committee extremely unlikely and asked for a second choice, Russell replied, he was to recall, that he didn't have one—that "if I can't be on Appropriations, I'd prefer not to be on any committee."

In a normal year, the result of such an ultimatum would probably have been disastrous, but Robinson was shortly to become aware that there would in fact be no fewer than five open Democratic slots on Appropriations. Nineteen thirty-three, moreover, was a year in which Louisiana's Huey Long was tormenting Robinson and disrupting the Senate with hours-long harangues and the introduction of legislation more liberal—or radical—than President Roosevelt was proposing, thus repeatedly forcing Democratic senators into uncomfortable positions. Russell's unexpected defeat of the respected Charlie Crisp, together with exaggerated descriptions of the young, reforming Governor's devastating campaign style, had given Capitol Hill a totally mistaken impression—as Russell would put it years later, still quietly laughing at the idea—that he was a second Huey Long, "a wild-spoken man like Huey." Intimidated by the prospect of a second rebellious southern demagogue raising havoc with inflammatory speeches, Robinson decided, as Russell was to put it, "to buy his peace with me"—by giving him one of the five Appropriations seats.* And hardly had Russell been put on Appropriations when, through an even rarer coincidence, he was made chairman of one of its most important subcommittees: the Subcommittee on Agricultural Appropriations. Seniority would have given that post to the subcommittee's senior Democratic member, Cotton Ed Smith of South Carolina, but the cantankerous Smith had for years been engaged in a bitter feud with Appropriations Chairman Carter Glass. And Glass had quickly become fond of Dick Russell. "Old Ed Smith thinks he's gonna get it, but he's not worth a damn and I'm not going to give it him," Glass told Russell. Instead, he told Russell, he was giving it to *him*. In a normal year, Glass wouldn't have been able to do this, and, had Smith insisted on the seniority rule, Glass wouldn't have been able to do it now, but Smith, perhaps because he had just received not only the chairmanship of the full Agriculture Committee, for which he had long yearned, but also three other key Standing Committee memberships—no one can any longer recall the reason—was willing to be placated with *ex officio* membership on the subcommittee.

This concatenation of one of the greatest upheavals in Senate history with one of the most bitter feuds in Senate history had placed Russell at one of the narrows of senatorial power, one of the strategic passages through which bills, great and small, had to pass before they could emerge into the broader waters of the full Appropriations Committee, and from there onto the Senate floor. In 1933, one-third of the nation's families still lived on farms, and agricultural appropriations were vital to almost every senator not only because of the big programs—the New Deal's AAA, soil conservation, crop rotation, parity, and the like—which affected farmers en masse, but because of the small programs, minor items tucked away in the vast Agriculture Department budget, that were not minor at all to a senator's constituents, and therefore to a senator's future: laboratories for research into local crop or animal diseases; soil conservation or wildlife experimental stations; an emergency grant for funds to inoculate sheep or cattle against a fatal disease that had suddenly struck a rangeland; the creation of a salary line for a federal agricultural agent for a county that needed one. Approval of a senator's pet project by the Department of Agriculture meant only that the project was approved, not that it was funded; funding— an appropriation—had to be approved by the Appropriations Committee, and the committee almost invariably approved only appropriations previously approved by its subcommittees. At a stroke, the youngest senator had become a powerful senator.

Russell fully understood that power had come to him so quickly only by a very unusual coincidence. "I got to be [subcommittee] chairman, in my first

---

*Another went to Russell's fellow freshman Theodore Francis Green. They thus became two of only five senators who had received seats on Appropriations immediately after coming to the Senate. The others, all of whom were also appointed during the 1930s, were Joseph O'Mahoney and Pat McCarran (both 1934) and Republican Styles Bridges (1937).

year, which was a great rarity, because of a feud," he was to say. Having been given the power, however, he made the most of it, displaying in Washington as in Atlanta an impressive intellect—along with an equally impressive willingness to use that intellect, to devote his life to his work—that quickly gave him an unusual grasp of the workings of the national government. Most of the invitations that flooded in on a new senator—particularly a charming young bachelor—were declined; he wrote his mother that he was keeping his acceptances "to a minimum as I have to work late nearly every day." His small hotel room was big enough for a desk, and at it, as at the Governor's desk in Georgia, Richard Russell would spend evenings alone, bent over a book.

There were then twenty-two formal Senate rules; Russell memorized them—word for word. Quickly realizing that the Senate was governed more by the precedents which over the years had modified the rules than by the rules themselves, he borrowed the book of precedents from a Senate Parliamentarian, and studied it—all 1,326 pages of it—"until he knew it backward and forward." After Charlie Watkins was appointed Parliamentarian, Russell would sit in Watkins' office for hours, discussing the precedents, learning their origins and the reasoning behind them—and the ways they could be used or circumvented. Soon, senators conferring in a committee room began to realize that if they were wondering what the parliamentary procedures might be on some legislation in which they were interested, they no longer had to send for Watkins: there was someone right in the room who knew the answer. And Richard Russell, they began to realize, didn't know only the procedures; he knew the legislation—*their* legislation. He had studied the bills they introduced: he knew what they were trying to accomplish with them—and, not infrequently, he knew a better way to accomplish it, a way to make a subtle modification in the language, to add an amendment, to delete a clause that might cause a conflict with some other bill passed years before.

And Russell was studying more than procedures. Newspapers from all over the United States were kept in the Marble Room, so that senators could read their home-state papers. Russell would sit in the Marble Room for hours, reading newspapers from other states. Senators came to realize that he understood not only their bills but the reasons they had introduced them; he possessed a remarkably detailed knowledge of political and economic conditions in their states. And sometimes Russell would comment on some bill that had been discussed before a committee of which he was not a member; senators would realize that he was familiar with the hearings, that he must have read the transcript. A legend began to arise that Richard Russell read the entire *Congressional Record* every day.

Equally impressive was his ability with people. After he had been in the Senate for a quarter of a century, *Time* magazine was to report that "Russell does not have a single personal enemy" in it. The head was tilted back, but the blue eyes looking down from it could be warm and friendly, as was his gentle, musical southern drawl. If he accepted you, he had a way of making you feel you belonged. Margaret Chase Smith, the lone woman senator, knew she belonged the first time Dick Russell gave her the nickname by which he would always refer to her thereafter: "Sis." He generally ate lunch at the big round community table in the senators' private dining room, and often other senators would delay their lunch until they saw Russell heading for the dining room, so that they could sit with him. The faces of senators already seated at the table would light up when they saw Dick coming to join them. That soft southern drawl could produce gleams of quiet humor, sometimes about his hairline, which by his mid-thirties had receded completely off his forehead and was inexorably making its way up his head; when a younger senator, concerned about *his* growing baldness, was having his photograph taken with Russell, and asked if they could change positions so that the camera would catch "my better side," Russell remarked, "You're lucky to still *have* a better side." He never volunteered an opinion as to what a senator should do about a problem that was troubling him, but if a senator solicited his opinion, not infrequently Russell had it already prepared—a startlingly well-informed opinion. "Well, if I were representing your state," he would say, "I guess I might think about . . ." And when Russell was unfamiliar with the problem, he would tell his colleague he would think about it—and when the senator saw Russell next, the senator could usually tell he *had* thought about it, seriously, deeply and empathetically. "In addition to being great" in many fields of legislation, recalls Sam Ervin of North Carolina, who served in the Senate with him for twenty years, "Dick Russell was great in his personal relationships. . . . He was a congenial companion, he was a man that had what I call an understanding heart, he understood the problems of other senators and other people. . . . "

If there was affection for Dick Russell, there was also respect—respect that would become exceptional, perhaps unique, within the Senate in its universality and depth.

This respect was a tribute not only to Russell's knowledge and expertise— of the Senate, of the individual states, of parliamentary procedure, of tradition and precedent—but also to the integrity with which the knowledge was employed. When a senator, wavering on a bill in which Russell was interested, asked Russell about it, he knew he would be told *all* about it. Quietly, dispassionately, Russell would make sure the senator understood not only the reasons why he should take the same position on the bill that Russell was taking, but the reasons why he should take an opposing position. Both sides of the issue would be given equal weight. Asked years later "[To] what would you attribute his ability to sway votes and opinions in the Senate?" Ervin would say: "I would attribute it to the fact that he told the truth. . . . People had so much respect in his intellectual integrity they knew that he was telling the truth when he described what the contents of a bill were or what the effects of that bill would be."

Russell's name was almost never mentioned by the press during the long, bitter fight in 1935 over Roosevelt's huge four-billion-dollar relief proposal, which had been stalled in the Senate over the demand of pro-labor senators that the government be required to pay relief workers the prevailing wage scale for private projects. But when the bill finally passed the Senate, Arthur Krock of the *New York Times* asked Roosevelt's floor leaders to give him the inside story of the fight. And after they did so, Krock reported that the real "hero of the drama" was the "very unobtrusive young man from Georgia. . . . The winning compromise in each instance was Mr. Russell's own idea."

As if displeased with even this meagre amount of publicity, Russell took further pains to cloak his Senate work in anonymity, often, after he had devised a compromise amendment, asking another senator to introduce it so that the other senator would be given the credit. So successful was he in keeping his name out of newspapers that he was frequently not even mentioned in connection with bills passed only after he had worked out the compromises which made passage possible. Within the world of the Senate, however, his ability to untangle legislative knots was widely recognized. As legislators from rural Georgia counties had come to him to air their problems, hear them analyzed, and be presented with solutions, now United States senators came to him. And, as his biographer notes, "When he spoke to them . . . they listened."

DURING HIS YEARS AS A SENATOR these abilities were placed at the service of great causes.

One was the nation's military strength. Russell was for twenty-six years either Chairman or dominant member of the Senate Armed Services Committee, which oversaw the battle readiness of the nation's far-flung legions and armadas. As senators of Rome had insisted that, regardless of the cost, the legions must be kept at full complement because the peace and stability of the known world—the *Pax Romana*—depended on their strength, Russell believed that the peace and stability of his world—the *Pax Americana*—depended on America's strength. Before World War II, listening to Senate isolationists, he knew that they simply had not read their Livy or their Gibbon, and as a member for twelve years of Armed Services' predecessor Naval Affairs Committee, he had insisted that America's Navy must be strong enough to control not one but both of the world's great oceans, and had been one of the earliest senatorial advocates of the construction of the most gigantic new machine of war: the aircraft carrier. During the war, he had spent months touring the battlefields around the globe on which American soldiers were engaged; he was not impressed with the performance of America's allies. Upon his return, he told the Senate—almost every seat in the Chamber was filled during his speech— that the world was becoming smaller and that America must have a presence in all of it; the bases on foreign soil purchased "with the blood of American boys" must be retained after the war was over. To liberal criticism—retaining the bases was inadvisable, *The New Republic* said, unless America intended to become the "greatest imperialist power of all time"—Russell replied that "call it what you will," retaining the bases would "prevent another generation of Americans . . . from being compelled to pay again in blood and treasure in taking those islands back." As the Romans had believed that the conquered Gauls must be made to *feel* conquered, Russell believed that the enemies of the United States must be made to feel its full vengeance; standing in the ruins of the German cities after V-E Day, he was satisfied that the Hun had felt it, but Japan must not be allowed merely to surrender, for if it was insufficiently humiliated, its "barbarism" would return; he rose in the Senate to demand that Emperor Hirohito be tried as a war criminal. When, three months later, the first atomic bombs were dropped, he exulted in the havoc they wreaked, and told Truman that if the United States did not possess more atomic bombs, "let us carry on with TNT and fire bombs until we can produce" more, and then use them—until the Japanese "are brought groveling to their knees" and "beg us" to be allowed to surrender. Even Japan's unconditional surrender did not satisfy him; he again urged the ouster and public trial of the Emperor, and advised Truman to parade a large army through the streets of Tokyo; having Admiral William Halsey ride the Emperor's white horse in the parade might give the "Japs" the message, he said.

In the years that followed, "There was," a fellow senator said admiringly, "no more ardent cold warrior in Congress than Dick Russell." Convinced that the conflict between Russia and the United States was simply a Manichean battle between evil and good, he opposed almost every suggestion for relaxing tensions or for disarmament or for a reduction in expenditures for military preparedness. Once, Senator Milton Young of North Dakota said to him, "You people in the South are much more militarily minded than in the North." "Milt," Russell replied, "you'd be more military minded, too, if Sherman had crossed North Dakota." Others might see non-military foreign aid as a key to world peace; to Russell, the key was military might, and foreign aid only drained away funds that could better be spent on troops and weapons. Important though he considered governmental economy and a balanced budget, those were not the most important considerations to Russell. America's security came first. "I want to see the planes first, and then consider the cost in dollars," he said once. And on Capitol Hill, Russell's views were the views that counted. "In the field of national defense, Russell is recognized as pretty much the voice of the Senate," journalist Jack Bell wrote accurately during the 1960s—and he could have written the same words accurately during the 1950s or the 1940s. "He is considered to be the greatest living expert on the military defense and establishment of the United States," another congressional observer said, and as such, he was "largely responsible for shaping military budgets during the Cold War," for keeping America militarily strong.

Another of Russell's great causes was that of America's farmers. Believing that "Every great civilization has derived its basic strength and wealth from the soil," and that the primarily agricultural character of the Old South was a principal reason that its culture was so superior to that of the North, with its pounding assembly lines and soot-covered cities, he felt fervently that unless America revived the dignity of farm life, it would decline as Greece and Rome declined. Passing through an almost empty Senate Chamber one day while Hubert Humphrey was giving an ardent speech on the importance of agriculture, Russell suddenly stopped as he was almost out the door to hear what Humphrey was saying. Walking back into the room, he sat down at a desk right in front of the fiery Minnesotan and looked up at him as he talked, and then began to say, in rhythm with Humphrey's points, "That's right." "Yes sir, that's right." "He's absolutely right." As a reporter wrote, "It was a little like a prayer meeting." And seeing that the American farmer was being driven from his land by economic forces too big for him to fight alone, for thirty-eight years Richard Russell tried to bring government to the farmer's side. He was fighting for farm price parity—the parity that he regarded as simple justice for farmers—in 1938, and again in 1948 and 1958. Decade after decade, he played a major role in providing funds for rural electrification, soil conservation, and government-insured mortgages to help farm families buy or keep their land. Year after year, behind the closed doors of conference committees, or of his subcommittee, he quietly inserted funds for agricultural research in appropriations bills. The 1937 legislation creating a Farm Security Administration to make land and equipment loans to impoverished farmers was called the Bankhead-Jones Act, but the key figure in making the FSA viable was Russell—whose name was never publicly associated with the legislation. Without his support, Bankhead was to admit years later, the measure, unpopular in the North, would not have passed in the Senate. Every year thereafter brought attempts to abolish the FSA or slash its appropriations. Year after year, in subcommittee and conference committee, Russell beat back those attempts.

Of all his battles for the farmer, Russell was proudest of his fight for a national school lunch program which would aid farmers by reducing the country's huge agricultural surpluses while providing nourishment for needy children. As one reporter noted, "He kept [the program] alive for nine years by stubbornly putting it into the appropriations bill," until in 1946, it was finally enacted into law. Yet the National School Lunch Act bore no senator's name although, as Gilbert Fite notes, it "was essentially the Russell bill." Not one of the agricultural bills for which Russell maneuvered and argued—not one of the bills which he rewrote and amended until he was in effect their author—bears his name. But so many of them bear his imprint that an admiring fellow senator could say that "throughout the late 1930s and early 1940s, farmers owed their direct parity payments, soil conservation payments, and loans from the FSA more to Russell than to any other single leader in Washington." And although in 1962 he was to surrender his chairmanship of the agricultural subcommittee to devote the bulk of his time to the Armed Services Committee, he was never to stop fighting for the rural families he regarded as the bulwark of democracy.

THE CAUSE MOST PRECIOUS to Richard Russell, however, was the cause that was not his country's but his Southland's.

In defending that cause, Russell was outwardly very different—in appearance and in arguments—from racist senatorial demagogues like Cotton Ed Smith and Theodore (the Man) Bilbo, who ranted on the Senate floor about "niggers" and the "Negro menace" and the intellectual and moral supremacy of "the pure and undefiled Caucasian strain," and who blocked every attempt to pass civil rights legislation with filibusters during which they read telephone books and recipes for pot likker and southern delicacies into the record for hours as if to show their utter contempt for "Northern agitators."

A Russell of the Russells of Georgia would not stoop to what Richard Russell called "nigger-baiting"; "he considered it unworthy of people in his class," his biographer wrote, and seldom used the word, never in public. He maintained firmly that he was not a racist. "There are no members of the Negro race in my state tonight," he said on the Senate floor in 1938, "who would say that any official or personal act of mine had resulted in any unfairness to the Negroes." "I was brought up with them. I love them," he said on another occasion. And, despising a Bilbo, the short, red-faced, pot-bellied, profane son of an impoverished mill-hand, for the pot-likker filibusters that made Russell's beloved Southland appear backward and foolish, he himself based his defense of the filibuster on the Constitution's concern with protecting the rights of minorities in this case, the minority being the eleven southern states—and on the Senate's provision to protect that right: the right of unlimited debate. And while, from his early days in the Senate, he opposed—as the Bilbos and the Smiths opposed—virtually any bill designed to ameliorate the condition of black Americans, in his arguments against these bills Russell took the high ground. He invariably based his arguments on constitutional premises: that the proposed legislation would violate either the constitutionally guaranteed sovereign rights of the individual states, or, as he put it, "the rights of private property and the rights of American citizens to choose their associates," or of American businessmen to hire and fire whom they wished.

He employed this rationale from his earliest days in the Senate. During the 1930s, lynching was the most urgent civil rights issue, and twice, in 1935 and 1938, liberal senators attempted to bring major anti-lynching bills to the floor, where, they felt, the bills would pass; the 1938 measure bore the sponsoring names of no less than seventy senators. Both times the Senate was blocked from voting by southern filibusters, in which Bilbo and Smith and Connally and Maybank pouted and postured—and in both of which Richard Russell delivered full-dress speeches, closely reasoned, calm in tone. And it was noticeable that when Russell spoke, "more colleagues were present to listen than at most Senate sessions" because "they considered Russell something of a moderate on this issue" and therefore "had unusual interest in what he had to say."

Standing, erect and dignified, fingertips resting on his desk, he dealt with the proposed bills on broad, philosophic grounds. The bills had grave implications, he said. They were attacks on principles—sacred principles: the Constitution was sacred; the constitutionally guaranteed sovereign rights of states were sacred; passage of the bills would shake the very bedrock of American government. And they were attacks as well, he said, on a way of life, on a whole civilization; they would, he said, "strike vital blows at the civilization of those I seek to represent."

This civilization—the southern way of life, gracious, civilized—was eminently worth preserving, he said. And, he said, it was based on a harmonious relationship between the races. It had not been easy to achieve this harmony, he said. It had "been evolved painfully through seventy years of trial and error, suffering and sacrifice, on the part of both races." It was based on segregation. "We believe the system of segregation . . . is necessary to preserve peace and harmony between the races." This system, he said, benefited not just whites but blacks; it "promotes the welfare and progress of both races." Just look, he told his fellow senators in one speech, how much the system had done for blacks: "In a short space of time the race that had only known savagery and slavery had been brought into a new day of civilization, where education and opportunity had been provided for them." In another speech, he said, "I challenge all human history to show another instance where in the brief span of seventy-five years as much progress has been made by an uncivilized race as has been made by the southern Negro." And he assured the Senate that not only southern whites but southern blacks agreed with this. "The whites and blacks alike in our section have learned that it is better for the races to live apart socially," he said.

> We have worked hard and painstakingly down through the years to evolve a plan of having the Negro in our midst with the least possible friction, and we have made remarkable progress in adjusting to inevitable problems and conflicts which arise when two races live side by side.

Of course problems still existed, he said, but the problems were not nearly as serious as they were portrayed. Lynchings, for example, were undeniably deplorable. No one could defend that practice; certainly he was not defending it. But, he said, in a 1938 speech, the problem of lynchings was greatly exaggerated. Lynchings, he said, had been nearly eliminated. The North, with its outbreaks of gangland murders, was more violent than the South. Federal anti-lynching legislation was therefore not only unconstitutional but "unnecessary and uncalled for." Furthermore, federal legislation would be "an unjust reflection on the people of the South" since it would "pillory" a "great section of this country before the world as being incapable of its own self-government." The South was itself eliminating lynchings, he said; nonetheless northern liberals were saying to it, "You are a clan of barbarians. You cannot handle your own affairs unless we apply to you the lash and the spur of federal power." And the proposed solutions, he said—not only the anti-lynching bills but the anti–poll tax bill and other anti-segregation legislation—would only aggravate the problem. Many of these proposals could be administered only by force: federal troops. "I'm as interested in the Negro people of my state as anyone in the Senate," he was to say once. "I love them. But I know what's going to happen if you apply force—there'll be violence." The poll tax and lynching bills were opening wedges of a program designed by northern liberals to change the political structure which had kept the two races living together in harmony; "if it were adopted in its entirety, [it] would destroy the white civilization of the South."

And finally, he said, these bills would violate a great principle—one which he was sure no senator, thinking of his own state's interests, would want violated. The federal government was forbidden by the Constitution from interfering in the internal affairs of any state, and if the Senate allowed such interference, no state would be safe. The poll tax might be unwise, he said—but it would be far more unwise to abolish it by federal law: "Let the poll tax be repealed, if it should be, at the proper place. We have not yet come to the state of affairs in Georgia where we need the advice of those who would occupy the position of the carpetbagger and the scalawag of the days of Reconstruction to tell us how to handle our internal affairs."

IN THIS SPEECH, and in scores of others during his thirty-eight years in the Senate, Russell indignantly defended himself against implications of racism. Once, after listening to northern liberal senators denounce southern racism, he said in an impassioned reply: "I don't know those people they're talking about. I just don't know the South they talk about. I have no greater rights because I am a white man. I'm proud of being a white man and I'll do all I can to encourage any other race to be proud of itself."

In scores of speeches he reiterated that he was interested in progress, and opposed only to attempts to force progress too rapidly by means of outside—federal—interference, which, he said, would only inflame passions and make the situation worse, not better. And in scores of speeches he assured the Senate that outside interference was not necessary, because the South was solving its problems itself—was, in fact, well on its way to solving them. As his biographer was to summarize: "Russell did not deliver racist diatribes. His tone was moderate, and he never said anything malicious about blacks. He aimed to educate and convince northern [senators] that the South should be left alone to handle racial problems."

And he did convince them. At the close of Russell's 1938 speech against lynching legislation, Borah of Idaho walked over to him and congratulated him—and then took the floor himself to echo Russell's argument that the bill was a violation of states' rights. (Whereupon Russell rose in his turn to say, "The people of the South will ever revere the name of William E. Borah.") George W. Norris—even Norris—said that the southern arguments had convinced him to vote against cloture.

He convinced northern liberals that he was not a racist, that he didn't hate the Negro, that he was a moderate who truly wanted progress in racial relations—convinced them so thoroughly that for decades descriptions of Richard Russell by the predominately liberal corps of Washington journalists were couched in terms that verged on idolatry. In a 1963 cover story—typical of twenty-five years of such descriptions—*Newsweek* informed its readers that "Richard Russell is at opposite poles from the stereotype some Northerners hold of a Deep-Dixie segregationist—the gallus-snapping, Negro-baiting semi-illiterate. Senator Russell . . . is a courtly, soft-spoken, cultured patrician, whose aides and associates treat him with deferential awe. Modest, even shy, in manner, devastatingly skilled in debate, he has a brilliant mind, encyclopedic learning. . . ."

This respect was based on the belief that, as *Newsweek*'s longtime chief congressional correspondent, Samuel Shaffer was to state flatly, "Russell was not a racist," and that he had "an essential reasonableness in this prickly area." "Russell's view must be respected," Shaffer wrote. "He did not say 'no' to change but tried to regulate the pace of change to prevent the disorder he believed would follow upon change forced down the throats [of the South]." Harold H. Martin wrote in the *Saturday Evening Post* in 1951 that Russell's opposition to civil rights legislation, "honest and unshakable," was based on his conviction that such legislation, "if passed, would lead to rioting and bloodshed in the South." Journalists clothed his opposition in a romantic view of the South. In an admiring cover story in 1957, *Time* explained that "Dick Russell's roots lie deeply and inextricably in the long-lost dream of the Old South. He was brought up . . . amid a smoky Georgia haze of swollen, mud-yellow streams and blowing red dust, of pine-cone fires and fireflies and summer thunder, of white new-blown cotton and wild peach blossoms and slow mules dragging their lazy load." And Russell epitomized the best of that heritage, *Time* said. "Dick . . . admired and respected [Negroes] in that special, paternal Southern way."

The Washington press corps and northern liberals paid Russell, in fact, what for them was their ultimate compliment: they assured their readers that, no matter what Dick Russell was forced to say for the record, his heart was in the right place. As Martin put it in that 1951 article: "Civil righters who like Russell personally and who note that he bears no resemblance in speech or manner to the classic Northern concept of the Southern demagogue are inclined to think that he is far more liberal in his heart than he is in his votes." And Martin added, "Russell, indeed, feels none of the demagogue's hatred toward the Negro, and he despises the Ku Klux Klan mentality which looks upon the Negro as something less than a human being. . . ."

His opposition to proposals to allow black Americans to vote, and to protect them from lynch mobs—his opposition, in fact, to any and all civil rights proposals—was, these journalists said, opposition he was forced to make for political reasons, because otherwise he could not be re-elected. His speeches, they said, were speeches made only for the consumption of his constituents. Dick Russell, they said over and over, year after year—as year after year, decade after decade, Dick Russell fought civil rights bills—Dick Russell didn't really mean the arguments he was making.

He was such a decent man, they said—he *couldn't* mean them.

BUT OF COURSE the high ground is generally the best ground from which to fight—and never more so than in twentieth-century senatorial battles for the Lost Cause. The South, with its twenty-two votes, was as outnumbered in the Senate as it had been in the Civil War. It needed allies to win. And potential allies—non-southern senators sympathetic to the southern position or at least willing to support it in return for southern support for pet causes of their own—didn't want to be labeled as racists. If they were to be bound to the Cause, its racial aspects had to be toned down, so that votes against the poll tax or anti-lynching laws could be cloaked in loftier—constitutional—principles, in philosophy rather than prejudice. Richard Russell's rationalizations made it easier for non-southern senators seeking rationalizations to vote with the South; his approach, so different from that of the Senate's racist demagogues, was vastly more effective in defending the cause that was so precious to him. And the more perceptive of the southern senators realized this. As Sam Ervin was to put it: "Dick Russell always carried on his combat in such a knightly fashion that he never aroused the antagonism of the people most determined to overcome his efforts. He had an uncanny capacity to do that. . . . Most southerners possess that capacity more or less to a limited degree, but Dick Russell possessed it to an unsurpassed degree."

And the South was not only fireflies and peach blossoms and white new-blown cotton, not only gentility and graciousness, not only a sturdy Jeffersonian yeomanry, not only the gallantry of Longstreet and Pickett and of staunch Stonewall on the ridge, not only a place of—in the words Richard Russell spoke on the Senate floor—"peace and harmony between the races." As

Richard Russell could hardly have avoided knowing, since at least two incidents that somewhat disproved those words occurred not just in Georgia, and
not just in Barrow County, but right down the road from his home.

In 1908, when Dick was an eleven-year-old boy in Winder, a young Negro
was arrested in Winder and charged with assaulting a "respected white
woman." A judge in nearby Gwinnett acquitted him after a witness testified that
the accused had actually been at another location at the time of the alleged
crime. Upon his return to Winder, however, the black youth's train was met at
the station by what the *Winder News* called "a reception committee of unknown
parties." Taken to "a secluded spot," he was given 175 lashes with a buggy whip
to "persuade" him to leave town. ("During the persuasion," the newspaper
said, the youth "admitted" his guilt.) No one was prosecuted for the crime.
In 1922, when Dick was already in the State Legislature, a black resident of
Winder, Jesse Long Reed, was charged with the attempted murder of a twenty-
three-year-old white woman ("He . . . left the black bruises of his hands on her
white neck," the *Winder News* reported). Arrested as he was eating in a local
restaurant, Reed was taken to jail, where "people from all directions began
gathering" and "there was talk of lynching." A county judge ordered the sheriff
to "get the negro out of Winder." As he was driving his prisoner to Atlanta,
however, the sheriff "found the road completely blocked with five or six automobiles" about three miles outside town. "About 25" masked men armed with
pistols dragged Reed from the car, hung him from a pine tree and riddled his
body with bullets. "For hours people gathered to view the negro as he hung by
the neck," with some families building fires, spreading blankets, and eating picnic dinners. The sheriff said he could not identify any of the lynchers because
they wore masks, and no one was ever prosecuted for the crime.

Russell had arrived in the Legislature to find the Governor, Hugh M.
Dorsey, and a group of legislators attempting to pass anti-lynching legislation—since during the past four years alone there had been fifty-eight lynchings in Georgia. Russell did not participate in this attempt. During his ten years
in the Legislature—the last five as Speaker of the House—there were other
lynchings in Georgia. There is no record of Russell's views on the subject.
There is only the fact that in the House that he headed, no anti-lynching legislation was passed. He "avoided," in his biographer's careful term, "inflammatory and emotional issues such as lynching. . . ."

When Russell was elected Governor, he became chief executive of a state
whose criminal justice system was considered something special even for the
South, in the harshness with which its courts and prisons treated those who
came within its purview, the overwhelming majority of whom were black.
"Georgia exceeds in size and wealth most of the nearby states, but its prison
system must be placed at the bottom of the list," the National Society of Penal
Institutions declared. Russell was very proud of that rigor, and of the role he
played in maintaining it—so proud, in fact, that when, in 1969, a reporter inter-

viewing him about his pre-Senate career neglected to raise the subject, Russell raised it himself.

"I suppose I was the harshest Governor on criminals" in the history of Georgia, he said. "All the statistics the last time I saw [them] showed I pardoned and paroled fewer people than any Governor they ever had." Even as harsh a governor as his successor Eugene Talmadge (known as "Whippin' Gene" because he said that while he had never actually been a member of the Ku Klux Klan, "I used to do a little whippin' myself) had, Russell said, pardoned three times as many criminals as he had. Georgia's criminal justice system as a whole, Russell said, was exceptional in the fairness with which it dispensed justice. Pointing out that he had been a criminal lawyer in his early career, he said, "I had never seen a man I knew was innocent, convicted."

The incident during his governorship that brought him, for a brief time, into the national spotlight revolved around the harshest aspect of that system. In 1932, America was stunned by the publication of *I Am a Fugitive from a Georgia Chain Gang*.* Its author, Robert E. Burns, a young white New York accountant, successful before the First World War, had emerged from the war shell-shocked and unable to hold a job, wandered south to Georgia where, "so hungry I was seeing things," he was partly persuaded and partly intimidated by two men into joining them in robbing a grocery store of four dollars and eighty cents. Arrested in 1922, he was sentenced to six to ten years in the Georgia chain gangs, where men wore a heavy iron shackle on each ankle and were manacled together at work all day, and in their bunks at night—those of them lucky enough to be in bunks and not in the notorious "cage wagons." Burns saw men tortured in medieval stocks, beaten with heavy leather straps, and worked to death until, within a year, he escaped.

During the next several years, he became a reporter and then the editor of *Chicago* magazine, before Georgia detectives showed up in his office in 1929. Georgia prison officials promised him a release or a parole within ninety days if he returned voluntarily. As soon as he returned, however, the promise was broken; he was remanded to the same chain gang to complete his full sentence. Escaping within a year again and making his way to New Jersey, he wrote his book, which received respectful reviews. The "real importance" of this "breathtaking and heart-wrenching book . . . lies in the baring of Georgia's incredible penal system . . . which manages to defeat essential justice and outrage humanity," said the *New York Times*. "The conditions he describes there, the filth, the starvation rations, the inhuman shackles and chains, the body-breaking labor, the vicious cruelty, would be almost unbelievable if it were not that . . . investigators . . . substantiate what he says." And the *New York Herald Tribune* said, "One would like to hear the answer of Georgia authorities to this burning book."

---

*That same year, the book was made into a movie, with the same title, that became one of the most famous of its time.

The answer came from Georgia's Governor. Demanding that Burns be extradited to serve the remaining years of his full term, he dispatched a team of state prosecutors, armed with somewhat unconvincing affidavits from convicts defending conditions in the chain gangs, to bring him back. When New Jersey's Governor, Arthur H. Moore, refused to allow him to be extradited, the Georgia Governor reacted to the refusal with rage. The New Jersey decision, he said, was "a slander on the State of Georgia and its institutions." And, he said, it was unconstitutional, a violation of the rights of a "sovereign state." "The Governor of New Jersey, nor anyone else has any right to wantonly and deliberately insult the state of Georgia and her people by declining to honor an extradition for a convict on the ground that our State is uncivilized and backward, inhumane to prisoners and barbarous in their punishments." As for "charges that our penal system is barbarous and inhumane," the Georgia Governor said, they must "be denounced for what they are: absolutely false and unfounded. . . . Prisoners are well fed and treated humanely, but are not coddled nor maintained in luxury."

The Governor, of course, was Richard Russell, and the response of northern newspapers to Russell's statements was summarized by one editorial which said, "The State of New Jersey . . . is telling the world that something is rotten in the State of Georgia," but "The State of Georgia, far from bowing its head in guilty shame, is taking the offensive and lashing out at New Jersey and its Governor with both fists. We can see how Georgia feels about it all in the statements of its Governor. . . ." But when, a decade later, articles about now-Senator Russell began appearing in national magazines, they contained no reference to his defense of a system that defeated essential justice and outraged humanity. The flattering cover stories in *Time* and *Newsweek,* the long profiles in the *Saturday Evening Post,* that celebrated the progressive reforms of Russell's governorship, never even mentioned the Georgia Chain Gang incident; in fact, if there was a single mention of the incident in even one of the scores of profiles of Russell that appeared in newspapers and magazines during the 1940s and '50s and '60s, the author has been unable to find it.

Nor did any of the articles mention that the southerner who said that anti-lynching legislation was "unnecessary and uncalled for," who said that the South was a place of "peace and harmony between the races," had had, very close to his home, at least two lynchings for which no one was ever convicted or even prosecuted. None mentioned that the southerner who asserted so passionately that the South could take care of the lynching problem itself had done nothing to take care of it as Speaker or Governor. None mentioned that he had, in at least one respect, been the harshest Governor in the history of a very harsh state—none mentioned any of the aspects of his career that might have hinted at the existence of feelings other than the "love" for black Americans of which he talked, and the "fairness" and "moderation" for which he was so widely praised.

. . .

AND IF RICHARD RUSSELL'S SENTIMENTS were kept on a lofty plane so long as he, and the South he loved, were winning, and winning easily, when winning became more difficult there did indeed begin to surface hints of feelings that might have surprised those who were sure that Richard Russell was "not a racist," that he had "an essential reasonableness" about race, that he was not trying to prevent change but merely to "regulate" its pace, that "he is far more liberal in his heart than he is in his votes," that he "admired and respected [Negroes] in that special, paternal Southern way."

Winning became harder because of the Second World War. Turning back civil rights measures in the Senate had been easy in 1935 and 1938, but the great buildup for the oncoming war brought huge defense plants to the South (ironically, to Georgia more than any other state, thanks to the influence of Russell and his House counterpart, Carl Vinson, on congressional Armed Services Committees; more than twenty-five thousand workers would be employed on the assembly lines at the great bomber plant at Marietta alone), and in 1941 President Roosevelt established by executive order a Fair Employment Practices Commission and empowered it to move legally against defense and war contractors who discriminated on the basis of race, color, or religion.

As a result of this order, and of the fact that there were not enough white workers to fill the jobs, northern blacks, unaccustomed to, and resistant to, the rigidities of southern segregation, flooded into the South. The haste with which the plants had to be geared up and manned made it unfeasible to build separate facilities, so that suddenly, in the very heart of the Southland, whites and blacks were eating together, using the same bathrooms and drinking fountains, sharing the same hospital wards. And there were also the huge new military training camps in the South, in which black men and white men were sleeping together in the same barracks.

Distressed by the fact that, by creating the FEPC through executive order, Roosevelt had bypassed the Senate, where the creation of the new agency could have been blocked, Russell saw it as an agency actively working to end segregation and thereby end the southern way of life. And then, in 1942, the House of Representatives passed a bill to eliminate poll taxes. Declaring that such efforts to use the war "to force social equality and the commingling of races in the South . . . are doomed to failure," Russell blocked the House bill from coming to the floor of the Senate—but he was aware that the vote on cloture, generally so lopsidedly pro-southern in the past, had been much closer this time. And in 1944 there was another anti–poll tax bill, and further attempts to expand the funding and jurisdiction of the FEPC. "I am afraid we are going to get licked," Russell wrote a friend, and although he wasn't, the vote by which he defeated cloture this time was uncomfortably close; forces generated by the war were threatening the South he loved.

At first, the veil under which Russell's feelings had been cloaked fell away only in private. There had always been scattered hints in private; years before, while he was professing on the Senate floor that "I have no greater rights because I am a white man," he had written in a letter marked "confidential": "Any southern white man worth a pinch of salt would give his all to maintain white supremacy." Now the tone in his letters sharpened when he wrote about whites and blacks using the same hospitals on Army bases. "It is a terrible mistake and I hope we will be able to convince the Army of it before it is widely advertised and becomes a serious issue," he wrote in 1942. The races were even sharing the same maternity wards! "A deplorable situation," he said. And there might be even worse situations. When, in 1942, a Savannah woman, indignant over the presence of black soldiers in nearby Army camps, wrote him that "It is not necessary to point out to you, a Southern gentleman, the tragic possibilities which this situation holds," possibilities which she said "will be inevitable," Russell replied that it was indeed not necessary. "I am fully aware of the very dangerous implications attending the concentration of negro troops from northern states in the South," he said. "I feel about this matter just as any other Southern white man does, and certainly hope that we can avoid trouble."

The whole question of blacks in the armed forces was troubling to Russell. Blacks had a limited usefulness in the military anyway, Russell felt; didn't people realize that black soldiers were not as physically courageous as whites?—"In the last war in France . . . the use of colored troops for heavy fighting was not very successful." For that matter, he was to say, they were not even as courageous as soldiers of some other non-white races. After the war, complimenting the Japanese-American Nisei units that had served with the American army for not "fading away in the face of enemy action," he said, "It is a great pity that other minority groups do not emulate their example instead of fading in the face of enemy action." Of course, he said, blacks should not be inducted into elite units like the Marine Corps, in which courage was especially essential. Not that blacks were not violent—"These people," his sister Patience heard him say, "when they get mad, they kill. And they will kill without being provoked, to a great extent"—it was just that they were not brave. As one study of his racial views puts it: "In spite of an enviable battle record of some blacks in World War I, Russell refused to accept the idea that blacks were not inherent cowards." And the commingling of black and white troops created other problems; it was not a matter of racial prejudice at all, he was to explain—at issue, rather, was the "health and morals of hundreds of thousands of American boys." "There is no more intimate human relationship known to men than that of enlisted men serving together at the squad level," he said. "They eat and sleep together. They use the same sanitary facilities." And, he said, "the incidence of syphilis, gonorrhea, chancre and all other venereal diseases is appallingly higher among the members of the Negro race." Not only is this difference true in civilian life, he said, but "it is likewise great between the units in the Army as compared with the white units, though both races have available identical systems of instruction and of hygiene to prevent venereal diseases." Having whites and blacks serve in the same units "is sure to increase the numbers of men who will be disabled through communicable diseases." Special camps should be created for blacks "who do not meet the health requirements" to cure them of VD before they are allowed to join the rest of the Army.

And it wasn't merely *killing* by blacks that Russell feared—as becomes apparent from a draft of a speech that he would later dictate to a secretary. In the draft he referred to newspaper stories from Portland, Oregon, about a fifteen-year-old white girl, the daughter of a Portland businessman, who had gone to a dance with a thirty-year-old black man, and was then abducted by him, held captive for ten days, and raped repeatedly by him and four other men.

"All of the men charged with the attack were past thirty years of age, and most of them were past forty," Russell dictated. "All of them were Negroes." He regretted, he said, that the *Congressional Record* did not print pictures. It was a shame that "the pictures of the defendants appearing at the head of the article cannot be printed in the *Record*." Moreover, he said, there have been "other cases of a similar type . . . outside the South," but they "are too sickening for the *Record*." And, he said in the draft, it is "the system of social intermingling of the races that gives rise to these cases."

This speech, however, was only dictated, never delivered; his opinion that "these people, when they get mad, they kill" was an opinion expressed only to friends and family. Russell almost never forgot the overriding strategic consideration: that, if the South was to win, it needed allies, and opposition to desegregation must therefore be made as respectable as possible in the North, respectable to Republican senators.

Nevertheless, the threat to the southern way of life grew steadily more serious during the war. Russell foresaw that blacks who had worked in defense plants and served in the armed forces were not going to return without protest to their prewar second-class citizenship. He saw all too clearly what was coming. Let the dikes be breached once, and the torrent would begin. "There is no such thing as a little integration," he was to say. "They are determined to get into the white schools and into the white restaurants and into the swimming pools."

He salvaged a 1944 Senate battle, the battle in which he was "afraid that we are going to be licked," but only by a brilliant appeal to Republicans whose votes had earlier that year defeated his amendment to halve the FEPC appropriation. Pointing out—"scathingly," Allen Drury wrote—"that for a party which condemned bureaucracy they were certainly inconsistent in wanting to leave the FEPC unchecked," he "successfully embarrassed enough Republicans into changing their votes" so that on a second vote his amendment carried. And during this fight he wrote a friend that the growing strength of northern efforts to force schools, swimming pools and other public places to accept both races was bringing "our southern civilization" to the verge of collapse. "I am sick about it," he wrote. He jotted on an office notepad that if the North had its way, even "baseball [and] football teams would have to play negroes." And, it was at this time, too, that a new word began to creep into his private correspondence: "miscegenation."

It was also at this time that he began to see a new, red tinge in the black menace. A letter he wrote in 1944 claimed not only that the FEPC was administered "almost entirely by negroes"—but by Negroes with ties to the Communist Party. FEPC Chairman Malcolm Ross, he said, was "a wild-eyed radical lionized by the *Daily Worker*." "The agitation to repeal the poll-tax laws was started by the *Daily Worker*," he was to say.

Never forgetting that in the Civil War, the South had won battle after battle, only to be worn down at last by superior numbers, he feared that the pattern was being repeated in the Senate. He was able, year after year, to slash FEPC appropriations; he was never able to legislate the agency out of existence entirely. The margins of his victories were growing steadily narrower. And Richard Russell's public statements as well as private letters were beginning occasionally to show less of the "moderation" and "restraint" that had always characterized them in the past, as if the veneer were cracking, just a little but enough to reveal what lay beneath. It was on the Senate floor now that Russell charged that an FEPC ruling against racial discrimination in hiring by the Philadelphia transit system—a ruling which touched off a strike by Philadelphia transit workers—was actually a Communist plot against the South; the strike, he said, had been deliberately instigated by the FEPC so that the Army could be called in to break the strike, thereby giving an "object lesson" to discourage others (meaning southerners) from resisting FEPC rulings. In 1948, racial tensions were rising sharply in the South. Demagogues running on "white supremacy" platforms had won postwar primaries in several states. Herman Talmadge, Eugene's son, had won Georgia's governorship after promising that "no Negro will vote in Georgia for the next four years." Crosses were burning again on southern hills: Ku Klux Klan activity in general was increasing, as were the beatings and whippings of black men. President Truman demanded passage of legislation to make the FEPC permanent. And in 1948, with the threat more serious than ever, Russell's rhetoric on the Senate floor sharpened.

Needing to make opposition to the FEPC bill respectable to win nonsouthern support, he argued, as always, that the bill was not necessary—the charges that Negroes in the South were discriminated against in employment were greatly exaggerated, he said; "this bill does not address itself to any condition which exists today in the United States of America"—and that there was no racial motive behind the South's opposition to it.

The cry of discrimination, he said, is a "cry of 'wolf, wolf.' . . . There has never been a greater fraud perpetrated upon the American people than the deliberate attempt that has been made to create the impression that we are opposing economic equality in fighting this bill." Discrimination, he said, worked against the best interests of the South—and the South was well aware of that. "It is said that southern Democrats are opposing [the bill] because they want to grind down and hold in subjection the Negroes." Actually, "there is not a southern Democrat who does not know that the welfare of his people and the progress of his state are inseparably intertwined with the welfare and progress of the Negro population." All the South wanted was the continuation of the system whose efficacy had already been proven: the separation of the races. "I am in favor of giving both the whites and the blacks equal rights, but not together. We are merely fighting to sustain in our country a way of life which both the white and the black man approve as being essential to harmony in racial relations in the South." And it was precisely this that the bill was really intended to destroy, he said. "Those who drew the bill, those who gave it life, and those who gave the distortedness to the American people know that the main purpose back of this measure is to make it a force bill, to break down the segregation of the races which we have found essential. . . ."

He also used the other argument most effective in appealing to conservative Republicans: that the FEPC was a Communist plot, "the entering wedge to complete state socialism and communism." "There was a great build-up for the bill over the radio and through the columns of the press," he said. "Every left-wing group in this country had each of its cells carefully instructed as to how to spread the propaganda in support of the measure. If the desire is to nationalize industry, here is the chance. . . ."

But amid these familiar arguments, there were hints of other feelings—even if a hint might be only a single hyphenated adjective. "Mr. President," Richard Russell said, "I do not mean to say there has been no imposition on any Negro in my section of the country, because I know there has been. There have also been semi-civilized Negroes who outraged the sense of decency of all white and colored peoples in their community by committing outrageous crimes." He even raised publicly subjects he knew were better avoided, such as intermarriage between the races. "That, Mr. President, would mean a mongrel race," which, he said, "would result in destroying America, because there has never been a mongrel race that has been able to stand." And there would be other hints that emerged as if despite himself. Once he had assured the Senate of his belief that "I have no greater rights because I am a white man." Now he told it: "Any white man who wants to take the position that he is no better than the Negro is entitled to his own opinion of himself. I do not think much of him, but he can think it."

ON JULY 25, 1946, on a lonely dirt road near Monroe, Georgia, in Walton County, about eleven miles from Richard Russell's home, two young black couples, both recently married, were being driven home by a white farmer who had just posted six hundred dollars' bail for one of the black men, twenty-seven-year-old Roger Malcolm, who had been accused of stabbing his white employer in the arm during a fight. As the farmer drove onto a little wooden bridge, he saw a car blocking its far end, and as soon as he stopped, another car drove up behind him, its bumper nudging his, trapping him on the bridge. Other cars drove up, and about twenty white men got out, carrying rifles and shotguns. They had not bothered to wear masks. They took Malcolm and his friend, a twenty-six-year-old war veteran who had served in Africa and the Pacific— his discharge button had, by chance, arrived at his mother's home that same week—out of the car, tied their hands behind them and marched them away. They were apparently going to leave the women unharmed, but one of the women, crying, called out to one of the attackers by name, so that he became afraid she would identify him, and they were pulled out of the car and led off, too. Then the four blacks were lined up in a row, each wife beside her husband. Three times the white leader counted, "One, two, three," and there were three volleys; the bodies, riddled with more than sixty bullets, were scarcely recognizable.

The incident might have embarrassed another man who for years had been assuring the Senate that in the South blacks and whites lived in "peace and harmony," and that anti-lynching and voter-protection legislation was unnecessary—as he might also have been embarrassed by the announcement a few days later from the head of the Georgia State Police that "we can't cope with the situation" because neither the farmer nor any of "the best people in town" would "talk about this" (and by the subsequent finding by a coroner's jury that the blacks had met their deaths at the hands of "persons unknown"). It didn't embarrass Richard Russell. When California Senator William Knowland inserted an article describing the lynching in the *Congressional Record,* Russell rose in indignation. "Mr. President," he said, standing at his desk, as dignified, reasonable and sincere as ever, "no member of the Senate deplores for a moment more than I do the murders which are said to have been recently committed in my state. . . . I know the people of Walton County. . . . The people of that county are law abiding and upright, and would be as much opposed to any murder as would the people of any other county in this country. There are no better people than the people of Walton County. I have no doubt that the State authorities of Georgia will prosecute to the full extent of their powers any person who may be charged with the commission of that crime." There was, he said, no excuse for a senator to insert in the *Record* a newspaper article insulting to the State of Georgia. "Crimes of this nature are not confined to the State of Georgia," he said. "I doubt not that if I were to peruse the newspapers of California I would find that there have been brutal crimes committed by people of that State."

On July 30, 1946, a black farmhand was flogged to death by six white men near Lexington, Mississippi; on August 3, in Gordon, Georgia, a black mine worker was shot to death; on August 7, a black veteran was hung near Minden,

Louisiana. And also in 1946, a young black sergeant, discharged from the Army just three hours before at a demobilization center in Atlanta, boarded a bus for South Carolina. When the driver refused to let him use the lavatory, the sergeant argued with him, and at the next town, Batesburg, South Carolina, the driver called the police. Two policemen dragged the young veteran, still in uniform, from the bus, took him to jail and ground out both his eyes with a blackjack. That year, not only in Georgia but in other southern states, there were also uncounted beatings—with fists and baseball bats and bullwhips; not fatal, they were not classified as lynchings—of black veterans who, in the words of one Alabaman, "must not expect or demand any change in their status from that which existed before they went overseas." As one act of violence after another went unpunished, the demand for federal legislation intensified. In 1946, President Truman appointed, by executive order, a blue-ribbon committee to study the civil rights problem in all its aspects, and the committee's report, "To Secure These Rights," called not only for a permanent FEPC, abolition of the poll tax, and federal laws against lynchings but also for the establishment of a permanent Commission on Civil Rights in the Executive Office of the President, and for an end to segregation in education, in housing, in health services—for an end to racial discrimination in the broadest terms. Firmly endorsing the recommendations for these "new concepts of civil rights," Truman told reporters afterwards, "I mean every word of it—and I am going to prove that I do mean it."

Never—never, at least, since Appomattox—had the threat been more ominous. Lee studying maps in his tent and watching, night after night, the arrows that signified the huge, well-equipped northern armies closing in on Atlanta, had seen doom no more clearly than Russell saw it now—now that a President of his own party had decided to join the "South haters." He was convinced that the motive behind Truman's decision, and the northern agitation in general, was strictly political: a coldly calculated political decision "to alienate Southern Democrats in exchange for the black vote" in the politically crucial big cities of the North. But that was a strong motive. Moreover, he knew that the President was not the only politician counting black votes: senators of the other party, and some of the once-staunch midwesterners of his own party, were counting them, too.

Russell's anger against those who, for such sordid reasons, were determined to "harass" and "hellhack" his beloved Southland, to make its people "a special object of obloquy," boiled over in private. In a letter to a Florida man, he pointed out that there were forty-three counties in Georgia in which blacks outnumbered whites. White people in these counties, he said, "cannot be expected to turn their children . . . over to schools that are run by negroes, or to live in counties that have negro sheriffs, county school superintendents or other officials." Occasionally it boiled over in public. Calling Truman's bill a "Gestapo" approach—"the most outrageous affront to the people of our section that we have had to face since Reconstruction Days"—he predicted that even-

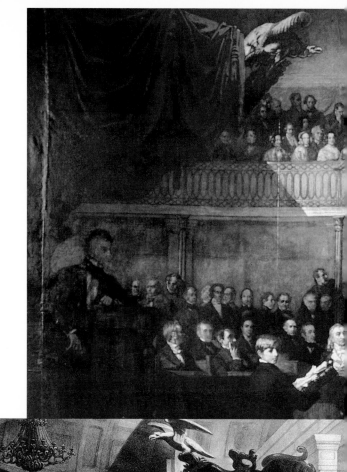

Above: Webster Replying to Hayne, by George P. A. Healy. Vice President John C. Calhoun, at far left, presides in the old Senate Chamber, January, 1830.

Opposite: The United States Senate, A.D. 1850, engraved by Robert Whitechurch after a painting by Peter Rothermel. Henry Clay presents his compromise to the Senate, presided over by Vice President Millard Fillmore. Calhoun is to the right of Fillmore, and Daniel Webster is seated at left, head in hand.

Above: Senate as a Court of Impeachment for the Trial of Andrew Johnson, 1868, after Theodore Davis. *Below:* Keppler's *The Bosses of the Senate, Puck* magazine, 1889

The Senate Four: left to right, Orville H. Platt, John C. Spooner, William B. Allison, and Nelson W. Aldrich, at Aldrich's Newport, Rhode Island, estate, 1903

Senator Henry Cabot Lodge, right, talks to newsmen during Senate debate over the Treaty of Versailles, 1919.

A Russell of the Russells of Georgia

Richard Brevard Russell Jr. being sworn in as Governor of Georgia by the Chief Justice of the Georgia Supreme Court, Richard Brevard Russell Sr., June 27, 1931

Russell and Johnson at a Washington Senators baseball game in 1955

The Orator of the Dawn: Hubert Humphrey, the fiery mayor of Minneapolis, fighting for a strong civil rights plank at the 1948 Democratic National Convention

Congresswoman Gahagan Douglas
emerging from the voting booth

Below: The Texas delegation in Washington
to attend Lyndon Johnson's January, 1949,
inauguration ceremony. At Johnson's right
are Justice Tom Clark and the senior Senator
from Texas, Tom Connally.

New Senator Lyndon B. Johnson allows new Senator
Robert Kerr to take center stage. Senator Clinton Anderson
is at right.

The Johnsons at home, August, 1948

Opposite: Johnson joins the Senate Armed Services
Committee, January, 1949. From left, Democrats
Lester C. Hunt, Estes Kefauver, Lyndon B. Johnson,
Virgil Chapman, Richard B. Russell, Chairman
Millard E. Tydings; Republicans Styles Bridges,
Chan Gurney, Leverett Saltonstall, Wayne Morse,
Raymond E. Baldwin, and William Knowland.

Christmas photographs. *Above,* 1949: from left, Lucia, Rebekah Baines, Josefa, Rodney on Sam Houston's lap, Becky Alexander, Rebekah Bobbitt, O. P. Bobbitt, and their son Phil. *Below,* 1955, at the Johnson Ranch: Aunt Jessie Hatcher, Lucy, Ramon, Sam Houston, Lyndon, Lynda, unidentified

Johnson with Walter Jenkins en
route to the office. Congressman
Homer Thornberry is in the middle.

Johnson and John Connally
at the Austin airport

Christmas, 1950, photograph of staff
for *Collier's* magazine. From left,
Warren Woodward, Mary Rather,
Johnson, Dorothy Nichols, Horace
Busby, Glynn Stegall.

At the ranch with his family, after his heart attack, August, 1955

The press conference, with Sam Rayburn (left) and Adlai Stevenson, September, 1955

"Lyndon Johnson Day" at his alma mater, Southwest Texas State Teachers College, November, 1955

On the ranch

Fording the river to get to the ranch

tually it would mean that blacks and whites would "attend the same schools, swim in the same pools, eat together, and eventually, intermarry." But with the threat so serious, a public display of these emotions was a luxury the South could not afford, and generally in public—as in a nationwide radio address he made on behalf of the southern senators—Russell tried to keep his tone reasonable and moderate, and to concentrate on issues more palatable to northern ears, saying that if the proposed expansion of federal power was adopted, not merely southerners but all Americans would find they had lost some of their freedoms to "hordes of federal bureaucrats" who would in effect be "federal policemen." On the floor of the Senate, the personality of Richard Russell was as grave, deliberate, judicious, reasonable as ever.

He tried to make the entire Southern Caucus adopt the same tone and arguments—a job made easier by Cotton Ed's defeat in 1944 and Bilbo's death in 1947. The last holdout was Tom Connally, and in one of the meetings of the Caucus in Russell's office, the Georgian faced the old Texan down, in a bitter confrontation in which one man was loud, and the other quiet—and the quiet man won. Over and over, Russell would try to make the other southern senators understand what he understood—that the tactics he was proposing were the best tactics for their cause, and that much as they might personally enjoy picturesquely defying the world, the Cause was all that mattered. Racist pejoratives and stalling tactics antagonized northern senators and inflamed anti-Southern opinion, he said. The South didn't need antagonism; it needed allies. Furthermore, such tactics made the South, their beloved South, look foolish—foolish and backward. "We've got a good case on the merits," he said at one meeting of the Southern Caucus. "Let's keep the arguments germane. Let's see if we can keep our speeches restrained, and not inflammatory."

The big table at which the Caucus met was round—Russell didn't want to be at the head of a table—but wherever he sat *was* the head of the table, and the references to blacks as "niggers" and "coons" died out of the Senate debate. The demands that the entire *Journal* of the previous day's session be read and amended were abandoned. Instead, states' rights and other constitutional issues (in particular the right to unlimited debate in the Senate, the right that made filibusters effective), along with the argument that civil rights agitation was Communist-inspired—an argument that had proved effective with conservative non-southern senators—became the staples of southern senatorial rhetoric.

And these tactics were indeed the most effective tactics for the South. When during one debate a northern senator sneeringly asked Russell "whether the Senator is going to devote his attention to a discussion of the bill or to the question of the *Journal*," Russell was able to reply with quiet dignity, "I have discussed only the bill and I have no other purpose." His discussion was, he always assured the Senate, "without reference to racism." His voice rang with sincerity when he assured the Senate that interference in the affairs of the South was not necessary, saying, "We've had our problems, but we've solved them pretty well."

Journalists took note of the change in southern tone. As one article put it: "The Negro, who is at the heart of the Civil Rights issue, is never mentioned, and none of the Southern coalition . . . ever breaks into the demagogic ranting of a Bilbo or Rankin. Discussion swirls around the parliamentary procedure at issue, and the speeches, though interminable, are germane." The journalists approved the change. As this article said: "Under Russell, filibuster oratory has improved greatly in quality"—as if it was the oratory that mattered, not the cause in which it was employed. There was little fundamental difference between the racial views of Richard Russell—those views expressed with a courtliness and patrician charm that made men refer to him as "knightly"—and the rantings of a Bilbo or Cotton Ed Smith, however much this Russell of the Russells of Georgia might feel that demagoguery was beneath him. The difference lay in their effectiveness. The knightliness accomplished what Richard Russell wanted it to accomplish: made it more difficult for the foes of his beloved Southland to prevail.

AS EFFECTIVE AS RUSSELL'S TACTICS was his personality, for it drew from his colleagues respect as deep as ever. In 1949, when Lyndon Johnson came to the Senate, Richard Russell was fifty-one. The outlines of his once-thin face were beginning to be blurred by flesh, and a paunch was starting to show beneath his senatorial blue (or, on a wild day, dark gray) suits. But there had been no softening of the dignity and reserve that had always, along with the grave, thoughtful demeanor and unfailing courtesy, set him apart from his peers—they were as rigid as ever. The backward tilt of the head had become more pronounced, and since the front of his head was now completely bald, his nose was even more prominent than when Richard Russell had been young; journalists described him in the same terms as had been used years—decades—earlier. "Senator Russell's almost Roman presence is enhanced by more than a suggestion of the eagle in his profile, and, on most occasions, by a marble rigidity of posture and an august manner of speech," Frederic Collins was to write in the *New York Times Magazine*. "His projection of himself toward those he wishes to sway is not chummy but Olympian." He was very conscious of the Senate's position in American political life, and of his position in the Senate—and he brooked no affront to either of them. Once, in 1957, a thirty-year-old reporter newly arrived in Washington, Tom Wicker of the *Winston-Salem Journal,* jokingly repeated in a group including Russell and newly elected Senator Frank Church the explanation Church had given him for his recent upset victory: that he had been "in the middle between two nuts," Idaho's right-wing Senator Herman Welker and the left-wing former Senator Glen H. Taylor.
"No one laughed," Wicker was to recall.

Russell's face froze ominously. I could see Frank Church looking for a way to go through the floor. I had forgotten that both Herman Welker and Glen Taylor had been United States senators. No matter what their politics had been, they were not in Richard Russell's presence to be referred to as "nuts" by a young whippersnapper from the press . . . or a junior senator from Idaho.

The son of the man who had said, "You can always be honorable," had what a friend calls "a monumental sense of honor," and it merged with his monumental patriotism. He regarded his responsibility for America's fighting men as a sacred trust. Once, after his Armed Services Committee had held a closed hearing on confidential military information, committee member Wayne Morse, looking for headlines, leaked a piece of that information. When reporters asked Russell to comment, he said he would comment not on the information but on the leak; his comment was one simple word: "dishonorable." Colleagues' confidences were safe with him—always. As his biographer wrote, "His colleagues considered him absolutely trustworthy." When Richard Russell died, a reporter was to say, "a thousand Senate secrets would die with him." When he gave a commitment on a piece of legislation, there was, his colleagues said, never an excuse given later; the commitment was kept. Estes Kefauver, whom Richard Russell despised, had to admit that Russell's "word is his bond." For many senators, Richard Russell embodied what they wanted to be: the quintessential Senator, in all the highest senses of that title. "He was incomparably the truest Senate type," William S. White was to write.

BEHIND THE PERSONALITY was the power—the senatorial brand of power.
Russell's dominance on the Armed Services Committee, a dominance that lasted for more than a quarter of a century, gave him a full measure of power in dealing with other senators—at least with any senator whose state contained an Army camp or an airfield or a naval base (or indeed any defense-related installation), or a major defense contractor. That power was magnified by his role on the Appropriations Committee (of which he would also later become dominant member and then chairman). In 1949, he was still, as he had been since 1933, Chairman of Appropriations' agricultural subcommittee—so that he still stood athwart that strategic Senate narrows, in a position to exact tribute from any senator who needed funding for an agricultural project. Magnifying his power further was his leadership of the Southern Caucus, which of course included in its ranks guardians of other senatorial narrows: chairmen of other two Appropriations subcommittees, other chairmen of Standing Committees, so the power of the South—the power exercised at Russell's command—was interwoven between committees and subcommittees into a very strong web indeed.
If further magnification was needed, it was provided by his role within his party. Richard Russell was the only senator who sat on both the Democratic Policy Committee, which controlled the flow of legislation to the floor, and the Democratic Steering Committee, which controlled the party's committee

assignments. Nor was Russell's power limited to his party's side of the aisle, for the conservative coalition was not limited to one side of the aisle. "I remember so well how Bob Taft had a working relationship with Dick Russell on certain issues," Hubert Humphrey was to recall. The relationship was very discreet—it was once said that Russell and Taft ran the Senate "with a wink and a nod"—and very effective. "Dick Russell would outmaneuver the Republicans five times a day, but he was always getting them when he needed them." When compromises were being worked out on controversial legislation, it wasn't merely Democrats but Republicans who were told to "Check it with Dick." An observer was to write in the 1960s—in words that would to a great extent have been applicable also to the 1940s and 1950s—"No major compromise can be concluded in the Senate without submission to his professional hand." His power was senatorial power: informal, vague, unwritten—and immense.

The use of this power to help other senators is documented in letters, and in senatorial reminiscences—as is the graciousness, the unpretentiousness, even diffidence, with which the assistance was tendered. A freshman senator was to recall how, standing at his desk, he was watching in despair as a bill vital to his future was being voted down on the floor when suddenly the famous Senator Russell, with whom he had hardly ever exchanged a word, was standing beside him. He had read the bill, Russell said, and he thought it was a project worthy of support; he was wondering if he might give a little help with it. Certainly, the freshman senator replied, wondering what Russell could do. Well, Russell said, why don't you bring it up again after the afternoon recess? The young senator wasn't sure what good that would do, but he said he would. When the bill was called that afternoon, he noticed that the Senate floor wasn't as empty as it had been earlier. He recognized the faces of the newcomers: the southerners had arrived. One by one they voted; all the votes were "aye." The young senator was to recall Russell's embarrassment when he sought him out to express his gratitude, and how quickly the older man tried to walk away. "He actually seemed embarrassed to be thanked," the freshman said. Russell never referred to the incident—not even when he wanted the young senator's vote on a matter of his own.

Another freshman senator, newly elected and nervous, was to recall how he told Russell that he had been warned that if he opposed certain legislation, a number of powerful senators might punish him by opposing projects for his state. After listening intently to the freshman's reason for his opposition, Russell said, "Well, I want to say that you ought to go ahead with this cause, and to the best of my ability, I'll see to it you don't get hurt." When a senator asked for help in securing passage of a pet project, Russell would often say no more than, "We should be able to put this over." But of course, "this" was indeed "put over," and the freshman was indeed not "hurt"—Russell's power might be vague, hard to define, but, as his biographer Fite notes, "Scores of other senators . . . turned to 'Dear Dick' for help in getting local projects approved and funded" because they knew that it was his decision that would determine the projects' fate. And the help was invariably given with graciousness and dignity. He was, Fite said, "everybody's favorite uncle."

RUSSELL'S USE of his immense power to punish senators instead of to help them was very seldom referred to—perhaps because it was exercised with the same diffidence; Richard Russell rarely if ever used the direct threat. But, as Meg Greenfield of the *Washington Post* was later to write, "It has not escaped the notice of other senators who are interested in projects for their districts or in good committee assignments for themselves that Russell, like the Lord, has the power both to give and to take away."

And the power *was* used to punish. Senators knew that—and acted accordingly. The number of individual votes that were, over the years, changed by the unspoken threat of its use, no one can know—but combined with Russell's knowledge of and use of the Senate's rules and precedents, and the indefinable, but monumental, power of his personality, the number was enough. Russell may have been afraid that he was going to be "licked," but he wasn't. With Russell as the "General" of the southern forces fighting civil rights legislation against long odds, the South had won in 1942 and 1944; in 1946, even with a President of Russell's own party determined to put through legislation, the South won again.

The South did suffer one defeat during the balance of Harry Truman's first term, but it was not on a piece of legislation. With Truman determined to integrate the armed forces, Russell countered with an amendment to the Selective Service Act that would allow draftees the option of serving in units made up only, as he put it, of "men of their own race and kind." (It was then that Russell raised the spectre of venereal disease: was not the Senate aware of its prevalence among Negroes?; "I could not bear, Mr. President, to confront some young man who would carry through life the marks of some disease contracted by him, through no fault of his own.") Russell couldn't get that amendment through the Senate, but he could keep the Administration from getting *its* amendment through; the President was finally forced to achieve integration through an executive order.

Of all Truman's other proposals—on desegregation of public facilities, on the FEPC, on the poll tax—not one got through the Senate in 1946, 1947, or 1948. With Russell basing his arguments on constitutional grounds ("We are not defending the poll tax as such. We are defending the rights of the States to govern their own elections and to keep Federal police and the Federal government away from the voting places. . . . The passage of these laws will strip the once-proud States of their last remaining rights . . ."), most proposals did not even make it to the floor; outmaneuvering the liberals with a parliamentary tactic they did not understand until it was too late, Russell ended the fight on the poll tax without it even coming to a vote.

As for the anti-lynching bill, what would be the sense of passing it in the House, asked the chairman of the House Judiciary Committee, since "it would be impossible to put [it] through in the Senate?" The anti-lynching bill died, and as southern prosecutors declined to indict and southern juries declined to convict, the policemen who gouged out the eyes went unpunished, as did the mob that shot the wives as well as the husbands, and the mobs that did not kill but only whipped and kicked. Under the leadership of Richard Brevard Russell Jr. the Senate was indeed the place where the South did not lose the Civil War. The great gifts for parliamentary rhetoric and maneuver, for personal leadership, of the "knightly" Richard Russell—his courtliness and graciousness, his moderation, his reasonable, genteel words—their cost had to be reckoned in tears and pain and blood. His charm was more effective than chains in keeping black Americans shackled to their terrible past.

OFTEN, DURING THE 1940S (as would also be the case during the 1950s and 1960s), Washington journalists would liken Richard Russell to the great general of the Lost Cause, the general who had been the young Dick Russell's hero, the general after whom a barefoot boy in Winder had named his fort. "A thin gray line is once again deployed against superior forces to resist what the Old South regards as an unwarranted assault on its way of life," as the *New York Times* put it during one senatorial civil rights battle. "The field general is a man whose dignity, integrity and high principle are recognized even by his opponents." Like "the Confederate commander of a century ago, Robert E. Lee, Richard Brevard Russell of Georgia is also a master of tactics and strategy and a much respected, even beloved adversary."

Russell accepted the comparison. His speeches were filled with what one reporter called "the words of war": "surrender," "treason," "appeasement," "retreat." "If we are overwhelmed," he said once, "you will find me in the last ditch." To Sam Ervin, he wrote, "Our position is desperate, for we are hopelessly outnumbered. But we are not going to yield an inch." And the comparison was apt—in more ways than some of the writers apparently realized. Lee was indeed the best of generals, military generals—but he was fighting in the worst of causes. Russell was the best of parliamentary generals.

But his cause was the same cause.

8

"We of the South"

THERE WAS ANOTHER motif as pervasive in Richard Russell's life as power, and it was loneliness.

Within the Senate world, there would for years be speculation about the reason that this man, who possessed "that persuasive charm that no woman can resist" had never married. Some said the explanation was Dick Russell's never-fading adoration for "the greatest woman I've ever known." At least one remark he made lent plausibility to another theory: that the explanation lay partly in his intense ambition, personal and political, both for himself and for his family, which had made him raise up early and never let drop the fallen banner of the Russells. Asked, when he was old, why he had never married, Russell replied to a reporter friend: "That's a question I've been asked many times, and I've asked *myself* many times. I think it was because I was too ambitious to start with. I wanted to be Governor of Georgia younger than any man had ever been in history . . . so I didn't marry until after I was elected, and somehow after that I didn't get around to it, didn't have time."

The denouement of the single episode in which Russell broke his lifelong pattern of "shying away from serious relationships" was viewed as support for this theory. During the 1930s, Russell and Patricia Collins, an Atlanta-born attorney for the Department of Justice in Washington, dated for three years, and were, acquaintances recall, obviously deeply in love. They set a wedding date. And then on the very eve of the wedding, it was canceled; Russell telephoned the editor of the *Atlanta Constitution,* which had already set the wedding announcement in type to run the next day, to ask him not to print it. Ms. Collins was a Catholic. In the highest circles of Georgia politics there were whispers that, at the very last moment, Richard Russell had finally bowed to the reality that, no matter how popular he might be, in a state with a Baptist-dominated, Catholic-hating Bible Belt, marrying a Catholic might end his political career. Russell and Ms. Collins continued to date frequently in Washington for several more years, and then less frequently, although they were still seeing each other when, in 1947, she told Russell she was going to marry someone else.

Nobody really knows the reason Dick Russell never married—perhaps not even he knew. But he knew the cost. When he was old, that reporter friend asked him whether perhaps it was fortunate that he had never married, and so had been able to concentrate fully on his work, and Russell answered, "Well, no—well, it certainly has permitted me to have more hours to work . . . but I would not recommend it to anyone. If I had my life to do over again, I would certainly get married."

In Winder, where his mother kept his room furnished as it had been furnished when he was a boy, and where, during the months he lived there every year, he often wandered around the house and the yard barefoot, as he had liked to wander barefoot as a boy, he had his family. His father, still Georgia's Chief Justice, had died in 1938, at the age of seventy-six—of a heart attack following a long day studying cases in his judicial office—and on a gentle hill behind the house, in a clearing surrounded by pines and red oak trees, Russell erected a gray granite obelisk, monumental in sleepy, small-town Barrow County, and wrote the inscription himself: "Richard Brevard Russell—Son of the Old South, Defender and Builder of the New." And he took his father's place at the head of the family table. At the sprawling Russell family gatherings, to which the other twelve children, each of them without exception a success in his or her chosen field, would bring their own children, "Uncle Dick," surrounded by scores of nephews and nieces, would preside—patriarch of the Russells, once again one of the first families of Georgia. He remained very close to his brothers and sisters; of his brother Robert E. Lee Russell, manager of his early political campaigns, he was to say, "We were about as close as two brothers could be." As for his mother, the flow of tender letters that had begun between them during his youth didn't stop when he was a senator. In 1952, the town of Winder held a parade in Ina Dillard Russell's honor; it was then, as her son rode beside her in an open car, that the newsreel camera for once caught, as pride and joy conquered reserve, a broad smile on Richard Russell's face. When she died, in 1953, to be buried with her husband under the same tall tombstone, he would draft her inscription: "There has never been a married relationship more tender than existed between this noble woman and her eminent husband." Thereafter, on his visits to Winder he lived alone in the big white frame house, tended by the family's elderly black housekeeper, and frequently walked up the hill in back, through pines and holly bushes, to the graveyard, and puttered around it for hours, plucking out weeds and neatening the plots, or just sitting there and thinking. He could think best there, he told a friend, close to his family. When years later, the Senator lay dying in Walter Reed Army Medical Center in Washington, and his brother Henry visited him, Dick told him of a thought that was comforting him—that perhaps dying meant that "we could run jump up in God's lap like we used to run jump up in Mother and Dad's lap when we were little boys."

And in Winder he had friends. So at ease was he in his hometown that, clad in a sweatshirt and stained dungarees, he would sit on a curb with old friends and chat with them for hours. "He just likes to talk," the editor of the *Winder News* explained. "If he has an enemy in Barrow County, I've never heard of it."

But Richard Russell seemed at home and at ease nowhere except in that little town. "He had warm feelings for individuals, but, outside of his family, he did not express them," says his biographer, Gilbert Fite. "He was not a man" who could talk about "his personal feelings." In Georgia—where he had been Speaker and Governor, and now, as senator, was known as "the Georgia Giant," where he was so respected that no politician dared to run against him—"he had a host of acquaintances and casual friends, and friends who would do almost anything for him," but "very few close or intimate friends."

And in Georgia, Dick Russell had been young. In Washington, he was growing older, and traits sometimes deepen, harden, as a man grows older, no matter how much he may wish them not to. "He became," as his biographer says, "somewhat more aloof."

"I had always been taught that if decent people asked you to come to their house you had to go," he was to recall, and for a few years after arriving in Washington in 1933, he accepted at least some of the invitations to parties and dinners that poured in on a bachelor senator. And, his hostesses said, when he wanted to be, there was no one who could be more urbane and charming. But gradually he accepted fewer and fewer invitations, and by the early 1940s he had all but stopped going to parties except for ones given by or for Georgians. Once, during the 1950s, a Washington reporter asked him exactly how often he did go to a party—cocktail or dinner. Leafing through his desk calendar, Russell discovered that he hadn't been to one for six months.

He stopped attending other social occasions, too. He had enjoyed hunting, for turkey, quail or deer—bird hunting was his favorite sport, and he owned five or six shotguns—and had regularly gone on hunting parties with old friends from Georgia. And he had enjoyed golf. But gradually he began finding excuses to decline invitations to hunting trips. "Frankly, I have no desire to kill more deer as I have killed more than twenty in my time," he said in response to one invitation. Gradually, he stopped playing golf. It took too much time, he said. As a young man, he had been a ladies' man; now he was an older bachelor. He still had dates, but less and less frequently.

With members of his staff, the reserve of this man so conscious of the dignity of a senator of the United States was especially marked. During his early years in the Senate, he had made attempts at camaraderie with his assistants and secretaries, but they were forced and didn't work out very well, and, year by year, they became fewer and fewer. Finally, he almost never joked with them, or even came out of his private office to wander around their work area; he was very formal in dealing with them. Women employees, his biographer says, "were 'Miss Margaret' or 'Miss Rachel' in the best traditional southern manner." Some of the members of his staff idolized him; they didn't want to leave him alone in the empty office, and although he never asked them to, when he stayed until six-thirty or seven, as he did most weekday nights, at least one of them would stay in case "the Senator wanted something." But when he would finish for the day, and take a bottle of Jack Daniel's out of his drawer and pour himself a drink, he almost never invited one of them in to have a drink with him. Occasionally, one of them would muster the courage to invite the Senator home for dinner; the acceptances were rare and the invitations grew rare, too.

With his fellow senators, he was invariably courteous, friendly, even cordial. But, more and more, as year followed year, that friendship also had a limit: the point at which intimacies, personal confidences, might have been exchanged but were not, because of the barrier around Richard Russell which was never lowered. He seemed unable to express affection, unable to talk about personal matters, to bridge the distance between himself and even a colleague he liked. The grave demeanor, the judiciousness and reserve, might bring him the respect of his colleagues; it did not make any of them his intimates.

He loved baseball, had in his head the day-to-day batting averages, not only of the Washington Senators but of an impressive number of players around the American League. A longtime tradition of the Senate was that on the season's opening day, senators who liked baseball (and a few selected functionaries such as Secretary of the Majority Felton [Skeeter] Johnston) would attend the game as a group. Russell, his aides say, had a wonderful time going to Opening Day with other senators, but, of course, that was a formal occasion, with the invitations made without any participation on his part being necessary. As for the rest of the season, members of his staff could have gone to games with him, just as they could have invited him to their homes, but one social occasion was as rare as the other. Sometimes the Senator went to a baseball game alone. It was embarrassing for such a man to be alone. If he was the renowned Richard Brevard Russell, the most powerful man in the Senate, why didn't he have anyone to go with? Would some colleague or staff member or acquaintance see him—and feel sorry for him, or tell people that Dick Russell went to baseball games alone? So Russell went to few baseball games.

WHEN THE SENATE was in session, of course, Russell's life was crowded with committee hearings and discussions about legislation and floor tactics, with professional give-and-take with his colleagues. But the Senate wasn't generally in session in the evenings, or on weekends.

The respect—almost awe—in which he was held made it difficult for his colleagues to invite him to their homes. He himself lived, during most of his years in Washington, in a small, two-room hotel suite, first in the Woodner

Hotel, then in the Mayflower; finally, in 1962, he moved into a small apartment, furnished as impersonally as a hotel room, in a cooperative apartment house on the Potomac.

In his hotel room or apartment, he would spend long hours reading, often with a cigarette and a glass of Jack Daniel's at hand, sometimes with the radio on. He still read the *Congressional Record* every day, and after he became a member of the Armed Services Committee he read not only the transcripts of the endless hours of testimony that the committee had taken, but the exhibits— the analyses and studies and charts—that witnesses had entered into the record to supplement their testimony, as well as classified Army, Navy and Air Force internal reports and memoranda. His apartment was filled with books, including a steady stream of books he requested from the Library of Congress; on many Fridays, a stack delivered from the Library for his weekend reading would be on the corner of his desk in the Senate, ready for him to take home. In the apartment, books, some opened, some with slips of paper sticking out of them to mark passages to which he wanted to refer, would be piled on the desk, on chairs, on the floor—mostly history and biography; during his early years in Washington, he read—again—Gibbon's complete *The Decline and Fall of the Roman Empire,* and in his later years, he read it through a third time.

His life fell into a pattern. He would arrive at the Senate early—at eight or eight-thirty in the morning—and eat breakfast alone in the Senate Dining Room. He would stay at the Senate late. After a day filled with Senate business, and punctuated by lunch at the round table in the dining room, the center of respectful attention whenever he spoke, he would return to his office at four or five o'clock to go through his mail, draft or dictate letters, and return telephone calls. By six-thirty or seven, he would be finished, and would take out the Jack Daniel's and water, and sip a drink or two while listening to the evening news on the radio, or, in later years, watching it on television. When the news was over, he would get up and leave, often through the door from his private office which opened directly onto the corridor, so that he would not have to make conversation with his staff. He generally ate at O'Donnell's Seafood Grill, on E Street, sitting alone at the counter. Then he would go back to his small apartment—that apartment where books were stacked on chairs on which no one ever sat; that apartment in which, unless he turned on the radio, there was no human voice—to spend the evening alone, reading.

"The Senate is my life and work," he told a reporter once. "I don't have any family or home life. If I don't get home till late, that's all right."

AFTER LYNDON JOHNSON'S DISCUSSION with Bobby Baker ("Dick Russell is *the* power"), in late December 1948, Johnson abruptly dropped his requests for a seat on Appropriations. There was, he would explain, only one way to get close to a man whose life was his work: "I knew there was only one way to see

Russell every day, and that was to get a seat on his committee. Without that we'd most likely be passing acquaintances and nothing more. So I put in a request for the Armed Services Committee." There was less demand for that committee than for Appropriations (or for Foreign Relations or Finance) and four vacant Democratic seats on it, and when, on January 3, the Senate was organized, and the list of Democratic Steering Committee assignments was read, he was given one of those seats. (His other committee was Interstate and Foreign Commerce, which under the chairmanship of Ed Johnson—"Mr. Wisdom"—supervised the oil and natural gas industries vital to Texas, and on which Johnson had an assignment to carry out for those industries in 1949.) Johnson threw himself into the Armed Services Committee's work, and he began dropping by Russell's office to discuss it.

At first, he would drop by only in the late afternoon, after the Senate had adjourned for the day. He was very deferential and formal in his approach. He would not ask the receptionist to tell Senator Russell he was there; instead, he would write a note asking if it would be convenient for Senator Russell to see Senator Johnson, and ask her to take it in. And he would keep the conversation focused on the committee's work, asking Russell questions about it, asking advice on how best to carry out some committee assignment he had been given. And he would listen to the answers, and listen hard. "If you saw them together, you would not see Johnson walking back and forth, and talking, like he usually did," John Connally says. "Russell would be doing the talking. He [Johnson] would be sitting quietly, listening, absorbing wisdom, very much the younger man sitting at the knees of the older man." Had the chairman of Johnson's other committee been given a nickname? The chairman of this committee wasn't neglected. Richard Russell, Johnson began saying, was "the Old Master." The phrase was used frequently—often to the Old Master himself. When Russell offered him a piece of advice, Lyndon Johnson would say, "Well, that's a lesson from the Old Master. I'll remember that."

After a while, the conversations no longer took place only in Russell's office. Russell would be drafting a committee report, or reading over one that he had assigned Johnson to work on, and there might be more work to do on it. Or there might be a line of questioning to be worked out for witnesses in the next day's hearings. Johnson would be helping. Why didn't they finish over dinner? he would suggest. Lady Bird had dinner waiting for him. It would be no trouble at all for her to put on another plate. It would make things easier all around. "You're gonna have to eat somewhere anyway," he would say. And after a few such invitations, Russell accepted one.

When the dinner guest at Thirtieth Place was Richard Russell, Lyndon Johnson's table manners would have pleased even his mother. Says Posh Oltorf, who was occasionally a fellow guest, "He was an entirely different person with Russell than he was ordinarily. There was no reaching, no slurping. Johnson was on his very best behavior."

At Thirtieth Place, moreover, Johnson had his great helpmate, and she was as valuable with Russell as she had been with Rayburn. The help was of a different kind, of course. The bond between Lady Bird Johnson and Sam Rayburn—lovingly daughterly on the one hand, lovingly paternal on the other—was the bond between a fierce, stern man whose fierceness and sternness concealed a terrible shyness and a young woman whose unwavering smile concealed a shyness and timidity just as terrible. And she saw Rayburn, whose portrait was the only one she would place in the living room of the Johnson Ranch, as the exemplar of all that was great in the common American people from which she, her husband, and the Speaker all sprang. Talking of "the Speaker," she says, with a passion very unusual for her: "He was the best of *us*—the best of simple American stock."

Richard Brevard Russell wasn't one of *us,* and had no desire to be, and Lady Bird's keen eyes saw it all in an instant. "I early knew that his father was, I think the chief judge in Georgia, and I remember a very patrician picture of him swearing in his young son, Dick Russell—and I would hear stories [from Georgians] of seeing the Russell family drive into town on a Saturday afternoon with Mrs. Russell sitting very erect and very starched, and extremely well groomed. . . . They were quality." When an interviewer from the Lyndon Johnson Library tries to suggest that her husband and Russell were intimates, Mrs. Johnson quietly sets him straight. "Senator Russell was always—there was a certain aloofness in him, it's my feeling," she says. "Although he had humor and he could have warmth, he was something of a loner. There was an aloofness, and you would be presumptuous to say, 'He's my best friend.' . . . He was a great friend, a dear friend, but he was not the sort of person with whom you could broach intimate things. . . ."

But the love Lady Bird Johnson had for Rayburn was no deeper than the respect she had for Russell. "He was a patriot right through and through," she says. "In appraising him I think you would have to get in the words, 'enormous sense of integrity.' . . . If he told you something, that was so." He was, she says, "a towering person. . . . I never looked at him without admiration." And of course Mrs. Johnson was a very southern woman, very devoted to the ideals and philosophy of the South, and, as she puts it, "Dick Russell was the archetype and bellwether of the South." And, in a way, the help Lady Bird gave her husband with his third *R* was the same she gave him with his second. No one, no matter how reserved, could remain untouched by the warmth with which Lady Bird Johnson would say, as she bid a guest good-bye, "Now you all come back again real soon, you hear." In both cases, her warm graciousness made a man who seldom visited other people's homes feel at home in hers, sufficiently at home so that he would come again and again.

The wisdom of Johnson's choice of committees—his insight that the only way to get to know Russell was to work with him—was documented, for, as Mrs. Johnson says, "As far as trying to sign him up for a dinner party three months in advance, I doubt if I'd have had much luck, or if I would have had the nerve to try. . . . He was always much sought after for parties, you know, and very unlikely to go. . . . He was our visitor so many times, but it was much more likely to be on the spur of the moment. They'd be working together on something and they would not be finished with it, and Lyndon would say something about, come on and go home with him, and Lady Bird will give us some— whatever we had. That was the way it usually happened." And when he got to the Johnsons, there would be, no matter what the hour, that wonderful welcoming smile.

If the hour wasn't too late, Lynda Bird and Lucy Baines would be awake. "He was always very nice to them and apparently at ease with them," Mrs. Johnson says. "And they remember him with affection." They called him "Uncle Dick" (their parents encouraged them to do so). But there are different types of uncles. "It was with just respect and affection, not intimacy," Mrs. Johnson says. "He did not wish to have too strong a tie to [people], in my opinion. Ties of family, dear Lord, he had them strongly and lovingly, but he just didn't go around becoming intimate with men, women or children." (Speaking of the entire twenty-year relationship between Richard Russell and the Johnsons, during which Russell made scores of visits to the Johnson home, the interviewer from the Johnson Library asked, "Did he ever bring little token-type gifts? I was just wondering, over the years did he bring any kind of little remembrance to you or the children?" "No, not that I remember," Mrs. Johnson replied.)

And after Spring arrived, occasionally, in the late afternoons, Lyndon Johnson would make another suggestion, one to which Russell always responded with uncharacteristic enthusiasm. Asked years later what drew the two men together, Russell mentioned first the sport he loved. "We both like baseball," he explained. "Right after he came to the Senate, for some reason we started going to the night baseball games together." Sometimes Lady Bird was invited to accompany them. "They would buy hot dogs . . . and sit and watch and talk about the prowess of this player or that player." And, she noticed, at baseball games Russell was less "aloof. . . . He really liked that." If no box seats were available, they would sit in the grandstand above the boxes—two tall men in double-breasted suits and fedoras, hot dogs in hands, sitting close together, talking companionably and laughing together.

Johnson's sudden interest in baseball surprised people aware of his previous total lack of interest in any type of sport. "I doubt that Lyndon Johnson had been to a baseball game in his life until he heard that Dick Russell enjoyed the sport," John Connally says. Connally, the only one of Johnson's aides who dared to joke with him, would say, " 'Well, I see you've become a baseball fan. Do you know the pitcher from the catcher?' He [Johnson] would smile and laugh, and say, 'You know I've always loved baseball.' I said, 'No, I've never been aware of that.' " But Connally understood: "He knew Dick Russell liked baseball games, so he went to games with Russell."

He began spending time with Russell not only after the Senate recessed for the day but before it convened. Although Johnson had generally eaten breakfast in bed ever since, with his wedding ceremony, he had acquired someone to bring it to him, he now began rising early and breakfasting in the senators' private dining room—as it happened, at the same hour that Russell ate breakfast there. More and more frequently, the two senators had breakfast together, discussing Armed Services Committee business.

And, more and more, he was spending time with Russell on weekends. Not many senators worked on Saturdays, but Russell did, of course, and Johnson did, too. Years later, he would say:

> With no one to cook for him [Russell] at home, he would arrive early enough in the morning to eat breakfast at the Capitol and stay late enough at night to eat dinner [at O'Donnell's]. And in these early mornings and late evenings I made sure that there was always one companion, one Senator, who worked as hard and as long as he, and that was me, Lyndon Johnson. On Sundays the House and Senate were empty, quiet and still, the streets outside were bare. It's a tough day for a politician, especially if, like Russell, he's all alone. I knew how he felt for I, too, counted the hours till Monday would come again and knowing that, I made sure to invite Russell over for breakfast, lunch, brunch or just to read the Sunday papers.

This necessitated some juggling because once Sam Rayburn had been the older man having brunch and reading papers with Lyndon, but the juggling was made easier by the fact that there was more than one meal on Sundays. During his last years in the House, Johnson had begun inviting a number of New Dealers—most of them Rayburn's friends, like Supreme Court Justice William O. Douglas and Tommy Corcoran and Jim Rowe—to Thirtieth Place for Sunday dinner. At seven o'clock he would switch on the radio so that they could all snarl at Drew Pearson's revelations about congressional activities. Rayburn enjoyed being one of that group, and had begun coming for dinner instead of brunch, so now Russell was invited for brunch, Rayburn for dinner. Frequent guests at Thirtieth Place noticed that, as Oltorf says, "You never, ever, saw them at Lyndon's house together." "Lyndon didn't want his two daddies to see how he acted with the other one," explains Jim Rowe.

Not all the time Johnson and Russell spent together on weekends was spent working, or reading the papers. For Russell found that this new senator from Texas shared—enthusiastically—some of his own interests. Those new enthusiasms that Johnson now revealed were as surprising to his assistants as his love for baseball. One, for example, was the War Between the States. All his life, Johnson had displayed a distaste for discussing history as intense as his antipathy for any subject that required reading: a feeling that went beyond lack of interest, and was disdain. That feeling had included the Civil War. Attempting to convince Lady Bird to marry him, he had assured her that "I shall take you . . . when you are mine" to the Civil War battlefields "and all of those most interesting places"; during the fifteen years since their wedding, she had been trying—in vain—to persuade him to take her at least once. Now Johnson told Russell that he had heard that Russell had a great familiarity with the battle-fields. He himself was fascinated with the tactics and the heroism that had been demonstrated on them, he said; the next time Russell visited one of them, he would certainly consider it an honor to be allowed to accompany him. And, on more than one occasion, he was.

Discussing in later years his early relationship with Russell, Johnson gave it a patina of generosity. "He was my mentor and I wanted to take care of him," he said. But contemporary witnesses to that relationship "snickered behind their hands," in the words of Bobby Baker, who says that Johnson was "press-ing an ardent courtship on" Russell. "He flattered him outrageously." Had Senator Russell been a woman, "He would have married him." But Johnson's courtship of older men had been the subject of snickers at San Marcos and in the House of Representatives, and those courtships had achieved their ends.

And, with Russell, too, as Baker also says, "there's absolutely no doubt that his campaign worked." When, years later, it was suggested to Russell that he and Johnson were dissimilar personalities, the Georgian replied, "Well, I suppose that's the public impression. Johnson and I had a good many things in common. . . . We just hit it off personally together." (The things they didn't have in common, and that might have repelled Russell, Johnson's iron self-control kept to a minimum when they were together; the inhaler, for example, was never in use in Russell's presence.) Within a remarkably short time after he was sworn in, this freshman senator was spending far more time than any other senator with the Senate's most powerful member.

But Russell wasn't Rayburn. Rayburn hungered, yearned, for love—for a wife, for children, in particular for a son. It wasn't a son that Richard Russell wanted, it was a soldier—a soldier for the Cause. Johnson may have made Rus-sell fond of him, but fondness alone would never have gotten Johnson what he wanted from Russell. As another southern senator, John Stennis of Mississippi, was to put it, Russell "wasn't a bosom friend with anyone when it came to . . . serious matters of government and constitutional principles." For Johnson to get what he wanted from Russell, he would have to prove to him that they had the same feelings on the issue that dominated Russell's life.

So Johnson's early efforts with Russell also included a speech. Delivered on Wednesday, March 9, 1949, it was his first speech on the Senate floor, and it was a major one: it took him an hour and twenty-five minutes, speaking in deliberate, grave tones, to read the thirty-five double-spaced typewritten pages that had been placed on the portable lectern that had been put on his desk. And it was delivered as a centerpiece of a southern filibuster against Truman's proposed civil rights legislation that would have given black Americans protection against lynching and against discrimination in employment, and that also would have made it easier for them to vote.

First, he defended the use of the filibuster. The strategy of civil rights advocates, he said, "calls for depriving one minority of its rights in order to extend rights to other minorities." The minority that would be deprived, he explained, was the South.

"We of the South who speak here are accused of prejudice," Lyndon Johnson said. "We are labeled in the folklore of American tradition as a prejudiced minority." But, he said, "prejudice is not a minority affliction: prejudice is most wicked and most harmful as a majority ailment, directed against minority groups." The present debate proved that, he said. "Prejudice, I think, has inflamed a majority outside the Senate against those of us who speak now, exaggerating the evil and intent of the filibuster. Until we are free of prejudice there will be a place in our system for the filibuster—for the filibuster is the last defense of reason, the sole defense of minorities who might be victimized by prejudice." "Unlimited debate is a check on rash action," he said, "an essential safeguard against executive authority"—"the keystone of all other freedoms." And therefore cloture—this cloture which "we of the South" were fighting—is "the deadliest weapon in the arsenal of parliamentary procedures." By using it, a majority can do as it wishes—"against this, a minority has no defense."

Then he turned to the substance of the legislation. Racial prejudice was not the issue, Lyndon Johnson said. Prejudice, he said, is "evil," and "perhaps no prejudice is so contagious or so dangerous as the unreasoning prejudice against men because of their birth, the color of their skin, or their ancestral background." And, he said, he himself was not prejudiced. "For those who would keep any group in our Nation in bondage, I have no sympathy or tolerance." But, he said, prejudice was not the reason that the South was fighting the civil rights bills.

> When we of the South rise here to speak against . . . civil rights proposals, we are not speaking against the Negro race. We are not attempting to keep alive the old flames of hate and bigotry. We are, instead, trying to prevent those flames from being rekindled. We are trying to tell the rest of the Nation that this is not the way to accomplish what so many want to do for the Negro. We are trying to tell the Senate that with all the sincerity we can command, but it seems that ears and minds were long ago closed.

He himself was opposed to the poll tax, Lyndon Johnson said, but the Constitution gave the states, not the federal government, the right to regulate elections, and Truman's anti–poll tax proposals were therefore "wholly unconstitutional and violate the rights of the States." He himself, "like all other citizens, detest[ed] the shameful crime of lynching," he said, "but we"—the southern senators—are trying to tell the other senators "that the method proposed in the civil rights legislation will not accomplish what they intend"; lynching is dying out; "I want to remind senators of the changing character of the South: an enlightened public already has rendered such a law virtually unnecessary even if it were not unwise in its scope."

At times, Johnson's rhetoric grew so impassioned that he went even further than the other southerners. He denounced the proposed FEPC, for example, in terms that seemed to suggest that it might lead to a return of something not far from slavery.

> It is this simple: if the Federal Government can by law tell me whom I shall employ, it can likewise tell my prospective employees for whom they must work. If the law can compel me to employ a Negro, it can compel that Negro to work for me. It might even tell him how long and how hard he would have to work. As I see it, such a law would do nothing more than enslave a minority.

So harmful would the proposed FEPC legislation be (it "would necessitate a system of Federal police officers such as we have never before seen. . . . It would do everything but what its sponsors intend. . . . It would do nothing more than resurrect ghosts of another day to haunt us again. It would incite and inflame the passions and prejudices of a people to the extent that the chasm of our differences would be irreparably widened and deepened") that, Johnson said, "I can only hope sincerely that the Senate will never be called upon to entertain seriously any such proposal again." And he presented one ingenious new rationale—a "novel argument," the *Washington Post* called it—to support the right to filibuster. In the recent presidential election, he said, Harry Truman had been far behind. "But there was no cloture rule on the man in the White House. There was no rule limiting him to an hour's debate because two-thirds of the Nation thought they had heard from him all they could hear, or all they wanted to hear." So Truman had kept talking. Because "Mr. Truman . . . dared to keep speaking, because Mr. Truman [did] not bow before the opinion of the majority . . . the people were listening and were changing their minds."

In general, however, his arguments were calm, reasonable, moderate. They were based on the constitutional rights of states and senators—in particular, in the case of senators, on the right to unlimited debate—and on the contention that civil rights legislation was not needed because the South was solving its racial problems on its own, and that such legislation would only inflame passions.

In later years, some journalists and historians would make much of his statements in his maiden Senate speech that his opposition to civil rights legislation was based not on racial prejudice but on constitutional grounds, that, as *Time* magazine put it, "He had no quarrel with the aims of civil rights advocates, only their methods." He had indeed said this—but so had Richard Russell. Johnson's arguments in his maiden speech closely mirrored the arguments Richard Russell had made familiar, the arguments Russell had persuaded southern senators to adopt, the arguments, reasonable-sounding but unyielding, that if accepted would leave southern black Americans as unprotected as they had always been against mob violence and intimidation, against discrimination in the workplace and in the general conditions of life, as unable as they had always been to vote as freely as white Americans.

Russell was very pleased with Johnson's speech. He had been given a copy of it on the previous day, and after reading it, he had contacted the other southern senators—telephoning many of them personally—to tell them he would appreciate their presence on the Senate floor when Johnson spoke. He had insured a high attendance in the Press Gallery by telling reporters that Johnson's maiden speech would be, as reporter Leslie Carpenter put it, "worth a story." When Johnson had finished speaking, and was standing for a moment taking sips of water from a glass a page had placed on his desk, the southern senators hurried over to congratulate him. A "long line" of southerners "formed to shake [Johnson's] hand," a reporter wrote. Russell was the first man on it. Johnson's speech, Russell was to say, was "one of the ablest I have ever heard on the subject."

LYNDON JOHNSON'S MAIDEN SPEECH was delivered during one of the century's most bitter civil rights battles, for Truman's dramatic 1948 election victory—after a campaign during which his commitment to civil rights never wavered, a campaign, furthermore, in which black voters played a newly important role in key northern cities—had combined with the Democratic recapture of Congress and the arrival on Capitol Hill of aggressive civil rights advocates like Hubert Humphrey and Paul Douglas, plus a rising public outcry against Jim Crow, to give liberals confidence that the long-awaited day of social justice was at last at hand, that Congress's Southern Bloc could no longer stand in its way. "The President can get most of his program, and without so much compromise, if he constantly calls upon the great public support manifest for him in this election," the liberal columnist Thomas L. Stokes wrote. Even Arthur Krock agreed that this time "it seems improbable that" the southern citadel could stand.

But as the southern senators realized when they caucused on January 13, their general was ready. He saw the cause in which he was fighting as holy, and he was ready to battle for it. Yes, Richard Russell told a reporter, the odds against the South were indeed long. "It is clear that the only thing we can do now is to gird our loins and shout the cry of centuries: 'The enemy comes: to our tents, O Israel!' " And he was armed with more than battle cries. No sooner had Truman won than Russell had begun throwing up his breastworks; even before the Senate convened, his aides were drawing up a list of all federal laws that would expire during the first six months of 1949 so that, as he would later explain, he would "know if there are any of them of any importance that will build up a logjam of discussion behind . . . the civil rights bills"—in other words, any whose passage the Administration could not afford to have delayed, so that threat of delay in general Senate activity by a civil rights filibuster would be more effective. And this scouting expedition found pay dirt: federal rent control laws—the only protection against exorbitant rents for millions of families in northern cities—were scheduled to expire on March 31. If the southerners could hold the floor into March, pressure would mount on northern senators to surrender on civil rights so that a bill extending rent control could be brought to the floor and passed. And there were other Administration proposals—to repeal Taft-Hartley, to continue the European Recovery Program, to strengthen NATO—that could not move along the legislative path so long as southerners held the floor, and that could therefore be held hostage to civil rights; Russell "made it clear that if Truman and his legislative leaders pushed any plan to [impose] cloture, the President's entire legislative program might be in jeopardy." The great general renewed his old alliances, including the one that consisted of a "wink and a nod." The fervently isolationist Robert Taft wanted something: the defeat or reduction of Truman's proposals for international cooperation and mutual aid. Although Russell was, of course, no isolationist, *The Nation* now reported that "a number of former influential internationalists and interventionists are modifying their position" to conform to Taft's; these internationalist senators were southerners. When an amendment was introduced to reduce Truman's proposed budget for the European Recovery Program, Senate observers understood at once that the vote on this amendment would be crucial, for, as one wrote, "it will forecast the Senate's position on other questions of foreign policy." And the amendment's sponsors were Taft—and Russell. The price for Russell's support, *The Nation* was to explain, was "Taft's help in scuttling the civil rights program."

Taft was the bellwether for about half the Republican senators; the bellwether for the other half was Vandenberg. As the Senate's president *pro tempore* in 1948, Vandenberg, citing those loopholes in Rule 22, had said that "the integrity of congressional procedures" gave him "no alternative" to ruling against liberal attempts to impose cloture. He said that while cloture could be applied on a debate on a bill that was already on the floor, it could not be applied on a debate on a motion to bring a bill *to* the floor (a ruling which of course made the threat of cloture almost totally ineffective).

The way to keep Vandenberg as an ally, Russell told his southerners, was to make the 1949 cloture vote a vote on the validity of Vandenberg's 1948 ruling, which the Republicans who respected the old senator would be reluctant to repudiate. Moreover, so long as Vandenberg held to his position on cloture, his towering reputation would give other Republicans the screen of parliamentary complexity when they voted against cloture, and their support would allow the southerners to hold the floor. Therefore, Russell told his troops, the emphasis in the 1949 battle must be kept on the point that Vandenberg had emphasized: the right of unlimited debate. Their self-discipline must be tighter than ever; in their speeches they must limit the irrelevancies. As soon as the Administration brought up any motion to make the civil rights bill the pending business of the Senate, or to strengthen Rule 22, the southerners must take to the floor—and keep the debate on that one point. Russell's strategy worked. As the Administration's plan to reverse the cloture ruling became apparent, *The New Republic* would report that Vandenberg was "working busily behind the scenes to vindicate his original decision."

In addition, like the incomparable legislative strategist he was, Russell made his first stand not on the civil rights bill, and not on the motion to take up the bill. Majority Leader Lucas, with the full weight of the White House behind him, had made a motion to change the Senate rules to allow cloture to be applied on a motion to take up a bill. The southerners launched a filibuster on *that* motion. This gave the South one additional line of defense. Should it be lost, there would still be two other positions to fall back to.

And the South didn't lose. Public pressure for cloture—for civil rights—mounted steadily. There were black faces in the Senate corridors. The NAACP announced that its secretary, Walter F. White, "has virtually moved to Washington to talk with the necessary people." Editorialists raged. But somehow the votes to invoke cloture were never there, and after weeks of skirmishing, the focus was shifting to the implications of the filibuster for rent control and other bills, and Lucas was confessing that the "logjam" on Senate business was intolerable. "The filibuster could go on for weeks," the Majority Leader said, and while it was going on, "rent control would go out the window"—and other major bills might not come to a vote, either.

Then, the day after Lyndon Johnson gave his maiden speech, Vice President Barkley, presiding over the Senate, ruled that cloture could be applied to a motion. Russell instantly appealed, called for a vote, and, reading previous cloture precedents, said that Barkley was wrong and Vandenberg right—that Vandenberg's ruling had in fact been a model of statesmanship and wisdom. Vandenberg then rose to reply to Barkley, and said that while he was in favor of civil rights legislation and wanted to change Rule 22, the way to change the rule was "not simply to disregard what it clearly meant," as Barkley had done. "Under such circumstances there [would be] no rules, except the transient, unregulated wishes of a majority," he said. The only way to change the rules, he said, was through the method authorized by the rules—Rule 22, actually—through a two-thirds cloture vote.

With that speech, the fight was over. Walter White heard it "with sinking heart." "Mr. Vandenberg has . . . given an aura of respectability to those who wanted an excuse," he said. When the vote was taken on Barkley's ruling, Russell had twenty-three Republican votes to go with twenty-three Democratic votes, for a total of forty-six. The pro–civil rights vote was forty-one.

The embattled group of southern senators had won—and they knew whom they owed their victory to. "With less than 25 percent of the membership of the Senate, the Southerners have won one of the most notable victories in our history," Harry Byrd wrote Virgil Chapman. "The credit goes mainly, of course, to our great leader, Dick Russell. . . . I do not think that even Robert E. Lee . . ."

A great general does not allow a vanquished enemy to escape from the battlefield, and with the votes in his pocket, Richard Russell was in a position to exact vengeance on those who had dared to try liberalizing the cloture rule. Suggesting "to his cohorts that the opposition be taught a lesson," as one writer put it, he pushed through the Senate a "compromise" on cloture. Under it, cloture could in the future be applied to motions as well as to bills. But under it, also, cloture would no longer require only the votes of two-thirds of senators present, which had been the requirement in the past—a requirement that would, if only a bare quorum of forty-nine senators were present, have allowed cloture to be imposed by as few as thirty-three votes. Under Russell's "compromise," cloture would now require, no matter how many senators were present, the votes of two-thirds of the entire Senate—sixty-four votes. After Truman's victory, after all the rising hopes for civil rights, not only did the Senate citadel against civil rights still stand, its walls were actually higher than before.

In later years, it would become an accepted part of the Lyndon Johnson legend that, apart from his maiden speech, he distanced himself from the southern fight in 1949. He gave the impression—an impression accepted by historians—that he refused to become part of the Southern Caucus that met under Russell's leadership. After her extensive conversations with Johnson, Doris Kearns Goodwin wrote that "he decline[d] Russell's invitation to join the Southern Caucus." In their biography of Johnson, Evans and Novak wrote that "In his first weeks as a Senator . . . Johnson made clear that he would not attend the Southern Caucus." And this belief is understandable, not only because of the convincingness with which Johnson made his statements, but because of statements by William H. Darden, who was one of Russell's secretaries from 1948 to 1951 and later became an ally of Johnson's. (As President, Johnson appointed Darden a judge.) Darden said flatly in an oral history interview with the Lyndon Johnson Library that "Senator Johnson did not participate in that Southern Caucus." And when the author interviewed him in 1986, he said flatly, "I was the one who would notify the southern senators of the meetings. Russell always told me to say there will be a meeting of the 'constitutional Democrats.' I would not call Lyndon Johnson. Russell would tell me who to call."

Because of his determination to become President, Johnson was certainly desperate to avoid being identified with the Caucus. Once, returning to his office at about the time a Caucus meeting ended, he was unexpectedly confronted in the corridor outside the main door to 231 by an Associated Press reporter. When the reporter began asking him about the Caucus, Johnson moved past him and opened the door. When the reporter began to follow him through it, Johnson pushed it shut and held it closed against the reporter's efforts to open it. An astonished Connally and Busby saw the Senator bracing himself against the door while saying loudly, "No, no. No, no." "After he got the door shut," Busby says, "he turned and went into his [private] office." Summoning Busby, he explained, "That little shit from the AP wanted me to comment."

But Johnson's later contention that he had refused to join the Southern Caucus would have come as a shock to Richard Russell, had he been alive to read it. While Russell *was* alive—in 1971, shortly before his death—an interviewer said to him, "I read where he [Johnson] would not attend your southern conference." Russell interrupted to correct him. "Yes, he did," he said. "Yes, he did. He did attend it. He attended all of them until he was elected Leader."

Russell furnished the interviewer with details of his typically unpressuring invitation to Johnson to attend. "I called him and said, 'Now we're having this meeting on this and I don't want to embarrass you—I don't know what your views are on this, but I want to tell you about the meeting and invite you if you want to come, but if you don't want to come, nobody but you will ever know that I ever called you.' Well, that made a tremendous impression on Johnson—he hadn't been accustomed to that kind of policy . . . well, he came to the meeting. . . ."

In fact, it appears that Russell was mistaken in saying that Johnson attended all the Southern Caucuses. After one, on January 12, 1949, Russell told *New York Times* reporter Clayton Knowles that Johnson had not attended because he was "at another committee meeting." There is, however, reason to believe that Johnson attended at least some meetings of the Southern Caucus. The Russell Library in Athens, Georgia, says that Russell's papers contain no lists of the names of the senators who attended the various Southern Caucuses, and the author has not been able to find a list in any newspaper. And the total number of senators who attended each meeting not infrequently varies from newspaper to newspaper. But after one caucus in February, 1949, the *New York Times* reported that "twenty-one [Southern Democrats] met in Russell's office." The *Times* did not name the twenty-second southerner, but all news accounts agree that the liberal Florida Senator Claude Pepper was never invited to Southern Caucus meetings. During the 1949 fight, a second southerner—Estes Kefauver of Tennessee—announced that he would not support the southern stand on cloture. The *New York Times* article on the next Southern Caucus did not specifically give the number of senators who attended, but said, "The caucus counted two of the twenty-two southern senators—Pepper and Kefauver—

as lost and gone over to the . . . opposition." The *Washington Post* article said, "Southern senators caucused," and "some twenty Southern senators are" united against cloture. And while it may (or may not) have been true that Judge Darden didn't call Johnson's office, *someone* called. Mary Rather would make an entry on Johnson's Desk Diary when she was notified that a Caucus was scheduled. In the early days of 1949 alone, she made such entries for February 11, February 24, March 1, March 5, March 11, March 14 and March 15, sometimes entering them as "Meeting of Southern Senators," sometimes referring to them by the phrase Russell preferred: for example, "Saturday, March 5—10:30 AM, Constitutional Democrats Meeting." And she told the author that while Johnson didn't attend all the southern meetings, "I'm sure he attended some of them."

And Johnson's contention would have come as a shock to journalists who, over the years, interviewed southern senators about him, for these senators told them that Johnson had attended some of the Caucuses. In 1958, members of *Time* magazine's Washington bureau interviewed a number of southern senators for a cover story on Johnson, and the story dealt with the matter this way: "During his first Senate days he was invited to a Southern caucus by . . . Russell. There was an argument over Southern strategy in fighting a proposed change in the Senate's cloture rule, and Johnson sided with Russell, who was both pleased and impressed." *Time* correspondent James L. McConaughy had been told about the same incident in 1953, apparently by Russell himself. He reported that "Russell knew little about Johnson until he invited him one day to attend a caucus of Southern senators . . . There was a fight over strategy; Johnson sided with Russell." In 1963, journalist Margaret Shannon was to write in the *Atlanta Constitution* that "authoritative sources say"—she does not identify the sources, but from the story they appear to be sources close to both Johnson and Russell—that Johnson had, at one early meeting of the Caucus, seen with his own eyes (and been deeply impressed by) the accuracy of Bobby Baker's statement that "Dick Russell was *the* power." Shannon wrote that "At the first Southern Caucus that Johnson attended, Senator Russell had occasion to chew out Texas' then senior senator, Tom Connally, as no other Texan would have dared to do and as perhaps no other senator would have dared to, either."

The contention that Johnson was distancing himself from the southern fight would also have come as a shock to the southern senators; on March 7, 1949, John Stennis, for example, replied to a correspondent who inquired about Johnson's role: "Senator Lyndon Johnson is cooperating fully with us in this fight to prevent the adoption of the cloture rule."

ALL THROUGH 1949, the fight went on. Victory did not lessen Russell's vigilance; look what had happened at Antietam! And in June, the need for vigilance was demonstrated. Another anti-lynching bill, Russell noticed, had been quietly slipped onto the Senate Calendar. The general decided to post sentries.

"In view of our experience in the past when one of these bills was almost passed by unanimous consent due to the absence from the floor of all Senators opposing it . . . one Senator from the South" must be "responsible for watching the floor each day to see that no legislative trickery is employed to secure the passage of any of these bills," Russell wrote to the members of the Southern Caucus. The schedule for this "guard duty," Russell said, would be drawn up by his aide William Darden. Johnson was one of those sentries. "Relative to my 'guard duty,' I will do my best when Mr. Darden notifies me," Johnson replied. And even on the most controversial measures, Johnson's vote was a vote of which Russell could be confident. In May, for example, he voted for the passage of an amendment, proposed by Bilbo's successor, James Eastland of Mississippi, to the District of Columbia Home Rule Bill. The amendment would have made segregation by race mandatory in public accommodations in the nation's capital.

And, of course, during all these months, not only while the Senate was in session but in the evenings and on weekends, Richard Russell was spending a lot of time alone with Lyndon Johnson. We do not know what these two men talked about, but we do know that Russell, a notably sharp-eyed observer of his colleagues—and a man who on racial matters was the most suspicious of men—had no suspicions at all about Lyndon Johnson. He had not the slightest doubt about Johnson's feelings about civil rights, about his loyalty to the Cause. "This great movement to [restrict] cloture—Johnson stood right with us on that," Russell was to say. "Our political philosophy was very closely parallel."

All that year, moreover, there were the baseball games, the dinners and Sunday brunches at the Johnson home, the outings to the Civil War battlefields. All that year, the two men were working together on Armed Services Committee matters. And when Johnson had a problem in some other area of Senate business, he would ask Russell's advice. "In a way without boasting because he was a new senator then and I had been there for years, he kind of put himself under my tutelage, or he associated himself with me you might say—that sounds better, I hope you can use that," Russell would tell an interviewer.

Johnson's attentions to him, his courtship, flattered and pleased Russell not only emotionally, of course, but, more importantly, in an intellectual, dispassionate way. Russell, after all, had himself zeroed in on power in the Senate from the moment of his arrival there, and was, in his coolly rational way, very aware of his own position in the Senate. He understood Johnson's tactics and appreciated them. "Senator Russell was extremely favorably impressed by how he just got started on the right foot and seemed to know where the sources of power were, and how to proceed," Darden would say.

Russell was also impressed by other qualities that Johnson possessed: his diligence, for one. Russell had little patience with colleagues not familiar with all the facts regarding a piece of legislation. Men had said of Richard Russell that he read the *Congressional Record* every day; now men were saying that about Lyndon Johnson. No one could fool a senator who worked as hard as did Russell about how hard another senator was working, and he saw that now, at last, there was another senator who worked as hard as he. He was impressed— this general who worried that he was letting down his Cause by not being sufficiently in tune with the modern age—by "how well-organized his [Johnson's] office was"; he was impressed by Johnson's energy and drive, by how he got things done.

Lyndon Johnson, Richard Russell was to say, "was a can-do young man." He had played tutor or patron to other young senators, he was to say; Johnson "made more out of my efforts to help him than anyone else ever had." The master legislator, the matchless parliamentarian, knew that there was another master in the Senate now.

9

Thirtieth Place

WHEN LYNDON JOHNSON called Lady Bird to tell her he would be bringing Dick Russell home for dinner in a few minutes, she always had something ready for them to eat. She had something ready every evening, no matter how late the hour, for she never knew when Lyndon would call to say, "I'll be home in twenty minutes. We've got four guests for dinner," and when he got home, he didn't want to be kept waiting. As he walked through the door, he would say without preamble, "We're hungry, Bird. Let's get dinner on the table." He had been doing this for years, often calling just as he was leaving his office, four guests—or six or eight—in tow.

Having something ready was easier now, for with the money rolling in from the Austin radio station they had bought in 1943, they had hired a cook, a young African-American woman from Texas, Zephyr Wright. But Johnson had begun bringing guests home before 1943—before they had even owned a house, in fact: while they were still living, without any domestic help, in an apartment on Connecticut Avenue—and Lady Bird had always had something ready then, too, along with her warm, welcoming smile. And often her husband didn't want a simple dinner. "I'm bringing four guests home tonight," he would say. "Let's have something special." And if he didn't consider it special enough, his temper would boil over. One year, he had announced in advance that he would be bringing Sam Rayburn home on the Speaker's birthday. "The dinner was turkey hash," recalls the journalist Margaret Mayer, who was temporarily working for Johnson and living at Thirtieth Place at the time, "and Lyndon flew into a rage—a *rage!* 'What do you mean serving turkey hash for Mr. Sam's birthday?' " (Mr. Sam said, " 'If I had my choice of anything I could have, there is nothing I'd rather have for my birthday than Zephyr's turkey hash,' " Ms. Mayer recalls. "That stopped *that* explosion.") And there were the meals with staff members—his own staff, or lower-ranking officials in government agencies whom Johnson needed for something at the moment; "Lady Bird makes me feel as important as Chief Justice [Frederick] Vinson when she introduces me to him," one lower-level bureaucrat commented. On Sundays, of course, Russell would come for brunch, and Rayburn for dinner—along with the group of Rayburn's friends—and if the men stayed up in the study after Drew Pearson's broadcast talking politics into the evening, Lyndon would come to the top of the stairs and shout down, "Bring us up some sandwiches, Bird." ("By God, he's gonna kill her!" Rayburn once muttered to his nephew Robert Bartley but, holding the husband-wife bond sacrosanct, he almost never interfered between the Johnsons.)

The relationship of Lady Bird (that nickname had been given Claudia Alta Taylor at the age of two by a black nurse because "She's purty as a lady bird") and her husband was, in 1949, the same as it had been since their marriage in 1934—although there were reasons why it might have changed. Readers of the earlier volumes of this work will perhaps remember her painful shyness and loneliness as a young girl. (Her mother had died when she was five; her father, a tall, coarse, ham-handed cotton gin owner, the richest man in his East Texas town, had little interest in his daughter.*) In high school, she was to remember, "I hoped no one would speak to me"; she dreaded so deeply the prospect of standing up in front of an audience that she prayed she would finish no higher than third in her graduating class since the first two students had to give speeches—she prayed that if she did finish first or second, she would get small-pox so that she wouldn't have to speak. (She finished third.) At college, she was a lonely young woman—plain and almost dowdy in dress—who, a friend says, was "so quiet she never seemed to speak at all," and as the wife of Congressman Lyndon Johnson her shyness had kept her from giving even the brief talks expected from a congressman's wife; at the mere suggestion that she give one, friends recall, there was real panic in her face; when she could not avoid standing in a receiving line, her friends winced at the effort it cost her to shake hands with strangers, so rigid was the bright smile she kept on her face. She played almost no part in her husband's political life; he didn't even tell her he was going to run for the Senate in 1941 until after he had announced the fact to the rest of the world in a press conference. And readers may remember the contempt, indeed cruelty, with which her husband treated her, humiliating her in public, this woman who had an almost visible terror of having attention called to herself—how at parties he shouted at her across crowded rooms ("Bird, go get me another piece of pie." "I will, in just a minute, Lyndon." *"Get me another piece of pie!"*), how he publicly mocked her appearance, often comparing her to her friend, John Connally's beautiful wife Nellie ("That's a pretty dress, Nellie. Why can't you ever wear a dress like that, Bird?" "You look so muley, Bird. Why

---

*Johnson's previous serious romances had been with two young women whose fathers had each been the richest men in *their* respective towns. At college he had boasted so openly about his determination to marry money that that desire was recorded in print in the college yearbook. While a congressional assistant, he proposed to Lady Bird on their first date.

can't you look more like Nellie?" "Get out of those funny-looking shoes, Bird. Why can't you wear pretty shoes like Nellie?").

And for years there had been that extramarital affair that was so special in Lyndon Johnson's life. The fact that Alice Glass was the lover (and later the wife) of a man as important to Johnson's career as Charles Marsh was one reason that the few men and women aware of the affair between Lyndon and Alice felt, as did John Connally, that it was "unlike any other" in which he engaged. They agree that it juts out of the landscape of his life as one of the few episodes that ran counter to his personal ambition. "Knowing Lyndon, I could hardly believe he was taking a chance like that," says Harold H. Young, a member of the Longlea "circle," who was later to marry Alice's sister, Mary Louise Glass. "It just didn't fit in with the Lyndon Johnson I knew." And then there was the fact that, as John Connally was to recall, "He guarded the secrecy of that relationship. He never talked about her, never revealed his feelings—that alone set it apart. It was the most intense and longest-lasting of any affair he engaged in." Noticing that Lyndon came to Longlea weekend after weekend, sometimes with Lady Bird and sometimes with Lady Bird remaining in Washington, and seeing the young congressman, normally so restless, sitting quietly staring at Alice as she read poetry, the members of the Longlea circle speculated that Alice's feelings were reciprocated and that she had reason for her belief that Lyndon would divorce Lady Bird and marry her.

In 1941, the alacrity with which Johnson jumped into the Senate race made Alice feel that her lover's political ambitions would always be put ahead of his feelings. In 1942, Johnson, a lieutenant commander in the Naval Reserve, went to the West Coast, leaving with his staff and constituents—and with Alice—the impression that he was en route to active service in a Pacific combat zone. He invited Alice out for a visit, however, and she realized that in fact combat service was not in his plans. In a letter years later, she told a friend, "I can write a very illuminating chapter on his military career in Los Angeles, with photographs, letters from voice teachers, and photographers who tried to teach him which was the best side of his face." An idealist who had believed that Johnson was an idealist ("She thought he was a young man who was going to save the world," her sister says), Alice "was disgusted, just disgusted with him after that trip." The intense, "sexual side" of their relationship ended, Mary Louise says, although all during the 1950s he would from time to time make the hour-and-a-half drive to Longlea. And it was in 1945, of course, that Lyndon met Helen Douglas. Lady Bird was, in the opinion of the Longlea circle, a drab little woman whom no one listened to.

Readers may also recall, however, that throughout Lady Bird Johnson's life, there had been hints of something more—of ambition, of determination, and of dignity: when her husband would bellow orders at her across a room or insult her, she would say simply, "Yes, Lyndon," or, "I'll be glad to, Lyndon," and would carry out his request as calmly as if it had been polite and reasonable, doing so with a poise that was rather remarkable in the circumstances. And there were hints of courage as well: suddenly thrust into her husband's political world when, after Pearl Harbor, he went into the service and she was forced, on one day's notice, to take over his congressional office, she not only did so, but did so very well, nerving herself to deal with constituents and Cabinet officers, pestering them when necessary ("The squeaking wheel gets the grease, I learned") to get things done for the district that Lyndon would have gotten done. Sometimes when Lady Bird had to call someone like "that formidable man, Mr. Ickes," Mary Rather, glancing into Lyndon's office, would see her staring at the telephone on Lyndon's desk, "looking as if she would rather have done anything in the world than pick up that phone and dial," but she always picked it up and did what had to be done, and did it with an unexpected graciousness and poise—and efficiency—that led constituents to joke that maybe she should be the congressman, and that led Nellie Connally to say, "She changed, but I think it was always there. I just don't think it was allowed out."

After Johnson returned to Congress, it was again not allowed out. Notably unamused by the jokes—obviously jealous—he not only relegated her to her old housewife's role, but took pains to put to rest the notion that her role in his office had been significant. Asked once if he discussed political problems with her, he said that "of course" he did. "I talk my problems over with a lot of people," he added. "I have a nigger maid, and I talk my problems over with her, too." After the purchase of radio station KTBC, while for public consumption Lady Bird was listed as the station's president and was said to be in charge of its operations and responsible for its success, in reality the success was due to Johnson's political influence, and to the fact that he sold that influence to individuals and corporations in return for their purchase of advertising time on the station. In truth, he oversaw, in detail, every aspect of KTBC's operations, often during these years without consulting more than cursorily with his wife. At the same time that he was telling the public that she was running the station, he was telling their friends—often in her presence, as she sat silently, not contradicting—that he was running it, making clear that her role in it was a minor one.

Now, in 1949, with Lyndon Johnson in the Senate, Lady Bird's duties hadn't changed. She no longer brought him breakfast in bed every morning, but she still laid out his clothes, unbuttoning his shirts so that he wouldn't have to perform that chore himself, put in the collar stays and cuff links, filled his fountain pens and put them in the proper pocket, filled his cigarette lighter and put it in its pocket, and put his handkerchief and money in their pockets. While he was shaving, she took dictation. Her other duties, too, remained the same as ever. As soon as he left for Capitol Hill, she would call his office to ask "Who's in town from Texas today?" If any of the visitors merited a tour, she would take them on it; she was to say that she had stopped counting her trips to Mount Vernon when the number passed two hundred. Or she might invite other visitors to lunch.

Nor had there been any change in Lyndon's treatment of her, which was still so abusive that people who witnessed it say, "You couldn't believe it." Orders were as brusque as ever. "Bird, go in and fix us something to eat," or, if he wanted her out of the room when a delicate political matter was being discussed, a dismissive "See you later, Bird." If, on a day on which he had told her in the morning that they were having guests to dinner, she ventured to call his office in the evening to ask when he might arrive, the reaction was swift. "Goddammit, tell her that I'll be leaving when I'm done here," he would snarl to Jenkins or Rather. "Tell her to quit calling every fucking five minutes. Now go phone her and tell her that." When, at Thirtieth Place, he wanted something from her and she wasn't in the room, he would shout for her—"Birrrrdd!"—in a voice one guest likened to a hog call. He told stories about her to amuse his friends, some the kind that many husbands tell about their wives, except that Johnson told them with a cutting scorn in his voice. Once when she got home from a shopping expedition after he was already there and talking with some friends, he said, "Well, Bird, did you wear out another four dollars' worth of shoe leather shoppin' around to save a dime?" He still mocked her appearance in front of friends, comparing it unfavorably to theirs. "Look at your hair, Bird," he said once, in a tone of disgust. "You look like a tumbleweed. Why can't you look nice, like Mary Louise here?" "He said it right in front of everyone," Mary Louise said. "I couldn't even look at her." "His attitude towards her was utter contempt," says his fellow congressman, the West Texan O. C. Fisher. In comments that are typical of many made by social friends of the Johnsons, Wingate Lucas of Fort Worth, who was elected to Congress in 1948 and saw them frequently, says, "Lady Bird was charming, but she was the most beaten-down woman I ever saw. You immediately felt sorry for her. Her husband was so mean to her, so publicly humiliating. He would dismiss what she said with a disgusted wave of his arm: 'What do you mean, Bird? That's ridiculous.' He'd shout across the room at her at parties of Texas people—friends of hers—and just order her to do something." Says her friend Mary Elliott: "He'd just click his fingers. *'Bird!'* She'd have to stop whatever she was doing, and just come running. I never saw anything like it." The tone he used with his wife was, in short, the same as he used with the staff in his office on Capitol Hill; he treated her as if she had been just another member of that staff—and not a particularly valuable one at that. "The women liked her," Nellie Connally says. "Every woman sympathized with her. If they didn't like her for herself—and they did—they liked her because they saw what she had to put up with. It made what they had to put up with not so bad." A researcher trying to get a picture of the Johnsons hears, over and over, the same phrase: "I don't know how she stood it."

But she did stand it, and in fact her devotion to him—her love for him—seemed only to grow stronger. He had only to put his arm around her for her face to grow noticeably happier. There was obviously a strong physical tie between them. Stuart Symington was struck by two incidents that occurred in

1951 while he and the Johnsons and Mary Rather were having dinner in the little back yard behind the Thirtieth Place house. "Lady Bird said, 'Stu, have another little piece of chicken,' and I said, 'Thanks but I've had all I can eat,' and she said, 'Oh, please, have just one more piece'—and Johnson blew. '*Goddammit,* Bird, leave the man alone! Didn't you hear what he said? Goddammit, the man doesn't want any more chicken! *Goddammit!*' And I never forgot it, he was so brutal with her." But that same year, Symington visited the Johnsons in Texas, and they drove out to the Hill Country for a picnic and while they were sitting on a blanket, Lyndon "said to her, putting his arm around her, 'Let's jest do a little 'spoonin' '—and the light in her face was something to see." Whatever the reasons, her adoration for her husband was visible to everyone. Once her biographer, Jan Jarboe Russell, asked her if she resented doing menial chores for him—bringing him breakfast in bed, etc. "Heavens, no," Lady Bird replied. "I was delighted to do it. I adored him."

THE MODEST HOUSE on Thirtieth Place seemed too small for its furniture. Not long after the Johnsons had purchased it, Lyndon, annoyed by the amount of time Lady Bird was taking to pick out furniture, went to an auction one day and purchased an entire houseful. But the furniture—large, heavy Victorian pieces—was evidently from a much larger house. Lady Bird had thereafter decorated "every inch of that house," as Elizabeth Rowe would recall; in the rather small dining room, for example, not only the windows but a wall mirror were hung with heavy red draperies. And the house seemed too small for all the people who lived in it—not only the Johnsons and their two girls but also Zephyr Wright and a changing cast of staff members and visitors from Texas who slept up on the third floor; "Texas friends descend on them all hours of every day, and stay for a drink, a meal, or a week," a journalist wrote. "Lady Bird takes it in stride." And it seemed too small for the man around whom life in it revolved.

The clock radio beside Lyndon Johnson's bed was set for seven-thirty, but on most days the bedside buzzer with which he called for breakfast rang down in the kitchen well before that time; it wasn't an alarm that jerked Lyndon Johnson out of sleep. He would often have made several calls to his assistants during the night when he thought of things that needed doing, and he would wake up thinking of more; as he lay in bed eating the breakfast that Ms. Wright had brought up on a tray—usually a Texas grapefruit, toast, and a big plate of spicy Hill Country sausage—drinking innumerable cups of coffee, and lighting the first of the day's cigarettes, he would be telephoning assistants at their homes and, at about eight, telephoning SOB 231 to see what the morning's mailbag had brought. And he would be reading: not only the *Washington Post and Times-Herald,* and the *New York Times,* but the *Congressional Record.* (Each day's *Record,* covering the previous day's activities, was printed at about six o'clock in the morning, and he had asked for it to be delivered to his home; five days a week a green truck from the Government Printing Office pulled up on the quiet street at about seven o'clock and a gray-uniformed GPO employee would lay a copy at the Johnson front door; sometimes the ink would still be wet and would smear Lyndon Johnson's fingers as he read it, turning the pages very fast but focusing on them very intently.) He would tear out articles as he read. As he shaved in the bathroom—with an electric razor because he considered it easier than a straight blade on his tender skin, and because he considered an electric razor faster, and he didn't want to waste time—and combed his hair, concentrating on covering a growing thin spot on the back of his head, he would be dictating letters, memos, and reminders to himself to Lady Bird, who was sitting on the bed with her stenographer's notebook. By eight-thirty or so, Walter Jenkins or Mary Rather would have arrived to take more dictation, and tension and haste would sharpen in Lyndon Johnson's voice as he put on the clothes his wife had laid out for him. The upstairs doorknobs were decorated with knotted neckties; believing that tying a tie each day wrinkled it— and also took too much time—he simply loosened his ties to take them off at night, and hung them, knots intact, on doorknobs, ready to be slipped on again. By nine, he would be out the door, and driving down Connecticut; sometimes, if he wasn't picking up Congresswoman Douglas, he would pick up Mary Rather and drive her to work, weaving in and out of cars, shouting at their drivers, mingling dictation and diatribes, gearing up for the day ahead. He wouldn't return home until after the Senate had adjourned for the day at five or six o'clock, and after he had attended Rayburn's Board of Education and had done several hours' work in his office, and then he would often bring last-minute guests.

Sometimes, he wouldn't have finished all his office chores when he had to get home to greet guests. The huge stack of letters that his staff had churned out that day might not all be reviewed and signed, for instance. Then that work would be done at home. While his guests were talking and having a cocktail in the living room, he would sit in a corner, a tall stack of papers in front of him, talking along with them but reading and signing as he talked.

THERE WERE, of course, two individuals at 4921 Thirtieth Place who did not fit into that routine: Lynda Bird Johnson, age five in 1949, and Lucy Baines Johnson, age two.

During the first nine years of their marriage, Lady Bird Johnson had become pregnant three times, but had suffered three miscarriages. In 1943, she had conceived again. Lyndon Johnson badly wanted a son—and apparently had no doubts that his wishes would be answered. Writing on November 22, 1943, to congratulate L. E. Jones on the birth of Jones' baby, he said, "You may be interested to know that I am expecting a boy in March." Talking to friends in

Washington, with Lady Bird present, he seemed so convinced of this that Jim
Rowe had felt called upon to inject a note of caution, writing him on March 4,
1944, "I do assure you, as a gentleman who desperately wanted a son and never
told his wife about it either before or after the event, that if your fate is the same
as mine you will in three months' time no more think of having a son instead of
a daughter than of voting with Pappy O'Daniel." This caution was reinforced
by Rayburn, and it apparently had some effect, for when Jones wrote Johnson
the next week, "Here's hoping it's a boy," Johnson wrote back, "I hope I'll be as
lucky as you, but at this point I'm not as particular about a boy as I was at first."
Lynda Bird Johnson was born, on March 19, 1944, only after twelve torturous
hours of labor, and doctors, as readers may remember, strongly advised Mrs.
Johnson not to become pregnant again; and when, in 1946, this advice was
disregarded, its wisdom was almost tragically proven—as was Lady Bird's
courage. She knew she was miscarrying again, yet she insisted that Lyndon go
to the office although she was in intense pain and running a high fever. She
called the doctor as soon as he had driven away, but before an ambulance
arrived she began to hemorrhage badly. As she was being carried out of the
house on a stretcher, she asked a visiting friend from Austin to mail an important letter to Texas, told her how much postage to put on it, and insisted that
a dinner party the following evening, to which she had invited Rayburn and
two guests, not be canceled, saying, "Lyndon has to eat anyway, and they're
already invited," and requesting that her friend act as hostess in her place. Her
condition was listed as critical for more than a week, but she recovered—and
became pregnant again. "We're waiting for baby brother," Lyndon told friends.
On July 2, 1947, Lucy Baines Johnson was born, in a delivery so difficult that
when the doctor held her up for the first time, he said, "I never thought I'd see
you." Johnson never stopped expressing his desire for a son; "You know I
always wanted a boy," he would tell his secretary Ashton Gonella. In an interview with Stewart Alsop published in 1959, he said, "I've always wished Lady
Bird and I had a son. If we had [had] a boy, I'd want him to be a politician or a
teacher or a preacher. . . . Someone who . . . has an influence on events."

On the days Johnson went to his Senate office, he was telephoning, giving
dictation, and reading the newspapers and the *Record* from the moment he
awoke, so he had little time in the mornings to spend with his two daughters.
Since he rarely returned before they were asleep, they seldom saw him during
the evenings of the days on which he went to his office. And since those days
were six of the seven in the week, their time with him was necessarily somewhat limited. There remained Sundays, of course, but as Lynda Bird was to say
during an interview in 1989, "Daddy was the kind of man who believed it was
more important to invite Richard Russell . . . over for Sunday breakfast than to
spend the time alone with his family."

It might have been expected that this gap in the lives of the two little girls
would be filled by their mother, who had taken such risks to bear them—

particularly since she was a woman with such seemingly boundless warmth and patience for her husband's colleagues and constituents. But this was not the case. Men and women who lived for a time at Thirtieth Place during 1949 and the early 1950s couldn't believe Lady Bird's attitude toward her children. "I never saw a mother-daughter relationship like it," recalls Margaret Mayer. "Lady Bird let everyone know that, no matter what, Lyndon came first." She spent her days with his constituents, her evenings accompanying him to Washington social events. When she was gone, the girls' baby-sitter was one of Johnson's secretaries, Willie Day Taylor, a gentle woman who Lady Bird says "became almost a second mother." Sometimes, Mary Rather, or Ollie Reed, the Johnsons' next-door neighbor, would act as baby-sitter. "The little Johnson girls are being raised by committee," another neighbor said. "I felt deprived," Lucy would admit years later. "I wanted a normal life. I wanted a father who came home at a reasonable hour, and a mother who made cookies. That wasn't what we had." "Why are you always going out, Mama?" Lynda Bird would ask. Their mother was going out because she had made her choice. "You either have to cut the pattern to suit your husband or cut it to suit your children," she was to say. "Lyndon is the leader," she was to explain to a journalist. "Lyndon sets the pattern. I execute what he wants. Lyndon's wishes dominate our household." Her friends could hardly credit the faithfulness with which that pattern was followed. "Lady Bird was so subservient and so under the spell of Lyndon Johnson that it made it difficult for the kids," one says. Another, B. A. Bentsen, wife of Congressman (and later Senator) Lloyd Bentsen, talking about Lynda, says, "It was just so sad. She wouldn't cry, but you could just tell she wished things were different."

10

Lyndon Johnson
and the Liberal

ANOTHER QUALITY THAT LYNDON JOHNSON had displayed on each stage of his march along the path to power was an utter ruthlessness in destroying obstacles in that path.

The obstacle in his path now was a man named Leland Olds, the chairman (and, in *The New Republic*'s phrase, "the central force and will") of the Federal Power Commission, the five-member body that licensed and regulated facilities to create power from natural resources as well as the sale of that power to the public.

The furniture in the chairman's office on the seventh floor of the FPC Building on Washington's Pennsylvania Avenue was federal bureaucratic standard issue, but not much else in that office was. On the big desk, near a rack holding several hickory pipes, lay a mathematician's slide rule, worn with use. In a corner stood a cello, with classical scores open on a stand; Olds was considered one of Washington's most accomplished amateur cellists. On the bookshelves, alongside the bound volumes of FPC regulations, were stacks of poetry magazines and dog-eared volumes on philosophy and history, one of which Olds might have been reading while coming to work that morning; he took the trolley instead of the bus because it was smoother, and he could read on it. On the coatrack would be a rumpled tweed sport jacket and the old felt fedora he had worn to work, tipped jauntily down over one eye. He would wander in shirtsleeves through the offices of the younger staff members: a brisk slender figure with a shock of graying hair, and lively pale blue eyes behind wire-rimmed spectacles, puffing on a pipe—"jolly, witty, completely informal, not at all aloof or reserved like the other commissioners, ready to talk about anything, like a professor talking with his students," one staff member recalls. And when Leland Olds got caught up in a subject (as he often did when the talk turned to the morality behind the Commission's policies or to the social benefits those policies could provide farmers or the poor), he would talk faster and faster, the words tumbling over each other in a very boyish enthusiasm that sometimes made it seem as if the professor-student role had been reversed. He seemed less like a high-level federal bureaucrat than a scholar or a writer or—when he was talking about morality or social justice—like a social worker or a minister. And those four professions had indeed been Leland Olds' professions until he was forty-one years old.

The son of a mathematics professor at Amherst, George D. Olds, who became the college's president, and Marion Leland, the daughter of a prominent Boston family, Leland Olds, born December 31, 1890, "liked fun," a college friend was to recall. Just under six feet tall, thin and wiry, with wavy dark brown hair and those striking blue eyes in a gaunt, high-cheekboned face, he was an ardent outdoorsman, a guide and blazer of trails in New Hampshire's White Mountains, a tennis player good enough to reach the finals of the Eastern State College Championships, a long-distance runner who once, on a bet, ran and walked the almost forty miles from Amherst to Williamstown and arrived before the kickoff of a football game, and a brilliant student who graduated *magna cum laude* in mathematics. But perhaps the formative experience of Lee Olds' college years occurred not on a campus but in a slum—during the two summers he worked at a vacation school that had been established by Grace Church in the nearby industrial city of Holyoke, Massachusetts. There the books by Riis and Dreiser and Norris came to life. In Holyoke, he was to say, "I learned at first hand the impact of the industrialism of that period on the lives of the children of wage earners." Those summers of watching children work all the daylight hours in sweltering, windowless rooms gave him a determination, as he was to put it, to be "of service," and after graduating in 1912, "I searched for some pursuit which would have some effect toward mitigating the evil of poverty."

At first, the search took him into social work—on the staff of a settlement house in the South Boston slums. But a year of seeing the horrors of the sweatshop and hearing the tuberculosis coughs through the thin walls of the railroad flats taught him, he was to say, "a great deal . . . about the limitations of social work as a means of mitigating poverty."

Then he turned to organized religion—to the growing Social Gospel movement in which some Protestant clergymen were attempting to secure social justice for the poor by adding a moral element to the reform movement, reminding businessmen, for example, that sweatshops were antithetical to Christian teaching. Olds had been quietly but deeply religious at college—he won Amherst's Bond Prize for the best talk given at chapel—and his year in South Boston had led him, he was to recall, to believe that the evils of the new industrial order "were not going to be cured by economic and political measures alone, although these must not be neglected, but by what would be in the nature of a religious revolution" in which "people really applied the principles of Christianity to their everyday business." After studying for two years at New York's Union Theological Seminary, he was ordained as a Congregationalist minister of a small church in a working-class parish in Brooklyn.

Leland Olds never talked much about the disappointments he suffered in that parish. One of his grandchildren was to write that he came to feel "that the church was not actively enough involved with the problems that faced society at that time," but Olds himself would say only, "My experience suggested that I might accomplish more through teaching." He enrolled in graduate school at Columbia University, studying European history, which he later taught at Amherst.

During World War I, however, he was hired as a low-level statistician by the government's Industrial Relations Commission, and assigned to study the level at which wartime wages should be set. Going beyond the scope of his assignment to satisfy his own curiosity, and displaying a startling gift for analyzing huge masses of raw economic data, the former mathematics honor student concluded that the root cause of the poverty he hated so passionately was the fact that labor was not receiving its fair share of the nation's increased productivity and wealth, and that labor unions must be given the right to bargain collectively. He realized that he wanted to teach not college students but the labor union activists who were closer to the front lines of the fight for social justice. He became the head of the research bureau of the American Federation of Labor, which was striking against the powerful Pennsylvania steel companies and railroads.

In one Pennsylvania steel town after another, Olds witnessed the brutality with which the strikes were suppressed; he himself was shot in the leg as he was watching police break up a demonstration. For the rest of his life he was to remember his shock at the discovery that the "great railroads were deliberately contracting out their locomotive repair work in order to create unemployment among their own employees." He was to remember how the children of the railroad workers were hungry. And he was to remember, also, an "inspiring" conversation with a white-haired Roman Catholic priest in Braddock, Pennsylvania, who had allowed striking steelworkers to meet in his church, until mounted police rode their horses into it to break up the meeting.

The Pennsylvania struggle ended in defeat—the companies were simply too strong for the unions, Olds was to say—and he emerged from it convinced that labor's only hope lay in the intervention of government on its side, that "railroad workers . . . must look forward either to government ownership of the railroads or to the political influence necessary to secure protective labor legislation," that if workingmen were ever to earn a living wage, they must be guaranteed the right to organize—and that if government did not secure them that right, the American system of government would perish. "The preservation of the American democratic system required" this "evolution" of democracy, he believed—and to educate labor's "rank and file" about this necessity, Olds turned from research to writing.

Because "the labor angle on news of strikes, negotiations and so forth was not adequately covered by the general press," a wire service, the Federated Press—similar to the Associated Press and the United Press, which supplied articles for general-circulation periodicals—had been established in 1918 to provide labor-oriented articles. Most of its eighty subscribers were union newspapers and magazines such as the *Locomotive Engineers Journal* and the *Seattle Union Record,* although among its other subscribers was the Communist *Daily Worker.* The Federated Press had no money to hire an additional staff writer, but Olds' brilliance as an economic analyst had attracted the attention of liberal and Progressive leaders, and, eager that Olds' analyses continue, the civil rights activist Roger Baldwin persuaded a liberal foundation, the Garland Fund, to pay part of his $3,600 salary. In 1922 he went to work as Federated's "industrial editor."

It was the Twenties—the Twenties of Harding and Coolidge and Hoover, the Twenties of "normalcy" and complacency, the Twenties in which the federal government and courts, high and low, seemed to regard themselves as allies of Big Business, allowing corporations to break strikes and unions, relaxing even token regulations on business, and abandoning social reform. In the Twenties, tariffs and profits and the stock market rose and rose again—and wages, so inadequate to begin with, fell further and further behind, so that workers received a steadily smaller share in the prosperity their toil had helped to create.

In 1919, when reformers' hopes for a fundamental redistribution of wealth and power—for a new social order—had been high, President Wilson had advocated "a genuine democratization" of industry; a "cooperation and partnership based upon . . . worker participation in control" of industry; unions and Progressives had more specific—and radical—planks: for nationalization of the railroads, and public operation—"along socialistic lines," in William Allen White's phrase—of natural resources like oil, water, and mines. In New York, Governor Alfred E. Smith was proposing not only a minimum wage law and an eight-hour day for women but state ownership of hydroelectric power. The AFL was urging nationalization not alone of railroads but of all key industries. So many liberal dreams had, for a moment, seemed within reach. Now, in the Twenties, labor was asleep again; the union movement, grown cautious and conservative, represented mainly the skilled crafts; the vast majority of America's overworked, underpaid workers were not members of any union. Dreams had faded. Liberal intellectuals responded by revolting against traditional liberalism, becoming, in their frustration and discouragement, more radical, many believing that a fundamental transformation of American society was required if individualism was to be rescued from its entrapment by a society based on the profit motive. Attracted by the model of the Soviet Union, and feeling that America's choice was between the ruthlessness of untrammeled private enterprise and a planned, governmental, collectivism, some advocated varied forms of democratic collectivism—perhaps a national economic council representing business and labor as well as government—to preserve what was good in the American tradition.

Leland Olds was a part of this new, radical, liberal current. His gift for economic analysis and his outrage over social injustice fused in the articles he poured out, at least five a week, for the Federated Press between 1922 and 1929. When President Coolidge refused to cut the sugar tariff because of the "hardships" of sugar beet companies, Federated's industrial editor analyzed the companies' annual reports and found that their true annual profits were as high as 32 percent. And then, turning to Labor Department studies—studies all but totally ignored by the "general press"—he contrasted the profits with the human cost that had created them. These studies showed mothers and children as young as six working up to fifteen hours a day at dangerous jobs in the sugar beet fields, he wrote in a Federated Press article published on July 1, 1925; at night, families "huddled together in shanties which were not even water-proof, and with practically no decent provision for sanitation." The Sugar Trust's "exorbitant profits," made "at the expense of women and little chil-dren . . . reveal the hypocrisy of President Coolidge in his apology for refusing to cut the sugar tariff."

He saw the power of big money everywhere—in universities, whose investment portfolios were filled with railroad and oil stocks. ("Needless to say, the dependence of universities on these securities for their incomes influences their view of the economic problem"), and in the church. When a Methodist bishop publicly boasted about his stock market profits, the indignation of the idealist who had once become a minister to help the poor boiled over. The bishop's financial speculations are "just another proof of the decay of the church as a religious institution and its transformation into a handmaiden of the capitalist system," he wrote. Religions now preach "the principles of the exploiting class." Pointing out that while securities given as gifts represented a substantial portion of colleges' and church portfolios, they represented a very small portion of the wealth of those who made the gifts, he wrote bitterly: "Give till it hurts means nothing to the money princes who govern industry, endow education, and generally distribute royal gifts to the Glory of God and the admiration of the populace. They simply can't give till it hurts. They have too much."

And of course, he saw the power of big money in government. When a keynote speaker at the 1928 Republican convention boasted that the United States had achieved a 25 percent rise in gross national product at the same time that labor costs were falling by 10 percent, Olds said, the boast was "hollow . . . unless he shows what the party has done for the millions of workers laid off in the process. Never was it more clear that the Republican Party is the party of big business, the party which represents the closest alliance between industrial rulership and political administration."

Not that the Democrats were much better, he wrote; the problem lay in the political system as a whole. The belief that "a political system created in a much simpler economic era still affords the people effective control through their votes over the complex industrial state which has come into being" is a popular delusion. "Politicians must perpetuate this idea, for their jobs depend on it," but "a true keynote speech would reveal the political government handling certain administrative details for an immensely powerful ruling class."

Only a complete transformation of the American economic system—"the complete passing of the old order of capitalism" with its *laissez-faire* government and unfettered economic individualism—would cure the problems, Olds said. The old ideal of democracy had become perverted; the idea of political freedom had resulted in the loss of the economic freedom which alone could really insure political freedom. "Without such a transformation," he wrote, "to millions of workers . . . the Fourth of July will loom as anything but the birthday of liberty."

Such a transformation had already begun in other countries, Olds said, as was shown by the rise of unions in England—and the resultant general strikes there. Changes were coming from both the right and the left, Olds said. He detested Fascism, but even in Fascist Italy, "supposed bulwark of capitalism," the state—Mussolini—had enacted laws against exorbitant rents and profits, and had begun jailing landlords and shopkeepers who violated them. "Here is certainly a breach which may widen until the sanctity of private property in the capitalist sense follows the divine right of kings into the discard. Inevitable changes in the economic organization of society are exposing it as just another myth. . . ." As for Communism, he had always distrusted it; "in my opinion, the very theory of Russian communism represents a negation of democracy," he was to say, and his distrust was reinforced by his religious convictions: "I rejected the approach of Karl Marx because I felt that the road to harmony must recognize spiritual values and that ambition for power was an unwholesome influence in human affairs." Seeing—more clearly than many American liberals in the Twenties—the danger that Communist infiltration posed to American liberalism, and to the American labor movement, when he attempted briefly during this period to help form a new, progressive party in Illinois, he was so concerned "to keep Communists from infiltrating" that he wrote into the party's "Qualifications for Membership" a statement that "no person who advocates the overthrow of the Government by force or violence or who supports organizations having that end in view will be accepted," and into its constitution a statement that "The new party must . . . build on the fundamentally American tradition that all are entitled to the right to life, liberty, and the pursuit of happiness. Importation of theories and influences not germane to American life must be ruled out"—as must "slogans and formulas produced by the struggle in other lands." Yet along with so many liberals of the time, he saw various innovations in Russia—vacations with pay, still relatively rare in America; improved working conditions for children—as significant social advances. By reducing child labor, he wrote in 1926, Russia "leads the world in its attempt to guarantee every child a chance to flower."

But whether the transformation of the American system came from the right or the left, Olds wrote, it was coming.

> The attempt to run twentieth-century industrial states with governmental machinery designed in the eighteenth century is breaking down. This is the significance of revolutionary events in Russia, Italy and England.
>
> Lenin knew what would take the place of political partyism when he made his bid for power in Russia with the slogan "All power to the Soviets." Mussolini . . . saw it when he moved to constitute in Italy under his dictatorship a government composed of the industries rather than regions, with the dominant branch of Parliament composed of representatives of organized labor and capital.
>
> Already in other countries a new age is being born which will succeed capitalist political democracy. The parliamentary systems are decadent.

The changes in America would have to take a different form from those in other countries, Olds wrote, or the particular—and precious—values of the American democratic system would be lost. "Theories developed to meet European conditions fail to include the values the American worker is seeking," he said. What democracy would evolve into was not yet clear, he wrote. "The new order will be a world order, but not the ideal world order envisioned either in capitalist America, Fascist Italy or Socialist Russia." A "promise, answering the yearning of people in an American environment," is needed—and "so far it has been lacking." But evolve democracy must, he wrote in article after article—or democracy would die.

So vast were the social inequities in the present system that the changes in that system would have to be equally vast, he wrote. Despairing—as many liberals during the decade of outward prosperity under *laissez-faire* capitalism despaired—that government would ever rein in capitalism, so powerful had it become, he saw no solution in the case of giant industries but nationalization or some other drastic reorganization: since the power of the Coal Trust was effectively preventing the United Mine Workers from bargaining collectively, the miners have only "two alternatives: to develop, along with the rest of organized labor, political power sufficient to put over nationalization, or to seek control by the workers themselves under a worker government." In the case of the giant utilities, Olds (again in conformance with the prevailing liberal theory of the 1920s; it was not Leland Olds but Governor Franklin Roosevelt of New York who said, "The water power policy of the Democratic Party is socialistic, if you like," but "I want the government of this State to develop the power sites of this state, because the Government can do it better than anybody else") advocated nationalization or some more imaginative alternative such as operating utilities "as giant consumer cooperatives."

DURING HIS WARTIME YEARS in Washington, Olds had met, and later married, Maud Spear. The daughter of a teacher in government schools for Indians, she had been raised on Indian reservations all over the West; then, at Oklahoma A&M, had become one of the first women in the United States to earn an advanced degree in civil engineering, and had been working in Washington with the War Department. During the 1920s, the Oldses had four children. They were quite poor, of course—their only income was his $3,600 salary—and when they moved to Northbrook, Illinois, a little working-class town near Chicago, for the Federated Press job, with his own hands Olds built a house for his family; until he could teach himself wiring, the house had no electricity. The only heat was that provided by a big kitchen stove; hanging blankets in a square around it, to keep its heat concentrated, Maud would gather the children inside the square.

The sacrifices they were making didn't bother Lee or Maud, but increasingly they felt as if the sacrifices were for nothing. In working-class Northbrook, Olds was to say, "I had an opportunity to observe the difficulties faced by many of my friends and neighbors as a result of protracted periods of unemployment which occurred even during the Golden Twenties." He felt that the solutions he was advocating in his articles could have reduced unemployment, but the solutions were not adopted—nor, he felt, even listened to. His articles changed nothing. The strikes for which he did research and wrote bulletins were defeated. The labor movement in which he had believed so deeply, and to which he had dedicated so much of his life, was, as it grew steadily more conservative and more timid, no longer something he believed in very deeply. His voracious reading had convinced him that, as he was to tell a friend, "Even men supposed to have shaped history were in the hands of something stronger than they were, and that applies equally to Napoleon and the man in the ranks." He had, he felt, been looking all his life for a cause worth fighting for, and he had not found one.

And then he did.

IN THE SUMMER OF 1929, with the Federated Press unable to continue paying its share of his salary, Olds accepted a lucrative offer with an economic consulting firm, but there was something he wanted to do first. He had come to feel, he was to say, that he was not sufficiently knowledgeable about a significant American business: the electric power industry. One of the country's great business libraries was Chicago's John Crerar Library. So, Olds decided, before starting his new job, he would "take a month's vacation" and spend it in that library, "studying the power and utility situation in all its aspects."

That "situation" made clear the chasm between America's dominant belief in Big Business and liberals' conviction that the business ethos had degraded the nation they cared about. Most of America's power was hydroelectric, generated by the water of its rivers; in the opinion of liberals, such a natural resource does not belong to any private interest. As the author John Gunther was to ask: "Who and what should own a river, if not the people as a whole?" In the America of the 1920s, however, not only did the people not own this power, they had to pay dearly for the use of it—and to much of America's people, it was not available at any price.

Most of the nation's hydroelectric power was controlled by a very few private companies, for the local operating electric companies had been absorbed into holding companies, and then the holding companies had been absorbed into other, larger holding companies, and then absorbed again—until by 1929, when Leland Olds sat reading in the Crerar Library, holding companies had been piled atop operating companies in layer after layer. Since holding companies were interstate, they were largely beyond the reach of state utility commissions, and in the pro-business atmosphere of the Twenties, the agency that had been created to provide federal regulation of interstate hydroelectric development— the Federal Power Commission—was notably unenthusiastic about doing so.

Effectively free of governmental restraint, the holding companies milked the operating companies, selling them materials and management and engineering services at grossly inflated prices, and watered their stocks until stock prices soared far beyond their real worth. These extra costs were passed back to the operating companies—and the operating companies passed them back to the consumers, in the form of rates so high that they deprived low-income urban and small-town families of money for other purposes. And for rural customers the consequences were far worse. Because holding companies saw little profit in rural electrification, which required the building of long power lines into sparsely populated areas, in 1929 more than 6 million of America's 6.8 million farms did not have electricity. Decades after electric power had become part of urban life, farmers had to perform every farm chore by hand; their wives had to haul up endless buckets of water from wells, and, without the vacuum cleaners, dishwashers, washing machines, and electric irons that had freed city women from much of the drudgery of housework, worked from dawn to dark as if they were peasant women in the Middle Ages.

Insulating private utility companies from government regulation was an impenetrable financial structure. Owen D. Young of General Electric, a brilliant financial innovator in his own right, was to say that when "I begin to examine" the utilities' complicated structure, "I confess to a feeling of helplessness."

But Olds' natural gift for mathematics had been honed by years of analyzing masses of statistical material for the AFL and the Federated Press; at the end of his month's "vacation" in the Crerar Library, he possessed a rare—in the opinion of men who worked with him later, a unique—understanding of holding companies' financial complexities and manipulations. This understanding enabled him to determine the true cost to consumers—the rate they should, under state regulation, actually be charged—which meant he was finding formulas under which electric rates could be drastically lowered. Moreover, the refusal of utility companies to provide electrification in rural areas was based on their contention that farmers could not afford to buy electrical appliances; that farmers' usage of electricity would therefore be low, and rural electric rates that would therefore have to be too high for farmers to afford.

Making detailed analyses of rural areas that *had* been electrified, Olds proved that this vicious circle could be broken—by lowering rates. In the rare instances in which they had been lowered, he demonstrated, farmers had invariably found that they could afford to use more electricity; they bought more appliances, used still more electricity, and rates could be reduced still further. The principle was not new, of course. Henry Ford had demonstrated it: the cheaper a company prices a needed product, the greater will be the company's profit. All that was necessary, Leland Olds said, was to apply the principle to rural electrification. And if it was applied, he said, electricity would transform the lives of farm families: a farm wife would no longer have to do her wash by hand, stooping over washtubs, but could simply push a button on an electric washing machine.

Olds' studies, in other words, had the potential to accomplish what he had decided so long ago he wanted to accomplish with his life: to be "of service"; to "mitigate the evil of poverty"; to "help human beings." As one of his associates was to explain: "All his life Lee Olds was concerned with the means for decreasing poverty and injustice." Now, at last, he had found the means. "His preoccupation with obtaining low-cost electricity was only an expression of his belief that low-cost energy would open the door to a more decent world." And at the end of that month's vacation, just as he was about to enter private employment, Leland Olds received a telephone call. Looking back at that call years later, he would tell a friend, "I haven't selected what I would do; things have selected me."

The telephone call was from Frank P. Walsh, an old Progressive who was now Chairman of the New York State Power Authority, and an admirer of Olds' articles. Walsh said that New York's new Governor, Franklin D. Roosevelt, was planning to use the State Power Authority to break the hold of the state's private utilities and to develop public power for the people. Governor Roosevelt, Walsh said, wanted stricter regulation of utilities, and lower rates, rates based on new formulas. A commission was being established to make recommendations to accomplish these aims, and there was an opening for a staff expert on it. Would Lee be interested in the job?

Lee said he would, and sometime in 1929, he was invited to visit Roosevelt in the Executive Mansion in Albany, and after dinner Roosevelt talked about a farm family in Dutchess County that couldn't obtain electricity because, as the Governor's counsel, Samuel Rosenman, was to recall him saying, "the damned old electric corporation says they can't afford the expense of the line."

"That farmer's wife still has to pump her water by hand, and sew by oil lamp, and cook by wood. The farm chores and household chores take so much time that they have no chance for rest and leisure. I want to get cheap electricity out to that farm. . . . Now, tell me what you think. . . ."

Olds told him. Although he was thirty-nine years old, he was still strikingly thin, and with his hollow cheeks and his eager, intense eyes behind wire-rimmed spectacles, still very much the young radical. And he still, when he became excited, talked too much and too fast. But now—at last—he had found someone who would listen, and who, in fact, spurred him on with more questions ("question and answer, until after midnight," Rosenman would recall), until the final question: "Tell me, what would you recommend if you were Governor?" As Olds replied, Rosenman, after listening for a minute or two, quietly pulled out a pad and pencil, and began taking notes—as fast as he could write. "Many of the ideas expressed that night found their way into a series of messages which the Governor sent to the Legislature in 1929 and 1930," Rosenman was to recall. And when, in 1931, Olds' ideas were codified in legislation expanding the powers of the New York State Power Authority, Roosevelt appointed Olds its executive secretary.

DURING THE TEN YEARS he held that job, Olds proved to be an unusual bureaucrat. To determine the cost, best location, and engineering feasibility of a proposed hydroelectric dam across the St. Lawrence River, he not only commissioned surveys but did some of the surveying himself—living in a tent, camping out on the banks of the broad river, sometimes taking his family along. Back in his office, he worked his big slide rule making pioneering analyses of electric rates. He drafted bills that, over last-ditch Republican resistance in the New York State Legislature, gave the State Public Service Commission new authority over utility rates—and that, in a new tactic to force rates down, authorized municipalities to construct their own plants and distribute power themselves. When New York City Mayor Fiorello La Guardia, angered by rates he considered onerous for the city's low-income families, proposed building a municipal power plant to establish a yardstick by which the utilities' rates could be measured, Olds worked with La Guardia's office on it—and exulted when, as he was to recall, "just one day before the Mayor went before the Board of Estimate for authorization," a power company official sullenly announced substantial rate reductions. And he exulted a year later, when the same official admitted that after the reduction electric usage had increased so greatly that the company's profits had risen instead of fallen.

During these ten years, Roosevelt became President (his successor as Governor, Herbert H. Lehman, continued his policies) and the New Deal changed Leland Olds' views in areas other than electricity. He had believed that there was no alternative to the corporate domination that was destroying the dream of "economic democracy" and social justice in America except the "complete passing of the old order of capitalism," that in the Industrial Age it had become impossible to reconcile economic and political freedom. Roosevelt taught him that he was wrong: that there were other alternatives—within the existing order. Olds had believed that there was no way of curbing the power of giant corporations and monopolies except by having them taken over, either by the government, by labor unions or by some form of consumer cooperatives. Roosevelt taught him that there was a way: government regulation. Olds had been led to believe by the bitterness of his own experiences that there was no hope that unions would prevail against corporate power; the New Deal taught him that there was hope—that government could enact laws that protected workers' rights to organize, and to bargain collectively. Olds had believed that under the old order of capitalism, wage earners and their families could never have security against unemployment and old age. Now at least a measure of that security had been given them—and Olds was confident that more would come. He no longer felt it was necessary for the capitalist system to be eliminated; he now felt it could be improved, restored, and preserved. Thanks to Roosevelt, real progress had been made toward the "new age" of which Olds had dreamed; the evolution of democracy which he had long thought impossible was in fact occurring—in the measures of the Hundred Days, and of the hundreds of days which followed during the New Deal. "The great reforms of the 1930s," Olds was to say, "completely changed the old *laissez-faire* capitalism into a new model." And those reforms changed Olds, too. His radicalism was transformed. Like many another passionate radical of the 1920s, Leland Olds became, in the 1930s, a passionate New Dealer—a liberal of the new, vibrant liberal faith.

Olds idolized FDR. Seeing no basic difference between the two parties, he had never been active in Democratic politics, but he became active now—to support the President who was, he said, "the greatest leader democracy has ever produced." When, in 1937, conservative Democrats in New York's Rockland County, where Olds now lived, sought to mobilize opposition to the "dictatorship" of Roosevelt's Supreme Court–packing proposal, Olds went to a meeting called to support the President, and jumped up in the audience, without preparation but with all his usual eloquence, to deliver an impassioned attack on "the real dictatorship" of "corporate interests" and "reactionaries" which was greeted, the *New York Times* reported, with "thunderous applause"; "people crowded forward, tipping over benches, to clasp his hand."

With conservative New York Democrats, including the powerful Tammany Hall organization, rebelling against the New Deal, labor leaders founded the American Labor Party. Olds joined it—because it had been founded to support Roosevelt. Delivering the keynote speech at its 1938 convention, he said the ALP would be the President's own party; it "invites all who would support the leadership of President Roosevelt, all who recognize the need for party realignment, all who believe that the re-establishment of economic democracy is essential to the preservation of political democracy in our age, to join its ranks . . ."—and remained active in it for a year, resigning when it became infiltrated by Communists. And in June, 1939, the President brought him to Washington as a member of the Federal Power Commission, of which in January, 1940, he became chairman.

BEFORE OLDS ARRIVED at the FPC, the agency had not been making the progress Roosevelt had hoped toward reducing private control over natural resources—in part because young staff members trying to ascertain utilities' true financial condition found themselves unable to unravel the tangled web of the giant holding companies' finances, in part because the commissioners seemed intimidated by the vast new powers they had been given and uncertain how to utilize them. The staff was disorganized; in striking contrast to the situation at most of the New Deal agencies, morale was low.

Olds' arrival changed that. The staffers who had been daunted by holding companies' finances found that, as one of them, Melwood W. Van Scoyoc, assistant chief of the FPC's Bureau of Finances, recalls, "Mr. Olds understood it all so well that he could make it very simple for you."

Olds provided these young men with not only technical skills but inspiration. The long columns of figures, he made them see, weren't just figures—they were the key to a better life for tens of thousands—hundreds of thousands, *millions*—of farmers and their wives and children. He made his assistants understand that if they could get electric rates down, farmers would be able to alleviate the terrible drudgery of their lives. And he made the young men understand that if they could understand the figures, the rates *would* come down. "He saw (public) power as a means to an end, as an important means of lightening the burden of man," says Alexander Radin, a young FPC staff member who would later become general manager of the American Public Power Association.

He not only made the young staffers feel they were part of a great cause, he made them feel he was fighting beside them. FPC staff counsel Reuben Goldberg recalls spending "an entire winter" in Butte, Montana, with a handful of FPC attorneys and accountants fighting a big team of high-priced attorneys for the Montana Power Company in a proceeding designed to force down the company's rates. One day, without any advance notice, there in that Butte courtroom was their boss. He had made the trip from Washington "just to see how we were doing," Goldberg recalls. "He just stayed a day or two, and had lunch and dinner with us, and was friendly and approachable like always—and let us know it was a very important job we were doing."

And he inspired them also with his own example. Leland Olds was in his fifties now; the shock of hair had turned gray on the sides. He was a little stooped, and arthritis in his right hand was making it difficult to play tennis or the cello. But while the young men would work late with him in his office, he would eventually send them home; glancing back as they left, they would see him still bent over the masses of figures. Returning to the office the next morning, sometimes they would, Radin recalls, "find him asleep at his desk—he had worked all night." Some of these young New Dealers were very bright men—bright enough to know how bright Lee Olds was. So broad was Olds' knowledge of economics, James M. Kiley says, that "His concentration on electric systems was a conscious narrowing of his sweeping, broad interest—like Einstein teaching elementary math to freshmen in college." They also admired Olds' sense of justice. "He was very fair-minded," Goldberg says. "While he was very much consumer oriented, he was also very much aware that you had to be fair to the utilities—that they were entitled to a reasonable return on their investment. Because their financial integrity was necessary to enable them to provide the service to the customers that should be provided. He was constantly reminding us that you don't help the consumer by destroying the utility. When you hurt the utility, you're really jeopardizing the consumer." Under his leadership, the FPC pressured electric utility companies to extend power lines into neglected rural areas, to encourage the increased use of electricity through low rates, and to reduce inflated capitalizations. But the pressure was never draconian. And although he sometimes threatened recalcitrant companies with government takeover—or with the creation of competing consumer cooperatives—behind the threats was a belief that unless the utilities instituted these reforms themselves, the public would demand that *government* take over their functions. The FPC program, he felt, was actually protecting private enterprise. As Olds told electric power company executives during a 1944 convention, "Many of you have probably heard the work of the Federal Power Commission . . . attacked as aimed at the destruction of private enterprise and furthering of public ownership. Actually we believe the effect of [federal] enforcement is just the reverse."

IN THE OTHER PRINCIPAL FIELD of FPC activity—natural gas—Olds insisted on enforcing the Natural Gas Act of 1938, in which Congress had given the FPC broad powers to regulate the price of gas brought by pipeline from Texas and other southwestern states to consumers in the big cities of the North. And he disallowed several accounting devices employed by natural gas companies to hide illegal profits. But his fairness and his belief that only through effective regulation could the private enterprise system be preserved were equally obvious, and he would almost invariably carry the other FPC commissioners with him.

When, in 1944, Roosevelt nominated him for a second five-year term, the articles he had written for the Federated Press during the 1920s were brought up by Senator Edward Moore, a rabidly right-wing Oklahoma oilman, who quoted from them to show that Olds was "Communistic," as well as a "reformer" and a "zealot" (those last two terms being given equal weight) who was "opposed fundamentally to private enterprise." Roosevelt had sent up the renomination on May 25, less than a month before Olds' term expired on June 22, and Moore, a member of the Commerce Committee subcommittee to which the renomination had been referred, delayed hearings until July 6, so that Olds was without a job. But when the hearings were held, the subcommittee's other members gave Olds an opportunity to explain ("I think my ideas have been going through a constant process of change. . . . I think it has been my continuous philosophy . . . that this country has got to work out its solutions in terms of its own traditions; that one of the great things in democracy is that it has the possibility of assimilating change, so that instead of . . . break-ups you have a constant evolution of the system") and found his explanations so convincing that they quickly reported his nomination favorably to the full committee, which, after the usual Senate delays, sent it to the Senate floor. When, on September 12, 1944, it was taken up there and Moore repeated his attack, subcommittee chairman James M. Tunnell of Delaware said, "I do not think anyone [in the subcommittee] believed Mr. Olds was a Communist. I do not think the Senator from Oklahoma believed Mr. Olds was a Communist. I do not think anyone believes that." Declaring that "any statements he [Olds] had made some years before would be rather immaterial, incompetent and irrelevant," Lister Hill said, "he has a record now of six years of service, and that record" is what he should be judged on, and Tunnell noted that that record "has been reviewed and re-reviewed"—and always approved—by Congress. "The Senator [Moore] must go back approximately twenty years in order to find some ground on which to attack Mr. Olds." Senators who had been governors—George Aiken and William Langer—and who had worked with Olds in their states rose to praise him, and when Moore demanded a roll-call vote on the renomination, not a single senator was willing to second even that request, and Olds was confirmed for a second term by an overwhelming voice vote of "ayes." Although the confirmation occurred almost three months after Olds' term had expired on June 22, the new term for which he was being confirmed had begun on June 22, so his back pay was restored to him.

IN 1944, however, natural gas had still been merely a by-product of the oil industry, a by-product whose price was low because the supply far exceeded demand. During the war, the government laid gigantic pipelines—including the picturesquely named "Big Inch" and "Little Inch"—more than a thousand miles northward to defense plants, and after the war those pipelines were available to link the urban and industrial markets of the Northeast and Midwest to the Southwest's natural gas fields. Demand multiplied, and multiplied again. Prices and profits could obviously be greatly increased, and private companies built more pipelines. A company established by Herman and George Brown, Texas Eastern Transmission, was allowed to purchase the Big and Little Inch—thanks to Lyndon Johnson's intervention—for a cash investment of $143 million, a fraction of what it had cost to build them. Although Olds allowed price increases, increases viewed as generous by impartial analysts, he kept prices far lower than the companies would have set them. And the 9.5 percent return on their investment that the FPC allowed producers, while high enough so that the stocks of natural gas companies were among the most attractive investments on Wall Street, was far lower than what the producers wanted. The cost of the FPC policies to the oilmen was immense; it was estimated that an increase of five cents per thousand cubic feet in the price at the wellhead would increase the value of the holdings in Texas alone of the Phillips Petroleum Company by $389 million. As for Texas Eastern Transmission, it had sold 118,000,000 cubic feet of natural gas in 1948 at prices between seven cents and ten cents per thousand; deregulation would enable the Browns to charge several times those figures. And Texas Eastern had recently received FPC permission to build a new pipeline to New England, with a capacity of 200 million additional feet. Hundreds of millions of dollars were at stake. During 1948 and 1949, natural gas producers lobbied furiously for an end to federal regulation, and supported a deregulation bill introduced by Moore's successor, Robert S. Kerr (a major stockholder in Phillips Petroleum). But in March, 1949, after Olds had testified against the Kerr Bill—testified not only convincingly, but, as one historian put it, "courageously," since his renomination for a new five-year term would soon have to be confirmed by the Senate—President Truman, whose respect for Olds was as deep as President Roosevelt's, vetoed the bill. A single figure was standing between the big producers, already the possessors of great wealth, and wealth far greater. Herman and George and their friends raged against him in letters to Lyndon Johnson. Olds "would establish 'social responsibility' in place of the profit motive. That is conclusive proof that he does not believe in our form of government," Hugh Roy Cullen of Houston wrote. "There is nothing more important to the welfare of the natural gas industry in Texas" than that Olds' confirmation be defeated, Charles I. Francis, a Brown & Root attorney, declared.

It was important for Johnson not only that Olds be defeated, but that he, Johnson, be given credit for that defeat. The oilmen had never been enthusiastic about Johnson; they had poured money into his 1948 campaign only because of Herman Brown's personal assurances that he could be counted on. He would need their money for his 1954 re-election campaign—and for the campaigns he saw beyond. It was essential that he demonstrate to them that they could depend on him—that he could be counted on not just to work in their behalf, but to work effectively—and Olds' renomination process was the ideal opportunity for such a demonstration.

"Olds was the symbol of everything they [the oilmen] hated," recalls the former Texas legislator Posh Oltorf, who had now become Brown & Root's principal Washington lobbyist. "He was just anathema to them because of his philosophy." And because of something more important to these men than philosophy: money. Says John Connally, who would shortly leave the Wirtz law firm to become oilman Sid Richardson's attorney: "This [Olds' defeat] transcended philosophy, this would put something in their pockets. This was the real bread-and-butter issue to these oilmen. So this would prove whether Lyndon was reliable, that he was no New Dealer. This was his chance to get in with dozens of oilmen—to bring very powerful rich men into his fold who had never been for him, and were still suspicious of him. So for Lyndon this was the way to turn it around: *take care of this guy*."

AND LYNDON KNEW how to take care of him. In 1944, the charges that Leland Olds was a Communist had not been taken seriously. But times had changed since 1944. China was being "lost"—and there was a steadily mounting crescendo of accusations that it had been lost because of the treachery of men in the American government. All through the summer of 1948, the House Un-American Activities Committee was holding hearings at which Whittaker Chambers was testifying to the existence of a Communist spy ring within the government, and in December of 1948, the microfilms of "documents of enormous importance" were found in a hollowed-out pumpkin on a Maryland farm—just where Chambers had said they were hidden. And all through 1949, there would be trials in New York not only of Alger Hiss for perjury but of eleven leaders of the American Communist Party for conspiracy to overthrow the government—and that trial would end in October with their conviction. In 1944, the Senate had not believed that Leland Olds was a Communist. It would be easier to make the Senate believe it now.

In the summer of 1949, Johnson asked Interstate Commerce Committee Chairman Ed Johnson for the chairmanship of the subcommittee that would look into Olds' renomination—he had no difficulty obtaining the assignment; no one else was particularly interested in it—and he then persuaded "Mr. Wisdom" to allow the subcommittee to hold hearings on the renomination. And then he set about arranging the hearings.

First, there was the research. "He [Johnson] suggested that we bring in various experts," recalls Representative John Lyle of Corpus Christi, a baby-faced congressman with a southern stem-winder's gift for loud stump oratory, and a keen understanding of the importance of serving his constituents—particularly his district's natural gas moguls, one of whom, Maston Nixon, the reactionary multimillionaire head of the Southern Minerals Corporation, had directed him to give Johnson any help he needed. The expertise required was in one particular field: Lyle was soon in communication with skilled investigators from the staff of the Communist-hunting House Un-American Activities Committee. A memorandum was prepared summarizing the information about Olds in the committee's files. Supplementing these efforts with those of his own men ("We called in several of the brilliant young lawyers who were associated with Lyndon at that time in various matters," Lyle was to recall), Johnson coordinated the overall effort.

Some of the research was in the area that, five years earlier, the Senate had agreed was the only relevant area: Olds' long record in the job to which he was now being renominated. Ten years of formal FPC reports, drafts of reports, and internal memoranda were combed for evidence of anti-industry bias and for instances in which Olds had gone beyond the intent of Congress. That area proved unrewarding; it was, it was decided, better to avoid Olds' record. But there were other areas of research—most particularly the area that, five years earlier, Lister Hill had said, and the Senate had agreed, was "immaterial" and "irrelevant." The research into this area, Lyle recalls, was "very thorough." Johnson's investigators combed through bound volumes of scores of "newspapers that had come out during the 1920s," Lyle was to recall. "We made copies of every statement that he [Olds] had made and every article that he had written."

The coordinating of the research was done in Austin, Texas—by a master: Alvin Wirtz, who was the Austin lobbyist for many Texas oil and natural gas companies. One of the reasons that Wirtz was a feared figure to those who had had dealings with him was the combination of cruelty and guile that he possessed. The big, burly man with a broad, ever-present smile was gentle in manner but, a fellow lobbyist—a friend—says, "He would gut you if he could. But you would never know he did it. . . . He would still be smiling when he slipped in the knife." And those qualities were very evident in a courtroom, where his agile mind ("slow in his movements, slow in his speech, but a mind as quick as chain lightning") made him a fearsome cross-examiner who, with his soft voice and reassuring manner, excelled in leading witnesses into traps from which they could not extricate themselves.

The material assembled in Washington was loaded into Brown & Root's DC-3 and flown down to Austin, and Wirtz and Johnson began consulting daily by telephone as the attorney hammered the evidence into shape.

Selectivity was the key. During his years with the Federated Press, Olds had written more than eighteen hundred articles. Out of them, Johnson and the investigators had selected fifty-four which, they felt, would most effectively influence senators against the nominee. And out of those fifty-four, they had selected portions—a paragraph from one, a sentence from another, sometimes merely a phrase—that highlighted what they wanted highlighted, and now, consulting with Johnson, Wirtz refined these into a presentation to be made to the subcommittee.

And finally there was the selection of the witnesses who would make the presentation.

Johnson, of course, could not be a witness; as chairman of the subcommittee, he had to appear impartial. So he decided that Lyle would be the main witness. Not only was Maston Nixon's man on the Hill an effective public speaker, he was especially effective when speaking for a cause in which he believed, and he believed deeply that Red Russia was threatening America's very existence. Now, Lyle recalls, the necessary "information" had been collected, and Lyndon Johnson "could translate that information into an effective weapon," and he, Lyle, had no qualms about using that weapon; he could, in fact, hardly wait to use it. And Lyndon Johnson coached him on its use: "we spent hours and days discussing it."

In selecting other witnesses, Johnson worked mostly through Wirtz, whose principal client was Brown & Root, and Ed Clark (himself the owner of forty thousand shares of Texas Eastern stock, purchased at seven cents a share) who was on retainer from oilman Clint Murchison, so that these clients would be told how hard their new senator was working on their behalf. (The two attorneys were in some respects very different. Clark, bluntly candid, unwilling to cloak his actions in some noble purpose, would have no patience with Johnson's hints that what they were doing was to protect America from Communists. "He [Johnson] would call early in the morning—'Communists! Communists!' Bullshit! Communists had nothing to do with this, and he knew it, and I knew he knew it," Clark says. On September 20, talking to Johnson's secretary Mary Rather, Clark said, "I don't care anything about these Communists. I wouldn't look under the bed for Communists but I might look down there and hope I would find a blonde. The only reason I am interested in this hearing is on account of Mr. Murchison. . . ." Wirtz, on the other hand, hated Reds almost as intensely as he did blacks.)

The two key attorneys sent lists of potential witnesses to Johnson in Washington—Clark, disdainful as always of consequences, put them in writing; Wirtz, always cautious, used the telephone—and from these lists, and from suggestions made by Maston Nixon and by Brown & Root's Charles Francis, Johnson culled the names he wanted, interviewing some potential witnesses in person to determine their suitability for his purposes, and coaching them—sometimes at considerable length—on their testimony.

A FINAL ELEMENT in Johnson's strategy was the element of surprise. This was vital. Not merely the Commerce Committee but the full Senate would have to be persuaded by the hearings to vote against the President's nominee, a nominee with whom many senators had worked, a nominee of whom many senators were fond. The hearings must therefore be convincing—and at them Olds would have to be allowed to reply to the accusations that were going to be made against him. The accusations dealt with the fifty-four articles—some concerning complex economic issues, so a reply would have to be rather detailed. Adequate time to research the reply was therefore necessary; a witness who attempted to handle complicated issues without careful preparation was seldom convincing. Some of those articles had been written a quarter of a century earlier; Olds could hardly be expected to be familiar with them, or to answer questions about them in a convincing manner. And while only fifty-four articles were going to be introduced into evidence, they were part of a body of eighteen hundred articles. Were Olds to attempt to answer a question about one of the fifty-four, some of those other 1,746 articles might be quoted against him to ostensibly refute his replies, to make them appear evasive or misleading, because he had not taken them into account in his answer. With time to read the articles he might be able to answer convincingly, but unless this reading took place before the hearings, it would not be effective. Reading such a mass of material took time, and once damaging testimony was given, it had to be answered quickly, otherwise, the charges would take root in the consciousness of the senator-judges and their newspaper-reading constituents. And since the hearings would take only a few days, if Olds did not answer quickly, the hearings would be over, his fate decided. If he was to defend himself, he had to have time to prepare—and he couldn't prepare unless he knew what was coming. So it was crucial that he not know.

Surprise was also vital because if Olds became aware of the scope and intensity of the attack that was to be launched on him, he might arrive at the subcommittee hearing with an attorney—an attorney experienced in such hearings and unintimidated by senators, an attorney who might, for example, request a recess if unexpected charges were suddenly made about writings or events that had occurred so long in the past that the witness needed an opportunity to familiarize himself with them before he answered questions about them. Many liberal Washington attorneys would have been willing to represent Leland Olds at the hearings. "He was a hero of mine," the great liberal advocate Joseph L. Rauh was later to say; "I would have gone in a minute" had Olds asked him. So it was important that Olds not become aware.

Finally, there was potentially a great deal of support for Olds—not only from officials of rural cooperatives all across the country for which he had helped to obtain electricity, and from governors and mayors whose constituents' natural gas bills had been reduced as a result of his efforts, but also from major figures of the New Deal aware of Olds' role in implementing FDR's policies. This support could be effective if it was organized and mobilized—as it would be should the seriousness of the threat to Leland Olds be recognized. So it was important that it not be recognized.

FOR A WHILE, keeping Olds and his liberal supporters from knowing what was coming was easy, for they believed that Lyndon Johnson was on their side.

The link that most strongly bound together the particular inner circle of

New Deal liberals of which Johnson had been a part was the fight that had been a central element of both Leland Olds' career and Johnson's—the fight to break the power of private electric utility companies and bring electricity to farms: in Olds' case, to all America's farms, in Johnson's to the farms of Texas' Tenth Congressional District. Tommy Corcoran and Ben Cohen had drafted the legislation that broke up the utility monopolies and created the REA, Jim Rowe had been their young assistant in that drafting; Abe Fortas had devised the strategy that enabled the PWA to defeat the power companies' lawsuits. And Johnson's victory in his difficult fight to "bring the lights" to the Hill Country had seemed to this group to be a wonderfully concrete realization of the goal—"public power"—for which they had been fighting. If as a senator Johnson had backed the Kerr Bill, well, that was a necessary requirement for any senator from Texas, and it hadn't anything to do with electric power, after all—and as for Lee's renomination, surely Lyndon, the passionate advocate of public power, would not oppose one of public power's greatest champions. In fact, Johnson had had dealings with Olds when he brought electricity to his district, and in these dealings, the two men had been in accord; Leland Olds felt that Lyndon Johnson was not only his ally but his friend. There had been a disagreement early in 1949, but only a brief one: Olds had rejected a Johnson request for a waiver of an FPC regulation that was causing complications on a Brown & Root construction project, but Johnson had quickly retreated. Olds believed that they were still basically on the same side—and that in the subcommittee hearing, he would have a friend in the chair. He believed, too, as did his friends, that these 1949 Senate hearings would be similar to the 1944 Senate hearings: the charge of "Communist" would be made; no one would take it seriously; even should the subcommittee vote against the nomination, his support in the full Senate was so overwhelming that he would certainly be confirmed.

For as long as possible, Johnson did nothing to disabuse the liberals of this notion. The nomination certificate from President Truman arrived at the Commerce Committee on June 5, and Olds assumed at first that renomination would be rather simple; "in fact," he wrote a friend, "I am hoping that confirmation will be possible before June 22, when my present term expires." A liberal Washington attorney who wrote to ask Olds, "What can I do to help out?" said that Johnson "is a good friend of mine but I would assume" he is "already convinced," and that was the general assumption of the letters that arrived at Johnson's office from such New Deal figures as Morris Cooke, the first REA administrator. Much of Washington's liberal community was present on June 14 at a cocktail party for Americans for Democratic Action, and a steady stream of friends came up to Olds to congratulate him on being renominated; they regarded Senate confirmation as a matter of course.

Although June 22 passed without Johnson setting a date for the subcommittee hearings, for some time neither Olds nor his friends saw any significance in the delay. It seemed only a repeat of the 1944 renomination scenario, when his nomination had not been confirmed for almost four months after President Roosevelt sent it up, and almost three months after his term had expired—and, with the exception of Moore's opposition (which proved to have no real significance), the explanation for the delays had been simply the usual Senate foot-dragging. Confirmation of appointees after their terms had expired was not, in fact, unusual in the Senate even for non-controversial candidates. During the summer, however, disturbing rumors began to be heard: that a whispering campaign was being carried on against Olds—and that the whispers were having an effect. In August Olds wrote a friend that there was a "good deal of opposition." Ben Cohen had lunch with Lyndon Johnson, and then reported on the lunch to Tommy Corcoran—and afterwards Corcoran said he was "afraid of the decision now."

Even then, however, the depth of Johnson's opposition was not understood. Olds still believed, as did most liberals, that the leader of the Senate opposition was Oklahoma's Kerr. They felt that Johnson's opposition would be limited to the *pro forma* statements and vote against the nomination obligatory for a senator from the nation's largest natural gas producing state. On August 18, Estes Kefauver spoke to Committee Chairman Ed Johnson, who, as Kefauver related to Olds, "rather agreed" that the "White House could probably bring Lyndon around." A column by Thomas Stokes on August 25 carried a warning of "serious danger" to the confirmation, but did not even mention Lyndon Johnson's name. It was only very gradually, as Summer turned into Fall, that Olds and his supporters began to suspect that a key figure in the opposition was the senator Olds had thought was his friend—the chairman of the subcommittee before which he would be appearing.

And then, on September 16, 1949, almost three months after his term had expired, Olds was finally notified of the date the subcommittee hearing would begin—September 27, just eleven days away; the first day would be brief and largely devoted to scheduling the roster of witnesses; the hearing would get under way in earnest on September 28. And in September, too, Johnson apparently let the mask drop away in a conversation with Olds, after which Olds wrote a friend that Johnson has "shown open hostility." And in that month, also, the door to the trap that Lyndon Johnson had been preparing was revealed. When, earlier, it had first been announced that the hearing would be held, a five-member subcommittee had been named, and its membership seemed innocuous; one of the two Republican members, in fact, was Owen Brewster of Maine, who was well acquainted with Olds' work, and admired it. Now it was revealed that the membership had been changed. There were to be seven members, not five, and Brewster was not one of them; instead, the three Republican members were three of the Midwest's most rabid Communist haters: John W. Bricker of Ohio, Homer Capehart of Indiana, and Clyde Reed of Kansas. After sounding out Bricker about Olds' nomination, White House aide Tom McGrath reported back that the Ohioan was "unalterably opposed." The White House did not even bother sounding out Capehart and Reed. Several of the Democratic senators on the full Commerce Committee—Francis Myers, Charles Tobey, Brien McMahon, and Lester Hunt—were sympathetic to Olds. Not one was on the subcommittee. Its Democratic members, in addition to Lyndon Johnson, were Ed Johnson, Herbert R. O'Conor of Maryland, and Ernest W. McFarland of Arizona, all of them as rabidly anti-Red as the Republicans. White House emissary Oscar Chapman, returning from an attempt to persuade McFarland to at least keep an open mind, reported that their conversation had been "unsatisfactory," mentioning "wild goose talk about commissions interfering with private business." Wanting the subcommittee's decision to be conclusive in the full, thirteen-member, committee, Johnson had enlarged the subcommittee so that if it was unanimous, the opinion of the rest of the committee wouldn't matter; by the time the full committee considered the Olds nomination, a majority of its members would already be committed against him. And he had made sure that the subcommittee's opinion would *be* unanimous. Not only had the witnesses been selected with care, so had the judges who would be hearing their testimony. The job had been done with Lyndon Johnson's customary thoroughness. The subcommittee was stacked, completely stacked. Leland Olds would not have a single ally on it.

EVEN AFTER the subcommittee's new membership had been announced, Lyndon Johnson maintained his pose when talking with liberal senators. Francis Myers of Pennsylvania visited his office to remonstrate about the "stacked [sub]committee," but Johnson told him that conservatives had been put on it in the hope that when they heard the testimony, they would come to support Olds. And it was the chairman who ran a subcommittee anyway, he reminded Myers—and he was the chairman. Myers, evidently reassured, reassured Clark Clifford, who reassured Olds—as is shown by the note Olds made after his conversation with the White House counsel. "Lyndon going to do judicial job," the note said.

The pose was successful. Olds finally began attempting to round up witnesses, writing a few old allies. "I am in a real fight," he told Adolf Berle, an old New Deal friend from New York. "They are going to avoid the main issue and try to pin the communist or near-communist label on me. . . . I am wondering whether you would feel that you could come down to tell the Committee that I am a reputable citizen." But not only was Olds writing these few letters—writing them at the last minute—after the campaign against him had been going on for months, the letters reveal that he was still unaware of the extent of that campaign, and of what the hearings would be like. While "the subcommittee is rather stacked against confirmation," he wrote Berle, "the administration is going all out" and "I am confident of winning in the long run."

Similar unawareness—and confidence—was still prevalent in Washington's liberal community, where, despite warnings such as the one in Stokes' column, the prevailing opinion remained that while there might be a tough fight, it would certainly end in victory. The President was committed; indeed, as Marquis Childs wrote, "seldom has such zeal been shown in behalf of a presidential nominee." The confidence extended to liberal senators. Paul Douglas didn't even bother to attend the hearings. "We thought it was going to be routine," recalls his administrative assistant, Frank McCulloch. "We had no reason to know what was coming."

No one, including Leland Olds, had any idea of what was in store for him when, on the morning of September 28, 1949, accompanied only by his wife and a single FPC aide—without an attorney, without having any idea of what evidence was to be presented against him (and, indeed, without having seen most of that evidence for more than twenty years)—he walked into the Senate Office Building, and came to the place of his hearing.

11

The Hearing

ROOM 312, on the third floor of the Senate Office Building, was a high-ceilinged room of white marble and tall windows and gold brocade draperies and sparkling chandeliers, but it was not one of the building's larger rooms, so that the wings of the raised horseshoe-shaped dais at one end ran halfway down the adjoining walls, and the room was dominated by the dais's dark, heavy oaken façade. It loomed over the small table, set between the wings, at which witnesses would testify.

Only a few witnesses, spectators, and reporters—uninterested reporters, since the hearings were not expected to generate much news—were sitting in the three or four rows of folding chairs that had been set up in the other half of the room. Coming in with Maud, Leland Olds saw John Lyle sitting among the waiting witnesses. The Congressman was holding a large briefcase on his lap. Olds didn't know what was in it, or why Lyle would be testifying, but then Lyndon Johnson, sitting at the center of the dais, rapped a gavel to open the proceedings and said, "We have with us Congressman John Lyle of Texas. Congressman Lyle, do you have a prepared statement?" and Lyle, taking the chair at the witness table, opened the briefcase, took out a thick stack of white-on-black photostats of the Federated Press articles, and said that Olds' reappointment would be "utterly unthinkable."

"I am here to oppose Mr. Olds because he has—through a long and prolific career—attacked the church," Lyle began. "He has attacked our schools; he has ridiculed symbols of patriotism and loyalty such as the Fourth of July; he has advocated public ownership; he has reserved his applause for Lenin and Lenin's system. . . ."

His stem-winder's voice ringing through the room, Lyle looked up at the senators on the dais. "Yes, unbelievable as it seems, gentlemen, this man Leland Olds, the man who now asks the consent and approval of the Senate to serve on the Federal Power Commission, has not believed in our Constitution, our Government, our Congress, our representative form of government, our churches, our flag, our schools, our system of free enterprise."

Olds had never believed in these things, Lyle said. "What manner of man is this Leland Olds?" he asked. He had discovered the answer, he said, in the fifty-four articles stacked before him; "they provide a clear and definite pattern of Leland Olds' alien economic and political philosophy." Many of them, Lyle said, had been published in the *Daily Worker,* "official organ of the Communist Party," and even those that had been published in other publications, Lyle said, had followed the Communist line. In reading them, he said, "I found he was full in his praise for the Russian system. I found that he advocated radical and alien changes in the things that all of us believe in, live for, and fought for." In the articles, Lyle said, Olds "commends Lenin"; conforms to the "Marxian doctrine"; "praises the Russian system as the coming world order and as a model for the United States; preaches class war; echoes the Communist doctrines of class struggle, surplus value, exploitation, downfall of capitalism, and international action by workers, as proclaimed by Karl Marx in his *Communist Manifesto* and *Das Kapital.*"

And Olds still didn't believe in the Constitution or the American flag, Lyle said. He has an "established contempt for the fundamentals of American philosophy," he said. Olds had merely concealed his true feelings in recent years, he said. "One of Mr. Leland Olds' particular and peculiar talents is the ability— like a chameleon—to be many things to many men." And he had concealed his feelings from dark motives. "Leland Olds has seen fit—even in very recent years—to resort to the gymnastics of expediency to remain in a position of power where his advocacy can retain the influence of high position."

But now that he himself had read those articles, Lyle said, Olds' true feelings were all too clear. "Now I can understand Mr. Olds, can understand his manner of doing things, his easy turn-about without reason, his easy advocacy of either side of a question, using the same artful, deceitful and sly tactics so evident from his writings which I have assembled." These articles, he said, "provide a clear and definite pattern of Leland Olds' alien economic and political philosophy. They unmistakably show that his objectives are basically hostile to our American way of life."

He would prove this, Lyle said, with the photostats he was holding, those photostats of Olds' own articles—with "words from his own pen," most of them words published in the Communist *Daily Worker.*

One by one, Lyle went through the articles that Leland Olds had written during the 1920s—or, to be more precise, through the fifty-four articles that had been selected. With each one, Lyle first summarized the key point: "Mr. Chairman, I have before me here a photostatic copy of the *Daily Worker,* July 16, 1925, wherein Leland Olds claims that educational institutions are subservient to the 'money princes who govern industry.' . . . I just briefly call your attention to a few lines: 'Give till it hurts means nothing to the money princes. They simply can't give till it hurts. They have too much. . . .' " Or: "I have before me, Mr. Chairman and gentlemen, a photostatic copy of the *Federated Press Labor News,* July 20, 1929, wherein Leland Olds hails the 'decay of the church. . . .' "

Early on, there was an interruption. Senator Charles Tobey of New Hampshire had been considered too sympathetic to Olds to be placed on the subcommittee. Assured by Johnson that the hearings would be routine, he had given him his proxy for the vote in the full committee. But he had stopped by to watch the hearings, sitting in one of the empty chairs on the dais, and as the thrust of Lyle's testimony became apparent, he could not restrain himself. As Lyle was calling Olds a "chameleon," Tobey interrupted. "A man has a right to change his mind; does he not?" he asked Lyle. "Did you not ever change your mind on issues and men?" When Lyle replied, "Yes, sir," Tobey said, "Does that not qualify what you are talking about now?" But before that line of questioning could continue, Lyndon Johnson intervened, asking that Lyle be allowed to read his prepared statement without interruption. "The Congressman . . . will be very glad to have any questions asked of him when he concludes, and I should not be surprised if some members of the Senate change their mind if they are willing to indulge him a courteous hearing. . . . If the members will bear with us, at least for a few minutes until the Congressman completes his prepared statement, the Chair will appreciate it."

The only further interruptions were occasional brief exclamations of approval from subcommittee members for Lyle's thoroughness, and a ritual began. Picking up a photostat, Lyle would identify it—"Here is a photostatic copy of the *Daily Worker,* July 5, 1928. There is an article in here entitled 'Imperialism and the Fourth of July,' by Leland Olds." He would read in a voice full of indignation a marked paragraph, sentence, or phrase from the article which he said summed it up. "That, gentlemen, was written by Mr. Leland Olds, who wants your permission to serve in high public office, your consent: 'The Fourth of July will loom as anything but the birthday of liberty.' " Then, rising, he would extend the incriminating photostat—"with a flourish," one observer recalls—to a committee clerk. "Without objection, the article appearing on page 5 of the *Daily Worker* of July 5, 1928, entitled 'Imperialism and the Fourth of July,' will be incorporated in the record at this point," Lyndon Johnson would say.

Occasionally, Lyle would deliver himself of an editorial comment. "Here is an interesting one, gentlemen," or "Perhaps I am naive, gentlemen, but this is one that shook me"—or

Here is one you gentlemen will enjoy, I am sure, because it concerns you. I will summarize it here. According to Mr. Olds, the Government of the United States is nothing more than a servant of business. He views it as a popular delusion that a political system created in a much simpler economic era still affords the people effective control through their votes over the complex industrial state, which has come into being. He says "politicians must perpetuate this idea, for their jobs depend upon it, but the true view," he says, "would reveal the political government handling administrative details for an immensely powerful ruling class."

I am quoting him from that statement wherein he relieves you gentlemen of the responsibility of thinking, the responsibility of acting. All you have to do is handle administrative details for the powerful ruling class.

Occasionally, Lyndon Johnson himself made a brief comment. When Lyle handed up the "administrative details" article, the chairman said, "Without objection we will perform one of those details now and insert this in the record." Usually, however, Johnson simply repeated, over and over, "Without objection it will be made part of the record." And that thick stack of photostats, of the very words that Leland Olds had written, that Lyle handed up so methodically, lent an air of authenticity to the Congressman's testimony. So thoroughly had the articles been deconstructed, in fact, that ideas had been found in them that Olds had not even expressed. At one point Lyle cited five articles to show that Olds had been a propagandist for the "surplus value" theory. "Surplus value," he reminded the subcommittee, is "the fundamental doctrine, you know, of Karl Marx and his Communist followers." As it happened, not one of the five articles contained the incriminating phrase, but Lyle explained that that point was of no significance. "Expressions" used in the articles showed that Olds "adhered to the surplus value" doctrine, the Congressman said. Recondite points had been noted, and now were called to the committee's attention. None of the fifty-four articles contained the word "gravediggers," but that fact was also of no significance. While Olds had not used the word, it had appeared in a headline above one of his articles—in a headline written by some editor in one of the scores of newspapers that printed the article—and Lyle gravely explained the implications to the subcommittee: "The word 'gravediggers' is of interest in view of Karl Marx's statement in the *Communist Manifesto,* page 42. I am quoting from Karl Marx: 'Before all, therefore, the bourgeoisie produces its own gravediggers. Its downfall and the victory of the proletariat are equally inevitable.' " ("Without objection, it will be made part of the record.")

Lyle testified for ninety minutes, and those sentences extracted from Olds' articles—"A new age is being born which will succeed capitalist political democracy"; "Lenin knew what would take the place of political parties when he made his bid for power in Russia with the slogan 'All power to the Soviets' "; "Child labor, and the employment of mothers" are "features of the economic order developed under private capitalism"—read to the accompaniment of Lyndon Johnson's ritualistic drone, "Without objection the article referred to will be made part of the record," painted a convincing picture.

The photostats produced the desired effect, in part because Lyle, by omitting the fact that the articles had been published in the *Daily Worker* only because the Communist newspaper was a subscriber to a press service for which Olds worked, created the impression that Olds had written them specifically for the *Worker* and was employed by it. At the conclusion of Lyle's testimony, Lyndon Johnson asked for questions from the subcommittee. "Mr. Chairman, I have not any questions to ask," Senator McFarland said. "I am shocked beyond words at these articles. . . . I am not a reader of the *Daily Worker,* and frankly I did not know that such articles as these are going out through the United States mail." He had worked with Olds, McFarland said, and "I have had a rather affectionate attitude toward him," but "I think that these are most serious charges, the most serious that I have ever heard made in Congress." Senator Tobey had no questions either. As the recitation of Olds' articles had unfolded, Tobey, who had said an early word in his defense, had quietly left the hearing room, not to return.

THE FIRST ATTACK on Olds had come from John Lyle. The second came from Lyndon Johnson.

At the completion of Lyle's testimony, Johnson thanked him and said, "Mr. Olds, will you come forward," and Olds walked up to the witness table and took his place before the high dais and the senators behind it. Like Lyle, Olds had a prepared statement, a twelve-thousand-word statement he had been writing for several weeks—he had given Johnson a copy the previous day—and he placed it before him on the table. It was, however, to be quite some time before he was allowed to read it.

While Olds' statement did not address Lyle's specific charges—Olds, of course, had not even known that Lyle was going to testify—it happened to deal with the substance of those charges. By sheer coincidence, Olds had composed the most effective answer possible to Lyle's attacks on his philosophy, for his statement was an explanation of his philosophy—an explanation of how it had evolved during his career first as a social worker, minister, teacher, writer, and then as a member of state and federal regulatory commissions; how, for example, it had evolved from a belief that only public ownership could control great corporations into a belief that they could be controlled by government regulation while remaining in private hands. In effect a twelve-thousand-word autobiography, the statement documented, quite thoroughly, the fact that during the twenty years since the last of the Federated Press articles had been written, his thinking had, under the influence of Franklin Roosevelt, changed considerably. It was a closely reasoned, persuasive description of the evolution of his beliefs from the radical liberalism he had espoused during the 1920s to the New Deal liberalism in which he had, during the intervening two decades, come so fervently to believe. And, almost incidentally but quite convincingly, the statement documented the fact that never, not even in the most radical moments of his youth, had Leland Olds believed in Communism. As a young man, the statement said, he had "rejected the approach of Karl Marx" as "unwholesome," and, the statement said, "I still believe that." It noted that throughout his life, as in his determination during the 1920s to "keep Communists from infiltrating" a new political party, he had not merely rejected Communism but had fought Communism. It pointed out that he had never—as Lyle had insinuated—written for the *Daily Worker* but that that newspaper had merely been one of eighty newspapers, almost all of them non-Communist, that subscribed to the press service for which he worked.

Olds' statement dealt not only with his philosophy, but, quite specifically and in detail, with his record: the record he had compiled during the twenty years since he had written the last of those articles—the twenty years during which he had served as a public official. It documented, in detail, the faithfulness and effectiveness with which he had implemented Roosevelt's policies (and, later, the similar policies of Lehman and Truman) in both New York and Washington—in Washington as those policies had been modified by Congress. His statement pointed out that Congress must have approved of his record; during his ten years on the Federal Power Commission, the statement noted, his work "has been an open book to Congress"; he had appeared before congressional committees scores of times; "Congress has had an opportunity to know me, my conception of the FPC's work, and what I was seeking to accomplish"; and, for ten years, again and again, Congress had approved what he was doing. If the statement had been read without interruption, it would have been an effective rebuttal of Lyle's charges.

So he would not be allowed to read without interruption.

Olds had hardly begun when Senator Capehart began firing questions at him. When Lyle's testimony had been interrupted—by Tobey—Johnson had quickly intervened, asking the senators to defer their questions until he had finished, and Lyle had thereupon been allowed to read his prepared statement without interruption.

When Olds' statement was interrupted, the Chairman did not intervene. Intervention finally came from McFarland, who despite his shock at the articles seemed unable to forget completely his onetime "affection" for Olds. Capehart's cross-examination was continuing—with Olds' statement still lying unread on the table before him—when McFarland said, "Mr. Chairman, may I suggest that the testimony offered here this morning has been of such a serious nature that I personally feel Mr. Olds should be given the opportunity to make his statement in chief without interruptions."

"Let us put it this way," Lyndon Johnson replied. "Let us hope Mr. Olds can proceed with his statement with a minimum of interruptions."

After Olds had been reading again for about six minutes, however, Johnson himself broke in. Olds' statement focused on his philosophy, on his record. Johnson wanted the focus on Marxism, and Leninism, and the Communist Party. And he knew how to get the focus there—by linking Olds with the name, instantly recognizable in Washington in 1949, of the head of that party.

Had he not, Johnson demanded of Olds, once spoken from the same platform as Earl Browder?

"It may be the case," Olds replied. "I do not know. I just do not remember. I remember once speaking before the Trade Union and Educational
League. . . ."

That gave Johnson an opening. "When you accepted that engagement with
the Trade Union and Educational League," he asked, "you did so with the full
knowledge and purposes of that organization?"

A stack of photostats—not Lyle's photostats but photostats with which *he*
had been provided by Wirtz—was lying before Johnson. Holding up the first
one, he brandished it in front of Olds. Didn't you know, he demanded, that the
Trade Union and Educational League was "cited by Attorney General [Francis]
Biddle as an affiliate of the Red International Labor Unions?" The document in
his hands, he said, was a page from an edition of the *Daily Worker* of March 29,
1924, reporting on the meeting at which Olds and Browder had both spoken.

"It was my understanding that the purposes of that organization were to
develop the organization of the unskilled and semi-skilled workers in industry
through the forming of unions on an industrial basis," Olds replied. But, he
said, even if he had known back then that the League was an affiliate of the Red
International Labor Unions, and even if he had known that Browder would be
among the other speakers, he would have spoken anyway. "I just want to say I
made it a principle, and I made it a principle all through my life, to accept
speaking invitations no matter who invited me," even if he did not agree with
the organization's views, even in fact if his speech would be "totally alien to
what they thought." How else, he tried to explain, could people be provided
with information that might change their opinions?

With Johnson's continued questioning, the dam broke. Capehart demanded
an answer—"Did you ever speak with Browder?" And McFarland asked, "You
surely do not mean that you would speak before any group no matter what their
objectives were, do you, Mr. Olds?"

"I would not speak in such a way as to further their objectives," Olds
replied. But, he said, he would speak. "Even though those organizations were
communistic or communistically inclined?" McFarland asked. "I think the
situation has changed," Olds said. "I do not think that the point of view of
Communist, or communistically inclined, was so prevalent in the days when I
spoke before the Trade Union and Educational League, as it has been since the
war in this country. I do not think we were thinking in those terms so much as
we are today."

AT LAST, Olds was allowed to resume reading, but he was not to be afforded
that luxury for long. When he reached his experiences with the "brutal suppression" of the Pennsylvania steel strikes, he tried to explain to the subcommittee,
"I am telling this so you will know what kind of *laissez-faire* capitalism I was

writing about during my years as industrial editor of the country's only labor paper during the years 1922 to 1929," but interruptions became continuous, and when Olds attempted to explain the evolution of his regulatory philosophy, Johnson was ready again.

As he asked his questions, Lyndon Johnson's demeanor, observed by the few spectators present, was as calmly senatorial as his dark blue suit or the high, massive dais at which he sat. His right hand, holding a pencil, was poised above a stack of papers, to which, putting on his horn-rimmed glasses, he would frequently refer. His face, normally so mobile, was unusually devoid of expression; what remained was grave and judicious. His voice was low and quiet—"very, very controlled," Busby says—and seemingly all the quieter because of the contrast with the louder voices of his fellow subcommittee members, and with Capehart's bellowing. But the members of his staff had learned that, terrible as were Lyndon Johnson's tantrums, it was the things he said in that low, quiet voice that made them flinch, and hurt most deeply. And there was a force in his voice now that made his Texas twang even more pene-trating than usual; it seemed to fill the room. Though the tone in which the questions were asked was neutral and judicious, moreover, the questions were not. His line of questioning had been developed for him by the great cross-examiner. Ralph Yarborough, in 1949 a lawyer in Austin, was to recall visiting Wirtz's office there during the Olds hearings when the phone rang. "Wirtz picked up the receiver and talked for almost a half hour; his talk consisting almost entirely of questions of the type a lawyer might ask in court. 'First ask him this—,' he said into the phone. 'Then ask him if he—' " Hanging up, Wirtz told Yarborough he had been talking to Lyndon Johnson. "He explained that Lyndon called him every day to report on the proceedings and to get more questions to be thrown at Olds. . . ." And they were effective questions. Olds might have been attempting to explain the evolution of his philosophy, but Johnson wanted a somewhat simpler reply.

"Is it correct to state for the record that you have advocated public owner-ship of railroads and public ownership of utilities and public ownership of coal mines?" he asked.

Johnson wanted, he was to tell Olds a moment later, a " 'yes' or 'no' " answer to that question—and either answer, in that simple form, would have served his purpose. If Olds said no, Johnson could simply point to the sen-tences in the 1920s articles which, read alone, would appear to give the lie to that denial. A yes answer would create the headlines—"OLDS FAVORED PUBLIC OWNERSHIP"—which would further the impression that he was a Communist. And if Olds replied yes, but said that he had changed his mind since he wrote the articles, that reply could be used to support Lyle's charge that Olds was a "chameleon" who changed positions to remain in power—which, as Lyle had reminded the subcommittee (already, even without the reminder, well aware of the fact), was a typical Communist trick.

Olds felt that the question—"Have you advocated?"—was too broad to be

answered accurately, since it seemed to apply to his entire career, and his position on the subject had changed during that career, and had never, even at the
beginning, been as simple as the question implied. He didn't want to answer
the question without explaining that while he had at one time advocated public
ownership, that advocacy had taken place in a context so different—the context
of the 1920s—that what he meant by public ownership could not be understood
if it was defined only in the context of 1949. And "public ownership" was in
itself a misleadingly simplistic term, he felt; for example, he was later to say,
what he had been advocating for utilities was cooperative ownership (such as
the Pedernales Electric Co-op that Representative Lyndon Johnson had formed
in Texas) and he did not consider that "as representing what we today mean by
public ownership." When Johnson asked, "Is it correct to state for the record
that you have advocated public ownership?" Olds replied, "No, sir, I do not
think that is a correct generalization." He said he could "discuss that later at
greater length"—evidently meaning in his prepared statement.

But Johnson was having none of that. "Have you advocated public ownership?" he demanded. "The answer then is no; is that right?"

"Not generally speaking," Olds said. "For the last twenty years—" he
started to say.

But Johnson did not allow him to finish the sentence. Leaning forward, he
asked in the low, quiet voice: "Will you tell me whether you have advocated it
or not? . . . I would like to know. I am not talking generally. I think you can say
'yes' or 'no.' "

Well, actually, Olds tried to explain, he couldn't say yes or no. As "a generalization covering the whole of my active life, it could not be said that I had.
I do think that probably during the twenties—"

That sentence was cut off, too. "I do not want to cover any period of time,"
Johnson said. "Have you ever advocated to your knowledge the public ownership of railroads, utilities and coal mines?"

Olds replied, "I think I have advocated it to the extent that those articles
that were read this morning indicated." When Johnson read a sentence from
one of those articles that he regarded as damaging, Olds said, "I assume that is
a correct statement of my position at that time. . . . According to my writing
during the twenties, they were certainly radical writings; there is no question
about that."

Senator Reed chimed in. "Mr. Olds, cannot you make a direct reply to the
Chairman's question?" he asked. Olds said, "No, I cannot, Senator, for this reason. My thinking in this is not so simple as the Chairman's question would
indicate." Furthermore, he said, it had been twenty years since he had last read
the articles that Lyle had put into the record; he didn't remember them. "I
would have to have them before me to analyze it to tell you just exactly what I
meant." He asked for time to read them. "I would be glad to take them and give
you the answer."

But time was not something Olds was going to be given. The other subcommittee members now seemed freed from all restraint. "It was a lynching party," says Melwood Van Scoyoc, the FPC aide who had accompanied Olds. To Olds' request for time to read the articles, Reed replied with more attacks, and, dissatisfied with Olds' replies, shouted, "I am talking about your evasion on these questions. . . . You have about run the gamut from one extreme certainly from the left-wing extreme, you have been there, according to your own statement."

Johnson had arranged to have a duplicate stack of Lyle's photostats, with the incriminating sentences clearly marked, placed before each of the senators. (No photostats had been given to Olds.) They read the sentences to Olds accusatorially, giving him little chance to reply. Capehart, particularly infuriated by Olds' statement in a 1927 article that Russia was leading the world in attempting to end the exploitation of children in industry, shouted, "You felt that the communistic system in Russia was a great thing." Olds tried to explain that he didn't think the system was a great thing—"I have never thought their method of doing it was right"—yet their efforts on behalf of children were right, but before he could finish that thought, Capehart was on to another sentence, which compared the British trade union movement with labor in Russia. "What you were doing was boosting the Russian system, the communistic system in Russia." "I had no intention of boosting the Russian system in Russia," Olds said, but Capehart was already lifting the next photostat off the pile. Reed appeared to have difficulty understanding Olds' points—referring to a sentence in a 1928 article in which Olds used the phrase "accumulators of wealth," the Kansas senator said: "I want to ask you what you meant . . . when you own your own house you have accumulated some wealth. Are you going to take protection away from householders . . . ?" And he appeared to have difficulty understanding the job Olds had held; he referred to the time "while you were on the *Daily Worker* in charge of the federated department."

OLDS WENT ON SAYING that he wanted to explain his positions, and that his prepared statement would do so. But the statement remained unread on the table before him. For long minutes, the subcommittee's chairman made no attempt to allow him to read it. Nor did he intervene to allow Olds to finish his answers to the senators' questions; indeed, when their attack faltered, the chairman urged it on.

"I am surprised," Lyndon Johnson said, "that Mr. Olds, who is writing this over a period of many years, does not remember what he advocated and does not say, 'Yes, I advocated it. I do not share that view now, but I did say it.' . . . You advocated taking over the electric industry and operating utilities as cooperatives. . . . I do not want somebody to drum up some charges here and say you advocate nationalization. . . . I just want to know what your mind was at that time. . . ."

"I want you to know what my mind was at that time," Olds tried to explain. "The reason I did not answer the question as far as utilities was concerned, perfectly direct, was because I do not consider the statement as it was read in the record, cooperative ownership, as representing what we today mean by public ownership."

But Johnson did not lose sight of the point. "Have you ever advocated public ownership of utilities?" he demanded again. And he finally did obtain a one-word answer. When Olds, after several further exchanges, said, "Do you want me to tell you what I advocate today?" Johnson said, "I want you to answer that question 'yes' or 'no.' " "No, I do not," Leland Olds said.

A few minutes later, Johnson said, in a statement somewhat at variance with the fact that he had organized the hearings around those twenty-year-old articles, "The important thing for this committee to determine—and I hope we will this week—is not what is represented in those articles twenty years ago. They are here and speak for themselves. It is the views of the nominee as represented before this committee today, and I regret that you find it necessary to somewhat generalize, hedge on what happened twenty-five years ago. . . . What those reports contain, what happened back in 1920, 1921, we can accept those. Let us get down to the question of what you think now."

And Johnson's efforts left the senators with the impression he wanted them to have. A comment by Senator Reed showed how clever Wirtz's trap had been—and how Olds did not really have the option of saying he had once advocated public ownership but no longer held that view. "Let me make a little comment there, Mr. Chairman," Senator Reed said. "Mr. Olds is a very able and very clever man who wrote a lot and talked a lot; probably assumed a lot of different positions throughout his career." (Later that day, Reed would make another comment. He made this one to a reporter for the United Press. "Here is a man who is a full-fledged, first-class Communist," he said.)

EVERY TIME OLDS TRIED TO EXPLAIN, the senators sitting above him on the dais would interrupt—almost in alternation: Capehart, then Reed, then Johnson, then Capehart again, two senators known as conservatives, one senator known as a liberal, refusing to let Olds explain. Two senators shouting—Capehart's round face red in his rage—one senator speaking in a soft, emotionless voice, all three tarring him over and over with the same brush.

And the interruptions had an effect on Olds. A reporter wrote that "as committee members frequently interrupted" him, he "rocked back and forth in the witness chair." Busby, who had only seen Olds once before and briefly, was to tell the author that Olds had "a nervous tic—his head would jerk." But Olds did not have a nervous tic, and Van Scoyoc understood. "He kept trying to explain, trying to explain," Van Scoyoc says. "And they wouldn't let him. Every time he started, they would interrupt him: Didn't you appear with Browder? Didn't you write for the *Daily Worker*? Didn't you say Russia had a better system for educating children? It was like they were punching him over and over. He'd keep trying to start, and every time they'd shout him down. And after a while, every time they'd start to shout, his head would jerk back."

RETURNING TO HIS OFFICE after the luncheon recess, Johnson found on his desk two Washington newspapers that had appeared that morning with columns about the renomination fight, both apparently based in part on what the columnists had heard about the "whispers" being circulated on Capitol Hill.

In one, which appeared in the *Star* under the headline "OIL AND GAS INTERESTS SEEN OUT TO HANG LELAND OLDS IN SENATE HEARING," Thomas Stokes told his readers that "it is often the secret maneuvering and manipulations of little groups of men, your elected public servants ostensibly, that decide great issues here that deeply and directly affect your public welfare." A "proved and outstanding champion of the public interest" is on trial before a subcommittee "which obviously is packed against him," he said. (The column had been written the previous day, before Johnson had begun questioning Olds, and it revealed the success with which Johnson had concealed his maneuvering; Stokes wrote that Johnson, "hitherto regarded as a progressive," now "is lined up against Mr. Olds and appearing somewhat uncomfortable in that role.")

Shying away from repeating the charges against Olds—as if reluctant to clothe them with the authority of print—Stokes identified them only as "the usual baseless sort of insinuations so carelessly made these days against progressive figures," but the *Washington Daily News'* Frederick C. Othman was less squeamish. "The opposition made much of the fact that pieces by Washington's leading amateur cellist used to appear in the *Daily Worker,* the Red newspaper," he wrote. "The implication was that if Olds weren't a Communist, he came close." And, Othman said, "If I were a referee, I'd call this hitting below the belt. Olds . . . used to write in his youth for the Federated Press, a kind of press association for labor newspapers. It sold news to hundreds *[sic]* of dailies and weeklies, most published by labor unions. One of its cash customers was the *Daily Worker*. [Olds] couldn't help that."

When the hearings resumed after lunch, there was a dramatic change in Johnson's tone. In part, this may have been because most—perhaps all; the hearing transcript is unclear—of the subcommittee's other members were absent, at a vote in the Senate Chamber, so there was no one present who had to be persuaded of Olds' radical propensities. And the explanation for the change may in part have lain in Johnson's attempt to keep from completely burning his bridges to the liberal community, the same attempt that had led him to downplay the hearings, keeping journalistic attendance low, so that his tactics would not receive a lot of attention in liberal columns. The Stokes and Othman columns were a reminder of how dangerous it would be for these tactics to become widely known. And at least one liberal columnist, Elmer Davis, startled by reports of the morning's hearings, had telephoned Johnson during that luncheon recess to ask if Olds was indeed being called a Communist. Assuring Davis that he was not, Johnson had invited him to attend the afternoon session to see for himself (whether Davis did or not is not known), and Johnson felt that other columnists might attend.

For a while, therefore, the chairman's afternoon tone of voice was as warm and sympathetic as the chairman's morning tone had been cold and threatening—particularly on the point that Othman had termed "hitting below the belt." Making clear that *he* certainly understood that Olds had never been a Communist, Johnson asked Olds, "So far as you know, it was not a prerequisite of the *Daily Worker* for a man to be a member of the party in order that his articles might appear; was it?" (Olds replied, "I judge not. I certainly was never a member of the party. . . .") Olds was even allowed to read his statement for a time without interruption, and, discussing his Federated Press articles, he said, "Frequently I made statements showing that capitalism should be reformed. In the light of the changes which have taken place in the world and my own experience, some of the statements in retrospect have seemed to carry an unfortunate connotation." Johnson, in his new tone, and with a question that revealed a dramatically improved understanding of Olds' point, said: "Reformed, but never destroyed or eliminated; is that right? Just reformed?" Between the chairman on the dais and the witness at the table below a dialogue even ensued. "That [reform] is generally what I had in mind," Olds replied.

> While I would not depart from the basic principle that great institutions such as our corporations must recognize their social responsibility as a moderating influence on the quest for private profits, I think it is pretty generally recognized today that the acceptance of such responsibility is not only a corporate duty, but that in the long run it benefits, through increased prosperity, the corporate owners themselves.

Johnson said, "I think that is a better way to put it than it was put in some of these articles," and Olds said, "I agree with you, Senator. I did not think then, and do not think now, that private enterprise in the 1920s was providing a decent family wage or assurance of security or even protection for the modest savings which small investors entrusted to it."

SENATOR JOHNSON.   Do you think it is now?
MR. OLDS.   I think it is coming much closer to it, Mr. Chairman. I think there has been tremendous progress made in the direction of the reform of capitalism.

And Johnson allowed him to make the point that while once he might have favored government takeover of utilities, for more than twenty years he had been in favor of government regulation. Johnson even allowed him to say:

> I want to answer categorically any contention that I was writing for the *Daily Worker*. I was doing so no more than writers for any press service which that paper takes today may be said to be writing for it. Actually, my articles were appearing in papers as widely separated as the *Seattle Union Record* and the *Brotherhood of Locomotive Engineers' Journal*. . . .

And Johnson was shortly to imply what Olds until recently had believed—that in at least one important area of FPC activity, not natural gas but electricity, they were on the same side. "I thought I had some slight experience with electric utilities with which I think you are personally somewhat familiar," Johnson said. The columnists' charge that Olds is being opposed by the utilities, he said—"the columnists are probably directing that at some [other] members of the committee because I have not tried to conceal the fact, both in and out of the Senate, that I had some interest in public power projects and exerted myself along that line in many instances, but I guess I just do not know what is happening here, and apparently you do not, either. Somebody has some information we do not know anything about."

This new tone didn't last long, however. The vote in the Senate Chamber was over, and the other members of the subcommittee began returning to the hearing. And Olds' statement, read without interruption, was too convincing on points on which Olds could not be allowed to be convincing.

On one crucial point, for example—the implication that Olds had Communist sympathies—the statement showed that this was demonstrably untrue even for the period, the 1920s, during which his radicalism had been strongest. The concrete proof was those provisions that Olds had during the 1920s personally written into the constitution for a proposed new labor party—the provisions designed to keep Communists out of it—and Olds, reading those provisions into the record, said: "This should make it clear that . . . I never believed in nor supported the Communist movement."

The provisions did make that point clear, so without warning Johnson switched the subject to another party. As Olds was saying, "I never believed in nor supported the Communist movement," Johnson abruptly demanded: "What date did you become a member of the American Labor Party?"

The effectiveness of having kept Olds in ignorance of the subjects to be covered in the questioning was again proven, because he did not at once know the answer. "I think I was a member of it for about a year, around 1938," he said, and he tried to explain that "At that time it was not the American Labor Party as it is today. . . ." But as Johnson pressed him, he had to admit, "I do not remember the precise time when I actually [resigned]," and Johnson then asked several questions designed to create the suspicion that Olds had remained in the ALP after it had become infiltrated with Communists, that he was trying to hedge and dodge around that fact—that perhaps he had never resigned from that party at all.

"You did notify them?" he asked.

"I am quite sure I did," Olds said.

"I wonder if you have a copy of that notification," Johnson said. "I think it would be important at this point if you have it."

Olds' recollection was accurate. That night he went home, dug through old boxes of papers, and found his letter of resignation, dated September 18, 1939. But his inability to remember the date at the moment he had been asked for it—an inability that was a dividend of the secrecy in which Johnson had cloaked his tactics—hardened the suspicions of the senators about his truthfulness, and about his Communist sympathies.

And Johnson's sympathetic tone of voice vanished completely when Olds, reading his statement, said, "I come now to the period of my life which I believe is really material to the Senate's consideration of my reappointment for a third term as a member of the Federal Power Commission": his record, a ten-year record, during his first two terms. Johnson couldn't let him talk about the record. The chairman again became sarcastic, Van Scoyoc recalls, "a mean, insulting tone . . . firing questions which made it difficult to answer them, and making it difficult to make sense. . . ."

Hardly had Olds begun talking about FPC policies when Johnson interrupted—to turn the discussion to FPC personalities. He had been quietly telling his fellow senators that Olds had been sowing dissension on the FPC, maligning fellow commissioners who did not agree with him, and now he tried to lead Olds into testimony that would reinforce that impression. At first, Olds replied with an answer that was true to his character. When, abruptly changing the subject, Johnson asked, "I gather you do not share the opinion frequently expressed that maybe some members of the commission are too friendly with utilities?" Olds replied, "I do not think along those lines. I try to assume that every man is good. . . ."

And when Johnson did not let the subject drop, but asked, "You are aware, of course, of the insinuation that has been made about other members of the Commission?" Olds replied: "I did not know there were many insinuations about the members." ("I did not say many," Johnson said. "I do not remember," Olds replied. "You do not remember having seen or read any of them?" "I just do not remember, that is the answer I can give.")

"All right," Johnson said, but it was all right only for a few minutes. Then he returned to the point, with questions designed to reinforce the impression, as well as the impression that he had been spreading that Olds considered himself an "indispensable man." And this time the questions were much sharper, for this was a point that would weigh heavily with senators who hated bureaucrats who assumed more power than Congress had delegated to them. The questions were asked in the quiet, carefully controlled voice, but though that voice, and the face the spectators saw, was carefully empty of emotion, that was not true of the part of Lyndon Johnson's body the audience couldn't see, the part hidden by the dais. As his dialogue with the witness continued, he began to hunch further and further forward, leaning on his arms in his intensity, until his rear end actually rose out of his chair, all his weight on his arms now—leaning further and further forward almost as if the lip of the dais in front of him was a barrier keeping him separated from the witness, a barrier he would very much have liked to cross.

> SENATOR JOHNSON.   You do not think the other members . . . can be actively counted on to pursue a policy of active regulation?
> MR. OLDS.   I think there would be a change in the policy of the Commission if the . . .
> SENATOR JOHNSON.   Why don't you answer my question?
> MR. OLDS.   I am trying to answer it.
> SENATOR JOHNSON.   You are evading it.
> MR. OLDS.   I do not, I frankly do not . . .
> SENATOR JOHNSON.   That is what I want you to say, if that is what you think. I do not want you to hedge and dodge and get away from it and make a speech on another subject.

Johnson began trying to get Olds to admit that the Commission's policies would remain the same even if Olds were no longer a member. Had not even Commissioner Nelson Smith (Kerr's man) concurred in the policies? he demanded, cutting Olds off when he tried to reply.

Olds finally protested against Johnson's tactics. "Unless I can answer these questions in such a way as to make the record intelligent, I cannot answer them," he said.

"I will judge whether it is intelligent or not," Lyndon Johnson said. "You want to make a speech. I have no objection to your making the speech after you answer the question. Were they on the Commission when you accomplished this? . . ." Olds tried to explain. "Was Mr. Smith on the Commission?" Johnson demanded. "Did they agree with you? Were they opposed to the policy?"

Finally, Olds got to reply. No, he said, Smith had not agreed with him. "I was going to tell you that Commissioner Smith issued a minority opinion." In as sharp a statement as Leland Olds made during the hearings, he said to the commanding figure above him on the dais, "That is what I started out to tell you, and I wanted to give you the background. That was the basis of the answer I was going to give you."

Johnson's attitude had again unleashed Homer Capehart, who now gave Olds perhaps more credit for the overall growth of international Communism in the twentieth century than he deserved.

Don't you feel, Capehart asked, that "as a result of the articles . . . in which you praised Russia . . . that made some contribution to the fact that the world pretty much is going communistic today and socialistic?" Olds said he didn't think so, but Capehart would not allow such false modesty to go uncorrected. Olds' article on the Soviet system being "beneficial to children . . . You do not think maybe that had some effect on helping to communize that portion of the world which had been communized or socialized?" ("We have a lot of it in this country," Capehart said. "A lot of what?" Olds asked. "A lot of people who believed in the so-called Soviet system." "I have not seen many of them, Senator." "You have not been looking for them, but there are a lot.")

LELAND OLDS WAS EVENTUALLY allowed to finish reading his statement—every word of it. For over an hour that afternoon, as Capehart and Johnson cross-examined him, the remaining pages lay unread before him. When the cross-examination was completed, Capehart rose and left the hearing room, along with the other senators who had been present. The dais was empty except for Lyndon Johnson. There was no other senator present to hear Olds' statement. And then Johnson allowed him to read.

After a while, as he was reading, some of the other senators returned. But by this time, Olds was dealing not with Communism but with his record on the FPC. As they sat on the dais, the senators chatted with each other, or leaned back and whispered to their assistants. As *The New Republic* commented: "Olds' FPC record was of so little interest to committee members that they scarcely listened to his prepared testimony."

AFTER OLDS FINALLY COMPLETED HIS TESTIMONY, Johnson began calling other witnesses. Those testifying on Olds' behalf received treatment no more sympathetic than the Chairman had given the man they were defending. When Olds' fellow FPC commissioner Thomas C. Buchanan testified that Olds was "a good judge," who "listens patiently, considers soberly, weighs wisely, and judges impartially," Johnson asked: "Do you really believe that last statement you made?" And when Buchanan said he did—"very much so"—Johnson's response was to try to show that Buchanan hadn't known Olds very long. (Actually, Buchanan said, he had known—and worked with—him for ten years.) When the elderly George S. Reed, a longtime member of the New York State Power Authority, said that he had worked with Olds for fifteen years and praised his "single-minded devotion to the ideals of democracy," Johnson could scarcely contain himself and tried to make Reed say that he held an opinion equally favorable about other FPC commissioners. (Refusing to be bullied, Reed said, "Well, I was speaking particularly on account of Mr. Olds.")

.   .   .

JOHNSON GOT the newspaper coverage he wanted. Only a handful of reporters had attended the hearings, and most newspapers relied on the article from the United Press. Reprinted the next morning—Thursday, September 29—in newspapers across the country, it led with Senator Reed's statement that Olds was "a full-fledged, first-class Communist," and used the word "admits," with its implication of guilt, in describing Olds' testimony, referring to "articles which Mr. Olds admitted writing. . . . Commissioner Olds, confronted with the documents, admitted they were 'radical.' . . ."

And over the article were the headlines Johnson wanted—headlines which contained the key word. "SENATOR REED HITS OLDS AS COMMUNIST," reported the country's most influential newspaper, the *New York Times,* above a subhead: "FPC Member, Up for a New Term, Admits 'Radical' Writing of 1929." In the *Washington Post* headline the key word was shortened: "SENATOR SAYS WRITINGS POINT TO OLDS AS RED."

Olds' friends had anticipated that the "Communist" charges brought up in 1944 would be raised again. "The money [natural gas profits] involved, was so big that you couldn't believe that these people were going to let it go," John Gunther (the ADA lobbyist, not the writer) recalls. Even so, largely unaware of Johnson's pre-hearing maneuvering, they felt the attack would again fail, and hadn't taken the hearings seriously. But on that Wednesday afternoon, Gunther received a telephone call from a fellow liberal, who asked, "Were you at the hearings this morning?" Gunther said he had not been. "My God!" the friend said. "They're taking Olds' hide off. They're really out to get him."

Late that afternoon, a group of Olds' admirers met and discussed plans for his defense. The next morning's newspapers had not yet appeared, and for a few hours they were optimistic. "We still hadn't had McCarthy," Gunther says. (Joe McCarthy's speech in Wheeling, West Virginia, which brought his Red-hunting career to national attention, would not be given until February, 1950.) "So I thought, This [Johnson's attack] isn't going to work. The guy [Olds] is too well-respected for this. They [the other senators] are not going to take this seriously." The optimism was briefly reinforced the next morning by the *Washington Post*'s editorial, which attacked "Representative Lyle's despicable and preposterous attempt to smear Mr. Olds as a Red," and by Lowell Mellett, perhaps the only columnist besides Othman to attend the Wednesday hearings, who ridiculed the point introduced by Johnson. After reporting that "I found the hearing had been launched as a trial of Mr. Olds as a former and perhaps unreformed communist," that "the air was charged with emotion or a reasonable appearance of same," and that "the subcommittee members were being 'shocked,' to their manifest delight, by the Federated Press articles," Mellett wrote sarcastically that "there was something worse."

The *Daily Worker* reported his appearance once on the same platform with Earl Browder, the chairman of the Communist Party. That really hit the Senators hard.

"I am shocked," said Senator McFarland of Arizona. "Shocked beyond words!" Which in the case of a Senator, could be a third-degree shock, possibly fatal. But the sturdy Arizonan rose to his feet and departed for the Senate chamber, apparently not wishing to hear any more.

If Senator McFarland had detoured by way of the Congressional Library and asked for a copy of Elizabeth Dilling's book, *The Roosevelt Red Record and Its Background,* he'd have got a shock that would have finished him. On page 59 he would have found a picture of Earl Browder taken with four men with whom he had just shared the platform at a meeting of the American Youth Congress. And who is the smiling gentleman sitting in the middle? None other than the senior senator from Ohio, Mr. Taft.

But their optimism (which of course vanished as telephone reports about the newspaper coverage across the country came in) was not shared by Leland Olds. In front of the subcommittee, Olds had maintained an air of confidence. When, late that afternoon, he got back to the FPC Building, however, he went into his office with his wife and his assistant, and shut the door. "And then he slumped in his chair," Melwood Van Scoyoc recalls. "He was always such a buoyant guy, but he just sat there, slumped, as if he was defeated." He asked Maud not to come to the hearings the next day, but she insisted that she would.

LATE THAT AFTERNOON, Lyndon Johnson shut the door to *his* office, because he had some telephone calls to make. Olds' inability to remember the date of his resignation from the American Labor Party, which many senators believed was a Communist front, had hardened the suspicions of the senators on the subcommittee—and Johnson wanted the circle with suspicions to be widened. Telephoning other senators, he said he was calling just to keep them informed on the hearings, and included in his information the fact that the man they were being asked to confirm had been a member of the ALP, and that, while Olds contended that he had resigned, he somehow couldn't say when. Johnson left the impression that Olds was lying, his tone by turns joking and confidential; Busby and Jenkins, opening the door, saw him with his feet up on his desk, big hand around the receiver, laughing as he described how the witness had squirmed when asked for a date. (If, after Olds had provided the date the next day, Johnson telephoned the senators again to correct the impression, none of his staff heard him do so.)

THE NEXT DAY'S HEARING—the final day scheduled—began with the testimony of pro-Olds witnesses. Johnson hurried them along, and at the conclusion of each witness's testimony, simply thanked him, asking no questions. As the pro-Olds witnesses testified, Johnson's bearing was impatient; several times he pulled out a large stopwatch and looked at it ostentatiously.

This technique was successful because of the thoroughness with which the subcommittee had been stacked, so that there was not even one senator present who was sympathetic to Olds. Joseph P. Harris, a University of California political scientist who was later to analyze the Olds hearings in detail, wrote that "witnesses favoring the nomination were treated politely, but were usually asked no questions. Quite a different public impression would have been made had there been a single member of the subcommittee to ask searching questions of both sides. . . ."

One of the witnesses refused to be hurried. She was Anne K. Alpern, who during seven years as Pittsburgh's city attorney had earned a reputation as a determined opponent of utility monopolies. Noting that the Senate had confirmed Olds twice before, she told the senators: "You have the same set of facts now as then. There is nothing new. Nothing is involved but the same set of facts. They have been brought up here, they have been hashed and rehashed and regurgitated. I think it is unfair. . . ." Aware that a telling point was being made, Johnson tried to cut her off—"If we spend our time considering what happened in 1940 or 1944, we will never get through. Proceed, Miss Alpern." But she faced him down. "Well," she said, "I hope that the senators will ask me some questions, because I think the only way by which anyone has an opportunity to present a point of view is through questions." As she proceeded to praise Olds as "a courageous public servant" ("The courageous ones are the ones who are decapitated. . . . That is why I think this confirmation is so very important. . . . If you do not confirm Mr. Olds . . . men in high positions will be fearful of . . . taking a stand"), other subcommittee members asked hostile questions. Johnson pulled out his watch and kept it out, staring at it as she talked. Then, breaking into her argument and giving her a "hard stare," he said, "Miss Alpern, you have consumed the time allotted to you."

Staring back at Johnson, Miss Alpern said: "Well, Senator, my time has been divided a little unequally between me and the members of the committee." Johnson then allowed her to finish. "We, the consumers of the country, have a great deal of difficulty in fighting utilities matters—we do not have the money; we do not have the staff; we need men like Mr. Olds," she said.

Some of the pro-Olds testimony was quite eloquent. After explaining that Olds' efforts had forced natural gas companies to refund the more than $8 million they had overcharged Kansas City residents in their monthly bills, city attorney David M. Proctor quoted a recent *Kansas City Star* editorial: "Human memory and gratitude are short, but a few persons in this area have reason to remember Leland Olds." The testimony came from witnesses representing both labor unions (William J. Houston of the American Federation of Government Employees called Olds "a man of humanity") and farmers ("Any criticism . . .

reflects more on the critic than on Mr. Olds," said J. T. Sanders of the National Grange). Recalling the hearing years later, Van Scoyoc was to write of the "numerous expressions by persons in his [Olds'] favor." But, Van Scoyoc was also to write, these expressions were "overwhelmed" by "expressions of hatred." For the witnesses who supported Olds were followed by the witnesses who opposed him, the witnesses Lyndon Johnson had selected with such care, the witnesses he had secretly met with and coached. Lyndon Johnson wanted words in headlines equally as devastating as "Communist" or "Red." And in these witnesses he had men who would provide headline writers with the words he wanted.

Two of them, South Texas attorneys linked to natural gas interests, were as unlike in appearance as they were similar in their violent anti-Communism. William N. Bonner of Houston, burly and braggadocious, had a beaming grin; Hayden Head of Corpus Christi, stony-faced and thin-lipped, kept his hair cropped close to his skull and his posture as rigidly erect as if he were constantly at attention in a military drill. Already known throughout corrupt South Texas as "the man with the black bag" because of his political fund-dispensing activities on behalf of Maston Nixon of Southern Minerals and other ultra-conservative Rio Valley moguls, Head was rabid in his racism ("We never celebrate Lincoln's birthday," he boasted) and in his hatred of Reds, which would lead him to found Citizens Alert, an organization to remind America of the threat of world Communism. (Johnson had been particularly impressed with Head; after a long interview with the attorney, he had wired Maston Nixon: "Am sure he will be invaluable.") Johnson had spent a lot of time coaching Bonner, but now, when he called Bonner to the witness table, he looked around the room as if he had never seen him before. "Mr. William N. Bonner," Johnson said. "Is Mr. Bonner present?"

As it happened, Mr. Bonner was, and taking his seat at the witness table, he testified that Leland Olds was "a traitor to our country, a crackpot and a jackass wholly unfit to make rules," that the Federated Press was "a communistic sheet whose articles were published each week by the *Daily Worker*," and that Olds "does not deny speaking from the same platform with Earl Browder."

"Every public utterance which this punk has uttered, every final position which he has taken, shows beyond cavil that he would, if permitted, substitute 'security' and 'statism' for freedom and opportunity," Bonner said.

Hayden Head had been saved as the last witness—for Head was the climax. He said Olds was a Communist, and also an intellectual (which made him "all the more dangerous. . . . He is a much greater threat to the American way of life than he would be if his brain were less agile")—and Head implied, sitting at attention in the witness chair, that Mr. Olds might also be something more: a Communist *agent* who had turned from writing to bureaucratic administration to accomplish his aims from within the government, an agent using the power he had obtained as a high governmental official to advance the Communist conspiracy—to destroy free enterprise, the capitalistic system and "American freedom."

"Do you realize, gentlemen of the committee," Head asked, that "Leland Olds, clothed in the mantle of respectability, of high public office, both State and Federal, has continued without appreciable intermission the pursuit of those objectives which he advocated twenty years ago in the columns of the *Daily Worker*? . . . He has done it slowly, yes: but insidiously, delicately, step by step, but relentlessly and persistently."

And, Head declared, Olds had already "accomplished much" of his agenda. "The entire history of his administration in the Federal Power Commission can well be characterized as a bite-by-bite process. . . . How far away is the last juicy bite, the destruction of the 'myth of private property'?"

During his ten years on the FPC, Head declared, Olds had been "indoctrinating" the FPC "with the tenets of, shall we say, communistic, or, shall we say identical with communistic thoughts, that is evident in his writings of the twenties. . . . Why should Mr. Olds continue to write for the Federated Press, for the *Daily Worker* (for Industrial Solidarity) when he can write for the Federal Power Commission and accomplish much more? Mr. Olds is boring from within; Mr. Olds is a termite; Mr. Olds is gnawing away the very foundations upon which this Government exists."

Who knew, Head asked, how far such hidden communistic influence might extend? "The elements in this country which support the philosophy which Mr. Olds represents are stronger than I had realized," he said. There was, for example, the *Washington Post,* "which, as I understand, is what is called one of your more advanced papers."

"In the *Post* there appear the writings of a man by the name of Childs," Head noted. Marquis Childs' attacks on the Natural Gas Act, he said, "seem strangely reminiscent of the words of Mr. Olds" and are part of "the greatest organized campaign of propaganda . . . that I have ever witnessed." Not only Childs but "a man by the name of Mellett, I believe, and another man by the name of Stokes have been in the forefront of the attack."

And, Head declared, "this morning the apex of misrepresentation occurred." He was referring to the editorial in the *Washington Post* which called John Lyle's testimony "despicable" because of its attempt "to smear Mr. Olds as a Red." The editorial, Head said, was "the culmination of this propaganda campaign, waged by Mr. Olds' machine. . . . No greater pack of lies has ever existed than that."

THE *POST* EDITORIAL had evidently struck a nerve not only with Head but with the subcommittee's chairman. And Mellett's column was a danger signal. What if other liberal columnists—the columnists who had believed that Lyndon Johnson was a liberal—appeared at the hearings, and saw what Mellett had seen? To telephone calls from liberal friends Wednesday evening inquiring about the reports they had been hearing, Johnson assured them that the reports were incorrect: Olds had indeed been labeled a Communist, he said, but not by him. On the contrary, he told the callers, he had attempted to stop such smears. He told the callers to come to the hearings and see for themselves.

Lyndon Johnson's behavior that Thursday morning was, for a time, as studiously impartial as it had been—for a time—after Wednesday's Stokes and Othman columns had appeared. He repeatedly attempted to document the even-handedness with which he had conducted the hearings by emphasizing that any witness—whether pro- or anti-Olds—would be allowed to appear: "I just want to be sure that the record shows that every man who wanted to say anything had his say," he declared at one point. He even attempted to distance himself from the most violent aspects of Bonner's testimony, thereby decrying in public the very words he had approved in private. "Now, Mr. Bonner," he admonished him at one point during his testimony, "there is no testimony before this committee that Mr. Olds was a member of the Communist Party. . . . There is no one who testified that he is disloyal to his Government. As a matter of fact, we had witnesses all day yesterday who talked about how loyal he had been." (Bonner would shortly be writing to "Dear Lyndon" to "compliment you on . . . the very able manner in which the entire hearing was conducted," and to gloat over his testimony's success in producing headlines. "Half the states . . . quoted my own statement . . . particularly the expression 'punk' which I used").

During the testimony of anti-Olds witnesses the chairman's stopwatch remained in his pocket; even though Head's testimony consumed more time than he had requested, Johnson made no reference to "time consumed." And during Bonner's testimony, the chairman departed from his previous practice. The Houston attorney had come equipped with his own photostat: a typed four-page summary—provenance unknown—of information from the files of the House Un-American Activities Committee: "Subject, Leland Olds." Bonner, holding the photostat out to Johnson, asked that it be made a part of the record. When other witnesses had presented exhibits with a similar request, Johnson had simply said, "Without objection, it will be made a part of the record," and had indicated that the documents should be handed to a committee clerk. But with this exhibit—perhaps because Senator Bricker, who was particularly susceptible to HUAC information and who had been out of town, had just made his first appearance at the hearing, and could not be relied on to read through the transcript of previous testimony—Johnson, before handing this exhibit to a clerk, said, "For the benefit of the committee, I will read the article [sic] into the record"—and did so, every word. Only after ten minutes of his recitation—"In Report 1311 of the Special Committee on Un-American Activities, dated March 29, 1944, the Federated Press was cited as a Communist-controlled organization. . . . In the report of the Special Committee on Un-American Activities, dated January 3, 1939, the Trade Union Educational League was cited as a project put under control of and made amenable to the central executive committee of the Communist Party of America"—did Johnson add a disclaimer. "Now I will say that the testimony yesterday by Mr. Olds covered most of the references. . . . Mr. Olds testified that he never belonged to the Communist Party. . . ."

He got the reaction from Bricker he wanted—both then ("He did not deny any of this charge, then, on page 4?") and at the end of the hearings, when Head was winding up his testimony. "In conclusion, I say this," Head declared. "Leland Olds is a fraud, he is a fraud on his friends who appeared here in his behalf; he is a fraud on the consuming public whom he fills with misleading statements. He is a fraud on the press, whom he fills with misleading statements, and he is a fraud on the people of the United States of America." "It is a good, strong, positive statement, certainly," said Senator Bricker.

And Johnson again got the headlines he wanted. Newspapers in states across the country did indeed, as Bonner boasted, carry some version of his statement; a headline in the *Houston Post,* for example, said: "LELAND OLDS LABELED CRACKPOT AND TRAITOR." The attorney's colorful phrases—along with Head's—provided rich grist for newspapers predisposed to be hostile to Olds, enlivening the articles under the headlines; the first sentence in the *Philadelphia Inquirer*'s article informed readers that "Leland Olds, President Truman's choice for a third term on the Federal Power Commission, today was branded a 'punk,' a 'crackpot,' a 'jackass' and a 'traitor' by a witness before the Senate Commerce Committee." "Denounced as a traitor to his country," reported the *Chicago Tribune.*

JOHNSON HAD ALLOWED only two full days for the hearings, and his emphasis on dispatch was perhaps explained by a remark he made to other subcommittee members Thursday afternoon: "The rumor has gone around today that maybe the proponents would like to continue the hearing on into next week some time until they get some more articles written, and things like that." By taking Olds' supporters by surprise, he had kept them from mobilizing support behind the embattled commissioner. He didn't want to give them time to mobilize now.

A stumbling block now appeared in the road to speedy conclusion, however. Olds asked for a chance to reply to the charges against him.

He had asked on Wednesday, as he was rising from the witness chair, and Johnson had said, "I think that can be worked out."

Johnson's idea of "working it out," however, involved speed. The rest of the hearings would wind up Thursday afternoon; Olds could reply, Johnson said, on Saturday morning. But when, on Thursday, Olds asked the committee clerk for the transcript of Lyle's testimony, and the exhibits upon which it was based—the fifty-four Federated Press articles—he was informed they would "not be available" until sometime Friday.

Olds thereupon wrote to Johnson requesting a postponement until the following Wednesday. "The material selected by Representative Lyle purports
to be selected from articles which I wrote more than twenty years ago and
which . . . number some 1,800," he said. "To have such material thrust upon me
at a moment's notice and without an opportunity to relate the selected articles
to my work, placed me in a position in which I could make no adequate comment. . . . I am, therefore, writing you . . . to renew my request for opportunity
to study the record and to make such answers as I believe necessary in a public
hearing."

Reasonable though Olds' request may have seemed, however, it was not to
be granted. Rather than replying to Olds himself, Johnson had a Commerce
Committee clerk, Edward Cooper, do it. At seven o'clock Thursday night,
Cooper telephoned Olds that the schedule would not be changed: his reply was
still scheduled for 10 a.m. Saturday. And Cooper made clear that there would
also be no change in the schedule for providing him with the transcript on
which the reply would be based: that would still not be available until sometime Friday. Olds was being given twenty-four hours—or less—to prepare his
defense.

There was what Olds was to call a "big heap" of Federated Press clippings
in his house on McKinley Street in northwest Washington, but he hadn't looked
at them in years, and they had just been tied together haphazardly; merely to
sort through them and to arrange them in some kind of order would take hours.
And he knew he didn't have many—perhaps most—of the articles Lyle had
cited; it had taken teams of investigators weeks of sorting through copies of old
newspapers in libraries to compile a complete file for the prosecution. Following Cooper's call, Olds worked until midnight Thursday sorting through the
clippings, and arose to continue at five-thirty Friday morning—still without
having seen the transcript to which his defense was supposed to reply. As the
impossibility of preparing an adequate defense by Saturday became apparent,
Olds telephoned Johnson to plead for more time. "I had asked for Wednesday," he said; if that was impossible, "I feel that in justice I should have until Monday to get this answer ready. I am appealing to you to let me have until
Monday. . . ."

"I talked to the [sub]committee before I called," Johnson replied. "Some
of them will be out of town Monday. They suggested you take Saturday. . . ."

When Olds obstinately balked at this suggestion, Johnson casually
unveiled a threat. Of course, he said, if Olds insisted on submitting additional
material, Lyle would testify again—and submit additional material himself.
"He said he had some pretty recent statements and will come back with some
more comparisons," Johnson said. "Said he had some more of your views he
would like to read into the record." And Johnson insisted firmly on his own
point of view. When Olds mentioned the "voluminous record" he had to study,
Johnson said the issue was actually quite simple. The subcommittee's "view-

point," he said, "is that there are some fifty articles and that you either wrote them or you did not. It shouldn't take any time to decide that." When Olds said that the White House "want[s] me to deal with this thing as fully as I think I ought to," Johnson replied: "You either wrote the article or you did not. We put the page and paragraph and you can check them." "It is not as simple as that," Olds said.

It was not he who objected to delay, Johnson said, but other members of the subcommittee: "As far as I am concerned I will have no objection. I will recommend it. I want to be as fair as I can. . . . I will treat you just as I would want you to treat me if the positions were reversed. I will talk to them and if I can get them to be agreeable I will let you know. . . ."

Later, Johnson called back, and said that the subcommittee had agreed to the Monday date. "Well, you are very kind," Leland Olds said. "And I appreciate what the others did very much, too." He wouldn't have the five days he had asked—a meagre enough time to defend a lifetime's work—but at least he would have a whole weekend.

"AT THE OUTSET I want to state simply and categorically that I am not a Communist," Olds said on Monday morning. "I never was a Communist. I am and always have been loyal to my country. I am and always have been a profound believer in democracy. In my opinion the very theory of Russian communism represents a negation of democracy.

"I did write radically during the period publicized by Mr. Lyle," Olds said. "I did so because I believed radical writing was needed in the 'golden twenties' to shock the American people, and particularly labor, out of social and political lethargy. . . . I felt that unless the American people were aroused to do something about it, the American way of life would be in real jeopardy."

Olds' prepared statement then would have gone on to analyze, one by one, the articles which Lyle claimed showed his "alien" philosophy. But Johnson may have been working that weekend, too, with the man who said, "First ask him this—" "Then ask him if he—" Hardly had Olds begun reading this analysis when Johnson cut him off—cut him off with questions that applied to the articles as a single group, and in the broadest, most simple (or, to be more precise, simplistic) terms. "Mr. Olds," he demanded, leaning forward across the dais and speaking in a very soft tone in which every word was carefully enunciated, "do you repudiate those writings?" And when Olds said he didn't, Johnson asked: "Do you reiterate them? Do you reassert them?"

> MR. OLDS. I am going to discuss those writings in terms of Mr. Lyle's presentation and tell you exactly what those writings mean.
> SENATOR JOHNSON. We are going to be able to judge what they mean. We will be glad to have your viewpoint upon what they mean,

but the question I want to ask you: Do you still feel as you did when
you wrote those articles?

MR. OLDS.   No. I have indicated that the change in the circumstances in this country, and the change in my thinking that has gone
along with it, would lead me to write some of those articles in a
somewhat different way today.

SENATOR JOHNSON.   But there has been a change in your thinking
since those articles were written?

MR. OLDS.   There has been a change in my thinking.

SENATOR JOHNSON.   Then you do repudiate certain things you said
then?

MR. OLDS.   I do not repudiate them as said at that time in terms of
my relationship to that period in which I was writing.

Repeatedly, as Olds attempted to explain the points he had been trying to
make during the 1920s, Johnson would cut in, demanding that he either "repudiate" or "reassert" them. Repeatedly, Olds would try to explain to Johnson that
the situation was not as simple as the question made it appear. His thinking had
changed, he said over and over, but those writings represented what his thinking had been at the time. He still believed that they represented his thinking at
the time. For example, "I did not think then, and I do not think now, that private
enterprise in the 1920s was providing a decent family wage or assurance of
security or even protection." And, he said, he therefore could not honestly repudiate them.

But simplicity was what Johnson was interested in. Over and over, when
Olds attempted to explain what he had meant by an article, how it related to the
times in which it had been written, or how its meaning had been altered by
changes in political or economic conditions, Johnson would cut in, demanding
that he either "repudiate" what he had written or "reiterate" it.

Whoever framed that question—Alvin Wirtz, Horace Busby, Lyndon
Johnson himself—could be proud of its effectiveness, for it placed Olds again
in a trap. Refusal to repudiate a specific article could be interpreted to mean
that the witness still held the beliefs expressed in it. If he said he did repudiate
the article, his repudiation could be taken as proof that he was indeed a
"chameleon" willing to express any view that would keep him in power—so
that he could further his secret communistic aims.

Had Olds been allowed actually to deal with the articles Lyle had quoted,
his answers would have been definitive. The articles may have been "carried in
the *Daily Worker*," he said, but they had not been written *for* the *Daily Worker*,
but for the Federated Press subscribers in general, and many other, non-
Communist, papers had carried them. (In a further demonstration of Johnson's
sophistry—and of Johnson's sensitivity to criticism—when Olds said this, the
chairman turned to the other senators, made a palms-up gesture of injured inno-

cence, and said, "The committee has not charged him, and so far as I know no other witness has charged him, with being an employee of the *Daily Worker*. And we do not want the country to get the impression that he has been so charged.")*

But Olds almost never got to make his points in an uninterrupted, coherent way. When, for example, he attempted to explain what he had meant when he wrote during the 1920s of the necessity for labor to obtain increased political power, Johnson said: "I am not asking you what you meant. I am asking you what you said."

"I made that statement, yes," Olds replied.

"You repudiate it today?" Johnson demanded.

"I repudiate it in the sense in which it is understood by you gentlemen," Olds said.

"I am not saying what the understanding is. I am asking, do you repudiate or do you reiterate it?"

"I would repudiate it," Olds said. ". . . What I was trying to describe is still going on, but I think I would repudiate today the way I said it then. I would say it in different terms today, if that is what you mean."

More than an hour after Olds resumed the witness stand, with his written statement barely begun, Johnson was still employing this tactic. ("The question the committee is considering is, What did you say? Did you say it? If so, Do you repeat it today? . . . If you said them, say so. If you believe them, say so. You have a right to say that and thank God in this country a man can still exercise some free speech.") At that point, Senator McFarland stepped in, as he had done on the first day of Olds' testimony, saying, "Mr. Chairman, I was just going to suggest that probably the best way would be for us to, nearly as we can, let Mr. Olds finish his statement in chief and then we would go back and bring up anything that we wanted in the nature that the chairman has suggested. . . . I believe that he ought to get in the record, in any way that he wants to, his explanation and then come back to the questions." Only then did the pace of the interruptions slacken—they never stopped completely—sufficiently so that, two hours later, Olds could get to the end of his statement.

The "repudiate" or "reiterate" tactic was effective with conservative journalists. Some of them, like nationally syndicated columnist Gould Lincoln, felt they knew how to interpret Olds' refusal to "repudiate."

Mr. Olds himself told the Senate Committee that he would have written the articles differently today—but he did not recant.

*Olds said that he had not even written one article Lyle had cited, charging that in it Olds had "publicized a school for Communists, urging the comrades to attend." That article was indeed damaging, Olds said. But, he said—in a statement never thereafter challenged by Lyle, the HUAC investigators, Lyndon Johnson, or anyone else—he had not written that article; he had never seen it before.

This raises again the issue whether the Administration is inclined to be soft with the Reds and fellow-travelers. . . .

Other conservative journalists felt Olds *had* recanted—and they knew how to interpret *that*. Calling him "chameleon-minded," the *Dallas Morning News* editorialized that he "no longer thinks along radical lines" only because he is in power. But "what guarantee have we of what his thinking will be tomorrow?" the editorial asked.

The tactic was effective also with the subcommittee members. As a *Time* correspondent explained, some of its members felt that "he is a radical and that he switches position and policy with rapid facility" while others were angered by his refusal to switch—"He had plenty of chances to renounce his inflammatory writings . . . but he declined to do so—That did weigh heavily against him."

THE SUBCOMMITTEE had been carefully selected for its susceptibility to testimony about Leland Olds' radicalism, and the effect of that testimony had been as powerful as even Lyndon Johnson could have wished—as was proven when, the following morning, Tuesday, October 4, its seven members met in Lyndon Johnson's office to cast their votes on the nomination. For the President had decided to fight for his nominee. After hearing a summary of the previous day's testimony, he had written a letter to Commerce Committee Chairman Ed Johnson, and the Coloradan read it to the subcommittee.

"I am aware of the efforts that have been made to discredit Mr. Olds before your committee," Harry Truman wrote. And it was because of those efforts that he was writing—"because of the nature of the opposition that has been expressed to his confirmation."

"Nothing has been presented in testimony there which raises any doubt in my mind as to his integrity, loyalty or ability," Truman said. "Much that has been said about him is largely beside the point. The issue before us is not whether we agree with everything Mr. Olds may have ever said or even whether we agree with all of his actions as a member of the Federal Power Commission. The issue is whether his whole record is such as to lead us to believe that he will serve the nation well as a member of the Federal Power Commission."

On that issue, Truman said, the record is clear. During ten years on the Commission, "he has served ably, and loyally. . . ." He is "a nationally recognized champion of effective utility regulation; his record shows that he is also a champion of fair regulation." During those years, Truman said, Olds has "made enemies. . . . Powerful corporations subject to regulation by the commission have not been pleased with Mr. Olds. They now seek to prevent his confirmation for another term. It would be most unfortunate if they should succeed. We cannot allow great corporations to dominate the commissions which have been created to regulate them."

Ed Johnson had received Truman's letter the previous evening, had discussed it with Lyndon Johnson, and a reply had been drafted. It might have been (and perhaps was) drafted by the same hand that had drafted Lyle's testimony, so closely did it follow its theme.

The President might feel, "Mr. Wisdom" wrote him, that Olds' articles were "beside the point," but the subcommittee begged to disagree. "The subcommittee," he said, "was shocked beyond description by the . . . views expressed by Olds some years ago." He would, he said, "include herewith a few excerpts"—and he quoted several of the paragraphs Lyle had quoted.

Certainly, Olds had sounded sincere in claiming that his views had evolved, Ed Johnson said—that was another reason for distrusting him. "The committee found Mr. Olds glib of tongue and very convincing. Like many crusaders for foreign ideologies he has an attractive personality and is disarming to a very high degree." Despite the presence of four Democrats, members of the President's party, on the subcommittee, its vote on a resolution, introduced by Lyndon Johnson, to report the presidential nomination to the full committee with the recommendation that it be rejected was a unanimous 7–0. The next day, as the *New York Times* reported, "President Truman's earnest appeal for the confirmation of Leland Olds for a third term as Federal Power Commissioner fell on deaf ears again" when the full Commerce Committee "voted 10 to 2, against the nominee."

WHEN A TELEGRAM ANNOUNCING the committee vote was read to a meeting of the International Petroleum Association of America in Fort Worth, the eight hundred oil and natural gas producers in attendance broke into cheers and rebel yells.

The reaction was different in Washington—in those precincts of Washington in which Lyndon Johnson had for so long held himself forth as a liberal, as the protégé of Franklin Roosevelt, as a crusader against the forces of conservatism in Texas.

The first reaction was shock—for so thoroughly had the preparations been concealed that it was only as the subcommittee and committee took their votes that the liberal community woke up fully to what had been done. "What a subcommittee!" *The New Republic* exclaimed. "It's been packed. They even brought in Bricker and Capehart. If we were a defendant in Russia and saw such a mackerel-eyed bunch as that looking down at us from the bench we'd start writing confessions quick."

Then there was outrage over the way in which it had been done: over the method used to reject Olds—the Communist smear. As *The New Republic* put it: "Olds, shouts the Senate committee shaking the yellowed pages of newspapers 20 years old, is the glib salesman of a foreign ideology. Who, then, are the Americans? Olds is the product of New England's Protestant conscience, of social work in Boston slums and of Pennsylvania steel strikes, of Frank Walsh and Franklin Roosevelt. . . ." The views Olds had held in the 1920s were views so many liberals had held, liberals pointed out. "I know of few men worth their intellectual salt who didn't have some of the doubts Olds had at the time," Max Lerner said. In an editorial in the *Washington Post*, Alan Barth wrote that "Like many a young man, he [Olds] was in a great hurry to reform the world [and] said some extravagant things in his column 25 years ago. Taken out of context and looked at in the light of today's relationship between left and right, they may be made to seem extremely radical. But the social conditions of 25 years ago invited radicalism. A man could denounce open-shop capitalism in those days without being called a Communist or being considered disloyal to the United States. The elder La Follette did so."

And Olds' views were not the true reason for the campaign against him, which was, *The Nation* said, actually a "vendetta . . . a flagrant attempt by vested interests to exclude from office a man who proved too 'consumer-minded' to suit their purposes." The real issue was the immense profits to be made from natural gas, I. F. Stone explained. "This is the reason for the fight on Olds. If he had been willing to knuckle under on the issue, he would have been forgiven the authorship of *Das Kapital* itself." But, these liberal writers knew, the campaign had been successful, frighteningly successful. As Lerner put it: "Once the issue of Olds-as-onetime-devil was raised, no one dared line up on his side. The hunting of dangerous thought has overridden every other quest. None of the Senators dared to take a chance that someday an opponent would accuse him of having voted for a man who had once criticized our master-institution of corporate power." And these writers understood the larger implications of that success. "No one in the government service is safe unless he played an intellectual Caspar Milquetoast from the moment he left his teens," Lerner declared. The Olds case was teaching Washington that "all a lobbyist has to do is dig up something vaguely pink or crimson in a recalcitrant official's past to ruin him," I. F. Stone said. As the *Christian Science Monitor* reported: "It is hardly surprising that the case of Leland Olds has embittered Washington as few such cases have in recent years."

And, as awareness grew of Lyndon Johnson's role in the campaign, increasingly the liberals' bitterness began to be directed against him—for many of them were now coming to believe that Lyndon Johnson had betrayed them. The awareness had grown slowly. His friends had not previously focused on the fact that he was the chairman of the subcommittee against which they were raging, but now, criticizing the subcommittee for being "so hostile to Olds that it resembles the House Un-American Activities Committee under J. Parnell Thomas," *The New Republic* rectified the omission—with a vengeance. In an editorial entitled "The Enemies of Leland Olds," the magazine said that "Against Olds is a onetime liberal Senator, Lyndon Johnson, born into the family of a poor farmer, brought forward by the New Deal, and carried into office by liberal and labor support. Johnson, who saw his first backer, Aubrey

Williams, hounded out of government on charges of Communism, now is hounding Olds out on the same charges—Johnson, who boasted that 'Roosevelt was a Daddy to me.' How Roosevelt would have scorned such backsliding!" Increasingly, in newspaper articles and editorials, the subcommittee was identified as "Johnson's subcommittee."

Over the weekend during which Olds was sorting frantically through ancient clippings, trying to assemble his defense, a new issue of *Fortune* magazine appeared on Washington newsstands with an article whose timing was, from Johnson's point of view, unfortunate. Among the photographs accompanying the article—on the "Big Rich" of the Texas and Louisiana Gold Coasts—was a picture of the two Brown brothers, Herman and George, and the article reminded the capital that "a tremendous item in which they [the Browns] have big holdings is Texas Eastern Transmission Co., owner and operator of the Big Inch and Little Inch pipelines. . . . Although they are pretty sure that there is no such thing as good publicity, they are well known in select circles. These include potent people in Washington. They once put up $100,000 to back Lyndon Johnson for Congress. . . ." ("This," Lowell Mellett commented in the *Washington Star,* "may explain the strange tangent taken by the subcommittee under Senator Johnson's chairmanship.")

The sense of betrayal was sharpest among those who had thought they knew Lyndon Johnson best: the small circle of liberal friends who for years, at their dinner tables, had heard him talk so eloquently about cheap electricity ("Public power was a passion with him") and about the rapaciousness of the private utilities. This circle, in fact, included some of the lawyers who had helped him circumvent the law to keep the Senate seat he had won in such questionable circumstances, because they had believed that by helping him win, they were helping to bring a strong new liberal voice to the Senate.

Decades later, Jim Rowe, who had long been tied psychologically as well as politically to Johnson's career, and who in many interviews with the author had defended unpleasant episodes in that career, at first tried to do the same with the Olds episode. In his thoughtful, understated manner, he said that he understood the reason for Johnson's determination to block Olds' renomination: "Because he wanted to solidify himself with the oil crowd in Texas. You could not *be* a senator from Texas without making your peace with them. I don't think he liked [doing] it, but he was a pragmatic fellow. . . ." After talking in this vein for several minutes, however, Rowe paused and stared down at the desk in his paneled law office—and the pause lasted for some time. When he resumed talking, he did so in a different vein. While he could have accepted Johnson's blocking of Olds, he said, he had always found it difficult to accept Johnson's tactics. Speaking very slowly, with long halts between words, Rowe said, "He grabbed onto the goddamned Commie thing and just ran with it and *ran* with it." There was another pause. "Just *ran* with it," Rowe said. "Ran it into the ground for no reason we could see."

Rowe's partner, Tommy Corcoran, Johnson's chief fund-raiser in liberal circles but a man tied psychologically to no cause but his own, was to say: "I told him [Johnson] to his face one day . . . that I thought it was the rottenest thing he'd ever done, and that he could take it or leave it. . . . The [Commerce] Committee did as dirty a job of trying to crucify this guy à la McCarthy as I have ever heard." Corcoran's sidekick, Ben Cohen, was always less loquacious than Tommy the Cork, but he could, in his quiet way, be equally eloquent. When asked about Johnson's tactics in the Olds fight, Cohen replied in a single word: "Shameful."

For some other leading Washington liberals, less under Johnson's spell than Rowe or Corcoran, the shock was less severe, for his "We of the South" speech in March had forewarned them that all was not as they had believed. Joe Rauh, who in 1948 had worked all night—along with Rowe and Corcoran—on the legal briefs that persuaded Justice Hugo Black to issue the last-minute ruling that saved Johnson's election, says he had been "disgusted" by the speech, so that when Johnson's maneuvers against Olds were revealed, "I wasn't surprised. I already knew. The tide had turned with Lyndon Johnson."

Rauh was not alone. He recalls that even before the Olds hearing "there were discussions. What's happened? This is not the shining New Deal fellow. . . . The lustre of winning the [1948] election went off pretty fast." Nonetheless, the speed, and thoroughness, of the transformation—as made clear in the Olds case—was startling; the election had, after all, been barely a year before. During the court fight over the contested election, Rauh recalls, "Corcoran called to get me on the defense team and said, 'This wonderful congressman . . .' In [Abe] Fortas' office these people were talking about what a great man we were defending. I just sort of automatically assumed it. . . . But it soon became clear that Johnson was not the shining knight that I was led to believe, that he was a totally different political figure . . . than he had been in the Roosevelt days. . . . I was quickly disabused of the notion that this was a New Deal guy. But it was the meanness of the use of these things [Olds' 1920s articles] that so attracted my attention." Leland Olds "was a great American," Joe Rauh says. What Johnson did to him was "really vicious . . . one of the dirtiest pieces of work ever done." Rauh says that "I sort of felt dirty, and double-crossed by Tommy. I goddamned Tommy for getting [me to] help. . . ." Opinion had turned even among the wives of the New Deal set who had been so charmed by the tall young congressman. "My, I wish I could have my campaign contribution back," Elizabeth Purcell, wife of SEC Chairman Ganson Purcell, said at one Georgetown party.

LIBERALS ATTEMPTED TO ORGANIZE. The effort had already started in the White House, with Truman's letter, and now the President ordered Clark Clifford to mobilize support from New Deal "names." Clifford asked Olds who he thought might help, and on a notepad on his desk, Leland Olds scribbled an address, 29 Washington Square West, New York, N.Y.—the address of the widow who bore the greatest name of all. And Clifford reported Eleanor Roosevelt's response: "Enthusiastic—will do it at once and discuss it later."

Olds was evidently not sure that Mrs. Roosevelt even remembered him. Writing her, at Clifford's direction, to give her details on the renomination battle ("The main line of attack has been an all-out effort to picture me as a communist. . . . Unfortunately our old friend Lyndon Johnson is supporting [that] point of view"), he added a reminder of battles long past, as if feeling it necessary to identify himself. "You may recall that we presented the evidence which . . . enabled Governor Roosevelt to start successful regulation in New York State," he wrote. And the letter's final sentences are sentences written by a man who, in dark days, is trying to remind himself of a time when days had been bright.

> I had the never-to-be-forgotten privilege to play a small part in your husband's great work. I look back with a sense of happiness to the one or two instances when you invited us to join the family luncheon at the Executive Mansion when Frank P. Walsh and I were seeing the Governor on the St. Lawrence project.

Mrs. Roosevelt's next "My Day" column showed that she remembered.

"I knew Mr. Olds when my husband was governor of New York State," she wrote. "He started his battle then for sound utility and power policy. . . . Mr. Olds' work must have been well done because it brought about changes in the state. . . . A program of effective [national] regulation was later . . . secured by the Federal Power Commission when Mr. Olds, himself, was chairman of the commission."

She had nothing but scorn, Eleanor Roosevelt said, for those who had raised the Communist issue. "The horrible fact has been brought out that he once spoke on the same platform with Earl Browder. I don't know what that proves. . . . Can't our senators and representatives see thru this opposition and recognize honest public servants? Must they swallow such an obvious Red-herring allegation on Communism?"

Other friends were attempting to mobilize, friends who would have been working for Olds for months had someone contacted them: New York's Governor Lehman, under whom Olds had served; Morris Cooke of the REA; Angus McDonald of the National Farmer's Union, Donald Montgomery of the CIO, Walter Munro of the Trainmen—men whose support could have weighed heavily with senators. Many great names from the farmers' movement and the labor movement and from the New Deal had, as the tenor of the subcommittee hearings became clear, been telephoning the White House, wanting to help. And there were editorials in leading liberal newspapers around the country—

some quite eloquent. "Certain senators," the *Louisville Courier-Journal* said, "have been able to make patriotism appear to be disloyalty, and to make protest against wrong seem an act of revolution."

But it was too late. The hearings—and the subcommittee and committee vote—were already *faits accomplis*. The surprise had been total. Men who would have testified had not done so. Jerry Voorhiis wrote a long statement on behalf of the National Cooperative League, but he wrote it after the hearings were over. Thanks to the thoroughness with which Johnson had selected the subcommittee's membership, moreover, there was no Senate supporter of Olds familiar with the testimony, and, now, with the hearings over and the vote of the full Senate imminent, there was no senator who was organizing support to make an effective presentation on the Senate floor. During the same conversation in which Clifford told Olds that "many want to do something," the White House aide also told Olds that his friends had "no place to plug in." At one point, in a remark that points up vividly the disparity between Lyndon Johnson's operation and the effort the Olds supporters were attempting to start, Clifford had to remind Olds of the "importance of accurate poll[ing]" of the senators.

And more time might not have helped. Max Lerner had been correct when he wrote in the *New York Post* about senators not "daring" to support Olds once the "Communist" issue had been raised. Senator Tobey's abrupt departure—and failure to return—to the hearing room had been a straw in the wind. On the day after the hearings, reporters polled senators—and found only twenty-nine who said they would vote for the President's nominee, a shockingly small number in a Senate containing fifty-four members of the President's party.

Truman thereupon ordered Democratic National Chairman William M. Boyle Jr. to send telegrams to all members of the Democratic National Committee and to state Democratic chairmen urging them to contact their senators and ask them to support Olds. Predictably, that maneuver backfired, for the Senate viewed Truman's effort as an attack on its cherished independence—"a brazen effort," Andrew Schoeppel of Kansas called it. Terming it "a deliberate effort to threaten and coerce the members of the Senate," Harry Byrd said, "President Truman appears to believe that the United States Senate should be an adjunct to his own office, whereby he can issue orders as he pleases." So predictable was the Senate's reaction that more than one observer speculated that, in the words of *Time* magazine, Truman must have "deliberately courted trouble." Reporters' polls showed that after Truman's attempt the number of senators willing to vote for Olds dropped to twenty-four. Leland Olds' nomination was dead—a simple voice or roll-call vote would have killed it.

But Lyndon Johnson didn't want a simple vote—for while he had won the Olds fight, he had not yet reaped from it the reward he wanted: recognition by the oil and natural gas industry that he was its savior and champion. The necessity to appear impartial in his role as subcommittee chairman had forced him to disguise the fact that he had organized and stage-managed the hearings—and the disguise had been so successful that his role had not been broadly publicized. Newspaper articles on the hearings had quoted Lyle, or Bonner, or Head—or, when they quoted senators, the senators were Reed and Capehart. Johnson himself had not yet given them much to quote. And he needed a better stage—the Senate floor. At his request, a debate on the nomination was scheduled—for an evening, Wednesday, October 12, since the Senate's evening sessions were particularly dramatic. He himself would deliver a major address during it; he told Leslie Carpenter that it would be the "most important speech of my life."

12

The Debate

PAUL DOUGLAS, not a member of the Commerce Committee and preoccupied with other issues in which he was taking a leading role, wanted to speak in support of Olds, although, his administrative aide, Frank McCulloch, recalls, "because of past attacks on Douglas himself [as a left-winger], he suspected he might be a target himself" if he did so. He had been waiting to hear from the nomination's floor manager, until, on the very day of the debate, he realized that there was no floor manager—that little or no planning had gone into Olds' defense. "In the afternoon, I made a canvass, found there was literally no one to speak for Olds," he was to recall. Attempting to round up speakers proved difficult; "as the hour for the vote approached, a number of liberals suddenly discovered out-of-town engagements." Exactly four other senators—Morse of Oregon, Aiken of Vermont, Langer of North Dakota, and Humphrey of Minnesota—were willing to take the floor for the nominee.

The five liberals who had the courage to rise in the Senate that evening knew they were going to lose. The natural gas industry "is moving heaven and earth to get Mr. Olds off the commission," Morse said, and would succeed in doing so. "I realize that Mr. Olds is not going to be approved by this body; I think there is no doubt about it," Aiken said. The forces moving against Olds were too strong, and "there are those who hope to see Mr. Olds destroyed. . . ." They had decided to defend him, the five speakers said, because of their outrage at the injustice that was being done to him. "When we are determining whether to reapprove a person who has been in public office, I think we should judge him by his work as a public official during the time he has been in office," Aiken said. "I do not think any of us would like to be judged entirely by what we did or said or wrote twenty or thirty years ago. . . . I do not think Mr. Olds is going to be hurt by those who would crucify him, but I think a great many other folk are going to be. I think the effects of what is being done here tonight will echo down far through the years ahead of us. . . . Certain public utilities are out to destroy a man for performing his duty. I do not know of anything worse than that." Langer said that the hearings held by "a subcommittee headed by the distinguished senator from Texas" had brought out "nothing new." Old charges were "dug up and dusted off again." Olds' long record in positions of public responsibility had been all but ignored. "I challenge senators to read the record from first page to last. They will not find a single word reflecting on his record."

Hubert Humphrey was particularly eloquent. Olds had indeed criticized the American free enterprise system during the 1920s, Humphrey said—and, he said, "In the 1920s the American enterprise system should have been criticized. If there is any room in heaven for a politician, the politician who will be in heaven is the one who had the courage to stand up and condemn the exploiters of child labor and of adult labor, the exploiters of the widows who put their money into phony stocks." Humphrey's voice rang with passion as he spoke. "If Mr. Olds had the courage to stand up in the 1920s and say that he did not like that kind of rotten business practice, God bless him. Those who should be on trial tonight are those who sat serenely and did not raise a finger of protest when millions of people were robbed, families were broken, homes were destroyed, and businesses were bankrupted. All they did was to talk about some kind of business confidence, and prosperity around the corner, and split up the loot. If there is any divine justice those men will fry, and Mr. Olds will have a crown."

And then, at 11:20 p.m., the subcommittee's chairman rose, laid his speech on a lectern that had been placed on his desk, and began to read.

He took a moment to praise the impartiality with which he had conducted the hearings ("Every person who sought a hearing received a hearing. I believe Senators will find the record is complete") and to raise the standard of senatorial independence against Truman's attempted intervention. And then he turned to Leland Olds—forgetting, as he did so, to be "senatorial," so that the rest of Lyndon Johnson's speech, which lasted fifty minutes, was delivered in a hoarse shouting voice.

Johnson repeated all the charges that had been made against Olds: that the FPC chairman had schemed to substitute his own views for those of Congress; that he had substituted "confiscation" for regulation; that he had "advocated the assumption of complete Federal control" of natural gas producers; that he had made "vile and snide remarks" to "undermine and discredit" members of the FPC who did not agree with him, conducting an "insidious campaign of slander." Seizing on the remark he had finally elicited from Olds that if he was no longer a member of the Commission, and the anti-regulation commissioners thereby became the majority, the Commission would not carry on "as active a regulation policy," Lyndon Johnson quoted that statement to the Senate, and interpreted it. "This, indeed, is a strange position," he shouted. "Here is a man declaring publicly and proudly that his colleagues on the Commission are virtually unworthy of the public confidence; declaring that he, and he alone, is capable and willing to defend the public interest."

Then he turned to the hearings, portraying them in a light that would have been startling to anyone who had been present at them—as if their focus had not been natural gas at all but rather electric power, defining the words "special interests" and "power interest" and "utilities" as if the interests involved were not oil and natural gas but electric cooperatives and companies.

By using this definition Johnson was able to say that the "power interests" had not opposed Olds as newspapers had charged, but rather had supported him. "During the hearings," he said, "not a single representative of power interests appeared to oppose Mr. Olds; the only representative of any utility who did appear came to testify in behalf of Mr. Olds. Hundreds of telegrams and letters have come to my office the past few days opposing Mr. Olds' confirmation; not one has been signed by a representative of the electric utilities." But, Johnson said, these "forces . . . have been at work on behalf of Mr. Olds. . . . Is it not self-evident that for favors granted, for services rendered, these 'dragons of special privilege'—which Leland Olds supposedly combats three times daily and twice on Sundays—are now log-rolling in the oldest of Washington traditions, seeking for Leland Olds what both he and they so desperately need. . . . An attempt has been made to blackmail Congress into accepting his appointment through the simple device of charging all who oppose Leland Olds with being tools of 'special interests'—many of which are actually supporting his nomination, and he knows it."

And then, a few minutes after midnight, Lyndon Johnson came to the heart of his speech.

It began with a disclaimer—"I do not charge that Mr. Olds is a Communist"—but continued with phrases that were clearly intended to keep that possibility alive in the minds of his listeners.

"I do not charge that Mr. Olds is a Communist. No member of the subcommittee made any such accusation. I realize that the line he followed, the phrases he used, the causes he espoused resemble the party line today; but the Communist tie is not the tie that binds Leland Olds' writings of the 1920s to his doctrines of the 1940s." Rather, Johnson said, that "tie" was an "unmistakably clear purpose." "Leland Olds had something in mind when he began to build his political empire across the Nation; he had something in mind when he chose to force a show-down with the Senate over his power to write laws of his own; he had something in mind when he chose to disregard the clear language of the Natural Gas Act and plot a course toward confiscation and public ownership."

The purpose, Johnson said, had become clear in the 1920s. Leland Olds chose, Johnson said, "to travel with those who proposed the Marxian answer. His choice was not dictated by necessity; the company he chose, he chose of his own free will. He spoke from the same platforms [sic] with Earl Browder. He accepted subsidy from the so-called Garland Fund, a fund created and expended to keep alive Marxist organs and Marxist groups."

And "why did these writings stop in 1929?" Johnson asked. Only, he said, "because Leland Olds, the advocate—Leland Olds, the man with a purpose," found he could advance that purpose more successfully from within the government. "There he has been ever since," Lyndon Johnson told the Senate. "From 1929 to 1949, discretion has stilled Leland Olds' pen; his purpose and his methods have found sanctuary in the legalistic prose of commission opinions—prose which affects many more men than the Federated Press affected. . . ."

"There can be no question about the environment, the trend of thought, the bent of mind of Leland Olds," Johnson said. The issue, he said, was clear-cut:

"Shall we have a commissioner or a commissar?"

LYNDON JOHNSON'S SPEECH put the finishing touches on the portrait of Leland Olds that he had been painting for the Senate. "The debate, as is seldom the case, did change some minds," one reporter wrote. Aired not in private or in a subcommittee hearing but on the Senate floor, the charges echoed with a heightened authority. And Johnson's new hint that Olds might have had some insidious plot in mind, that he had stopped writing because he could more effectively accomplish "confiscation and public ownership" from within the government, evidently made some liberal senators who had determined to stand up for Olds, whatever the consequences, reconsider. "It took a brave senator to vote for a man who had been fingered, as Johnson fingered Olds in a committee and as he now did again, even more brutally, in the closing hours of that day on the Senate floor," Robert Sherrill was to write. Says Professor Harris: "Most senators were far less interested in determining the accuracy of every accusation against Olds than they were in letting the public know and having the record show that they themselves did not vote for a man who was accused of being a communist." While Johnson was speaking, with his accusations—"Marxian," "Earl Browder," "Marxist," "Commissar"—rolling across the rows of Senate desks, a number of liberal senators quietly rose and left, and did not return for the vote. When the clerk called the yeas and nays, only thirteen Democrats voted yea, along with two Republicans. Leland Olds' renomination was defeated by a vote of 53 to 15.

When the clerk announced those figures, a reporter wrote, "There was a moment of stunned silence [at] the overwhelming size of the vote." In what the *Washington Star* said was "about as severe a political licking as any President ever got on a nominee," Truman had been able to persuade only fifteen of ninety-six senators to support the official he recommended—an official who had already held his job for ten years, an official whose work many senators had come to know and to respect, as, over ten years, they had come to know and respect the man himself.

. . .

ON CAPITOL HILL, and throughout political Washington, the vote was viewed as a personal triumph for Lyndon Johnson. "It's not just every day in the week that a freshman senator can oppose his President, the chairman of his party, governors, mayors, national committeemen and others, and come out with a 53–15 victory," one senator told a reporter. "Lyndon Johnson almost alone was responsible for the defeat," Joseph Rauh said. "And he did that as a freshman senator." John Gunther, making his rounds of Capitol Hill offices to lobby for ADA causes, said, "During the next couple of weeks, walking around the Hill, it became clear that people were a little scared of Lyndon Johnson. All of a sudden, he was big."

One aspect of the triumph made it especially significant. Dissatisfied with the attendance as Johnson was rising to speak, the two giants from Georgia glanced at each other, and then rose and walked together out of the Chamber to summon other senators. Before long—and well before the crucial "commissar" line was uttered—the number of senators listening to Johnson (even after the discreet liberals had left) was quite respectable.

After the speech, Richard Russell was beaming. As always, he hung back, but Walter George, the Senate's most renowned speechmaker, hurried over, and told Johnson, "I've never heard a more masterful speech against a nomination." And southerners (along with some conservative Republicans) lined up to shake Johnson's hand, as they had done after his maiden speech in March.

The strident anti-Communism of Johnson's rhetoric may have grated on liberals, but it didn't grate on southerners, most of whom were as fervently anti-Communist as even Johnson could have wished. During his first year in the Senate, Johnson had delivered two major speeches. The first, in March, had announced his enlistment in the ranks of the southerners who ran the Senate. The second had demonstrated that he could be an effective leader in their causes. "In the minds of many," Lowell Mellett wrote, "the shame of the Senate, in the session now ending, has been written in oil . . . by a sneak attack on [Leland Olds'] personal reputation, the surefire smear technique of labeling him a Communist or Communist sympathizer. . . ." But the columnist's analysis also noted that "the Southern bloc emerged from the session stronger than ever."

"VICTORY" WAS A WORD used in banner headlines all over Texas, and, the state's newspapers made clear, it was Lyndon Johnson's victory. In a score of articles he was identified as "Lyndon Johnson, who led the fight against Leland Olds."

And, the newspapers told Texans, it was a victory that had required great political courage. In his speech, Johnson had portrayed himself as a lone crusader fighting overwhelming forces: the President, the Democratic National Committee and, of course, those "dragons of special privilege" bringing immense pressure to bear for Leland Olds. "The lash of a party line can be painful," he said. "I do not relish disagreeing with my President and being unable to comply with the chairman of my party, but I can find no comfort in failing to do what I know is right." The big Texas newspapers, many of whose publishers had substantial oil and natural gas interests, took the point. "The outstanding feature of the present session of Congress has been the courage displayed by Sen. Lyndon B. Johnson of Texas in opposing confirmation," the *Dallas Times-Herald* said. "It was a whopping triumph for Sen. Lyndon B. Johnson of Texas . . . who led the Senate revolt against pressure attempted in Olds' behalf by the Democratic national committee," David Botter wrote in the *Dallas Morning News.* The headline over an editorial in the *Houston Post,* which stated that "left wing columnists and commentators" and the Truman Administration "exerted all possible pressure," was "PRINCIPLE VS. PRESSURE." Principle had won, the *Post* said, because Johnson had made the issue clear: "The question" was indeed, the *Post* said, "Shall we have a commissioner or a commissar?"

As was often the case, Leslie Carpenter, correspondent for a number of Texas newspapers, was the most enthusiastic writer of all. "At 11:10 PM [*sic*] on the night of Oct. 12," his story began, "Texas' lanky 41-year-old Junior Senator Lyndon B. Johnson stepped to the front of the historic Senate Chamber to begin what he considered the 'most important speech' of his public career. . . . When Johnson—who had sat patiently without saying a word while the Olds' partisans spoke—began speaking, it was evident that the responsibility for proving the case against Olds rested upon the Texas Senator. The Texan spoke calmly, deliberately. . . ." At other points in his narrative, Carpenter said, Johnson spoke "soberly," "firmly." "Patiently," Carpenter wrote, "Johnson unfolded the record." His opponents, Carpenter said, had been routed. "Columnists and commentators, who had been defending Olds by assailing Johnson, remained silent and said nothing further against Johnson."

The Texas newspapers lauding Johnson included many which had, a year before, opposed his campaign for the Senate. Now they confessed their error. Said the state's most influential newspaper, the *Dallas Morning News:* "The junior senator from Texas very properly stands up to this pressure and stands up to his duty as he sees it. The *News* believed and believes that Senator Johnson obtained office as the result of an election by a slender majority counted in his favor in violation of law. . . . Without retracting anything that has been said, it is possible to commend the Senator de facto for what is certainly personal and political courage in the performance of duty." The Leland Olds fight had given Johnson the newspaper support he had previously lacked. A hundred articles portrayed him as the senator who had stood up against a President and against subversion—and when he returned to the great province in the Southwest (in a symbolically appropriate chariot, Brown & Root's new DC-3), he did so as its hero, on a triumphal tour across the vast state on which he spoke before cheering audiences.

.   .   .

THE TOUR GAVE HIM an opportunity to achieve another goal—one he had been trying to achieve since the day Franklin Roosevelt died. As long as his great patron had been alive and lavishing favors on him, Johnson had been identified as a New Dealer, but in the four years since FDR's death, he had been attempting to make Texans understand that, as a friendly reporter wrote after a 1947 interview, while "People all over Texas formed an impression over the years that Lyndon Johnson personified the New Deal . . . it would be an error to tag Johnson now as a strong New Dealer." (In that interview Johnson himself said that the tag would always have been an error, saying "I think the term 'New Dealer' is a misnomer. . . .") Nonetheless, doubts had lingered—were still lingering despite his sterling record in the civil rights and Leland Olds fights; he intended the speeches he made on this tour to lay those doubts to rest. His instructions to Busby were specific, and the young speechwriter, sending Johnson a draft of one talk, attached a note saying he hoped he had succeeded in complying with them. "I hope it is sufficiently conservative. I merely wrote things I do believe, and think you do, too."

The strongest argument that Lyndon Johnson was not now and had never been a liberal, of course, was a record of militant anti-Communism, and he selected a dramatic setting to remind Texas of his victory over the FPC "commissar": the annual meeting, held in 1949 in El Paso, of delegates from southwestern rural electrification cooperatives—many of them men who had been assisted by Leland Olds in their battles to establish those co-ops.

In his speech, Johnson told the delegates that during the renomination fight, an REA spokesman—"a man purporting to speak for all of you"—had endorsed Olds. And in allowing this man to do so, Johnson hinted, the delegates had been used as tools by Communists. The argument that Olds was opposed by the power lobby, Johnson said "was simply not true—it was the same old smokescreen behind which many men hide when they need to hide their records. If Joe Stalin were nominated, I suppose his pals would try to arouse support by shouting that the power lobby was against him. You have a bigger job to do than serve as a tool of the smear artists and the propagandists. . . ." Johnson warned the delegates—who were acutely aware, of course, that their co-ops' continued expansion depended upon Washington's approval of their loan applications— that their error in judgment had better not be repeated. "The graveyard of good intentions is filled with the remains of individuals and organizations who nosed into affairs which were not their own," he said. "For your political life as for your business life, I recommend a four [*sic*]–word slogan: 'Stay out of the Red!' " He warned the delegates not to "permit REA to become the lambskin in which the wolves of alien radicalism cloak themselves."

The most significant meetings Lyndon Johnson held on this tour, however, were not the public ones but the private. When the Brown & Root plane delivered him to Texas, it delivered him first to Houston, where a Brown & Root limousine met him and took him to the Brown & Root suite in the Lamar Hotel.

Waiting for him there, in Suite 8-F, were men who really mattered in Texas: Herman and George Brown, of course, and oilman Jim Abercrombie and insurance magnate Gus Wortham. And during the two months he spent in Texas thereafter, the Senator spent time at Brown & Root's hunting camp at Falfurrias, and in oilman Sid Richardson's suite in the Fort Worth Club.

These meetings were very private. During his stay in 8-F, a Houstonian—important but not important enough to be part of the 8-F crowd—telephoned Johnson's office in Washington to try to arrange an appointment, but Busby was careful not to let him know even that Johnson was in Houston. When Johnson was at Falfurrias—the most private place of all—even high federal officials couldn't reach him, not even his longtime ally Stuart Symington, who was told the "Senator cannot be reached by telephone"; the Secretary of the Air Force was reduced to leaving a message for Johnson to call him. To the extent possible, his whereabouts were concealed from everyone in Washington—even from members of his staff there. During his week at Falfurrias, Busby attempted to reach him through his Austin office; Mary Louise Glass, in that office, would tell him only that "Mr. Johnson has just advised me that he is taking a vacation himself—on a ranch—and cannot be reached until he comes out of the shinnery." Even the most urgent communications from Washington—the envelopes from Walter Jenkins to Johnson marked "personal and confidential"—were held in Austin by Mary Louise instead of being forwarded.

THE BROWN BROTHERS had been assuring their conservative friends for years that Lyndon wasn't really a liberal, that he was as "practical" as they were, and now they were almost gloating in this proof that they had been correct. As their lobbyist Oltorf recalls, "Even after everything Lyndon had done—even after the Taft-Hartley and the way he fought Truman on the FEPC and all that—they [independent oilmen] had still been suspicious. They still thought he was too radical. But now he had tangibly put something in their pockets. Somebody who put money in their pockets couldn't be a radical. They weren't suspicious any more." Herman Brown was a businessman who wanted value for money spent. As George, who echoes his brother's thinking, says, "Listen, you get a doctor, you want a doctor who does his job. You get a lawyer, you want a lawyer who does his job. You get a Governor, you want a Governor who does his job." Doctor, lawyer, governor, congressman, senator—when Herman "got" somebody, he wanted his money's worth. And now he had gotten it—gotten it and more. The men associated with Herman Brown had gotten it, too. A long time ago, in 1937, when Lyndon Johnson had first run for Congress, Ed Clark had decided to "buy a ticket on him." Now that ticket had paid off big.

The Leland Olds fight had paid off for Lyndon Johnson, too, and he knew it. He had known for years that he needed the wholehearted support of the oilmen and of men like Clark for the money necessary if he were ever to realize his dreams. Now, at last, he had that support, and he was as happy as his aides had ever seen him. "It is a real pleasure to be around him when he is feeling this way," Warren Woodward wrote Busby. Back in the house on Dillman Street in Austin for Christmas, Lyndon Johnson wrote a letter to Justice William O. Douglas. "This has been one of the finest years—perhaps the finest—of our lives," he said.

AND WHAT ABOUT the effect of the fight in another house—Leland Olds' house in Washington on McKinley Street?

There was very little money in that house. By October, Leland Olds had not received a paycheck for four months, and the Oldses' meagre savings were almost exhausted. President Truman wrote him, "Of course, I felt very badly about your situation. I sincerely hope that it will work out all right for you individually." And the President tried to make it work out as well as possible. Telling reporters he "would still like to find a government job for Olds"—one that would not require Senate approval—he thought he had found one: as a consultant to his nominee as Secretary of the Interior, Oscar L. Chapman. But there were delays. Although Olds' appointment did not need Senate approval, Chapman's did, and Democratic National Chairman Boyle told a reporter confidentially that although Olds "is in desperate financial straits," his appointment could not be announced "until after Chapman's confirmation for fear it would cause Chapman grave difficulties with the Senate." Olds could not hold out. In January, 1950, the President created a Water Resources Policy Commission, headed by Morris Cooke, apparently primarily to provide Olds with a salary; he was the Commission's only paid member, with a salary drawn from a presidential emergency fund. The following year he was shifted to a salaried post on an interagency committee studying the development of natural resources in New England.

After January, 1953, however, there was no Truman in the White House—and no job in government for Leland Olds, now sixty-two years old. He would never hold a government job again. On the advice of friends and admirers, he established a consulting firm, Energy Research Associates, with two employees—himself and a secretary—in a small office on K Street furnished with used furniture. Rural electrification cooperatives and public power systems retained him for research projects for which, recalls the American Public Power Association's Alex Radin, "He charged modest fees."

Speaking at conventions of rural electrification organizations, Olds imparted his philosophy to the organizations' young officials—the new generation of crusaders for public power—and they came to revere him. When, in 1984, the author arrived at Alex Radin's office in Washington to interview him, he noticed open on Radin's desk a black-bound book he recognized. It was the bound transcript of the 1949 hearings on Leland Olds' renomination. "Yes,"

Radin said, "I've been reading the Lyndon Johnson hearings." During the interview, even while Radin was discussing other subjects, his eyes kept glancing toward the transcript. Finally, he reached out for it, and showed the author the page—142—to which it was open. "Johnson is trying here to get Olds to say the members of the FPC who opposed him [Olds] were tools of the private power companies," Radin said, "and Olds replies, 'I do not think along those lines. I try to assume that every man is good.' All the time I knew him, that was how he acted about Lyndon Johnson, and the others who attacked him. I never once heard him express one word of recrimination." Then, so that the author could read the exchange for himself, Radin handed him the transcript. It was battered and dog-eared. "Yes, I've read it and re-read it many times," Radin said.

While the young officials could give Olds work, however, the fees they could pay were modest. After he lost his FPC post, says a friend, "He was a poor man the rest of his life."

AND THERE WERE worse things than poverty.

Maud Olds had insisted, over Leland's objections, on attending the subcommittee hearings. "My mother sat there with my father all day long," their daughter Zara Olds Chapin says, listening to witnesses call her husband a traitor and a jackass and a crackpot, listening to Lyndon Johnson sneer at him and demand that he "answer that question 'yes' or 'no,'" and stop hedging and dodging."

"It was a very bitter time," Zara says, "a very hurtful time for my mother.... You just can't believe that human beings can turn on you like that." And, of course, every morning her mother had to open her front door, where the newspapers were waiting, with their headlines.

The hurt was deepened by the behavior of some of her neighbors—particularly as, a few months after the hearings, McCarthyism began to cast its pall over Washington. More than one couple on McKinley Street whom the Oldses had considered friends—"people we had had to our house for dinner," Zara says with an indignation undimmed after four decades—became noticeably reluctant to be seen talking to them. "They wouldn't even come into our yard," she says. One neighbor, in the past, would always stop if she saw Maud outside and chat with her. Now the neighbor passed by without stopping, and finally she told Maud—as Maud related—that "she didn't dare" to stop and talk.

"That was the atmosphere in Washington then," Zara says. "They were afraid they would be tainted if they were seen talking to someone who had been called a Communist. They said they didn't feel *he* was a Communist, but that their career in government might be hurt. That was the atmosphere in Washington then. Mother understood that, but it hurt Mother very much."

Maud had always been what her family and friends call "high-strung," "intense," and in 1944, she had suffered what they describe as a "nervous breakdown." She had been recovered for years, but now, after the hearings and the snubs in the street, "she became very upset," Zara says. During the months following the hearings, she lost twenty-five pounds. Sometimes someone walking into a room in the Olds house which they had thought was empty would find Maud Olds standing there, silently weeping.

It took a long time for Maud Olds to recover, her daughter says, and in some ways, she never recovered. "She always was wishing there was something she could do to get back at the people" who had hurt her husband, Zara says. "She just never stopped wishing that." She lived until the age of ninety, and, says Zara, "she died hating Lyndon Johnson. Until the day she died, she could hardly say his name."

As FOR THE EFFECT of his renomination fight on Leland Olds himself, he tried not to let anyone see it. Alex Radin, who often traveled and talked with him, says, "I never once heard Leland Olds mention Lyndon Johnson. . . . I think he sort of buried that part of his life." But while friends and colleagues who had known Olds before the hearings use words like "bouncy," "cheerful," and "enthusiastic" to describe him, men and women who met Olds only after October, 1949, use adjectives like "restrained," "tense."

"My father never really talked much about the hearings," Zara recalls. "Never really very much at all. He was a stiff-upper-lip kind of guy." That pose was effective with her for three years after the hearings, but then, returning home for her first extended stay since the hearings, she saw beneath the pose. "It wasn't anything he said," she recalls. "But he had lost all his buoyancy. My father had always had so much energy. He wasn't enthusiastic, and all the other things he always was."

Her father, Zara was to say, had loved his work with a consuming passion. He had never lost his enthusiasm for analyzing huge masses of data and finding the significant implications in them: time had always passed unnoticed when he was involved in such work; when he finally went home at night, he was always eager to get up and start at it again the next day. And he loved the fact that in that data lay the possibility of improving people's lives. "One of my father's driving things was to make a dent in history by helping human beings," Zara would say. "I was taught from the time I was a child that the important thing was to get cheap electricity for the common people." His work with the FPC, she says, was the work he was born to do.

Now, at the age of fifty-eight, that work had been taken away from him forever. To Zara, the saddest part of her return home was that in the evenings her parents "would go out to dinner and the movies like other people. Daddy had never had time to go out like that."

And then, of course, there was another poignant aspect of the situation. To replace Olds, Truman appointed Mon Wallgren, a former senator and crony, who, in 1952, *Fortune* magazine was to call "quite possibly the least effective chairman, or even member, the FPC has ever had. . . . A lazy fellow [and] too preoccupied with politicking to pay proper attention to FPC business." During Wallgren's chairmanship, the policies and regulations that Leland Olds had instituted to break the grip of the private electric utilities and natural gas monopolies were, one by one, reversed.

Zara would never forget one visit she made to the McKinley Street house in late 1953 or early 1954. She and her parents and her sister Mary were sitting around the dining room table listening to the evening news when suddenly the announcer was talking about yet another policy change that had been announced that day by the FPC, a change that eliminated a regulation for which Olds had once fought. Someone jumped up and switched off the radio, as if it hurt too much to listen. Years later, recalling the incident to the author over the telephone, Zara said she realized in that moment that "My father had seen all the things he'd worked for broken.

"I have to hang up. I'm crying now," she said.

Writing years later about the hearings, Senator Paul Douglas was to say that "Olds was crushed by the experience, and I do not think that he and his family ever recovered from the blow." The experience, Joseph Rauh says, "killed Olds. I don't know how many years he lived after that, but he never really recovered himself."

ONE OTHER INCIDENT connected with the hearings perhaps deserves mention. It occurred during a brief recess. Leland Olds was standing in the corridor outside the hearing room, talking to his wife and Melwood Van Scoyoc, when Lyndon Johnson emerged and started to walk by. Then he stopped, came up behind Olds, and put his hand on his shoulder.

"Lee," he said, "I hope you understand there's nothing personal in this. We're still friends, aren't we? It's only politics, you know."

LELAND OLDS DIED, after suffering a heart attack, on Sunday, August 5, 1960. There were tributes in the Senate—a few tributes: by 1960, few senators remembered Leland Olds. Senator James Murray of Montana said, "A great American passed away last week. He had his enemies, but I wish to state on the floor of the Senate that I believe we owe to Leland Olds a debt of gratitude which was not paid, and may never be paid, but which I wish to acknowledge at this time." One of the tributes was from the Democratic presidential nominee, John F. Kennedy, who said, "In a sense . . . developments such as the St. Lawrence Waterway and power projects are a permanent memorial to him," and added that Olds established "the foundation for the giant power systems that will soon be serving America."

There was no comment from the Democratic vice presidential nominee.

13

"No Time for a Siesta"

WHEN RICHARD RUSSELL congratulated him on his victory over Leland Olds, Johnson replied: "I'm young and impressionable, so I just tried to do what the Old Master, the junior senator from Georgia, taught me to do." And his note to the master included the most potent of code words: "Cloture is where you find it, sir, and this man Olds was an advocate of simple majority cloture on the gas producers." Of all the spoils that Johnson reaped from his victory over Olds, perhaps the most valuable was the fact that it reinforced, and indeed heightened, Richard Russell's favorable opinion of him, and not just of his philosophy—Communism was, of course, second only to civil rights on Russell's list of the plagues that beset mankind—but of his potential.

In a previous engagement—the Civil Rights Battle of March 1949—and in the many small skirmishes of a Senate year, Johnson had shown Russell that he would be a loyal soldier for the Cause. Now, in the Olds engagement, Johnson had not only organized the forces against Olds, but had planned their strategy and tactics, led them on the field of battle. And the engagement had ended in victory—in the utter rout of the liberal forces. Was the South's great general now beginning to feel that perhaps he had found not merely a soldier for the Cause, but something more: a leader for the Cause, a new general—someone who might one day be able to pick up its banner when he himself finally had to let it fall? It would not be for another year or so that Richard Russell began to hint at such a feeling, but there was, almost immediately after the 53–15 vote, impressive testimony to at least the warmth of his feelings for Johnson. The Senate adjourned for the year on October 19, six days after the Olds vote. Before he left for Texas, Johnson extended an invitation to Russell to join him there on a hunting trip in November. And Russell, who had turned down so many invitations to hunting trips, accepted this one.

Their destination was "St. Joe," as it was known to the select few who were invited there—St. Joseph Island, the twenty-one-mile-long island in the Gulf of Mexico that had once been a fishing resort but had been purchased by

Sid Richardson and turned into his own private island, on which he built a hunting lodge so luxurious that its cost embarrassed even him and he never revealed it.

Johnson had arranged a week-long stag party on St. Joe, and the stags were some of the biggest in the Texas business herd: not only Richardson but Clint Murchison, Amon Carter, Myron Blalock and, of course, Herman Brown. It was a group that held views quite similar to Russell's on Communism and labor unions and Negroes and the importance of ending government interference with free enterprise, a group that had long considered Russell the leader of the good fight on these issues and had been looking forward to meeting him. Although none of them was noted for an interest in books, Russell found he had a lot to talk about with them, that conversation was, in fact, relaxed and easy, for they shared an interest, these hard, tough men who wanted so much from government, in politics. And with Herman Brown in particular—Herman who loved to talk not only about politics but about issues (and who didn't want to talk about them with "some damned radical professor"), Herman who loathed Negroes and unions because Negroes were lazy and unions encouraged laziness in white men, Herman who called New Deal programs "gimmes" because they gave government handouts to lazy men who were always saying "gimme"—with Herman in particular Russell got along famously. And, of course, not only the perfectly arranged duck hunting and the strolls, in total privacy, along the beautiful beaches in the sun, but also the luxury of the accommodations, the deferential black retainers everywhere, the lavish dinners prepared by a chef flown in from New Orleans for the week, the long evenings after dinner in which a lot of Old Weller was consumed, added to the pleasantness of those days in the Gulf. For Dick Russell, who had just spent ten months in Washington with very little warmth in his life, it was a week basking in warmth, and in admiration—and the thank-you note he sent to Johnson from Winder showed how pleasant the week had been. "Dear Lyndon," he wrote. "Ever since I reached home I have been wondering if I would wake up and find that I had just been dreaming that I had made a trip to Texas. Everything was so perfect that it is difficult to realize that it could happen in real life."

And when, the next year, a great opportunity suddenly appeared, and Lyndon Johnson grabbed for it, Russell saw to it that Johnson got it.

THE FIRST HALF OF 1950 WAS SLOW. The desultory, now-familiar, Senate routine resumed—as did the extra-senatorial routine: the lunches and dinners at Bill White's and Dave Botter's to cultivate the press; the lunches and dinners to cultivate Rayburn (most notably a birthday lunch for the Speaker that Johnson, along with Representative Wright Patman, persuaded President Truman to attend as a surprise guest, and a boisterous dinner the Texas delegation threw for the Speaker at the Mayflower); the lunches and dinners to cultivate Ray-

burn's nephew, FCC Chairman Robert Bartley: when the Congressional Club
had a ladies' tea, it was Ruth Bartley who was Lady Bird's guest. (And there
was the evening that Lyndon and Lady Bird, just the two of them, spent at the
Speaker's apartment, eating a dinner he had had sent in from Martin's—a very
happy evening for Mr. Sam.) Sunday brunches were still devoted to Russell,
but during the first half of 1950 there was little Russell could do for him. Johnson's main effort in the Senate, apart from routine Armed Services Committee
work, ended in frustration when, in April, Truman vetoed a natural gas deregulation bill.

Making the first half of the year more difficult was the tension at the
Georgetown dinner parties of his old circle caused by the Leland Olds hearing,
and now aggravated by the stands he continued to take on civil rights issues—
his vote, for example, against cloture when Truman tried again to make employment practices more fair. His relationship with the President, never warm,
had been further chilled by the Olds fight. The White House, during the reign of
Roosevelt so open to him, was now a place he visited only when the Speaker
brought him along, which during the first six months of 1950 was exactly once.
Otherwise, apart from a few group occasions like the Rayburn lunch, Lyndon
Johnson saw Harry Truman mainly up on daises—on Capitol Hill as the President delivered his State of the Union address, at the National Guard Armory at
the Jefferson-Jackson Day Dinner. He had come a long way, but he had a long,
long way to go—and, it seemed, in that slow, slow Senate, as if it was going to
take a very long time to get there; if there was a shortcut, he hadn't found it.
The buzzer summoning aides to his private office was sounding less often; he
was starting to brood in there again; when he telephoned Tommy Corcoran or
Jim Rowe, his voice was beginning again to be flat, a little listless.

FOR A FEW MEN IN WASHINGTON, the news came late Saturday night, June 24,
in telephone calls like the one Assistant Secretary of State Dean Rusk received
during a dinner party in Joseph Alsop's home in Georgetown. Watching as
Rusk listened to the message, Alsop saw "his face turn the color of an old-
fashioned white bed sheet," although all Rusk said, as he asked his host to make
his apologies, was that there had been a rather serious "border incident" in
South Korea. For the rest of Washington, including freshman Senator Lyndon
Johnson, the news came, as the news of Pearl Harbor had come, on a quiet Sunday morning, in headlines and radio bulletins.

When Johnson telephoned Horace Busby's house in suburban Chevy
Chase that morning, Busby heard the difference in the Chief's tone immediately. "He called me at ten, and we were still talking at noon," Buzz would
recall. "All of a sudden, he was energized. He came to life. Because he knew
the territory. He was a creature of war. His whole life had been shaped in the
buildup to World War II. He felt he knew what was necessary. He talked about

China—would China come in? Would Russia come in? He knew the territory. He was back in command."

Johnson's involvement was not immediately requested, however. When, on Tuesday, with North Korean tanks rumbling down through South Korea, the President invited some forty congressional leaders to the White House, to inform them that he was dispatching United States air and naval forces to support the South Koreans, Johnson was not among them. He was just one of the crowd of senators and representatives who cheered the President's statement when it was read on Capitol Hill, and he did not participate in the Senate debate on the "police action," which took place on Wednesday.

But if you do everything, you'll win. Johnson had already done something. The White House was concerned about adverse congressional reaction to Truman's failure to ask congressional authorization to send in troops. In the event, despite tense moments—Robert Taft declared that the President had "usurped the power of Congress"—substantial reaction did not materialize; several senators were to write letters to the President expressing their support. Johnson did everything he could to make sure *his* letter would have the strongest possible impact on the President.

On Tuesday night, Busby recalls, "He called me at home and said I want you to draft a letter from me supporting him." The tone of the letter had to be *perfect,* he said. And it had to get there first, before a letter from any other senator. He would get to the office early Wednesday morning, he told Busby, "and I want that letter on my desk when I get in. I want it on Truman's desk when he gets there in the morning." And, Busby says, "he called someone in Truman's office to make sure the President would see it the minute he got in."

Beginning "My dear Mr. President, I want to express to you my deep gratitude for and admiration of your courageous response yesterday to the challenge of this grave hour," the letter spared no adjectives. Your leadership, Johnson told him, had been "inspired"; it would, he said, "be remembered as the finest moment of American maturity." It "gives a new and noble meaning to freedom. . . . For the decisions you must face alone, you have my most sincere prayers and my total confidence. Under your leadership, I am sure peace will be restored and justice will assume new meaning for the oppressed and frightened peoples of the world." And Truman replied in a "Dear Lyndon" letter with a tone more cordial than that in which he had responded to previous Johnson overtures. Some months later, talking with Johnson, the President would say, "I remember: you were the first Senator to support me." "The *first* was very important," Busby says. Although the relationship between Johnson and Truman would never be particularly warm (Margaret Truman says that her father "never quite trusted him"), a moderate thaw, with occasional reverses, can be dated from this exchange.

But getting closer to the President, important though that was, was not nearly as potentially significant as another opportunity Johnson saw in this moment—and for which he reached just as quickly. Still an obscure senator, he saw within hours, perhaps even more quickly, that America's entry into the Korean War was a chance for him to assume the same role that had propelled Harry Truman into national prominence when *he* had been just an obscure senator.

Of course, Johnson knew the story: how Truman, just beginning his second term, still known only by the derisive title "the Senator from Prendergast," had in January, 1941, become concerned about waste and mismanagement in America's defense mobilization program and had persuaded the Senate to create a special committee to investigate the program, and, after Pearl Harbor, the war effort; how the "Truman Committee" had, with remarkable rapidity, become a national byword for its fairness and lack of partisan bias, as well as for the revelations it produced; so that when in 1944 Franklin Roosevelt was looking for a running mate, the chairman of "the most successful congressional investigating effort in American history" had sufficient stature to be chosen for the vice presidency that became the presidency. Everyone in Washington knew the story. *Truman of the Truman Committee* was the title of an inspiring political Horatio Alger saga. And, in a city in which so many men viewed great events at least partly through the lens of personal opportunity, many men— including many senators—saw very quickly how a new war, or even a "police action," could provide the backdrop for a repeat version of the same scenario. But no one saw the opportunity as quickly as Lyndon Johnson. And no one moved as quickly—or as deftly—to take advantage of it.

Speed was necessary, for the odds against him getting the job were very long. For one thing, an investigation might well fall under the jurisdiction of the Senate's Committee on Expenditures in Executive Departments, chaired by John McClellan. Had the powerful and prickly McClellan moved to assume jurisdiction, no senator would have opposed him. But McClellan didn't move. Johnson did: he had an emissary, Truman's Secretary of the Air Force, Stuart Symington, respectfully point something out to the President: Expenditures' ranking Republican member, who would play a prominent role if that committee investigated the Administration's war effort, was Joe McCarthy. With an election coming up and the Democrats by no means certain of retaining control of the Senate, McCarthy might, in fact, soon be the committee's chairman. That possibility should be eliminated before anyone focused on it. Truman took the point. He was soon on the phone to Majority Leader Scott Lucas, to, in Busby's words, "get an investigation started, and started quick, and put it in the Armed Services Committee."

That move reduced the odds against Johnson only slightly. Grasping the potential in such an investigation, Armed Services Chairman Millard Tydings wanted to head it himself. At that very moment, however, Tydings was getting bad news from the home front—*his* home front, the state of Maryland, where he would be up for election in November. He had been chairman of the Senate's

Select Committee on McCarthy, which, earlier that year, had brought to light the lack of proof, and of truth, behind McCarthy's Wheeling speech, and McCarthy, out for revenge, was planning to campaign against him. Tydings had survived a 1938 purge attempt by Franklin Roosevelt, but this threat, his advisers were telling him—more and more urgently each day—was worse; he was in a fight for his political life, and had better concentrate on his re-election campaign. Still, Tydings tried to keep his options open. Although, formally staking Armed Services' jurisdiction over the investigation, he emerged from a committee meeting on July 17 to announce that, pursuant to a resolution introduced by Senator Lyndon Johnson, the committee had established a seven-member "Preparedness Investigating" subcommittee "similar to the one headed during World War II by President Truman," the announcement did not name the subcommittee's membership, much less its chairman; Tydings apparently intended either to take the chairmanship himself after he had been re-elected or to return jurisdiction to the full committee which he chaired. And if Tydings did not take the chairmanship himself, of course, the committee had several senior senators (most notably Russell, the Senate's leading expert on military readiness) who would be more logical choices than a freshman senator.

Seeing his precious opportunity slipping away, Johnson pleaded for a chance to talk to Tydings in person—"Millard, as indicated twice today, I shall be delighted to discuss my position with you at any time . . . that may be convenient for you"—a chance he was apparently not given. In a letter he wrote Tydings on July 19, there was, before the requisite disclaimer, a note of desperation. "I believed that I would be named chairman of the group authorized by the resolution I introduced. Since this would only be in line with the usual practice of the Senate, I thought I had some right to expect this. I have no political ambitions to further, however, so I have no intention of objecting if you want to name yourself chairman." In a July 25 memorandum, Johnson sought to reassure Tydings that the subcommittee would pose no threat to his authority as chairman of the full Armed Services Committee, or to his ability to take credit for the subcommittee's findings. As chairman of the parent committee, Tydings would have full authority over the subcommittee's expenditures, the memo said; its expenses and the salaries of its staff, which would be limited to a mere $25,000, "shall be paid . . . upon vouchers approved by THE CHAIRMAN OF THE COMMITTEE." (The crucial words were capitalized.) Tydings would have full authority over the subcommittee's staff—not that there would be much staff. "You would designate such members of our [Armed Services Committee] professional staff as you saw fit to be the nucleus around which additional investigators could be employed when, and if, they were needed," Johnson promised. "You would be expected to designate and approve any additional investigators." And it would be Tydings, not the subcommittee's chairman, who, the memo promised, would have full authority over the subcommittee's reports—and the right to release them: "The subcommittee would submit all reports, recommendations, etc., to the full committee—not to the Senate or to the public. The full committee then would decide what, if any, reports would be presented to the Senate by the chairman of the full committee." And the memorandum closed with a note of urgency. "In view of the fact that other resolutions are now being introduced calling for similar investigations by other and special committees, I think it is important that announcement of the [membership] of our subcommittee should be made at the earliest possible date."

Attempting during the long, frustrating week following the July 17 committee meeting to enlist Truman's influence on his behalf, Johnson issued a number of statements designed to reassure the President that he need not fear criticism from any subcommittee headed by Lyndon Johnson. Pointedly reemphasizing in one statement that establishment of the subcommittee would "cut off other indiscriminate investigations of the emergency [defense] effort," he added, "I personally do not believe we have time for criticism at the present moment."

If Truman intervened, his intervention was not sufficient: the President's influence on Capitol Hill was on the wane. Tydings refused to budge. For a freshman senator to get this prized subcommittee chairmanship, he would need an ally—a patron—more influential within the Senate than the President.

And this freshman senator had that ally. "He had talked it over beforehand with Senator Russell and asked his help in convincing [Tydings] to give him the subcommittee despite his lack of seniority," a journalist familiar with the situation was to recall. Although Russell had agreed to help, he had hitherto not thrown his full weight into the scales. Now he did so—and with Russell on his side, Lyndon Johnson didn't need anyone else. As Symington was to put it, "Russell was for him. There were no other factors that mattered."

While Tydings may not have been talking to Johnson, he now began talking with Russell, in the secrecy of the Marble Room. The details of those conversations are not known—because, as always with Russell, they took place in confidence—but their outcome was clear. "As was generally the case in delicate maneuvers involving Russell, there was no rancor, no controversy; but it somehow came to pass that Tydings, faced with the rigors of a difficult campaign, decided that he did not want to take on additional time-consuming duties," John A. Goldsmith wrote. Saying privately that he would assume the subcommittee chairmanship himself when, with the re-election threat disposed of, the Senate reorganized in January, 1951, Tydings, on July 27, 1950, simply announced that Lyndon Johnson would be chairman.

The significance of the appointment to Johnson's career was instantly apparent. "Senator Johnson of Texas today faces opportunities for fame, public service and political advancement almost without equal for a senator serving his first term," Leslie Carpenter wrote. "Those opportunities are fundamentally the same as those that confronted Senator Truman . . . in 1941. And no one has to be told what happened to Truman." And, Carpenter pointed out, Truman had been in his seventh year in the Senate when he was given his great opportunity. "Johnson is only in his second year." As *The Nation* reported, "With the outbreak of the Korean War dozens of Congressmen recognized that the impact of a tremendous rearmament program would open up new fields for legislative investigation and that national reputations could be built by skillful employment of the power to probe." Dozens had recognized it; one had gotten it— thanks largely to his third *R*.

AND ONCE LYNDON JOHNSON had the opportunity, he made the most of it—displaying gifts more rare than the ability to court an older man.

The Senate as a whole—and most senators individually—may not have grasped the importance of staff, of a new kind of staff suited to the new, more complicated postwar world, but Lyndon Johnson had grasped it from the day he arrived in the Senate. And now, assembling a staff for the Preparedness Investigating Subcommittee, he set out to create what he had had in mind.

He had promised Tydings that the "nucleus" of the subcommittee's staff would be the staff of the parent Armed Services Committee, but that staff consisted of former career military officers, not at all what Johnson had in mind. So from the moment he got what he wanted from Tydings—the chairmanship—the promises he had given Tydings were moot.

Assembling part of the subcommittee's staff was easy, for it was already on his payroll. The "best man with words" whom he knew—Horace Busby— was simply moved out of 231 and down the hall to a little cubicle in the Armed Services suite, and on the cubicle's door was painted the title "Editor of Subcommittee Reports." Another man of unusual abilities was on a payroll that Johnson treated as his own: that of Alvin Wirtz's Austin law firm. John Connally had thought that he had finally found a refuge from Johnson there, but Wirtz now informed Connally that while he would remain on salary with the firm, he would also have assignments from the subcommittee.

Assembling the rest of the staff was hard, for Johnson wanted men with ability and expertise equal to that of the bright young professionals of the executive agencies "downtown." For a committee or subcommittee to "borrow help" from "downtown" was strictly against Senate rules, for the use of executive branch personnel violated the Senate's cherished independence and the principle of separation of powers, and also threatened the Senate's institutional authority, since personnel not on the Senate payroll were not bound by Senate rules or subject to Senate discipline. Alarmed by the proliferation of "borrowing" under wartime necessity, the Senate had given the rigid longtime regulations prohibiting the practice the force of law by codifying them in the Legislative Reorganization Act of 1946. Since passage of the Act, an internal Rules Committee memorandum would report in 1950, the number of borrowed personnel had been sharply reduced, and "nearly all" had been merely low-level clerical or administrative employees or FBI investigators. The sole exception—the only administrator of more than low rank borrowed from an executive agency since the war—had been an assistant to an agency commissioner.

Lyndon Johnson had a different level of help in mind: was the "best man with words" on the subcommittee staff?—he wanted the "best man with numbers," too. That man, Donald Cook, a trained accountant as well as a very sharp lawyer, was not a commissioner's assistant but a full commissioner, vice chairman of the Securities and Exchange Commission, in fact—at that very moment, in fact, under consideration for the SEC's chairmanship. Johnson wanted him instead to run the Preparedness Subcommittee's day-to-day operation. And he got him. Cook didn't want to leave the SEC—the chairmanship, as a stepping-stone to the wealth that was his goal, was what he had been aiming at, hitherto with Johnson's support. But he wasn't given a choice; Johnson had arranged his career—the positions with Tom Clark's Justice Department; the SEC commissionership—and, it was made clear to him, Johnson could stop arranging. Cook was told—in so many words—that if he wanted Johnson's future backing for the SEC chairmanship, he would first have to be chief counsel of Johnson's subcommittee.

In hiring Cook, Johnson circumvented the strictures of the Legislative Reorganization Act, seemingly insurmountable to other senators, with astonishing deftness. Calling Cook's appointment "temporary," he said it would be only an unpaid, part-time job; Cook would continue to hold his post, and draw his salary, as SEC vice chairman. In reality, however, despite the "temporary" designation, Cook would devote most of his time to the subcommittee for almost two years (at which point he would in fact be rewarded with the SEC chairmanship). No one challenged the appointment—since he was drawing no salary from the Senate, it did not require approval from Tydings or anyone else—and at the subcommittee's organizational meeting on July 30, Cook was named its chief counsel. Cook's dual role—a vice chairman of an executive branch regulatory agency on the staff of a legislative subcommittee*—clearly violated both Senate custom and federal law, but Johnson had found a way to maneuver around custom and regulations, had pushed the tactic to the limit (beyond, so far as can be learned, the point to which any other senator had ever gone) and, as had so often been the case with his unprecedented maneuvers, had succeeded with it.

Drafting Cook brought other benefits besides his incisive intelligence. The subcommittee's budget, including salaries for its staff, was of course only the modest $25,000 that the Armed Services Committee had approved. At the SEC, however, Cook had been planning to hire an "Assistant to the Vice Chair-

---

*When, years later, Cook's appointment was mentioned to an expert on Senate hiring practice—Donald A. Ritchie, associate historian in the Senate Historical Office—he refused at first to believe it had occurred.

man," and a salary line had already been created for that job. Offering it now to a young, Yale-educated SEC attorney, Gerald W. Siegel, who had caught his eye, Cook made it clear that while his salary would come from the agency, his work would be for the subcommittee.

As important as money was space, always in short supply in the Senate Office Building. It was not unusual for congressional committees to use offices in the vast regulatory agency buildings, but under federal regulations rent had to be paid for them. With the vice chairman of an agency on your staff, however, that was a problem easily solved. Six rooms on the second floor of the SEC Building on Second Street were given rent-free to the subcommittee, and filled with SEC accountants and typists whose salaries were still paid by the agency, but who were actually working for the subcommittee. To deflect objections to all these arrangements from the other SEC commissioners, Senator Russell had a quiet word with Senator Maybank, whose Appropriations subcommittee oversaw the SEC budget, and the agency's annual appropriation was increased by some $200,000.

Johnson filled up his new space seemingly overnight. It was the Preparedness *Investigating* Subcommittee; he needed investigators. He wanted the best—which he considered to be investigators from the Federal Bureau of Investigation. And he wanted them to be supervised by someone experienced at supervising FBI investigators—an official who, as he put it, had been "high up" in the FBI. He got him, too. J. Edgar Hoover gave him the name of Lyon L. (Slug) Tyler, the former deputy chief of the bureau's investigative division, who had recently resigned to enter private law practice. Although Tyler idolized Hoover, he had said no to Hoover's attempts to retain him, and when Lyndon Johnson first telephoned him, he said no to him, too. His first thought, he was to recall, was: "I ain't for Capitol Hill. I'm trying to get a law practice started." When Johnson asked him to at least come in and talk, he said there was no point.

But "no one said no to Lyndon Johnson." Since his call to Tyler himself had failed to produce the desired result, he made other calls—to Tyler's old friends at the FBI. And he gave them a potent argument to use with a man who worshiped his old boss. "I began to get calls from my friends," Tyler would recall. "They would tell me that because I had refused to even consider Johnson's offer, the Senator was pestering Hoover to find someone else. They would say, 'At least go up there and talk. All you got to do is go up there, and you'll get Hoover off the hook.' "

When he went "up there"—when Mary Rather ushered him into Johnson's private office and shut the door behind him—Tyler found himself being offered not only good money (the same top civil service salary he had been earning at the FBI) and good staff ("He had three top people coming in that day—one from ONI [the Office of Naval Intelligence]; he was a great man for borrowing people. And he told me to bring in men from the FBI: the best men I knew"), but inspiration. "We need you! Your country needs you! Put a staff together,

and get 'em rollin', and you can go on your way. But right now, we need
you. We're at war! This is a big world war we're getting into, and we need some
top-class help. This is gonna be the Truman Committee of the Third World
War!" So deeply affected was Tyler that when he walked out of 231 he no
longer had one idol but two. "Lyndon, I thought, had great, great strength,"
Tyler says. "He could talk you into anything. Listen—he had to me some of the
drive of J. Edgar Hoover. What more can I say?"

By August 15, two weeks after the Preparedness Subcommittee had held
its first organizational meeting, the subcommittee's staff—lawyers, accountants, researchers, stenographers, investigators—numbered twenty-five, three
times as many as the staff of Tydings' parent committee. Lyndon Johnson, still
in his second year in the Senate, had assembled a staff not only larger than that
of most other senators—perhaps larger than that of *any* other senator—but
more qualified. In just two weeks, in that small-scale Senate of 1950, Lyndon
Johnson had created his own little empire, and it was an empire of talent.

HAVING ACQUIRED A STAFF with remarkable speed, Johnson used it with
remarkable speed.

Speed was essential. Tydings' intention of taking over the defense mobilization investigation after his re-election in November gave Johnson less than
three months to compile a record so impressive that his chairman would find it
embarrassing to supplant him, and in fact he had even less time than that. A
number of House committees were beginning their own mobilization investigations; at least one senior senator, Homer Ferguson, was making noises about
forming a special Select Senate Committee, and the committee that produced
the first newsworthy result would have the important first public identification
as the investigating body. Johnson needed to have a report ready fast—and he
did. Most of the subcommittee's staff reported for work on August 15. The subcommittee's first report was released to the press three weeks later.

Johnson was able to produce a report so quickly because much of it was
simply a recycling of a report that had been all but completed—by another
Armed Services subcommittee he had been chairing—before the Korean War
began: a routine study analyzing the implications for America's rubber supply
should some future major war break out in the Far East, source of the world's
natural rubber. The bulk of the Preparedness Investigating Subcommittee's
report—issued on September 5—was simply a rewriting of that earlier study
which had found that war in the Far East would be "an obvious threat" to
America's rubber supply and had advocated reactivating America's World
War II synthetic-rubber-producing program. There was nothing particularly
new or significant in the report; in fact, by the time it appeared, the Administration had already begun reactivating the program.

The rest of the September 5 report dealt with the government's surplus-
property disposal program, under which, since World War II, it had been shut-

ting down defense plants and selling them off to private industry. The report said that the Preparedness Subcommittee had found "a number of instances in which plans were going ahead for the 'surplus' sale" of plants "which appeared to be essential to our current mobilization needs," including a synthetic rubber plant in Akron, Ohio. The day after the subcommittee was formed, Stuart Symington told Johnson that that plant, closed since the end of World War II, was in the process of being sold by the Reconstruction Finance Corporation to a private company, which was planning to reopen it. Johnson wrote RFC Chairman Harley Hise, urging him to cancel the sale, and to keep the plant closed and available for defense use. There was nothing particularly exciting in this, either; Symington had informed the White House at the same time he told Johnson, and by the time the report was issued, the sale had already been canceled, as had plans for putting three other rubber plants on the market. Nor was the case for such cancellations clear-cut. A body of expert opinion held that such plants might be better prepared to produce rubber for defense purposes if they were reopened and running, and had only to be converted from civilian to defense use, than if they remained closed and had to be reconditioned from scratch. With the public in an outcry over the country's lack of readiness for war, Truman appears to have ordered the plants retained, and the overall synthetic-rubber program increased (by a token 80,000 tons per year) as the simplest way to avoid a controversy in which he could hardly have helped looking bad. But the cancellation of the Akron sale allowed Johnson to claim a victory in the subcommittee report, which stated: "Because of this [the subcommittee's] intervention, fortunately, the Government still has this essential plant."

The most significant aspect of the first report of the Senate Preparedness Subcommittee was not its contents but the way it was presented. During his entire career, Lyndon Johnson had demonstrated, again and again, a remarkable proficiency in the mechanics of politics, in the lower-level, basic techniques that are essential to political success but that some politicians never seem to learn. Lyndon Johnson had never *had* to learn these techniques. From the moment he entered politics—from those first Hill Country campaigns, now so many years behind him—he had seemed to *know* them, to know them instinctively, and to practice them with a rare ingenuity, a resourcefulness, a sureness of touch, as unerring as it was untaught. In a democracy, the bedrock of political power is public support, so one of the most basic requirements for a public official is the ability to influence public opinion, and the journalists who mold it. None of the lower arts of politics is more essential to the politician than the ability to obtain favorable publicity, and the subcommittee's first report demonstrated that its chairman was a master of that art. Although most of what the report said was neither new nor significant, Johnson made it *seem* new and significant—by saying it in phrases brilliantly calculated to catch the journalistic eye.

Some of these phrases were written by Johnson's little wordsmith—

contained in the draft report Horace Busby brought into Johnson's office. Some were Johnson's own, written onto the draft in his bold handwriting, the phrases of a great storyteller who all his life had displayed a gift for the dramatic. Phrases like *"darkest days," "business as usual," "too little and too late"* leapt out of the final report. "During the darkest days of the Korean crisis, evidence was found of a 'business as usual' attitude in some quarters charged with responsibility in the preparedness program," it said. "We must not have too little and be too late in our rubber program." The report was infused with a sense of drama: the subcommittee, it said, was trying "to make certain that we are not continuing to demobilize with one hand while trying to mobilize with the other." The subcommittee, it said, "has fought at every Government level for a maximum reactivation of our synthetic-rubber producing program. The word fought is used advisedly." Its prose was aggressive. Noting that the subcommittee had asked the National Munitions Board to discuss the rubber program, and "to date no reply or acknowledgment has been received," it said: "Either the Munitions Board has a program or it has not. If it has a program it could readily be described. If it has no program it should be candidly admitted." There was urgency in the report—a shout of warning, a call to arms: "We face the distinct threat of a war of attrition. . . . Not only the Nation's security but its very existence is challenged. . . ." And Johnson had thought up one phrase that was particularly original and vivid, and Busby happily included it in the press release he handed to newspapermen along with the report: "If we find in the other fields into which we move the same siesta psychology that we found in surplus disposal and rubber, our work is certainly cut out for us."

The next morning Johnson's phrase was on front pages all over the country. " 'SIESTA PSYCHOLOGY' LAID TO DEFENSE DEPT" was the headline in the *New York Herald Tribune*. (The *New York Times* felt its readers needed the term defined: "In Mexico—and in some parts of south Texas—the Spanish word 'siesta' defines a habit of halting all work and taking a long nap every afternoon.") The following morning it was on editorial pages. "No Time for a Siesta" was the headline over the lead editorial in the *Washington Star*. On Sunday the subcommittee was the darling of the feature pages. "SENATE PREPAREDNESS UNIT GETS OFF TO ROARING START—Successor to Truman Committee Stirs Up Federal Agencies with Its Recommendations," the *Star* said. And in the *Washington Post* on the following Sunday, accompanied by a big picture of Johnson, was an article by Robert C. Albright which told readers that "If waffle-bottomed Washington is beginning to rise out of its swivel chair, a new Congressional Committee may have something to do with it. . . . The Senate's 'Johnson Preparedness Committee' is a new version of the old Truman Committee. It . . . puts quiet inquiries . . . ahead of headline hunting. So anonymously hush-hush had it worked that its recent preliminary report caught Washington by surprise, serving notice that the postwar 'siesta' is over." Arthur Krock called the report "a model of its kind," "an example of Congress at its best."

. . .

AND THAT WAS JUST THE FIRST REPORT. During the next two years, the Preparedness Subcommittee was to issue forty-three more. Most were even shorter on substance than the first. The second, for example, released on November 20, returned to the subjects of surplus disposal and the rubber stockpile, but in two months the subcommittee had been able to find no governmental mistake even as significant as that of the Akron plant; the example most prominently cited in the new report was the sale in August of an alcohol plant in Kansas City to Schenley Distillers, Inc.—and as a Schenley spokesman pointed out when reporters contacted him, the plant, which had stood idle for five years, had been cannibalized of its equipment and was useless unless someone purchased it and re-equipped it; Schenley had agreed to do so, and had contracted to sell the government the alcohol the plant produced, should the government need it. Some of the forty-three reports, following the pattern of the reports on rubber, contended that the government had similarly failed to provide for sufficient stockpiles of strategically important materials such as nickel, tin, tungsten, and wool. Others showed that the government was continuing to sell, as surplus, equipment needed by the armed forces. Underlying the subcommittee's emphasis on stockpiling, however, was its chairman's belief, not shared by the Administration or, for that matter, by many defense experts, that the United States should maintain stockpiles adequate not merely for the Korean conflict and any short-term enlargement of that conflict, such as Chinese involvement, but for an all-out global war. The subcommittee's report that stockpiling of the "critical" nickel supply was "lagging seriously"—and that the government agencies involved were guilty of "complacency" and "a very leisurely approach"—ignored the fact that the stockpile was actually larger than it had been during World War II.

Mundane in substance though the reports may have been, however, that was not the case with their prose. The second report may have been scant on specifics; it was long on phraseology that was grist for a reporter's typewriter or for a headline writer, as was demonstrated by the lead paragraph in the story about it, on page one, in the *New York Times:* "Government agencies in charge of disposing of so-called military surpluses were accused today by Senate investigators of acting with 'less prudence than they would display in operating a charity bazaar.' " And there was, from Busby's typewriter and Johnson's editorial pen, more to delight the journalistic eye: America's mobilization was only a "paper preparedness"; Government bureaucrats seem to think the surplus disposal program is "a compulsory giveaway." Cries of alarm (America was facing "a natural rubber 'Pearl Harbor,' " the report said) were mingled with vows of vigilance: "As far as the Preparedness Subcommittee is concerned, policies that look good on paper aren't good enough. Wars aren't won with memoranda. We intend to see that future performances live up to present promises." And rolling off the subcommittee's mimeograph machines and rushed to the Senate Press Gallery by Busby were press releases about vivid individual examples that made front pages all by themselves, like the East Texas farmer who, in November, told the subcommittee that he had purchased 168 unused aircraft fire control instruments for $6.89, and then, after the Korean War broke out, sold them back to the Air Force for $63,000.

Busby's determination to preserve what was left of his psychological independence had not abated, however, and he was planning to leave Johnson's staff early in 1951, whether or not a replacement had been found. Then, at a party given by Dave Botter of the *Dallas Morning News,* he noticed that the United Press reporter who had been covering the subcommittee, George Reedy, was roaring at Johnson's jokes. "He responded to Johnson very well," Busby was to recall. Some days later, when Reedy telephoned Johnson's office to get information for an article he was writing, he was told that the Senator was in Walter Reed Naval Hospital in Bethesda with one of his chronic bronchial infections, but that he had left his phone number and was hoping Reedy would call him there. When Reedy did, and had finished asking his questions, Johnson said, in what Reedy recalls as "a joking way, 'I want you to get over on my side and work for me where you belong.' " Thinking Johnson was joking, Reedy said, "Make me an offer," and when Johnson did—$9,688 per year, almost double what he was earning at the United Press—Reedy accepted and succeeded Busby in April, 1951.

Although Reedy was as liberal as Busby was conservative, for Johnson's purposes they were interchangeable tools, and the catchy phrases continued without abatement. One of the first reports Reedy wrote assailed the Army for assigning tens of thousands of able-bodied men to desk jobs. This was also not new; the high proportion of administrative to combat personnel in modern armies was, as one military expert commented, "inevitable," given the complexity of modern war and the public's insistence that America's soldiers be given the best support possible. "A good many others have made similar discoveries before," he said. But the subcommittee's discovery made headlines, because never before had desk-assigned soldiers been categorized in a phrase as vivid as the one in the Johnson Subcommittee's report: "the Chair Corps."

"It's all right with me that Lyndon Johnson is junior Senator from Texas instead of being a rival Washington columnist," syndicated columnist Holmes Alexander was to say. "The guy can write." What you notice right away about these Johnson reports is that they're low in federal gobbleygook and high on the peppy turns of phrase which make for public understanding. . . . This stuff Johnson puts out is written to be read."

And it wasn't just the writing that was getting Lyndon Johnson headlines—for he was playing the press like a master. Understanding that the most effective means of burnishing the subcommittee's image (and that of its chairman) would be identification with the renowned Truman Committee, Johnson wanted the ultimate identification: for journalists to call his group "the new Truman Committee." But in that desire lay a pitfall: one word of public disapproval from the man whose name was in that title would end any possibility of that identification—and Johnson almost fell into that pit with his first step, when, drawing up his subcommittee's agenda, he made it so broad in scope that Truman felt it might impinge on his Administration's conduct of the war. The President reacted—luckily for Johnson only in a private memo of which Johnson was made aware—with anger.

Hastily pulling back from the edge, Johnson soothed the President—in what was, even for him, a masterstroke of flattery. A "Statement of [Subcommittee] Policies and Procedures" was drafted, and it reassured the President—not surprisingly, since the key points were virtually his own words, words Truman had written ten years before to guide *his* committee. Truman, for example, had written, "The function of generals and admirals is to fight battles and to tell us what they need to fight battles with." Johnson's statement said, "We were not created to tell generals and admirals how to fight battles, but rather to make sure that they and the men fighting under them have what they need to win those battles." Had Truman decreed that his committee would not investigate "military and naval strategy"? Johnson's statement said that his committee would not investigate "battlefront strategy."

Other passages were designed to allay any fears Truman might have had that the subcommittee would criticize his Administration. Pledging that "We will not hunt headlines," the subcommittee stated, in phrases that also echoed those of the Truman Committee, that it was not concerned with past mistakes. "What's done is done. Most important, I think this subcommittee must be extremely diligent not to establish—or attempt to establish—itself as a Monday morning quarterback club." Having marked the passages that echoed Truman's words, so that the President couldn't miss them, Johnson sent him the statement and delivered further reassurances in person—Johnson's appointment with the President on August 8 was the first time he had been in the White House since January—and the desired effect was evidently achieved. Returning to his office, Johnson recounted details of the meeting to one of his staff, who wrote that the President had read the statements "and approved them heartily as some of the finest ever to be made by a Senate committee. . . . He said go right ahead, on the charted course; if anything is wrong, come and tell him about it and it will be remedied. Senator said it was the 'finest meeting' that could possibly be had."

With the President's support assured, there was seemingly no interview Lyndon Johnson gave in which the magic title was not invoked, and the press took the point. "A NEW 'TRUMAN COMMITTEE' EMERGES" was the headline in the *Washington Post*. After talking with Johnson, Robert Walsh of the *Washington Star* wrote that the two committees are "like father, like son." The Johnson subcommittee, the article said, is the Truman Committee's "natural heir." It has

Truman's "paternal blessing." Truman "has made it abundantly clear to all around him that he is 'cooperating' with the committee," Walsh wrote.

FREQUENT AS WERE the comparisons between the Johnson and Truman bodies, however, there were significant contrasts between their respective chairmen's methods of operation—contrasts which reflected the differences in their personalities, and which foreshadowed the differences between their presidencies. But these methods also helped Johnson in his playing of the press.

One was a difference in control. The genesis of the Truman Committee was very much the work of one man. Disturbed by reports of profiteering and waste in the vast military buildup begun in 1940 and by the possibility that his home state of Missouri was not receiving its fair share of defense contracts, Senator Harry Truman decided to try to find out the truth for himself—by leaving Washington, alone in his old Dodge automobile, and driving to military installations and defense plants from Florida to Michigan, covering perhaps ten thousand miles. It was his speech to the Senate on what he had found on this personal inspection that led to the creation of his committee, and even after it was formed in April, 1941—until his nomination for the vice presidency in July, 1944—Truman would make other trips, sometimes by plane, sometimes in that old car, usually not saying who he was unless he was asked, lying awake at night in hotel rooms in strange cities and little towns worrying over the course of the war. But Truman also went to great lengths to involve the committee's six other senators in its work, encouraging their active participation, generously sharing the limelight with them. Throughout the war, committee members—sometimes all six—would accompany him and committee investigators on cross-country tours. "They would put down at a city or military base, go through their routine for a day or so, and then be off again, like a roadshow, everybody by now knowing just what to do," David McCullough has written. "War plants were inspected, hearings held in local hotels."

Participation was not encouraged on the Johnson subcommittee; steps were, in fact, taken to discourage it.

Cook and Busby had long since learned the inadvisability of conducting long conversations with their boss's colleagues. Busby was very adept at turning aside senators who dropped by his cubbyhole to discuss a subcommittee report. The group's three Democratic members were not especially eager to participate. Fellow freshmen Estes Kefauver and Lester Hunt, both ambitious, were preoccupied with their own subcommittees; without encouragement they wouldn't give more than cursory attention to Johnson's; Kefauver, in fact, signaled his lack of interest by giving Johnson a blanket proxy to use "whenever I am not present." And Virgil Chapman, a big, bald Kentuckian who considered Johnson his friend because they had served in the House (and had been "Sam's boys") together, was sliding rapidly down a very steep alcoholic slope. One of the three Republican members, Leverett Saltonstall, so amenable that he was known as "Old Oil on Troubled Waters," certainly wasn't going to make trouble by poaching on another senator's preserve. The second Republican, Styles Bridges, was known for his receptivity to the *quid pro quo*. A freshman senator with an infant subcommittee with a tiny budget might seem to have little to offer the ranking GOP member of Appropriations, but Johnson had recognized that Bridges was building his own empire: what one observer calls "an apparatus all over Washington; he had guys stashed away in every agency." Johnson told Bridges that he would value his "guidance" in filling two positions on the subcommittee staff. And, he made clear, while these men would be paid by the subcommittee, they would not be required to work for it; they would take their assignments not from him but from Bridges. In return for the *quo,* Johnson got his *quid:* Bridges' support on subcommittee actions, and a free hand in running it. The real problem was the third Republican, Wayne Morse of Oregon, independent, intelligent, opinionated, and hungry for publicity—and to solve this problem Johnson went to considerable lengths. Morse was facing a re-election fight in Oregon, where there was considerable apprehension about Russian designs on Alaska, separated from the USSR only by the fifty miles of the Bering Strait. Telling Morse that "Alaskan defense," and indeed the defense of the entire Pacific Northwest, should be one of the subcommittee's central concerns, Johnson asked him to head a special one-member task force on the subject. Morse was dispatched on this mission with pomp—his "work will take priority over all our other work," Johnson told reporters; "Senator Morse has been insistent that adequate defense be given the Northwest"—far enough away from Washington (he was soon holding publicity-rich hearings in Oregon) so that, at least until November, his interference with other subcommittee work was kept to a minimum.

ANOTHER CONTRAST between the two bodies was in the openness with which their work was conducted.

The Truman Committee had been characterized by a notable openness. Its work had centered around its hearings, meetings of the subcommittee at which witnesses testified. These hearings were remarkable not only for their number—during the just over three years that Truman was chairman the committee held 329 hearings, or about 104 per year, hearing approximately eight hundred witnesses——but for the fact that even in a wartime atmosphere, Truman leaned over backward to make as few of them as possible "executive" or closed sessions, closing them only for genuine security concerns or to afford officials criticized in a draft committee report an opportunity to refute the criticism before it was made public. More than half the hearings—194 of the 329— were open to the press and public. Held in hotels, in the committee's hearing room and, as interest grew and crowds mounted, in the great Senate Caucus

Room itself, these hearings produced what McCullough calls "memorable days of testimony": when a great steel company official was forced to admit under oath that the company had falsified test results on steel used in Navy ships, when an inspector for Curtis-Wright, who had two nephews in the Air Force, broke down at the witness table and sobbed as he confessed that the company was selling the Air Force airplane engines it knew were faulty.

A characteristic of the Johnson Subcommittee was its secrecy. On-the-spot inspection trips were not a luxury in which Johnson indulged himself; during the two and a half years in which he was chairman before the Republicans gained control of the Senate in November, 1952, he ventured no farther afield on such a trip than New York. And it was not a luxury in which other members of the subcommittee, with the exception of Morse, were encouraged to indulge, so there were few hearings in other cities.

And there were few in Washington (except on a single project for which Russell, to further a pet proposal of his own, used the subcommittee as an arm of his full committee so that it was acting more under his direction than Johnson's*). Aside from that project, during the two and a half years of Johnson's chairmanship, Preparedness held forty-one hearings, in contrast to the more than one hundred per year of the Truman Committee, about sixteen per year. And in even sharper contrast only nineteen of Johnson's hearings were open, or about eight per year. (Truman had held about sixty-five open hearings per year.) The rest of the Johnson Subcommittee's hearings were executive, or closed,

---

*The proposal was for the establishment of a system of Universal Military Training, a cause for which Russell was the longtime champion on Capitol Hill and for which Russell had introduced legislation (Senate Bill S.1) in 1948, 1949, and 1950. It had been carried forward in those years by the Armed Services Committee because he wasn't yet chairman, and could therefore adhere to his lifelong practice of avoiding the spotlight on legislation in which he was interested. Not being the "point man" on this legislation was particularly important to Russell because he was simultaneously proposing a bill that would have fostered segregation in the armed forces by allowing draftees to elect to serve in racially segregated units; knowing that this bill would be defeated, he didn't want UMT entangled with it. After Tydings' defeat in 1950, however, Russell became Armed Services' chairman, so he "delegated" the UMT hearings in January, 1951, to its Preparedness Investigating Subcommittee, and extensive hearings were held on S.1. But this delegation was in name only; as Richard T. McCulley, Historian of the National Archives' Center for Legislative Archives and author of *A History of the Senate Committee on Armed Services,* writes, "On S. 1 the Preparedness Subcommittee was functioning as an arm of the full Committee . . . rather than as an [independent] investigative entity." Russell, McCulley says, was using the subcommittee "to facilitate the work of the full Committee and to meet his own political needs." In contrast to all its other work, in this lone instance the "Investigating" subcommittee wasn't even investigating; in what Russell's aide William Darden calls an "unusual" step, Russell had given "an investigative subcommittee a legislative job": analyzing the merits of a specific bill. The hearings were in all but name hearings by the full committee, even down to the fact that the key staffers involved were not the ones Johnson had hired but two regular Army officers, General Verne Mudge and Colonel Mark Galusha, whom Johnson had not wanted for Preparedness, and who had been working on UMT for Russell for years. In other

sessions, held in its meeting room, SOB 212, with a uniformed Capitol police-man stationed in front of its closed doors to keep out the public.

Public hearings, with witnesses' upraised hands as they took the oath, the rap of the gavel, the popping glare of flashbulbs, the senators and counsel hunching forward for cross-examination, the dramatic moments of testimony, the murmur and hush of the audience, the reporters' scribbling pencils, the wire service men jumping up and hurrying toward the door to send bulletins—public hearings with their constant potential for the controversy and confronta-tion that makes news—were one of the surest devices for bringing recognition to a senator, the device used by most senators seeking publicity. But the public hearing is always a risky device, with ample possibilities for mishaps; it is, after all, not only the chairman to whom the committee horseshoe offers a forum: senators can disagree with each other. The witness table, too, can be a forum—a national sounding board for a witness who disagrees with the chair-man. Controversy and confrontation do not always play out according to a chairman's script.

Lyndon Johnson didn't want any mishaps. He wanted to minimize the chance of controversy and confrontation—wanted to have publicity without, so far as possible, the danger of bad publicity. And he succeeded: by making not hearings but reports—the forty-four printed, formal reports issued by his sub-committee during his chairmanship—the basis of his subcommittee's work.

These reports, based either on investigations by the subcommittee staff or, in not a few cases, on work previously done by other government agencies (several were simply rewritings of studies that had been carried out by the research service of the Library of Congress) were drafted (or rewritten) by Siegel and then redrafted by Cook and Walter Jenkins. Then they were rewrit-

aspects, too, the subcommittee was acting less under Johnson's direction than Russell's, and its procedures in this instance were in sharp contrast to the rest of its work. Not only the subcom-mittee's members but other members of the full committee sat in on the hearings: Russell, Ralph Flanders of Vermont and John Stennis of Mississippi, for instance, sat on the dais, questioned witnesses and made statements. The hearings were not even funded under the Senate resolution providing funding for the subcommittee but rather under the resolution providing funding for the full Armed Services Committee. And when the bill came to the floor, although Johnson was called its floor manager, it was actually Russell who, as his biographer Gilbert Fite says, "skill-fully guided the bill through the Senate. He granted interruptions and time to key supporters. . . ." When a conference committee met to reconcile Senate and House versions of the bill, Russell was its chairman. (The bill eventually provided that it would become effective only if Congress approved an implementation procedure to be proposed by a special commission; since Congress never did so, the bill never went into effect.) "The UMT thing—that was a Russell operation, not Johnson's," Horace Busby said. A similar situation existed with four "task forces" estab-lished by the Armed Services Committee during the Eighty-second Congress. Although they were called "task forces" of Preparedness, "Chairman Johnson chaired no Task Force and attended no Task Force meeting," McCulley writes. Some of them included senators who were not even members of Preparedness, and not Johnson's men but Mudge and Galusha handled the bulk of the staff work.

ten again by Busby or Reedy, two experts in summarizing findings in pithy introductions and summaries. (And, of course, they were then edited by the senator-editor who was an expert himself.) Only then would the galleys printed by the Government Printing Office—generally the fourth set of galleys, so much reworking had been done—be shown to the other senators on the sub-committee, an inescapable step since their signatures were needed on it to show that the report was approved by a majority.

Around these reports was drawn a curtain of secrecy. Cook and Jenkins and Busby knew better than to talk with newspapermen, and now the new members of the subcommittee staff were informed of this in a staff meeting—informed unforgettably. "If you get any calls [from reporters]," Lyndon Johnson said, "refer them to George or to Walter. I'll talk for Preparedness. No one else talks." Then he paused, as if considering whether he had said enough, and then, evidently concluding he hadn't, went on—this time in a low, quiet voice almost throbbing with threat. "Remember," he said, "no one speaks for Lyndon Johnson except Lyndon Johnson. *No one!*" One of the new staff members, a big, tough former FBI agent named Daniel F. McGillicuddy, recalls: "He looked around that room at each one of us, looked into our eyes, looked into our eyes to see that we understood. We *understood*. That was the first time I had ever met Lyndon Johnson. I walked out of that room knowing one thing for sure: I didn't *ever* want to tangle with that guy."

Precautions were taken to guard against anyone letting a journalist see the galleys. Only a few copies—"fifteen, maybe, no more," McGillicuddy says—of each draft were printed, and staff member Wally Engel "had to guard them with his life." The galleys were kept in a safe in the subcommittee's offices, and each copy was numbered in the upper right corner so that Johnson could, if necessary, trace its circulation.

It would, of course, have been possible for journalists to wait outside the room in which the subcommittee was meeting or holding a hearing and ques-tion senators or witnesses as they emerged, but that would have required the reporters to know there was a meeting or hearing going on, and often they didn't, for Johnson didn't announce a schedule. A reporter who asked would be told the time, of course, but Johnson would explain to him that the subcommit-tee would be covering classified information, and in the patriotic atmosphere of the time, that statement would generally be sufficient to dissuade a reporter from pressing for admission. "We just didn't do anything to encourage reporters to come around," Busby recalls, and not many did.

These measures gave Johnson an unusual degree of control over the news-paper coverage his subcommittee received. That coverage had to be based mostly on the printed reports—the final reports, from which all areas of dis-agreement had been removed, all controversy smoothed over. "Johnson wanted the press only after the whole thing was done," Busby says. "You just ran the mimeograph machine, and handed it out." Moreover, these measures helped to ensure that news about the subcommittee would have to come from Johnson, and from Johnson alone.

The secrecy which surrounded the reports gave Johnson another great advantage in dealing with the press. It infused the reports with an aura of importance, as if information so tightly guarded must be significant. A journalist lucky enough to be given advance information about a report's contents could tell, and convince, his editors that the findings were significant because he believed they *were* significant. And, of course, it made the reporter look good to his editors: he was the one who had gotten the scoop; he was the one who had, his bosses back in New York now knew, that valuable Washington commodity, access. It made journalists eager to obtain advance information about the reports; grateful if they got the information, and less disposed to evaluate it with a critical eye, particularly since they would want to be given an advance look at the next report.

And advance information was available, for one of the most important of the lower arts of politics is the leak. Lyndon Johnson's mastery of this art had been displayed so early—and long before he had substantial ammunition to work with—that his gift for it was obviously natural, instinctive, innate. At the age of twenty-five, still only an assistant to a junior congressman, he had used it to defeat a quiet attempt by the Vice President of the United States, as tough and canny a politician as Texas had ever produced, Cactus Jack Garner, to grab federal patronage from the twenty-one Texas congressmen. Awed by the Vice President's power and legendary ruthlessness, the congressmen were resigned to the loss of the patronage—until Johnson, through his congressman, Richard Kleberg, told them they didn't have to lose, that he had a strategy. And a key to the strategy was a leak—his secret disclosure of Garner's maneuver—not to a Texas newspaper whose publisher, friendly to Garner, might not have printed it but to the Associated Press (through a young reporter from Texas, William S. White, with whom he was acquainted), and the resultant nationwide publicity had forced Garner into a hasty retreat. So impressed had the Vice President been that, as White was to recount, he repeatedly asked, "Who in hell is this boy Lyndon Johnson; where the hell did Kleberg get a boy with savvy like that?"*

Now, in 1950, Lyndon Johnson had ammunition to work with—*real* ammunition. He used it with a flair, infusing it with drama, emphasizing to favored reporters the risks he was taking in letting them see one of the still-secret reports. Handing an advance copy of one to Frances Levison of *Time*'s Washington bureau on a Friday afternoon, he made her understand that he was able to give it to her only because no one would be looking into the subcommittee's safe over the weekend—and that Levison *must* get the copy back to him before the safe was opened again, so that the leak couldn't be traced.

*For a fuller account of this incident, see Volume 1, *The Path to Power*, pp. 266–68.

"PACKETING ADVANCE COPY OF SENATOR JOHNSON'S SUBCOMMITTEE PROG-
RESS REPORT ON RUBBER, FOR TUESDAY RELEASE," Levison cabled her editors
in New York. "THIS PARTICULAR COPY MUST BE RETURNED AFTER WEEKEND,
BECAUSE IT IS SPECIALLY SIGNED FOR COMMITTEE FILES."

The excitement and feelings of complicity—of alliance—that journalists
felt at being involved in such intrigues comes through in their memos. "NOT
FOR USE, WE HAVE READ THE PRELIMINARY DRAFTS OF LYNDON JOHNSON'S
COMMITTEE REPORTS ON MILITARY PROCUREMENT, WHICH WILL START ISSU-
ING IN ANOTHER TWO WEEKS, POSSIBLY TEN DAYS. THEY SHOW UP GLARING
DELAYS IN PROCURING 3.5 BAZOOKAS," Frank McNaughton of *Time*'s Washington bureau cabled New York. And evident also is the extent to which this
leaking influenced journalists who might otherwise have been skeptical to
accept the evaluation Johnson put on the leaked information. Giving a journalist a look at a report in private provided Johnson with an opportunity to
"explain" its significance, and the fact that the report would remain secret until
the journalist printed it meant that an evaluation of the explanation could not be
obtained from anybody else. The "glaringness" of the delays the preliminary
draft "showed up" was, it would later turn out, a matter of debate, but the
debate would not take place until the report had already been published in a
prominent position in *Time*. And by the time doubts as to the true significance
of a subcommittee report surfaced, the subcommittee would be on the verge of
issuing a new report—and no one was better than Johnson at making a reporter
believe that the report to come would be *BIG!* Even when a promised Johnson
"bombshell" fell far short of expectations (as was the case with the procurement report), he was adept at explaining away the shortfall—and in a way
that redounded still more to his credit. He had been privately promising
James L. McConaughy major revelations about lagging defense deliveries;
when the revelations proved less than major, he told McConaughy, as
McConaughy reported in his weekly memo to his editors: "Trouble is, the committee can't figure out a way to tell the public just how bad the situation is
without revealing information damaging to security."

And if the *quid pro quo* was unstated, it was nonetheless implicit. If Johnson liked a publication's treatment of his subcommittee, and of him, there
would be other tidbits—juicier tidbits. For a publication as influential as *Time,*
in fact, it was not only copies of reports that were available; so were the transcripts of the subcommittee's tightly closed executive sessions. And no conversation, not even one in the Oval Office, was off limits, as was made clear by a
telex from John Beal, a member of *Time*'s Washington bureau, to his editors in
New York.

Had a long bull session with Lyndon Johnson this afternoon in
which he told of some recent off record conversations with Truman.
Johnson was pleased with *Time* story this week and wanted us to

know about Friday's committee sessions. He supplied me with a transcript which I have sent by packet to NA [*Time*'s National Affairs section].

Please return the transcript to Washington Bureau for return to Johnson.

NOTHING WAS TOO GOOD FOR THE PRESS. Lyndon Johnson rationed out his news, soothed reporters who had not been the beneficiary of his latest leak by telling them he had no idea how the information had gotten out, someone else on the subcommittee must have done it, and promising that he would try to make it up to them. "He worked at keeping the press on his side," comments Marshall McNeil of the *Fort Worth Star-Telegram*. "He made a point of seeing all newspapermen, and everyone left thinking that he was Lyndon's best friend."

And he kept it on his side. *Time,* preparing an article on the first subcommittee report, sent John Beal to get the story of the chairman's life for a brief biography, and Johnson spent hours telling a story, and while much of it wasn't true, all of it was charming. "I think that everything considered he deserves a good sendoff in this introduction to *Time* readers," Beal cabled his editors. The editors, several of whom had themselves been charmed by Johnson at dinner parties, agreed. The magazine sent him off with a nickname, embodied in the headline "TEXAS WATCHDOG"; with a paragraph of *Time*speak ("The Senate's new watchdog committee on U.S. preparedness uttered its first warning growl. After just a month's sniffing through the U.S. mobilization effort, Texas' sharp-nosed Lyndon Johnson had caught the strong scent of 'business as usual' "); and with the observation that "The work that [he] had cut out for himself was just the kind that lifted Missouri's Senator Harry S Truman out of obscurity." (*Time* also said he "had set himself a commendable set of rules: don't spend time looking for headlines.") The other object of his special attentions, the *New York Times,* had him on its front page three times before the end of 1950, and all across the country newspapers and magazines followed the *Times'* lead. "Mild-mannered but determined" Lyndon Johnson "is beginning to get considerable national publicity," *The Nation* said. By the end of the 1950 session, *Collier's* was reporting that Johnson's "prominence is the undisguised envy of many a member who was his senior in service. Numerous senators are pounding their temples in fury because they did not think of reviving the committee first."

THEN HE GOT A BREAK.

His temporary lease on the subcommittee chairmanship was running out, and, as Horace Busby recalls, "It was expected that when Tydings won re-election, he would take back the subcommittee." Even if Johnson's triumphs made it too embarrassing for the arrogant Marylander to supplant him directly, his chairmanship of the subcommittee's parent committee, his unchallengeable authority over the subcommittee's funding and staff, his right (which was, in a way, only logical, given the centrality of the subject to the committee's work) to make preparedness the business of the full committee and not just of a subcommittee would have assured that Johnson would no longer have the preparedness spotlight to himself.

But, suddenly, Tydings wasn't going to be returning to the Senate. It was in the 1950 elections that the ferocity and efficacy of Joe McCarthy's tactics were demonstrated for the first time, and nowhere were they demonstrated more vividly than in Maryland, where Tydings' opponent was a political nonentity. Raising big money (much of it from Texas ultra-conservatives like the men who had walked the beach on "St. Joe" with Lyndon Johnson; Clint Murchison alone gave ten thousand dollars), the Wisconsin senator assailed Tydings in bitterly vindictive speeches, and arranged for the creation of an effective anti-Tydings tabloid that was distributed across the state; it featured a "composite"—in reality, a totally fake—photograph in which Tydings was shown apparently listening attentively to Earl Browder. (It was the second time that Browder had been of use to Johnson.) When the campaign was over, so was Tydings' career. The new chairman of the Armed Services Committee was Richard Russell, who reappointed Lyndon Johnson chairman of Armed Services' Preparedness Subcommittee, and increased its annual budget to $190,000. "When Tydings lost," Horace Busby recalls, "that's when people began to say that Lyndon had a charmed life, or was a genius—mostly, that he was a genius."

14

Out of the Crowd

THE JOHNSON SUBCOMMITTEE had far less impact on the defense effort than the Truman Committee had had, and not only because the police action in Korea was not the Second World War but because, unlike Truman's work, so much of Johnson's was based not on original research—on-the-spot inspections—but on previously compiled documents simply reworked in the interests of publicity. Dan McGillicuddy, who was to work for Preparedness for thirteen years, eventually as its assistant chief counsel, came to feel that "The whole thing was to get Johnson's name in the papers." And, McGillicuddy says, Johnson wasn't any too particular about how he did it. "He was looking for the sensational," McGillicuddy says. "Hell! Twenty-six reports in one year! These things weren't being carefully researched. They'd get a report from somewhere, and Reedy would wrap it up in catchy phrases, and they'd put it out, and hope it caught on. He [Johnson] was fishing for a program of national interest." The Army colonel who later became the committee's staff director, Kenneth E. BeLieu, echoed McGillicuddy's feelings in an interview; then, asked if the subcommittee's impact during these two and half years had been significant, BeLieu smiled and said, "No, not really."

Sometimes this search for the sensational led down false alleys, out of which Johnson was able to scramble only by employing considerable ingenuity. After an unexpected rush of enlistments during the Christmas holidays at the end of 1950, senators' mailbags began to contain complaints from enlistees' parents about conditions at overcrowded Lackland Air Force Base, near San Antonio, at which sixty-eight thousand men were receiving basic training. In the middle of the coldest winter on the Texas plains in forty years, parents wrote, their sons were sleeping in unheated tents, with inadequate blankets, clothing, and food. There were reports of suicides and deaths from a pneumonia epidemic. Summoned to a closed session of the Armed Services Committee, Air Force officials said that they had heard the rumors, had already begun investigating them, and that rumors were all they were. There was no epidemic of pneumonia, or any other illness, at Lackland, they said; every man on the base had adequate blankets, clothing, and food. The base was indeed over-crowded because of the rush of enlistments, and some men were indeed sleep-ing in tents, but none of the tents was unheated—and, after all, these officials noted, it would not be the first time in history that soldiers had slept in tents. Construction of twenty-five new, centrally heated barracks, and of a new air-field equipped for basic training—Sampson Air Base in Romulus, New York—was being rushed; Sampson's completion, due within two months, would end the overcrowding. In the interim, the officials said, the Air Force had already curtailed enlistments and Lackland's population was being reduced daily as men were shipped to other camps for their basic training. The senators were urged not to add fuel to the rumors. As Air Force Secretary Thomas K. Finlet-ter was to say in a letter to Johnson:

> We are all extremely solicitous of the welfare of our young men but with large numbers of them now in combat we feel that others should not be encouraged to make public complaint because of minor discomforts and inconveniences. During a period of emer-gency some very minor hardship must be considered normal. False or exaggerated reports can cause unjustified worry or apprehension on the part of parents and others when they become public issues.

On January 27, 1951, however, Johnson emerged from an Armed Services hearing to announce that the Preparedness Subcommittee was rushing a team of four investigators to Lackland, and on January 31, escalating the sense of urgency, he told reporters that the four investigators were, as the *New York Times* put it, "to make a personal check tonight," to draw the same "blankets and sleeping gear issued to any recruit," to "sleep in separate, unheated tents along with the recruits," to eat with them—and to telephone him personally in Washington in case emergency measures were necessary. And urgency perme-ated his instructions to the crack team he had selected for the mission—Lyon Tyler, Colonel Mark Galusha, and his two Texas aces, John Connally and Horace Busby. He sent them into battle with an inspirational battle cry: "We've got to tell these mothers something!"

"Get down there right away and find out what's going on," he told Tyler. "He points his finger at me, and says, 'You're an FBI man. *Find out what's going on!*' " There was no time to be lost, Johnson said. Mothers were worried about their boys. Busby, snug in a public relations berth in Austin, could hardly believe the telephone call that was sending him out into a tent on the freezing Texas plains, but Johnson had no patience with his attempt to beg off. "Listen," he said, "this is important. *We've got to tell these mothers something!*"

The initial headlines—"INVESTIGATORS SLEEP IN LACKLAND TENTS," the *Dallas Morning News* said—were as dramatic as any senator could have desired, particularly because on the day the investigators arrived, a Texas storm swept across the plains, and temperatures plummeted to fifteen degrees. And so were the initial stories from Texas reporters who rushed to the camp because of Johnson's announcements. "An estimated 20,000 new recruits sleeping in tents at Lackland Field in subfreezing temperatures had company Tuesday night when four investigators crawled in with them," said the *Morning News*. "Chairman Johnson had the four draw GI clothing, sleep outdoors in unheated tents and eat every meal at a different mess hall," said the *Austin American-Statesman*. Within the stories, however, were statements of a different tone. Writing that "Lackland officials emphatically deny [the] rumors," Jerry Banks of the *Morning News* added that the denials appeared accurate. He reported that as he was leaving one tent, "an older recruit—perhaps twenty-four—stepped up and said: 'Don't pay any attention to these kids. . . . I was in the Army before, and it was the same then as it is now.' " In fact, Banks found, it was. "For the most part, the gripes of the recruits are the same ones their older brothers had in World War II and their fathers in World War I."

That was also the finding of Johnson's own investigating team. Even on that fifteen-degree night—the coldest night of the year—on which they had slept in the tents, the four investigators had, as Busby was to write in the report summarizing their findings, experienced "no undue cold or other discomfort." What's more, Busby's report stated, there had been no suicides at Lackland, absolutely none. There had been no pneumonia epidemic; in fact, there had been not a single death from pneumonia. "During the past 18 months, there have been only two deaths on the base—one from cancer, one from an automobile accident." The average daily sick-call attendance at the base was actually lower than it had been when the Korean War began. "The enlistees at Lackland were generally well-clothed. . . . Food was good." Morale problem? "No morale problem was found. . . . The men were generally in good spirits." And Johnson was informed of the true situation by a telephone call from his own investigators the next day, February 1.

Reassuring though this news would have been to the recruits' relatives, however, it was not news to which they were immediately given access. Somehow, the urgency about telling mothers *"something"*—giving them some form of comfort—disappeared. In fact, the Johnson Subcommittee told them nothing for almost three weeks (during which, the *Fort Worth Star-Telegram* reported, "many parents, relatives and friends of the enlistees . . . made special trips to [Lackland] because of rumors about conditions there"). Not a single word came from the subcommittee on the subject of the Lackland Air Force Base until February 19.

And when news did come, it was presented with the Johnson touch. The facts that disproved the rumors—that "There have been no suicides at the base as alleged," no pneumonia "epidemic," "no morale problem," and plenty of clothing, blankets, heat and food—were certainly all in the subcommittee report. But while these facts would have provided reassurance for parents, they would have caused embarrassment for Lyndon Johnson, who by casting doubt on the Air Force's reassurances—reassurances which had turned out to be true—had helped make the rumors a "public issue." And these facts were not the main purport of the February 19 newspaper stories. For Johnson's report presented the facts from a different angle, emphasizing not the points on which the Air Force could not be criticized but rather a point on which it could: the fact that it had accepted more enlistees "than it was capable of processing" at Lackland. In its Conclusion, the report called the Air Force policy on enlistments "irresponsible" and charged, with only the scantiest documentation, that the resultant "overcrowding" had resulted in "the total breakdown of training."

And if the report's Conclusion was much stronger than the facts contained in the body of the report, the interviews which Johnson gave about the report—before it was issued—were much stronger than the Conclusion. These interviews were designed to influence journalists, who of course had not yet seen the report, to place on it the emphasis that Johnson wanted. Since a critical evaluation of the document might have resulted in articles embarrassing to him, he called in first—for an exclusive, nationally syndicated interview—a journalist he could be confident would not give it such an evaluation, Marshall McNeil, who during the 1948 Texas senatorial campaign had written not only articles for the Scripps Howard chain of newspapers but speeches for Lyndon Johnson. The day before its release, Scripps Howard's millions of readers were prepared for it by McNeil's story that predicted a "blistering report that tans the hides of high Air Force Commanders." In other interviews Johnson said the report would be "sizzling," and explained that "It was the greed of the Air Force for the best of the nation's available manpower" that had led to overcrowding at Lackland. These interviews created the impression that Johnson wanted, even though it would turn out on closer examination that the "total breakdown" meant little more than that the overflow of enlistees had had to be sent to other bases for their basic training.

And the press followed the script he had written. "GREED FOR MANPOWER CHARGED TO AIR FORCE BY SENATE INQUIRIES" was the headline in the *Washington Star;* "LACKLAND MESS LAID TO AF 'GREED,' " the headline in the *Washington Times-Herald;* "SENATORS HIT MANPOWER HOARD BY AF—Blistering Report Says Policy Brought 'Total Breakdown in Basic Training,' " the headline in the *Washington Post.* Front-page articles across the country were dominated by the words "blistering," "sizzling," "greed," "irresponsible," and "total breakdown." It was not in the headlines or the lead paragraphs but only further down in the articles that the reader would discover statements like: "Reports of epidemics, deaths, bad food, inadequate shelter and clothing . . . were found to be completely unwarranted."

Coupled with the report was the promise of another report to come, a report that, Lyndon Johnson said, would be even more significant than this one.

There was, as always, the guarantee that this was only the beginning, that bigger revelations were just around the corner. Shocked by the overcrowding at Lackland, Johnson announced, the Preparedness Subcommittee had already launched investigations of other induction centers. "I want the parents of our young men to know that this committee is at present conducting a first-hand investigation of indoctrination camps for all three of the services all over the nation," he said. "We want to find out what the services are doing and not doing."

That report would be issued on April 15. Its conclusion was that "all branches of the armed services . . . are doing a generally commendable job at the indoctrination and training centers." But that report, preceded by no leaks or adjectives, received relatively little publicity.

IF THERE WERE STRIKEOUTS, however, there were also home runs. With complaints increasing that in the vast buildup of the armed forces, inadequate provision was being made for housing servicemen's families, so that families that wanted to accompany soldiers to their military bases were being exploited by civilian landlords, in July, 1951, Johnson dispatched three two-man investigating teams to military bases across the country. And, as McGillicuddy was to recall years later, "We hit pay dirt." In Morganfield, Kentucky, near the Army's huge Camp Breckenridge, for example, the investigators found that servicemen's wives and children were forced to live in unsanitary hovels, often without electricity or indoor plumbing, for which they were charged outrageous rents. Some residences had become so notorious among Breckenridge recruits that they had acquired nicknames. There was the "Doll House," which had once been a playhouse, fourteen feet wide and nine feet deep, built for a civilian family's children on the back lawn of their home, and which now, divided into four cubicles that the landlord called "rooms," housed a sergeant, his wife, and three children, who cooked their meals on a two-burner hot plate since there was no room for a stove, and drank water carried by bucket from the landlady's house. There was the "Chicken Coop," which "had once been just that, and now housed a family of three. There was the aptly named "Rat House."

McGillicuddy showed his photographs of these dwellings to Reedy, who said happily, "This will catch them." And Reedy made sure that the pictures did indeed catch the attention of the press and public, writing that they were evidence of "cruel indignity, irresponsible greed and casual disdain for the self-respect of our men in uniform. . . . Men who have been called into the service of the country have been forced to house their dependents in places not fit for human habitation." On the morning of Monday, July 19, the release date on the Twenty-eighth Report of the Preparedness Subcommittee—"Interim Report on Substandard Housing and Rent Gouging of Military Personnel"—those pictures "were on front pages *everywhere*," McGillicuddy recalls. Legislation to provide on-base housing for the dependents of military men had already been introduced—by Senator Wherry—and the subcommittee's findings played a major role in the passage of the Wherry Housing Act. In later years, McGillicuddy would be proud that "when you go to an Army base and see the housing with a nice playground in the middle of it—well, you can thank us for that."

(At the time, McGillicuddy's sense of accomplishment was tempered by Lyndon Johnson's response. The ex-FBI man assumed, as did the five recently hired subcommittee investigators who had also gone on the inspection trips, that their boss would be pleased by the front-page headlines and when, on the morning on which the headlines appeared, the six men were summoned to Johnson's office, "we were joking, as we walked up the hill from the SEC Building, that we were going to be decorated." But that was only because they had never dealt much with Johnson. "I ask you to go out and do a simple investigation," Lyndon Johnson said. "I ask you to go out and get pictures. Half of my team comes back with pictures. Half of my team comes back with *promises!* They'll get pictures all right. *In ten days! IN TEN DAYS!!!"*

Life magazine, it turned out, was contemplating a major story on the subcommittee report, but it needed additional pictures, some from other bases, and when Johnson had asked Tyler about more pictures, he had been told it might take as long as ten days for the investigators to fly to bases, locate suitably photogenic housing, take the pictures and get them back to Washington. Johnson "was snarling," McGillicuddy says, "just *snarling*. 'I want you all out of this town by *tonight!!* Take cameras, take film, take whatever you need—but get out of town, and get me the pictures.' He had been shouting. His voice got low, and he just snarled: *'By tonight!'* ")

THE WORK OF THE SENATE PREPAREDNESS SUBCOMMITTEE, and in particular the forty-four formal reports it published before the Republican victory in 1952 removed Lyndon Johnson from its chairmanship, demonstrated another aspect of Johnson's political ability, one that went beyond the technical—and was revealing of his personality. For each one of the reports was signed not only by him but by every one of the subcommittee's other six members.

There were the strongest of political reasons for the subcommittee's chairman to want seven signatures on every report. *Unanimous* was a word that carried a lot of weight with a Senate bitterly divided, even hamstrung, by party divisions, and with journalists, particularly when they were writing about a group whose membership was divided, 4 to 3, along party lines; unanimity would be regarded as proof that the subcommittee's decisions, being bipartisan, were above politics, that they were based on higher, more objective considerations.

And there were the strongest of personal reasons as well—reasons that had governed, and would always govern, Lyndon Johnson's life. Years later, in 1960, when he was running for vice president, his campaign train was backing into the New Orleans train depot. Standing beside him on the train's rear platform was his fellow senator, George Smathers. Seeing the huge, cheering crowd in which, Smathers recalls, "there had to be at least a thousand signs, 'Kennedy/Johnson, Kennedy/Johnson.' " Smathers thought "we were doing great"—until Johnson "jumped like he was shot," whirled on him, and said, " 'Look at that son of a bitch! Look at that sign there!' There was one [unfavorable] sign! It wasn't a foot high. There were thousands of signs, and that was the one he picked out. 'Goddammit it! Look at that sign!' I thought, this is the damndest fellow I had ever seen in my life, here we had all this, and all he could see was [that one sign]. But that was typical Johnson. . . . It had to be unanimous as far as he was concerned."

It had always had to be unanimous—starting, years before, in Johnson City's Courthouse Square, where a gangling boy barely into his teens would refuse to stop arguing politics with older barbershop hangers-on so long as there remained one man who was not subscribing to his point of view: on that small, bare stage it had been clear that the young Lyndon Johnson was so starved for respect that he needed every last taste of it he could get; that the psyche of this son of ridiculed parents had been rubbed so raw that to him disagreement was also disrespect, so that anything less than total agreement burned like salt in his wounds. "If there was an argument, he *had* to win, just *had to*. . . . he just wouldn't stop until you gave in." And now, watching Lyndon Johnson's unwillingness to allow even one member of his subcommittee to refuse to sign a majority report, Gerald Siegel realized the depth of the forces behind Lyndon Johnson's insistence on seven signatures, every time. "Any kind of criticism"—even a single negative vote on a subcommittee report—was unbearable to him, Siegel says. "He really wanted one hundred percent, and anything short of that was a great blow. He was a man who, for some reason, seemed to want unanimity in acceptance of himself." To Lyndon Johnson, those seven signatures were a sign of approval not merely of the report but of *him,* and not merely of approval of him but of the respect and affection for which he hungered.

Unanimity was easier to obtain on this subcommittee than it might have been on some others, for the reports' subjects were in general such easy targets as "waste" and "mismanagement" and "gouging," and they were being issued against a national backdrop of frustration and anger over what the public was convinced was the nation's lack of proper readiness. Landlords exploiting servicemen were fair game for Democrats and Republicans alike. Nonetheless, the subcommittee included both the staunchly liberal Hunt and the rabidly conservative Bridges—and Morse, who was known to disagree for the sake of disagreeing, and for the publicity involved. It would be, a journalist would write, "a real challenge for any chairman to bring such a group to consensus." But

Lyndon Johnson had to have unanimity, *had to*. And to get it, this reader of men read his six members, and read them well, particularly their weaknesses, and used what he read.

With Kefauver and Hunt preoccupied with their own subcommittees, Johnson could concentrate on his remaining Democrat, Virgil Chapman, whose weakness for alcohol made him particularly vulnerable.

"Drinking makes you lose control," Johnson told Bobby Baker, and control was something he never wanted to lose. In 1950 and '51, he made a show of being a heavy drinker, in the accepted, senatorial, one-of-the-boys, manner, and indeed he was—sometimes. But usually he wasn't. "Drinking makes you let your guard down," he would say, and he didn't want his guard down, ever. When, therefore, he was drinking along with another man, he had as many drinks as the other man—but his were weaker. In his own office, the instructions were strict: the other man's drinks were to be made regular strength—two or three one-ounce jiggers of whiskey per drink—but, unknown to the other man, Johnson's own drinks, Cutty Sark Scotch and soda, were not. Says his secretary Ashton Gonella, who mixed them for years: "His drinks could have no more than an ounce of liquor in it, and if there was more than an ounce, you were in trouble." In public, at the cocktail receptions that were so much a part of Washington life, he would dispatch Bobby Baker, whom he had begun to bring along to receptions, to fetch him a drink, and would order him to "make it weak." If the bartender mixed it too strong, he would grow so angry—"You trying to make an ass of me?" he snarled at the young page once; on another occasion, Baker recalls, "the Senator thundered: 'Bobby, you tryin' to sandbag me so I'll make a fool of myself?' "—that Baker took to tasting each drink himself before bringing it over to Johnson.

When Johnson discussed subcommittee business with Chapman, the discussions would be held in the late afternoon or evening, in 231's inner office, over drinks. Feet up on his desk, his body extended so fully in his chair that it seemed almost parallel with the carpet, the host was seemingly totally relaxed as he drank along with his guest, holding out a long arm to a secretary whenever his glass was empty and rattling the ice cubes for refills—frequent refills. But while the host didn't get drunk, the guest did, and, a happy, friendly drunk, the chubby Kentuckian was soon agreeing to whatever Johnson wanted. Sometimes—not often—at the next formal subcommittee meeting, Chapman might raise a question about some part of a subcommittee report, only to be told that he had agreed to it the previous afternoon—a statement which never failed to end his objections. Chapman's alcoholism was rapidly growing worse. His round face with its heavy double chin seemed almost invariably flushed with drink now, and, more and more often, when he waddled through the tall door of the subcommittee's meeting room, he would be too inebriated to follow the proceedings, and would ask Busby to sit behind him and signal him when his vote was needed, by touching him on the right shoulder for an "aye" vote, on the left shoulder for a "nay." Busby did so—always on the right shoulder; nay votes were not wanted. "I'd tap him on the shoulder; he'd jerk awake, and in this big voice boom out, 'Vote "AAAH!" ' "

Republican Saltonstall, the epitome of the dignified New Englander, had both a manner that Johnson wanted to emulate, and weaknesses that Johnson could exploit. He had learned, as he told his assistants, that the lantern-jawed Boston Brahmin, "as trustworthy and straight as he looked," had a total lack of understanding of the more sordid aspects of politics, and of life in general ("Why, you could be screwing every secretary in his office and he wouldn't have any idea that anything was going on," Johnson told Booth Mooney), as well as a patrician aversion to disputes or controversy that made him "shrink from quarreling." When Saltonstall disagreed with some aspect of a subcommittee report, Johnson would call on him and discuss it. The situation was so complicated, Johnson would say; solving it was so difficult; he had tried to accommodate all the different sides; wouldn't Saltonstall help him on this? I'd really appreciate it if you could see your way clear to helping me on this, he would say. I sure need your help. Putting the issue on such a personal basis made continued refusal to help almost a personal matter, the kind that might lead to a quarrel. Lyndon Johnson never became strident with Saltonstall; his argument would be made in a calm, courteous voice, and would be interspersed with jokes and anecdotes to prove his point. But the arguing wouldn't stop. Johnson had correctly deconstructed the Saltonstall text: if he didn't stop, eventually Saltonstall, to avoid what might escalate into a serious disagreement, would give in.

With Morse safely off in Oregon, the remaining GOP text was Bridges. The New Hampshire Republican was too powerful and shrewd to be gotten around, so Johnson, who had already given him two staff positions, now gave him anything else he wanted, including help with his constituents. New Hampshire manufacturers of wool blankets were demanding that their senator do something about recent increases in the price they had to pay for wool, increases that were reducing their profits. Following an inquiry by the subcommittee staff, Bridges was able to give them the good news that the Office of Price Stabilization would shortly be setting a ceiling on the price of wool. And when Bridges wanted help *against* some of his constituents, Johnson gave him that, too—as is made clear by the transcript of a closed subcommittee session that was held one Monday morning, July 9, 1951, in the Armed Services Committee room.

Local opposition to a proposal, dear to Bridges' heart, to construct an Air Force base near Manchester, New Hampshire, was infuriating him—and he wanted to find out who was behind it. It was possible, he said, that the opposition came from people who simply didn't want an airfield near their homes, but he doubted that explanation; there were, after all, Communists even in New Hampshire. Perhaps, he suggested, "some investigator from our committee" should go up and find out . . . whether there might be some people with rather deeper feelings who don't believe in preparedness in our country that are behind it. . . . Who is behind it? People very prominent, for instance, in the American Legion tell me they think very deeply there is something beyond just ordinary opposition."

Although Bridges didn't push the suggestion—"I don't think I am ready to ask that it be formally investigated yet, but I may"—Johnson leapt at the opportunity to be of service. After an "off the record" discussion (off the record even for a closed session), Cook told Bridges, "whenever you tell us that you would like that investigation made we will send somebody up there immediately and get to the bottom of it." Who could ask for more than that? "Thank you very much," Senator Bridges said. A rapport sprang up between Johnson and Bridges, and often in the late afternoons they would have a drink together in one of their offices.

THESE LATE-AFTERNOON SESSIONS had one aspect which Horace Busby, adoring Lyndon Johnson though he did, found disturbing—for the young speechwriter had grown fond of Virgil Chapman.

By late afternoon, he says, Johnson and Bridges could be sure Chapman would be drunk. Johnson would telephone Chapman's office, "and a secretary would answer and say the Senator was taking a nap."

"Johnson would say—this was a part of Johnson I didn't like—well, 'Wake him up!' and when he [Chapman] would come to the phone, Johnson would have him come on up. He would come rolling in, and they [Johnson and Bridges] would keep pouring him drinks. Some people think it's good sport."

(On March 8, 1951, Virgil Chapman was killed when the car he was driving collided with a tractor-trailer on Connecticut Avenue at two in the morning. His replacement on the subcommittee was John Stennis of Mississippi.)

DILIGENT AS WAS THE CHAIRMAN'S CULTIVATION of his six subcommittee members, however, occasional disagreements arose—if not over some philosophical issue then over some proposed criticism of an industry or a defense contractor of which some senator felt protective—and one or more of the senators would let the chairman know that he wouldn't be able to sign the report, or even that he wanted to issue his own, dissenting, minority report.

But the chairman would not allow disagreement. Considerable rewriting by Cook and Siegel and Reedy would already have gone into the numbered drafts which had been circulated to the six senators, and one of the principal objectives of these revisions had been to remove material to which some senator objected. Now, if a senator wanted something else rewritten, the draft would be returned to the three staff members for more work. And if problems still remained, Johnson would personally discuss them with the objecting senator. Then he would try to find a way of modifying the report yet again to meet the objections while not modifying it so much that some other subcommittee member might object. In seeking such compromises, he was notably amenable to his colleagues' points of view, so much so that staff aides—not Cook or Siegel, perhaps, but others less closely tied to Johnson—came to feel that he cared less about the content of the report than about the fact that there *be* a report. Says McGillicuddy: "Sometimes, if there was something there a senator didn't like—a sentence, a paragraph, a whole page—it would be deleted. All he [Johnson] wanted was a report to show action." Occasionally, however, the views of two of the subcommittee's members seemed irreconcilably opposed. Johnson would shuttle back and forth between their offices, talking first to one and then the other, editing, altering, trying to persuade them to a compromise that both could sign.

During these negotiations, he would compliment the senators, with that gift for the perfect compliment. Says Colonel BeLieu, who sat in on many such sessions: "He'd tell one of them that he knew he wanted to help his country, that he was a real patriot, so many times that the guy thought he *was* a patriot." He would charm them: if one of the senators complimented him back, Lyndon Johnson would grin, with a warm grin that crinkled up his big face, and say, "Well, Ah sure do wish mah parents had been here to hear you say that, Senator. Mah father would have enjoyed it. And mah mother would have believed it."

He used his stories, those wonderful stories, told in that persuasive Texas drawl, to make points—whatever points needed to be made. If he wanted the subcommittee to accept a recommendation made by the military, and one subcommittee member was refusing to go along, he might tell him an anecdote about Rayburn. "During the war, the Army was just *determined* to have Mr. Sam get on a plane and go all the way down there to some base and inspect these new tanks they were building. This whole bunch of generals comes to his office to tell him he's just *got* to go, and give them his opinion. And Mr. Sam, he just looks at them and says, 'Well, gentlemen, if you all can't tell about those tanks better than I can, we've sure been wasting a lot of money at West Point.' "

If, on some other matter, he wanted the subcommittee to criticize the military, he would tell a different story—to make the point that testimony from lower-ranking officers couldn't be trusted because military protocol forbade them to disagree with their superiors. "You hear about the latest computer that the Army's using?" he would ask. "Well, this general puts in a question. The question is this: 'Will there be peace or war in our time?' The wheels whir. The lights flash. The machine grinds out the answer: *Yes.* The general is upset. He feeds back the question: 'Yes, what?' The answer comes: *Yes, sir!*"

If the compliments and the stories didn't work, he would cajole and plead

with a senator for his signature, would work from the high ground (a unanimous report would demonstrate that the subcommittee members weren't motivated by partisan considerations, he would say, and with a war going on, that
was important; "Hell, we've got boys *dyin' out there"*) and from lower ground
(framing his arguments in pragmatic political terms, he would explain to a colleague precisely how a proposed report would strengthen him in his own state,
displaying a remarkably detailed familiarity of that state's political situation).
He would use every variety of argument, all couched in sentences whose very
rhythms infused them with a force and persuasiveness that made them hard to
resist: telling one of the subcommittee members that he was the only one still
refusing to sign a report, he would say, "Ah talked to Styles. He's goin' along.
Ah talked to John. He's goin' along. Hell, even ol' Wayne's goin' along."
Implied, if not stated, was the question: Do you want to be the only member
standing in the way of the subcommittee's work?

　　And most significantly, if, despite all the charm and the cajoling and the
pleading, one senator still continued to refuse to go along, said he simply could
not sign the report, that would not be the end of the matter.

　　Perhaps the senator had made clear that he didn't want to discuss the matter any further, and had done so in terms so firm it would have been a mistake
for Lyndon Johnson to try to schedule yet another meeting with him. In that
case, no new meeting would be scheduled—although one would in fact occur.
Alone behind the closed door of his private office, Johnson would prepare new
arguments, forecast the senator's replies to them, prepare his own responses to
those replies, rehearse his delivery. Through the door his aides would hear the
Chief's voice: "Now, Styles, you've got a real strong point there, but here's the
thing. . . ." He would, in Doris Kearns Goodwin's words, fashion "a detailed
mental script from which he would speak—in a manner designed to seem
wholly spontaneous—when the meeting took place. . . . The meeting itself
might seem like an accidental encounter in a Senate corridor; but Johnson was
not a man who roamed through halls in aimless fashion: when he began to wander, he knew who it was he would find."

　　For a recalcitrant subcommittee member, even home offered no sanctuary.
The telephone would ring, and on it would be the subcommittee's chairman,
wanting to discuss the matter again. If the senator continued to disagree, Johnson would telephone him again—later in the evening or on a weekend. In these
conversations, he never threatened—he had nothing to threaten with, of
course—or demanded. He was respectful, deferential—humble, even. But he
was also untiring. Other senators wanted to spend time with their wives and
children. They had other things they wanted to do besides talk about a subcommittee report. But if he did not have agreement—the signature he needed to
make the report unanimous—Lyndon Johnson would not stop talking about the
report.

　　"Most chairmen—if some senator kept insisting on filing a minority report, they'd finally say okay," Ken BeLieu explains. "Johnson would keep saying, 'Let's talk about it.' Home, family, Lady Bird—all this was strictly secondary with him. And the thing is: he got them to change. He got them to change, even guys who had said flatly they weren't going to change. The reason was that he was going to invest more time than they would." No matter how much time a man was willing to spend arguing with Lyndon Johnson, Lyndon Johnson was willing to spend more. "He would just wear you down. Finally you'd agree—anything to get it over with. You'd agree just to get rid of him." *He just wouldn't stop until you gave in.* He hadn't stopped in Courthouse Square, and he didn't stop now, wouldn't stop, because he couldn't stop. He *had* to win, *had to.* "One way or another, he just refused to have a single vote against him," BeLieu says.

And he didn't have one. "This unanimity is especially remarkable because the group is a cross-section of Senate political opinion," one journalist said.

ALL THROUGH 1951, Lyndon Johnson drove his subcommittee. After Congress recessed in September, the corridors of the Senate Office Building were even quieter than usual, but in the second-floor corridor outside the Armed Services Committee suite, the clatter of Reedy's typewriter could still be heard, announcing, after President Truman signed the new defense appropriations bill, that the Preparedness Subcommittee was—as Sen. Lyndon B. Johnson (D-Tex.) said today—set to guard the new defense spending against "chiselers, spendthrifts, grafters and blue sky artists"; announcing that the subcommittee was—as Sen. Lyndon B. Johnson (D-Tex.) disclosed today—subpoenaing Biloxi's mayor and police chief about slot machines on the wide-open Mississippi Gold Coast which were fleecing airmen at Keesler Field of their pay; that Senator Johnson was concerned about the "inexcusable failure" by the Army and the Department of Agriculture to coordinate their specifications for food purchased for the armed forces despite Preparedness Subcommittee warnings. ("Our reports are not written as literary exercises," Senator Johnson declared. "We expect our recommendations to be implemented or we expect to be shown the reason if they are not.")

Johnson had flown back to Texas, and was to remain there for three months, but every day, of course, his staff was telephoning him from Washington with a report on the day's mail, and if there was a possibility in it, he grasped it in an instant. When families of servicemen in Korea wrote him wondering if there would be enough warm clothing for the frigid Korean winter ahead, Johnson telephoned Army Secretary Frank Pace, and as soon as Pace assured him that there would be, Johnson rushed to reassure the parents—in an announcement, typed by Reedy, that made front pages across the country.

It was a great show. And it got great reviews. "Congress has gone home, but . . . Preparedness keeps grinding out its detective stories, which are invariably the despair of guilty or sloppy operators and the delight of anybody who enjoys seeing such miscreants put to witty and delicate torture," columnist Holmes Alexander wrote. The subcommittee's work, he said, is "like watching a super vaudeville show with pratfalls and belly laughs coming faster than it's easy to count. . . ."

If 1950 had been, for Lyndon Johnson, a year of bold black headlines in newspapers, 1951 was a year of color photographs, illustrating long articles about him in national magazines. They were the kind of articles about which a politician dreams. In a *Collier's* article accompanied by a full-page picture of a smiling Johnson being fed a piece of birthday cake by Dorothy Nichols as Busby, Woodward, Stegall, and Mary Rather looked on adoringly, and by a picture of his wife in a red dress and his two little girls in matching blue pinafores sitting in their pale green living room, Leslie Carpenter reported that "Johnson has surprised many of his colleagues by emerging as a national leader for the millions of Americans who believe their government failed miserably in meeting the challenge of the Korean War." In the *New York Times Magazine,* there was "JOHNSON OF THE 'WATCHDOG COMMITTEE.' " ("He Is Interested in Results, Not Headlines," the subhead said.) "He is tall, dark and handsome," Eliot Janeway wrote. "He inhabits an oral universe of discourse . . . and from 6:30 a.m. to the small hours of the next day, he ranges across it, arguing, listening, 'needling,' explaining, compromising, chain-smoking and chain-telephoning. Yet out of this whirl of extroverted activity Johnson has distilled the seemingly contradictory virtues of patience and tolerance." The subcommittee's unanimity reflects his "placing of patriotism above party," Janeway said.

Even the *Saturday Evening Post,* which, as one newspaper put it that year, "never says anything kind about a Democrat if it can avoid it," couldn't avoid it. While Paul Healy's *Post* article mentioned Johnson's treatment of his "underlings" (who "jump like marionettes") and of motorists on Connecticut Avenue (whom he "continually addressed in unparliamentary language") and, after quoting his statement that Roosevelt "was like a Daddy to me," mentioned that "He says much the same thing" of Rayburn, Fred Vinson, Carl Vinson, and Alvin Wirtz, Healy also admitted that "In Washington, Johnson is given the major share of the credit for keeping this investigation nonpartisan and devoid of a circus atmosphere. . . . He succeeded in getting a unanimous vote from his committee every time." Healy called him "dynamic," with an "extraordinary quick and incisive mind" and "a willingness to work like a dray horse." Johnson "is a student of human nature," the article said. "He reads other senators like a psychologist." And, it concluded, he was

> just about the hottest young senator in the Capitol, in terms of legislative results. One senator says Johnson is the most effective freshman he has seen. . . . [R]eally fervent admirers, such as his good friend W. Stuart Symington . . . call him a "man of destiny."

These articles created a particular image of the young senator. When, Carpenter wrote, a visitor to Johnson's office commented, "Why, you have one of the most beautiful views in Washington from your window," Johnson "turned his head," looked out, and said, "I'd never noticed before." John Connally told reporters that when he suggested they go to see a Lana Turner movie, Johnson replied, "Who is Lana Turner?" When a reporter mentioned Johnson's golfing afternoons at Burning Tree, Johnson emphasized that he played golf only as a means of advancing some purpose with Symington or some other influential partner. "He confesses privately that he does not enjoy the game and can't waste the time it would take to really learn it." He had no interest in life other than his work, these interviews suggested. "Leave Lyndon Johnson alone in a room with a telephone and he will make a long-distance call," his staff member Arthur Perry told Carpenter. And Busby, as always, had a vivid anecdote ready. Meeting his boss at an airport, he recalled, he found him pacing back and forth near a row of three telephone booths. "Watch those phones!" he yelled, as he started toward the newsstand. "I've got a long-distance call working in each one."

The image was summarized in Healy's lead paragraph, which said that "the junior United States Senator from Texas maintains the most rigidly one-track mind in Washington. Johnson is entirely preoccupied with the science of politics, which for him is an exact science and one which he has mastered superlatively. Politics is, naturally, Topic A for most social circles in the national capital. But for Johnson it is Topic A-to-Z. . . . He refuses to be trapped into thinking about or discussing sports, literature, the stage, the movies, or anything else in the world of recreation."

IN NOVEMBER, the yearlong flood of publicity reached its crest. This time, when a photographer—Ed Wergeles of *Newsweek* magazine—arrived at Lyndon Johnson's office to take his photograph, he wasn't satisfied to pose him just behind his desk or against a wall. He had to have a better background, Wergeles said, for unless some breaking major news story erupted during the next two or three days, this photograph was for the cover.

Johnson had bid for the cover—the cover of a national magazine with a circulation of more than two million—with the tried and true technique of which he had, during this year, so repeatedly demonstrated his mastery: a leak of a still-secret subcommittee report. He had privately assured a *Newsweek* correspondent that this report, the thirty-fifth the subcommittee had issued, was its most significant; it revealed, he said, that America's overall defense production program—deliveries of planes, tanks, ships and guns—was lagging "dangerously behind schedule." He had given the magazine not merely a draft of the report but the final version, signed by all seven subcommittee members and already in the final printed form in which it would be released to the rest of the press on November 29. And he had given it to *Newsweek* well enough in advance so that the magazine could use it in its issue that would appear on newsstands on Wednesday, November 28.

Even George Reedy, author of the report's Introduction and Conclusions, and of the accompanying press release, was to admit later that "That report was not very substantive." But Reedy's written words at the time—particularly a phrase designed to catch the journalistic eye—certainly made it seem substantive. The reason for the lag, he wrote, was that "We didn't have the courage to put guns ahead of butter." In the press release, Johnson said: "This report spells out for the American people the payoff for the wasted months that have been spent in a fruitless search for a formula that will give us both butter and guns in ample quantities. The results have been excellent in terms of butter. But unfortunately butter—even fortified butter—is not enough to stop Communist armies. That takes guns and when it comes to the production of guns, our formula has not worked out well."

During the week before the cover story was scheduled to appear, Johnson received a letter that might have raised concerns among *Newsweek*'s editors had they learned about it. One of Johnson's key contentions for some weeks had been that America's "dangerous lag" in defense production included production not only for American troops but for those of NATO nations. To document his point, he had cited what he said was a shortfall behind various schedules. But on Wednesday, November 21, Acting Secretary of Defense William C. Foster wrote Johnson that he was confusing two schedules: that for NATO arms deliveries scheduled for 1951, and that for 1951 fiscal appropriations for NATO arms which required substantial "lead time" to design and had never been intended to be delivered that year. Furthermore, Foster said, there was no need for these arms to be delivered in 1951, since they were intended for use by NATO units which had not yet even been formed. Johnson did not release that letter, nor show it to any other member of the subcommittee. And, although Johnson was in frequent communication with *Newsweek* reporters during this week, he never let them know about it, either.

Wergeles' prediction had made Johnson hopeful that he might attain the cover, but the prediction was conditional, and Johnson, who had left Washington for the ranch shortly after the photograph was taken, spent several days filled with anxiety over the possibility of some major news development. Finally, on Tuesday, unable to bear the waiting, he telephoned Walter Jenkins and told Jenkins to get an advance copy that very night, he didn't care how; Jenkins apparently flew to New York to get one.

Jenkins still had not telephoned, however, when Johnson and Lady Bird had to leave to go out to dinner with some neighbors. While they were gone, the call came—to Mary Rather in Austin. Mary typed a note to Johnson, and a car sped out of the city on the lonely road through the dark hills to the Johnson Ranch, and when the Johnsons returned, the news was waiting for them. "Walter says the cover is a beautiful picture in color," Miss Rather wrote. "Very vivid. The background is that Scotch plaid blanket. . . . You are leaning forward with your hands up to your face—head resting on right arm and cigarette in left hand. Underneath the picture: 'Watchdog in Chief.' " The next morning copies of *Newsweek* arrived in Johnson City, and there he was, on the newsstand in Fawcett's Drugstore, where Sam Ealy Johnson's credit had been cut off so that his son had had to stand by watching while his friends charged purchases to their fathers' accounts.

The articles that accompanied the cover (under the headline "TOO MUCH BUTTER, NOT ENOUGH GUNS") were equally satisfying. *Newsweek*'s editors, who, an editor's note said, had given the "Johnson Report" a "searching examination," accepted it without reservation, saying "When the Senate Preparedness Subcommittee calls the armament lag 'dangerous,' it is not just indulging a taste for rhetoric." Noting that the subcommittee had found American air strength to be "below what the American public expects," *Newsweek* said that "If the Korean War continues and the Chinese decide to challenge American air supremacy, the result could be a military disaster for America."

And there was a separate article on the subcommittee, and on him. The subcommittee, the editors said, "has been likened to the Truman Committee." Actually, the editors said, it was better than the Truman Committee.

> The [Truman Committee] sought to correct mismanagement and eliminate corruption by holding open hearings, which exposed them amid explosive newspaper headlines. The resulting clamor usually brought about reforms, and drove the grafters to jail.
>
> In contrast, the Preparedness Subcommittee holds few public hearings. And it doesn't wait for a situation to become a public scandal before investigating.

As for its chairman, "Johnson has made a great and growing reputation," *Newsweek* said. "His manner is quiet and gentle, and everything he does, he does with great deliberation and care. Yet, when he believes the facts warrant it, he can be two-fisted and tough."

NO SOONER HAD HIS WORK on the report been completed than George Reedy, who had never before participated in the subcommittee's in-the-field investigations, abruptly found himself dispatched on one—to one of the most isolated military installations in the United States: Goodfellow Air Force Base southeast of San Angelo in the remote prairies of West Texas.

Arriving there, Reedy quickly saw that the trip was a waste of time. "There had been some complaints about the quality of the training," he was to recall, but "even I could see that most of the complaints were absolutely nothing except the standard sort of thing that bobs up at any military post." He couldn't understand why he had been sent until he saw the *Newsweek* cover. "He got me out of town deliberately on that one because he sensed that I would be opposed to what he did," Reedy was to recall. "He literally got me out of town. . . . When I came back I discovered they had wrapped up this *Newsweek* deal."

Johnson was correct in thinking that he would have been opposed, Reedy says. "You really can't do anything much worse than that. If you're going to give a newspaperman or a magazine . . . an exclusive, for the love of God don't make it a formal committee report. It's too obvious, among other things." It would infuriate other journalists, he knew. While they had not subjected any of the previous thirty-four subcommittee reports to intensive scrutiny, they would scrutinize this one, he felt. And, he felt, this "not very substantive" report would not hold up under scrutiny.

Reedy's premonitions were well founded. Even a master of an art can sometimes overreach himself, and by thus stretching the leaking technique to its limit—leaking an entire formal report for a cover story while describing the report in exaggerated terms—Lyndon Johnson had overreached. Analyzing a Preparedness report in depth for the first time, the press now found what some subcommittee staff members felt it would have found about many of the sub-committee's previous reports had it analyzed *them* in depth: that the promise of the catchphrases was not fulfilled by the content.

"He got this cover of *Newsweek* . . . and in return for that he had the enmity of every economics writer in Washington," Reedy was to explain. "And they all set out to prove the report was a phony, and they did.

> Oh, Lord, I'll never forget when that storm broke. They [John-son's subcommittee] were not able to come up with one single demonstration of a gun or a weapon system or anything needed by the armed forces that had been delayed in production because a higher priority had been given to any civilian need or desire. Oh, the thing was ridiculous! I can recall at one point arranging one of these off-the-record conferences where facts could be used but nobody's name could be cited, with Don Cook and some of his hotshots. And, Lord, though, the press tore him to pieces. . . . It became apparent to everyone very quickly in Washington that the report did not have any substance to it and that he [Johnson] had used it as bait to get this cover on *Newsweek* magazine.

As outcry over the report mounted, so did embarrassment. After an official of the Office of Defense Mobilization demanded to know "one instance where materials or equipment . . . needed for the Korean fighting was not available," reporters asked the subcommittee to name such an instance, and the subcom-mittee proved unable to do so. Releasing Acting Secretary Foster's letter to Johnson, the Department of Defense charged that Johnson "sat on it"—delayed releasing the letter—until after the *Newsweek* article had appeared. Confronted by reporters holding copies of the letter, a flustered Jenkins disappeared into Johnson's private office to telephone the Senator in Texas. Emerging, he said that the charge was "unfair," and that Johnson would respond to it the next day. The response was as aggressive and headline-catching as always— characterizing Foster's statements as "doubletalk," Johnson made a new charge, in a new colorful phrase, saying, "It certainly does the public confidence no good to find that the Department of Defense, behind a cloak of security, keeps for all practical purposes a double set of books"—but the Defense Department refused to retreat, saying, as the *Herald Tribune* put it, that "the Texas legislator just didn't know what he was talking about," and in effect defying Johnson to provide one example of double bookkeeping—an example Johnson did not provide. For a year and a half Johnson had been claiming, as proof of his subcommittee's fairness, that it always afforded departmental officials the opportunity in executive session to rebut any negative findings in a draft report so that the report could, if necessary, be modified in its final version. It was now clear that in preparing this report, at least, Preparedness had never spoken to a single departmental official—either to give him a chance to put the department's side of the story on the record, or for any other reason.

More damaging still, the press now began to look beyond the specific report and to examine for the first time the subcommittee's work as a whole— and the examination yielded decidedly mixed results. As the *Herald Tribune* reported: "People in Washington differ on the merits of Sen. Johnson and his committee. Undoubtedly some of his reports are extremely valuable, and have struck the Administration at vulnerable points. Others, however, while making good headlines, have apparently not stood up to later examination."

In addition, the subcommittee's work as a whole amounted in effect to a demand for greatly expanded mobilization, a placing of the nation on an all-out war footing almost as if it were engaged in a global conflict. There began to be, for the first time, an examination of this premise also, and even such a staunch Johnson redoubt as the *Washington Post* editorial page said that "if rearmament is directed at the long pull," the balance between civilian and military goods "makes sense. It is of course important to correct bottlenecks. But before the country is pressured into what would be tantamount to full mobilization, it needs to assess both the external danger and the probability that despite the bottlenecks it will soon have military equipment running out of its ears."

The *Post* now assigned one of its most respected reporters, Alfred Friendly, to look thoroughly into the current defense effort, and Friendly's study, a seven-part series that was perhaps the most searching contemporaneous journalistic examination of the mobilization situation, would find that "with respect to the charge, could we have had more guns if we had less butter?, despite loud and general cries in the affirmative no compelling proof has yet been adduced, Sen. Johnson to the contrary notwithstanding. . . . It is a fact, and has not been denied, that no military production schedule fell short of accomplishment because an insufficient allocation, out of the total available supply, was made to the military use."

The Truman Administration had decided against full immediate mobilization, Friendly wrote, not because of any lack of toughness or of concern about the Russian threat but partly because such a mobilization "cannot be maintained over a long period in the absence of war itself." Furthermore, Friendly said, immediate massive mobilization would have meant producing weapons that would shortly be outmoded instead of creating new production facilities to produce "a new generation of weapons," so that, as he summarized, "if war did not come until three or four years later, the nation would be less, rather than better, able to win it." While Johnson and other critics had conveyed the impression that the Administration had decided not to go all-out in military production, the fact, Friendly said, was that the Administration had decided not "to go all-out in the production of models it believed were rapidly being rendered obsolescent."

As to Johnson's specific contention that the United States was losing air supremacy in Korea—that contention, Friendly found, was false. "Although the critics seem to be conveying the impression that it was otherwise, the fact is that we, not the Communists, have the superiority in Korea. . . . It is our planes, and not the Reds', which bomb the supply lines. The MiGs do not come over our lines and bomb our troops." And Friendly's overall conclusion was harsh. "From the cries of the calamity-howlers it might be concluded that the national defense program has fallen flat on its face and that, as a consequence, the Kremlin is giving us a military trouncing," Friendly wrote. Of course, the Russian forces greatly exceed our own in terms of men and planes alone. "But it is not true that we are suffering military defeats. Nor is there evidence to suggest that we have been going so slowly and taking it so easy that we are losing our chance to achieve our supreme goal, the prevention of war."

ONCE THE PRESS had taken its first hard look behind the catchphrases, it would never again view Lyndon Johnson's Defense Preparedness Subcommittee in quite the same way. Coverage of the subcommittee reports that followed the "Guns and Butter" embarrassment was notably less enthusiastic than had previously been the case. So dramatically was the perception of the subcommittee altered that by 1953, Time's James McConaughy would report confidentially to his editors that while he himself considered the criticism unjust, the subcommittee was in fact "often criticized as too publicity seeking." Another Time reporter, Clay Blair, summed up its work as "much ado about nothing."

Not that there was, after "Guns and Butter," all that much ado. From the moment the subcommittee received its first widespread criticism, Lyndon Johnson showed little enthusiasm for its work. Its production declined: in 1951, it had issued twenty-six reports; in 1952, it would issue nine, one of which was merely a summary of the year's activity. The clearest sign of Johnson's declining interest was the fact that in May, 1952, he allowed Don Cook to leave for the SEC chairmanship.

If the changed perception had a crippling effect on the subcommittee, however, it had no such effect on Lyndon Johnson's career.

He had, after all, already gotten out of the subcommittee a great deal of publicity—a favorable national image, even a cover story in a national magazine. He had gotten it because of the rare political gifts he possessed. To obtain the chairmanship, he had not merely grasped the potential in the post and reached for it faster than any other senator, he had maneuvered for it more sure-handedly, had won it against very long odds (what odds longer than a desire by his committee's chairman, Tydings, to head the subcommittee himself?). Although the success of his maneuvers had been made possible by the backing of a single powerful older man, that fact did not diminish the impressiveness of the speed and the sureness of touch. Once he had the chairmanship, he used it with the matchless talent for the practical aspects of politics he had displayed during his entire life, assembling, seemingly overnight, a staff of a caliber unique on Capitol Hill, and then wielding that staff with brilliant ingenuity, demonstrating an instinct for publicity, and a skill in obtaining it, possessed by very few even in a city filled with men avid for publicity. If—because a police action was not, after all, a war—his image was not as strongly imprinted on the national consciousness as Senator Harry Truman's had been, it was imprinted there nonetheless. And Truman had been fifty-seven years old when he created his Preparedness Committee. Johnson was forty-two. Twenty years earlier, when, fresh out of college, he had displayed the skills and sureness of a master politician, he had been called "the wonder kid" of Texas politics. No one now called him the wonder kid of the Senate. But that was what he was. In less than a year and half—if one dates the golden era of his Preparedness chairmanship from July, 1950, when he was named to it, to November, 1951, the month of the *Newsweek* cover—he, a senator hitherto all but unknown to the general public, had been on the front pages of newspapers not just in Texas but in every state in the country—over and over again. His life—or, to be more precise, the life he portrayed—had been described at length in *Collier's,* in the *Saturday Evening Post,* in *Time,* in *Business Week,* and in *Labor.* The man who could not stand—"just could not *stand*"—to be merely "one of a crowd" had been one of a crowd so long. Now he would never be one of a crowd again. He was "Johnson of the Watchdog Committee," the "Watchdog in Chief." In a single great leap—with a single issue, preparedness; with a single instrument, a brand-new subcommittee—he had thrust himself up out of the mass of senators.

THE SIGNIFICANCE of the damage to the subcommittee's image was also diminished by another factor, moreover. Even in the midst of that great leap, even as Lyndon Johnson had still been directing the subcommittee, issuing the reports, holding the press conferences, his eyes had been focusing on something else.

Lyndon Johnson's political genius was creative not merely in the lower, technical aspects of politics but on much higher levels. And if there was a single aspect of his creativity that had been, throughout his career, most impressive, it was a capacity to look at an institution that possessed only limited political power—an institution that no one else thought of as having the potential for any more than limited political power—and to see in that institution the potential for substantial political power; to transform that institution so that it possessed such power; and, in the process of transforming it, to reap from the transformation substantial personal power for himself. Lyndon Johnson had done that with the White Stars. He had done it with the Little Congress. He had done it with the Democratic Congressional Campaign Committee. And now the eyes of Lyndon Johnson were focused on another institution: the Senate of the United States.

Part III

LOOKING
FOR IT

15

No Choice

LEADERSHIP POSITIONS in the Senate were hardly among the prizes of American politics—with good reason.

The Constitution had provided that there be a Speaker for the House of Representatives, and during the century and a half since its ratification, a succession of forceful Speakers had buttressed that office with rules and precedents that made it strong. Over the Senate, however, the Founding Fathers wanted no one to have authority, and the Constitution they wrote therefore provided only that it be presided over by the Vice President (who "shall have no Vote, unless they be equally divided") or, in his absence, by a president *pro tempore*. And the Senate's rules limited the powers of the Vice President or any other presiding officer so strictly that they were little more than figureheads. "The Senate shall chuse their other officers," the Constitution said, but the only officers to be chused were administrative subordinates: a Secretary of the Senate, a Sergeant-at-Arms, a Chaplain. The Senate had certainly chosen no "leaders"; why would the ambassadors of sovereign states want to be *led*? A senator referred to as a "Leader"—Majority Leader or Minority Leader—was therefore leader not of the Senate but only of his party's senators, elected not by the Senate but by them in a party conference, or "caucus," to chair the caucuses and "lead" their parties on the Senate floor.

During the first 124 years of the Senate's existence, there were no "leaders" even in this limited sense. Until 1913, when newspapers mentioned Senate "leaders," they were referring, as one study states, to "leadership exercised through an individual's oratorical, intellectual, or political skills, not from any party designation, formal or informal." The chairmen of Standing Committees "were generally the ones to move that the Senate consider legislation reported by their committees"; the scheduling of legislation was coordinated—when and if it was coordinated—by party "policy committees." As Woodrow Wilson wrote in his 1885 classic, *Congressional Government,* "no one is *the* Senator. No one may speak for his Party as well as himself; no one exercises . . .

acknowledged leadership." When, during the Gilded Age, the GOP instituted tight control of its senators, the control was group control; the Republican Senate bloc was run not by one senator but by the "Senate Four"—and even then only through their domination of the larger party Steering Committee. After the turn of the century, as the ascension of America to world power and of Wilson to America's presidency necessitated increased coordination of activities within the Senate, party caucuses began to regularly designate caucus chairmen who were sometimes called "leaders," but there was still no official designation of a floor leader. "No single senator exercised central management of the legislative process," Walter Oleszek states. "Baronial committee chairmanships" still "provided the chamber's . . . internal leadership." In the opinion of most students of the Senate (so murky is the body's administrative history that there is little general agreement on the subject), it was not until 1913 that one of the caucus chairmen, Democrat John Worth Kern of Indiana, was generally referred to as a "Majority Leader," although, as Floyd M. Riddick, the longtime Senate Parliamentarian, puts it, Kern still lacked "any official party designation other than caucus chairman." (In 1913, also, the Democratic caucus elected an Assistant Leader, called a "whip," after the "whipper-in" of a British fox hunt who is assigned to keep the hounds from straying, whipping them back into line if necessary.")*

Kern and the Majority Leaders who came after him—five Democrats (one of whom, Oscar Underwood of Alabama, became, in 1920, the first officially designated "Democratic Leader," as well as the first Leader to sit at the front-row center-aisle desk) and four Republicans—had no formal powers. The Senate had given them none. In the forty rules that were designed to govern all its activities there is not a single mention of a Majority or a Minority Leader—of a leader of any type. Riddick's 1,076-page volume, *Senate Procedure,* published in 1974 to expand and amplify the rules, contains exactly one reference to "leaders"—an explanation that custom had established the practice of "priority of recognition": if more than one senator was requesting the floor, recognition should be granted first to the Majority Leader, and then to the Minority Leader.

The Democrats had decided to designate a Leader in 1913 primarily because Wilson, and progressive senators, felt that the President's program would have a better chance of passage if the party's senators were united under a single senator. Kern acted primarily as Wilson's agent, following the President's dictates in scheduling Senate business. Nor was Kern Wilson's only agent in the Senate; indeed, at times the President seemed to be dealing more with the powerful committee chairmen than with the supposed Leader; and as the President's power waned, so did Kern's, since his authority as Leader was

---

*He was J. Hamilton Lewis of Illinois, known as "the biggest dude in America" because of the stylishness of his clothes.

merely a function of presidential backing (Kern was in fact defeated for re-election in 1916 when Wilson failed to carry Indiana). And the same was true of the Majority Leaders who followed Kern, even though the best known of them, Joseph T. Robinson of Arkansas, would be a memorable figure on the Senate floor, pounding his desk and flailing his arms; "he roars his sneers, and shouts . . . and bellows until" his opponents "are drowned out by the volume of sound and the violence of enunciation," Alsop and Catledge wrote.

Elected Democratic Leader in 1925, Robinson was Minority Leader until 1933, when the Roosevelt landslide made him Majority Leader, and he ran his party with a firm hand, dividing up Senate patronage, appointing as Senate employees men loyal to him, disciplining rebellious senators. But he ran it on behalf of the President—no matter who the President happened to be. During the first ten years of his leadership, it was Coolidge and Hoover, and Robinson supported, and had Senate Democrats support, many Republican policies.*

Robinson's leadership of the Senate coincided, moreover, with one of the most distressing periods of Senate impotence. During the Depression years of 1930, 1931 and 1932, Democrats held a *de facto* majority in the Senate, but when Wagner, La Follette, and Norris proposed measures, many of them backed by a majority of their party, to alleviate America's pain, Robinson stood not with them but with President Hoover. In 1931, for example, his party, together with progressive Republicans and independents, favored a massive drought relief program for America's desperate farmers—and, at first, so did Robinson, himself the son of an impoverished farm family. But when Hoover insisted on a more modest program—a program so meagre as to be all but useless—Robinson abruptly switched to the President's side, calling the liberal proposal "a socialistic dole," in an abject surrender that a fellow southern Democrat, Alben Barkley, called "the most humiliating spectacle that could be brought about in an intelligent legislative body." In 1932, with America still begging for congressional leadership, Robinson said, "I know there is great unhappiness and dissatisfaction, but I do not think any legislation can secure correction." "He has given more aid to Herbert Hoover than any other Democrat," Al Smith declared. It was only after the President was Franklin Roosevelt that corrective legislation began to pass.

During the Hundred Days, journalists glorified Robinson for the speed with which he rushed bills through; the humorist Will Rogers said that "Congress doesn't pass legislation any more; they just wave at the bills as they go by." The bills going by, however, were not Robinson's but Roosevelt's, and increasingly they were bills for which Robinson, at heart a typical southern conservative, had a deep distaste.

---

*For example, he helped Coolidge kill government operation of Muscle Shoals, supplied enough Democratic votes to pass the Hoover tariff, and cut off a proposed Senate investigation of the Power Trust.

When he tried to explain his doubts to Roosevelt, however, the President—
"not interested," as the author Donald C. Bacon writes, "in Robinson's views
on matters of policy"—barely listened. FDR expected him simply to follow
orders, and Robinson followed orders, continuing to push the President's
program—in part because "his loyalty to presidents . . . had always been
strong," in part, perhaps, because this President kept dangling before him the
Supreme Court appointment that was his heart's desire. "Joe's job is to keep the
Senate pleasingly obedient" to the "commands" of "his beneficent master,"
Alsop and Catledge wrote in 1936. And although the next year Robinson began
to show signs of a new independence, that was the year he had his fatal heart
attack as he was fighting for the Supreme Court–packing bill Roosevelt hadn't
even bothered to tell him about in advance. Even this Senate Leader of whom it
has been written that "He did more than any predecessor to define the potential
of party leadership" defined it primarily in terms of the program of the Executive Branch; "forceful" and "effective" though he may have been, he was forceful and effective only when he was doing the President's bidding and was
backed by a President's power. In creating and developing public policy, his
role was, in fact, less than minor, since the legislation he advanced was, on balance, legislation of which he deeply disapproved. And the extent to which his
power was based on presidential backing was demonstrated when he tried to
exert authority on internal Senate matters about which the Administration had
no interest—then his vaunted authority seemed strangely diminished; Huey
Long "drove Joe nearly mad," Alsop and Catledge wrote. "He was outskir-
mished by Huey again and again in guerrilla warfare on the floor." It was partly
Robinson's fear of having another Huey Long on his hands that led him to
capitulate to the freshman Richard Russell's demand about a committee assignment. With the single exception of Robinson, at the time Lyndon Johnson came
to the Senate in 1949, the great names of the Senate—not only the great names
before the formal post of Leader was created (Clay, Calhoun, Webster, Benton,
Sumner) but the great names after the post was created (La Follette, Norris,
Borah, Byrnes, Vandenberg, Taft)—had not been Leaders, which may have
been why they were great names. And even Robinson's performance in many
ways confirmed that a Leader possessed power largely to the extent that he was
an agent of the White House; if the vividness of his performance covered up
that bleak reality, reality it was nonetheless.

WITH THE PASSAGE OF YEARS, in addition to "priority of recognition," a few
other prerogatives had accreted, through custom rather than formal rules,
around the majority leadership: by 1949, it had, for example, become the custom for the Leader to be the only senator who made the motions that called
bills off the Calendar (the list of bills eligible for consideration by the Senate)
to the Senate floor, where they could be debated and voted on—a custom which

in theory allowed him to determine the order of business and thus the priority in which bills were considered. If there was any moment at which the Majority Leader appeared to be truly directing the Senate's business, it was during this "Call of the Calendar," when, standing at the Leader's front-row center desk, he made the motions that called bills to the floor.

The realities of Senate power, however, robbed these prerogatives of most of their significance. The Majority Leader's control over the Calendar, for example, was exercised only as an agent of his party's Policy Committee; that committee determined the schedule by which bills were considered on the floor, and told the Leader which bills to call off. And since that committee included some of the party's most powerful senators, a Leader was exercising that control only as one, and not the controlling, member of that committee. And while a Majority Leader might be able to call a bill off the Calendar, he could not put it *on* the Calendar: in the case of virtually all significant bills, that power, like so many other real powers in the Senate, belonged to its fifteen Standing Committees; a bill could go on the Calendar only after a committee voted to report it out. And over those committees a Leader had no authority at all. He had no control over their membership, determined as it was by seniority and by his party's Committee on Committees (called by the Democrats their "Steering Committee"), of which he was a member (on the Democratic side, the chairman) but on which the southerners and their allies had a majority, so that it was they or *their* Leader ("You had to see Russell on committee assignments") who determined those assignments. (The party Leader's inability to reward or punish senators by making or withholding assignments also meant that he had no authority in an area vital to senators.) The Leader could not set the agenda of a Standing Commitee, or intervene in any way with the committee's workings; that was the province of its chairman, who was chosen by seniority, and only by seniority, not by a Leader. A Leader couldn't make a chairman put a piece of proposed legislation on the committee's agenda for hearings, and couldn't make him have the committee vote on the bill so it could be reported out to the Calendar, which meant that the Leader did not in fact control what legislation came to the floor. And, as William S. White was to say, "woe to any Majority Leader who goes to [a chairman] to 'demand' anything at all. This is simply not done in the Senate." On the rare—very rare—occasions on which it *was* done, the affronted chairman could count in his resistance to the demand on the support of the other fourteen chairmen, wary of the establishment of a precedent that might one day be used against *their* power in *their* committees. In 1949, the chairmen were as baronial as ever, secure in their committee strongholds; the Majority Leader was only a first among equals—and, often, not even all that first. The so-called Senate Leader was an official not of the Senate but only of his party, and even within that party he had little power to lead.

This situation was particularly frustrating for a *Democratic* Senate

Leader. The Democratic Party was, in the public mind, the more liberal of the two parties, and the Democratic presidents—Roosevelt and Truman—who had held the presidency since 1933 had sent to the Senate, year after year, liberal legislation. Since the Democrats were the majority in the Senate for all but four of those years, and since there was a large Democratic liberal bloc there (in 1949, no fewer than nineteen or twenty Democratic senators bore a liberal label), and since this bloc was very vocal, with eloquent speakers who continually demanded the passage of that liberal legislation, the public and the press expected the Democratic Leader not only to fight for, but to achieve its passage.

The Senate Democrats were divided by a seemingly unbridgeable chasm, however, and the power in the Senate—virtually all the power—was not on the liberal side of that chasm. The committee chairmen who held that power were almost all southern and/or conservative. A Democratic Leader trying to pass Administration legislation found himself trapped on the wrong side of an angrily divided party. And the situation was similar in the Senate GOP, even if less acute because the Republicans, being in the minority, were not *expected* to get legislation passed. Both parties were dominated by their conservative elders; it was they, not the Majority and Minority Leaders, who held senatorial power.

A Senate "Leader" had little power to lead even on the Senate floor. Because of the tradition of unlimited debate, even after he had brought a bill to the floor, any one of his ninety-five colleagues could halt consideration of the measure merely by talking. Since, as White wrote, "No one may tell any senator how long he may talk, or about what, or when," a Majority Leader "cannot even control from one hour to the next the order of business on the floor." Any attempt to do so—to limit the debate in any way—would raise in the minds of southerners and conservatives the spectre of a threat to the sacred. Any Leader contemplating an attempt to break the filibuster that was the tradition's ultimate expression would know that he would have White's "eternal majority" firmly against him. And even when there was no filibuster, White noted, "there remains the quicksand of rules that were made for deliberation, and even for obstruction, but never for speed and dispatch. A Senate Leader may wheedle and argue; he may thrash about and twist and turn in his frustration. But he does not successfully give 'orders' unless these happen to be welcome to the ostensible 'followers.' " His "party associates may thumb their senatorial noses at him just about as they please." The title of "Leader" brought with it no power that would have made the title meaningful; any attempt to truly *lead* the Senate was almost foreordained to end in failure.

WHICH LED to another unpleasant aspect of the leadership. Failing to understand the realities of Senate power, press and public thought a "Leader" was a *leader,* and therefore blamed the Leaders—particularly the "Majority

Leader"—for the Senate's failures. As White wrote: "A large part of the public has come to think that it is only the leaders . . . who somehow seem to stand, stubbornly and without reason, against that 'action' which the White House so often demands." And heaped atop blame was scorn. Many Washington journalists were liberals, eager for enactment of that liberal legislation which seemed so clearly desired not only by the President but by the bulk of the American people and impatient with the Majority Leaders who, despite the fact that they were leading a *majority,* somehow couldn't get the legislation passed. Not understanding the institutional realities, the journalists laid the Leaders' failure to personal inadequacies: incompetence, perhaps, or timidity. This feeling was fed by liberal senators, some of whom seemed to comprehend the intricacies of Senate power little more than the reporters, and who continually assailed the Leaders in speeches and interviews. The journalists mocked the Senate Leaders—in print, so that the job carried with it the potential not merely for failure but for public humiliation on a national scale.

LYNDON JOHNSON HAD had a ringside seat as potential became reality. His arrival on Capitol Hill as a young congressman in 1937 had virtually coincided with Robinson's beleaguered, and disastrous, last stand on the Senate floor, and he had seen what happened to the Majority Leaders who succeeded Robinson: Democrats Alben Barkley of Kentucky and Scott Lucas of Illinois, and Republican Wallace H. White of Maine.

Barkley had been forced on the Senate by Roosevelt, whose arm-twisting had given him the leadership by a single vote over the conservative favorite, Pat Harrison of Mississippi, and the Senate didn't let him forget it. The southerners routinely embarrassed Barkley on the Senate floor, jeeringly calling him "Dear Alben" in mocking reference to the salutation in Roosevelt's letters which gave him his marching orders. Hardly had he been elected Leader—leader of the largest majority in the Senate's history—when he lost on a routine motion to adjourn; attempting the following year to round up Democratic votes to support an Administration tax bill, he managed to marshal exactly four; "a public humiliation for Senator Barkley," one newspaper called it. Barkley felt (as Kern and Robinson had felt) that his primary responsibility was to pass the Administration's program; that was why he often simply recited speeches written by the White House. But his first four years as Leader were four years, 1937 to 1941, during which not a single major Administration bill was passed. Some journalists called Harrison "the real leader of the Senate majority," others said it was Jimmy Byrnes of South Carolina; on one point, however, all observers were agreed: the leader was not the man who held the title of Leader.

Each of Barkley's defeats—and there were many defeats—was chronicled with glee by the Washington correspondents, who competed in mocking him, nicknaming him "Bumbling Barkley" and claiming that he consulted the White

House even before he salted his soup. In March, 1939, *Life* magazine asked reporters to name the ten most able senators; the Majority Leader did not make the list. "As the unhappy Barkley has too often learned," Joseph Alsop wrote in 1940, "the slightest misstep will allow a committee to make the wrong report, or tangled parliamentary procedure to bring the wrong business before the Senate, or a debate to go the wrong way, or an important roll call vote to be lost."

When the Leader did attempt to assert his authority, the result was fiasco. Unable to enforce attendance by normal methods—with absenteeism so widespread that obtaining a quorum had become an almost daily problem—Barkley first appealed to his colleagues, telling them indignantly in 1942 that "the least they could do" was "remain at their desks and try to give the impression that they were doing their duty whether they were or not." Finally Barkley ordered the sergeant-at-arms to bring absent senators to the Chamber. Asked "Do you mean Senator McKellar, too?" he replied, "I mean *everyone!*" Roused from his hotel room, McKellar was escorted to Capitol Hill. The enraged Tennessean, whose seat in the Chamber was next to Barkley's, refused to speak to him for a year, and at the next Democratic caucus, to teach the Leader a lesson, nominated for caucus secretary his own candidate, who defeated Barkley's.

In 1944, driven to desperation by yet another demonstration of Roosevelt's contempt for the Senate, Barkley resigned as Majority Leader. The Democratic caucus quickly re-elected him, thinking, as one senator put it, that "Now he speaks for us to the President," but Barkley shortly resumed his role as a presidential flag-carrier, even after the flag became Truman's.

Barkley had learned his lesson, however. While he still presented Administration proposals, he no longer tried particularly hard to force his colleagues to vote for them—because he knew now that he had no power to do so. "I have nothing to promise them," he explained plaintively. "I have nothing to threaten them with." This attitude, together with his amiable personality, restored his popularity with his colleagues, but so completely did he relinquish the field to the conservative coalition that liberal senators and commentators routinely referred to the Senate's "leadership vacuum."

As the Democratic Leader of the Senate became the butt of jokes, so did Wallace White, leader of the Republican minority from 1943 to 1946 and Majority Leader in 1947 and 1948. Although White had the title, Vandenberg, and conservatives Bridges, Eugene Millikin of Colorado and Robert Taft, had the power. White's candor about his lack of authority (he told reporters who asked about GOP plans, "Taft is the man you want to see") didn't save him from ridicule. Watching from the Press Gallery as he frequently looked two rows back at Taft for guidance, journalists suggested, in print, that a rearview mirror be placed on his desk, and named him "Rearview White."

Taft's influence led *Time* to call him "boss of probably the most efficiently organized GOP Senate the nation has ever seen" (a rather drastic oversimplification, since it ignored the GOP Senate of William Allison and Nelson

Aldrich), but during the Forties Taft's only formal party post was chairman of its Steering Committee. He didn't want the job of Leader, with its scheduling and other responsibilities; he had, as one observer put it, "no desire to monitor the often dreary floor debate." And he had no sufferance for fools. He placed many of his party colleagues in that category, but, as Leader, he would have had to plead for their votes. Vandenberg, Bridges and Millikin didn't want the job either (although Bridges would later take it—on condition that it be only for one year; Taft finally accepted the post in January, 1953, but he died just four months later), just as the most influential figures on the Democratic side of the aisle—Walter George, Carl Hayden, and of course Richard Russell—didn't want it. When Lyndon Johnson arrived in the Senate in 1949, it had been for some years a well-known fact that any of these men—particularly Russell and Taft—could have had the leadership job for the asking, but that they had all refused to accept it. And if Johnson needed any proof of the wisdom of that decision, all he had to do was to watch, during his first two years in the Senate, the fate of the man who *had* accepted it.

WHEN HE HAD INTRODUCED JOHNSON as "Landslide Lyndon" at the Democratic caucus in January, 1949, Scott Lucas was the newly elected Majority Leader, a well-tailored, self-confident man whose classic Roman profile and taste for the spotlight had earned him the sobriquet "the John Barrymore of the Senate." Eager for the job, which he thought would bring him the national attention he openly craved, he seemed well qualified for it, being both popular with his colleagues and tough. "Formidable in debate," he had "a quality of playing for keeps," William White said. "Nobody goes out of the way to take him on." His political philosophy qualified him for the job, too: Russell approved him for it not only because his ancestors came from the South but because, as Rowland Evans and Robert Novak put it, while his "postures were liberal, his visceral instincts often tended to be conservative—particularly on matters concerning civil rights." And he was smilingly certain that he could handle it. He presided at his first caucus with an air of satisfaction, which seemed to increase perceptibly as he strode from it to the Majority Leader's long black limousine that stood waiting for him in the portico beneath the steps in front of the Capitol's north wing.

But his confidence didn't last long. Every Monday morning, the limousine brought him to the White House, where he, along with Assistant Leader Francis Myers of Pennsylvania and House Democratic leaders, received from Truman a list of legislation that the President wanted passed. Then the car returned him to Capitol Hill, where the southerners, who chaired the committees that would handle the legislation, let him know—quietly, courteously but firmly—that it would not be passed.

As the Democratic President pressed insistently for civil rights, compulsory health insurance, and other Fair Deal legislation (and for a bill repealing Taft's Taft-Hartley Act), the Democratic Leader tried to at least bring this legislation to the floor—and found himself caught between the southern senators, who had begun viewing him with anger, and liberal senators, who assailed him on the floor for not pushing the bills with sufficient enthusiasm. And as the liberal legislation remained stalled, the press kept demanding that he pass it by exercising the "powers" of the leadership—powers that did not exist. Within three months, Lucas had become an object of scorn in liberal journals like *The New Republic,* which referred to him as the "ever more futile Majority Leader." Reporting in April that "there are rumors that [Lucas] has already had enough" and would resign, the magazine added "Such a move could only be for the best." By July, the more sympathetic White was writing about Lucas' "worn and haggard" look. By the end of his first year as Leader, Lucas had national attention, all right, but not the kind of which he had dreamed. While "it now seems certain history is going to remember his name, what history is going to say about him is" much more debatable, *Collier's* said. Trollope's Plantagenet Palliser did not dread the morning newspapers more than this once-confident man who had been so proud of what he had thought was a thick skin. "The hostile estimates of his leadership were so incredible to him that he knew no way even to begin to cope with them," White wrote. He had developed, in the words of another reporter, a "perennial look of a man whose finger is caught in a mousetrap," a new habit of writing little poems to remind himself of the inadvisability of losing his temper ("Senators who preside / Shouldn't rhyme, shouldn't chide")—and a bleeding stomach ulcer that required hospitalization.

The second year was worse. Goaded by President and press into gingerly trying to bring up the FEPC, Lucas confronted a southern bloc so completely in control of the Senate that it defeated the bill without even bothering to filibuster. His efforts to liberalize an anti-Semitic, anti-Catholic displaced-persons bill antagonized conservatives of both parties. Once, when he stepped off the floor for a few minutes, the arch-conservative William Langer of North Dakota made a motion to adjourn, and the Senate did so—without the Majority Leader even being aware of that fact. Rushing back to the floor in a rage, Lucas called Langer a "snake." Chaos erupted, with liberals and conservatives shouting epithets at each other, and for the rest of the year, a year in which Lucas was often in pain from his ulcer, the floor was the scene of repeated angry outbursts. *The New Republic* appealed to Taft for help because "the Democratic Majority Leader is completely out of control of the situation."

And two years was as much time as Lucas was to have, for his senatorial term expired in 1950. All that year, the formidable former congressman Everett Dirksen had been campaigning against him back in Illinois, dramatizing his absence from the state by "debating" an empty chair on which sat a big placard: "Reserved for Scott Lucas." As early as January, reporters were writing that Lucas was in "a serious fight for his political future." All that year, he was warned that he had better get back home and campaign. He was, however, trapped by his leadership responsibilities. He felt—correctly—that he would be criticized if he left Washington before the Senate had completed the minimum business necessary to keep the government in operation, but he could not persuade the Senate to complete that business. The Senate did not adjourn until September, two months before the election, which Lucas lost. Years later, just another lobbyist in Washington, he would confide that his two years as Majority Leader of the United States Senate had been the most unhappy years of his life.

There was even a small footnote to this demonstration of the risks involved in becoming a member of the Senate's Democratic leadership. Lucas was not the only member of the leadership who had run for re-election in November, 1950. Assistant Leader Francis Myers had also been running. And he had also lost.

LYNDON JOHNSON, who so dreaded failure and humiliation, had thus seen with his own eyes, in close-up, the probability of failure and humiliation for anyone who took a Senate leadership position. He was under no illusions about those positions; knowing—this son of Sam Johnson—the cost of illusions, as always he wanted facts, and he asked the Legislative Reference Service of the Library of Congress to list the powers of party floor leaders; when he received the list it contained exactly one item: "priority in recognition" by the chair. He then directed George Reedy, as Reedy recalls, to conduct his own search "of the records, the precedents and the memories of old-timers," but priority of recognition was "the only thing I could find." Other than that, Reedy concluded, party leaders possessed no authority whatsoever; senatorial power was held by the same forces—the Southern Caucus, the conservative coalition, most of all by the committee chairmen—that had held power for so long. And there seemed no realistic possibility that the situation would change. The leadership was weak because the committee chairmen wanted it weak—and the chairmen had the power to keep it weak.

But what alternatives did Lyndon Johnson have? The road to a chairmanship for himself was seniority, and it was a long road—too long.* Leadership positions were the only positions in the Senate for which length of tenure was not an inflexible requirement. During the last months of 1950, Johnson's life was filled with the activity of his Preparedness Subcommittee, but, increasingly, the activity wasn't satisfying him. More and more often now, in the late afternoons, the staff in the front room of 231 would again hear the click as the corridor door to the private office opened and shut, and the creak as the big

*Johnson was correct in this assessment. Had he remained on the two committees, Armed Services and Interstate and Foreign Commerce, on which he was serving in 1950, he would not have become chairman of either committee until 1969.

chair took the weight of the big body, and then, for a long time, the silence. And now, again, when the buzzer finally sounded on Walter Jenkins' desk, often he would open the door to find no lights on, and his Chief slouched deep in his chair in the gathering gloom, his face hidden behind his hand. Looking back on this period in his life, Lyndon Johnson would tell Doris Kearns Goodwin that he had felt an "increasing restlessness." He simply couldn't stand, Jim Rowe was to recall him saying, to "just wait around again" as he had done in the House—as he had done in the House for so many years. Becoming a part of the Democratic floor leadership would be a risk, a gamble—to this man who feared humiliation as well as defeat, a great risk, a great gamble— but he had taken great risks before; he had gotten to the Senate on the greatest gamble of all, running against the unbeatable Coke Stevenson. And the alternative was to wait, and keep "taking orders." He couldn't bear to do that. Sometime in November or December, 1950, as Goodwin was to put it, "He told Russell that a leadership position was one of the most urgently desired goals of his life."

RUSSELL, OF COURSE, could have had the now-vacant Democratic leadership—the majority leadership, since the Democrats would have a two-vote majority in the incoming Eighty-second Congress—had he wanted it, but he didn't, for the same reasons that had kept him from taking the job in the past. As his aide William Darden puts it, "With him, the scheduling problem would have been the big [problem]. Senator Russell was a person who just didn't want to be bothered with details. He didn't want people saying to him, 'Please don't vote this afternoon—my wife is sick, etc.' " And there were political considerations. Russell felt, his aides say, that a Majority Leader had an obligation to give at least a modicum of support to a President of his own party, "and there were a lot of things in the Truman program that he didn't want to have to support." In addition, the attacks from the liberals were louder than ever. When, that November, a letter from Alabama's John Sparkman urged him to accept the leadership because "You could bring [it] into a new position of prestige and power," Russell wrote back: "You and I both know that as a general rule the South is blamed for everything which does not meet with the approval of our critics," and to have a southerner as Majority Leader "would cause criticism of his acts to fall upon the South as a whole." To forestall such criticism, Russell felt, the new Leader should not be a southerner but a friend of the South, someone who would keep the Senate on its present, southern course, without rocking the boat.

Ernest W. (Bob) McFarland of Arizona fit that bill. A chubby, ruddy-faced, easygoing man of fifty-six with a habit of running both hands through his mop of gray hair when he was puzzled (a gesture he made rather frequently), he was shy but genial and friendly and not at all a boat-rocker. He was a middle-of-the-roader—except on the issue that mattered most: his record against cloture and civil rights was rock solid. And, "perhaps yearning for a few moments in the political sun," as Evans and Novak speculated, McFarland accepted the job, although his Senate term expired in two years, and he would have to run for re-election then.

The choice of McFarland dismayed liberals. He is "an amiable, inoffensive, genuinely likeable ex-judge," said columnist Lowell Mellett. "He is my friend and everybody's friend." But he is "no leader"; during his ten years in the Senate, "he had just gone along . . . content to be led."

> The country is crying out for leadership. . . . [This is] a time of crisis in our country's and the world's history. How well our country meets this crisis will depend greatly on the United States Senate, and that will depend on how well the Senate is led. So it is proposed that it shall not be led at all.

But although liberal senators decided to unite behind Joseph O'Mahoney of Wyoming, there was no chance that they would have the votes when, in January, 1951, the forty-nine Democratic senators convened in caucus. The southerners and their allies would have the votes—and votes to spare. During the two months between Election Day and the caucus, Russell didn't have to devote much time to the question of the majority leadership.

Nor did he have to devote much time to the question of Assistant Majority Leader, or "whip," which was after all a job of even less significance. To Johnson's request for a "leadership position," he replied that the whip's job was his if he wanted it.

As a Senate historian was to summarize, "Johnson had no claim to the position, except that he had the backing of Dick Russell." But that backing was all he needed. "Once he had Russell he had the whole South," recalls Neil MacNeil, who was covering the Senate for *Time* magazine. "The [Democratic] caucus [was] simply a formality to ratify those privately selected with Dick Russell's assent," Evans and Novak were to write. When Johnson telephoned Senator William Fulbright of Arkansas to ask for his support, MacNeil, who had been talking with Fulbright, recalls that the Senator's "eyebrows went flashing up, he was so startled that Johnson wanted the job. It wasn't a job that people wanted. And he [Fulbright] was startled that someone would campaign for it. You didn't campaign for it; you were drafted." But Fulbright said he would go along with whatever Russell wanted. When Johnson telephoned John Stennis in Mississippi, Stennis told him that, as he was to put it, "Lyndon, you might have known that I wasn't just going to promise a whole lot out of the clear sky. . . . Senator Russell and I are very close and . . . I would naturally consult with him before I would give a final answer to anyone." "You must think that I am foolish," Johnson replied. "I wouldn't have been calling you or anyone else about . . . this position unless I already had a firm position from Dick Russell that I am the man."

On January 2, 1951, an article in the *Washington Star* on the Democratic caucus, which was to be held that morning, said that "The Democrats also must elect a whip, or assistant leader, but there has been little interest in the post." As Evans and Novak wrote: "The world outside . . . had little interest in the Senate Democrats' tribal ritual. . . . The official Senate leadership was an unwanted burden, stripped of power and devoid of honor." Walking down a Senate Office Building corridor to Room 201, the big corner conference room in which the caucus would be held, Russell told Johnson that he had decided to nominate him himself, and after McFarland had been elected Leader by a 30–19 vote, Russell did so. Liberal Paul Douglas tried to nominate Sparkman, but Sparkman could hardly withdraw fast enough, and when no other names were proposed, Russell said that in that case, he supposed that Lyndon was the whip, and there was no dissent.

No detailed analysis of Johnson's selection as Assistant Democratic Leader—at the age of forty-two and after just two years in the Senate—is necessary. He had gotten the job for the same reason he had gotten the chairmanship of the Preparedness Subcommittee: because of the support of one man. But he had gotten it.

16

The General
and the Senator

DURING THE TWO YEARS—1951 and 1952—that Lyndon Johnson was Assistant Democratic Leader, the Senate would have a moment of glory, an episode that would show what the Senate could be at its finest—and why Russell was, in aspects other than racial, the personification of that ideal.

The episode almost became one of America's gravest constitutional crises. "It is doubtful if there has ever been in this country so violent and spontaneous a discharge of political passion as that provoked by the President's dismissal of the General," Arthur Schlesinger and Richard Rovere wrote. "Certainly there has been nothing to match it since the Civil War."

Flying home in April, 1951, after his dismissal by President Harry Truman from his proconsulship in the Far East and his command of the empire's armies in Korea, General Douglas MacArthur was uncertain of the reception he would receive in the United States, and timed his arrival in San Francisco so that his plane, the famed chariot *Bataan* (named for one of the many battles with which his name was indelibly linked), would set down after dark. But as he stepped out of the plane's door, suddenly the battered gold-braided cap and the familiar old trench coat were bathed in massed spotlights. He had prepared a brief speech, in case it was needed, but no one could hear it. In the dark beyond the spotlights an Army band was playing; cannon were firing—a thundering salute to the hero who had, for so long, held the empire's perimeter against its enemies, to the hero who, forced into terrible retreat, had promised "I shall return" (and who *had* returned, and had conquered), to the hero who, until the moment of his sudden dismissal, had been fighting against the empire's new enemies. California's Governor was waiting to greet him, and San Francisco's Mayor, but they were swept away by the crowd that surged through police lines to try to touch the hero's hand. From the airport, it was fourteen miles to his hotel; the journey took more than two hours; the streets were lined with half a million San Franciscans. The next day MacArthur flew across the continent to Washington—flew over hundreds of towns in which flags were being flown at half-mast or even upside down, flew over hundreds of towns in which the President was being burned in effigy and automobiles were blossoming with bumper stickers that read "Impeach Truman," in which people were parading carrying banners with the same two words; *Life* magazine was not exaggerating when it said that "The homecoming of the legendary MacArthur was like nothing else in American history." His arrival in Washington had been preceded by a tidal wave of mail; Senator Richard Nixon of California had received six hundred telegrams, most of them advocating impeachment of the President, during the first twenty-four hours after the dismissal ("the largest spontaneous reaction I've ever seen," he said happily); the White House admitted that of the first seventy thousand letters and telegrams it received, those critical of the General's recall outnumbered those in favor twenty to one; at that point it stopped counting. Truman had tried to keep the welcome at the airport as low-key as possible—his only emissary was his military aide, General Harry Vaughan, "a gesture," as *Life* put it, "strictly according to protocol but less than cordial"— but the Joint Chiefs of Staff and a crowd of congressmen and VIPs had also shown up, and when, after midnight, the *Bataan* touched down, a cheering crowd charged out of the shadows with a great roar, engulfing Vaughan, Chiefs, and congressmen.

The next day, April 20, was the day of the General's speech to a joint session of Congress, in a Chamber so full that even some senators had to sit on the floor. When the doorkeeper shouted, "Mr. Speaker, General of the Army Douglas MacArthur," and he appeared in the door, erect, impassive, dressed in a trim jacket without medals or ribbons except for the five stars of his rank, a nation's elected representatives leapt cheering to their feet. And as he spoke, the cheers came again and again—thirty times in thirty-four minutes. All his life, Douglas MacArthur had been holding audiences spellbound, and now he had his largest audience. "Most Americans listened, and 30 million or more watched on television as he spoke, and they were magnetized by the vibrant voice, the dramatic rhetoric and the Olympian personality," *Life* said. The speech was an unapologetic argument for his policies, and a defiant denunciation of the policies of the civilian Administration, and they were couched in the phrases of a master phrasemaker. He said that his policies—to blockade China, to bomb the Chinese forces in Manchuria, to place no limits on his war against the North Koreans—were absolutely necessary: "Once war is forced upon us, there is no alternative than to apply every available means to bring it to a swift end. War's very object is victory—not prolonged indecision. In war, indeed, there can be no substitute for victory." He said that "practically every military leader concerned with the Korean campaign, including our own Joint Chiefs of Staff," had agreed with those policies. And he said that those who had not agreed— those who he said were mainly civilians in the Truman Administration—were wrong. "History teaches with unmistakable emphasis that appeasement but begets new and bloodier wars. . . . Why, my soldiers asked of me, surrender military advantage to an enemy in the field?" There was a dramatic pause, and the General's voice dropped to a husky whisper. "I could not answer." The last words of the speech were unforgettable words. "The world has turned over many times since I took the oath on the Plain at West Point," he said, and his "boyish hopes and dreams have long since vanished." But, he said,

> I still remember the refrain of one of the most popular barrack bal-
> lads of that day, which proclaimed, most proudly, "Old soldiers never
> die. They just fade away." And like the soldier of the ballad, I now
> close my military career and just fade away—an old soldier who
> tried to do his duty as God gave him the light to see that duty.

And the last word of all was spoken in a whisper—a whisper into a great hush: "Good-bye."

AS MACARTHUR LEFT THE PODIUM he "stepped down," in William Manchester's prose, "into pandemonium." Representatives and senators "were sobbing his praise, struggling to touch his sleeve." In a voice that could be heard in the Press Gallery, Representative Dewey Short of Missouri shouted, "We heard God speak here today, God in the flesh, the voice of God!" Across the country, the congressmen's constituents, who had been glued to their radios or television sets, were just as moved. When a reporter asked Herbert Hoover for a comment, he called MacArthur "a reincarnation of St. Paul into a great General of the Army who came out of the East." MacArthur left the Capitol for the Washington Monument, where he was to give another speech. During his progress down Pennsylvania Avenue before a quarter of a million cheering onlookers, Air Force jets screamed overhead and a phalanx of growling motorcycles and armored personnel carriers carrying helmeted soldiers preceded the open car in which he stood at rigid attention, as Manchester wrote, "a senior officer in full uniform contemptuously defying a President and a Constitutional Commander-in-Chief and undertaking to force an alteration in the highest decisions of the civil government." It was a parade more fitting for the capital of a South American republic ruled by a junta than the capital of a democracy.

Covering that parade for the United Press, in his very last assignment before joining the staff of Lyndon Johnson's Preparedness Subcommittee, was, George Reedy would recall, "the only time in my life that I ever felt my government to be fragile. . . . I'll never forget watching him go up Pennsylvania Avenue. I had a very strong feeling that had he said 'Come on, let's take it' and had started to charge toward the White House. . . . [T]he adoring crowds that

thronged the streets would have gone with him." More thoughtful observers
could not avoid, at least at the moment, the same thought. As William S. White
walked with one of his senatorial friends—"one of the most balanced and
soundest public men I have ever known"—back toward the Senate side of
the Capitol after MacArthur's speech, the sound of the pandemonium fading
only slowly behind them, the Senator said, "This is new to my experience; I
have never feared more for the institutions of my country. I honestly felt back
there if the speech had gone on much longer there might have been a march
on the White House." The next day, the General pushed on to New York. That
city's monumental homecoming parades, in which Lindbergh and Pershing and
Eisenhower had ridden down the skyscraper-lined Canyon of Heroes through
blizzards of swirling confetti, had been the nation's most memorable and exuberant welcoming receptions. MacArthur's parade was, in *Time*'s words, "the
greatest and most exuberant the city had ever seen."

Republican senators—a delegation led by Taft and Wherry had called on
MacArthur at the Waldorf Towers in New York—had already demanded a full-
scale senatorial investigation, and Democrats, not only southern Democrats
who held a brief for many of the General's views but even liberal Democrats
who did not, knew one had to be held. MacArthur's arguments had to be
countered, his hold on the public imagination weakened. While fears of Truman's impeachment or of a march on the White House might be exaggerated,
other concerns were more realistic. The next presidential election was only a
year and a half away, and even were MacArthur not to be the Republican
candidate (and, at the time, the odds seemed good that he would be), every
cheer for MacArthur was a jeer for Truman—as was demonstrated at the Washington Senators' opening game, when he became the first President to be booed
(and the booing was long and loud) since Herbert Hoover in the depths of
the Depression. And if in 1952 the Democratic Administration remained
as discredited by MacArthur's speech as it was at the moment, the re-election
chances of Democratic senators and representatives would be hurt as well. And
other concerns went beyond the political. The outpouring of admiration for
MacArthur was to a large extent an indication of the emotional appeal to
Americans of the General's belief that wars were meant to be *won*—by whatever means necessary. Around the erect, heroic figure of MacArthur of Cor-
regidor, MacArthur of Inchon, had coalesced the national impatience over the
long-drawn-out stalemate in Korea, and his speech—with its defiant "There is
no substitute for victory" and his insistence that a refusal to use all the force
available amounted to "appeasement"—was a call, a call that had seemingly
mobilized a substantial segment of American public opinion behind it, for such
options as blockading China, bombing Chinese sanctuaries in Manchuria,
crossing the Yalu River, unleashing Chiang Kai-shek's troops to invade mainland China, and even the use of nuclear weapons. Around him also had coalesced the simmering discontent with the organization that, as much as

Truman, was tying his hands. In April, 1951, there was, William White was to report, "an almost runaway movement toward rejection of the United Nations." And the most serious threat was to a principle basic to democratic government: the blurring of the lines between civilian and military authority. While he was still in Korea, MacArthur, in defiance of Truman's policies, had suggested that he meet on his own authority with the enemy commander to discuss a truce; now *Life* magazine actually asked: "What was bad about that? In ordinary circumstances a field commander might have no business talking as MacArthur does. But these are extraordinary circumstances, created not by him but by the timidity of his bosses." The United States, White felt, was in "perhaps the gravest and most emotional Constitutional crisis that the United States had known since the Great Depression. . . . The issue was the supremacy, written and unwritten, that a century and a half had given to the civil government over the military." "Popular emotions," George Reedy was to recall, had been raised "to a fever pitch and it was obvious that they could not be cooled by pretending that nothing had happened. Congress had to do something that would respond either affirmatively or negatively to the widespread belief that a patriot with a program to end a war was being shoved aside by an Administration that was incompetent and possibly infested with traitors."

BUT, REEDY WAS TO RECALL, there seemed to be at that moment "absolutely no anti-MacArthur sentiment in the country worth noticing." The fury of editorial writers was still rising, and so was the flood of mail—rising to an unprecedented crest; by one estimate, senators alone received some two million letters, postcards, and telegrams. Only one senator, Robert Kerr, dared to "get up and make speeches attacking MacArthur," Reedy recalls, and "Boy, you could just feel the hostility in the gallery. They hated Kerr at that moment." And Kerr, a freshman senator still largely unknown outside Oklahoma and Washington, did not possess sufficient stature. Liberal senators with stature, critical though they might be of MacArthur in private, were notably reluctant to take on the General publicly.

As for the Senate hearings, Marshall would have to testify—and Acheson. The Republicans would have these two favorite targets before them—and on the defensive, on an issue on which the public was overwhelmingly against them, on an issue on which it seemed clear that by preventing MacArthur from taking the more aggressive measures he wished to take against the Chinese Reds, they had indeed been too "soft" on Communism. The Republican primitives would, it was widely believed, use the hearings to tear Marshall and Acheson apart—would make the hearings the great forum they had always wanted to criticize Democratic foreign policy from Yalta to Korea. Who could keep the primitives under control? What senator possessed enough personal fortitude, and enough power within the Senate, to keep the hearings from turn-

ing into a great witch-hunt—to allow the other side to be heard? Who possessed prestige and respect so invulnerable that he could stand up to the right-
wingers without being himself tarred as "soft"? Equally important, who could
not only control the right-wingers but defeat them? When votes were taken
within the investigating committee, who could persuade southern conservatives
to vote for moderate proposals, and thereby, together with Democratic liberals,
create a majority in the committee? Who could at the same time align with
Democrats enough moderate Republicans so that the hearings would not turn
into a merely partisan fight that would only further inflame public opinion? No
liberal possessed the necessary power and prestige. Who did? Who would lead
Congress in doing what it had to do? MacArthur's arguments were sweeping
the country, but there were arguments on the other side. Who would bring them
out? Who would dare to stand against the tide?

THIS WAS ONE of the moments to which Hugh Sidey was referring when he
wrote that "when the U.S. got into trouble . . . Russell would . . . stick a forefinger into his somber vest and amble down those dim corridors to see if he
could help his country. Everybody watching felt better when he arrived."

Republican senators, who would be in the minority no matter which Senate body conducted the hearings, wanted them chaired by a Democrat they
could count on to be nonpartisan, impartial, fair. They petitioned Russell to
have the Armed Services Committee hold the hearings, so that he would be
chairman. As for Democratic liberals, they were aware that unless the hearings
were run with a very firm hand, they would become merely another stage on
which MacArthur would star, bolstered this time by a chorus of approval from
the GOP's Neanderthals. On international issues, if not domestic, they knew,
the firmest, and fairest, hand was that of the Senator from Georgia. No other
senator, the Democrats felt, could defuse this most explosive of situations. And
certainly none of the liberals wanted the chairman's gavel for himself, no matter how great the potential for publicity contained in that piece of wood; it contained also the potential for the political destruction of the chairman, who
would, in having to gavel down MacArthur and his allies, be standing in the
face of overwhelming public opinion. Democratic liberals also wanted Dick
Russell—Russell and no one else. When Tom Connally claimed jurisdiction for
his Foreign Relations Committee, the Senate, confronted with a jurisdictional
dispute, ruled that the two committees would hold joint hearings, but that the
chairman of Armed Services, not the chairman of Foreign Relations, would
preside. Although Russell, "leader of the Southern bloc," was regarded as the
Enemy by most liberals, "that did not prevent them from running to him for
shelter" when MacArthur returned, Reedy says. "It was rather amusing to see
the speed with which the Senate just automatically gravitated to Russell."

Russell knew the necessity of holding hearings. Admiring though he was of MacArthur the battlefield technician and even of MacArthur the theater commander, he understood the terrible dangers of the policies of MacArthur the global strategist. And he was very aware of the danger inherent in MacArthur's challenge to the President's authority; Russell had, Reedy was to say, "a deep sense of the vital necessity of reestablishing the principle of civilian control over the military." And he understood as well the role of the Senate: that the Senate could not be hurried, could not be stampeded—that the Senate was uniquely insulated against the phrensy of public opinion, that the Senate was equipped to be calm, judicious, fair. The hearings, he felt, must not be one-sided. Heated argument was not what was necessary; what was needed was a cool look at all sides of an exceedingly complex issue. "Russell believed . . . that what was happening here was a tremendous upsurge of emotion, and that if time was given to look at the MacArthur position, that the ridiculousness of it would eventually become apparent, but would *not* become apparent if there was an adversary investigation. . . . So therefore it was a question of gaining time, gaining time so that the American people would really look at it. . . ."

Russell knew, moreover, that he was the best man to preside over the hearings. He had no false modesty about his expertise on the military and on global strategy; no false modesty about his knowledge of Rome and of Greece and of all the great empires of the past, nor of his ability to evaluate this controversy in the light of history. And he had no false modesty about his stature in the Senate. "He believed," says his biographer, Gilbert Fite, "that he had enough power and influence to direct the investigation along the lines that would be most useful to the country."

And he knew he had no choice but to preside over the hearings; he had to do it: it was his duty, he was a Russell of the Russells of Georgia; *noblesse oblige*.

HARDLY HAD RUSSELL accepted the chairmanship when a dispute erupted that seemed to make utterly impossible the nonpartisan, impartial, calm inquiry he had planned—a dispute over whether the hearings would be open to the press and the public, or closed.

Part of Russell's desire to keep them closed was as political as that of other Democrats, who, as *Time* put it, "were anxious to keep General MacArthur's thundering rhetoric out of earshot of the microphone, and his dramatic profile off the screen of 12 million television sets." But there was something more. The hearings, Russell knew, would center around America's deepest-held military and strategic secrets. "We are entering doors that have been barred, we are unlocking secrets that have been protected in steel safes," he was to say. When it was suggested that he invoke Truman's support for his position, he said there was no need to do so; he knew he was right, he said; never talked to Truman about "whether closed or open," he scribbled on a telephone notepad. When the Republicans—not the Republicans on his committee, moderate internationalist Republicans like Lodge and Saltonstall, but midwestern right-wingers like Wherry and Capehart—demanded that the hearings be open, he rose on the floor of the Senate to argue against them in words that could have been written by Madison: "I have been disturbed in recent days because of the way we are running the government, by taking action here in response to a quick expression of uninformed desire." It was not, he said, a question of hiding facts from scrutiny; there would be facts spoken and documents discussed about which the Communists should not know. "There is something here that is more important than continued tenure in the Senate or even the election of the President of the United States in 1952." Four times the Republicans forced a vote; each time it was close, but each time Russell won.

He wanted as many of the facts as possible released, since he felt that if the public was permitted to see all sides of the argument, the weaknesses in MacArthur's position, and the menace of nuclear war which it posed, would become obvious, and the emotionalism would die down, the Administration would be vindicated, and the cause of world peace advanced. To accomplish this, while safeguarding strategic secrets, he announced that as the stenotypists in the Armed Services Committee room finished typing each page of the testimony, the page would be taken to an anteroom, where two censors—one from the State Department, one from Defense—would read it, cutting out any information that shouldn't be released. The edited transcript would then be run off on a mimeograph machine in the anteroom, and handed to reporters, who thus could read the testimony, shorn only of sensitive information, within minutes after it had been given.

THE HEARINGS were scheduled for 10 a.m. in Room 318 of the Senate Office Building, the great Caucus Room, on Thursday, May 3, 1951. General MacArthur arrived almost twenty minutes late ("Couldn't get him down from the Cross," one Democratic senator growled under his breath), and strode with a casual wave through a crowd of secretaries and reporters as photographers' flashbulbs popped; the tall doors of the Caucus Room slammed shut, three uniformed Capitol policemen stationed themselves in front of them. Gaveling the hearings to order, Russell welcomed MacArthur in the most complimentary of terms. "On the permanent pages of our history are inscribed his achievements as one of the great captains of history. . . . But he is not only a great military leader, his broad understanding and knowledge of the science of politics has enabled him to restore and stabilize a conquered country and to win for himself and for his country the respect and affection of a people who were once our bitterest enemies." And then, as *Time* put it, "for three amazing days, Douglas MacArthur sat at the center of the stage to make his case against the foreign policy of his Commander in Chief."

He made his case as well as it could be made, with the forceful, colorful rhetoric of which he was such a master. His strategy would not enlarge the war, he argued; on the contrary, it would lead to the defeat of the Chinese Communists, force Mao Tse-tung to sue for peace, and thus produce a clear-cut "victory." Of course, he didn't propose invading China with American troops, he said; "no man in his proper senses would advocate throwing our troops in on the Chinese mainland." He hadn't been opposing the Administration's policy, he said; "I was operating in what I call a vacuum. I could hardly be said to be in opposition to policies which I was not even aware of. I don't know what the policy is now. . . ." "There is no policy! There is nothing, I tell you, no plan, no anything." And, he said, by continuing to fight "indecisively," America would incur staggering casualties. "It isn't just dust that is settling in Korea, Senators; it is American blood." The Truman Administration's attempt to make war "piecemeal" would lead to a broader conflict, as "appeasement" always did. As to the risk that by bombing Manchuria, blockading China, and using Chiang's troops to invade it, America would push China into the war on a full scale and perhaps Russia, too, he said that the risk of that was small, but that no matter how large it might be, it was a risk that should be taken. "I believe if you let it go on indefinitely in Korea, you invite a third world war." And, he said, and he said it very firmly, the Joint Chiefs of Staff agreed with this view. "I am not aware of having had any differences with the Joint Chiefs of Staff on military questions at all. . . . The position of the Joint Chiefs of Staff and my own, so far as I know, were practically identical." To support this contention, he quoted a JCS study which recommended, among other things, removal of "the restrictions on air reconnaissance of Chinese coastal areas and of Manchuria."

But when the General had finished, the chairman had some questions. Some were about MacArthur's contention that his position had been "practically identical" with that of the Joint Chiefs. Senator Russell asked mildly, "There is quite a difference between reconnaissance and attack, is there not?" "Yes, sir," MacArthur replied. "Did the Joint Chiefs ever suggest in addition to reconnaissance that these bases be attacked?" Russell asked. "Not that I know of."

Some of the questions—by Russell and other senators, including moderate, internationalist Republicans like Henry Cabot Lodge Jr. of Massachusetts and Brien McMahon of Connecticut (and Lyndon Johnson, in his role as a member of the Armed Services Committee; he had also loaned Reedy to Russell for the hearings, since Russell did not have an adequate public relations man of his own, and Donald Cook and Gerald Siegel were drafting questions for committee members)—were about the specific proposals MacArthur was making, and they brought out some implications that MacArthur had not mentioned.

Russell's questions were asked in the most courteous of tones. "I do not understand exactly what you would have done about [Chiang Kai-shek's] Nationalist troops [on Formosa]," he said, and when MacArthur replied, "I recommended to Washington that the wraps be taken off the Generalissimo," the Senator had another question. "General, would you mind advising the committee and the Senate what you think is the real strength of the Generalissimo's forces on Formosa?" MacArthur said there were half a million "excellent" men, "exactly the same as these Red troops I am fighting." Then, Russell said, you feel that if they were landed on the mainland, they could maintain themselves without American help? This question MacArthur did not answer directly, and Lodge brought up another implication of the proposed "unleashing," brought it up also in the most courteous of tones. "What would happen with regard to Formosa if Chiang were to land on the mainland and then be wiped out?" Lodge was asking if America would have to then defend Formosa itself, but MacArthur said, "Senator, that is a hypothesis that is very difficult to speculate upon."

In his dramatic speech, MacArthur had assured the Senate that if the Chinese were driven out of Korea Mao Tse-tung would sue for peace. But, he was asked now, what if Mao didn't sue for peace? Suppose when the Chinese were chased back across the Yalu River, they refused to sign a treaty—what then? What if they massed near the river, on their own territory, forces that could be used for a new offensive in Korea. MacArthur refused to take that premise seriously. "Such a contingency is a very hypothetical query. I can't quite see the possibility of the enemy being driven back across the Yalu and still being in a posture of offensive action," he said. But the senators did not let the matter drop, and by the end of that line of questioning, it had begun to be clear that at least a strong possibility existed that MacArthur's proposals would have drastically widened the conflict.

And, of course, China was not the only opponent that might be drawn into the war if MacArthur's policies were followed, as Russell, speaking in his calm, courteous voice, brought out. Tell me, General, he said, if the United States were—hypothetically, of course—to have to aid Chiang's troops on the mainland of China; if hypothetically, the United States were to be forced to assume the defense of Formosa, if the United States was busy fighting China— what would happen if Russia then attacked Japan? And when MacArthur said, "I do not believe that it would be within the capacity of the Soviet Union. . . . I believe that the disposition of the Soviet forces are largely defensive," Russell asked quietly, "How about the submarine strength of the Soviet in that area?"

And, Russell asked, what if Russia, seeing her allies being defeated, decided to enter the war on a larger scale? What if she attacked in Europe? What if she launched an atomic attack? "If we go into all-out war, I want to find out how you propose in your own mind to defend the American nation against that war?"

"That doesn't happen to be my responsibility, Senator," MacArthur replied. "My responsibilities were in the Pacific."

Did the General know the number of atomic bombs the Russians possessed? McMahon asked. No, MacArthur said, he did not. "Do you think that we are ready to withstand the Russian attack in Western Europe today?" McMahon asked.

"Senator," Douglas MacArthur said, "I have asked you several times not to involve me in anything except my own area. My concepts on global defense are not what I am here to testify on. I don't pretend to be an authority now on those things. . . . I have been desperately occupied on the other side of the world." "That was the point," McMahon said. "The Joint Chiefs and the President of the United States, the Commander in Chief, has to look at this thing on a global basis and a global defense. You as a theater commander by your own statement have not made that kind of study, and yet you advise us to push forward with a course of action that may involve us in that global conflict."

By the end of the three days, even *Time* had to admit that "When General MacArthur replaced the hat of a theater commander with the hat of a global strategist, he seemed less sure of his ground." "Among themselves," as William Manchester reports, "the committee members agreed that MacArthur's bold proposals were . . . unrealistic."

And when MacArthur had completed his testimony—with, of course, a compliment from the chairman, who praised his "patience, thoroughness and frankness" (there was no praise for his wisdom)—another General of the Army, George Catlett Marshall, entered Room 318 to sit before the senators. He was dressed in a civilian's gray suit, as if to symbolize, as *Time* put it, "the civilian authority of the Secretary of Defense," and he testified for five days, calmly, carefully, even ploddingly, in "a flat, unemotional voice and sparse phrases that contrasted sharply with his antagonist's flow of words and orotund delivery," and that fit in perfectly with the judicial atmosphere the chairman had established. By the end of the five days, the Secretary's testimony, and the senators' questions, had made clear that, at the very least, the question of escalating the war in Korea was far more complex than it had seemed when MacArthur first charged "appeasement" and said there was "no substitute for victory," "no policy . . . no plan, no anything." Russell led Marshall through testimony that showed that the Administration did have a policy: "To contain Communist aggression in different fashions in different areas without resorting to total war." That policy, Marshall said, had worked in Berlin, it had worked in Greece, and it would work in Korea. Despite MacArthur's ridicule of limited war, Marshall said, MacArthur's proposals "might well mean formal Soviet intervention." Contrary to MacArthur's contention that the Soviets did not have sufficient forces in the Far East to pose a real threat, Marshall said they had plenty: not only a submarine fleet but "a considerable force in the vicinity of Vladivostok, Darien, Port Arthur, Harbin." In a very quiet voice, Russell asked Marshall to tell the committee "what might occur if the Soviet intervened," and with Marshall's reply there were suddenly, in the Caucus Room, new realities. "That would immediately involve the defense of Japan, Hokkaido in particular,

attacks on our air all over Japan, all over Korea . . . and we couldn't accept that
without the maximum retaliation on our part which inevitably means a world
war. . . ." And a world war might well mean nuclear war—and the end of
mankind. "My own view was—and I think it is similar to that of the Chiefs
of Staff—that we were risking a hazard that had such terrible possible consequences that what we would gain was not comparable to what we were
risking. . . ."

THE CONTEST BETWEEN these hearings and the usual headline-hunting Senate investigation could hardly have been greater. The method of releasing
quickly edited transcripts turned what could have been a circus—the typical
senatorial investigative circus—into what White was to call a "proceeding . . .
quiet, unruffled, orderly and strangely at variance with the investigative habits
of the Institution." The hearings, White was to say, in an opinion echoed by
Rovere and other Washington correspondents, dramatically increased the public understanding of the Korean War, of the Cold War as a whole, and of arguments for and against a policy of containment as opposed to that of all-out war.
And this detailed presentation of facts and complexities had the effect of calming the waves of public indignation stirred up by MacArthur's clarion call.
Soon Rovere was writing that "it is possible to discern a slight dropping off of
interest in the hearings. . . ."

The calm would, during succeeding weeks of testimony, be maintained by
Richard Russell.

Never had the respect in which he was held within the Senate been more
evident, and more significant for America, than during these weeks, in which
other generals followed Marshall to the witness table. Every outburst of rage by
the Republican reactionaries, every maneuver they attempted as they saw they
were losing, shattered against it. When Senator Wiley, attempting to drag Truman more directly into the controversy, demanded that General Omar Bradley,
head of the Joint Chiefs, reveal the contents of his conversations with the President about the Korean War, Bradley refused, and Wiley, Knowland, and the
other conservative Republicans exploded. "I am asking the chairman to rule
that my question . . . should be answered," Wiley said angrily. But the chairman
ruled, calmly, that a "private conversation between the President and the Chief
of Staff as to detail can be protected by the witness if he desires." Wiley's rage
boiled over; accusing the Democrats of a "frantic desire to cover-up and white-
wash," he was to charge that Russell's support of executive privilege had drawn
an "iron curtain" over the investigation. Wiley said he would demand a vote by
the committee. But his demand was not supported by Lodge, or Saltonstall, or
by another Republican, H. Alexander Smith of New Jersey, who said that he
wanted to "compliment the chairman on conducting the hearing on the highest
possible plane of fairness." The vote upheld Russell, 18 to 8.

The leaking that would normally have accompanied closed hearings had been drastically reduced by the committee's new method of releasing the testimony, but in the early days, some sensitive information did find its way to the press. "Every half hour or so," Rovere noted, Senator McCarthy "pops out of Room 318 . . . to brief his favorite correspondents."

Russell reduced it further. When some of Marshall's censored testimony found its way into newspapers, Russell said he wanted to say a few words to his colleagues. All the testimony except that which would endanger American men fighting in Korea was already being released through those edited transcripts, he said. He was sure, he said, that no committee member—that no senator of the United States—would deliberately give a reporter, and thus the enemy, information that would endanger American soldiers, but of course there was always the chance of "a careless word, a slip of the tongue." And if American soldiers were endangered by such carelessness, he said, neither "God nor our fellow citizens will ever forgive us." He paused for a moment, and the full power of Richard Russell's personality was there in the Senate Caucus Room. "Nor would we deserve forgiveness," he said.

Russell led Bradley, a World War II general almost as respected by the American public as MacArthur, slowly and carefully through an explanation of the flaws in MacArthur's proposals, and, thanks to the transcript-release method, Bradley's testimony was carried in newspapers across the country. On the sixth day of that testimony, Bourke Hickenlooper said he had a proposal: the hearings were consuming so much time, he said, why not skip the other three Joint Chiefs? "In doing so," as *Time* reported, "Hickenlooper conceded . . . that the Republicans had just about abandoned their hope that the hearings would find the Joint Chiefs siding with MacArthur against the President."

The proposal might well have carried the day had another senator been chairman of the joint committee: its conservative members had a political interest in cutting the testimony short; as for the others, they had already been hearing testimony for almost three weeks, and it was becoming apparent that more long weeks of testimony, weeks during which their presence would be required, lay ahead. But, as *Time* reported, "Russell put it up to the committee, and the committee, by a 14–11 vote, decided nothing doing; it would keep going down the line of witnesses in turn."

The Chiefs of Staff who followed Bradley—Hoyt Vandenberg of the Air Force, Forrest Sherman of the Navy, and J. Lawton Collins of the Army—made clear that MacArthur's claim of their support was, by the most charitable interpretation, a misunderstanding on his part. "One by one," William Manchester writes, "officers who admired MacArthur seated themselves before the senators and sadly rejected his program for victory." Day by day, as *Time* put it, "The glamour, excitement and anger of the first weeks of General MacArthur's return subsided; the public, or at least a large part of it, admitted that things were more complicated than they had seemed."

It was Russell's demeanor, rather than any specific vote or ruling, that

made the tone of the hearings thoughtful, judicious—senatorial. It was difficult
for even a Wiley or a Hickenlooper to shout for long when the chairman was so
quiet and courteous and considerate of every point of view, when he introduced
each witness with so glowing a recitation of his accomplishments and qualifications. When, in mid-June, the time for Dean Acheson's testimony arrived,
"Capitol corridors were charged with political tension," *Time* reported. " 'Wait
until we get Acheson,' the more partisan-minded Republicans had crowed. . . .' "
But, as *Time* reported, "once the committee doors swung shut, Acheson's ques-
tioners, Republican as well as Democratic, settled into the attitude of grave
decision that had dominated the investigation from the start. The Republicans,
however noisy the blood cries of their colleagues outside, were courteous, dispassionate and earnestly in search of answers. . . . A calm seemed to settle over
the hearing room. Not in years had an investigation in which feelings ran so
high been conducted in so temperate and fair-minded a fashion."

The torrent of mail that had inundated Capitol Hill became a stream, and
then a trickle, decreasing as rapidly as if it had been water turned off by a tap.
The onlooking senators in the audience melted away, and then the attendance
of members of the joint committee began to decline; by the last week in May,
when, *Time* said, "the dramatic thunder and lightning of the big MacArthur
hearing had settled into a steady drizzle of repetitious questions and answers,"
and testimony was nearing "the million-word mark, and there were still many
witnesses . . . to come," the Caucus Room was no longer needed, and the hearings were moved into the Armed Services Committee's room—where, small
though that room was, there were soon vacant seats. As for the tenor of public
opinion, a baseball game was again the barometer. In April, before the start of
the Senate hearings, President Truman had been booed at one for firing
MacArthur. Now, in June, MacArthur attended a game at the Polo Grounds in
New York, and left between innings, to the strains of "Old Soldiers Never Die,"
striding briskly across the diamond toward the centerfield exit—until one fan
yelled in a Bronx accent, "Hey Mac, how's Harry Truman?" and the crowd
burst into laughter and applause. A group of Texas oil barons flew him to Texas
for a speech, in a seventy thousand–seat stadium, that was supposed to be the
kickoff to a MacArthur presidential boom, but only twenty thousand of the
seats were filled.

There was one more triumph—one more quiet triumph—for Russell. It
came over the question of a formal committee report on the hearings. He didn't
want one. He had attempted to keep the hearings as free as possible from political controversy, and to a remarkable extent he had done so. A report was the
last minefield; it "can only serve as a textbook for political arguments," he
scrawled on his desk calendar. So what he did, at the conclusion of the hearings, was, essentially, nothing. Pleading his work on the agricultural appropriations bill as an excuse, he did not convene a committee meeting to consider
the question of a formal report until August 17, almost two months after the

hearings had ended. At this meeting he advised against issuing a report, saying that it would inevitably reflect a division of opinion, and that any division might affect truce negotiations in Korea. Knowland, Wiley, and three other Republicans objected; the vote against them was 18 to 5. On a motion by Saltonstall, the committee then decided to simply "transmit" the hearing transcript to the full Senate without comment. Eight of the committee's eleven Republicans later issued a statement criticizing the conduct of foreign affairs in the Far East; it received relatively little public notice. No formal report, or any other action, resulted from the long investigation. Yet the investigation had had a profound effect. As William White was to put it, "Without rejecting outright a single MacArthur policy, without defending at a single point a single Truman policy, without accusing the General of anything whatever, the Senate's investigation had largely ended his influence on policy-making. It had set in motion an intellectual counterforce to the emotional adulation that for a time had run so strongly through the country." It had done, in short, precisely what the Founding Fathers had wanted the Senate to do, what their Constitution had designed it to do: to defuse—cool off—and educate; to make men think, recall them to their first principles, such as the principle that in a democracy it is not generals but the people's tribunes who make policy. "It was, in all truth, a demonstration of what the Senate at its best was capable of doing," White was to say.

And the Senate, as Samuel Shaffer said, had been at its best largely because of Richard Russell. It was his "power and prestige . . . employed at a moment of great crisis in America" that had calmed a country that was "as close to a state of national hysteria as it had ever been in its history." He had displayed, *Life* magazine said, "firmness, fairness and dignity almost unmatched in recent Congressional history."

LYNDON JOHNSON PLAYED a minor role in the MacArthur episode, a role that had no relationship to his new post as Assistant Leader. He had assigned his two Preparedness attorneys, Donald Cook and Gerald Siegel, to analyze each evening that day's testimony and prepare a list of questions for Russell to ask the next day. Before the hearings, Russell had not understood about "staff" in the modern sense. But for weeks now, when he arrived at his office in the morning, there on his desk had been the analysis and the list, tools prepared not by old-style Senate staffers, not by tired old military officers put to pasture on Capitol Hill, but by keen legal minds. Before the hearings, Russell had not understood about public relations in the modern sense. But Johnson had suggested that George Reedy each evening write a statement that Russell could deliver at the opening of the next day's hearings. For weeks now, Reedy's opening statements had been there on his desk.

Russell now understood, moreover, that staff could mean more than questions and press releases. Richard Russell had never had an assistant like George Reedy. Sometimes they would be alone together in Russell's office in the evenings, and Russell found himself discussing the strategy for the hearings— not specific questions or press releases, not matters of tactics, but the overall *strategy*—and he found that Reedy was worth discussing strategy with, that it helped to bounce ideas off him, to get other sides of the issue. Reedy, the flaming Wisconsin liberal who had always despised Russell because of the Georgian's views on civil rights, had come to realize that Russell was not only "the preeminent senatorial tactician" but that he possessed "a grasp of history that was equaled by very few politicians in my memory." And Russell realized that Reedy, too, possessed quite a grasp of history. He came, almost despite himself, this senator who had never relied on staff, to rely on Cook and Siegel and Reedy. One day, noticing that Russell never delivered the opening statements he was preparing, Reedy didn't bother to write one. "George, please do it," Russell said. "You don't realize something. I may change it. I may not use it at all, but it gives me a sense of reassurance to know that when I come down that that statement is going to be there." Reedy did so, of course, and he began to see that while Russell might not deliver the statement as written, he managed, in making his own statement, to incorporate most of Reedy's points—just as, in asking questions of MacArthur and Marshall and Bradley and Acheson and the Joint Chiefs, he either used or incorporated the questions prepared by Cook and Siegel. By the conclusion of the MacArthur hearings, Russell understood the importance—the *necessity*—of staff, of the way in which it could enable a senator, could enable the *Senate*, to deal with new complexities, the complexities that had been overwhelming senators and Senate. He understood the importance of this tool in modern politics.

He understood because of Lyndon Johnson—and he had seen that Johnson was a master in the use of this new tool, as he was a master in so many other new tools. He saw that Johnson was capable of adapting the Senate to the new age.

And, of course, during those weeks in which Russell had been using the questions and statements provided by Lyndon Johnson's staff members, it had only been natural for him to discuss them with Johnson. The two men had worked over them together at breakfast in the Senate Dining Room, and, often, in the evenings, so that they often had not only breakfast but dinner together. Their relationship, already close, had become even closer. "By the end of 1951," George Reedy says, "the Russell-Johnson relationship was a very, very close relationship." And it was about this time that Richard Russell paid Lyndon Johnson quite a compliment. In an undated memorandum that appears to have been written in November or December, 1951, a *Time* reporter informed his editors in New York that "Russell has soberly predicted that Lyndon Johnson could be President and would make a good one."

17

The "Nothing Job"

THE PRESIDENCY, OF COURSE, was never far from Lyndon Johnson's mind. Just after his election as Assistant Democratic Leader in January, 1951, Leslie Carpenter had written that "To Johnson and his admirers his selection as majority whip was just one more step on the road to the Vice-Presidency—and perhaps one day to the White House itself. The Texan makes no particular secret of his ambitions in that direction." But the path ahead was still a very long one, and if Johnson had few illusions about the position of Democratic Leader, he had even fewer about the position of Assistant Leader. "The whip's job is a nothing job," he told journalist Alfred Steinberg. If he was to advance along that path, however, his progress during the next two years at least was going to have to be through that "nothing" job. So he had set about making, out of nothing, something.

While, during these two years, 1951 and 1952, the Senate had, in the MacArthur Hearings, a moment of glory, over the rest of those years hung a miasma of gloom. The century-long decline in its power and prestige accelerated. Hardly had the Eighty-second Congress convened in January, 1951, when President Truman announced that he was sending, "without reference to Congress"—and without any emergency to justify the decision—"four more divisions to reinforce the American army in Europe." This was not sending a few Marines to some Latin American banana republic; this wasn't a murky question of whether the dispatch of troops was interposition or intervention; "never before," as Arthur Schlesinger was to write, "had a President claimed constitutional authority to commit so many troops to a theater of potential war against a major foe."

Truman didn't merely claim the authority, moreover; he flaunted it. Even while Senate business was being dominated by a "Great Debate" over whether or not to give him permission to do what he had already done, the President said of Congress, "I don't ask their permission; I just consult them." Not, he added, that he was required even to consult "unless I want to. But of course I am polite, and I usually always consult them."

Opening the debate, Robert Taft said the "President simply usurped authority, in violation of the law and the Constitution, when he sent troops to Korea," and "without authority he apparently is now attempting to adopt a similar policy in Europe," but Tom Connally replied that the President had "authority . . . as Commander-in-Chief to send the Armed Forces to any place required by the security interests of the United States." For eighty-six days the debate rolled back and forth, but when Dwight Eisenhower, who had been the Supreme Commander of Allied Forces in Europe during World War II and was considered an unchallengeable authority on military questions, testified to the Senate Armed Services Committee that there was "no acceptable alternative" to the "defense of Western Europe" but to send the four divisions, the debate was effectively over. Attempting to save some face, the Senate resolved that it was its "sense" that Congress should be "consulted" before future presidential decisions to send troops abroad ("What this foggy final paragraph meant no one seemed to know," one observer commented), but it approved Truman's decision, and, as *Fortune* put it, "The effect was to loosen still more Congress' none-too-firm grip on the sword, thus bringing about a definite relinquishment of some of its constitutional authority."

These two years were years of investigation; Johnson's Preparedness Sub-committee and Estes Kefauver's Organized Crime Subcommittee were only the most famous of a score of congressional investigating groups actively looking into Truman's Administration, into atomic spying, into a host of other areas, and hardly had Russell's hearings, which burnished the Senate's reputation, concluded when Joe McCarthy removed the luster and lacquered on tarnish by speaking, on the Senate floor, of a "conspiracy so immense"—and thereafter, throughout these two years, McCarthy's influence on the Senate grew. With the Korean War still dragging on, Congress at least passed some foreign affairs leg-islation, authorizing increased military expenditures and nonmilitary aid. On the domestic front, as one observer noted, "Mr. Truman's Fair Deal program scarcely got discussed." When the national legislature finally ground to a halt in October, 1952, it had, the *Washington Star* said, "completed less work than the 80th Congress, the Congress called 'the worst' by Truman." The *Washington Post* reported that "almost as many major bills have been sent back to com-mittee as have been reported to Congress in the first place." In the House, there was at least some leadership, thanks to the commanding figure of Rayburn; the Senate was in almost total disarray. "Congress is being overcome by its own inertia," said *Fortune;* "the legislative machinery, which is the heart of democ-racy, is breaking down." The era's most authoritative work on Capitol Hill, the 689-page *The Legislative Process in Congress,* was being written even as the Eighty-second session was going forward. Its author, the political scientist George B. Galloway, concluded that "Many people are losing faith in American democracy because of its repeated and prolonged failures to perform its implicit promises."

Although both houses of Congress were indicted for failure, the focus of criticism was shifting gradually to the Senate. In part, this was because of its larger role in foreign affairs. "Now that the United States has become the leading democratic world power, the future of the Senate is a subject of general concern," Galloway wrote. "The quality of its performance and the nature of its output have worldwide repercussions." And in part, it was because of its role in domestic affairs. The absenteeism that had plagued Majority Leaders Barkley and Lucas was even worse under McFarland, so the body couldn't even pass urgently needed domestic legislation on which both parties agreed. When, for example, increased federal financing of medical facilities—a measure supported by both parties and favorably reported by the Senate Labor Committee—was brought to the floor, so few of its supporters were present that it was defeated. The passage of time had had its inevitable effect on the seniority problem. The Senate Appropriations Committee had become a particularly notorious bottleneck because, as Drew Pearson reported, "Tennessee's never-say-die Kenneth McKellar, grandpa of the Senate, is now so feeble that he can no longer run the Committee, which passes on all the funds for the entire government. Yet he is so jealous of his powers as chairman that he won't let another senator run it." And then there was the Senate's peculiar institution. The responsibility for Congress' failures, Galloway wrote, "lies in large part at the door of Senate filibusters. . . . Filibusters have delayed for decades the enactment of social legislation passed by the House of Representatives and desired by a majority of the American people."

Neither Galloway nor any other realistic observer saw any substantial hope of even modifying, much less abolishing, the sacred senatorial tradition of unlimited debate—or of passing other needed procedural reforms. Despite almost universal disapproval of the seniority system, Senator Mike Monroney was only expressing another universal sentiment when he said that any Senate Majority Leader who suggested a substitute for that system "would be cutting his political throat."

Mounting concern was expressed on the Senate floor. "The Senate of the United States has in recent years been losing its hold on the confidence and respect of the American people," Senator Morse said. "The complaint is universal." Condemning the "blind rush" to pass legislation in the session's closing days, the Acting Minority Leader, Republican Guy Cordon, said, "We are mighty close today to acting not as a parliamentary body but like members of a group in a riot. . . . I feel that I am part of a vast failure of public duty." There was even being heard, still faintly but with increasing insistence, the suggestion that perhaps America no longer needed a Senate, that in a modern world a Senate might be an anachronism, as Galloway put it, a "relic of the days when checks and balances were needed to prevent tyranny," that perhaps the Senate's powers should be reduced—or that perhaps the Senate should be abolished entirely. That, Galloway pointed out, would only be in keeping with a worldwide trend: "the decay of second chambers and the trend toward unicameralism in the democratic constitutions of the post-war world are widespread phenomena"; twenty-nine democratic countries now had unicameral legislatures. And perhaps that would be the fate of America's Senate, too. "The obsolescence of the Senate, so the argument runs, together with its tolerance of unlimited and irrelevant debate and its frequent absenteeism, may lead the American people in time to recognize that their second chamber is not indispensable," Galloway wrote.

THE PREDICTIONS THAT INOFFENSIVENESS and amiability would prove insufficient qualifications for the job of Senate Majority Leader had been borne out—embarrassingly—at Ernest McFarland's very first encounter with the press following his election to the post. When the reporters crowding around the four Democratic congressional leaders—House Majority Leader John McCormack and whip Percy Priest, McFarland and Johnson from the Senate—as they emerged from their first Monday conference at the White House asked likable old "Mac" for a statement, he stammered for a moment, and then said, "Uh, John is more experienced at this than I am." McCormack and the reporters reminded him that the statement traditionally came from the Senate Leader. Well, McFarland finally said, "The President expressed confidence in Congress and what we can get done in the next two years." Only when reporters pressed him did he think to add that of course "I share his confidence. I think we will be able to work out a unity that will be good for the country." McFarland seemed to have forgotten a piece of news that the conference participants had agreed should be told to the press. When Lyndon Johnson whispered a reminder, McFarland told him to make the announcement himself, and Johnson thereupon stated that his "Preparedness Committee" would start hearings on the Selective Service Bill that week, and that "General [George] Marshall will make the first statement." Only then did McFarland remember what he had been supposed to say to demonstrate Democratic unity on the draft issue: "The President emphasized that General Marshall's proposal will be an Administration proposal, and Marshall will speak for all departments and agencies of the government. If you hear any rumors to the contrary they are not true." And he delivered that message with the air of an actor trying to remember difficult lines. McFarland was not to improve with practice; it was soon an open secret on Capitol Hill that Old Mac just couldn't think very fast on his feet. Nor was this man who said, "I just try to get along with people," adept at the exercise of power. When a senator—even one whose vote was crucial—told him that he was going to vote against an Administration proposal, McFarland's standard response was: "That's all right. I'll never ask you to vote against your convictions." As William White was to say: "There are not many times when a Senate leader can afford to 'get tough.' To McFarland there was no time at all."

And, of course, had Old Mac wanted to exercise power, he didn't have much to exercise. Though he was called the Democratic Leader, more than half the Democrats took orders not from him but from Richard Russell, and should it come to a showdown involving the entire Senate, a majority would take orders from Russell and Taft; the conservative coalition, not the Administration, had the votes in a crunch. Liberal senators and the President might insist that he get a bill out of a committee that was letting it die by inaction, but what was he to do when the committee chairman flatly refused even to put the measure on the committee's agenda? Obtaining a majority vote for a motion to discharge a bill from a committee would be all but impossible. And if a liberal measure *did* somehow reach the floor, what was the "Majority Leader" to do then? Once, with Truman demanding that a bill giving home rule to the District of Columbia be brought to a vote, McFarland gingerly raised the subject with the southerners—who informed him that should the bill reach the floor, they would discuss it "at length," because, as one southerner put it, home rule would open the door for "a 'Nigra' mayor of Washington." And where was McFarland to find the votes to shut off the filibuster? He let the home rule bill die—he had no choice but to let it die—in committee. Day after day, the genial, inoffensive Arizonan had to listen to the Douglases and Lehmans pillory him to his face for inaction, had to read, day after day, that "McFarland was simply ineffectual" or that "Majority Leader McFarland was no leader at all"; there was nothing he could do about it.

The number of senators on the floor—for years so disgracefully small—grew smaller; endless quorum calls were required to round up enough senators to conduct even routine business. In August, McFarland convened a caucus of his Democratic senators. At the Senate's present pace, he said mournfully, "we'll be here until Christmas." The "useless quorum calls," he said, "were wasting the equivalent of "one day a week. It's got to stop." Not an hour after the caucus adjourned, he went to the Chamber; the first voice he heard when he opened the doors at the rear was that of one of his Democrats—calling for a quorum. When he did manage to get a measure to the floor, even a non-controversial measure on which no one wanted to filibuster, he could not put a halt to speeches, often on some unrelated topic, designed for home consumption. In September, with the *Washington Post* saying that "Congress is taking longer to pass fewer bills than it ever did in recent history," he took the floor, and as the *Post* reported, "pleaded with senators to stop talking and start voting 'so that we can get out of here.' " He is, the *Post* said, "getting positively plaintive about it." By the end of his first year as Leader, McFarland was a figure of ridicule in the Senate, and in national publications as well.

ALTHOUGH THE FAILURE of the congressional "leadership"—in particular, of the Senate leadership—was a theme much emphasized as the Eighty-second Congress drew to a close, the leadership referred to was that of McFarland and the committee barons. None of the criticism included Lyndon Johnson, for he

was not considered part of it. His title, "Assistant Leader," had always been little more than honorary; journalists had the impression that the whip's job was
still the "nothing job" he himself had called it.

Johnson was careful not to disturb that impression. While he was still
photographed emerging from the White House, after that first Monday morning
he seldom if ever again made the mistake of injecting himself into the
exchanges between the Leaders and journalists; he stood silently in the background with his House counterpart, Priest, as McFarland and McCormack
answered—or tried to answer—reporters' questions. When reporters called
him off the Senate floor, or interviewed him in his office, he took stands on no
subjects other than those that dealt with preparedness. Sometimes he would be
asked, by the White House or by McFarland, to persuade a senator to vote for
an Administration measure, but he almost invariably demurred. Resurrecting a
sobriquet from Johnson's past, Drew Pearson wrote that he "has adopted a
policy of antagonizing no one—a policy which has won for Lyndon the nickname of 'Lying Down Johnson.' " But that barb was drowned in the wave of
publicity for the Preparedness Subcommittee and for the Watchdog-in-Chief;
1951 was the year of the long profiles that climaxed in the *Newsweek* cover.
Most of those articles concentrated on the subcommittee chairmanship; almost
no attention was paid by the press to Johnson's other job, as party whip; that
job was not, in fact, so much as mentioned in the *Newsweek* article.

But within the private world of the Senate—in the cloakroom and the
Marble Room and behind the tall closed doors of the offices in the SOB—
attention was beginning to be paid. For, without the press noticing it, the job
was changing.

Part of the change was simply a matter of information.

Senators wanted to know—needed to know—at what time a roll call vote
would occur, so that they could be present, and have their vote recorded. They
needed to know what day a bill in which they were interested would come to
the floor, so that they could arrange to be present to argue for or against it; to
offer, or oppose, amendments. Not infrequently, they needed to know at least
the approximate hour it would come up, which meant knowing if amendments
would be introduced to bills on the schedule ahead of it, and how much time
might be consumed discussing those amendments. They needed to know if
a Monday or Friday session would be, as was so often the case, only a brief
pro forma session without roll-call votes, in which case their weekend fence-
building trips back home could be extended.

McFarland often didn't know. Overwhelmed by the responsibilities he had
accepted, he seemed increasingly helpless as the pace of the session picked up
and the backlog of bills mounted. And during the second year of his term, worried about his re-election campaign, he spent more and more time back in
Arizona.

Lyndon Johnson began checking with the chairmen on the status of bills before their committees, and when senators asked about a particular bill, he knew the answer, or said he would find out. And in talking with senators, he acquired as well as provided information. His colleagues found him an attentive listener as they told him about amendments they were planning to introduce, in committee or on the floor. And Johnson was therefore able to provide information to the Democratic Policy Committee, of which, as party whip, he was an *ex officio* member. When that committee discussed issues, he was silent, and followed Russell's lead in voting. But when the committee turned to schedules, all of a sudden the discussions were no longer as haphazard as they had been in the past. Johnson could report what amendments were going to be introduced, and who was planning to speak for or against them, and how heated, and how long, the discussion on each amendment was likely to be. And when the schedule had been decided on, he could bring more precise information back to individual senators. There began to be, in the Democratic cloakroom, a realization that now, when a senator needed to know when a certain bill would come to the floor, there was, suddenly, someone he could ask.

THE INFORMATION wasn't only about schedules. It was also about votes.

The White House needed to know if it had the votes for a bill it wanted brought to the floor. A senator needed to know if there would be sufficient support to pass a measure he had introduced. "Vote-counting"—predicting legislators' votes in advance—is one of the most vital of the political arts, but it is an art that few can master, for it is peculiarly subject to the distortions of sentiment and romantic preconceptions. A person psychologically or intellectually convinced of the arguments on one side of a controversial issue feels that arguments so convincing to him must be equally convincing to others. And therefore, as Harry McPherson puts it, "Most people tend to be much more optimistic in their counts than the situation deserves. . . . True believers were always inclined to attribute more votes to their side than actually existed."

Lyndon Johnson had seen firsthand the cost of wishful thinking, of hearing what one wants to hear, of failing to look squarely at reality, when his father, that "man of great optimism" sentimentally attached to the old Johnson Ranch, purchased it for a price higher than was justified by the hard financial facts. Lyndon Johnson had felt firsthand the consequences of romance and sentiment every time the reins of the fresno bit into his back. And Lyndon Johnson had been a master of the vote-counting art for a long time. Of all the aspects of his political talent that had impressed the group of fast-rising young liberal pragmatists of which, as a young congressman, he had been a member, none had impressed them more than this ability. These men, to whom politics was life, were uninterested in party games; at Georgetown parties, while others played charades, they would go off and amuse themselves by trying to predict the exact vote on some bill that would be coming up in Congress that week.

And they learned that, as Jim Rowe recalls, "He was a great counter. Someone would say, we've got so many votes, and Johnson would say, 'Hell, you're three off. You're counting these three guys, and they're going to vote against you.' " Says Abe Fortas: "He would figure it out—how so-and-so would vote. Who were the swing votes. What, in each case—what, exactly—would swing them."

Now Lyndon Johnson's counting was not a social pastime but an exercise in hard political reality—and he was still "a great counter." He kept his counts on the long, narrow Senate tally sheets on which the ninety-six names were printed in alphabetical order in a column down the center with a blank line on either side of each name, on the left side for the "yea" votes, on the right for the "nays." When he knew which way a senator would vote, he would write a number—the number that the new vote raised the tally to—on the appropriate side of the senator's name. And no number was written until he *knew,* knew for sure. To a staff member who, after talking with a senator, said he "thought" he knew which way the senator was going to vote, he snarled, "What the fuck good is *thinking* to me? Thinking isn't good enough. Thinking is never good enough. I need to *know!*" Often, he didn't know. He had no power to make a senator tell him which way he was going to vote, and some senators didn't want to be asked. Pat McCarran, asked once by Walter Jenkins, warned Jenkins never—ever—to do it again. And he never tried to persuade a senator to vote one way or the other; it was information, not votes, that he was collecting. But if he didn't *know,* he didn't guess: the lines flanking the senator's name stayed blank.

In this collecting of information, there had been an important development, what Evans and Novak call the "ripening of the relationship between Lyndon Johnson and Bobby Baker." Owing a favor to a political operative from the South Carolina hamlet of Pickens, Senator Burnet Maybank paid it in 1942 with the offer of an appointment to the Senate's corps of teenage pages, and the man recommended Bobby Gene Baker, the fourteen-year-old son of a Pickens mailman. Bobby was working in a drugstore; he had been hired six years before to sweep out the place, but, as he was to say about himself, he was "an eight-year-old boy who had it in him to hustle," and the store's owner was to say that it wasn't long before Bobby was "doing everything but filling prescriptions." One of his teachers said he was "so vivacious, just a little trigger. If you wanted something done, you gave it to Bobby and you knew it would be done."

For the first ten nights the boy was in Washington, he wrote in his diary each night, "I'm so homesick," but when one of his Pickens teachers, hearing of his loneliness, wrote him an encouraging letter, Bobby's reply, scrawled on a lined piece of paper from a notebook, was "Miss Hallum, Bobby Baker don't quit," and he got ahead in the Senate as he had gotten ahead in the drugstore: in his words, by "hard work and hustle." The twenty-two pages, all boys, wore dark blue knickers, went to school each day in a special school in the Capitol, and, on the floor, filled the inkwells and snuffboxes in the Chamber, "brought the senators public documents, newspapers, telephone messages, or anything they desired. To call us, they'd snap their fingers and we'd scurry to them." He carried out such errands eagerly, and sought more: "I [learned] to anticipate what each senator might require. . . . When I learned that a given senator would be making a speech on a given day, I stationed myself nearby to quickly fetch some documents or materials or fresh water as he might need." (His favorite senator was Truman: "Not once did I see him act imperiously toward lowly page boys. 'Young man,' he would say—not 'Sonny' as so many called us—'Young man, when it's convenient, could you please get me a glass of water?' ") Before long, senators were asking for him by name, and giving him another type of assignment. " 'Bobby, I'm having a rubdown in the gym. Can you hold the vote for half an hour?' I then would go to another senator, explain the situation, and ask him to request a time-consuming quorum call. . . ."

He loved the institution; wandering around the floor, he would open the drawers of the desks so that he could read the names burned or carved into the wood, "running my fingers over the names—Daniel Webster, Stephen Douglas, Andrew Johnson—and marveling that I stood where they had stood." He was "very early" intrigued by "the give and take of Senate debate." When a parliamentary maneuver was underway, and he didn't understand it, he would later approach Parliamentarian Charles Watkins in his office; "He was a kindly, gracious man from Arkansas and he patiently educated me." So earnestly did he ingratiate himself with senators that at the age of sixteen he was named chief page, and at eighteen he was given a title on the Senate staff so that he, unlike the other pages, "might remain on the Senate payroll even after Congress had adjourned for the year." When he married, it was to a woman from the Senate world: Dorothy Comstock, one of Scott Lucas' secretaries.

Bobby "made the Senate his home," an article stated. "[He] experienced the major episodes of a young man's life under the great dome of the Capitol itself. There he grew into long pants, had his first shave, went to high school, received his diploma . . . met his wife and courted her. His wedding reception in 1948 was held in the Capitol. . . . Other boys have aunts and uncles beaming at their receptions. Bobby had five United States senators." He was truly, reporters said, the "child of the United States Senate." When a senator, Walter George, told him to upgrade his name, he did so. "A gentleman of the old school who enjoyed being thought of as an elder statesman, he responded to elaborate courtesies. 'Bobby,' he said, shortly after I had turned twenty-one, 'you've got a boy's name and now you're a man. It doesn't have enough decorum or dignity. I'd strongly advise you to change it.' " His father was offended when he changed Bobby to Robert, Baker was to relate, but "Senator George . . . was delighted and thereafter treated me in the warmest possible fashion." By 1951, everyone around the Senate knew him, everybody talked to him freely; he knew a lot of Senate secrets. And Baker worked at knowing secrets; as the writer Evan Thomas was to put it, he "made it his business to know things: who owed whom a favor, who was drunk, who was on the take, who was sleeping with his secretary." If an instrument was needed for obtaining information in the Senate world, it would be hard to find a better one than this twenty-two-year-old page.

And for Lyndon Johnson, Bobby Baker made clear, he would be a willing, eager instrument. The waiter who brought them sandwiches at their first meeting had felt that Baker seemed "drawn to LBJ by some invisible magnet," and thereafter the attraction had only increased. "I found him fascinating from that first talk in 1948," Baker was to recall. "I was, indeed, beguiled by him." He flattered Johnson unmercifully, implored him to give him chores to carry out. Says one of Johnson's staff: "He was an unabashed lackey, a bootlicker. He'd think of all manner of excuses to come in the office and see Johnson, and he'd tell him about all the things he was doing for him, all the little ways he was helping him." "A bootlicker, but an agile one," Evan Thomas was to call him. He carried out Johnson's errands efficiently, and as quickly as he could—often at a trot. "He would scurry around the Capitol corridors, often scribbling notes as he walked," his biographer would write. "He hunched a bit as he moved, and as a result some people began to call him 'the mole,' " a description made more exact by his face, which was narrow, with a very large nose (which he later had altered) and a forehead and chin which both receded sharply, giving him a pointed-face look. He tried, somewhat unsuccessfully because he was much shorter and stooped, to stand in Johnson's commanding attitude, and to walk as he walked; he had better luck talking like Johnson: "His voice seemed to take on a bit of the Johnson twang," his biographer wrote. He was to name not one but two of his children—Lynda and Lyndon John—after him. Johnson's response was all that Baker could have wished: "You're like a son to me, because I don't have a son of my own," he told him.

When Lyndon Johnson asked Bobby Baker what was going on around the Senate, the young man always had a lot to tell him. And Johnson took steps to make sure Baker would have even more to tell. He took the unusual step of inviting a Senate staffer to the small dinner parties at Thirtieth Place at which the other guests were senators and journalists. "In the intimacy of the dinner table," as Evans and Novak were to write, "the men spoke frankly and unguardedly." Sometimes at such parties, there would be three or four tables. Johnson could hear only what was said at the table at which he was sitting; with Baker present, and at another table, Johnson had a pair of sharp ears there, too.

There was another venue in which senators let their guard down, and Johnson installed Baker there, as well. Sometime in 1951, Johnson casually mentioned to McFarland and to Maybank, that Bobby had been doing such a good job, didn't they think it would be nice to give him some sort of meaningless title? Johnson even suggested one: Bobby could be an assistant to Skeeter Johnston; he could be called "Assistant, Democratic Cloakroom." The duties of

Baker's new job were nebulous, but the title freed him from the status, and duties, of page. And whatever the duties might be, they certainly had something to do with the cloakroom—which meant that Bobby now had a reason to spend a lot of time there.

For Bobby Baker, the cloakroom was a fertile field, because, as he himself was to put it, senators felt safe there. "No prying newsmen," no constituents, apart from a few exceptions no staff members "need apply for admittance behind those sacrosanct doors," he was to recall. "Safe in the cloakroom senators opened up their heads and their hearts. . . ." And now, when heads and hearts were opened, a very sharp pair of ears was listening.

> It was here I first heard direct from the horse's mouth what senators were considered to be for hire, and to what extent, and to whom; I learned one could not presume that just because two senators shared a common ideology or a common state that they were soul mates. Jealousies played a part, and all the other human factors entered in: competing wives, distaste for another's lifestyle, class differences, clashing personal goals.

Two years earlier, Lyndon Johnson had summoned Bobby Baker to his office because he had heard that Baker knew "where the bodies are buried." During the intervening two years, Johnson had learned that Baker was willing to tell him where the bodies were buried. Now he had placed Baker in ideal vantage points to observe the burials. And of course the information Baker thus obtained gave him insight into how senators were likely to vote on a particular bill. The counting of votes on the Democratic side had been the province of Skeeter Johnston, the punctilious, dignified Secretary for the Majority. Skeeter still counted votes, still gave the counts to Lyndon, still thought it was his counts on which the leadership was basing its decisions. But it wasn't. Bobby Baker had quietly begun making his own counts. He was a very good counter, and not only because of the information he had collected. Bobby, McPherson says, was no "true believer"; he was not one of those who "just can't help but feel that the issue is so clear on their side that the people must vote that way. . . . Bobby didn't let that kind of consideration affect him, maybe because he didn't have terribly strong convictions himself."

It was important to Lyndon Johnson that the information—Bobby's information and the information he himself had collected—on those long tally sheets be accurate. Eyeglasses perched on his nose, he would hold a sheet in one hand, and the thumb of the other hand would move down the list of names, name by name, pausing on each line, making sure that no numbers were skipped or repeated, and that he knew—*knew*—that each senator would vote as the sheet showed he would vote. The thumb moved very slowly. Sometimes it would pause by a name for quite some time while Lyndon Johnson reflected, and it would not move down to the next name until those reflections had been completed. The tall young senator standing with a tally sheet in hand, head bowed over it, sometimes seemingly lost in the numbers on the sheet, oblivious to the world around him, was a picture of concentration. He was a picture of determination—of a man resolved not to make a mistake.

If these predictions of upcoming Senate votes were never complete, if the sheets usually contained more than a few blanks, they were nonetheless the best predictions available—by far. The White House learned that if it wanted to know what would happen if it pressed for a vote on some major Administration measure, the best person to ask would be the Assistant Leader. Senators learned that if they wanted to know what would happen on a vote on some minor issue, some intra-state issue important only to them, the best person to ask would be the Assistant Leader. In the world of the Senate, in which, for years now, nobody had known what was going on, an awareness was gradually growing that now, at last, somebody did.

Baker was also a source of other information, more routine but nonetheless vital. Votes needed not only to be counted but to be produced. If an Administration measure was coming up, it was the Leader's responsibility to know where the bill's supporters could be reached—in their offices, at their homes, in a mistress's apartment, on the golf course, in a bar—so that they could be summoned to the floor in time to vote. More often than not, McFarland didn't know. But when he was back in Arizona, the responsibility fell to the Assistant Leader. Lyndon Johnson told Bobby Baker he wanted him to know the whereabouts of every Democratic senator at all times. Soon, recalls McFarland's administrative assistant, Roland Bibolet, "whenever some senator went someplace, Bobby would always have a phone number where he could be reached. Or where he couldn't be reached, and why he didn't want to be reached." During his two years as Democratic whip, Johnson forged a tool for his use—a tool perfectly fitted to his hand.

THE CHANGE IN THE WHIP'S JOB was a matter of more than information.

One of the Majority Leader's routine responsibilities was scheduling activities in the Senate's "morning hour," the period—actually two hours long—at the beginning of each day's session during which routine resolutions and petitions and certain "unobjected to" bills could be introduced. With McFarland often in Arizona—and, when he was in Washington, uninterested in so mundane a chore—resolutions, petitions, and bills were piling up.

Johnson was very politic about moving into the realm of actually scheduling Senate business, however unimportant. Not wanting to do so when McFarland was in Washington, he would, when the Leader was in Arizona, check on his schedule with Roland Bibolet. "He wanted to know precisely the moment Ernest would be back on the Hill," Bibolet recalls. If he was unable to get an answer from Bibolet during the day, he might call during the night. The phone would ring in the darkness of Bibolet's bedroom, and a voice would say, without preamble, "Roland, I've tried and tried, and tried, and I can't find McFarland." Bibolet would try to protect his boss: "I know he got the message, and I'll bet anything he'll call you first thing in the morning." Realizing from evasiveness that McFarland's return was not imminent, Johnson would draw up the morning-hour schedule for the next few days. Democratic senators began to realize that the easiest way to get on that schedule was to ask Lyndon. And at the end of April, 1952, with the Calendar in chaos and the Leader away, the Assistant Leader took a firmer hand.

Calendar Calls were being invariably delayed, or interrupted, by senators' speeches on unrelated matters. Johnson persuaded Bridges, who was serving his year as GOP leader, to agree that when the Senate convened on May 1, the Calendar would be brought up first, and that only "unobjected to" bills would be considered, so that a large number of them could be disposed of. Then he told a number of Democratic senators who wanted to make *pro forma* speeches, less than five minutes in length, about these bills that if they came to the Chamber at noon on May 1, they would be able to give the speeches and leave fairly quickly. And when, as was all too usual, a senator, in this case Republican James Kem of Missouri, who had not been advised of the agreement, wandered onto the floor and said, "Mr. President, I ask unanimous consent to make a short statement on an unrelated topic," Johnson, standing not at his own desk but at the Majority Leader's front-row center seat, was firm. He told Kem that under his agreement with Bridges, speeches on unrelated topics were out of order. Since Kem had not known about the agreement, he said, he would allow him to speak nonetheless—but only if he agreed to limit his speech to five minutes; if Kem didn't agree, Johnson said, he would regretfully be forced to object to him speaking at all. Kem started to bridle at that, but Johnson addressed him with a disarming smile: "I know the Senator does not desire to place himself ahead of other senators. I have told the Senator of the agreement made by the leaders of both sides. In view of that agreement, certain Senators were asked to come to the chamber. . . . I hope the Senator will confine his request to five minutes. If he does, there certainly will be no objection." Kem acquiesced—and for once a substantial number of bills were called off the Calendar and enacted.

Democratic senators began asking Johnson if the party's Policy Committee could schedule a certain bill to be called off the Calendar and brought to the floor, or if another bill could be held on the Calendar and kept off the floor. Johnson would say that he would be glad to see what could be done. He very delicately started asking McFarland—or at least as often, Russell—whether it would be possible to report out, or to delay reporting, various bills. The bills he asked about in 1951 and 1952 were never controversial bills, never major bills, but their enactment (or delay) was important to individual senators, and when he told a senator he had intervened on his behalf, the senator was grateful. In addition, McFarland or Russell would almost invariably accept Johnson's suggestions, and word got around: if you had a bill you wanted moved, Lyndon was the guy to see. The Assistant Leader was no longer only providing information about schedules; to a small, but growing, extent, he was *making* schedules—and he was reaping benefits from that seemingly routine role: gratitude and debts, small but debts nonetheless, from his colleagues.

Then there was "pairing"—one of the more indefensible of the devices by which senators were allowed to veil their attendance and voting records from constituents. A senator who was absent on the day of a vote but didn't want to be recorded as absent, or a senator who was present but didn't want to have his vote recorded on a controversial bill yet didn't want a future opponent to be able to accuse him of not voting on that issue, would arrange to be "paired" with an absent senator on the opposite side of that issue. The Leader, or the Assistant Leader, or the bill's floor manager would then announce before the vote that the senator, "who is necessarily absent," was "paired on this vote" with the other senator. "If present and voting," the Leader would say, "the senator . . . would vote 'nay,' " and the other senator "would vote 'yea.' " In a variation of this device—a variation known as a "live pair"—an absent senator would request a senator who would be present, as a personal favor, to refrain from voting and instead to be announced as a "pair."

Pairing is strictly "a voluntary arrangement between individual senators," *Senate Procedure* states. Pairs are not included in the official tabulation of roll-call votes. Neither the clerk calling the roll nor the presiding officer so much as mentions them during or after the roll call. The two senators are listed in neither the "yeas" nor "nays" column, but as "not voting." But the Leader's announcement of pairs is recorded in the *Congressional Record,* and a paired senator can therefore later excuse his absence by saying that he had balanced the loss of his vote by removing one from the other side. As Bobby Baker puts it:

> When accused of nonaction on the bill by some future opponent, they could bluster of how they'd "been recorded" on the bill—either for it or against—no matter that they'd had absolutely no influence on it. It would take the opponent six days to explain the parliamentary deceptions involved, by which time he'd be speaking to empty chairs or dark television sets. Such tricks are important in the political game, and politicians do not forget those able to arrange them.

Senate legend had it that some past Senate leaders had taken on themselves the responsibility for pairing, but for at least a decade, and probably for several decades, it had not been, as McFarland's assistant Bibolet says, "a strategic thing." Either "two fellows would arrange their pairs between themselves, or one could call Skeeter [Johnston], and say, 'I'm going to be out of town. Get a pair for me.' Skeeter would call around and arrange the pair." Or, although Bibolet does not say this, during McFarland's careless regime, Skeeter might forget to arrange it, or find it too much trouble. On the long voting tabulation sheets that the Leader carried, the spaces beside some senators' names—sometimes many senators' names—would remain blank. No one would care, until, as his next re-election campaign drew closer, a senator would suddenly realize that his failure to vote on some bill might be used against him—in which case the *Congressional Record* would be "corrected" to show him not absent but paired. The awareness among senators that they could do this added to the laxness and confusion with which the Senate operated.

But now, whenever McFarland was back in Arizona, that practice was changing. Lyndon Johnson didn't want blank spaces on the voting sheets; he wanted every vote accounted for. So, more and more, the job was turned over to Bobby Baker, Bobby who would "always have a phone number" even when a senator had left for someplace where he "didn't want to be reached."

Arranging pairs, arranging schedules, getting minor bills called off the Calendar—mundane chores that no one wanted to do, mundane chores that, left undone, clogged the schedule and slowed the Senate down, little chores that, for many years, no one had done with any diligence. They were being done with diligence now.

If you do everything . . . The days were long days, and the nights were not just for sleeping. The counting didn't stop then, the planning didn't stop. On the night table beside Walter Jenkins' bed, there lay, every night now, a yellow legal pad, so often did the telephone jangle in the bedroom's darkness. And it was not only in the homes of Lyndon Johnson's own assistants that the phone would ring in the night. More and more frequently, "sometimes at three a.m." Bibolet would be jolted awake. *"Roland, I can't find McFarland."* No one could remember a whip ever really working at that "nothing job" before, but Lyndon Johnson was working at it now. And he was making it into something it had never been before.

AND THOUGH MOST of Lyndon Johnson's activities as his party's Assistant Leader were matters merely of scheduling and vote-counting, there were, at times, signs that he was capable of doing more: flashes of something that was beyond just hard work or flattery—and beyond just talent, too.

One came in 1952, during the annual end-of-session struggle over foreign aid. The Administration was losing the struggle that year—losing in a year when losing would be particularly disastrous, since Western Europe, attempting to unite to meet the threat of Communist aggression, badly needed to feel that the United States was solidly behind NATO. President Truman had requested seven billion dollars for aid to NATO's members. The House had reduced the amount to six billion. Dwight Eisenhower, now NATO commander, had warned that the alliance might be able—barely able—to live with that lower figure, but that any further reductions would cripple it. Yet Senate isolationists and conservatives, led by Taft and Herman Welker, were determined to make further reductions—big ones. "We've already poured seventy-five billion dollars down a rathole and still are losing people by the millions to Communism," Welker said. "Unless we call a halt to this crazy spending and these give-away programs . . . we will revert to the Dark Ages." And the conservatives had the votes to make those reductions—partly because of what the *Herald Tribune* called "heavy absenteeism among northern Democrats and liberal Republicans" who, with the Senate on the verge of adjourning for the long summer vacation, had left Washington and were not willing to return; among the fifteen absent senators were eleven who might have supported the Administration. Welker, "sensing the weakness of his opponents," in *Newsweek*'s words, offered an amendment to cut an additional half billion dollars from the House figure, Russell Long offered one to cut $400 million, and both amendments seemed certain to pass.

In the Senate Chamber, before galleries as full (of summer tourists) as the floor was empty, the famous internationalist orators raised their voices in support of the Western alliance, Walter George telling his colleagues in majestic, organ-like tones that "Nothing less is involved than the will of free men, especially in Western Europe, to stand up and integrate themselves in a federation which is the hope of the free world. . . . If we overcut here, it would discourage the very people in Europe we hope to encourage at the time of their greatest need." Tom Connally, managing the bill in his swan song in the Senate, was making his final performance memorable. Thumping his chest, his voice quavering in imitation of old-fashioned stump speakers, he advised his opponents sarcastically to cut the entire appropriation—"Then you can go home and strut your stuff before your constituents and make Fourth of July speeches and tell them 'I saved seven billion dollars and let the free world go to hell.' Then go out and beat your breasts while war is breaking out in Europe," and as he spoke his fellow senators laughed out loud in appreciation, and the galleries roared. Richard Russell, customarily in favor of cutting foreign aid, understood that this time the cutting had gone too far; he was talking privately, gravely judicious yet passionate in his conviction, to individual senators in the rear of the Chamber. But Welker, Taft, and William Jenner were pressing for a vote—and the Administration knew it didn't have the votes. Of the eighty-one senators still in Washington, forty-one were committed to cutting foreign aid, and available to cast votes. Even if every one of the other forty senators was persuaded to be present, the Long and Welker amendments would still be passed. Standing at the Leader's desk, McFarland was running his hands through his hair in frustration. Internationalists felt, as *Newsweek* reported, that "without a minor miracle, they could never muster enough votes to hold the line."

Then the double doors to the Democratic cloakroom swung open and the party's tall young whip came through them. He said something to Russell, and Russell nodded, and Lyndon Johnson strode down the center aisle and spoke to McFarland, and McFarland walked over to old Matt Neely and asked him to hold the floor for the rest of the day's session, and Neely did so for the full hour and a half—which gave Johnson eighteen hours to work with before the Senate convened the next day. And when the Senate adjourned, Lyndon Johnson went with McFarland to McFarland's office, and told him what he thought they should do with those hours.

If there were too many votes against them, Johnson said, the only thing to do was to get rid of those votes. And that could be accomplished, he said, by using live pairs. If they could persuade isolationist senators who were still in Washington and who were planning to vote for the aid-cutting amendments to agree to pair with absent senators who would have voted against the amendments, each senator who agreed to do so would be depriving the amendments of one vote. And pro-amendment senators *would* agree, Johnson said, for the usual reason—to do a colleague a favor by saving him the embarrassment of being recorded as absent on an important vote. The only reason they wouldn't agree, as Johnson was later to explain, was if they realized that the ordinarily routine pairing device was being used for a very unroutine reason. And, as he was to explain, they *wouldn't* realize unless someone on the other side checked around and found that an awful lot of live pairs were being arranged. And this checking would have to be done in advance: once a senator had assured a colleague that he would pair with him, that assurance was considered an unbreakable promise.

The pair that Johnson focused on first was the absent internationalist Warren Magnuson, back home in the distant state of Washington and unwilling to return, and Joe McCarthy, an adamant opponent of foreign aid. The two bachelor senators were dating buddies. "If Magnuson wasn't going to be present, you've lost his vote anyway," McFarland's assistant Bibolet explains. "So if you can get a live pair with Magnuson, you've cut out an opposite vote." Johnson asked McCarthy to save his friend "Maggie" from embarrassment with a live pair, and McCarthy agreed. And then Johnson focused on Guy Gillette of Iowa and Kerr of Oklahoma, two other senators who didn't want to return, and on McMahon of Connecticut, who couldn't, because of illness.

The next day, the unsuspecting Russell Long called for the yeas and nays on his amendment, and the yeas and nays were ordered. But just before the clerk called the roll, a number of his amendment's supporters asked to be recognized for brief statements.

"On this vote, I am paired with the senator from Washington," Joe McCarthy said. "If he were present and voting, he would vote 'nay.' If I were permitted to vote, I would vote 'yea.' I withhold my vote." Olin Johnston said: "I am paired on this vote with the senator from Iowa. If he were present and voting, he would vote 'nay.' If I were permitted to vote, I would vote 'yea.' I withhold my vote." John Stennis said: "On this vote I have a pair with the senior senator from Oklahoma, who if present would vote 'nay.' If I were permitted to vote I would vote 'yea.' I withhold my vote." A. Willis Robertson said: "On this vote I have a pair with the senior senator from Connecticut. If he were present and voting he would vote 'nay.' If I were permitted to vote I would vote 'yea.' I withhold my vote." The Long Amendment therefore received not the expected forty-one yeas, but only thirty-seven. There were forty nays, so it was defeated. It fell four votes short of passage—the four votes Lyndon Johnson had stripped from it by using live pairs.

All that day, other amendments to reduce foreign aid would be offered—and all that day Administration supporters fought them off, armed with live pairs. In the evening, Administration opponents finally passed an amendment, but only for a $200 million cut. And that was their only victory. At first, Welker had been puzzled. "I am concerned by the number of pairs," he said at one point. "What is this—legislation by absenteeism?" Then, realizing that he had been outsmarted, he strode over to McCarthy, whom he had been defending against attempts to discipline him for breaches of Senate rules. "From now on, let Magnuson defend you," he said, in a snarl that could be heard in the Press Gallery above. "McCarthy turned white," *Newsweek* reported. But McCarthy's reaction was the only satisfaction Welker could obtain from a day he had been confident would bring major victories. When he asked other pro-amendment senators to stop pairing, they told him they couldn't do so—that they had given their promise. As Robert Albright was to report in the *Washington Post,* "By adroit 'pairing' of missing votes with a few 'live' (supporters of the amendment), the Democrats managed to stave off a serious cut." Absenteeism had been crippling the Senate, and no one had seen a solution to the problem. And then suddenly someone *had* seen a solution—had seen a way, in fact, not only to solve the problem but to turn it to his party's advantage. Within the clouds of legislative gloom that had shrouded the Senate for so many years, there had suddenly flickered, very brief but very bright, a bolt of legislative lightning.

AND OTHER CHANGES WERE also taking place during Lyndon Johnson's two years as his party's Assistant Leader in the Senate.

These changes had no relationship to the Senate's internal workings. They were, however, to have a very significant relationship to the Senate's future. For their relationship was to power.

Leader after Leader, Democratic and Republican alike, had complained about their lack of anything to "threaten them with," of anything to "promise them"; about the paucity of sources of intimidation or reward that would give a Leader enough power so that he could truly lead. Their frustration was understandable. Generations of gifted parliamentarians, determined that the Senate not be led, had done their best to ensure that it couldn't be, designing an institution in which there existed few levers with which a Leader could move it.

But of all Lyndon Johnson's political instincts, the strongest and most primal was his instinct for power. The man who was to say "I do understand power. . . . I know where to look for it" was looking for it now. There were few places within the Senate where a Leader could find it—so he looked for it outside the Senate.

One place he looked was not on the Senate side of the Capitol at all but on the House side, in the little hideaway room on the ground floor with an unmarked, unnumbered door—the room that journalists called Sam Rayburn's "Board of Education" but that Rayburn himself called simply "downstairs."

Lyndon Johnson had become a "regular" in that room when he first came to Congress, a twenty-eight-year-old freshman hoisting a glass with the great House barons every afternoon after the House recessed for the day. His betrayal of Rayburn in 1939 had resulted in his exclusion from the hideaway for almost three years—"I can get into the White House; why can't I get into that room?" he had shouted in frustration to House Parliamentarian Lewis Deschler in 1941—but on his first day back in Congress after his return from the Pacific in 1942, Rayburn not only had invited him to "come downstairs" but had even handed him the most prized of status symbols on the south side of the Capitol: his own key to the hideaway door.

Lyndon Johnson was a senator now, but he still had that key—the only senator who had one, the only senator who was a regular at Rayburn's "Board Meetings"—and that key meant power if it was used correctly. Senate passage of a bill vital to a senator was only half the action required on Capitol Hill; the bill also had to be passed by the House, and in the House, Rayburn ruled. It was during this era that, angry over the defeat of a bill he favored, he simply announced that there would be a second vote, and, calling twenty freshmen representatives to his office, flatly ordered them to vote for it—which they did, so that the measure was passed. It was during this era that, the night before the vote on a controversial resolution, he said, "I don't want one word said against this resolution on the floor"—and not one word was said. Sometimes, when he was up on the triple dais, his stocky body, massive, totally bald head and grim, unsmiling face dominating the Chamber, a member would attempt to raise a perfectly legitimate point of order. "The Chair does not desire to hear the gentleman on the point of order," Rayburn would say—and would stand there, impassive, unmoving until the gentleman sat down.

Walter Jenkins had one assignment that took precedence over all others: to notify Johnson—*immediately*—when the House adjourned for the day. Johnson would usually set out on the long walk to the south side of the Capitol as soon as Jenkins' call came; on the rare afternoons on which he was delayed, Rayburn would telephone 231, without identifying himself would bark, "Tell Lyndon I'm waiting for him," and slam down the phone, as if embarrassed at this admission of need. When Johnson was told that the Speaker had called, he would abruptly cut short whatever he was doing, and hurry out of the Senate Chamber or the cloakroom. As he walked along an arcaded passage and then around a small, colonnaded rotunda, a tall figure, alone and intent, he would be leaning forward in his haste, his ungainly but very long stride eating up the bright blue and gold tiles, his arms swinging stiffly and out of rhythm with his steps. He had to walk almost the whole length of the long Capitol, and as he reached the immense central Rotunda beneath the dome, and then, beyond the Rotunda, Statuary Hall, he would sometimes break into an awkward, gangling trot, his suit jacket flaring out, as he crossed their wide spaces, past the statues of Benton and Houston and La Follette. Reaching the House side, tiles now red and white, he would check his stride, though still walking very fast, pass the Speaker's Lobby, crowded in the late afternoon with members who could not go where he was going, run down a flight of stairs two at a time, and enter the unmarked door.

Sometimes he seemed to resent these trips as if they were journeys to Canossa. One afternoon he was talking to Jim Rowe when Jenkins' call came. "I've got to go over there to the Board of Education and kiss his ass again, and I don't want to do it," Lyndon Johnson said. But this feeling was never in evidence in the "Boardroom." He came through its door every afternoon with a smile on his face so broad that, as one of the other regulars says, "Every time Johnson saw Rayburn he would light up like I do when I see my grandson." House members in Rayburn's hideaway for the first time—intimidated, as most men were intimidated, by the stern, unsmiling Speaker—were astonished at what Johnson did next. Walking over to the huge mahogany desk at which Rayburn sat, he would bend over and kiss the Speaker on the top of his bald head. Sometimes he would say, in a loving, deeply solicitous tone, "How are you, Mr. Sam?" And sometimes he would say, "How are you, my beloved?" ("Mr. Rayburn would play gruff.") Other men watched how Johnson "handled" Rayburn. "In that room, he [Rayburn] was boss, and Johnson acknowledged that," one says. Says another: "It was never 'Sam.' It was always 'Mr. Sam,' or 'Mr. Speaker,' and 'Lyndon.' There was never a feeling that they were equals. Never." Says another: "Johnson was quite deferential to him. He would argue with him, but always in such a way that you knew who was the boss." Another sums up Johnson's tone and demeanor simply as "Sirring." Occasionally Rayburn would grow irritated with Johnson. "Lyndon couldn't sit still," one regular says. "He was always jumping up and walking around. And the Speaker would say, 'Sit down, Lyndon. You're making me nervous.' " Johnson might ask him for an opinion, or a decision, on some matter, and Rayburn would give it. And if Johnson tried to argue, Rayburn would simply repeat what he had said—repeat it in exactly the same words. "That was the conclusive remark. That was the end of that conversation."

The regulars also saw that Rayburn acted very differently toward Lyndon Johnson than he acted toward any of them. After the betrayal, his affection for Johnson was never again uncritical. Talking about the younger man, he at least once used the phrase "vaulting ambition." Ramsey Clark says, "He understood

Johnson. I've heard him talk about Johnson and his ambition. I don't think it was blind love at all." Says Richard Bolling: "A constant refrain was about [Johnson's] arrogance and egotism. He [Rayburn] said to me several times the same words: 'I don't know anyone who is as vain or more selfish than Lyndon Johnson.' " But these men agree that although the "love" was no longer "blind," love it certainly was. Says Rayburn's assistant D. B. Hardeman: "It was a father-son relationship, with all that implies. . . . Johnson would just infuriate him, but he would defend Johnson against all comers. He loved him in the way: I'd like to wear the bottom of his britches out." He loved him—and wanted to help him in any way he could. So when Lyndon asked for a favor—such as House passage of a bill vital to some individual senator—Rayburn would usually grant it.

Other senators soon came to realize this crucial fact of Capitol Hill life, and to ask for Johnson's intercession with the mighty Speaker. A bill vital to Clinton Anderson was passed in the Senate, but, Anderson wrote Johnson, "Our . . . problem is to get action in the House," where it would go before a committee whose chairman was sponsoring his own, competing, proposal on the subject. "I have written Speaker Rayburn," Anderson wrote, but he knew that his letter wouldn't be enough, so he also wrote Johnson: "I hope to enlist your continued interest in piloting this legislation to enactment." Even the most powerful Senate committee chairmen—Allen Ellender of Agriculture, for example—would ask. "You put a little note on Lyndon's desk and ask him kindly to get in touch with our friend the Speaker on the Sugar Bill," Ellender told Dorothy Nichols over the phone one day. "It has been pending there for quite some time. We want to clear up the decks. Put a little note on his desk and let him talk to Sam Rayburn."

When Johnson used his influence with Rayburn on a senator's behalf, he made sure the senator knew it. After writing Anderson that "I appreciate the difficulties which may arise in moving the measure through the House [and] I shall be glad to do what I can to be helpful in this regard," he let Anderson know the minute the bill had been passed. "I want you to know I have spoken to Speaker Rayburn," he wrote Ellender, whose bill also passed. Few emotions are more ephemeral in the political world than gratitude: appreciation for past favors. Far less ephemeral, however, is hope: the hope of future favors. Far less ephemeral is fear, the fear that in the future, favors may be denied. Thanks to Sam Rayburn, Lyndon Johnson now had, at least to a limited extent, those emotions on his side in dealing with senators; he had something to promise them, something to threaten them with.

ANOTHER SOURCE of power was money.

Lyndon Johnson had been using money as a lever to move the political world for a long time—ever since, as a young worker in a congressional campaign, he had sat in a San Antonio hotel room behind a table covered with five-dollar bills, handing them to Mexican-American men at the rate of five dollars a vote for each vote in their family.*

For years, men had been handing him (or handing to his aides, for his use) checks or sometimes envelopes stuffed with cash—generally plain white letter-size envelopes containing hundred-dollar bills—for use in his own campaigns, or in the campaigns of others. His first campaign for Congress, in 1937, was perhaps the most expensive campaign for a congressional seat in the history of Texas.† During his first campaign for the Senate, in 1941, envelopes stuffed with cash cascaded into Texas from Washington attorneys and the New York City garment district unions. Some of these campaign contributions were carried in a more casual fashion. Recalling one trip on which he brought between $10,000 and $15,000, Walter Jenkins says, "I went down to Texas carrying this money in bills stuffed into every pocket." The amounts of cash heading south were so large that Johnson sometimes lost the personal control over its use that was important to him. Corcoran "went up to the garment district and raised money for Johnson, and we . . . sent it to Texas," Jim Rowe was to say. "Johnson called and said: 'Where's that money? I need it!' " When Rowe told him who was carrying it, Johnson exploded, apparently because the courier had authority to distribute funds on his own. Rowe recalls Johnson saying: "Goddamn it—it'll never get to me. I'll have to meet him at the plane and get it from him." And money was being raised in Texas, too. Because campaign contributions were not a deductible business expense, Brown & Root distributed to company executives and lawyers hundreds of thousands of dollars in deductible "bonuses" and "attorneys' fees," which Internal Revenue Service agents came to believe were then funneled, in both checks and cash, to the Johnson campaign—contributions on a scale unprecedented at the time even in the freewheeling world of Texas politics. A tax-fraud investigation of Brown & Root launched by the IRS was cut off only after Johnson had solicited the personal intervention of President Roosevelt.‡ During Johnson's second—1948—Senate campaign, hundred-dollar bills had been given to his aides in stacks so large that sometimes letter-size envelopes couldn't hold them. Picking up $50,000 in "currency" in Houston, John Connally had to bring it back to Austin in what he calls a "brown paper sack like you buy groceries in" (which he left in a booth in an all-night diner, the Longhorn Café, where he had stopped for a bite to eat with fellow Johnson assistant Charles Herring, so that the two attorneys rushed back to the diner in a panic that was assuaged only when they saw the bag still lying in the booth). A paper bag Connally brought back from Houston on another occasion contained

*See *The Path to Power*, p. 277.
†See *The Path to Power*, pp. 408–9.
‡See *The Path to Power*, pp. 684–85, and pp. 716–18, 742–53.

$40,000.* "They were spending money like Texas had never seen," Ralph Yarborough, later a United States Senator from Texas but in 1948 an activist Democratic politician in Texas, was to recall. "And they did it not only so big but so openly."

Lyndon Johnson's use of money in other politicians' campaigns had also been instrumental in his rise. It was money given to other candidates that, in 1940, had furnished him his first toehold on national political power. Obtaining an informal post with the moribund Democratic Congressional Campaign Committee, he had arranged for newly rich Texas contractors and independent oilmen, anxious to enlarge their political influence in Washington, to make contributions to the committee, with the stipulation that they be distributed at his discretion.

That was when the checks and the envelopes stuffed with cash began to pour into his office in Washington—not into his office in the House Office Building because of federal strictures against receiving contributions on federal property, but into a five-room suite he rented in an office building on E Street, the Munsey Building, to circumvent those regulations: to circumvent not their spirit, which was to discourage the sale of political influence, but their technical letter. Tommy Corcoran handed him several cash-filled envelopes, filled with bills from the New York garment-center unions, and trusted couriers from Texas, including William Kittrell, the veteran Texas lobbyist, handed him others. To circumvent another federal law, the Federal Corrupt Practices Act, which prohibited any political contributions from corporations and set a limit of $5,000 on contributions from individuals, Herman and George Brown arranged to have business associates—subcontractors, attorneys, an insurance broker—send $5,000 each, in their own names, to the Congressional Campaign Committee.† On the scale of political contributions of the time, these contributions had a substantial heft. When six of these checks arrived at once, Lyndon Johnson had provided, through Brown & Root, more money than the committee received from any other source. And more and more checks came in, from Brown & Root, and from other Texas oilmen and contractors.

Lyndon Johnson was quite frank about why businessmen should be happy to make these contributions. When, the following year, removed in a power struggle from a formal job at the Congressional Campaign Committee, he became exasperated by the stinginess of some contributors, and by Sam Rayburn's failure to understand why they should be more generous, he wrote the Speaker that "These $200 droplets will not get the job done." What was needed, he said, was to "select a 'minute man' group of thirty men, each of whom should raise $5,000, for a total of $150,000." And, he added, "There isn't any reason why, with the wealth and consideration that has been extended, we

*See *Means of Ascent*, pp. 274–75.
†See *The Path to Power*, pp. 633, 635.

should fall down on this." *Wealth and consideration*—the favors, the political influence that had provided FCC licensing favors that had let radio station owners grow rich, and federal oil depletion allowances that had let oil field operators grow richer; that had procured federal contracts to build and provision military installations in the Tenth Congressional District for favored Austin businessmen, and much larger contracts—such as the contract (it eventually grew to $357,000,000, then one of the largest in Navy history) that the Navy gave to Brown & Root early in 1941 to build sub-chasers and destroyers, despite the fact that, at the time, Brown & Root had never built a single ship of any type (and, as George Brown was to say, "We didn't know the stern from the aft—I mean the bow—of the boat").* Johnson was asking for contributions, in other words, on grounds of naked self-interest: political contributions should be given in return for past government help in acquiring wealth and upon the hope of future government protection of that wealth, and of government assistance in adding to it.

That argument was evidently persuasive. The droplets again became a gusher, and the needed money was again raised—although because Johnson felt himself unwelcome in Campaign Committee headquarters, some of the envelopes came into his House office, and the money they contained was distributed from there. Lyndon Johnson's first national political power was simply the power of money, used as campaign contributions; it had given him whatever small taste of power he had for a year or two enjoyed in the House.

Now, in the Senate, the cascade of cash continued. Some insight into these contributions would be furnished years later, and almost by accident, because of a 1975 Securities and Exchange Commission lawsuit against the Gulf Oil Corporation that grew out of an investigation not into Lyndon Johnson but into the Watergate scandal. Testifying in this lawsuit, Claude Wild Jr. said he had become Gulf's chief Washington lobbyist, reporting to the company's general counsel, David Searls, on November 1, 1959. "Do you recall your first assignment?" he was asked. "One of the first assignments I had resulted from a commitment that" Searls "had made to then Senator Lyndon Johnson," Wild replied. "The commitment was that Gulf Oil would furnish $50,000 to Senator Johnson for his use, and . . . I was furnished $10,000 on five separate occasions which I delivered to Walter Jenkins, who was Senator Johnson's primary aide." The money, Wild testified, was in "cash." No one asked him at the time the denominations of the bills, or how they were carried, but in 1987 he told the author of this book that "probably it was hundreds," carried in "plain white envelopes." He said that the money could have been given either to help finance Johnson's 1960 presidential campaign, or to help Johnson finance other senators' campaigns—"it was for whatever he wanted." He also testified that he had later made another payment, twenty-five thousand dollars, to Johnson "staff members" for "his or his dele-

*See *Means of Ascent*, p. 75; *The Path to Power*, p. 664.

gate's use in assisting members of Congress whom he hoped to see elected or re-elected."

And Wild's contributions were not the largest being delivered to Johnson. Men familiar with this aspect of Texas politics agree that his most important fund-raisers were Tommy Corcoran; John Connally, who carried cash given by, among others, Sid Richardson; Ed Clark, courier for, among others, Clint Murchison, Brown & Root, and the Humble Oil Company; and, on occasion, George R. Brown himself. By the time the author learned about the cash-filled envelopes, Brown had died, so the author could not ask him about them. But he did discuss them with both Connally and Clark, and both men spoke freely—indeed, somewhat boastfully—about flying up to Washington with envelopes tucked into the inside breast pockets of their suit jackets. And both Connally and Clark, as well as intimates familiar with the fund-raising efforts of these two men during the 1950s, agree that they brought to Washington amounts far larger than those about which Wild testified. Asked if the largest amounts he carried were of the same scale as the forty- or fifty-thousand-dollar contributions he had transported in a sack in 1948, Connally shook his head no, grinned, and said that the amounts he carried increased, particularly after he became Richardson's personal attorney in 1951. "I handled inordinate amounts of cash," he said. Clark, moreover, points out that Wild didn't go to work for Gulf until 1959. Before that, contributions to Johnson were made by Chief Counsel Searls. Searls had died before the SEC began its investigation of Gulf, and therefore did not himself testify, but he worked closely with Clark for years; it was, for example, primarily Searls to whom Clark was referring when he explained how he had persuaded Gulf to purchase Lyndon Johnson's political influence by purchasing advertising time on Johnson's radio station, KTBC: "I had friends there. I spoke to them about it, and they understood. This wasn't a Sunday school proposition. This was business."* Clark didn't put anything in writing about his association with Searls; the "Secret Boss of Texas" never put *anything* about money in writing, but in every instance in which one of Clark's statements could be checked against something in writing, the statement proved to be accurate, and when he was asked about Wild's testimony, he said, "I knew about that fifty thousand. I knew about two *hundred* thousand." And Gulf was only one oil company—and there were non-oil businesses in Texas, too.

Some idea of the free-and-easy atmosphere that surrounded Lyndon Johnson's fund-raising relationship with Texans would be documented in transcripts of telephone calls made in early 1960. "I have some money that I want to know what to do with," George Brown said in a call to Johnson's office on January 5. "I was wondering . . . just who should be getting it, and I will be collecting more from time to time." (The answer to Brown's question is not transcribed.)

*See *Means of Ascent*, p. 103.

Ed Clark was raising so much that some of it had to stay in Texas to await the next trip down before Jenkins or some other Johnson aide could pick it up. "Woody," Jenkins wrote Warren Woodward on January 11, "Ed Clark tells me that he has received some assistance from H. E. Butt. I wonder if you could go by and pick it up and put it with the other [we] put away before I left Texas." Clark says that Brown's money was for the presidential run for which Johnson was gearing up that January, and that Butt's was for Johnson to contribute to the campaigns of other senators, but that often he and the other men providing Johnson with funds weren't even sure which of these two purposes the funds were for. "How could you know?" Ed Clark was to say. "If Johnson wanted to give some senator money for some campaign, Johnson would pass the word to give money to me or Jesse Kellam or Cliff Carter, and it would find its way into Johnson's hands. And it would be the same if he wanted money for his own campaign. And a lot of the money that was given to Johnson both for other candidates and for himself was in cash." "All we knew was that Lyndon asked for it, and we gave it," Tommy Corcoran was to say.

This atmosphere would pervade Lyndon Johnson's fund-raising all during his years in the Senate. He would "pass the word"—often by telephoning, sometimes by having Jenkins telephone—to Brown or Clark or Connally, and the cash would be collected down in Texas and flown to Washington, or, if Johnson was in Austin, would be delivered to him there. When word was received that some was available, John Connally recalls, he would board a plane in Fort Worth or Dallas, and "I'd go get it. Or Walter would get it. Woody would go get it. We had a lot of people who would go get it, and deliver it. The idea that Walter or Woody or Wilton Woods would skim some is ridiculous. We had couriers." Or, Clark says, "If George or me were going up anyway, we'd take it ourselves." And Tommy Corcoran was often bringing Johnson cash from New York unions, mostly as contributions to liberal senators whom the unions wanted to support. Asked how he knew that the money "found its way" into Johnson's hands, Clark laughed and said, "Because sometimes I gave it to him. It would be in an envelope." Both Clark and Wild said that Johnson wanted the contributions given, outside the office, to either Jenkins or Bobby Baker, or to another Johnson aide, Cliff Carter, but neither Wild nor Clark trusted either Baker or Carter. In Baker's own memoir, *Wheeling and Dealing,* a book he wrote with Larry L. King, Baker was to call himself the "official bagman" for Senate Democrats, but Clark was to say he "was the only person in Washington I ever recoiled from," and Wild was to call him "a crook." (As would a Federal District Court jury: in 1967, Baker would be found guilty of seven counts of theft, fraud and income tax evasion, in a case that did not involve Johnson. The jury found that in 1962 he had accepted one hundred thousand dollars in "campaign donations" intended to buy influence with various senators, and instead had pocketed the money himself. Jurors told reporters that they felt Baker had lied under oath. Sentenced to one to three years in federal prison, he served sixteen months.) So the two Texas fund-raisers almost always gave their contributions to Jenkins, "but sometimes," in Clark's words, "Walter were [*sic*] not available, or it were not convenient to do that," and on such occasions they would be given directly to Johnson. Asked if the envelopes were always handed over outside the office, Clark replied, "Usually. Not always." He said that Johnson was less cautious with him and with Brown and Connally and Wild than with other contributors because "We had had wheelings and dealings for a long time." Wild responded by noting that before going to work for Gulf in 1959, he had been the Washington representative for the Mid-Continent Oil and Gas Association, "and they had a much more casual way of doing things" than Gulf. During this period, he said, he had given Johnson "quite a bit" of money—he said he had no idea how much—for the campaigns of other senators, sometimes giving it to Johnson "personally," in his office. Money also found its way into Johnson's hands by other means. In 1956, for example, Richard Reynolds of Reynolds Tobacco telephoned Juanita Roberts, one of Johnson's secretaries, and said, according to a memo Roberts wrote, "He has $500.00 he'd like to contribute toward the Senator's expenses." After Gene Chambers, one of Johnson's assistants, picked up the money, it evidently passed through Johnson's hands. "Sen. J handed it to A.W. [Moursund] to take care of," Roberts noted.

If Johnson was in Texas, he might collect the money himself. Shortly after Joe M. Kilgore had been elected to Congress in 1954, Kilgore says, Johnson came up to him after a meeting in San Antonio and "asked me if I was going to Washington."

"When I said I was," Kilgore recalls, "he said, 'Here, take this.' It was an envelope. Inside was ten thousand dollars. 'Give it to Arthur Perry.' I had never had ten thousand dollars before. Jane and I didn't have ten thousand dollars [to our name]."

Kilgore patted his breast pocket with a nervous gesture. "All the way up I kept [patting] to make sure it was still there. I was sure everyone knew I had it. When I got to Washington, I called Arthur Perry. I was going to make sure he counted it in my presence to make sure I hadn't taken out one of those hundred-dollar bills." As it turned out, however, "he [Johnson] had called Earle Clements, and Clements was in the office when I arrived. I made them count it in my presence."

So many envelopes were being filled with cash in the Lone Star State that Kilgore was not the only man who transported them to Washington despite a lack of familiarity with such chores. "Twice I personally carried packets of a hundred hundred-dollar bills, the common currency of politics, to Jenkins," Booth Mooney, whose customary duties were in the speechwriting field, wrote in his book *LBJ: An Irreverent Chronicle.* "This money came from [oilman H. L.] Hunt, who said substantial contributions were also being sent to Washington by other oilmen and business people in Dallas and Houston."

. . .

No MATTER HOW MUCH MONEY WAS RAISED, "it was never enough for
Johnson—never," Ed Clark says. "How much did he want?—he *wanted*,"
Claude Wild says. "He wanted all you could give and more." And to get as
much as possible, Lyndon Johnson took a very direct role in raising money.
Clark would for years—decades—be regarded in Texas as the state's most
skilled political fund-raiser, but, Clark says, there was someone better at that
art than he. "No one was better at raising money than Lyndon Johnson," he
says. "He would get on the phone and call people, and he knew just what to
say."

What he said sometimes dealt bluntly with "the wealth and consideration
that had been extended." Texas was home to businessmen much smaller than
Sid Richardson or Herman Brown, and if some of them were reluctant to contribute, or to contribute as much as Johnson thought they should contribute, he
would get on the phone with them personally. One of Clark's clients, Theo
Davis of Austin, owned a wholesale grocery company which had been given
contracts to supply central Texas military installations, and he wanted to keep
those contracts, and, Clark says, Johnson would "get on the phone with him"
and "remind" him what he had to do to keep them, and, Clark says, "He gave
Johnson five thousand dollars at a time." Johnson had John Connally make him
lists, Connally recalls—"We called them 'John's Special Lists' "—of how
much certain businessmen and lawyers could give, and why they should give it.
With some of these targets, the reasons were philosophical. "Good Democrat"
Connally would write by a name. "Old Roosevelt man." But with others, the
reasons related more to "wealth and consideration." One Leonard Hyatt would
be good for $1,000 partly because he was a "Good Democrat" but also because
"You have helped him on Bracero matter," Connally wrote on one such list. An
attorney, Floyd McGown Sr., who "can give and raise" $1,500, had been helped
by Johnson years before—"represents Frederick Refrigeration & some other
employers since War Labor Board days." Next to another name, that of Johnson's Fredericksburg ally Arthur Stehling ("500 to 1500"), Connally wrote,
"Had a good year—Two pretty good capital gains transactions"—which, Connally explains, meant two transactions Lyndon had helped Arthur with.

If a more general type of coaxing was required, Johnson was adept at that,
too, as is shown by the transcript of a telephone call he made to wealthy oilman
Dudley Dougherty, who would be Johnson's opponent in the 1954 election but,
at other times, his ally. He complained about organizational difficulties to
Dougherty until Dougherty said, "Let me see if I can dig up five thousand dollars for you."

"If you can—don't you get in any hurry," Johnson said soothingly. But, in
fact, he wanted to firm up the arrangement. "You let my boy Warren Woodward
in Austin, he is a mighty good boy, or John Connally—they will fly down to

your place. If you can help us, I'll sure appreciate it." And when it didn't firm—when Dougherty was apparently going to hang up without any further word about the money—Johnson said, "You tell me when you want Warren Woodward to come down there."

And sometimes, in the raising, Johnson took a very personal hand indeed, as is shown by two incidents that occurred at the Democratic National Convention in Los Angeles in 1960.

The first, recounted in Booth Mooney's book, occurred in an empty clothes closet in Johnson's hotel suite. The suite "was filled with people," Mooney was to write, so Johnson led him into the closet "and shut the door. 'This won't take long, Booth,' he said urgently. 'I just want to tell you we've got a lot of bills to pay here and other places. I have to raise a pile of money. Will you talk to Hunt and tell him he'll never regret it if he'll contribute ten or twenty to help us get square?' "

Hunt declined to give that help, Mooney says, but Johnson had more success with another appeal, this one recounted by Bobby Baker. "LBJ," Baker was to say in *Wheeling and Dealing,* "wore a sad hound dog's look as he said, 'Bobby, we're broke and we owe $39,000 for a hotel bill out here. See what you can do.' . . . I went to Bart Lytton, president of Lytton Savings and Loan, with the sad tale. He required persuading. 'I don't have that much available,' he said. 'Even if I did I wouldn't want it on record that I'd given it.' I assured Lytton that he'd be protected and stressed the benefits of incurring LBJ's goodwill. 'On the other hand,' I said, 'he can be a miserable prick if he feels someone has let him down.' Bart groaned, but motioned me into a public men's room nearby." In one of the stalls, Baker was to write, Lytton "gave me two $10,000 personal checks made out to cash. I delivered them to LBJ, who took one look and said, 'Hell, Bobby, this is just a little over half of it.' " Nonetheless, "Senator Johnson pocketed the checks, though grumbling under his breath. . . ."

Johnson sometimes also took a personal hand in distributing money to other senators.

"On one occasion," Baker was to write, "I was asked to transmit $5,000 from Lyndon B. Johnson" to Styles Bridges. "As was the Washington practice, Johnson handed me the boodle in cash. 'Bobby,' he said, 'Styles Bridges is throwing an "appreciation dinner" for himself up in New Hampshire sometime next week. Fly up there and drop this in the kitty and be damn sure that Styles knows it comes from me.' " On another occasion, in 1957, Joe Kilgore relates, Johnson gave a contribution to William Blakely, who had been appointed to Texas' other senatorial seat to replace the retiring Price Daniel, and was running for the permanent seat in a special election.

"He [Johnson] called me to come over to his office," Kilgore says. "When I got there, he said, 'Come on, I'm meeting Bill Blakely down on the sidewalk.' We left his office and went down in an elevator. While we were in the elevator, he said, 'Here, hold this,' and stuck something in my hand. I looked down and it was a big wad of money. When we got out of the elevator, we went into a closet—I think it was a janitorial closet. He told me to count the money. It was twenty thousand dollars. In one-hundred-dollar bills. I knew why he wanted me to count it. He wanted a witness. So that he could prove that he had given this money. He gave the money to Blakely, saying, 'I just want you to know I'm on your side.' "

Johnson's use of money to help finance the campaigns of his colleagues had begun even before he became whip. In 1950, he had funneled Texas cash into the campaign of an old House acquaintance who was trying to move to the Senate, Earle Clements of Kentucky. Now, in 1952, there were senatorial elections again, and Johnson used financing on a broader scale. And Johnson's financing of colleagues' campaigns was not limited to money he distributed himself. Stuart Symington, making his first try for the Senate in 1952, had wealthy financial backers in Missouri, but as one of them was to write, "We can't raise money in the quantities you Texans can." In September and October, 1952, Johnson raised it—largely from Herman Brown. "I gave him some money and I sent a man down to help him at Lyndon's instigation," Brown would recall years later, after he had become enraged by Symington's refusal to vote for further natural gas deregulation. "But Symington has very little ability, the least of any of them. I've got a nigger chauffeur who's got more ability than Symington—although maybe I shouldn't express myself so frankly."

How much did Brown, and other Texans, contribute at Johnson's instigation to Symington's 1952 Missouri senatorial campaign? In a painful interview with the author in 1982, Symington at first attempted to minimize the amount and to contend that it had been given only in the form of checks, checks that, as legally required, had been reported. The author then showed him contradictory information. "Well, I remember Johnson sent my campaign manager somewhere to get money for me. It wasn't much—five thousand or ten thousand dollars—but it was a nice gesture." The author asked if the amount might have been higher. "I'm pretty certain it wasn't fifteen thousand," Symington said. "Maybe it was ten thousand. Nobody could buy me for ten thousand dollars." Asked if the money had been cash, Symington said, "I don't know. My worst characteristic as a politician was my inability to raise money." The money—at least much of it—*was* in cash: in hundred-dollar bills. And the amount may have been far higher than Symington's estimate. Ten thousand dollars—in cash—was the amount contributed to Symington in 1952 by oilman Wesley West alone. Arthur Stehling, one of Johnson's lawyers, was to recall sitting in Johnson's ranch house during the fall of 1952, listening to Johnson discuss over the telephone the financial needs of various senators: "He would say, 'Well, I've got twenty for him, and twenty for him and thirty for him.' Symington was always the highest." Twenty or thirty thousand dollars were paltry amounts by the fund-raising standards that would be in place at the end of the twentieth century; they were quite substantial amounts by mid-century standards. And Johnson's use of money, like his use of Rayburn, was getting him what he wanted, as Ed Clark saw. "Roosevelt would pay people off in conversation or speeches," Clark says. "Johnson went right to the heart of it. The nitty-gritty. 'How much do you have to have to make this campaign go?' " When senators returned to Washington after the 1952 elections, there was a new awareness on the north side of the Capitol. There was a vast source of campaign funds down in Texas, and the conduit to it—the only conduit to it for most non-Texas senators, their only access to this money they might need badly one day—was Lyndon Johnson.

Lyndon was the guy to see if you wanted to get a bill off the Calendar, Lyndon was the guy to see if you were having trouble getting it passed in the House, Lyndon was the guy to see for campaign funds. There wasn't anything Lyndon was using these facts for as yet. But in ways not yet visible, power was starting to accumulate around him—ready to be used.

WITH HIS COLLEAGUES, still, no favor was too small for Johnson to perform, no favor too big. Nothing was too much trouble. In March, 1952, Harry Byrd's thirty-five-year-old daughter, Westwood, died after falling from her horse during a fox hunt. Her funeral was to be held in Winchester, Virginia, near the Byrd family home, Rosemont. Byrd had always treated Johnson with notable reserve, a reserve that sometimes seemed to border on dislike, and Winchester was seventy-two miles from Washington, but Johnson decided to attend.

Not wanting to go alone, he persuaded Warren Magnuson to accompany him, telling Maggie he would pick him up at the Shoreham and drive him down. When the morning of the funeral dawned with heavy rain, Magnuson tried to demur, but Johnson told him he had no choice but to go, that "everyone in the Senate is going to be there—including the Republicans."

But, as Lyndon Johnson was to report to Horace Busby when he telephoned him later that day, "You know how many United States senators were there? Two! Maggie and me!" When he saw that, he told Busby, he had "almost got cold feet" and decided it might be better to simply turn around and go home. But he stayed, and he and Magnuson stood in the cemetery, holding their hats in their hands in the rain, on the other side of the grave from the Byrd family, directly across from the Senator, whose head was bowed in grief. And suddenly, while the minister was reading the service, Harry Byrd looked up and saw them. "He looked at us, and then he looked back at me," Johnson told Busby. "I don't know what that look meant, but I'll bet a dollar to a dime that was a very important look."

BECAUSE JOHNSON WAS WHIP, he had a reason for doing what before he had needed excuses for doing: for meeting and talking with other senators, for making friends with them, for selling himself, man to man, one on one.

He sold on the Senate floor. No longer did he have to sit at his desk in the

Chamber with only Horace Busby for company, hoping that some senator would "come by and say something to him." Senators wanting information, senators wanting favors—he had plenty of senators coming by to say something to him now. And he made the most of the opportunity.

It wasn't only senators from his own party who came by. During his early days in the Senate, Republican leaders had ignored him; he had not been important enough. Now, however, he was Assistant Democratic Leader, and often in charge of the Democratic side of the floor. Most Democrats ridiculed the Republican Leader, Kenneth Wherry of Nebraska, one of Dean Acheson's "primitives," for his malapropisms on the Senate floor ("Indigo China"; the "Chief Joints of Staff"; India's fierce soldiers were "gherkins"; not infrequently he would refer to a colleague as "the senator from junior"), and were careful to keep out of his way, not only because in private life Wherry was an undertaker who loved his work, and if one were not careful, one found oneself listening to unpleasantly intimate details of the embalming process, but because so intense was Wherry's "hatred" for Democrats that he was likely to take offense at some innocuous remark a Democratic senator made in conversation, and, when he was thus offended, he would delight in objecting to, and thereby blocking, the offender's most precious private bills. Several older senators advised Johnson to avoid Wherry. But avoidance would not suit Johnson's purposes; instead, he threw himself in Wherry's path as often as possible, employing on him his customary techniques—as Alfred Steinberg was to write: "Johnson made it a point to be diffident in Wherry's presence"—and demonstrating that their effectiveness was bipartisan. Wherry began to wander across the center aisle to talk to Johnson with evident fondness. And when during an evening session convened to pass a Truman Administration bill, Wherry announced that he was going to block it by objecting to every private bill on the Calendar to stall the Senate and block consideration of the President's measure, Johnson, who had one of the private bills, approached the Nebraskan and said, in a tone that a listener described as "a plea to a superior": "You know how I never do anything except Senate work." Tonight, he said, he had made an exception and had promised to go to one of Gwen Cafritz's dinner parties. "So couldn't you just let my one little bill go through?" Acquiescing with a smile, Wherry added, "I'd rather do business with you than anybody else on your side, Lyndon." Sometimes, in fact, Lyndon Johnson would even have a conversation with Bob Taft. In McFarland's absence, Johnson would be sitting in the Leader's front-row seat on the center aisle. Taft, managing some piece of legislation on the floor, would sit at the Republican first desk directly across the aisle—temptingly near. At first, the proximity did Johnson no good; the dour Taft resisted every Johnson device to draw him into conversation. So Johnson came up with a ploy irresistible unless Taft wanted to be blatantly discourteous. Leaning across the center aisle, holding a copy of the bill that was under discussion, Johnson would whisper that he had forgotten his eyeglasses, and, with an apology for his constant forgetfulness, would ask Taft to read a particular paragraph to him. Taft would do so, Johnson would be very grateful, and brief exchanges sometimes ensued. Although Johnson wasn't close to the key Republican yet, he was getting closer.

He sold in the Democratic cloakroom, where the now-familiar tableau was still being repeated almost every day—Walter George pontificating from an easy chair, Lyndon Johnson, in the adjoining easy chair, listening reverently. Chatting with other Big Bulls in the cloakroom, often in similar, one-on-one conversations in adjoining armchairs or on a sofa, Johnson's tone was as soft and calm as ever, his attitude as humble. Advice was still being sought: "I need your counsel on something," or "I want to draw on your wisdom on something," or "I need the counsel of a wise old head here." Assistance was still being offered—with Senator Byrd, for example, assistance in counting. The Virginia squire was the most fervent of believers in a conservative economic policy, and when he was pushing a tax or budget proposal, he was anxious to know what the vote would be, but, patrician to the core, he had never been able to bring himself to ask a colleague how he planned to vote. After Johnson became whip, Byrd got this information without asking; Johnson had Bobby Baker ask, and then would relay the finding to Byrd—always offhandedly, subtly, as if he didn't know how anxious Byrd was.

And in the cloakroom now, there was also, sometimes, a new tableau. Lyndon Johnson would be standing in the center of the long, narrow space between the couches. Senators wanting favors or information would be coming up to him, Bobby Baker would be darting to his side, whispering something in his ear, darting away again, working the telephones. Often, the Assistant Leader would be holding one of the long Senate tally sheets, and he would be writing numbers on it; sometimes, a telephone page would run up to him excitedly, saying that the White House was on the phone; Johnson would go over to one of the booths, take the call, and report what the numbers were. And, more and more frequently—when he was talking not with George or Byrd, but with one of the less powerful senators—as he talked, one of Lyndon Johnson's long arms would come up and drape itself over his colleague's shoulders, in warm camaraderie.

If the other arm wasn't gesturing, it stayed by his side. In 1951 and 1952, Lyndon Johnson wasn't grabbing lapels.

Not yet.

AND AS, more and more frequently, senators needing something dropped by his office, he sold there, too. There the subject was politics and only politics, for to many senators, including the host, politics was the most important thing in life, and even senators who regarded themselves as experts on politics came to realize that Lyndon Johnson was worth listening to. When senators returned to Washington after a recess to report, in relation to the President's constantly fluctuating popularity, "Harry's up" or "Harry's down," Johnson's explanation of the trend was so cogent that senators would repeat it to others as if it had been their own. When Truman offered to back Eisenhower for the Democratic nomination, and when Eisenhower refused and then resigned from NATO, and speculation arose that he would seek the GOP nomination against Taft, Johnson always seemed to know the inside story. When speculation arose as to when Congress would adjourn for the year, it was Johnson who had the best overview of the business that still needed to be transacted—and how long it would take. When discussions of strategy arose, "Johnson would say, If you do *x*, then so-and-so will do *y*, and then such and such is likely to happen." To Lyndon Johnson, some of his colleagues were beginning to realize, politics was a chess game, and he had the ability to see quite a few moves ahead. "Sometimes it was just amazing to listen to him," Stuart Symington says.

Amazing, and, in Elizabeth Rowe's word, *fun*.

Lyndon Johnson's sentences were the sentences of a man with a remarkable gift for words, not long words but evocative, of a man with a remarkable gift for images, homey images of a vividness that infused the sentences with drama. A special interest group—organized labor in Texas, say—was never merely weak, it was "not much stronger than a popcorn fart." In the Johnsonian lexicon, a House-Senate joint committee was not merely a meaningless legislative exercise; "Hell," he would say, "a joint committee's as useless as tits on a bull." About a Republican senator expounding on NATO, he said, "He doesn't know any more about NATO than an old maid does about fucking." He would say that one man was "as wise as a tree full of owls," that another was "as busy as a man with one hoe and two rattlesnakes." Glancing out the window of 231, he would say, "It's raining as hard as a cat pissing on a flat rock." Ridiculing a Republican senator who thought he was making a national reputation with his expertise on economics, he said, "Making a speech on economics is a lot like pissing down your leg. It may seem hot to you, but it never does to anyone else."

And, of course, the sentences would often be strung together in stories, many of them set in the Hill Country. They were about drunks, and about preachers—there was one about the preacher who at a rural revival meeting was baptizing converts in a creek near Johnson City and became overenthusiastic. One teenage boy was immersed for quite a long time, and when his head was lifted out of the water, one of the congregation called out from the creek bank, "Do you believe?" The boy said, "I believe," and the preacher promptly put his head under again. Again, when he emerged, someone shouted out, "Do you believe?" and again the boy said, gasping this time, "I believe." Down he went again, and this time, when the preacher lifted his head up, someone shouted, "What do you believe?"

"I believe this son of a bitch is trying to drown me," the boy said.

Then there was the preacher who became irritated because every time he came to Johnson City, one farmer would sit in the front row, promptly go to sleep, and snore very loudly through the preacher's sermon. "He finally got tired of it," Johnson would say, "and decided to play a little joke on this farmer, and while he was sleeping, he said in a rather low voice, 'All of you people who want to go to heaven, please stand,' and everybody stood except the fellow in the front who was sleeping. And when they sat down, the preacher said in a very loud voice, 'Now all of you folks that want to go to hell, please stand,' and that stirred the fellow, and he waked up, and he heard the preacher say, 'Please stand,' so he jumped up, and he looked around and saw that no one else was standing with him, and he said, 'Preacher, I don't know what you're voting on, but you and I seem to be the only two people for it.' "

And the stories were about himself. An unhappy childhood can be a novelist's capital, and it was Lyndon Johnson's capital, too. If he was as sensitive as a novelist in reading other men, he was as vivid as a novelist in depicting the hardships of his youth, in describing the blisters he got from chopping cotton ("The skin would come off your fingers like a glove," he would say, seeming to peel off the skin from his fingers as he did so), or the Hill Country farm wives ("Those ol' women—their faces jes' like prunes from the sun"), or in talking about his family's poverty. And he embellished his stories with a license so broad it might have been literary. "He frequently talked about the things that they didn't have when he was a young boy," George Smathers recalls. "They didn't have firewood on certain occasions when they would get cold. I remember one time when we were in Florida and it suddenly turned cold. We were out on a boat and we couldn't get warm, and I remember Johnson saying something to the effect that 'I haven't been this cold since I was a kid living back on the Pedernales.' I said, 'My God, did it get this cold?' 'Oh, sure it got this cold,' but, he said, 'the thing about it was we didn't even have heat of any kind. We just had to huddle up around whatever firewood we could gather.' He said, 'That was pretty tough getting warm when six of you were trying to back up to one fire.' He would talk about things like that." No such scene had ever occurred in the Johnson home, poor though it was, but the description of it, and of other exaggerated scenes of his boyhood poverty, had the desired effect. It was, Smathers says, because of "things like that" that "I think he was very much inspired to lift himself and his family out of those conditions."

And few novelists could have been more perceptive in their insights into human nature.

One afternoon in Johnson's office he told a story about "the judge down in Texas during the Depression."

"They called him up one night—this [state] senator did, and said, 'Judge, we just abolished your court.'

"He said, 'Well, why'd you abolish my court?'

"The senator said, 'Well, we got to consolidate the courts for economy reasons, and yours was the last one *cre*-ated.'

" 'Well,' he said, 'you didn't do it without a hearing, did you?'

"The senator said, 'Yes, we had a hearing.'

" 'Well, who the devil would testify *my* court ought to be abolished?'

" 'Well,' he said, 'the head of the State Bar Association.'

"The judge said, 'Let me tell you about the head of the State Bar Association. He's a shyster lawyer, and his daddy ahead of him was.' "

At this point, the men listening to Lyndon Johnson started to smile, but he had only begun.

" 'Well, the mayor of the city came down and testified against you.'

" 'Well,' the judge said, 'let me tell you about that mayor. He stole his way into office. He padded the ballot boxes. He counted 'em twice. Who else testified?'

" 'Well,' the senator said, 'the banker.'

" 'Well, he's been charging usurous rates jest like his daddy and his grand-daddy ahead of him did.' "

The men in Lyndon Johnson's office would be laughing now, as he paused. Then he resumed. The state senator, he said, now told the judge, " 'Well, Judge, I don't think we ought to talk any longer. You're gettin' your blood pressure up, and you're all excited, and it's late tonight. I just thought I'd tell you that the Legislature has adjourned. Somebody *did* offer an amendment to abolish your court, but we didn't have a hearing—I was just kidding you— and nobody came down and testified against you at all. But I fought the amendment and killed it, and the bill's gone to the Governor, and he's signed it, and you're safe, and I just thought I'd call you up and make you feel better.' The judge said, 'Thank you, Senator, but *why* did you make me say those *ugly* things about three of the best friends any man ever had?' " As Johnson leaned back in his chair, his feet up, his arm holding the glass out for a refill, his listeners would be roaring with laughter.

MOST OF THE STORIES WERE, of course, about politics. They were about political history, about scenes he had witnessed, or, to be more precise, that he said he had witnessed: about the scene in Sam Rayburn's office when the call came that FDR was dead; about Huey Long, angered by the dirty campaign that the Arkansas political machine was waging in 1932 against elderly Hattie Caraway, the only woman senator at the time, shouting on the floor of the Senate (Johnson said he had seen this scene from the gallery), "I'm going down to Arkansas and pull those big bullies off that poor old woman's neck." Or they were about current political situations—he seemed to have a story apropos every one. Once a group of senators were talking about a colleague who might have had trouble winning re-election except that his opponent was as inept a campaigner as he was, and Johnson said, "That reminds me of the fellow down in Texas who says to his friend, 'Earl, I am thinking about running for sheriff against Uncle Jim Wilson. What do you think?' His friend says, 'Well, it depends on which of you sees the most people. If you see the most, Uncle Jim will win. If he sees the most, you will win.' "

Johnson's gift for mimicry made his listeners *see* the characters he was describing, Huey Long or Harry Truman or FDR; his big, ungainly frame brought to life his preachers and drunks and good-ol'-boy Hill Country ranchers. There was a natural rhythm in his words that drew his listeners into the story, caught them up in it, a rough rhetoric that nonetheless relied on devices such as parallel construction that might have been used by a highly educated orator, as well as the timing—unhurried, perfect—of a master narrator. And as Lyndon Johnson spoke, his face spoke, too, expressions chasing themselves across it with astonishing rapidity; his huge, mottled hands spoke, too, palms turned up in entreaty or down in dismissal, forefinger or fist punching the air for emphasis, hands and fingers not only punctuating the words but reinforcing them. He had what Busby called "the schoolteacher habit of laying his fingers down to make his points—one, two, three." And, of course, his piercing dark eyes, those Bunton eyes, the eyes that the Hill Country said "talked"—they were speaking, too. His whole body spoke, with expressive posture and gestures; once, he was telling a few senators about a horrible embarrassment that had occurred to Bob Kerr, who maintained that he was a teetotaler, and whose political support in Oklahoma was indeed heavily dependent on the temperance vote in a largely dry state. Kerr, giving a barbecue in Washington, had had several steers butchered on his ranch and flown up to provide the meat, but a typographical error in the Associated Press dispatch on the event had informed Oklahomans that Kerr had had several "beers" flown up. And, as Johnson got to that point in the story, his face breaking into a wide grin, he threw up both arms and ducked behind them in a boxer's defensive gesture against a big punch. Afternoon after afternoon, the staff in the outer office of Suite 231 would hear warm, delighted laughter from behind the closed door of Johnson's private office. "People like to laugh, and he made the senators laugh," Warren Woodward says. "So it was just natural that they liked Mr. Johnson."

And Lyndon Johnson's stories did more than merely charm his listeners. "I like to make points with jokes," he would say, and he was very effective doing so, so effective that Evans and Novak were to speak of his "genius for analogy." To emphasize the importance of the Democrats presenting their image as a compassionate party, he would tell a story that showed that the GOP's image was quite different, saying that a Texan who needed a heart transplant was given his choice of three hearts: one from a healthy twenty-three-old skiing champion who had just been killed in an avalanche; one from a healthy twenty-year-old football player who had just died of a football injury. "Of course," the surgeon added, "there's also this seventy-nine-year-old Republican banker who's just passed away." The man thought a moment, and said he would take the banker's heart. When the surgeon asked why, the man said, "I just wanted to make sure I was getting a heart that had never been used."

18

The Johnson Ranch

DURING THESE TWO YEARS—1951 and 1952—Lyndon Johnson was trying to make something out of nothing in Texas, too. He was trying to make the Pedernales Valley "Johnson Country" again.

There was a lot of Johnson sweat in that valley—and a lot of Johnson tears. In the 1860s and '70s, the Johnson Ranch had been the largest on the Pedernales, and indeed the largest in that whole area of central Texas, its corrals stretching for miles along the northern bank of the little river. The original Johnson brothers, Sam Ealy and Tom, who had ridden into the Hill Country determined to make themselves "the richest men in Texas," had seemed for a while on the way to realizing that goal, driving huge herds north to Abilene and returning with their saddlebags filled with gold, with which they assembled even larger herds and bought land not only along the Pedernales but in Austin and Fredericksburg as well. But the last of those drives had been three-quarters of a century before. Sam and Tom were Johnsons—romantics, unbusinesslike and impractical, dreamers of big dreams, dreamers unwilling to be bothered with details, and in the Hill Country's opinion, too "soft" for that hard land. In a very short period of time—two or three years of cattle-killing drought, Comanche horse-stealing raids, and disastrously unlucky cattle drives—they had lost everything. Tom died in 1877, according to family legend flat broke. Sam had married a Bunton, and that saved him from his brother's fate. Eliza Bunton was a tall woman with "raven hair, piercing black eyes and magnolia-white skin" who was not only one of the very few women to ride on the long cattle drives north through Indian territory but who rode, rifle in hand, out ahead of the herd to scout. She was known for the canny bargaining with which she sold her eggs and chickens, and for an expression she was given to repeating, an expression that might have been the Buntons' motto: "Charity begins at home." In 1887 Eliza and Sam Ealy had scraped together enough money to move back to their beloved Pedernales, to a 433-acre tract, on which they raised a few cows but mostly cotton, near the land that had once been the Johnson Ranch. In August, 1907, their eldest son, Sam Ealy Johnson Jr., had brought his bride, Rebekah Baines of Fredericksburg, to this new "Johnson Ranch," to a little "dog-run" cabin, two boxlike rooms on either side of a breezeway—not far from his parents' house. Their first child, Lyndon, was born there a year later, and the family lived there until 1913, when they moved fourteen miles down the river into Johnson City, an "island town" cut off from the rest of the world, a tiny huddle of houses in the midst of a vast and empty landscape. Sam Ealy Jr., the idealist and romantic—in the Hill Country's opinion too much a Johnson with not enough of the tough Bunton practicality—dreamed of expanding this holding, of re-creating the great "Johnson Ranch." When his parents died, their other children wanted to sell the 433 acres, for which they had been offered a good price, but Sam Jr. wouldn't hear of selling the family heritage, and to keep it in the family, to keep his dream alive, he outbid a wealthy in-law, paying far too much for the property, and in 1919 moved back to his parents' house, planning to raise cotton for a few years and then to start up a herd again. But in that valley the reality was the soil, which wasn't as fertile as Sam Ealy guessed it was, not fertile enough to support cotton or cattle, and the reality was the weather, which didn't produce enough rainfall to support either. And cotton prices fell instead of staying high, as he had been sure they would. During the years in which Lyndon was twelve and thirteen and fourteen years old, his father was going broke on the Pedernales. These were the years during which, Lyndon was to say, his family fell so rapidly "from the A's to the F's"—during which the Johnsons "dropped to the bottom of the heap." His father lost the 433 acres in 1922 and fell into debt so deep that he would never be able to pay it off; he and Rebekah, and their five children— Lyndon, his younger brother, Sam Houston Johnson, and three sisters—moved back to Johnson City, into a house which he was able to keep only because his brothers, out of charity, paid the interest on the mortgage. During the intervening years, there was no Johnson Ranch on the Pedernales. When Lyndon and Lady Bird were in Texas, they lived in Austin, in a house on Dillman Street.

Now, early in 1951, Lyndon was told that his Aunt Frank—one of his father's sisters, who had been given a man's name because her parents had been hoping for a son, and who had married a prosperous attorney, Clarence Martin—wanted to sell her house on the Pedernales, which was on a 233-acre piece of land that adjoined the farm that Lyndon's father had lost.

The Martin house resonated with reminders of the Johnsons' terrible fall. A narrow two-story stone structure, originally built by a German family in about 1893, it had been bought by Martin in 1906. He was a prominent figure in the Hill Country, a member of the Texas Legislature and then a District Court judge, and he had tried to pull his brother-in-law, Sam Ealy Jr., who was two years older than he, along in his footsteps, encouraging him to run for the seat he had held in the Legislature, and, after Sam was elected to the first of his six terms, helping him in his first big legislative project, the acquisition and preservation of the Alamo. As the Johnson house, only a wood dwelling, reflected Sam's failures, becoming more and more run-down, the Martin house, just up the road, grew grander and grander with white-frame additions to the stone structure: a large master bedroom, a music room, even an indoor bathroom, one of the first in the area, so that the Johnsons felt more and more like poor relations. The house was the gathering place for family get-togethers at Christmas and Thanksgiving and Easter; at Christmas, each child would have to stand on the raised hearth of the big fireplace in Judge Martin's living room and perform—sing a song, do a dance, or give a speech (in Lyndon's case it was always a speech)—before he was allowed to take his present from the big pile in front of the fireplace. Feeling that Frank patronized her, Rebekah deeply resented both her sister-in-law and the judge. After Sam, forced out of the Legislature by his need to earn a living, had had to move his family back into Johnson City, they would still drive out to the Martins' for family gatherings, and when Sam was penniless, Judge Martin got him a job with the state—a two-dollar-a-day job as a road inspector. The Martin house "was the *big* house on the river," Lyndon's cousin Ava Johnson Cox would recall. "That was how we thought of it. When we were children, Lyndon used to say to me, 'Someday, I'm going to buy the big house.' " After Judge Martin died in 1936, the house fell into neglect and disrepair. (The Martins' only child, Lyndon's cousin Tom, died of a heart attack in 1948, at the age of fifty-four—yet another Johnson male dead young of a heart attack.) In 1951, Aunt Frank was seventy-eight years old and ailing. Anxious to move into Johnson City, where medical help would be more readily available, she was looking for a buyer for her home. One weekend, when Stuart and Evie Symington had joined Lyndon and Lady Bird for a few days on the Wesley West Ranch, Lyndon suddenly said—without any advance notice to his wife—"Tomorrow Lady Bird and I are going down to look at a piece of property I'm thinking of buying. Would you like to go?"

Driving from the West Ranch, Lyndon stopped the car at the top of a rise, and the two couples got out and looked down. Below them was the valley, with the little river meandering its way along in gentle curves. To their left as they looked at the valley was an unpainted, sagging three-room shack, not the house in which Lyndon had grown up—that had been torn down not long after the Johnsons moved out—but a structure that had been built almost on the same site, largely with boards from the old house. To the right—about a half mile to the right, also along the narrow, graveled Austin–Fredericksburg road—was the white-painted, gabled Martin house. Green meadows sloped from both houses down to the river. At the river's edge was an orchard of about two hundred pecan trees, and on the old Johnson property a grove of wide-spreading live oak trees, their leaves a bright dark green against the paler green of the grass and the blue of the water. In their shade stood a group of small pink granite tombstones—the old Johnson family cemetery. Other live oaks—some of them two centuries old—dotted the meadows, as did a few grazing cows.

Beyond the river, the gray-and-white spire of a little country church rose in the distance. It was a peaceful, bucolic scene, but when they drove down and entered the Martin house, Lady Bird had no difficulty understanding why Aunt Frank wanted to sell it. After years of neglect, the rooms were dark and dirty, the floors sagged; "to make the picture complete," she was to recall, a colony of bats was living in the chimney. "It looked like a Charles Addams cartoon of a haunted house." She knew she didn't want to buy it. "Oh my Lord, no!" she thought. "I knew the old stone ranch house would take *so* much work to fix up. I could hardly bear the thought of it!" Evie Symington was to say that when they walked in, "Bird seemed appalled, and frankly I shared her feeling." But, Lady Bird was to recall, "To my horror I heard Lyndon say, 'Let's buy it!' "

"How could you do this to me? How could you?" Lady Bird screamed when they got home. In subsequent conversations with her husband, she tried to be firm. "You're not going to get me out there with all those bats!" she said. Her wishes received their customary consideration, and a week or so later, the Johnsons purchased the ranch, paying Aunt Frank twenty thousand dollars, and giving her the use for her lifetime of the Johnson house in Johnson City.

Almost as soon as the closing took place—on May 5, 1951—it became apparent to Lady Bird that her husband had bigger plans. He began talking about buying other properties along the banks of the Pedernales, not only the adjoining ranch on which he had been born and raised—watching his father go broke—but others beyond it, stretching toward Johnson City, which would make him the owner of a substantial part of the original Johnson Ranch. He quickly purchased one thirty-acre tract, but the rest of these plans would not be realized for some years, because the owners didn't want to sell, not even the owner of the adjoining land. The sagging shack made from the boards of his birthplace was being rented to a family of Mexican field-workers. But Lyndon changed the name of the Martin property—to the "LBJ Ranch"—and began to transform it.

Knowing what needed to be done on a ranch in that land of alternating drought and floods, of worn-out eroded soil, wasn't hard. Water had to be provided, and controlled, the soil had to be restored to its earlier richness. But doing it was hard—impossible, in fact—for most Hill Country ranchers, for doing it was expensive, costing far more than most ranchers, including Lyndon Johnson's father, could even think of spending. Sam Johnson had never had enough money to do it, in large part because of the way he viewed his government position. Among the reasons—optimism, an overly romantic view of life—that this idealistic Populist had gone broke was his passionate belief that the influence he had as an elected official was something to be used to help people caught in "the tentacles of circumstance," and not only to get a road built for them or to get them government loans for seed when they were trapped by recession, but to help them personally. To secure elderly men the pensions they deserved as Civil War veterans or Indian fighters, Sam would spend a lot of time in libraries searching through old files to find their service records, and more time driving them, over rutted Hill Country roads, into Austin to apply for their pensions, and then driving them home—all to the neglect of his own affairs.

Lyndon Johnson, of course, had an additional use for political influence: to amass wealth—first to obtain favorable rulings from the FCC that made KTBC a dramatically more effective place on which to advertise, and then to let businessmen and their attorneys and lobbyists who needed favors from the government know that the way to enlist his influence on their behalf was to purchase advertising time. So successfully had he made such sales that by 1951, that station—the station his wife had bought in 1943 for $17,500—was earning the Johnsons more than $3,000 per week. That was an enormous amount of money in the impoverished Hill Country—enough to let him do what needed to be done on the ranch. And in 1951, he and Lady Bird—and a coterie of very hard-eyed Washington lawyers—were already looking toward the acquisition of a Johnson television station (they would buy it in 1952) that would multiply those profits.

Water was a key—water of which there was usually too little in the Hill Country, and sometimes, all at once, too much. It was a land in which, Lyndon was to remember, sometimes "the Pedernales used to run dry as a bone, not a trickle," while crops and cattle died under a burning sun, and then suddenly heavy thunderstorms would cause fierce "gully washers" to sweep down ravines and riverbeds, washing away crops and precious topsoil, destroying barns and hard-earned farm equipment.

The answer, for every farmer or rancher along the Hill Country's little rivers, was to build low dams across them. The lake that would form behind a dam would provide water in times of drought, and in times of flood would hold at least some of the water that would otherwise leap the banks and wash away everything in its path. Obvious though the answer was, almost no dams were built in the Hill Country, for, as the first foreman on the new LBJ Ranch, Oliver Lindig, was to explain, a dam might cost ten thousand dollars or more, "a very expensive proposition" for someone trying to get money out of the Hill Country. But Lyndon Johnson was getting his money out of a radio station, so it wasn't an expensive proposition for him. He tried nonetheless to bargain down Marcus Burg, a Stonewall contractor—"He tried to talk like he was a poor boy," Burg recalls—until that stubborn Dutchman told him to "get someone else to do it." Eventually he agreed to Burg's price, and for two weeks Burg and a crew of six men stretched a nine-foot-high concrete dam across the Pedernales below the Martin house while Lyndon Johnson sat on the riverbank watching and chatting. The dam was "the first thing . . . we built," Lady Bird was to recall. "Then the road and all the irrigation tanks followed in quick succession before we did anything to the house." With the dam in place, enough pressure was created so that pumps could pump water up to irrigate the fields, and irrigation lines, eighty-foot-long sections of lightweight pipe, perforated so that water sprayed out either side, were linked together and run from the newly formed lake up into the fields on the hills behind the Martin house.

With enough water for the soil, it was possible to try to restore its fertility. When Lindig, who had a college degree in agricultural management (that was one reason Johnson hired him), arrived at the ranch in 1952, he saw how difficult this would be. "This was old, old soil," he would recall. "Highly eroded soil. Hill Country farming was a very tough business. A lot of restoration would be necessary." But he also saw that his new employer was determined to do whatever was necessary. Crops that would build up nutrients in the soil were planted over the two hundred acres and then plowed under so that the nutrients would work more efficiently. And so that the invigorated soil would not be washed away in those thunderstorms, big bulldozers and other earth-moving equipment were brought in to terrace and contour-plow the fields. This was also a "very expensive proposition" in Hill Country terms—but not when measured against a radio station's income. The fields were then planted with a type of grass called "coastal Bermuda," which was very costly but grew very fast and put down long roots to hold the soil. And finally cattle—only thirty at first— were brought in to graze, and there was a new Johnson herd on the Pedernales.

An Austin architect, Max Brooks, was designing the restoration of the "haunted house." Whatever her original misgivings about the project, Lady Bird had as usual dismissed them in the interests of what her husband wanted. "The ranch is Lyndon's spiritual home . . . so I have a tenderness for it," she was to say. "His roots are there for three generations. After I came to sense how completely Lyndon was immersed in the rocks and hills and live oaks of this, his own native land . . . I gradually began to get wrapped up in it myself." "Horror turned to blessing and we put hand and heart to it to build it into a small, productive, operating ranch." The heart of the house was the old section with its eighteen-inch-thick stone walls and the enormous fireplace, large enough to hold four-foot-long logs, on whose elevated stone hearth the children had once performed. Into this living room Lady Bird put antiques, and functional and roomy sofas and chairs—one with a big pillow on which was embroidered, in big letters, "LBJ"—and paintings of Hill Country scenes. And one touch that was particularly her own: a photograph of Sam Rayburn; if a guest failed to comment on the photograph, she would do so, pointing out that "there is only one picture of a person in this room." New floors and ceilings were installed in that section, and in the white-frame additions that were already there, and new additions, painted white, were built out from it, rambling off in all directions; in a year or two, there were two master bedrooms downstairs, one for the Johnsons, one for guests, and five bedrooms—each with its own bathroom— upstairs, for guests and staff members. By 1952, down on the north bank of the Pedernales, only a half mile from the little weather-beaten shack reminiscent of the house in which Lyndon Johnson had been born, was a very different house: large, gracious, impressive, pristine white, surrounded by green fields bordered by pristine white fences. "We love it," Mrs. Johnson would say with a happy smile. Guests had started to arrive from all over the country, to be served ribs or large hamburgers by white-hatted chef Walter Jetton, "the Leonard Bernstein of the barbecue": wanting the hamburgers to be shaped like Texas, Lyndon had had a mold made in that shape, but he had come to feel that the shape was too asymmetrical and at lunch would wander among his visitors, telling them to "eat the Panhandle first."

The host would take them on tours, gunning his big car down rutted dirt paths or across fields at speeds which kept the occupants jouncing in the seats. He would drive the car right up to cows to stir them into activity; if one remained lying down, he would honk his horn at it and gun the engine, and if it still wouldn't get up, he would nudge it with the car's fenders until it did. He would show his guests flocks of wild turkeys strutting across a ridge; herds of white-tailed deer—once a visitor counted thirty-five in a single herd—would flee gracefully over a hill as the car approached. "Now look across yonder," he would say. "See that church steeple over there in the valley? Where you going to find a prettier view than that?" His initials were on everything: from the pillow in the living room to a flag he designed, and which hung, beneath the flags of the United States and Texas, from an extremely tall flagpole in front of the house, a deep blue pennant with a white "LBJ" in the center, surrounded by a circle of white stars. On the two big stone pillars that flanked the entrance to the ranch were two big "LBJ"s in wrought-iron script. And on the day Marcus Burg laid the last concrete in the wide walkway from the entrance gates up to the front door, Lyndon Johnson couldn't contain himself. "Do you have a long nail?" he asked Burg. Burg handed him one, and with it, in the still-wet concrete, Lyndon Johnson scratched, in large sprawling letters, "Welcome—LBJ Ranch." Then, giving Burg a hug that astonished that phlegmatic man, he bent down again and wrote in small letters in a corner: "Built by Marcus Burg."

Lyndon Johnson was very proud of his ranch. The Symingtons were annual visitors until there was a break between the two senators in 1956, and after the ranch had become an impressive showplace, they could understand Johnson's pride. The pride was, to this sophisticated and wealthy couple, less easy to understand in 1951 and 1952, "when it wasn't much."

ON SEPTEMBER 16, 1952, with Lyndon away in South Texas, there would be a violent reminder of how destructive nature could be in the Hill Country. A line of fierce thunderstorms rolling across the vast Edwards Plateau caused what old-timers called a "hundred-year flood," the highest waters in a century. Marcus Burg's dam couldn't come near containing the Pedernales. That morning, when Lady Bird had driven Lynda Bird, then eight years old, across a little concrete bridge to catch a bus to her school in Johnson City, the river had been rising, and the rains were getting heavier. Knowing the bridge would soon be under water, Lady Bird had telephoned Lyndon's cousin Ava, who lived in the town, to pick up Lynda. The water rose high over the dam and over the shore—washing away every one of the Johnsons' two hundred pecan trees (the live oaks, whose powerful roots stretch out horizontally far in either direction, held firm, as they had been doing for two centuries). It crept up the sloping meadow toward the Johnsons' house. The telephone went dead. At 8:45 that evening, the lights went off and the electric clock stopped. The power line had been swept away. "Lucy and I sat in the house and watched topsoil from our neighbors' farms just float on by, right out to the Gulf of Mexico, and livestock—cattle and horses—were swept away, too," Lady Bird was to remember.

Lyndon had contacted Arthur Stehling, who arrived at the Johnsons' after a horseback ride from Fredericksburg, saying that he had been sent to take one of their cars out of the garage and drive Lady Bird and Lucy to a ranch on higher ground; it was a harrowing trip along a washed-out road lined with uprooted trees. Returning home the next day after the waters had receded, Lyndon found a bright spot in the situation. Wesley West had told him that building a dam would be useless because it would have to be anchored in the river's banks and therefore would be washed away in a flood. Burg had assured Johnson that the dam would hold—and it had. When West telephoned the Johnson Ranch now, and asked Lyndon, "Well, where's your dam now?" Johnson was able to reply: "Just where the Dutchman said it would be!"

THE FLOOD was a happy memory for Lucy, too. When the lights went out, Lady Bird had lit a coal-oil lamp and read her stories. And, Lucy was to recall, "my mother heated up a can of tomato soup and spread peanut butter on saltine crackers. It is the only time in my life I remember her cooking just for me. There was no one there—no staff, no other family—except the two of us. I thought it was great fun."

AS SOON AS THE LBJ RANCH was in good enough shape to be shown to journalists from Washington and New York, Johnson began to invite them down, because he wanted to use the ranch to create a picture of himself in the public mind—the picture of a self-made man who had pulled himself up in life by his bootstraps, of a man who, no matter how high he had risen, still had his roots firmly in his native soil. He wanted his image to be that of a westerner, or to be more precise a southwesterner—a Texan; a true Texas image: a rancher with a working, profitable ranch.

The image was fashioned with his customary skill. He soon had a horse—a tall Tennessee walking horse named Silver Jay—and he liked to pose astride him, wearing or waving his big gray Stetson. His clothing was in keeping—tan twill and cowboy boots, although sometimes, freed of Washington restraint, he would show up for lunch or dinner clad in a cardinal-red lounging suit or in one that led a journalist to call him "the jolly green giant." And his tours of the ranch helped—showing off his crops and cattle to reporters while dispensing western wisdom and witticisms. He had purchased a prize bull named Friendly Mixer to sire the herd he was planning on. Driving a visitor around the ranch, he would get out of the car, and, walking over to the bull, would note his good points ("Look at that flat back") and heavy withers. "But that's not why I bought him," he would say with a grin, lifting up the bull's tail to display his huge testicles. (Johnson might then be reminded of a Swedish congressman from Minnesota, Magnus Johnson, who had served with him in the House. Magnus was not too bright, Lyndon would say, and would, in a broad Swedish accent, tell how Magnus had once made a speech on the House floor in which he earnestly declared, "What we have to do is take the bull by the tail and look the situation in the face.") Driving a little further, Johnson would come to a group of steers. "You fellows know what a steer is," he would say. "That's a bull who has lost his social standing."

The tidbits of philosophy he dispensed to journalists were western philosophy. Working with nature was good for a man, particularly for a public official, he would explain. "Every man in public life should own a plot of land"—it gave him a practical knowledge of agricultural problems, and it rooted him in the realities ordinary Americans have to face. "All my life I have drawn substance from the river and from the hills of my native state," he would say. When he was in Washington, he would say, "I am lonesome for them almost constantly."

ONE KEY PART of the image—that the ranch helped him to relax and reflect, that he was a different man down there from the frenzied, driven Lyndon Johnson whom they knew in Washington—was cultivated with great assiduity. A hammock was part of it; he liked to have magazine and newspaper photographers take his picture when he was lying in it, a beatific grin on his face. "I haven't thought one time today about what would happen if Western Europe fell," he told Margaret Mayer, now working for the *Dallas Times Herald,* when she visited the ranch. "People tell me I look better than they have seen me in a long time—no circles under my eyes." As soon as he arrived, he was a happier man, he would tell reporters, because he was back among "the best people, climate and all-the-way-around best place on earth to live." He was back among friends, he would say; "I have the best neighbors anyone could ask for. Most of them lived right here when I grew up as a kid." So convincing was his performance, that Tom Wicker, who had moved from the *Winston-Salem Journal* to the *New York Times,* was only expressing the universal journalistic sentiment when he wrote, after a visit to the LBJ Ranch during Johnson's presidency, that Johnson had an "essential ease" there—"the comfort of certainty, the assurance of belonging." On the ranch, Wicker wrote, "the President is elemental in a different fashion" from what he was in Washington: "The West dominates him—this big, breezy, rough-cut man of the plains—the grass and the dust of the arid Texas hills. . . . Down on the ranch, on the old home place . . . LBJ is all wool and a yard wide. In tan twill and leather boots he is at home, at ease—serene as a restless Westerner can be."

The reality was very different, however; very different, and very sad.

There was a gully on the ranch, a deep crevasse that had been cut into the earth, and then worn deeper and deeper, by decades of heavy Hill Country thunderstorms. Beginning almost at the top of the ridge that was the ranch's northern boundary, it ran diagonally southeast across the meadows that sloped toward the Pedernales and then abruptly slashed its way straight south into the river—a ravine almost a half mile long, thirty yards wide in places, fairly shallow in some spots, but in other places, where the rains had cut not only through the soil but into the rock beneath, so deep that, Lindig recalls, "If you had elephants in there, you wouldn't have been able to see anything but their backs." Filling that ravine was a very expensive proposition. Soil—a lot of soil—had to be purchased, trucked in, then pounded down into the ravine with heavy equipment and reshaped so that grass could be planted in it so that its roots would hold the soil in place. In order for the grass to grow in that arid country, irrigation would be necessary: the laying of pipes up from the river all along the ravine's half-mile length; the use of big electric pumps that could pull the water all the way up to the ridge. But Johnson said he wanted to grow feed for his cattle and sheep in the gully, and by the time Lindig arrived, he had already filled the ravine in twice. The first time, a thunderstorm had struck before the grass could take hold, and washed all the soil down into the river; the second time, the grass had taken hold and seemed stable, but only until the "hundred-year flood." When, some weeks after the flood, Lindig arrived, the gully was as deep and as wide as ever, and Johnson told his new foreman to fill it up again.

Filling the gully wasn't necessary for any practical reason that Lindig could see, for Lyndon Johnson wasn't growing crops on the ranch to support its operation, and feed could be purchased for a fraction of the cost of filling the gully. The cost of filling it was disproportionate to other expenditures Johnson was making on the ranch grounds. But Johnson insisted that it be filled, and it was, and it washed out again. "We finally got [the erosion] stopped, but only because we ran the irrigation pipe right over into the ditch and watered it, and fertilized it, over and over until the grass got established," Lindig recalls. He couldn't understand why Johnson was so insistent on filling it, but he saw that he was; "He had this fixation about gullies," he says.

Lyndon's cousin Ava understood, however, and so did Lyndon's brother, who knew him so well, and who understood that the "most important" thing for Lyndon was "not to be like Daddy." It had been a gully—one not far from this one and very similar in length and width—that had symbolized his father's struggle to make the Johnson Ranch pay, and his failure. For Sam Johnson, it *had* been necessary to fill his gully—desperately necessary; a lot of cotton could be planted in it, and Sam needed all the cotton he could grow. Time and time again, in labor that must have been backbreaking for a man in his forties, Sam had taken a wagon down to the Pedernales, shoveled up into it the richest river-bottom soil he could find, and then shoveled the soil into the gully and planted cotton seeds in it—and every time, before the seeds could take root, a gully-washer had washed the seeds and soil away again. "He planted it and planted it," Ava was to say. "And he never got a crop out of it. Not one." For Lyndon Johnson, his ranch on the Pedernales was a place of memories. No matter where he walked, there was a reminder: the sagging "dog-run" that looked so much like the shack in which he had been born and spent much of his boyhood; the family graveyard, with the tombstones of his father and grand-father, both of whom had failed on the Pedernales; the weather-beaten little schoolhouse nearby, where as the youngest child in school he had sat on the teacher's lap (and scrawled on the blackboard, in letters as large as he could make them: "LYNDON B. JOHNSON"). The very sky was a reminder, for his first years on his ranch—1952, '53, and '54—were years of a terrible drought in central Texas; he could look up at the sky—the beautiful "sapphire" Hill Coun-try sky, that heartbreakingly empty Hill Country sky—and search for clouds that gave hope of rain, just as he had watched his father and mother look up at the sky and hope for rain.

Sometimes, he would drive into Johnson City. That little town was so unchanged; almost every house was still occupied by the same family that had been living in it when he had been growing up there, so almost every house held memories for him. Kitty Clyde Ross (now Kitty Clyde Leonard) was still living in Johnson City—Kitty Clyde, with whom, as a high school senior, Lyn-don had been "in love," but whose father was one of the merchants who had written "Please!" on the bills he sent to Sam Johnson every month and who, to break up her romance with Lyndon, had allowed another suitor to drive her around Courthouse Square in the Rosses' new Ford sedan. ("I saw how it made Lyndon feel when that big car drove by. . . . I cried for him," Ava recalls.) Tru-man Fawcett still lived in Johnson City, Truman Fawcett, who had been sitting on his uncle's porch when Lyndon walked by, and who had heard his uncle say, "He'll never amount to anything. Too much like Sam."

He had proven Johnson City wrong, had amounted to quite a lot. But memories still shadowed his time on the ranch. And there were other shadows of the past, for often he would be visited at the ranch by his mother, and his brother and sisters, who had gone through that childhood with him.

The marks of those years remained indelible on the Johnsons. In the *Family Album* she wrote after her eldest son had become a national figure, Rebekah Baines Johnson portrayed her harsh life in soft colors, but a more accurate gauge of her feelings was what she did on the day—October 24, 1937—of her husband's funeral. The night before Sam Ealy Johnson was buried in the Johnson family cemetery, she had packed her clothes and whatever else she wanted to keep, and immediately after the funeral she was driven to Austin—without returning to the house. "She went away that very night," her eldest daughter, Rebekah, was to say. After a night in Austin, she took a train to Washington, where three of her children—Lyndon, Sam Houston and Rebekah—were living, and after a month or two there came back to Texas, first to Houston for some months, then to Corpus Christi, and finally back to Austin, where she rented an apartment. She was to live in Austin for the rest of her life. If she ever lived again in the house in which she had raised her children, it was not for very long. By January of 1938, the house had been rented. In March of that year, Lyndon Johnson wrote the tenant that his mother was reluctant to sign a long lease since "there is a very slight possibility that she will want to return to Johnson City after a year's time," but that he had suggested that she sign because "I seriously doubt that she will want to move back." In fact, say both her daughter Rebekah and Sam Houston, she never did. "Mother never went back into the house after Daddy's funeral," her daughter said. Asked if that statement was to be taken literally, both she and Sam Houston said it was. "Mother never could stand Johnson City," her daughter said. Sam Ealy had died without making a will—he had very little to leave, beside his gold watch and chain*; the house was mortgaged to close to its value—and in 1940, his five children relinquished to their mother any claim they might have had to the property. In 1942, Lyndon bought it from her for a token payment of ten dollars, assuming the mortgage and tax payments; this was apparently done so that she could have the rent from the house without having to make the payments.

The complexity of the relationship between Lyndon Johnson and his mother would be demonstrated for the rest of his life; during the twenty years until she died of cancer in 1958, he would help support her, adding monthly payments to the income she received from Social Security and renting the Johnson City house, but except for very rare occasions, he wouldn't write her; if, during his youth, there had been a steady stream of letters between them— his desperate for encouragement and reassurance, hers providing them with an unstinting hand—during the years since he had first gone to Washington in 1931, the correspondence continued, but with one difference: while his mother was still writing him ("I have been highly incensed all day over Drew Pearson's hateful thrust. . . . Courage and forthrightness are synonomous with your name"; "You are a fighter, darling, you have right on your side; you are doing a

---

*Lyndon's sisters insisted it go to Sam Houston; Lucia told Lyndon, "Daddy wanted him to have it. We all know that." In 1958, however, Sam Houston gave it to Lyndon. (See *The Path to Power,* pp. 543–44.)

wonderful selfless task for your government and for humanity, so keep up a
brave heart, my wonderful son, right will triumph again! My dearest love,
Mother"), he wasn't writing her; almost all the letters—hundreds of letters—
signed by him were written by members of his staff, for a while by Herbert
Henderson, for a while by Walter Jenkins, for some years by Gene Latimer.
"He used to say, 'Write two long pages. Put in a lot of bull. Just fill it up with
everything that happened this week,' " Latimer recalls. Unlike his other correspondence, these letters were not letters he read, corrected, and sent back to a
staffer for rewriting; "He never sent any back that I remember," Latimer says,
and during his Senate years, after Latimer and Jenkins had learned to duplicate
his signature, they were often letters he didn't even sign. The staff was consci-
entious about this chore ("Next Sunday is Mother's Day. Shall I wire her a
greeting? '. . . Darling: Mother's Day just one of three sixty-five I give thanks
for you annually. Lyndon' "), but it was one in which he seemed to have very
little interest. That he saw as much of her as he did was largely due to Lady
Bird. Rebekah had been very hurt that her son's wedding had been so hastily
arranged that she was not invited to it, but Lady Bird understood her ("She was
a college graduate and accustomed to more luxuries than she had living out
there on a farm, where the going was rough"), and the two women had similar
interests; when Lyndon's mother came to Washington (the invitations were
often issued by Lady Bird), the two women would visit antique shops and go
"kinship hunting" in Virginia and Maryland. "We would case the county seat
for a good place to have lunch, and spot the antique shops, before heading into
the big old courthouse" to examine birth and marriage certificates, Lady Bird
would say. The two women became friends. "I *liked* her so much," Lady
Bird was to say. "If I had an extra hour in Austin before I had to catch a plane
or train to Washington, I would think of all the friends I could call, but I usually
decided I would rather go and see Mrs. Johnson. We would sit together and talk
about books, about household decorating, about family. We were very good
friends, and that is probably better than loving one's in-laws." Lyndon's mother
often stayed overnight at the big white ranch house. Visitors from Washington,
meeting the gracious, white-haired woman and seeing the affection with which
she treated her grandchildren, and the rapport between her and her daughter-in-
law, had a hard time understanding why, when she was around, her normally
loquacious son sometimes fell into such long silences.

HIS THREE SISTERS and his brother were sometimes at the ranch, too.
      All four had a nervousness, a fragility of temperament, that was striking to
people who met them as adults. Three of them—Sam Houston Johnson and his
two oldest sisters, Rebekah and Josefa—developed serious ulcers while they
were in their early thirties.
      Two of them—Rebekah and Lucia—were to live relatively stable lives.

Rebekah was a tense, high-strung woman; by 1950, her mother, writing about her to Lyndon, would describe her health as "highly precarious." She married Oscar Price Bobbitt, who went to work for the Johnson radio station as a salesman and eventually rose to be senior vice president of the Johnson television station. Lucia married Birge Alexander, who became area manager of the Federal Aviation Agency in Memphis.

The lives of the other two Johnson children were quite different. While Josefa, who was born in 1912, was still an undergraduate at San Marcos, bright, tall and strikingly beautiful, stories about what the Hill Country calls her "looseness" or "wildness" in sexual matters began to spread, and continued to spread after college. So did tales of her drunkenness; Arthur Stehling, the powerful Fredericksburg attorney who kept Gillespie County in line for Lyndon Johnson, was called on more than once to intercede after she had been brought to a sheriff's office or police station in some small Hill Country town because of complaints about a drunken party in a hotel or motel. She was married to an Army lieutenant colonel in 1940, and Lyndon got her a job with the Texas NYA, but the job didn't work out—that year Lyndon wrote to his mother that if Josefa refused to learn to type, other arrangements would have to be made—and neither did the marriage; by 1945, she was divorced, and more than once Horace Busby, who in 1948 was delegated to "deal with" the "Josefa situation," had to deal with the fact that she was in a hospital alcoholic ward. Fascinated by politics, she worked in Lyndon's 1948 senatorial campaign, and on the Texas Democratic Executive Committee in the 1952 presidential race, and the kind of stories that had followed her at San Marcos reemerged. Says a woman reporter who watched her at conventions and executive committee meetings in those years, "If there was a man to be picked up, Josefa picked him up." The Josefa Johnson who came to the LBJ Ranch in 1951 and 1952 was a woman with trembling hands and few traces of her former beauty, and what Horace Busby was to call "a frighteningly low opinion of herself; when someone important came into the room, sometimes she would jump up and run out as if she felt they didn't want to be bothered talking to her."

During their boyhood, there had been a great closeness between Lyndon Johnson and Sam Houston Johnson, five years younger than he, who would say that he would never forget "those wonderful conversations (monologues, really) that ran through the long Saturday afternoons and Sundays" when he would visit his big brother at San Marcos, and would sit "listening with wide-eyed admiration as my brother" talked of his political stratagems—"even now, I can still visualize him restlessly moving back and forth . . . his eyes gleaming with anticipation and his deep voice tense with emotion." This idolatry lasted into adulthood. "He worships you and will do anything for you," their mother wrote Lyndon in 1937. "You are his hero." But there was also a great competitiveness, and this, too, lasted into adulthood. Six-foot-one, very handsome and very charming, with a crooked, engaging grin, Sam Houston seemed to some friends to have a brilliant mind (Bill Deason says, "He was smarter 'n Lyndon in some respects"), particularly about politics, a field in which Sam Houston had the same ability Lyndon had—Sam Houston said they both got it from their father—to see several moves ahead on the political chessboard. "More than any man I have ever known he loved politics for its own sake," Booth Mooney was to write. "His greatest pleasure was to set up intricate, devious schemes for bringing about the discomfiture of any Texas or Washington politician who dared to oppose his brother." Graduating from San Marcos at fifteen, he received a law degree from Cumberland College in Lebanon, Tennessee, at nineteen, and it seemed for a while as if he would follow in his brother's footsteps: when in 1935 Lyndon left his job as Richard Kleberg's chief assistant to become Texas NYA director, he persuaded the Congressman to hire Sam Houston to succeed him.

But what Sam Houston made of that position was very different from what Lyndon had made of it. He loved to party, loved to drink, and to grandiosely pick up the check when he was out with friends. And he was always buying expensive clothes, for which he couldn't pay. So that he would have more money, the indulgent Kleberg had him put on the payroll of his family's King Ranch as a public relations consultant, but Sam used the money to rent an expensive apartment and hire a valet, and his debts only increased. In addition to his own money problems, Sam Houston was creating some for Kleberg. Says Russell Brown, who was a friend of both men, "He didn't pay much attention to office business. Bills would come in, and instead of methodically compiling them and getting them paid like Lyndon used to do, he would throw them away. . . . He stopped paying anybody." A school board in Kleberg's congressional district actually filed suit to force the Congressman to pay unpaid school taxes. To cover his own debts, Sam started to write checks that bounced, one, to a custom tailor in Washington, for quite a substantial amount.

Sam Houston tried but failed to become Speaker of the Little Congress, as Lyndon had been. When he lost the election, he and some friends devised an amendment to the organization's bylaws that gave "power over all social functions" to a five-man committee, which elected him chairman. He then organized a trip to New York for the organization's members, obtaining free train tickets from one lobbyist, and liquor from another. The staffers nonetheless ran up bills at New York hotels so high that they couldn't pay them, and a scandal that would have had repercussions for the staffers' congressional bosses was only narrowly averted. The money situation within Kleberg's office started to get uglier; there was at least one tailor's bill, for two hundred dollars, that Sam Houston had the Congressman pay—although some members of the Kleberg family felt the bill was for one of Sam Houston's suits. And he became involved in an angry dispute over some sexual liaison in the office—the details have been lost in time—that infuriated Kleberg's wife. Sam left Kleberg's office for a post—also arranged by Lyndon—as a regional director for the

NYA. But the same pattern—of drinking (Sam once spoke of waking up almost every morning in an "alcoholic haze") and debts and office romances that all seemed to end unpleasantly—repeated itself. Criminal charges were threatened by creditors who had gotten the bad checks. By 1940, Alvin Wirtz, then Undersecretary of the Interior, was trying to procure a job for Sam with the Federal Housing Administration in Puerto Rico to get him far enough away so that he could no longer embarrass Lyndon. "When [the proposed appointment] was announced in the paper, . . . his creditors began really protesting, and he didn't get the position," Brown recalls. ("Amusingly enough," Brown says, "he said he had made a terrible mistake giving those hot checks. He should just have charged things and not paid for them, then he couldn't have gotten into any trouble. They could just sue him but they couldn't bring criminal charges against him. But with the hot checks they could file criminal charges.") Sam was married that year, to Albertine Summers, a secretary to an Illinois congressman, and had two children, Josefa in 1941 and Sam in 1942, but there was soon a divorce—Albertine remarried—and he seemed to feel little responsibility for the children; in 1956 young Sam was watching the Democratic National Convention when the camera focused on a box reserved for Lyndon Johnson's family; Sam Houston was pointed out to the boy; it was the first time he had seen his father since infancy.

After the war, Lyndon gave Sam Houston a job ("I was just a flunky," he was to say) in his congressional office, but the drinking and irresponsibility had grown worse, and he would disappear for weeks at a time on drunken sprees. He had an affair with one of his brother's secretaries, and in April, 1948, in Biloxi, Mississippi, they had an illegitimate child, a boy who would be named Rodney. The parents had intended to put Rodney up for adoption at birth ("the 1948 campaign was coming up, and he [Sam Houston] was afraid someone would find about me," Rodney was to say), but his aunt Josefa, who was unable to bear children, said she wanted to adopt him, and she did. The Johnson family tried to conceal (not only from outsiders but from their mother) the fact that Josefa's adopted baby was actually Sam's child, but, as Rodney was to say, "I looked so much like Sam Houston that there was no concealing it"; at one family Christmas celebration, Cousin Oreole made the parentage clear even to Rebekah Baines Johnson when she said, pointing at Rodney, "Well, that's the Bunton in the family right there." (Rodney would die of AIDS in 1989.)

When Johnson was elected to the Senate, he put Sam Houston on his staff, but again, as Sam complained, "I was still just a flunky in Lyndon's office." His desk was just inside the front door, next to the receptionist's, not in the room behind it, in which Connally, Busby, and Jenkins sat. He went to Mexico, disappeared for months and came back terribly thin; at one point he weighed only 120 pounds. Meeting him for the first time, Booth Mooney found himself looking at a man who was "so much like a shrunken version of the Senator that I would have known who he was even if he had not referred early and often in that initial conversation to 'my brother. . . .' " His health had broken; his ulcer seemed never to heal; he kept drinking. About the time that Lyndon and Lady Bird were buying the ranch, Sam Houston was in and out of hospitals, sometimes for treatment of alcoholism, sometimes for what appear to have been nervous breakdowns. "It was a great relief to learn that Sam Houston is under hospital care," Rebekah Baines Johnson wrote Lyndon once. "I am so glad you put him where he can rebuild his shattered nerves."

When Sam Houston wasn't in a hospital, he was often at the new Johnson Ranch. Josefa, who had moved back to Fredericksburg, was often there, too, along with Rodney. So when Lyndon was there, so was his sister, about whom all the stories were told, so was his gaunt, hollow-cheeked, sunken-eyed brother, and so was his brother's illegitimate son. The Hill Country was religious country—hard-shell, hellfire, revivalist, Fundamentalist, Old Testament religious. No drinking at all was allowed. "Sneaking a beer by Jesus is like trying to sneak daylight by a rooster," one of Lyndon Johnson's high-school classmates, John Dollahite, would explain. The fierceness of the region's prejudices and the rigidity of its intolerance led one of Johnson City's more enlightened residents, Stella Gliddon, to call it "almost a Puritan town." Sam Ealy Johnson, Lyndon's father, had never been a drunk, but he did like a drink, and these good people had known what would come of that. Sam Ealy "was nothing but a drunkard," Dollahite says. "Always was." Sam Houston's drinking, and Josefa's—and the other things that decent people didn't mention—were staples of Hill Country conversation now, and Lyndon Johnson, child of the Hill Country, knew it, and knew what the Hill Country must be saying. He knew that the Hill Country, in a sneer at the Johnsons' attempts at respectability, was calling Rodney "Little Sam Houston." And to the Hill Country ranchers, breeding was significant, of course. During Lyndon Johnson's youth, he had had to live with the fact that as "a Johnson" he was regarded as a member of a shiftless, no-account clan; "I don't want you getting mixed up with those people," the father of Carol Davis, the girl he had wanted to marry at college, had told her. Lyndon Johnson's home now was big, gracious and gleaming white. But it was as filled with shadows as if it had been a dog-run, and relaxing there was very hard. He arose even earlier than he did in Washington; during his first years on the ranch, the rural route carrier delivered the mail to his mailbox—it was across the river, up toward Stonewall—about six-thirty, and not long thereafter Johnson would drive across the "low-water" dam and down the dirt road to pick it up; sometimes he would be waiting at the mailbox when the mailman drove up. Waking up early was, of course, routine in the country, where people went to bed early, but while Lyndon Johnson went to bed early, he didn't sleep any better than he did in Washington, as Mary Rather realized the first time she stayed the night at the ranch. Sometime during the night, hearing a noise outside, she looked out her window. For a few moments, she couldn't see anything in the darkness. And then she saw a tiny red glow; it brightened and faded. It was the glow of a cigarette—her boss's cigarette. Lyndon Johnson was standing there in front of his house, smoking. "He didn't sleep very well there either," Ms. Rather was to say. There were, in the Hill Country as on Capitol Hill, still the terrible rages, sometimes over things whose significance to him his assistants couldn't understand, like a coil of barbed wire left near the bottom of a tree ("That's bad ranching," he snarled at a ranch hand who had left it there. "You don't want a cow to get tangled up in that. That's *bad ranching!* What do you think— that I spend all this money on cows so you can give them blood poisoning, you ———") or an irrigation line running when it shouldn't be ("You know that line's uncapped out there? You're washing my soil away out there! Get on it!"). There was as much urgency in Texas as in Washington; Lady Bird had filled the living room with antiques; he filled it with telephones and typewriters. A second line was run into the house, and then a third; telephones were installed in almost every room; visitors were constantly tripping over the wires. He had his desk in the living room, and now a bridge table was set up for a secretary to work at, and then a second bridge table, for a second secretary. And the telephones were snatched out of their hands as if they were all still back together in SOB 231. The wristwatch alarm was always going off to remind him of a call he wanted to make or was expecting to receive.

Even while visiting journalists were writing about how relaxed Lyndon Johnson was on the ranch, members of his staff knew that when journalists weren't around, Lyndon Johnson's behavior was in some areas as frenetic in Texas as in Washington. George Reedy was to write that he would sometimes embark on "a wild drinking bout. He was not an alcoholic or a heavy drinker in the commonly accepted sense of those words. But there were occasions when he would pour down Scotch and soda in a virtually mechanical motion in rhythm with the terrible tension building visibly within him and communicating itself to his listeners. The warning signs were unmistakable and those with past experience tried to get away before the inevitable flood of invective. As they found out, it was rarely possible." Reedy wrote that "there did not appear to be any relationship between the locale and the episode. It could happen in his Capitol office; in the living room of his ranch"; other members of his staff say that it actually happened more often on the ranch, both because in Washington he felt more need to keep his guard up and not "lose control," and because in Texas he didn't have Bobby Baker measuring the drinks.

His behavior in Texas was similar to his Washington behavior in other ways. The journalist Hugh Sidey would write about Lady Bird: "Her constant pacification of the beast in her husband was her greatest achievement. . . . He caressed other women in front of her." In Washington, there was in these public "caresses" at least some restraint. In Texas, there was less. Horace Busby was to recall sitting in the back seat of Johnson's car while Johnson was showing the ranch to a friend of Lady Bird's who had come to visit. Johnson was driving, with Lady Bird in the front seat at the window and the friend sitting between them. Leaning over the front seat to ask a question, Busby saw that Johnson had his hand "under the woman's skirt and was having a big time, right there in front of Lady Bird." (Busby says that "Lady Bird didn't say a word," but "after a while" the woman "slapped his hand.") The journalist Eliot Janeway was to speak of Johnson's "harem," saying that "one way you could visualize Lady Bird is as the queen in *Anna and the King of Siam*. It worked that way; you know the scene where she sits at the table and all the babes— Lady Bird was head wife."

19

The Orator of the Dawn

BACK IN WASHINGTON, Lyndon Johnson, as the Democrats' Assistant Leader, was having ample opportunity to "read" his party's senators—to learn what it was they wanted, *really* wanted—and to make use of what he learned, and into one senator he was reading very deeply indeed. It was during 1951 and 1952, William White was to say, that "Lyndon Johnson fixed his restless, reckoning eyes on Hubert Humphrey."

If Johnson were to become Democratic Leader, he would find himself faced with the problem that previous Democratic senatorial Leaders had been unable to solve, and that had been a major cause of their failure and humiliation: the hostility-filled chasm between the party's ardent liberals and defiant conservatives that kept a Leader from presenting a unified front. For him to avoid his predecessors' fate, he would have to find a bridge over that seemingly unbridgeable gulf, some means of compromise between two factions so bitterly divided that no compromise seemed possible. And since he was regarded as a conservative and would be a Leader placed in power by the conservative bloc, the instrument of compromise would have to be found on the liberal side of the chasm.

As Nathaniel Hawthorne said of Andrew Jackson, "His native strength . . . compelled every man to be his tool that came within his reach; and the more cunning the individual might be, it served only to make him the sharper tool." No man, in 1951, would have seemed less likely to be an instrument of compromise than the senator Johnson chose; no senator, indeed, would have seemed less likely to be anyone's tool. But the more cunning the man, the sharper the tool—the more uncompromising the man, the better tool he would be for the making of compromises.

Hubert Horatio Humphrey had burst on the national stage as the very symbol—courageous, passionate—of unwillingness to compromise, as the defiantly unyielding champion of a noble cause.

The stage was the 1948 Democratic National Convention, the last non-air-

conditioned convention ever held by either major party, and the temperature on
the podium in Philadelphia's Convention Hall was ninety-three degrees. It was
the convention's third day, the day scheduled for President Truman's renomination and acceptance speech, but the delegates' mood, dispirited and downcast
because Truman was considered to have no chance to win (in the hall, Alben
Barkley was to recall, "the very air smelled of defeat"), had turned angry, over
civil rights.

Party leaders, up to the President himself, had concluded that if any
slim chance of victory existed, that chance rested on the only section of the
country that, in good times and bad, remained solidly Democratic, and they
felt that that chance would disappear completely if the party antagonized
the South. They had, therefore, agreed that the platform's civil rights plank
would be bland and unspecific enough to satisfy the South; it even contained
a sentence—"We call upon the Congress to exert its full authority to the limit
of its constitutional powers to protect these rights"—particularly agreeable
to segregationists, who could, as journalist Irwin Ross was to put it, "interpret
[it] as meaning that little federal action was possible, for in their view Congress' constitutional powers were severely limited by the doctrine of states'
rights." And the convention's organizers had tried to muffle dissent over the
civil rights plank by including only about twenty liberals (and only four from
the militant Americans for Democratic Action) on the 108-member Platform
Committee.

Refusing to bow to the committee's majority, however, these liberals had
held out during the first two days of the convention for a much stronger,
uncompromising, civil rights plank, one that endorsed the proposals Truman
himself had made two years earlier. They had even rallied some support in the
committee, largely because of Humphrey, the thirty-seven-year-old Mayor of
Minneapolis, Minnesota, who seemed to have a devotion to civil rights, and
who, as Mayor, had not only secured in his city the passage of the nation's first
effective Fair Employment Practices ordinance, but had also worked doggedly
to erase the city's previous reputation as "the anti-Semitism capital of America."

When, fifteen months earlier, sophisticated eastern liberal leaders had gotten their first look at Humphrey during an ADA Midwest organizational conference in Chicago, he had seemed very unimpressive, with his overly somber
black suit, a Phi Beta Kappa key dangling ostentatiously from a gold chain
across his vest, and a penchant for farmyard anecdotes so corny they made the
Ivy Leaguers wince—until he rose to speak. Decades later, Harvard-educated
Joseph Rauh could still recall how "dazzled" he had been by the young Mayor's
passion and sincerity, how he had brought the audience to its feet, applauding
and cheering, and how, during the long evening of talk that followed, Humphrey
had won their hearts. As uncompromising on the page as on the platform, he had
demanded in an article he wrote for the *Progressive* that the Democratic Party
and the Administration "lead the fight for every principle" in the "To Secure

These Rights" report. "It is," he wrote, "all or nothing." And now, in a steaming meeting room in Philadelphia's Bellevue-Stratford Hotel, he still wouldn't compromise, fighting so unflinchingly against party leaders for a stronger civil rights plank that, after one heated exchange, Senator Scott Lucas of Illinois muttered angrily, "Who does this pip-squeak think he is?"—the first of a dozen times Lucas was to use that word, sputtering with anger, in the angry hours that followed. At first, only four or five other committee members supported Humphrey, but as the hours passed and he kept fighting, sweat dripping down his thin, pale face, others began to be swayed by arguments that were not only moral but political; didn't they understand, he demanded of the stony-faced party elders on the committee, that the black vote was becoming pivotal in the North's big cities, and that, if the Democratic Party didn't stand up for a strong plank, they might lose that vote? The battle went on for two days and nights; Humphrey's friends, knowing that when he got involved in a fight, he forgot about eating, sent him in food (he was, despite their efforts, to lose eighteen pounds from an already thin frame during the convention). At the end, the liberals' proposals lost by a big majority, and the "moderate" plank was adopted; calling it "a sellout to states' rights," "a bunch of generalities," Humphrey said that when, the following day, the platform was brought to the convention floor for ratification, the liberals would offer a minority plank, and ask the convention as a whole to adopt it instead of the moderate proposal.

Over and over again, that evening and all through the night, the liberals were warned about the fate of the Democratic Party if they persisted, that the southerners might even walk out of the convention and form their own party, that at the very least the party would be split wide open and the last hopes of victory would vanish. And warnings were issued also about the fate of Humphrey, who the liberals all assumed would lead the floor fight, for, as one of his biographers was to put it, only his oratory could "give them a chance . . . on the convention floor." Pulling Rauh aside in a hotel corridor, Truman's assistant for minority affairs, David K. Niles, laid it on the line: "Joe, you won't get fifty votes on your minority plank, and all you'll do is ruin the chances of the Number One prospect for liberalism in the country." Another member of the Administration was angrier: "You ADA bastards aren't going to tell us what to do," he said.

Humphrey was told to his face that speaking for the minority plank would ruin—permanently—his own career; that, as Ross reported, "he was sacrificing a brilliant future for a crackpot crusade. 'You'll split the party wide open if you do this. You'll kill any chances we have of winning in November.' " And for many hours of that night, Rauh recalls, Humphrey "was not at all sure what to do. . . . He was reluctant to make a big fight and speech on the floor." He was well aware that, "personally," as Ross put it, "he had much at stake"—starting with his own upcoming bid for the Senate. "If he won, he was likely to be one of the national leaders of the party. . . ." And, as Ross puts it: "Humphrey's personal sympathies were firmly engaged in the cause, of that his colleagues never had any doubt; on the other hand, he was a professional politician who was being asked to challenge the entire national leadership of the party."

Humphrey himself was to recall that "It was sobering . . . we were opposed by all of the party hierarchy." He was well aware, he was to say, that the customary course in such a situation was to compromise. "I knew that the traditional thing to do was to make a gesture toward what was right in terms of civil rights, but not so tough a gesture that the South would leave the Democratic coalition."

But, Humphrey was also to say, some issues were beyond compromise. "For me personally and for the party, the time had come to suffer whatever the consequences." At about five o'clock in the morning, after he and a small group of liberal friends had been talking for hours in a hotel room, he said abruptly, "I'll do it." His friend Orville Freeman recalls him saying, "If there is one thing I believe in in this crazy business, it's civil rights. Regardless of what happens, we are going to do it. Now get the hell out of here and let me write a speech and get some sleep." And the next afternoon, after the majority plank had been proposed, Hubert Humphrey, in a stifling hall (the Secret Service had closed all the doors in anticipation of Truman's arrival to accept the nomination) packed to the rafters with hot, bored delegates impatient to hear the President—many of them hardly knew who Humphrey was—stepped to the microphone.

For once he paused for a long moment before beginning to speak, as if he was gathering himself, a very thin figure perspiring so heavily under the glare of the lights that sweat made his black hair glisten and ran down his high forehead; and his face, as David McCullough puts it, was "shining," with sweat and sincerity. "No braver David ever faced a more powerful Goliath," Paul Douglas, who was sitting in the throng below him, was to say twenty years later. "I can see Hubert still, his face shining with an incandescent inner light." And as he began to speak, his words slashing across the murmur of the restless throng, "the audience," as one writer put it, "grew quiet, suddenly aware that someone they wanted to listen to was talking."

For once his speech was short—only eight minutes long, in fact, only thirty-seven sentences.

And by the time Hubert Humphrey was halfway through those sentences, his head tilted back, his jaw thrust out, his upraised right hand clenched into a fist, the audience was cheering every one—even before he reached the climax, and said, his voice ringing across the hall, "To those who say that we are rushing this issue of civil rights—I say to them, we are one hundred and seventy-two years late.

"To those who say this bill is an infringement on states' rights, I say this— the time has arrived in America. The time has arrived for the Democratic party to get out of the shadow of states' rights and walk forthrightly into the bright sunshine of human rights."

"People," Hubert Humphrey cried, in a phrase that seemed to just burst out of him. "People! Human beings!—this is the issue of the twentieth century." "In these times of world economic, political and spiritual—above all, spiritual—crisis, we cannot and we must not turn back from the path so plainly before us. That path has already led us through many valleys of the shadows of death. Now is the time to recall those who were left on the path of American freedom. Our land is now, more than ever before, the last best hope on earth. I know that we can—know that we shall—begin here the fuller and richer realization of that hope—that promise—of a land where all men are truly free and equal."

ALL HIS LIFE, Hubert Humphrey had had a voice that could bring people to their feet, that could make them raise their banners and march, and people came to their feet now, banners raised, marching.

The Minnesota delegation's seats were surrounded by those of Georgia to their left, Louisiana to their right, Virginia behind them, and Kentucky in front of them, so that when the Minnesotans jumped up, the first delegation to do so, coming shouting to their feet as Humphrey shuffled his papers together and turned away from the podium, their banners were surrounded by the seated, glaring delegates of the South. But their banners were not alone for long. While Humphrey had been speaking, there had been something else that Paul Douglas would never forget: "hard-boiled politicians dabbing their eyes with their handkerchiefs." Turning to Ed Kelly, the Mayor of Chicago, who was seated beside him, Douglas said, "Mr. Mayor, that was a great speech." Mr. Mayor, he said, we can win now. "If Illinois will lead a parade," we can win. "We will fall in behind you." Kelly had been adamantly opposed to the stronger civil rights plank because he thought it had no chance of passage and would only divide the party. "Paul," Kelly said now, "we ought to have a parade, and Illinois ought to lead it. I would like to do so. But I am getting old, my legs are tired, and I couldn't hold up under this terrible heat."

"He paused for a moment," Douglas was to recall, "and then he said, 'But, Paul, I want you to lead the parade.' " Lifting the Illinois standard from its socket, Kelly handed it to Douglas, and then turned to the delegation, pointed at Douglas, and motioned them to follow him. The towering, white-thatched figure moved down the aisle. A forty-piece band that had been organized by James Caesar Petrillo, president of the American Federation of Musicians, had been kept hidden under the podium because it was not supposed to begin playing until President Truman appeared in the hall later that evening to give his acceptance speech. But Petrillo had been staring up at Hubert Humphrey as Humphrey spoke, and suddenly now, Petrillo motioned the band to begin playing. As Douglas led Illinois forward, the big California delegation fell in behind it. "Then New York, overcoming the caution of its Tammany leaders . . . Delegation after delegation joined us. . . . Here and there groups of sullen Southerners and conservative Northerners remained stubbornly in their seats, but the main mass of Democrats was moving with jubilant feet toward a better and more equal America."

In the vote on Humphrey's minority plank, Truman's Missouri, Barkley's Kentucky, Democratic Chairman Howard McGrath's Rhode Island, and of course the southern delegations all voted no. But Illinois's sixty votes, which had been controlled by Kelly and which had been counted in the southern camp, were cast for the minority plank. And then came the states of the Northeast: the thirty-six votes of New Jersey, the ninety-eight votes of New York, the seventy-four votes of Pennsylvania ("the latter," Irwin Ross writes, "an implied repudiation of the chairman of the platform committee, Pennsylvania's own Frank Myers"). The vote, 651½ to 582½, was for the minority plank. A huge roar of triumph filled the hall. Later, analyzing the victory, Humphrey would say it could be explained "in part by conscience, in part by political realism." The bosses of the Northeast "probably supported us because they wanted something to attract the votes of liberals, Negroes, minorities, and labor. Maybe they wanted to protect us from the appeal on the left of Henry Wallace's Progressive Party. . . ." And, "they reflected, and our victory reflected, a deep current running in the party and in the country." But that evening, there was no analysis, there was only triumph. "All we knew was that we, a group of young liberals, had beaten the leadership of the party and led them closer to where they ought to have been." Leaving the hall, Minnesota's National Committeewoman Eugenie Anderson heard a reporter say, "Can you beat that? The ADA has licked the South."

"AT THE WHITE HOUSE," as McCullough has written, "angered by the turn events were taking, Truman spoke of Humphrey and his followers as 'crackpots' who hoped the South would bolt."

Southerners did walk out during the balloting for the presidential nominee, but only some southerners: the Mississippi delegation and half of the Alabama delegation. Those that remained decided at the last minute to nominate their own candidate (Russell), but he received only 263 votes (to Truman's 947½). Delegates from four southern states eventually formed a Dixiecrat party and nominated their own candidate, Strom Thurmond, but in the November election those four states, with a mere thirty-nine electoral votes, were all that Thurmond carried. And, as McCullough writes, "The fact was the convention that seemed so pathetically bogged down in its own gloom had now, suddenly, dramatically, pushed through the first unequivocal civil rights plank in the party's history; and whether Truman and his people appreciated it or not, Hubert Humphrey had done more to reelect Truman than would anyone at the convention other than Truman himself." A crucial element in the President's stunning upset victory in November was the allegiance of blacks in the big cities.

At the time, there were not a few comparisons between Humphrey's speech and what has been described as "the only convention speech that ever had a greater impact on the deliberation of the delegates"—William Jennings Bryan's "Cross of Gold" oration of half a century before—but later events were to blur the memory of Humphrey's speech so that today it is all but lost to history. Nothing, though, could ever dim the memory of that speech for those who were there to hear it. "It was the greatest speech I ever heard," Paul Douglas would say a quarter of a century later. "He was on fire, just like the Bible speaks of Moses." Recalling the "magnificent" line about moving out "into the bright sunshine of human rights," Douglas would say, "To me, he will always be the orator of the dawn." And at the time, the speech, and the national acclaim it brought him, gave a boost to Humphrey's career. Although no Democrat had ever won popular election to the Senate in Minnesota, he had entered the race against the formidable incumbent, Joseph Ball. Now, arriving back in Minneapolis after the convention, he was hoisted to the shoulders of a crowd that carried him through the streets, and he went on not only to win, but to win in a rout. His arrival in Washington in January, 1949, as a senator-elect was heralded on the cover of *Time* magazine, on which the "glib, jaunty, spellbinder with a 'listen-you-guys' approach" was portrayed as a whirlwind spiraling into the capital. The "Number One prospect for liberalism in this country" was greeted by Washington liberals as a man who, as *The New Republic* said, "has a well-knit liberal philosophy and a powerful urge to right wrongs"—as a politician whose beliefs were so firmly held that he was willing to fight for them without compromise, and who, in the face of long odds, could win.

The subject of the cover story considered this image accurate. His victory at the convention, the victory he had won without compromise, had apparently made him believe that his ideals could become reality without compromise. In his autobiography, *The Education of a Public Man,* published a quarter of a century later, he would recall his feelings after the Democratic convention: "I had taken on our establishment and won. It was a heady feeling. But it confirmed something I felt and hoped. You *could* stand for a principle in politics and you could move an unwilling party toward a necessary goal."

But in the next sentence of that autobiography, Hubert Humphrey wrote, "How slowly and with what difficulty you kept it moving I was yet to learn."

It was the Senate that taught him.

HUBERT HUMPHREY came to Washington determined to right the wrongs he hated so deeply, and, euphoric because of his convention victory, and because of Truman's, which liberals viewed as a mandate for progress in civil rights, he was understandably confident that he could defeat the establishment in Washington as he had defeated the establishment at the convention—overconfident, in fact, so that his stridency, always annoying to new acquaintances until they had had a chance to discern the sincerity and passion beneath it, was at its most irritating.

Arriving to be greeted by journalists' predictions that, despite the liberal victory, Congress would again stall civil rights legislation, the freshman senator called a press conference (a well-attended press conference) to inform reporters that "there are enough votes in Congress" to pass the legislation "if [members] are honest and sincere—and I warn them that if they are not honest and sincere they may have trouble in the future." Friends tried to facilitate Humphrey's entrée to the capital's Democratic establishment and took him to lunch with one of its pillars, Jim Rowe, at the august Metropolitan Club. "My God, I was shocked," Rowe would recall. "This guy was just awful. He knew everything about everything." Dining at a nearby table was Arthur Krock, and when Rowe pointed him out to the newcomer, Humphrey said that Krock was always too hard on civil rights advocates. But now, Humphrey said, he had arrived in Washington and "I'll knock his block off." When Krock wrote a column criticizing him, he replied in a letter to the *Times* that attacked the columnist by name, as well as "the unholy alliance of the Republican party with the conservative wing of the Democratic party." He employed similarly uncompromising terms in a speech to a black audience at Howard University, denouncing the filibuster not only as "purely and simply an undemocratic technique to permit rule by a minority" that "will fail because history is against them, the people are against them, the times are against them" but also as a "rotten political bargain" between Republicans and southern Democrats. Even worse, he showed up at the Senate Dining Room one day with a black member of his staff, Cyril King, and when the headwaiter, himself a black man, told them they could not be served (one can only cringe at the thought of one black man forced to tell another that because of his color he was not welcome as a guest), Humphrey first softly, and then loudly and angrily, kept insisting that he and King were going to eat together, until at last they were allowed to do so. Worse still, he accepted the national chairmanship of the ADA, an organization regarded by the "unholy alliance" with hatred and scorn, accepted it because, as he was later to say, he felt that by doing so, "I would be more than a freshman senator . . . I would become a national leader."

The Senate, whose new Majority Leader, Scott Lucas, was the man who in Philadelphia had called Humphrey "a pip-squeak," responded in typical Senate fashion. When Humphrey rose on the floor (much too soon, by Senate standards) to deliver his maiden speech, he chided the Senate for its slow pace ("Sometimes I think we become so cozy—we feel so secure in our six-year term—we forget that the people want things done") while supporting Senator James Murray's proposal for the creation of a Missouri Valley Authority that would "do for the dust bowl what the Tennessee Valley Authority has done for the hillbilly hollows of the South" and would be as well "a symbol of liberalism to the large majority of Americans who voted liberal last November and in other Novembers." A symbol it was, and the Senate referred it to, and buried it in, committee, as it did, in 1949, bills embodying improvements in the minimum wage and health care, repeal of the Taft-Hartley Act, and other pledges made at the Democratic convention. And 1949 was also, of course, the year of the civil rights battle in which Lyndon Johnson gave *his* maiden speech—the battle Richard Russell won decisively, cementing the "undemocratic technique" into place more firmly than ever.

If that was the Senate's response on governmental issues, there were responses on a more personal level, responses for which Humphrey, unable to hold a grudge, was, as he would later say, "unprepared." (Although he might have been prepared, given the fury still raging against him in the South; an editorial in the Dothan, Alabama, *Register* said: "His name is anathema. It will remain for history to tag him as the demagog he is.")

Scott Lucas, Humphrey was to realize, "still had not forgiven me for Philadelphia"—and neither had the southeners who had placed Lucas in the majority leadership. Humphrey's requested committee assignments were Foreign Relations and Agriculture. While there was no opening for a freshman on the former, there was one on the latter, and it might have seemed logical for Humphrey since he was from an agricultural state. He was assigned instead to two of the least desirable committees, Government Operations and Post Office, and, in a peculiarly senatorial version of a covert sneer, he was, as one of his biographers was to put it, placed in "the juniormost seat on the Labor and Welfare Committee, whose ranking Republican member was Taft, author of the law Humphrey was committed to repeal." (Humphrey responded by writing an article for the *American Political Science Review* in which he attacked the seniority system as "the most sacred cow in the legislative zoo" and tendered the Senate some additional advice: to "give the spirit of youth a larger place in our legislative halls.") "The extra perks of office that [Lucas] could deny, he did deny." Since Humphrey was deeply interested in foreign affairs, the Majority Leader didn't appoint him to any of the many congressional delegations that traveled to foreign countries between sessions. Humphrey requested a seat on a new Select Committee on Small Business, but he was not one of the freshmen appointed to it. Vice President Barkley intervened to add Humphrey's name to a Senate group traveling to Germany, and, with President Truman's backing, persuaded Lucas to add him to the Small Business Committee, but he could do nothing about a dozen other slights Lucas managed to inflict. Humphrey despised Lucas (who, he was to say, "of course always voted with us on civil rights [in the Senate] . . . because it wasn't going to pass anyway"). As he had proven in Philadelphia, he could defeat Lucas in open combat, but in the Senate nothing was open.

And there were other personal responses particularly hurtful to a man of Humphrey's open and gregarious nature.

The Senate was such a convivial place, a place of pats on the back and hearty handshakes and warm, welcoming smiles, of banter and friendly exchanges. But there were few pats and handshakes for Hubert Humphrey, and few smiles, either. Paul Douglas would smile, of course, and Estes Kefauver, and Jim Murray, but not other senators, including the most influential, the ones who were the center of the chatting groups in the cloakroom or on the Senate floor. When Humphrey walked into the cloakroom or out onto the floor, there would, in fact, often be a turning away by these men, just slightly but enough to discourage conversation. It began to be noticeable that he was, in fact, being snubbed outright by the southerners and many of their allies.

And there were responses more hurtful than snubs. There were *sotto voce* comments about him, little jokes. Once, when Humphrey, still a freshman, was speaking yet again on the Senate floor, William Jenner whispered that Humphrey reminded him of some tomatoes he had once planted "too early in the spring and the frost got them." Some of the whispers got back to Humphrey.

And there were remarks pitched loudly enough for Humphrey to hear. Richard Russell was always polite except when someone was trying to improve the lot of the black man in America, and Hubert Humphrey, who had made those unforgivable statements in Convention Hall, simply would not stop trying in the Senate to improve the black man's lot. One afternoon, Humphrey was to recall, "I walked from the Senate chamber past a group of Southern senators. They ignored me and I moved silently on, but not out of earshot, and one of them, Senator Richard Russell of Georgia, said, obviously for my benefit: 'Can you imagine the people of Minnesota sending that damn fool down here to represent them?' "

Late in 1949, staff members of Harry Byrd's Committee on Reduction of Non-Essential Federal Expenditures quietly "analyzed" the cost of every bill that Humphrey had introduced in the 1949 session, came up with estimates—inflated estimates—that put the total at thirty billion dollars, and leaked the figures to right-wing columnist Fulton Lewis Jr. and to newspapers back in Minnesota. Republican senators then used the figures against Humphrey on the Senate floor, Kenneth Wherry saying sarcastically: "That is how he believes in economy." In retaliation, Humphrey introduced a resolution to abolish the Byrd Committee, which, he charged, "is merely used as a publicity medium" by Byrd, its work virtually duplicating that of a Government Operations subcommittee. He added that its "very existence is a wanton waste and extravagance" and the appropriation for its staff and printing costs "stands as the Number One waste of the taxpayers' dollars."

Humphrey's charges had substance, as most of the Senate might privately have admitted—Byrd's committee had not even met since 1947—but a public attack by a junior senator on one of the pillars of the Senate club was a tactical mistake. And, in a violation of Senate protocol, Humphrey had unknowingly made the charge when Byrd was away from Washington visiting his ailing mother. The counterattack came six days later, and when it began, the Senate Chamber was, as one of Humphrey's biographers was to put it, "ominously full." Byrd's patrician accent had never been softer as the ruddy-faced Virginia apple-grower begged the Senate's permission to "correct some misstatements" by Humphrey about his committee. When he had finished, he said, "I have mentioned nine misstatements in 2,000 words. This is on average one misstatement in every 250 words—and the Senator speaks like the wind." Harry Byrd's drawl grew even more pronounced. "As the Senator from Minnesota is a publicity expert himself," he said, "his statement, although not intended as such, could be regarded as a compliment from one who welcomes and has been signally successful in creating publicity for himself and his objectives. If he has ever hid his light under a bushel, I am unaware of it. And I have not observed any indication that he is of the shrinking violet type evading publicity." The Senate in its wisdom could, if it so desired, abolish his committee, Harry Byrd said. If the Senate thought that best, he would not oppose so many colleagues whose opinion he deeply respected. But, he said, "I do not want it done as the result of misinformation such as that which has been presented to the Senate."

Byrd's attack, biographer Carl Solberg was to write, was only "the initial salvo of a verbal barrage that has seldom been equalled in modern Senate history." One by one, southern and conservative senators defended Byrd—and assailed his attacker in personal terms that verged on the vicious. Rising at his front-row desk and turning to stare directly at Hubert Humphrey, Walter George said that of course the Byrd Committee should not be abolished. It was "doing a magnificent job." The attack on the committee was, he said, "the height of reckless irresponsibility."

Personal attacks were supposedly forbidden on the Senate floor, and Humphrey tried repeatedly to get the floor to make that point, or to respond, but Barkley, in the chair, refused to recognize him, and Humphrey finally gave up, and sat slumped at his back-row desk as one after another of his colleagues assailed him. When, after four hours, Byrd's allies finally yielded the floor, Humphrey rose to reply. As he did so, Byrd and every one of his supporters turned their backs on him and strode out of the Chamber.

Humphrey tried to fight back by publishing a letter in the *Times,* and accepting an invitation to debate Byrd before a liberal group in Richmond. When Byrd declined to appear, President Truman wrote him: "The senator from Virginia wouldn't have dared to debate with you." But in the Senate, the hostility to him became increasingly overt. Following an angry debate in the radio studio in the Senate Office Building, Homer Capehart called him a "Commie," and tried to shove him out the door. Humphrey was only stopped from punching the burly Indianan by an aide who wrestled him away. When news of this undignified display was brought to the Democratic cloakroom, Barkley knew immediately who was to blame, and made a crack, playing on the name of Minnesota's senior senator, Edward Thye, that within minutes was circulating all over the Capitol: "Minnesota is a great state—first they send us their Ball, then they send us their Thye, and now they send us their goddamned ass."

Such remarks, which invariably seemed to make their way to Hubert Humphrey's ears, would be seared into his memory. Talking to an interviewer in 1977, not long before he died, he could still recall how he had felt when he heard Richard Russell call him a "damn fool." "I just felt sick. . . . This hurt me more than anything in my private or public life, anything." Humphrey would call those first years in the Senate "the most miserable period of my life." They were, he would say, "dark days. . . . I despaired." *Despair* was a word Hubert Humphrey would, in the last years of his life, use frequently in describing those first years in the Senate, *despair* and *bitter*—and, most of all, *lonely*. He "just couldn't believe" the way he was treated, he would say. "I was prepared for the normal political opposition you could expect to encounter," and of course he was aware of the South's anger at his convention speech, but "I always worked on the basis that when the election was over, you didn't hate anybody, and you sort of shook hands and you went to work." And, he would say, "I was a more than normally gregarious person, who wanted to be liked," and "I wanted to do well, and I knew that my political intensity, my personal enthusiasm, needed a friendly environment to blossom. I didn't feel any comradeship, any friendship. Nobody showed us around. . . . We didn't go to many parties and the few we went to weren't very helpful." He envied, he was to say, freshmen like Johnson, Kerr, and Long. "They had friends in the South," he was to say. "That's all you needed. I had nothing. Absolutely nothing. No friends anyplace."

At the time, of course, he tried not to let his hurt show. "I hated to expose my feelings. . . ." And, except to his wife ("Without Muriel, I might have given up. . . . She was never too tired to listen . . ."), he didn't let his hurt show. His broad smile was always in place in public. But that was in public. In the evening, after the Senate day, he would get into his old Buick and drive home to Chevy Chase. And sometimes, driving home, he would cry—Hubert Humphrey, the youngest, and perhaps the best, mayor in the history of Minneapolis, elected to the Senate at the age of thirty-seven in a landslide, Hubert Humphrey who had brought a Democratic convention to its feet with the greatest speech since the Cross of Gold, Hubert Humphrey, as brave as any David who ever faced a Goliath, driving up Connecticut Avenue in the stream of rush-hour cars, with tears running down his face.

DURING HIS EARLY YEARS IN THE SENATE, Humphrey was to say, "Johnson and I had virtually no contact, reflecting, I suppose, the general attitude of the senators toward me." Johnson's attitude toward him was, in fact, distinctly chilly. Then, one day in the spring of 1951, Humphrey came out of the underground door of the Senate Office Building to catch the subway to the Capitol, and Johnson and George Reedy were standing on the platform. During the ride, the two senators sat together, and a surprised Reedy heard Johnson speaking warmly to Humphrey. As Reedy was to recall it, Johnson said, "Hubert, you have no idea what a wonderful experience it is for me to ride to the Senate Chamber with you. There are so many ways that I envy you. You are articulate, you have such a broad range of knowledge, you can present it with such absolute logic." And then, in what Reedy describes as "a sudden change of voice," Johnson said harshly: "But goddamn it, Hubert, why can't you be something but a gramophone for the NAACP? Goddamn it, Hubert, why can't you make a speech about labor for once? Goddamn it, Hubert, why can't you make a speech about farmers?" And Johnson ended by saying, "Goddamn it, Hubert, why can't you do something for all those people *and* the NAACP besides talking about them? You're spending so much time making speeches that there is no time left to get anything done." Reedy does not record Humphrey's reaction to the harshness, but it evidently reinforced whatever it was that Lyndon Johnson's reckoning eye had seen in him. It was in the spring of 1951 that, Humphrey would recall, "He started to show some interest in me. He didn't treat me as if I was a pariah." He began, in fact, "to invite me to his office for talk and frequently for a drink."

"I found him fascinating right from the beginning," Humphrey would recall. "A marvelous conversationalist in private conversation. Told a lot of stories, a lot of human interest stuff. He had been close to Roosevelt, who was my political hero. And he knew the operations of the House, and he knew all the personalities. And he knew all the little things that people did. He was a great mimicker, too, you know." To hear Hubert Humphrey recall those talks in 231 is to hear a man utterly charmed by Lyndon Johnson.

Charmed—and impressed. Humphrey had a master's degree in political science, and had been the mayor of a major American city, but in these conversations with Lyndon Johnson, Humphrey was learning a political science that couldn't be learned in college, or even in City Hall. Beside Lyndon Johnson, Hubert Humphrey was only a student, and he knew it. A note he wrote Johnson at the time says, "I am learning a great deal from you. You are one teacher who makes a fellow like what he's taught."

Some of the lessons that Johnson taught about politics were pragmatic, basic. "Johnson said the first lesson of politics is to be able to count," Humphrey would recall. "I have never forgotten that." Some were about personalities. "From the very beginning, it seemed to me, he understood the most intricate workings of the Senate. It seemed that he got there aware of the backgrounds of most of the members, and he took the trouble to find out about the ones he didn't know about. He was like . . . a psychiatrist. He knew how to appeal to every single senator and how to win him over. He knew how to appeal to their vanity, to their needs, to their ambitions." And some of the lessons were at a higher level. With every conversation, it seemed, Hubert Humphrey was becoming increasingly aware that Lyndon Johnson was operating on a level of politics of which he himself had been only dimly aware. "He knew Washington as no other man in my experience. He understood the structure and pressure points of the government, and the process and problems of legislation. He understood . . . the appointed officials. He knew the satellite worlds of Washington: the business lobbyists, the labor movement, the farm and rural-electrification lobbyists, the people interested in health research and social security. . . ."

"I was always fascinated by his knowledge of politics," Hubert Humphrey was to recall. "If you liked politics, it was like sitting at the feet of a giant."

HUMPHREY WAS IMPRESSED not only by Johnson's politics but by his personality. The words and phrases with which he describes that personality—words and phrases sprinkled through Humphrey's autobiography, and through the texts of interviews he gave to writers and to oral history interviewers—reveal an admiration that verges on awe.

Big is a word that recurs frequently in these descriptions. "You have just almost got to see the man," Humphrey says. "He'd get right up on you. He'd just lean right in on you, you know. Your nose would only be about—he was so big and tall he'd be kind of looking down on you, you see. . . ." "He was like a plant reaching out for water," Humphrey says. "Like a tree. And his whole demeanor was one great big long reach." He talks about Johnson's hands— "those great big hands of his. I can still see him clap them." Recalling Johnson's use of Hill Country maxims to make a point, Humphrey says: "One of his favorite expressions was 'If you're going to kill a snake with a hoe, you have to get it with one blow at the head.' And he'd give a dramatic expression of what he meant with his hands, those hands that were just like a couple of great big shovels coming down."

Strong is a word that recurs frequently—along with words that are evocations of strength. "This fellow is a very strong man, strong willed, strong of body," he said of Johnson; "he was a muscular, glandular political man."

In describing Lyndon Johnson, Hubert Humphrey describes him as subtle. "He was a born political lover. It's a most amazing thing. Many people look upon Johnson as the heavy-handed man. That's not really true. He was sort of like a cowboy making love." He describes him as fierce: "a lion . . . clever, fast and furious when he needed to be and kind and placid when he needed to be." He describes him as an elemental force of nature. "He'd come on just like a tidal wave sweeping all over the place. He went through walls. He'd come through a door, and he'd take the whole room over. Just like that. Everything."

In describing Lyndon Johnson, Hubert Humphrey paints with his own words—unwittingly, perhaps, but vividly—a portrait of two strong personalities in interplay, and of one, strong though it was, coming more and more under the spell of the other.

OF ALL JOHNSON'S QUALITIES, none impressed Hubert Humphrey more than the fact that, as he was to say, "Johnson was always able to take the measure of a man. He knew those that he could dominate; he knew those that he could out-maneuver. Right off the bat he sized you up."

Did Lyndon Johnson "size up" Hubert Humphrey? Were these talks be-hind the closed door of Johnson's office a perusal, a studying—a reading, by a master reader of men, of a very difficult text?

It is possible that Lyndon Johnson never had a more difficult text to read, for the interplay between him and Hubert Humphrey was very complicated. It was, after all, not only Johnson whose life was fired by burning ambition; that quality was blazoned as boldly as idealism across Humphrey's life; with his characteristic frankness, he had once asked a group of Minneapolis supporters, "What's so un-American about being ambitious? Of course I'm ambitious." Both men were, in fact, fired by the same ambition, reaching for the same dis-tant goal. Joe Rauh, who first met Humphrey in 1947, recalls that "From the moment we met, he was talking about how he was going to be President some-day." In fact, about a month before the 1948 Democratic Convention, when he was still only a young mayor—utterly inexperienced in national affairs, and lit-tle known outside Minnesota—he persuaded Rauh and two other ADA friends who were acquainted with Eleanor Roosevelt, Eugenie Anderson and James Loeb, to travel up to Hyde Park and ask her if he should skip the Senate race against Joe Ball and instead follow the course her husband had taken in 1920, when he ran as Vice President on a losing ticket, and try to go on Truman's ticket (which virtually all the experts expected to also be a losing ticket) as a prelude to a later presidential run. (Mrs. Roosevelt replied that "Of course [if you run for Vice President] you're going to get better known.") It was only after the utter impossibility of obtaining the vice presidential nomination became apparent to him that he settled down to concentrate on the Senate race. That great goal was to glimmer before Humphrey, always out of his reach but always to be sought for, throughout his life. He was to make three all-out tries for the presidency—in 1960; 1968, when he received the Democratic nomination and almost won the election; and 1972—and he was about to make a fourth try, in 1976, when the realization was borne in on him that he was about to be defeated this time by cancer. These were two men, almost the same age, who never took their eye from the same target. It was not only Lyndon Johnson who was so driven that his quest was filled with "energy" that made other men, even men of great energy, marvel; it was not only Lyndon Johnson who brought to his quest a willingness to sacrifice sleep and family and so many other considerations that influence other men. And if Lyndon Johnson was strong, what was the man Paul Douglas had been moved to liken to the Bible's heroic David? Hubert Horatio Humphrey, a spindly youngster with a sunny smile and a strikingly open, bright cheerfulness that "made you feel good when he was around," was the son of a small-town druggist who struggled to make a living in a series of the little towns that dot the windswept prairies of Minnesota and South Dakota; he got himself to college, but then was forced to drop out for six years and work behind the counter to help his father survive in a Depression-ravaged area where their farmer-customers had no money to pay their bills; he eventually returned to graduate and then get a master's degree through sheer determination. And as Mayor of Minneapolis—elected at thirty-four, he was the youngest mayor in the city's history—he was uncompromising in ramming through measures for social justice: when even the publisher of the city's leading black newspaper urged him to drop his fight for a municipal FEPC because of the bitterness it was engendering, he replied, "To hell with that, it's right and it's going through"; while he was Mayor, a mayor who hung two big portraits of Franklin Roosevelt in his office, Minneapolis became not only the first city with an effective FEPC but the first city to offer free chest X-rays to those who couldn't pay for them. And he was so tough in ending police brutality toward blacks and union strikers that when he died, Thurgood Marshall, the great black attorney, would say that of all Hubert Humphrey's achievements, none had impressed him more than "what he did with the police." When Hubert Humphrey and Lyndon Johnson sat talking behind the closed doors of Johnson's office, it was not only one of those two men whose life was a study in determination and strength of will.

Difficult though the text may have been, however, Johnson read it—and made use of what he read.

It is possible to know why Lyndon Johnson befriended Hubert Humphrey, for in later years Johnson would boast about the use he had made of him, and because of a memorandum "written" during those Senate years by George Reedy but virtually dictated by Johnson, that spelled out, in considerable detail, Humphrey's usefulness to him.

Humphrey could, Johnson saw, be the bridge to the northern liberals which he needed. They acknowledged the Minnesotan, as much as they acknowledged any man, as their leader; they viewed Johnson as a typical southern conservative, but if Humphrey came to like him and trust him, he would, should Johnson become Democratic Leader, be a link between Johnson and the liberals; there would be at least a beginning of unity among Senate Democrats. He might, indeed, be the only bridge possible; as the "Reedy" memo put it: "Senator Humphrey is about the only force that is able to control the [liberal] extremists."

Johnson wanted, in fact, to use Humphrey as an emissary between the two senatorial camps, as an instrument of compromise, someone through whom could be worked out the compromises necessary for unity, necessary to at least soften the antagonisms in the party, the compromises necessary for a Leader to have a chance of success. Such an emissary, to be effective, would have to believe, first, that compromise was desirable, and second, that it was possible. He would have to believe that at bottom there existed some common ground between Lyndon Johnson and the liberals, that their aims were not, after all, totally dissimilar. And, moreover, Johnson wanted Humphrey to be a friendly, sympathetic instrument, so that in negotiating for compromise, he, Lyndon Johnson, would be negotiating through someone who liked and trusted him. Reedy wrote that there was a reason that Humphrey, seemingly so uncompromising, might be such an instrument—because he believed deeply and sincerely in what he was fighting for, and therefore victory in the fight was very important to him. "There are compulsions upon Senator Humphrey—both of conscience and of constituency—which force him to lead a civil rights fight. But he is not going to win a civil rights fight by splitting the Democratic Party. The only way he can win the fight is to drum up enough votes on his side and soften the opposition on the other side."

Johnson wanted Humphrey not only to bring southern and northern Senate blocs closer together, but to bring *him,* Lyndon Johnson, closer to the northern senators. For him to become President, he needed the North. Viewing him as a typical southern conservative, however, northern liberals, even those of them who were beginning to like him personally, still deeply distrusted his philosophy and aims. He needed the liberal senators to trust him, or at least to feel they could work with him; he needed them to be convinced that at bottom they shared some of the same goals. The best way of convincing them would be to have someone within their own camp who would argue for him. And who better to do that than Humphrey? If the Minnesotan liked and trusted him, he would be the best possible means to the personal rapprochement required for the realization of Lyndon Johnson's great ambition.

And, lastly, and perhaps most importantly, what Lyndon Johnson wanted in his dealings with Hubert Humphrey was to modulate that great voice. Of all the liberals who could rise on the Senate floor and embarrass—humiliate, in the Johnsonian lexicon—a Democratic Leader by demanding that he pass liberal legislation which he was in fact not able to pass, no one could do so nearly as eloquently and effectively as Humphrey. No senator could enunciate liberal aims more persuasively, could arouse liberal emotions more dramatically, could mobilize national liberal opinion against a Senate Leader more effectively than that mighty orator from the plains, and Johnson knew it, as "Reedy's" memorandum makes clear: "The most compelling reason" for making Humphrey a link between the two sides, the memorandum states, "is that a running battle between Senator Humphrey and the leadership will place the leadership in the public mind as a 'sectional southern' leadership continually battling the northern liberals." Humphrey, the memo said, is "a national figure around whom" liberals can rally; if he continues fighting the southern senators, "it would split the party. He has sufficient prestige and sufficient standing that he may do precisely that." He had to be brought to Johnson's side.

And Johnson, capable of making every man his tool, knew how to use Humphrey to attain the ends he wanted. Was there, shining out of that text, ambition? Knowing now that Humphrey wanted the same thing that he did, wanted it perhaps almost as badly as he did, Lyndon Johnson used that knowledge—used it so skillfully that the intensity of Humphrey's ambition would serve only to make him a better tool for realizing Johnson's ambition. Since a rapprochement with the liberals would strengthen Johnson's position in his run for the presidency, and Humphrey was of course smart enough to see this, Johnson made Humphrey believe that ultimately it would be to his own benefit for Johnson's position to be thus strengthened. For Humphrey to believe that, he had to believe that Johnson was no threat to his presidential dreams, and, that in fact, building up Johnson's support would wind up helping him more than Johnson. And Johnson made him believe that.

The exact words he employed we do not know, for there is no record of these conversations. But we do know the general nature of the arguments he employed—for Humphrey believed them and later repeated them to others. There was no point in trying to convince a man as intelligent as Hubert Humphrey—and Johnson fully understood the keenness and depth of Hubert Humphrey's intellect—that Johnson didn't want the presidency. Instead, Johnson acknowledged to Humphrey that he wanted the presidency but said he knew he would never get it—and he convinced Humphrey that he would never get it, explaining to him, with apparently deep conviction, why no one from the South could be President. And he convinced Humphrey as well that since Johnson couldn't get the nomination it was to his advantage to build up Johnson as a candidate, make him as strong a candidate as possible, because his strength would eventually go to whomever Johnson wanted—and so long as he and Johnson were allies, it would eventually go to him. Humphrey, believing him, was to explain all this in a strictly off-the-record conversation with Robert Manning, then a reporter for *Time* magazine, who relayed Humphrey's words to his editors in a confidential memo: "Nobody can love politics as much as Johnson does, and not want to be President," Humphrey told Manning. But, Humphrey also said, "for all his political sagacity and influence on party affairs, even if he guns for it, he's not repeat not going to be nominated." In fact, Humphrey explained to Manning, Johnson's ambition would end up helping him, Hubert Humphrey, receive the nomination, since "Johnson votes [the votes from southern states] could very well determine who else gets the nomination," and those votes "could very well go to Humphrey." During those chats behind the closed door in 231, Johnson was not the only one of the two young senators who was trying to use the other. If Johnson needed the North if he was ever to become President, and saw Humphrey as a means to obtaining it, so did

Humphrey need the South—and see Johnson as a means of obtaining it. And Johnson made sure that Humphrey kept seeing him that way. Carl Solberg, the author of the only thoroughly documented biography of Humphrey, concludes that in his dealings with Lyndon Johnson, Humphrey was thinking that only one of them was going to be President—and that he was going to be the one; that he had a better chance because he wasn't from Texas; that while Johnson might be under the impression that he was using him, in reality, he was using Johnson.

Was there, shining out of that text, idealism? Personal admiration—awe, even—could never be a decisive influence with a man who believed as deeply in principles, in moral goals, as did Hubert Humphrey. "Our little group of 25 [*sic*] or so liberal senators were very suspicious of Johnson, in those early years, very suspicious of him!" Humphrey was to recall. *He* was very suspicious of Johnson. In order for him to ally himself with Johnson, he would have to be convinced that the alliance would not involve any betrayal of principle— that, in fact, the alliance would improve the chances for realization of those goals.

Humphrey's recollections of the conversations in 231 give some hint as to the methods Johnson employed to make him believe that they shared the same principles. One was for Johnson to identify himself with the President who to Humphrey had been the supreme embodiment of these principles. Like the great storyteller he was, Johnson brought alive those two paintings on Humphrey's office wall, talking endlessly about his private dinners and breakfasts with FDR. Humphrey could never get enough of these stories, and to him they did indeed validate Johnson's liberalism. "Johnson was a Roosevelt man," Humphrey says. "That was his greatest joy. To remind people that Roosevelt looked upon him as his protégé. A hundred times I heard him mention that, you know. That was his great moment. . . . This made him in a sense, in his contacts with many people like myself, a sort of New Dealer." And Johnson talked also about Ben Cohen and Tommy the Cork and other almost legendary New Dealers with whom he was friends. "David Dubinsky was another one of his heroes, and the ILGWU, and how he and David always worked together." And Johnson also talked, as only Lyndon Johnson could talk, about the episodes in his life in which he had fought for the things in which liberals believed, about fighting the private utilities to bring electricity to the Hill Country, about the months he had spent in Cotulla. "I knew he was very sympathetic to the Mexican-Americans," Humphrey says. "Johnson never forgot that he was a schoolteacher down there."

Humphrey could see with his own eyes that Richard Russell also regarded Lyndon Johnson as his protégé, that the senators with whom Johnson was on the most intimate terms were the southerners, but Humphrey felt, after those talks with Johnson, that he understood that. "Johnson never was a captive of the southern bloc," he says. "He was trying to be a captain of them, rather than a

captive. . . . He was, I think, biding his time, so to speak, and building his contacts." He was not yet fully convinced of Johnson's liberalism, but he was convinced that there was much more liberalism in his new friend than he had
previously believed.

Was Johnson also reading in Humphrey his loneliness, the loneliness of a
gregarious man, shunned in the Senate, who badly needed a friend? Of all the
things that Lyndon Johnson made Hubert Humphrey believe, in those years
when one was not yet President of the United States and the other was not yet
his Vice President, one of the most important in binding Humphrey to him was
to convince Humphrey that Lyndon Johnson was his friend.

Johnson liked him, Humphrey would say, he was sure of it. "We were hitting it off." Looking back at those Senate years in 1972, from a very different
vantage point, he would say, "I really believe that Lyndon Johnson looked upon
me—I've tried to think about this even after the Vice Presidency and all—I
think it's fair to say he liked me as an individual, as a human being." He
thought he understood why. "Johnson had a sense of humor, and he could kid
with me," he would say. "Johnson didn't enjoy talking with most liberals. He
didn't think they had a sense of humor." And there was in Johnson's attitude an
implicit assumption that they were comrades-in-arms, friends fighting for the
same cause. He not only showed Humphrey a mountaintop—that both of them
would rise (although because he, Johnson, was unlucky enough to be from
Texas, Humphrey would rise higher)—but that they would be on the mountaintop *together*. Once, on the Senate floor the day after one of the huge Democratic Jefferson-Jackson dinners, he told Humphrey in a low, confidential voice
that he was tired of "the same old phonograph records of yesterday" that had
been played at the dinner. "We've many fine governors and members of Congress, fresh faces, who weren't heard from," he said. "We need new voices.
Someday we'll give our own party."

In letters he wrote to Humphrey from Texas during the long Senate
recesses, he used over and over again the word Humphrey wanted to hear. "I
have been sorely missing your wise advice and friendly counsel," he wrote in
1953. "I am looking forward to many more years of service with a good
friend," he wrote in 1954. In a letter at a crucial point in their relationship, in
1956, he wrote assuring him, "You will be on the scene as a national leader
long after the others are forgotten.

"And you are my friend."

"You are a wonderful friend, and I will never forget it," he wrote in 1957,
and, also in 1957, "My deep thanks go to you for . . . being my everlasting
friend."

And Humphrey responded with the same word. "The privilege of your
friendship is a priceless gift," he wrote. "Thanks so much for your warm words
of friendship," he wrote.

And there was one further key element in the Humphrey text, one element that to Lyndon Johnson, to whom personality was all-important, may have been the most important of all. It was a quality that could have been discerned, at this stage of Hubert Humphrey's career, only by an unusually gifted reader of men, for at this stage Humphrey was regarded as a very strong man, strong and tough enough to have stood up to the South. But Lyndon Johnson was just such a reader. Hubert Humphrey may have been strong and tough, Johnson saw, but he wasn't strong *enough* or tough *enough*. Most importantly, he wasn't as strong, as tough, as he himself was.

At the bottom of Humphrey's character, as Johnson saw, was a fundamental sweetness, a gentleness, a reluctance to cause pain; a desire, if he fought with someone, to later seek a reconciliation, to let bygones be bygones, to shake hands and be friends again. And to Lyndon Johnson that meant that at the bottom of Humphrey's character, beneath the strength and the ambition and the energy, there was weakness. Years later, he would define this crucial difference between them with Johnsonian vividness of phrase. At the time, they were both in a dispute with labor leader Walter Reuther, whose right arm had long been permanently crippled by a would-be assassin's gunshot. Reuther had come to Washington to meet with them individually, and Johnson told an assistant: "You know the difference between Hubert and me? When Hubert sits across from Reuther and Reuther's got that limp hand stuck in his pocket and starts talking . . . Hubert will sit there smiling away and thinking all the time, 'How can I get his hand out of his pocket so I can shake it?' When Reuther sits across from *me*," Lyndon Johnson said, "I'm smiling and thinking all the time, 'How can I get that hand out of his pocket—so I can cut his balls off!' "

Hubert Humphrey was trying to use him, just as he was trying to use Hubert Humphrey. Lyndon Johnson knew that. But he knew something else, too. If two men were each trying to use the other, the tougher one would win—and he, Lyndon Johnson, was the tougher.

LYNDON JOHNSON BEGAN, although he was still only Assistant Leader, to prepare the way for the time when, as Leader, he would be able to make use of what he had learned about Hubert Humphrey. Of all the political science lessons taught in SOB 231, the most important, for the teacher's purpose, was about the need for compromise.

To convince Humphrey of the efficacy—indeed, the necessity—of compromise, Johnson played on one of the Minnesotan's deepest desires: his wish not only to fight for social justice, but to win; to help, instead of merely talking about helping, the poor and underprivileged, the "people! Human beings!" that he saw as the main issue of the twentieth century; on Humphrey's desire for genuine accomplishment.

As Humphrey would later relate, Johnson would often telephone him in his office at about seven-thirty in the evening. "Hubert, come over. There's something I want to talk to you about," he would say. If Humphrey protested that his family was waiting, Johnson would say, "Damn it, Hubert, you've got to make up your mind whether you're going to be a good father or a good senator." And when Humphrey arrived, Johnson would, evening after evening, play variations on the same theme: "Your speeches are accomplishing nothing," he would say. Humphrey should learn to compromise. "Otherwise, you'll suffer the fate of those crazies, those bomb-thrower types like Paul Douglas, Wayne Morse, Herbert Lehman. You'll be ignored, and get nothing accomplished you want." Humphrey, the man who had refused to compromise, not only came to believe this—"Compromise is not a dirty word," he would say. "The Constitution itself represents the first great national compromise"—but to believe it with all the fervor of the convert, the convert who is the most enthusiastic of believers. Not only, he was to say, was compromise not a dirty word; those who refuse to compromise are a threat; "the purveyors of perfection," as he came to call them, "are dangerous when they . . . move self-righteously to dominate. There are those who live by the strict rule that whatever they think right is necessarily right. They will compromise on nothing. . . . These rigid minds, which arise on both the left and the right, leave no room for other points of view, for differing human needs. . . . Pragmatism is the better method." The fact that some of his fellow liberal senators were to come to look upon him as, in his own words, one of the "unprincipled compromisers" bothered him for a while, he was to say; "it doesn't bother me any more at all. I felt it was important that we inch along even if we couldn't gallop along, at least that we trot a little bit."

THE CONVERSATIONS IN 231 were in a way a testing—a test (of which Humphrey was evidently unaware) of whether Humphrey could and would be the means to Johnson's ends—and Humphrey evidently passed. Slowly but steadily Johnson began to move Humphrey into a position where he could one day be a bridge between liberals and conservatives, and an instrument of compromise.

During that 1951 session, Johnson began telling Walter George, "Senator, Hubert isn't such a bad fellow, you know." He told George how interested Humphrey was in foreign affairs. When Humphrey walked into the cloakroom, Johnson would bring him over to George's armchair and begin discussing foreign affairs; Humphrey by this time had realized the necessity of listening when George was pontificating, and he listened. And when he himself occasionally interjected a thought, George listened, too; it was difficult to be in a conversation with Hubert Humphrey and not be aware of his intelligence. And of his warmth; the more Walter George saw of Humphrey, the more he began, despite himself, to like him. Simultaneously, Johnson was working on Russell, telling him that Humphrey's views on agriculture were remarkably like his own—which was, in fact, the case; "the South and the Midwest have always been together on farm legislation," Humphrey would say. "We needed each other." Once or twice, when Johnson invited Humphrey over for a drink and a talk, Russell would be there, too. Then Johnson told Russell that Hubert would appreciate having his opinion on an agricultural bill he wanted to introduce. "Humphrey utilized this opportunity to show deference by his repeated 'sir' to Russell when they discussed the measure," Steinberg relates. Russell, too, as John Goldsmith puts it, "came to appreciate Humphrey's intelligence." And he came to appreciate his sincerity; Russell had a passion to help the poor farmers of the South, Humphrey had a passion to help the poor farmers of the Midwest, and this shared passion brought them a little closer together. And always Johnson was putting in a good word for Hubert with Russell.

"Johnson was actually becoming a bridge for me with some of the more conservative members of the Senate," Humphrey was to say. Their feelings about him had eased to a point at which Russell Long of Louisiana, his neighbor in Chevy Chase, felt able to bring him one day to the round table in the senators' private dining room. "Since there was seldom talk of issues or legislation, lunch was usually a relaxed social hour of storytelling, chatter about the sports page, whatever was not political or controversial." The southern senators started to get to know Hubert Humphrey not as a fighter for civil rights but as a human being. And, like most people who got to know Hubert Humphrey as a human being, they liked him. And Humphrey knew who had gotten them to like him. "My apprenticeship of isolation drew to a close as I got to know Lyndon Johnson," he was to say; it was Johnson who brought even "Dick Russell around to look with some favor on me." He knew that his relationship with the southerners— his key to acceptance in the Senate, to the end of his time as a "pariah"—was due to Lyndon Johnson. He knew that Johnson had given him a great gift. And, being an intelligent man, he knew that what had been given could be taken away.

IF IN 1951 AND 1952, Hubert Humphrey was charmed and impressed by Lyndon Johnson, friends with him and eager to stay friends, he was nevertheless still the dominant figure in the Senate's liberal bloc and not at all disposed to relinquish that role. His loyalty to that bloc was as undivided as ever. On controversial issues, his views and those of Johnson and the conservatives were not similar, and Johnson didn't try to modify his views. Nor did Johnson make any attempts during those two years, the years when he was only Assistant Leader, to make use of Humphrey's new understanding of the virtues of compromise, nor of Humphrey's new, easier relationship with the southerners, a relationship that would have made it easier for Humphrey to deal with them on the liberals' behalf. And if Johnson had made such attempts, they would not have succeeded. Humphrey was aware that whatever Johnson's true philosophy might be, the Texan was very much part of the southern bloc and represented its interests. While during those years, Johnson, as Doris Kearns Goodwin puts it, "seemed to foresee that someday Humphrey might be useful to him," that day had not yet come. For it to come, an additional, final ingredient would have to be added to the relationship between the two senators: power, more power than an Assistant Leader possessed.

20

Gettysburg

NINETEEN FIFTY-TWO, of course, was a presidential election year. Lyndon Johnson would not be forty-four years old until August of that year, and he was still a first-term senator, but neither of those facts precluded a try for the great goal which never left his mind. An interview published in January demonstrated that, and demonstrated also that he viewed the Senate as only a way station on the road to that goal.

The interview was conducted—symbolically—in the Capitol's glittering President's Room, with Johnson and Alfred Steinberg, who was writing an article on the House and Senate whips for *Nation's Business* magazine, sitting, under the immense gold-plated chandelier and the richly colored Brumidi frescoes, in two low, deep-burgundy leather armchairs on wheels.

Johnson, Steinberg recalls, "was outraged when he learned he would be only one of four men featured in the article." Wheeling his chair so close to Steinberg's that their knees touched, and leaning forward so that their noses were only inches apart, he pressed the reporter back at an uncomfortable angle, seized one of his lapels to hold him steady, and asked loudly, "Why don't you do a whole big article on me alone?" When Steinberg asked ("from my strange sitting position"), "What would the pitch be?—that you might be a Vice-Presidential candidate in 1952?" Johnson said, this time in a whisper and after a glance around to make sure that no one else was present, "Vice President, hell! Who wants that?" His voice boomed out again. "President! That's the angle you want to write about me."

Steinberg recalls that when "I smiled at the obvious impossibility of Johnson's ever becoming President," Johnson said, "You can build up to it by saying how I run both houses of Congress right now." And when Steinberg asked for an explanation of "this extraordinary remark," Johnson said, "Well, right here in the Senate I have to do all of Boob McFarland's work because he can't do any of it. And then every afternoon I go over to Sam Rayburn's place." One of Johnson's hands was still firmly gripping the reporter's lapel, but Johnson's other hand had been unoccupied. Now, for emphasis it took a firm grip on one of the reporter's thighs. "He tells me all about the problems he's facing in the House, and I tell him how to handle them. So that's how come I'm running everything here in the Capitol."

Other journalists were aware of the same ambition. After an off-the-record conversation with Johnson, a member of *Time* magazine's Washington bureau informed his editors in New York that "despite his Southern origins," Johnson "is interested in the Number 1 spot."

But 1952 was to be the year Richard Russell ran for President himself.

Although Russell's "sense of the sweep of history" made him feel, as George Reedy realized during their long conversations together, "that the only way to ever really put an end to the Civil War, to heal the breach, would be to elect a Southerner President," the Georgian also appears when he first entered the race to have been aware that, as *Time* said on March 19, "Russell has as much chance of being nominated as a boll weevil has of winning a popularity contest at a cotton planter's picnic." "The chances of any Southern Democrat residing at 1600 Pennsylvania Avenue during our lifetime are very remote," the Senator had written a friend a few months earlier; when, in December, 1951, John Stennis urged him to run, Russell replied, "I'm under no illusions about any Southerner being elected President of the United States."

He appears to have begun running more for the South than for himself. The South's great stronghold was Capitol Hill, the keys to the stronghold were the House and Senate committee chairmanships, the southerners would hold those chairmanships so long as the Democrats held the majority in Congress—but holding the majority wasn't going to be easy. Foreseeing who the Republican candidate would be, Russell was uneasily aware of the genial Eisenhower's popularity. A large Eisenhower plurality might sweep the GOP into the majority in Congress; Democratic unity in the face of this threat was crucial. The party could simply not afford to be split again, as it had in 1948, over the civil rights issue. And beyond the political considerations were the historical: his desire to make the South part of the United States again. Should the Democrats renominate Truman, or nominate another candidate with similarly unacceptable views on race, the South would break away from the party again, thereby reemphasizing the gulf between it and the rest of the country. The candidate might, in fact, be Estes Kefauver, who, detested though he was in the Deep South, was viewed by the rest of the country as the "southern" candidate. A Kefauver victory at the Democratic Convention—an event which in the Spring of 1952 seemed more likely with every passing week as he won a string of primaries—would trigger another walkout by southern delegates, and Russell believed that this would weaken the South by revealing the split within its own ranks. The way to avoid these scenarios would be for the South, a unified South, to have a candidate who would arrive at the convention with a bloc of votes large enough so that even though the candidate himself might not be able to win the nomination, he would have sufficient influence to force the selection of a candidate, and the writing of a platform, acceptable to the South. Russell knew that the old Confederacy would unite behind him, and that he would be its strongest candidate; it seems that he began running more to keep the South and the party together than because he felt he could win the nomination.

Nonetheless, illusions came, particularly after Truman, buffeted by seemingly endless revelations of corruption in his Administration (nine of whose members, including his appointments secretary, would go to prison), by his inability to end the war in Korea, and by "soft on Communism" allegations, was defeated by Kefauver in the New Hampshire primary in March and then announced that he would not run for re-election. Entering the May 6 Florida primary against Kefauver to prove that he, not the Tennessean, was the true candidate of the South, Russell won an easy victory. The announced candidates—Kefauver, Vice President Alben Barkley, and New York Governor Averell Harriman—were hardly formidable. The big-city bosses whose machines had been embarrassed by the Kefauver investigations were determined that he would not get the nomination, no matter how many primaries he won. Barkley, at seventy-four, was considered too old, Harriman had never run for national office. Truman had in mind another candidate, Adlai Stevenson, landslide victor in the 1948 race for the Illinois governorship and a noted orator, but Stevenson had declined the President's offer of support in language so firm that the *New York Times* said in April that he "has to all intents and purposes taken himself out of the race." When Russell, fresh from his Florida victory and "exuding optimism," spoke to the National Press Club on May 8, the assembled journalists realized to their shock that he had come to believe that he could win the nomination, and the general election as well. "That," Russell told the Press Club, "would destroy a fable of long standing that no citizen from the southern part of our nation can be elected President."

His optimism, at least about the nomination, was, in some ways, understandable. With 1,230 votes to be cast at the Democratic Convention, 616 were needed for nomination, and Russell could count on the votes of every Confederate state but Tennessee: 262 votes, a solid base. And he was counting on a substantial number of nonsouthern votes because of the support of senatorial colleagues. Big Ed Johnson of Colorado had agreed to be his national campaign manager, Pat McCarran of Nevada had enthusiastically endorsed him, and not a few senators from the Midwest and West, while not actually endorsing him, had spoken warmly of his candidacy: having lived for almost twenty years in a world in which these men possessed genuine power, Richard Russell could be excused for assuming that they possessed it in their states as well. And senators from farm states had been appearing for years before Appropriations' agricultural subcommittee asking for his support for their projects; pointing out that "Those in the Midwest who are concerned about agriculture would be wise to support Russell," Senator Milton Young of North Dakota now said that "if the Democrats have sense enough" to nominate the Georgia Giant, he, although a Republican, would support him.

Calculations relating to the general election, and to Dwight Eisenhower's immense popularity in the South, were also feeding Russell's belief that his party would turn to him. There were 146 electoral votes, vital to Democratic chances, in the thirteen "contiguous" states—the eleven Confederate states plus border states Kentucky and West Virginia—and polls were showing that, as Russell put it, "I am the only Democratic candidate who can defeat a certain military personage" in those states. And if he did so, he said, "it will only be necessary to obtain an additional 118 votes from the other 35 states to win in . . . November."

Beyond such rational calculations there was the euphoria produced by a national campaign: the enthusiastic applause from audiences in Florida, and the rolling cheers from the huge throng that lined the streets of Atlanta as he paraded through it, seated high atop the back seat of an open convertible as the bands marching before it played "Rambling Wreck from Georgia Tech," a song to which new words had been written: "The Senator from Georgia / Dick Russell is his name— / Will Take His Place among the Great / of U.S. History's Fame. / His Years of Public Service Devoted to our Nation / Will Lift him from his Senate seat / the Presidential station!" (Flying down from Washington that morning for the parade, Russell had landed first in Winder, so that he could visit his mother [who so long ago had written him that she had not brought "my R. B. Russell, Jr." into the world "to ever *fail* in anything he might undertake"].) For so many years now, his colleagues had been telling him that he was the man in Washington best qualified to be President, and that they hoped that one day he would be. He still kept close to hand the cherished note Harry Truman had written him in 1945: "Dick: I hope you [will] be recognized next. And you will be." Was Truman's prediction to come true at last?

In addition, once Russell had entered the race, Johnson had put his own ambitions on hold, and thanks to him the Georgian's campaign organization was of impressively high caliber. Although John Connally was now working for one of Eisenhower's most generous financial backers—Sid Richardson had, in 1951, hired him away from Alvin Wirtz's law firm—he was a key part of it; Johnson had persuaded Richardson to lend Connally to the Russell campaign, because, Connally explains bluntly, "We felt that he [Russell] was going to be a power in the Senate, win, lose or draw." Furthermore, "Richardson regarded Russell as one of the greatest public servants this country ever developed"; had he won the Democratic nomination, Richardson "would have supported *both* [him and Eisenhower]." Although Atlanta banker Erle Cocke Sr. had the title of Russell's "convention manager," most of the contacts with individual delegates were handled by the young Texan whose political competence was already well known in Washington. And, thanks also to Johnson, working in offices near Connally's at Russell campaign headquarters in the Mayflower

Hotel were two speechwriters whose competence Russell admired: Reedy and the conservative Booth Mooney. Johnson had arranged for ample supplies of money as well as talent. Russell's Georgia campaigns hadn't required much money, and he was astonished and at first daunted by the amount required for a presidential campaign. This, he wrote to a supporter, was "a new league." It was, in fact, Johnson's league, and he made playing in it easy for Russell, arranging for lavish financing by ex–Texas regulars H. R. Cullen and E. B. Germany, and by the three conservatives whose wallets were always open to Johnson: Richardson, Murchison, and of course, Herman Brown. The dignified Georgian didn't even have to soil his hands. When at one point the campaign ran short of ready cash, Connally simply flew down to St. Joe Island and returned with an envelope, and, Connally says, Russell may not even have known about the trip.

Johnson was, in fact, working very hard for Russell in every area of the campaign. The Texas Democrats were split, with liberals supporting Kefauver, but Johnson, in alliance with the state's Dixiecrats, including reactionary Governor Allan Shivers, arranged for the announcement, the day Russell won the Florida primary, that Texas' fifty-two votes would be cast for him as a block. All through the campaign, Johnson would use his contacts across the nation on Russell's behalf, always making sure that Russell knew he was doing so, and in Chicago, his tall figure was conspicuous as he roamed hotel corridors and convention floor, draping an arm around delegates' shoulders and urging them to vote for Russell. Johnson even provided Russell with a campaign slogan, which he said had been coined by a Texas constituent: "Let's Hussle for Russell." ("A number of others have suggested the same slogan, though they spelled it differently," Russell wrote back.) The staff, the money, the national contacts—all these added to Russell's optimism.

A MEETING WITH TRUMAN on June 10, a meeting Russell requested in an attempt to translate the President's 1945 sentiment into a 1952 endorsement, might have made the Georgian recognize the folly of his hopes. Russell came as close as he could to pleading. "I told him [Truman] that I would like to have his support and that with a little more help than I now had there was no question about my nomination and election. He then said, substantially: 'I would give my right eye to see you President, but you know that the Left-Wing groups in Chicago, New York, St. Louis and Kansas City must be kept in the Democratic Party if we are to win and they will not vote for you. We must keep these groups in the party.' " According to Russell, Truman also said: "Dick, I do wish that you lived in Indiana or Missouri. You would be elected President hands down. We have differed on a great many issues but we have always understood each other. You are a great Democrat and I respect you. . . ."

But Russell was by this time beyond the reach of logic. His aide William

Darden says that "When he started [his campaign], he was realistic. But as he progressed, and had a little bit of success here and there, and nobody else pulled out of the pack, I think he got a little bit of hope in a way that was very uncharacteristic of him." John Connally says that "He had convinced himself he had a chance. Any man who [runs for President] has convinced himself there is a way he can be successful. And he had convinced himself." Deriding the idea that a southerner could not be elected President "as more a fixation of timid politicians than it is any widespread feeling on the part of the American people," Russell told reporters that he expected to arrive at the convention with between 300 and 400 votes, that neither Kefauver, Barkley nor Harriman would be able to amass the necessary 616, and that by the seventh or eighth ballot, he would win. The depth of his hopes can perhaps be measured by the fact that, in an effort to remake his image with liberals, he even attempted for a time to portray himself as a "moderate" on racial issues, stating that he was for "constitutional" government and that the Constitution "enumerated the basic and fundamental rights which are the heritage of every citizen without regard to race or creed." His long opposition to the FEPC, he added, was not based on racial considerations but on his opposition to government interference in private business. ("He could not," however, as his biographer Fite notes, "muster enough moderation to criticize segregation," and the attempted makeover didn't last long. Pressed by reporters to comment on segregated food counters at Washington drugstores, Russell said that he was "American enough to believe that, if a drug store owner wants to serve only red-headed people with brown eyes, he can do it." Even his desire to be President couldn't overcome his prejudices. After Kefauver said he would feel "morally bound" to accept a strong FEPC plank, reporters pressed Russell on what he would do if the convention adopted such a plank; he would, Russell said, ignore it.)

Then, in the latter part of June, Russell made the same mistake that Lee had made—the mistake that led to Gettysburg. He took his campaign into the North.

The Democratic Party officials and convention delegates whom Richard Russell met on this trip responded to his personality as people always responded to his personality. One of the men who met him in Maine, Edmund Muskie, who would later be that state's Governor and a United States Senator, was then a young county committeeman meeting all the potential candidates for the first time. "Of all of them, Russell made the biggest impression on me," Muskie would recall years later. "He had the look of an eagle. There was strength there. He knew he was coming to a Northern state. He made no apologies. He was coming so we could see what he was. When he walked into a room, instantly you knew here was a man you could trust. You knew from his demeanor, the way he moved: that quiet projection of authority, authority in the sense of knowing what they're about, who they are. And when he spoke—Russell's intellect was very impressive."

Impressed though they were by the personality, however, the northern Democrats did not forget the principles for which Russell stood. When he met with "the New Jersey leaders," George Reedy was to recall, "he got the same reaction from all of them: 'My God, Senator, we'd like to support you. You're the best man around, but we can't support a southerner.' " There was to be no support for Russell in Maine, none in New Jersey, and none in the other northern or western states—New York, Pennsylvania, Wyoming, California, Colorado—to which he traveled. He had thought Big Ed Johnson's support would give him Colorado, he had counted on Colorado. But when he arrived in Denver, Big Ed had to give him bad news: there was no hope that the delegation would support him; the only possibility of keeping Colorado's votes out of the Harriman column would be to persuade the delegation to vote for a favorite son on the early ballots. Then the two senators walked out on a stage together before the delegation; despite Ed Johnson's immense popularity in his home state, there was little applause, and even some scattered boos. From Colorado, Russell flew to California, where he had hoped for a bloc of votes in California's big delegation. The response in California was very cold.

ARRIVING AT THE CONVENTION that was being held in the International Amphitheatre, near the Chicago stockyards, a week after Eisenhower had ended forever Robert Taft's dream of following his father into the White House (and had chosen as his running mate thirty-nine-year-old freshman Senator Richard M. Nixon), Russell and his Georgia supporters still believed he had a chance to win. Walter George himself was going to deliver the nominating speech, the great Walter George whose speeches could change votes in the Senate. "They thought Walter George could work a miracle," John Connally recalls. More dispassionate observers were startled at their optimism. Visiting Russell's campaign headquarters, two Georgians with experience in national politics and an awareness that by this time Russell had no realistic "expectations of getting the nomination," Chip Robert, the knowledgeable Georgia national committeeman, and Roy V. Harris, publisher of the *Augusta Courier,* got what Harris calls a "surprise." Harris recalls convention manager Cocke saying, " 'Now, we're going to get so many votes on the first ballot, and . . . on the seventh ballot Dick will be nominated. This state will come, and this state will come.' And I scratched my head, and I'd look at Chip and he'd look back at me. . . . We found out they were serious. We found out Dick was serious. . . ."

The jammed Amphitheatre was not the Senate Chamber; Walter George tried in vain to make himself heard as the hundreds of delegates would not stop talking among themselves. With only a handful of exceptions, the only marchers in the parade for Russell (in which, one article stated, "Senator Lyndon Johnson was among the most enthusiastic paraders") were southern delegates. The convention's decision had in fact become a foregone conclusion on the day before George spoke, for on that day the Governor of the host state had spoken, welcoming the delegates—and had demonstrated vividly why *he* was known as a great orator. "In one day," the *New York Times* reported, "all the confused and unchannelled currents seemed to converge upon the shrinking figure of Governor Adlai Stevenson as the one and only, the almost automatic, choice of the Convention," and Stevenson had finally agreed that if he was chosen, he would run.

Even so, Russell refused to give up hope. After the second ballot, on which he had received 268 votes, only five more than he had received in 1948 when he hadn't campaigned and almost all of them again from the South, "things began to fall apart," says Ernest Vandiver Jr., a Georgia politician working on Russell's staff, and the Arizona delegation (which in loyalty to Carl Hayden had added twelve votes to the southern total) "came to me asking me if I could release them from their pledge so that they could vote for the winning candidate, so . . . I called the Senator and told him the situation and he said, 'No, I won't release. No, I want them to stick in there. You can't ever tell what might happen.' " On the second ballot, the move to Stevenson began, and he won easily on the third, with Russell receiving 261 votes.

FOR A MAN WHO LOVED and idealized his "Southland" as deeply as did Richard Russell to be told to his face that no southerner could be President was, in Goldsmith's phrase, a "visceral blow." He "had indeed known, rationally, that he could not be nominated. Before campaigning in the North, however, he had not heard political leaders . . . tell him to his face that he was obviously the best-qualified candidate, but that they could not support a Southerner." As George Reedy says, "It's one thing to know something academically; it's another to have it hit you in the face."

He had planned to go on a fishing vacation off the Florida coast arranged by George Smathers—Lyndon Johnson and two or three other senators would be along—following the convention, but now he said he wouldn't be going. He returned to Winder for a while. For the first time, he began to complain about his health, talking about a pain in his left shoulder, a cough, headaches.

Johnson arranged for Russell to go to the Mayo Clinic, where a week-long physical examination found his health "excellent." Although he was still only fifty-five years old, however, aides would notice, from this time on, a loss of what they called "energy," and when, that fall, he visited the Johnson Ranch, Lady Bird noticed the same thing. "Energy; it's my feeling that after 1952 he did not exhibit as much of that," she says. And her sharp eyes noticed other changes, which she felt she understood. "I have a distinct feeling" that the 1952 campaign "was sort of a benchmark in his life," she was to say. "It was the time when he really put his chips in and tried, and not receiving the nomination probably caused him to retreat into the ivory tower . . . sort of withdrew him from the field of battle to some extent." Upon his return to Capitol Hill, some journalists noticed the change, although none of them would do more than hint at it in print until after his death in 1971. Samuel Shaffer of *Newsweek* would write at that time that "Something happened internally to Richard Russell after the 1952 campaign." He "lost some of his zest for legislative battles." And George Reedy, who often heard Russell refer to that campaign "with some bitterness," began to notice creeping into Russell's conversation "a little querulous tone" that had not been there before. "He had just been hurt so deeply."

This bitterness was to have a significant effect on Lyndon Johnson's career. It made Russell more determined than ever that one day the North would accept the South back into the nation in the most dramatic manner possible, by electing a southerner to be its President. He wouldn't be that southerner, he knew that now; he would never try for the presidency again, he told people around him. But by the end of 1952, it was becoming clear to a number of these people that Richard Russell had settled on the southerner it was to be.

Russell's growing affection for Lyndon Johnson had now been cemented by gratitude—gratitude for Johnson's help in his campaign. "He [Johnson] worked very earnestly in my behalf," Russell would say. "He did everything in the world—everything he could. . . . He really meant it when he supported me in '52." And beyond these personal considerations—and far more important to Russell in matters vital to the South—during the campaign Lyndon Johnson had demonstrated a political qualification that the Georgian, from his own experience, now understood was essential for any southerner who wanted to become President.

Watching Johnson talking familiarly at the convention to delegates and political leaders from New York, from Chicago, from Montana—from all across the North—Russell had seen that these men knew the Texan and liked him, these men whose feeling toward most southerners was contempt. What other southern senator was a friend of Dubinsky? What other southern senator *knew* Dubinsky? He was already, of course, aware that in Washington Johnson was a member not only of southern but of New Deal circles, a pal not only of John Stennis and Lister Hill but of Tommy Corcoran and Abe Fortas—one of the relatively few men in Washington to have a foot firmly in both camps. Before he had taken his campaign north, Richard Russell might not have realized fully the importance of such a national acquaintance, an acquaintance on both sides of the Mason-Dixon Line, but he realized it now. If his goal—to make a southerner President—was to be realized, that southerner, while absolutely committed to "constitutional principles," would have to be someone with whom northerners, even northern liberals, were nonetheless comfortable. With at least one southern senator committed, Russell believed, to "constitutional principles," northerners were comfortable already.

Johnson possessed other qualifications that Russell now understood to be essential. A national campaign, he had learned, was indeed "a new league," requiring financing on a scale of which he had previously been unaware. Johnson, he had seen, had access to such financing—easy access. Watching Johnson discuss politics with northern delegates, Russell had seen that he understood their states' internal politics. Russell's knowledge of, and ability to relate to, intra-state politics across the country had been unequaled by that of any other senator. There was, he now saw, another senator who knew, and could relate to, these politics perhaps as well as he.

And there were yet other qualities, vaguer to define but even more important. During the campaign, Richard Russell and Lyndon Johnson had spent many hours in conversation not about senatorial or Armed Services Committee strategy but about political strategy on a national scale. Who can recognize a master of politics better than another master? As succeeding years were to make clear, Richard Russell was indeed beginning, if very gradually and hardly perceptibly at first, to withdraw from "the field of battle." But he was not abandoning the field to his enemies, to the enemies of the South. He believed that he had found a new champion, younger, with more "zest," who would, relying always on his advice and counsel, take the field in his place. Not long after the campaign, Richard Russell, who so much wanted a southerner to become President, began to make his feelings clear in confidential conversations. A year before, he had "soberly predicted" that "Lyndon Johnson could be President and would make a good one." Now, shortly after the 1952 election, George Reedy "became aware that Russell wanted to make Johnson President."

"Russell made no bones whatsoever" about that, Reedy recalls. "He was quite open with me. He was determined to elect a southerner president. And he could not see any other southerners that could be elected president except LBJ. He talked about that to me as early as 1953." As to his reasons, it is impossible today to know with certainty what they were, or what weight to give to each. Reedy says that Russell saw Johnson "as an instrument of this purpose—to heal the breach so the South would no longer be a separate part of the nation." But did he also mean something more—something darker? By far the best book on the Russell-Johnson relationship is a little-known work, *Colleagues,* by John A. Goldsmith, who began covering the Senate for the United Press in 1946 and was head of its Senate bureau for almost twenty years. In his book, Goldsmith speaks of Russell's "hope that Johnson might . . . become a President attuned to southern culture." What does that last phrase mean? Did it mean attuned to southern culture in the best sense, in the sense of civility and graciousness and tradition and the political creativity that made southerners principal architects of America's system of government? Or did it also mean attuned to that worst aspect of southern culture—that blacks had to be kept in their place? Had Johnson convinced Russell that in his heart he believed that? When one reads words spoken at the time by members of Russell's Southern Caucus, the senators to whom the Georgian explained his reasoning to secure their support of Johnson, it is difficult to escape that suspicion. In 1957, Herman Talmadge would arrive in the Senate as a new senator from Georgia, and receive Richard Russell's explanation of why he was supporting Johnson for the presidency: because "Johnson would be more favorable to the South's position on States' Rights and local self-government." In Talmadge's view, that statement was not about breach-healing, as became apparent when the author interviewed Russell's fellow Georgia senator in January, 2000. Johnson, Talmadge said, "gave me the impression" that his views on the appropriate relationship between white and black Americans were the views of the southern senators. And what were Johnson's views, Talmadge was asked. "Master and servant," Talmadge replied. Didn't Johnson have any sympathy for the plight of blacks? "None indicated," Talmadge said. "He was with us in his heart," he said—and, he said, that was what Russell believed. It was when he was asked if Russell was boosting Johnson for President out of friendship that John Stennis replied that Russell "wasn't a bosom friend of anyone when it came to . . . constitutional principles." The concept of segregation—continued segregation—was of course deeply embedded in "States' Rights," "local self-government," and "constitutional principles." A Georgia friend once told Russell, "You're just fighting a delaying action." Russell replied: "I know, but I *am* trying to delay it—ten years if I'm not lucky, two hundred years if I am." A delay of some decades would be a considerable victory. And, during those decades, a lot could happen. The mood of the country could change, could become more conservative, more supportive of the southern way of life, or at least less overwhelmingly determined that that way be changed. A long enough delay might almost be the equivalent of victory for the South. Did Russell feel that one way of ensuring a long enough delay would be to make Lyndon Johnson President? Whatever the reason, Richard Russell, Reedy says, "was very determined to elect Lyndon Johnson President of the United States."

THE LESSON OF RICHARD RUSSELL'S DOOMED, quixotic campaign of 1952 was not lost on Lyndon Johnson, for whom it had the deepest implications. After all the acknowledgments that Russell was the best qualified candidate for the presidency—acknowledgments that had come from the North as well as the South—he had received virtually no northern votes at the Democratic Convention; the fact that he had never had a realistic chance of winning his party's nomination, much less the presidency, had been made dramatically clear. And if the strongest possible southern candidate had never had a chance, *no* southern candidate had a chance. If Lyndon Johnson had ever entertained a hope of winning the nomination as a candidate identified largely with the South, Russell's fate demonstrated conclusively the futility of such a hope. In order to attain his great goal, Johnson would have to make the party and the nation stop thinking of him as a southerner.

And this hard fact created for Johnson the most difficult of dilemmas.

Being linked with the South would keep him from rising beyond the Senate. Yet being linked with the South was the only way in which he could rise within the Senate.

DURING THE 1952 CAMPAIGN, the Red Scare and the inability to win in Korea stirred up the class and ethnic resentments that were never far below the surface of the American electorate. Republican charges that the Democrats were "soft on Communism" and that in fact the Roosevelt-Truman years had been "twenty years of treason," and Joe McCarthy's references to "Alger—I mean Adlai" and his statement that if he got onto the Democrat's campaign train with a baseball bat, he would "teach patriotism to little Ad-lie," resonated with the electorate. And so did the personality of the Republican candidate, about whom British Field Marshal Bernard Law Montgomery, no fan, had once remarked: "He merely has to smile at you, and you trust him at once." Journalists, attracted by Stevenson's wit and dignified, issue-oriented campaign, were slow to understand this, and polling was not as exact a science as it would later become (and pollsters, burned in 1948, may have been hedging a bit), so that the predictions were summed up in the *New York Times* headline the morning before the balloting: "ELECTION OUTCOME HIGHLY UNCERTAIN." But Dwight Eisenhower, America's greatest military hero, who had smiled at the American people—and promised them "I shall go to Korea"—was swept into office with 55 percent of the vote, and 442 electoral votes to Stevenson's 89. Stevenson retained his sense of humor (after the election, he asked a friend, "Who did I think I was, running against George Washington?" and said of the results, "I'm too old to cry, but it hurts too much to laugh"), but Eisenhower's overwhelming victory pulled so many Republican candidates into office with him that the GOP won control of both houses of Congress, the Senate by a single vote; over the Christmas holidays, Capitol maintenance men unscrewed Senate desks from the floor of the Chamber and rearranged them, so that there were only forty-seven on the Democratic side of the center aisle.

Among the missing Democrats would be Ernest McFarland. Once, McFarland had been a fixture in the Senate, a sure bet for re-election. Then he became Leader—and identified in Arizona with the unpopular Truman Administration. Scant his leadership responsibilities though he would, moreover, they had nonetheless cut into the time he could spend back home campaigning. He had been defeated by a forty-three-year-old Phoenix city councilman, Barry Goldwater.

His loss had re-emphasized the perils posed to a Democratic Leader, particularly one who would be up for re-election in less than two years: Scott Lucas had accepted the leadership in 1949 and been defeated in 1950; McFarland had accepted it in 1951, and been defeated in 1952. The job had cost both men their careers. With a Republican in the White House, the Democratic

Leader would no longer be forced to support unpopular presidential programs, and, as the party's highest elected official, he and the Speaker would assume a larger importance in national affairs, so that the leadership became in some respects more desirable. But during the campaign, liberals had been so infuriated by the refusal of southern Democratic senators (including, notably, Lyndon Johnson) to campaign enthusiastically for Adlai Stevenson that the old hostility between the liberal and conservative wings in the Senate had been dramatically inflamed, and on balance the problems that would confront the next Democratic Leader loomed more menacingly than ever. But although Johnson's senatorial term would be up in two years, he wanted the job. One Democratic senatorial aide recalls that when McFarland lost, "the liberals began musing on what they would do when they got back to Washington, whom they were going to support." But long before they got back, Johnson had begun to move. The dawn had just broken in Boston, and after a long, tense night, young John Fitzgerald Kennedy had just learned that he had defeated Henry Cabot Lodge Jr., when he got a call and Kennedy aide Lawrence F. O'Brien heard him say, "Well, thank you, Senator, thank you very much." Putting down the phone, he told O'Brien, with what O'Brien described as "a puzzled expression": "That was Lyndon Johnson in Texas. He said he just wanted to congratulate me." It was an hour earlier in Texas. "The guy must never sleep," Kennedy said. Kennedy's puzzlement over the call disappeared when, a few hours later, the final Arizona results were reported. With the Democratic leadership suddenly vacant, "Johnson wasn't wasting any time in courting Kennedy's support," O'Brien was to explain.

Richard Russell could either become Leader himself, or decide who would. According to some sources, the Arizona results had hardly been tallied when the Brown & Root DC-3 was in the air, carrying Johnson to Winder. According to others, the two senators met in Washington, on November 9. Evans and Novak, who interviewed the two men that month, reported that Johnson, in his first telephone call that morning after Election Day, suggested that Russell be Leader, and volunteered his support, saying, "I'll do the work and you'll be the boss." Russell declined; since the Georgian had been turning down the job for years, "Johnson," they wrote, "must have had a strong suspicion that this was precisely what Russell would do." Russell then suggested that Johnson himself should take the job. Quickly agreeing, Johnson set one "condition": since he would be constantly needing the Old Master's advice, he said, Russell would have to change his desk in the Senate Chamber so that he would be sitting directly behind the Leader's desk.

Matters were settled quickly. Bobby Baker was called out of class at the American University law school to take a telephone call from Texas, and when he told Johnson, "All you've got to do is convince one man and you're home free," Johnson told him that that man had already been convinced, and that Bobby should let his sponsor, Burnet Maybank, know it. When the South Carolina Senator told Baker, "I'm a Dick Russell man first, last, and always, if he wants it," Baker assured him that Russell didn't want it, and was supporting Johnson, and Maybank agreed to send a telegram to Johnson pledging to support him unless Russell became a candidate. When Johnson telephoned John Stennis in Mississippi to ask for his support, the conversation was a reprise of the one that had occurred between the two senators two years earlier, when the topic had been the assistant leadership. "I very frankly told him that if Senator Russell was interested at all, that I would support him, Senator Russell," but Johnson said "he had already checked it out with Senator Russell," so "I told him I'd support him gladly." North Carolina's Clyde Hoey, who had already publicly suggested Russell for the job, now wrote the Georgian that while "I was strong for you, as I would be for you for anything," in deference to his wishes "I shall do all I can for Lyndon Johnson." To every senator who telephoned Russell to ask him to take the leadership, Russell replied that he didn't want it, and that he wanted Johnson to have it. And these calls did not come only from southern senators, for Russell's influence was not confined to them. The eighty-five-year-old Theodore Francis Green of Rhode Island was one caller, and when he said, "A southerner should be the Leader," Russell told him who he would like the southerner to be. Some senators who didn't telephone Russell were telephoned by him instead, and on November 10, he wrote on his desk calendar in the Senate Office Building: "Saw L. Johnson—buttoned up leadership for him." That afternoon, in a very rare gesture, he invited reporters into his office so that he could make the stamp of approval public. "A number of senators have highly honored me by suggesting me for the post," he said, but "Senator Johnson is my choice for the place and I shall support him. . . . In my opinion, he will be chosen." Johnson's selection "is practically certain," the astute James L. McConaughy wired his editors at *Time*. "Dick Russell's endorsement means that it is as good as in the bag already." In fact, by November 10, just eight days after the election, Johnson was assured of the support of a majority of the forty-seven Democrats.

A MERE MAJORITY was not what Lyndon Johnson had in mind, however. Becoming Leader with purely conservative support and the liberals solidly opposed to him would exacerbate the hostility between the two factions which had hamstrung past Democratic Leaders. Only by creating a new unity among the party's senators could he avoid the fate of McFarland and Lucas and Barkley. Besides, were he to win the leadership almost entirely with southern votes, the press would identify him as the candidate of the South. Lyndon Johnson needed not a simple majority, but a big majority—one that included enough liberals so that he would not be tagged with that label so destructive to his future hopes.

Such a majority was going to be very difficult to achieve, Johnson saw.

Russell couldn't help him get it—couldn't help him with Douglas or Lehman or Hennings or Kefauver or Murray or Monroney, or with newly elected liberals such as Kennedy, or Jackson or Mike Mansfield or Albert Gore. In fact, although Green had at first told Russell he would be guided by his wishes, the elderly Rhode Islander was now under pressure from his fellow liberals—and was declining to make a public statement of his preference. As many as twenty senators might line up behind a liberal candidate for Leader. So Lyndon Johnson began campaigning himself, telephoning other senators, listening, trading, selling.

Some of the selling was on philosophical grounds—to Hayden, for example, who wanted assurances that a new Leader would support the cherished right of unlimited debate. And some was done on grounds more pragmatic. The question of committee assignments for the newly elected senator from Massachusetts was being handled at what was, for the Kennedys, the highest level. Jim Rowe had been contacted by Joe Kennedy himself about "a good assignment for Jack." Rowe contacted Johnson. What was said—or promised—is not known, but on November 13 Jack Kennedy wrote Johnson that "I want you to know that you will have my full support."

In the case of Pat McCarran the grounds may have been more pragmatic still, for Nevada's Silver Fox had a problem that went beyond the political. His long-rumored ties to Las Vegas and Reno underworld gambling syndicates had recently been noted in legal papers, in which the Senator was named, along with several prominent mafiosi, in a suit brought by Hank M. Greenspun, the crusading editor of the *Las Vegas Sun,* who charged them with attempting to drive him out of business because of his criticism of the "McCarran Machine." If the suit escalated into criminal proceedings against the underworld figures, not only would McCarran's re-election prospects be threatened but a whole new group of legal and public relations problems would be opened up, and the pre-trial hearings were not going well for him.

The solution to many of the senator's problems might lie in the appointment of his protégé, James W. Johnson Jr., whom McCarran had previously installed as Nevada's Democratic state chairman, as the state's United States Attorney. In the lawsuit, Greenspun's attorney had implied that McCarran had urged James Johnson's nomination "to get a more friendly United States Attorney in Nevada."

President Truman hated McCarran, but through an oversight had sent James Johnson's appointment to the Senate in a large group of nominations. While McCarran was rushing it through the Judiciary Committee, the White House was made aware of the situation, and when the commission, approved by the Senate, had been sent back to Truman in July, 1952, for the normally *pro forma* signature, Truman had refused to sign, and had made it clear he never would. McCarran was one Senate elder who had never been particularly charmed by Lyndon Johnson, but now he apparently asked Johnson if he would intervene with the President if he was elected Leader; Johnson said he would, and McCarran agreed to support him.

As he was making the calls, Johnson was counting votes and making lists. The first lists were drawn up, as it happened, on a notepad from the Carlton Hotel, where Brown & Root maintained a suite, with Johnson making a large, firm checkmark next to a senator's name when he was sure of his vote. The later lists—of the names of all forty-seven Democratic senators, from "Anderson" to "Symington," typed in two double-spaced columns in alphabetical order—were on plain white paper.

This was vote-counting by the son of a man who had fooled himself with wishful thinking. On the typed list Johnson would write a number to the left of the name of each senator who was for him, to the right of the name of each senator who was against him, and no number was put on the left until Lyndon Johnson was absolutely sure he could count on that senator's vote. Senators about whom he had any doubts—even senators who had promised him their vote but about whom he still had some trace of uneasiness—were put in the "against" column. Optimistic though he may have been that Harry Byrd would support him, a number "1" was written against Byrd—to the right, to the right along with Douglas and Lehman and Humphrey. Russell may have assured him that Theodore Francis Green would be for him, but he himself had not heard from Green, and against Green the number "7" was written, on the right. He had been told that Willis Robertson of Virginia was certain, but after listening very carefully to Robertson on the phone, he felt that Robertson was not certain enough. He marked an "L" for "leaning" on the right of Robertson's name, not on the left.

The first of the lists—they are undated, but this first one was apparently made on November 11—had twenty numbers or marks to the right; the numbers on the left (including, by this time, McCarran's) ran only up to twenty-seven. About noon on that day, Johnson talked again to Robertson, and afterwards wrote a "28" to the left of the Virginian's name, but there were still nineteen names with numbers on the right—too many—and among them were names whose opposition would not look good in the newspapers: Matt Neely, for example, and, still, Green. The oldest senator was staying at the Vanderbilt Hotel in New York. On November 12, Johnson took the train to New York, returning the same day, and went to 231 to clean up some work. A few minutes after he had disappeared into his inner office, Green's administrative assistant, Eddie Higgins, came through the door of the outer office carrying a press release. Walter Jenkins snatched it from his hand, and read its first sentence even as he buzzed in to Johnson, "I am happy to join . . . in endorsing Senator Lyndon B. Johnson of Texas for Minority Leader." Attached was a note to Johnson that Higgins had written: "At the direction of Senator Green, I am releasing the attached statement to the papers immediately." Johnson dictated a wire to the Vanderbilt: "THANKS FROM THE BOTTOM OF MY HEART." Scratching out the negative number to the right of Green's name, he wrote instead a

"29." He not only had another vote, but a vote which was, as the *New York Times* noted the next day, from a senator "identified with the Fair Deal wing of the party in the North." And another piece of good news had been waiting for him when he got back to Washington, a memo from Jenkins telling him that "Senator Clements tried to page you on the train to tell you that he had talked to Albert Gore and that Albert Gore is going to be for you." And John Pastore and Neely were, at last, firm in their support. "30," Johnson wrote. "31." "32."

THIS LEFT A POSSIBLE FIFTEEN VOTES against him—fifteen liberal votes, still too many. And the opposition was hardening. Analyzing the upcoming selections of Rayburn and Johnson, William White wrote in the *New York Times* that both were southerners and their selection therefore "suggests . . . the almost indestructible power of the Southerners" in the Democratic Party; Rayburn's selection, however, "will be hailed with fervor by the 'regular' [liberal] Democrats because in the recent presidential election Mr. Rayburn risked forty years of political prestige in a vain effort to hold Texas for the Democrats." Johnson's selection, White wrote, "will not [be hailed] for the reason that he is [too] close to the intransigent southerners. . . . The Democrats of the Senate are about to choose as their Leader . . . not only a Southerner but a Southerner whose state went to General Dwight D. Eisenhower. . . ." Liberal senators, as Hubert Humphrey was to recall, were "upset" by that prospect. They were also, as a memo from *Time*'s Washington bureau put it, "worried about their own problems back home, if they were being led in Washington by such a person." On November 13, Jim Rowe telephoned Johnson's office to warn him that "some of the liberals are getting ready to try to knife you" by nominating their own candidate when the Democratic caucus met on January 2 to formally select a Leader.

"Humphrey wanted it, but he couldn't get the votes," Bobby Baker was to recall. Fond though some of the southern senators had become of him personally, that fondness would obviously not extend to supporting a civil rights champion for Leader, so, as he himself realized, his candidacy was unfeasible. Humphrey was therefore asked to organize the liberals and find a candidate to block Johnson.

The liberal effort was a study in ineptitude. When, in mid-November, eighteen or nineteen senators finally got around to meeting—at Drew Pearson's home in Georgetown—they decided that since no militant liberal could win southern votes in the caucus, "their only hope of success was to support Lister Hill, the most moderate southerner," as Doris Kearns Goodwin put it. They telephoned Hill at his home in Alabama, only to be told that he was already committed to Johnson. They finally settled on seventy-six-year-old James Murray.

The Montanan's frailness, which had just begun making itself apparent at the time of Johnson's arrival in the Senate in 1949, was more marked now. His step was increasingly uncertain; at moments he seemed almost to totter. Murray had long been a courageous fighter for the New Deal, but his mind was no longer as strong as his heart, and more and more it dwelt in the past. "He had perfect memory of everything that took place under Franklin Roosevelt, but not as much more recent," an aide says. But he was still capable, at least on most occasions, of holding his own on the Senate floor. And he was still a great favorite with the press, a noted New Deal "name." While his candidacy was not a genuine threat—twenty-four votes were needed for election as Leader, and Johnson had thirty-two commitments—it could receive publicity, publicity that would work against Johnson's objective.

The possibility of the press focusing on the leadership fight would of course be increased if speculation arose about the attitude of the Democratic standard-bearer in the recent election, and in mid-November, Adlai Stevenson, speaking to several Democratic senators—not Johnson—from Chicago said he was planning a trip to Washington to discuss party policy in a meeting with Democratic congressional leaders.

Johnson did not want that. Who knew where a Stevenson visit to Washington might lead? It might revitalize the Senate liberals. It had to be headed off. Although Lady Bird Johnson was in the Scott and White Clinic in Temple, Texas, for a gynecological procedure, her husband did not leave Washington until the Stevenson visit *was* headed off—which was accomplished in a telephone conversation with Stevenson at 4:10 p.m. on November 20, with Mary Rather on an extension, without Stevenson's knowledge, taking down every word.

"I was hoping to get a chance to see you some time and talk to you a little bit," Stevenson said, and when Johnson said he would shortly be leaving for Texas, Stevenson asked if "you couldn't stop off here on your way." Or, he said, he would be in New Jersey on December 3 and in Washington on December 4. Perhaps they could meet there.

Johnson was very diplomatic. He gently let Stevenson know that the leaders had already met. He, Russell, Clements, and Kerr "all had a very fine discussion the other night," he said. They were all "very much in agreement." And, he said, one thing they had agreed on was that there should not be any public meeting "until after we get this Senate organization behind us, because some of the speculators might attempt to inject you into it and we know that would be an embarrassing thing. . . . They would be saying that you were injecting yourself into it." "We kinda concluded that probably we would get that behind us on January 2." After it was behind them, he said, we "would try to work out a meeting. . . ."

When Stevenson responded that he had thought the matter of the leadership had been settled ("I was under the impression . . . that there wasn't any question but what the Democrats would elect you"), a warning, still diplomatic but slightly firmer, was delivered. "There is not any [question]," Johnson said. But, he said, "there are some pretty strong feelings on the other side." And "up until the time they actually make the decision, you know, you are taking a little chance in having conferences. The first thing the press says is that the Governor is telling the Senate what to do. Or that I was asking the Governor to get these boys in line."

Stevenson seemed to take the point. "That is that," he said. "The last thing I want to do is to get in any way entangled with the selection . . ." and Johnson then assured him, "You are the head of the Democratic Party. You must remain so. You are our leader. You are the most popular one we have had. You made a great campaign. . . ." But, it turned out, Stevenson had not yet grasped Johnson's feeling that there should be no meeting at all, not even on general party policy, before the leadership election. "I would like to talk to you off the record in Springfield rather than Washington," he said. "They always know in Washington." Johnson replied that "I'm afraid that if I go to Springfield they will [know] too. I am afraid the construction will be placed on it that I am seeking Governor Stevenson's intervention. I think that would be bad. The denial would never catch up with the original stories. I think if we do it early in the year that would be better." And when Stevenson persisted—"I don't want to cause any commotion, but if I could talk to you a bit. And I think I would like to talk to Dick Russell"—the warning became firmer still. "I know he [Russell] feels very much that we should talk and he would be very glad to participate, I feel sure. I feel sure, too, that we oughtn't to endanger a possible division in the Senate and get you involved." Finally, after several other exchanges, Stevenson acceded. "Maybe it would be better if we didn't try to have any further talks for the present," he said.

THE NEUTRALIZATION OF STEVENSON quashed the liberals' last hope of blocking Johnson. Even some of the senators who had met at Pearson's home had not agreed to vote for Murray. The liberals were not giving up, however, as was revealed by their spokesman, Humphrey, when, on December 15, 1952, he appeared on a radio show, *Reporters' Roundup,* and was asked if he was supporting Johnson for Leader. Humphrey said he was not, "although I do have a great respect for Lyndon Johnson as a person." "For the good of the Democratic Party," he said, "it would be better to have someone that wasn't so clearly identified with a sectional group." Pressed on the point, he said he believed that "if the Democratic Party . . . intends to be the great national liberal party . . . it must emphasize the broad national program on a liberal basis."

But Johnson did not want any vote at the caucus at all. A vote was a fight, and a fight not only meant newspaper stories, in which he would be labeled the southern candidate, but also an increase in tensions that would later make unity harder to achieve. And of course it meant there would not be unanimity, the unanimity that was psychologically so important to him that "anything less than one hundred percent was a great blow."

So he made more calls. What Lyndon Johnson said during these calls we don't know. Was he appealing to these men on personal grounds—playing on their affection for him or on their admiration for his abilities? Was his approach more pragmatic: was he delicately or forthrightly reminding them—with the help of Jenkins' files—of favors he had done them in the past, hinting—or speaking bluntly—about favors he could do for them in the future? We don't know. We only know that some of the calls were to senators and senators-elect—men like Tom Hennings and Stu Symington and Scoop Jackson—who in the past would have been firmly in the liberal column, on Lyndon Johnson's lists with the numbers on the right side of their name, but who had been recipients, during their election campaigns, of financial assistance from Lyndon Johnson. And we know that on Lyndon Johnson's lists, there were fewer and fewer numbers on the right side.

BUT JOHNSON didn't want any numbers there at all.

The key to the unanimous vote he wanted was the liberal who was organizing the liberal forces, and who was giving no indication of quitting just because the fight was hopeless. "Hubert can't win," Johnson told Bobby Baker, "but I don't want him gumming up the works for me. If he fights to the bitter end, then I won't have a cut dog's chance to be an effective Leader. The Republicans will eat our lunch and the sack it came in."

Johnson sent Baker to "promise" Humphrey what Baker was to call "candy"—the candy that, from his reading of Humphrey, Johnson knew would be sweetest to his taste. "I know that Senator Johnson will be looking to you as the spokesman for the Senate liberals, and for the national constituency you're building," Baker told him. And, knowing also Humphrey's desire to be a member of the Senate "club," he offered him that candy, too. "I wouldn't be surprised if he brought you into the leadership circle," Baker said. And when that somewhat vague offer didn't produce the desired effect, Johnson made a more direct one himself. Telephoning Humphrey at home, he asked for his support and, Humphrey relates, "When I said I had already made a commitment and couldn't support him, he said he was sorry, in part because he was considering me for the minority whip job."

Charmed and awed though he may have been by Johnson, eager though he was for his friendship, Humphrey would not abandon his fellow liberals. Despite this "exhilarating" offer, he tried to bargain with Johnson, telling him that the only way for him to obtain liberal support was to offer liberals additional seats on the Democratic Policy and Steering Committees. And the next day, he and fellow liberals Hunt of Wyoming, Lehman of New York, and Paul Douglas came to Johnson's office "prepared to trade our support."

But Humphrey was trying to bargain with a Lyndon Johnson who now, for the first time in their relationship, held all the cards. He had little patience with them. After letting them talk—"briefly," to use Humphrey's word—he told them he wasn't going to bargain with them. "He wasn't in the mood to make concessions." In fact, he said, the talking was over. "I've got the votes in the caucus, and I'm not going to talk to you." And then, "politely but curtly," he "dismissed us." And then, as soon as Humphrey had returned to his own office from "that awful meeting," Johnson telephoned him and told him to come back alone—and when he returned, Humphrey found himself in the presence of a different Lyndon Johnson from any he had seen before, not "quiet and gentle" but, in Humphrey's euphemistic phrase, "in a take-charge, no-nonsense mood," a Johnson whose tone was "stern" as he showed Humphrey that he had not yet fully absorbed the political lessons he had given him, and that he had still more lessons to learn.

"How many votes [for Murray] do you think you have?" Johnson asked, and when Humphrey replied, "Well, I think we have anywhere from thirteen to seventeen," Johnson "stared at me for a quiet moment and said, 'First of all, you ought to be sure of your count. That's too much of a spread. But you don't have them anyway. *Who* do you think you have?' "

Humphrey handed him a list of names, and Lyndon Johnson looked at it. "*He* isn't going to vote for him," he said. "*He* isn't, and *he* isn't. These fellows are going to vote for me."

"I can't believe that," Humphrey said, saying that the senators Johnson named had already promised him or Douglas that they would vote for Murray.

"Well, you'll find out," Lyndon Johnson said. And then he said, "As a matter of fact, Senator Hunt, who was just in here with you, is going to vote for me."

AT ABOUT TEN O'CLOCK in the morning on Friday, January 2, 1953, the forty-seven Democrats in the Senate of the United States began filing into Room 201 of the Senate Office Building, on whose door a painter had, the previous day, changed the gold lettering from "Majority Conference" to "Minority Conference." Ernest McFarland called the caucus to order and said that the first order of business would be to elect his replacement as Leader, and Richard Russell rose to nominate Lyndon Johnson of Texas.

Russell's notes indicate the points he wished to make about Johnson. "Courage," the notes say. "Character. Ability. Experience. Tolerance. LJ is Democrat. Record of party loyalty in Congress. In elections tried by fire. FDR. Supported party programs not slavishly but because believed. High degree of courage. Tempered with judgment. Against rash decisions. Patience and tolerance. No secret differences. No peer as conciliator. Complete confidence in his ability both to serve the party to which we adhere and the country and people we seek to serve." Mary Rather, who heard about the speech from Johnson, was later to call it "very wonderful." The seconding speeches were given by Chavez of New Mexico, speaking for the West, and Green of Rhode Island, speaking for the East.

After Murray was nominated, McFarland called for the vote. Humphrey was to recall that "Senator Murray had his own vote and mine, plus three or four others," and those, despite the list in Humphrey's pocket and the promises he had received, were all he had. (He did not have Hunt's.) "You'll find out," Johnson had warned Humphrey—and now Humphrey had found out. "I'll never forget it," he was to say. "He was just as right as day. They voted for Johnson." He quickly moved that Johnson's election be made unanimous without a formal vote, and it was.

Humphrey was to explain later that he had made that motion because "Number One, I didn't want to have Murray embarrassed . . . by getting only a handful of votes from his colleagues. . . . For an old gentleman who had been there all those years, that didn't look good at all." But that was only Number One. Humphrey had learned a lot about Lyndon Johnson (although, as would in later years become apparent, not nearly enough). He had seen that Johnson was not a man to forgive and forget, to let bygones be bygones, to tolerate opposition. He had seen in Johnson a determination to make opponents pay for their opposition, and pay dearly. And that last, "stern," interview—in that new, "take-charge," tone—had reinforced that insight; he had seen a side of Lyndon Johnson he had not seen previously, and an element of fear, of intimidation, had been added to their relationship, as is revealed by the rest of Humphrey's explanation for wanting to dispense with a formal vote: "Number Two, I knew that Johnson would keep book. I mean, when that roll call came he'd watch to see who each one of them was." Whatever the explanation for Humphrey's motion, however, it gave Johnson not merely unity but unanimity.

After the caucus, Johnson summoned Humphrey to 231, and told him to come alone: "Don't come down here with any committees."

When Humphrey came—alone—Johnson asked him: "Now, what do you liberals really want?" Humphrey was to recall that "The dialogue was brief and to the point. 'The first thing we want is some representation on the Policy Committee.'

" 'All right, you'll have it. Who did you want?'

" 'Well, I think it ought to be Jim Murray.'

" 'I don't think he's the right man, because he's older and he won't be effective, but if that's who you want, that'll be done. What else do you want?'

"I listed our other requests [formerly demands]" for liberal representation on a number of committees, Humphrey was to recall, and Johnson agreed to them. And then Johnson said, "Since you had enough sense not to drive it to a vote down there and made it unanimous, I am perfectly willing to deal with you." But, the new Leader said, "I don't want you bringing in a lot of these other fellows. When you've got something that your people want, *you* come see me. I'll talk to you. I don't want to talk to these other fellows. Now you go back and tell your liberal friends that you're the one to talk to me and that if they'll talk through you as their leader we can get some things done."

What Johnson was offering Humphrey now was power—the first power Humphrey had had in the Senate. Those "other fellows" would be told that if they wanted something from their party's Leader (and of course they would all, at one time or another, want something from the Leader), they would have to ask Humphrey to approach him on their behalf.

Humphrey understood the offer, and its significance for him. "I would be the bridge from Johnson to my liberal colleagues." He would hold the power only at Johnson's pleasure. "I had become his conduit and their spokesman not by their election, but by his appointment." As long as he and Johnson got along—but only as long as he and Johnson got along—he would keep that power.

And he accepted the offer. He was to say in his autobiography that he accepted it in the interests of getting things done. "I knew clearly by then that I had no chance of influencing legislation in any major way without the help of the . . . Leader. With his influence, I might get the necessary votes for legislation I was interested in." But, as time would make clear, he had accepted it also in his own interest. For whatever reason, the offer was accepted, and in accepting it, Humphrey was in effect pledging his allegiance to Lyndon Johnson.

The significance of this pledge for Johnson's prospects as Leader can hardly be exaggerated. He had needed to unify his party, which meant bringing the liberals to his side. Now he had succeeded in bringing the liberals' leader to his side, in binding him there quite firmly.

IN JANUARY, 1953, Lyndon Johnson was forty-four years old, and he was therefore not only the youngest senator in history to be elected either Majority or Minority Leader, but the youngest by quite a margin. Neither party had ever before elected a Leader who was in his forties; the average age of the seven previous Democratic Leaders at the time of their election was fifty-eight; the average age of the six Republicans who had been elected before 1953 was sixty-two.* In addition, Johnson had been elected Leader while still in his first term; in an institution in which seniority was considered so vital, only once previously had a first-term senator been elected Leader, and that was the first Leader, John Worth Kern (who had been elected at the age of sixty-three).

---

*The Leader the Republicans elected on the day that Johnson was elected, Robert Taft, was sixty-three. Before Johnson, the youngest Leader of either party had been fifty-three-year-old Joe Robinson.

When he had been young, Lyndon Johnson had come along his path so fast, and then, for seven years, he had stopped. Now he was coming fast again.

On the day they had been sworn in, several members of the Class of '48 had seemed far more likely than he to advance within the Senate. But Douglas and Humphrey had chosen the public route, becoming spokesmen for liberal causes, using the Senate floor as a national forum, as a pulpit for ringing speeches. Kefauver had chosen as his arena not the Senate floor but the television screen.

Lyndon Johnson had, in his defense preparedness work, sought national recognition as avidly as they, as avidly as any senator, but by a very different route: a route to publicity that was, up to the final moment of the press release or the leak about the press release, remarkably unpublic—the preparation, behind tightly closed doors, of subcommittee reports. And publicity had not in fact been a major factor in his advancement within the Senate. If the Douglases and Humphreys had chosen the outside route, he had chosen the inside route: the Senate route. And the key to his advancement had fit the pattern of his entire life: as he had done at San Marcos and in the House of Representatives, he had identified the one man who had the power that could best help him, had courted that man, had won his support, and through that support, had been given the opportunity to attain the position he sought. But if that was how he had been given the opportunity in the Senate, he had made the most of the opportunity, by following not the pattern of his previous life—the pushing, the grabbing—but rather the pattern of the Senate. The work that had been most significant in his Senate advancement had been quiet chats behind closed office doors; he had concentrated not on the podium but on the cloakroom and the Marble Room. It was in these private precincts of the Senate that he spent most of his time and energy.

These places suited him. In a way, Lyndon Johnson had never before been at home anywhere in his life—certainly not in the Hill Country, the trap he had longed to escape; not in the NYA, from which he had wanted to escape back to Washington; not in the House of Representatives, where he had been just one of a crowd. He was at home now. The Senate was his home. He had fit into it. His tone, his mannerisms, had been transformed utterly—transformed into the Senate tone, the Senate mannerisms. He had become the true Senate man.

Now that he had the leadership, there were, also with remarkable speed, hints of new mannerisms. Hubert Humphrey had noticed a new tone: "take-charge, no-nonsense, stern." Late in the afternoon of the day of the Democratic caucus, Drew Pearson encountered Johnson in a corridor. "He had just been made Democratic floor leader by the Southern reactionaries, and he felt supremely in the saddle," Pearson wrote in his diary. As Johnson brusquely dismissed a Pearson request, the columnist wrote, he could not help remembering "the days when Lyndon used to call me from Texas saying he had a tight primary fight and asking me" for help. The next day, the Senate convened before the usual packed galleries of opening day, and reporters in the Press Gallery, looking down at the new Democratic Leader at the front-row center-aisle desk, saw a new Lyndon Johnson. He wasn't so much sitting in his chair as sprawling in it, sprawling, as Evans and Novak were to write, "almost full length . . . legs crossed, laughing and joking . . . the picture of self-satisfaction."

21

The Whole Stack

Now that Lyndon Johnson had become the Leader of the Democratic senators, his personal ambitions were bound up with that divided and disorganized band. The bond was unbreakable: for him to use the leadership as a stepping-stone to his real goal, he would have to be an effective Leader—and he could be an effective Leader only to the extent that his Senate Democrats were an effective party.

Johnson's personal fortunes had been interwoven with institutions before, when he had been leader of the White Stars, or of the Little Congress, or of the Democratic Congressional Campaign Committee. Each of these entities had also in its own way been so disorganized and ineffective that in order for him to use them as vehicles for his personal, political advancement, it had been necessary for him not merely to make them more efficient but to change them completely, to transform them into institutions capable of accomplishing a political purpose. Each time, so creative was his political genius that he *had* transformed them. Now, however, the institution to which he was linked was not a college or staff members' social club or a political fund-raising committee but the Democratic Party in the Senate of the United States; now Lyndon Johnson's personal fortunes were bound up inextricably with the fortunes of something far larger than anything he had ever led before. This link carried with it, moreover, a threat, one that was terrible to a man who feared humiliation as much as Lyndon Johnson feared it, for every recent Democratic Leader had *been* humiliated, made a figure of public ridicule. And this institution had been insulated against change. Not only did a Senate Leader have little power—"nothing to promise them, nothing to threaten them with"—to cajole or force his party's senators into line behind him, the Senate's rules and customs had been designed to prevent him from acquiring any.

The link carried with it another threat to Lyndon Johnson's greater ambitions. Difficult though the acquisition of power would be for any Senate Leader, it would be especially difficult for him—because of the place from which he had come, and the place to which he wanted to go, because his true objective lay not in the Senate but beyond it. Power in the Senate was held by the southern senators who were his allies, and who had made him Leader. The natural human reluctance to surrender power would be reinforced in the southerners' case by their devotion to the institution and the region that were both sacred to them. Since their power was derived from the Senate's rules and precedents and constitutional prerogatives, bound up in the body's very fabric, any reduction in their power would entail drastic change in an institution they were determined to keep unchanged. And reinforcing that determination also was the fact that it was their power that made the Senate the South's stronghold, so that any reduction would also weaken the South. They would never give up their power voluntarily. Nor could they be forced to give it up—it was fortified far too strongly for any Leader to take it away. Lyndon Johnson's only hope of obtaining the power that the southerners now held was to persuade them to give it to him, and he would be able to do that only if they didn't realize that they were giving it to him—if he was able to conceal from them the implications of what he was doing.

Difficult though this would be, however, what would be even harder than getting the power would be what he would have to do with it once he got it. Power in the Senate might be in southern hands, but it was northern hands that held the prize at which he was really aiming. He could reach it only with northern support, and to get that support, he would have to make the Democratic Party in the Senate more responsive to northern wishes, would have to advance liberal causes. He would have to use the power that he took from the South on behalf of causes that the South hated.

But if senatorial power was the South's to give, the South also had the power to take it back. Even if he succeeded in enlarging a Leader's powers, the South not only would still hold its committee chairmanships but would still command a majority in the Democratic caucus. The South had made a Leader; the South would be able to unmake a Leader. If in furthering the causes of the North, he antagonized the South, the South could, in a very few minutes—in the time it took to take a vote in a caucus—make sure that he had no power to further anybody's causes, including his own. So he couldn't antagonize the South. Not only would he have to take power from the southern senators without them realizing what he was taking, he would have to use that power without them realizing how he was using it.

This would be very difficult, for deceiving the southern senators meant deceiving men who were expert parliamentarians, expert legislators, masters of their craft.

Masters. But not geniuses.

IN FRONT OF THE CAPITOL, during the first two weeks of 1953, scores of carpenters were hammering into place the stands for the presidential inaugural.

Pennsylvania Avenue was draped with red, white, and blue bunting, the full panoply that accompanies the transfer of executive power in America.

The hammering couldn't be heard down Delaware Avenue, where, on the second floor of the Senate Office Building, in Suite 231, the door to Lyndon Johnson's private office stayed closed, hour after hour, during those two weeks, while, on the four-button telephone on Walter Jenkins' desk, the left-hand button, the one that was lit when Johnson was using his phone, stayed lit hour after hour. Behind that door, Lyndon Johnson was attempting a transfer in legislative power, a transfer without precedent in American history; he was taking a gamble that would, if successful, change the nature of power in the Senate, a gamble in which the odds against him were very long—and in which the stakes were so high that, describing the maneuver later, he was to say, "I shoved in my whole stack."

Of all the barriers between a Senate Leader and genuine power the highest was the seniority system. The committee seats so vital to senators' careers were assigned according to that fixed rule, so a Leader had no discretion over the assigning, no power to use committee seats as instruments of threat or reward. And because the system enabled the southern senators, with their greater seniority, to monopolize seats on the better committees, it exacerbated the resentment of excluded northerners and thus sharpened the hostility between the party's two wings and made it all but impossible for a Democratic Leader to unite the party behind him. In addition, not only did the seniority system keep the Democratic Leader from being as strong as he might be, it kept the Democratic Party in the Senate from being as strong as *it* might be: filling vacant seats on the basis of longevity rather than expertise or ability meant that the party didn't make full use of that expertise or ability. But no Senate custom was more sacred than the seniority system, the system that "the Senate would no more abandon than it would abandon its name." Behind that door, over that telephone, Lyndon Johnson, in his first act as Leader, was trying to change the seniority system.

IN A WAY, he was working with a giant chessboard. It had 203 squares, the 203 seats on the Senate's fifteen Standing Committees.* In theory, ninety-four of them were his to play on, for the Democrats, in the minority in the Eighty-third Congress, would be allowed to fill that many seats. Actually, however, eighty-seven of the squares were already occupied by Democratic senators, so he had only seven to play on, and only four of these were on major committees.

By tradition, moves on the chessboard would be governed almost entirely by seniority. Into the four major committee seats would move the most senior

---

*In all the previous postwar Congresses, fourteen committees had had thirteen members, Appropriations twenty-one members, for a total of 203.

of the senators desiring them. Their moves would vacate four places. Into *them* would move the most senior senators wanting them. There would be other moves. Occasionally—not often, for a senator who moved from one committee to another had to start accumulating seniority with that committee from scratch—a senator would move from one committee to another of approximately equal importance. And of course there were always vacancies in the least desirable spaces: seats on the least important committees. They would generally be filled with newly elected senators who had no seniority at all. Seniority had never been the only factor in the filling of committee seats. Liberals, for example, would almost never be appointed to Finance, the committee which wrote tax laws like the oil depletion allowance which meant money in the pockets of oilmen and other business interests who backed conservatives. A disproportionate number of them found themselves relegated to the Post Office and Civil Service Committee or to the equally impotent Labor and Public Welfare. And sometimes, defeat or death would empty an unusual number of seats, and freshmen found themselves on important committees, as had been the case in Richard Russell's appointment to Appropriations in 1933. But for generation after generation, seniority had almost invariably been the governing factor. If more than one senator wanted to move into a vacant space, the one with the most seniority was the one who was allowed to move.

PLAYING THAT CHESS GAME in his private office, behind the closed door, sometimes he would be sitting in his big black leather chair behind the desk at the far end of the office, phone in hand, hunched forward in concentration. Sometimes he would be standing behind the desk. One mottled hand—the left hand if things were going well, the right hand if they weren't—would be wrapped around the black receiver he was holding to his ear, the receiver looking unexpectedly small in that huge fist. The other hand would usually be holding a cigarette. He lit one cigarette from the end of another, often not bothering to stub out the first, and the ashtray on his desk and the standing ashtray next to it were overflowing with butts, some still burning.

Often, for long minutes, the only words Lyndon Johnson spoke were words to encourage the man on the other end of the wire to keep talking—so that he could better determine what might bend the man to his purpose, what arguments might work. For long minutes, the only movements Lyndon Johnson made were to raise the cigarette to his mouth and take a long, deep drag. The hand gripping the telephone would not move, the lines of the normally mobile face would not move, the eyes next to the phone, narrowed to unblinking slits, gleamed black with concentration through a slender column of smoke while another column or two rose from the ashtrays, their lazy upward spiral accentuating the intensity of the big figure behind them. Lyndon Johnson would stand or sit that way for a long time, motionless, intent, listening—pouring

himself into that listening, all his being focused on what the other man was saying, and what the man wasn't saying; on what he knew about the other man,
and on what he didn't know and was trying to find out.

And then, when he had decided what arguments might work, Lyndon
Johnson would begin to talk, and as he did so, he would begin to circle the
desk, prowling restlessly around it in front of the fireplace that was so delicate
alongside his tall, burly frame. His voice would be soft, calm, rational, reasonable, warm, intimate, friendly, telling the stories, explaining the strategy, shoving in his whole stack. And whether he was listening or talking, the room was
filled with Lyndon Johnson's determination, with the passion and purpose radiating from him. Then the call would be over. He might immediately make
another one, the index finger so big in the dial. Or instead he might drop back
down into the big chair and sit for long minutes motionless, slouched down on
his spine, the relaxed pose of the body belied by the fierceness of the concentration on the face, the hand holding the cigarette rising again and again to his
lips. Or, turning his back on the room, he would stand behind the desk, staring
at the window whether the blinds in front of it were open or closed, stand there
unmoving except for the hand in his trouser pocket. There would be no sound
in that office at all except for the jingling of coins. Sometimes, then, he would
take out a white handkerchief from his other pants pocket and mop it hard over
his brow. And sometimes, lighting yet another cigarette, he would bend over in
his chair, head low as he took his first drag, "really sucking it in," in Jenkins'
phrase, and sit like that, head bowed, cigarette still in his mouth, for a while, as
if to allow the soothing smoke to penetrate as deeply as possible into his body,
as if trying desperately to relax for a moment. And then he would reach for the
phone again.

HE SOLD WITH LOGIC—some very unpleasant logic.

It was based on two new facts of political life that had been revealed
by that November 2 election, and that Lyndon Johnson, down on his ranch,
had grasped very quickly. One was the previously unappreciated depth of
America's affection for Dwight David Eisenhower. The other, demonstrated in
some hard numbers in the election returns, was that, even beyond Eisenhower's
personal victory, the national balance of power might be tipping against the
Democrats. The foundation of Eisenhower's victory had been his overwhelming margins in the suburbs, and it was suburbia, traditionally GOP suburbia,
that was the fastest-growing part of America. As for the cities, the longtime
Democratic strongholds, the Democrats had, almost incredibly, lost Chicago
and almost lost New York—an indication of what analysts called "the total
decay of the old Democratic city machines." The significance of these facts, as
well as their all-too-likely implications for the Senate Democrats, was spelled out
in a three-page memorandum Johnson had had George Reedy write on Novem-

ber 12. Eisenhower's victory, the memo said, "was a personal triumph and *not* a Republican victory," as was proven by the fact that despite "one of the most astounding votes in history," he had been able to pull into office with him only slim majorities in Congress. But, as Reedy added, it would not be difficult for Eisenhower to "turn his personal victory into a party victory. . . . He has a mandate almost unmatched in American history. If he has the ability, he can use that mandate to do anything he wants." And "should he have a truly successful administration," he could "bring in large Congressional majorities in 1954. . . . The balance of power will certainly shift from Democratic to Republican." The current tenuous Republican edge in the Senate would be made firm—and it would stay firm for a long time.

Johnson had had the memo written—ostensibly to himself—to lend an air of objectivity and authority to a key argument he wanted to make. After making the argument to a senator over the telephone, he would say that it was Reedy's memo that had persuaded him of its validity, and that he would have George drop off a copy so that the senator could read it, and then he would phone back to draw the senator's attention to specific points. Before January 2, he had had to be discreet in explaining the implications for the seniority system because he wasn't yet Leader, but now he could do so, and he did, not that much explaining was needed with the master politicians who were reading it. The men to whom he was speaking had been committee chairmen for a long time, but now, suddenly, they were no longer chairmen, and a successful Eisenhower Administration would mean that they would not be chairmen again anytime soon. Their best hope of regaining their lost power—their gavels and their patronage—was to create in the Senate a Democratic record strong enough so that Republican gains in the next election would be kept to a minimum—so that perhaps the Democrats might even become the majority in the Senate again.

And that, Lyndon Johnson said, would require the Senate Democrats to change the system by which they assigned committee seats.

The Foreign Relations Committee, on which there were two of the seven Democratic vacancies, was a key illustration he used to explain what he meant. Foreign Relations was going to be a focal point of the Republican attack, he said. Anyone could see that: the rumors that Taft himself was moving from Labor to Foreign Relations had just been confirmed, and Taft always went where he was going to attack, as he had moved to Labor in 1947 so that he could push through Taft-Hartley. And Taft was bringing with him Ferguson, Knowland, and Langer, Old Guard haters of the Marshall Plan and the China policy. This move presaged an all-out attack on the Roosevelt-Truman foreign policies that the Old Guard felt had not only drained America's coffers to provide foreign aid for untrustworthy Europe, that had not only handcuffed the noble MacArthur when he had tried to wage the Korean War the way it should have been waged, but that had also given the world the Yalta Conference; the Old Guard had always felt that even the Yalta agreements that had been announced publicly, those agreements that had allowed the Russians to enslave Poland and the other Eastern European countries, were unconstitutional because they were actually treaties and had never been presented to the Senate for ratification. And the Old Guard believed as an article of faith that other, secret agreements had been made at Yalta. Now Taft would try to use the power of the Foreign Relations Committee to obtain those secret texts at last, and thereby document once and for all the Democratic Party's "softness" on Communism, an attack that could be devastating both to the party's future, and to the Roosevelt-Truman hopes for the containment and ultimate collapse of Communism, and for peace. And the Old Guard would want a formal vote in Foreign Relations, and then in the Senate as a whole, to repudiate all the Yalta agreements, secret and public alike, and to amend the Constitution to ensure against any future circumvention of the treaty process. Moreover, the Old Guard had always felt that Truman had acted unconstitutionally in sending those four divisions to Europe to be part of NATO; now was the chance to end that commitment, too.

If Foreign Relations was going to be the main point of the Republican attack, Lyndon Johnson said, Democratic defenses on that committee should be especially strong, but they were, in fact, weak. They should be shored up by senators with the expertise in foreign affairs, and the force, to stand up to Taft. He had two senators in mind who fit that description perfectly, Johnson said, but one, Hubert Humphrey, was in his first term in the Senate, and the other, Mike Mansfield, was in his first week. And both were liberals besides. Under the old system, there was no chance that they would be given the coveted Foreign Relations seats, but, Johnson said, the Democrats couldn't afford *not* to give those seats to Humphrey and Mansfield. Hubert could hold his own against any senator, even the dreaded Taft, in debate, or, equally important, in the cut and thrust of committee deliberations, and he had already demonstrated considerable interest in foreign affairs. Mansfield had been not only a professor of Latin American and Far Eastern history but a leading, and very respected, member of the House Foreign Affairs Committee. "Mansfield out-knows Taft, and Humphrey can out-talk him," Lyndon explained, over and over, on the phone.

And, he explained, Foreign Relations was only one example of what he was talking about. Another newly elected senator was Missouri's Stuart Symington. The Democratic Party might once have had the luxury of relegating a former Secretary of the Air Force, one of the nation's foremost authorities on the armed services, to the District of Columbia Committee; the party couldn't afford that luxury now. The Democratic minority in the Senate had to be made as strong as possible all across the board, Lyndon Johnson told the men on the other end of the telephone. A host of talent was already going to waste; men of real ability like Clements, Hennings, Monroney, Smathers and Pastore were wasting that ability on minor committees. And among the newly elected senators were other men besides Symington and Mansfield who could step right in and make strong records, make the Senate Democrats a real fighting force, if they were just put on major committees.

He sold with humor—some very pleasant humor.

What he was proposing was only fair, he said; it was unfair to allow a few senators to monopolize the more desirable committee seats while other senators had no desirable seat at all; that was why no senator should be given a second major seat until every senator had at least one. And he made this point with one of his wonderful Texas anecdotes.

"When I was a young fella," Lyndon Johnson would say, "the Crider boys were just about my best friends. Ben was the older one. He was kind of strong and self-reliant—always goin' off somewhere. Otto—well, he was more shy and retiring. One day I was over there at the Crider house. Ben was away somewhere, and I was playing with Otto, and it was the weekend and no school the next day, and we asked Miz Crider if Otto could come sleep over at my house for a couple of nights. And Miz Crider, when we asked her, she said, 'No.' No reason. Just 'No.'

"Well, Otto, he was real upset. And you know what he said? He said, 'Mama, why can't I go? Ben, he's already been twowheres, and I ain't never been nowheres!' "

The new senators had to be given at least one place, Lyndon Johnson said, before more senior senators, who already had one good committee seat, got to go "twowheres." To do otherwise, Lyndon Johnson said, wouldn't be good for the party, wouldn't be good for the Senate, wouldn't be good for the country.

He sold with whatever he thought might work. The self-interest of the southerners who had been committee chairmen dovetailed with the larger interests of the South, and he made sure they understood that: the South's last stronghold, the last and best defense of its peculiar, and sacred, institution, was those chairmanships; the South had to get them back. The best way to accomplish that was to make a strong Democratic record, which required unifying and strengthening the Senate Democrats. And, he pointed out, since no senator was being required to give up a committee seat he already held, the major committees would still be stocked, three or four deep, with southerners.

Another argument he never mentioned to the southern senators—but he didn't have to. Some of them had become aware of Russell's grand design, to make Lyndon Johnson President, a plan that required that Johnson be made acceptable to the North. "While he didn't say it in so many words, LBJ very early, in private conversations, started taking advantage of a growing belief that he might be a presidential candidate," Reedy says. "I think it started right there. And what he was saying is that he had some northern senators who were Democrats and he just had to get them on something besides the Capitol committee on roofs, domes and skylights. . . . I think the primary thrust was their [southern senators'] recognition that LBJ had to have some leeway in order to get national recognition. . . ." When Lyndon Johnson told Harry Byrd or Walter George or Jim Eastland, "I've just got to give those damned red-hots something to get them off my back," they understood what he was *really* saying.

And, of course, over and over again Johnson emphasized that since no one was being forced to give up anything, nothing fundamental was really being changed. Everyone would be able to stay right where they were if they wanted to, he said. Southerners could still control every major committee, he said. Years later, during his retirement, Lyndon Johnson would explain his maneuvers to Doris Kearns Goodwin, and Ms. Goodwin, summarizing his explanation, would write that although the seniority system "was the foundation of power and the principal determinant of the conduct of Senate business," in seeking to change that system, "Johnson dissembled his aim in such a way that his request for change seemed more like a trivial departure which did not threaten the governing mores of the Senate."

THE FIRST SENATOR he had to persuade, of course, was Russell; if he didn't persuade Russell, there was no sense in going on. Johnson appealed to the qualities in Russell that were as noble as his racial feelings were ignoble, to his loyalties not only to his beloved country ("You're a patriot, Dick"), which couldn't afford to have America's international commitments voided, but also to his beloved party, to his beloved Southland—and to his beloved Senate. Giving freshmen who already had expertise in particular fields seats on the important committees that had jurisdiction in those fields would make the Senate a stronger, more effective institution, and would start them early on the road to being, in the highest sense of the title, *Senators of the United States.* "We'll be making real *senators* out of them," he told Russell. And Russell proved much easier to persuade than might have been anticipated, in part perhaps because of his plans for Lyndon Johnson, in part perhaps, as John Steele was to speculate, because his own early experience as a brand-new senator (that fortuitous, immediate assignment to Appropriations) had taught him "that a leg up in committee could help a new senator's career tremendously." In fact, Evans and Novak relate, "when Johnson broached his revolutionary idea, Russell surprised him by replying that he, too, had always favored giving new senators one good committee assignment." While warning Johnson of the risks in what he was planning ("You're dealing with the most sensitive thing in the Senate," he told him. "[You're] playing with dynamite"), Russell did not forbid him to make the attempt. While he would not actively support Johnson's plan, Russell said, he would not oppose it, either. If Lyndon could persuade the other senators to go along, he would go along.

GETTING THEM TO GO ALONG was a problem of such difficulty that it seemed all but insoluble.

If the problem before him resembled a chessboard—with the spaces representing committee seats, the chessmen the senators who moved among those spaces—the seven vacant spaces available to him, only four of them on major committees, were not nearly enough to allow him to make the moves necessary to accomplish his purposes. The senators who now occupied the other desirable spaces would not want to move off them. And senior senators had already filed with Walter Jenkins their claims to the four desirable seats. Their appointment to those committees did not fit into Lyndon Johnson's plan, but they were entitled to those seats by seniority—and would not be at all inclined to surrender their claims.

Foreign Relations was a particular sticking point. Getting Humphrey and Mansfield onto it required first of all the approval of the Committee's former chairman (now its ranking Democrat member) Walter George, who never wanted liberals on his committees, and of other elders of the conservative coalition. Johnson gave his explanations of the strategic importance Foreign Relations would have in the months ahead, how Mansfield could "out-think" Taft and Humphrey could "out-talk" him. He received, from these elders, as he had from Russell, at least tacit permission to go ahead with his plans for the two empty seats on Foreign Relations—if, of course, and only if, the senior senators who had prior, higher, claims to those spaces agreed to surrender their claims.

One of these senior senators was Harry Byrd, whose surrender was easy to obtain, for his interest in a Foreign Relations seat was not passionate. It was made easier by his fondness for Johnson—a fondness that had begun when he had looked up at his daughter's funeral and seen the Texan there. When Johnson explained why he needed the Foreign Relations seat, Byrd said he could have it. That, however, was not the case with the three senators with the greatest seniority who had formally applied for those seats, whose names Lyndon Johnson had written in the "Requests for Assignments" column on the papers on the desk in front of him. Warren Magnuson, Spessard Holland, and Matt Neely wanted those prestigious seats, wanted them badly, and expected that, in the order of seniority, they would be given them.

Magnuson, first in seniority for one of the two seats, not only Johnson's Senate ally but a power in the Senate, had been unmoved by the "out-talk, out-think" arguments, in part because he felt that he himself possessed those qualifications, in part because he felt that under the seniority system he was entitled to a seat on the most desirable committee available whether he possessed them or not. He had entered his name for two committees, Foreign Relations and Appropriations (the only committee more desirable than Foreign Relations), but since there were no vacancies on Appropriations, he was demanding Foreign Relations. Warren Magnuson was not a man ever to give up something he was entitled to. He wanted Foreign Relations, and he intended to have it. No matter how many times Johnson had approached him, he had been very firm, so firm that on his lists Johnson, surrendering, had scrawled the name *Magnuson* on one of the blank lines under "Foreign Relations." And on the other line he was going to have to write *Holland* or *Neely*. There seemed no way to get Humphrey or Mansfield where they were needed.

Then he got a break. The GOP's new leader, Taft, had a problem: Wayne Morse, disillusioned with Eisenhower, had bolted the Republicans during the campaign, and was listing his party affiliation as "Independent." He had agreed to vote with the Republicans on organizing the Senate, so the Republicans would still hold a 49–47 edge on those votes. But thereafter Morse would be voting as an Independent. With the party ratio so close, the Republicans would only have a one-vote majority on the committees on which Morse sat, so if Morse didn't vote with them, they wouldn't have a majority. And they would have this problem no matter which of the fifteen committees they put Morse on.

To solve their problem, the Republicans had proposed a simple solution: that a Republican be added to each committee to which Morse might be assigned. But Johnson didn't want a simple solution. *For other men, nights were for sleeping.* . . . It was at four o'clock one morning, Lyndon Johnson was to recall, that he had suddenly seen that the Republican problem could solve his, that if he handled things right, he might even come out of the situation with the only thing that could persuade Warren Magnuson to give up his claim to a seat on Foreign Relations—a seat on Appropriations. He told Taft that if these new extra seats the Republicans wanted were added, the Democrats should get some seats *they* wanted. And he had the leverage to make the argument stick: the old Senate leverage. The number of seats on a committee could be changed only by changing the official Senate rules, and such a change could easily be blocked. A series of very complicated negotiations ensued. At one point, on January 7, Taft asked unanimous consent for a new rule. Johnson did not consent. Reserving the right to object, he said he wanted to sit down with the distinguished Majority Leader for further discussions, and when the discussions were over, there was a new, even more complicated fomula, under which the membership of nine committees had been enlarged, and four had been reduced, by either two or four members. (The size of two committees remained the same.) Johnson kept the negotiations friendly. Taft felt he had gotten what he wanted. So impressed was he with Johnson's cooperation that on Inauguration Day, he would write a friend, "So far everything has gone well in the Senate, with an amount of harmony which is almost unprecedented." But under the new formula, the number of spaces on the chessboard had been increased from 203 to 209, and the Democrats had gotten three of the six new seats, and among the new seats was one on Appropriations. Johnson offered the seat to Magnuson, and Magnuson accepted. What Johnson said to Holland and Neely we do not know—he appears to have promised Holland that if he would surrender his claim to Foreign Relations, he would be given the *next* empty seat on Appropriations; he may have placated Neely by allowing him to continue to be one of only three Democrats who would be allowed to sit on three committees, although his ranking membership on one of them would normally have disqualified him from three assignments—but both senators agreed to step aside, and he could recommend to the Steering Committee that Humphrey and Mansfield be moved into the empty spaces on Foreign Relations.

LYNDON JOHNSON WAS VIEWING the chessboard as a whole now, and since the pieces on the board were men, he knew all the moves. He didn't want to make any move merely for the sake of that move alone: he wanted one of those Foreign Relations moves to make possible other moves—to give him more of those strategic vacancies that he had to have. And the reader of men, having read Hubert Humphrey, knew how to do it. Johnson didn't tell Humphrey he could have a seat on Foreign Relations, he told Humphrey he could have a seat on Foreign Relations if he gave up his seats on Agriculture and Labor. (He could retain his seat on the Government Operations Committee, Johnson said.)

While Humphrey wanted Foreign Relations, he didn't want to make the sacrifice that Johnson was demanding. The price, he said, was too high. After all, he said, he had to run for re-election in Minnesota in two years. In his oral history recollections—recollections confirmed in essence by Johnson aides—Humphrey was to write that he told Johnson: "Mr. Leader, you know at home my constituency is Democratic Farmer-Labor Party. You're asking me to give up Labor." That, Humphrey said, he might be able to do because "I've got strong support in the labor movement." But "Our farmers, they need me on that Committee on Agriculture. There isn't anybody from my part of the country on the Democratic side on . . . Agriculture. . . . For me to back off now, the Farmers Union and the people out there that are the liberals in the agriculture area would never understand it."

But Lyndon Johnson knew what Hubert Humphrey really wanted. The Foreign Relations seat would, Bobby Baker was to say, give Humphrey "a forum from which to bolster his national ambitions." Johnson couched his appeal in terms of duty, telling Humphrey, "You can fight for the farmers down here on this floor and you can fight for the laboring man, but we've got some serious foreign policy issues coming up, and they're going to be major." Ticking the issues off on his fingers, he added, "This is one time where you're going to serve your country and your party. You're going to have to drop those two other committees." And when Humphrey agreed—he exacted one condition: that should, in future years, another seat open up on Agriculture, he would get it—Johnson had not only shored up the Democratic position on Foreign Relations, he had also created two new vacancies, two new open squares, one on Agriculture and one on Labor. Suddenly, the chessboard was beginning to open up. Earle Clements of Kentucky wanted Agriculture badly. There hadn't been a vacancy on Agriculture, but there was now; Johnson told Clements he could have it—if *he* gave up two committees, Public Works and Rules. That opened up two more squares.

. . .

THERE WERE DOZENS of other moves to be made in order for his purposes to
be accomplished. The moves were no longer governed by the objective, inflexible seniority rule, and he had promised that everyone could stay right where
they were if they wanted to, that no one would be forced to give up a seat. So
each move had to be sold individually to the senators concerned.

Some of the arguments with which Lyndon Johnson sold were pragmatic.
The vacancy he was most anxious to create was on the Armed Services Committee. Each of the seven seats on the Democratic side of the committee table
was already filled; he had to empty one of those seats, so that he could put
Symington in it.

Russell Long had one of those seats, and he liked Armed Services, but
Johnson knew that for a senator from Louisiana, rich in oilmen anxious for
government tax breaks, Finance was a better committee. And there was an open
Democratic spot there. Long had not bothered to apply for it, since he had so
little seniority, but Johnson told him he could have it—if he gave up Armed
Services. And Johnson may have pointed out to Long—at least Johnson aides
believe he did—an extremely pragmatic consideration. Although Long was
only thirty-four years old, on Armed Services there were three other young senators ahead of him, and even Chairman Russell was only fifty-five. On Finance,
whose chairman, Byrd, was sixty-six, there was no other Democratic senator
younger than forty-nine; Long would be the committee's youngest member by
a full fifteen years; given the reality of the human life span, he could expect to
be chairman one day of the crucial tax-law-writing body. Long moved to
Finance; the open seat thus created on Armed Services was filled by the senator
best qualified to fill it.

Some of the arguments with which Johnson sold were *very* pragmatic.
If Foreign Relations would be one focal point of the Republican attack, the
other was just as easy to predict—and was also vulnerable. Government Operations had always been regarded as a minor committee, but now its chairman
was going to be Joe McCarthy. With a chairman's authority—and staff—
McCarthy was going to make life very difficult for the Democrats. Only one
Democratic seat on Government Operations—John McClellan's—was filled
by a senator tough enough to stand up to the Wisconsin demagogue. Two seats
were empty, but on a list of requested committee assignments on his desk in
231's inner office Johnson had scrawled: "McCarran requests Govt. Operations." Pat McCarran wanted one of the seats not to oppose McCarthy, but
because, a rabid Communist witch-hunter himself, he wanted to be part of
McCarthy's anti-Communist crusade. McCarran had a full twenty years of
Senate seniority to back up his claim, and, as Alben Barkley had learned to his
sorrow, it was unwise for a Democratic Leader to cross Judiciary's coldly ruthless chairman.

Back in Nevada, however, McCarran's problems—political and legal, both—were growing more serious. After years of dominating the state's Democratic politics, the Silver Fox had in 1952 backed one of his law partners for the party's nomination for the other Senate seat—only to see him lose the primary, in a stunning upset, to a crusading young lawyer. Although the lawyer had himself been defeated in November by the Republican incumbent, George (Molly) Malone, the young upstart was hinting that in 1956 he was going to run against McCarran himself. And in that troubling lawsuit alleging ties between McCarran and shady Las Vegas casino interests, pre-trial depositions were not going well; the Senator had already been forced to admit that he had interceded with the Internal Revenue Service in a tax case involving a casino. The appointment of a "friendly" United States Attorney was more urgent than ever.

But Truman's resistance to signing the necessary appointment form was as strong as ever; in November, Johnson, keeping his promise to McCarran, had raised the issue with the President, but on January 1, 1953, the *Washington Post* reported that the Senator's nominee "is not going to get" the appointment as long as Truman was in office. His replacement by the Republican Eisenhower on January 20 would, of course, make the appointment even less likely. In November, Johnson's request to Truman had been on behalf of a single vote for Leader; when, going to the White House on January 13, Johnson again asked Truman to sign the appointment form, the stakes were high not just for him but for the Democratic Party. "All right," the President finally said. "I'll give this to you, Lyndon. But if that old so-and-so doesn't produce, you bring it back to me." Signing the form later that day, Truman had a White House courier deliver it not to McCarran as was customary, but directly to 231, and on it the President attached a note to Johnson marked "Personal and Confidential": "As you know, I am doing this under protest. It is your 'baby' from now on." Johnson carried the appointment form up to McCarran's big office on the fourth floor, and when he returned to his own office, Johnson drew a line through "McCarran requests Govt. Operations." A seat that under the seniority system would have gone to McCarran stayed vacant; two were still empty on Government Operations. Johnson managed to empty a third, which had been held by the mild-mannered Mike Monroney. What good was a Monroney against Joe McCarthy? Johnson moved Monroney into a vacancy on the more prestigious Commerce Committee. He wanted the three seats filled by senators who possessed certain qualifications: as Evans and Novak were to put it, "None of them wrapped in the orthodox liberal mantle, and none of whom would have to run for re-election for six years" (a qualification that would presumably encourage them to stand up to McCarthy). When he filled the seats with Symington, Scoop Jackson, and John F. Kennedy, he felt he had the kind of freshmen on the committee that he wanted, although Kennedy's position on McCarthy would prove to be equivocal.

Some of the arguments with which Johnson sold were idealistic, personal.

To McClellan, who was already in fact not only twowheres but threewheres, since he was not only ranking minority member of Government Operations but a member of both Appropriations and Public Works, to McClellan who was so intimidating to most senators but whose farmer father had named John's brothers after Democrats who had fought for farmers, Johnson said that McClellan had to help protect the New Deal programs that had helped the farmer, that McClellan had to keep the Democrats in the Senate strong—and that he, Johnson, had to find a good seat for Albert Gore, the newly elected senator from Tennessee, and that he wanted to put Gore on Public Works, since that appointment would strengthen his position in his state because of what a member of that committee could do to protect TVA. And Johnson said that McClellan's Government Operations seat might well be the key Democratic post in the whole Senate, because the ranking member would be the Democratic point man against McCarthy—that job would be a full-time job in itself, Johnson said. Johnson didn't actually suggest that McClellan resign from Public Works so that Gore could take his place; McClellan, after listening to Johnson, made the suggestion himself. There would be six Democratic freshmen senators in the new Congress; McClellan's resignation had allowed Johnson to find desirable committee assignments for five of them. When he put the sixth, Price Daniel, on Interior, every freshman had a place on a major committee.

It was not only freshmen he was helping, it was liberals—at least some liberals: neither Paul Douglas nor Estes Kefauver, both of whom had voted for Murray for Leader, received a committee assignment he requested. As he moved senators around the chessboard, more and more spaces opened—and he made the most of them. In previous years, the southerners had consigned Lehman to Interior as a punishment for his liberalism; now Johnson found a space for the New Yorker on the committee he wanted: Banking. Onto Interior moved a senator for whom Interior was not a punishment but a reward: Clements—Clements who had of course surrendered Public Works for Agriculture.

And it was not only liberals. Somehow, as Lyndon Johnson shifted senators around, desirable spaces were found for southerners Olin Johnston and George Smathers; little bulls who were now, suddenly, well along the road to becoming Big Bulls.

ANY MOVE HE WANTED to make would have to be approved by the party elders who dominated the Democratic Steering Committee, of course, so every move had to be sold to men to whom seniority had always been sacred. Any move, furthermore, had to be approved by the former—and, it was hoped, future—chairmen of the Standing Committees involved, and sometimes dealing with the chairmen was harder than dealing with the senators he was moving around. Hour after hour, behind the closed door of 231, Lyndon Johnson was on the telephone with Harry Byrd and Carl Hayden and Ed Johnson, as well as with the senator who, in the past, "you had to see" about committee assignments.

Sometimes, through the office wall, Walter Jenkins or Mary Rather would hear Lyndon Johnson's voice in a different tone, a tone he used when he was talking not to someone else but to himself. They knew what the "Chief" was doing then. They had heard him doing it in the automobiles in which he had been driven around Texas during his campaigns. As his chauffeur on some of those trips puts it, "It was like he was having discussions with himself about what strategy had worked or hadn't worked," when he had tried to persuade someone, "and what strategy he should use the next time." And not just discussions. Behind that closed office door, Lyndon Johnson would be playing out a conversation: what he would say; what the other senator would say in response; what *he* should then say—"He would be in there rehearsing, doing it over and over, trying to get it right," Walter Jenkins recalls. And then, after a while, the left-hand button on Jenkins' telephone would light up—the Chief would be making the call he had rehearsed. And sometimes the rehearsing wasn't for a call, for a call wouldn't be enough. Sometimes, when the rehearsing stopped, Jenkins and Rather would hear the door to Lyndon Johnson's private office open and close. Bursting out of his room, he would run up the nearby stairs, or lope down the corridor with those long, fast strides until he got near the office for which he was heading. Then, abruptly, he would slow, perhaps even stop for a moment, gather himself together, get himself into a relaxed posture, and, easygoing, respectful, deferential, calm, polite, ask a Bill Darden or a Colonel Carlton if the Senator was in, and could he possibly spare a minute?

With some of the older senators—particularly Walter George and McClellan—Johnson played on their paternal feelings toward him, telling them that he wanted to be a good Leader, but it was sure a big job, he was worried about whether he would be able to handle it, he needed help, and part of the help he needed was to have Stu Symington on Armed Services. Most of all, he said, he needed to be able to give desirable seats to those damned northern crazies, so that they wouldn't always be tearing at his flanks as they had torn at, and destroyed, ol' Scott and ol' Bob McFarland.

Over the telephone and in the offices, he used his memo and his "twowheres" story. He appealed to his Democrats on grounds of party. Taft was moving, he would say; he had ascertained that that rumor was true. Taft was going to Foreign Relations. You know what that means, he would say. He's going to bring up Yalta. "Bob Taft is loading up the committee. They're going to try to tear down everything that Roosevelt and Truman did, everything the Democratic Party has stood for for twenty years." We've got to put our best young fellows on there, he said. We've got to put Humphrey and Mansfield on. And Government Operations, he said. "McCarthy's going to go wild there if we let him. All we're gonna be hearing for the next two years is 'The Party of Treason, The Party of Treason.'" McClellan and Humphrey and Clyde Hoey had been talking about leaving Government Operations; who wanted to be a minority member on a McCarthy committee? Well, he told McClellan and Humphrey and Hoey, you *can't* leave Government Operations. We need you on there. We need real fighters on there; we need guys that McCarthy can't intimidate. And, he said to those senators—and to the Big Bulls—wouldn't you feel better with Stu and Scoop on that committee? McCarthy won't be able to make Stu or Scoop back down.

He appealed to them on grounds of policy. The Republicans had been aching for years to dismantle rural electrification, he told senators who had spent their lives fighting for the farmer. They all knew that. Now, with a Republican President and a Republican Congress, would be the Republicans' chance to do it, to turn TVA over to private interests, to give the goddamned private utilities more of the power generated by the great dams of the West. Those proposals would have to move through either Public Works or Interior. Those committees must be shored up; vacancies on them should be filled with Democrats who not only believe in public power but who know how to *fight* for public power. We can't think only of seniority now, he said; we can't afford to. He appealed to them on pragmatic grounds. The major committees would still be solid, three or four deep, with southerners, he reminded them repeatedly. He appealed to them on whatever grounds would work—watching their eyes, watching their hands, listening to what they said, listening to what they didn't say, "the greatest salesman one on one who ever lived"—trying to make a very big sale.

And then, on January 12, the new Democratic Leader convened a meeting of the Democratic Steering Committee, and almost the first assignment he suggested was of Symington to Armed Services, and some of the committee members looked out of the corners of their eyes at Russell, and Russell gravely nodded in approval. "Now I'm going to hit you with cold water," Lyndon Johnson said. "Mike Mansfield for Foreign Relations." The pause then was long, for Walter George loved to hold the center of the stage, but when George finally spoke he said only one word, "Excellent." Everyone nodded, and then Lyndon Johnson reeled off the rest of his lists, and everything went very fast. Of all the archaic rules and customs and precedents that had made the Senate of the United States an obstacle to progress, the seniority system had been the strongest. For decades men had been saying that no one would ever be able to change the seniority system. Lyndon Johnson had changed it in two weeks.

WHEN, shortly after the Steering Committee had adjourned, George Reedy dropped on the long wooden table in the Senate Press Gallery copies of a press release announcing the new committee assignments, veteran journalists quickly grasped the significance of Johnson's achievement. "I still remember how all of us in the Press Gallery that day felt it was a real change," John Goldsmith of the UPI was to recall forty years later. "We said, 'Gosh, a lot of good people are going to go on good committees right away.' If that had ever happened before, none of us remembered it."

Their articles, and the columns that followed during the next few days, reflected a sense almost of wonder over the fact that the brand-new Democratic Leader had, as *Time* put it, "dared to violate the traditions of seniority." "A remarkable feat," Doris Fleeson wrote. The *Washington Post* gave the feat a headline—"FRESHMAN DEMOCRATS RECEIVE MAJOR COMMITTEE ASSIGN-MENTS"—and several journalists gave it a name, saying that the "seniority rule" had been replaced by the "Johnson Rule." Johnson has "rather miraculously persuaded fellow Southerners with seniority to step aside in favor of liberals and newcomers," the Alsops declared. Writing about the new appointments to Foreign Relations, journalists could barely contain themselves. "Extraordinary action . . . a break with tradition," William White wrote in the *New York Times* about the assignment of "an out-and-out 'freshman,' Mr. Mansfield," explaining that now when Taft began to make his charges about Yalta and the sellout of Eastern Europe, facing him across the committee table, serious and intent, ready to respond, knowledgeably and eloquently, would be Humphrey and Mansfield, "two of the most advanced internationalists in Congress. To make" such moves "possible, it was necessary in some cases for Southern members with greater priority" to give up their claims, White wrote. "One of the principal citadels stormed in this movement was the Finance Committee," to whose aging Democrats had been added youthful, energetic Russell Long.

Journalists explained to their readers how Johnson had dramatically strengthened his party as a whole by giving "to the liberal wing a degree of representation that it had not known in many years." Barely two weeks before, Marquis Childs pointed out, congressional Democrats had been in disarray, the gap between northerners and southerners seemingly more unbridgeable than ever, not least because of the selection of the southerner Lyndon Johnson as Leader, a selection which, as Childs put it, "was greeted with solemn foreboding . . . by Northern Democrats," who felt that they would be left more than ever "to shift for themselves." Now, he wrote, "almost the exact opposite has happened," because of Johnson's "shrewd and skillful leadership." For the first time in years, Senate Democrats showed signs of becoming a unified party.

And liberals had particular reason to rejoice over that fact, Childs said.

> Realists for the Democrats knew they must build an alternative [to Eisenhower Republicanism]. They know . . . how hard is the job ahead with a party suffering from attrition and decay at the end of a long tenure of office. . . . But the Democrats in the Senate feel that at least they have taken the first step.

Time's McConaughy told his editors in New York that "In barely two weeks Lyndon Johnson has emerged as a crack minority leader. . . . In fact, he may turn out to be the best Democratic leader in recent Senate history."

Lyndon Johnson's ascension to the leadership had suddenly brought his narrow personal interests into conjunction with the larger—the largest—interests of the Democrats. His first major moves as Leader had done a lot for his party.

AND HE had done a lot for himself.

By giving the liberals desirable committee seats, he had not only made them feel more a part of the party, he had also made them less likely to attack its Leader. And the newcomers like Mansfield and Symington and Jackson who had been expecting to waste years on minor committees had instead been put at once on major committees—and they knew who had put them there. "Dear Lyndon," wrote Jim Rowe, Mansfield's longtime intimate. "Re: Foreign Relations Committee—I don't know *how* you did it, but I know *who* did it. And so does Mike." They would, within the limits of politics, be grateful. And if the coin of political gratitude is a currency subject to rapid devaluation, the political fear that is the coin's obverse has more stability. Its value might even increase as the implications of what had been done sank in: men who knew who had given, would know also who could refuse to give. Barkley and Lucas and McFarland, like the Leaders before them, had had little to give, and therefore little to refuse. That was not the case with the new Leader. Lyndon Johnson had something to promise them now, and something to threaten them with. "We've got a real leader," Bobby Baker told his friends. "He knows what makes the mule plow."

And Lyndon Johnson had obtained more subtle means of threat and reward as well. Every senator was aware of his long-standing friendship with the new member of Appropriations. With "Maggie's " appointment, as Bobby Baker was to say, Johnson all at once had "more control over the purse strings. Dissidents might not so easily attack Johnson if they knew a word from him might determine whether their pet projects would be funded." All at once senators no longer had merely to consider "What will they do to me in Appropriations?" They had to consider "What will *he* do to me in Appropriations?"

It wasn't merely praise that Lyndon Johnson had obtained in just two weeks. He had obtained power, too.

THESE DEVELOPMENTS HAD implications for the Southern Caucus that might become quite profound indeed. In the past, it had been the southerners—through the Democratic Steering Committee they controlled and through their leader Russell—who decided on committee assignments. Freshmen had been told that if they wanted a certain committee, they had to "see Russell." Now, in those first two weeks of 1953, freshmen had been told that it was Lyndon Johnson they should see.

The southerners, in particular Russell, had been consulted at every step, of course. Lyndon Johnson had, day after day, run back and forth to their offices to clear with them what he proposed to do. No step had been taken without their approval—without, in particular, Russell's approval. Lyndon Johnson had done this so diligently, and with so much deference, that neither Russell nor any other southerner appears to have realized that a great change had occurred. But it had.

AND, DURING HIS FIRST WEEKS AS LEADER, it was not only the seniority system that Lyndon Johnson was changing.

The two party "policy committees" created in 1946 in the hope—political scientists' hope—of narrowing the rifts within both parties that contributed so greatly to the Senate's paralysis, and of creating more clear-cut party ideologies and positions, thereby defining issues and giving voters a "definite choice" between parties, had not fulfilled that purpose—or, indeed, any significant purpose. Since the Republicans were somewhat more cohesive in their views, their Policy Committee, which had a staff of twelve, at least met fairly frequently, after which Taft or Knowland "would," as one writer puts it, "emerge to announce Republican opposition to the latest Democratic spending program" or to some other New Dealish proposal. The main function of the three-person staff of the Democratic Policy Committee, housed in Capitol Office G-18, a small two-room suite next to the Press Gallery, was to record senators' voting records on index cards. "All we got out of the Policy Committee in those days were the little white cards," George Reedy would recall. "No one quite knew what to do with it."

But no one had known what to do with the Democratic Congressional Campaign Committee, either.

Assembling a new staff for the Policy Committee wasn't easy. Johnson wanted Donald Cook to head its legal activities, but Cook, having worked for Johnson before, wouldn't work for him again. (Cook would *never* work for Johnson again; he kept finding excuses to turn down Johnson's repeated job offers; in 1964, Johnson, now President, would offer the brilliant attorney, by then president of a major utility company, the post of Secretary of the Treasury, but Cook declined.) Now, in 1953, leaving the Securities and Exchange Commission to make room for Eisenhower's choice, he excused himself by saying, disingenuously, that he had made a commitment, impossible to break, to join a private company. Johnson wanted Bryce Harlow to head the committee's non-legal side, but Harlow was still unwilling to accept the "blacksnake." (He would remain unwilling; he, too, would turn down repeated job offers from Johnson.) Johnson then offered the post to Jim Rowe, only to be turned down again. Nonetheless a staff was assembled—a competent staff, if not an outstanding one. George Reedy and Cook's self-effacing, mild but diligent deputy, Gerald Siegel, were brought over from the Preparedness Committee, and Johnson also hired Roland Bibolet, who had been McFarland's aide. Suddenly there were six desks crammed into G-18's outer room, and the Senate's Democratic Party had a staff capable of performing the new functions that the Democratic Leader had in mind for it.

These functions were not at all what the political scientists had envisioned, for Lyndon Johnson didn't want clear-cut positions or issues, or a "definite choice."

His reasons were partly personal—that deep aversion to issues that had manifested itself throughout his entire political life; and that desire for unanimity which Gerry Siegel had observed on the Preparedness Subcommittee and which he was now to see again. His reasons were partly strategic. Raising issues could only divide the party, Johnson felt. How could a Douglas and an Eastland, a Lehman and a Stennis, ever be reconciled?—the gap was simply too wide to be bridged. The mere raising of many issues would spotlight the Democratic schism, would foster dissension and the disunity that would undermine a Leader's authority, and ultimately make him an object of derision. He wanted unity, and he made clear to his newly formed Policy Committee staff that it was their job to take the preliminary steps necessary to produce it.

The lawyerly Siegel would analyze the drafts of legislation that senators were planning to introduce, and he or Reedy would solicit comments from the other senators interested in the same subject. "We'd call individual senators who were objecting to something in a bill, and we'd explore their thinking and determine what would meet their objections." Then Siegel would set to work, to, as he puts it, "make the changes . . . necessary to adjust to the reality. . . ." The staff's job, in other words, was to devise compromises within the party, to see that dissent was muffled before it became open. Then Lyndon Johnson would confer—in person or over the phone—with the senators involved, and try to win their agreement to the compromise.

This procedure, of course, had profound significance for the Senate. The Senate had always been the citadel of individualists, of independents, of ambassadors from sovereign states negotiating with each other—from positions of sovereignty. Although there had always been exceptions, senators had to a considerable extent negotiated, either in person or through their assistants, directly with each other—had negotiated among themselves. Now, gradually— very gradually at first, almost imperceptibly—a change was taking place. Senators were still negotiating with each other, of course, but now they were also negotiating through Lyndon Johnson. He—or his Policy Committee staffers— were representing senators' opinions to other senators. He was telling one senator what an opposing senator was asking for—and what he would really settle for. He was telling Gerry Siegel what wording to put in the next draft of a senator's bill. The beginning of this change can be dated precisely: the first meeting of the transformed and revitalized Democratic Policy Committee—the Lyndon Johnson Policy Committee—on February 3, 1953. Its evolution and growth would for some time be unnoticed by those—the Democratic senators—whom it was most directly affecting. But it had begun.

. . .

DISSENT ON THE POLICY COMMITTEE was muffled also by his selection of its nine members. On *this* committee, seniority was followed, for its four holdovers—Russell (of course), Green, Hill and Kerr—were allies on whose support he could count. He and his compliant Assistant Leader Earle Clements of Kentucky were *ex officio* members, and he filled the seventh seat with "Mr. Wisdom." That left only two seats. To fulfill his pledge to Humphrey, Johnson had to fill them with liberals, but the infirmities of the liberal Humphrey had named, Jim Murray, were worsening so badly that Bobby Baker would describe him as "an echo who would do Johnson's slightest bidding"; his vote could be counted on "to solidify Johnson's control in party matters." And if Murray was dependent on Johnson because of age, the other liberal he selected, Tom Hennings, was in a similar position because of alcohol.

Johnson wanted, in fact, unanimity on the Policy Committee. He didn't want it to recommend a Democratic policy, throw its weight behind any Democratic bill or resolution, or issue any statement unless the stand was endorsed by, in Bobby Baker's words, "one hundred percent—or at least ninety percent—of the Committee." Exercising such caution "makes sense," he explained to Baker. "If we can get our team solidly behind a bill and pick up scattered Republicans, we'll win. Otherwise, we'll lose. We're a *minority* party, remember." One hundred percent was the figure on which Johnson insisted in practice. "Unless there were *no* real serious objections, he wouldn't come out of the Policy Committee with any decision," Siegel says. But often, thanks to his selection of the committee's members, there *were* no serious objections; the nine senators voted as one. Asked to describe the committee, George Smathers of Florida, who joined it in 1955, replied, "Lyndon Johnson . . . was really it. He ran it."

Johnson's use of the committee also muffled dissent. Practically the first piece of substantive legislation that it discussed—at its second meeting, on Tuesday, February 17, 1953—was the Hawaiian Statehood Bill, which Johnson reported would soon be brought to the floor by the GOP. Liberals were anxious to make the bill a party issue, believing that it was clear-cut. But the South saw the bill differently, feeling that admission to the Union of racially mixed Hawaii would mean another two votes in the Senate for cloture, and Russell raised objections in the Policy Committee, which, as the minutes tersely reported, finally took a position that blurred the issue: "The Committee discussed the Hawaiian Statehood Bill, and generally agreed that an effort should be made to amend that bill by granting statehood to Alaska as well."

Other issues—virtually every issue, in fact, that came before the Democratic Policy Committee during Lyndon Johnson's time as the Democratic Leader—were handled the same way.

The committee's meetings, held every other Tuesday over lunch in the inner room of the G-18 suite, were the epitome of the traditional senatorial

bonhomie and clubbiness. Its nine members were all members of the Senate
"club," and they were easy with each other. They would stroll into the staff
room, "usually late, with the air of a man dropping into another's office to have
a drink and, having nothing better to do at the moment, to pass the time of day,"
William White was to say, and head toward the tall open door in the rear where
the courtly Skeeter stood to welcome them. Nothing could have been more
pleasant than to see the youngest member of the committee, the youngest by
half a dozen years, who happened to be its chairman, walk through the room
with a gently guiding hand on the elbow of Murray, whose gait seemed more
unsteady at each meeting, or stand listening deferentially and appreciatively to
Green or Russell. Just inside the door there would be the hand-shaking, the
backslapping, the "Glad to see ya's," the "Those were great remarks you made
down there," the rough, masculine joking before, with Skeeter firmly closing
the door against any eavesdropping, the senators sat down, beneath the glittering senatorial chandelier, to the fruit cocktails embedded in ice and the thick
sirloins served on the starched white tablecloth that had been spread over the
long table flanked by the tall senatorial bookcase and the elegant senatorial
fireplace and gilt mirror. Unless Russell brought up some matter he felt
required lengthy discussion, the talk wouldn't touch on serious matters until
dessert (usually ice cream), when the chairman would turn to the agenda. Since
the Democrats were in the minority, they had no responsibility for the scheduling of bills to be brought to the floor; Johnson might say that Taft or Knowland
was planning to place a particular piece of legislation on the Calendar, and ask,
"Does anybody have any objection?" and if one of the committee members did,
the matter would be discussed.

The Republicans were, in 1953, issuing statements of purpose for their
Policy Committee, rules for its operation. Johnson wanted no statements and
no rules—nothing in writing. Political scientists who attempted to analyze its
activities found themselves baffled. "Nowhere have the Democrats set down
the functions for their Policy Committee," Professor Hugh Bone of the University of Washington was to note in 1958. Journalists were baffled, too. "From
that committee there were no leaks, none at all," one recalls. Reporters would
be reduced to waiting in the corridor outside G-18 in the hope that Johnson
would emerge at the end of the meeting to tell them what Democratic "policy"
had evolved. And often there was no policy to report at all. Nothing could have
been more informal, more relaxed—more in the traditional Senate way—than
the operation of the Democratic Policy Committee.

Under the bonhomie and the backslapping, however, behind those tall
doors where nine men met seemingly as friends, developments were taking
place that would have deep significance for the party, for the Senate, and, it
would turn out, for the United States. Lyndon Johnson's Democratic Policy
Committee was not reconciling but ignoring conflicts among Democrats, not
clarifying party policy but blurring it. The committee was being turned into a

device to discourage the discussion of issues. Liberals were angered by that turn, as Bobby Baker was to say. They "saw the Democratic Policy Committee as Johnson's private rubber stamp—which it was—and they accused LBJ of using the [committee] as a ploy to place on the back burner those bills he did not want called up. They were not entirely wrong. 'I don't see any profit,' LBJ told me, 'in calling up bills so that Jim Eastland and Herbert Lehman can insult each other, or so that Paul Douglas and Albert Gore can exercise their lungs. Why should we cut ourselves up and then lose . . . ?' "

And it was a very effective device. Democratic Party councils—notably, the caucus—and the Democratic side of the Senate floor had always been platforms for the liberals' demand for social justice, for social change, for the calls for equality from Douglas and Humphrey and Lehman. There were no liberal orators on the Democratic Policy Committee. Of the many impressive liberal senatorial voices in the party, not one was on the committee that enunciated the party's policy. Room G-18 was an ideal place in which to kill an issue quietly; behind its closed doors there was no voice to keep the issue alive. As a result, the Democratic Party now appeared far more unified than it had in the recent past, but the unity was a unity that was, for the first time, imposed by the Democratic Leader. The transformation of the Policy Committee therefore had the same side effect as did the transformation of the seniority system: an increase in Lyndon Johnson's power. Moreover, since the committee was supposedly setting party policy, he could say there was less need for party caucuses. During the first four years that he had been in the Senate—before he was Democratic Leader—the Democratic Caucus had met twenty-one times, or about five times a year. Under his leadership, that changed. For six of the first seven years that he was Leader, the caucus met only once a year. During the other year—1956—it did not meet at all. In only one year that he was Leader—1960—did the caucus meet more frequently—four times—and then only because of political considerations relating to Johnson's run for the 1960 presidential nomination. After Johnson left the leadership, Democratic Caucuses were again held more frequently: five times each in 1961 and 1962, four in 1963, eight in both 1964 and 1965.

AND LYNDON JOHNSON was making other changes that involved the Policy Committee, changes more subtle—and more far-reaching.

The first two topics raised by the committee's new chairman at the committee's initial, February 3, luncheon meeting were the schedule of future meetings (twelve-thirty every Tuesday) and the method of paying for them ("A fund was established, to be financed by a $25 contribution from each member," the minutes reported. "You know Dick," Lyndon Johnson joked. "Dick wants to know who's paying for these steaks.") The third topic was presented just as casually—although a great deal of not-at-all-casual thought had gone into it.

"Senator Johnson (Tex.) . . . explained that there was a need for liaison between the Policy Committee and the Democratic members of [Standing] Committees," the minutes reported. He "presented a draft of a letter to be sent by him to each of the ranking Democratic members on standing committees, requesting that they work out an arrangement whereby either some senator on the committee or some minority staff member keep the Policy Committee staff advised as to what is going on in the various committees."

Johnson had, of course, "counseled" with his Policy colleagues beforehand, and as soon as he made the suggestion, Senator Hill said at once "that he thought it an excellent idea." Senator Russell agreed, but suggested, possibly by prearrangement, that the liaison be kept on the staff level. "There being no objection, Senator Johnson (Tex.) stated that the letter would be redrafted, in accordance with the suggestions," and the next day the ranking Democrat on each of the fifteen Standing Committees received the letter:

> The Senate Democratic Policy Committee is in need of regular information upon the activities of the various Legislative Committees of the Senate. I have been requested by the Policy Committee to ask your help in meeting this problem.
>
> If you could designate a staff member of [your] Committee . . . who could contact Roland Bibolet . . . on a weekly basis, it would be greatly appreciated. Bill analyses are not requested, but a report upon the status of legislation pending in your Committee that affects the Senate Democrats as a whole and the probable timetable for action on this legislation would be of great value.
>
> With assurances of high esteem and respect, I am,
>
> Sincerely yours,
Lyndon B. Johnson

No suggestion could on its face have been more logical, simply more conducive to the efficient operation of the Senate and to the unity of the Democrats in the Senate. If a single senator glimpsed the possibility of further implications behind the seemingly innocuous request, there was no indication of it. By Policy's next meeting, Johnson could report that "replies furnishing the names of committee staff members" were coming in at a rapid rate.

But there *were* further implications. In the past, each of the Senate's Standing Committees had operated as a totally independent barony, generally advancing its bills without more than cursory reference to other committees' bills—not infrequently, in fact, advancing bills whose contents conflicted with other committees' bills. Some of the more irascible chairmen were, in fact, prone to give notably short shrift to inquiries about schedules, or bill content, from the party leadership. This lack of coordination contributed to the Senate's inefficiency: it was one of the primary reasons for the traditional end-of-session logjam in which major bills from many different committees arrived on the floor at the same time. It also contributed to the committees' independence, to their almost absolute freedom from any outside control—and therefore to the power of their chairmen. Now, with that February 4 letter, the situation was changed. An outside entity, the Democratic Policy Committee, would henceforth be advised weekly on the status of bills within the Standing Committees. The Policy Committee could notify the committees' ranking members (the same senators who would be the chairmen again when the Democrats took back the majority) of potential scheduling conflicts, could suggest that a bill be moved forward or held back, could by doing so intervene in the all-important strategic timing of action on legislation. The Policy Committee would, after that letter, also be regularly apprised of the content of proposed legislation, including legislation that was still under discussion by a Standing Committee or one of its subcommittees—legislation that was still in the early stages of being formulated or reshaped. Policy staffers Reedy and Siegel and Bibolet—and their boss— would be much better able to analyze the legislation, to "call individual senators, explore their thinking," mediate between opposing points of view; to perform, in short, a role hitherto performed only by the mighty chairmen, and *their* staffers.

The chairmen had, in fact, been to some degree removed from this new arrangement. It was not they with whom the Policy Committee—and that Leader who controlled the Policy Committee so absolutely—was communicating, but rather a member of their committee's staff.

And while the degree was small, it was to become larger. Lyndon Johnson made it larger. By the mid-1950s, after Bobby Baker had been promoted to being Skeeter Johnston's assistant, Baker had begun meeting, on behalf of the Policy Committee, with the fifteen committee staff directors *as a group,* ostensibly to encourage them, urge them forward, but in those meetings he of course not only inevitably learned more about the inner workings of their committees but also made them feel more comfortable about answering his specific, more detailed, more pointed questions when he would call them later on the phone. By the mid-1950s, in fact, *Lyndon Johnson* would be taking the unprecedented step of meeting himself with the staff directors as a group. The fifteen men were invited from their rooms in the Senate Office Building to the Capitol, where, over coffee, in the words of one staff director, "he came in and massaged us, about how important we were and how we should get back and get our chairmen cracking and get those bills out of committee." "Of course it helped him to deal directly with the staff," Bibolet says. "Sure it did. He couldn't control chairmen. He could control staff. And he dealt with staff, or Baker and Reedy did, more and more."

The change was gradual—very gradual during 1953 and 1954, because the Democrats had only a minority party's input into legislative scheduling and content. But even in 1953 and 1954 the change was taking place. One of the constants in the Senate of the United States had always been the total independence of the chairmen barons. In 1953 and 1954, these senators still thought they were totally independent, but in reality a bit had been gently slipped into their mouths, a bit attached to a checkrein. Committee schedules—the chairmen's schedules—had never been coordinated before. Their schedules were being coordinated now. In the past, discussions with the Policy Committee about the content of "their" bills, the bills before their committees, had been held, when a chairman deigned to allow the holding of them at all, only by them. Now the content of their bills was being discussed with the Policy Committee by members of their staffs. These staffs were consulting not just with them but with George Reedy, and with Reedy's boss. In 1953 and '54 the bit was hardly noticeable. The reins were still loose.

But they would be tightened.

LYNDON JOHNSON'S TRANSFORMATION of the seniority rule and the Policy Committee combined to give him so much new power that the entire old order of affairs on the Democratic side of the Senate was substantially altered, both for liberals and for conservatives.

This alteration had greater implications for the conservatives, of course, for in the old power structure the power had been theirs. During the days in which the alteration was occurring—during the earliest weeks of Lyndon Johnson's leadership, in January and February, 1953—had there arisen an understanding among any of the party's "Big Bulls" of its implications, it could have been easily stopped. Had even one of the mighty chairmen realized the long-term effect of what Lyndon Johnson was doing, and explained it to others, Lyndon Johnson would not have been able to do it.

If, however, even a glimmer of any such understanding arose, there is no evidence of it. On the contrary, the reaction of the Senate's barons to the changes that would eventually drastically reduce their cherished power and independence was only praise: "Excellent," said Walter George, "Excellent," said Lister Hill. The southern conservatives were loudest in their praise. They saw the changes Johnson had made in the Policy Committee as a means of muffling the liberal firebrands. They appear not to have realized the implications of those changes for *them*.

Did even the wisest of them—the shrewdest, the most astute parliamentarian of all these astute parliamentarians—realize the implications? Richard Russell could of course have stopped the changes with a word, with a shake of his head, with a wink, but he supported the changes, and if Russell was for them, who would be against them? If Russell was for them, who, indeed, would even bother to analyze them, to think about them in the detail required to understand their long-term consequences?

We can never know definitively the extent to which Russell and the other southern barons supported these changes because they wanted Lyndon Johnson to be President, believing that if he became President, he would help prevent radical change in the nation's racial laws; or because they wanted Johnson to have power in the Senate; or because they thought the changes would improve the Senate; or because they thought the changes would strengthen the Democratic Party. The extent to which Johnson kept the senatorial barons from understanding the true implications of the changes—the extent to which he may have tricked them—will also never be known definitively. But after long discussions about these very changes with Johnson, Doris Kearns Goodwin wrote that

> He accomplished this almost without conflict or opposition precisely because authority and influence of this kind had been of no significance to the exercise of Senate power and were not perceived as a potential threat to those who ruled. It did not occur to his powerful associates—respectfully consulted in every move—that from such insubstantial resources Lyndon Johnson was shaping the instruments that would make him arbiter and, eventually, the master of the United States Senate.

THE CHANGES LYNDON JOHNSON had effected in the seniority system and in the Policy Committee had increased his power—but at the same time they had increased the power, and the effectiveness, of his party. That was why these first weeks after he was elected Democratic Leader were a watershed in his life. With only a single major exception—the bringing of rural electrification to his congressional district—his previous use of power had created power mainly for himself. Now, in 1953, for the first time, with his election as Leader, his fate had been linked indissolubly with something far larger than himself, something that transcended the boundaries of a single congressional district. Attaining power for himself without attaining power for his party had been impossible. His political genius had always been used only for himself; now it had been used for the Democratic Party in the Senate—and it had transformed both the Senate Democrats and, to a lesser extent, the Senate itself.

Part IV

USING IT

22

Masterstrokes

AND NOW THE LIFE of Lyndon Johnson was to become linked with something larger than a party or the Senate. The chorus of approval that greeted Hubert Humphrey's motion in the Democratic Caucus of January 2, 1953, to make Johnson's election unanimous had installed him as his party's leader in one of the two houses of the national legislature, and his party was the opposition party; there was no Democratic President to whom he had to defer; that vote in the caucus made Lyndon Johnson one of the two or three most prominent and influential Democrats in America. His life was now to be indissolubly entwined with his country's. And, within a very short time after that link was soldered fast, it became apparent that Lyndon Johnson's political gifts were not limited to the institutional or to the tactical—that they could operate on levels far above those.

THE ENTWINING HAD BEGUN, of course, before January 2, had begun with the maneuvering to win the leadership, and with the planning of his strategy for using the leadership, which had taken place on the ranch, and on his trips to Washington in November and December, 1952, when he had grasped so quickly the fact and the implications of Eisenhower's popularity.

Eisenhower's first moves after the election had demonstrated that he might become more popular still: fulfilling his campaign pledge to "go to Korea," he went there even before his inauguration, and his actions on the trip reminded Americans of his calm decisiveness before D-Day. General Mark Clark, commander-in-chief of the UN forces in Korea, and South Korean President Syngman Rhee had developed plans for an all-out new offensive; Eisenhower gave them no chance to present them. Instead, as his biographer Stephen Ambrose writes,

> for three days, Eisenhower did what he had done so often during World War II; he visited frontline units and talked with the senior

commanders and their men. Despite the bitter cold and snow-covered ground, Eisenhower bundled up in a heavy pile jacket, fur-lined hat, and thermo boots to see for himself. He flew a reconnaissance mission over the front. He studied the artillery duel with his binoculars, chatted with troops, ate outdoor meals from a mess kit. . . .

Plans for an all-out offensive, he concluded, were irrational. The situation was intolerable, he said; the only solution was to end the war on honorable terms as soon as possible, and get the troops home. America nodded in agreement.

And as the new President's personality impressed itself on America, America was coming, day by day, to love it more and more. While some columnists had expressed disappointment over the failure of Eisenhower's Inaugural Address to speak to domestic issues—it dealt almost entirely with foreign policy—and while the speech had not been nearly partisan enough for the more rabid Republicans, even the liberal columnist Richard Rovere had to call it "statesmanlike" and admit that it "was appreciated by most people and fervently admired by some." And the most significant moment of the Inauguration had occurred not during the Address but in the moment before it. Repeating the oath of office after Chief Justice Fred Vinson, Eisenhower wore a serious, determined expression, but as he said "I do," he turned toward the huge crowd below and suddenly shot his arms up high over his head in a wide V-for-victory sign, and he grinned, and as his great wide smile beamed over the crowd, the cheering began, and the warmth of it was enough to make even hardened politicians and observers understand, some of them for the first time, just how much America liked Ike.

As the implications of the size of Eisenhower's margin had sunk in on Democrats, along with the figures from the suburbs and even from the cities that had once been Democratic strongholds, many Democratic leaders had come to "privately fear that the November vote may represent a more or less permanent shift in the party balance of power," the Alsops wrote. While Johnson had still been down on the Pedernales, and making his quick trips back and forth to Washington to sew up the leadership, a feeling almost of panic set in among Democrats, a feeling that centered on the Senate. As the Alsops wrote, "The great movers and shakers of the recent past, the chairmen of powerful committees—Southerners almost to a man—are movers and shakers no longer. Accustomed to page one in the newspapers, they now find themselves among the want ads—if they are lucky." Senatorial barons who had for decades dispensed patronage with a lavish hand suddenly found many of the elevator operators, doorkeepers, file clerks, secretaries, and committee staffers who had depended on them out of work. And even the most cursory look ahead at 1954 showed that the situation was likely to remain unchanged. "A whole series of shaky Democrats are up for re-election, while only two or three Republicans need worry. . . . [T]he Senate will remain Republican." The southerners bitterly blamed northern liberals for their plight, and the liberals, with equal bitterness, blamed the South. The Democrats were a party in disarray, a party, as *Time* would put it, "looking for an excuse to fly to pieces," a party reeling and bloody amid the wreckage of a battlefield on which they had suffered a great defeat.

But that was not how Lyndon Johnson saw the defeat, not even in its first, worst, moments. He had grasped the unpleasant facts of the election very quickly, of course, as was shown by the analysis he made in the "Reedy" memorandum of November 12. And while he had had to delay using these facts to support his plan to change the seniority system, waiting until after his election as Leader was a *fait accompli* to reveal his potentially controversial plans for the system, no such discretion had been necessary in using those facts to propose an overall strategy for the Senate Democrats. And he had also seen, almost immediately after the election, that those facts had a deep significance for such a strategy, a strategy that went far beyond the seniority system— because while Eisenhower was popular with voters, in the Senate it was not the Eisenhower wing of the GOP but the Taft wing that ruled, and with those Old Guard senators Eisenhower was not popular at all.

It was still in November, 1952, that Dallas-based public relations man and political speechwriter Booth Mooney received a telephone call from Walter Jenkins asking him to come down to Austin for a job interview with his boss, who, Jenkins said, was going to be elected Democratic Leader when the new Congress convened. The "interview" lasted for three and a half hours, and, Mooney was to recall, "He talked nearly non-stop. We left his office only once, to go to the men's room, and he continued to talk as we stood side by side" at the urinals. And the gist of Johnson's monologue, Mooney was to recall, was that if he was elected Democratic Leader, he would have a great opportunity, "an opportunity to lead his colleagues in support of the Republican President."

Mooney was not the only person to whom Lyndon Johnson tried to explain that Dwight Eisenhower's popularity could be not a disaster but an opportunity. It could be an opportunity for himself. "The way he [Johnson] looked at it, about half the voters of Texas were against him," Mooney recalls. "He had to make a dent in that large body of citizens before 1954, when he would be up for re-election. . . . He wanted to—he must—project a more conservative image," and what better way to do that than by supporting a Republican President? And it could be an opportunity for his party as well.

Since Eisenhower was so popular, Lyndon Johnson explained, whoever was supporting him would be on the popular side. The Democrats, he said, could be on the popular side—particularly if they were supporting Eisenhower and the Republicans weren't.

And, Lyndon Johnson said, if they handled things right, the Democrats *could* be supporting the President against his own party. At a time, between the

election and the Inauguration, when the prevailing opinion not only of Democrats but of commentators of all shades of political opinion was that mounting
a comeback in any near future would be difficult if not impossible for the
Democrats, Johnson said that that opinion was wrong—that, in fact, mounting
a comeback in the near future would be easy.

It would be easy, he said, because the first issues that were going to come
up in the Eighty-third Congress would be foreign policy issues, and in foreign
policy the dominant Republicans in Congress (and in particular in the Senate,
which would, because of its treaty-approving power, be the focus of foreign
policy debate) were not Eisenhower's natural allies but his natural enemies. It
was the support of the eastern, internationalist wing of the party that had given
Ike the presidential nomination over Taft, but the Taft wing consisted mostly
of Republicans from the Midwest, bedrock of isolationism. The Ohioan's
midwestern allies—Jenner, Bourke Hickenlooper, Welker, Ferguson, Molly
Malone—had yearned for years to dismantle the Roosevelt and Truman policies that the liberals thought were so wonderful. Now, they felt, their time had
come at last. They would, Johnson was certain, move at once to repudiate Yalta,
slash away at the Marshall Plan, and loosen or sever America's ties with the
United Nations and with NATO. But Eisenhower was not merely a supporter of
NATO; he had been *commander* of NATO. Says George Reedy, who was down
on the ranch with Johnson and was familiar with his thinking, Eisenhower "had
actually spent most of . . . the preceding twenty or thirty years in virtual support
of the foreign policies of Roosevelt and of Truman. The Republicans . . . under
Taft were opposed to that policy, [so] he and the congressional Republicans
were just bound to be at loggerheads." All the Democrats had to do was "take
advantage" of the situation.

JOHNSON SAID THIS FIRST, of course, to Rayburn and Russell in long telephone calls from his paneled, comfortable study in the white house near the
Pedernales, and both *R*s agreed, wholeheartedly.

With one, the reasons for agreement included the personal. Sam Rayburn
knew Dwight Eisenhower, and he liked him. Eisenhower had been born in
Denison, a town in Rayburn's district, and although his family had moved to
Kansas when Ike was still a baby, that meant something to Rayburn. "He was a
wonderful baby," he would say with a grin. And Eisenhower's parents had been
poor, and that meant more. And Rayburn admired the General, not only for his
wartime leadership but for the candor of his testimony during his frequent
appearances before congressional committees; Sam Rayburn, who put such a
high premium on truthfulness, regarded Dwight Eisenhower as a truthful man.
Besides, he trusted Ike's judgment on international affairs and defense. He
would soon be writing a friend that "I told President Eisenhower . . . that he
should know more about what it took to defend this country than practically

anyone and that if he would send up a budget for the amount he thought was
necessary to put the country in a position to defend ourselves against attack, I
would promise to deliver 95 percent of the Democratic votes in the House. . . ."
As for domestic programs, Rayburn said, he would oppose Eisenhower if the
President tried to undo "the good things we Democrats did" in the New and
Fair Deals, but would provide the votes if the President tried to expand them.
Beyond this, the adage that the opposition's duty was to oppose was not Rayburn's adage. He didn't want to oppose simply for the sake of opposing. "Any
jackass can kick a barn down," he said. "But it takes a good carpenter to build
one."

With Richard Russell, the personal paled before the patriotic. Russell,
who had studied the generals of Rome, considered Eisenhower a great military
leader, and was happy to rely on his judgment in defense matters. And, as
Evans and Novak were to write, this "old-fashioned patriot" was "genuinely
worried about the impact on the rest of the world if the Democratic Congress
should be openly hostile to the Republican President."

Convincing the rest of the senatorial Democrats was more difficult. Hour
after hour, with senator after senator, repeating the arguments over and over
again ten times, twenty times, in a single day, Lyndon Johnson tried to make
them understand how popular Eisenhower was, and that, as Reedy puts it, "to
announce right at the start that, by God, we're going to give Eisenhower a battle down the line would have been just suicide," whereas if they supported the
hero, they would be on the popular side, and if they supported him more firmly
than the Republicans, the Republicans would, as Reedy puts it, "look cheap
and partisan, whereas the Democrats would resemble statesmen willing to put
petty issues of partisanship aside to battle for the public good." "He spent hour
after hour in personal conferences" trying to make them understand that the
popularity of the man who had vanquished the Democrats could mean not
doom but hope for the Democrats, that it could in fact be the very key to a
Democratic resurgence. When the Democrats gathered in a group—at the
January 2 caucus, at which they elected him Leader—the acceptance statement
he read to them repeated these arguments. "I have never agreed . . . merely to
obstruct," he said. Instead, he said, the Democrats should support "a program
geared NOT just to opposing the majority but to serving America." When, in his
State of the Union address on February 1, Eisenhower said that foreign policy
"must be developed and directed in the spirit of true bipartisanship," Johnson
had Reedy draft a response which he read to the Policy Committee at its February 3 luncheon. "Americans everywhere have been gratified by the President's
call for 'true bipartisanship,' " it said. "The issues of war and peace are far too
serious to be settled in the arena of narrow, partisan debate. They can be solved
only by the united wisdom and efforts of all Americans regardless of political
affiliations." The Policy Committee approved the statement unanimously. It
wouldn't be merely in the Foreign Relations Committee that the Democrats

were going to line up on Ike's side. All-out defense of the international agreements, of NATO, was going to be the stance of the Senate Democrats on the
floor as well.

Foreign policy was indeed the area on which the Republican Old Guard
focused first—and the very first target in their sights was Yalta.

Isolationism was back on Capitol Hill, and it was back strong. Journalists
who remembered the America First Committee filling the Senate galleries in
1940 and 1941 saw what Richard Rovere called a "resurgent isolationism" in
the way the galleries were filled in 1953 when Joe McCarthy was scheduled to
speak. The thunderclap of Pearl Harbor may have demolished in an instant the
arguments of the Borahs and Nyes, the thunderclap of Hiroshima may have
made it even clearer that in an age of nuclear weapons and modern air forces,
the oceans were no longer moats; but those thunderclaps seem to have been
heard only faintly in Senate Republican councils, in which the views of quite a
sizable bloc (including, of course, the Republican leaders, the defiantly isolationist Taft and the suavely isolationist Bridges) sometimes seemed to resemble
the views of the Republican senators who had helped Henry Cabot Lodge Sr.
defeat the Treaty of Versailles.

Yalta gave these throwbacks a focus for their rage, for it symbolized so
much of what they detested and feared: the usurpation of the sacred constitutional powers of Congress by the hated Roosevelt; the "softness" on Communism that had left Eastern European nations under Stalin's heel; not to mention
the treachery implicit in those "secret" agreements that they were certain
existed. The isolationists had dreamed for years of having the Senate repudiate
the public agreements, unearth the secret ones, and initiate the constitutional
amendment process that would prohibit any future President from ever entering
into such agreements. And they wanted action ("the form of which," as Ambrose
comments dryly, "was unspecified") to liberate the enslaved satellites. As Sam
Shaffer, Newsweek's chief congressional correspondent, was to recall years
later, "It should have been so easy for Republicans . . . to translate the dream into
reality. . . . All that was needed to make the dream come true was a sweep in
which a Republican Congress and a Republican President could join hands in
repudiating the Yalta Agreements as soon as possible after taking the oath of
office on inaugural day. It is difficult to comprehend today how intensely the
Republican politicians clung to this article of faith." Now their faith had been
rewarded; the sweep had occurred; it seemed in the weeks following the
November elections that nothing could stop them from realizing the dream—
and thereby, they felt sure, becoming, once again, America's majority party.

During the campaign, despite his role as implementer of Roosevelt's
agreements, Eisenhower had let the Old Guard believe that he acquiesced in
their hard line, but as President he was not disposed to continue doing so, particularly after the State Department reminded him that it was at Yalta that the
Allies had been given their occupation rights in Berlin and Vienna, and that if

America could repudiate the agreements, so could Russia. His attempts to explain this to the Old Guard met with a response so stony that, on February 7, the new President noted in his diary, "Republican senators are having a hard time getting through their heads that they now belong to a team that includes rather than opposes the White House." Nonetheless, he would not give them what they wanted. Instead of disavowing the Yalta accords, the resolution he proposed to Congress on February 20 merely rejected "interpretations" of the accords that "have been perverted to bring about the subjugation of free peoples." On the subject of freeing the satellites, the President only "hoped" that they would "again enjoy the right of self-determination." The Republicans' new President did not even mention the "secret" agreements that they had for so long been certain existed; Secretary of State John Foster Dulles had investigated, and had found that they simply didn't exist.

As congressional Republicans realized that Eisenhower was not repudiating the accords but only accusing the Russians of subverting them, their fury boiled over. Taft proposed an amendment that said, "The adoption of this resolution does not constitute any determination by Congress as to the validity or invalidity of any of the provisions of the said agreements," and Taft's allies on the Old Guard–controlled Foreign Relations Committee—Hickenlooper, Langer, Ferguson, and Knowland—were planning to offer other amendments, far harsher than Taft's, in a closed-door committee hearing that had been scheduled for February 24.

On the eve of that meeting, however, a new voice was suddenly heard—a Democratic voice, the voice of the Senate's Democratic Leader. Late that evening, Lyndon Johnson telephoned William White of the *Times* to say that the resolution the Democrats wanted was the resolution Eisenhower had proposed—without any changes. Senate Republicans, he said, would face a fight from the Democrats if they tried to amend it. He read White a statement: "President Eisenhower's proposal to serve notice on the world that the United States will not acquiesce in the Soviet enslavement drive is one that all Americans can embrace. There is in the President's resolution no trace of the partisanship that could lead to discord and disunity. Congress should be able to respond in the same high spirit. It is to be hoped that the resolution—as written by the President and his advisers—will receive the unanimous approval of the Senate and thereby serve to notify mankind that Americans are united against Soviet tyranny."

Pointing out at the Foreign Relations hearing that "it would not be in the national interest to repudiate agreements such as those establishing American rights to be in Berlin or providing free elections in Poland," Dulles pleaded for a unanimity behind the Eisenhower resolution that would present a united front to the Russians. "If the resolution is going to be controversial, if it were to pass the Senate by a narrow margin, it would be an absolute detriment to what we are trying to do," he said. The committee adopted the Taft Amendment nonetheless.

Telephoning Johnson in an effort to head off harsher amendments that would dramatize to the public the deep rift between the White House and the Republican Old Guard, Dulles attempted to persuade him and the Democrats to support the Taft Amendment—which was, after all, relatively mild—but got a flat refusal. It was Eisenhower, not Taft, whom Johnson wanted to be supporting. "How can we criticize the Russians for perverting understandings if we refuse to admit their validity?" he asked Dulles.

Stalin's death on March 4 was providential for the Republicans, since it allowed them to declare that in such unsettled times it served no useful end to pass a resolution that would make it harder to establish a relationship with the new Soviet leadership. When Eisenhower told a news conference that all "I really want to do is put ourselves on record . . . that we never agreed to the enslavement of peoples that has occurred," Taft admitted that it was probably better "to forget the whole thing." But the Republican rift had been revealed; it could no longer be papered over. And neither could the fact that the Democrats were on the President's side of the rift. Johnson had positioned his party precisely as he—he alone—had wanted it positioned, and the wisdom of his strategy was dramatically apparent. Grand in scale, this overarching political plan that he had conceived down on the ranch in a flash of inspiration had proved to be a political masterstroke. As George Reedy was to say: "The picture before the public was that of a great war hero and a very popular President under attack by a disruptive Republican Party while a constructive Democratic Party was rushing to his defense." In addition, by creating an issue on which most Senate Democrats were on the same side, Johnson had also increased his party's unity and strength, particularly since the issue was one especially close to the hearts of the liberals who had been most suspicious of his leadership. And he had increased *his* strength. The forty-seven Democrats he led had—for a moment, at least—been a unified group.

The strategy had another, larger, result—one that, just a few weeks before, might have seemed all but impossible. Johnson had held back a rising isolationist tide that, had it washed away the Yalta agreements, might next have swept unchecked toward the Marshall Plan, NATO, the United Nations. In his first battle as Democratic Leader, Lyndon Johnson had scored a major triumph not only for himself and his party, but for his country as well.

AND THAT MAJOR VICTORY was almost immediately followed by a minor one that nonetheless was significant in its own right.

If they couldn't win on the broad Yalta front, the Old Guard seemed to feel, at least they could take revenge on someone associated with it—even though his association had been in one of the most innocuous roles possible. Charles (Chip) Bohlen, a career foreign service officer, had been only an interpreter at the Crimea conference. He had since become widely recognized as one of America's most knowledgeable experts on the Soviet Union, but when Eisenhower nominated him as Ambassador to Russia, his expertise was not what the Old Guard focused on. "Chip Bohlen was at Yalta," Everett Dirksen said, shouting. "If he were my brother, I would take the same attitude I am expressing in the Senate this afternoon. He was associated with the failure. Mr. President, in the language of Missouri, the tail must go with the hide. I reject Yalta. So I reject Yalta men." Despite a Foreign Relations Committee recommendation that the Senate advise and consent to the nomination, Bohlen's name remained on the Executive Calendar for the next two months under the heading "Nominations Passed Over," while on the floor Pat McCarran accused Secretary of State Dulles of concealing FBI files that would be damaging to the nominee, and Joe McCarthy, elaborating on that point, said that he had seen the files—and that they contained damaging information about Bohlen's "family life," a euphemism for homosexuality. He demanded that Dulles make the files available to the Senate.

Fearing it would set a damaging precedent, Eisenhower refused to open the files and also refused to retreat from his support of the nominee, dealing with the rumors in his own oblique fashion. Telling a press conference that Bohlen was "the best-qualified man for the post," he added: "I have known Mr. Bohlen for some years. I was once, at least, a guest in his home, and with his very charming family. . . ." And he refused to let Dulles retreat, informing him that he had checked, and was "confident that Bohlen had a normal family life." When McCarthy responded to Dulles' assurance that the FBI files contained no damaging material on Bohlen by demanding that the Secretary of State submit to a lie-detector test, Taft—in a rare event—chastised the Wisconsin senator and announced his support of the nominee. A compromise was worked out: one senator from each party, Taft and the Democrats' John Sparkman, would be allowed to examine the files, and would then report back to the full Senate. Taft's report gave the lie to Tail-Gunner Joe. "There was no suggestion anywhere by anyone reflecting on the loyalty of Mr. Bohlen in any way or any association by him with Communism or support of Communism or even tolerance of Communism," he said. Nonetheless, when Bohlen's nomination came to a vote, eleven members of Taft's party continued to oppose him. Johnson had marshaled his troops into almost unbroken ranks, 45 to 2. The Republican vote was 37 to 11—which meant, as the press pointed out, that Democrats had lined up more solidly than Republicans in favor of the nomination made by the Republican President.

"THE HIGH-WATER MARK of the isolationist surge in the 1950s came upon what was known as the Bricker Amendment," George Reedy was to recall. John W. Bricker of Ohio, stately and handsome, possessed of a full head of meticulously waved senatorial white hair and a consciousness of his senatorial dignity so profound that it was said that he always walked "as if someone was carrying a full-length mirror in front of him," was a fervent admirer of Taft, whom he had three times backed for the Republican presidential nomination, and of McCarthy, whom he would support to the last, and a fervent hater of foreign aid, the United Nations, and all those he lumped with Eleanor Roosevelt under the contemptuous designation of "One Worlders." He was the embodiment of the GOP's reactionary Old Guard, and his amendment, introduced as a joint resolution—"S.J. Res. 1"—at the opening of the Eighty-third Congress was the embodiment of the Old Guard's rage at what it viewed as twenty years of presidential usurpation of Congress's constitutional powers. And fueling the conservatives' anger now was their fear that treaties and international agreements such as the United Nations Charter and Human Rights Covenant might not only provide a legal basis for the extension of federal control over matters previously regulated by the states, but might nullify specific state laws, such as the southern segregation laws. S.J. Res. 1 struck at the heart of executive activism by calling for a constitutional amendment to restrict the President's power in foreign affairs.* Although the amendment would, in Ambrose's words, go through "a complex and incomprehensible series of changes," its continuing substance was that no international compact could be binding on the United States without the passage of positive legislation not only by Congress but in many cases by the legislatures of the individual states as well. Declaring that it would cripple an Administration's ability to conduct negotiations with other nations by "making it represent forty-eight [state] governments in its dealings with foreign powers," Eisenhower said privately that it was "stupid, a blind violation of the Constitution by stupid, blind isolationists." In the American heartland, however, it touched a deep chord. The American Legion, the Daughters of the American Revolution, the *Chicago Tribune,* the Committee for Constitutional Government, all leapt to support it. A newly formed organization, Vigilant Women for the Bricker Amendment, quickly obtained more than half a million signatures on petitions, mail running nine to one in its favor was pouring into Congress, and sixty-three senators joined Bricker in sponsoring it, enough to give S.J. Res. 1 the two-thirds of the Senate needed for passage even if all ninety-six senators voted. Among the co-sponsors were not only forty-five of the Senate's forty-eight Republicans but nineteen Democrats, including many of the party's southern hierarchy. And although the names did not include Walter George, the Senate's bellwether on foreign affairs felt that "Many of our people are fearful and suspicious of the way the treaty-making power and the President's power to make executive agreements have recently been used," and let it be known that while some refinements in S.J. Res. 1 might be necessary, he was in agreement with the philosophy behind it; without some new constitu-

* A constitutional amendment requires passage by a two-thirds vote of both houses of Congress, and ratification by three-quarters of the states.

tional check, George was to say, the country might "one day know one-man rule."

"An incredible momentum built up behind the amendment," Reedy would recall. "In all the years that I've been around the Congress . . . I don't know of any other single legislative issue that has aroused such emotion. It . . . became apparent from the start that it could not be defeated on a straight-out vote. No one could vote against the Bricker Amendment with impunity, and very few could vote against it and survive at all—at least, so they thought." Only the most liberal senators—no more than fifteen or twenty of them, not nearly the necessary one-third plus one—would vote against it. "There was no hope of stopping it through direct opposition."

To Lyndon Johnson, S.J. Res. 1 was, as he said to Bobby Baker, "the worst bill I can think of," for reasons that included not only the political (it was, after all, a slap at *Democratic* presidents, and its passage would be a major Republican victory) but the philosophical (if there was a single tenet he held consistently throughout his political career it was the necessity for broad latitude in the exercise of executive power) as well as the personal: the strongest of personal reasons for this man who wanted the world to think of him as "LBJ" and was certain that one day it would—at which time his connection with executive power would no longer be merely theoretical. S.J. Res. 1 "ties the President's hands, and I'm not just talking about Ike. It will be the bane of every President we elect," he told Baker.

Trying to stop the Bricker Amendment would, however, be extremely risky for Johnson. Among its most fervent supporters were not only a large majority of his Texas constituents but his key Texas financial backers, as Eisenhower suspected; once, when his aide W. Bedell Smith asked who was financing the avalanche of pro-Bricker "propaganda," the President replied, "Probably those two millionaires from Texas"—by whom he appears to have been referring to the two oilmen who had contributed so lavishly to both his campaign and Johnson's, Sid Richardson and Clint Murchison (although the President could also have been referring to H. R. Cullen and H. L. Hunt, who had also contributed heavily to both campaigns). And also among its supporters were Johnson's key senatorial allies: Russell and virtually the entire Southern Caucus. It could be dangerous for him to oppose the Bricker Amendment if oilmen, press, and public became aware of what he was doing.

The best insurance against such awareness was to have someone else, preferably someone prominent, out in front in opposition—and who better than the President?

Having tried and failed to persuade Bricker to drop the whole thing, or at least to modify it, Eisenhower had realized that the Senator would not be budged, and had then tried to make the proposal look silly, telling his Cabinet that "Bricker seems determined to save the United States from Eleanor Roosevelt." The "people *for* it," he told Attorney General Herbert Brownell, "are our deadly enemies." But the President, trying to avoid emphasizing the split within his party, had made most of his comments privately. To Dulles' suggestion that he speak out more directly, he replied, "There was nothing fuzzy in what I told Bricker. I said we'd go just so far and no further." "I know, sir," Dulles replied, "but you haven't told anybody else."

Eisenhower's stance sufficed for a time. Growing ambivalent about the resolution, Taft had his allies on Judiciary hold it in committee (to the growing annoyance of the committee's chairman, Jenner, who said that "a secret revolutionary corps" was working against it). But on June 10, Taft, dying, turned the majority leadership over to Knowland, one of S.J. Res. 1's true believers, and just five days later Judiciary reported it out, with a favorable 9–5 vote. Afraid that it would be brought to the floor and passed before Congress adjourned, Johnson got into his big limousine, which pulled away from the Senate steps and headed for the State Department. The purpose of the trip was to keep the President standing firm against the amendment, and Johnson therefore wanted to relay, through Dulles, his ally on the issue, Taft's judgment on the situation, in which he knew the President had come to trust. That afternoon Dulles sent Eisenhower a memo:

> Lyndon Johnson was in to see me today. In the course of the conversation he mentioned the Bricker Amendment. He said he expected you would stand firm against it. He was confident it would be defeated unless you gave in. He added that Senator Taft had told him he did not think it would be brought up at this session unless you did give in on the matter.

Eisenhower thereupon not only announced publicly his "unalterable opposition" to Bricker's text, but also had Brownell draw up a substitute resolution, and asked Knowland to introduce it—and the preliminary skirmishing over the new proposal insured that no action on the floor of the Senate had been taken when Congress adjourned for the year on August 4.

All that Fall and Winter, the Bricker Amendment stayed on the front pages of the nation's newspapers, but statements on the issue came strictly from Republicans. The only word from the Senate's Democratic Leader—made in a radio broadcast over an intra-state Texas network—was the innocuous hope that the Republicans would resolve their differences over "technicalities" and agree on a compromise text. Otherwise, from down on the Pedernales there was only silence.

But all through that Fall and Winter, Lyndon Johnson was sitting for hours every day in the big reclining chair in the study of his ranch, slouched and silent, in his hand a cigarette, on his face the expression that meant he didn't want to be disturbed. Sometimes he would lunge up out of the chair, and, pushing open the study's screen door, would walk outside along Marcus Burg's concrete walk to the front gate, and as he passed the living room window, Reedy and Rather and Lady Bird could see the same expression on his face. Beyond the gate was the dirt path down to the little river, and the family cemetery and the site of the house in which he had been born, and he would walk along the path, one hand holding a cigarette, the other deep in a pants pocket. Sometimes he would stop and stand, motionless except for the hand jingling the coins in his pocket, a tall figure in rancher's khaki staring unseeing toward the river or toward the hills. All that Fall and Winter, Lyndon Johnson was trying to deal with the knot of tangled political implications that the Bricker Amendment posed for him.

It was a knot of almost incredible complexity.

Defeating the amendment and thereby preserving the power of the presidency—his first objective—could not be accomplished even if he united his party's liberal and moderate senators against it; there simply were not enough of them. He would have to turn conservative senators against it too, conservatives who were at the moment wholeheartedly for it—and not just Democratic conservatives but at least a few members of the Republican Old Guard.

Even if he somehow managed to turn enough conservatives against it, however, that feat—difficult though it would be—would not accomplish his other purposes, for the public would then be presented with a picture of the President and at least some of his party's Old Guard as allies, and Johnson didn't want them allied; he wanted the public to see a clear, vivid picture: the President, the trusted, idolized President—the beloved Ike—being fought by the Old Guard tooth and nail. And Johnson also wanted the picture to contain another dramatic element: the rescue of Ike from the Old Guard by his true friends, the Democrats in the Senate. He wanted the Senate Democrats to get the credit for defeating the Bricker Amendment and preserving the powers of the presidency.

Nor did the complications end there. He wanted credit not merely for his party, but for himself—a substantial share of the credit from liberal press and public for the amendment's defeat. He wanted to be seen, and portrayed, as the general who had led the senatorial cavalry to the President's rescue. But getting such credit would be especially difficult because of the situation in his own state. He could not appear, in the eyes of the conservative Texas constituency and of key supporters like Richardson and Murchison, and, most of all, in the eyes of Herman Brown, to be opposing limitations on the hated executive power. He would have to emerge from the coming battle in a position to convince these men—one of whom, Brown, was extremely hard to fool—that he had not opposed limitations but had supported limitations. He would have to be able to claim (and to allow southern conservatives in his own party to claim) that he and they had supported a constitutional amendment that would prevent future Yaltas.

So tangled and twisted together were all these strands that they composed a knot that might have been thought to be as beyond untying as the one Gordius wove together in Phrygia. But Alexander had solved the Gordian knot by simply slashing through it. Johnson solved his the same way—with a single slash. By the time Congress reconvened, he had conceived of the political masterstroke that would do the job. Turning conservatives against the Bricker Amendment seemed all but impossible, but Johnson thought of a way—perhaps the only way—to do so: by turning against it the senator most influential in foreign affairs with conservatives of both parties.

Not that persuading Walter George simply to oppose the Bricker Amendment would accomplish all of Johnson's objectives. George's opposition might move some of the Old Guard to oppose Bricker, but then the picture the public saw would be the somewhat blurred picture—of Ike and some Old Guarders on the same side—that Johnson didn't want. He would therefore have to persuade George not only to oppose the Bricker Amendment but to offer an amendment of his own. The new amendment would have to split the GOP. It would have to still be strong enough—still contain sufficient curbs on presidential authority—so that the Old Guard would support it and Ike would oppose it, so that Ike would still be on one side of the issue and the isolationists on the other, but it would have to be less stringent, more moderate than the Bricker Amendment—moderate enough so that moderate Republicans who had been united with Ike in opposing Bricker would break away from him and support this new amendment. The GOP would therefore be split—and if the GOP was split, the balance of power in Senate voting would shift to the Democrats. If moderate Democrats supported the George Amendment, Senate Democrats would be in the position Johnson wanted: Democrats would be saving Ike from the Bricker Amendment—saving him from the isolationists in his own party. Moreover, the George Amendment would be a Democratic amendment. A Democratic proposal would become the focus of activity and interest. Although they might be in the minority, the Senate Democrats—the Democrats and their Leader—would have seized the initiative on the most prominent political issue of the day.

There would still be complications. The Democratic amendment—the George Amendment—would have to be popular with the public, and the popular side of the issue, as demonstrated by the overwhelming public support for Bricker, was the strong side, so the George Amendment would have to be a stringent curb on presidential power. But Johnson himself didn't want a stringent curb. He would have to make certain, therefore, that the George Amendment, the amendment he had persuaded George to introduce, did not receive the necessary two-thirds vote. He had to persuade George to introduce an amendment—and then he had to make sure the amendment was not passed.

Which created *another* complication. He would need George's support in Senate councils of the future as he had needed it in the past. He would never have it again if the old man felt humiliated by the reception of the proposal

Johnson had persuaded him to introduce, and a defeat might well make George, who wasn't used to defeats, feel humiliated. Johnson had to make sure that the defeat was not decisive, that the final vote was close. He decided that the George Amendment should pass by a majority—no one, not even Walter George, would feel humiliated by a majority vote—but not by the necessary two-thirds.

There was a final complication. At the end of the ensuing fight, Johnson's reactionary Texas backers would have to be convinced that he himself had supported restrictions on presidential power. He would have to make sure that although he was arranging for the George Amendment to fail, he would be able to tell his constituents that he had worked earnestly for it to succeed. But, Johnson saw, that complication would be solved only if the George Amendment contained strong restrictions. If it did, and if he, along with Democratic conservatives, supported it, at least in public, he would be able to tell Richardson and Murchison that although the amendment had been defeated, he had personally supported it.

TANGLED AS WERE THESE COMPLICATIONS, the mind working down on the Pedernales was equal to them. By the time Lyndon Johnson returned to Washington on December 28, 1953, and Bobby Baker mentioned the Bricker Amendment to him, he was able to tell Baker: "We've got to stop the damn thing, and I think we can."

The single necessity, of course, was Walter George's agreement to stop supporting Bricker's amendment and introduce his own. That was the masterstroke, the only way to cut through the Gordian knot. None of Johnson's plans would work without George's agreement. Johnson set out to get it—to persuade the senator who never changed his mind to change it this time.

"To get George to take on Bricker, that was quite an undertaking," Hubert Humphrey would recall. Johnson did it in part with a memorandum, written by Gerald Siegel and analyzing, in Siegel's dry style, the flaws in S.J. Res. 1. And he did it in part—after what Siegel calls "just a quick reading of the memo"—with a demonstration of his persuasive powers.

"He called me into a meeting that was going on between himself, Bill White, and Walter George," Siegel recalls. "I sat there and watched one of those really stellar performances of persuasion that he was so capable of with the dean of the Senate. . . . Walter George was still a formidable guy. He was getting a little old but . . .

"I sat there and witnessed Johnson . . . persuade Walter George that he should not . . . favor the Bricker Amendment. It was a rapid-fire, almost uninterrupted monologue. It wasn't a give-and-take discussion. It was the Senator expressing just about every point of view that he thought would be effective. . . . Finally, after long discussion, Senator George . . . agreed to introduce a substitute for the Bricker Amendment."

The substitute contained only two clauses. The first provided that no provision of a treaty could supersede the Constitution; the second that no "international agreement other than a treaty"—such as an executive agreement or the United Nations Charter—could become effective "as internal law in the United States . . . except by an act of Congress."

Innocuous though the George Amendment may have been, however, it accomplished Johnson's purposes. Since it contained none of the provisions to which internationalists had objected most strongly, it instantly attracted liberal and moderate support. And by reasserting the primacy of the Constitution over any treaty, it still contained a sufficient check on executive power so that the Old Guard—or at least all of it except its most rabidly isolationist members—could support it. Moreover, its wording, as Reedy was to say, "sounded very much like the language of the Bricker Amendment," so it provided "a safe harbor to which Senators could flee who felt uneasy about the Bricker Amendment but who also felt compelled to vote for it under constituent pressure." And its very introduction, on Wednesday, January 27, accomplished two of Johnson's purposes: to move the Democrats to center stage on the issue, and to do so in the sympathetic role of presidential rescuer. "Within five minutes of the formal opening of the Senate's long-awaited debate on the issue," Walter George "momentarily seized the initiative for the Democrats," White wrote in the *Times*. "Some Democrats privately said that Mr. George not only had moved ahead of the Republicans for the moment on the issue, but also that the effect of his effort would be greatly to reduce Republican embarrassment. Until today, the fight, in public at least, had been almost exclusively between the pro-Bricker and the pro-Eisenhower Republicans."

Eisenhower was at first elated. "DDE not only has no objection to the George Amendment but actually believes it could work out to our advantage," one of the President's secretaries noted. "DDE believes this will get what we want on bipartisan basis." Republican legislative leaders, feeling themselves rescued from an intra-party fight, breathed a sigh of relief. After calling on Ike the next morning, Ferguson, Millikin, and Majority Leader Knowland emerged from the White House full of optimism that "a broadly backed agreement was at hand."

But the man who got what he wanted was not Eisenhower or Knowland but Lyndon Johnson. The Republican leaders arrived back at the Senate to find an enraged Bricker on the floor assailing the President for even considering replacing his amendment with George's—and Bricker's speech was so bitter that, White wrote, it "burned the last stick of any conceivable bridge remaining between his forces and the Eisenhower Administration." And as the likely impact of newspaper coverage such as White's sunk in, general Republican enthusiasm for the George proposal faded rapidly. At 4:57 p.m. on Thursday, Bedell Smith reported to Eisenhower that Senate "Republicans now feel they cannot accept the George Amendment and have it said that the Democrats had to save the GOP from fight on Bricker Amendment." Republican senators, the author Duane Tananbaum wrote, "were reluctant to let Democrats claim that they had saved President Eisenhower and the nation from extremists in the Republican Party."

By Friday, Eisenhower himself was concerned over the same point. In a telephone call that afternoon, the President complained to Brownell that "pretty soon, Republicans will have nothing of their own to put in." After Brownell raised an additional concern with the President—the possibility that the George Amendment, broad though its language might be, might one day be construed to limit a President's powers to make war, or to prosecute a war as Commander-in-Chief—Eisenhower told his Attorney General to tell Knowland, "We couldn't possibly accept the George Amendment without some qualifying language to protect power of the Pres. to carry out his duties as prescribed in the Constitution." Knowland and Ferguson were trying to placate their fellow Old Guarders by working out a compromise text that retained some of Bricker's language, but Eisenhower angrily rejected each attempt; he was, he told Press Secretary Jim Hagerty, "getting so tired of the name [of Bricker]. If it's true that when you die the things that bothered you most are engraved on your skull, I am sure I'll have there the mud and dirt of France during [the] invasion and the name of Senator Bricker." And each angry outbreak on the Senate floor re-emphasized the fact that, as White put it, "The fight was fundamentally . . . between the Eisenhower wing of the Republican party and the Old Guard"—an Old Guard which would not compromise; Bricker said his supporters' differences with the Administration reflected "fundamentally different philosophies of government."

THE ANGRY SHOUTING MATCHES on a relatively crowded Senate floor were, for the next month, to be succeeded by day after day of the more familiar Senate tableau, with only a handful of senators present while negotiations went on behind the scenes. The political reality, however, was not what was happening on the floor but what the press said about it, and as James Reston noted, "The headlines make it appear that an exciting debate is in process here. The papers are full of well-argued charge and countercharge, and it is easy for the reader to imagine 96 Senators all in their places and crowded galleries listening to an eloquent debate. . . ." For an entire month, the "Bricker Debate" was on the front pages day after day—in the light Lyndon Johnson wanted it portrayed, as an exciting story of a no-holds-barred battle between a beleaguered President and his party, a battle in which the Democrats were coming to the President's aid.

And when, on February 26, the day of voting finally arrived, the rest of Lyndon Johnson's objectives were attained.

THE FLOOR OF THE SENATE CHAMBER wasn't empty that day, and neither were the cloakrooms, for this was the showdown.

In the Republican cloakroom were more than a normal complement of representatives from the White House, for so great was the importance the Administration attached to the preservation of executive power that seven or eight of its congressional liaison men had divided the forty-eight Republican senators among them, and each was keeping an eye on his charges until the moment they pushed through the swinging cloakroom doors and went out on the floor to vote. Every few minutes, it seemed, the liaison men huddled and counted votes together.

In the Democratic cloakroom only one man was counting. Few counts that he had made in his life were more crucial.

Three proposals for a constitutional amendment were scheduled to be brought to the floor: the first was Bricker's; the second was a brand-new proposal cobbled together at the last minute by Knowland and Ferguson with limits on the presidential power so minor that Eisenhower had privately agreed he could accept it; and the third was Walter George's.

The first two were Republican, and Johnson didn't want either of them to receive the necessary two-thirds vote. He wanted the final vote to be on a Democratic bill, the George Amendment, so that it would remain clear to press and public which party had taken the initiative. He had arranged therefore that when the Knowland-Ferguson Amendment was called, a Democratic senator would make a motion to substitute the George Amendment for it. That substitution motion required only a majority vote, and Johnson wanted the motion passed, to give Walter George the necessary pride-saving victory. Johnson didn't want the George Amendment itself to pass, however, since it would reduce presidential powers that he wanted to keep unreduced. He wanted the amendment to win on that first vote, but lose on the last vote: the vote on passage of the amendment itself. Passage required not merely a majority but a two-thirds majority. Johnson didn't want it to get the two-thirds.

Counting the Bricker Amendment vote was relatively simple, for many conservatives who had once supported it now preferred Walter George's bill. When S.J. Res. 1 had initially been introduced a year before, nineteen of its sixty-four co-sponsors had been Democrats; Johnson and George between them had persuaded thirteen of those Democrats to defect, and there were enough additional Republican defections so that when, after the year's delay that Johnson had arranged, the clerk finally called the roll on the measure, it failed of passage, 42 votes to 50; not only did the Bricker Amendment, once seemingly so certain of passage, not receive the necessary two-thirds of those voting, it did not receive even a simple majority.

The rest of the counting was much harder.

The vote to substitute the George Amendment for the Knowland-Ferguson Amendment had to be favorable, and it had to be favorable by a big margin— that was necessary for the party, to cement the Democratic initiative, and it was necessary for Walter George's pride. But if the George Amendment had to be substituted, it then had to be defeated, by failing to get the necessary two-thirds vote.

Johnson had, as *Newsweek* later put it, "passed the word to all party members: Vote for the George Amendment as a substitute, whether you are for or against the idea of changing the Constitution. Then after this gambit has succeeded in shunting aside . . . the Knowland substitute, do what you wish. . . ." This, Lyndon Johnson felt, would ensure enough defections from Democratic liberals and moderates on the final vote—the vote on passage of the George Amendment itself—so that the measure would not receive the necessary two-thirds. But that final count was going to be uncomfortably close to two-thirds, and he couldn't be certain which way some Republicans would vote—he tried to prepare for every eventuality, to guard against any unforeseen development. Although they personally disapproved of the George Amendment, a number of liberals from states in which opinion strongly favored a curb on presidential power were reluctant to vote against it. Johnson had obtained commitments from three such senators, Lister Hill of Alabama and Washington's two senators, Magnuson and Jackson—all of whose seats were safe enough, and whose next election was far enough off—that although they would vote in favor of the George measure as a substitute, should their votes be needed to defeat it on the final vote, they would then switch and vote against it. A number of southerners personally opposed to the George Bill did not believe they could survive the next election if they were *ever* recorded voting against it. Johnson had persuaded Alabama's John Sparkman and one or two other southerners that if necessary, they would absent themselves from the floor on the final vote so that, while not actually voting against George, their votes could not be part of the necessary two-thirds. But he was still worried. Standing in the center of the crowded Democratic cloakroom, senators milling around him, Bobby Baker darting to his side and away again, he kept nervously pulling the long tally sheet from his pocket and studying it through his glasses, counting and recounting. There were so many switches back and forth that he wasn't putting numbers next to the senators' names, since each switch would mean renumbering; he was using checkmarks instead. And sometimes, as a senator spoke to him, or Baker whispered something in his ear, or a piece of intelligence came to him from the Republican side, he would take a pen from his pocket and scratch out a checkmark on one side of the list, and make one on the other side, and then count again.

And, as it turned out, his caution was not unwarranted. Although Eisenhower's aides, as one historian of the event has written, "continued, right up to the final vote" to lobby against the substitution of the George Amendment for the Knowland-Ferguson Amendment because the Administration wanted the final vote to be on a Republican bill, the substitution was approved, 61 to 30, and the only constitutional amendment left before the Senate was then the Democratic amendment. But the substitution vote showed the threat to Johnson's ultimate objective to be quite grave. The sixty-one votes George had received *was,* with ninety-one senators voting, the necessary two-thirds. As the vote was announced, wire service reporters ran up the steps of the Press Gallery and teletype machines began clattering out the prediction that on the next roll call the Senate would almost certainly approve the George Amendment as a constitutional amendment.

A switch of a single vote would block the George Amendment, and Johnson, in his caution, had those three liberal votes available to switch. That had seemed like enough, but as senators were milling around the well of the Chamber waiting for the final vote, there was a development that no one had predicted or even considered. Red-faced and waving his arms, William Knowland was suddenly standing at his desk—the front-row, center-aisle Majority Leader's desk—shouting for recognition from Vice President Nixon, above him in the presiding officer's chair. And when Knowland got it, he strode to a desk in the third row, and said, "Mr. President, I have left the desk of Majority Leader because I wish to make it very clear that what I say is not said as Majority Leader, but is said in my capacity as an individual Senator"—and what he said was that he had just decided, "because of the very real need for some steps to be taken to curb . . . the gradual encroachment by the Executive on the legislative power of the Congress," and because the only amendment left on the floor was George's, that he would not vote against the George Amendment, as he had done on the first vote, but instead would switch sides and vote for it. Tumult erupted on the floor—not only would Knowland's vote, added to the sixty-one votes that the George Amendment had received on the previous roll call, raise its total to sixty-two, but other Republican conservatives would probably follow their leader into the pro-George camp.

Herbert Lehman, who earnestly believed that "if we are not to accept a position of isolation," the President must have the same freedom to conduct foreign affairs as he had had in the past, and who believed that the amendment to end that freedom was on the verge of passage, said, "Mr. President, what we are doing is one of the most dangerous and inexcusable things that any great legislative body can do." Infuriated southerners and members of the Republican Old Guard started shouting, "Vote! Vote! Vote!" to drown him out, but Lehman said, "This is an important matter, and I will have my say on it." Wringing his hands in his distress, the stocky little New Yorker began to speak again, wandering up and down the center aisle. A furious Burnet Maybank demanded a point of order. "The Senator who is speaking must stand at his desk," he shouted. Lehman returned to his desk, but a moment later, carried away by his emotions as he spoke, he forgot himself and stepped away again— to be admonished again. As he continued speaking, flushed and angry, he was interrupted repeatedly by the shouts of "Vote! Vote!" but he refused to yield until he had finished his statement. Walter George, rising to make a final plea— "Mark my words, now, gentlemen: you are going to [pass] a constitutional amendment. . . . You will do it now, or you will do it later. This is the best amendment which can be worked out"—was saluted by Bricker, and saluted Bricker in return, weeping, so emotional had he become, and Nixon finally called for the yeas and nays.

The Minority Leader's desk was vacant. Lyndon Johnson was in the cloakroom, calling in his commitments. Hill, Magnuson, and Jackson lived up to them, switching to vote against the bill. There was also an unexpected Republican switch—by Ralph Flanders—against it. But two Republicans, Millikin and Robert Hendrickson, did indeed follow Knowland and switched to vote for it, so that there were still only thirty votes against it—and sixty for it. The margin was precisely the two-thirds necessary for passage. Johnson was standing just inside the cloakroom doors with Sparkman, who had voted for the bill, ready to throw him against it; he was gripping Sparkman's arm, on the verge of pushing him through the doors to vote; Sparkman would remember for a long time how hard Johnson's big fingers grasped his biceps. But Johnson had another card to play before it would be necessary to play that one, reluctant as it was. Harley Kilgore of West Virginia, a Democratic opponent of restrictions on the President who had voted against the George Amendment on the previous ballot, had not voted on this one because he wasn't present. Because of the effects of either alcohol or influenza, he had fallen into a very deep sleep on a couch in his office. Men had run to get him, and had finally, with difficulty, brought him to the Chamber, and the oak and bronze doors in the rear swung open, and there he was. Nixon looked at him expectantly, but all Kilgore did was stare groggily back. He said nothing, Nixon said nothing. For a long moment, the Chamber was still, staring at Kilgore. Johnson was in the Chamber now, moving fast. Grabbing Magnuson, he whispered: "Stall." "Mr. President," Magnuson shouted, "how am I recorded voting?" A clerk studied the voting list, and of course said what everyone already knew, that Magnuson had been recorded against the resolution. While that charade was being enacted, Kilgore was pulling himself together and finally he nodded at Nixon. "The Senator from West Virginia," Nixon said.

"Mr. Kilgore," the clerk said.

"No," Kilgore said. He walked slowly and deliberately down the center aisle and sank into a seat in the front row, as the clerk turned and handed the tally sheet up to Nixon. "On this roll call," the Vice President said, "the yeas are sixty, the nays are thirty-one. Two-thirds of the Senators present not having voted in the affirmative, the joint resolution is rejected."

THE CASTING OF THE DECISIVE VOTE by a Democrat emphasized the crucial role the Democrats had played in defeating the amendment that would have curbed Dwight Eisenhower's power. They had supplied more of the "nay" votes that had kept the George Amendment from passing than the Republicans:

sixteen Democratic nays, only fourteen Republican (Independent Morse had also voted nay). Republicans had, in fact, voted for the amendment—and against their own President—by a margin of 32 to 14. Eisenhower had won a big victory in the battle that had begun with Bricker's introduction of S.J. Res. 1, for he had defeated the Old Guard isolationists. But Lyndon Johnson had won a bigger victory.

Johnson had hit, in fact, every target at which he had aimed in the battle. Wanting to show the public a hero President, unparalleled in his knowledge of foreign affairs, being opposed in foreign affairs by his own party, and being rescued from that party by the Democrats, he had succeeded in doing exactly that. Wanting to demonstrate that despite GOP control of both White House and Senate, the Democrats had taken the initiative on the issue, he had, by arranging for the final vote to be not on a Republican but on a Democratic bill, done exactly that. He had wanted the Bricker Amendment defeated, and it had been defeated. He had wanted the George Amendment substituted, at first, and it had been substituted. He had wanted the George Amendment blocked at last, and at last it had been blocked.

Moreover, it had been blocked by a single vote. That was a feat dramatic in itself. But even more dramatic was the fact (which the public never learned) that had that single-vote margin not materialized—had, for example, Harley Kilgore not been able to make it to the Chamber—Lyndon Johnson would still have won. His hand had been on John Sparkman's arm; he could have sent Sparkman out to switch. And if Sparkman's vote had not been sufficient, Lyndon Johnson had had other votes ready. He had had almost no margin for error—and he hadn't made any errors. The man who a long time before, when he had still been young, had won the reputation of being "the very best at counting" had shown that the reputation was deserved.

LYNDON JOHNSON WAS HAILED for the results of the fight on the Bricker Amendment, and for the other victories he had masterminded—on Yalta and on Bohlen—over the future shape of American foreign policy. The praise was justified. His initial overall decision not to oppose but to support a President of the rival party was political strategy of the highest order. It helped his party, and it helped himself.

But it was a masterstroke on levels higher than the political. As Stephen Ambrose has written, the Republican Old Guard "wanted major policy and structural changes . . . a flat repudiation of the Yalta agreements," a constitutional amendment banning future executive agreements, action "to free the East European satellites. . . . For the nation and the world, these were matters of transcendent importance." In these matters, the defeat of the Old Guard was accomplished at least in part—and not in small part—through Johnson's maneuvers. Through them, he increased his party's popularity and his personal power. But through them also, he helped defend and make possible a continuation of a foreign policy that had produced the United Nations, the Greek and Turkish alliances, the Marshall Plan, NATO, the strategy of containment—the policy that had shaped the postwar world. Anyone who believes that the history of that world would have been the same had the senatorial Old Guard triumphed in the aftermath of the Republicans' 1952 election victory has only to look back to the time, after the first Great War, when the Senate was run not by Lyndon Johnson but by Henry Cabot Lodge. The isolationist Old Guard had felt sure that the 1950s would be their time, and liberals had felt uneasily that the Old Guard was right. Whatever the motives behind Lyndon Johnson's strategy, that strategy had helped ensure that the 1950s would not be such a time.

The icing on this triumphal cake was Johnson's success in achieving his objectives without awareness of what he had done from supporters who disapproved of those objectives. He himself, of course, had voted for the George Amendment, and he told his reactionary bankrollers that he intended to keep on doing so. On March 3, he wrote Ed Clark, the attorney and lobbyist for many of them: "We had a mighty close one last week on the George Amendment, losing by one vote. It will be taken up again, and we hope the final result will be different." And over dinner on St. Joe or at Falfurrias, or over drinks in 8-F, he assured Herman Brown, and Richardson and Murchison and Cullen and Hunt, that he had been fighting all along for some measure that would prevent further usurpation of power, and they believed him.

23

Tail-Gunner Joe

WHILE LYNDON JOHNSON'S STRATEGY on foreign policy dovetailed with his country's interests from his first days as Democratic Leader, on domestic issues, and in particular on the dominant domestic issue, his arrival on the side of the angels was delayed, and came only after there was little risk involved.

It had been in February, 1950, that Wisconsin's junior senator told a women's club in Wheeling, West Virginia, "I have here in my hand a list of 205" State Department employees "who have been named as members of the Communist Party . . . and who nevertheless are still working and shaping the policy of the State Department," words that touched off the decade's Red Scare.

The national bonfire thus ignited by Republican Joseph R. McCarthy—a bonfire that was to consume or sear, leaving scars that sometimes never healed, the reputations of thousands of innocent Americans—was to blaze for four years and ten months, and during virtually all that time, a period longer than America's participation in the Second World War, not only liberals and concerned journalists but more than a few Democratic senators argued that the Senate should take a stand against him. It was in the Senate that a stand should be taken, they said, for McCarthy was using the Senate floor as his platform (it was the fact that many of his charges were made in the Senate that gave them a veneer of respectability), and his Senate chairmanships—of the Government Operations Committee and its Permanent Investigations Subcommittee (Roy Cohn, chief counsel)—as his base of operations. And in his abusive language about targets and colleagues on the Senate floor, and his misuse of senatorial powers of investigation and privilege, it was not merely basic human tenets of fairness and justice that were being violated, again and again, by the man who was, in Robert Sherrill's words, "the most influential demagogue the United States has ever produced," but specific Senate rules of decorum and civility. It was therefore under Senate rules that he could most fittingly be brought to book, and the tarring, month by month, of innocent Americans halted. From the time of that first speech in February, 1950, there were attempts to move in the Senate against this consummate liar (among his inventions was a war record for himself: he claimed to have been known in the Pacific as "Tail-Gunner Joe," and in 1951 asked for, and received, a Distinguished Flying Cross for flying twenty-five combat missions, although he had never been a tail-gunner but rather an intelligence officer whose primary duty was to sit at a desk and debrief pilots upon their returns from missions). When, several weeks after his Wheeling speech, he repeated on the Senate floor his charge that "there are presently in the State Department a very sizable group of active Communists" (although not, apparently, as sizable as had been the case before: the number was reduced from 205 to 57; it would thereafter fluctuate from speech to speech), the Senate established a special subcommittee, headed by Millard Tydings, to investigate his allegations, and after extensive hearings concluded that they were "a fraud and a hoax" not only on the American people but on the Senate itself. And, as Robert Byrd has written in his history of the Senate, "from the day he gave his address in 1950 . . . McCarthy was constantly under fire" from liberal senators—from liberals on both sides of the aisle. When, on June 1, 1950, Margaret Chase Smith delivered on the Senate floor her "Declaration of Conscience" ("Recently [the Senate's] deliberative character has too often been debased to the level of a forum of hate and character assassination, sheltered by the shield of congressional immunity"), six fellow Republicans supported her. And repeatedly Johnson, as whip first and then as leader of the party opposed to McCarthy's, was asked by liberals both in and out of the Senate to take steps to at least put the party on record against not only McCarthy but McCarthyism, the technique of guilt by association and innuendo that was poisoning the nation's political dialogue. "Something, somebody, has got to stop this man McCarthy," Bill White said to him in 1951. "You simply must put the Democratic party on the attack against him." But no help from Lyndon Johnson was forthcoming.

Considerations against going on the attack were understandable. Not a few senators agreed with McCarthy. His fears of Communist infiltration of the government were no more paranoid than those of Republican reactionaries like William Jenner or Homer Capehart, or of Molly Malone, who walked into a Washington cocktail party one evening, and loudly announced: "I'm for the son of a bitch and I'm for his methods. And I don't want to talk about him any more tonight." In addition, as long as the Wisconsin demagogue confined his attacks to Democratic targets, his party regarded him as a considerable asset in congressional elections in the Midwest. It was for a combination of these reasons that in 1950 Robert Taft told reporters that McCarthy should "keep talking and if one case doesn't work out, he should proceed with another one." And among the senators who agreed were more than a few of the conservative, ardently anti-Communist southerners who were the base of Johnson's support.

Many senators feared McCarthy—with reason. Instead of retreating in the face of the Tydings' subcommittee report, he attacked, going into Maryland to campaign against the patrician Senator, using a fake photograph that "showed" Tydings listening intently to Communist Party leader Earl Browder. In 1938, Tydings had turned back Franklin Roosevelt's attempt to purge him; he couldn't turn back McCarthy's. In November, 1950, he lost to the obscure John Marshall Butler by a startling forty thousand votes. The lesson, underlined by the unexpected victories that November of two Republican candidates for whom McCarthy had campaigned, Herman Welker of Idaho and Wallace F. Bennett of Utah, was not lost on the Senate. After observing the early days of its 1951 session, William White wrote: "There was a time, only a few months ago," when many Republican senators "snubbed" McCarthy—when they "quietly arranged matters in their daily routine so as never to pass close to the desk of their colleague, Joseph McCarthy of Wisconsin. With a seeming casualness they avoided any public friendliness. . . . The desk of Senator McCarthy of Wisconsin is not, these days, avoided very often by his Republican associates. Senator McCarthy is, by any standards, the most politically powerful first-term senator in this Congress." Nor, White reported, was the fear confined to the Republican side of the aisle. At the first Democratic conference that January, 1951, "there ran through the caucus" a "general expression of fear that what had happened to Mr. Tydings could happen to any other man in the Senate. 'For whom does the bell toll?' one Democrat asked. 'It tolls for thee.' " The extent to with which McCarthy had intimidated the Senate was definitively demonstrated during a speech in which he was presenting his "evidence" of Communist infiltration of the State Department, standing behind a lectern piled high with documents on the various "cases" that proved his point, and saying that any senator who wanted to examine the evidence was free to do so. One senator tried to take him up on the offer. With his funny waddling walk and his heart full of courage, Herbert Lehman came over to McCarthy's desk and stood in front of it, his hand held out for the documents. Then, as Stewart Alsop wrote,

> the two men stared at each other, and McCarthy giggled his strange, rather terrifying little giggle. Lehman looked around the crowded Senate, obviously appealing for support. Not a man rose. "Go back to your seat, old man," McCarthy growled at Lehman. The words do not appear in the *Congressional Record,* but they were clearly audible in the press gallery. Once more, Lehman looked all around the chamber, appealing for support. He was met with silence and lowered eyes. Slowly, he turned and walked [back to his seat]. The silence of the Senate that evening was a measure of the fear which McCarthy inspired in almost all politicians. . . . Old Senator Lehman's back, waddling off in retreat, seemed to symbolize the final defeat of decency. . . .

To traditionalist senators of both parties, moreover, the idea of taking action against a colleague because of his political views was anathema. "At that time, there was a feeling that if the people of a state wanted to send an SOB to the Senate, that was their business," George Reedy was to write. "It is difficult, in this place so devoted to debate, for the Senate to think of disciplining a member for what he *says*," William White said.

Other considerations may also have been holding Johnson back, some of them strategic. If the issue became a partisan one—if the attack on McCarthy was almost entirely a Democratic attack—Republicans, as Evans and Novak were to write, "would be forced as an instinctive partisan reaction to come to McCarthy's defense. Beyond that, Johnson had a deeper fear that if the entire Democratic establishment in Congress, led by himself, turned against McCarthy now when he still had a dangerous and powerful hold on millions of Americans, it might appear that the Democrats were moved by self-interest in trying to cover up some unspeakable wickedness in the Truman Administration."

There may have been personal considerations as well. Lyndon Johnson was, after all, unusually well qualified to appreciate the strength not only of the issue McCarthy was using but of some of the specific tactics McCarthy employed; who knew better than Lyndon Johnson the efficacy of linking an opponent to Earl Browder—even if he himself had used not a photograph but photostats of an old newspaper article? It had been a bare six months before the Wheeling speech that Johnson himself had employed the issue, and the link, himself—had employed them so effectively that in August, 1949, the Senate, at his instance, had refused to consent to the reappointment of Leland Olds; if McCarthy had not hit on a single epithet as damaging as "Commissar"—well, McCarthy was not as gifted a phrasemaker as Lyndon Johnson. The issue was not one on which it was wise to be on the wrong side. If Johnson tried to fight McCarthy in the Senate, it was a fight he well might not win.

The fight was also one for which he had little stomach—for Lyndon Johnson had read not only the polls but the man, and he was very, very wary of the man. "Joe will go that extra mile to destroy you," he said privately. And he may have been worried that if McCarthy decided to go that mile against him, the Wisconsinite already knew which route to take. On one of Arthur Stehling's trips to Washington, a lobbyist had taken Johnson's Fredericksburg attorney and McCarthy to dinner, and at the dinner McCarthy had asked Stehling, as Stehling was to relate, "about how Johnson made his money, how he treated his office help, and whether he trifled on Mrs. Johnson." And, Stehling was to relate, "he [McCarthy] said enough to make me suspect that he knew at least a little about the money part." The Senator from Wisconsin seemed particularly conversant with a factor in Johnson's rise of which Johnson was not anxious that Washington be reminded. After being introduced to Herman Brown at a cocktail party, McCarthy told Johnson the next day: "Well, I met your sugar daddy." As Evans and Novak were to say: "Johnson, it seems clear enough, wanted to strike at McCarthy—but not until McCarthy could be brought down. He knew how dangerous McCarthy was." Bobby Baker heard Johnson telling men he could trust, "Joe McCarthy's just a loudmouthed drunk. Hell, he's the sorriest senator up here. Can't tie his goddamn shoes. But he's riding high now, he's got people scared to death some Communist will strangle 'em in their sleep, and anybody who takes him on before the fevers cool—well, you don't get in a pissin' contest with a polecat."

These considerations were especially strong in Texas, where McCarthy's popularity was high in 1951 and 1952, not only with the public but with some of the most reactionary—and richest—of the state's oil barons, who felt that their country and their fortunes were threatened by Communism. The largest single contributor to McCarthy's enterprises was Hugh Roy Cullen, and among his other major supporters were H. L. Hunt and Clint Murchison.

Johnson had to run for re-election to the Senate in 1954. By 1953, his courting of the Texas establishment, all-powerful in the state's Democratic politics, had been cemented by the federal contracts he obtained for their companies, and by his defense of the depletion allowance and other tax breaks for the oilmen, and of course by his destruction of Leland Olds and his support of legislation that would free their natural gas enterprises from government regulation. Johnson's presence in the Senate meant millions of dollars in their pockets, and they knew it, and any possibility of a challenge to him in the Democratic primary was discouraged; the only candidate to enter the field against him would be the extremely wealthy—and extremely eccentric—thirty-year-old Dudley Dougherty, who was regarded, as Ed Clark was to put it, as "a little bit of a nut"; Reedy said that "Dougherty is just a screwball" who "could be equated with no opposition at all"; he would campaign against Johnson from the back of a red fire truck in which he toured the state, would describe Eleanor Roosevelt as "an old witch" and Roosevelt and Truman as mental incompetents, and would tell voters that with the single exception of himself, all Texas politicians were "afraid of sinister, hidden powers." Dougherty's candidacy, George Reedy was to say, "is the sort of thing you dream and pray will happen" if you are the incumbent. "Johnson made only a single speech in Texas during that whole campaign," Reedy would recall. "He never mentioned Dudley Dougherty's name, did not put out any campaign literature, and he took out only one ad"—and he defeated Dougherty by more than half a million votes—883,000 to 354,000. While Johnson did not have to worry about re-election, however, he had to worry about losing the future support of the oil barons, many of whom were his financial supporters as well as McCarthy's—and whose financial support he would need for a presidential bid; in moving against McCarthy, he had to walk a very thin line so as not to alienate them.

When liberals—liberal senators, liberal journalists, liberal Washingtonian insiders like Abe Fortas and Ben Cohen and Tommy Corcoran—asked him to put the Democratic senators "on the attack" against McCarthy, he told them that the time wasn't right, that McCarthy was still too popular, the issue too potent. When Bill White said that McCarthy was "destroying civil liberties in this country," Johnson replied: "Bill, that's a good point, but let me explain something to you. If I commit the Democratic Party to the destruction of McCarthy—'what he meant was an attempt at something like censure'—first of all, in the present atmosphere of the Senate, we will all lose and he will win. Then he'll be more powerful than ever. At this juncture I'm not about to commit the Democratic Party to a high school debate on the subject, 'Resolved, that Communism is good for the United States,' with my party taking the affirmative." It was while explaining to Hubert Humphrey that it was necessary to wait until victory was certain, for they might get only one chance at McCarthy, that he warned "that to kill a snake . . . have to get it with one blow." Recalls Gerald Siegel: "He kept saying to those people who were impatient, 'Now just wait a minute. The time will come, and when we've got enough votes to be sure we'll win, we'll move.'"

HE DIDN'T "MOVE," HOWEVER—didn't commit the Democratic Party in the Senate—even when, in the opinion of many liberals, he *had* enough votes, even when, in their opinion, the time was right at last. He had told Humphrey, back in the early days of the Red Scare, what he was waiting for. Attacks on McCarthy by liberals were useless, Johnson said, both because it was easy for McCarthy to destroy them by calling them "soft" on Communism ("He just eats fellows like you. You're nourishment to him"), and because they didn't have enough power in the Senate. Only when the Senate Bulls took the field against him could he be stopped, he said. "The only way we'll ever get Joe McCarthy is when he starts attacking some conservatives around here, and then we'll put an end to it."

What Johnson said he was waiting for began to occur in April, 1952, in George Reedy's opinion because McCarthy failed "to realize the fundamental toughness of the senior members of the establishment. It had never occurred to him that politicians who had survived two or more Senate contests must know something about political warfare. They had said nothing about him and he thought they were keeping silent out of fear. That was a serious misunderstanding." That April, McCarthy, speaking on the floor of the Senate, attacked one of Carl Hayden's faithful retainers, Darrell St. Claire, chief clerk of Hayden's Rules Committee, charging that in a former job—as a member of the State Department's Loyalty Board—St. Claire had voted to give security clearance to an economist who was the subject of "twelve separate FBI reports." Hayden, in his usual quiet voice, defended his aide, saying that St. Claire's name "has been dragged into this dispute without any basis of fact at all." McCarthy, who,

George Reedy says, regarded Hayden "as an old, blind, fuddy-duddy," then almost casually took a swipe at the Senator himself. "God," Reedy was to say, "that was a stupid thing for him to do. . . . Carl Hayden was one of the toughest creatures that ever walked the face of the earth." Speaking to some reporters that night, Johnson said, "Joe has made a lifelong and powerful enemy in Carl Hayden, and Carl is not a man who forgets easily."

Looking back on the McCarthy affair years later, George Reedy, praising Johnson for his "superbly developed sense of timing," would say that "the Hayden episode really sealed Joe McCarthy's doom although it did not come until many many months later." But superb though Johnson's timing may have been, it was also slow. Although he became Democratic Leader in January, 1953, he neither spoke against McCarthy nor raised the matter in the Policy Committee until July, 1954. The number of months that would elapse between the Hayden episode and the Senate's censure resolution on McCarthy was, in fact, thirty-two months—more than two and a half years, years during which scores of men and women were destroyed by the Wisconsin demagogue's charges, and hundreds, possibly thousands, more were destroyed by charges brought by local vigilantes emboldened by the national atmosphere of fear and distrust that McCarthy went on creating. During these years, thousands of government workers would be fired under federal loyalty decrees and hundreds of others lost their jobs—in Hollywood, in schools, in colleges, in unions—and were prevented by blacklists from finding others.

During this period—beginning, in fact, just a few days after the Hayden episode—more cracks in McCarthy's aura of invincibility appeared in the very spots that Johnson had told Humphrey would be crucial. In April, 1952, Richard Russell, while reiterating his warnings about the threat of world Communism, also took an obvious slap at McCarthy, warning about "hucksters of hysteria" who, in criticizing those who disagreed with them, undermined "the American system of fair play." He predicted that these "salesmen of infamy" would fall because of the common sense of the American people. To some liberals Russell's remark was the signal they had been waiting for: that the conservative southern senators were no longer solidly behind McCarthy, and that Democrats could begin to move against him in the Senate. Then, in July, 1953, the chief investigator of McCarthy's subcommittee, J. B. Matthews, in an article in the *American Mercury* entitled "Reds in the Churches," assailed Protestant clergymen, including Bishop G. Bromley Oxnam, Methodist bishop of the District of Columbia—and a friend of Harry Byrd's. Minority Leader Johnson was reading wire service stories that had been clipped from the teletype machines in the Senate lobby when he came across the story on Matthews' attack. "Come on over here," he shouted to Hubert Humphrey, and, showing him the article, said, "This is the beginning of the end for Joe McCarthy. You can't attack Harry Byrd's friends in this Senate, not in this Senate." McCarthy, he said, had made "a fatal mistake. Harry Byrd is going to take this personally. And that is going to be a fatal blow."

A blow was, in fact, to be struck—but it wasn't fatal, and it wasn't struck by Lyndon Johnson. After a furious Byrd, his round cheeks flushed as bright a red as his apples, demanded on the Senate floor that Matthews "give names and facts to sustain his charges or stand convicted as a cheap demagogue, willing to blacken the character of his fellow Americans for his own notoriety and personal gain," not only liberals but southerners Stennis and Maybank attacked McCarthy, and McCarthy's own subcommittee voted 4 to 3, with Democrats McClellan, Symington, and Jackson joined by Republican Charles E. Potter of Michigan—to dismiss the subcommittee investigator. The Senate had taken its first significant step to rein in McCarthy, and the move, as McCarthy biographer David Oshinsky was to write, "tarnished the myth of inevitability so vital to his fortunes. . . . He seemed more vulnerable and less menacing than before." And, perhaps most importantly, the Matthews affair had, as Oshinsky writes, "hurt [McCarthy] in the Senate"—the place where his fate would be decided.

The Senate move had been made, however, without the help of the Senate's Minority Leader, and indeed the Minority Leader may have tried to head it off. It was during this period, Stuart Symington was to recount, that Johnson began trying to convince him that it was still too early to take on McCarthy. Symington disregarded the advice, and, he was to say, "the fact that I took on McCarthy, Johnson didn't like at all; I've never quite known why. I think it's probably because so many important, I guess it's fair to say wealthy, people [in Texas] were backing McCarthy." Also, midway through 1953, McCarthy abandoned his uneasy accommodation with President Eisenhower, and his salvos began falling on Republican as well as Democratic targets. Previously McCarthy had described the Roosevelt and Truman administrations as "twenty years of treason." Now, a year into Eisenhower's presidency, he began speaking of "twenty-one years." And Tail-Gunner Joe said, "You wait. We're going to get Dulles's head." Taft's feelings began to change. While publicly continuing to support some of McCarthy's attacks, "behind the scenes he gave his rambunctious colleague no encouragement," Taft's biographer says, and when McCarthy started moving against liberal professors in universities, the Republican Leader said, "I would not favor firing anyone for simply being a Communist." But if Taft's sense of responsibility was moderating his support for McCarthy, that was not the case with the Senate's "Taft wing," and after Taft's death in 1953, his successor as GOP Leader was Knowland, a McCarthy supporter.

But the Taft wing amounted—by the most generous calculations—to no more than half the Republican senators. The November, 1952, elections had brought to the Republican side of the Senate not only Potter but Prescott Bush of Connecticut and Thomas Kuchel of California; there were additional Republican recruits now for the views that Margaret Chase Smith and six other Republicans had expressed three years before. Democratic liberals felt that bipartisan support for a move against McCarthy—the support that Lyndon

Johnson had been saying he was waiting for—was surely present now. As for their own party, McClellan's vote on the subcommittee, coming after the attacks on McCarthy by Russell, Hayden, Byrd, Maybank, and Stennis, was a signal that the Democrats' southern conservatives had had enough of McCarthy and were prepared to take action against him. Confident that with the exception of Pat McCarran and perhaps one or two other Democratic conservatives—and perhaps two or three Democratic senators with large Catholic constituencies—the forty-seven Democrats would be lined up against McCarthy almost solidly, liberals pleaded with Johnson to bring the issue before the Democratic Policy Committee, so that the party could take a course of action, or at least go on record, against the demagogue. But if during this period he did so, the Policy Committee's minutes do not reflect it. Herbert Lehman asked Johnson to support a resolution condemning McCarthy—Johnson, who had been assuring liberals that he would move when "we have enough votes." They felt there were certainly enough votes to pass a resolution, but no support was forthcoming from Johnson, and the resolution never reached the floor. When Maury Maverick wrote him that "Everybody in the Government is scared to death . . . and as the leader of the Senate Democrats I hope you will do your part to stem the tide," Johnson replied with words that in one form or another he had repeated so often that they had become a refrain, his mantra on McCarthyism. While he regretted the "hysteria around the country and in the government," he said, "You have got to realize that atmosphere can be dispelled only by letting it run its course so that people can see for themselves what is really behind all the noise."

Lyndon Johnson had determined on the course of action that should be taken. Sometime in 1953, he told a group of friendly reporters, in an off-the-record talk: "If I were the Majority Leader, I know what I'd do about McCarthy. I'd appoint a bipartisan select committee, and I'd put on our side the very best men we have, men who are above reproach, the wisest men in the Senate and the best judges, and I'd ask 'em to make a study of McCarthy and report to the Senate. With the men I'd pick, the Senate would accept their judgment and that would be the end of it." But, Evans and Novak were to report, "he was *not* Majority Leader. And McCarthy was Bill Knowland's problem, not his." Knowland remained reluctant to move against McCarthy, but liberals were increasingly skeptical of Johnson's reasoning. So substantial had anti-McCarthy sentiment become within the Senate, they felt, that there would be a majority for disciplining the Wisconsin senator if that sentiment were only mobilized behind some specific Senate action, and the mobilizing did not necessarily have to be done by the Majority Leader. There was among these liberals considerable feeling, in fact, that the more obvious senator to do the mobilizing was the leader of the party opposed to McCarthy's party—the Minority Leader. But the Minority Leader continued to decline every opportunity to do so. Without such an action, senators remained too timid to act alone. In January, 1954, only one senator—William Fulbright—cast a vote for what would have been the rare move of denying funding for a subcommittee McCarthy chaired.

THEN, IN FEBRUARY, 1954, as the McCarthy era entered its fifth year, the Wisconsin senator picked a new target—the United States Army—and the climate began to change. Nineteen fifty-four would be the year of Irving Peress, an Army dentist who had received a promotion despite the fact that he had taken the Fifth Amendment when asked if he had ever been a Communist, a fact which, when McCarthy got hold of it, caused a furor so great that it produced a large *New York Times* headline: "WHO PROMOTED DR. PERESS?" (No one, as a matter of fact; the promotion had been automatic.) It was the year of General Ralph Zwicker, the officer who had had the bad luck to be Peress' commanding officer at the time of the promotion, and who McCarthy said was therefore "not fit to wear the uniform"—although the uniform was covered with medals; Zwicker was a battlefield hero of World War II. It was the year of Roy Cohn, smirking and vulpine, and of Private G. David Schine, Cohn's handsome friend, for whose training-camp comforts Cohn had exerted pressure on the Army. It was the year of the "chicken lunch" in Everett Dirksen's Capitol hideaway, at which Secretary of the Army Robert Stevens was tricked into signing a "memorandum of understanding" that gave McCarthy so much of what he was asking for that the *Times* of London said: "Senator McCarthy this afternoon achieved what General Burgoyne and General Cornwallis never achieved—the surrender of the American army." And it was the year of the March 9 *See It Now* documentary that was advertised in a small ad paid for by Edward R. Murrow and his co-producer Fred Friendly because CBS would not pay for an ad, and that was, in David Oshinsky's phrase, "chillingly effective" because Murrow and Friendly let the film clips of McCarthy speak for themselves—and they did, showing McCarthy terrorizing a witness before his subcommittee, chuckling over his "Alger—I mean Adlai" remark, and belching and giggling his high-pitched, uncontrollable giggle. Murrow ended the program by saying, "This is no time for men who oppose Senator McCarthy's methods to keep silent. . . . We cannot defend freedom abroad by deserting it at home," and reaction poured in on the reluctant network. CBS had to hire dozens of operators to take an estimated fifteen thousand calls—which ran about ten to one for Murrow and against McCarthy. McCarthy's popularity began to fall; in January, 50 percent of the public had a "favorable" opinion of him; only 29 percent were "unfavorable." By March, the margin had been tightened to 46 percent to 36, and by April, the balance had tipped the other way, with 38 percent "favorable" and 46 percent "unfavorable." And then, on April 22, 1954, before McCarthy's own subcommittee—recusing himself, he appointed his closest friend in the Senate, Karl Mundt, as chairman—began the "Army-McCarthy Hearings."

Understanding the lesson of *See It Now* (as another very savvy—if very different—politician also understood: "Ike wants hearings open and televised," Jim Hagerty wrote in his diary), Lyndon Johnson had told John McClellan, the subcommittee's senior Democrat, that no matter what concessions the Democrats made to the subcommittee's Republicans, they must insist that the hearings be televised. "He knew that what McCarthy was doing was a very dangerous thing for the country," Sam Houston Johnson was to say. "And he knew that the newspapers alone and two minutes a night on television during the Army hearings wasn't enough. McCarthy had to be seen day after day during the entire hearings on the Army. He thought that would make people see what the bastard was up to." And television did indeed let millions of Americans see for themselves another "doctored" photograph—this time, a figure had been cut out rather than added—and heard Roy Cohn maintain, even with the two pictures displayed in front of him, that the picture had not been "changed." Television let millions of Americans see for themselves McCarthy's black-jowled sneer as he whined, "Point of order, point of order, Mr. Chairman," and witness the brutality with which he bullied witnesses—and it let America contrast him with the Army's courtly, puckish counsel, Joseph Welch. It let America see McCarthy's black-jowled smile as he brought into the hearing the name of a young attorney, Fred Fisher. A member of Welch's Boston law firm, Fisher had originally been a member of the Army legal team, but when he told Welch that during the 1940s he had belonged for a time to the National Lawyers Guild (learning of its link to a local Communist organization, he resigned), Welch had said that Fisher had better not work on the Army case because if he did, "one of these days that will come out and go over national television and it will hurt like the dickens." And now millions of Americans saw Welch's distress as McCarthy said, "Mr. Chairman . . . I think we should tell him that he has in his law firm a young man named Fisher whom he recommended, incidentally, to do work on this committee, who has been for a number of years a member of an organization which was named, oh, years and years ago, as the legal bulwark of the Communist Party. . . . I am not asking you at this point to explain why you tried to foist him on this committee." They saw Welch's face contorted with dismay as he tried to stop McCarthy—"Senator, may we not drop this? We know he belonged to the Lawyers Guild. . . ." They saw the despair on Welch's face when he realized he wasn't going to be able to stop him. "Let us not assassinate this lad further, Senator. You have done enough. Have you no sense of decency, sir, at long last? Have you left no sense of decency?" When McCarthy kept talking about how Welch had tried to "foist" Fisher on the committee, millions saw how even Mundt felt impelled to try—to try repeatedly—to correct him: "The Chair would like to repeat that he does not believe Mr. Welch recommended Mr. Fisher as counsel for this committee." And they saw how Welch finally had to say, "Mr. McCarthy, I will not discuss this further with you. You have sat within six feet of me, and could have asked about Fred Fisher. You have brought it out. If there is a God in heaven, it will do neither you nor your cause any good." Leaving the hearing room, the Boston lawyer, weary, grim-faced, said, "I never saw such cruelty." Millions of Americans had seen what Welch had seen; television had let them see it. By the time the Army-McCarthy hearings ended on June 17, McCarthy's favorable rating had dropped to around 30 percent—where it was to remain for the rest of the year. McCarthy's great weapon had been his mass support. "That weapon," as Oshinsky writes, "was gone now, and gone for good." And that fact was promptly underlined in terms that senators could grasp. In 1950 and '52, McCarthy's support in elections for the Senate had been a fearsome weapon. In 1954, he sponsored—and arranged for the financing of—a primary campaign against Margaret Chase Smith by a personable, dynamic young candidate whom he called "that Maine boy who is going places." The Maine boy carried exactly two, small, precincts. The legend of McCarthy's political invincibility had been destroyed.

Upon the conclusion of the Army-McCarthy hearings, Vermont's Republican Senator Ralph Flanders introduced a resolution to censure McCarthy for conduct that violated Senate traditions and brought the body into disrepute, and liberal organizations, including the National Committee for an Effective Congress, urged Senate Democrats to support the resolution or in some other way to take a broader position to demonstrate that their party was opposed not only to McCarthy but to McCarthyism. Johnson refused to take any action at all, and indeed he did not take any action until after his primary victory over Dougherty on July 24—and until after his hand had been forced by Knowland's announcement that he was about to bring the resolution before the Senate for a vote.

WHEN LYNDON JOHNSON FINALLY moved against Joe McCarthy, he did so with his customary effectiveness—both with strategy and with men. He didn't want the Democrats to take a party position on McCarthy, and on the very day before the vote, he staved one off. On July 29, at his call, the Democratic Policy Committee finally met to discuss McCarthy, for almost four hours. Johnson had invited five liberals who were not members of the committee to present their views, and Lehman said that he had "never subscribed to the thesis that this [Senator McCarthy] is a Republican responsibility. Every man in the Senate has a responsibility. . . . I very much hope that the Policy Committee will decide that it is a matter of our concern. I very much hope that Senator Johnson will take the lead in censuring Senator McCarthy. I think the Democratic Party will suffer if it does not take a stand." Symington said that "A vote against McCarthy is a vote against evil." But Johnson, supported by Clements, Kerr, Murray, Ed Johnson ("This should not be a partisan issue and therefore I do not think the leadership should be asked to deliver votes"), and Russell ("The Policy Committee has got no right to commit Democratic members on issues of this kind"), persuaded the committee not to formulate a Democratic position.

He had lined up support for the move he wanted, the appointment of a select committee—a *bipartisan* select committee—by consulting with such key Republicans as Earl Warren and General Jerry Persons, head of the White House congressional liaison team, and on August 2, the Senate voted, 75 to 12, to refer the Flanders resolution to a select committee of three members from each party, which was directed to report back to the Senate before it adjourned for the year.

Knowing that the committee had to be sufficiently respected so that its report would pass, Johnson had devoted a great deal of thought to selecting its members—and a great deal of craft to making Knowland think *he* had selected them. "Knowland theoretically appointed the Republican members, but Johnson appointed every one of them," White was to recall. "I was present in his office one day when they had their final conference on this." Johnson would suggest "some Republican he knew Knowland detested. He'd say, 'Now, Bill, I'm sure you want so-and-so.' Knowland would say, 'Oh, no! Good God, no, I don't want so-and-so!' and he'd wind up naming the man Johnson wanted." Johnson didn't want liberals, who would be "just grist" for McCarthy's mill, but conservatives, and conservatives tough enough to stand up to McCarthy, and he had read his men. On the Democratic side he wanted Stennis ("It had never occurred to me that anybody as gentle as John Stennis could actually get up in across-floor debate and not only hold his own but mop up the floor with an Irish brawler like Joe McCarthy, which Stennis did," George Reedy was to say. "I think Joe McCarthy was cleaning blood off himself for two weeks after he made the mistake of trying to tangle with Stennis"); and Ed Johnson, who hated McCarthy because of an old personal feud; and Sam Ervin, because Ervin had been a state supreme court judge in North Carolina, and, as Evans and Novak say, "it was essential that the country accept the select committee as juridically qualified" to render a verdict on McCarthy. As Republicans he wanted the same kind of senators, and he got them—Frank Carlson of Kansas, Francis Case of South Dakota and, as chairman, Watkins of Utah, very quiet and very tough. All, except Case, belonged to the Senate's "inner club," and respected its rules and traditions, which McCarthy had so flagrantly broken. The Select Committee's report, as Oshinsky would note, "left an awful lot unsaid." It was a condemnation not of McCarthy's long inquisition—"There was hardly a word about his anti-Communist crusade"—or of his use of classified information and "senatorial privilege" to destroy innocent people. It recommended his censure—or, to be precise, "condemnation"—only because of conduct "contrary to senatorial traditions" that "tended to bring the Senate into dishonor and disrepute" and to "impair its dignity." But when the report was delivered to the Senate, Johnson lined up behind it forty-four of the forty-seven Democrats. Two were paired with Republican senators who were unavoidably absent. So only one Democratic senator—John Kennedy, who was hospitalized in Boston recovering from a serious back operation—was not announced for

McCarthy's condemnation. The GOP split down the middle, with twenty-two moderate and liberal Republicans voting in favor of condemnation and twenty-two old Taft partisans overwhelmingly opposed. Independent Morse voted yea, so McCarthy was censured, 67 to 22. (Republican Wiley was absent and unrecorded, and McCarthy himself voted "present.") He was to spend his last three years in the Senate—before his death in 1957—increasingly in the throes of alcohol, wandering the halls, prone to tears, often unshaven, fawningly anxious for a kind word from his colleagues. Once Reedy was standing on a sidewalk in Washington when a mud-encrusted automobile pulled up, "and something black and round and squiggly forced its way out the front door and rolled up to me. . . . It took me about thirty seconds to realize that this was the remnant of Joe McCarthy—unshaven, needing a bath, bloated from too much booze, almost inarticulate."

"The size of the majority," as Oshinsky notes, "was impressive indeed." Lyndon Johnson had lined the Democrats up in a solid front—from Lehman to Eastland. He had achieved Democratic unity on still another issue, and thereby helped end McCarthy's reign of terror. "Whatever you say about his delaying and delaying, well past the point when it was necessary, and allowing this inquisition, with all its human suffering to go on," nonetheless Johnson "in rounding up those votes" accomplished something "that was really difficult," Paul Douglas' administrative aide, Frank McCulloch, was to say. Douglas himself was to call Johnson "splendid on McCarthy." Yet the censure, as Oshinsky notes, was voted "on rather narrow grounds." "We have condemned the individual, but we have not yet repudiated the 'ism,' " Herbert Lehman said.

Moreover, the condemnation vote was taken on December 2, 1954; the vote to bring McCarthy's career to a conclusion was taken only after that conclusion was foregone. Oshinsky says that McCarthy "could have been stopped rather quickly"—and almost certainly he could have been stopped far more quickly than he was. By the time the censure vote was finally taken, McCarthy's support from the American people was very low—and, except for the Taft wing, so was his support in the Senate.

His Senate support had, indeed, been low for some time. The attitude of the three Democratic subcommittee members at the Army-McCarthy hearings had demonstrated that in April. Scoop Jackson had confronted McCarthy's staff on the doctored photograph, and Symington had confronted McCarthy himself on so many occasions, and so directly and uncompromisingly, that an enraged McCarthy had called him "Sanctimonious Stu" to his face. And if these two Democratic moderate liberals had clearly shown their hostility to McCarthy, so had the subcommittee's Democratic conservative member, the ironbound McClellan, who more than once turned down the table and lectured McCarthy in terms quite harsh by Senate standards, going so far as to tell him bluntly, on one occasion when he had reversed the names of two witnesses, "Get your names straight," and on other occasions telling him flatly that he was breaking the law in revealing classified information, and that he, McClellan, would not allow him to do so. Between Jackson, Symington, and McClellan, all segments of the Senate Democrats had been represented at those hearings except for the most "ardent" liberals—who were, of course, McCarthy's bitter enemies. Had Lyndon Johnson not been so efficient and persuasive in lining the Democrats up behind a censure resolution, there might conceivably have been a few Democratic votes against the resolution, but only a very few: Democratic liberal and moderate support for curbing McCarthy had been evident well before April. Given Republican moderate support for curbing McCarthy— support also evident well before April, 1954—Senate opposition to a resolution was effectively limited to the GOP's Taft wing. Despite the mounting toll of McCarthy victims month after month, Johnson had waited to move against him until it suited his purposes to do so. He had acted not as a mobilizer or enunciator of opinion against the unprincipled demagogue who was using the Senate as his platform, but only as a coordinator by which that opinion, already formed, could be expressed.

He had had his reasons. If he had moved against McCarthy too early, he might have lost—and increased McCarthy's strength. If he had moved before a substantial number of Republicans had become disillusioned with the Wisconsin demagogue, the issue might have become a partisan one, with the Democrats on the less popular side of the issue. Feeling, moreover, that "Joe will go that extra mile to destroy you," and that McCarthy might have been made aware, through the Texas oilmen who were his allies, of damaging information about his finances, he was very wary about taking him on until he had been sufficiently discredited that an attack from him would not cause as much damage as it had previously. If he had played too prominent a role in the opposition to McCarthy he might have alienated the oil barons who were McCarthy's principal financial supporters, and thus jeopardized the future financial support he himself would need. For all these reasons, Lyndon Johnson didn't move against Joe McCarthy until the time had come when moving wouldn't hurt him, and when he did move, he stayed sufficiently behind the scenes so that his own alliance with the Texas reactionaries would not be weakened. Johnson biographer Robert Dallek acknowledges that "Johnson's role in ending McCarthy's influence should not be exaggerated." In the McCarthy affair, Lyndon Johnson had demonstrated his legislative skill—and had demonstrated how this skill was subordinated to pragmatism.

24

The "Johnson Rule"

JOHNSON'S STRATEGY OF BIPARTISANSHIP was vindicated in the November, 1954, elections. The Democrats regained control of the House. In the Senate, rather than lose additional seats—the fate that had been widely predicted two years previously—they gained one, giving them forty-eight to forty-seven for the Republicans.

The key to control of the Senate was therefore the ninety-sixth senator, Wayne Morse.

Morse had been feuding with Johnson—it had been only a few months since he had said derisively, "Lyndon Johnson represents Lyndon Johnson"— but if the former Republican would vote with the Democrats in organizing the new Senate, they would have a majority. The time for feuding was over; it was time for a deal. Telephoning Morse, Johnson said that Morse could have any committee assignment that a *Majority Leader* had to offer.

Morse understood the proposal, but said he would have to think it over. Johnson facilitated his thinking. While he was still in Texas, he said that "Morse never should have been kicked off his committees"; upon his return to Washington, he told a group of reporters, "I don't know what Senator Morse may want, but whatever he wants, he's going to get it—if I've got it to give." What Morse wanted was Foreign Relations. Johnson checked with the committee's ranking Democrat, Walter George—and, as always, with Richard Russell. With a chance to regain their lost chairmanships, what did their dislike—contempt, in fact— for the Oregonian matter? Morse announced he would vote with the Democrats; Johnson announced Morse's assignment not only to Foreign Relations but to Banking and Currency as well, and added that he would also keep his seat on the District Committee. "He would serve with distinction in any post, and we decided to give him three," Johnson said. On January 4, 1955, Lyndon Johnson was re-elected—by acclamation—to the leadership of the Senate Democrats. As he had become, at the age of forty-four, the youngest Minority Leader in the history of the United States, so he was now, at forty-six, the youngest Majority Leader in the history of the United States.

· · ·

AND NOW THAT LYNDON JOHNSON was Majority Leader, the Majority Leader was powerful.

For two years, Johnson had had the power of a Minority Leader—but only of a Minority Leader—over scheduling: over determining the order of business on the floor, over deciding when a bill vital to a senator's career would be allowed to come to the floor, over deciding *if* the bill would come to the floor. He had been able to make suggestions or requests—but only suggestions or requests—to the Majority Leader about holding back one bill or speeding up another, about coordinating, and making rational, the arrival of legislation on the Calendar and on the floor. His party's minority status had restricted him to monitoring bills' progress; he couldn't direct it. Now he had the power of a Majority Leader, who had the privilege of first recognition, who could use that privilege to schedule, who alone could say, and have his words assented to: "I move that the Senate proceed to the consideration of . . ."

The scheduling power of previous Majority Leaders had been diluted by the degree to which they exercised that power merely as agents—rubber stamps, in effect—of their party's Policy Committee. But Johnson had made the committee his "private rubber stamp."

For previous Majority Leaders, the scheduling power had been further diluted by the power of the Standing Committees, whose chairmen had moved bills forward and finally brought them to a vote within their committees at their own pace, so that the bills' arrival on the Senate Calendar was at the chairmen's discretion. Furthermore, since they arrived in the form the chairmen wanted, all too often troublesome amendments would not be thrashed out until the bills were on the floor, which made realistic advance scheduling impossible. But Johnson's intervention, as Minority Leader, in the internal workings of the Standing Committees had created an unprecedented intra-party mechanism for monitoring bills' progress within committees and for bringing them to the floor with disputes already ironed out. And now, with his party in the majority, the committee Democrats with whom he was dealing were no longer merely ranking members; they were *chairmen*. He would be able to play a role greater than any previous Majority Leader in determining the schedule on which bills emerged from committee, the schedule on which they were placed on the Calendar, the schedule on which they were called off the Calendar and brought to the floor. Awareness of this new reality came quickly, as is shown by the new tone in the letters he began receiving from his colleagues almost from the moment that he became Majority Leader:

> Dear Lyndon:
>   I respectfully request your assistance in scheduling S. 2345, a
> bill that I consider of grave importance to me and to my constituents.

Dear Lyndon:

   I would consider it a great favor if you could help me to achieve postponement of the textile bill. As it is now written, it poses enormous problems for the textile industry in my state and I have promised them that I will obtain a delay until at least next month so they can study it further.

Dear Lyndon:

   Four measures of primary importance . . . are ready for action, and inasmuch as I have charge of them, I would deeply appreciate an indication of when they might be taken up.

   I will deeply appreciate your cooperation to make certain that none of these measures is lost in the closing congestion of the session.

He would be able to play a role greater than any previous Majority Leader not merely over the scheduling of legislation but over its content.

During his two years as Minority Leader, Johnson had been intervening more and more in the internal give-and-take among the Democrats on the Standing Committees, using Siegel and Reedy and Bibolet to ascertain the points of disputes between senators, and then mediating the disputes so that Democratic positions within the committees were unified. His three aides would ask a committee's staff about Democratic bills—who was objecting? why were they objecting? Then Johnson's aides would go to the senators involved: ask what would satisfy them, work out possible compromises. Then Johnson himself would telephone or visit, or summon, the senators: reason with them, cajole or threaten them in private—persuade them to accept the compromise. The content of legislation still before the Standing Committees was therefore being altered—altered sometimes in extremely subtle ways—not only by those committees but by the Leader. More and more, during those two years, proposed Democratic legislation had become the product of bargains, trade-offs, rewordings, of additions, excisions, that had been made not by a committee or subcommittee chairman but by him. More and more, it had become the product of temporary alliances—often very complex alliances— that he had woven together. And, more and more, since the bargaining process was not only so complex and detailed but so private only the Leader knew the trade-offs between senators which had been made, or rejected—and the reasons why they had been made or rejected. Sometimes, the persuasion used involved some other, unrelated issue; in exchange for a senator's agreement on one bill, Johnson might have promised the senator something he wanted on a different measure—perhaps one that was being considered not by his committee but by some other committee. Previously, the committees had been separate, proudly independent baronies; there were threads—slender but strong—between them now. And only the Leader knew all of those threads, and how they had been tied together. Only he knew the promises that had been made, the threats that had been withdrawn. The myriad legislative matters of a single Senate session made up a vast tapestry in which a thousand threads were interwoven in a complex, intricate pattern; only Lyndon Johnson knew that pattern. When a senator demanded a change in a bill, only Johnson could tell him why such a change was possible or not possible. And often, since the reasons might be very private to the other senators involved, the senator demanding the change could not even learn if what Lyndon Johnson was telling him was true.

And, of course, after a compromise had been worked out in a Standing Committee, it was submitted to that "private rubber stamp." During the Democrats' two years in the minority, Johnson's control of the Policy Committee had had only limited significance: although never before had a party Policy Committee intervened so extensively with respect to bills still within the Standing Committees, those bills had been minority bills, generally not the bills finally reported out of the committees to the floor. Now Democratic bills—the bills whose final form he was playing such a decisive role in determining—would be the actual legislation on which the Senate acted.

That fact made his control of the Policy Committee very significant in the history of the Senate. For decades, the Majority Leader had been, even at his strongest, no more than a first among equals—the equals being the mighty chairmen, impregnable in their committee strongholds, with their absolute power over the bills their committees were considering, the bills that "in reality the Senate does little more than approve or disapprove . . . practically as they are reported." In the nearly century and a half since the committee system had been solidified in 1816, no Leader had been able to curb the chairmen's power.

Now, in 1955, that was no longer true. Two years earlier, Lyndon Johnson had gently slipped a bit between the teeth of the Democratic senators who had once been committee chairmen, and who would be chairmen again, so gently that the chairmen had hardly noticed it was there, and the reins attached to it had been kept loose. But it was there. And now the reins were being tightened.

THEY WERE being tightened in other ways as well. Was Lyndon Johnson already arranging with the chairmen the schedule of when their bills would reach the floor? Now he began suggesting to some chairmen that he manage the bills on the floor.

In the past, chairmen had managed major pieces of legislation on the floor except when they assigned one to a committee member with a particular interest in it. Says Floyd Riddick, who in 1955 was the Senate's assistant parliamentarian, and had been observing the Senate, in one capacity or another, for almost twenty years: "In the past the chairmen would never have let the Majority Leader do that. *They* managed their bills on the floor." But some of the chairmen—not only Finance's seventy-seven-year-old Walter George but Interior's seventy-eight-year-old Jim Murray and Rules' eighty-seven-year-old Theodore Francis Green (whose eyesight, hearing, and mental faculties had all declined to a point at which he sometimes required an aide's assistance even to find his way around the Capitol hallways)—were elderly now, and it was no longer easy for them to manage controversial or complicated measures. They had grown accustomed to Johnson's assistance in so many matters; George and Green were now quite appreciative of the way in which, when they were confronted with a crowd of question-shouting reporters as they emerged from a White House foreign affairs briefing, Johnson, standing between them, would field the questions. Fielding questions on the Senate floor seemed only a logical extension. Furthermore, their paternal fondness for Johnson made his offers of assistance seem the offers of a loyal young friend, eager only to help. Johnson was not exaggerating when he told Doris Kearns Goodwin that these elderly senators were as grateful for the offers "as for a spring in the desert."

With younger chairmen—William Fulbright of the Banking and Currency Committee, for example—Johnson would use a different tactic. He would point out that unwanted amendments would be offered on the floor. The chairmen would realize that while they had been able to squelch those amendments within their committees, the Leader would be in a better position to squelch them on the floor and keep the bills in the form they wanted. And Johnson would use his power to keep the bills as intact as possible.

Once, for example, after a long battle in committee, a bank regulatory bill emerged in a form favored by Chairman Fulbright and by the bill's proposer, the committee's ranking Democratic member, A. Willis Robertson. Robertson told Johnson that while Fulbright had been able to force the bill through the committee, some of its members were determined to introduce major amendments on the floor, and that some of them would pass. Fulbright couldn't do anything about this, but Johnson could. He told Robertson to tell the would-be amenders that in that case the bill wasn't going to come to the floor, that he would not make a motion to have the Senate consider it unless Robertson gave him "assurance that . . . no amendments will be offered." Robertson relayed this message to the dissidents, and some of them, eager for the bill to pass, agreed to drop their amendments. Three would not. "The nearest I can come to your request" would be to reduce the number of amendments to three, Robertson wrote Johnson, but he also reported that all three could be voted down quickly on a voice vote. That was good enough for Johnson—and for Fulbright. Johnson had, by negotiating on his behalf, obtained most of what the chairman wanted.

Noting such developments from his seat on the dais, Riddick saw their significance. "Now, for the first time, you had a Leader who's going to keep it [a bill] intact. . . . They [the chairmen] went along [with letting Johnson manage their bills] because by letting him take over the management of the bills, they knew they would get what they wanted," Riddick says. "Out of loose consideration of legislation was emerging leadership control [of legislation]—control by Lyndon Johnson. Johnson just gradually pulled the management [of bills] out of the hands of the chairmen. They were surrendering their powers—not intentionally, but it was a growth process. There was gradually growing an attitude, 'Let Lyndon do it.' You don't realize you're losing power, you don't realize that things are changing. You think the Leader is only helping you. But the first thing you know, he's integrating everything. He knows everything about every bill, he can change one thing for another with different senators. Things *were* changing."

HE WAS ALSO USING other powers he had acquired, or created, as Minority Leader, and he was using them with less restraint.

Majority Leader or not, he still needed the support of the old Democratic Bulls—of Russell, George, Hayden, Byrd, Ellender, Eastland, McClellan, three or four others; while Walter George, elected President *pro tempore* at the Senate's 1955 opening session, was laboriously ascending the dais to accept the gavel, a reporter in the Press Gallery above muttered, "Save your Confederate money, boys. The South is rising again." With southerners as chairmen of six of the nine most powerful Senate committees (and its ally Hayden ascending, thanks to McKellar's death, to the chairmanship of a seventh, Appropriations), "its hold seems even stronger than previously," Thomas Stokes wrote. Were the Big Bulls to turn against Johnson, they could wreck his leadership as easily as they had wrecked McFarland's and Lucas' before him—and to the Big Bulls Johnson was as deferential as ever. He praised them publicly at every opportunity, telling one reporter, "We have the master craftsmen in the legislative field in the Democratic Party," noting to another that these chairmen "have been twenty-five years in Congress, on the average. Hell, every one of 'em's an old pro." In private, he was as obsequious, as fawning, as ever. "He didn't rant and rave at the Harry Byrds of the world," Senator George Smathers of Florida would say. "Oh no, he was passive, and so submissive, and so condescending, you couldn't believe it! I've seen him kiss Harry Byrd's ass until it was disgusting: 'Senator, how about so-and-so? wouldn't you like to do this? can't we do this for you?' "

But with the Big Bulls solidly behind him, the addition of his new powers made the support of the rest of the Democrats less important to him; they needed him much more than he needed any one of them. For the first time since college and the NYA, Lyndon Johnson had direct power over other men. And as soon as he got it, he showed how he was going to use it. Power, Lord Acton said, corrupts. Not always. What power *always* does is *reveal*. And now there began to be revealed a Lyndon Johnson who would have been familiar to those who had known him in college.

It began quickly—in his first action as Majority Leader: the making of committee assignments. In the appointment calendar on Johnson's desk the pages headed January 6, January 7, and January 8 were blank except for a numeral he had scrawled large across each one: "231." His office in the Capitol was too accessible: once again, in the first days of a new Congress, Lyndon Johnson was operating from behind a closed door in his old suite in the SOB; once again, the left-hand button on Walter Jenkins' telephone console glowed yellow-white; once again, by the date of the Democratic Steering Committee's first meeting—this year on Monday, January 10—the Standing Committee checkerboard was already filled, and Steering Committee ratification had been arranged. There was, however, a difference between the telephone calls Lyndon Johnson was making now and the calls he had made two years earlier. Throughout his two years as Minority Leader, despite the power over committee assignments that had been ceded to him by the Steering Committee, he had, in making and explaining controversial assignments, hidden behind that committee, telling disappointed or angry colleagues that it was the committee that decided, that he was only one of its members. Though that veil had become increasingly transparent, he had nonetheless kept it in place, and to some extent it had softened the harsh reality of his wielding of power. Now the veil was allowed to fall.

A number of younger senators had accumulated sufficient seniority to expect seats on major committees, seats for which they were well qualified—in some cases, extremely well qualified. But their committee assignments were not going to be made on the basis of seniority or of qualifications. Their assignments were going to be made on the basis of their personal allegiance to Lyndon Johnson. And Johnson let them know it.

Estes Kefauver, for example, had been trying for four years to get on the Foreign Relations Committee or the Policy Committee (making, in regard to the Policy Committee, the argument, strong in traditional Senate terms, that Tennessee had historically had, in McKellar, a Policy seat), and Johnson had always told him in the past that these selections were determined by the Steering Committee. On Tuesday, January 11, 1955, Kefauver learned that he had again been passed over for Foreign Relations. The makeup of the Policy Committee had not yet been announced, and he telephoned Lyndon Johnson and, with Walter Jenkins listening, mouthpiece unscrewed, taking notes, said, "Lyndon, I want to be a member of the Policy Committee."

"Well, Estes," Lyndon Johnson replied, "I appreciate your wanting to be there." But, Johnson said, you're not going to be there. And in explaining why, Johnson didn't bother to cite the Steering Committee. The pronoun he used was the first person singular. "The man I selected hasn't been you," he said.

When Kefauver began to argue—"Lyndon, you remember I started trying to be a candidate for [the Policy Committee] when Tom Hennings got it . . ."—Johnson reverted to traditional terms, mentioning the need for geographical diversity on the committee, and the requirements of seniority, and Kefauver attempted to swallow his chagrin. "Of course, if it is already settled . . ." he said. "I was of course kind of disappointed about Foreign Affairs. . . . How about keeping me in mind?" And when Johnson replied this time, he made things clearer. There were no more traditional terms; instead the new reality was spelled out—in the "new tone" that Hubert Humphrey had heard. "I will sure keep you in mind," Lyndon Johnson said. But, he said, "I have never had the particular feeling that when I called up my first team and the chips were down that Kefauver felt he . . . ought to be on that team." The price of his favor was stated. "If you feel you ought to be and want to be [on my team], it is the best news I have ever had," Lyndon Johnson said. "I will meet you more than fifty percent of the way. I will push you into every position of influence and power that you can have. . . . If you and I can ever get on that basis . . ."

Kefauver began to plead a little. "As far as I am concerned, I have always wanted to be on that basis," he said. "I will let my hair down on this point, Lyndon: honestly, you have never given me a break since you have been the Leader." But Johnson was having none of that. "Maybe I just felt like I wasn't positive you wanted me to be the captain—that's letting your hair down," he said. Proof, clear proof, of Kefauver's willingness to be on the Johnson team—and to let Johnson be the captain—would be required, Johnson made clear. "You have got to have a lot more than desire on these committee appointments," he said. Kefauver had not provided such proof in the past, he said. "You just look through your documents and see when you have said to Johnson that you were on my team. . . . There's no use in our kidding each other."

Johnson apparently felt there was at least a chance that Kefauver could be brought to heel. With liberals like Lehman and Douglas, uncompromising in their principles, there was no such chance, and Johnson knew it. So with them he was more brutal. Long determined to end the injustice and prejudice codified in existing immigration laws, Lehman badly wanted a seat on Judiciary, the committee with jurisdiction over those laws. His seniority for that seat was sufficient, his expertise unique: not only did he represent the state which, as Drew Pearson put it, "was more concerned with immigration than any other," possessing as it did, New York City, lodestar of immigrants, he had been that state's governor for ten years. But he didn't get the seat, and when he asked Johnson why, Johnson gave as his reason, as he later told reporters, that Lehman was not a lawyer, an excuse so transparent (no Senate rule made a law degree a requirement for membership on the committee; degreeless Earle Clements had only recently been serving on it) that he obviously did not care whether or not it was believed.

Lehman's qualifications for Judiciary were equaled by those of Douglas for Finance, and since Johnson had proclaimed expertise a criterion for committee appointments, it was assumed that he would not dare to continue keeping the Senate's most respected expert on taxation off its tax-writing committee, particularly since it had not one but two vacancies to be filled (and since, as Evans and Novak were to write, although Douglas was opposed to the oil-depletion allowance, "the Finance Committee was already so stacked in favor of the oil and gas industry" that one vote on it could not affect its decisions). "It had been assumed that he [Douglas] would get it up to the time the lists were made public," Thomas Stokes was to write.

But Johnson had another plan for the economist, one with a particular sting in it. There was a committee with the word "Economic" in the title: the Joint Economic Committee. But whereas Finance had vast power, this committee had no power at all; it was authorized only to issue reports. "I'm gonna name him chairman of the Joint Economic Committee," Johnson told Bobby Baker. "It can't do a damn thing. It's as useless as tits on a bull. But it'll give Professor Douglas some paper to shuffle." And for Douglas' exclusion, Johnson vouchsafed no explanation at all.

In 1955 as in 1953, every newly elected senator received an assignment to a major committee, and columnists were once again full of praise for the "Johnson Rule." "Johnson at his best again," Doris Fleeson wrote. "Senator Johnson has once again quietly worked a revolution in the ancient system." All but unremarked by journalists, however, was the fact that the nature of the revolution had changed. No longer was it only the assigning of freshmen, or the use of expertise as a criterion. Added to the Johnson Rule now was another factor—one which did indeed prove that Johnson ruled.

HE WAS ACQUIRING NEW POWERS, too—and using them with little restraint.

The Democrats' recapture of majority status gave the party more patronage slots to distribute, and that meant more work for its Patronage Committee. And the committee's chairman, the seventy-seven-year-old Hayden, was also becoming chairman of Appropriations. He was, in the words of one aide, "just not as interested in patronage as he had been." And he had become very fond of Lyndon Johnson. He was increasingly willing to listen to Johnson—the party's Leader, after all—on party matters; patronage, the aide says, "just sort of wandered into the hands of the leadership." Realization of that development came quickly, too—as was shown by a letter from Burnet Maybank to Skeeter Johnston a few days after the November, 1954, election: "I know you feel better about Tuesday's results—I certainly do. Hope you get the opportunity to talk to Lyndon Johnson about the patronage situation in the Capitol. It appears to me with us having a majority we are certainly entitled to more positions. Of course as you know, my appointees were laid off. . . . Do let me know what Lyndon thinks about the patronage."

What Lyndon thought was that Maybank's appointees should be restored to their former places, and they were. And that was not the case—at least in several instances—with appointees of senators who were not on his "team."

Neither Kefauver nor Albert Gore was on its roster. Now both Tennessee senators sought to intervene on behalf of an elderly Tennesseean, Walker Toddy, who had been dismissed after twenty-nine years on Skeeter Johnston's staff. "Mr. Toddy has given 29 years of loyal and faithful service to the Democratic Party and to the Senate of the United States," Kefauver wrote Johnson. Toddy was not well off financially, and Kefauver noted that one more year would make him eligible for a higher pension. "I am very hopeful that Walker can secure some worthwhile place in the new senatorial setup"—even if only in a position as lowly as that of Bill Clerk. "I know that a lot of senators feel as I do," Kefauver wrote, but one of those senators was not Lyndon Johnson, and Toddy was not given any place. Watching which senators received patronage slots—and which senators didn't—Democrats were again reminded that it was better to be on Lyndon's team.

For a senator who was not on the team, the cost of such independence might have to be reckoned not only in seats and slots, but in space—for Hayden's move to Appropriations had left the chairmanship of the Rules Committee, allocator of office suites, in the hands of the "ailing" Theodore Francis Green, and Johnson assured Green that he would remove this "burden" from his shoulders.

Paul Douglas learned this new fact of Senate life during that same week in January. Johnson wanted more, and better, office space, and now that he was Majority Leader, he set out to get it. One January afternoon, he told Walter Jenkins to go down to the Senate custodian's office and come back with the master keys that would open every door on the Senate side of the Capitol. That evening, Johnson waited until most senators and their staff had gone home, and then he began to walk through the empty Capitol, opening every door. On the top floor, near the head of a flight of stairs leading up from the gallery, he found what he wanted behind a door marked G-14, "Joint Economic Committee." Inside, in the outer room of the two-room suite, sat its staff director, Grover Ensley, working late. Suddenly, without a knock or any other warning, the door swung open, and the startled Ensley found himself facing the tall figure of the Majority Leader.

Without a word, Johnson walked in and began looking around. The two rooms were rather small but elegant; from their high ceilings hung two chandeliers impressive even by senatorial standards; they had hung in the White House in Theodore Roosevelt's time. In the inner office was a working fireplace, which, in Ensley's memory, was probably lit that evening; he made a point of lighting it every afternoon. "It was very comfortable and cozy," he recalls. The inner office was a corner room, and Johnson pulled aside the heavy draperies in front of its windows, and there was a view "right down the Mall to the Lincoln Memorial and across to Arlington Cemetery." And what made the office perfect was that it was the office of the Joint Economic Committee. "The next day I got a letter from the Rules Committee," Ensley recalls. It said that G-14 was going to be the new office of the Majority Leader. Having relegated

Douglas to a committee whose only amenity was its office, Evans and Novak were to write, Johnson had now taken away the office, and "the Senate took notice. It was a dramatic sign of the consequences of a lack of rapport with the Majority Leader." For other rapport-lacking senators, the signs were less dramatic, but decipherable nonetheless. Every time a senator had to walk a long way to reach the Capitol subway—and knew that other senators, with more conveniently located offices, had a shorter distance to walk—he was reminded of what Lyndon Johnson could do for him, or to him. "After a while," as Doris Kearns Goodwin wrote, "insiders could recognize Johnson's allies by one look at the roster of office suites—the larger suites . . . were reserved for friends, the smaller . . . were allotted to 'the troublesome ones.' "

THERE HAD BEEN a façade of courtesy in his dealings with other senators, even those senators who were not part of the team. Now that façade dropped away. In the pile of message slips on his desk, there would be notations that "Senator Lehman called—please call him back," "Senator Douglas called—please call him," "Senator Kefauver called—would like to speak to you." When he saw such slips, a thin smile would cross Lyndon Johnson's face. Crumpling them up, he would throw them in his wastepaper basket. Or Walter Jenkins would be reading off the messages from his yellow legal pad, writing beside each one Johnson's instructions for dealing with it. When he got to one from a senator who wasn't on the team, there would be a silence. Jenkins would read the next message. "He wouldn't return Lehman's phone calls for days on end," recalls Lehman's administrative assistant, Julius Gaius Caesar Edelstein.

He might not return them at all. And his men—Clements, Skeeter, Bobby Baker—wouldn't return them, either. When, in 1955, this first began happening, Lehman, himself the soul of courtesy, a man who, as Governor, would never have dreamt of snubbing even an avowed enemy, could hardly believe it was intentional. But after one incident in 1955, he had no choice but to believe. He first had difficulty reaching Johnson, who was at the ranch, being "told he was out hunting," as he was to recall. When he finally spoke to him, Johnson promised that he would deal with the matter "immediately" and that either he or Earle Clements would call him back. "I even gave him the number of my [hotel] room and told him that if I should be out, he or Earle should leave word that they had called, and I would call back as promptly as possible," Lehman was to tell Edelstein. Neither Johnson nor Clements ever called.

The façade dropped away in the cloakroom, too. Johnson would be standing in the middle of it, talking, laughing with a group of senators. A Lehman or a Douglas or a Kefauver or another senator not on the team would walk in. Johnson would turn away so that he wouldn't be facing them, so that they couldn't become part of the group. And some of the other senators, men attuned to nuances of power, would take their cue from the Majority Leader.

Edelstein was to recall what it was like to be walking with Herbert Lehman after it became clear that he was in the Leader's disfavor. "You'd walk into the cloakroom. People would fall silent. You'd walk down the hall, and there would be an averting of eyes so that they wouldn't have to say hello." The façade dropped away on the Senate floor as well. "Lehman would begin making a speech, and if Johnson was on the floor he would walk out to the cloakroom, just ostentatiously enough so you knew it was deliberate. And other people would drift—leave—the floor." Or they would not come out onto the floor, as they otherwise might have done. While Lehman or Douglas or Kefauver was speaking, a senator would wander into the cloakroom, intending to go out on the floor. Bobby Baker would be standing by the swinging doors leading from the cloakroom to the floor. He would say to the senator, "Why don't you stay in the cloakroom for a while?"

There were methods of humiliating a senator on the floor as well. Johnson would go over to Douglas' desk, while the Illinois senator was sitting with one of his assistants. He would lean over and chat with the assistant, ignoring Douglas.

And there were methods less public than these, but, with certain senators, equally effective. "Skeeter would routinely have the boys back to his office at five or six o'clock," Douglas' administrative assistant, Howard Shuman, recalls. The invited senators would walk through the tall, dark door into those cheery rooms beyond, their arms around each other's shoulders, chuckling or laughing. Other senators would see them going in. It was hard not to see; Skeeter's office was just outside the cloakroom. "Paul was almost never invited," Shuman says. "In fact, once, when he was, he told me about it." In the telling, Douglas tried to make a joke of the situation, "but," Shuman says, "it didn't come off too well."

"Oh, they did a lot of things to diminish Paul, Paul and the others," Shuman says. "They went out of their way to diminish them. William S. White wrote that the way to get into the [Senate] Club was to be courteous and courtly. Well, that's nonsense. Lehman was the most courtly man in the world, and he wasn't part of the club. It didn't have anything to do with courtly. It had to do with how you voted—with whether or not you voted as Lyndon Johnson wanted you to vote." Says Neil MacNeil, a longtime congressional correspondent for *Time* magazine: "The Senate was run by courtesy, all right—like the longshoremen's union."

Assistants to non-team members were constantly being reminded of their bosses' lack of status. "He [Johnson] was cutting [to me]," Edelstein recalls. "With other staff people he was very verbose. But when I said hello, he'd be very curt and turn his back on me." Sometimes Johnson would be chatting, outwardly relaxed, in the cloakroom when he would notice, standing nearby, an assistant to one of the senators who was not on the team. "What the fuck do you want?" Lyndon Johnson would say. "Nothing, Senator," the aide would answer.

"Then get your fucking ass out of here," Johnson would say. Or he would give these aides instructions for their senator in a tone that left no doubt as to where the senator stood in his estimation. Says Harry Schnibbe, administrative assistant to John A. Carroll of Colorado, elected to the Senate in 1956 and never a member of Johnson's team: "Most of the time he ignored you. But he might say, 'I want you to tell Carroll to get over here. Get on the phone and tell him! I need senators over here on this debate! You're over here listening to this. Where the hell is *he*?' " Or he might simply tell Schnibbe, in a low, threatening tone: "Get your fucking senator over here right away!"

"I'd say, 'Yes, sir!' like I was a page," Schnibbe recalls. "I'd almost salute. He terrified me. To tell you the truth, if I went in the cloakroom and Johnson was in the cloakroom, I left. I'd say, 'Oh, shit, I'm not staying here.' We all operated in total terror of Johnson."

IN OTHER WAYS, too, the humility of Lyndon Johnson's first term fell away, to be replaced by characteristics that would have been familiar to students at San Marcos—to students, that is, who hadn't been on his team there.

G-14 had been refurnished—almost instantly, it seemed, thanks to the efficiency of the Senate Cabinet Shop—in the traditional Senate mode: turn-of-the-century desks and a visitors' bench, refinished and polished until it glowed, from the Old Supreme Court Chamber; a nineteenth-century painting of "Rebecka, daughter of the mighty Powhattan, Emperor of Attaboughko-mouck." Johnson had admired portraits of John Nance Garner and a former Texas senator, Morris Sheppard, that had been hanging in Skeeter's back office; now they were hanging in Johnson's office. At the end of the day, Johnson would, after (or, increasingly, instead of) a session in Skeeter's office, invite a few chosen senators or journalists to G-14 for a drink and a chat. Unbuttoning his double-breasted suit, he would put his feet, clad in either gleaming black shoes or gleaming, elaborately hand-tooled "LBJ" cowboy boots, up on the desk, and buzz a secretary to bring drinks. A *You ain't learning nothin' when you're talking* plaque had been installed on the mantelpiece, but now, in sharp contrast to his first six years in the Senate, Lyndon Johnson paid markedly little attention to his father's advice—as little attention as he had paid before those six years.

The most notable characteristic of these gatherings was the extent to which the conversation at them was dominated by one man. The talk was fascinating, but its dominant theme was the smartness, or, to be more precise, the shrewdness, of the host. Once, for example, on January 13, 1955, the day the committee assignments were announced, he was in the middle of a monologue when he abruptly interrupted himself. "My God," he said, "I forgot to call Senator Stennis and congratulate him." Snatching the phone out of its cradle, he tucked it between his shoulder and his chin, and dialed Stennis' home. And when Mrs. Stennis, answering, said that her husband was not home, Johnson said, "Well, I must tell you, ma'am, how proud I am of your husband and how proud the Senate is, and you tell him that when he gets home. The Senate paid him a great honor today. The Senate elected your husband to the Appropriations Committee. That's one of the most powerful committees in the whole Senate and a great honor for your husband. I'm so proud of John. He's a great American. And I know you're proud of him, too. He's one of my finest senators. . . ."

A number of aspects of the monologue Johnson was conducting with Mrs. Stennis—a monologue that went on for quite some time—were worth noting. The first was the attention to detail—to doing *everything*. Giving Stennis the Appropriations seat had put the Senator in his debt; a telephone call like this would add a little to the debt—so, late though it was, long though Johnson's day had been, the call was made, and the call was not cursory; Johnson's conversation was not hurried, but slow and as drawlingly gracious as any Mississippian could have desired. Another was the use of the "I" and the "my"—as Rowland Evans, one of the reporters listening, was to put it, "implicitly he was belaboring the obvious—that it wasn't the Steering Committee or the full Senate that was really responsible. It was LBJ." But the most significant aspect of all was that as Johnson talked to Mrs. Stennis, buttering her up, he would, as he poured it on, wink and nod to his listeners, grinning at them over what he was doing. Although his words seemed sincere, he seemed to want his listeners to understand that they really weren't. It seemed to be important to him that they know that.

THE VERY RUTHLESSNESS with which Lyndon Johnson used his power helped him to amass more of it. The story of how Bernard Baruch's contribution had never reached Paul Douglas had gotten around, and everyone knew how Douglas' office had been taken away from him without warning or excuse. The ostracism of Herbert Lehman had been noted. And aides gossiped. It was an open secret now that some senators couldn't even get their phone calls returned. The United States Senate contained men adept at reading power and they had no difficulty in drawing from these ongoing actions a unifying lesson.

And new lessons were constantly being provided for their edification.

A single attempt at independence could end an alliance with Lyndon Johnson forever—even if the alliance had been as long in duration, and as intimate, as that between Johnson and Stuart Symington.

Symington had no jealousy of the Texan with whom he had spent so much time and exchanged so many favors. "I thought he was a man of destiny," he was to recall years later. And he had thought they were friends. "I was awfully fond of Lyndon B. Johnson," he was to say. But after Johnson put Symington on the Armed Services Committee, the experience and expertise—

true expertise—in military matters of the tall, handsome Missourian became apparent at Armed Services Committee hearings, and Johnson's aides became aware that he resented it. Johnson began to say, when Symington's name came up during private conversations, "He's not a team player." For a while Johnson remained amiable when talking to Symington in person, but Symington, detecting a subtle change in Johnson's attitude, decided it was simply that "I was getting too much prominence." He decided to play a less prominent role in future hearings, he was to recall; he didn't want anything to break up the friendship. But 1954 was the year of the Army-McCarthy hearings, and of Symington's courageous challenge to McCarthy, after Johnson had told him not to challenge McCarthy, "and," Symington says, "Johnson didn't like that at all. I've never quite known why. But it [standing up to McCarthy] was something that just had to be done, and I did it." And then, Symington recalls, "I found out that if you crossed him—well, the one word that was foremost in his mind was power, and if anyone stood in his way—well, no one stood in Lyndon Johnson's way." Then Symington realized something about Johnson that he had not understood before: that "there was a sort of cruelty there."

He found out the hard way—in public. Because of the role he had played in building up Texas defense contractors, it had become a tradition for Symington to be invited to luncheons given by Texas' congressional delegation for prominent visitors from the state. Walking into a luncheon shortly after his confrontation with McCarthy, Symington strode over to his friend Lyndon as he always did, and Lyndon turned his back on him. "I did not realize he was breaking with me before that," Symington recalls. "My goodness, only a few years before he had introduced me [at a Texas delegation luncheon] as 'the Greatest Texan of Them All.' And he did it so that everyone saw it. Cruelty."

Then Johnson did it so that everyone in the Democratic cloakroom saw it. In the past, whenever Bobby Baker circulated through the Democratic cloakroom at the end of the day inviting senators to drop by the Leader's office, Symington would be one of the senators invited. Now, one day, he was standing with two senators when Baker approached. Taking the arms of the other two senators, Baker said to them, "The Leader wants you in his office." He walked away. Symington realized he hadn't been invited. And for some years after that, he never was invited. "He [Johnson] was deliberately leaving me out—and he was doing it in such a way that everyone would know. No one crossed Lyndon Johnson."

"Senators mutually recognize the primary natural law of political survival," Neil MacNeil, a very perceptive observer, was to write. When a senator was asked for a vote, an excuse invariably accepted by most Leaders was that it would be politically harmful in his home state. "Hell, I know what it takes to get elected," one of Johnson's predecessors as Leader would explain. Even very pragmatic men recognized this law, and accepted it. That was why, Scoop Jackson would later say, that if, despite President Kennedy's persuasiveness with a senator he had invited to the Oval Office, "the senator said his people [constituents] wouldn't go along, Kennedy would finally say he was sorry they couldn't agree but he understood."

Johnson wouldn't understand. He would refuse to understand. Considerations important to the Senator—even the consideration of political survival—did not divert him from his purpose. "He could charm you or knock your block off, or bribe you, or threaten you, anything to get your vote," Jackson would explain. "And he'd get it. That was the difference."

THE LESSON KEEN-EYED SENATORS drew from what happened to Kefauver and Douglas and Lehman was spelled out by one of the keenest, Russell Long. Lyndon Johnson, Long said, "could not bear to have anyone operating outside his camp. When he saw this developing, he would either reconcile or isolate them." And this made senators all the more anxious to be in his camp, anxious to be on his team. Men learned from watching what happened to Symington what Symington had learned the hard way. "As for Senate loners," Russell Long said, "he could make their lives miserable." Seeing what had happened to Symington, men made sure they didn't make Symington's mistake and cross Lyndon Johnson. As Frank Van der Linden of the *Richmond Times-Dispatch* put it, "When somebody is ruthless like that, and has the power, and is willing to use it, weaker men get out of his way."

AND LYNDON JOHNSON, looking for power over the Senate, had found another instrument with which power could be created. It wasn't a new instrument. First employed in 1845, it had been formally embodied in the Senate Rules (Rule 12, Paragraph 3) since 1914, and previous Senate Leaders had used it in a number of different ways. Never, however, had it been used as this Leader used it. His use of it was, in fact, perhaps the most striking example of the creativity that Lyndon Johnson brought to the legislative process.

The instrument was a "unanimous consent agreement," a procedural device under which the Senate, by unanimous consent, agrees to limit the amount of time that a particular bill can be debated; to divide that time between the bill's proponents and opponents according to a prearranged formula incorporated in the agreement, and to place the allocation of that time under the control of one or two specific proponents and opponents of the measure; to limit the number of amendments to the bill that can be introduced, and the amount of time each amendment can be debated, and to place that time, too, under the control of specific senators.

Prior to World War II, most unanimous consent agreements had come near the end of a session, when the bill in question had already been debated for days, if not weeks; the Senate would then agree that after a certain number of additional days of debate, a vote would be taken. The mounting impatience after the war with the Senate's inefficiency had led to increased use of these agreements, but they still had generally been employed only after substantial debate on a measure had already occurred, and they still generally allowed additional time for debate. The 119 bills that had become the subject of agreements between the end of the war and the end of the 1954 Senate session had been debated for an average of six days before the agreements were instituted—and the agreements had allowed an average of three additional days of debate, so that a total of nine days of discussion had been allowed before the vote.

Lyndon Johnson wasn't allowing nine days; sometimes, in fact, he wasn't allowing even one.

Traditionally, says assistant parliamentarian Riddick, who had begun drafting more of the agreements as parliamentarian Charlie Watkins grew older, "It was sort of a practice to allow them to consider [debate] the bill a while to see if they anticipated a long debate"; it was only if they saw that one could be expected that they would try to restrict debate. "After Mr. Johnson came to the forefront," however, the agreements began coming earlier and earlier in the legislative process; "you would get an agreement on some [bills] before you even started debate." Johnson would decline to call some bills—including some quite major bills—off the Calendar onto the floor until a unanimous consent agreement had been worked out setting a strict time limit; the total debate on a bill might be only six, or four, or, in some cases, two hours. Nor was that the only difference. Until Johnson became Majority Leader, Riddick explains, most agreements were "loose—just general agreements," many dealing only with time limits. "Often they just set the number of hours, or a set time at which they would vote—that was all many of them contained. You didn't work out all the details." Now the agreements became much stricter, and much more detailed. "What Mr. Johnson did was introduce the use of . . . a detailed agreement as to . . . how long each amendment would be debated; how long the general debate of the bill would last; whether all amendments had to be germane to the bill, and details of that nature. This was all reduced to unanimous consent agreements, even specifying the hour that you'd proceed to the consideration of said bill; and the hour that you'd vote on it."

Among the details now included, moreover, was the identity of the senators who would control the allocation of time to other senators who wanted to speak for or against the bill. In the past, the time given to a bill's supporters had usually been controlled by the senator who had introduced the measure (the "mover"), or by the senator who was managing it on the floor, or by the chairman of the committee from which it had emerged. Now, in more and more unanimous consent agreements, a new figure was named. *Ordered by unanimous consent, that . . . debate shall be limited to four hours, to be equally divided by and controlled by the mover of the bill and the majority leader,* an agreement might say. *Ordered that on the question of the final passage of such bill debate shall be limited to six hours, to be equally divided and controlled, respectively, by the majority and minority leaders,* said another. Sometimes, in fact, the time allotted to a bill's supporters was divided and controlled by the Majority Leader alone.

Because of Lyndon Johnson's unprecedented intervention in committee work, the wording of the bills was often to an unprecedented extent a creation of the Majority Leader. He would previously have acted as a mediator between individual senators, or between blocs of senators, who were in conflict over an issue. Once the conflict would have been thrashed out on the Senate floor, but now Johnson would meet alone with each of the senators, or get them together privately, explore their differences to find areas of agreement, and finally would ask, and if asking did not work, would urge, and if urging did not work, would demand, and, finally, if all else failed, would use his raw power to threaten the senators to force them to consent (and to produce the consent of their allies) to the compromise he proposed—would, one way or another, arrange some wording on which they could agree, and for which he felt he could line up a majority of the Senate for passage. He would have been able to do this because of the power—the power of Rayburn, the power of campaign funds, the power of scheduling, the power of office space—with which he had previously surrounded himself. The *quid pro quo* was seldom stated, seldom precise, seldom the offer, of, say, a dam in return for a compromise on a specific bill. But the senator who needed the dam, or the campaign funds, or a private bill called off the Calendar would know that the man asking for this favor had the power to grant the other favor. Now the bills that were already the creations of the Majority Leader, creations made possible by his new powers, would under this additional new power be managed on the floor by the Majority Leader.

And Lyndon Johnson made sure, in each instance, that he had that power, beyond any question. When he resolved a point with a senator, he—or Reedy or Siegel—took notes on what the agreement entailed. Then the notes would be formally typed up. Recalls Riddick: "Johnson would come up to me: 'Now look, I want you to type an agreement.' And he would tell me what he wanted in it. For example: 'And I want to make sure there are no non-germane [amendments].' . . . I would go down to Skeeter's office [and have the agreement typed up]. Then I would find him, and give it to him. He would read it, and he might say, 'Well, now, change this so it will do so-and-so.' " In words that would equally apply to Johnson's maneuvers on the Gulf of Tonkin Resolution ten years later, Riddick says:

> Johnson wanted everything written to back him up as a record. He would get us [the parliamentarians] to sign the damned thing. He wanted it written down so he would be able to say [if anyone objected], "Well, you *gave* me this power."

And, Riddick says, Johnson would take the formal document "around and show it to senators. He would say, 'I hope you won't object. . . .' " He would make it very difficult for a senator to object; everyone else had agreed, he would say; we can't waste days debating this bill; we've got to make the Senate function. After he had secured everyone's consent, he would go to his front-row center seat and stand by it—never for very long—until the presiding senator said, "The chair recognizes the distinguished Majority Leader."

"Mr. President," Johnson would say, "I ask unanimous consent that a proposed unanimous consent agreement, which is offered on behalf of myself and the distinguished Minority Leader, be read." He would hold out the order that Riddick had typed, and a page would hurry over, take it, and give it to one of the clerks on the lower dais, who would read it into the record. "Is there any objection?" the presiding officer would ask. "The chair hears none. Without objection, so ordered."

LYNDON JOHNSON'S USE of the unanimous consent agreement to drastically limit debate ran contrary to the principles on which the Senate had been founded, and to the customs which had, during the previous century and a half of its existence, been most fundamental in its functioning. Unlimited debate had been sacred Senate custom, the device by which, more than any other, it fulfilled the Founding Fathers' vision of it as the bulwark against the "fickleness" and "transient impressions" of the majority, as the guarantor of the sovereignty of the individual states. And it was debate—in its highest sense: unhurried, thoughtful discussion to educate first the Senate and then the people, to raise issues and examine them in depth and at length—that had made the Senate a great deliberative body. Johnson's agreements limited debate so drastically that with their increased use the very nature of the Senate was altered. From the moment a motion for one of his agreements was made on the Senate floor, the body's normally loose functioning was transformed into something very strict indeed.

Amendments to a Unanimous Consent Agreement—Out of Order is the laconic title of the section of Senate precedents relating to the matter. That means *all* amendments. "There is," the precedents state flatly, "no rule providing for amendment of unanimous consent requests." And not only can the agreement therefore not be modified, once the agreement has been approved ("Without objection, so ordered"), there is no appeal from it except by unanimous vote ("A unanimous consent agreement can be set aside" only "by another unanimous consent agreement")—by a vote that would be unobtainable should even one of the proponents of the original agreement want it to stand intact.

As for the measure—the bill itself—covered by a unanimous consent agreement, its consideration is hedged about by rules very different from the normal Senate procedure which allows virtually unlimited amendments and virtually unlimited debate. What if the senator who had introduced the bill now, listening to even the limited debate allowed, had a new thought—and, contrary to his earlier belief, realized that the bill should be amended? Under many agreements, no new amendment whatsoever could be introduced. Even in the rare cases in which new amendments were in order, they could only be introduced, not debated—which meant that their purpose could not be explained or discussed on the floor. Most Senate precedents dealing with unanimous consent agreements say that amendments "must be presented and voted on without debate." What if a senator who has introduced an amendment on the floor before the agreement was ordered thinks that this proposed new amendment, modifying his, is a good idea? That does not change anything: even "Where an amendment proposed by a Senator to an amendment is accepted by the mover of the first amendment as a modification, further debate on such latter amendment is not in order." And in the even rarer cases in which discussion is in order, it could only be cursory; the time for debate on the "modification" of an amendment had to be subtracted from the already meagre time—often a single hour—already allotted to the amendment.

As employed by Lyndon Johnson, the unanimous consent agreement was even eliminating the tradition that a senator could introduce an amendment on any subject he wished, at any time he wished. Under Rule 14, one of the Senate's supposedly immutable rules, "germaneness of amendments to bills is not required."* Nothing was more important to the guardians of the Senate traditions than that tradition. "Russell held that the sacredness of Senate procedure was that you could amend anything," Riddick says. "You could tack anything onto a farm subsidy bill, for example. . . . There were no restrictions." But among the few exceptions to Rule 14 was the unanimous consent agreement. "If a unanimous consent agreement . . . contains a provision for germaneness of amendments, an amendment not germane is out of order." Most of Lyndon Johnson's unanimous consent agreements contained that provision. *No amendment that is not germane to the provisions of the bill shall be received,* Riddick would type.

And the provisions of an agreement which gave control to a single senator—and, more and more, that senator was Lyndon Johnson—were, more and more, designed to ensure that that control was firm. Once the agreement was voted, the presiding officer no longer had authority to recognize a senator. "A Senator cannot be recognized unless time is yielded to him by one of the Senators having control," the Senate Rules state. So firm were such provisions that, as Riddick's chief assistant, Secretary to the Parliamentarian Murray Zweben, puts it,

---

*Except in the case of general appropriation bills, or of bills being considered under the cloture rule.

Because of the unanimous consent agreements he devised, he [Lyndon Johnson] could keep major legislation from coming up. A senator could not introduce himself a major bill with provisions Johnson didn't like, because Johnson wouldn't let it come to the floor. And he [the senator] couldn't offer it as an amendment to a different major bill because of the unanimous consent agreement [on that bill].

As for minor legislation, a senator had little hope of the amendment making its way into law by that route either—thanks to Johnson's power over scheduling. Johnson would simply not allow that bill to come to the floor; "If a senator offered it [the amendment] to some piddling minor bill, that bill was dead," Zweben says.

The unanimous consent agreements were a culmination of all the powers that Lyndon Johnson had created over scheduling, over the content of bills, over the managing of bills, over committee assignments. The agreements were made possible—senators had no choice but to accept them—because of the combining of these internal powers with the powers he brought to bear from outside the Senate: the power of Rayburn, the power of money. And the agreements cemented his power, made it formal, as formal as the wordings of the Senate orders in which the agreements were embodied. "Of course any senator could block unanimous consent and keep the debate going," Evans and Novak were to say. "In fact, however, few did. Debates grew shorter—and ever less important. . . . Thus did Lyndon Johnson revolutionize the Senate, severely modifying its proud heritage of unlimited debate without changing a single rule."

MAJORITY LEADER LYNDON JOHNSON may have been limiting debate on the Senate floor; he was not eliminating speeches. He wanted speeches, and he wanted plenty of them, the longer the better. Speeches—which he, and his aides, and most journalists persisted in calling "debate"—had their uses for him. The Lyndon Johnson version of "debate," however, was not at all what the Founding Fathers had intended.

The Founders had envisioned debate—thoughtful discussion—as an indispensable part of the Senate's main work. For Johnson, "debate" was a device to divert attention from the main work, and to buy time for him to do it. As George Reedy explains, "As long as somebody on the Senate floor is talking, the Senate cannot vote." From the time he became Majority Leader, therefore, Johnson began using talk on the floor as what Reedy calls "a diversionary device, which enabled him to stay out of the spotlight while horse-trading," as a smoke screen for the maneuvering that was taking place in the cloakrooms, or, more and more, in his top-floor Capitol office, as a method of stalling the Senate to give him time to work out his deals.

There were of course senators who liked—loved—to talk, and he used them. "Hubert prepares for a major address by taking a deep breath," Johnson was to say, and "whenever Johnson needed extra time for horse-trading and a vote was inconveniently near, he invariably sent out Hubert H. Humphrey, who could stand up and deliver a discourse" of two hours or more "without previous preparation," Reedy recalls. Another was Molly Malone, that "relic of Smoot-Hawley days," who could still rise at his desk to deliver a passionate—and lengthy—explanation of the need for high tariffs. Although Johnson held the opposite view of tariffs, when he needed to buy time because he didn't yet have the necessary votes for an upcoming vote on some non-tariff measure, he would often encourage Malone to give his views; "it was the interlude he wanted, not the message," Harry McPherson says.

While the quorum calls and speeches were droning on meaninglessly on the Senate floor, therefore, the action that mattered was taking place off the floor. When it was completed—the compromises made, the deal closed, the unanimous consent agreement in place—the time for talking was over, and Johnson had little patience with any senator who failed to understand that. A senator heading onto the floor to discuss the upcoming bill would be inter- cepted by Bobby Baker. "Keep it short, keep it short or the Leader will be mad," Baker would say. If the senator failed to take the hint, the Leader, seeing him raising his hand for recognition, would hurry over to his desk. "We've got the votes, don't talk, don't talk," he would whisper. "Under Johnson, the Senate functions like a Greek tragedy," Paul Douglas was to say. "All the action takes place offstage, before the play begins. Nothing is left to open and spontaneous debate, nothing is left for the participants but the enactment of their prescribed roles."

THIS CHANGE IN THE NATURE of the Senate had a further implication. It was offstage, of course—in secret—that Lyndon Johnson himself liked to work. Debate was about goals, issues, about "principled things." "It is the politician's task to pass legislation, not to sit around saying principled things," he said, repeating that credo over and over. George Reedy was to write that "He [John- son] regarded public discussion as dangerous to the conduct of government. . . . He was absolutely convinced that achievement was possible only through care- ful negotiations in quiet backrooms where public passions did not intrude." And, as Reedy notes, "This attitude left no room in the LBJ philosophy for the Senate as a *deliberative* body in which speeches could change the outcome of legislation or as an educational body in which speeches were intended to inform the public on the issues of the day. . . . The role of public debate in securing popular assent to policies and, ultimately, national unity was a con- cept he could not grasp."

Under this cloaking of Johnson's methods in governmental philosophy, however, lay something personal—and deeper. The unanimous consent agreement, the key device by which Lyndon Johnson was changing the fundamental character of the Senate, was, in Doris Kearns Goodwin's words, "a natural extension of his personality. Because he himself felt uncomfortable in larger groups and formal debate, he gradually shifted senatorial and public attention away from the floor to the places where he felt most at home—the cloakroom, the office, the hallways."

Some of his assistants understood this fact. "Discussions of goals and ethics were merely exercises in posturing, and he had no patience with such goings-on," Reedy was to write. "He abhorred dissent to a point where he sought to quell it long before protagonists had talked themselves out." Disagreement, to this man to whom everything was personal, was disagreement not with his point of view but with *him*—and, Colonel BeLieu says, "he had zero tolerance for disagreement." He *abhorred* dissent. He had *no patience* with discussions of goals and ethics. Even the loyal McPherson was to acknowledge that "His constant pressure for unanimous consent agreements . . . often came close to harassment."*

Other thoughtful men were as concerned as Paul Douglas about the consequences of this pressure. "Lyndon Johnson did not believe it was a function of the Senate to inform and instruct the public," Julius Edelstein says. "He believed it was the function of the Senate to pass legislation. But of course the Senate had always been the forum of the nation. The great tradition of the Senate was the tradition of Norris, and Borah and La Follette. . . ." Such concern no longer had much significance, however. Lyndon Johnson had looked for power in the Senate, and had found it—and now that he was Majority Leader, he was using it. During his first six years in the Senate, he had concealed certain aspects of his character, adapting his personality to the institutional personality of the Senate, but now, in the seventh year, he was forcing the Senate to adapt *its* personality to his.

The adapting was, furthermore, taking place with remarkable rapidity. By June, 1955, within six months of his election as Majority Leader, the unanimous consent agreements that were the legislative embodiment of Lyndon Johnson's personality had become, as Howard Shuman observes, "the standard operating procedure . . . on all big Senate bills." Debate "beyond a sparse allotment of time became a favor which a Senator had to request from the Majority Leader," Goodwin writes. The right to offer amendments? "If Lyndon Johnson didn't want your amendment, you couldn't even offer it," Shuman says. He hated

---

*Although McPherson adds, "But I could not fault him. Senators who raised objections had frequently benefited from his power. Complaints about limiting debate . . . often turned out to be based on a plaintiff's annoyance that he must either miss a vote or forgo a speaking engagement back home. And besides, who knew better than liberals the enervating consequences of unlimited debate?"

debate, and now in the Senate, once the very home of debate, debate was no longer important. In what had once been called the greatest deliberative body in the world there was now very little real deliberation. So creative was Lyndon Johnson's political genius that it had transformed every political institution of which he had been the Leader. Now it had transformed the United States Senate—remade that body, seemingly so immutable, in his own image. He could run it now, run it as he wanted to run it.

25

The Leader

ON THE SENATE FLOOR, LATE EACH MORNING, a clerk might be desultorily shuffling papers on the dais, pages might be strolling through the deserted arcs of desks, laying out the Daily Calendar and the drafts of bills, one or two senators might be standing chatting near the door of each cloakroom, down in the well a little knot of journalists, assembled for the daily briefing by the party leaders, might be listening to Minority Leader William Knowland talk, in his ponderous, droning way, about the day's schedule—the Senate Chamber was the sleepy, slow-moving place it had always been.

And then, shortly before noon, the tall double doors at the rear of the Chamber's center aisle would swing open—wide open, so hard had they been pushed—and Lyndon Johnson would be coming through them. As they swung, he would, without pausing, snatch the brown file folder Gerry Siegel was holding out to him, and toss an order to George Reedy out of the side of his mouth. And then he would be coming down the aisle's four broad steps with a long, fast stride. Seeing the journalists' heads turn, Knowland, realizing Johnson was approaching, would stop talking. He would sit down at his desk, waiting to hear what the Majority Leader had to say.

Johnson would stand by his desk, in the center of that broad semi-circle of shining mahogany. Since he was on the first step, six inches higher than the floor of the well where the journalists were standing, he would be looking down at them from a height even greater than his own, and he also looked even taller than he was because the desk was so small. His thinning black hair was slicked down smooth, so that as his face turned to one side, there was nothing to soften that massive skull, or the sharp jut of the big jaw and the big nose, and when the face turned back, his eyes, under the heavy eyebrows, were those intent, intense dark eyes, always wary, that could in an instant narrow into slits and become so intimidating. And under the eyes was the grim tough line of Lyndon Johnson's mouth. "He would stand there very erect, so tall and confident, just the model of a take-charge man," recalls one of the journalists.

"There was a nervous vitality that just poured out of him, almost an animal energy."

And his physical presence wasn't the only reason he seemed so big.

Other Majority Leaders who had met with reporters before each day's Senate session had traditionally been accompanied by assistants to fill in the details of the answers to the reporters' questions. No assistant accompanied Lyndon Johnson: he didn't need any; he knew the details himself. The file folder that Siegel had prepared contained the day's agenda, the Calendar of Bills, with notes on senators' views about various bills, and brief statements Johnson was to give. In the memory of the reporters who met with him regularly, Lyndon Johnson never—not once—opened that folder. "Somebody might ask him about some minor bill," one reporter says. "He'd say, 'Oh, that's Calendar Number so-and-so.' He knew the numbers without looking. Or he'd say, 'That's not been discussed in committee yet. Looks like it might be coming out of the subcommittee this week.' He knew where each bill was—exactly where it was." He knew the activities that had occurred in the various committee and subcommittee hearing rooms that morning—the arguments that had been made, the actions that had been taken—as if he had been present in every room. "If you said, 'Look, such-and-such committee just amended that amendment,' he would say, 'That new amendment is there because . . .' He seemed to know every aspect of everything the Senate had done or was going to do." Says another reporter: "He knew the Republican strategy, too—how we didn't know. He might say, 'Now, we're going to debate an hour on this. However, the other side will try to amend the amendment. . . .' "

He knew exactly what he wanted to say—what he wanted the journalists to know—and he said nothing more. As the journalists looked up at him, the clock over the double doors at the rear of the center aisle was in their line of vision, so they were constantly reminded that the bell would ring, bringing the Senate to order and their time to ask questions to an end, precisely at noon. "He not only had his physical, dominating presence, but the clock behind him," one of the reporters recalls. Not that he needed that assistance—or any assistance. "There would be little time for questions," Booth Mooney would recall. "Nor any need for them, in Johnson's opinion. The Majority Leader of the Senate had given them a basis for their stories. What more could they ask?" If there was a question that annoyed him, recalls one of the journalists, "he would answer the question. But he would put a spin on it, so he would be saying it his way." That was the only way he answered any question. "You didn't get any more than Lyndon Johnson wanted to tell you," a journalist says. "Never. I don't think, in all those years, he ever slipped up. He knew exactly what he wanted to say—and that was what he said. Period. I never felt in all those years that he ever lost control [of one of those press conferences in the well]. He was always *in charge*."

Part of the aura that surrounded Johnson as he stood front-row center in the Senate Chamber was, as some of the reporters acknowledge, "the buildup, the accrual—the knowledge we had of what this guy *had* done, of what this guy could do. Of what he wanted to be." It was an aura of triumphs won, of triumphs anticipated. But the aura was more than reputation. "Power just emanated from him," another of the reporters says. "There was that look he gave. There was the way he held his head. Even if you didn't know who he was, you would know this was a guy to be reckoned with. You would feel: don't cross this guy. He was so *big*! And he would look around the Chamber—it was like he was saying, 'This is *my* turf.' " More than a century before, a rider encountering big-eared, blazing-eyed John Wheeler Bunton on the Texas plains wrote of his unusual "bearing," others spoke of his "towering form" and "commanding presence." For more than a century, those words and phrases had been applied to generation after generation of Buntons. Now they were being applied to the Bunton who had become Majority Leader of the Senate. "He had the bearing of a man on a pedestal," one of the reporters in the well recalls. "He had the bearing of a man *in command*."

Then, at noon, the bells would ring, and the gavel of the senator in the chair—the senator Lyndon Johnson had put in the chair—would rap, and the Senate would convene. And Lyndon Johnson would still be in command.

The first words from Richard Nixon or Walter George, or whoever was presiding in their place—after the chaplain's prayer and the ritualistic "The Senate will be in order"—were "The chair recognizes the Senator from Texas," and for some time thereafter, Johnson, standing at his desk in the center of the first row, would be the only senator recognized. It would be he who, after disposing of the parliamentary preliminaries ("On request of Mr. Johnson of Texas, and by unanimous consent, the reading of the Journal of the Proceedings of May 25, 1955, was dispensed with"), made the requests—the requests that only he could make—for permission for committees or subcommittees to meet although the Senate was in session. ("On request of Mr. Johnson of Texas, and by unanimous consent, the Subcommittee on Judicial Improvements of the Committee on the Judiciary was authorized to meet during the session today"), the requests that had once been automatic but that were no longer so automatic, that were an exercise of his power. It was he who ordered up the executive session ("Mr. President, I move that the Senate proceed to the consideration of executive business." "Without objection, so ordered"), and it was he who, during that session, shepherded the Senate through the Advise and Consent functions on nominations ("The Chief Clerk read the nomination of Admiral Arthur William Radford to be chairman of the Joint Chiefs of Staff. . . . The Chief Clerk read the nomination of General Maxwell Davenport Taylor to be Chief of Staff, United States Army. . . . The Chief Clerk read the nomination of General Nathan Farragut Twining to be Chief of Staff, United States Air Force . . . MR. JOHNSON of Texas: "Mr. President, I ask unanimous consent that the nominations be confirmed en bloc." "Without objection, so ordered") and on treaties as well ("Mr. President, I ask unanimous consent that these treaties be considered as having passed through their various parliamentary stages up to and including the presentation of the resolutions of ratification, that the Senate take one vote on the treaties, and that President Eisenhower be notified of the Senate's action." "All those in favor of ratification, please stand and be counted. . . . Two-thirds of those senators present having voted in the affirmative, the resolutions of ratification are agreed to"). It was he who ended the executive session, and moved that the Senate return to legislative business. It was he who ordered up the morning hour, with its speeches, "subject to the usual two-minute limitation," and it was he who ended the morning hour. And it was he who, after the morning hour, stood again at his desk to recite the formula—the formula that, by Senate custom, only he could recite—that was so vital to senators: "Mr. President, I move that the Senate proceed to the immediate consideration of Calendar No. 394, Senate Bill 2080, a bill for the relief of Oakley F. Dodd"; "Mr. President I move that the Senate proceed to the immediate consideration of S. 2083, a bill to authorize a preliminary examination and survey of the channel leading from Indian River Bay to Assawaman Canal, Delaware." After each of these Calendar Calls, the legislative clerk had to participate in the ritual, stating the bill by its full title ("A bill [S. 2083] to amend the Water Pollution Control Act in order to . . ."), and if the clerk was not reading fast enough, Johnson would become impatient. As he stood beside his desk, he was separated from the clerks on the second level of the dais only by the few feet of the well, and his eyes were on a level with theirs. "C'mon, c'mon, let's get going," he would say to the clerk facing him across the well, and a few bills later, "C'mon, *GET GOING!*" Senators watching Lyndon Johnson intone the ritualistic words that called a bill off the Calendar would know that *they* had bills over which they wanted—needed—that ritual intoned, and that only Lyndon Johnson could intone it.

It was Lyndon Johnson who called up the non-controversial bills that had been reported out of committees, moved their consideration and shepherded them efficiently through the process of passage. After the presiding officer had ordered a clerk to "state the bill by title for the information of the Senate," and had then said, "The question is on agreeing to the motion of the Senator from Texas," Johnson would either have the committee chairman briefly explain the measure—"I call the motion to the attention of the distinguished senator from Oklahoma"—or would briefly explain it himself.

And it was Lyndon Johnson who gave the Senate its schedule—in a tone of authority that let the Senate know that it was he, and he alone, who was establishing that schedule.

"Mr. President," he would say, "I wish the Senate to be on notice that the Senate will consider on next Tuesday the State Department Appropriation Bill. The mutual security bill probably will be reported to the Senate by then and be available for consideration on that day. It is my understanding that the Committee on Banking and Currency hopes to report a housing bill. If it is reported as expected, it is my hope that the housing bill be considered sometime next week. If action can be had on the minimum wage bill, it is my plan to schedule it for consideration by the Senate as soon as it is reported out of committee." He would make verbal gestures toward those who presumably were also involved in the scheduling process—"If the committees will report the bills—and I do not urge them to do so until they have thoroughly considered them and have reached full accord on them—the Policy Committee, and I am sure the Minority Leader will cooperate as he has in the past, will schedule the bills quickly." But at the slightest hint that some other member of the Senate was daring to interject himself, no matter how slightly, in the process, Johnson reminded him who was in charge. In May, 1955, for example, Republican Charles Potter of Michigan, whose state was vitally interested in an early vote on the Great Lakes Fisheries Convention, a treaty with Canada, ventured to press Johnson a bit too hard on when the vote might be taken.

"When did [the Majority Leader] say he would call up the Convention?" Potter asked.

"The distinguished senator from Michigan has spoken with me on several occasions about the Fisheries Convention," Johnson replied. "I am anxious to cooperate with him, as he has always cooperated with the Democratic side of the aisle, particularly with the leadership. If it is possible to call up the Convention on next Tuesday, it will be done." On such occasions, Johnson's tone indicated clearly that if it wasn't possible, it wouldn't be done. And senators hearing the exchange could hardly help being reminded of what might have happened to Potter's cherished treaty if he had not "always cooperated with . . . the leadership."

THESE MATTERS OF SCHEDULING were mostly routine, on non-controversial bills. But there were also the controversial bills, the major legislation. Passage of such legislation—winning on the major bills—was as difficult for Lyndon Johnson as it had always been for Majority Leaders, for he was in as precarious a position as any of his predecessors; what position, indeed, could be more precarious than that of a Leader with a one-vote margin, particularly when the party that was supposed to provide that margin was divided as deeply as his was divided? The Senate as a whole was divided on almost every major issue; with blocs of senators—Mountain States senators, Prairie States senators, Northeast urban votes, Southern Caucus votes—certain to oppose one issue or another, there were few proposals on which a majority vote was certain.

Because of these divisions, passage of most significant legislation required putting together, for each bill, a new, unique, collection of votes, and the margin would always be narrow—every vote counted. And Lyndon Johnson needed on each separate major bill votes not only for the bill but for the unanimous consent agreement that alone could insure that the bill could be brought to a vote, and that the differences between voting blocs and between individual senators had been sufficiently bridged so that when the votes were counted he would have a majority. So each major bill was the subject of countless negotiations.

Some took place in the Chamber, on the Senate floor—on that floor on which, for generations, the prevailing pace had been the slow, hesitant steps of old men, on which the prevailing attitude had been the extremely dignified, or overdignified, senatorial pomposity, on which the prevailing parliamentary procedure had often seemed to be the quorum call, the prevailing sound the drone of insignificant rituals.

Now Lyndon Johnson was in charge of that floor. One moment he would be sitting down beside Kerr or Anderson on one of the couches in the rear of the Chamber, the next, he was up buttonholing a senator who had just entered, joking with him, draping an arm around his shoulders, and then talking confidentially to him, bending close to his ear. Then, seeing another senator come in, he would be off to greet him, crossing the long Chamber. He would be throwing himself into the chair next to Richard Russell and talking with him out of the side of his mouth, or sitting down next to Walter George, and, leaning forward, be bringing him up to date on the activities of the day, or, jumping up, would be heading across to another senator. Sometimes he would throw himself down in his own chair, and, stretching his long legs out into the center aisle, or crossing them, would lean far back into the chair and slouch down until he seemed to be resting on the nape of his neck and the small of his back. He might sit like that, lost in thought, for several minutes. And then, having arrived at some decision, he would lunge up out of the chair and stride rapidly over to some senator and begin talking to him.

Even standing still, Lyndon Johnson was somehow always in motion, rocking back and forth on the balls of his feet, restlessly shifting his shoulders, one big hand plunging into a pants pocket to jingle coins or the keys on his big key ring, the other scratching his back—or scratching other parts of his body, too, for some of the motions Lyndon Johnson made front-row center on the great stage of the Senate floor were those intimate motions that embarrassed other men even in the relative privacy of Johnson's office. The reporters in the Press Gallery would nudge each other and giggle when, jamming a hand into a side pocket of his pants, the Leader quite openly scratched his crotch, bending one leg and leaning far over as he did so, one shoulder much lower than the other, the better to reach hard-to-reach recesses of his body; sometimes, taking out his inhaler, he would tilt his head so far back that he was staring straight up at the ceiling, and shoving the inhaler far up his nose, he would snort so vigorously as he inhaled that the snorts were clearly audible up in the Gallery. Sometimes, standing there, he might jam both hands into his pockets and rise up on his toes as he glanced around the Chamber with that air of command.

As the day wore on and the routine business was disposed of, and the crucial votes began to loom closer, his conversations would take on more intensity. Grasping a senator's arm, he would take him off to the side of the Chamber for a quiet talk. One of his arms would be firmly around his colleague's shoulders, and after a while, his other hand would begin to jab, jab toward the other senator as he made his points. The jabs would no longer stop in midair; Lyndon Johnson's long forefinger would begin to poke into the other senator's chest. Or that hand—the other arm would still be around the shoulders, lest the senator try to get away—would reach out and take the senator's lapel, gently at first, but then harder, grabbing the lapel, pulling the senator closer or pushing him back. And Lyndon Johnson's big head would be down in the other senator's face, or, twisting and cocking, coming up into that face from below.

And he would be moving faster and faster, throwing himself down into a chair beside one senator to whisper urgently to him for a moment, then bounding up the steps to talk to another at the rear of the Chamber, then, seeing another on the far side of the Chamber, crossing the center aisle, hurrying through the Republican desks with those long strides, leaning forward in his haste. Or he would beckon Bobby Baker over to him, lean far down to whisper right in Baker's ear so that no one else could possibly hear, and Baker would dart away. Or Baker would rush out of the cloakroom and over to Johnson and whisper up into his ear, and Johnson would rush up to the cloakroom. "And even if he was just standing there jingling the coins, you couldn't take your eyes off him," says Robert Barr of *U.S. News & World Report*. "If you were a spectator and you didn't know who he was, you would wonder [who he was]— because of this unbelievable restless energy that emanated from him." The Senate Chamber which had been so sleepy and slow, was now, suddenly, a room filled with energy and passion.

THEN THE UNANIMOUS CONSENT AGREEMENT would be almost finalized— almost but not completely. Or, if the agreement *was* finalized, the times fixed in writing at which the roll would be called on the amendments and the final bill, he might have almost enough votes for passage—almost but not enough. And all too often in that divided and stubborn Senate, it seemed as if he would not be able, despite all his efforts, to get enough. And he *had* to have enough, *had to* win.

Striding up the aisle, Lyndon Johnson would push open the double doors to the Democratic cloakroom. Bobby Baker would hold out a tally sheet; Johnson would snatch it out of his hand. And Baker, who had been trying to make sure that all Johnson's votes would be on the floor when they needed to be, would also have lists of the senators whom he had been unable to locate, or who had other commitments and had said they couldn't be present, or who, for one reason or another, did not want to vote "with the leadership" on the upcoming bill. And he would have information for Johnson about disputes between two senators, or about the bill—amendments on which there was still no acceptable compromise.

"Get 'em on the line for me," Johnson would say, and Baker would give the numbers to the telephone clerks, and the first call would go through into Booth Ten, the telephone booth closest to the clerks' desks.

The matter to be discussed might be only one of attendance, and then Johnson might only say into the telephone: "Lister, we're gonna motion up the District bill tonight, and Ah want you to be standin' by. Ah'll need you over here. Ah'm not even gonna tell the Republicans until Ah bring it up. And Ah want you guys to be ready."

But the matter might be more delicate. Then the door to Booth Ten would close, and a senator or aide passing by would see Lyndon Johnson hunched over the phone inside. One hand would be holding a cigarette, from which he would take frequent deep drags. The other would be holding the receiver, and Johnson's mouth would be very close to it. As he spoke into it, he would sometimes rise to his feet, his tall body filling the booth, or he might remain seated and hunched over on the little seat, but, standing or sitting, if he was having difficulty persuading the senator on the other end of the line to his way of thinking, Lyndon Johnson's whole being would be poured into that persuasion. His head would be bowed low over the mouthpiece, and sometimes as he talked and he became more and more wound up in his effort, he would lower his head until it was beneath the receiver, and then it would cock to one side and come up under the receiver as if it was the senator's face.

Sometimes Johnson would want to make sure that nobody could hear what he was saying. "If you stepped out of Booth Ten you could see the whole cloakroom," one of the telephone clerks recalls, "and he would stand up, open the door [of the booth] and look around the corner to see if anyone could hear." Then Lyndon Johnson would duck back into Booth Ten to say the things he didn't want anyone else to hear.

What he said might have the desired result, and he would replace the receiver, step out of the booth, and snatch up the phone in the next booth, where the clerks had another senator waiting on the phone. Or it might not have the desired result. Then, as the conversation came to a close, Johnson, still inside the booth, door closed, might kick the booth as he hung up, or pound his fist into its wall. In the cloakroom, men would watch the booth shaking with the Leader's rage. Or, stepping out of the booth after hanging up the phone, his face the "thundercloud" that men feared, he would kick the outside of the booth, "viciously," as one Senate staffer puts it, or slam the door.

By this time, there would be lights, signals that senators were waiting for him on the line, over several booths. "He would go right down the row, getting his players lined up," the telephone clerk says.

Often, while he was talking to one senator, a call he needed to take immediately would come in on another line. A clerk would tap timidly on the door of the booth in which Johnson was talking, and tell him the other senator was ready. Stepping out of the booth, the telephone still in his hand, the cord stretching with him, Johnson would reach into the other booth and take that receiver, and then stand between the two booths, with the cords stretching out from them to his hands. Or he might want to talk to two or three or even four of his "players"—senators with disagreements about the same amendment—at the same time, and he talked to them at the same time, on two or three or four phones, standing in the narrow aisle between the two rows of phone booths with a receiver, or two receivers, grasped in each big hand, talking first into one receiver, then into another, long black cords stretching out from his tall figure in all directions.

Sometimes this telephone persuasion would be successful. Then, moving from booth to booth, Johnson would slam the receivers back into their cradles, a thin smile of satisfaction on his face. Sometimes it wouldn't. Then, with a grimace of disgust and fury, Johnson would drop the receivers, or hurl them to the floor so hard that they bounced and their cords would still be quivering when a clerk scurried to pick them up. He would smash his foot into one of the booths so hard that it shook, and as he strode out of the cloakroom back entrance to collect himself in the corridor outside, the telephone area still vibrated with Lyndon Johnson's rage.

"Or," the clerk recalls, "he might look around the corner of Booth Ten to see if anyone was in the cloakroom that he wanted to work on." If there was, Lyndon Johnson would go over to him, to persuade in person.

The quarry might be seated on one of the leather couches that lined the cloakroom walls. They were low and soft—ideal locales for persuasion, in the words of the clerk "good places for him to pin a senator into so that he couldn't get away."

Approaching the senator, Johnson would lean over him, perhaps chatting amiably for a moment or two about inconsequential matters, but with his weight resting on one hand that had been placed on the back of the couch, close by the senator's shoulder. Then, switching to the real subject of the conversation, Johnson would sit down beside him. The hand would remain on the back of the couch, so that when Johnson, continuing to talk, leaned forward to look the senator more directly in the face, his arm would be stretched out beside the other man's head. In the urgency of his appeal, Johnson would lean further forward, sliding to the edge of his seat, and twist his body so it was more in front of the senator. Then he would cross the leg furthest from the senator over the knee closest to the other man. Already faced with the difficulty of pushing up from those deep, soft cushions, the senator would find the difficulty increased by the fact that not only was there a big arm like a bar on one side of him, but also a big leg like a bar in front of him. If the senator exhibited signs of restlessness, Johnson would grab the ankle of that leg with his free hand, so that there were in effect two bars in front of the senator, not to mention a size 11 shoe in front of his face; "the poor guy," the clerk notes, "couldn't get out."

With the senator's continued presence thus assured, the first Johnson arm, the one that had been resting on the back of the couch, would stretch along it, so that the senator was almost completely surrounded. And the trap would be tightened. As Johnson talked faster and faster, that heavy arm would come down around the senator's shoulders, hugging them. His hand would grasp the senator's shoulder firmly. He would lean further and further into him, the hand that had been on his own ankle now on the senator's knee or thigh. "I can still see those big meaty hands," the clerk would recall decades later. "One would be massaging the poor guy's shoulder, and the other one would be grabbing his leg. I can still see Johnson leaning into him." His face would be very close to the senator's now, pushing closer and closer, his head coming up under his companion's so that the senator's head was often forced back against the back of the couch. No matter how much he may have wanted to retreat further, he couldn't, and as he was held helpless, Johnson would talk faster and faster, pleading, cajoling, threatening.

Some of these sessions on the cloakroom couches—or in the deep, soft cloakroom armchairs, better even than the couches for Johnson's purposes, since by sitting down on one armrest and stretching an arm across to the other, he could imprison its occupant more effectively—lasted quite a long time. He had to win, and to win he needed the senator's vote. And he wasn't going to get up until he got it. "I've seen him devote an hour to work on one senator," the clerk says.

Then that vote would be secured. Lyndon Johnson would be up off the couch, standing in the center of the cloakroom, dispatching Humphrey or Molly Malone to hold the floor with a speech ("Don't quit talkin' 'til you see me back in there"), asking Russell or Eastland to exert his influence with one of their conservatives or Humphrey to exert his influence with one of his liberals, going over the tally sheets again, reading—quickly but with great care—the latest text of an amendment, ironing out the last details of the unanimous consent agreement, and then sending Baker on the run to have Floyd Riddick's fastest typist type it up. And then he would have the agreement back, and, holding it in one hand, and shoving open the double doors with the other, Lyndon Johnson would come back out on the floor to announce it—or, if he had not been able to get an agreement, to push the Senate to a vote without it, with, in his hand, the tally sheet that almost invariably showed that the vote was going to be very close.

IF HE HAD THE VOTES, debate—even the limited debate permitted under the unanimous consent agreement—could only hurt, could allow opponents to realize what he was up to, could give Knowland time to get a more accurate count, could give men whose minds he had changed with his relentless persuasion time to change their minds back, to think better of what they had agreed to. He wanted the question called, and called fast; although the unanimous consent agreement allowed a certain number of hours or minutes for debate, he wanted to be able to yield his time back, and have his opponents yield *their* time back.

"Don't talk, we've got the votes. Don't talk, we've got the votes," Bobby Baker would whisper, standing at the corridor door to the cloakroom as the senators came through on the way to the Chamber—which, with a vote imminent, was beginning to fill up. Some senators didn't get the idea and insisted on speaking. "I'd go up to him [Johnson] on the Senate floor and say Senator Lehman would like to have the floor as soon as possible," Julius Edelstein recalls. "He'd say" (and as Edelstein shows Johnson's response, his face twists into a snarl), " 'Well, he can have the goddamned floor!' " Rushing over to Edelstein, Gerry Siegel said: "I know Lehman has to talk for his constituents, but make it short. Make it short! Otherwise, it'll make the Leader mad."

As a supporter of a measure was rising to speak, Johnson would go over to the supporter's desk and growl, "Make it short. I've got the votes for it." The reminders would continue during the senator's statement. Once, Richard Neuberger of Oregon was giving an impassioned statement at a moment Johnson considered propitious for a vote. Johnson whispered to him to stop, but Neuberger didn't. Circling Neuberger's desk—in John Steele's words, "like a coon dog does a treed animal"—Johnson whispered to him "from in back and then to the right side to tell Neuberger to knock it off." Olin Johnston's southern drawl was so slow! "Olin," Johnson whispered urgently, "get the lead out of your ass!" "Lyndon," Johnston said calmly, "you know I always read slow." Says a Senate staffer who was standing nearby, "Then Olin goes back to reading. I thought Lyndon was going to have a fit." Looking on another occasion at a speech that Olin was insisting on reading, Johnson saw to his dismay that it covered quite a few pages. "Two minutes, that's all I can give you," he said. "You've got to hold it to two minutes." Johnston kept refusing. "Olin," Lyndon said, forcing a comradely smile to his face, "why don't you speak for two minutes and tomorrow you can put your whole speech in the *Congressional Record* and you can mail it to all the folks in South Carolina, and they won't know the difference." "Well, I guess that's all right, Lyndon," Johnston said, and read only a small part of the text—"so quickly," an observer said, "that he scarcely could be understood."

The long arcs would be filling up now—senators coming in and walking along them to their desks, and then standing talking quietly with a colleague or sitting listening to the debate on the proposed bill—as if a painter, having finished the background, was putting in the figures. Other senators would have congregated in the well, bantering with each other in the relaxed senatorial way. The Chamber floor would be the familiar, still Senate tableau.

Except that, on that floor, there would be one figure who, now, with the vote coming closer, seemed never to be still.

He was prowling the big Chamber now, ranging restlessly up and down, side to side. He rarely listened to the debate, except occasionally for a moment or two to see if the speaker was saying anything he hadn't anticipated. Rather his eyes would be constantly roaming the Chamber, "seeing how things were going—seeing *if* they were going," as one aide put it.

What was going on in the Republican cloakroom? How could he find out? What could he read in the faces of the senators coming out of that cloakroom? Where were *his* senators: why weren't they all here? Raising his hand over his head, he would beckon Bobby Baker or one of Baker's aides, or, if they didn't see him, snap his fingers loudly to get their attention, and order them to see that the senators were on their way. Were two or three on whom he had counted likely to be absent? He'd hurry across the floor to arrange live pairs. Was something going wrong? Was the chairman of Public Works drunk again, confused and rambling as he tried to manage one of his committee's bills? Striding across the floor to another senator, he would whisper, "You ready to do five or ten minutes on Defense? I want to get Denny off the floor." Then, forcing himself to move slowly so as not to attract attention, he'd walk down the aisle to where Chavez was standing, take his arm—if that wasn't enough, take his lapel and put his other arm around his shoulder—whisper, "Denny, I'd like to talk to you outside for a minute," raise a hand for recognition, tell the presiding officer, "Mr. President, I'd like to suspend discussion, and if it be the will of the Senate, take up the Defense Appropriations bill, and we will bring Public Works back in a few minutes," and then lead Chavez up the aisle and out the door. Did he catch a glimpse, as the doors to the Republican cloakroom swung open, of a GOP senator on whose vote he was counting, talking inside the cloakroom, in a suspiciously cordial manner, to a White House liaison man? Waiting until the senator came out on the floor, he would check to see if the vote was still firm, and if it wasn't he'd be moving quickly to some other senator, to try to replace it.

With the vote all but upon him now, he seemed always to be in motion, and the motion would be faster, almost frenzied. As he talked to senators, his hands never stopped moving, gesturing expressively, chopping the air with that snake-killing gesture, opening a palm to illustrate a point, punching the air with a fist, jabbing a lapel with a finger, patting a senator's shoulder, straightening his tie, grabbing his lapel, hugging him if he agreed to the proposition being made.

If he dropped down into his own front-row center chair, he might sprawl down in it, stretch out both long legs across the aisle, or lean far back, crossing them. But he wouldn't stay in any pose long. "Jiggling, scratching, crossing and uncrossing his legs," leaning back in his chair with a hand up to his face as he whispered to Russell close behind him or to a senator who had approached with information or an inquiry, pulling out a tally sheet, writing something on it, tucking it back in his pocket, "he seemed," in the words of one reporter, "simply unable to sit still for a moment." Abruptly, galvanized by a sudden thought, he would leap out of his seat, "going from slouched to almost frenetic in an instant," as another reporter put it, to rush over to a senator. "You'd see him with the finger right in the face. He'd be over on the Republican side as much as the Democratic. Then he'd be back across the floor, pulling someone else off to the side," a slash of vivid movement through the senatorial still-life.

And if something was going wrong, Lyndon Johnson would be moving even faster, moving so fast that, Neil MacNeil reported, "his baggy-cut, almost zoot suit flies open." Once, when Johnson was away from the floor, a number of senators unexpectedly began proposing one controversial, contradictory, and often confusing amendment after another to a routine Post Office appropriation bill being managed by Olin Johnston. The mere discussion of those amendments would plunge the Senate into the kind of angry debate that, in past years, would have brought it to a halt for endless days, Steele wrote; passage of any of the amendments would result in a certain Eisenhower veto. "The Senate was in a turmoil. The babble on the floor prevented senators from hearing and being heard. There were amendments to amendments; amendments offered and withdrawn; senators arose to protest they couldn't hear the debate, didn't understand what was transpiring."

Then, into this "mixed-up mess" roared Lyndon Johnson. "Quickly sizing up the situation, he began to act. He paced from one side of the Senate Chamber to the other, moving at a loping gait, the coat tails of his gray flannel suit winging out behind. He whispered with Bill Knowland, with Frank Carlson, the Administration's spokesman on postal matters; he conferred with Olin Johnston and Johnston's aide; he talked with Russell Long, Ev Dirksen, Parliamentarian Charlie Watkins, with Dick Russell; he slipped to a phone, one equipped with a baffled mouthpiece, in an alcove just off the Senate rostrum. He snapped his thumb and second finger with the retort of a firecracker to summon a page for water. . . . The Senate Majority Leader was ready to straighten things out.

"It would take some straightening out—seven different maneuvers. . . . Johnson was running the whole show. From his Majority Leader's desk, he hand-signalled the various players in the drama. He peremptorily cut senators off to seize the floor. He barked harsh orders to Jack Kennedy in the presiding officer's chair to put this question, make that ruling. He pleaded with senators to defer speeches, he whispered to aides to summon this or that senator, he snapped his fingers like a whip to fetch more water. He sped to the cloakroom for a conference and back to his desk. He ranged the aisles. . . . A legislative catastrophe [was] averted."

And that was on a non-controversial, relatively minor bill. On a bill on which the vote was going to be close, and the result of genuine political significance, the frenzy of Lyndon Johnson's actions escalated another notch. As the moment approached for the roll call—the call that would determine the actual, irrevocable winning or losing for this man who had to win—Lyndon Johnson's orders grew sharper, more punctuated with fury.

Some of his votes, votes he had counted on, were missing. There was no more "Sure, I understand, I hope he feels better"—*"By God, I got to have his vote!"* he rasped to Hennings' assistant Bernard Fensterwald. *"Get him IN HERE!"* To other senators' aides there was a single sentence, delivered in a low, threatening snarl: "Get your fucking senator *over* here." Once, in the well, he dispatched Baker to the cloakroom to make a call; Bobby, walking away from him, didn't move fast enough. With one long step, Lyndon Johnson caught up to him, grabbed each of Baker's narrow shoulders in a huge hand and shoved him violently up the aisle. Once, Humphrey told a reporter, Johnson, after ordering him to do something and to "get going," was so impatient that he actually kicked him—hard—in the shins to speed him on his way. (The reporter, Robert S. Allen, thought Humphrey must be exaggerating until "he [Humphrey] added, 'Look,' and he pulled up his trouser leg and, sure enough, he had some scars there. He had a couple of scars on his shins where Lyndon had kicked him and said, 'Get going now.' ")

Some of the senators he needed on his side were still planning to vote the other way. On one vote, the recalcitrants included John Pastore. Talking to the little Rhode Islander, Johnson led him into the cloakroom, where they could not be seen from the galleries. Then he took each of Pastore's lapels in a hand, pulled the hands together, and lifted them up so that Pastore was held motionless on tiptoe while Johnson brought his face down to stare into his eyes and deliver the argument that way.

The Leader was hurrying back and forth across the Chamber, prowling the aisles, charging up the stairs to the cloakroom—and then, suddenly, the moment was at hand, the moment for which he had been waiting: the number of votes on the tally sheet in his hand was—at last—the number he needed. He would win—if nothing changed. If the senator in the chair was not a thoroughly loyal Johnson man, he quickly put someone in the chair who was. And, prompting him across the well, he hurried the new presiding officer through his paces. Standing next to his Leader's desk, he would mutter along: "No further amendments. . . . Third reading of the bill. . . . The clerk will call the roll. . . ." There might be interruptions from the floor from opponents. The muttering would become a growl—sometimes audible in the gallery. "Out of order!" Lyndon Johnson would prompt. *"Out of order!"* "Out of order," the senator in the chair would say. "Call the question," Lyndon Johnson would prompt. *"CALL THE QUESTION!"* The question would be called. "Yeas and nays have been ordered. The clerk will call the roll."

And with those last words, the words that signaled the actual vote, the power of Lyndon Johnson as Majority Leader was fully revealed, for during the six years of his leadership, the Senate of the United States presented, during close and crucial votes, a spectacle such as had never been seen before during the century and a half of its existence.

If all his senators were present when the roll call began, and he could see that there were absentees on the other side, he wanted the roll to be called at a fast pace. If he didn't have all his men there—if some stragglers hadn't been found yet—then he wanted the roll call to be slow. And during the years when he was Leader, the roll was called at precisely the pace he desired.

Standing at his front-row center desk, facing the presiding officer and clerk calling the roll, Lyndon Johnson would raise his big right hand, and with a pen or pencil, or simply with a long forefinger, would make those "revving-up circles in the air" that meant, as was said in the Introduction, "hurry up—he had the votes and wanted them recorded" before something changed. When, however, "he didn't have the votes but would get them if only he had a little more time," he would make the downward pushing motion with his open hands that meant "slow down." As senators hurried into the Chamber, many walked down to the well to talk with their colleagues. Standing at the edge of the well, towering over men in it, Lyndon Johnson would raise his long arm over them, making those big circles, like "an orchestra conductor," leading the United States Senate—the Senate that, for so long, had refused to be led.

Sometimes he would indulge in an even more blatant manifestation of his power. Somehow the vote hadn't worked out as he had thought it would; he was a vote or two short of victory. So a vote or two would be changed—right out in the open. Johnson would walk across the floor to a senator who had been in opposition, and whisper to him, and the senator would rise and signal the clerk that he had been incorrectly recorded. "You would see votes changed right in front of your eyes," the Senate aide says. Neil MacNeil, who knew the Senate so well, could hardly believe what he was seeing. "He did it in front of God," MacNeil was to recall. "It didn't happen much, but it happened. He was absolutely brazen about it. He put the arm on guys right on the floor."

Sometimes Johnson would not even bother to walk across the floor. Once he yelled across the well to Frear, who was sitting at his desk: "Change your vote, Allen!" The Senator from Delaware did not immediately respond, so Johnson yelled again, in a shout heard, in the words of one writer, by "more than eighty senators and the galleries": *"Change your vote, Allen!"* Allen changed his vote. Small wonder that Hugh Sidey, remembering years later the "tall man" with "his mind attuned to every sight and sound and parliamentary nuance," who "signaled the roll calls faster or slower," who gave another "signal, and the door would open, and two more guys would run in," would say, "My God—running the world! Power enveloped him."

SOME OF THE TOUCHES that Johnson brought to the role of Leader were merely for dramatic effect. "Often these shows were carefully orchestrated and perhaps even a shade melodramatic," Bobby Baker was to recall. "He [Johnson] was not only a fine actor but a fine director and producer as well. He delighted in striding about the Senate floor, conferring and frowning and giving the impression of great anxiety, while the packed press gallery and the visitors' galleries buzzed and hummed with tensions, even though he knew—and I was one of the few people who knew—that he had three decisive votes hidden in some Capitol nook and would produce them at the most effective moment. The Republicans would snort at losing another cliff-hanger, the newspapers would trumpet a new Johnson miracle, and Lyndon Johnson would go off to a fresh Cutty Sark and soda to laugh and laugh." But, Baker was also to say, "I see nothing wrong" in such "trickeries. . . . Lyndon Johnson knew that the illusion of power was almost as important as real power itself, that, simply, the more powerful you appeared to be, the more powerful you became. It was one of the reasons for his great success."

Some of the more perceptive journalists realized that some of the drama they were reporting was staged drama. "Lyndon Johnson *played* Leader," Sidey says. But he played the part well—played it better, far better, than anyone had ever played it before, played it as if he was made for it, as if he had been born for the role. And however he got the power, he got it. Doris Kearns Goodwin was not the only writer who was to call Lyndon Johnson "the Master of the Senate," because that was what he was.

26

"Zip, Zip"

AND WITH THIS POWER, Lyndon Johnson made the Senate work. Thanks to his intervention in the Standing Committees, his coordination of their schedules and his prodding of their chairmen, bills were emerging from committees faster than in the past. And since they were emerging with most points of contention already resolved, on the floor they were being passed faster than in the past.

The reciprocal trade bill was one example. For decades—after the Second World War as before it—the bill's arrival on the floor had caused the Senate to grind to a halt, sometimes for weeks, as free-trade senators fought protectionists and the protectionists fought among themselves, no fewer than twenty states having products they insisted be protected by tariff, and with the rates of each tariff the subject of separate bargaining.

In 1955, the bargaining had—thanks to Johnson—taken place within the Finance Committee, where the logrolling went far more smoothly than it would have done in public. And with the necessary compromises agreed, he had been able to secure a unanimous consent agreement to limit debate. There was still another hurdle, a high one for previous reciprocal trade bills: there was traditionally a roll call on the measure, since there always seemed to be some senators who demanded one, and protectionist senators privately in favor of a bill often voted against it to avoid having to explain an affirmative vote to their constituents. The hurdle was removed for the 1955 bill. Putting a supporter of the bill in the chair, Johnson armed him with a surprise parliamentary tactic. Instead of calling for the yeas and nays whenever there was a show of a few hands requesting one, the presiding officer responded to the request by invoking Article I, Section 5 of the United States Constitution, which said that yeas and nays should be ordered only "at the desire of one-fifth of those present." And Johnson made sure that there were always enough senators present with instructions not to vote for the roll-call request so that the necessary one-fifth was never achieved. The Reciprocal Trade Act of 1955 passed in three days.

Reciprocal trade was only one example. The Upper Colorado River Reclamation Bill—one of the most vital but controversial measures among westerners—had been brought up in session after session, hotly (and often lengthily) debated, but never passed. In 1955, it, too, passed in three days. The Paris accords, which, as Stewart Alsop wrote, "could have been expected at the very least to have elicited a lot of oratory for the folks at home," were passed in less than two hours of floor debate. Then there were the dozen departmental appropriation bills, those measures that had been stalling Senate machinery for years—decades, in fact. "Traditionally," as Alsop wrote, "the agriculture appropriation bill, touching as it does many sensitive farm pocketbooks, is the subject of loud, long and angry argument." In 1955, "it passed, all but unnoticed, after exactly an hour of debate."

The other appropriation measures were handled with comparable dispatch—even one, the bill covering the Departments of State and Justice, that was being handled by an Appropriations subcommittee whose chairman, Harley Kilgore, was one of the few chairmen who had refused to coordinate, or even discuss, his subcommittee's deliberations with Johnson because he viewed such discussions as an infringement on his independence. Despite Kilgore's secretiveness, Johnson knew exactly what was going on in his subcommittee, and when, near the close of Senate business at the end of one May week, Kilgore suddenly appeared on the floor to announce that his subcommittee had completed its work and had a bill prepared, Johnson was ready. He asked a question to which he already knew the answer: "Was the subcommittee report a unanimous report?" "It was a unanimous report," Kilgore replied. In that case, Johnson said, the bill would be brought up at the earliest possible moment the next week. He had already discussed that schedule with "the distinguished Minority Leader," he said; the distinguished Minority Leader had agreed. As for routine business, in a single day, as *Newsweek* reported, "the Senate passed 90 bills, confirmed an ambassador and a Federal Trade commissioner and then knocked off because it had temporarily run out of business. The elapsed time: four hours and 43 minutes. Washington was jolted to attention." The first session of the Eighty-fourth Congress, Alsop wrote, "is certainly the most efficiently run session in recent memory." In less than six months as Majority Leader, the youngest Majority Leader in its history, Lyndon Johnson had tamed the untamable Senate.

ALTHOUGH THE SENATE was running more efficiently, however, it sometimes seemed to be running in opposite directions. But underlying most of its significant actions was a single principle that determined which legislation would be passed—and which wouldn't. The principle was the ambition of its Leader. As Leader of the majority instead of the minority, Lyndon Johnson's personal interests affected America's interests more directly than ever before, and when they conflicted, his interests came first.

Richard Russell had by now made most of the Southern Caucus understand that the way to make the South part of the United States again, "to really put an end to the Civil War," would be to elect a southerner President, and they understood that their beloved Dick, giving up his own dream, had anointed Lyndon as that southerner. With the unbeatable Eisenhower expected to run again in 1956, victory that year would probably not be possible, but the Democratic nomination might be, and the nominee in 1956 would be a front-runner for the 1960 nomination. And they understood—to those of them slow in grasping the fact, Russell had *made* them understand—that in order for Johnson to attain the nomination he would first have to be perceived as a strong and successful Senate Leader, and that therefore he would have to have a unified party behind him, and they must bend their views to support him and not simply oppose the Leader's every attempt to pass even moderately liberal legislation; that they must, in fact, even allow him at times to, in George Reedy's words, "engage in maneuvers" that would facilitate the passage of legislation with at least a tinge of liberalism, legislation they would never have permitted another Leader to pass.

This understanding had allowed Johnson, again in Reedy's words, to obtain "elbow room from the Southern Democrats" in his attempts to establish at least a modicum of rapport with Senate liberals. "The Southern dons of the Senate, the conservative men with seniority and power . . . regarded him with pride as their boy," Booth Mooney says. "The southerners did not always agree with their Leader, but they wanted him to do well, and when it was necessary, were usually willing to stretch their own convictions to support him." As Johnson advanced toward a more liberal position, his rear and his flank had therefore been protected against the southern attacks that would normally have made that advance impossible. There was even a symbol of that protection; the fact that as Lyndon Johnson sat in the Senate, the desks directly to his rear and at his side were manned by Russell and Walter George, the two most important southerners. Some of the less senior southerners had even made sacrifices (short-term sacrifices for which they had been assured they would be recompensed in the long term): to help him do well, to help him achieve the unity with liberals he needed, they had agreed that young liberal senators be appointed to committee seats into which they themselves would otherwise have moved through seniority; they had allowed the entrance of Humphrey into high party councils (some southerners still couldn't understand how they had been talked into *that*: Harry Byrd said to Johnson one day, "Lyndon, I'll never understand how in the world you got me to liking Hubert Humphrey so much"). And there were more subtle means of assistance: Johnson was no longer placed in the embarrassing position of attending, or declining to attend, meetings of the Southern Caucus; he simply was no longer invited.

On a number of issues, however, "Dick Russell and His Dixieland Band" would alter their position not an inch—and on those issues, Lyndon Johnson marched to their tune.

On the issue that mattered above all others, the southerners were, as Strom Thurmond's aide Harry Dent puts it, "just as sure as ever that in his heart he was on their side"—a confidence that was understandable, since added to his eighteen years of votes on their side and his other actions of support for them in the past were the actions he was taking now, in 1955, as Majority Leader.

Almost the first major policy issue that confronted Johnson upon his assumption of the leadership was the issue that would make possible progress in civil rights: the long-dreamed-of change in Rule 22. The Senate liberals who had fought for the change in the past hoped that the liberal Democrats elected in November, 1954, would provide the reinforcements needed to vote it through at last. "We had [a] chance for a significant step forward," Paul Douglas was to recall. But Johnson crushed the hope, in part, in the opinion of some observers, by making it clear to the newly elected senators that his offer of choice committee seats was contingent upon their support of "the leadership" in the Rule 22 fight (Walter White of the NAACP was to blame the defeat on "shrewd horse-trading over committee memberships"); in part by using Hubert Humphrey to sabotage the liberal caucus from within. After listening to Humphrey argue, with his customary eloquence, that the liberals should "abandon the devil theory of history," stop thinking of Johnson as the devil and give him, now that he was equipped with the new powers of the majority leadership, "a chance to see what he could do with the South," and to fight for civil rights not through "a frontal assault" on the rules but through the regular Senate committees," Douglas went along with Humphrey's pleas to shelve the rules-change motion. He knew almost at once that "we had made a bad mistake," Douglas was to say. "There was no change in Johnson's opposition to civil rights and not the slightest softening in the attitude of the South," which, in fact—emboldened by Johnson's success—"sharply stiffened its opposition." Humphrey's persuasiveness, Douglas was to say with bitterness, may not have resulted in any gains for blacks but it resulted in gains for Humphrey; his "role in this matter sealed his alliance with Johnson." (Douglas was not alone in this opinion. John Steele informed his editors that in the Rule 22 fight, "behind Humphrey stood the off-stage figure of Lyndon Johnson.")

Thwarting a new liberal attempt in 1955 to attain another long-sought objective—statehood for Hawaii—was easy for Johnson, but in May came an assault more threatening to those who believed in separation of the races. The black congressman from New York, Adam Clayton Powell Jr., attached to one of the South's—to one of Richard Russell's—most cherished proposals, the military reserve bill, an amendment to ban racial segregation in reserve units, and the House of Representatives passed it. The bill was before Russell's

Armed Services Committee, and there it stayed, for as much as Russell wanted a reserve system adopted, the threat to separation of the races was too grave; the Senate might pass the bill without the amendment, but the bill would then eventually be returned to the House, which might reinstate the amendment. Elated by the success of the maneuver, liberals were planning to attach a similar amendment to the school construction bill; House conservatives had responded by holding that measure in committee.

Attacking Powell's military reserve amendment publicly, Lyndon Johnson said: "The issue that is now holding up passage of this crucial measure is one that has been settled in a number of different forms by the courts and by the executive agencies. Congress is no longer a meaningful forum for such debate. I sincerely hope that this issue can now be worked out and that we will not imperil the existence of our Nation by raising issues which can have no meaning in terms of results." And Johnson maneuvered privately as well, getting Eisenhower out front on the issue as he had gotten the President out front on the Bricker Amendment. After Johnson urged him to do so, Eisenhower spoke against the practice of attaching anti-segregation amendments to major bills, saying, "If you get an idea of real importance, a substantive subject, and you want to get it enacted, then I believe the Congress and I believe our people should have a right to decide upon that issue by itself, and not be clouding it with amendments that are extraneous." As for the reserve bill amendment, Eisenhower said, "It is entirely erroneous to try to get legislation of this character through by tacking it onto something that is so vital to the security of the United States." Neither of the Powell amendments was enacted into law.

Another aspect of Johnson's strategy—and its coordination with the strategy of the South—had been dramatized in January, at the conclusion of Eisenhower's State of the Union address. As the President stepped down from the dais, Knowland had hurried over to congratulate him, but Johnson had moved faster, and had been the first to reach Eisenhower's side, thereby, as Frank Cormier of the Associated Press put it, winning "the informal Capitol Hill footrace" to congratulate him. During the months since January, the considerations that had motivated Johnson to thus demonstrate his solidarity with the President had only been strengthened. In late spring of 1955, with the economy booming, the Formosa Strait crisis ended. With the world generally at peace, "millions of Americans" had, in Stephen Ambrose's words, "a feeling of near-euphoria," and Eisenhower's promise of peace, progress, and prosperity seemed fulfilled. Johnson was more convinced than ever that opposing Ike would be politically unwise. Proposals were made repeatedly by Democratic senators for investigations of questionable Administration activities such as the Dixon-Yates "giveaway" of hydroelectric power to southern power companies. The proposals were shunted by the Democratic Leader into the Democratic Policy Committee, from which none of them ever emerged.

The Senate's southern barons likewise had strong reasons for not opposing the President, not only because of the similarities in their philosophies but because of something that Lyndon Johnson and the barons never discussed in public. As *The New Republic* was to state:

> It is difficult to document, yet the deans of the Senate, men like Walter George and Harry Byrd and Richard Russell and John McClellan, show a profound disinterest in whether or not a Democrat moves into the White House in 1957. These Southern veterans . . . already have their chairmanships and their committee patronage. The Administration is forced to clear important bills and appointments with them. No Democratic successor to Mr. Eisenhower could be more deferential to their prerogatives. In fact, a Democratic President might even cause a great deal of discomfort by prodding for more progressive and less moderate domestic legislation.

Though these barons were called Democrats, they were unenthusiastic about the leading Democratic presidential contenders—Stevenson, Harriman, and Kefauver, all liberals—and may have preferred another four years with the safely moderate Eisenhower in the White House. By cooperating with the President on such issues as the tariff and foreign aid and by hamstringing investigations that might have embarrassed the Administration, Johnson was acting not only in his own interest but in their interest as well.

The "cooperation" issue was raised publicly in April, in a very dramatic setting. Washington's great annual Democratic gathering, the black-tie Jefferson-Jackson Day Dinner, was usually held in a hotel ballroom, but the guest of honor in 1955 was the man whom the Associated Press called "the beloved 'Mr. Sam' of legions of Democrats." No ballroom in Washington could accommodate the more than thirty-seven hundred Democrats from across the United States, the largest such crowd in history, who were coming to pay tribute to Sam Rayburn, and the dinner had to be moved to Washington's National Guard Armory. Facing the audience above the dais was a gigantic cartoon of Jefferson and Jackson welcoming Rayburn to the Democratic pantheon, and the cartoon was flanked by huge portraits of FDR and of the most famous living Democrat, Harry S Truman.

Following tributes to Rayburn by Eleanor Roosevelt ("My husband counted on him and never found him wanting") and Adlai Stevenson ("He was there when the record was made"), and Rayburn's characteristically humble response ("I accept this honor feeling my inadequacy"), Lyndon Johnson, in his speech, repeated the statement he had made so frequently: that Democrats wanted a "party of moderation" in 1956. But when the seventy-one-year-old Truman spoke, assailing the GOP's "cynicism"—the "most cynical political behavior" since the Harding era—in the familiar Truman rhythms, suddenly the audience, chanting "Give 'em hell, Harry," louder and louder, seemed to remember that the Democratic Party, in leading America out of the Great Depression, and in fighting for social justice, had not been the "party of moderation" at all. And the next morning, in his suite at the Mayflower, the ex-President gave William White an interview in which he made clear that it was not only Republicans who he felt had recently been guilty of "cynical political behavior."

He did not want to criticize the Eisenhower Administration's Formosa policy, Truman said, because "I haven't got a great deal of information on the subject." But, he said, he did want to criticize one aspect of the situation: "that," as White put it, "the Senate had not adequately debated the subject. Had there been such a debate, the former President observed, he would have felt no anxiety at all over the ultimate decision, whatever it might have been." And Truman made clear, with Trumanesque vividness of phrase, whom he blamed for the lack of debate—and for other aspects of recent Democratic policy as well. "I have got tired a long time ago of some mealy-mouthed senators who kiss Ike on both cheeks," he said. "Mr. Truman did not name these senators," White wrote. "The implication seemed inescapable, however, that he was far from satisfied with the restrained partisan activity of the present Democratic leadership of the Senate headed by Lyndon B. Johnson of Texas."

Arrangements had been made earlier for Truman to pay a nostalgic visit to his old Senate desk ("My heart has always been at this desk," he said, adding that his ten years in the Senate had been "the happiest years of my political life"), and to be honored by Senate leaders at a luncheon in the Capitol on Monday. Johnson had no choice but to deliver the Senate's formal welcome, written by Reedy: "This is a better Senate because he was part of it. Welcome back, Harry. The latch string is always out when you pass this way." Then he had to stand next to Truman as reporters asked the former President to confirm the quotes White had used, and he did so, quite firmly. He had to pose beside Truman at the luncheon (from which several southern senators were noticeably absent), and ride beside him on the Senate subway as photographers took pictures. Truman seemed in high spirits; Johnson's smile was noticeably wan.

Truman had told White that he had only one remaining political purpose in life: "to keep" the Democratic Party "over on the liberal side." And his trip to Washington had at least succeeded in reminding some liberals that that was the side the party was supposed to be on. Reporting that "many Democrats were stirred by his [Truman's] fighting speech—partly because they got so little of the same from the party's actual presidential hopefuls," John Steele commented specifically on Johnson's call for a "party of moderation." "Some thought this was a strange Democratic doctrine," he said. And following that April weekend, the attitude of liberal journalists underwent an abrupt and dramatic alteration. "Some Democrats feel the party is compromising with principle," Doris Fleeson wrote in May. Her column of June 3 said: "Southern senators are sensitive to the charge that they are perfectly satisfied to let Eisenhower continue in the White House. The record they make in support of the President proves, however, that they certainly aren't unhappy. And it is under Southern leadership that all investigations of the Administration have faltered and no majority program has been approved." *The New Republic* had come to realize that despite the Senate's new efficiency, there was little political gain in the bills it had passed, and because of the dearth of senatorial investigations of the Administration, "there will be . . . no heavy ammunition for the Democrats' candidate for the White House" in 1956. Columnist Roscoe Drummond began referring to Lyndon Johnson as "malleable." In Drew Pearson's columns he was again being called "Lyin' Down Lyndon."

IF, HOWEVER, Lyndon Johnson's interests always came first with Lyndon Johnson, there were times when those interests coincided with America's interests—with the highest of America's interests, the great liberal cause, the cause of social justice. And when they did, the cause advanced.

In some areas, conservatives and southerners would not give Johnson "elbow room," but in other areas they would. And when Johnson had it, he used it. In June, 1955, in a single week, as the attacks on him by Fleeson and other liberal commentators were continuing to escalate, there arrived a moment in domestic legislation comparable to that which had occurred two years before with foreign legislation: a moment in which Johnson's ultimate ambition did not conflict with, but instead coincided with, the aspirations of the liberals who had been attacking him. And, in that week, he accomplished—suddenly and without warning—gains the liberals had not believed possible.

He did it on two days of that week: Tuesday, June 7, and Wednesday, June 8, 1955.

On that Tuesday, the Senate voted on housing.

The conditions in which America's poor and lower-middle-class families were housed had been a national disgrace for decades, and the situation was growing not better but worse, in part because in 1954 the Republican majorities in Congress had brought to a near standstill even the meagre low-rent public housing programs then in existence. Witnesses before the Senate Banking and Currency Committee, which had jurisdiction over housing, had testified earlier in 1955 that more than ten million American families were living in substandard dwellings, that the number was growing by hundreds of thousands of families each year, and that at the current rate of construction by the private real estate industry, the number was going to grow even faster.

The Eisenhower Administration's 1955 public housing proposal was to fund 70,000 units over two years—a mere 35,000 per year—but Banking and Currency was one of the few Senate committees with a strong liberal bloc, and after hearing Philadelphia's Mayor, Joseph Clark, testify that his city alone had 70,000 substandard units, the committee reported out a bill authorizing the construction of 540,000 units over four years, or 135,000 per year.

The very concept of public housing was anathema to Senate conservatives, who regarded it as pure "socialism." And it provoked particular opposition from southern conservatives, because so many of the families that would be helped by this particular form of socialism would be black. Liberal housing bills had been reported to the floor before and had been killed or drastically scaled back there, and conservatives were confident that this one would be scaled back, too. The Indiana Neanderthal, Homer Capehart, had introduced an amendment reducing the number of units to the Administration's original 35,000-per-year figure, and the amendment's passage, George Reedy recalls, "was taken for granted." An extremely careful head count by the real estate lobby, which, as Sam Shaffer put it, "exercises genuine power in virtually every congressional district," had concluded that it would pass by a margin of 51 to 37. Capehart's and Knowland's counts were approximately the same, although, trying to be cautious, they were predicting victory by only eight votes.

Johnson reinforced the prevailing feeling. When reporters asked him about the eight-vote prediction, he said, with an air of dejection, that that was about right; his own count, he said, showed that the margin would be seven. Liberals, as Evans and Novak would recall, "had no hope at all"; Lehman and Douglas "were resigned to fighting" yet another "lonely, futile battle for public housing." And the liberals knew who was to blame. That very weekend, the ADA had again assailed Johnson for "affably acquiescing to the Republican assault upon liberalism" and thereby "betraying the Democratic party's traditional claim to be the party of the people." The Majority Leader, the ADA said, "has consistently used the pretext of 'party unity' to avoid action on liberal legislation."

But Johnson's pessimism was only a mask—behind which he was preparing a surprise. His opponents' head counts had as a matter of course included all the Senate's twenty-two southerners with the exception of public housing advocates Sparkman, Hill, and Ellender (Sparkman was, in fact, the author of the 540,000-unit bill), and by traditional Senate standards that count would have been accurate. But in 1955 there was a new, non-traditional element: the southerners' desire to help Johnson look liberal if they could do so without damage to their basic principles or to their popularity with their conservative political constituency. And at the last moment—over the long Memorial Day weekend before the Tuesday vote—Johnson had thought of a way in which they could vote against the Capehart Amendment without such damage.

It was true, he told the southerners, that the amendment cut back on public housing. But, he said, it nonetheless still authorized those 35,000 units per year. A vote for the amendment might be hard to explain to their constituents; it could make them vulnerable to some rabble-rouser back home who would charge them with voting for public housing; trying to explain that it was a reduced bill, he said, would be like saying, "My daughter is only a little bit pregnant." Why vote for public housing at all? Johnson asked them. It wasn't necessary to do so. All they had to do was vote against the Capehart Amendment, and then vote against the overall bill—that way, he pointed out to the southerners, they could assure their constituents that they had voted against *all* provisions for public housing.

"ONE OF THE ADVANTAGES of dealing with the Southern Bloc in those days was that its members knew how to reach complete and binding agreement without any word of their intentions leaking to the outside," George Reedy was to recall. No one—including Homer Capehart or William Knowland—had the slightest inkling of what was in store. That very Tuesday morning, *Time*'s John Steele had bumped into the Indianan in a corridor outside the Senate Chamber, and had asked if the eight-vote margin was still firm. It sure was, Capehart said. At that moment, Lyndon Johnson walked by. "Lyndon," Capehart said loudly, with his customary gift for the elegant phrase, "Lyndon, this time I'm going to rub your nose in shit." Johnson's reply, delivered in a rueful tone, was, "Okay, I guess you've got me."

The debate, which began at about one o'clock that afternoon, was enlivened by a touch of drama. There was no more ardent supporter of public housing, of course, than the onetime pioneering mayor of Minneapolis, but months earlier Hubert Humphrey had scheduled an important speech in Minnesota for Monday evening, and the earliest he could return to Washington was via a seven-thirty Tuesday morning plane scheduled to arrive in the capital at about two o'clock. Johnson had promised him to delay the vote until that time, and had obtained Knowland and Capehart's agreement on the grounds of collegial courtesy. But now Johnson's staff, checking with National Airport, was told that the flight, delayed by inclement weather in the Midwest, was running more than an hour behind schedule.

Otherwise, the debate proceeded along the expected lines. After Sparkman had introduced and explained the Banking Committee's bill, Paul Douglas, who had been fighting for public housing for so many years, stated his position forcefully. "Anyone who walks into any city of any size in this country, away from the central business district, will find in nearly every case a slum—streets without trees, houses that are many years old and in disrepair, and children growing up in circumstances that are very difficult." Some of those children, Douglas said, grow up into fine men. "All credit to men like that and all credit to families like that." But, he said, "Most children growing up under those conditions swim against the tide." Over and over again, since almost "my maiden speech in the Senate," "I showed that the death rate in the slums was very much above the average of the community; that the sickness rate, particularly from tuberculosis and other diseases, was very much greater than the average for the whole community. I showed that the fire rate was high, that the crime rate was high, and that the juvenile delinquency rate was high.

"After all," Paul Douglas said, looking around at the few senators who were on the floor, "juvenile delinquency is just a fancy name for kids getting into trouble."

And, he said, "the slums are expanding. . . . The cities need help. . . . The people for whom we are speaking on the floor of the Senate this afternoon are the low-income people. They are inarticulate. It is difficult for them to voice their needs. We provide aid and assistance to virtually every other group. . . . We provide assistance to private builders, real-estate groups . . . subsidies galore to those who do not need them, but none, or little to those who most need assistance.

"Mr. President, this is the noblest country on earth, but we have two great blots upon us: One is our treatment of the Negro and the other is the slums in our cities. . . . Mr. President, we all want a nobler country, a better country. One of the things we must do is cut out the cancer of the slums. . . . So I hope, Mr. President, that the Senate will reject the amendment of the Senator from Indiana."

By about four o'clock, all the scheduled speeches had been delivered, Humphrey had still not appeared, and Capehart and Knowland were insisting on an immediate vote. Afraid to leave the floor lest a vote be called, Johnson prowled restlessly around the Chamber, glancing at his watch, throwing his troops into the breach—Sparkman rose to provide a lengthy overview of the whole history of public housing—embarking on a series of maneuvers: quorum calls accompanied by the palms-down motion to direct clerks to read the names slowly; a reversal of his previous refusal to allow Prescott Bush to introduce a last-minute amendment that would assist a local Connecticut housing authority (since discussing the amendment would take time). But Capehart couldn't be stalled much longer. Walking back to the cloakroom door, Johnson shouted to a telephone clerk to get National Airport—not some airline clerk at National Airport but an air traffic controller in the airport's control tower—on the phone. When the telephone clerk had done so, Johnson, saying, "Mr. President, I must leave the Chamber for a few minutes," rushed into the cloakroom and grabbed the phone. "Damn it, I've got a senator up there," Johnson shouted to the controller. "He's two hours overdue and I want him down quick. He's got to vote. You better be awful sure he's not stacked up there." The controller said that Humphrey's plane was indeed stacked up, in a holding pattern over Pittsburgh; a lot of planes were stacked up in the pattern, the controller said. Johnson stopped shouting. His voice grew quiet and threatening. "Well, you better be goddamned sure none of those planes comes in before his comes in," he said. After checking to make sure that a Capitol police car was waiting at the airport to rush Humphrey to the Chamber, he returned to the floor, where the debate was droning languidly on. At 5:13 p.m., Humphrey appeared on the floor. A quorum call was in progress; Johnson twirled his index finger, and the names came out faster and faster, and after the call was completed, the vote on the Capehart Amendment began.

Capehart was sitting complacently at a front-row desk, without a clue to what was about to happen, until the clerk reached the name of Senator Price Daniel of Texas, a staunch opponent of public housing whose vote, Capehart was sure, would be in favor of his amendment.

"Senator Daniel," the clerk called.

"No," Senator Daniel replied.

"Capehart's head jerked around so rapidly I was afraid his neck was going to snap," George Reedy recalls, and what he saw was another shock. The last time Capehart had looked around, most of the Democratic desks had been empty. They weren't empty now. Sitting at them were the southerners who he had been certain would support his amendment. And the shock was intensified by their votes, as Capehart's face showed. "For once it was the literal truth to say that a man's jaw dropped as southerner after southerner voted against him," Reedy recalls. Not only Daniel but Ellender, Ervin, Fulbright, George, Gore, Johnston, Kefauver, Kerr Scott, Sparkman, and Stennis (and, of course, Lyndon Johnson himself) voted "No." Russell and Eastland, of whose votes Capehart had also been confident, abstained. (Had Johnson needed their votes to defeat the amendment, they would have voted "No.") Smathers, Long, and McClellan had already been lost to Capehart through pairs. Capehart had expected to get eighteen or nineteen votes from the Southern Bloc. He got five. His amendment was defeated, 44 votes to 38.

"As the vote was announced, ponderous Homer Capehart, who had spent the day predicting his own victory by eight votes, was a slumped-down hulk, a pale-faced man in a rumpled suit at his Senate desk," John Steele was to report. "Bill Knowland, his face a fiery red, stared stunned at the telltale tally sheet in front of him."

Then came the vote on the overall housing bill. Many of the southerners voted against that measure, also, but while their votes on the amendment had been decisive, on the bill itself their opposition had no significance, so over-whelmingly was the rest of the Senate in favor of the measure. It passed 60 to 25. "As soon as the vote was announced," Reedy recalls, "the Southern Democrats . . . hastened to the Senate recording facilities where they had them-selves plugged in to radio stations all over their home states. There they explained to their constituents that they voted against the Capehart Amendment because it still represented socialism—35,000 units [per year] of it."

Liberal senators remained on the Senate floor, because they had some-thing they wanted to say there. Hubert Humphrey thanked "both sides of the aisle" for "making it possible for me to vote in favor of a progressive and decent housing bill," but said that "most particularly I desire to express pro-found thanks to the distinguished Majority Leader, my friend, the senior Sena-tor from Texas."

"The Senator from Texas," Humphrey said, "is a genius in the art of the legislative process." And, Humphrey said, his genius was being used "in behalf of an effective Democratic Party liberal program." "I know," he said, "that the purpose of the Senator from Texas is to direct Congress so that its legislative behavior is a humanitarian one, consistent with the basic tenets of the New Deal and the Fair Deal."

Fulsome praise of Johnson from Humphrey had become routine in the Senate, so that the words of the next speaker were more meaningful. For the next speaker was Paul Douglas, Douglas who so distrusted Johnson, Douglas who believed that Johnson's motives were not at all liberal, Douglas who had been denied his rightful committee assignments by Johnson. "I am frank to say I did not think it would be possible to defeat the Capehart Amendment," Paul Douglas said. "I do not know the precise methods by which the Capehart Amendment was defeated, but it was due to the extraordinary political virtuosity of the leader of the Democratic party in the Senate, and I wish to thank and congratulate him."

And more meaningful still was the scene in G-14 an hour or so later, where Johnson was holding court. Among those present were the regulars at such celebrations: Humphrey, Bobby Baker, several members of the Southern Bloc, two or three chosen journalists. But also present was a senator who had not been invited to G-14 since Johnson had evicted him from it.

Paul Douglas had not wanted to accept Johnson's invitation, but he felt he *had* to accept it. He had been fighting for so long for decent apartments to help "the low-income people, the inarticulate people"—to help them "swim against the tide"—fighting without success. Now at one stroke more than half a million apartments had been provided, and, being Paul Douglas, he had to give to the man responsible what he knew the man wanted.

While Johnson was holding forth, with Baker and Humphrey and the others laughing, loudly, at his jokes, Paul Douglas kept his distance, standing just inside the door. But when Johnson, gloating over the details of his triumph, looked over at Douglas and said, "Well, Paul, you got what you wanted, didn't you?" Douglas walked over to Johnson's desk so that he was standing directly in front of him, "grave and dignified," as Evans and Novak wrote, and said, "I didn't think you could do it, and I will never know *how* you did it, but you did it, and I'm grateful."

THE NEXT DAY, Wednesday, June 8, the issue was the minimum wage, which hadn't been increased in six years—it was still the same seventy-five cents per hour it had been in 1949—and neither had the coverage, which liberals had been trying to extend to low-paid employees in the retail and service industries.

The Eisenhower Administration had proposed a 20 percent increase to ninety cents per hour, but had declined to broaden coverage. Conservative senators like Spessard Holland opposed even that modest increase. Since the Labor Committee subcommittee handling the matter was chaired by Paul

Douglas, it was expected that the bill that would be reported out would both broaden coverage and raise the minimum to $1.25. If it did, the bill would therefore contain two provisions that conservatives would not accept, and the bill would therefore not pass and there would be no improvement in the financial situation of low-paid Americans.

Lyndon Johnson didn't wait until the bill reached the floor, or even until it reached the full Labor Committee. He began working instead on the subcommittee, where he had only seven senators to persuade, and he convinced them to report out a moderate bill calling for a one-dollar minimum wage and no broadening of coverage.

With liberals determined to hold out for $1.25 and broader coverage and many conservatives opposed even to the one-dollar figure (one conservative, Republican H. Alexander Smith of New Jersey, was preparing an amendment that would raise it only to the ninety cents the Administration wanted) there were enough liberals and conservatives opposed to the bill so that it appeared that the 1955 minimum wage scenario would follow the scenario of previous years, and that at the end of the day, no bill would be passed.

The scenario was to be rewritten in 1955, however, thanks to those eyes that "missed nothing" on the floor.

That Wednesday, trying to avoid a floor fight that would not only split the Democrats but dramatize the split to the world, Lyndon Johnson had been working for a compromise—passage of Smith's proposed ninety-cent amendment and of the rest of the Labor Committee bill, with its *status quo* coverage—and had been trying to get enough votes for this strategy by playing on the worst fears of both sides, telling liberals that he had counted votes and if they didn't settle for ninety cents, there would be no increase at all, telling conservatives that he had counted votes and if they didn't settle for ninety cents, they might find the minimum wage increased to $1.25. "The cloakroom was just jammed. . . . We knew what he was telling both sides, but there was just enough credibility in it—he was a master," says one Senate aide. And he had apparently succeeded. The Smith Amendment, and the rest of the Labor Committee bill, was going to pass.

And then, all at once, Lyndon Johnson, standing next to his desk as he managed the bill under the unanimous consent agreement he had negotiated, noticed something. Under that agreement, two hours had been allocated to discussion of the Smith Amendment. The Republican arguments in favor of it had been completed, but the Democratic hour was just beginning. Not expecting a vote for an hour, senators had begun wandering on and off the floor. All at once, although there were still a substantial number of senators on the floor, that number did not include most of the liberals who opposed the Labor subcommittee bill—or most of the conservatives who opposed the bill. By coincidence, at that moment the bill's strongest opponents all happened to be gone at the same time, leaving on the floor mostly moderates who were willing to settle for an unamended bill—no broadening of coverage but an increase to one dollar in the wage—in the form the Labor Committee had reported.

"I think we'll pass that minimum wage bill now," he told Hubert Humphrey, with whom he had been talking.

It happened very quickly.

"Mr. President," Johnson said. The presiding officer recognized him. "I yield myself such time as I may require," Johnson said, speaking fast. "The committee considered this question long and thoroughly. I am hopeful that we shall not start amending the bill. I yield back the remainder of my time, and ask for a vote."

"All time on the amendment has been used or yielded back," the presiding officer said, and called for a vote. It was a voice vote, and the amendment was defeated. Suddenly, the pending matter was the unamended bill itself. "The bill having been read the third time, the question is, Shall it pass?" the presiding officer said. No Republicans were waiting to speak, and Knowland yielded back his remaining time. "Mr. President," Johnson said, "I yield back the remainder of my time." A voice vote was taken, and the chair announced that the bill was passed.

"Zip, zip," Humphrey was to recall. "He called it up, and it passed just like that—voice vote—zip." Lister Hill, the Labor Committee Chairman, was in the cloakroom at the time, and did not even know what was happening. Herbert Lehman happened to wander onto the floor as the clerk was announcing that the bill had passed. "What's the vote on?" he asked. Told that it had been on the minimum wage bill, Lehman was "speechless." Spessard Holland wasn't. "Boy, oh, boy, Spessard Holland came charging out of the Senate dining room, and he wanted to know what had happened here," Humphrey would recall. "Oh, he was just jumping, screaming, hollering and pounding the desk. Johnson said, 'Well, Spessard, I had a little vote. If you fellows aren't on the job around here, I've got legislation to pass.' He just slipped it right on through there. Zip! Oh boy, they were furious with him."

While both sides were furious, however, the fury of the liberal side was tempered by the realization that not only had an increase in the minimum wage finally been achieved, the increase to a dollar was higher than the ninety-cent increase that the Administration had proposed. As Reedy was to say, "Obviously we were proceeding on the 'half a loaf' theory. But it seems to me that the scoffers must be men and women who have never been hungry."

Among those who agreed was old Matthew Neely, whose state of West Virginia was home to tens of thousands of coal miners who had just had their wages increased by a third. Rising stiffly at his desk, Neely said, "This has been a senatorial red-letter day for labor. With a minimum of debate, a maximum of efficiency and a majestic measure of humanity, we have [increased] the minimum wage from 75 cents to a dollar an hour. This action will cause rejoicing in thousands of American homes."

"Some of us had hoped the amount would be somewhat larger," Hubert Humphrey said. "But surely, by this very decisive action in the Senate, we have raised the economic levels of vast numbers of persons." And among those who agreed was Paul Douglas. Passage of the minimum wage bill had confirmed the feelings about Lyndon Johnson that Douglas had expressed the previous day after the passage of the housing bill. "I was against him for Leader, but I think I was wrong," he told his administrative assistant, Frank McCulloch. "I think now he's the best man for the job."

The last time a minimum wage bill had been before the Senate, Lyndon Johnson had voted against increasing it. Now he had fought for an increase in the wage—and the wage had been increased. Whatever the reason for his change on that issue, he *had* changed—and had made the Senate change with him. Whether or not Lyndon Johnson talked about "principled things," or believed in "principled things"—and in both the public housing and minimum wage fights he had all but ignored the issues and concentrated on maneuvers— he had won principled things, for hundreds of thousands of Americans who needed those things. The slickness of Johnson's maneuver had senators laughing among themselves as they walked out of the Chamber, but the liberals had much more reason to laugh. Lyndon Johnson had not only made the Senate work, he had, in at least two areas of social welfare legislation, made it work on behalf of that legislation. For so many decades—generations—the Senate had stood against such legislation like a dam. The dam was being breached now.

"THE TALK OF POLITICAL WASHINGTON today is the way Lyndon Johnson runs the Senate," Leslie Carpenter wrote in his column on June 12, and the talk, and the print, now ranged all across the political spectrum. Conservative Gould Lincoln's "The Political Mill" ground for him in the *Washington Star*. Under the headline "LYNDON MOVES MOUNTAINS," Lincoln wrote that "The Senate, which so often has been the stumbling block over which legislation has fallen by the wayside, has set a pace rarely equaled—All this hasn't just happened. There's a tall Texan in the saddle. . . ." The *Wall Street Journal* ordered up a long article on "the Texas-sized Texan" who "RUNS THE SMOOTHEST DEMOCRATIC SHOW IN YEARS." Johnson had been enjoying praise from conservatives all year, but now, following the passage of the housing and minimum wage bills, liberals joined them on the Johnson bandwagon. "On several occasions in the past this newspaper has been critical of Senator Johnson's leadership," the *Washington Post* editorialized. "We are happy to say that in this session of Congress, he has exhibited a remarkable amount of finesse, understanding and restraint [and] has served the national interest." Declaring that Johnson had "snatched victory from defeat" with "brilliant political technique," Doris Fleeson added: "Admiring spectators suggested that all that remains is for him to do his next triumphs to music." Drew Pearson praised "the deftness of [his] lead-

"The Frantic Gentleman from Texas," *Saturday Evening Post,* May 19, 1951

The Monday Meeting: President Harry Truman poses at the White House with his congressional leaders. Seated: Senate Majority Leader Ernest McFarland, Truman, and House Majority Leader John W. McCormack. Standing: Senate Whip Lyndon Johnson and House Whip Percy Priest, January, 1951.

Leland Olds, September, 1949

The cover Johnson wanted

With the Republican leaders. *Above:* Robert Taft of Ohio. *Below:* William Knowland of California

President Dwight D. Eisenhower with Johnson and Senate and
House leaders, on the White House steps, 1955

In the middle: Johnson with Hubert H. Humphrey and Richard B. Russell

WORKING
THE PHONES

Bobby Baker

Theodore Francis Green

Allen Ellender

Leverett Saltonstall

Scott Lucas

THE JOHNSON
TREATMENT

Sam Ervin
(seated, Alan Bible
and Herman Talmadge)

Johnson campaigning in 1954 with George Reedy and Dorothy Nichols

Democratic National Convention, August, 1956: Estes Kefauver, Truman, Adlai Stevenson, and Johnson

Questioning a
witness at a
subcommittee
hearing

Strolling the halls after the 1958 State of
the Union Address, with William Knowland;
ahead of them are Vice President Richard
Nixon and Senator Carl Hayden.

Conferring with Bobby Baker

Lunching with the Democratic Policy Committee

The Southern Caucus meets in Richard Russell's office to discuss strategy for the civil rights bill, July 26, 1957. From left foreground: James Eastland, Strom Thurmond, John Sparkman, Sam Ervin, Kerr Scott, Allen Ellender, Russell, Herman Talmadge, John Stennis, Olin Johnston, Spessard Holland, Russell Long, Lister Hill, Harry Byrd, and Willis Robertson (back to camera).

Frank Church, Joseph O'Mahoney, Johnson, Estes Kefauver, and Richard Russell, after the passage of the jury trial amendment, August 1, 1957

Happiness: on August 27, 1957, Johnson's forty-ninth birthday and the day the House passed the Senate's civil rights bill, Johnson hugs Angel Macios, whose Monterrey, Mexico, team had won the Little League Baseball world championship.

On August 29, 1957, still Majority Leader because of William Proxmire's election, Johnson emphasizes a point after Proxmire was sworn in. Left to right: John Kennedy, George Smathers, Hubert Humphrey, Proxmire, and Johnson.

Dedication of Henry Clay's portrait in the Senate Reception Room: Senators Hayden, Kennedy, and Johnson, March, 1959

President-elect John Kennedy bids good-bye to his dinner guests, Vice President–elect Johnson and family, November 27, 1960.

ership." A long *Newsweek* article on June 27 called him "THE TEXAN WHO IS JOLTING WASHINGTON."

As the Senate prepared to recess for the long Fourth of July weekend, moreover, the lionization by the press was about to take a new turn—the turn Lyndon Johnson had been waiting for.

The South had begun to throw out its skirmishers for a Johnson presidential candidacy in 1956. The lack of enthusiasm south of the Mason-Dixon Line for a second campaign by Adlai Stevenson was more than equaled by the South's distaste for the men northern liberals were mentioning if Stevenson were not to be the candidate: the New Yorker Harriman or the apostate Kefauver. The man the South wanted was the man the South always wanted, of course, but now Richard Russell withdrew from consideration in terms so unequivocal that they would have been called "Shermanesque" had not that adjective been particularly inappropriate, and the conservative columnist Bascom Timmons wrote that "Johnson will inherit much of the support which was given Senator Russell last time." Immediately after Russell's withdrawal, a chorus of such support began to issue from the southern citadel on Capitol Hill. Taking the Senate floor on June 30 with the *Newsweek* article in his hand, Harry Byrd himself read into the record the magazine's prediction that Lyndon Johnson would be President one day.

And over the Fourth of July weekend, the press was going to join in the chorus, as Johnson knew. George Smathers had given him an advance copy of a front-page editorial scheduled to appear in Florida's *Orlando Sentinel* on Saturday, July 2, an editorial that would say that "only the nomination of Lyndon Johnson" could "put solidarity back in the once solid South" and save the Democratic Party from another defeat, that only his nomination "can extirpate and expiate the shameful and disgraceful insults heaped upon the South at the last convention. . . . He is the one man who . . . can win back such states as Florida, Tennessee and Texas. . . . The Stevenson-Kefauver-Harriman liberals are through. They bear the stamp and stigma of the leftwingers and big city political machines." Johnson had also seen the advance text of a Liz Carpenter article that was going to appear on July 3. "This super-sensitive political town began speculating this week" about "the first rumblings of a Johnson presidential bandwagon," the article said. *The New Republic*'s July 4 issue would carry what would be described as an "exuberant panegyric" of Johnson by Senator Richard Neuberger. And, most significantly, Robert Albright's "Gallery Glimpses" column, scheduled to appear in Sunday's *Washington Post* (which would, as Evans and Novak put it, "be on every Sunday breakfast table in the capital"), contained the words that Johnson so much wanted to read: "Lyndon Johnson last week emerged as something more than a highly skilled legislative technician. Unless bystanders missed their guess, he was riding a presidential boom." Having obtained an advance look at the Albright column, Johnson was telling colleagues to be sure to read it Sunday.

. . .

BUT LYNDON JOHNSON HIMSELF was not to read those articles on Sunday. On Sunday, July 3, 1955, he lay, as his father had once lain, under an oxygen tent in a hospital, having heard a doctor say to him what a doctor had said to his father: the words he had always dreaded hearing.

27

"Go Ahead with the Blue"

AS THE PACE OF THE 1955 session had accelerated and, with the increased press and public focus on Lyndon Johnson's role as Leader, the stakes had grown larger (and, with each success, the expectations for further successes— and the danger of resultant disappointment and criticism—had become greater), the frantic quality to Johnson's efforts had intensified. His days grew longer. His alarm was set for 7:30 a.m., but he was almost always awake when it went off; it wasn't an alarm that was jerking Lyndon Johnson out of sleep. Often the long black limousine would be pulling away from Thirtieth Place by eight o'clock, with Johnson in the back seat dictating to Mary Rather and leafing through the morning newspapers at the same time. And no matter how early he arrived in 231, the morning was never long enough for all the private meetings that senators had requested, for all the telephone calls that had to be made or answered. Every time Walter Jenkins appeared in the doorway of the inner office, more pages of the yellow legal pad he held in his hand would be filled with urgent requests for a moment of the Leader's time. There were committee meetings at which he had to put in appearances. Afternoons were spent in the unremitting tension of the Chamber and the cloakroom, every minute seemingly filled with a task that couldn't be postponed. Lunch would often be a hamburger, placed on his office desk by Mary or Ashton as he was talking to someone in person or on the telephone. He would gobble a bite or two, put it down, resume talking—sometime later, cold now, the rest of the hamburger might be eaten, or it might not. Or Jenkins would bring a hamburger to the cloakroom and hand it to him, and as he talked Johnson would absentmindedly put it down on the little desk along the wall. An hour or two later, the Leader's hamburger would still be sitting there. One day, Johnson ordered his staff to set aside an hour for a late lunch at the conference table in his private office with Arthur Krock. The *Times* columnist was very important to him, but as he was leaving the Senate floor, a matter unexpectedly arose that required him to stay to resolve it, and he arrived a half hour late. He had instructed Jenkins that he was not to be interrupted except for calls that simply could not wait. During the lunch, there were eight such calls, three of them on matters sufficiently complicated so that, as Krock put it, "it was essential to talk at length." Johnson would return to the table, resume talking to Krock. Suddenly, he would remember something he had forgotten to say—some instruction he had forgotten to give, some instruction he had given that might be misunderstood without further explanation. In the middle of a sentence, or a bite, he would jump up, grab the phone, make sure everything was clear, every base covered. And then Jenkins was buzzing in to say that the important delegation he had agreed to see had already been waiting in the outer office for some time, and the lunch had to be ended, half the meal uneaten.

Trying to cram everything in, he would run from place to place. "More than once I saw him literally run the few steps from a doorway in the Senate Office Building to his car waiting at the curb," Ashton Gonella would recall. As he was managing a Senate debate, the car would be waiting outside in the portico beneath the Senate steps, and his driver, Norman Edwards, would often have the motor running, for there was no time: "for a 3:30 plane, he left at 3:30," with Ashton or Mary Margaret Wiley or Jenkins on the phone to the airport to ask them to hold the flight until he got there—"Senator Johnson is on his way."

When the Senate recessed, at 6 p.m. or later, it was across the Capitol—often at a dogtrot—to the Board of Education, and then back to G-14, to put on the day's events the spin he wanted for the voracious journalists waiting there. And before he went home, there would be the next day's session to arrange. "It has become almost a commonplace for friends to receive telephone calls from him as late as ten o'clock at night and to find that he was still at his Capitol Office," Robert Albright was to write. One evening in June, he didn't arrive home until after midnight. So ashen was he with fatigue that Lady Bird took one look at him, told him to get into bed, and brought dinner to him on a tray. And the nights were not for sleeping; in Walter Jenkins' recollection, there was hardly one now during which his telephone did not ring at least once. And in other houses in quiet Washington neighborhoods, too, in the homes of senators as well as staffers, a phone would ring in the early-morning darkness and a man, jolted out of sleep, would reach groggily for the phone, to hear the Leader's voice on the line.

The antidotes with which he tried to relieve the tension he took with a frenzied compulsiveness. His secretaries were still mixing his drinks weak, but, coming back to G-14 after the Senate recessed for the day, sinking into the big chair and having a glass placed in his hand, he would throw back his head, empty the glass in a single gulp, immediately hold it out and rattle the ice cubes for another Cutty Sark and soda, and another and another. More and more, the man who wanted never to be "out of control" because of drinking was out of control. Nicotine was, as always, the antidote he relied on most. His fingers were stained yellow with it; no matter how often Ashton and Mary Margaret emptied the ashtrays in his office, they were soon filled again; there was a feverish impatience in the way in which, in the middle of a tense conversation, he would reach for the open pack on his desk, pull out a cigarette, and fumble to light it; sometimes, sitting in one of the soft armchairs in the cloakroom, he would light a fresh cigarette and bend low over it, inhaling deeply as he took the first, long drag. Smoking was not allowed in the Senate Chamber: if Johnson had to be present, but didn't have to be at his desk, he would stand in the rear of the Chamber, just in front of the cloakroom doors, with his hand cupped around a hidden cigarette.

He was too wound up to stop talking, and, at dinner parties at which the drinks were not mixed weak, all inhibition was gone. Russell Baker was to describe him at one party—four or five tables, guests of the Dean Acheson and Abe Fortas caliber—in the garden of William White's home, "chain-smoking one cigarette on top of another and pouring down Scotch whiskey like a man who had a date with a firing squad. During the drinking hour before dinner, I watched him taking in rivers of smoke and whiskey and waving his hands and weaving his long, skinny torso this way and that, all the while talking nonstop to a group of four or five who seemed enthralled by the performance."

Baker, who had recently returned from a stint with the *Baltimore Sun*'s London bureau, was seated next to Johnson at dinner. "As food arrived, he stubbed out a cigarette, lit another, finished his Scotch, called for another, and asked how the House of Commons compared" with the Senate. When Baker replied that he had been "surprised" at the lack of "debates in the Senate," Johnson, who "had taken only two or three mouthfuls of food . . . shoved his plate aside, stubbed out his cigarette in the food, lit another smoke, drained his whiskey, and called for another." He gave Baker a lecture. "Speechmaking didn't count for anything when it came to passing bills, he said. What mattered was who had the votes. . . . 'You want to hear a speech? I can get somebody to make any kind of speech you want to hear. What kind of speech do you want? . . . You want to hear a great speech about suffering humanity? I've got Hubert Humphrey back in the cloakroom. I've got Herbert Lehman. I've got Paul Douglas. . . . You want to hear about government waste? I can give you Harry Byrd. . . .' " And all the time Lyndon Johnson was talking, Baker was to say, he never stopped smoking and drinking, ignoring the rest of his dinner, waving away dessert, stubbing out cigarette after cigarette in his food, motioning for another drink again and again. "I had seen people smoke and drink dinner before," Baker was to say, but Lyndon Johnson "did it like a man trying to kill himself."

When he ate at home, Johnson's dinners were usually the heavy southern staples he preferred, and he insisted that the portions be big—huge heaps of black-eyed peas and tapioca pudding—and he shoveled the food into his mouth, head bent low over his plate, so greedily that even the adoring Bobby Baker said he ate "like a starving dog." While he may have been "skinny" at White's dinner party, during the 1955 session his weight rose with almost incredible rapidity—from the 185 pounds it had been when he returned from his annual checkup at the Mayo Clinic in February to 195, to 200, to 210, 220, 225.

EVERY PREVIOUS CRISIS in Lyndon Johnson's career had been accompanied by a crisis in his health—and in every crisis he had refused to allow the illness to interfere, had refused so successfully that colleagues and friends and assistants had scarcely believed in the illnesses, had felt he must be exaggerating them, since if they were genuine, how could he possibly keep working so hard, keep driving himself so mercilessly: how could a man have such energy if there was something seriously wrong with him?

For weeks during his first, desperate campaign as an unknown candidate for Congress in 1937, he had complained of severe stomach cramps, often doubling over in pain. He couldn't eat; every time he tried, he gagged or vomited. But he refused to cancel a single speech, drove every day for hours over bumpy Hill Country roads—had kept campaigning at the pace that made tough Ed Clark say, "I never thought it was *possible* for anyone to work that hard"—and his aides had stopped taking the complaints seriously. And then, during a speech two days before the election, he could no longer, even by holding on to a railing in front of him, stay on his feet, and he consented at last to be taken to a hospital, where doctors, rushing him to an operating table, found his appendix on the point of rupturing.

During his second desperate campaign—the "last chance," "all or nothing" gamble he had taken against the seemingly invincible Coke Stevenson in 1948—the depth of Lyndon Johnson's need to succeed, and of his determination to do so, had once again been illuminated by the way he dealt with illness. He began that campaign suffering from an infected kidney stone. Not only did it produce a 104-degree fever and make it impossible for him to eat, forcing him to vomit over and over until finally he could only retch because there was nothing left in his stomach, but it also caused pain—gripping, radiating cramps in the back, groin, and testicles—that physicians describe as "agonizing" and "unbearable," classifying it as one of the most intense pains a human being can suffer. One of his doctors would say that he "didn't know how in the world a man could keep functioning in the pain that he was in." But Lyndon Johnson, bearing the unbearable, not only kept functioning, he kept campaigning, day after day driving hundreds of miles between Texas towns and cities, walking the streets for hours shaking hands, making speech after speech, and although, while lying on the back seat of his car, racked with fever and chills, he would gasp in agony, and in bathrooms he would double over, clutching his groin and panting for breath, he never cut a line out of a speech or left a hall afterwards without shaking, with a smile, the hand of every person who wanted to shake his hand. And when, finally forced into a hospital, he was told by doctors that the danger of permanent damage to his kidneys was very real, that an immediate operation was imperative—that postponing the operation in the hope that the stone might pass naturally could prove fatal—Lyndon Johnson nonetheless insisted on postponing it because the operation, and the six-week recovery period, would have brought his campaign, and perhaps his career, to an end, costing him his last chance. He waited for three days, each day the doctors warning him he must wait no longer, and finally insisted, against their advice and against prevailing medical practice because of the great risks involved, that they attempt a still-experimental procedure to avoid the operation—insisted with an implacability that raises inescapably questions whose answers lie buried within Lyndon Johnson's labyrinthine personality: whether, if he didn't attain his goal, he didn't care what happened to him; which choice he would make, if the choice lay between death and failure.

And now, in 1955, as the stakes grew higher, there were again warnings of illness—this time of illness even more serious than an infected kidney stone. And again Lyndon Johnson refused to let them interfere.

LOOKING BACK LATER, colleagues could see how clear the warnings had been. But at the time, the warnings were ignored, ignored not only by other men but by Lyndon Johnson himself—although fear of a heart attack had been one of the great constants in Lyndon Johnson's life.

In May, while managing a foreign affairs bill on the Senate floor, he suddenly clutched his chest for a moment, but when he was asked if anything was wrong, he said impatiently that he merely had a touch of indigestion. Then on Saturday, June 18, he and George Smathers were scheduled to drive down to Brown & Root's Virginia estate, Huntlands. They had lunch in the Senate Dining Room, where, Smathers was to recall, "he ate his usual double meal and gulped the food," and got into the big limousine which Norman Edwards was driving. They had just crossed the Memorial Bridge into Virginia when Johnson clutched his chest, and "gasped out, 'It's killing me. I've got indigestion.' " He had Edwards pull over at a gas station and bring him a Coca-Cola, Smathers says, "but even after he drank it, he didn't feel better," and Smathers says, he was still complaining about the pain during a dominoes game at the Brown estate.

"Finally, he went to bed, and the next morning he said he was better," Smathers recalls. "But he didn't look better." When Smathers asked him to see a doctor, however, "he kept saying, 'No—no,' as though I was looking for trouble." He did, in fact, submit to a cursory examination by the Capitol physician,

Dr. George Calver, on Monday, but nothing wrong was found, and Johnson's pace only intensified, although several times each day he would say he felt very tired, statements discounted by whoever heard them because the pace of his activities never slackened. Sometime in late June, telling two or three reporters about his fatigue, he said that he had had a bad pain and "a flutter" in his chest the last time he had had sexual intercourse with Lady Bird. "All I could think was, Who the hell would say something like that," one of the reporters recalls. "Nobody took it [the symptoms] seriously." On Friday, July 1, the eve of the Fourth of July weekend, George Reedy told John Steele that he felt Johnson was "near the edge of sheer exhaustion," and that evening, when Johnson went out to dinner with Sam Rayburn and Stuart Symington (Rayburn was trying to effect a rapprochement between the two men), Rayburn became worried. "He [Johnson] seemed very tense, seemed to want to talk politics all during dinner," Symington was to say. "He was uptight." Rayburn took the two senators home in his limousine, and after they dropped Johnson off, said to Symington, "He just can't think, eat or drink anything except the problems he has as Majority Leader. He won't relax."

The next day, Saturday, July 2, Johnson was again to go to Huntlands for the weekend, and it had been arranged that Posh Oltorf would drive him down with George and Alice Brown on Saturday morning, but there turned out to be too many things to be done before he could leave, and he said Norman would drive him down later in the day.

A score of urgent senatorial matters that he had not been able to attend to during the week had to be resolved (one, involving Senator Francis Case, resulted in four separate visits from Case to G-14 that morning), and during the course of the morning Johnson made seven other telephone calls on Senate business—and there was also a trip to his tailor, Sam Scogna, that in its own way was urgent, too, since thanks to the thirty-five or forty pounds he had put on in the last five months, his suits no longer fit, and he was being measured for two new ones—one dark blue, one brown, both double-breasted and cut very full. He had told Reedy to have reporters from the three wire services in G-14 at three o'clock for a briefing, out of which Johnson was hoping for articles summing up the Senate's accomplishments thus far in the session and making it clear that there would be more accomplishments, as major bills still before the various committees began to emerge onto the floor. The beat of one of the reporters, John Chadwick of the Associated Press, included the Judiciary Committee, however, and Chadwick brought up a bill Johnson had been hoping the press would ignore: proposed liberal legislation to alter the McCarran-Walter Immigration Act.

"I don't know anything about it," Johnson replied curtly. "Still in committee."

Chadwick, a soft-spoken, notably well-mannered journalist, waited until Johnson had finished discussing the status of other bills, and then returned to the subject, saying, as he was to recall, "Can't you tell us anything about the immigration bill?" and when Johnson replied, "I told you I don't know anything about that—it's still in committee," said, "Well, what's the difference between that bill and all these other bills you've been telling us about? They're still in committee, too." With a violence that another journalist present, William Theis of International News Service, was to say "shocked" the reporters—"I'd never seen him lose his cool in public in a way like that"—Johnson shouted: "Goddamn you, don't you ever tell me how to answer questions! You can get the hell out of here!"

Theis, who felt Johnson was "obviously not well, out of control," says he "just blew his stack completely." The other reporters defended their colleague for a moment, saying there had been nothing improper about his question, and then, in Theis' words, "broke the thing up right away," and left Johnson's office.

Stalking out a few minutes later, Johnson went down to the senators' private dining room. Seeing Mike Monroney having lunch there alone, he joined him, bolted down a plate of frankfurters and beans, and half a cantaloupe, and got into his limousine. There was one more stop to be made: at the Mayflower, for a visit to Walter George, who had been confined to his apartment with a respiratory infection—and it was a quarter to five before Johnson came out, climbed into the back seat of the big limousine, and told Edwards to head for Huntlands. He was alone except for the chauffeur: Lady Bird was later to say that she had remained behind because Saturday was Lucy's birthday and was planning to come down on Sunday.

"I remember it suddenly began to seem terribly close, and I told Norman to turn on the air conditioner," Johnson was to say. "He said it was already on, and I said to turn it on full steam, and he said it was already on full steam, and was getting very cold."

He was late, Johnson was to say, "and I was trying to make it up, and there was this sense of pressure. My chest hurt." At first, he was to say, "I thought to myself, if only I hadn't eaten that cantaloupe at lunch," and "I belched a little and felt better." But as the car headed deeper into the Virginia hunt country, "my chest really began to hurt." It felt, he was to say, "as though there were two hundred pounds on it."

By the time he arrived, George Brown was taking a nap, and Posh and Alice were leaving to take a swim in a neighbor's pool. When they asked him to come with them, he said he didn't feel well, that, Oltorf recalls, "he had terrible indigestion" and "heartburn." They brought him some baking soda, and he said he felt better and would lie down on a couch in the living room and take a nap, too. As he was lying there, however, "I got this feeling that I couldn't breathe," he was to say. When Posh and Alice returned, George met them at the door. "Lyndon is sick," he said. He had given him more baking soda, "but he says he's got these pains, and I'm worried about him. It might be his heart." At this time, Clinton Anderson, who was on his way to a friend's house in Virginia, dropped by. Lyndon tried to tell Anderson he had indigestion, but Anderson had had a heart attack, and when Johnson mentioned the pressure on his chest and said that his arms felt "heavy," he said "Lyndon, I think you may be having a coronary." He should see a doctor at once, he said.

Johnson's reaction was rage. "He was furious about that," Anderson was to say. "He didn't want any doctor. . . . He knew there was a story coming out in the *Washington Post* about him as a possibility for the presidency. He didn't want to knock it in the head, kill it right at the beginning." When Anderson told Brown that a doctor should be called, Brown said, "Now, Clint, Lyndon doesn't want us to do that." As Anderson detailed the similarities between Johnson's symptoms and those of a heart attack victim, Johnson became, in Oltorf's words, "more and more frantic." But Anderson insisted that a doctor be called, and Oltorf, who had of course spent a lot of time in the area, at Longlea, located one, James Gibson of Middleburg, and after Gibson had examined Johnson he told him that he had the symptoms of a heart attack, "and a bad one." The doctor said that there were no local facilities to treat it properly. He knew Johnson was in a great deal of pain, he said, but he suggested that Johnson try to get back to Washington. "You'll probably go into deep shock in about an hour and a half," the doctor said, "which just gives us time to get you back into town." That would be the best course, he said, "if you feel like you can do it."

AND THEN POSH OLTORF, who had known Lyndon Johnson so long, saw, for the first time, the true strength of Lyndon Johnson.

Johnson's usual reaction to physical danger, real or imagined, and to minor pain or illness, was dramatic; at San Marcos, he had had the reputation of being "an absolute physical coward," and all during his life after college, whenever he had encountered minor physical problems—the only physical problems Oltorf had ever seen him encounter—he had become "frantic."

But there had been other episodes in his life, episodes that Oltorf had not witnessed. To avoid service in a combat zone during the war, Lyndon Johnson, a reserve officer, had spent months traveling up and down the West Coast on an ostensibly Navy-ordered tour on which the Navy often could not even find out where he was. But when inquiries from constituents and reporters made it imperative that he at least give the appearance of entering a combat zone, he persuaded President Roosevelt—"for the sake of political future," as one of Roosevelt's aides wrote—to send him to Australia as an "observer." And when, in Australia, he realized that he could not, "for the sake of political future," return without at least saying that he had witnessed combat, he flew as an observer on a bombing mission on which his bomber was attacked by Japanese Zeroes. It was only a single bombing mission; the next day he left the war zone as quickly as possible. But on that mission, while he was watching Zeroes heading straight at his plane, Lyndon Johnson had not been frantic but "cool as a cucumber." Although he had avoided for as long as possible being at the scene of battle, once he was at it, his conduct had been calm and courageous, nonchalant in the face of danger. And, of course, when, during the 1937 and 1948 campaigns, there had been not minor sickness but grave illness, and great pain, Lyndon Johnson had not let it interfere with his work. All his life, whenever courage had been needed, it was there. This, now—the pain in his chest, the heaviness in his arms, the words "heart attack"—was what he had always dreaded. But what was required now was calm. And, instantly, there was calm. Oltorf, who had seen Lyndon Johnson "complain so often, and so loudly" about indigestion, now saw a doctor tell Lyndon Johnson that this time the "indigestion" was a heart attack—and Oltorf saw Lyndon Johnson's demeanor change.

Yes, Johnson told Dr. Gibson, if it was best for him to get to Washington, he could do it. The place to take him, he said, was the Bethesda Naval Hospital. He wanted his people to be at the hospital to meet him, he said, and he told George Brown who they were, and to get them there: Lady Bird; Walter Jenkins; Earle Clements, so that he could give him instructions about the Senate's upcoming work; George Reedy, to handle the press. He wanted someone he knew—someone responsible to *him*—with him at all times, and he asked Oltorf to accompany him in the ambulance. When it arrived—Middleburg's "ambulance" was actually a hearse, with the undertaker driving—the doctor took a seat in front, Johnson lay on the floor in the rear, and Oltorf sat in the rear with him, on a sort of jump seat that pulled out from the wall, "so that I was sitting right over him."

From that vantage point, Oltorf saw not only calmness but courage. The chest pain would "come and go," Oltorf recalls, and about halfway to Washington, it got worse. "I can't stand this pain," Lyndon Johnson told the doctor. "You've got to give me something for it." The doctor said, "I can give you a shot if you want, but we'll have to stop, and it's going to take some time, and time means a lot to you."

"If time means a lot, don't stop," Lyndon Johnson said. "Keep going."

"It was a very hectic ride," Oltorf was to say. "It hurt him desperately." But between bouts of pain, he and Oltorf talked. "It was an amazing conversation," Oltorf felt. "He was extremely courageous and brave. I always thought, you know, that if he had a toe ache, he'd complain about it . . . and expect a great deal of sympathy. He was just the opposite with this serious thing."

Oltorf watched him running over things in his mind. "I think he definitely felt there was a possibility that he'd die before he got there," Oltorf says, and at one point, "he reached up to me," and said, "Posh, if something happens, I want to tell you where I think my will is." He said he thought it was in the bottom drawer of his desk at the radio station in Austin, that he had drawn it up when he went off to war and had not seen it in a long time, but thought that it was there. "If it's not," he said, "I just want to tell you what I want. I want Lady Bird to have everything I have. . . . She's been a wonderful, wonderful wife, and she's done so much for me. She just deserves everything I have. That's what was in my will."

There was another matter Johnson mentioned, and Oltorf did not allude to it in the oral history he gave the Lyndon Johnson Library, although he included it—or at least part of it—in his interview with the author. "Then he asked me did I ever see Alice [Glass]. That was something he very seldom asked me. And I said [I saw her] off and on. He said, 'How is she?' and I said all right, and then he said something I didn't tell you and I don't think I'm going to."

And there was another important matter. "Doctor," he said, "let me ask you something. Will I be able to smoke again if this is a heart attack?" The doctor said, "Well, Senator, frankly, no," and Johnson, with what Oltorf recalls as "a great sigh," said, "I'd rather have my pecker cut off."

At the emergency room entrance to Bethesda, attendants lifted Johnson onto a stretcher and carried him into an elevator, which took them up to the seventeenth-floor cardiac treatment section. Lady Bird, Walter Jenkins, and George Reedy were in a waiting room there (Clements had not been located), and they saw Johnson carried past its doorway into an examining room, and doctors took them to the private room he would have as a patient. After about a half hour he was brought in, and lifted onto the bed. "He looked very, very bad," Walter Jenkins says. Johnson said the doctors had told him he had had a serious heart attack, and that they would be coming to "put him under" in a few minutes. Lady Bird was Lady Bird. "She didn't break down or cry or carry on or anything of that nature, as some women do," Jenkins says. "It's not her nature to do that. She just said, 'Honey, everything will be all right.' " Johnson told Reedy to notify the press about the attack, and not to minimize its seriousness, to tell them it was "a real bellybuster," and that Clements would take over for him. He gave Reedy instructions for Clements. He told Jenkins "where his will was" and reminded him about the cash in the secret compartment in his desk, and told him to give it to Lady Bird. "I really felt that he did not think he would live through the night," Jenkins would recall. "He was preparing himself for not being there anymore. . . ."

He told Lady Bird to stay with him in the hospital, not to leave him. He handed her his wallet and keys. He mentioned the two suits he had ordered that morning. "Tell him to go ahead with the blue," he said. "We can use that no matter what happens." He asked for a cigarette, and when Lady Bird said he couldn't smoke anymore, he said if he could have one last cigarette, he would never have another. Someone handed him one. "It was very sensuous," Mrs. Johnson recalls. "He looked at it like, 'This is the dearest thing.' " Then he went into shock. Mrs. Johnson saw him turn gray, "just about the color of pavement." He was "motionless as stone and cold to touch." After a while, the doctors came to see her. They said her husband had had a very serious heart attack, that his chances were fairly good, but that only time would tell. The first twenty-four hours, they said, would be critical.

28

Memories

LYNDON JOHNSON HAD SUFFERED a myocardial infarction, the death or damage (infarction) of part of the muscular substance of the heart (myocardium) because the flow of blood to the heart had been interrupted by a blockage of an artery.

He was kept sedated for forty-eight hours, but there were intervals of consciousness, during one of which it became apparent that sedation had not dulled his ability to obtain information that someone did not want to give him. Lady Bird may have been determined not to let him know the doctors' estimate of his chances of survival during this initial period following the attack, but he got the information from her anyway. She had been sitting almost constantly at his bedside, but she left the room for a few minutes, and when she returned, he spoke as if doctors had visited him during her absence.

"I've just heard the bad news," he said.

"What news? What do you mean?" she said.

"I know the doctors feel I only have one chance in ten of pulling through."

"Nonsense!" she blurted out. "They say it's fifty-fifty."

With this type of heart attack, however, the patient's chance of survival increases dramatically with each day he survives without another attack and without increased damage to the heart from the first attack, and by the fourth day, although he was still permitted no visitors other than his wife, doctors told the press that while the Majority Leader had suffered "a myocardial infarction of a moderately severe character," X-rays had shown no further damage to the heart, "his condition is stabilized," and "he is resting comfortably." "He was quite critically ill following the attack, but his recovery has been satisfactory," they said. Any immediate return to work was out of the question, the statement said. "He cannot undertake any business whatsoever for a period of months. However, if there are no further attacks of a severe character and his recovery continues to be satisfactory, he should be able to return to the Senate in January."

The damage to his chances of reaching his great goal appeared for some time, however, to be as severe as he had feared it would be when Clinton Anderson had first told him he was having a coronary.

"The immediate political casualty of the Majority Leader's heart attack is the Johnson boom for President," which previously "had been coming along on schedule," Doris Fleeson wrote, and in the days following the Fourth of July weekend, the prevailing view in newspaper articles and columns was that the damage might well be permanent. A headline over an Associated Press analysis said "HEART ATTACK DROPS JOHNSON FROM WHITE HOUSE HOPEFULS," and in an era before the later dramatic advances in the understanding and treatment of heart disease, that analysis did not apply merely to 1956. "Although when he recovers he may have a long and useful life as a senator, uncertainty is the greatest certainty about the life of a man who has had an attack," the article declared. "Anyone who has had an attack and seeks the presidency starts under a political handicap: the voters are conscious of the risk in picking him over an opponent who has never had his first heart attack." Johnson's attack therefore "just about eliminates the 46-year-old Texan" permanently "from consideration as a presidential candidate." Some journalists speculated that the attack might eliminate him from the leadership as well. While the doctors had said Johnson should be able to return to the Senate, they had declined to express such optimism about a return to the leadership; "It might be six months before it would be possible to say whether he could resume the leadership," one of his physicians said. The AP said it is "questionable that when he returns his doctors will let him resume as Senate leader, preferring he go back to the less demanding role of senator."

Lyndon Johnson fell into a depression. The doctors had told Walter Jenkins and George Reedy that depression was common among heart attack victims, but they also told the two aides that this one seemed unusually severe. Jenkins says he understood why: "He felt . . . if he had any chance to be President or Vice President or something, that this had ended it. . . . He became quite despondent at times." Neither antidepressant medication nor the arrival of his mother (whose trip to Washington was her first airplane flight) seemed to help. For some days, he lay in his bed—"just wouldn't talk, wouldn't have anything to do with [anyone]," in Jenkins' words—while his centrality in his assistants' lives was dramatized. Bobby Baker got the news over the telephone at the New Jersey seashore, where he was vacationing with friends. Returning from the telephone, he was, recalls one friend, "white as a sheet. 'The Leader's had a heart attack,' " he said. Rushing to Bethesda, he was told that Johnson was allowed no visitors except Lady Bird. He went down to the lobby and waited— day after day. "For almost ten days I stayed at the hospital almost around the clock, leaving only to grab a few random hours of sleep and to take showers," he was to recall. "Though there was little I could do, I felt it my duty to be there." Once he went down to the Capitol to see Sam Rayburn, seeking solace, but didn't get any: "Speaker Rayburn was disconsolate and near tears." And when, finally, some days after Baker had returned to work at the Capitol, Lady Bird telephoned to say that Lyndon wanted to see him, Baker found "a quiet and sober man who talked of how close he'd come to death, of how he would be forced to curtail his activities, and of how he might no longer be able to act as Senate Majority Leader." Saying he might resign from the Senate, he asked Baker if he would resign, too, and manage a radio station in Brownsville he was thinking of buying. "You're my Leader, and I'll follow where you lead," Baker replied.

And then, one day, Reedy's telephone rang and it was Jenkins. "For the love of God, do you know what's happening?" Walter asked him, and told him to go to the hospital, and Reedy recalls, "When I got to the hospital, I couldn't believe it!"

Letters—almost four thousand of them—had been pouring into Johnson's office from friends and the public, and Lady Bird had been reading them to him. For days, Johnson had shown little response. And then one morning, immediately upon awakening, he had told Lady Bird that he wanted the letters answered—all of them, each answered not with a form letter but with a person- alized note. Lady Bird should send handwritten notes to personal friends, he said, and as for the rest—he told her to have Booth Mooney come to the hospi- tal, and when Mooney arrived, "he had a project for me," a project Mooney was to call "Project Impossible."

"We're going to answer all of them," Johnson said. "Every one has to have a personal reply." And when Mooney, "aghast—*four thousand* letters"—tried to protest, saying that "all the newspaper people know you're not up to dictat- ing letters; it would look fake," Johnson said he had figured out a way around that problem. The letters would be signed by Lady Bird, he said; Mooney would dictate them at the office, and after they had been typed, would bring them out to the hospital for her to sign. "Make 'em short, just a few lines, but tender and grateful," Johnson said. And, Johnson said, he had a few letters he wanted to dictate himself; a stenographer should be sent out from his office. By the time Reedy arrived at the hospital, a desk had been set up in Lady Bird's room next to Lyndon's, and she was writing at it as fast as she could. "Two or three stenographers" were sitting at the physicians' station in the corridor, and they were "out there with those typewriters going full blast. He took over the corridor, installed a couple of typewriters there, he was dictating letters, he was just going full speed."

His physicians, J. C. Cain of the Mayo Clinic and cardiologist Willis Hurst, had prescribed complete rest, with absolutely no excitement, and had banned radio, television, and newspapers from his room. That morning John- son had told Hurst that he missed country music, and had asked for a radio so he could listen to some. Hurst agreed, on condition that Johnson not listen to any news broadcasts. Once he had the radio, of course, Johnson listened *only* to the news, switching from station to station. One radio was not enough; he got a second, a small transistor with earphones, so that he could listen to two newscasts at once. And when a newscaster's wording did not please him, he shouted back at the radio, and, as Reedy put it, "his nurses reported that they almost immediately acquired larger vocabularies." A television set was installed in his room; a visitor found him "simultaneously watching TV, listening to the news through an earphone receiver on a tiny transistor radio, and carrying on a lively conversation with a nurse." Visitors from the political world had also been banned, but Johnson insisted that Reedy and Jenkins be constantly on call, and then Rayburn was sent for, and Russell, and Earle Clements. The Senate wasn't doing much in his absence, but, Jenkins says, "he really kept his oar in in the sense of being certain that he understood what was going on." (Not that, as Reedy explains, Clements was trying to make the Senate do much; "By that time the Lyndon Johnson legend had become so overpowering that I pity anybody that had to step into his shoes.") Baker was sent for again, and this time when he arrived his Leader was the *Leader* again, "demanding that I bring him all the news and gossip. Who was absent from roll calls? Who'd been drunk recently? Tell Senator Kerr this. Tell Speaker Rayburn that. Bring me a copy of this committee report or that *Congressional Record*. Johnson seemed pleased when I told him that not much was happening in the Senate, that it was conducting a mere holding action until he could return to work." One day, Baker was rushing down the seventeenth-floor corridor toward Johnson's room, his arms filled with papers he had demanded, when he encountered Rayburn, who had just been in to visit the patient. "His old face split into a rare grin," Baker recalls. "I'm happy to see you taking him all that work," the Speaker said. "It would kill him if he relaxed. I know he's getting better because he fussed at me." And "Project Impossible" had proved possible after all. On July 18, a Jenkins memo told Johnson: "We in the office know that having all your mail answered means more to you than any gift which we would give you. Therefore we have stayed here tonight to see that every letter is answered and filed. I am glad to report all of the letters about your illness—almost 4,000 to date—have now been answered." Johnson had also decided to have letters written to the publishers of every newspaper that had carried a complimentary editorial about him during his illness, and to have those editorials inserted in the *Congressional Record*. That also had been done. More and more visitors came—including some from the GOP, like Knowland and Bridges. Dr. Hurst had tried to set a limit on the number of visitors per day, but when he told Johnson that the limit had been exceeded, Johnson replied, "Oh, now, look, Doctor, you're not going to count Republicans, are you?" One day, the door opened, and the President was standing there, his great smile beaming into the room. "Why, Lyndon," Ike said, "you look a lot better than I thought you would." The Vice President came, for what had been intended as a brief visit but which lasted for more than an hour, as Richard Nixon and Lyndon Johnson fell into a serious conversation, one that was to mark the beginning of a close relationship between the two future presidents which is only now beginning to be glimpsed by historians. One rule on which Hurst had insisted was that no more than two visitors be in Johnson's room at a time, and one day Harry Byrd sat patiently on a bench in the seventeenth-floor corridor for more than thirty minutes while Sid Richardson and Richardson's lobbyist, Bill Kittrell, were talking inside.

Hurst and Cain did not object to Johnson's activity because, alarmed by the depth of his depression, they had had a long discussion with Lady Bird, and as a result they had a better understanding of their patient, and of his inability to do anything in moderation. "If he was sitting on the porch at the LBJ Ranch whittling toothpicks, he'd have to whittle more than anybody else in the country," Dr. Cain was to say. They explained to Reedy that, in Reedy's words, "to cut down his schedule would be worse than adding to it" because "his psychology was such" that the "frustrations" of idleness would be more likely than work to lead to "another heart attack." And for a while, as he turned the seventeenth floor of the Bethesda Medical Center into an uproar, Lyndon Johnson was his old self. As Jenkins wrote to Mary Rather on July 23: "Mary, you would be real happy if you could see how well the Senator is getting along. He is just as cheerful and chipper as he can be."

LYNDON JOHNSON'S OLD SELF had been characterized by violent mood swings, however, and they persisted in the hospital, so that from day to day Jenkins and others on his staff would not know whether they would find Johnson cheerful and chipper or lying flat on his back in his bed, speaking only in monosyllables and monotone, unwilling to take an interest in anything anyone told him. One antidote to his depression was the letters and editorials. Sitting next to his bed, Lady Bird read them to him. She put the best of them into acetate sheets in gold-tooled leather scrapbooks, and left them beside the bed. And Lyndon Johnson read them.

He spent hours reading them, reading them, in Reedy's words, "over and over and over again," putting his fingers on them as if he needed to touch them, becoming, in Reedy's words, "absolutely obsessive about them." In a way, Reedy and Jenkins and Mooney felt, his illness had deepened his lifelong need for reassurance that he was loved, and the letters and editorials seemed to assuage that longing. "There was sort of an unspoken yearning of his that could be felt all the way down to the Senate for that kind of reassurance, and he got it," Reedy says. "Oh, he was just basking in those letters."

The Senate had stood for a moment of silent prayer for him on the first day it met following his attack—Herbert Lehman had asked it to do so—and then there had been one laudatory speech about him after another. Lady Bird had told him about these eulogies at the time, but he hadn't seemed interested. She had put the pages of the *Congressional Record* containing the speeches in a scrapbook, and now he read them, slowly, carefully, devouring every word. And there were letters from senators. "Give Lyndon my best," Harry Byrd wrote to Lady Bird. "Tell him the Senate is not the same without him." The longest letter was from Humphrey, of course; it said in part: "I miss having you get after me; I miss your good humor. Yes, we're just lonesome for you." One day, Johnson said with a grin, "Everybody loves Lyndon, I found out." And then, in a lower, very serious, almost unbelieving tone: "Nobody run out and left me."

THE OTHER ANTIDOTE was the woman who read him the letters and editorials.

When he had arrived at the hospital that first night, and the doctors were about to put him under, he had said to his wife, in a voice that Walter Jenkins says was the "pleading" voice of "a small boy": "Stay with me, Bird." When, the next day, he emerged for a moment from the sedation, he said it again: "Stay with me, Bird."

She did. She was there, sitting by the bed, when he woke—every time he woke. "Lyndon wanted me around him twenty-four hours a day," she was to recall, and that was how many hours she was there. "At first," her friend Ruth Montgomery was to write, "Bird would not leave him even long enough to go out for a meal." It was a week before her friends Eugene and Ann Worley persuaded her to go out to a restaurant; Ann Worley would never forget how, when Lady Bird first saw them, she said, "optimistically," as if to convince herself, "Everything's going to be fine"; she would never forget "how determinedly gay and cheerful Bird was" all that evening; she would never forget the smile that never left her face.

Her husband would remain at Bethesda for five weeks, periodically falling back into that terrible depression, a pit of despair so dark that at times Jenkins "did fear that he would kind of give up, maybe wouldn't make the effort to [recover]. I thought maybe he would just say, 'This is it. I've had it.' " For a few days, Jenkins says, Johnson would be "all right, but then he'd have these periods." The doses of "despondency medicine" would resume, "and then he'd be all right for a while, and then he'd have another period of despondency." During those five weeks, Lady Bird Johnson left the hospital to go to her home—where, of course, there were an eleven-year-old and an eight-year-old daughter living—exactly twice.

DURING THOSE FIVE WEEKS in the hospital, Lyndon Johnson was displaying other characteristics that had been prominent features of his old life.

One was that incredible will. Cigarettes—sixty cigarettes or more each day, lit one from the end of another—had been so desperately important to him for so long. Now Cain and Hurst confirmed what Dr. Gibson had told him in the ambulance: the smoking must stop immediately and completely. Lyndon Johnson tore the wrapper off a pack of cigarettes, opened the pack and pulled one cigarette halfway out of it. Then he put the pack on the night table next to his hospital bed, and the pack stayed there, open but untouched, the cigarette sticking out, for the rest of his hospital stay. When he got home, he put a pack on his night table there, and there would be another one next to his bed on the ranch, and they all remained untouched. Once, in 1958, one of his secretaries, Ashton Gonella, asked him if he didn't miss smoking. "Every minute of every day," he replied. But except for occasional lapses—all seem to have involved no more than a cigarette or two—Lyndon Johnson did not smoke another cigarette for fifteen years, not until, in 1970, he had retired from the presidency and was back permanently on his ranch, when he began smoking copiously again.

If there was another substance that had been as important to him as nicotine, it was caffeine. From breakfast, which had often consisted of several cigarettes and several cups of black coffee, through the rest of his day, "he had seemed," in Jenkins' words, "to live on cigarettes and coffee." Now, since caffeine was dangerous for heart attack victims, he was told to cut out caffeinated coffee, too, and he did—completely, drinking only decaffeinated.

He had to cut out a lot more. Excess weight is a burden on the heart, and doctors told him he should weigh about 185, which would mean losing about forty pounds. So he went on a diet—with Johnsonian thoroughness, the thoroughness of a man who believed in doing "everything." He announced he would lose even more weight than the doctors wanted, saying he would get down below 180, by reducing his daily intake of calories not to the 2,000 the doctors had recommended but to 1,500, and, Reedy says, "he became the goddamnedest diet fanatic that ever lived." To make sure he kept the calories below that figure, he insisted that on every tray brought to him at the hospital there be a list of the calories in each dish on it. And since studies had begun showing that, as one article put it, "a fatty substance known as cholesterol is suspect in connection with heart disease," the list must, he said, include a count not only of the calories but of the fat grams in each dish.

The responsibility for the list was assigned to Lady Bird (who for years thereafter would be referred to by some irreverent members of the Johnson staff as "the keeper of the weight"), and her husband tolerated no mistakes. Since he couldn't seem to make himself eat small portions—although the portions were notably smaller than before—it was important that he eat foods very low in calories, and since a slice of cantaloupe contains only 45 calories, he became, Jenkins says, "a cantaloupe nut." Once his tray arrived with a slice of watermelon instead, and he asked how many calories it contained, and, as Reedy recalls, "Bird incautiously said 65, and he insisted they look it up," and when it turned out to contain 145, "you would have thought that the world had come to an end or he'd been betrayed." Sometimes, determining the fat grams was difficult; "I'm either going to have to turn registered chemist or jump out the window," Lady Bird said. But his methods worked. "I've given up eating and smoking at the same time," he said, "and if any of you all have tried giving up just one of them, you'll know how hard [giving up] both could be." But by the time he left the hospital and returned to Thirtieth Place on August 7—to be greeted by a group of neighbors standing on his front lawn, a "WELCOME HOME" telegram from J. Edgar Hoover, who was out of town, and an enthusiastic welcome from Little Beagle Johnson—he weighed 179.

FOR THE REMAINDER OF THE YEAR, as he rested at his Washington home until August 25, and then, two days before his forty-seventh birthday, went back to the ranch in Texas for a four-month stay, reporters were told that Lyndon Johnson was resting, concentrating on regaining his health, and that he had learned to relax—that he had changed his philosophy of life.

His illness was dramatized with the customary Johnson flare—reporters who interviewed him in Washington and then at the ranch found him talking in slow, calm phrases interrupted by frequent pauses and walking, as one article reported, with "agonizingly slow steps"—but so was the fact that, he said, doctors had assured him that if he took care of himself, he would recover from the illness and be able to return to his duties, to *all* his duties, "as good as new." He wanted therefore to create the image of a prudent man taking care of himself, and he made sure reporters understood that he was doing so. He told them how much he had weighed when he had stepped on the scale that morning, emphasized that he was getting his weight down even lower than the doctors had ordered. The doctors had told him to take a nap every day; he took *two* naps, he said. The doctors had told him to get plenty of sleep at night; "even here," as one article reported, "he tried to beat par. When the doctor told him to get eight hours sleep a night, Lyndon insisted on getting nine." And he said he had resolved never to go back to his old driving ways; "I've thrown out the whip." In fact, he said, he had developed a whole new philosophy of life, which was codified in an article, "My Heart Attack Taught Me How to Live" (written by Horace Busby), which appeared over his byline in *The American* magazine, and in dozens of interviews with reporters.

"During nearly 25 years of political life I drove myself and others at headlong pace," the article said. "I never learned how to relax." "Now," he said, "I've got something I never had before in my life—something I always wanted, too—and that is time." And, he said, he had learned to use that time. "It took a heart attack to make me cut my cloth to the pattern of contentment God has given me, but now I know the lesson well," he said. "I began consciously looking for some of the good things I had been missing."

One of those good things, he said, was *nature*. He loved to walk in plowed fields, "just to feel the dirt under my feet," he said. He loved to "walk down the road with a view of my fat cows grazing on the one side and my beautiful river flowing on the other."

Another of the good things—"high on the list of those good things," he said—"was getting acquainted with my two daughters. They had come to be 11 and 8 years of age, and I hardly knew them at all." For example, "I had always been too busy to join with the girls in observing their birthdays." Now, he said, there was time to get to know them, and "I found myself falling into a happy relationship with Lynda Bird and Lucy Baines." They played dominoes together, "took turns reading aloud from their books," and he found, he said, "Why, they liked me!" On Sunday mornings, he said, "after a leisurely, chatty breakfast, little Lucy suddenly threw her arms around my neck and hugged me hard. 'Daddy,' she said, 'it sure is nice to have you around the house so much.' "

He portrayed his new life as one of reading and thoughtful contemplation. Although in truth his refusal to read books was as adamant as ever, plenty were scattered about, some of them open as if he had just put them down, when reporters arrived for interviews. Booth Mooney recalls that "stories began to appear which I scanned in utter disbelief. The Johnson who once had admitted or even boasted that he doubted if he had read as many as half a dozen books all the way through since leaving college was said now to be deep into Plato, not to mention innumerable volumes of American history." After interviewing Johnson in his bedroom at Thirtieth Place, Mary McGrory reported that "There are books all over the room," including Plato's *Republic* and Machiavelli's *The Prince*—"and the Senator is taking the unusual opportunity to do a little reading." As the months passed, his thirst for the arts appeared to broaden. Arriving at the ranch for an interview in October, *Newsweek*'s Sam Shaffer found Johnson "sprawled in a hammock, a book on his lap. Strauss waltzes floated into the air from a record player." As he talked to Shaffer, "He touched the book on his lap, and recalled that he'd always been too busy to read books before; he probably hadn't read more than six all the way through from the day he left college until the day of the heart attack, and now he was reading that many a week. He listened to the music and said: 'You know, until the attack, I just never listened to music. I don't know why. I just didn't.' " Lady Bird chimed in, telling another reporter that Lyndon was reading "innumerable history and biographies." He certainly was, Lyndon said: at the moment, he was deep into Douglas Southall Freeman's massive, three-volume *Lee's Lieutenants* and "enjoying it immensely." And it was wonderful, he said, with a deeply thoughtful expression, to "have time at last just to sit and think."

The image he wanted was the image he got. Sarah McClendon wrote of his new, "easy-going, relaxed peace." Mary McGrory, noting that "a man who has been 'in a hurry all my life' is learning to slow down," and that he is "something of a model patient," added: "It would perhaps be too much to say that the Senator is finding sweet the uses of adversity, but there have been advantages."

But in reality he wasn't resting, and he wasn't relaxing, and he wasn't at peace. He couldn't be—particularly not back on the ranch.

He took off, on Wesley West's private jet ("whose owner he declined to name"), from bustling National Airport outside Washington, but he landed at the tiny Fredericksburg airport, which consisted only of a landing strip, a wind sock, and a shed that was used as an office. There "representatives of both local newspapers and the United Press were on hand to chronicle in story and picture the return home of the famous native son," and also present was a shocked Mary Rather, who was to recall that, as she watched him come off the plane, "He was the thinnest thing you have ever seen, and his clothes were just hanging on him. And of course Mrs. Johnson looked bad too." Ranch hands had a station wagon there, and they drove him along the Pedernales Valley, with the houses further and further apart, to the ranch. And there, on the first morning, he was awakened at dawn by the mooing of a cow demanding to be milked, the same sound that had awakened him on the ranch as a boy—and instantly Lyndon Johnson was back in his first home, back ill on the ranch where his father had been ill, and where his father, who had had such great dreams, had failed; back on the ranch where his grandfather, whose saddlebags had once been filled with gold, had come to live out his life in poverty after his great dreams had been brought to nothing; back on the ranch where the heroine Eliza Bunton Johnson, who had dared to ride out ahead of the herd to scout, had come back to live when she was old—old and poor and paralyzed, with a stroke-twisted face that lived in Lyndon's nightmares. Sometimes in the morning, he would walk along the river to the Johnson family graveyard, and there, under the spreading branches of a big live oak, inside a rickety little fence, were the tombstones: of Eliza Bunton Johnson, Sam Ealy Johnson Sr., and Sam Ealy Johnson Jr. He would stand there for long minutes, staring at the names. And one morning, thinking that no one was watching him, Lyndon Johnson drew with his shoe an X in the ground in that graveyard: the spot for his own grave.

His brother, Sam Houston Johnson, had come back from Washington to live at the ranch that summer, so Lyndon was back with that broken, wretched man. Josefa was living in Fredericksburg, so he was back with the sister who had brought the family into even deeper disgrace. He was back with his mother, who kept telling people how much like his father he was. If he walked past the graveyard, he soon came to the site of the house in which he had been born—on which another battered, ramshackle dog-run cabin now stood. Lyndon Johnson painted, and journalists repainted, a picture of a relaxed, almost idyllic existence on the tranquil banks of the Pedernales, but the reality was far different. "It was way out in the country and it was so quiet and still," Mary Rather was to recall, and during the first few weeks, "it was a real quiet, long, lonesome, sad kind of a fall." His nightmares came back, worse than ever.* And not

---

*"They got worse after my heart attack," he was to tell Doris Kearns Goodwin.

long after his arrival, he fell into a despair deeper even than his despair in the hospital.

FOR A WEEK, Lyndon Johnson sat in the big recliner in the ranch's rock-walled living room, the chair tilted all the way back so that as he slouched down in it, he was lying almost flat, with his feet at the level of his head. He would sit there for hours, staring at nothing, and saying nothing. When someone—his wife or daughters—attempted to engage him in conversation, he would reply in monosyllables or not at all. Little Beagle Johnson would jump up, and lie in his lap. From time to time, he would lick Lyndon Johnson's face, wagging his tail frenziedly and barking. There would be no response. As the dog licked his face, his master wouldn't even move. Dr. Hurst, who had begun to understand his patient, had warned Mary Rather that, in her words, "some days he might want to see the mail that came in, and the next day I might have it all ready for him, and he wouldn't look at it." Ms. Rather, who knew the talismanic significance that the mail held for her boss, had not taken Hurst seriously, but the doctor's prediction turned out to be correct. For a day or two, Johnson refused even to pick up the telephone when Walter Jenkins called to give him the news from Washington. She told Sam Houston, "He's going into a very deep depression, and we don't know what it is."

Sam Houston, who knew his brother so well, knew what it was. "I said, 'Well, if you had one office you aspired to all your life, and . . .' " And he knew what the cure was—the only cure. Telephoning the nationally syndicated political columnist Holmes Alexander, a close friend, he asked him to write a column saying that the heart attack would not prevent Lyndon Johnson from becoming President. When Alexander demurred, Sam Houston recalls, "I said, 'Here I've been giving you scoops for years. If you can't take a chance on helping me save my brother, then the hell with you.' "

Alexander agreed to write it, and on September 1, there in the *Austin American-Statesman* were the magic words: "The Senator is now almost restored in health. He is a serious candidate for the Democratic nomination, either in 1956 or 1960, depending on which is more propitious. It's hard to see how the party so united in praising him when he was ill, can divide against him now that he's bushy-tailed and ambitious once more. This may be the first time in history that a man was virtually nominated by his press clippings." Sam Houston gave the column to his brother as he lay on the recliner, and not long thereafter the beagle jumped up on Lyndon's lap and went into one of his face-licking, tail-wagging, barking frenzies. And after a while, Lyndon Johnson laughed—the first laugh Mary Rather had heard him utter since he arrived at the ranch—and went for a walk.

And that same day brought another development. At Jim Rowe's suggestion, Johnson had decided before the heart attack to put on his staff a new assistant, one who would be a living reminder of his early link with Franklin Roosevelt, which Johnson considered essential to mending his fences with liberals. Now that assistant would be a reminder also that Roosevelt had suffered a serious illness but had become President nonetheless. And when Grace Tully arrived in Texas, she knew just what to say. "Many things about the senator reminded her of FDR," one article reported; for example, Roosevelt had been deeply interested "in conservation and natural resources," and Johnson's improvements to his ranch show that he, too, "takes a great interest in the land." "JOHNSON AIDE SAYS TEXAN IS LIKE FDR," proclaimed a headline in the *San Antonio Express*.

There would be other spells of depression while Johnson was in Texas, but none as serious as the first one.

DURING LYNDON JOHNSON'S REMAINING MONTHS on the ranch in 1955, there was no recurrence of the heart problem, no pain or any other symptom. The bottle of digitalis, a heart stimulant that doctors had given him in case of another attack, remained unopened next to the pack of cigarettes on his night table. For the rest of Lyndon Johnson's life, however, he lived in terror of another heart attack. He never wanted to sleep alone, so that there would always be someone to help him if he suffered an attack during the night, and if Lady Bird was away, he would dragoon an aide or a friend into sleeping in the same room with him. Years later, in the White House, asking an assistant, Vicky McCammon, and her husband to stay overnight, he would insist that they sleep in Lady Bird's dressing room next door to his bedroom; "The only deal is you've got to leave your door open a crack so that if I holler someone will hear me." But that fear wasn't as strong as the fears, born of his boyhood insecurities and humiliations, that haunted him throughout his life. Now he was back on the ranch that was a constant reminder of those boyhood fears, and he fled from them as desperately as ever—more desperately, in fact.

During the rest of his months on the ranch, the "sad, quiet" spells of depression alternated with periods of frantic activity. During these frenzied periods, he poured himself into recovering his health. Following doctors' orders to get plenty of rest was easy on the isolated ranch. The Johnsons and their staff kept farm hours, going to sleep at nine and rising early, when the cows started to moo; the rural mail carrier left the mail and the morning newspapers in the box across the Pedernales around 6 a.m., and Mary Rather would walk across the concrete bridge to bring them back. Every afternoon there was the long nap, and Johnson spent a lot of additional time lying in the recliner.

The doctors had told him to relax. Massages relaxed him, so his favorite masseur from the Senate gymnasium, Olaf Anderson, was dispatched to Texas, and installed at the ranch for the duration. The sun relaxed him, so he would spend hours lying in the sun with his shirt off, his pale skin gradually turning bronze. The doctors had told him to get plenty of exercise, and specifically to walk a mile each evening after dinner. Using a pedometer, he measured various walks he might take. The little home of his elderly spinster cousin, Oreole Bunton Bailey, he determined, was just over a half mile away, so if he visited her each evening, he would be doing more than the doctor ordered. Those walks became a legend among Johnson's staff. "Oh, he loved to talk to Cousin Oreole about old times and kid her about her boyfriends, which she didn't have, just tease her." This pastime was less enjoyable to his staffers than to him, but he insisted that everyone accompany him on the walks, and stand around while he shouted at the elderly lady in the faded Mother Hubbard—she appeared to be, Jenkins recalls, "about as stone deaf as you could be"—and then walk back.

For additional exercise, a kidney-shaped swimming pool was built in the front yard of the ranch house. It was a Johnsonian pool—large, nine feet deep at the deep end, expensive, personally supervised ("Every shovelful," George Reedy says. "That swimming pool became one of the great construction projects of history"), equipped with every technological innovation, including a huge, elaborate heater, kept constantly at full blast, that kept the pool as warm as a bathtub because he did not like cold water ("I myself hated that pool," Reedy says. "I didn't go into it unless he absolutely forced me into it, because I want water to be cold"), and surrounded by a lawn of grass as smooth and lush as a carpet. "Telephone outlets make it possible for Johnson . . . to conduct business neck-deep in the warm water, while piped-in music [from speakers placed in the live oaks] soothes his nerves and those of his guests; and while secretaries and assistants scurry about the pool, obeying an endless stream of instructions," one visiting journalist reported. Strauss waltzes were played only when journalists were present; at other times the repertoire was strictly "elevator music." How much exercise the pool gave him is doubtful (aside from a few sidestroke laps every day, he spent most of his time in it in a floating reclining chair, a drink in his hand), but it did give him a new means of control: Reedy at least was tall, other assistants were shorter, and when Johnson was swimming with a shorter assistant, he would wait until the assistant was at the deep end of the pool, and then stop and stand still while he was between the assistant and the shallower water. Years later, five-foot ten-inch Joseph Califano, newly attached to the White House staff, would describe how President Johnson outlined a multi-part domestic program in the pool with "his finger poking my shoulder as though it were punctuating a series of exclamation points." ("I nodded, treading. He was so close to me, almost nose to nose, that I couldn't move around him so I could stand on the bottom of the pool. [I was] breathless from treading water as his finger against my shoulder kept pushing me down. Not until months later, as I got to know him, did I realize that for this early exchange Lyndon Johnson had instinctively and intentionally picked a depth of the pool where he could stand and I had to tread water.") Johnson spent hours

lying on an immense chaise lounge that had been placed beside the pool, sip-
ping lemonade made with sugarless sweeteners, and yelling "Bird! Bird!" into
an intercom, in a voice that one visitor likened to a "hog call," whenever he
wanted something.

Then there was the diet, and as time passed, it grew increasingly difficult
to keep Johnson on it. A dietitian, Juanita Roberts, was brought to the ranch,
and installed there, and she devised dishes—a low-fat tapioca pudding made
with Sucaryl, for example—with which Johnson could cram himself without
ingesting many calories; his weight stayed between 175 and 180. Lady Bird
had to supervise this area of his activity, too. "When this is over," she told a
friend, "I want to go off by myself and cry for about two hours." Lyndon might
"get along all right," she wrote another friend. "I don't know whether I'll make
it or not."

And he poured himself into the recovery of his career. Part of the day was
rest, but the remainder was politics as usual—the Lyndon Johnson brand of
politics. Wanting, in Reedy's words, to "generate attention—keep people aware
of his presence," he began dictating letters to Lady Bird and Mary Rather, dictating so many that they couldn't keep up with him, and they were joined by a
recent addition to the staff, Mary Margaret Wiley, a twenty-six-year-old University of Texas graduate, dictating so many that the three women, working at
card tables set up in the rock-walled living room, couldn't type them up in the
perfect style he wanted fast enough, or to cross-index them for the files, and the
letters were sent off for typing ("On new stationery with pretty typewriter—
Hurry Please!") in big packages to the larger staff in the Washington office,
which also couldn't keep up. (The letters were to foes as well as allies, and all
were written with the Johnson touch: "Dear John: I have been sitting here on
my Ranch looking over the Country in which I was born and just relaxing and
enjoying myself thoroughly. Every prospect pleases except one—the distance
from my close personal friends in the Senate. One of the reasons that I am so
very anxious to recover completely is so I can return to Washington in January
as good as new and thank all of my friends on both sides of the aisle. One of the
first hands I want to shake is that of John W. Bricker.") He began telephoning,
and was soon demanding that the calls be stacked up waiting for him; so many
new telephone lines had to be installed that the long cords grew tangled on the
living room floor. To the clatter of typewriters, a clatter which, a visitor says,
"never seemed to stop," that drifted out of the open windows of the living room
and down across the lawn and the meadow to the placid Pedernales was added
the ringing of telephones, a ringing that also "never seemed to stop." The stacks
of letters and telegrams on the card tables grew higher. A former secretary,
Dorothy Palmie of Austin, who had been reading in the newspapers about the
calm, restful atmosphere at the ranch, drove out for a visit and found him
"going full-blast. Mary Rather and Lady Bird were beating their brains out
with all these little details and tasks and chores." A team headed by Reedy set

up an office in the United States Courthouse in Austin, Jenkins remained in Washington with the rest of the staff, and the three offices were in constant communication. By mid-September, the reports from the Senate Preparedness Investigating Subcommittee began to flow again, as did the glowing promises of future reports ("Watch for the SPSC to try to make headlines this fall with a searching probe of undue cuts in the Defense Department's aircraft and missile programs," *Newsweek*'s "Periscope" declared. "Senator Lyndon Johnson is personally laying out the agenda for this while recuperating in Texas") and the leaks (Reedy, in Austin, to Siegel, in Washington: "I had another talk with the Senator about [reporter] Jack Anderson and I think we should do something for him as soon as possible. Can you find anything in the Preparedness Committee files that I could slip to Jack in a hurry and that would make him a pretty good story? . . . I think that we could make some real 'hay' with Jack"), and other means of influencing the press, including the orchestration of a "spontaneous" letter-writing campaign to try (unsuccessfully) to persuade *Time* magazine that Lyndon Johnson should be its "Man of the Year." The planted stories began again ("Dear Senator, All right! I have followed your instructions. I have just finished and mailed to Texas a five-page story on Grace Tully—Affectionately, Liz"), as did the pressures on government officials for favors for Johnson's friends.

With the loneliness becoming unbearable to him, Johnson began to invite visitors to the ranch—senators and journalists, and others important to him; the first visitors would be Adlai Stevenson, still the leading candidate for the Democratic presidential nomination, who was going to speak at the University of Texas on September 29, and Sam Rayburn, who would introduce him—the two men had agreed to drive out to the Johnson Ranch after the speech and spend the night. So many people were invited that the five upstairs bedrooms, several of which were already occupied by staff members, would not be sufficient; while the pool was still being built, another construction project was begun: a four-room guest house.

Johnson had, furthermore, resumed, as avidly as ever, his quest for money. He did it with his customary circumspection. When E. L. Kurth gave him a prize Brahma bull, named "Johnson's Manso," the papers were sent not to him but to A. W. Moursund, and Moursund was at the ranch almost every day. And he did it with his customary energy. During this period, while he was publicly proclaiming—over and over—his devotion to rest and relaxation, he was working at a headlong pace to add new advertising revenues for his radio and television stations, calling Edwin Weisl Sr., Hearst Newspapers counsel, in New York to bring pressure on some advertisers, using Jenkins to bring pressure on others ("I don't want to leave the impression that we muscled people to come [as advertisers], but we did try to call it to their attention that we had the space available or the time available and could use the programming," Jenkins would say). And he was adding new stations. "That summer he had a little time on his hands, of course, and we decided that we wanted to go and buy another station or perhaps two stations," Jenkins recalls. The station Johnson decided to buy was KANG in Waco, and he conducted the negotiations for that property with the old Johnson touch, bargaining with the owners for a favorable price while gently obtaining from compliant FCC Chairman Bartley advance knowledge of upcoming FCC decisions that would make KANG much more profitable for him than it would ever have been for them, and keeping that knowledge secret so that they would sell to him at a lower price. "Lyndon made a lot of money that summer," Arthur Stehling says. And he was entering new fields as well, buying up stock in the Johnson City Bank and other little Hill Country banks. He took his naps religiously, but woke up from them running—as fast as before. His pace, in fact, seemed to be even faster now. Asked years later, "Did the heart attack slow down Johnson?" George Reedy replied: "It speeded him up if anything."

THEN, IN SEPTEMBER, the political landscape changed—dramatically. Dwight Eisenhower was at the very peak of his enormous popularity. In July, at a top-level conference in Geneva with British Prime Minister Anthony Eden, French Premier Edgar Faure, and the two Russian leaders, Nikita Khrushchev and Nikolai Bulganin (Winston Churchill had coined a word for such a meeting; he called it a "summit"), Ike's broad, open grin and his apparent candor and earnest desire for peace had won the hearts of Europeans, and his proposal for an "Open Skies" aerial inspection treaty to reduce the threat of nuclear war had captured the world's imagination. As he was flying home in triumph aboard the *Columbine,* Gallup pollsters were finding that no less than four out of five Americans approved of his performance as President. And then, on September 24, he suffered a heart attack while on a golfing vacation in Denver.

Ike's attack, a coronary thrombosis, was more serious than Johnson's, and Eisenhower, just three weeks short of his sixty-fifth birthday, was almost eighteen years older. The Democratic National Convention was less than a year away, and the general assumption in Washington, an assumption that endured for months, was that the President would not run for another term. Lyndon Johnson, who during the next three days would telephone Eisenhower's press secretary, Jim Hagerty, two or three times a day to express concern and ask how the President was doing (thereafter, he would be given daily reports by Jerry Persons), was almost instantly running for the prize he had always sought.

The strategy he evolved—in talks with no one, lying deep in thought on the recliner or walking deep in thought along the path next to the Pedernales— was the strategy Richard Russell had used in 1952, but with a crucial difference. With Russell having removed himself from the picture, Johnson believed he would be the candidate of a solid South, with its 262 votes in the 1,200-vote convention. And he believed that because of the firm ties he had forged with western and border-state senators, he could do what Russell had not been able to do—collect enough votes from these states to give him a substantial bloc at the convention.

At the moment, Stevenson had most of the southern votes, as the least of three evils, the others being Kefauver and the New York liberal Harriman. If none of these three men could get a majority of the convention, it would be stalemated, and the nomination could well go to a fourth, "compromise," candidate, if this candidate had a substantial, solid bloc of votes behind him.

The first requirement was that southern support be stripped away from Stevenson. That would be accomplished by Johnson's entry into the race. The second was that both Stevenson and Kefauver be stopped—preferably that they kill each other off. The third was that Johnson position himself to be a candidate. And there was an additional, urgent, requirement: that Johnson do so without becoming a candidate openly. An announcement that he was running would rouse northeastern Democrats and liberals across the country, distrustful of him because of his past pro-southern positions, to organize a "Stop Johnson" movement and effectively destroy his candidacy before the convention so that he would not be able to become a compromise choice there. His effectiveness as the Democratic Senate Leader would be undermined as well; as Tommy Corcoran was to explain, "If his colleagues thought he was pushing all those programs to get a track record for a presidential race, they'd scatter every time he called a caucus." He should go to the convention, he decided, as Texas' favorite-son candidate. That way, his name would be placed before the convention—but in such a fashion that he could claim he was not a serious candidate but was only trying to hold his state's vote until its delegation determined which of the other candidates to support. And to make sure he held the delegation's vote, he decided, he should also be its chairman.

By COINCIDENCE, the perfect opportunity to implement this strategy was immediately to hand: that already scheduled visit, just five days after Eisenhower's heart attack, by Adlai Stevenson and Sam Rayburn.

The visit had originally been thought of—by both Johnson and Stevenson—as little more than a courtesy call. Now, however, there were consequential matters to discuss. Johnson wanted them discussed in secret, but someone in Austin learned that Stevenson and Rayburn would be going out to the Johnson Ranch after the speech, and George Reedy had to telephone Johnson from Austin to inform him that a large contingent of reporters could be expected the following morning.

Johnson's reaction was rage: an old-time explosion that "could be felt all the way to Austin," that was so violent that Reedy "started being afraid that he was going to bring on another heart attack and die," and that didn't subside for hours; at midnight, Reedy got another call—from Lady Bird, "just begging me

to keep the press from going out to [the ranch]." "She was just crying, just crying. Apparently the people out at the ranch were like a family would be during
the Black Death in Europe." Explaining that while reporters could be barred
from the ranch itself—"That's private property"—nobody could keep them
from standing on the public highway right outside the gates "and talking to
people going in and out," he advised her to allow them on the ranch instead of
letting them "use their imaginations as to what happened."

Rayburn, Grace Tully (along for symbolism), Stevenson, and Stevenson's
aide Newton Minow arrived about eleven o'clock at night, expecting to find a
man recuperating from a heart attack already asleep. Instead he was waiting for
them in front of his house. And the discussion among the three leading figures
in the Democratic Party, held on the porch, under a huge Hill Country moon
and a sky filled with stars, lasted until well past midnight.

Among the subjects of discussion was how to handle the press the next
day. The reporters, Johnson said with his usual hyperbole, "think that you,
Adlai, and you, Mr. Sam, and I are here plotting to take over the government
while Ike is dying. We're not going to let them do that." And the next morning
was, to Reedy, who had spent a very worried night, another "Lyndon Johnson
paradox," with his boss the most gracious of hosts. Coming out onto the front
porch at 6:30 a.m., while his guests were still asleep, Johnson found a crowd of
newsreel, newspaper and radio reporters on his front lawn. "Are you going to
throw me off, Senator?" Dave Cheavens asked. "Of course not," Lyndon Johnson said, with a laugh and a broad smile. Walking over to his station wagon and
saying, "Hop in," he took a half dozen reporters, with the others following in
their own cars, on a forty-minute tour of the ranch. When they returned,
Stevenson was outside, and Johnson beckoned him to come over to the barn,
then walked ahead of him, noticeably faster than usual with his long strides so
that Stevenson was forced to trot to keep up. He loaded Stevenson into an electric golf cart, in which the two men zoomed along the concrete walk past the
herd of white-faced Herefords near the river, and when Rayburn emerged from
the house, the three men had a Texas ranch breakfast: orange juice, Pecos cantaloupe, scrambled eggs, bacon, venison sausage, hominy grits, popovers, and
coffee. "Please," said Stevenson after the meal. "Let's skip lunch." Then they
sat down on three chairs on the lawn, the journalists crowded around, and a
press conference was held.

Rayburn didn't do much talking, sitting with no expression at all on his
face, declining to smile for the cameras, and Stevenson wasn't required to do
much, either. When, asked if he thought Texas would return to the Democratic
column in 1956, he started to reply, Johnson cut him off. "I think Mr. Rayburn
and myself are in a better position to answer that question," he said. "Texas will
be in the Democratic column." "Who am I to contradict?" Adlai said with a
smile. When, at the end of the conference, a reporter asked Stevenson if he was
planning to return to Texas, he said, "I'd like to come back to Texas and either

talk or listen—whatever they'll permit me to do." All three men said that they had agreed not to take advantage of President Eisenhower's illness. Johnson and Stevenson said the visit had been just a purely social call. Stevenson had the grace to make the statement with a slight smile, which seemed to suggest that everyone there knew he was saying what had to be said, and when pressed on whether any politics had been discussed, he said, "I am in the presence of politicians, and it is possible the talk may have reverted to politics." Johnson, however, insisted that *his* statement be believed. "It was purely a social visit with an old friend," he said firmly, and his elaboration on this point was summed up by *Time:* "No politics had been discussed, said Johnson, and as far as he was concerned none were going to be. The visit had absolutely no relationship to any political situation arising from Eisenhower's illness."

The visit had not been purely social, naturally. Stevenson had been "pointedly advised by Senator Johnson," as William White was later to report, that he must contest Kefauver in at least one or two state primaries in order to prove he was more popular. This course might well lead Stevenson into a trap "in the light of [Kefauver's] demonstrated skill in that type of campaigning," White noted; should Stevenson "fail to score heavily in the primaries, he then would be only one of several candidates" and "no longer the odds-on favorite at the convention." Aware of that danger, Stevenson told Minow on the flight back to Chicago that "I'm not going to do it. If the party wants me, I'll run again, but I'm not going to run around like I did before to all those shopping centers like I'm running for sheriff. The hell with it." Johnson's "advice," however, had been accompanied by a subtly worded warning about what might happen if it was not followed: in White's phrase, if Adlai entered the primaries, "no all-out 'Stop Stevenson' movement would be likely to arise at the Convention." And in the event, the advice was followed.

Texas' powerful and reactionary governor, Allan Shivers, had expected to be chairman of the state's delegation, but Johnson had on his side the only man in Texas capable of breaking Shivers' hold on the state, and Sam Rayburn was willing to do so because, he believed, Shivers had in 1952 committed the sin that was unpardonable to this man to whom "there are no degrees in honorableness—you are or you aren't": he had broken his word to him, promising to support Stevenson and then throwing the state to Eisenhower. After Stevenson left the ranch, Johnson apparently told Rayburn—Rayburn was shortly to repeat the conversation to Tommy Corcoran and Jim Rowe when they visited him on his ranch in Bonham—that he knew he couldn't win the Democratic presidential nomination, but that he wanted to try for it at the convention so that he would be in a stronger position to get the vice presidential nomination—which would put him ahead of the field for the top spot in 1960.

Feeling that Stevenson had the nomination sewn up, and aware of the depth of liberal antipathy to Johnson, Rayburn was not enthusiastic about Johnson's candidacy, believing it would split his beloved party after fate—Dwight

Eisenhower's heart attack—had handed it a chance to retake the White House. Although he had little more respect for Stevenson than Johnson did, he wanted a short, harmonious convention. In addition, loving Johnson, he didn't want him running so soon after his heart attack.

But, loving Johnson, Sam Rayburn knew what Lyndon really wanted (not for a minute, Corcoran and Rowe understood, did Mr. Sam believe that what Johnson was aiming for was the second spot on the ticket), and he knew how much he wanted it. He agreed to help. Rowe was to write Johnson in a very confidential letter that at Bonham "he spoke of you, as he often does to me, with a certain amount of pride in you and also with some hedging, like an over-fond uncle who thinks his favorite nephew should get a lot more spankings than he does." Rayburn told the two Washington insiders that he had "regretted agreeing" to Johnson's proposals "as soon as he left" the LBJ Ranch. "He made it clear that . . . he wants a quick convention giving the nomination to Stevenson, so that the Democrats don't get themselves in a first-class row. . . . He felt that you were making a serious error in forming the Southern coalition because it meant that you would become the prime target of the Northerners." And Rayburn told the two Washingtonians that if what Johnson wanted was really the second spot, "he, Rayburn, could get it for you by himself and without any trouble." (Tommy Corcoran asked him how he would do that. Years later, Tommy the Cork would recall Rayburn's reply. "Sam just looked at me, for a long time, and said, 'I will go to him [Stevenson] and ask him for it.' But it wasn't what he said, but the way he looked when he said it. That was the end of that conversation. I thought, 'God help Adlai if he tries to take on Mr. Sam.' ") In his contemporaneous letter reporting the conversation with Rayburn, Rowe, who was not given to reporting facial expressions, wrote Johnson that Rayburn had said "he would go to Stevenson and demand it and he knew he would get it." But he *had* agreed to Johnson's proposals, had given his word. Shivers was loudly vowing to fight for the delegation chairmanship; Sam Rayburn simply said to reporters, "Lyndon will be Texas's 'favorite son' for President at this year's convention and he will also serve as chairman of the Texas delegation to that convention." And that was the way that, after a brutal fight, it turned out.

THE REACTION TO Dwight Eisenhower's heart attack emphasized to Lyndon Johnson the gulf between where he was and where he wanted to be: the fact that while a Senate Leader might be big news in Washington, and to some extent in New York, he was decidedly less big—indeed, not even particularly well known, compared to the President—in the rest of the country. The Dow Jones Industrial Average plummeted, in its most disastrous day since the Crash of 1929; losses were estimated at more than $12 billion. There had not been a tremor in the stock market on the news of his own attack. He had been so proud that the number of letters and telegrams he had received had eventually risen to seven thousand. The White House received tens of thousands of letters and telegrams every day. Bulletins about the President's condition were on newspaper front pages day after day; his cardiologist, Paul Dudley White, of Boston, became the most famous physician in the country, his every pronouncement analyzed and reanalyzed by columnists for clues as to whether Ike could run again. (Question: "Is your answer yes?" Dr. White: "I would say that it is up to him." Question: "Did you say he would be physically able to do it?" Dr. White: "Oh yes. . . . But many things are possible that may not be advisable. If I were in his shoes I wouldn't want to run again, having seen the strain.") After an Eisenhower press conference on January 8, 1956, newsmen would conclude by four to one that Ike would not stand for re-election; not until later that month did the President begin to hint that he would run again.

And all during that fall and winter of 1955, the jangle of telephones and the clatter of typewriters were not the only additions to that still, quiet Pedernales landscape; there were plumes of dust in the air, fast-moving plumes from cars carrying visitors from the Austin and Fredericksburg airports to the LBJ Ranch along unpaved Hill Country roads. The flow of visitors increased: Russell, Clements, Symington, Fulbright, Price Daniel, George Smathers, John Connally, Bobby Baker—so many that Reedy could tell Johnson that his ranch had become his party's "political capital." Polls were telling Johnson one story, Gallup's reporting that Stevenson was the favorite of 39 percent of Democratic voters, Kefauver of 33 percent, Harriman of 6 percent, and Johnson of only 3 percent, several other polls listing him only among the "other candidates" favored by less than 1 percent of the respondents. A survey of Democratic county chairmen showed him far behind Stevenson and Kefauver even among the 573 chairmen in the South. In the rest of the country he was the favorite of hardly any county chairmen at all: of only four out of 567 in the Midwest, of only six out of 214 in the West. And of the 142 chairmen in the East, not one preferred Lyndon Johnson for President. But he was telling himself another story. "The backing and filling around the candidacy of Adlai Stevenson . . . is by this time not merely obvious but blatant," Doris Fleeson wrote. "Its basic cause, of course, is that Democrats now think they can win," but not with Stevenson as the candidate. If the South's county chairmen were not solidly behind Johnson, the South's senators were, and other elements of a southern–border-state–western coalition seemed to be falling into place. Asked during a visit to the LBJ Ranch if Oklahoma might join Texas in making Johnson a favorite son, Senator Bob Kerr replied that "Outside of football, there is no state Oklahoma would rather go along with than Texas and no subject on which it would be easier to reach agreement." Montana's Mansfield said it was a "reasonable assumption" that Johnson "might become a figure around whom Southern and Western Democrats could rally." "Here [on the Johnson Ranch] is where the southern bloc is being organized," Richard Strout wrote in *The New Republic*. "Before the Roosevelt Revolution, the South had a two-thirds convention rule that gave Dixie something of a veto power over the candidate. Now the effort is being made to organize the same device, in effect, through the offices of Senator Johnson." White wrote in the *Times* that "Some of the Democratic professionals are maneuvering to gain for the South and conservatives generally an extraordinary and conceivably even a decisive influence on the Democratic national convention next year. The unofficial and unlabelled headquarters for this effort is the LBJ Ranch on the Pedernales River."

THE REACTION OF DEMOCRATIC LIBERALS—"growing resentment," in a *Times* phrase—to these reports reinforced Johnson's conviction that they would organize against him if he became an open candidate, and his denials were piously emphatic. Attacking "unjustified presumptions" in the press, he declared that his ranch "has not been a meeting place for discussions or evaluations or planning the strategy of any Democratic nominee," and added that "It would be unfair and improper for a trustee of the party to set himself up as a kingmaker."

Corcoran had come to the ranch bearing the offer of a substantial gift— from a man who had the power to make one: Joseph P. Kennedy Sr. In a meeting in New York, the Ambassador instructed Corcoran to tell Johnson that if he would publicly enter the race for the nomination, and would privately promise that if he won, he would select Jack Kennedy as his running mate, Joe Kennedy would arrange the financing for the ticket. If Johnson was not running, the Ambassador said, he would support Stevenson.

This offer revealed at least two drastic underestimations on the Ambassador's part: first, about the extent of Johnson's own financing, and, second, about Johnson's political acumen. No sooner were the words of the offer out of his mouth, Corcoran saw, than Johnson understood the reasoning behind it: old Joe Kennedy was betting that Eisenhower would run again (in which case he would, of course, win again). The Democratic vice presidential nomination would give young, relatively unknown Jack Kennedy the national recognition he needed to give him a running start at the 1960 presidential nomination. And it would be more desirable for that candidacy to be on a Johnson rather than on a Stevenson ticket; Adlai, old Joe felt, would lose in a landslide, and an overwhelming defeat would be attributed partly to the Catholicism of his running mate, a belief which would damage Kennedy's chances in 1960. Johnson, the Ambassador believed, would lose, but in a much closer race.

Johnson didn't believe that Jack Kennedy would have a serious chance in 1960. "He never said a word of importance in the Senate and he never did a thing," he was to recall later. And the young senator was also, in Johnson's words, obviously seriously ill, "malaria-ridden and yellah, sickly, sickly." But there was no point in improving Kennedy's chances—and it was important that his own candidacy in 1956 not be made public. "Lyndon told me he wasn't running, and I told Joe," Corcoran recalls. Joe then telephoned Lyndon himself, making the same offer, and was turned down; Johnson was to recall telling the Ambassador that "I did not wish to be a candidate."

"Young Bobby [Robert F. Kennedy] was infuriated," Corcoran was to recall. "He believed it was unforgivably discourteous to turn down his father's generous offer." Jack, Corcoran was to recall, was more circumspect. He called me down to his office. . . . 'Listen, Tommy,' Jack said, 'we made an honest offer to Lyndon Johnson through you. He turned us down. Can you tell us this: Is Lyndon Johnson running without us? . . . Is he running?' " " 'Of course he is,' " Corcoran replied. " 'He may not think he is. And certainly he's saying he isn't. But I know goddamned well he is. I'm sorry that he doesn't know it.' "

He *did* know it, of course. He was running harder than ever—so hard, in fact, that his doctors, worried, tried to slow him down. When Dr. Cain did not hear from Johnson for "three or four weeks," he understood why—"I am sure his reluctance to write is related to the fact that he knows I might fuss at him for doing too much. . . . He is doing too much and thinking too much"—and, finally, on November 19, he wrote him. "Lyndon, you have come along very well following this heart attack and, as I have said all along, I have every hope that you are going to be completely all right." But, he said, "I just want to offer a word of warning and a suggestion that you slow down some."

But they couldn't slow him down. One of Reedy's memos had spoken of a need for Johnson to demonstrate that he was "back in the saddle again." The phrase caught Johnson's fancy, and he provided the demonstration by returning to the national stage with a speech, his first since his heart attack, in the little Texas town of Whitney (as he appeared on stage, a band struck up the song "Back in the Saddle Again"). The speech announced his program—he called it "A Program with a Heart" (get it?)—for the upcoming congressional session, a list of thirteen proposals which he said would be submitted to the Democratic Policy Committee "in the hope that they can be brought before the Senate, considered and acted upon by the Senate." Twelve of the proposals were acceptable to liberals—broadening of Social Security coverage, increased federal funding of medical research, school construction, highways and housing, for example—including the one civil rights proposal that southerners would tolerate: a constitutional amendment to eliminate the poll tax. The thirteenth, listed as Number 7 because Johnson believed that if it was buried smack in the middle of the list it had its best chance to escape notice, was the price he was paying for the Texas conservatives' support: "A natural gas bill that will preserve free enterprise." (Johnson said that "of course" the bill would also provide protection to consumers.) A number of editorials noted that, as the *Baltimore Sun* pointed out, "on a good many of the issues the Republicans have already been there," and somehow liberals managed to find, and understand, even Number 7: "Senator Johnson's 'of course' will not be accepted by many of his colleagues in the Senate who feel that the 1955 Johnson natural gas bill . . . was just a gim-

mick to make Texas gas millionaires richer at the expense of northern consumers," the *Washington Star* commented. On the whole, however, his return
from death's door was greeted so enthusiastically that Dorothy Nichols, mail-
ing a packet of press clippings to the ranch, wrote, "It looks like in the eyes of
the press and the nation you have reached a spot where you can do no wrong.
How fine!"

Johnson had said repeatedly that he would defer a decision on resuming
the majority leadership until after a complete checkup by Dr. Hurst at Emory
University Hospital in Atlanta on December 14 and then by a team of doctors at
the Mayo Clinic in Rochester, Minnesota. But he couldn't wait. More and more
senators—Kerr Scott of North Carolina, Humphrey, Styles Bridges—were
coming to the ranch, as were television executives and lobbyists like Scoop
Russell of NBC, and when they returned to Washington, they reported, as
Robert Albright wrote in the *Washington Post* on November 27, that Johnson
"is talking in terms of the same personally run floor show he successfully conducted last year. . . . Delegations of authority will be few. To friends who
inquire if he is well enough, Johnson retorts that he would 'rather wear out than
rust out.' " And the private meetings grew only more numerous: day after day,
pilot Reg Robbins would put down on Wesley West's landing strip, where no
unwanted eye could see, and keep the engines idling. The big white Lincoln
Continental would pull up, and the tall, gangling figure of the Majority Leader
of the United States Senate would climb out and climb aboard, and the Brown
& Root DC-3 would take off, for the quiet conferences in 8-F in Houston or in
the messy suite at the Fort Worth Club, or for Fort Clark or St. Joe. And at least
once, on November 29, Robbins headed west to California, where Lyndon
Johnson gave a speech before the American Hotel Association ("The Democrats will take everything from the courthouse to the White House," he predicted), then met in the Beverly Hills Hotel with a representative of Howard
Hughes, with whom he was on a "hard cash, adult basis," and who had to be
made to understand that five thousand a year wasn't what was needed now—
that "real money" was going to be required in 1956—and on the way back the
DC-3 made a stop in Las Vegas, to see Hughes himself.

The private maneuvering behind the Senate scenes intensified, too. In late
November, Estes Kefauver arrived at the ranch, where, on a hunting trip with
Johnson, the Tennessean got a ten-point buck "right through the heart" at about
three hundred paces with a rifle with a telescopic lens. Outwardly, all was
friendliness but, unknown to Kefauver, Johnson was taking steps to deny him
the position from which he was hoping to garner publicity during the upcoming
Senate session. Judiciary Chairman Harley Kilgore had promised Kefauver the
chairmanship of the subcommittee to investigate monopolies, which Kefauver
could use to investigate the Dixon-Yates contract. But now, Drew Pearson
reported, Johnson "laid down the law to Kilgore": if Kefauver was given the
subcommittee chairmanship, Judiciary's budget would be cut to the bone.

So caught up was Johnson in the race he was running now that, once again, as for most of his life, dates meant nothing to him; trying to set up a conference with Adlai Stevenson or his campaign manager, Tom Finnegan, he scribbled a note to Stevenson: "I'd like to see you or Finnegan [on] Dec. 25th." If there was a reason that the December 25 page in his appointment book had been blank, the reason didn't seem to cross Lyndon Johnson's mind.

THERE WAS ONE ADDITIONAL REMINDER of his youth that autumn. The 1955 Homecoming Day celebration of Southwest Texas State Teachers College at San Marcos had been named "Lyndon Johnson Day" and the college's "most illustrious graduate" gave the principal address in Cecil E. Evans Auditorium, and afterwards sat on a reviewing stand as floats, decorated by fraternities and sororities, chronicling his triumphant political career passed by. Johnson's feelings on that day may not have been solely of triumph, however. On the platform with him were the two former deans, Tom Nichols and H. E. Speck, who had with razor blades cut out of every copy of the 1930 college yearbook, *The Pedagog*, they could find the pages that referred to "Bull" (for Bullshit) Johnson, and that set down in print other aspects of his fellow students' disdain for him. Also on the platform were several fellow members of the Class of 1930 who had used that nickname freely to Johnson's face—and whose feelings, in some cases, had not been blunted by time; the member of the class selected to give a talk about Johnson was Vernon Whiteside, who took delight, every time he met Johnson, in reminding him of mean tricks he had played or elections he had stolen during his student days. Also on the platform was the college's librarian, Ethel Davis. She was the sister of Carol Davis, daughter of the richest man in San Marcos, whom Lyndon Johnson had courted avidly, with a determination to marry for money so unconcealed that *The Pedagog* had mocked it in print, but whose father had held the Johnson clan in contempt—Carol Davis who had broken with Lyndon because "I knew I couldn't go against my father's wishes."

ON DECEMBER 11, three days before the "definitive" medical checkups, the DC-3 took off from the Wesley West airstrip, but not to either Atlanta or Rochester. Lyndon Johnson, accompanied by his wife, cook, masseur, dietitian, and chauffeur, was flying to Washington. He had dinner at Thirtieth Place with Richard Russell. The next day, Gene Williams drove him down to Capitol Hill, the first time he had returned there since his heart attack, and he held a standing-room-only press conference attended by 125 reporters. The reporters were astonished by the transformation in Johnson's physical appearance. Tanned, trim (he weighed "about 170 pounds"—about fifty-five pounds less than he had weighed the last time they had seen him) and handsome, he seemed bursting with energy and confidence. Edward J. Milne of the *Providence Bulletin,* who interviewed him in G-14, described how Johnson sat "with his feet crossed on the desk top as if to prove how relaxed he is, but with a frequent tapping of fingers on chair arm hinting at all the old, restless tension." Before the press conference, he had met with Senators Murray, Mansfield, Hayden, and Anderson, with lobbyists Clark Clifford, Corcoran, and Rowe, and with columnist Fleeson. After the press conference he met with Justice Douglas, then had dinner with Averell Harriman. Only then did he fly to see his doctors, accompanied by Reedy and Russell and talking presidential strategy all the way. After examining Johnson, the doctors reported that he had fully recovered. "Senator Johnson is now active, and his reactions to activity are normal," they said. "His blood pressure is normal, his heart size is normal, and his electrocardiogram has returned to normal." They said that they had advised Johnson that "extraordinary pressures and abnormal tensions should be kept to a minimum," but that so long as he maintained "carefully regulated hours of work and rest," the Senator could resume the leadership.

TWO ASPECTS of Lyndon Johnson's life changed during the six months he spent recovering from his heart attack.

One was his relationship with his wife.

He had asked her never to leave his bedside until he was out of danger, and she hadn't left. "Every time I lifted my hand, she would be there," he was to recall. After he left the hospital, Ruth Montgomery was to write, "Lyndon could scarcely bear to have Bird out of his sight." On the ranch, Mary Rather says, "whatever Lyndon did, Lady Bird did with him. How she managed to run the house, attend to her children, talk to visitors and still take care of her husband, I sometimes wondered." Chores that took her away from him were done while he was sleeping. Whenever he woke and asked, "Where's Bird?" she "was always near enough at hand to answer for herself: 'Here I am, darling.' " Their daughters, Ms. Montgomery was to write, "sensed a subtle change in their parents. . . . They seemed closer to each other than ever before." "Of course, what happened, it deprived the girls even more of her presence and her motherhood," George Reedy was to say. "I think they spent almost all of that time with Willie Day." (Wherever they spent their time, Ms. Rather says, "They weren't there at the ranch a great deal.") An exception was the trip to California, on which the Johnsons took Lynda and Lucy along, and where they spent a day with them at Disneyland; the girls "had the time of their lives," Ms. Rather says.

And as Lyndon recovered on the ranch, Lady Bird was happy, happier than anyone could remember her being.

"I never saw a woman more obviously in love with a man and more obviously grateful that he had been rescued," George Reedy says. "In her face, you could see it. I remember once when we were walking down the path, she just reached over and gave him a quick hug. You could almost feel the joy bubbling in her veins that he was still alive. I think she forgot and forgave all the times that he'd made life miserable for her, which he did very often." Among the hundreds of letters from strangers to Lady Bird was one from a woman who wrote that "Some of the happiest days of our lives were *after* my husband's heart attack." At the time she first read the letter, Lady Bird was to recall, she was "puzzled" by what the woman had written. But later, she was to recall, "I came to understand."

Her every thought seemed to be for his comfort and peace of mind; she would tell guests at the ranch to laugh as much as possible—Lyndon liked people to laugh, she would say—and to be careful not to say anything about how loosely Lyndon's clothes hung on him; "she knew how susceptible he was to the dispositions of those around him." There was no longer any resistance to his suggestions about her own clothes. "I begrudge making a career out of clothes, but Lyndon likes bright colors and dramatic styles that do the most for one's figure, and I try to please him," she was to say. "I've really tried to learn the art of clothes, because you don't sell for what you're worth unless you look well." Accompanying him on his diet, keeping him on it with soft-voiced diplomacy (to his demand for a banana one afternoon, she said, "Let's each have half a banana"), she herself reduced her weight from 132 to 114. The only task she undertook without success was the one Lyndon's mother had failed in when he was a boy: to get him to read books. She was finally reduced to doing what Lyndon's mother had done so many years before: find a portion of a book she felt would be helpful to Lyndon, and read it to him, in the very small doses which were all he would tolerate. (Jim Rowe, familiar with Lyndon's reading tolerance, sent Benjamin Thomas' new biography of Abraham Lincoln to Lady Bird with a note: because "Lyndon has a lot to learn from Lincoln," he wrote, "I am sending it to *you,* not Lyndon, with instructions that you should read it to him for one-half hour a day and no more." Lady Bird replied that "I promise to siphon as much of the most significant parts as I can to Lyndon, choosing the opportunities whenever they come along.") She collaborated with her husband in concealing what he wanted to conceal: because her first excuse for her absence at Middleburg—the fact that she had stayed in Washington for Lucy's birthday party—emphasized that Lucy's father had not stayed, she changed the excuse, telling journalists now that she had stayed because Lucy had a slight fever. She helped him to create the image he wanted, telling journalists that Lyndon's illness had given him time to read and that "he has been rediscovering the printed word in magazines and books"; that he had no presidential ambitions ("I firmly believe that he does not," she told journalist Irwin Ross. "If he does have such ambitions, they are so subterranean that I don't know about them").

And now, gradually, Lyndon Johnson's treatment of Lady Bird began to change. Not that it became, by normal standards, considerate or even polite, but he began to allow her a role in his life, the life from which he had so largely excluded her ever since, in 1942, she had proven she could be effective in it. ("Politics was Lyndon's life, not mine.") The "See you later, Bird" dismissals continued, but, now, only when the politics under discussion was very pragmatic. More and more, for other discussions—of issues and strategy—she was allowed to remain. So long as other politicians were in the room, she sat quietly, concealing her thoughts. After they had left, however, and she was alone with her husband and perhaps an assistant, he began to ask for her opinion, and Booth Mooney noticed that, more and more, when she gave it, "He listened to her." He was particularly observant of her opinion on how a speech or issue would "play" to the general public. "Somebody else can have Madison Avenue. I'll take Bird," he was to say. He began to praise her publicly. During interviews with journalists, he would, more and more often, point to her picture on his office wall and, as Irwin Ross put it, "deliver some tribute to her wit or wisdom." Even at home, although he still ordered her in the old bullying tone of the past, to run the most menial errands, more and more his orders to her would have at least a veneer of courtesy.

And in response, Lady Bird changed—in a change that was slow but sure and would eventually be so complete that it would amount to a transformation from the shy young woman who had once been terrified of speaking in public to the poised, dignified, gracious Lady Bird Johnson whom the American people were to come to admire in later years. "If ever a woman transformed herself—deliberately, knowingly, painstakingly—it was she," Mooney was to say. "A modest, introspective girl gradually became a figure of steel cloaked in velvet. Both metal and fabric were genuine." When she was seated on a dais, her face, while her husband was speaking, would still be tilted upward and toward him as unmovingly as ever, and her expression would be approving. But it was not long after their return to Washington in December, 1955, that she began, when her husband had been haranguing an audience for a long time, to slip him little notes as he stood speaking. And once, Mooney, picking up a note after a speech, read, with astonishment, the words she had written: "That's enough." Then Mooney began to notice that the notes appeared to have an effect; sometimes, after receiving one and glancing at it, Johnson, about to launch into another area of discourse, would visibly check himself, thank the audience for its attention, and sit down. And once, when a Lady Bird note had had no effect, Mooney, from his vantage point on the dais, saw something even more astonishing: Lady Bird reached out, took the tail of Lyndon's jacket, and tugged at it, and "soon afterward he stopped talking and sat down." And there were other signs of the transformation. When, at cocktail parties, Johnson began pouring down Scotch and sodas at his old methodically intensifying rate, she would say a quiet word to him. Once Lyndon replied that "My doctor says Scotch keeps my arteries open." "They don't have to be that wide open," she said with a smile.

Her encouragement and reassurance were constant and extravagant. Once, not seeing her at a public function, he demanded, with something of his old snarl, "Where's Lady Bird?" and she replied, "Right behind you, darling. Where I've always been." At a conference at which he became agitated, she slipped him a note. "Don't let anybody upset you. You'll do the right thing. You're a good man."

THE CHANGE IN LYNDON JOHNSON'S TREATMENT of Lady Bird did not extend to sexual fidelity.

Until the guest house at the Johnson Ranch was completed near the end of 1955, Lyndon's guests and his secretaries and assistants stayed in the five bedrooms on the second floor of the main house. Johnson made frequent nocturnal visits to that floor. During one visit, Corcoran and Rowe were sharing one of those bedrooms, and, both men recall that, in Rowe's words, "Next to us was a [bed]room in which a good-looking girl was sleeping." As the two men were preparing to turn in for the night, they heard footsteps—"clearly identifiable as Lyndon's"—coming up the stairs and going past their door to that bedroom. They heard the door to that room open and shut. Later, Johnson "barged" into their room, exchanged a few sentences of idle conversation, and left. The next day, Rowe, Lyndon, and Lady Bird happened to be swimming in the new heated pool together, and Rowe without thinking said jokingly, "You know, a guy with a heart attack isn't supposed to be climbing so many stairs."

"Lady Bird asked Lyndon, 'Were you up on the second floor last night?' " Rowe recalls, and, suddenly realizing his mistake, "I almost sunk under the water with mortification at what I had said." As he was sinking, however, Rowe heard Johnson say, "I just went up to see that Tommy and Jim had everything they needed."

Rowe then understood, he says, why Johnson had barged in on them: "So that he could say, 'I just went up to see that Tommy and Jim. . . .' " His feelings were confirmed after Johnson had returned to Washington in January, 1956, and his affair with the "good-looking girl" became, in Corcoran's phrase, "common knowledge" around the capital.

But Lady Bird had, years before, at Longlea, learned to reconcile herself to this aspect of her husband's behavior, and she hadn't forgotten that lesson, as was proven during a conference among his physicians down at the ranch. Lady Bird was present, as was a single staff member, George Reedy, when the doctors again advised Johnson that he had to relax more, to do things he enjoyed, and Johnson told the doctors that "he enjoyed nothing but whiskey, sunshine and sex." Reedy found the moment "poignant," he was to recall. "Without realizing what he was doing, he had outlined succinctly the tragedy of his life. The only way he could get away from himself was sensation: sun, booze, sex." It was "quite clear," Reedy was to say, that Johnson was not talking merely about sex with his wife, and there was an "embarrassed silence." It was broken by his wife, speaking to the doctors in a calm voice. "Well, I think Lyndon has described it to you very well," she said. In later years, when more details of her husband's sexual affairs emerged, she would sometimes be asked about them. She finally evolved a stock reply: "Lyndon loved *people*," she would say. "It would be unnatural for him to withhold love from half the people." And the reply was always delivered with a smile.

THE OTHER ASPECT of Lyndon Johnson's life that changed after his heart attack was his relationship with his staff, or at least the rages that had been a centerpiece of that relationship. Tension and anger were among the gravest threats to a heart attack victim, his doctors had warned him. Some causes of tension and anger would, to Lyndon Johnson, still be unavoidable, as would become apparent quite soon after his return to Washington. But anger at subordinates was not one of them. Some of his obscenity-laced tirades at his assistants and secretaries had been rages into which he deliberately worked himself as a means of control; there were other methods—simple ones—of controlling subordinates, and more and more he used these instead. Other tirades, not planned, had simply reflected a refusal to control himself. Now, with anger at subordinates a luxury he could no longer afford, indulgence in that luxury was reduced, quickly and effectively. "He became . . . less hard to get along with," Walter Jenkins says. "Up to that time, when things didn't go just to suit him, he had a tendency to fly off the handle, at little things. . . . It seemed to me that he was able to ignore these things more after the heart attack."

Not that the rages ended. There were, at intervals, still the sudden, vicious, obscenity-filled explosions. Men and women who had not known the pre–heart attack Lyndon Johnson would still, witnessing one of these explosions, say they had "never seen anything like it."

Fearsome though they were, however, they were not the rages of old. There was a reduction in frequency, in duration—and in intensity. While they had lost nothing of their viciousness and ability to hurt, their relative quietness made them less emotionally draining. "Now he *had* to control himself, and he did," John Connally says. "In those early days, he would be just wild, *wild!*, raging, ranting, screaming, totally out of control. Now, you could almost see him sometimes checking himself, reining himself in, as if he was saying, 'I'm not going to have a heart attack over George Reedy.' "

29

The Program
with a Heart

ON THE OPENING DAY of the 1956 session of Congress, ninety-one senators were at their desks when, after the chaplain's prayer, the Majority Leader rose to ask for recognition so that he could request a quorum call. Before Vice President Nixon gave him the floor, however, he said, "The Chair knows that he expresses the heartfelt sentiments of all the members of this body when he says that we are most happy to see the senator from Texas back in his accustomed seat." All along the four arcs of desks, senators stood and applauded. "You don't know how glad I am to stand at this desk again," Lyndon Johnson said quietly. After the quorum call had begun, he walked out to the lobby to pose for photographers. Nixon came out and put his arm around him. Walter George and Harry Byrd crowded up to him, not to get into the picture but to say hello, and Theodore Francis Green was not far behind. As they talked to Lyndon, the old men's faces lit up and their eyes were warm behind their thick glasses. Hubert Humphrey bustled over to shake his hand, with a broad, warm smile on his face, and it was no broader than Bill Knowland's. When, later that week, the Democratic Policy Committee held its first meeting, Johnson began by expressing his "everlasting gratitude" to Earle Clements and all the committee members for "carrying on so admirably" during his illness. "It was a labor of love for all of us," Clements replied, and the heads around the table—Jim Murray's and Lister Hill's and Bob Kerr's and Carl Hayden's as well as Dick Russell's—nodded vigorously in agreement. Lyndon Johnson, who had spent his life searching for affection and a sense of security, was back in a place where he had found as much of those commodities as he was ever likely to find anywhere. He had just spent five months in the valley in which he had been born and raised, but he was back in a place, on a hill, that was much more a home to him than the Pedernales had ever been.

. . .

SPEAKING AT THE WOMEN'S NATIONAL PRESS CLUB "Welcome to Congress" dinner in the Hotel Statler that evening, tall and rangy, his deeply bronzed face dramatic above the black and white of his evening clothes, Johnson said that his heart attack had been "a wonderful way to gain a little perspective. I think I learned lessons of humility and of proportions—when to put forth the maximum effort and when to let troubles go by." Assuring reporter John D. Morris of the *New York Times* that he was going to follow his doctors' orders, he said, "I'm going to be sensible. I'm not going to try to do everything."

James H. Rowe, the highly respected lawyer and political insider, who had known Lyndon Johnson for almost twenty years, was aware that, as he was to say, Johnson would always use "whatever he could" to "make people feel sorry for him" because "that helped him get what he wanted from them." But that awareness didn't help Rowe when the person from whom Johnson wanted something was *him*. Johnson had been trying for years to acquire Rowe's full-time services. He was aware of something known to very few people in Washington. Capital legend had bestowed much of the credit for Harry Truman's 1948 victory on a memorandum written to the President before the campaign, at a time when his chances appeared hopeless. The memo proposed a campaign strategy, and it did so with great specificity and pragmatism; every one of its recommendations was based not on ideology but on what the memo called "the politically advantageous thing to do." Truman had reputedly kept the document—thirty-two single-spaced typewritten pages—in the bottom drawer of his desk all during the campaign, using it as a blueprint for his come-from-behind victory. The memo, which had acquired an almost talismanic significance in the capital's political circles, had been presented to the President by Clark Clifford, his legal counsel, and its authorship was publicly attributed to him, but Johnson knew that except for some editing changes the author was actually Rowe. Having read the memo—and having observed how closely Truman adhered to its strategy—Johnson believed that the President had relied on it heavily, and that its brilliance had been proven by Truman's victory. He felt that Rowe could do the same for him: could give him, too, a blueprint for reaching the goal that flickered always before him. He had, George Reedy was to say with more than a touch of envy, "an almost mystical belief in Jim's powers. He thought Jim might make him Pope or God knows what." But while Rowe had always been available to help Johnson with advice, having observed how Johnson treated people on his payroll, he had always rejected Johnson's offers to join his staff. During that first week in January, however, Johnson renewed his overtures—with a new argument—and when Rowe refused this time, he wouldn't let it drop. "I wish you would come down to the Senate and help me," he said in a low, earnest voice. And when Rowe continued to refuse, using his law practice as an excuse ("I said, 'I can't afford it, I'll lose clients' "), he found that Johnson was telling other members of their circle how cruel it was of Jim to refuse to help to take a little of the load off a man at death's door. "People I knew were coming up to me on the street—on the *street*—and saying, 'Why aren't you helping Lyndon? Don't you know how sick he is? How can you let him down when he needs you?' "

Johnson had spoken to Rowe's law partner, Rowe found. "To my amazement, Corcoran was saying, 'You just can't do this to Lyndon Johnson!' I said, 'What do you mean I can't do it?' He said, 'Never mind the clients. We'll hold down the law firm.' " Johnson had spoken to Rowe's wife. "One night, Elizabeth turned on me: 'Why are you doing this to poor Lyndon?' "

Then Lyndon Johnson came to Jim Rowe's office again, to plead with him, crying real tears as he sat doubled over, his face in his hands. "He wept. 'I'm going to die. You're an old friend. I thought you were my friend and you don't care that I'm going to die. It's just selfish of you, typically selfish.' "

Finally Rowe said, " 'Oh, goddamn it, all right' "—and then "as soon as Lyndon got what he wanted," Rowe was forcibly reminded why he had been determined not to join his staff. The moment the words were out of Rowe's mouth, Johnson straightened up, and his tone changed instantly from one of pleading to one of cold command.

"Just remember," he said. "I make the decisions. You don't."

THROUGHOUT THE 1956 SESSION, Johnson used his heart attack to get what he wanted from senators, too. Bobby Baker would remind senators recalcitrant on one issue or another that they shouldn't upset the Leader, that he was a sick man, that they should try to make things easier for him—arguments that had particular resonance in 1956 for a group in which, that year, the shadow of death was particularly dark. In February, Harley Kilgore died of a stroke, and in April, Alben Barkley, giving a speech at a college in Virginia, had just proclaimed, in one of his trademark religious references, "I would rather be a servant in the House of the Lord than sit in the seats of the mighty," when he clutched his chest, collapsed, and died of a heart attack. And all through that year, Eugene Millikin, once tall and vigorous but now pale and gaunt, was forced to attend Senate sessions in a wheelchair because of an illness that he called arthritis but that his colleagues suspected was something worse; in July, Millikin announced that he would not seek reelection that November.

Johnson did, indeed, act like a heart patent for a while, following his doctors' orders. He took a nap in the midafternoon, on the couch either in G-14 or in Skeeter Johnston's inner office, or, occasionally, in the Marble Room, with an aide stationed outside the door to make sure he wasn't disturbed. Because the ordinary sofa was too short for him to stretch out, he had Senate cabinetmaker Renzo Vanni make a number of new couches, seven feet long, extra wide, so big that Vanni called them "battleship couches"; one, called by others the "Johnson Couch," remains in the Marble Room to this day. And for a while these naps were not to be interrupted. He would tell Skeeter's assistant, Dorothye Scott, "how soon to call him," and tell her he wasn't to be disturbed until then.

But only for a short while. After a week or two, when he came through Skeeter's outer office, Ms. Scott recalls, "he would walk in his great, big strides, like an antelope, and by the time he would get from my outer office into the inner office he would have said about seven things he wanted me to do." And long before the time he had told Ms. Scott to wake him, the door to the inner office would burst open, and he would stride out, asking her if the things had been done. More and more days were uninterrupted by any nap at all. Clements was in trouble in Kentucky, where he would have to stand for re-election in November against a very popular Republican, tall, handsome Assistant Secretary of State Thruston Morton. By February, the Assistant Leader was spending a lot of time back home, and Johnson asked George Smathers to be "acting whip." The suave Floridian knew Johnson the senator, but he didn't know Johnson the boss, and he quickly found out that, as he was to put it, Johnson "was very, very difficult to work for." Senator though he might be, Smathers found himself treated as if he were a member of Johnson's staff, and he learned that when Johnson gave an assignment, no excuses were accepted. "He used to say, 'I want only *can do* people.' That was one of his favorite expressions. 'I only want *can do* people around. I don't want anybody who tells me that they can't do something.' " If the assignment was to obtain a senator's vote, "Johnson was very unsympathetic" if that vote was not forth-coming. Once "Quentin Burdick . . . didn't vote like Johnson wanted. 'Why didn't you get on that, goddamn you, so-and-so and so-and-so two weeks ago!' " And the assignments never stopped coming. "He demanded not just one hundred percent of your time, but more than that," Smathers recalls. Every morning, early, "Lyndon came by my house on Garfield Street," and I was with him until ten-thirty at night. As soon as we walked into the Capitol, he started his sixty-cylinder engine, and he didn't slow up during the entire work-day." He wanted Smathers to be available until he left for home, and "Then it seemed like only a few hours later [that] Lyndon and his limousine were back at my front door to start a new day." There was no time to nap, or to slow down, because the first major business Lyndon Johnson put before the Senate, within three weeks after the session began, was the part of his "Program with a Heart" that he considered the most significant for his political future: that proposal he had tried to conceal in the middle of the program so that no one would notice it.

DURING THE SIX YEARS that had passed since 1949, the Senate's refusal to advise and consent to the reappointment of Leland Olds had had the desired effect on the Federal Power Commission. Olds' replacement by the malleable

Mon Wallgren meant that three of the FPC's five members were consistently reluctant to stand between the wealthy natural gas producers and the still greater wealth they coveted—understandably reluctant, in Paul Douglas' view. "All know the great pressure which has been exerted by the big producers on the Commission . . . and the punishment which has been meted out to those who took an opposite stand," Douglas wrote in 1956. "Since this is a real world, it is not to be wondered at that the majority of the Commission have chosen to play it safe." Not only had the FPC reversed, one by one, the policies and regulations that Olds had promulgated to moderate the producers' greed, it had even taken the stance that its jurisdiction did not extend to the independent producers who sold gas to the pipeline companies—a stance which allowed the producers to claim steadily higher costs and to charge steadily higher rates— and when House liberals moved to formally give it that jurisdiction, the commission declined to accept it. During those six years, therefore, the price of natural gas had risen and risen again, from six cents per one thousand cubic feet of gas in 1949 to ten cents in 1955, and so had the profits of the natural gas companies, and the price of their stock: a share of Superior Oil Company stock sold for $150 in 1949; in 1956, it was selling for exactly $1,000 per share; since the Keck family owned 21,977 shares of Superior stock, it was easy to calculate the value of their holdings: $21,977,000. As for Herman and George Brown's Texas Eastern Transmission, a share of its stock, priced at $12 in 1949, was selling for $28 in 1955, which meant that the holdings of the two brothers— only a small share, of course, of their overall assets—was worth $8,379,000.

In 1954, however, the states of Michigan and Wisconsin, whose residents and factories constituted the captive market of gigantic Phillips Petroleum, were paying almost 40 percent more for natural gas than in 1949, took the FPC to court to force it to give consumers the protection that Franklin Roosevelt had created it to give them, and the Supreme Court, holding for the states, specifically ordered the agency to accept jurisdiction over the independent producers, and regulate their rates.

Responding to this verdict as slowly as it dared, the FPC issued its decisions on rate applications so slowly that they caused what *Fortune* called "the biggest logjam in the history" of any federal regulatory agency. Delayed though regulation might be, however, it was coming, unless something was done about the court ruling. Legislation was needed to supersede it. In October, 1954, therefore, the country's largest oil companies formed two committees. The activities of one, the "Natural Gas and Oil Resources Committee," would be public: an advertising and public relations campaign to create support for the legislation; the committee would spend $1,753,000 during 1955 "to educate the public." The activities of the other committee—budget and expenditures kept tightly concealed—were more private. Its educational efforts were directed not at the public but at members of Congress; it was formed, as a memorandum by the committee's attorneys was to explain, "for this express purpose." The funds for the lobbying carried out by this "General Gas Committee" were collected under the direction of another figure from the Olds hearings, Lyndon Johnson's old ally Maston Nixon of Corpus Christi, president of the Southern Minerals Corporation, and were distributed by two principal lobbyists: Johnson's former administrative assistant John Connally, and Elmer Patman, a loud, arrogant attorney from Austin, Texas, who was on Superior Oil's payroll. Early in 1955, a bill was introduced by Arkansas Representative Oren Harris to in effect nullify the Supreme Court decision by exempting independent producers from FPC regulation, and on July 28, 1955, after extensive lobbying by both public and private committees, it was passed, 209 to 203, by the House of Representatives. A companion bill, introduced by Arkansas Senator Fulbright, was reported out of the Senate Commerce Committee that same day.

BRINGING THE HARRIS-FULBRIGHT NATURAL GAS BILL to the Senate floor would angrily divide Democratic senators. The resulting split would run along geographic rather than the usual ideological lines: senators from the gas-producing southwestern and western states were adamantly in favor of deregulation; senators from the gas-consuming northern and eastern states adamantly opposed. The intra-party floor fight would be bitter, for not only were Democratic liberals against the measure, so were some of the party's many conservative senators—because the injustice was too raw for them. More than 70 percent of America's natural gas was owned by only forty-two companies, many of which were controlled by a small, often overlapping, group of individuals like Richardson, Murchison, Abercrombie, the Kecks, and the brothers Brown. It was this small group that was reaping, at the expense of more than 21 million familes, most of them middle or lower class, enormous, almost unimaginable profits. If there could be said to exist a "national interest" in natural gas regulation, it most certainly lay on the side of the consumers, not the producers. The producers, in addition, possessed a virtual monopoly over a natural resource which should, in the last analysis, belong to the people as a whole, and in the absence of federal regulation, the monopoly would only grow stronger, and the consumers would be only more and more defenseless against it. Millions of urban families owned gas-powered stoves, hot-water heaters and furnaces; purchasing new appliances run on other fuels would be expensive— too expensive for most of them. "Once the lines are laid, the homes hooked into the utility systems and the cooking and heating appliances bought, the chance for the users of gas to get any real protection against unfair producers' prices by competition is nil," Walter Goodman said. Speaking for the mayors of fifty American cities, Philadelphia's Mayor Joseph Clark told a Senate committee: "To eliminate controls . . . is to leave the consumer at the mercy of [a] small group of oil companies." The southerners on whose support Lyndon Johnson could usually rely were split. Brown & Root's Posh Oltorf would never forget his surprise when he learned that "Lyndon was having as much trouble with the conservatives as with the liberals—with Russell as much as Humphrey. They [leading conservative senators] were opposed to it [the natural gas bill]. They were for free enterprise, but this was just too much. They thought it was terrible. They thought it was a damned bonanza for the oil companies. We had a terrible time with Russell and Byrd. I remember my shock that they would be opposed to something for businessmen."

The stakes involved in passage of the bill were huge, however. Estimates of the short-term increases in gas prices that could be expected following its passage ranged between $200 million and $400 million per year, an increase that would boost the values of the producers' gas reserves by between $12 billion and $30 billion. In expectation of passage, immense quantities of gas were being held off the market so that it could be sold at higher prices. Divisive though the bill would be, Lyndon Johnson's cherished "unity" had to be sacrificed to higher considerations. To win the Democratic presidential nomination, he would have to become friendlier with northern liberals, and his principal financiers, rabid reactionaries almost to a man, would not ordinarily tolerate that. But the natural gas bill could be the key to greater tolerance, for these Texas tycoons held huge natural gas reserves. As the astute Oltorf was to explain, "This [the natural gas bill] transcended ideology. This would put something in their pocket. That's how they viewed politics. Any son of a bitch who makes me a million dollars can't be all bad. As long as you put dollars in their pockets, they'd forgive your ideology."

Divisive though the Harris-Fulbright Bill might be, therefore, in 1955 Lyndon Johnson had only been waiting for it to be passed by the House before bringing it to the Senate floor and passing it. With a majority of Democratic senators against the bill, he would have to pass it, over the wishes of his own party, with Republican votes—and he had been intending to do just that, with the support of Eisenhower, who firmly believed that the measure would liberate businessmen from unwarranted governmental restrictions.

Johnson didn't want these arrangements upset by his heart attack. When Acting Majority Leader Clements visited him at the Bethesda Medical Center in July, 1955, Johnson expressed himself, as Clements reported to the Democratic Policy Committee upon his return from the hospital, "very frankly"; "he [Johnson] would like the bill taken up yesterday and passed the day before yesterday."

Clements was not the man for so difficult a job, as he himself appears to have recognized. Telling the Policy Committee that "opponents were ready for extended discussion," he betrayed a lack of confidence that the bill could be passed without Johnson's personal participation in the fight, saying, "In January, we will have back with us our distinguished friend from Texas. He will be back with us strong. . . . I will be happy to have it come up as early as possible in January." The committee agreed that that would probably be best.

Now Johnson was back—strong. Opposition within his party had filtered into even his rubber-stamp Policy Committee. Trying to show, as he put it in a committee meeting on January 5, 1956, that "I wanted to lean over backwards so I could not be accused of ramming the bill down the throats of the Senate," he had invited the leading proponents and opponents of the natural gas bill to make their case before the committee, and Paul Douglas made the opposition case with his usual eloquence. The bill, Douglas said, shouldn't be passed, or even introduced, "under Democratic sponsorship." In 1954, Douglas said, one of the most effective Democratic issues against the Republicans had been the "giveaway to big business." If the bill "comes out under Democratic sponsorship," he said, "it is going to deprive our presidential, senatorial and congressional candidates of our strongest arguments. . . . If any Democratic speaker talked about giveaway favors to big business, it would be thrown back in his face. . . . This might well be a factor in our losing control of committees in both houses." Johnson tried to counter that argument, but as usual when he confronted Douglas in argument, he did not get the better of the exchange. "Senator Johnson said he had heard that [Douglas'] viewpoint expressed strongly in the Tidelands argument, but it didn't seem to have that effect on the 1954 elections," the Policy Committee minutes report. "Senator Douglas replied that the Tidelands Bill was brought up under Republican leadership." Conceding that "the majority of the Policy Committee" was probably against the natural gas bill, Johnson said, "the only question was whether it should be brought up." Was there any objection to bringing it to the floor? he asked. "I won't object, but I want to say that it will be very unfortunate in my state," Hennings of Missouri replied. Five of the nine committee members hadn't said a word during the discussion, and the committee finally looked where it always looked for direction. When "Senator Russell said his memory was" that in July the committee had agreed that it would be bought up "as early as possible in January," the committee agreed that it could be brought up.

IT WAS TIME for the first team. "They [the oilmen] sent their best men up," Posh Oltorf was to recall, in the tone of a Texas Homer relating the story of an historic battle. Across the crowded lobby of the Mayflower Hotel a big hand with two missing fingers waved to a friend, and, seeing that hand, Lobbyist Dale Miller whispered in awe to a friend, "Ed Clark's here." To get the legendary Secret Boss of Texas to Washington, the Humble Oil Company was paying him—in addition, of course, to the rent for his suite and all expenses— a fee of one thousand dollars per day, but, so that he wouldn't have to suffer the indignity of registering as a lobbyist, "it was arranged," as he would recall, "that although the 'Umble was paying me, it would be paid through Brown & Root," a construction firm ostensibly unconnected with any legislation then before Congress. And Clark, of course, had his private incentive for winning the natural gas fight: those forty thousand shares of Texas Eastern in his lockbox back in Austin. The broad-shouldered, big-bellied, squeaky-voiced, rumpled, coarse Clark was one of the two men the natural gas industry considered its most effective champions; the other—tall, slim, handsome, smoother than smooth, custom-tailored in pinstriped banker's blue—was also at the Mayflower. "John Connally had the entrées [*sic*]," Oltorf would recall. "He knew everybody from being on Johnson's staff. And everybody liked Connally. And he could really get his side across. He knew how to talk to senators. He would say, 'We'll *never forget* you. You will be doing a wonderful thing for your country, and I'll *never forget it.*' And, of course, that implies future support." The arrogant Patman had been supervising the General Gas Committee's lobbying efforts; he was informed that from now on, he would be reporting to Connally.

Other lobbyists, not of the stature of a Clark or Connally but heroic figures in the Texas oil industry nonetheless, took the field in the Natural Gas Battle of 1956: Charlie Francis, Colonel Ernest O. Thompson of the Texas Railroad Commission ("I remember seeing Colonel Thompson when I was a boy, in a tent in an oil field in East Texas," Dale Miller would say. "And he was up there in Washington in 1956—old and bent, but he was there"), Robert Windfohr of Dallas. Some wore into that battle the mantle of their fathers. Dale Miller's huge suite at the Mayflower—377—had been the suite of his late father, Roy Miller of Texas Gulf Sulphur, an almost mythical lobbyist possessed of so much power in Washington that, the *Saturday Evening Post* said, "For twenty years he has had the status of a quasi-public figure." The executive director of the Mid-Continent Oil and Gas Association, Claude Wild Jr., a very canny young political string-puller, was the son of Claude Wild Sr., the canny old pol who had pulled strings for Lyndon Johnson's early campaigns in Texas. And all these men knew that this battle would be remembered in years to come. Talking with the author decades later, some of them tried to ensure that their participation in it would be recorded for history. Claude Wild Jr. was discussing another matter when he interrupted himself to say, "You know, I was in charge of counting the votes for the natural gas bill." After a pause, he added, "You're not writing that down." And he waited until the author had made the desired note before continuing. During that battle, some of the oilmen even came up to Washington themselves, staying at the Mayflower. "I saw Hunt there today," Texans told each other excitedly. "Sid's here, too. I saw him. And Old Man Keck in his wheelchair." George Brown, suave and discreet, was seldom seen: his suite was not at the Mayflower but at the Hay-Adams.

And it was time for the captain of the team. Not only did Lyndon Johnson install Clark and Connally in the Democratic Policy Committee office—"at whoever's desk was vacant," secretary Nadine Brammer recalls—so that they could make their telephone calls right out of the Capitol Rotunda, not only did he allow them to use his private office when face-to-face lobbying was needed, he also threw his weight behind them. "He [Johnson] would call senators up and ask them to come in and see me," Clark says. And Johnson made sure that senators knew that when Clark and Connally spoke, they spoke for him.

Johnson, of course, was lobbying himself—"harder than anyone," Oltorf says—as well as mapping strategy and directing the overall campaign. Every evening, after the Majority Leader had finished his work on the Senate floor, Connally would be waiting for him in 231 to give him what Oltorf calls "daily reports." Then Connally would have dinner with Oltorf—who would relay the reports to Herman Brown in Houston.

And Johnson was not lobbying only in his office. In obtaining the necessary votes from the other side of the aisle, he needed more than Eisenhower's support, so he was deepening his alliance with the Republican senator who, as chairman of the GOP Policy Committee and ranking GOP member of the Appropriations Committee, held power over bills vital to GOP senators. The glue for part of that alliance was social: "He had Styles [Bridges] down [to Huntlands] during the natural gas fight," Oltorf recalls. Part was philosophical—to Bridges, of course, any assault on business had to be Communist-inspired—and part, as always in the Johnson-Bridges relationship, was pragmatic. The five thousand dollars in cash from Johnson that Bobby Baker carried to New Hampshire for Bridges was only one episode—in either October or November of 1955, Elmer Patman had made a "lobbying" trip to that state. And in the overall pattern of the Johnson-Bridges relationship, these were minor episodes. The key figures in the major episodes were Connally and Clark. Asked why Bridges would not only support the natural gas bill himself but would also bring the support of other Republican senators, Connally replied, "The reason was money." He said he did not recall the amount involved, but that it was large. "I told you, I carried inordinate amounts of cash," he said. Asked the reason for Bridges' support, Clark smiled and rubbed together his thumb and index finger in the gesture that means money. Asked how much money, Clark said he could no longer recall, but, asked if it might have been about five thousand dollars, he laughed. "It would have been many *times* five thousand," he said. "Styles Bridges was no piker." Nor was such "lobbying" confined to New Hampshire. Patman sent an emissary, John Neff, to pay visits to several Republican senators in the Midwest.

Whatever terrain he picked for his battle, Lyndon Johnson fought well. "I was worried," Claude Wild recalls. "It [natural gas deregulation] was not a popular issue. If you don't have a good champion there—well, it's awful easy for a senator to vote against it." But, Wild says, natural gas had "a real champion": not Rayburn ("I doubt he had any impression [of the stakes]. He had no idea what money was") but Johnson. "In Lyndon, we really had one." Says Oltorf: "He [Johnson] got Bridges. Johnson really wanted him involved—and he *got* him involved." Hardly had the Senate convened on January 3 when Johnson knew he had enough Republican votes to win.

The captain had devised a devastatingly effective strategy. Northern newspapers and magazines were already seething with outrage. The *New York Times* called the bill wrong "socially, economically and politically." *The Nation* called it a "gouge," saying that "the producers are convinced they will get away with it because of their power over Congress" (and reminding its readers that "oil interests helped to finance McCarthy's four-year anti-Democratic crusade"). *The New Republic* said that "the contention that natural gas ought to sell in a free market, like coal or wheat, loses some force when one notes that buyers of natural gas can never buy in a free market." Johnson kept debate on the Senate floor from turning the temperature up any higher. Proclaiming repeatedly that he would not "ram" the bill through, that of course there must be "full debate" on so important a measure, Johnson gave the northerners all the time they wanted—a full month, with the vote scheduled for February 6. His only request, he said, was that the debate be "gentlemanly." What he didn't give them was arguments, or opposition, or even an audience—anything that would furnish grist for the journalistic mill. When liberal opponents of the bill were speaking, there were few comments, or even questions, from the bill's supporters. There were, in fact, few supporters. Johnson had told them to stay away from the Chamber.

By thus arranging for the liberals to be ignored rather than answered, he had ensured that their speeches received less attention than would have been the case had there been controversy—newsmaking controversy—on the floor. And since many liberals had a natural reluctance to sit at their desks listening to someone else give a long speech, and they had no leader strong enough to ensure that they stayed on the floor anyway, liberals often found themselves speaking to a very small audience indeed. On January 25, for example, Paul Douglas took the floor for a long, carefully researched speech against the Harris-Fulbright Bill. There were only two other senators present, the presiding officer and Frank Carlson of Kansas. The presiding officer signaled to Carlson to take the chair, and, stepping down from the dais, left the Chamber himself. "That left Senator Douglas talking to four rows of desks" in which there was not a single senator present, Frederick Othman wrote. "In the press gallery, reporters were busy interviewing each other on the question of whether anybody remembered seeing a senator speaking to nobody at all. Even the oldest correspondent couldn't remember a time when at least two or three senators weren't on the floor."

Unwilling to blame themselves for the situation (which of course could have been at least partially improved had they simply been willing to sacrifice a little time to listen to one another speak), the liberals blamed Johnson. "For the sake of appearances it would seem that Senator Lyndon Johnson, who cleverly stage-managed this puppet show, would have arranged for more senators to . . . attend to make it look good from the galleries," Thomas Stokes said. As it was, Stokes said, the "farce gives itself away. Too slick was his careful arrangement of 'full debate.' . . . The scene in the Senate reflecting the apathy and cynicism of the elected servants . . . carries me back to the 1920s when big money was moving the pawns about here in Washington." But the strategy worked. While some of the arguments against the bill were eloquent—"the concentrated power of the great oil companies, wielded today to influence the decision of national Government by contributions to both parties in many parts of the United States, is a menace to the proper functioning of free government within this country," Hennings said—the arguments were delivered before galleries that were almost as empty as the floor. Writing angrily that "perhaps the most cynical aspect of Johnson's management of the issue was his pious decree that the debate must be 'gentlemanly,' " Doris Fleeson had to admit that the decree, "of course, had the effect of dampening tension and excitement, emotions that do sometimes communicate themselves to the Senate and the public and affect the outcome of debate." The *Washington Post* could only observe helplessly that because "senators have stayed away from the Senate in droves," the "arguments on the floor have attracted far less attention than they deserved." "Never in the many years I have covered Washington have I seen such a skillful job of backstage manipulation," Drew Pearson had to confess. So completely did Johnson feel he had the situation under control that in the middle of the debate, he left for a brief vacation in Florida—on a Brown & Root plane.

AND THEN, WITHOUT WARNING, the Natural Gas Bill of 1956 became a moral issue. On Friday, February 3, as the Senate was droning toward the weekend recess before the scheduled Monday vote on the measure, Senator Francis Case of South Dakota suddenly rose at his desk and announced that a lobbyist for a natural gas company had come to his campaign headquarters in Sioux Falls and left an envelope to be given to him—an envelope containing hundred-dollar bills, "twenty-five of them, in fact."

He had been planning to vote for the bill, Case said—"The principle of maintaining free enterprise appeals to me"—but the payment (which "would be the largest single contribution I could remember for any campaign of mine") reminded him of Hennings' warning that the oil companies' "money power" is "a menace to the proper functioning of free government."

"I object," Case said, to "doing something so valuable to those interested in natural gas that they advance huge sums of money as a down payment, so to speak, on the profits they expect to harvest." Since the bill evidently "has prospects of unusual monetary profit to some, and with that profit would go the means for a continuing effort to influence the course of government for private gain, I must vote" against it.

Suddenly the press had all the grist it needed. "SENATOR TELLS OF BRIBE ATTEMPT," headlines blared. Summoning Gulf Oil's chief lobbyist, David Searls, to his Mayflower suite, Ed Clark gave him some very serious advice. "You are in the wrong place today. I wouldn't want to be in Washington today."

There would almost certainly be an investigation of Case's charge, Clark said, and that investigation might easily expand to include other contributions. If Searls was in Washington, it would be easy to serve a subpoena on him. "And if you ever get called to testify, you're going to be in a position where you have to tell the truth or lie. And if you lie, you're going to be in danger of perjury. If it were me, I would leave *today*." Whether or not Searls himself followed Clark's advice is not known, but it was followed by so many others that the Mayflower found itself with an unexpectedly high number of vacant rooms that Friday evening: all that afternoon, the private planes had been taking off from National Airport, heading southwest.

John Connally was not nearly as tough as Clark. And he was far more immediately threatened by Case's bombshell. Although the Senator had not yet named the lobbyist who had offered him the cash, saying he wanted to do so not on the Senate floor but to some "properly constituted authority" such as the FBI or a Senate Committee, Connally knew that it was John Neff, a lobbyist for Keck's Superior Oil Company, and that the cash had come from Elmer Patman and the General Gas Committee, whose lobbying operations Connally was directing. And Connally didn't move as fast as Clark, either. When Tommy Corcoran rushed into Connally's suite at the Mayflower, he found him "white-faced," all the self-assurance gone in an instant. For an entire day, he "sat paralyzed," one of his biographers, James Reston Jr., was to write. Then he, too, left town. As Reston says, "The widely held rumor was that Lyndon Johnson had spirited his friend out of Washington for fear that Connally would be questioned and then implicated and indicted in the scandal." (In his own memoir, Connally says, in an attempt at exculpation that is unintentionally revealing: "No attempt had been made to bribe anyone. A contribution that would have been given routinely was handled clumsily, with atrocious timing. But this was unfortunately one of the quirks of character of people who lived and died in an industry where fortunes were made and lost almost overnight. Many oilmen of that period carried with them staggering amounts of cash, and they treated it as though they were tossing around chips in a Las Vegas casino.")

Lyndon Johnson wasn't paralyzed. His instant reaction was to rage at Case—"I think we ought to investigate the morals of some people in South Dakota for bringing this up," he said—and to try to make him seem like a guilty party in the matter. First, he tried to impugn Case's veracity by casting doubt on the truth of the story, saying (in a statement with no basis in fact) that it was based upon "a vague recollection of a lady clerk." The next day he said: "Thus far, Senator Case has declined to reveal the name of the man who left the money. Unless the senator from South Dakota voluntarily divulges the name of the fellow, and the impropriety, if any, the Senate is going to investigate." Then, when Case gave Neff's name—together with the envelope and the twenty-five hundred-dollar bills—to the FBI, Johnson switched to impugning Case's motives. Ignoring the fact that Case had been a supporter of the natural gas bill, and the fact that he had reported the contribution as soon as he realized it was connected with the bill, Johnson told reporters that he considered the timing of Case's revelation—so close to the date of the vote—a deliberate attempt to sabotage the measure, an attempt he said would not succeed; when several senators urged that the vote be delayed until, as Mike Mansfield put it, "a complete and thorough investigation" could ascertain "whether other senators had received similar offers," Johnson said there would be no delay. The vote, he said, would be held on Monday as scheduled.

ON MONDAY, on a packed Senate floor, several senators on both sides of the aisle called for a delay until, as Republican Potter of Michigan put it, it could be determined whether Neff's approach to Case had been an isolated instance or "just a small part of the big overall effort of certain people to influence the passage of this bill." But the Majority Leader was having none of it. "The Senate of the United States can ill afford to prostrate itself before phantoms," he said. "That is what we would be doing if we delayed the vote now at hand." When the clerk called the roll, the only senator who changed his vote because of the uproar over the Case contribution was Case, who voted against it. Every other senator voted as Johnson's tally sheet showed he was going to vote. And while Democrats voted against the bill, 24 to 22, Republicans supported it by a 31–14 margin. "The Senate, casting aside suggestions that it was voting under a cloud of suspicion, passed the natural gas bill tonight, 53 to 38," John Morris reported in the *New York Times*. "All signs indicate that President Eisenhower will sign it into law."

The calls for an investigation did not die away, however. In a coincidence that Johnson viewed as unfortunate, the Rules Committee had the previous year appointed a three-member subcommittee to look into the broad question of campaign financing. Not only was it the obvious body to conduct the investigation, but its chairman was Missouri's Hennings, who, facing a re-election campaign in November, had vowed to stop drinking, had in fact kept that vow for some months, and was therefore once again a dynamic and effective senator—and who, as a former District Attorney, knew how to investigate. Moreover, the other Democratic member was the lamentably independent Albert Gore. Surrounded by reporters, in the lobby outside the Senate Chamber, Hennings said his subcommittee would begin the very next morning a "thorough and complete look into the Case matter and every other damn matter in connection with it and get at the big boys if we can."

Lyndon Johnson could not allow such an investigation. The "big boys" in question were *his* big boys—Herman and George, and Sid and Clint and the other oilmen with whose lobbying efforts he had been so closely connected. They were Ed Clark and John Connally, who had worked right out of his office. Any "thorough and complete" investigation could hardly help turning up his name. It had to be stopped.

And he stopped it—on the next day, Tuesday, February 8, 1956, a day of fast-paced, and often brutal, maneuvering in the Capitol and the Senate Office Building. He was not the only senator who wanted it stopped, of course. Some of his colleagues had personal reasons. "What [Mr. Case] did was to raise in the Senate the whisper: 'Oil money,' " William White wrote. Campaign financing was a sensitive issue with many senators, and no aspect of such financing was more sensitive than "oil money." In "recent years," the issues "in which there were truly vast sums of money involved have concerned the oil and gas lobby." Who knew how many senators' names might be blackened in a probe of "oil money"? Others feared a blackening not only of themselves but of what Russell Baker described as the entire "political structure supporting them." There was "a growing uneasiness in the Senate about having itself subjected to a 'tough' investigation on this most delicate of issues," Baker said, a growing "doubt as to whether the voting public could stomach the facts of political life." And the mere fact of such an investigation might tarnish the Senate's image. "Nothing" disturbs "the Senate type" more than "evidence that the Senate may be losing the respect of the country," White wrote. For all these reasons, James Reston Sr. said, "If there is anything that exceeds the need for a fundamental investigation and revision of the present system of financing campaigns it is the unwillingness of many senators to encourage such an investigation." But Johnson was the senator most involved, and he was the senator who played the leading role in stopping the investigation.

Pleading with Hennings to restrict his subcommittee's investigation to the single contribution, Johnson pulled out all the stops. The agitation over the natural gas fight was causing his heart to act up again, he said; the doctor was even threatening to put him back on digitalis. "I felt as though I were being cast in the role of his murderer," a shaken Hennings would tell a friend the next morning. And when Hennings nonetheless tried to stand his ground, he abruptly found it opening beneath his feet.

As soon as the Senate convened on Tuesday, Johnson and Knowland, in a move which Johnson devised and to which Knowland acquiesced, jointly introduced a resolution, which passed unanimously, without discussion, establishing a "Select Committee for Contribution Investigation." Its four members were Democrats Walter George and Carl Hayden, and Republicans Edward Thye of Minnesota and Styles Bridges.

The Select Committee's mandate was as narrow as was implied by the lack of any plural in its title: the resolution empowered it to "investigate the circumstances surrounding" the "alleged improper" contribution to Case—and no other contribution. Included in the resolution was a budget—$10,000—adequate only for so narrow an inquiry. And in the committee's first meeting, held in Vice President Nixon's office, steps were taken to make sure that its investigation of that contribution would be the only investigation of that contribution.

Hennings had telephoned Senator Case that Tuesday morning to invite him to testify at two o'clock that afternoon before his Campaign Finance Sub-committee, and Case had agreed to do so. Johnson, learning of this, moved fast—with Nixon's help. In a formal ruling which the *New York Times* said was "without known example in the Senate," Nixon awarded the Select Committee exclusive jurisdiction over the Case investigation. A letter, hastily typed for Walter George's signature, and delivered to Case at 1:40, just twenty minutes before he was to appear before the Hennings Subcommittee, summoned him to testify before the Select Committee on Friday. The letter notified him of Nixon's ruling, and said that therefore "they [the Select Committee] respect-fully request that you appear before no other committee" prior to that time. The written request was reinforced by an oral communication, described by Arthur Krock: "Mr. George just sent word to Mr. Case that at two o'clock he was to come to the Vice President's room, where Mr. George's Select Committee was to assemble, and Mr. Case was to go nowhere else." And when Case arrived, he was told by George that his first public testimony "had better be to the Select Committee." He was not requesting Case to testify before the committee first, Walter George said; he was directing him to do so.

While Senator George was thus taking steps to keep the subcommittee from holding its hearing, Senator Johnson was taking his own steps, asking Senator Hennings to come to see him in his office, and then trying to persuade him, at length, to leave the investigation to the George Committee.

Johnson had wanted to see Hennings alone, but the Missourian had brought Gore along, and the three men were arguing heatedly when Gore told Hennings, "Let's go. It's after two o'clock and Case was scheduled to meet with us at two."

"Go ahead," Johnson said angrily. "I didn't invite you here."

The two senators went to the subcommittee room, but Case was not there. When the South Dakota senator finally did appear, he was carrying George's letter, which he read to the subcommittee to explain why he couldn't testify before it. And then Hennings and Gore were summoned to a hastily called closed meeting of their subcommittee's parent Rules Committee, and although they angrily protested the "unprecedented" Johnson-Knowland attempt to gag a senator, the rest of the committee said that, in view of Nixon's ruling, the George Committee had exclusive jurisdiction over the Case affair. Once again, all other arguments had faded before what Arthur Krock called "Mr. George's unique prestige." In a column bearing the accurate headline "IT DOESN'T PAY TO CHALLENGE MR. GEORGE," Krock wrote that "The old man doesn't hold with argument if he says a thing is so, or is to be done thus and thus. He doesn't hold with it even if he is acting in his individual capacity, which is pretty pow-erful. And that goes double when Mr. George has been deputized by the Senate leaders of both parties, and another Senator tries to put on the same show in another tent."

· · ·

THE SELECT COMMITTEE TRIED to keep the focus on the Case contribution, and on Case's motives for disclosing it and on the timing of the disclosure. Questioning the Senator for four hours, committee counsel Charles W. Steadman "bored in like a prosecuting attorney," the *New York Times* reported, so that Case "was cast somewhat in the role of a defendant." Nonetheless, it was impossible to avoid calling the man who had made the contribution, and asking where he had gotten the money, and as soon as Neff began to testify, the names of more senators began to surface.

Neff testified that he had gotten the $2,500 from Elmer Patman, and then Patman had to be called, and he testified that he had gotten it from Howard Keck. Asked the nature of his connection with Patman and Keck, Neff testified that he had been employed by Keck's Superior Oil Company to represent it not only in South Dakota but in Nebraska as well. The name of an "old friend" in Nebraska, Donald R. Ross, the U.S. Attorney, came up, and Ross was questioned by the Justice Department. He was shortly to resign, but before he did he stated that Neff had offered him $5,000 after receiving assurance that both of Nebraska's senators, Republicans Carl Curtis and Roman Hruska, would vote for the natural gas bill (as, in fact, both of them had). And, Ross added, Neff had offered to make additional contributions to Nebraska's Republican State Finance Committee. Then the chairman of that committee, Joseph Wishart, revealed that Neff had pulled out "this handful of money," had peeled off $2,500 and given it to him for the committee, and had said he wanted to make additional donations. And Ross also added that Neff had said his employers wanted to make contributions in other states where the people were not unfriendly to the natural gas industry. He had mentioned trying "to get in contact with somebody" in Montana, and had mentioned that he had also made trips to Wyoming and Iowa, and in Iowa had spoken to GOP national committeeman Robert K. Goodwin. It was impossible to avoid calling Goodwin, and he testified that Neff had indeed visited him, had told him that he "had $2,500 . . . to contribute to Senator Hickenlooper's campaign," and had "offered to leave one thousand dollars" with him "pending the time when he could see Senator Hickenlooper." Goodwin said he had turned both offers down because they "seemed like a down payment on a purchase." And then there was a development which made it seem likely that the names of other senators might surface. Goodwin said that when Neff had visited him, he had "apparently inadvertently" left behind a list of the ninety-six senators. Next to each name was written "For," "Doubtful," or "Against," and against the names of ten of the fifteen "Doubtful" senators a checkmark had been made.

It became obvious that more money might be involved than the amounts that had been mentioned. Testifying before the committee, Keck said that he did not consider $2,500 a "substantial" contribution. He said he could not say what other senators had received contributions—substantial or not—because he did not keep records. It became obvious that contributions were mostly in cash. Just as there had been an envelope with twenty-five hundred-dollar bills intended for Case, the money offered to Wishart had been in hundreds, and in an envelope.

Booth Mooney sat in on every hearing of the George Committee "on Johnson's orders, and gave him a detailed report at the end of each day's session," he was to recall. "He was worried, more deeply than I had ever seen him, that his name or John Connally's would come up in the course of the investigation." But somehow, Mooney wrote, "that did not happen," despite the fact that Connally had worked closely with Patman.

Nor was that the only subject unexplored. Neff had testified that "he had contributed to the 'personal campaign fund' of no Senator except Senator Case since last October." But, as the *New York Times* put it, "He was not asked to explain the qualification 'personal campaign fund,' and no attempt was made to determine whether he had made any contributions before last October." Editorials demanded that the Select Committee broaden its probe; ADA Chairman Rauh accused it of merely "scratching the surface of this scandalous incident." "Only the most naive would think that this is all the money involved," the *New York Times* said. Why was Case singled out, "or was the 'benevolence' one of many?" Arthur Krock asked. "The questions call for answers." But Senator George said, "Personally, I see no need for any further inquiry." The committee's hearings were adjourned on March 5. Noting that it "was limited in its scope and confined in its authority by the express direction of the Senate" to the Case contribution, its report, issued on April 7, kept within these limited confines. Commenting that it "left much unsaid," the *Washington Post* stated that its "strangest deficiency . . . lies in its failure to commend Senator Francis Case for his courageous exposure of what the gas bill lobbyists were up to. At the committee's hearings it sometimes appeared that Senator Case was the culprit rather than the people who tried to influence his vote by contributing $2,500. . . ." As for the other senators whose names had come up in the hearings, the committee's report mentioned them only in passing. It assailed Neff, Patman, and Keck, and said it was turning the transcript of the hearings over to the Justice Department to determine if any statutes had been violated. (Neff and Patman were later indicted for failure to register under the Lobbying Act and both men pled guilty, thereby avoiding a trial in which other names might have been mentioned; they were each given a one-year suspended jail sentence and fined a token—a rather whimsical token—$2,500.) And, saying that the Federal Lobbying Act and the Federal Corrupt Practices Act were "too vague and loosely defined," it contained the usual recommendations that Congress make a "thorough and complete" study of campaign financing laws.

THE NEXT EPISODE in the natural gas fight took place, on February 17, not on Capitol Hill but in the White House. President Eisenhower numbered many titans of the oil industry among his friends. He was as indebted to the industry for past campaign contributions as was Johnson—and, as he prepared for his re-election campaign, he was as hopeful of future contributions. He was philosophically committed to reducing, not increasing, government regulation of industry in general, and he was particularly committed to reduction in the case of this industry, for he had become persuaded of the validity of the argument that oil and natural gas exploration entailed great risk, and high profits were therefore necessary to encourage exploration. But to Eisenhower all those considerations were invalidated by the circumstances surrounding the passage of the Natural Gas Act. "There is a great stench around the passing of the bill," he wrote in his diary. It is "the kind of thing that makes American politics a dreary and frustrating experience for anyone who has any regard for moral and ethical standards." Announcing that he approved the bill's basic objectives but that because of the "arrogant" lobbying efforts on its behalf, he could not sign it without creating "doubt among the American people concerning the integrity of governmental processes," he vetoed it. Taking into account his approval of the bill's objectives, as well as the fact that the Republican Party was counting on millions in contributions from the oil industry for the coming campaign, "the veto was an act of some courage," Eisenhower's biographer, Stephen Ambrose, has written.

Lyndon Johnson issued a statement which said, "Since the President himself has regarded this bill as meritorious, his veto is difficult to understand."

NARROW THOUGH JOHNSON had kept the Select Committee investigation, he hadn't kept it narrow enough to accomplish his purposes. Despite his efforts, enough hints of the vastness of the oil industry's lobbying efforts had emerged to fuel indignation over the Senate's failure to police itself, and, in editorials in major newspapers in every section of the country except the Southwest, the indignation was laid at the door of the senator at which it belonged. The *Denver Post,* for example, told its readers that it was "Lyndon Johnson's slippery leadership of the oil bloc" that "has blunted one of his party's sharpest campaign weapons. He's helped turn what had the makings of a crusade against 'giveaways' into a Hollywood production interspersed with drawling commercials for Col. Johnson's banana oil. . . . The plunderbund was Mr. Johnson's victory."

Demands for a full investigation escalated. "The honor and dignity of the Senate require that it expose every aspect of the efforts of the gas lobby to influence the vote through political contributions—both those made recently and those made before the bill was under active consideration," the *Washington Post* said. Calling Senator George's inquiry "unsatisfactory," the *New York Times* said, "There is every reason for a much fuller investigation. . . . Even seasoned veterans of legislative battles have been astounded at the pressures brought to bear." And the indignation was summarized, eloquently, by a journalist who was rising to rare respect and influence in the capital.

Ever since Francis Case made his statement, James Reston Sr. wrote on

February 20, "this city has been full of the most disturbing rumors, not only that this kind of money is passed around by wealthy organizations that stand to gain by the enactment of certain legislation but that the leadership of the Senate is in cahoots to conceal the facts. The immediate question is whether the majority and minority leaders are going to use their power and influence to correct the evils they know to exist or whether they are going to try to conceal them and allow the rumors of widespread misconduct to stain the reputation of what they are fond of referring to as 'the world's greatest legislative body.' "

Given Johnson's plans for an imminent entrance onto the national stage, there was little alternative to authorizing a more complete investigation, and one was authorized—with appropriate fanfare. The day after the Reston column appeared, the Majority Leader took the floor. Declaring that he had been "unfairly, unjustly and almost unmercifully" portrayed as blocking a Senate inquiry, he said his whole purpose from the start of the controversy had been to have a full inquiry and not one confined to the Case contribution. "You senators and reporters—you better saddle your horse and put on your spurs if you're going to keep up with Johnson on the flag, mother and corruption," he said. Then he introduced a resolution, endorsed by Knowland and quickly passed, to create a new Special Committee that would conduct, he promised, a "far-reaching and thorough" investigation dedicated "to uncovering any wrong-doing of any kind and accomplishing something constructive." Instead of having the customary Democratic majority, half of its eight members would be Republican, which, he said, would "give no unfair advantage to either party"; it would have a full-size—$350,000—budget; it was assumed that its chairman would be Albert Gore, who, as the *Times* put it, lauding his appointment, "has been insisting on an intensive investigation" which he had intended to carry out through the Elections Subcommittee but which Johnson had now persuaded him could be better conducted by the Special Committee. The resolution was greeted enthusiastically by the press. "The lobbying investigation" promises "to become the year's liveliest," *Time* said.

Because of what a complete investigation might reveal, however, there was no alternative to making sure that the Special Committee did not actually conduct one. That insurance was put in place by naming to the committee, as the senior Republican member, the ubiquitous Bridges, who was totally unabashed by the revelation that he had been one of the senators visited in his home state by Elmer Patman and hence might himself be a target of the investigation. Gore had assumed that the chairmanship would carry with it a chairman's customary prerogatives, such as the right to appoint the committee's chief counsel and the rest of its staff, and to issue the subpoenas indispensable to any financial investigation. That assumption, however, now proved to be incorrect. At the committee's organizational meeting, at which Gore had expected the first order of business to be his election as chairman, Bridges said that since the committee was not a Standing but a Special Committee, the Senate's normal rules for a committee did not apply, and that new rules would have to be made. "Speaking for the Republicans," he said, an agreement on the rules would have to come "before we proceed to election of any personnel such as chairman." Among the rules the Republicans wanted, Styles Bridges said, was the right, should a Democrat become chairman, to name the vice chairman— him, Styles Bridges. And, he said, the vice chairman must have the right to co-sign all subpoenas. Furthermore, if the Democrats selected the chairman, the Republicans must have the right to select the chief counsel—who, he made clear, would be a Republican with whom he was personally comfortable. Since the Democrats did not have a majority in the committee, Gore was helpless. No chairman was elected, no counsel appointed, no subpoenas issued; after one meeting, *Newsweek* reported, Gore, "boiling with rage, ran out of the building and leaped into a cab before newsmen could catch up." Journalists' initial enthusiasm faded before reality. "Bipartisanship can play Jekyll-Hyde" and the Senate leadership "has found a way to frustrate the lobby investigation . . . and still remain on the side of the angels," *The New Republic* said on March 12. "The new 8-man Senate Committee on Lobbying . . . is headed by the Tennessee crusader Albert Gore. But there will be no Great Crusade here." (Bridges told reporters that his conditions were simply "reasonable proposals drawn up to prevent abuses by a "runaway committee.") The Republicans supported as chairman McClellan, whose Little Rock law firm represented several oil and natural gas companies, and who, as the *Times* put it, has "evinced little sympathy for Senator Gore's objectives." (Bridges was elected vice chairman.)

McClellan moved with deliberation. His first task, he said, on March 10, was the selection of a staff, "which might take some time." That prediction proved accurate. An entire meeting of the committee in mid-April was devoted, the *Washington News* reported, "to discussion of the qualifications of a lady applicant for the job of file clerk." That pace was maintained in all other aspects of the inquiry, which hardly touched on the specific revelations that had been made. Bridges, of course, was never asked about Elmer Patman's visit—or about whether the lobbyist had arrived bearing gifts. Hruska and Curtis were never asked whether they had received the $5,000 contributions, Hickenlooper was never asked about the thousand-dollar offer that "seemed like a down payment on a purchase." John Neff was never asked if any of the fifteen senators listed as "Doubtful" on his list had received funds—or about the significance of the checkmarks by ten of the names. No attempt was made to learn the full extent of the cash distributed by Keck and the Superior Oil Company—or by any other individual or oil company. Key figure though John Connally was in the natural gas lobby, closely though he had worked with Patman, he was never called as a witness. The interest of the press slowly but surely waned, and faded entirely when the national conventions came to dominate the news that summer. The investigation finally petered out in 1957.

·   ·   ·

LYNDON JOHNSON WAS NOT BLAMED by the Texas oilmen because the Natural Gas Act of 1956 did not become law. That, of course, was President Eisenhower's fault; Johnson, they felt, had done his job, and done it well. The man who was in charge of counting the votes for the natural gas lobby, Claude Wild Jr., had expected that after "the big to-do" over the Case contribution, "we would lose some votes," perhaps even enough votes so that the bill wouldn't pass. "But it passed," Wild says. "Only one vote was changed." And he knew who was responsible for such steadfastness. "I've got to give Lyndon Johnson a lot of credit," he says. "I think that was the finest piece of lobbying work I've ever seen." The money that had been promised to Johnson to finance other senators' campaigns in 1956 and in subsequent years would be delivered; Connally and Jenkins still brought envelopes stuffed with cash to Washington; Searls continued to carry cash himself. And it was after Wild succeeded Searls in 1959 that "as his first assignment, to meet a commitment Searls had made earlier to Senator Lyndon B. Johnson," he made the delivery, "over a period of months," of $50,000 in cash "to Mr. Walter Jenkins."

And indeed, despite the presidential veto, the oilmen had no reason to be dissatisfied with the attitude of the federal government. Even pro-business *Fortune* magazine found in 1959 that the Federal Power Commission still "shirks its statutory responsibility of regulating the price of gas in the interests of the consumer," and in that same year the Supreme Court, in a unanimous opinion, assailed the commission for having authorized a new high price for gas producers on "insufficient evidence." The price of the product which before 1956 had already risen from its 1946 level of four cents per million cubic feet to ten cents, had in the three years since 1956 doubled, to more than twenty-one cents—had risen, in fact, to as much as the market could bear; *Fortune* said that "in some areas, like New England, natural gas is close to pricing itself out of the market." The industry's revenues were not the $5.3 billion of 1956 but $10.7 billion. The value of the Kecks' stock was now $40,108,000. And as for Herman and George Brown, they were finding the business so profitable that when, in 1958, an immense new field, the Rayne Field, containing more than a trillion cubic feet of natural gas, was brought in in Texas, they had Texas Eastern Transmission buy up the entire field. By 1959, the annual profits of Texas Eastern would be $24,527,583, so that the Brown stock was worth $7,113,072. The company which had been formed twelve years earlier for an initial investment of $143,000,000 had assets worth more than a billion dollars.

GEORGE SMATHERS, Johnson's "assistant whip" during the Natural Gas Battle, was with him from early in the morning "until ten-thirty at night," and saw that this man who had suffered a heart attack "didn't slow up during the entire workday"—"I don't know how his body stood it." But Johnson not only stood it but thrived on it. At the conclusion of the natural gas fight, Dr. Cain of the Mayo Clinic wrote Tommy Corcoran, "I have had my fingers crossed during this whole trying period, for I know Lyndon must have been under a terrific strain." But when, on February 20, Lyndon underwent a complete physical examination at Bethesda, his heart showed no enlargement, and his blood pressure and other vital signs were actually better than they had been in December.

To the uninitiated, the first close-up look at Lyndon Johnson was astonishing. A new member of his staff, Nadine Brammer, couldn't believe the abuse he rained on the men and women in his office. "He could be totally charming, a lot of fun—he was always trying to put the make on me—but there was a rotten side to him. There was a lot of personal exhibitionism, a lot of hitting on women. It was like a family atmosphere, and he was the Big Daddy. He controlled everything. He ruled with fear—like a heavy-duty parent. Fear permeated the whole staff. Lyndon would jump on someone. Just make mincemeat of him. Tongue-lashing people. Walter was just always on pins and needles. I've seen Walter shake, just literally shake, when Lyndon was asking him questions. Walter was just stripped of any human dignity." Mrs. Brammer was to leave the staff the next year. "I just couldn't understand how they [the staff members] put up with it." Another new member of the staff wouldn't put up with it. Within a month after Jim Rowe, whom Johnson had recruited so ardently, came on board, he told Johnson he was leaving. He finally agreed to remain until the end of the 1956 session, and left then. But no aspect of Johnson was more striking to new staffers than his energy. "He worked us, he *worked* us," Mrs. Brammer says. "And he worked himself, *worked* himself. He had made up his mind to be President, and he was demonic in his drive."

LYNDON JOHNSON'S "Program with a Heart" had contained only one proposal anathema to liberals. Despite scandal and widespread outrage, he had rammed that proposal to passage in the Senate, in a vivid illumination of his power over that body. The fate of the program's other twelve proposals—all liberal proposals—was instructive because it illuminated the purpose for which he was using that power.

Five of those twelve proposals—poll tax elimination, immigration reform, disaster insurance, aid to depressed areas, and tax reduction for the poor—died quiet deaths during the Senate's 1956 session. Five more—for a federal water conservation program and for federal aid for medical research, and for hospital, school, and housing construction—passed in amounts so small or forms so diluted as to make them insignificant. Since President Eisenhower was supporting most of the same programs, the failure of these proposals in a Senate controlled by Johnson was an indication of the extent to which his heart was—or wasn't—truly in the program, of the extent to which the program had been proposed merely to blunt liberal criticism, and of the extent to which his first priority was not to appease liberals but to avoid antagonizing conservatives.

The fate of an eleventh proposal was particularly infuriating to liberals. It was a proposal that was actually more part of Eisenhower's program than Johnson's: the bill that became the basis for the Interstate Highway System. Organized labor had assumed that construction workers on the highway program would be covered by the existing Davis-Bacon Act, which required workers on all federal projects to be paid the prevailing local wage. But Herman Brown, who had started as a road builder and had never lost that image of himself, could not bear to have this most sacred area of free enterprise polluted by the hated unions and their endless "gimmes." "He laid down the law to Lyndon on that one," Ed Clark would recall.* When the Administration-backed highway program reached the Senate floor on May 28, labor unions were ready for a fight, and a union-backed measure was introduced to have wage rates set by the Secretary of Labor. UAW lobbyist Robert Oliver, who had been on what Evans and Novak call a "quiet campaign to soften Johnson's antipathy toward organized labor," warned the Majority Leader that opposition to the bill when it came to a vote the next day would be disastrous to his future relations with labor, and Johnson found a way to avoid the vote. He had been scheduled to leave for a checkup at the Mayo Clinic at 3 p.m. on the 29th; he moved up his flight to 10 a.m. so he wouldn't be present during the vote (which labor won). As the two journalists put it, "Johnson's absence saved him from another attack from the unions, but it scarcely won him their praise."

As for the twelfth proposal, that, too, seemed dead as late as July. But when, that month, Johnson began to feel that he had a real chance for the Democratic nomination for President, a softening of liberal antipathy became desirable. And since passage of the last remaining item in the "Program with a Heart" would advance both liberal objectives and his own, that item passed—in a form far more liberal than he had at first proposed.

In 1955, the House had passed a bill that would have changed the nature of the Social Security system, the first broad change since 1939 in that major New Deal achievement. Previously, Social Security had meant retirement benefits at age sixty-five and payments to widows and orphans. The House bill would have lowered the age at which women could begin collecting benefits to sixty-two, but, more significantly, it provided for the payment of benefits to totally disabled persons of both sexes at the age of fifty, a provision that would

---

*When, in 1955, Johnson, responding to Brown's edict, had pushed through the Senate an amendment exempting the highway program from Davis-Bacon (allowing senators to vote aye in anonymity by blocking Paul Douglas' attempt to get a roll-call vote), as telling to liberals as Johnson's maneuver had been his rationale for it—what Evans and Novak called his "quite sincere apprehensions about organized labor." In discussing the bill, they wrote, "He [Johnson] recalled his own experience" on the road gang. "Paradoxically, he remembered not his own low pay but the small profit margin of the contractor, his difficulty in financing new equipment and his trouble in meeting his tax liabilities"—and Johnson's resultant "sympathy for the small county contractor . . . colored his attitude" toward Davis-Bacon.

transform Social Security from a retirement and survivors' benefit plan into a vehicle for much broader social welfare programs, including the program that was the longtime dream of liberals and labor and the longtime nightmare of many doctors: Social Security–financed federal health insurance. Seeing the House bill as the thin end of the wedge for socialized medicine, the doctors' lobby, the immensely powerful American Medical Association (AMA), mobilized against it—confident of success: annoying though the House action may have been, there was still that firmer body that had been created to stand against radical innovations. And, thanks in part to its Majority Leader, the Senate had indeed stood firm in 1955. With Johnson declining to fight for the House bill, it had never even reached the Senate floor that year. By the time it came up in 1956, therefore, the AMA would have had "over a year to pressure fence-sitting senators—particularly those facing re-election" that year, one account noted. Johnson's "Program with a Heart" had mentioned Social Security, but mainly only to support the lower age requirement for women. It did not even mention disability benefits.

Now, however, it was 1956, a presidential election year. Johnson decided to support the House bill because, as he told Democratic senators, "it clearly differentiated them from Republicans." It was time to mend fences with labor, and this was the quickest way. "I happen to believe passionately in Social Security," he wrote AFL-CIO president George Meany. "I went through the Depression and saw what it did to our older people. A country that is as great as ours does little enough for them."

The floor debate on the measure went on for four days in July, and for four days the count on Johnson's tally sheet seesawed back and forth. "The Administration really put on the heat to defeat that bill," George Reedy says. "We'd wake up in the morning with about a ten-vote margin . . . and by two or three in the afternoon it would have dropped to about three, and then it would shrink to one." For four days, Johnson held the Senate in session; he had, he wrote Meany on July 19, spent "about twelve hours a day on the Senate floor for the last four or five days."

The vote was going to be very close, but Johnson had quietly obtained leverage over two senators on whom Eisenhower was counting. Conservative Republicans were of course opposed to enlarging the scope of Social Security, and the further to the right they were, the more adamant their opposition. Among the furthest right, however, was Molly Malone, and the Nevada senator also had a bill up for consideration in 1956: a guarantee of at least $69 million in federal purchases from Nevada's tungsten mines which was a blatantly unjustified giveaway of the public's money to an already wealthy special interest.

Little attention was being paid to the proposed guarantee, which was, after all, a rather minor item in the overall federal budget. Both the Eisenhower Administration and the Republican senatorial leadership opposed it, and most of those senators aware of it, even conservatives, were planning to vote against it. Liberals, of course, opposed it on principle. Since the tungsten interests were a major force in Nevada politics, without passage of the bill Malone had little hope of re-election, but there seemed no way for him to get the necessary votes.

Lyndon Johnson told Malone he would get him the votes, as many votes as were needed—in return for just one vote: Malone's vote in favor of the Social Security disability amendment. Malone agreed to the bargain. When the tungsten bill came up for a vote on June 18, only four Republicans voted for it—but so did twenty-eight Democrats, including liberals like Humphrey, Lehman, Kennedy, and Green who would normally have voted against it. Johnson had offered them no explanation for his request that they vote for Malone's bill, simply asking them to "support the leadership" on the matter. "Few if any Democrats connected tungsten with the Social Security bill," Evans and Novak were to report. "They were frankly puzzled," but the amount involved was small, and "if the Leader needed help, they were willing to give it to him." With little more than half the Senate voting, the bill passed by a 32–22 margin.

Then, on July 17, the Social Security bill came up for a vote. Malone, who had given no hint of his intentions to anyone but Johnson, was anxious not to "be importuned face to face with earnest arguments" by his own Leader, Knowland, who of course assumed his vote would be no. As Evans and Novak reported, "He stayed in the cloakroom, appearing only momentarily to call his 'aye' vote for the disability amendment, then fairly ran out of the Chamber— disappearing . . . before Knowland could get a crack at him."

Malone's vote made the count on Social Security 46 to 46. The proposal would fail on a tie; Johnson needed one more vote.

That vote belonged to Earle Clements. Of all the senators "loyal" to Lyndon Johnson in the way Lyndon Johnson wanted men "loyal," none was more loyal—"dog loyal"—than the Kentucky Senator, who was willing to "do anything" for the Leader. Clements was well aware by now that his re-election campaign against Thruston Morton, Assistant Secretary of State, was, in George Smathers' words, in "serious trouble." He had not dared to oppose the doctors, whose opinions carried great weight with the unsophisticated voters in the rural Kentucky counties that were his stronghold, and had flatly promised the AMA that he would vote against the disability amendment. "Bob, I'm not with you on this bill," he had told the UAW's Oliver, labor's chief representative on the issue. "I gave a commitment back home that I would vote against this bill." When Oliver started to protest, Clements cut him off. "I can't do it. I made a commitment."

But the doctors' support was not all Clements needed against the well-financed Morton. He needed cash—campaign financing on a scale far beyond what Kentucky would provide. Johnson had already provided some from Texas, and had promised Clements there would be more. Now, some weeks before the vote on the disability amendment, he told Clements he could have as much as he needed—but he said he might need something, too: Clements' vote in favor of the disability amendment. He didn't think he would need his vote, Lyndon Johnson said; the amendment was probably going to be defeated overwhelmingly, he said. But if it turned out that he *did* need Clements' vote, Johnson said, he wanted to know that he had it. Clements could vote against the amendment at first, Johnson said, but if the decision came down to one vote, Clements would have to change his vote on the amendment from "nay" to "aye." Clements told Johnson that breaking his word to the doctors might cost him the election, and Johnson was aware of that; "Johnson fully recognized that this would subject Clements to the full wrath of the doctors' lobby," Evans and Novak were to write. But Johnson refused to be influenced by this consideration, and Clements had no choice; he had to have the cash. Reluctantly he agreed that if Johnson needed his vote, he would have it. And now, as the roll call proceeded on the Senate floor, Johnson ordered Clements to stay close to hand. The bald old pro "was seated right next to Johnson and sweat was coming off his head," Bobby Baker recalls. "He was down there, just hoping and praying that" his vote would not be needed. But it was. Johnson told him to change it, and he changed it, and, as Baker says, "We won by Clements' vote."

Johnson provided what he had promised. He sent Booth Mooney to Clements' campaign headquarters in Louisville to provide speechwriting and public relations expertise—and more pragmatic assistance, as well. "He arranged, through me on a small scale and through Bobby Baker, on a much larger scale, for financial assistance to be pumped into Kentucky," Mooney was to write. "I remember Bobby Baker came down there one weekend with a suitcase just stuffed with currency for [the] Clements campaign. I think it was about sixty thousand bucks, which was a good deal then." But the money couldn't offset that "aye." Clements lost to Morton. The margin was less than five thousand votes; "no doubt about it, his vote on the disability provision defeated him," Evans and Novak wrote; the vote he cast in the Senate, to accommodate Johnson, "infuriated the doctors and resulted in their organized opposition to his reelection," Mooney says.

Even to someone as imbued with the pragmatism of politics as was Bobby Baker, this episode was something special. "Senator Clements had made a commitment to Senator Johnson that although it would destroy him politically, which it did, if he broke his word, which he did, that he would vote with us," Baker says. "Of all the votes that I've ever seen that was mean and cruel and defeated a man, it was that vote by Senator Clements to liberalize Social Security, contrary to his commitment to the doctors' lobby in Kentucky." *Senators mutually recognize the primary natural law of political survival.* Not this senator, not Lyndon Johnson. *Kennedy would finally say he was sorry they couldn't agree, but he understood.* If understanding stood in the way of Lyndon Johnson's aims, he wouldn't understand, would refuse to understand. He got the vote he needed from a senator, even though that vote cost the other senator, a senator "dog loyal" to him, his career.

(Baker, as always, was to try to excuse Johnson. "Johnson tried . . . to make up for Clements' defeat," he says. "He made him [campaign director] of the Democratic Senatorial Campaign Committee. . . . Johnson felt bad about that one vote the rest of his life, because he destroyed a man's political career." Johnson did indeed appoint Clements to the Campaign Committee post in 1957. In 1959, Clements resigned to become Kentucky's State Highway Commissioner, and to work in Johnson's presidential campaign. He resigned the highway job within a few months, at the age of sixty-three, and never again held a position in government. After a brief stint with the Democratic National Committee in 1960, he became a consultant to the American Merchant Marine Institute, and then a lobbyist for tobacco companies. Baker's view that Johnson "felt bad" does not jibe with the view of other Johnson aides and allies, including Booth Mooney, who over the years had sat in on many meetings between the two senators and who had been sure that "Johnson truly loved Clements." When a saddened Mooney returned to Washington after Clements' defeat, he had expected Johnson to be sad, too—at least a little sad. But Johnson simply congratulated Mooney on his work in Clements' campaign. And when "I . . . pointed out that obviously I had fallen short of attaining the hoped-for goal," Johnson said airily, "You shouldn't feel that way. Look at it this way. Your man ran way ahead of the national ticket. You did everything anybody could've done."

"Sometimes," Mooney wrote, "Lyndon Johnson could be downright surprising.")

THE SENATORS' APPROVAL, by a 47–45 vote, of the disability amendment to the Social Security Act showed Lyndon Johnson's power at (in the case of Molly Malone) its most subtle, and at (in the case of Earle Clements) its most raw. And that approval showed also the extent of his power, documented again that the Senate, a body designed so that it would never have a master, had a master now.

But the Senate was not what Lyndon Johnson wanted. It was only a step on the ladder to the goal, the only goal, of which he dreamed. So he had at last to come to grips with his great dilemma—which was also America's great dilemma: the plight of the sixteen million Americans whose skins were black.

Part V

THE GREAT CAUSE

30

The Rising Tide

IF AN AMERICAN CITIZEN of African descent—a "Negro," to use the term then in common usage—wanted to register to vote in Bullock County, Alabama, during the 1950s, he had to register under what the county's Board of Registrars called the "voucher system." He was required to bring with him a "supporting witness" (called by the Board a "voucher") to attest to his character, morals, and general "fitness" to be a voter. But only Bullock County residents who were already registered voters were eligible to be supporting witnesses, and no witness could vouch for more than three persons during each four-year term of the Board. And since, by inviolate Bullock County custom, no white person would ever vouch for a Negro, eligible "vouchers" for Bullock Negroes were in rather short supply.

For out of the county's eleven thousand Negro residents, exactly five were registered voters.

This meant, of course, that no more than fifteen Negroes could be registered during any four-year period, but even this number was apparently more than the Board was disposed to allow—as a small group of Negroes, perhaps a half dozen, learned when, on January 18, 1954, they showed up at the Board's office in the Bullock County Courthouse in Union Springs with their supporting witnesses. "What's your trouble?" Board Chairman S. B. Wilson asked them brusquely, and when one of them, Aaron Sellers, a forty-year-old farmer, replied that they were there to register, Wilson said, "Well, we're busy today. You all come back tomorrow."

They returned the next day. Wilson and his fellow Board members let them sit there for an hour, until finally another white man, Allen B. Tucker, "who," as a federal judge was to note, "was not connected with the board in any official capacity," came over to them, and asked the same question: "What's your trouble?" Sellers, speaking for the group, said, "We were here yesterday, and the chairman told us to come back today." Tucker asked them why they wanted to vote. Sellers said something to the effect that they wanted to vote because they were citizens, and Tucker said, "You all are citizens already—you pay taxes, don't you? If I were you, I would go back home." And when they didn't take his advice, but remained sitting—the Board continuing to ignore them—for perhaps another half hour, the veneer of civility, thin though it was, disappeared entirely. Returning to the room, Tucker stood over the Negroes and said in a low, threatening voice, "I thought I told you to get the hell out of here."

The Negroes were all aware not only of incidents of violence against members of their race who had defied white wishes, but of other forms of intimidation as well. "The white people in the town kept a list of the names of who was trying to vote, and they kept the list in their pockets for ready reference," Sellers would recall. There were many ways in which that list could be used. Word had been passed that "the banks were organizing" and might "stop lending colored people money," he says. The county's impoverished Negro farmers would shortly—in March or April—need "crop loans," money to buy seed and fertilizer to plant their cotton and peanut crops. And, as Sellers says, "you had to have a little to live on, too, you know," until the crops were harvested in October. Tucker's threat was effective. "We were all somewhat afraid," Sellers says. "We got up and left." When he decided to make another attempt—on February 1—he was able to persuade only three men to come with him, not that it made much difference. Their approach to the courthouse had been noted, and this time when they walked up the stairs and knocked on the door to the Board of Registrars office, there was no reply, and when Sellers finally worked up the nerve to open the door, the room was empty.

Encountering a white courthouse clerk in a corridor, the four Negroes asked where the Board was meeting, and the clerk, a smirk on his face, said he didn't know. Afraid to go looking in every office, the Negroes finally left the courthouse and stood outside, waiting for the registrars to come out and go to lunch; when they returned, they followed them to the unmarked office in the basement in which they had been meeting. But although all three members of the Board went into the room, when Sellers knocked on the door, only Wilson appeared, stepping through the door and closing it quickly behind him. And when Sellers told him that he and his friends wanted to register, Wilson, as Sellers was to recall, "told us he couldn't register us because he was alone and the law required two at least to be present."

They knew now that the Board was not going to allow them to register, Sellers was to say, so "we didn't go back anymore." Instead, they decided "to go to law," to sue the Board of Registrars for denying them the chance to vote. "We were citizens. We knew the law said citizens could vote," Sellers was to say. "We thought we would win." They found an attorney—Arthur D. Sholes of Birmingham, one of the handful of black lawyers in Alabama—who was willing to represent them, and Sholes brought suit in Federal District Court in Montgomery, the state capital, asking for a declaratory judgment that the Board had discriminated against them, and for an injunction prohibiting the

Board from such discrimination and ordering it to use the same criteria for registering Negroes as it did for whites. The Federal Bureau of Investigation had no difficulty in confirming their story—no sooner had an FBI agent, looking for witnesses, entered a pool hall in Union Springs and pulled out his badge than Tucker told him proudly, "I just run off a bunch a niggers who were tryin' to vote."

But then, having gone to the law, they found out there was no law that could help them.

The District Court judge, Charles Kennamer, ruled, in ringing words, that their cause was just. The Board's actions "whenever the plaintiffs appeared before them . . . amounted to discrimination . . . solely because the plaintiffs were members of the Negro race," he wrote. "The supreme law of this Republic" is that no voter can be discriminated against. "Therefore, let no Board of Registrars try to devise any scheme or artifice to do otherwise." The words didn't mean much, however—as even the judge had to admit. By the time he issued his ruling, it was irrelevant. While the trial was still going on, the three members of the Board simply resigned, and in his ruling Kennamer had to admit that "by virtue of their resignations, the defendants are now beyond the vale of an injunctive directive from this court." There was no point in ordering them to register Negroes; they *couldn't* register Negroes any longer. No one in Bullock County could register Negroes. In his ruling, the judge promised that "The court will grant injunctive relief . . . in the event . . . these defendants again become members of the Board"; the defendants did not again become members of the Board: they stayed resigned until their terms expired, in 1956. During this time, their posts remained unfilled. Vacancies were supposed to be filled by a state agency, but the state agency didn't fill the vacancies for more than two years—and Aaron Sellers and his friends were told that there was no law that could compel the state to fill them. And when, in 1957, a new, different Board of Registrars was appointed, and Sellers and his friends returned, hoping for a better result, they found the Board office again empty ("We couldn't find out where the Board were," he says) and they realized they would have to begin the same laborious legal proceeding all over again—with, almost certainly, the same result at the end of it.

ALL ACROSS THE SOUTH, the eleven states of the Old Confederacy that stretched in a great crescent from the Atlantic Ocean to the plains of West Texas, black American citizens being discriminated against—not only in voting but in housing, in employment, in virtually every aspect of life—were trying during the 1950s to turn to the law so that they could enjoy the same rights as white Americans. And all across the South, black Americans were finding what the blacks of Bullock County had found: that there was no law that could help them.

Once, long before, for a brief period, there *had* been such laws.

Some had been woven into the fabric of the Constitution that was America's highest law. The three great "Civil War Amendments" to the Constitution had been passed to give force to the concept of the equality of all men which had been proclaimed in the Declaration of Independence but which had then, in submission to the slaveholding South, been omitted from the Constitution itself. The Thirteenth Article *In Addition To, and Amendment Of,* the Constitution outlawed the institution of slavery; the Fourteenth made former slaves citizens, full citizens entitled to "due process of law," to "the equal protection of the laws"—to all the rights, the sacred "privileges and immunities," of citizens; the Fifteenth made specific that among the rights of these new citizens was the right to vote: the right on which all other rights rest in a democracy in which governmental powers were derived from the consent of the governed. "The right of citizens . . . to vote shall not be denied or abridged . . . by any State on account of race, color or previous condition of servitude," the Fifteenth Amendment proclaimed. Each of the amendments, or articles, had an identical final clause—"Congress shall have power to enforce this article by appropriate legislation"—and in the decade immediately after the terrible war, a vengeful Congress determined to "reconstruct" the South had exercised that power, accepted that responsibility, enacting specific national statutes to give teeth to those guarantees. In 1866 it passed the first Civil Rights Act, which enumerated, in provisions both detailed and sweeping, the "civil rights"—the specific rights, privileges, and immunities of citizens—which were not to be left to the varying whims of states but were to be protected by the sovereign central government. In 1867, it passed the First Reconstruction Act, which not only disbanded the governments of the rebel states but carved the South into five military districts subject to martial law to ensure that the black man's right to vote would be backed by federal bayonets. And when the South thereupon erupted in rage, and the men of the Old Confederacy donned the hoods of the Klan and rode out in the thousands to beat and maim and kill, Congress passed more laws—stiff election-enforcement bills—that prohibited the use of force or intimidation (or of bribery or fraud) to deter citizens from voting because of their race, and that ensured, as well, that, if necessary, those bayonets would be used. And in 1875 it enacted another Civil Rights Act, one that sought to guarantee Negroes the right to serve on juries and that also sought to free them from discrimination in the daily round of life, guaranteeing their rights to "the full and equal enjoyment" of "the accommodations of inns," of "theaters and other places of public amusement," and of public facilities and "public conveyances" of every type.

The Civil Rights Act of 1875 was the high point—and the end point—of the passage of such laws, however. In that very year, a series of rulings by the United States Supreme Court—very narrow rulings, in tune with the growing *laissez-faire* attitude of the time and in tune also with the popular feeling that perhaps the government had gone far enough in handing the freedman new rights—began drastically limiting the scope of the Fourteenth and Fifteenth Amendments; by the time, two decades later, that the Court had finished, the Amendments' guarantees had been held to apply only to actions by a state, not by the state's citizens, whether acting alone or in a group; in 1882, the Court, overturning the conviction of members of a Louisiana mob that had broken up a Negro political rally, in effect held that while a state couldn't break up a rally, it was legal for a mob to do so, unless there were prohibitions against such an action in the state's—not the federal government's—laws. (There were none in Louisiana law.) In 1883, in a ruling that in effect struck the 1875 Civil Rights Act from the statute books, the Court, acting under the same principle, struck down the prohibitions against discrimination by hotels, theaters, restaurants, and other places of business, and by "public conveyances." One individual civil rights law after another was found unconstitutional, until finally only three— all vague, ambiguous, and essentially unenforceable; mere "fragments of the original legislation," a Justice Department official was to call them—remained on the national statute books, so that Negroes were left with no federal protection against *de facto* segregation in the rounds of daily life.

During the many decades that followed, these invalidated laws against segregation were not replaced by other national laws. No civil rights legislation of any type was passed by the federal government after 1875. The national laws were replaced by state laws that allowed segregation—that in fact *required* segregation. As Richard Kluger wrote in his monumental book *Simple Justice,* the Supreme Court had "flashed the green light," and the eleven southern—and several border—states sped through it, passing legislation that made segregation a matter not merely of custom or tradition, but of law. In 1887, the Florida Legislature passed a statute requiring that white and "colored" passengers be separated on railroad trains, Mississippi adopted a similar law in 1888, Texas in 1889, and in 1890 Louisiana followed suit—with an act whose key phrase was to become widely adopted: "all railway companies carrying passengers in this State, shall provide separate but equal accommodations for the white, and colored, races, by providing two or more passenger coaches for each passenger train, or by dividing the passenger coaches by a partition so as to secure separate accommodations." Any passenger, white or Negro, not obeying the law was subject to a fine of twenty-five dollars and up to twenty days in jail. By 1895, every southern state had, by similar "separate but equal" laws, formally relegated Negroes to the front coaches that were nearest to the soot-belching engines. As Kluger wrote: "The Jim Crow era had begun."

It spread rapidly, particularly after the Supreme Court in its remarkable 1896 verdict in *Plessy v. Ferguson* ruled that the Fourteenth Amendment "could not have been intended" to give the Negro equality in social situations but only "before the law"—and that racially separate facilities were therefore legal so long as they were equal, and that social segregation was therefore not discrimination. By the beginning of the twentieth century, the legislatures of the southern states had written into statute books laws that, in Kluger's words, "officially designated" the black man as "a lower order of being"—laws that stipulated that not only in railway cars and stations, not only in hotels and restaurants but in courtrooms (where, in addition, restrictions were placed on the status of blacks as plaintiffs, witnesses, and jurors), in cemeteries, and in hospitals, in bathrooms and at water fountains, black people and white people would not mix. It was no longer the option of an individual restaurant or hotel owner whether or not to separate his clients by race; under the law, he *must* separate them. (Interracial dating and marriages were strictly forbidden, of course, and special emphasis was placed on separation in the schools, for what would be the inevitable result of letting white girls mingle all day with black boys but the most dreaded threat of all? Mississippi's United States Senator Theodore Bilbo spelled it out in 1947 in a self-published book, *Take Your Choice: Separation or Mongrelization:* better to see civilization "blotted out with the atomic bomb," he wrote, "than to see it slowly destroyed in the maelstrom of miscegenation, interbreeding, intermarriage, and mongrelization.")

The place of Negro citizens in the southern states' political picture had undergone a parallel transformation. Reconstruction legislation had sought to make the newly freed slaves a part of southern political life, but the protection of black voters from fraud, trickery, and the outright brutalities of mob intimidation at a thousand polling places throughout the South required an enormous number of troops. In 1876, Rutherford B. Hayes won the presidency with a razor-thin margin provided by the disputed electoral votes of three southern states, and as part of the negotiations under which he received those votes, federal troops were withdrawn from the South, and the vote began to be taken away from the new Negro citizens—so effectively that by 1889, a prominent southern editor would remark that "The Negro as a political force" was no longer a "serious consideration" in the region. In the 1890s, southern states passed laws to keep that *status quo.* They instituted poll taxes—often retroactive, sometimes to age twenty-one, so that the amounts involved might be prohibitive for poor people; by 1901, every southern state had its poll tax. In 1898, Louisiana passed a "grandfather clause" that made registration automatic for any man whose father or grandfathers had been registered before Reconstruction—meaning most southern white men—and that, through prohibitive property and educational requirements, made registration very difficult for any man whose father or grandfathers had not been registered—meaning most southern black men. By 1901, every southern state had its grandfather clause. The "white primary" was another effective means of evading the Fifteenth Amendment's wording that the right to vote should not be denied because of race or color by any *state.* Democratic Parties in the various states declared that the party's primary elections were not state functions but rather the mechanisms of a private organization for selecting its nominees, and that the parties were therefore allowed to exclude Negroes from membership, and hence from the right to vote in the party's primaries. So dominant was the Democratic Party in the Old Confederacy that Negroes were therefore excluded completely from the only election that mattered. The combination of these techniques was so effective that in the 1940 elections only about 2 percent of Negroes of voting age in the South, where most black Americans lived, cast votes.

For a moment, in 1944, it had seemed that the situation might change. In a suit brought by a black Texan, Lonnie E. Smith, against election judge S. E. Allwright, who had denied him the right to vote in the Texas Democratic Party's white primary, a Supreme Court made strikingly more liberal by Roosevelt appointments ruled that "the right to vote in such a primary . . . is a right secured by the Constitution." That ruling, coupled with the return of black veterans, led to a dramatic upsurge in Negro registration in the South. By 1948, some 750,000 Negroes, about 15 percent of the estimated five million Negroes of voting age in the South, had made it onto the election rolls; in that year, there were several unexpected victories by liberal state legislators over the conservative opponents who previously would easily have won in Democratic primaries. But black determination spawned white defiance: the wave of repression and violence that included the gouging out of Isaac Woodward's eyes, the riddling of the two young black couples in Georgia with so many bullets that they were unrecognizable, and countless incidents of physical or economic intimidation to discourage black Americans from trying to register, and to discourage those who *had* registered from actually going to the polls. The number of new Negro registrations, as John Egerton wrote, "was the warning siren . . . that caused white supremacists to purge voter lists, raise court challenges, adopt new laws and constitutional amendments—do anything, in short, to prevent the large African-American minority from regaining the power of the franchise." And, as Egerton notes, these tactics worked; their "success . . . would be borne out by one overriding fact: in spite of the increase in minority registration, fewer than half a million black Southerners—not even one of every ten of voting age—actually managed to cast ballots" in the 1948 elections. And after 1948, the situation grew worse. Southern legislatures began shoring up the South's defenses—passing laws that gave registrars new, and arbitrary, powers. The years after 1948 saw the proliferation of "literacy" tests—in which applicants for registration were required to demonstrate their "understanding" or "interpretation" of passages of state laws (or, ironically, of the United States Constitution) or to answer trick questions put to them by registrars whose decisions were purely subjective—and, according to the new laws, were not subject to appeal, so that even college graduates could be arbitrarily disqualified if their skins were dark. These years saw the proliferation of the "voucher" system in a hundred counties like Bullock.

Obviously, new, stronger, federal voting legislation was needed, and no fewer than thirteen separate voting bills were brought to the floor in the two

houses of Congress between 1946 and 1954, but every one was blocked. So
when in 1955 courageous Negroes attempted to invoke the law to obtain the
right to vote supposedly guaranteed them as citizens of the great Republic, they
found, as Aaron Sellers and his friends had found, that there was no law to help
them.

As a result, the surge in Negro voter registration in the South that had followed the *Allwright* decision slowed to a trickle. The figure was 750,000 in
1948; it would not reach a million until 1952. By that year, the number of
blacks of voting age in the South had risen to just under six million, so only one
out of every six eligible southern Negroes—about 16 percent—was registered
in that year, in contrast to 60 percent of southern whites. And the million figure
was misleading. So effective was the intimidation, economic and physical,
practiced by whites to keep registered Negroes from going to the polls that in
1952, the estimated number of black votes actually cast in the eleven southern
states was not a million but, at most, 600,000. Only one out of every ten
Negroes eligible to vote in those states actually voted. More than three quarters
of a century after the ratification of the Fifteenth Amendment that had been
intended to make America's black citizens truly part of America's political system, they were still not part of it; they were still that system's outcasts—
democracy's outcasts.

THE HUNDREDS OF THOUSANDS of black Americans who marched off to the
Second World War had gone into battle in defense of America's shining principles, so many of which—all of which, in the last analysis—rested on the decla-
rations that "all men are created equal" and that all men "are endowed by their
Creator with certain unalienable Rights," and that it is to "secure these rights"
that "Governments are instituted among Men, deriving their just powers from
the consent of the governed." And then these veterans came home, many with
medals, many with wounds, to be reminded not of America's promises, but of
America's practices.

Many of those coming home to the North rode through white neighborhoods in which they couldn't live, to housing projects, bleak and bare, that
were a constant reminder of their status in society, the projects that James Baldwin said they hated "almost as much as they hated the policeman." And when
they went looking for jobs, they learned anew that, war or not, there were so
very many jobs for which they could not apply. And for those coming home to
the eleven states of the South, in which, in 1946, two-thirds of black Americans
still lived, there were additional reminders. If they came home by bus, there
were the seats in front in which they couldn't sit. When the bus pulled into a
terminal or a diner parking lot for a rest stop, there were the water fountains at
which they couldn't drink, and the bathrooms they couldn't use: the fountains
and bathrooms labeled "Whites," as opposed to "Colored"—the label whites

had given them. If they wanted something to eat and went to the diner, there was the window out back at which they would be handed their sandwich, for only men whose skins were white were served inside. When they reached their hometowns, some of them, their awareness sharpened by their travels and experiences in the war, saw with a new understanding the paved streets and sidewalks in the white neighborhoods and the unpaved streets, unbordered by sidewalks, in the black neighborhoods. They saw, alongside these streets, the ditches running filthy with a stream of raw sewage because there was no sewage system in their part of town. If they took their girlfriend, or their wife, to a movie, for their first date after their long-awaited return, they had to climb, as they had had to climb before they left for war, to the balcony because the orchestra below was reserved for whites, and the screen itself was often a reminder—for so few of the faces of the stars upon the screen were black, and the demeanor of black actors in the movies made the couples in the balcony cringe. If they wanted to take their girls or their wives for a hamburger and a soda, or for dinner, there were so many places to which they couldn't take them. Their little brothers and sisters, who hugged them so tightly when they saw them again, were taller now than they remembered them, but the returning veterans still had to watch them trudge to school, trudge miles sometimes in the heat and the dust, because the school board wouldn't pay to transport them, while the buses carrying the white children sped past them. They had to watch them trudge home in the evening—tired girls and boys. And the men returning home knew what the schools were like, for they had attended the same schools, and they found that the schools hadn't changed. The ramshackle shanties that were Negro schools had raw, unfinished walls through which the wind whistled in winter as it did through the planks of the outhouse you used instead of a bathroom. Raw pine plank tables served as "desks," desks so rough it was hard to write on them because school boards wouldn't pay even for the sandpapering of desks in Negro schools. And the veterans could see new white schools—so shiny, so clean. Did any of the veterans ask their brothers or sisters, Do you still say the oath to the flag in the mornings?—the oath that pledged allegiance to the country that brought liberty and justice to all.

If they wanted the opportunity, supposedly given them by the G.I. Bill, to go to college, black veterans often found that there were too many of them— that with the doors of white colleges closed to them, there was no place left for them at black colleges. The big southern state universities taught whites—they wouldn't teach them. And for every one of them who went beyond college, who earned the graduate degree that made him a lawyer or a doctor, there were many who wanted to go beyond college but who couldn't, because in southern graduate schools there were almost no places at all for them. If they wanted to vote, to exercise the most basic right of citizens, they found that nothing had changed there either; there were still the literacy tests that were a humiliation even if the white registrar condescended to pass you. Did they think, some of them at least, about America's promises to its people—and about the faithless-ness with which America was keeping its promises to those of its people whose skins were black? Did others try not to think about that—because they couldn't bear to?

These hundreds of thousands of black veterans had fought to make the world safe for democracy, not Jim Crow, and upon their return, they deter-mined, many of them, to do something about what they found, to secure in their own country the freedoms for which they had fought overseas.

Among these Negro veterans, there was, in addition, a new sense of possi-bility, a sense that, as Egerton puts it, "things *would* be different—they had to be." Many joined an organization dedicated to making things different: the National Association for the Advancement of Colored People; by the end of 1946, the NAACP had more than a thousand branches, with a membership totaling nearly half a million. In the courts, in the years after the war, the effort to challenge school segregation in the South was steadily widening, and victo-ries were coming faster and faster—many of them won by a black lawyer, Thurgood Marshall, whose triumphs were beginning to turn him into a legend—and with each victory the feeling grew stronger that the argument should not be merely that separate facilities be equal, but that facilities should not be separate: that the lawyers should push the courts to declare illegal the very separation of the races itself. The momentum for faster change was sweeping before it those Negroes who had argued for moderation. "A lot of the black communities around the country had the bit between their teeth by then," said one of the leading black civil rights attorneys, William Hastie. "It would have been futile to try damming the tide of human emotion that had been let loose."

The tide was not rising only among blacks. Widespread though racism remained among white Americans, the war had made more of them aware of—and uneasy about—their country's broken promises. And their understanding had been given an intellectual underpinning: Gunnar Myrdal's monumental *An American Dilemma,* published near the end of the war, which documented the pervasiveness of white racism in America and disproved the clichés about the innate inferiority of Negroes on which that racism was based, and which made readers grasp the terrible gulf between America's behavior and the ideals on which America had been founded; and whose scathing import—that America had blamed the black man for what it had done to him—was working its way, gradually but steadily, into America's consciousness. And in 1947 their under-standing had been personified in a popular hero, a hero with dark black skin, gleaming white teeth, and a flaming will; even if you were white, when you saw the bat held high and then whipping through the ball, when you saw the speed on the base paths, and when you saw the dignity with which Jack Roo-sevelt Robinson held himself in the face of the curses and the scorn and the run-ners coming into second base with their spikes high, you had to think at least a little about America's shattered promises. The Brooklyn Dodgers were in the

National League, but three months later, rooting for the Washington Senators of the American League became less of an unalloyed joy for Richard Russell; if he wanted to watch the Senators play the Cleveland Indians, he had to watch a black man on the same field as whites: Larry Doby had joined Jackie in the big leagues. In 1950, Jackie Robinson would be on the cover of *Life* magazine— the first black on *Life*'s cover in all its seven hundred issues. Race was becoming, faster and faster, an open topic of discussion in America; there was, in Egerton's words, "a spreading sense of outrage that discrimination based solely on skin color was locking people out of jobs, housing. . . ." During the years since V-J Day, support for civil rights, for the end of Jim Crow, had been rising all across the North, the demand quickening. A tide of opinion for equality and social justice had been rising—rising slowly, but rising. And the tide had been swelled by a hard pragmatic consideration: Negroes in the North had much less difficulty in voting than those in the South, and, led by the newly militant, better-educated, black veterans, more of them were doing so, particularly in the big northern states whose electoral votes were crucial in political calculations.

During the first seven years of the postwar era, moreover, there had been a President in the White House who had been determined to harness that tide, a President who not only reiterated the requests of his predecessor, twice passed by the House but twice rejected by the Senate, for the creation of a permanent Fair Employment Practices Commission and for the abolition of the poll tax, but who had also proposed, in 1946 and 1947 and 1948, what Franklin Roosevelt had not—after commissioning the study that would be called, in a phrase out of the Declaration of Independence, "To Secure These Rights," this President whose "very stomach turned over" at the beating of Negro veterans, asked Congress to secure those rights by making lynching a federal crime, banning discrimination in schools, hotels, restaurants, and theaters, and passing legislation protecting the Negroes' right to vote.

But the tide had risen before, and had been blocked before, by the Senate, and now, as it rose again, the Senate blocked it again: with the defeat, in 1946 and again in 1947 and 1948, of the anti-lynching legislation and the anti–poll tax legislation and the anti-discrimination legislation, the tide broke helplessly against the dam that had stood athwart it for so long. And in the 1949 civil rights battle in which Lyndon Johnson had delivered his "We of the South" maiden speech which Richard Russell had called "one of the ablest I have ever heard," the dam had been made even stronger and higher than before by Russell's strengthening of the rules against cloture. And after that southern victory, when in 1950 and in 1951 and 1952, civil rights legislation had been proposed in the Senate, it had seldom even reached the floor.

DURING THE YEARS SINCE 1952, despite the presence in the White House of a new President whose lack of enthusiasm for civil rights made the Executive

Branch almost as high a barrier to the cause as the legislative, the rising tide had for a time apparently found another channel through which it could flow toward justice. All during the early 1950s, four separate school desegregation cases, which had been lumped together under the title *Brown v. Board of Education,* had been rising, slowly but steadily, through the federal court system toward the highest court. That court was scheduled to begin hearing arguments on the *Brown* case on December 7, 1953, and that morning, when the trolleys pulled up on Constitution Avenue and congressional employees stepped off and walked toward their offices in the Capitol, they noticed, through the winter-bare trees, in front of the smaller white marble temple of the Supreme Court Building to their left, a long line of men and women waiting for admittance to the Court's session that day. Most of them wore hats against the thirty-degree cold, and almost all of the faces under the hats were black. Some of those men and women had been in line all night. "I have a feeling that the Supreme Court is going to end segregation," one of them explained to a reporter.

For three days that December, the Supreme Court heard arguments on *Brown,* and five months later, on May 17, 1954, the Court ruled that separation of races in schools violated the Fourteenth Amendment's pledge of equal protection of the law, "that in the field of public education, the doctrine of 'separate but equal' has no place. Separate but equal facilities are inherently unequal. . . . To separate them [Negro children] from others of similar age and qualifications solely because of their race generates a feeling of inferiority . . . that may affect their hearts and minds in a way unlikely ever to be undone." The Court's Chief Justice understood as Lyndon Johnson understood the importance of unanimity, and Earl Warren had obtained it—even from Justice Stanley F. Reed of border-state Kentucky. Reed, who had been the last holdout, was looking down from the bench at Thurgood Marshall, who had led the fight in *Brown,* when Warren uttered the words, "So say we all." Reed "was looking me right straight in the face, because he wanted to see my reaction when I realized he hadn't dissented," the great black attorney would recall. The two men exchanged nods, barely perceptible. But there were tears on the Justice's face. All across the United States black men and women knelt to give thanks to God.

THEIR THANKS WERE PREMATURE. In education as in voting, determination spawned defiance. Against the Court's decision, the Old Confederacy rose in rage.

With the hooded Ku Klux Klan somewhat in disrepute because of its reputation for redneck violence, a new organization, the White Citizens Councils, sprang up, with a membership that included prominent citizens—the pillars of scores of southern communities—and with a philosophy that ostensibly repudiated violence and secrecy in favor of a new "reasonableness" (although its leaders' "reasonableness" was somewhat undercut by their rhetoric, which had an unfortunate tendency to slip back into a more-familiar mode; in a Council-published book that sold widely throughout the South, the movement's intellectual leader, Tom P. Brady, a Yale-educated Mississippi circuit court judge, denounced the Court's refusal to recognize the physiological differences that made Negroes unsuitable for education—"The Supreme Court refuses to recognize that it cannot by a mandate shrink the size of a Negro's skull which is one-eighth of an inch thicker than a white man's"—as well as its lack of appreciation of all the white man had done for the Negro. "The American Negro," he wrote, "was divorced from Africa and saved from savagery. In spite of his basic inferiority he was forced to do that which he would not do for himself. He was compelled to lay aside cannibalism, his barbaric savage custom. He was transported from aboriginal ignorance and superstition. He was given a language. . . . His soul was quickened. He was introduced to God! The veneer had been rubbed on, but the inside is fundamentally the same. . . . You can dress a chimpanzee, housebreak him and teach him to use a knife and fork, but it will take countless generations of evolutionary development, if ever, before you can convince him that a caterpillar or a cockroach is not a delicacy"). The first White Citizens Council was formed, in Indianola, Mississippi, two months after the *Brown* decision; within months, hundreds of chapters, with tens of thousands of members, had sprung up all across the South.

And with education as with voting, defiance was made law—formally written into statute books. Southern school boards, state legislatures, attorneys general and governors wrote laws and regulations designed to frustrate the Supreme Court ruling and keep white children safe from contamination by black children.

These laws and regulations accomplished their purpose. Although the border states moved at once to comply with the Court's ruling—by the fall of 1954, classes were widely integrated in Delaware, Maryland, West Virginia and Missouri; the next year, Kentucky began to comply—when, in May, 1955, a year after its first ruling, the Supreme Court decreed that its ruling should be implemented "with all deliberate speed," integration was still limited to the border states. And the reaction to that decree was the passage by southern legislatures of still more laws designed to frustrate it. Afraid that federal courts might attempt to accomplish integration by ordering the transfer of students to other schools, the South Carolina State Legislature in 1955 authorized local school boards to reassign transferred pupils to their original schools. The new law also stated that if a school accepted a pupil who had not been assigned by the school board—even if that pupil had been transferred there under a federal court order—the school board was authorized to deny state funds to that school. And South Carolina legislators boasted that if a federal court ruled unconstitutional this method of circumventing the Supreme Court decision, they would simply pass another law, authorizing the school board to close the school—or as many schools as it wished. A board could close *all* its schools, the Legislature explained. White parents would then have the option of sending their children to school in another—unintegrated—district. And if a suit was then instituted to force integration in *that* district, *that* district's board could then close its schools. As one writer put it, "A separate suit might therefore be required for every school district in the state." And of course, whites could always set up a private school of their own. Since blacks couldn't afford to follow suit, the end result of the integration suits would be that blacks would have no schools at all. In other southern states, there were even broader pieces of legislation. Georgia amended its state constitution so that it no longer required the state to maintain a public school system.

If laws were not sufficient to accomplish the purpose, other methods—"economic pressures"—were employed. In August, 1955, fifty-three Negroes petitioned the school board in Yazoo City, Mississippi, to allow their children to attend white schools. The local White Citizens Council published the names of the petition's signers, in a full-page ad in the *Yazoo City Herald*. One of the fifty-three was fired from his job. Another, who had spent twenty years building up a plumbing business, found that no white customer would hire him, and he lost his business. The day he had to close down, he tried to buy a loaf of bread in a store, and the storekeeper told him he had just tripled the price. Another signer, a grocer, found that his wholesalers would no longer supply him. A banker told him the bank didn't want his money, and ordered him to close his account. A woman who had signed tried to buy food, but when she got to the counter, the clerk refused to accept her money, and she had to return the food to the shelves. Soon there were only two names left on the petition, and the Yazoo City schools remained segregated. And there were more subtle methods. When a similar petition was filed in Jackson, Mississippi, Citizens Council leaders met in a Jackson hotel room, telephoned for room service, and let the Negro waiters who brought the food overhear them as they said that the petition's signers were going to be investigated by a grand jury. "That was the end of the petition," a Council leader said. "No fuss and fury. We're not trying to raise hell. We just want separate but equal schools."

This combination of methods was effective. When schools opened in September, 1955, three of the eleven former Confederate states had made token efforts at desegregation, so small as to be meaningless: a few hundred black children were going to school with white children in Tennessee, Arkansas, and Texas. The other eight states had made no gesture at all; the total number of black children in integrated schools in those states was zero. And officials in those states were pledging that that was going to be the number in years to come—in all years to come.

Obviously the best counterweight to this resistance would be the passage of federal civil rights legislation, national laws that would override states' laws. Understanding that the highest obstacle to the passage of such legislation was Senate Rule 22, with its cloture provisions, liberals had tried to loosen that rule at the beginning of each new Congress—in 1947 and 1949 and 1951—

only to see it made tighter instead. They had tried again in January, 1953. Thanks to the new Eisenhower-generated Republican majority in both houses of Congress, the southerners were no longer committee chairmen, and the liberals believed they had a chance at last. But the wink was given, and was answered by the nod: the vote in 1953 against liberalization of Rule 22 had been 70 to 21.

January, 1955, of course, was the month in which the Senate liberals, their ranks strengthened with new recruits, believed they had an even better opportunity—and it was the month in which, if they did have one, it was thrown away when Douglas and Lehman acceded (in the concession which Douglas soon realized was "a bad mistake") to Hubert Humphrey's request that they "give Johnson a chance." And with the filibuster still as firm as ever, there was no chance at all for the passage of civil rights legislation in the Senate in 1953 or 1954 or 1955. During those years, sixty-one separate civil rights bills were introduced in the Senate. Not one made it to the floor. The tide, whipped forward now by the wind of hope, had at last reached the top of the judicial branch. In some respects, as will be seen, it was rising within the executive branch. On Capitol Hill, however, it dashed as helplessly as ever against Congress, and particularly the Senate. Thanks to Lyndon Johnson, the senatorial dam had been breached on other liberal issues—housing and the minimum wage, for example. But on civil rights it was, thanks in part to Johnson, still standing, as strong as ever. The black Americans who had been denied justice for so long were being denied justice still. Their condition was still, in 1955, the great contradiction between the Republic's professed ideals, the ideals embedded in its Constitution, and the reality of the actual conditions in which sixteen million of its citizens still lived.

DURING THE SECOND HALF OF 1955—those months during which Lyndon Johnson was down on his ranch recuperating from his heart attack—dispatches had come to him which had made him aware that during the Senate's 1956 session, the fight in the north wing of the Capitol was going to be joined again. Liberals, ashamed of their meek surrender, were determined to redeem themselves. "In view of my error . . . I felt a special need to strengthen the fight," Douglas was to say, to go "much further than our past attempts." He directed his staff to draw up the most comprehensive civil rights bill ever to be presented to Congress, "encompassing a whole battery of proposals, from voting rights to an effective FEPC law."

During the Summer of 1955, moreover, there had been encounters on the battlefield itself—in the Deep South, hundreds of miles below Washington, where Negroes' rising determination to fight for their rights had been met by white fury at their effrontery.

Most of these encounters had been lonely skirmishes, and most had been

defeats. In Mississippi alone there had been four. Belzoni was known to Negroes as "a real son of a bitch town," but nonetheless the Reverend George W.
Lee had somehow gotten on the voter registration rolls not only himself but
some thirty other Negroes. The sheriff responded by refusing to accept their
poll tax payments, and ordering Lee to "get the niggers to take their names off
the book." And when Lee refused to do that, a car pulled alongside as he was
driving home one day, and a shotgun was fired at him at point-blank range.
"When I saw his body in the casket—I will not be able to forget how the whole
lower half of his face had been shot away," Ruby Hurley, who opened the first
permanent NAACP office in the Deep South, was to say. All through that summer, the NAACP tried to force the sheriff (that same sheriff who had refused
the poll tax payments) to investigate the murder—without success. He would
not even examine the lead shotgun pellets in Lee's face; they could, he said
"have been fillings from his teeth." The next event occurred in August, in
another little Mississippi town: Brookhaven. It took place in broad daylight, in
Courthouse Square, bustling with about fifty Saturday shoppers. Three white
men approached Lamar Smith, who during World War II had enlisted in the
Army at the age of forty-nine, and who now, having returned from the war to
build up a profitable farm, had enlisted in another battle: "He was determined,"
an admirer would say, "that his people would have a say in local government."
The three men warned Smith to stop encouraging blacks to register. When he
refused, one of the men drew a .38 caliber revolver and shot him dead in the full
view of bystanders. The three white men were arrested, but not one of the people who had been in the Square was willing to testify against them, and a grand
jury returned no indictments. Then, in November, in "son of a bitch" Belzoni, a
sixty-five-year-old Negro grocer, Gus Courts, who had been helping the Reverend Lee's registration efforts and had refused to stop even after he saw Lee's
half-destroyed face in the casket, and even after the White Citizens Council had
instituted a boycott against his store, was shot and seriously wounded by a gun-
man who fired from a car through the store's plate-glass window. "I've known
for a long time it was coming, and I'd tried to get prepared in my mind for it,"
Courts said. "But that's a hard thing to do. . . . It's bad when you know you
might get shot just walking around in your store." The sheriff made only the
most cursory investigation, the FBI interviewed the victim—once; the agents
never returned—and showed no interest even in examining the shotgun pellets
extracted from Courts' stomach; when a surgeon offered them to the agents, he
was told to "keep them"; Attorney General Herbert Brownell said that under
existing federal law, the Justice Department had no authority to prosecute—
and no one was prosecuted. Three shootings, one in broad daylight before a
crowd of onlookers, and no one had been brought to court, much less convicted. And making the murders grimmer still was the fact that, outside the
South, they were ignored. The *New York Times,* for example, ran exactly one
article about the Lee murder—three paragraphs long. About the Smith murder,
and the Courts shooting, it ran no articles at all. As David Halberstam was to

write about one of the shootings, in a paragraph that was applicable to all: "The nation's press paid no attention. . . . This was what Mississippi white men had always done, and therefore it was not news. Blacks in Mississippi seemed not only outside the legal protection of the police, but also outside the moral protection of the press."

But during the summer of 1955, there had been a fourth encounter, and while this, too, had been a defeat, it had been a defeat with a difference—a crucial difference.

In August, 1955, while a fourteen-year-old Negro boy from Chicago, Emmett Till, was visiting his mother's hometown, a hamlet named "Money" in the Mississippi Delta, he was playing one day with several local black teenagers outside a little country grocery store when he pulled from his wallet a picture of a white girl, and boasted that she was his girlfriend back in Chicago. The other boys scoffed at his claim, and one of them said, "Hey, there's a white girl [actually twenty-one-year-old Carolyn Bryant, who owned the grocery store with her husband, Roy] in that store there," and dared him to go in and talk to her. Emmett did, while buying two cents' worth of bubble gum. According to one account, he said, "How about a date, baby?" According to another, he said, "Bye, baby," as he was leaving, and gave a "wolf whistle." Talking "fresh" to a white woman was a violation of one of segregation's most basic rules, and whatever Emmett Till said, or whether or not he whistled, he was certainly, under those rules, guilty of that offense.

So he had to be punished. That night, Roy Bryant and his half brother, J. W. Milam, a violent man with a fearsome temper, known as "Big" Milam because he was six feet two and weighed 235 pounds, armed themselves with .45 Colt automatic pistols, drove in a pickup truck to the home of Till's uncle and aunt, Mose and Elizabeth Wright, where Till was staying, and, holding their pistols and shining a flashlight in Mose Wright's eyes, took Till away. They drove him to a two-room toolhouse, and beat him with their pistols, so hard that a black youth and his aunt who lived near the toolhouse heard the thuds of steel striking flesh and bone. At first, Till tried to be brave, but this only infuriated them, and they beat him until finally he was crying and screaming; the other youth made out some words: "Mama, Lord have mercy, Lord have mercy." One of his eyes was gouged out. Then Bryant and Milam ordered him to climb back into the truck, and drove to a cotton gin, where they had noticed a large exhaust fan, weighing about seventy pounds, that had been abandoned for scrap. They made him lift the fan onto the truck. They drove to the Tallahatchie River, parking about thirty feet from its steep banks. They forced Till to unload the fan and carry it to the very edge of the bank, and then to strip. When he was naked, he was beaten again with the pistols, so hard that one side of his forehead was crushed in. Then Milan shot him in the other temple. The two men tied the fan around his neck with barbed wire to weight the body down, and rolled it off the bank into the river.

The Wrights telephoned Till's mother to tell her that her son had been taken away, and that they didn't know what had happened to him. She contacted the Chicago police, who began telephoning sheriffs in the counties around Money. Accompanied by Mrs. Wright's brother, Greenwood Sheriff George Smith went immediately to the Tallahatchie; "We went by custom when something like that happened," the brother later explained. "That's usually what they done to them." The body was not found until three days later, however, when its legs, unweighted by the fan, popped up above water. It was badly decomposed, the face bloated, but not all the damage had been done by water. Only one side of the skull was intact; the other side had been crushed; one eye was dangling out of its socket, the tongue was swollen to many times its normal size. A policeman said it was the most badly beaten face he had ever seen. It was all but unrecognizable; Mose Wright was able to identify it primarily because Emmett's initialed ring was on one of the fingers.

UP TO THIS POINT, the episode was, tragically, no different from hundreds, thousands, that had occurred in the South, and that were still, in 1955, occurring in the South, without any more than cursory attention being paid to them outside the South—if, indeed, any attention was paid to them at all. After all, there were three other racially motivated murders—at least three—in Mississippi that year, and the national press had barely covered them. But this episode, unlike the others, was now to catch the attention of the nation, and, indeed, of the world.

It did so because the victim was not from the South but from Chicago, and because when the local southern sheriff wanted Emmett Till's body buried (quickly, with the casket closed) in Money, the boy's mother refused and insisted that it be returned to Chicago and opened so that she could be certain that the body inside was her son—and because when she saw what had been done to her son, she insisted that the casket remain open for three days before the funeral was held, so that "the world can see what they did to my boy." ("Have you ever sent a loved son on vacation and had him returned to you in a pine box, so horribly battered and waterlogged that someone needs to tell you this sickening sight is your son—lynched?" Mamie Till Bradley was to say.) The church in Chicago's great South Side black ghetto in which the casket lay held seventeen hundred people, but it wasn't big enough. Thousands upon thousands of black men and women lined up in the street outside and filed past it. Men's faces changed as they saw what was inside, women fainted, some women flinging up their arms in horror, covering their faces as if to shield themselves from the sight. Ruby Hurley, down in Mississippi, had not been able to forget the Reverend Lee's face, but very few people from the North had seen it. Thousands of people saw Emmett Till's face, and, *The Nation* reported, Chicago's black community "is aroused as it has not been over any similar act in recent history," and then the black magazine *Jet,* with a national circulation, ran a photograph of the face, and when Roy Wilkins of the NAACP spoke to a rally in Harlem to protest what the NAACP called the "jungle fury in Mississippi," ten thousand people jammed a street to hear him, and rallies were held in black communities all across the North, not only in Chicago and New York but in Youngstown, and Baltimore, and Cleveland and Detroit and Los Angeles, and the "Wolf Whistle Murder Case" was in big headlines in scores of black newspapers. And then articles began to appear in newspapers whose circulation was not mainly among Negroes, and while these stories were for the most part confined to inside pages, there were also editorials. For many reasons—the fact that Till was little more than a child; the brutality, documented in a photograph, of the murder; the public funeral not in a town in Mississippi but in one of the great cities of the North—the case became a *cause célèbre*. "Here," David Halberstam was to write, "was what the Northern press had been waiting for: a rare glimpse beneath the Deep South's genteel surface, at how the white power structure kept the blacks in line—using the rawest violence, if necessary."

Most of all, perhaps, the murder of Emmett Till caught the attention of the world because, unlike most similar murder cases in the South, in this one there was a witness who was willing to testify.

When the two half brothers, Roy Bryant and Big Milam, had come that night to Mose Wright's home, an unpainted cabin behind a cotton field, holding pistols and shining flashlights into his eyes and demanding that he produce "the boy who done the talkin' in Money," they had warned the sharecropper, a small man, five feet three inches in height and very skinny, against making any trouble. He had pleaded with them not to take his nephew, saying that the boy had acted badly because he was from Chicago—"He was raised up yonder. He didn't know what he was doing. Don't take him"—and his wife had offered to "pay you gentlemen for the damages," and then, after Milam had said, "You niggers go back to sleep," and was about to march Emmett off to the truck, one of the men had asked Wright, "How old are you?" and when he said that he was sixty-four, the man had said, "If you cause any trouble, you'll never live to be sixty-five." After the body was found, Wright was told bluntly that if he testified he would be killed, but when the Tallahatchie County District Attorney asked him if he would testify, he said he would—which meant that, even in Mississippi, there was going to have to be a trial.

The fact that there *was* a trial was, of course, unusual, but both the District Attorney, Gerald Chatham, and the judge, Curtis M. Swango, were unusual public officials in Mississippi, and Chatham pursued the case, and Swango presided over it, with exemplary fairness. In other respects, however, the trial was memorable for the vividness with which it furnished documentation of the totality of segregation in the South. Although 63 percent of the residents of Tallahatchie County were Negro, there were no Negro jurors; there couldn't be: only registered voters ("qualified electors") were eligible to serve on juries, and not a single Negro in Tallahatchie was a qualified elector; the county clerk, and

registrar of voters, had won re-election year after year by promising white voters "to keep vigilance over your registration books." The courtroom in the town
of Sumner was, of course, completely segregated, and most of the spectators
were white; it was only after all the white people who wanted to observe the
trial had been seated that blacks were allowed to fill in the back rows behind
them. The segregation extended to the press table. Fifty to sixty reporters,
many of them from the big cities of the North, had shown up to cover the trial,
and the white reporters were seated at the press table up front. Some of the
reporters, however, were black, from northern black newspapers. Tallahatchie's
sheriff, Clarence Strider, a huge man, at 270 pounds bigger even than Milam,
whose own sharecroppers lived in tiny shacks on whose roofs were painted
giant letters spelling out "S-T-R-I-D-E-R," declared that "There ain't gonna be
no nigger reporters in my courtroom," and when Judge Swango overruled him,
Strider sat them at two bridge tables far off to one side; entering the courtroom
one afternoon, he greeted them with a loud "Hello, niggers." A black congressman from Chicago, Clarence C. Diggs Jr., came down for the trial, and when he
arrived at the courtroom, all the seats allotted to blacks were already filled.
When a Negro newspaperman from New York tried to explain who Diggs was,
Strider and his deputies could scarcely believe their ears. "This nigger said
there's a nigger outside who says he's a congressman," one deputy said incred-
ulously. "A nigger congressman?" another deputy said in disbelief. After the
judge had ordered Diggs admitted, Strider said, "I'll bring him in here, but I'm
gonna sit him at you niggers' table." Also memorable was the atmosphere in the
steaming-hot courtroom in which everyone—spectators, attorneys, jury—
seemed to be drinking bottles of beer or Coke. "It was just like a circus," Ruby
Hurley was to say. "The defendants were sitting up there eating ice-cream
cones and playing with their children in court just like they were out at a picnic." Racist jokes made the rounds of the white spectators: Wasn't it just like
that little nigger to try and steal a gin fan when it was more than he could carry?

But nothing was as memorable as Mose Wright. The whites of Tallahatchie had been sure Mose wouldn't testify. Bryant and Milam had told him
he would be killed if he testified, and as soon as the two men had driven off
with Emmett that night, the elderly little sharecropper had put his wife on a
train to Chicago, and every day since she had arrived there, she had written him
begging him to join her, to leave Mississippi, to not testify. And since only he
could identify the two men who had taken Emmett, without his testimony there
was no case.

And then the district attorney called Wright to the witness stand, and he
came to the stand—in an act of heroism difficult even to contemplate.

The sharecropper looked very small as he sat there, dressed in a white
shirt and dark tie, on the stand, just a few feet away from Roy Bryant and the
massive Big Milam, so small that, to the journalist Murray Kempton, he was "a
black pygmy standing up to a white ox." And then the district attorney asked if

he could identify the two men who had taken Emmett Till away, and the "pygmy" stood up. He stood on his tiptoes, held his right arm out very straight, and spoke, in broken English, two words that were, nonetheless, adequate for the purpose. Pointing at Milam, he said: "Thar he."

"J. W. Milam leaned forward, crooking a cigaret in a hand that seemed as large as Mose Wright's whole chest, and his eyes were coals of hatred," Kempton wrote. "Mose Wright took all their blast straight in his face, and then, for good measure, turned and pointed that still unshaking finger at the man sitting next to Milam, and said: 'And thar's Mr. Bryant.' "

With those words, Kempton wrote, Wright "sat down hard against the chair-back with a lurch that told better than anything else the cost in strength to him of the thing he had done." And that was not the only courageous thing that the sixty-four-year-old sharecropper did on that witness stand. The district attorney, although he was on Wright's side, nonetheless addressed him without any prenom of respect, but only as "Uncle Mose." The manner of the defense attorney Sidney Carlton, one of the town's five lawyers, all of whom were representing Bryant and Milam *pro bono,* was, in Kempton's words, "that of an overseer with a field hand"; he "roared at Wright as though he were the defendant," and "every time Carlton raised his voice like the lash of a whip, J. W. Milam would permit himself a cold smile." And then, as Kempton wrote, "Mose Wright did the bravest thing a Delta Negro can do; he stopped saying 'sir.' Every time Carlton came back to the attack, Mose Wright pushed himself back against his chair and said 'That's right,' and the absence of the 'sir' was almost like a spit in the eye." Two other local black witnesses were to testify: the nineteen-year-old-youth who had heard the screams and thuds from the barn, and his aunt; their testimony was only peripheral, since they never saw Till; they had to be compelled to testify; the youth was so terrified that on the stand he could speak only in a whisper. And Emmett Till's mother testified. She had to—because the defense was claiming that the body was not really her son's, a contention bolstered by Sheriff Strider, who, in a somewhat unusual move for a law enforcement officer, testified for the defense. When Mamie Till Bradley, thirty-four years old, neatly dressed, a $3,900-a-year procurement clerk for the Air Force, entered the courtroom, the *Memphis Commercial Appeal* reported, "an expression of almost painful dislike swept across" the white spectators' faces. She was very calm as she recalled that she had tried to warn her son that he had to act "humble" in the South, that he had "to be very careful of how he spoke, and to say, 'yes, sir' and 'no, ma'am,' and not to hesitate to humble yourself if you had to get down on your knees," but that because Emmett had been raised in Chicago, he "didn't know how" to act that way. She lost her composure only once; when the district attorney held up before her a photograph of her dead son so she could identify it; then she took off her glasses and held a handkerchief to her eyes for a few seconds. But despite the testimony of these other witnesses, it was Mose Wright's testimony that made the case possible. His half hour on the stand, Kempton wrote, was "the hardest half hour in the hardest life possible for a human being in these United States." But at the end of it, "against Carlton's voice and Milam's eyes and the incredulity of an all-white jury he sat alone and refused to bow." It was as a result of his courage that two white men were on trial for killing a Negro, a trial in which, whatever the result, "there is a kind of majesty. And we owe that sight to Mose Wright, who was condemned to bow all his life, and had enough left to raise his head and look the enemy in those terrible eyes when he was sixty-four."

The result, of course, was the traditional result. Judge Swango had not allowed the jury to hear what the journalist I. F. Stone called "Mrs. Bryant's sexy whopper," that Till had grabbed her around the waist, made "unprintable" suggestions to her, and boasted, "I've been with white women before." But that didn't matter. After defense attorney Carlton had told the jury that if they found Bryant and Milam guilty, "your ancestors will turn over in their graves, and I'm sure every last Anglo-Saxon one of you has the courage to free these men in the face of that [outside] pressure," the jurors proved that they did indeed have that kind of courage: the verdict, after the jury had been out of the courtroom for an hour and seven minutes, was "not guilty"; the foreman told reporters that it wouldn't have taken that long "if we hadn't stopped to drink pop." In fact, it hadn't taken that long; jurors were to say later that they had delayed coming back into the courtroom to "make it look good." (The foreman was later asked what he thought of Mrs. Bradley's testimony. "If she tried a little harder, she might have got out a tear," he said.)

But although the verdict in the trial was simply one more in the long line of defeats for justice in the South, in a larger sense the Emmett Till trial was not a defeat. For the trial, and the verdict, had been brought to the attention of the world. Fifty or sixty print reporters had covered it, and outside on the court-room lawn there was, if not a forest, at least a small grove of tripods, support-ing television cameras. "For the first time," the *Delta Democrat-Times* noted, "a number of small local stations [in Mississippi and Louisiana] are staffing a news event." The interviews shot by some of the cameras reached more than local audiences. Planes chartered by the three major television networks set down every day of the trial in a field about seven miles away to pick up film, and while network television coverage was not extensive, there *was* coverage.

This coverage had an effect on blacks in the South. "We've got more phone calls from our listeners thanking us for having a man on the scene than anything we've ever done," said a radio reporter from a black station in New Orleans. The Till trial brought home to them with a new vividness the peril in which they lived. "Emmett Till's murder" instilled in Anne Moody, a fourteen-year-old black girl from Alabama, "the fear of being killed just because I was black." It was the senselessness of the murder of the fourteen-year-old boy that she couldn't get out of her mind, she was to say. "I didn't know what one had to do or not do as a Negro not to be killed. Probably just being a Negro period was enough, I thought." "The Emmett Till case shook the foundations of Mississippi, because it said even a child was not safe from racism and bigotry and death," recalls Myrlie Evers. It made southern blacks more willing to fight for their rights. Myrlie's husband, Medgar, "cried . . . over this particular vicious killing," Mrs. Evers says. "He cried out of the frustration and anger of wanting to physically strike out and hurt. Medgar made it his mission to see that word of it was spread as widely and accurately as possible. Publicizing the crime and the subsequent defeat of justice became a major NAACP effort." She says that the case helped provide a "frame of reference for us to move on to do more things, positively, to eliminate this from happening ever again. . . . Sometimes it takes those kinds of things to help a people become stronger and to eliminate the fear that they have to speak out and do something." Emmett's mother came back to Mississippi, and spoke, and when she spoke, the audiences were large and emotional, and when she asked for contributions to help her publicize her son's death, "Everyone poured out their hearts to her, went into their pockets when people had only two or three pennies, and gave . . . some way to say that we bleed for you, we hurt for you, we are so sorry about what happened to Emmett." The tide was rising even in the Deep South.

And not just in the Deep South. By the 1950s, millions of American Negroes had never lived in the South, and while they may have been intellectually aware of conditions there, of what segregation was like, they did not really *know* those conditions. James Hicks of the leading black newspaper in New York City, the *Amsterdam News,* had "covered the courts in many areas of this country, but the Till case was unbelievable. I mean, I just didn't get the sense of being in a courtroom. . . . When the people started coming into the courtroom, they filled up the white section, then the black filled up what was left." This, of course, was simply the normal court routine in the South, but now reporters like Hicks made northern blacks see it. And they responded. A new wave of mass meetings swept across black communities in the North, and the response came not only in cheers but in cash. Before the Till trial, the NAACP had been deeply in debt because of its legal expenses in the *Brown* trials. Now contributions to its "fight fund," the war chest to help victims of racial attack, soared to record levels.

Nor was the tide rising only among blacks. Large, influential newspapers like the *New York Times* and the *Washington Post and Times-Herald* had sent reporters to cover the trial, but while it was still going on, coverage was mostly on inside pages, as if the State of Mississippi, by bringing the killers to trial, had done what was needed, and as if the trial was not major news because conviction was a foregone conclusion. An editorial in the *Times* before the trial had said, "The fact remains that the Tallahatchie County grand jury, made up of white men, took this step against other white men for a crime against a Negro. . . . [This] prompt action . . . indicates that the people of contemporary

Mississippi are against this form of murder as against other forms of murder."
When justice failed, however, the story wasn't inside anymore, but on the front
page, in the Washington paper under a big banner headline, "TWO ACQUITTED
IN BOY'S KILLING." The acquittal was on front pages everywhere, and not only
in America, as if, as one account of the case put it, "both the wolf whistle and
the resounding 'not guilty' were heard around the world." "Scandalous," *Le
Figaro* said of the verdict; "The life of a Negro in Mississippi is not worth a
whistle," said *Das Frei Volk* in Düsseldorf.

White indignation rose, and with it, a white sense of responsibility. There
had really been two verdicts, not one, rendered at Sumner, I. F. Stone wrote.
One was the "not guilty" against Bryant and Milam. "The other, unspoken,
unintended, unconscious but indelible, was a verdict against the rest of us and
our country. . . . The murder and the trial could only have happened in a sick
countryside. Where else would a mother be treated with such elementary lack
of respect or compassion?" Stone urged Negroes to fight, to "rouse themselves
to make their indignation felt in some dramatic way." The "American Negro,"
he wrote, "needs a Gandhi to lead him, and we need the Negro to lead us—
into a better, more just, world." And the feeling expressed by Stone and Kempton was beginning to spread beyond the audience traditionally commanded
by the Stones and Kemptons. *Commonweal,* the magazine of liberal Roman
Catholics, said that the "moral disease" responsible for Till's murder was not
confined to Mississippi. "The same disease . . . created the Northern ghetto in
which he lived, [and] the southern shack from which he was taken to his death,"
Commonweal said. "The illness that ultimately killed him confines Negroes
to inferior homes, schools and jobs" in the North as well. And at least some
northern whites took the point. Now the rallies in the North demanding anti-
lynching legislation and other civil rights legislation—demanding justice—
were held not just among blacks, but among Jewish organizations and labor
organizations; a resolution adopted by the Jewish Labor Committee, which
represented half a million members of the American Federation of Labor and
the Congress of Industrial Organizations, denounced "this evil, bigoted act." As
David Halberstam was to write, "The Till case marked a critical junction for the
national media." The *Brown* decision had created "for the first time" a "national
agenda on civil rights. The national media was going to cover . . . the entire
South." And now, with the nation ready at last to read about the South, the Till
case had provided reading material more dramatic than school desegregation
lawsuits. "The educational process had begun"; the Emmett Till trial "became
the first great media event of the civil rights movement. The nation was ready;
indeed, it wanted to read what happened." Some Mississippians still thought
the episode was a joke. Two years after the trial, when John Bartlow Martin visited Sumner while researching a book on school desegregation, the head of the
local Citizens Council pointed to the Tallahatchie River, and, chuckling, said,
"You wouldn't come all the way down to Mississippi and not see Emmett Till's
River." But their laughter showed that they didn't understand. At a recess dur-

ing the trial, reporters had heard a white spectator say, nodding in the direction of the Tallahatchie, "That river's full of niggers," and they had reported the statement, had made America hear it. They had felt the depth of what the *Times* called the "controlled hostility" in Mississippi, and they had made America feel it; wrote Dan Wakefield of *The Nation,* "You lie in bed at night listening to the hounds baying, and during the day you see more men wearing guns than you ordinarily do outside your television screen. I am not ashamed to confess that I was afraid." Congressman Diggs was to call Mose Wright's unflinching "Thar he" inside that sweltering, hate-filled courtroom an "historic" two words, and they *were* historic, because thanks to Wright, there had been a trial. The brutality and injustice of white treatment of Negroes in the South was several centuries old, but now the entire nation—the entire world—had been able to read about it for itself.

AND THEN it could see it for itself.

In December, 1955, in Montgomery, Alabama, a quiet, dignified black seamstress, Rosa Parks, refused to move to the back of a bus to make room for a white passenger, and was arrested for violating the Alabama bus segregation laws. A meeting in the church of Mrs. Parks' pastor, a twenty-six-year-old black preacher named Martin Luther King Jr. who, as Taylor Branch has written, "looked and acted much older than his years," called for a boycott of the buses on the following Monday morning, but since many of Montgomery's blacks would have no alternative means of getting to their jobs except to walk for miles, no one was really sure the boycott would work. On Monday morning, the Reverend King's wife, Coretta, was looking anxiously out her window to see the first morning bus, which was usually jammed with Negro maids on their way to work. Then she saw it. It was empty. "So was the next bus, and the next," Branch reported. "In spite of the bitter cold, their fear of white people, and their desperate need for wages, Montgomery's Negroes were staying off the buses." That morning, there was another startling development. At the courthouse where Mrs. Parks was being tried—she would be fined fourteen dollars—the only spectators expected were the usual few relatives of the accused. Instead, when the door to the courtroom was opened, five hundred black Americans were standing in the corridor and spilling back down the stairs out onto the street. That evening, Martin Luther King Jr. was drafted as the first president of the Montgomery Improvement Association, and he made his first speech to the group. And with his first sentence, "We are here in a general sense, because first and foremost—we are American citizens—and we are determined to apply our citizenship to the fullness of its means," there was a murmur of assent, and when he said, "And you know, my friends, there comes a time when people get tired of being trampled over by the iron heel of oppression," there was a sudden, rising cheer, and when he cried, "If we are wrong—the Supreme Court of this nation is wrong. If we are wrong, God almighty is wrong! . . . If we are wrong—justice is a lie," a mighty leader was born. And the Montgomery Negroes made the boycott stick; at last southern Negroes had found a weapon—nonviolence—with which to challenge white supremacy, and had found the courage to use it. And again, as in the Till case, their courage, like Mose Wright's courage, furthered the "educational process." The bus boycott was in a big city, not an isolated hamlet, and it went on not for a week as the Till trial had, but for months. Television coverage increased. With the fuel from the Montgomery bus boycott added to the national fire started by the Till case, the furor in the North was not going away.

WHICH MEANT THAT IN JANUARY, 1956, Lyndon Johnson, returning to Washington after his heart attack, was going to have to make a decision, a decision that was to bring to the surface, within a character filled with deep contradictions, perhaps the deepest contradictions of all.

31

The Compassion
of Lyndon Johnson

LATER, WHEN HE WANTED his presidency to be remembered in history for its great civil rights legislation, Lyndon Johnson would often declare that he had, during his entire life, been free from racial prejudice. "I'm not prejudiced nor ever was," he told one biographer. "I never had any bigotry in me. My daddy wouldn't let me." His biographers took him at his word, and so did his assistants. In a typical comment—one of a hundred (one of hundreds, really) of similar comments from Johnson's aides—George Reedy says, "The man had less bigotry in him than anybody else I have ever met . . . Johnson had none in him . . . not racial, ethnic, or religious prejudices." So did his friends, or, to be more precise, those of his friends to whom he "talked liberal." "I'm telling you this man does not have prejudice," Helen Gahagan Douglas was to insist.

Like everything else about Lyndon Johnson, however, the question of his prejudice wasn't so simple. While in Georgetown he talked one way to men and women of liberal views, of tolerance toward human beings of other colors and persuasions, talked to them so passionately that they believed *he* was tolerant toward minorities, anxious to help them, waiting only for the right moment; talked so passionately that even civil rights crusader Virginia Durr accepted his response to her reproaches about his long silence on civil rights (a comradely hug and an assurance that "Honey, you're dead right! I'm all for you, but we ain't got the votes. Let's wait till we get the votes"), he talked quite another way in Suite 8-F of the Lamar Hotel in Houston to men of intolerance, to men who felt that Negroes and Mexican-Americans were inherently dumb, dirty, lazy, stupid, looking only for handouts ("gimmes," as 8-F's presiding spirit, Herman Brown, called black Americans) and talked to them, too, so passionately that they believed he shared *those* feelings, shared them fully.

Their beliefs about Lyndon Johnson, their descriptions of the way he talked to them, were not made a part of the journalism of the time, or of the history that has been written about it, because these men, unlike the George-town liberals, did not talk to journalists or historians—for more than twenty years after they became legendary figures in Texas, Herman and George Brown tried to avoid giving interviews, and every time an historian proposed writing a history of Brown & Root, they blocked the attempt. But their opinion of John-son's attitudes is just as strong as the liberals' opinion; and what they felt was that, while he had to be diplomatic and not express them publicly, his attitudes were the same as theirs. And although their names are not known to history as are those of the Washington liberals, they were just as close to Lyndon Johnson as the liberals were: Herman and George were the major financiers of his rise; Ed Clark, who "bought a ticket" on him in 1937, was his principal lawyer, and the man who kept Texas in line for him, for thirty years; when Johnson left Washington at the end of each congressional session, it was to the watering holes of these men—Falfurrias, St. Joe, Fort Clark—that he repaired, for the week-long, whiskey-soaked hunting trips that played so crucial a role in his political career. His rise was financed by men so bigoted that to talk to them when their guard was down was to encounter a racism whose viciousness had no limit; sitting in his apartment on Austin's Nineteenth Street on the day that signs went up with the new name the Austin City Council had given the street—"Martin Luther King Boulevard"—Clark was so filled with rage that as soon as the author of this book walked in, Clark told a "joke": "Did you hear about how the *Reverend* King went to Africa to look for his roots, but as he were climbing the tree, a baboon shat in his face?" During an earlier interview, Clark had been asked if Lyndon Johnson's views about Negroes and Mexican-Americans were any different from his own. Smiling a slow, amused smile, he replied in his East Texas twang, "If there were any difference at all, it were not apparent to me."

To take Lyndon Johnson at his word—his word that "I never had any big-otry in me"—it is necessary to ignore other words of Lyndon Johnson's: his own words, written, in his handwriting, in a private diary he kept (the only time he kept a diary) during the month he spent in the Pacific during the Second World War. To take him at his word, it is necessary to ignore still other words—words spoken in his own voice, and preserved on a tape recording made not in the Oval Office with an eye on posterity but by a Lyndon Johnson who thought no one was listening, not knowing that while he was talking to employees on his ranch over a radio telephone in 1967 and 1968, an Associated Press pho-tographer, Steve Stibbens, assigned to take photographs for a feature story on Johnson, had found himself, by accident, listening to the conversations, and had decided to record them because, as he recalls, "I was so shocked—I couldn't believe what I was hearing—I mean, this was the great civil rights President."

Crossing the Pacific in May, 1942, the big four-engine Coronado flying boat on which Lyndon Johnson was traveling would put down for refueling at small islands, and Johnson would observe the natives' behavior. On May 17, on the island of Nouméa, he wrote in his diary, in a neat, cramped script: "Natives very much like Negroes. Work only enough to eat." After he reached Australia, he was at an air base in Brisbane on June 4 when a violent incident involving black servicemen occurred. John Connally, with whom Johnson later discussed the incident, explained that it reinforced Johnson's belief that Negroes had a predilection toward drunkenness and violence. "Negro problem—no hard liquor as order Lieutenant," Johnson wrote in the diary. "Negroes and constables knife threat." The tape made during Johnson's presidency a quarter of a century later shows that he subscribed to some of the stereotypes about Mexican-Americans, too. Complaining about the laziness of Mexican-American workers on his ranch to Dale Malechek, his ranch foreman, he said, "I don't think Mexicans do much work unless there's a white man with them, so from now on I want a white man with every group."

A firm hand was necessary with Mexicans, Johnson felt. "I know these Latin Americans," he told the journalist Tom Wicker in 1964. "I grew up with Mexicans. They'll come right into your back yard and take it over if you let them. And the next day they'll be right up on your porch, barefoot and weighing one hundred and thirty pounds and they'll take that, too. But if you say to 'em right at the start, 'Hold on, just wait a minute,' they'll know they're dealing with somebody who'll stand up. And after that you can get along fine."

To accept Lyndon Johnson's contention, it is necessary to ignore notes taken by reporters on statements he made in off-the-record conversations—statements that never made their way into print at the time Johnson made them or during the more than three decades that have passed since, but that are available in the Lyndon Johnson Library yet are never included in any of the now-numerous biographies of Lyndon Johnson—statements that further document his acceptance of stereotypes: a belief, for example, that blacks are aggressive motorists. In a conversation with a correspondent for *Time* magazine on January 29, 1968, he explained why he didn't want to dispatch gunboats to protect vessels like the U.S.S. *Pueblo*. "If we started sending gunboats out to protect everybody gathering information we'd have a budget of five hundred billion dollars every year," Lyndon Johnson said. "That harassment is part of the job. It is just like you driving home at night and you come up to a stop light, and there's some nigger there bumping you and scraping you."

To accept Lyndon Johnson's contention that "I never had any bigotry in me," it is necessary to ignore certain phrases in his early speeches which revealed his attitude toward people whose skins were not black or brown but yellow. During the late 1940s, his public rhetoric was filled with references to "the menace of Eurasia." America must not surrender to "the barbaric hordes of godless men in Eurasia," he said during a speech in 1947. "Without superior airpower America is a bound and throttled giant; impotent and easy prey to any yellow dwarf with a pocketknife," he said during another speech the same year.

These were prepared addresses; his off-the-cuff speeches were not recorded, but persons who followed his campaigns say the speeches were filled with references to "yellow dwarves," "hordes of barbaric yellow dwarves," "sneaky yellow dwarves," and "godless yellow dwarves."

His remarks about African-Americans and Mexican-Americans before he was President were not isolated remarks. In conversations with friends, Johnson constantly employed the caricature shorthand for people of color—that they were dumb, that they were lazy, that they were prone to drunkenness and violence—to make points in casual conversation, as when, to show, as one man put it, "that he had no particular respect" for Lady Bird's opinion, he said "I have a nigger maid, and I talk my problems over with her, too." On other occasions, he made the same point by saying, "I talk my problems over with my nigger chauffeur, too."

Despite what he claimed, then, Lyndon Johnson was not without prejudice. Like millions of other Americans, he held stereotypes, and sometimes the stereotypes were expressed in racial terms. When, moreoever, Johnson was speaking to a Negro, he often used racial pejoratives. If Negroes were sufficiently subservient to him, he was kind and rather gentle with them, and used these words in a somewhat friendly manner. One afternoon in the mid-1930s, during Johnson's tenure as Texas director of the National Youth Administration, his old friend State Senator Welly K. Hopkins was talking with Johnson in his NYA office in Austin when a black employee came in. Hopkins was to tell an interviewer for an oral history that Lyndon asked the man what he wanted. "He said, 'Boy, what do you want?' Well, he said he wanted to borrow five dollars. 'Well, what do you want it for, boy?' " Hopkins said that "I could tell the President was going to let him have it"—and after the employee said he needed it so that he could get married, Johnson gave him the money. But sometimes those terms were not used in a friendly way. Lyndon Johnson possessed not only a lash for a tongue, but a rare talent for aiming the lash, for finding a person's most sensitive point, the rawest of his wounds, and striking it, over and over again, without mercy. With a black American, of course, the rawest point was likely to be the color of his skin, and the names by which he was addressed because of it: "nigger," for example, or "boy." And when Lyndon Johnson wanted to hurt a Negro, that was often where he aimed the lash. When the author asked Hopkins if Johnson always used the word "boy" in a joking or paternalistic way, Hopkins shook his head to say no, and related an incident that occurred in the NYA office, on another occasion when he was visiting Johnson. An employee, not of the NYA but of the office building—a middle-aged black man, "a porter or something, I think"—had done something that angered Johnson. "My God, I will never forget how he talked to that man," Hopkins said. "He would just rip him up and down, and the man would just have to stand there and take it. Lyndon would just keep calling him 'boy,' 'boy.' 'You understand that, *boy*? You got it now, *boy*? Do this, *boy*. Do that, *boy*.' "

Racial stereotypes sometimes governed Johnson's actions as well as his words. A stereotype that had currency in the Hill Country was that Negroes were terrified of all snakes. Sometimes Johnson or one of his Hill Country friends would catch a snake, sometimes a harmless snake, sometimes a rattlesnake. Johnson would put it in the trunk of his car, and drive to a gas station at which a Negro was working as the gas pump attendant. Pulling up to the pump to get gas, he would tell the attendant that he thought the spare tire in his trunk might need air, and would ask him to take a look at it. Often this practical joke was successful; relating this story, he said, about one Negro attendant, "Boy, you should have seen that big buck jump!" He went on playing this joke not only when he was in college, but when he was a congressional assistant—when he was a congressman, in fact. Once, when he played it while he was a congressman—in 1945 or 1946 at a service station at the corner of First Street and Congress Avenue in Austin—the joke had a different denouement. While Lyndon was "standing there laughing" at the attendant's shock, the black man picked up a tire iron and, threatening to wrap it around Johnson's neck, shouted, "I'll make you a bow tie out of this!" The manager of the service station had to hustle Johnson out a back door to get him away.

BUT THERE WAS A DIFFERENCE between Lyndon Johnson and all the other Americans who held racial stereotypes—and between Lyndon Johnson and all the presidents, save only Abraham Lincoln, who came before him and who came after him. Lincoln freed black men and women from slavery, but almost a century after Lincoln, black men and women—and Mexican-American men and women, and indeed most Americans of color—still did not enjoy many of the rights which America supposedly guaranteed its citizens; they did not—millions of them, at least—enjoy even the most basic right, the right to vote, and thereby choose the officials who governed them. It was Lyndon Johnson who gave them those rights. It was the civil rights laws passed during his presidency—passed because of the inspiring words with which he presented them ("*We* shall overcome," he said once as a Congress came cheering to its feet, and in front of television sets all over America, men and women of good will began to cry), and because of the savage determination with which he drove them to passage—that gave them the vote, and that made great strides toward ending discrimination in public accommodations, in education, in employment, even in private housing. Lincoln, of course, was President during the nineteenth century. In the twentieth century, with its eighteen American presidents, Lyndon Baines Johnson was the greatest champion that black Americans and Mexican-Americans and indeed all Americans of color had in the White House, the greatest champion they had in all the halls of government. With the single exception of Lincoln, he was the greatest champion with a white skin that they had in the history of the Republic. He was to become the lawmaker for the poor and the downtrodden and the oppressed. He was to be the bearer of at least a measure of social justice to those to whom social justice had so long been denied, the restorer of at least a measure of dignity to those who so desperately needed to be given some dignity, the redeemer of the promises made to them by America. He was to be the President who, above all Presidents save Lincoln, codified compassion, the President who wrote mercy and justice into the statute books by which America was governed.

LYNDON JOHNSON WAS ABLE to win these victories, to become this champion, in part because of where he came from.

Texas was in the South—one of the eleven Confederate states—but in a crucial respect, the Texas Hill Country wasn't southern. Because rainfall sufficient to grow cotton petered out just before its eastern edge, little cotton was grown there, and there were very few Negroes there—none at all in Johnson City. "There were no 'darkies' or plantations in the arid Hill Country where I grew up," Johnson was to recall. "I never sat on my parents' or grandparents' knees listening to nostalgic tales of the antebellum South." This was not to say that the Hill Country wasn't part of the South. "In Stonewall and Johnson City I never was a part of the Old Confederacy," he was to say. "But I was part of Texas. . . . And Texas is a part of the South. . . . That Southern heritage meant a great deal to me." Southern racial attitudes existed in the Hill Country—the word "nigger" was in common use—but with few Negroes to focus on, or to pose a threat, the attitudes were more casual than in the rest of the South; the atmosphere in which Lyndon Johnson was raised was not steeped in racism, and neither was he. He never exhibited, in word or deed, the visceral revulsion that southern racists like Bilbo and Eastland displayed at the very thought of Negroes and whites mingling together in social situations, or at work, or at the thought of them having sexual intercourse together or of racial intermarriage; never exhibited the conviction of a Richard Russell that "mongrelization" would lead to the end of civilization. Lyndon Johnson's use of words like "nigger" and "boy" to hurt or intimidate was primarily an example of the way the lash that was his tongue sought out the most vulnerable spot in everyone, not just blacks: in using those words, Lyndon Johnson was guilty less of racism than of cruelty. At least once, in fact, dealing with an African-American employee, he used these epithets, and the pain they caused, in a different way, to teach the employee the lesson Johnson felt everyone had to learn, a lesson Johnson felt would lead to an improvement in the employee's life: that it was necessary to accept reality, to face harsh facts and push beyond them, to be pragmatic, which in the employee's case meant to accept that he would always be the target of these epithets, would always be the target of prejudice, and that he had to accept that fact—because only by accepting it could he move beyond prejudice and achieve his ambitions.

The employee, a native of Wichita Falls, Texas, Robert Parker, was, indeed, ambitious. He would, during the 1960s, become *maître d'* of the Senate

Dining Room. During the 1940s and 1950s he was one of Johnson's "patronage" employees, holding down a Johnson-arranged job as a District of Columbia postman and being paid by the Post Office Department while earning his patronage by serving without pay as bartender and waiter at Johnson's parties, and, after Johnson acquired the use of the Democratic Leader's limousine, filling in as his chauffeur when Johnson's regular driver, Norman Edwards, had a day off.

"Yet for years," Parker would write in his autobiography, *Capitol Hill in Black and White,* Johnson "called me 'boy,' 'nigger,' or 'chief,' never by my name. . . ." Parker felt there were political reasons that could explain Johnson's use of these terms in public. "He especially liked to call me nigger in front of southerners and racists like Richard Russell," he was to write. "It was . . . LBJ's way of being one of the boys," and once, when "we were alone," Johnson "softened a bit" and said, "I can't be too easy with you. I don't want to be called a nigger-lover." But Johnson also used those terms in private. "Whenever I was late, no matter what the reason, Johnson called me a lazy, good-for-nothing nigger," Parker wrote. And there was an incident that occurred one morning in Johnson's limousine while Parker was driving him from his Thirtieth Place house to the Capitol. Johnson, who had been reading a newspaper in the back seat, "suddenly . . . lowered the newspaper and leaned forward," and said, " 'Chief, does it bother you when people don't call you by name?' "

Parker was to recall that "I answered cautiously but honestly, 'Well, sir, I do wonder. My name is Robert Parker.' " And that was evidently not an answer acceptable to Johnson. "Johnson slammed the paper onto the seat as if he was slapping my face. He leaned close to my ear. 'Let me tell you one thing, nigger,' he shouted. 'As long as you are black, and you're gonna be black till the day you die, no one's gonna call you by your goddamn name. So no matter what you are called, nigger, you just let it roll off your back like water, and you'll make it. Just pretend you're a goddamn piece of furniture.' "

Parker found that incident in Johnson's limousine difficult to explain—or forgive. Years later, as he stood beside Lyndon Johnson's grave thinking of all Johnson had done for his people, Parker would say he was "swirling with mixed emotions." Lyndon Johnson, he would write, had rammed through Congress "the most important civil rights laws this country has ever seen or dreamed possible." Because of those laws, Parker would write, he felt, at last, like a free man. "I owed that freedom to him. . . . I loved the Lyndon Johnson who made them possible." But remembering the scene in the limousine—and many other scenes—Parker was to write that on the whole working for Johnson was "a painful experience. Although I was grateful to him for getting me a job . . . I was afraid of him because of the pain and humiliation he could inflict at a moment's notice. I thought I had learned to fight my bitterness and anger inside. . . . But Johnson made it hard to keep the waves of bitterness inside. . . . But I had to swallow or quit. If I quit, how would I support my family? I chose survival and learned to swallow with a smile." And, Parker would write, "I hated *that* Lyndon Johnson." The words Johnson shouted from the back seat in the limousine that day—"As long as you are black, and you're gonna be black till the day you die, no one's gonna call you by your goddamn name"—those words, Parker was to write, "stuck in my belly like a fishhook for thirty years until I almost believed them." Yet that lesson Parker learned—that he had "to swallow" in order to get ahead—was taught to him in part by the man who shouted in his ear, "Let it roll off your back like water, and you'll make it. Just pretend you're a goddamn piece of furniture."

Lyndon Johnson was able to win these victories in part because of empathy—a deep sense of identification with the poor, including the dark-skinned poor; he understood their thoughts and emotions and *felt* their thoughts and emotions as if they were his own. And this was not surprising, for in a way they *were* his own. His empathy was deeply rooted in his personal experience, in blisters and sunburn and windburn and humiliation.

This empathy was also a product of the place from which he came. Because there were so few Negroes or Mexicans in the Hill Country and no money in that impoverished land to import Negroes or Mexicans to work the crops, when one of the few farmers who grew cotton needed it chopped or picked, "there wasn't any Mexicans or niggers to do it," as Lyndon's friend Otto Crider was to recall, "so everybody, including the kids, went out to do it," and one of the kids doing this work they called "nigger work" was young Lyndon Johnson.

One Texas chronicler was to call cotton "a man-killing crop." Chopping it—thinning out the rows by hacking out every other plant with a hoe—is hard, and when picking time comes, the pickers strap on kneepads and hang long burlap sacks around their necks, and all day long, from before daybreak until dark, under that broiling Hill Country sun, they stoop and crawl along the cotton rows, dragging after them the sacks that grow heavier and heavier as they are filled with the cotton bolls. After just one day of this work, even a young man, even a boy, has trouble straightening his back at night, and even work-hardened hands are raw and bleeding from the sharp-pointed cotton hulls. Lyndon Johnson's hands never became hardened; his soft white Bunton skin refused to callus but only blistered, one blister forming on top of another. Nonetheless, at the age of nine and ten, Lyndon Johnson was doing this work, out in the stony Hill Country cotton fields on his hands and knees, dragging the sack behind him. His older cousin Ava, who often worked beside him, remembers him whispering to her, "Boy, there's got to be a better way to make a living than this. There's got to be a better way."

When he was seventeen or eighteen, moreover, Lyndon Johnson worked on a Texas State Highway Department "road gang," gravel-topping stretches of the road between Johnson City and Austin. The workers on most such road gangs were Negroes or Mexicans; the work was brutally hard and the pay was only two dollars a day. This particular gang was all white, but the work it was doing was nonetheless "nigger work." At times, he would be half of a pick-and-shovel team, working with Otto Crider's brawny brother Ben. "He'd use the shovel and scoop the dirt up"—that hard Hill Country limestone caliche—"and I'd use the pick[ax] and pick it up, or vice versa," Ben recalls, and, he recalls, that work was "too heavy" for the skinny, ungainly teenager. At other times, Lyndon "drove" a "fresno," a heavy, two-handled iron scoop pulled by two mules. "Driving" a fresno meant standing behind the scoop, between its handles, with a hand on each handle. Since the driver didn't have a hand free, the reins were tied together and wrapped around his back, so that he and the mules were, really, in harness together. Lyndon would have to lift the handles of the heavy scoop, jam its front edge into the hard ground, and push hard to force the scoop through the rocky soil, as the mules pulled. When the scoop was filled with earth and stones, he would have to press down on the handles, straining with the effort, until the scoop rose off the ground. Then, still pressing on the handles as hard as he could, the reins still cutting into his back, he would have to drive the mules to the spot where he could dump the heavy load. "This, for a boy of . . . seventeen, was backbreaking labor," Crider says. In summer, working in the unshaded hills under that merciless Hill Country sun was almost unbearable, and the laborers worked with their noses and mouths filled with the dried soil the wind whipped into their faces. Winters could be so cold that the men had to thaw out their hands around a fire before they could handle their picks and shovels. Lyndon Johnson worked on that road gang for almost a year. All his life, he would hate the very thought of physical labor, and he never forgot what cotton picking and road-gang work—that "nigger work"—was like. Harry McPherson, who went to work for Lyndon Johnson in 1956, would comment that his new boss "did not pretend, as many Southerners did, that Negroes 'really enjoyed' the southern way of life," and that he didn't "romanticize" that life, including the menial work that was part of it. How could Lyndon Johnson have romanticized that work? He had done it.

But Lyndon Johnson's empathy for the poor and the dark-skinned came not from experience alone but also from insight. It was rare insight, provided by rare ability: his ability to read people so deeply, to look so deeply into their hearts and see so truly what they were feeling that he could feel what they were feeling—and could therefore put himself in their place.

During the first twenty years of his life, he had little contact with people whose skins were not white, but he spent his twenty-first year—from September, 1928, through June, 1929—teaching them, at the "Mexican school" in the little town of Cotulla on the flat, barren plains of the South Texas brush country.

There he saw into his pupils' lives. When "lunch hour" came, he saw that the children had no lunch, and were hungry. He went to visit their homes—on the "wrong" side of the tracks of the Missouri-Pacific Railroad that divided

Cotulla into Anglo and Mexican sections—and saw the tiny, unpainted, tin-roofed, crumbling hovels, with neither electricity nor running water, in which they lived. (Lyndon himself lived that year on the "Anglo" side of the tracks but in accommodations only marginally better: a room he shared with another, older boarder, in a small, shabby house on stilts next to the railroad tracks; at night he would be kept awake by the rumble of the long trains that passed endlessly, carrying bawling cattle up from Laredo.) He learned the slave wages that his pupils' fathers were being paid by Anglo farmers.

And he saw into his pupils' hearts. "I saw hunger in their eyes and pain in their bodies," Lyndon Johnson would say years later. "Those little brown bodies had so little and needed so much." He saw hunger and pain—and he saw more. "I could never forget seeing the disappointment in their eyes and seeing the quizzical expression on their faces—all the time they seemed to be asking me, 'Why don't people like me? Why do they hate me because I am brown?' "

And his own heart went out to them. Out of the insight came indignation—Cotulla's Anglos treated the Mexicans "just worse than you'd treat a dog," he was to say, and he was snarling as he said it. After the cotton fields, after the road gang, after Cotulla, there would be present amid the violently contrasting and clashing elements of Lyndon Johnson's personality one element that was as vivid and as deep as the cruelty, no matter how opposite it might be—an understanding of and sympathy for the poor, particularly for the poor whose skins were dark; a tenderness for them, a compassion for the very people to whom at other times he could be so callous.

Understanding the conditions of the children's lives, he understood the impact of those conditions. Even his most diligent students were often absent, and he knew why; all his life, he would recall lying in his room before daylight and hearing truck motors and knowing that the trucks were "hauling the kids off . . . to a beet patch or a cotton patch in the middle of the school year, and give them only two or three months schooling."

And because he understood that, the prejudices he had against Mexican-Americans, as with the prejudices he held against black Americans, while he expressed them in racial terms, were stereotypes less of race than of culture and class. His view of the characteristics that he thought he saw in blacks and Mexican-Americans—laziness and a predisposition to violence, for example—was very different from the view of southern racists, for unlike them, Lyndon Johnson did not feel that these characteristics were due to some innate, ineradicable defects in their genes expressed in the color of their skin. He believed that they were a product of the lack of education and opportunity with which America had shackled them, and that if that situation were changed, they would be changed: that if people of color were freed from these shackles, they would, in every way, be fundamentally the same as people whose skins were white. He often expressed this belief, often with his customary coarseness. In 1964, he told a Texas friend: "I'm gonna try to teach these Nigras that don't know anything how to work for themselves instead of just breedin'; I'm gonna try to teach these Mexicans who can't talk English to learn it so they can work for themselves . . . and get off of our taxpayers' back." The racists in 8-F were wrong about Lyndon Johnson, as wrong as the southern racists whose support he needed on Capitol Hill.

The clearest proof of the genuineness of his feeling that the stereotypical view of minorities would be changed if the circumstances of their lives were changed was how hard he tried, as a twenty-one-year-old schoolteacher, to change the circumstances of those Mexican-American children with whom he came in contact. He tried very hard. He was filled with a need to help. He had taken the teaching job only as a means of earning enough money to finish college, but he became a teacher such as Cotulla had never seen, not only arguing the school board into providing equipment so that his pupils could play games during recess but arranging for games with other schools—baseball games and track meets like the white kids had—and since the board declined to pay for buses to transport his kids to the meets, climbing hovels' rickety porches to persuade men to whom every day's work was precious to drive the children in their cars.

As I wrote in *The Path to Power,* "No teacher had ever really cared if the Mexicans learned or not. This teacher cared." He arrived at school early and stayed late. "If we hadn't done our homework, we had to stay after school," one of his students was to recall—and no matter how long that took, their teacher stayed with them. Insisting that they speak English, he not only handed out spankings to boys who lapsed into Spanish but, to give boys and girls practice in speaking English in front of audiences, he formed the school's first debating team.

He tried to inspire them. "I was determined to spark something inside them, to fill their souls with ambition and interest and belief in the future," he was to say. Recalls another student: "He used to tell us this country was so free that anyone could become President who was willing to work hard enough." He told them a story—"the little baby in the cradle," as a student would call it. "He would tell us that one day we might say the baby would be a teacher. Maybe the next day we'd say the baby would be a doctor. And one day we might say the baby—any baby—might grow up to be President of the United States."

And the passion of Lyndon Johnson was not limited by the job. Telling the school janitor, Thomas Coronado, that he should learn English, he bought Coronado a textbook to learn it from; before school opened and after it closed, he sat on the steps outside the school with him, tutoring him. "After I had learned the letters, I would spell a word in English. Johnson would then pronounce it, and I would repeat." The tutoring, Johnson made clear, must not interfere with Coronado's responsibilities. "He made it very clear to me that he wanted the school building to be clean at all times. . . . He seemed to have a passion to see that everything was done that should be done—and that it was done right."

The circumstances of the children's lives interfered with everything he was trying to do, and he saw that, saw that their lives were permeated with injustice.

"I swore then and there," Lyndon Johnson was to say, "that if I ever had a chance to help those underprivileged kids I was going to do it." It was at Cotulla, Lyndon Johnson was to say, "that my dream began of an America . . . where race, religion, language and color didn't count against you."

And Lyndon Johnson won these victories for America's downtrodden because he possessed not only the quality of compassion, but a rare gift for translating compassion into the only kind of accomplishment that would be meaningful.

As was shown in *The Path to Power,* that gift first became apparent in Lyndon Johnson's first governmental job—as a twenty-four-year-old assistant to a do-nothing Texas congressman from a district on the Gulf of Mexico, even further south than Cotulla. At a time when no one (certainly not the congressman) could think of a way to save from imminent foreclosure the district's hundreds of Depression-wracked farms which were so far behind in their tax and mortgage payments that they seemed hopelessly beyond the reach of the newly elected President Roosevelt, Lyndon Johnson thought of a way—a unique and complex refinancing plan—and persuaded banks, mortgage companies, and two federal agencies to implement it fast enough so that the farms were saved, sometimes only hours before the foreclosure sale began. And, as was also shown in the opening volume, the gift came to flower in Johnson's first elective office, after that victory he won as a twenty-eight-year-old congressman, when he brought electricity to thousands of lonely farms and ranches in the Hill Country—a victory, against seemingly impossible odds, that displayed not only a remarkable determination to mobilize the powers of government to help the downtrodden but a remarkable ingenuity in expanding and using those powers, in transmuting sympathy into action: governmental action. If Lyndon Johnson wanted to hurt, he also wanted to help—and no one could help like Lyndon Johnson.

LYNDON JOHNSON was not to become the champion of the poor, particularly the poor of color, solely because of his compassion or his governmental genius, however. Indeed, had his accomplishments on their behalf depended solely on those traits, they might never have become reality.

As his life proved.

Strong as was the compassion, the need to help, it was not the strongest force in Lyndon Johnson's life. His character had been molded by his youth in a tiny, isolated Hill Country town: by the interaction there of humiliation with heredity, by the impact of insecurity and shame on that potent inherited strain that gave him not only a huge nose and ears but also a huge need to be "in the forefront," to "advance and keep advancing." It was the fires of that youth that had made his needs, the imperatives of his nature, drive him with the feverish, almost frantic, intensity that journalists called "energy" when it was really desperation and fear, the fear of a man fleeing something terrible. And those fires had hardened the clay of his character, a clay hard in its very nature, into something much harder—into a shape that would never change. Compassion, sympathy—the desire to help, impulses that might be called noble—constituted one of those imperatives, a strong one. But during his youth, he had seen, and felt, the result of noble impulses; it was such impulses—his father's idealism—that had played such a large role in his family's fall "from the A's to the F's." It was therefore not compassion that most fully satisfied his needs, but rather power. It was not the desire to "help somebody" but to "be somebody" that drove him most strongly—that is the motivation mentioned most prominently not only by the companions of his youth ("If he couldn't lead, he didn't care much about playing") but of his more mature years as well. Unrelenting ambition—the need not merely to advance but to "keep advancing"—had been the trademark of generations of Buntons. And it was the strongest driving force of the man who had inherited—so clearly in the opinion of the Hill Country—the "Bunton strain." Sometimes the two forces—compassion and ambition—ran on parallel paths, but sometimes they didn't. And whenever those two forces collided, it was the ambition that won, as had been demonstrated at half a dozen turning points in his early career, even within his congressional district. "The best congressman for a district there ever was" lost much of his interest in helping his constituents when, following his defeat in the 1941 senatorial campaign, it appeared that he would never reach the Senate, and that his work for his district might not lead to political advancement but would have to be an end in itself.

When the element of race had been added to the collisions between the two forces—compassion and ambition—the collisions became more dramatic; the result was unvaryingly the same.

The foreclosure and electricity accomplishments had been achieved largely on behalf of white farmers. There had, however, been a period in Lyndon Johnson's early life—between July 26, 1935, when he left the congressional assistantship, and February 23, 1937, when he began running for a congressional seat of his own—during which his career had been intimately involved with blacks and Mexican-Americans, for during this period he was the director for the state of Texas of the New Deal's National Youth Administration, an agency whose goal was to extend a helping hand to young people of all races and colors.

The NYA had been created, in June, 1935, to help students stay in high school or college by providing them with part-time campus jobs that would allow them to earn enough—fifteen or twenty dollars per week—to continue their education, and to help young people who were not in school by creating small-scale public works projects on which they could be employed and thus earn some income while improving the civic estate.

Lyndon Johnson, at twenty-six the youngest of the NYA's forty-eight state directors (he may, in fact, have been the youngest person to be entrusted with statewide authority for any major New Deal program) and one, besides, who had absolutely no administrative experience and now was suddenly administering a multimillion-dollar statewide program, threw himself into his job with energy and passion, the passion "to see that everything was done that should be done."*

The young people of Texas whom Lyndon Johnson wanted to help included young blacks and Mexican-Americans. He was very anxious to help them. Sometimes, indeed, his outrage at society's indifference to their plight burst out of him, as if he could not contain it. Once, while he was waiting to explain NYA programs to a businessmen's luncheon club in San Antonio, one of the club's members tried to tell him that most of the programs were unnecessary. "All these kids need to do is get out and hustle," he said. Turning on the man, Johnson said sarcastically: "Last week over here I saw a couple of your kids hustling, all right—a boy and girl, nine or ten. They were hustling through a garbage can in an alley," looking for something to eat.

When he spoke to blacks and Mexican-Americans, he made them believe—believe completely—in his commitment to helping them. For Texas' black colleges, financially pressed in good times and in desperate condition during the Depression, NYA assistance was a blessing, and Johnson always telephoned the administrators of those colleges personally to tell them it was coming. "You have any boys and girls out there that could use some money?" he would ask. He made them believe, as well, that he was stretching the limits of his authority to help them, that he was giving them not merely their fair share of the NYA allocation for Texas, but more than their fair share. "He'd send us our quota of money," says O. H. Elliot, bursar of the black Sam Houston College in Huntsville. "Then, off the record, he'd say, 'I've got a little extra change here. Can you find a place for it?' " ("We could always find a place for it," Elliot adds, saying that part of the extra money was used for faculty salaries; "We couldn't have paid our faculty except for Mr. Johnson.") "It sorta sold us on him even before he ran for elective office," he says. "He cared for people." New Deal administrators from the NYA's Washington headquarters who visited Texas were taken on elaborate, carefully choreographed tours, and were impressed, not only by Johnson's overall accomplishment—after a trip to Texas in February, 1937, NYA Southwestern Regional Representative Garth Akridge called him "easily one of the best men directing one of the best staffs in one of the best programs with the most universal and enthusiastic support of any state in the Union"—but by his record on behalf of minorities. NYA Assistant Director Richard R. Brown, who was often in touch with Johnson ("He

---

*For an account of Johnson's work with the NYA that does not touch on its racial aspects, see Chapter 19 of *The Path to Power.*

always called me Mr. Boss Man," Brown recalls) and who visited Texas several times, says, "I think that Lyndon made every effort there to reach as many blacks as could be done. . . . I would say that for a Texan he had a rather broad tolerance for races." (The possibility that Johnson was making a special effort to leave that impression with Brown is raised by the fact that, while during other staff meetings he occasionally referred to blacks as "niggers," when, during a staff meeting attended by Brown, one of Johnson's assistants made a remark that was mildly racially disparaging, Johnson said, 'You can't use that term here.' " Brown was indeed impressed: "I felt that he was a very tolerant, a very broad-minded young man.")

At meetings in Washington, Johnson spoke to members of the NYA's headquarters staff with his customary eloquence; impressed with his desire to help black youth, they spread the word among prominent black figures in New Deal circles. One such figure, Robert C. Weaver, would later recall that an NYA administrator, Frank Horne, "kept talking about this guy in Texas who was really something. His name was Lyndon Johnson, and Horne said Johnson didn't think the NYA was for middle-class people; he thought it was for poor people, including Mexican-Americans and Negroes. . . . This guy in Texas was giving them [blacks] and Mexican-Americans a fair break. This made quite an impression on me." Praising his "energy" and "vigorous imagination," the NYA's dynamic black Director for Negro Affairs, Mary McLeod Bethune, was to describe Johnson as "one who has proven himself so conscious of and sympathetic with the needs of all people." Brown recalls that "whenever Lyndon's name came up she would say such things as, 'Well, he's a very outstanding young man. He's going to go places. He'll be a big man in this country.' "

AFTER LYNDON JOHNSON BECAME PRESIDENT, and during the decades since his death, this impression would be resurrected, and would grow, its growth fueled in part by the oral histories assiduously collected by the Lyndon Baines Johnson Library ("He never asked what *color* people were. If we had the money, we hired the kids. It was as simple as that"—Bill Deason), in part by Johnson's vivid, indeed fascinating, recollections of his NYA days, and in part by the fact that as President, he had indeed won great battles by fighting with all his might on behalf of minorities, a fact which understandably increased people's willingness to believe that he had been waging the same fight as a young man. The impression became a cornerstone of the Johnson legend. Biographers, understandably influenced by his later civil rights victories, painted a picture of a Lyndon Johnson who during his entire adult life had *always* battled wholeheartedly for minorities—who had done so, for example, as Texas NYA Director, fighting gallantly, in the face of southern bigotry, to give minorities more than their fair share of his resources. After her long exposure to Johnson's eloquence, Doris Kearns Goodwin was to write that "Johnson did put together special NYA programs for the black young, often financed by secret transfers of money from other projects that had been approved at upper levels of the bureaucracy."

In some respects, this picture is accurate, quite dramatically so. At Prairie View Normal and Industrial College, in Waller County, young black men built dormitories to house young black women. These young women worked two and a half hours a day and studied "domestic science" for four, learning how to cook, clean house, take care of children and do other household work, and this "domestic training" program was then expanded to four black colleges. A staffer from NYA national headquarters in Washington was to report back that in Texas "I have found what I have been hoping to find for colored girls. . . . I believe I know the Negro condition in the southern states, and no one would be more delighted to see them have the kind of training that Mr. Johnson is setting up in Texas. The Texas Director is doing what many of us are talking." And Johnson was to tell Ms. Goodwin that only his determination to circumvent NYA regulations on behalf of black colleges made the Prairie View project possible. The NYA's allocation for supplies and equipment, he told her, was supposed to be spent for "equipment, shovels, etc., and nothing for fancy things like dormitories. . . . What I did was to go around and get people to donate money for the equipment in white areas and then apply that saving to Prairie View and use it to build dorms which they so badly needed." Some projects must have given Lyndon Johnson great personal satisfaction. One was to transform the debris-littered vacant lot in front of Cotulla's "Mexican school" into a neat plaza; another NYA grant allowed the school to hire its first "library assistant."

On closer inspection, however, the picture is less clear, in part because of the most important appointment Lyndon Johnson made as NYA Director: the chairmanship of the Texas NYA's nine-member State Advisory Board.

Intent on having the NYA as decentralized as possible within the overall guidelines set up in Washington, its national director, Aubrey Williams, considered the state advisory boards "crucial." He wanted them to have not *pro forma* but active involvement in tailoring NYA programs to each state's different needs. And the chairman Johnson selected was Alvin Wirtz, whose racism was so virulent that he could not restrain himself even at a Georgetown dinner party at which Virginia Durr began advocating giving Negroes the vote. Wirtz responded, "Look, I like mules, but you don't bring mules into the parlor."

Having grasped, while he was still a congressional secretary, Wirtz's carefully concealed but immense behind-the-scenes power in Austin, Johnson had begun cultivating "Senator's" friendship at that time, with the success documented by Wirtz's inscription that he loved Lyndon "as if he were in fact my own son." Now, immediately after his appointment as Texas NYA Director, the cultivation was intensified. With the whole city of Austin to choose from, Johnson rented for the NYA office a suite on the sixth floor of the Littlefield Building, directly below Wirtz's law office on the seventh floor, and constantly—"daily, several times a day," Luther E. Jones recalls—ran up the stairs to seek the lobbyist's advice about NYA matters. And Johnson drew Wirtz closely into the NYA's work, not only consulting him constantly but even persuading him to accompany him on field inspection trips through the state.

And the picture is also less clear because of appointments Johnson didn't make.

Shortly after he was appointed to his NYA post, in July, 1935, he was told by NYA administrators in Washington that in a state with as large a Negro population—approximately 855,000—as Texas, there should be at least one Negro member of the State Advisory Board. Johnson did not accept the suggestion. Instead, he created a separate five-member Negro Advisory Committee (which he said would advise him on the best methods of using the money the Texas NYA was allocating to black youth programs). This committee, he was to tell the NYA administrators, was composed of "the outstanding members of the race," men, he said, "who enjoy the confidence of white people and who are respected by white people for their work and ideas."

The creation of a separate Negro committee did not satisfy the NYA administrators. In only a few states did the State Advisory Boards play a role as active as Aubrey Williams had envisioned for them. In most states, they had no significant function: they were indeed only advisory. In some states, they met only infrequently—Johnson's effort to get his board chairman to take a more active role was unusual. But the NYA headquarters staff in Washington considered the presence of a leading Negro citizen on the Advisory Board important, since it made blacks feel they had a role in the program, a voice in setting its policies, instead of merely receiving handouts from it. They pressed Johnson to appoint at least one black to the overall board, and when Johnson continued to decline to do so, the NYA's National Deputy Administrator, John J. Corson, telephoned him in early August and discussed the matter with him "thoroughly." On August 20, when Johnson came to Washington for a conference of all forty-eight state directors, Corson raised the matter again, telling him that the NYA administration was in agreement that the appointment should be made. When, on September 17, it still had not been made, Corson wrote Johnson, setting out formally the fact that there was a "large number of Negro youth in Texas" and that "in order that there may be just recognition of this group, we believe it would be advisable to give them the means of expression which the appointment of a Negro leader on the Advisory Committee would permit."

To this letter, Johnson responded with one of his own—long and eloquent. In five single-spaced and emotional pages, he told Corson that such an appointment would have a "disastrous result" both for what the NYA was trying to accomplish for Negroes and in terms of race relations in Texas. "The racial question during the last one hundred years in Texas . . . has resolved itself into a definite system of mores and customs which cannot be upset overnight," he said. "So long as these are observed there is harmony and peace between the races in Texas. But it is extremely difficult to step over lines so long established and to upset customs so deep-rooted, by any act which is so shockingly against precedent as the attempt to mix Negroes and whites on a common board."

Were he to "place a Negro on this Board," he said, "I know . . . and everyone acquainted with the situation in Texas knows, that . . . three results would be inevitable": every one of the board's present nine members "would resign immediately"; he himself would have to resign as state director because "my judgement would thereafter always be at a discount in Texas, and I would be convicted of making a blunder without parallel in administrative circles in the state. I might even go so far as to say that I would, in all probability, be 'run out of Texas.' " The third "inevitable" result of the appointment, he said, would be "to cost us the cooperation of Negro leaders in Texas." "To one unacquainted with conditions in Texas, this may seem paradoxical," Johnson wrote, "but I sincerely believe that an investigation will reveal that Negro leaders would have no confidence in any of their number who permitted his name to be proposed as a member of the Board, because of the friction they know would certainly ensue." The "turmoil" and "publicity" that "would inevitably follow" such an appointment "would react to the detriment of the Negroes and all their projects. . . . Both the whites and the Negroes would be thrust farther apart than ever by such a move." He himself had already launched programs to help Negro youths, he said, and "I feel confident that in these ways the NYA of Texas will be able to do vastly more to benefit Negro youths than by setting them on the firing line of public opinion in Texas, to be shot at by the whites and dodged by the Negroes."

Johnson's response, on its face no more than a concerned statement of the results that could well be expected from placing a Negro on a predominantly white board in a southern state, was evidently convincing. Corson, forwarding it to NYA Director Aubrey Williams on September 22, attached a memo saying "Under the circumstances, I have advised him that we will not press the matter at this time." Corson was shortly to leave the NYA, and the matter was not raised again. No Negro was ever appointed to the Texas NYA Advisory Board. In retrospect, however, the letter becomes somewhat less convincing—because of something that has gone unmentioned in any Johnson biography: at the very time he wrote the letter saying that an attempt to appoint a Negro to his state's Advisory Board would "inevitably" result in the calamitous consequences he enumerated, seven of the ten other southern states had already appointed Negroes to their advisory boards—with no such consequences. The other three states would all follow suit—also with no consequences. Even Alabama and Mississippi had Negroes on their NYA Advisory Boards, as did Arkansas, Florida, Georgia, Louisiana, North Carolina, South Carolina, Tennessee, and Virginia. In not one of those ten states did the appointment cause the rest of the board—or the state director—to resign. In not one was the director run out of

the state. In none of these states did the appointment result in the loss of cooperation of Negro leaders; in none of them did the appointment cause "turmoil."
Eloquent though Johnson's reply was, the results which he said were "inevitable" hardly seem to have been inevitable at all.

IT WAS NOT JUST to his Advisory Board that the Texas NYA Director declined
to appoint an African-American. The appointment of African-Americans to
high-level administrative and supervisory positions in the state NYAs was
important to the Negro Affairs Director, Mrs. Bethune, who was to explain to
the state directors that "It does not matter how equipped your white supervision
might be, or your white leadership, it is impossible for you to enter as sympa-
thetically and understandingly into the program of the Negro, as the Negro can
do." In February, 1936, seven months after Johnson had been appointed Texas
director, a report issued by the NYA's Washington headquarters stated that "In
those states where the Negro population is large, a Negro staff member has
been appointed to the state staff"—a salaried administrator, generally called
"Assistant to the State Director," who worked directly under the director at
state headquarters and oversaw all Negro programs. Those states included ten
of the eleven southern states—even Mississippi and Alabama. They did not
include Texas. Johnson did not appoint a Negro administrator, instead using the
five members of his Negro Advisory Committee as liaison with black organizations.

All five already had full-time jobs—two, Joseph J. Rhoads of Bishop College, and Mary Branch of Tillotson College in Austin, were presidents of black
colleges and highly respected educators in Texas' black community; two were
principals of black high schools, and the fifth was a home demonstration
agent—and their work for the NYA was not made easier by the fact that, unlike
members of Johnson's white Advisory Board, they were given little staff assistance. In March, 1936, the NYA's newly appointed Administrative Assistant in
Charge of Negro Activities, Juanita J. Saddler, took an inspection trip of Texas.
She found that the members of the Negro Advisory Committee were personally
very fond of Johnson, but upon her return to Washington, she reported that the
committee "feels . . . that they have been asked to assume heavy responsibilities . . . responsibilities that for the white group are carried by employed persons." She felt particularly the lack of a salaried black administrator, and wrote
Johnson:

> I was very much impressed with the splendid cooperation you were
> receiving from the Negro Advisory Committee. I feel however, as I
> said when I was there, that they are being asked to assume major
> responsibilities for the NYA program which, in view of the heavy
> pressures of duties involved in their own jobs, must put them under

an extra burden. Whereas they are doing a very splendid job, an employed person carrying full responsibility for the program for this group would assure greater development of the work.

NYA Regional Director Garth Akridge renewed the request for a salaried Negro administrator without results, and on August 3, 1936, after receiving a report on the situation in Texas, Akridge's supervisor, Richard Brown, the NYA's Assistant Director, put the request in writing, telling Johnson, "We feel very much the importance of having a well trained Negro Assistant to the State Director to look particularly into the program of the Negro youths of your state. In the fourteen states where these appointments have been made, the work among the Negroes has been most productive and satisfactory." Johnson's response was to ask for a face-to-face meeting on the subject, and, as the most detailed study of the Texas NYA puts it: "What was said at that meeting is unknown, but Johnson did not appoint a black assistant." He never appointed a high-level black assistant. No black administrator would be hired by the Texas NYA until Johnson had left the agency. "Apparently Johnson was not willing to take the politically damaging step of integrating his [headquarters] staff with one black member," this study says.

Johnson's reluctance to hire blacks may have extended further down the Texas NYA's organization chart than the "Assistant to the State Director." The racial background of the Texas NYA's more than two hundred administrators and supervisors is not given in the organization's records, and the author has found it impossible to determine—sixty years after the fact—how many were African-American, but contemporary statements hint that that reluctance may have included almost every one, if not every one, of the top administrative and supervisory jobs at his disposal. Enthusiastic though they were about the Freshman College Centers Johnson had created, at least two members of the Negro Advisory Board, Rhoads and Branch, were disturbed by the fact that although the students at the centers were overwhelmingly black, the two top supervisors of the College Centers program were white. Johnson established a Junior Employment Center in Fort Worth, at which hundreds of black youths would be interviewed by "counselors." When Ms. Saddler arrived at the Employment Center, she appears to have found that every counselor was white. In her report, she was to say that while the Negro Advisory Committee was planning a vocational guidance program, "it will not substitute for an efficient counselor attached to the employment office. . . . I hope that in time it will be possible to place a Negro counselor there." Upon her return from Texas, Saddler wrote Johnson that during her tour

I was asked on several occasions why there were so few supervisory positions available for Negroes. It was pointed out to me that even though the greater number of College Centers were for the colored group, the supervisors were white. . . .

Being a hopeful person, not always with justification, however, I look forward to the time when Negro Counselors can be assigned to interview Negro youth in connection with the new Junior Employment Service that has been established in Fort Worth. The fact that the Government is aiding and supporting various projects in the State, seems to me to allow leeway for liberal and tolerant groups and individuals in the community to try to make the social patterns more just and equitable for all the people in the community.

THE PICTURE of a crusading young Lyndon Johnson battling to get blacks more than their fair share of NYA assistance grows even more blurred when one looks—not through the prism of the great accomplishments of his presidency—at the share of NYA assistance that blacks actually received in Texas during Johnson's nineteen-month tenure as the agency's Director there. Examining the extent to which the moneys allocated to the Texas NYA went to blacks—looking not at rhetoric but at the actual figures—raises, in fact, not only the question of whether, during Johnson's tenure, blacks received, as he claimed, more than their fair share of such assistance but also the question of whether they received *even* their fair share.

The NYA, as the inspiration of Eleanor Roosevelt, was committed to a just and equitable distribution of its funds. Mrs. Roosevelt was insistent that it give a fair share to black youths. In the early days of the NYA, Director Aubrey Williams sought to ensure this by establishing a policy that state directors include blacks in NYA programs in percentages proportionate to the state's total population, but it was soon felt that since the program was intended to assist not all blacks but black *youths*, a fairer criterion would be to include them in percentages comparable to their percentage in a state's youth population; a 1936 bulletin from NYA headquarters declared that "Certainly the proportion of Negro youth aided should never fall below the percentage of the youth population." In Texas, Negroes comprised 27.8 percent of the youth population and 14.7 percent of the total population. In November, 1936, the sixteenth month of Johnson's tenure, the NYA's Division of Negro Affairs issued a report on "school aid"—the assistance given to students in high school and college—which was the NYA's major program. The report stated that "While in most states, Negroes have shared at least to the extent of their proportion of the total population, there are a number of notable exceptions." Six such exceptions were listed: Arkansas, Delaware, Louisiana, Mississippi, Tennessee—and Texas. And of those six states, the differential between a fair share for Negroes and the share they had actually been given was largest in Texas, where, the report stated, "Negroes comprise 14.7% of the total and 27.8% of the youth population, but receive only 9.8% of the school aid." By the criterion established by the NYA then, in the agency's major program Texas was the worst state in the country. (The report also stated that "Although accurate figures are not available, even larger discrepancies exist in the proportions of the amount of money actually expended.")

As for the Texas NYA's other programs—assistance to youths working on non-campus projects—determining the proportion of such assistance that went to black youths has proven difficult because racial breakdowns cannot be found in the National Archives or at the Lyndon Johnson Library, possibly because they have been lost, possibly because Johnson did not submit such break-downs, despite repeated NYA directives to all state directors to do so each month. In January, 1936, after Johnson had been in office for seven months, National Assistant Director Brown wrote him: "In going over the report of the activities of the Texas Youth Administration, we observe that you failed to report on the plans which are in progress regarding Negro activities. I shall appreciate a statement regarding this phase of the program in Texas, inasmuch as this is *a real problem in your state*" (italics added). From the scattered and incomplete figures that can be found for some months, it appears that the pro-portion of non-school aid that went to blacks was somewhat higher than cam-pus aid, but never high enough to raise the Texas NYA's overall aid to blacks up even to the 14.7 figure, much less the 27.8. During the nineteen months that Lyndon Johnson was Director of the Texas NYA, the proportion of its funds that went to black youths may never—not even once—have reached even the lower of the two figures below which "the proportion of Negro youth aid should never fall."* Lyndon Johnson may indeed, as he later claimed, have been quietly transferring funds from white schools to black schools and from white public works projects to black public works projects. But if he was doing so, he was nonetheless only shifting the funds out of allocations (allocations he himself had made) that were so inequitable—so far from the NYA purpose and guidelines as defined by its director—as to make the final allocations not fair, not nearly fair, but only somewhat less unfair.

THERE WAS IN TEXAS another racial minority almost as numerous as African-Americans and also desperately in need of the aid the NYA could offer.

Mexican-Americans did not have a separate division at NYA headquarters in Washington or a strong voice such as Mrs. Bethune's to prod state adminis-trators toward equal treatment, and for approximately seven hundred thousand Mexican-American citizens in Texas there was not only no seat on the Texas

---

*It should perhaps also be noted that those figures that *were* submitted by Johnson aroused skepticism at the time: in January, 1937, for example, a memorandum from the NYA's Area Statistical Office in Washington noted a "considerable difference" between the number reported by Johnson for "youth employed on projects" and the number recorded by the statisti-cal office. For example, the memorandum states that for July, 1936, Johnson reported 10,673 youths employed and the Statistical Office found only 7,050 employed.

NYA's Advisory Board, but no separate Advisory Committee, either. At other levels, however, their treatment within Lyndon Johnson's organization was comparable to that afforded Negroes. There was no high-level staff member at NYA headquarters in Austin to oversee Mexican-American programs and represent their interests within the agency. There was not a single individual with a Spanish surname on a list of the top thirty-seven Texas NYA staff. As for on-site supervisors for individual projects, even projects on which every one of the youths employed was Mexican-American, the skin color of those supervisors is a reminder of Johnson's feeling expressed three decades later on tape that "I don't think Mexicans do much work unless there's a white man with them." Separate statistics on Mexican-Americans were not kept within the NYA because the agency was determinedly classifying them as "white"; President Roosevelt had ordered all federal agencies to change their designation after Congressman Maury Maverick of San Antonio told him that the "colored" classification they had previously been given was reducing the participation of this loyally Democratic group in the southern states' white primaries. But if there were any Mexican-American supervisors, their number was very small— deliberately so. A Texas NYA directive looked for Spanish-speaking Anglo supervisors who "know how to handle men, with particular reference to Mexican boys, ages 18–25." In her book *LBJ & Mexican Americans: The Paradox of Power,* the most thoroughly documented analysis of the subject, Julie Leininger Pycior concludes that Mexican-American youths were "categorized officially as white but [were] treated as racially inferior" by the Texas NYA. Although they comprised almost 12 percent of the state's population, "they had no voice in administering the Texas NYA."

Determining whether Mexican-Americans received an equitable share of the Texas NYA's funds is impossible because of the failure to keep separate statistics of Mexican-heritage recruits. But Lyndon Johnson, using the NYA to set up what would be a statewide political organization—*his* statewide political organization—didn't want to antagonize local officials, so in Texas, in contrast to the practice in many other states, the NYA did not itself select those high school students who would receive its grants but allowed local school officials to do so. "It was up to the [school] superintendent to determine who needed it most," a Texas staffer was to say. And, as Dr. Pycior writes, "Thus the same people who enforced the segregation selected the trainees." Although no precise figures are available, Dr. Pycior says, "most of the Mexican-heritage trainees in the NYA worked as common laborers" on projects like the roadside parks that required only unskilled labor. "A few learned skilled jobs. . . . A small number received college aid. . . ." At the Residential Training Centers, she says, Mexican-American women were hired "in numbers far below their actual unemployment rate." ("These residential facilities barred black women," she adds.)

As Texas Director of the National Youth Administration, then, Lyndon

Johnson set up a statewide organization in a state more than a quarter of whose population—more than a million and a half people—had skins that were not white. But no member of the organization's Advisory Board, and, so far as can be determined, no member of its headquarters staff, had a skin that was not white. As for the deputy directors and other administrators out in the field across the huge state, "Johnson did not hire Mexican or African-American staff members," Dr. Pycior writes. If there were any blacks or Mexican-Americans among them, their number was certainly small. And that fact calls to mind the paternalistic condescension of Johnson's remarks about black Americans and Mexican-Americans in his diary and on the photographer's tape, for regardless of the amount of money he was allocating to young people of these races, very few members of those races were allowed to decide how the money was spent or to supervise its expenditure.

Lyndon Johnson certainly wanted to help black and Mexican-American youths in Texas—wanted very much to help them. His spontaneous outburst of anger at the San Antonio businessman—"I saw a couple of your kids hustling, all right"—and the fact that he threw himself into the creation of public works projects that would employ black youths as eagerly as he did into the creation of "white" projects, and that he showed as much energy and ingenuity in helping black colleges and black high school students as white, demonstrates that his heart was in helping them. But again, it had not been the heart that ruled but the head. The compassion, though genuine, had taken a back seat to calculation; the Texas journalist Ronnie Dugger, who covered Johnson for many years, was to write, in an incisive phrase, of his "real, though expendable, compassion." In Johnson's unending, silent calculations about the best way to further his career, it was the Alvin Wirtzes and the Herman Browns who were the key figures, not some powerless black leaders, and in his direction of the NYA program, it was not the philosophy that perhaps had captured his emotions which he followed, but the diametrically opposed philosophy of the Wirtzes and Browns. And, of course, the correctness of his course—if ambition was the guiding star—was proven when, on February 23, 1937, the congressman from the Tenth District suddenly died. Lyndon Johnson was in Houston, touring NYA projects there, when he saw a newspaper headline announcing the death. He was far from a logical candidate in a district containing many experienced, well-known politicians. Not only was his age a drawback but so was the fact that many of the district's political leaders—and most of its voters—had never even heard of him; on the day Johnson saw the headline, the *Austin American-Statesman* ran a list of possible candidates, a list that included not only the favorites but long shots as well, and Lyndon Johnson was not even mentioned. Speeding back to Austin, however, Johnson pulled up in front of the Littlefield Building and went not to the sixth floor but to the seventh, and asked Wirtz to give him the support he needed to enter the race. And Wirtz agreed on the spot.

. . .

THIS PATTERN WAS REPEATED after Lyndon Johnson had become a congress-man—in the single instance during his early congressional career in which his work as congressman became significantly involved with constituents whose skins were brown or black. Again there was a spontaneous, emotional, passionate outpouring of indignation and outrage, of sympathy and tenderness, of ingenuity to conceive a solution to the problem, and of energy to drive the solution to reality, and again this was followed, as soon as it became apparent to him that that solution would conflict with his ambitions, by a calculated, pragmatic drawing back that left in place the appearance of the solution but not the reality.

This conflict was precipitated by the passage, in September, 1937, a few months after Lyndon Johnson's election to Congress, of the Wagner-Steagall Housing Act, which made federal loans available for low-cost slum-clearance projects administered by local agencies.

At the moment that President Roosevelt signed the bill, Johnson was seeking every available source of funds for projects that would help his constituents, and the Housing Act seemed to provide an ideal opportunity. Some fifteen thousand Austin residents—the great majority of them Mexican-heritage or black Americans—were living in slum shanties, most of them without even electricity, running water, or indoor bathrooms. Johnson had, furthermore, won his seat in a special election in which blacks could vote, and he had carried most of the black vote, partly because of cash payments to leaders of the black community, but partly because of an emotional appeal he had made to other leaders of that community who were motivated by less selfish considerations. Meeting with them in the basement of a black Methodist church, with no reporters present—"It might have been dangerous otherwise," one of the group was to explain—the young candidate had told them, in the recollection of another member of the group, that " 'I think I can help you,' that if he got to Congress he could do such things as recognizing the Negroes for their votes, we together could recognize their voting rights. . . . He was very disposed toward us, and he was asking for our help." He had made his appeal so persuasively that, a third member was to say, "I'll never forget that meeting." The new Housing Act seemed to provide an ideal means of providing the help Johnson had promised.

At first, Johnson was fervently caught up in the idea of providing that help. Walking around the Austin slums when he returned to the city from Washington over Congress's Christmas recess in December, 1937, he was as filled with indignation and outrage and a desire to do something as he had been in Cotulla, and he told Austin Mayor Tom Miller, "Now look, I want us to be the first in the United States if you're willing to do this, and you've got to be willing to stand up for the Negroes and the Mexicans." When Miller agreed, Johnson gave a radio speech. Its title was "The Tarnish on the Violet Crown" (the short-story writer O. Henry had dubbed Austin "The City of the Violet Crown" because of the purplish haze which hung over the hills outside the city at dusk). And the title was no more vivid than his description, filled with heartfelt understanding, of the horror of what he had seen on a second walking tour, which he had taken on Christmas Day:

> Within five blocks, a hundred families, an old man with TB, dying, a child of eleven, all of them Mexicans. . . . I found one family that almost might be called typical living within one dreary room, where no single window let in the sun. Here they slept, here they cooked and ate, they washed themselves in a leaky tin tub after hauling the water two hundred yards. Here they raised their children, ill-nourished and sordid. And on this Christmas morning, there was no Santa Claus for the ten children, all under sixteen, that scrambled around the feet of a wretched mother bent over her wash-tub, while in the same room her husband, the father of her brood, lay dangerously ill with an infectious disease.

He poured himself into the project with all his energy; when the new United States Housing Authority announced its first three grants in January, 1938, they were to two large cities, New York and New Orleans, and one much smaller one, Austin, Texas—"because," Leon Keyserling, the Authority's deputy administrator, was to explain, "there was this first-term congressman who was so on his toes and so active and so overwhelming that he was up and down our corridors all the time."

When it came to spending the grant, however, passion ran into pragmatism—and passion lost without much of a fight. Far from being short of allies, the new congressman had solidly behind him on this issue not only the city's mayor but its only large newspaper, Charles Marsh's *Austin American-Statesman,* which ran story after story about families living in tents or in shacks made of tin cans. He even had surprisingly strong support from the community as a whole, for Austin was a very liberal city for Texas; at a public hearing before the City Council in January, 1938, every one of the 340 residents present voted to support the proposal. But it was not their views that were decisive. There was strong opposition from conservative realtors and businessmen, including Herman Brown, whose antipathy to "gimmes"—to "niggers" and "Meskins"—was intensified in this instance because he viewed federally subsidized low-cost housing as competition with private real estate enterprise (including profitable slum buildings, of which he owned more than a few in Austin). And on the other side also was Brown's lawyer, Alvin Wirtz. Lyndon had already convinced Wirtz and the Browns that, as George Brown puts it, "Lyndon was more conservative, more practical, than people understand. You get right down to the nut-cutting, he was practical. He was for the niggers, he was for the little boys, but by God . . . he was as practical as anyone," and he didn't want that impression weakened. Johnson named the top officers of the newly created Austin Housing Authority, which would administer the grant. As chairman he named E. H. Perry, but Perry, an elderly, mild-mannered, retired cotton broker was only a figurehead; the Authority would really be run by its vice chairman. To that post Johnson named Alvin Wirtz.

In the event, therefore, the Austin low-income housing program was not quite what Negroes and Mexican-Americans—or Austin's liberals—had hoped for. It was not only that the new housing units were segregated by race, although they were—strictly segregated; there were three separate garden-apartment developments, one for Mexicans, one for blacks, and one for whites. Some of Johnson's critics in Austin would later call the project "Housing for the Poor, by Race," but, given the fact that Austin was in some respects a southern city, this criticism was unfair. There was, however, another aspect of this low-income housing that was quite striking, given Johnson's desire to help African-Americans and Mexican-Americans—particularly, in regard to housing, Mexican-Americans, since his Cotulla experience had made him so sensitive to their plight. The federal Housing Authority generally adhered to a directive handed down by Interior Secretary Harold Ickes that its housing projects reflect "the racial composition of the neighborhood where they were located." Although the overwhelming majority—90 percent by some estimates—of the inhabitants of Austin's slums were blacks or Mexican-Americans, almost as much of this new housing was built for whites as for blacks and Mexican-Americans combined. In his speeches and talks with Austin leaders, Johnson had emphasized housing for the Mexicans and Negroes, the people he wanted to help. When the new apartments were built, there were 40 apartments for Mexicans, 130 apartments for Negroes, and 162 units for whites. As for other low-income public housing that would be built in Austin during Johnson's ten remaining years as the city's congressman—there wasn't any. Austin's slums grew steadily larger, but not a single new unit of low-income housing was built there.*

THE PATTERN WAS REPEATED in Lyndon Johnson's votes in the House of Representatives. Near the end of his eleven years in the House, he assured a constituent that he had "voted against all anti-poll tax, anti-lynching, and all

---

*The only public housing of any type built in Austin during these years was 1,641 units, not of low-income housing but of veterans' housing, created in 1946 and 1947 for returning World War II veterans and their families. These units were primarily barracks moved to Austin from deactivated Army camps and used to house veterans attending the all-white University of Texas. Twenty units—not barracks but trailers—were provided for a black college in Austin: Sam Houston College.

FEPC legislation since I came to Congress." He was not overstating the case. He routinely lined up on the southern side in votes on civil rights measures, excusing himself to liberal constituents by saying he was not "against" blacks but rather "for" states rights: he had a 100 percent record against not only legislation aimed at ending the poll tax and segregation in the armed services but even against legislation aimed at ending lynching. The votes he thus cast had little significance—none of the legislation would have passed had he voted the other way—and neither did the few speeches he made in the House, violent as was their language. In 1947, he denounced President Truman's "Fair Deal" program as "a farce and a sham," saying that it was "the province of the state to run its own elections," and that "I am opposed to the anti-lynching bill because the federal government has no more business enacting a law against one form of murder than another." What might have mattered more was not such public manifestations as votes and speeches but behind-the-scenes efforts in the House cloakroom or in the aisle at the rear of the Chamber, where members quietly buttonhole colleagues to argue for or against legislation, but the pattern held here, too. It was about civil rights measures as well as other liberal legislation that Johnson's liberal colleagues say he wouldn't take stands, that, as Edouard V. M. Izak of California put it, "He just simply was not interested. . . . He was very, very silent."

ALTHOUGH BOTH COKE STEVENSON, Johnson's major opponent in the 1948 race for the Senate, and the third man in the race, George E. B. Peddy, were segregationists and expressed themselves in racist terms, civil rights was not an issue in that campaign. Johnson ensured that it wouldn't be an issue with a statement about President Truman's civil rights program that he made in his opening rally on May 22, 1948, in Wooldridge Park in Austin. Repeating his attack on the program as "a farce and a sham," he added that it was "an effort to set up a police state in the guise of liberty. I am opposed to that program. I have voted AGAINST the so-called poll tax repeal bill; the poll tax should be repealed by those states which enacted them. I have voted AGAINST the so-called anti-lynching bill; the state can, and DOES, enforce the law against murder. I have voted AGAINST the FEPC; if a man can tell you whom you hire, he can tell you whom you can't hire."

During the 1948 campaign, Johnson occasionally reiterated this unambiguous opposition to the main tenets of the civil rights movement of the 1940s, but civil rights never became an issue. A survey of 147 Texas newspapers showed that civil rights "was hardly mentioned during the 1948 campaign."

Johnson received heavy majorities in African-American areas in Texas cities, in part because Washington figures like Mary McLeod Bethune and Robert Weaver sent word to African-Americans in Texas that Johnson was "really something," in part because African-American college and school officials who had met him during his NYA tenure felt he "really cared about people," in part because in meetings in small groups or one-on-one with black leaders of these areas, he convinced them that despite his public statements he was really on their side—but perhaps mostly because these leaders felt that, no matter what his true opinions, he was preferable to his two opponents. "For U.S. Senator, we have chosen Lyndon B. Johnson," the *Houston Informer* declared. "Though he is no angel, he is about as good as we have seen in the race." As one study put it, "Johnson was the best Texas minorities could get in 1948." Ed Clark was to say, "They had no choice. Where else were they going to go?"

AFTER HE BECAME PRESIDENT, Johnson wanted his image to be that of a man who had "never had any bigotry," who had been a longtime supporter of civil rights. The memory of the Wooldridge Park speech would blur that image, so he did his best to make sure it wouldn't be remembered. Stapled to the text of the speech in the White House files was the following admonition:

"DO NOT RELEASE THIS SPEECH—NOT EVEN TO STAFF, WITHOUT EXPRESS PERMISSION OF BILL MOYERS. As background, both Walter Jenkins and George Reedy have instructed this is not EVER TO BE RELEASED."

32

"Proud to Be
of Assistance"

IT WAS JUST EIGHT DAYS after Lyndon Johnson had been sworn in as a United States senator, in 1949, that the pattern—of true, deep compassion surrendering to true, deeper pragmatism—was repeated, in a fast-paced drama that revealed the pattern very clearly indeed.

The prologue to the drama had taken place more than three years earlier, in June, 1945, on Luzon Island in the Philippines, when a twenty-six-year-old Mexican-American private, Felix Longoria, a truck driver from a small South Texas town called Three Rivers, volunteered for a patrol and was killed in a fusillade of Japanese bullets, leaving a wife, Beatrice, and a young daughter. He was buried in a temporary military cemetery on Luzon for three years, and in December, 1948, his body was shipped home, and the Army notified his widow, who had moved to Corpus Christi. She said she wanted the body brought to Three Rivers for funeral and burial, and on Monday, January 10, 1949, she took a bus back there to arrange for her husband to be buried in his hometown. When, however, she arrived at Three Rivers' only funeral parlor, the Rice Funeral Home, the owner, T. W. Kennedy Jr., told her that she could not use its chapel for the service because "the whites won't like it."

Once, Beatrice Longoria might have simply accepted that edict, for before Pearl Harbor, Mexican-Americans in South Texas had generally accepted discrimination meekly, but during the war, Mexican-American soldiers had served not in segregated units as had blacks but alongside white soldiers (and had compiled the country's highest ethnic group representation in combat service and Medal of Honor awards), and had returned home in a different frame of mind, and in 1948, several hundred Mexican-American veterans in Corpus Christi had formed the American G.I. Forum to make sure they received the medical and educational benefits to which they were entitled under the G.I. Bill. As soon as Mrs. Longoria got back to Corpus Christi, she contacted the

Forum's president, physician and former Army major Dr. Hector Garcia. Dr. Garcia telephoned Kennedy, and told him that Mrs. Longoria wanted to use his funeral home. Kennedy repeated his refusal, at first simply giving the same explanation—"The white people just won't like it"—but when Garcia had the temerity to persist, saying, "But in this case the boy is a veteran, doesn't that make any difference?," he lost his temper and furnished additional reasons. "That doesn't make any difference," he said. "You know how the Latin people get drunk and lay around all the time. The last time we let them use the chapel, they got all drunk and we just can't control them . . . I'm sure you'll understand."

Dr. Garcia understood. Hanging up the phone, he sent seventeen telegrams to military officials, congressmen and senators, including one to the new junior senator from Texas, in which he asked for "immediate investigation and correction" of Kennedy's "un-American action" which "is in direct contradiction of those same principles for which this American soldier made the supreme sacrifice in giving his life for his country and for the same people who now deny him the last funeral rites."

The telegram was delivered to Suite 231 in the Senate Office Building at 8:49 the next morning, and was opened by either John Connally or Walter Jenkins (neither can now remember which one) and when Lyndon Johnson arrived at the office about an hour later, it was shown to him—and there was hardly a moment's pause before his response. "By God," he said, "we'll bury him in Arlington!" He told someone to get him the official in charge of Arlington National Cemetery, burial place of America's heroes, determined that indeed Private Longoria was eligible for burial there—any soldier, sailor, or marine who died in active service or held an honorable discharge could be buried there, with full military honors: three volleys from a firing squad, a bugler blowing taps, four uniformed flag-bearers holding the American flag over the casket as it was lowered into the grave, and then the presentation, by a soldier of the same rank or higher as the dead serviceman, of the flag to the next of kin, the soldier saluting and saying: "The Government presents to you this flag under which he served."

The Lyndon Johnson who called in his staff now was a Lyndon Johnson in the grip of his emotions. "You all get on the phone," he said, and his staff ran to obey, and within a few minutes after he had first read the telegram— "immediately, really," Connally was to recall—"not only I but Walter was on the phone arranging things." "His *immediate* reaction was he [Longoria] was eligible to be buried in Arlington," Connally says. "This was an instinctive thing—his instinctive sense of fairness and his basic feelings. . . . It had to do with outrage. Here was a veteran who died for his country and he can't be buried in his hometown." And no one could have translated that outrage into action more effectively. The decision to have the burial in Arlington was so *right,* so perfectly suited to correct an injustice. A veteran's hometown had refused to bury him with the ordinary honors that any dead soldier who died for his country deserved; so Lyndon Johnson had arranged that the veteran would be buried with full honors, in a place of deep symbolic significance. And his telegram back to Dr. Garcia, sent that afternoon after several calls to check to make sure that Garcia's account was accurate, was so right. "I DEEPLY REGRET TO LEARN THAT THE PREJUDICE OF SOME INDIVIDUALS EXTENDS EVEN BEYOND THIS LIFE," Lyndon Johnson's telegram said. "I HAVE NO AUTHORITY OVER CIVILIAN FUNERAL HOMES, NOR DOES THE FEDERAL GOVERNMENT," he explained. However, he said, that did not mean that he, or Beatrice Longoria, was without recourse—glorious recourse. "I HAVE TODAY MADE ARRANGE-MENTS TO HAVE FELIX LONGORIA REBURIED WITH FULL MILITARY HONORS IN ARLINGTON NATIONAL CEMETERY HERE AT WASHINGTON WHERE THE HON-ORED DEAD OF OUR NATION'S WARS REST." Or, he told Garcia, should the widow desire to have her husband's body buried nearer his home, "HE CAN BE REBURIED AT FORT SAM HOUSTON NATIONAL MILITARY CEMETERY AT SAN ANTONIO." Just tell him what was desired, Lyndon Johnson telegraphed. It would be done. "IF HIS WIDOW DESIRES TO HAVE HIM REBURIED IN EITHER CEMETERY, SHE SHOULD SEND ME A TELEGRAM." And Lyndon Johnson knew, because he knew the Mexican immigrants of South Texas, that the widow might be very poor. She should send her telegram collect, he said. And, he added, whichever cemetery she selects, she should not worry about the cost. "THERE WILL BE NO COST."

And there were still other sentences in Lyndon Johnson's telegram. "THIS INJUSTICE AND PREJUDICE IS DEPLORABLE," he said. "I AM HAPPY TO HAVE A PART IN SEEING THAT THIS TEXAS HERO IS LAID TO REST WITH THE HONOR AND DIGNITY HIS SERVICE DESERVES." After reading the telegram over one last time to make sure it accurately expressed his sentiments, he told Connally to send it out—at once.

Dr. Garcia had called an emergency rally of the G.I. Forum in a Corpus Christi elementary school for that evening, and when he walked out on the stage, before an audience of more than a thousand people, he was holding Johnson's telegram, and he read it to the audience, and as he did, men and women began to stand up and cheer, some of them with their fists in the air, and the whole audience cheered when Garcia announced that Beatrice Longoria had selected Arlington as her husband's resting place. She herself replied to Johnson by a telegram. It was addressed to "Senator Lyndon B. Johnson, House of the Senate, Washington, D.C." "HUMBLY GRATEFUL FOR YOUR KINDNESS IN MY HOUR OF HUMILIATION AND SUFFERING," the telegram said. "FOREVER GRATEFUL FOR YOUR KINDNESS," it said. And when, the next day, Walter Jen-kins drafted a reply—"IN VIEW OF YOUR DESIRE . . . HAVE COMPLETED NECES-SARY ARRANGEMENTS . . ."—Johnson was dissatisfied with the formality of its tone, which extended even to its closing sentence, a typical sentence from his form letter to constituents, which said that he was pleased to help. He sat there staring at Jenkins' draft for a long minute, and then crossed out that sentence and wrote in his own hand another sentence, which hinted at the depth to which his heart had been enlisted in the widow's cause. Instead of saying merely that he was pleased to help, the telegram now said that he was proud to help. "I AM PROUD TO BE OF ASSISTANCE," Lyndon Johnson wrote.

Johnson called in William S. White, and on January 13, the story was on the front page of the *New York Times,* under the headline, "GI, OF MEXICAN ORIGIN, DENIED RITES IN TEXAS, TO BE BURIED IN ARLINGTON," and with a quote from Johnson as perfect as the lines in his telegram; "I am sorry about the funeral home at Three Rivers," he had told White. "But there is, after all, a fine national funeral home, though of a rather different sort, out at Arlington." He telephoned Walter Winchell in New York. "The State of Texas, which looms so large on the map, certainly looks small tonight," Winchell told his national radio audience that evening. Newspapers across Latin America and the United States picked up the story—"U.S. TO BURY MEXICAN G.I., SPURNED BY TEXAS HOME," the headlines said; "G.I. DENIED REBURIAL IN TEXAS TO GET FULL ARLINGTON HONORS"—even newspapers in Texas, not in South Texas perhaps but in the rest of the state. "A ringing blow for Latin-American relations, downright Democracy and plain ordinary humanity was struck by Texas' junior Senator," the *Sherman Democrat* editorialized. "Felix Longoria will be buried at Arlington National Cemetery, that haven where America pays its highest respect for its outstanding battle heroes." "A WRONG IS RIGHTED" was the headline in the *Denison Press.* From New York City came a wire from a Veterans of Foreign Wars post saying that its members would consider it an honor and a privilege if the post's chaplain could officiate at Private Longoria's reburial. And if a note of pure grace were needed to this explosion of feeling, it was provided by a letter that Lyndon Johnson wrote to Beatrice Longoria on January 13, because he felt that, as he wrote her, "It was impossible for me to express to you in my telegram yesterday the deep sympathy I feel for you in this hour. I am honored to have some small share in making possible your husband's reburial in Arlington National Cemetery, where many of our most honored heroes lie buried. I know your heart would be warmed if you could read and hear the many, many kind and thoughtful expressions of unselfish sympathy which have come to my office today. . . . We want to be helpful to you in every way possible. . . . My only desire is to be helpful, whenever and however you call upon me. Your wishes will guide me in all that I do, and I will be glad to do all that I possibly can." Describing Johnson's feelings during the first days of the Longoria incident, John Connally was to say years later that "His reaction was outrage, it was outrage over injustice, it was instinctive, it was real—it was from his heart."

AND THEN, as John Connally was to recall, "We began to backtrack."

Although Connally and Jenkins felt that Johnson's initial reaction to Hector Garcia's telegram—the reaction that governed his responses completely for the first three days of the Longoria drama—was not calculation but outrage, the two aides were not blind to political advantages that would accrue from his decision to help Beatrice Longoria, since the returning Mexican-American veterans were becoming politically active in South Texas and Johnson's decision placed him firmly on their side. In that sense, Jenkins was to say, his decision "helped him immeasurably. I think they [the Mexican-Americans] felt like they had a friend maybe for the first time that would champion at least a small cause." In fact, Mexican-American leaders like Dr. Garcia felt that they might have for the first time a champion for causes that were not small. A United States senator had taken their part against the Anglos, had stood up for them against discrimination; might not that senator right other wrongs, help them pass the laws they needed so badly? A champion gave them someone to rally behind, and they rallied behind him. Members of the American G.I. Forum "were inspired, energized," Dr. Pycior recounts. "For the first time a Texas senator had treated them as full-fledged constituents, had responded to their call. Messages, money, and letters of support poured into the Forum headquarters. . . . From all over Texas Mexican-Americans were inundating their new senator with thanks and advice." In the Senator's office, recalls John Connally, "The phones were ringing off the wall."

The first significant sign of trouble came—on the morning of Wednesday, January 14, the fourth day of the drama—in one of the telephone calls, from United Press reporter Warren Duffee. He asked Horace Busby, who took the call, if Senator Johnson would care to comment on a statement just released by undertaker Kennedy and S. F. Ramsey, president of the First State Bank of Three Rivers and of the town's Chamber of Commerce, that denied that racial factors had been involved in the matter of Longoria's burial. Kennedy's statement said, "I did not at any time refuse to bury him or allow the use of the chapel," but that "I did discourage it"—not "because he was Latin American" but solely because "of friction that I heard existed between members of the [Longoria] family." He said, "I thought I was avoiding any trouble at the funeral home by asking Mrs. Longoria to use her house." He said he had written Mrs. Longoria to say that "If there was a misunderstanding on my part, my apologies are extended. If you still want use of our funeral chapel and want us to conduct services, we will be only too glad to be of service." Ramsey accused Johnson of having exploited the "misunderstanding" for political reasons. "It is our feeling that Johnson capitalized on this situation to further his own standing with the Latin-American population in Texas." Three Rivers, Ramsey said, was a town notably free of racial discrimination. "You'll find no town in South Texas that has enjoyed better relations between Latin-Americans and whites." (That was probably true.) "Our town is ashamed of the publicity we have received," he said. "We didn't deserve it."

Busby advised Johnson not to comment, saying "Any answer might cause the public to question just what your motives really were, and it would be less than dignified to enter a quarrel now," and for the moment that was the stance that Johnson adopted, but that afternoon, at the monthly meeting of the steering committee of the "Texas Exes," the Washington chapter of the University of Texas alumni association, in Dale Miller's suite at the Mayflower Hotel, a heated argument broke out over the Longoria incident, and during it Miller said, "It's too bad that one man down in Three Rivers could bring on an international incident. It's even worse, though, that some of the men in Congress would try to capitalize on it for their own political position." Connally put a typed report of the argument on Johnson's desk, with the diplomatically worded notation, "Senator, this is interesting." Johnson understood at once the seriousness of the report. Dale Miller, son of Roy, had succeeded not only to his father's sprawling Mayflower suite but also to his mantle as Texas' pre-eminent lobbyist, Washington representative of the Texas Gulf Sulphur Corporation, of an impressive array of oil and natural gas companies, and of business associations, including the Dallas Chamber of Commerce. Influential and popular, host for eighteen years of Sam Rayburn's annual birthday party, Miller was the very heart of the conservative Texas establishment. He had, moreover, consistently been among Johnson's staunchest supporters, persuading other conservatives to support him even when they were reluctant to do so, telling them that if they knew Lyndon as well as he did, they would be convinced of what he and his father had been convinced: that Johnson was "no wild-eyed liberal," that he in fact "gave the impression of being much, much more liberal than he actually was," and at least part of Miller's conviction was based on the belief that Lyndon was as "practical" on racial matters as he and his father, racists to the core. Dale Miller's reaction to Johnson's involvement in the Longoria affair was an indication of what the response of the Texas conservative establishment was likely to be.

The political factors in Lyndon Johnson's calculations began to change. As Posh Oltorf, who was shortly to become a major participant in the unfolding drama, puts it, Johnson now "realized" that "if he pursued" his original course in the Longoria affair, at the end "he would have gained a lot of new friends but would have lost a lot of old ones"—old friends whom he could ill afford to lose.

These old friends were the Anglo rulers of South Texas—of the impoverished, largely illiterate Mexican-American counties of the Rio Grande Valley that formed the border between Texas and Mexico, and of the counties that stretched north from the valley to San Antonio. While tens of thousands of Johnson's votes in both his 1941 and 1948 Senate campaigns had come, in margins as high as 100 to 1—some reported well after Election Day—from those counties, the explanation for those huge pluralities had little to do with the preferences of the Mexican-Americans. The overwhelming majority of their votes had been cast at the orders of the Anglo-Saxon border dictators called *patróns* or *jefes,* orders often enforced by armed *pistoleros* who herded

Mexican-Americans to the polls, told them how to vote, and then accompanied them into the voting cubbyholes to make sure the instructions were followed— if indeed the votes had been actually "cast" at all; in some of the Mexican-American areas, the local border dictators, in Texas political parlance, didn't "vote 'em," but rather just "counted 'em." In those areas, most of the voters didn't even go to the polls: the *jefes'* men would, as one observer put it, simply "go around to the Mexicans' homes. Get the numbers of their poll tax receipts. Tell them not to go to the polls. Just write in hundreds of numbers, and cast the hundred votes yourself," or, after the polls closed, would simply take the tally sheets and add to the recorded total whatever number was needed to give their favored candidate the margin he desired. "You get down on the border, and it didn't matter how people [the Mexican-Americans] felt," Ed Clark would explain. "The leaders did it all. They could vote 'em or count 'em, either one." It was not the Mexican-Americans of South Texas, then, but rather their Anglo *patróns* who had given Johnson the votes he needed to get to the Senate, and whose votes would again be needed in his re-election campaign. As for the "new friends" he might make—the returning Mexican-American veterans— their movement was still in its infancy, and confined to cities like Corpus Christi; there were no chapters of the G.I. Forum in 100–1 Duval or the other border counties. And since the returning veterans would not use the *patróns'* methods, they would never be able to deliver a bloc vote of such huge dimensions. It was the South Texas Anglo leaders whose support would still be crucial to Johnson. And subsequent developments made clear the extent to which his actions in the Longoria case had antagonized those leaders.

The next day—Thursday, January 15—the Three Rivers Chamber of Commerce intensified its attack, in two telegrams to Johnson. "WE DEPLORE YOUR ITCHY TRIGGER FINGER DECISION AND ACTION WITHOUT FIRST INVESTIGATING THE LONGORIA CASE," the first said. The second deplored "YOUR ACTION WITHOUT FIRST INVESTIGATING TRUE FACTS FROM RELIABLE SOURCES."

The "facts" to which the telegram referred were actually rumors, the rumors of "friction" within the Longoria family, and in their attempt to lend them credence, the Anglo leaders of Three Rivers revealed the depths to which they would sink. According to the rumors, sometime after Felix Longoria had been killed, Beatrice had dated another man, and Felix's family had been infuriated by this. Now Ramsey, together with Three Rivers Mayor J. K. Montgomery and City Secretary Bryan Boyd, came to the home of Felix's father, Guadalupe Longoria, a sixty-six-year-old man seriously ill with heart disease who did not speak English well, brought him down to Ramsey's bank (which they may have considered a persuasive venue because there was still an outstanding balance on a small loan the bank had made to Guadalupe), and began firing questions at him in English, some of which he had a hard time understanding. Then they put in front of him a typed statement which they asked him to sign. The statement said that "Felix's wife would not speak to me because I objected to the association she was having with another man," that she "did not want us [the rest of the family] to know when the body would arrive," and that he and the rest of the family did not want Felix buried in Arlington but rather in Three Rivers. "My family and I hope that our Three Rivers friends will help in getting his body brought here for burial." At the bottom of the statement was a blank line for Guadalupe Longoria's signature. A notary public was sitting outside Ramsey's office, waiting to witness it.

The line remained blank, however; Guadalupe Longoria refused, although the interview went on a long time, to sign; an article was to say that "his grief was not less than his daughter-in-law's, but neither was his honor, and he would have no part of this thing." That evening, the same three men came to Guadalupe's home, bringing with them the statement, which they again urged him to sign. He still wouldn't sign it. Guadalupe would later dictate—and sign, along with Felix's two brothers and three sisters—a slightly different statement: "I wish to state, contrary to reports published in some newspapers, my son's widow, Beatrice Longoria, and I have never had any personal differences. She, members of her family, and all members of my family including myself have always been on the best of terms. . . . To this day, my son's widow visits my home frequently and we still consider her, as we always will, as our own daughter." Beatrice and he had agreed together to accept "Senator Johnson's offer . . . to bury my son's body in Arlington," Longoria's statement said. And even if he had disagreed with her, Guadalupe Longoria said, he would have bowed to her wishes; "the widow . . . after all, has the final say in all these matters, and properly so."

"If any embarrassment has been caused by this case to anyone, I am sorry," Guadalupe Longoria added. "But after all I did not create a feeling of prejudice which seems to exist in many places in Texas. . . . I think that we would only be fooling ourselves to try to leave the impression that people of Mexican descent are treated the same as anyone else [in] Texas."

Guadalupe Longoria's refusal to sign their statement did not deter Three Rivers' leaders, however. They gave it to the newspapers as if he *had* signed it; "Lupe Longoria, Sr. still wants" his son buried in Three Rivers, according to Mayor J. K. Montgomery, the *Corpus Christi Caller-Times* reported. " 'If it were in my power, I would still have my son buried in Three Rivers,' Longoria told the Mayor"—the Mayor said. Undertaker Kennedy repeated the rumors for publication; in the January 20 issue of the *Three Rivers News,* he said: "There were reasons why I 'discouraged' the use of the funeral chapel. There is considerable evidence to the effect that there has been trouble between the wife of Felix Longoria and the rest of the family, including his parents. . . . I did not want trouble in the funeral chapel. . . ." His desire to avoid "family trouble," Kennedy repeated, was the sole reason he had "discouraged" Dr. Garcia, although, Kennedy said, "In the heat of the argument [I] undoubtedly made other statements which could possibly be misconstrued." (Some of them possibly could. Garcia had taken the precaution of having his secretary, Gladys Blucher, listen on an extension phone, and take shorthand notes, when he telephoned Kennedy, and the notes, later attested to in an affidavit, showed that Kennedy had indeed said "Latin people get drunk and lay around all the time. The last time we let them use the chapel, they all got drunk and we just can't control them.")

The Three Rivers Chamber of Commerce continued to deplore "the stigma of unfavorable publicity" which it said Johnson had caused, and Live Oaks County State Representative J. F. Gray, a key figure in the loose alliance of South Texas Anglo leaders, accused him of "pulling a grandstand play to try and embarrass somebody." ("Gray was bitter as hell—mean bitter," John Connally was to recall.) Anglo anger spread beyond Live Oaks' borders. "Dear Lyndon," wrote William F. Chesnut, a longtime Johnson loyalist from the town of Kenedy, in adjoining Karnes County, "I don't mean to be telling you what you should or should not do, but I would like to let you know what people are saying about you. . . . In the first place, there was a big misunderstanding of the whole thing. The funeral parlor at Three Rivers is rather small and the undertaker thought it would be better to hold the funeral service in the local Catholic Church. He had no sooner suggested this when right away, some hot-headed Latin-American jumped to his feet and hollered 'PREDJUDICE' [sic]. Now that is the whole truth of the matter . . . I have heard several comments on 'Why doesn't Johnson keep his nose out of this affair' . . . and still others which run mostly in the vein of 'I voted for him once but I'll be damned if I'll do it again.' "

The American Legion's Bexar County Central Council, which represented twenty Legion posts in and around San Antonio, passed a resolution, "to be sent to the Honorable Lyndon Johnson, Honorable Walter Winchell and Dr. Garcia," condemning "careless and immature actions by people in high and honorable places," which has caused "harmful humiliation and embarrassment . . . to the Kennedy family, Rice Funeral Home, the good people of the City of Three Rivers and the State of Texas by bringing nationwide publicity." Its own investigation, the Council said, had "not found the least trace of Un-American activities or racial discrimination practiced in this matter." The state's most influential newspaper, the right-wing *Dallas Morning News*, weighed in with the disclosure that "Many who sent abuse [to Three Rivers] are offering apologies" as more facts about the case became apparent. "There is good comradeship [in Three Rivers]. . . . The two groups of citizens mingle freely and do business with one another with no apparent thought of difference in race origin." The story, John Connally says, "became bigger than any of us had anticipated . . . became a furor." After making rounds of telephone calls, both he and Ed Clark, in Austin, reported to Johnson that anger against him was intensifying among South Texas leaders. Posh Oltorf, taking soundings in the Legislature, recalls that "they [Johnson and Connally] were concerned with keeping this from becoming a big issue where all the Anglos would turn against Johnson and the Mexican-Americans." But the calls coming in to 231 showed that that was exactly what was happening. "There were forces at work beyond our control," Connally says. "By this time, we wanted to engage in damage control as far as South Texas was concerned." Which is why, he says, "We began to backtrack."

THE BACKTRACKING BEGAN on the point which had most infuriated Three Rivers and many Texans: the fact that the case had received national attention because of the decision to bury Longoria at Arlington instead of in his home-town, or at least in his home state. This decision had been regarded as a par-ticular "stigma" by the town, which blamed Johnson for it, pointing out, accurately, that before he had made the suggestion no one else had thought of it. "Previous to your action," the *Three Rivers News* said in an "Open Letter to Senator Johnson," not "one word had been said in Three Rivers as to where this American soldier would be buried, other than the Longoria family lot in the Three Rivers Cemetery . . . in his own native town. . . . Therefore, Senator, you can very easily understand why the citizens of Three Rivers were so stunned when over the radio and in the papers came reports that you had made arrange-ments to have Felix buried in Arlington Cemetery." R. E. Smith, chairman of the Texas Good Neighbor Commission, the state agency responsible for improving relations with Mexico, implored Dr. Garcia to intercede with Bea-trice Longoria and persuade her to change her mind and allow her husband's body to be "brought back to Texas for burial at Three Rivers, or at least in Texas." If she did so, Smith assured her, "the Governor will do everything pos-sible to show her that he approves of this action." He urged her to "bear in mind that the reputation of Texas will be at stake in history's recording of this very delicate matter. . . . Bring the Hero's body back to Texas where it should be, and would have been had it not been for whatever action that caused all of this trou-ble. . . . Bear the thought in mind that Texas and all Texans and the children of Texans now living will feel the effect of the criticism, and we all know that none of them had anything to do with it."

Once, during the first few days after he had received Dr. Garcia's telegram, Lyndon Johnson had wanted his role in the decision to bury Felix Longoria at Arlington to be as prominent as possible. He had told Garcia he could read at the G.I. Forum meeting his telegram that "I HAVE TODAY MADE ARRANGEMENTS" for that burial; he had focused attention on Arlington by his remark that "There is, after all, a fine national funeral home, though of a rather different sort, out at Arlington." He had telephoned Bill White and Walter Winchell. Once, he had been "honored to have some small share in making possible your husband's reburial in Arlington." In the form letters with which he replied to letters praising him for his role, he had been "Honored to have this share in securing Felix Longoria the last rites befitting a hero"; "proud" that "I was able to make arrangements." He had done everything possible to empha-size his role in Longoria's burial there.

Now that tone changed. On January 16, the day after Three Rivers accused him of bringing the "stigma of this publicity" on the town, he tried to disclaim responsibility for the publicity. Telephoning Dr. Garcia, he asked the physician to remind reporters that it was he, not Johnson, who had released the telegrams. (Garcia, who had considerable political savvy—he would become a very effec-tive leader for Mexican-Americans in Texas—understood and agreed, cooper-ating with Johnson's wishes by not mentioning that Johnson had given him permission to release them. The *Corpus Christi Caller-Times* reported that "According to Garcia, Johnson asked publication of the fact that he did not release the telegram to the press himself. The release was made by Garcia.") While Johnson's staff continued to send out the "honored" and "proud" replies to congratulatory letters, a series of new replies was drafted, to be used in response to angry letters from Texas, and successive drafts revealed a growing desire to distance himself as much as possible from the national publicity and the Arlington burial decision—not that much distancing was possible, given the centrality of his role in the whole affair. In a letter of January 26, addressed to Glen Rabe of Three Rivers but intended as a general form letter for Texas constituents, Johnson tried to claim that he had played only a "small part . . . in the Longoria case."

"I did not release the story here, the entire publicity originated in Texas," he wrote—a statement that was, at best, disingenuous, given his initiation of the contacts with White and Winchell which had generated the national public-ity. "I had no control over it," he added. And, he said, "I had no desire to have any connection with the affair except to see that an American soldier was given a decent burial under honorable conditions"—which, he said, had not neces-sarily meant Arlington. "I sent a telegram advising the body could be buried" in either Arlington or Fort Sam Houston. "I made no recommendation of where the body should be buried." By January 28, in a telegram to Three Rivers Mayor Montgomery, Johnson was suggesting that, in fact, Arlington had been only one of *many* possibilities he had raised. "MY ONLY CONNECTION WITH LONGORIA MATTER HAS BEEN TO INFORM CONSTITUENTS THAT THEY HAD PRIVILEGE OF REBURIAL OF SOLDIER'S BODY IN <u>ANY</u> [emphasis added] MILI-TARY CEMETERY, INCLUDING FORT SAM HOUSTON AND ARLINGTON," John-son's telegram said. "I HAVE NOT AND DO NOT INTEND TO INFORM ANY PARTIES IN CONNECTION WITH THIS MATTER, AND MY PARTICIPATION WAS LIMITED TO DOING MY DUTY AS I SAW IT TO THIS CONSTITUENT."

LYNDON JOHNSON'S DESIRE TO AVOID, as far as possible, any further public-ity in connection with the Longoria affair was demonstrated by his actions when the Longorias arrived in Washington.

It might have been expected that when the family—Felix Longoria's widow, his eight-year-old daughter, and his mother, two brothers and a sister (his father, whose heart condition had worsened, in the opinion of his family because of the pressure from the Three Rivers leaders, was too ill to make the trip)—arrived for the funeral on February 15, the day before it was held, the senator who had, with so much fanfare, planned that funeral, would have invited the Longorias to visit his office, would have arranged for them to have their picture taken with him. No such invitation was extended, or arrangement made. Instead, John Connally, Horace Busby, and Warren Woodward met the Longorias at the airport, drove them around Washington on a sightseeing trip (which did not include the Senate Office Building), and dropped them at their hotel, where they stayed until the funeral.

At the funeral, Johnson's actions were striking—coming from a politician known among journalists for the pithy and dramatic statements he generally had ready for quotation in their articles, and for the way he invariably thrust himself into the center of photographs. Asked years later about the funeral, John Connally would say, "I don't recall if he [Johnson] went to the funeral. My guess is he didn't go." Connally's recollection was inaccurate. Johnson *was* present when Felix Longoria's body was laid to rest, along with the bodies of eighteen other servicemen killed in action, at Arlington on Wednesday, February 16. But it is easy to understand Connally's mistake.

A number of dignitaries attended the service, because of the attention that had, thanks to Johnson, been focused on it. President Truman sent his military aide, Major General Harry H. Vaughan, who arrived early and had a statement ready when reporters approached him. He was there, he said, "because of the stupidity of that undertaker." The First Secretary of the Mexican Embassy arrived carrying a large wreath, and there were representatives of the State Department.

Lyndon Johnson did not have a statement for reporters—did not, in fact, so far as can be learned, speak to any. There would be no quote from him in any of the newspaper articles that appeared on the funeral the following day. He did not arrive early, and after the ceremony he quickly shook hands with the family and left.

RETURNING TO HIS OFFICE FROM ARLINGTON, Johnson immediately wrote Dr. Garcia to urge him not to keep the matter alive. After commenting on the "impressive ceremony" and complimenting the Longoria family—who, he said, "seem to be exceptionally fine people"—and saying, "If there is any way in which I may be of further service to them, it will be a pleasure to do whatever I can," he added the following: "As I told you, I have not sought and do not seek any personal attention for my small role in this. I hope there will no further reason for this to linger in the newspapers or instigate unnecessary contention."

This hope was to prove fruitless. By a 104–20 vote, the conservative Texas House of Representatives, at the urging of the furious Gray and some of his fellow South Texas legislators, passed a resolution establishing a five-member committee to investigate "the truth or untruth" of the allegations of racial discrimination by Kennedy's funeral home.

Further "damage control" was therefore undertaken. Gray and his allies expected House Speaker Durwood Manford, a staunch conservative, to name only conservatives to the committee, which would then, they expected, exonerate Kennedy, finding that his refusal had been based only on the Longorias' "family troubles," and thereby clear Three Rivers' good name. And this fiction might well have been perpetrated—had not Manford been firmly under the thumb of Herman Brown and Ed Clark. When Manford announced the names of the committee members, only four were conservatives. The fifth, to the conservatives' shock, was the canny young liberal Frank C. Oltorf (still a legislator and not yet Brown & Root's Washington lobbyist). "Without Clark, there wouldn't have been a single liberal member on it," Posh Oltorf was to say.

Oltorf understood his assignment: to keep Johnson's name as inconspicuous as possible throughout the committee hearings. Each evening during the hearings, which were held that March in Three Rivers, he would telephone Johnson's office in Washington to report on the day's developments to either Johnson or Connally, and when it was Johnson who picked up the phone, "He [Johnson] would ask, 'Did they bring up anything about me?' " Oltorf understood Johnson's concern, and knew there was reason for it. "They [the South Texas Anglo leaders] would have liked to punish Johnson. They would have [liked to show] that he had meddled when he had no business to meddle. They [Johnson and Connally] were afraid of a complete whitewash [of the funeral home]—that the committee would find that there had been no discrimination, and it [the funeral] could all have been arranged quietly if Johnson hadn't interfered." But, the young legislator realized, the two men in Washington were more afraid of something else: that Johnson would be prominently "labelled an ally of the Mexican-Americans and all the [South Texas] leaders would then turn against him." Johnson could have been vindicated on the "meddling" point by the truth—proof that Kennedy's motives had been racial. But, Oltorf realized, proving that explosive point—with the resultant big headlines—would not accomplish Johnson's larger purpose. The Senator was less concerned that his role be vindicated than that it be minimized. "The thing they [Johnson and Connally] wanted was his name kept out," he says, in a recollection confirmed by Clark.

Oltorf's assignment was carried out successfully. In some ways, the hearings were blatantly stacked; the committee's four-member majority allowed Mayor Montgomery to testify that no discrimination against Latin-Americans existed in any form in Three Rivers, and did not allow testimony that would have disproved the Mayor's contention. (Although proof would have been quite convenient to hand. While the hearings were going on in the courthouse square of Three Rivers, a Mexican-American veteran attempted to get a haircut in a barbershop a few doors away; "We don't serve Mexicans here," the barber told him.) Thanks largely to Oltorf, however, testimony about the Longorias' alleged "family troubles" was, mercifully, kept to a minimum—as was the inclusion of Johnson's name. To every demand by a committee member that the "full story" of the Longoria incident be told, Oltorf would blandly reply that the committee had been authorized to look into only the initial "refusal or discouragement" of the use of Kennedy's funeral home. And "every time his [Johnson's] name was brought up, I would change the subject," Oltorf recalls. "I'd say, 'Well, that's not the issue.' " His job proved easier than he had expected, thanks to the power of the "Secret Boss of Texas." "There were times when you could see one of the other [committee] members was ready to start a fight [with me]," Oltorf says. "But then all of a sudden, they'd think better of it. He [Johnson] had Ed Clark behind him, and so I had Clark behind me, and believe me, in the Legislature no one ever wanted to cross Ed Clark—ever."

Assisting Oltorf in his assignment was attorney Gus Garcia, a law school friend of Connally's, whom Connally had enlisted to advise the Longorias during the hearings. Gus Garcia was an eloquent and flamboyant courtroom attorney, but eloquence was not what was required here, and Garcia understood that. At the close of the hearings, he would write Johnson, "Your name was bandied about a bit, but we managed to leave the correct interpretation in the record—namely, that you did nothing except follow Mrs. Longoria's instructions." He had had no choice, the attorney wrote Johnson, but "to introduce a letter from you to her, in which you stated that you would follow her instructions. You also expressed your sympathy in that letter, but there is nothing in it which would harm you politically." As for the telegrams that Johnson had sent in those first moments of the Longoria affair, the telegrams that said "I DEEPLY REGRET TO LEARN THAT THE PREJUDICE OF SOME INDIVIDUALS EXTENDS EVEN BEYOND THIS LIFE," the telegrams that said "I AM HAPPY TO HAVE A PART IN SEEING THAT THIS TEXAS HERO IS LAID TO REST WITH THE HONOR AND DIGNITY HIS SERVICE DESERVES," the telegrams that said "I AM PROUD TO BE OF ASSISTANCE"—Gus Garcia was able to assure Johnson now that he and Oltorf had been able to keep those wonderful telegrams from being introduced in the hearings (because, he explained in his letter, "Frank and I decided" that they "might be distorted by your political enemies"). When Dorothy Nichols, one of his secretaries, brought Gus Garcia's letter to Johnson's attention, he had her give it to Connally to draft a reply, with a note: "John—Senator says you'll have to answer this; be careful about it." And John was. The letter Gus Garcia received over Lyndon Johnson's signature was carefully noncommittal except for one sentence: "I trust that the incident will shortly be a closed chapter."

The committee's majority drafted a report that was the expected white-wash; "There was no discrimination on the part of the undertaker at Three Rivers," the draft concluded. A liberal state senator, Rogers Kelley, was to call the document "a slap in the face of more than one million Latin-American citizens of the State of Texas." The report was signed, however, by only four of the five committee members. Declaring that "I could not concur in their majority report without violating both my sense of justice and my intellectual honesty," Oltorf refused to sign it, and issued his own minority report which was so persuasive that one of the four later withdrew his signature, and, as one analysis put it, "the two dissensions so undercut the credibility of the majority report that the committee found itself on the defensive," and the report was quietly tabled without any action by the full legislature.

THE LONGORIA AFFAIR was a turning point—"a catalyst," the *Texas Monthly* was to say in 1986, "for the modern civil rights movement of the Mexican-Americans in Texas." Before that affair, Hector Garcia was to recall, the G.I. Forum "had nothing to do with civil rights. It was strictly a veterans affairs organization." By demonstrating so vividly how "prejudice and hatreds" poisoned "all aspects of our lives in the state of Texas," the affair broadened the Forum's focus to include all aspects of civil rights, and moved the organization into the political arena in which those rights could be secured. New chapters sprang into being; membership burgeoned. Almost two decades would have to pass before this new Mexican-American movement became as significant a force in Texas political calculations as the docile old Mexican-American bloc vote, but the birth of that new force dates from the Longoria affair. The furor over the burial of the Army private from Three Rivers galvanized the movement, and filled it with energy and purpose.

And it did so because of Lyndon Johnson—because of his compassion and his genius for making that compassion politically meaningful. Without him, the Longoria incident might simply have faded away—have become only one more quickly forgotten episode in the long history of racial discrimination in Texas. In an instant, hearing of the injustice to Felix Longoria, Lyndon Johnson's heart had been enlisted in the Longoria cause, and in that same instant he had found the perfect gesture, a grand gesture, to right the wrong that had been done, to right it gloriously—"By God, we'll bury him at Arlington!"—and the perfect words, the words of those stirring telegrams, that brought an audience to its feet and made it feel that it had a champion at last. It was his gesture and words that had taken a local incident, probably only one of a score of similar incidents that had gone unremarked outside the boundaries of the towns involved, and had made it, as one writer was to put it, "into one of those signal events that stir consciences" across an entire state.

The Longoria affair was not a turning point for Lyndon Johnson, however.

For a moment, it had seemed that it would be—a magnificent turning point. Prior to the morning on which Dr. Garcia's telegram arrived at the Senate Office Building, Johnson's record on civil rights had been, during his almost twelve years on Capitol Hill, almost entirely one of opposition. In the first hours after the telegram, he had galvanized the cause, seized its flag and charged to its fore. But as opposition mounted, the flag had been quickly dropped. On that night in the Corpus Christi elementary school, it had seemed that the Mexican-Americans of South Texas had found a champion, an Anglo leader who would lend his name to their cause. But Lyndon Johnson's concern had been to keep his name from being linked to their cause. Summing up the Longoria affair for the author of this book in 1986, John Connally would explain Johnson's "backtracking" by saying it was consistent with his entire life: "He never wanted to be a dead hero."

The damage control was effective. It didn't work with Representative Gray of Three Rivers, whose bitterness over the incident never abated. "He hated Johnson forever because of it," John Connally was to say. But most of the Anglo border county leaders remained Johnson's allies.

Nor did Johnson's backtracking in the Longoria battle hurt him with the rank and file of South Texas' Mexican-Americans. The dexterity with which he had handled his retreat from the field—simply removing his name, and his presence, from the fight without any dramatic public statement—meant that most of the Mexican-Americans who had cheered his earlier, dramatic championing of the Longorias' cause were unaware that he had stopped doing so. Realization that the Senator could have used the legislative hearings as a platform for their cause, or that a statement could have been issued from Washington, required a political awareness and experience still in short supply in 1949 within this newly militant group. Johnson's silence was as nothing beside the gesture he had made in having their compatriot buried in Arlington. The Longoria episode was to have a permanent and prominent place in the Mexican-American consciousness; Felix Longoria would become in a way a martyr, and the Senator who had arranged for the hero to be buried in a hero's grave became a hero himself. Teachers in South Texas' Mexican schools recounted the episode to their students. Accompanying Johnson on a 1953 swing through South Texas to shore up support for his 1954 re-election campaign, George Reedy would never forget the chant with which Mexican-Americans greeted his boss: "Olé Johnson, Olé Johnson! Tres Rios, Tres Rios, Tres Rios!"

As for the Mexican-American leader, Lyndon Johnson quickly began to bind Hector Garcia to him. Shortly after the legislature's investigation had been completed, he agreed to address Garcia's G.I. Forum, and the doctor was grateful: "He addressed our group, and of course it was a great occasion because at that time it was rare to have any politician or certainly a U.S. Senator addressing [a] Mexican group." When there was an opening on the U.S. Border Patrol or for some other minor federal job, Johnson began asking Garcia to recommend someone. And he did small favors for Garcia, the little favors that a federal officeholder could do for his constituents—but that no officeholder had been doing for South Texas' Mexican-Americans. The veterans who made up the backbone of the Mexican-American movement were entitled to veterans' benefits; Johnson saw that they got them. And once a mother of a Corpus Christi boy in the Marine Corps came to the doctor's office, saying that her son was in a guardhouse at Camp Pendleton in California, and that no one at the base would give her any information about him. "All I want is to talk to my son and find out what is happening to him," she said. "Perhaps he is dead. I am going to pieces, doctor." Garcia could see, he recalls, "that she *was* going to pieces." He called the base and got a major, who refused to give him any information, even after Garcia said, "You are doing a very cruel thing to this woman. A mother needs talking to her son."

"I got on the telephone, and I called Senator Johnson," Garcia recalls, "and five minutes after he hung up this major was calling apologetically." Garcia was a very adroit politician—his G.I. Forum was to become the largest Mexican-American organization in the country, with chapters in twenty-eight states—and he knew how much the fact that he could produce such assistance helped him retain a position of leadership with his people. "These are the favors I do for people, through people like Johnson," he would say. "I'm the helpful go-between." Explaining Garcia's adherence to Johnson, Dr. Pycior says: "He [Johnson] answers their letters. He treats them with dignity. It's pathetic that such small things can [mean] so much. But you've been beaten down for so long—to have a senator treat you like a human being, that means a lot."

Cementing the alliance between the two men further was the promise it might represent for the future of Hector Garcia's people. The physician was totally bound up with their cause, and Johnson convinced him that he, too, wanted to advance that cause, but that he would be able to do so only if he continued to hold power, and therefore he couldn't take steps that would hurt him politically. As Pycior wrote, "Garcia thought that Johnson could not afford to risk his political advancement by supporting controversial issues." For that reason, Garcia was to say, he understood why Johnson had had to back away from the Longoria affair. "Johnson . . . certainly may have been subjected to some of the pressures of state politics. . . . Yet his heart was all right."

Binding other Mexican-American leaders to Johnson was the same combination of patronage and promises. When Reynaldo Garza of Brownsville, whose ambition was to be the first Latin-American federal judge, was wavering over whether to support Johnson or Governor Shivers in intra-party maneuvering, Johnson put it to him flat: "Reynaldo, Allan Shivers is going to be out as Governor and I'll still be up in Washington, and I know I can do more for you than he can." ("After I got appointed federal judge some years later, I ran into Allan Shivers," Garza recalls. "He told me, 'Well, he was right, wasn't he? He could do something for you.' ") In a particularly dramatic example of what

Johnson could do for a leader, he arranged an attractive job with Brown & Root for Manuel Bravo, when Zapata County's feared *jefe* became tired of politics. And he convinced these leaders—convinced them absolutely—that he wanted to help Mexican-Americans, and was only waiting for the right time to do so. He kept reminding them—movingly—of his days in Cotulla. "Johnson had a real empathetic relationship with the Mexicans in Texas," George Reedy was to say.

A LOT OF BINDING was necessary. Although in later years—after the great civil rights achievements of Lyndon Johnson's presidency—Garcia would say that Johnson had consistently stood with the Mexican-Americans over the years, the records of the time show this to have been very far from the case. For if, when controversy erupted in the Longoria affair, their champion had vanished from the field, when he reappeared, it was not to be on their side.

Each harvest season, hundreds of thousands of Mexican farm workers crossed the Rio Grande into Texas to work on the huge South Texas farms owned by the powerful Anglo "growers." Some were imported legally under the "bracero" program, through which wages and hours were established by contracts (their terms unbelievably unjust to the migrants; wage scales were often set at about twenty cents per hour) approved by the federal government. Others simply swam or waded across illegally, and hence were called "wetbacks." Legal immigrants or illegal, however, these Mexicans were pitiful figures, working under the scorching South Texas sun for endless hours each day at "stoop labor," bent over the notorious "short hoe," crammed at night into hovels without electricity or running water. They had come because they had no choice: there was no work for them in Mexico; "exiled from [their] homeland by the threat of starvation, unselfishly hoping to mitigate the woes of [their] . . . relatives by sending them a few dollars each week or month." Once on those immense ranches—feudal domains, most of them—the migrant worker was, as one study put it, "entirely at the mercy of his . . . employers. Once within the walls or fences of . . . a ranch or farm, he has no recourse to appeal, no bargaining power, no protection of any kind. . . . If he expresses dissatisfaction with the treatment he receives, his employer can merely expel him, whereupon he will be caught by the officers and taken back to face worse privation in Mexico." Some of the worst of the growers, in fact, expelled these migrants anyway; they would wait until the harvest was completed, and then call the sheriffs or Border Patrol, report their workers as illegal aliens; they would be arrested and deported, without even the few dollars they had earned.

This exploitation of their countrymen made the bracero issue an overriding concern to the Mexican-Americans of South Texas on humanitarian grounds; they called the bracero program "rent a slave." And it was overriding on economic grounds as well: in the opinion of most Mexican-American leaders, it was the willingness of these Mexicans to work the same jobs they were working, and accept such low wages, that kept their own wages low. The unrestricted flow of migrant workers was held to be the principal reason why the rise of Mexican-Americans to the middle class had been so much slower than that of the Irish or other immigrant groups. If there was a single issue most important to Mexican-Americans in the 1950s, it was this issue. And on this issue, throughout the 1950s, Lyndon Johnson supported not them but their opponents. They wanted the government to require working conditions and wages in bracero contracts equal to those prevailing in the United States and to cut off the flow of illegal immigrants, both by increasing appropriations to the United States Immigration Service and by increasing criminal penalties for growers who knowingly hired illegal aliens. "Something must be done and I believe that charging a heavy fine to those persons who insist on hiring wetbacks . . . will do it," one Mexican-American leader wrote Johnson. But the Anglo *patróns* wanted a surplus labor supply, and it was these *patróns* who controlled the votes Lyndon Johnson had needed, and might need again. One of his first actions after becoming Democratic whip in 1951, therefore, was to muster Democratic support, crucial for its passage, for a bill renewing the bracero program with its harsh contracts. When it passed, on May 28, he wrote to a committee of thirty-three large growers: "Delighted to inform you that the Senate and House conferees have agreed . . . [o]n the Mexican labor bill . . ." J. C. Looney, one of the attorneys who represented the committee—and who had helped "coordinate" Johnson's 1941 and 1948 Senate campaigns in the valley—wrote Johnson to assure him that "the people in the valley who are handling the situation and who are certainly influential . . . know what you are doing." They would express their gratitude, he told Johnson, but "without . . . publicity that could backfire."

In 1951, and again in 1952, Johnson opposed bills that would have increased criminal penalties for hiring illegal aliens. With the wetback problem growing worse in 1953, Mexican-American leaders pleaded with Johnson to support a bill earmarking four million dollars for an intensified campaign by the Immigration Service against illegal importation of wetbacks. If the bill was defeated, they predicted, South Texas would be "flooded" with migrant workers, whose willingness to work endless hours for low wages would cause "suffering to native workers." Johnson led the opposition to the bill, which was defeated. This was too much even for the G.I. Forum, which passed a resolution noting that "whereas, Senator Johnson owes in large measure his position in the U.S. Senate to the vote of thousands of citizens of Mexican descent in South Texas . . . [h]is vote is in utter disregard of the friendship in which he has been held by [those] citizens." Claiming that his vote had been due only to the lateness, and excessiveness, of the Immigration Service's budget request, Johnson replied that "I am sorry that the friendship that I have shown throughout the years . . . should be . . . cast aside" because of a single vote. "There is no group for which I have done more and to whom I feel more friendly than the Latin

Americans," he added. "I have tried to show my friendship in a number of practical ways and I shall not be deterred from continuing to do so by resolutions which seem to me at least to be unfair."

The resolution did not have much impact on his actions. In 1953, the Eisenhower Administration attempted to stop the illegal importation of wetbacks, but Johnson opposed the program. On several other issues of major concern to the Mexican-Americans Johnson was also on the growers' side. During his first seven years in the Senate—1949 through 1955—he was willing to help the Mexican-Americans on any issue on which their interests did not conflict with the interests of the Anglos. When the two groups were in conflict, he almost invariably came down on the side of the whites. He kept the support of Hector Garcia and other leaders in part because he had convinced them that "his heart was right," in part because of the patronage and prestige he gave them—and in part because of another factor, which both John Connally and Ed Clark were to sum up in the same question: "Where else were they going to go?" The Republican Party had no power in Texas. Within the state's all-powerful Democratic Party the alternative was the party's Shivers wing, so right-wing and unapologetically racist that any enemy of that wing must be their friend. After Tom Connally, no friend to Mexican-Americans, left the state's other Senate seat, he was succeeded by Price Daniel, also no friend to Mexican-Americans. As Stanford Dyer wrote, "Johnson was aware that his civil rights record was the subject of much concern among Texas minorities. Yet he also knew that he had everything to lose and nothing to gain politically by supporting civil rights legislation. Texas minorities would continue to support him until some Texas politician promised them more, and this was not likely to happen in the near future." The Mexican-Americans of South Texas never stopped supporting Lyndon Johnson. They couldn't—as he was well aware: There was nowhere else for them to put their support. Although Forum leaders were "disappointed" with Johnson on some issues, Forum official Ed Idar Jr. was to tell Pycior that "we were not ready to make an enemy of the man." In 1954, they had no difficulty recognizing his opponent Dudley Dougherty's ineptitude, and had no wish to be allied in any way with that hapless political *naïf*. In that election Johnson received the overwhelming majority of Mexican-American votes in South Texas, whether those votes were merely "counted" by *patróns* or freely cast. After his victory, Johnson wrote Dr. Garcia, whom he called his "special friend": "Believe me, I am well aware of all you did to help make our great victory possible. I will never forget it. Please let me know when I can be of service—and I mean that from the bottom of my heart." After the lesson he had learned in the Longoria affair, however, Lyndon Johnson had not again—in 1949 or the next six years—taken the field on behalf of Mexican-Americans in any battle in which there was danger of antagonizing the South Texas Anglos. Having learned the cost of siding with the oppressed, he took his stance, over and over, on the other side.

He was on that side in Washington, too. It was less than a month after the legislative hearings on the Longoria affair, in fact, that Lyndon Johnson took the field not with the friends of social justice but with its foes by delivering, as part of the southern battle against President Truman's civil rights legislation, his "We of the South" maiden speech—the speech that Richard Russell called "one of the ablest I have ever heard" and that moved the Houston NAACP to telegraph Johnson, "The Negroes who sent you to Congress are ashamed to know that you have stood against them on the floor today." It was during that same 1949 battle that Johnson stood as a southern "sentry" against northern maneuvers for civil rights, and all during that year, the year of the Longoria affair, he repeatedly convinced Russell that he would be a loyal soldier in Russell's cause, even voting for the Eastland Bill that would, had it passed, have made segregation mandatory in public accommodations in the District of Columbia.

He had stayed on that side in the years since 1949, voting against FEPC and anti–poll tax legislation as well as against legislation to outlaw discrimination in unions, voting for legislation that would have allowed draftees to serve in segregated Army units—voting on the side of the South not only in 1949 but in 1950 and 1951 and '52 and '53 and '54 and '55. And in 1955, having won the majority leadership with southern support, he used the Leader's power to crush the hopes of Senate liberals for a change in Rule 22 and to turn back liberal attempts to ban segregation in armed forces reserve units. His empathy and tenderness for people oppressed simply because their skins were dark, strong though it was in his makeup, was not as strong as his need for power. The compassion, genuine though it was, had always—always, without exception—proven to be expendable. That had been true throughout his life before he got to the Senate—and it was true after he got to the Senate. The Longoria affair had been proof of the compassion—and of its expendability. The next seven years had been further proof. By the end of 1955, Lyndon Johnson had held positions of public authority—State NYA Director, Congressman, Senator—for twenty years, and for twenty years the record had been consistent. Whenever compassion and ambition had been in conflict, the former had vanished from the landscape of Lyndon Johnson's career. For it to become a permanent element of that landscape, it would have to be compatible with the ambition: compassion and ambition would both have to be pointing in the same direction. When the year 1955 came to an end, that had not yet occurred, and once again ambition had won.

Now, in 1956, it won again.

33

Footsteps

LYNDON JOHNSON HAD DETERMINED, down on his ranch during his heart attack summer of 1955, that the surest path to the presidency was to win the Democratic nomination for that job in 1956: then, even if Eisenhower decided to run again and that nomination therefore became worthless, he would, as the party's last standard-bearer, be the front-runner to win its nod in 1960, when Eisenhower would not be running. Almost ridiculously long as were the odds against his winning the nomination—favored (in the most favorable poll) by a meagre 3 percent of the country's rank-and-file Democrats, and by exactly twenty-nine out of 1,944 county chairmen outside the South—he had therefore spent the autumn of 1955 grabbing for the prize, flying across the country to rustle up financial support, forcing Adlai Stevenson into the primaries, accepting both the chairmanship and the favorite-son nomination of the Texas delegation, trying to blunt at least somewhat the knife edge of liberal antipathy toward him by passing the Social Security Bill.

Despite his overtures to liberals, however, the base of his support—the *sine qua non* of his candidacy—was the South: his strategy was to arrive at the Democratic Convention in August with most of that region's 324 votes; to add to that base some western support; to keep Stevenson from winning on an early ballot; and then, with the convention deadlocked, to become its compromise choice. And for the South, of course, one issue loomed above all others.

THAT ISSUE WAS LIKE A WOUND IN 1956, a wound that, as the year went by, gaped wider and wider, red and raw, across the bland face of peaceful, prosperous 1950s America.

Nineteen fifty-six had hardly begun when the scars of the Emmett Till case were abruptly ripped open anew—when the two murderers decided to tell the world their story.

They did so because, having been acquitted of Till's murder, they could not be tried again for the same crime—and because of greed. A journalist, William Bradford Huie, offered them four thousand dollars for their story, and Roy Bryant and Big Milam were broke and needed money, and in the Mississippi Delta four thousand dollars was a lot of money. And, they did so for applause. They were sure that if they told the world the whole story, explained the good reason they had had for executing the visitor from Chicago, people—not "nigger lovers" from the North, perhaps, but plenty of people—would understand, and approve. As Huie said in his article, published in the January 24, 1956, edition of the national magazine *Look,* Bryant and Milam "don't feel they have anything to hide"; rather, they felt they had something to boast about.

Their original intention, Milam explained to Huie, was to "just whip" the boy "and scare some sense into him"—that *had* to be done, of course; "when a nigger even gets close to mentioning sex with a white woman," stern measures had to be taken. But young Till had not been scared, Milam said. "We never were able to scare him. They had just filled him so full of that poison he was hopeless." Even after they drove him to the toolhouse, and beat him on the head with their pistols, he refused to be scared, Milam said. So, of course, he and his half brother Roy had no choice. "What else could we do? He was hopeless. I'm no bully. I never hurt a nigger in my life. . . . But I just decided it was time a few people got put on notice. As long as I live and can do anything about it, niggers are gonna stay in their place. Niggers ain't gonna vote where I live. If they did they'd control the government. They ain't gonna go to school with my kids. . . . Me and my folks fought for this country, and we've got some rights." That was the reason, he said, that he had told Till, "I'm going to make an example of you." That was the reason he and Bryant took the youth to the cotton gin, forced him to load the exhaust fan onto the truck, and then drove him to the bank of the Tallahatchie. That was the reason he shot him in the head.

The lawyers who had been so proud to defend Bryant and Milam were also quoted in Huie's article. They had advised their clients to cooperate with the journalist because they, too, felt that people would understand if only the reasons were explained. And, being men of higher education and broader outlook than their clients, they had an additional reason: they felt that the case should be publicized as widely as possible because it would make clear to the rest of America the futility of trying to impose desegregation on the South. Milam was not a pleasant person, one of the lawyers admitted to Huie: "He's got a chip on his shoulder. That's how he got that battlefield promotion in Europe; he likes to kill folks." But, the lawyer explained, there was a need for men like Milam and Bryant: to "keep the niggahs in line." And the country should understand, he said, that the "niggahs" were *going* to be kept in line. "There ain't gonna be no integration," he told Huie. "There ain't gonna be no nigger votin'. *And the sooner everybody in this country realizes it, the better.* If any more pressure is put on us, the Tallahatchie River won't hold all the niggers that'll be thrown into it." Publication of the true facts of the case would be valuable, therefore, to "put the North and the NAACP and the niggers *on notice*"; it might even force the repeal of school integration, "just like Prohibition." And the "true facts" did indeed reach audiences not accustomed to seeing how parts of the South kept blacks in line, because after *Look,* with a circulation of three million, published Huie's article, it was excerpted in *Reader's Digest,* with a circulation of eleven million—much of which was in the North's largely white suburbs.

THEN, STILL EARLY IN 1956, the wound was widened. In February, the Supreme Court ordered the University of Alabama to admit its first black student—and with that order, white fury spilled over. The Till atrocity and the Mississippi voter-registration murders had been violence by individuals. The Alabama incident escalated abruptly into violence by mob.

The would-be student was twenty-six-year-old Autherine Juanita Lucy. Quiet and shy, the young woman had been brought up on her father's farm in backcountry Alabama, her home an unpainted frame shack and her high school another unpainted frame shack, but she wanted to be a librarian, and had put herself through a small Negro college. She applied to the graduate program in library science at the University of Alabama at Tuscaloosa, but was not accepted because of her race. With the help of the NAACP, she sued for admittance, on the grounds that Alabama had established no institution, separate or not, in which blacks could obtain a library degree, and now, in February, her suit was granted, and the university's trustees complied, although, to avoid contaminating the otherwise all-white student body, she was barred from dormitories and dining halls so that the other students would not be forced to live or eat with her.

That restriction did not satisfy some students. For two days, Autherine Lucy went to classes, passing burning crosses on campus, amid what she was to call "hateful stares," and then, on February 6, came the "day I'll never want to live through again."

Ms. Lucy went from class to class in a dean's car that day, "chased from one building to another," a reporter wrote, "as though she was an animal pursued by a pack of hounds." At each building there was a mob, made up not only of students but of rednecks from the countryside and hard-bitten factory workers from the industrial plants near Tuscaloosa, and the mobs threw eggs and stones, smashing the car's windows, as they shouted, "Kill her! Kill her!" "There was murder in the air," the reporter wrote, but state highway patrolmen on the scene made no move to protect her, or to arrest any of the stone-throwers, reportedly on orders from Governor James (Big Jim) Folsom. As the mob grew larger and more menacing, university officials asked for city fire engines to be sent, so that fire hoses could be used if necessary, but no engines appeared. Finally, the mob trapped her in a building, and she had to stay there

("I could still hear the crowd outside") until, after a very long time, the police arrived. The disturbances spread from the campus to downtown Tuscaloosa; when the rioters spotted cars driven by Negroes, they blocked their paths, smashed their windows, and climbed on their roofs and stomped dents in them. The university's trustees reacted by suspending not the rioters but her, "for her own safety": had they not done so, they said, there was the possibility of a lynching. "God knows I didn't intend to cause all this violence," she said. "I merely wanted an education."

Going back to court, the NAACP charged that university trustees had conspired with the rioters, and a federal judge ordered the university to lift the suspension—whereupon the trustees expelled her permanently (for, they said, falsely accusing them of conspiracy). Promising to "keep fighting until I get an education," she moved to the Birmingham home of her brother-in-law, Ulysses Moore, where men with rifles guarded the porch ("I'm not going to have her snatched from my care as they did the Till boy," Moore said). But the phone rang constantly with callers saying, "We're coming after you," or "We'll get you this time," and she was unable to put from her mind the enraged faces that had pressed against the windows of the dean's car. "All I could do then was pray, and I thought, 'Am I going to die?' " Rioters whom the NAACP had named in its suit sued her for defamation, asking four million dollars. She flew to New York where Thurgood Marshall, glancing with evident concern at her tense, hollow-eyed face, told reporters at LaGuardia Airport, "She left Alabama because at this stage she's taken as much as a human being can take. . . ." A reporter asked if Miss Lucy had in effect lost the fight despite the court verdicts. "You and other American citizens have lost," Marshall replied. As the reporters pressed around her, she said to Marshall, "Please get me out of here." Then he drove her away, not to his office but to a doctor, who ordered her to take a long rest.

Some Alabama whites crowed that the riot had "worked," and in fact, by their definition, it had: it had restored segregation at the university. The trustees had expelled Miss Lucy "because the mob forced them to," said one student leader who was on her side. "The mob won." In addition, the South's indignation at the Supreme Court's interference in its affairs "woke people up like nothing else did," a spokesman for the White Citizens Councils said. Tens of thousands of new members joined; wrote a reporter at one huge Council rally, "They filed in the coliseum doors in long lines, millionaires mingling with farmers, as many women as men, all with eager looks on their faces like people going to a Billy Graham revival." There was no longer, said John Bartlow Martin, any doubt "that the South . . . has found in the Citizens Councils a flag to rally round. The Deep South was solid once more."

Yet it was not only in the South, not only among conservatives and racists, that the Autherine Lucy episode had stirred, and solidified, deep emotions. The death of her modest dream of being a librarian, like the death of Emmett Till, might on the surface have seemed like a victory for injustice, like simply another defeat for Martin Luther King's "great cause." But these victories were Pyrrhic, for in both cases, an entire nation had been reading about the injustice, had seen it all, stark and clear. Into the hearts of those willing to have their hearts opened had been brought home, with new vividness, the cruelty and inhumanity with which black Americans were treated in the South. These two episodes had hardened, among men and women of good will, a desire that, at last, something be done on behalf of these long-downtrodden people.

DRAMATIC AND SIGNIFICANT as were the Till and Lucy encounters, trumpet calls to rally Americans behind the banner of justice, they were not the most significant on the southern civil rights front of 1956. Justice marched that year not to a trumpet call but to a drumbeat—a soft, undramatic, but unfaltering drumbeat, that instead of fading away like a trumpet call went on all that year, month after month. It was a drumbeat of footsteps on pavement—the footsteps of maids and washerwomen and cooks, of garbagemen and yardmen and janitors. For, month after month, all through 1956, the Montgomery Bus Boycott went on.

"Come the first rainy day and the Negroes will be back on the buses," Montgomery's Mayor, W. A. Gayle, had predicted, shortly after the boycott began in December, 1955. He could hardly be blamed for his confidence. "To a largely uneducated people . . . [t]he loss of what was for many their most important modern convenience—cheap bus transportation—left them with staggering problems of logistics and morale," Taylor Branch has written. Their jobs might be five or six miles from their homes. Drivers in a hastily organized car pool, using cars loaned by blacks, took black workers to and from their jobs, but there were never enough cars, and many had no choice but to walk. Others had the choice but chose to walk anyway, preferring to "demonstrate with their feet" their determination to end the indignities and humiliation of bus segregation. Passing an elderly lady hobbling slowly and painfully home after her day's work, a car pool driver offered her a lift. Refusing, she explained: "I'm not walking for myself. I'm walking for my children and my grandchildren." There had been black bus boycotts before in other southern cities, but they had all ended quickly—perhaps the longest had been one in Baton Rouge, Louisiana, in 1953, that lasted two weeks—as their participants gave up and admitted defeat. But the Montgomery boycott didn't end. Rain came indeed, and cold, and, as the seasons changed, the heat of an Alabama summer, and Montgomery's blacks kept walking.

One reason they kept walking was their leader, that twenty-six-year-old preacher only recently come to Montgomery.

The Reverend Martin Luther King Jr. was one of the generation of new, better-educated, more confident black leaders who were beginning to appear in the South—one with unusual political sophistication. Hardly had he become minister of Montgomery's Dexter Avenue Baptist Church when he announced a goal: "Every member of Dexter must be a registered voter." Registered—and knowledgeable. Weekly forums discussed election issues; a political action committee was formed.

At Boston University, where the Reverend King had been studying for his Ph.D., the faculty, impressed by him, had urged him to become an academic, but, although attracted by that prospect, he rejected it in favor of a southern pastorship; "That's where I'm needed," he told his wife, Coretta. He was to discount his role in the Montgomery boycott. "I just happened to be there," he was to say. "There comes a time when time itself is ready for a change. That time has come in Montgomery, and I have nothing to do with it." But at the boycotters' nightly mass meetings, he echoed Douglass the Lion, who had said, "Power concedes nothing without a demand. It never did and never will"; said Martin Luther King: "Freedom is never given to anybody, for the oppressor has you in domination because he plans to keep you there." And he went beyond Douglass to espouse a doctrine of passive, non-violent resistance. "Hate begets hate, violence begets violence; toughness begets a greater toughness," King said. "Our aim must never be to defeat or humiliate the white man, but to win his friendship and understanding. . . . This is a nonviolent protest. We are depending on moral and spiritual forces." King's phrases were ringing, rhythmic, unforgettable; as the young preacher left the pulpit each evening, men and women who had walked for miles that day reached out their hands to touch him, and the next morning walked again. When, in January, 1956, Montgomery's white leaders arrested King for a minor traffic violation, thinking thus to break the boycott, he was very afraid. As he sat in the back seat of a police cruiser, his mind was so filled with thoughts of lynchings—crossing a bridge, he feared that a mob was waiting for him on the other side; he could not stop thinking about the river below—that when he finally saw the jail, he was overwhelmed by happiness that he was not going to be killed or mutilated. But even as he was entering the jail, carloads of Negroes were racing toward it, and the jailer hastily released him on his own recognizance. So many people attended that night's mass meeting in order to get a glimpse of him that it was announced that a second meeting would be held at another church, and when that was filled, a third meeting was announced, and then a fourth—seven meetings, packed with men and women who just wanted to see for themselves that the Reverend King was all right. And when he went home after the last meeting, he was accompanied by a group of young men who had decided they would guard him from then on whenever he left his house; he was too precious to lose.

Montgomery's blacks also kept walking because of themselves.

Though incidents on the city's buses had been increasing in recent years, they had invariably ended in defeat and humiliation for the black person involved. Boarding a bus with her arms filled with packages one Christmas, Jo Ann Robinson, a professor at Montgomery's black college, Alabama State, took a seat in the white section without thinking. Striding toward her, his arm up as if to strike her, the bus driver shouted, "Get up from there! Get up from there!" "I felt like a dog," Mrs. Robinson was to recall, and, crying, she left the bus. But when she asked friends to help her protest the incident, they demurred, saying that the driver's conduct was simply what one expected in Montgomery. Once, Martin Luther King's predecessor in the Dexter pulpit, Vernon Johns, had dropped his dime as he was trying to put it in the fare box. Although it rolled near the driver's seat, the driver ordered Johns to pick it up, saying, "Uncle, get down and pick up that dime and put it in the box." When Johns asked the driver to do it himself, the driver said that if Johns didn't do it, he'd throw him off the bus. Turning to the other passengers, all of whom were black, Johns said he was leaving and asked them to join him. Nobody moved.

But now, partly because of their new leader, partly because of a new determination, emblematic of the widespread new determination among southern blacks, Montgomery's blacks kept on walking even when ten thousand people attended a White Citizens Council rally in the Montgomery Coliseum—"the largest pro-segregation rally in history"—to hear Mississippi's senior United States Senator, James O. Eastland, shout that "In every stage of the bus boycott we have been oppressed and degraded because of black, slimy, juicy, unbearably stinking niggers . . . African flesh-eaters. When in the course of human events it becomes necessary to abolish the Negro race, proper methods should be used. Among these are guns, bows and arrows, slingshots and knives. . . . All whites are created equal with certain rights, among these are life, liberty and the pursuit of dead niggers." They kept on walking even when, after that rally, long caravans of cars filled with hooded men brandishing rifles and Confederate flags roamed the city. Montgomery's Negroes kept on walking even when the city fathers, who thought they were dealing with blacks from the past— ill-educated, easily divided, and without access to national publicity outlets— turned to the "get tough" policies that had always worked with blacks in the past, urging businessmen to fire Negro employees who came to work on foot instead of by bus, ordering police to break up for "loitering" groups of Negroes waiting for car pool pickups, and to give car pool drivers so many traffic tickets—Jo Ann Robinson got seventeen in two months—that the drivers faced the loss of their licenses and insurance. They kept walking even when a grand jury—an all-white grand jury, naturally—subpoenaed more than two hundred Negroes, and it became known that wholesale criminal indictments were being prepared under an obscure anti-boycott ordinance. They kept walking even when, in late February, after 115 indictments, twenty-four against ministers, had been returned by the grand jury but had not yet actually been served by police, the city commissioners called on the Reverend Ralph Abernathy, a key figure in the boycott, and delivered an ultimatum: a broad hint that the indictments would not be served if the boycott was called off immediately. "We have walked for eleven weeks in the cold and the rain," Abernathy replied. "Now the weather is warming up. . . . We will walk on. . . ."

They walked on even when the indictments were served—walked on, and found the courage not to be cowed by the indictments.

"For centuries," as Taylor Branch has written, "the jailhouse door had conjured up visions of fetid cells and unspeakable cruelties" for southern blacks. Now one of the 115 blacks indicted, E. D. Nixon, a rough-hewn rail-road porter, didn't wait for the sheriff's deputies to come for him, but walked into the county courthouse and said, "Are you looking for me? Well, here I am." Released on three hundred dollars' bail, he emerged, having removed a lit-tle of the terror from the act of being arrested. Then a dignified elderly black pastor followed Nixon, joking with the deputies as they were booking and fin-gerprinting him. News of what the two men had done spread across Negro Montgomery. A crowd gathered around the courthouse, shouting encourage-ment to the men and women who walked into it, applauding them as they came out. The furious sheriff came outside to shout, "This is no vaudeville show!" but that dreaded jailhouse door had begun to turn, in Branch's words, "into a glorious passage."

One of the ministers indicted was Martin Luther King. He was away when the indictments were handed down, and his father, a renowned black minister himself, in Atlanta, pleaded with him not to return to Montgomery lest he be killed. The Atlanta police chief told the younger King that that was a strong possibility: "I think you're in great danger," he said. "I think you're a marked man." There might be no bail for the boycott's leader—and if he was kept in jail, what might not happen to him there? King replied that he must go back, and he did—arrested, he was photographed as a criminal, with a number, 7809, under his chin. He was released on bond, but only after an early date had been set for his trial.

One evening not long thereafter, King was speaking at a mass meeting when, looking down from the podium, he saw a man hurry into the hall and say something to Abernathy, who quickly left the room, and, when he returned, seemed very upset and started whispering urgently to ministers near him in the audience. Then King saw other men come in, and he saw some of them start to walk toward the podium, and then hesitate and retreat, as if there was some-thing they didn't want to tell him. He saw some of them whisper something to Abernathy. Abernathy didn't come up either. Motioning Abernathy to come up to the podium, King whispered "What's wrong?" and Abernathy had to tell him. "Your house has been bombed," he said. When King asked, "Are Coretta and the baby all right?" Abernathy had to say, "We're checking on that right now"—he had been desperate to have the answer for King before telling him anything.

In front of King's home was a barricade of white policemen shouting to a huge crowd, a black crowd, to disperse, but the men in the crowd, yelling in rage, were brandishing guns and knives, and teenage boys were breaking bottles so that they would have weapons in their hands. King pushed through the crowd. The front porch, broken in two by the bomb, was covered with shattered glass from broken windows. He walked across it. Inside the front room, which was still reeking of dynamite fumes, were the Mayor and other city officials, whom King brushed past. In a back room was a crowd of neighbors; it was only when they parted to make way for him that he saw that at its center were Coretta and Yoki, unharmed.

And then, having made sure of that, Martin Luther King became very calm, with what Branch calls "the remote calm of a commander." Stepping back out on the porch, he held up his hand for silence. Everything was all right, he told the crowd. "Don't get panicky. Don't do anything panicky. Don't get your weapons. If you have weapons, take them home. He who lives by the sword will perish by the sword. Remember that is what Jesus said. We are not advocating violence. We want to love our enemies. I want you to love our enemies. Be good to them. This is what we must live by. We must meet hate with love."

The crowd was silent now, as King continued speaking. He himself might die, he said, but that wouldn't matter. "If I am stopped, this movement will not stop. If I am stopped, our work will not stop. For what we are doing is right. What we are doing is just. And God is with us."

The people left, the men taking their weapons home. The boys put down the broken bottles. "I owe my life to that nigger preacher," a white policeman said. That very night, floodlights were strung around the King home with its shattered porch, and for the remaining months of the boycott, men stood guard around it. They knew nothing must happen to the man inside. I. F. Stone had said that Negroes needed a Gandhi. They had a Gandhi now.

THE EMMETT TILL CASE had been the first great media event of the civil rights movement, but it had been a brief event—its centerpiece a five-day trial—and it had been primarily a story for the print media. The Montgomery Bus Boycott took place not in a hamlet but in a big city, and it went on for months—for almost all of 1956, in fact—a dramatic story from the start, with its basic theme of downtrodden people fighting for a very basic right; and with the arrest and trial of Martin Luther King, and the bombing of his home, the drama escalated and escalated and escalated again. The reporters from the big northern newspapers who had come together for the first time in Money now came together again in Montgomery, and were joined by many others. And even in the six months since the Till trial, television had grown immensely, and so had the importance of its news programs, and this story provided the raw material that television needed—dramatic, unforgettable pictures: of elderly women trudging wearily home from work, passed by the buses they refused to ride; of King's wrecked home; of mass meetings with hundreds, thousands of men and women lifting up their heads in defiant song. The days of setting down planes in fields were over; the networks set up direct feeds from Montgomery, for the boycott was on the news night after night.

Among the effects of this coverage was increased safety for the boycott's footsore troops. As David Halberstam says, "The more coverage there was, the more witnesses there were, and the harder it was for the white leadership to inflict physical hardship upon the blacks. In addition, the more coverage there was, the more it gave courage to the leadership and its followers. The sacrifices and the risks were worth it, everyone sensed, because the country and the world were now taking notice."

The coverage also affected the television viewers who were watching it, particularly, perhaps, those in the North. The "educational process" begun in the Till case was continuing, and intensifying. For people for whom "segregation" had been only an abstraction, disliked but vague, segregation was suddenly, night after night, a reality brought into their living rooms, in all its injustice and cruelty.

And this story had a hero. A keen sense of the possibilities of the media was combined in Martin Luther King with rare courage and a passionate desire for justice, and TV caught it all. An interview with that serious young man, who quoted Hegel and Nietzsche with evident familiarity, was memorable for reasons that went far beyond erudition. "Are you afraid?" an interviewer asked him after the bombing, and there was a pause, and then Martin Luther King said, very firmly, "No, I'm not. My attitude is that this is a great cause, a great issue that we're confronted with, and that the consequences for my personal life are not particularly important. It is the triumph of a cause that I am concerned about, and I have always felt that ultimately along the way of life an individual must stand up and be counted, and be willing to face the consequences, whatever they are, and if he is filled with fear, he cannot do it." His arrest and trial—on March 19, he was found guilty, sentenced to pay a $500 fine or serve a year at hard labor but was freed pending appeal—was front-page news everywhere. More and more, it was not just to Negroes that King was a hero. Arriving in New York to raise funds for his cause, he received what one newspaper called "the kind of welcome [the city] usually reserves for the Brooklyn Dodgers"; there were white people as well as black among the thousands who crowded into New York churches to hear him. White people as well as black came from all over the world on pilgrimages to Montgomery. A Swedish woman wrote, "I went directly from the airport to the by now world-famous car-pool lot. I stood across the street from it for a moment, and although I am neither a sentimental nor an emotional woman—we Swedes are neither—I don't mind telling you that my throat tightened as I watched the crowded station wagons entering and leaving the car park and as I watched the many gayly smiling people who waited so patiently for their turn to be brought home after a hard day's work. . . . I felt that somehow I was standing on historical ground." The Negroes of Montgomery, Alabama, had gained—had *won,* won by sacrifice, by determination, by courage—the attention, and, increasingly, the admiration of America.

AND, BEFORE 1956 WAS OVER, they would win more than admiration. They would *win.*

On November 13, 1956, Martin Luther King was sitting again at the defendant's table in a Montgomery courtroom. The city fathers had finally devised a maneuver that would cripple the boycott; they had asked for an injunction banning the car pool as an unlicensed transportation system, and the lawyers for his Montgomery Improvement Association had told King the injunction would be granted. If it was, the boycotters, with another winter approaching, would no longer have the car pool to help their fight—and to his wife Coretta, King confessed that without the car pool, "I'm afraid our people will go back to the buses. It's just too much to ask them to continue if we don't have transportation for them." On November 13, when the hearing began, "the clock said it was noon, but it was midnight in my soul," he was to remember.

But it was noon.

All that year, since long before the injunction suit had begun, another suit—brought not against the MIA but filed by the association itself—had been rising through the federal court system. Back in February, the MIA's leaders had decided that the fight should be not merely for more seats for blacks on buses, and for a section reserved for blacks from which they could not be ousted, but rather for the right to sit anywhere on a bus they wanted, and the association had therefore filed a federal lawsuit not to modify bus segregation ordinances but to eliminate them entirely, on the grounds that they were unconstitutional because they violated the Fourteenth Amendment. The suit had been filed not only against Montgomery's ordinances but also against Alabama's, so it carried the hope of a victory over all bus segregation in the state. (MIA attorney Fred Gray had been arrested for barratry for filing it.) The suit had been upheld by lower federal courts, and had reached the Supreme Court that fall. And it was that case—not the unlicensed transportation system injunction—that was decided first: on that very day, November 13, on which King was sitting desolate in court.

Pushing through the crowd, a reporter handed him a slip of paper that had just been torn off the Associated Press teletypewriter. It said: "The United States Supreme Court today affirmed a decision of a special three-judge U.S. District Court in declaring Alabama's state and local laws requiring segregation on buses unconstitutional."

Although the city went ahead with the injunction request, and the judge granted it, the Supreme Court decision made the injunction irrelevant. The Emmett Till and Autherine Lucy episodes had ended in defeat. Not the Montgomery Bus Boycott. On the morning after the Supreme Court decision, a bus pulled up at the bus stop near Martin Luther King's home and King boarded it. The driver, a white man, smiled at him. "I believe you are Reverend King," he said. "Yes, I am," King said. "We are glad to have you with us this morning," the driver said. Martin Luther King sat down—in the front row. All that year, black Americans had been proving they could fight. Now they had proved they could win.

SOUTHERN WHITES REACTED to this development with heightened fury. A shotgun blast was fired into the King home; snipers fired on the integrated buses, one volley wounding a pregnant Negro woman in both legs; a car pulled up to a bus stop at which a fifteen-year-old Negro girl was standing alone, and five men jumped out and beat her; the long Klan caravans honked through Negro sections of Montgomery, and Klansmen marched through the streets in full regalia; fiery crosses burned in the night. One night explosions rumbled across the city as four churches and two homes—one of them Ralph Abernathy's—were wrecked. Praying for guidance at a mass meeting the next day, King said, "Lord, I hope no one will have to die as a result of our struggle for freedom in Montgomery. Certainly I don't want to die. But if anyone has to die, let it be me." Two weeks later, while Coretta and Yoki were in Atlanta, something—he wasn't sure what—disturbed King during the night; leaving his home, he went to a friend's. A few hours later, a bomb exploded at his house; another—twelve sticks of dynamite—failed to explode; it was found at the house later. But the victory—a victory at last—had given southern blacks hope, and they met segregationist fury with increased determination. King and Abernathy established a permanent organization, the Southern Christian Leadership Conference, to launch civil rights protests all across the South. In one sense, the victory in Montgomery was confined to a single front. While it was no longer illegal on a Montgomery bus for someone with black skin to sit beside someone with white skin, the rest of the city was still rigidly segregated, and whites vowed to keep it that way, planning not only new tactics of physical intimidation but legal strategies that could keep such threats as desegregation of the schools ensnarled in perpetual litigation. In a larger sense, however, the victory elevated the fight for civil rights to a new level, in part because it had produced a leader whose greatness was equal to the greatness of the cause— Martin Luther King gave people "the feeling that they could be bigger and stronger and more courageous than they thought they could be," Bayard Rustin said—in part because of the powerful new weapon, non-violent resistance, that had been forged on the Montgomery battlefield. For perhaps the first time, and certainly the first time on such a scale, a black community had risen up in the heart of Dixie and defeated entrenched white power, and blacks had a new self-respect. After the Montgomery Bus Boycott victory, after they had proven they could endure, and could win, they were ready to move on to new fronts. They could sit beside white people on buses now; why couldn't they sit beside them in theaters, in restaurants? Why couldn't they live beside them in the same housing developments and apartment houses? Why couldn't they compete equally with white people for jobs? Why couldn't they vote in elections as easily as white people voted? Why was it that their children, whom the Supreme Court had ruled three years before could attend the same schools as white children—why were their children still not attending those schools? Fed, after Till and Lucy, by indignation, driven, after Montgomery, by hope, the tide was rising steadily now, southern black and northern liberal demand for equality combining to beat more and more powerfully against the political barriers that had, for so long, held it back.

And now, in 1956, some of these barriers were, all at once, no longer quite so solid as they had been. Southern Democrats on Capitol Hill had long been able to count confidently on support for their anti–civil rights stands from conservative Republicans (and not a few Democrats) from midwestern or Mountain States with negligible black populations. During the last two or three years, however, the years of *Brown* and Till and Lucy and Martin Luther King, that support, on the surface as solid as ever, was nonetheless being eroded.

To some extent, it was being eroded by conscience. Emmett Till's battered face and Autherine Lucy's haunted eyes and the weariness of Montgomery's cleaning ladies had now been brought into millions of American homes, including the homes of elected officials—and, in some cases, into their hearts. It had in the past been easy for congressmen and senators whose constituents included few blacks and for whom southern injustice was only a distant, remote issue, to ignore that injustice. It was less easy now.

To some extent, it was being eroded by embarrassment. Congressmen and senators who had traditionally been able to vote with the South without their constituents caring no longer enjoyed that luxury; constituents who had read about the Till case and had seen on television the mobs rampaging unchecked through the streets of Tuscaloosa, now began to ask questions of their elected representatives about their pro-southern votes, questions that were not easy to answer.

And to some extent, it was being eroded by calculation. After the Civil War, African-Americans had remained loyal to the party that had freed them—the Republican Party of Lincoln—for more than half a century, from Reconstruction to Depression. When the Depression struck, however, the heartlessness of Republicans—and of another Republican President, Hoover—changed that, particularly after the arrival in the White House of a Democratic President who demonstrated that government didn't have to be heartless. Unemployment compensation, Social Security, relief payments, strong unions, the chance, through WPA and PWA, to be back at work again—all these meant so much to the people hardest hit of all Americans by any economic downturn. Wooden-legged William Dawson of Chicago, during the 1940s the only African-American among the 435 members of the House of Representatives, had been raised in Georgia's Dougherty County, which was not far from Richard Russell's idyllic Winder, but his view of the area was not quite the same as Russell's. Dougherty County, Dawson was to say, "was just one step this side of hell. I stood guard with my father all one night to stop a lynching when I was fifteen." He had, he said, "hated the word Democrat when I came north," but the New Deal had changed his allegiance. Without FDR, he was to say, "Negroes would have died like flies." While Negroes didn't vote in the South, they voted in the North—and in 1956, they had, for more than two decades, been voting solidly Democratic, becoming one of the key elements in the coalition that had made the Democrats America's majority party.

And more Negroes were voting now—a lot more.

In bus depots and train stations throughout the South—in Mobile and Tallahassee and Raleigh and Nashville and New Orleans, and in a thousand small towns scattered across the countryside of the Old Confederacy—the same scene was being enacted day after day: whole families of black people, sometimes two or even three generations, clustered together, clutching their tickets (a ticket to the North usually cost more than a week's pay), waiting to get out of the South. Most of them were very poor; they carried their possessions in cardboard suitcases or cloth sacks or simply in bundles wrapped in string—and what they carried was often all they owned; "They went north largely without possessions and yet they left behind almost nothing," David Halberstam has written. And every evening, in the North's huge railroad terminals—in Chicago, the great railhead, due north of the Delta, but also in New York's Grand Central Station and Washington's Union Station and Detroit's Central Depot—another scene was enacted. The black families would step off the trains and buses to be met by relatives, who took them to their new homes in the fast-spreading northern slums.

African-Americans' vast migration from the southern countryside to the northern cities had surged during the two world wars, when jobs were opened up by the cutting off of immigration and the departure of white workers for the armed forces, but even between wars it had never really stopped, because as bad as were conditions in the North—and they were terrible: overcrowded schools; brutalization by police; cramped apartments in fetid slums or in the public housing ghettos they hated—they were nonetheless better than the conditions from which these people had come; as Nicholas Lemann says: "Money and dignity were indisputably in greater supply in Chicago than in the Delta." Since 1949 that migration had been accelerating dramatically, because the mass production of the mechanical cotton picker and the introduction of chemicals that killed the weeds between cotton plants which formerly had had to be laboriously chopped out made human hands largely unnecessary in the cotton field. During the 1940s, Chicago's black population, concentrated in its huge South Side ghetto, had increased by more than twenty thousand a year; during the 1950s, it was increasing by more than thirty thousand a year; by 1955, 17 percent of Chicago's population was African-American—and that inflow was being mirrored in a dozen industrial cities of the North. By 1956, the exodus of the Negro from the South to the North had become the largest American migration since the pioneers drove west in their covered wagons. In 1910, 90 percent of all American Negroes had lived in the Old South. By 1956, almost half— about eight million of the sixteen million African-Americans in the United States—lived in the North.

Huge as was this mass movement of millions of people, very little was being written about it. There was nothing very dramatic in the daily debarkation of twenty or fifty or eighty black people from a train, and in James Reston's words, journalists do a better job of covering revolution than evolution. But a public official was ignorant of these implications at his peril. Chicago Mayor Martin Kennelly failed to treat Congressman Dawson with respect despite Dawson's control of the five wards of the South Side; in 1955, partly at Dawson's instigation, Kennelly was supplanted by Richard J. Daley, and Daley, supported by Negro votes, was to hold the mayoralty until he died twenty-one years later.

Rising within the growing northern urban black voting bloc, moreover, was what the black journalist Carl Rowan described as "a new kind of Negro leader." In the past, all too many African-American black leaders had been complaisant puppets selected by a city's white power structure because of their willingness to be manipulated by strings held in white hands. The new Negro voters, their eyes opened by war service, by higher education, by the victory in Montgomery, wanted a new type of leader, and, in 1956, while there were still many of the old "Uncle Toms" left, there were more and more leaders of whom Rowan could say, "These men . . . are not the semi-literate ward heelers who used to sell Negro votes at $5 a dozen; these are articulate Negroes, moved by a passion for justice." These new leaders, and the new voters in their wards, saw, quite clearly, that the party they and their people had supported so faithfully for two decades was, despite Roosevelt and Truman, also the party that was in power on Capitol Hill—and was therefore the party that was denying their people justice.

When Democratic strategists sat down to analyze the 1952 election returns, they saw that while in city after city the African-American vote had still been overwhelmingly Democratic, it had not been as overwhelmingly Democratic as in the past. In black wards where once FDR and Truman had polled 80 or even 90 percent, Adlai Stevenson had polled 70 percent, or even less; his percentage of the country's overall black vote was 68 percent.

The Democrats' initial reaction had been to ascribe the slippage to Ike's popularity, and this was certainly part of the explanation, but when, their attention focused now on the black vote they had previously taken for granted, they began analyzing it more closely, they realized that the decline was also due to deeper, and much more disturbing, factors, for, they realized, it had actually begun not in the 1952 presidential election but in 1948, and, in some cities, in the congressional elections of 1946. Quietly but steadily, they realized, their party had been losing the Negro vote.

That fact had the gravest of implications. The Negro vote was concentrated in the big cities of the big industrial states of the North that cast the highest electoral votes. In fact, it was concentrated in the queen cities (Chicago, Philadelphia, New York, Detroit, Cleveland, Indianapolis, St. Louis, Newark, and Los Angeles) of the nine states (Illinois, Pennsylvania, New York, Michigan, Ohio, Indiana, Missouri, New Jersey, and California) which alone had a total of 223 of the 266 electoral votes necessary to elect a President. The bloc Negro vote in these cities had been a key reason that the Democrats had, in five consecutive presidential elections between 1932 and 1948, been able to count on those states—and therefore occupancy of the White House. The magnitude of the Eisenhower landslide had rendered the Negro shift relatively insignificant in 1952, but in a closer election it could be a decisive factor.

Nor was the significance of the slippage limited to the presidential level. Gerrymandering and other devices instituted by the white power structure made blacks' leverage in presidential, or statewide or citywide, elections greater than in elections for aldermen or congressmen; the House of Representatives, after all, still contained only three Negroes (Chicago's Dawson and Clarence Diggs, who had sat at the press table in Sumner; and New York City's Adam Clayton Powell Jr.). In no fewer than thirty-five congressional districts outside the South, however, the number of eligible Negro voters in 1956 was going to be greater than the winning congressional candidate's margin of victory had been in 1954, so that in these districts Negroes would hold the balance of power. And while every one of these districts had gone Democratic in 1954, as they had been going Democratic since 1932, in many of them the 1954 Democratic plurality had been, disturbingly, much narrower than in the past— uncomfortably narrow, in many cases.

The possibility of even greater slippage had been increased by the recent civil rights atrocities in the South. After years of unswerving Democratic allegiance, the loyalty of many northern Negroes in 1956 was going to be not to a party but to a purpose: to an insistence on justice for their embattled southern brethren. "We Negroes have got to think this year, because here in the North, we will be speaking for all the Southern Negroes who can't speak for themselves on Election Day," said an engineer interviewed by Rowan. "We'll be voting for Emmett Till and Miss Lucy and that preacher in Mississippi who was murdered because he wanted to vote."

The northern black urban vote was therefore a giant political plum ripe for the taking—and Democrats were not alone in seeing this. Republicans knew they had been presented with a great opportunity. Risks were involved. Enthusiasm for Eisenhower among southern white voters had enabled him to carry four southern states (Texas, Florida, Tennessee, and Virginia) in 1952; there had been additional signs of increased Republican strength in the once-solid South since then; Republicans were anxious to widen that beachhead; GOP support for civil rights jeopardized it. The southern stake, however, was dwarfed by the northern. Persuade Negroes that the Republican Party, rather than the Democratic, offered the best chance for justice for their race and the GOP might be able at last to get back the Negro vote. Get it back, and for years to come, even without an Eisenhower at the head of the ticket, it might be a Republican who occupied the White House. Get it back, and it might be Republican representatives and senators who wielded the gavels at the head of the green felt tables on Capitol Hill. In only four of the twenty-four years since 1932 had Republicans controlled Congress, and they hungered to do so again. Get that vote back, and the Republicans might become again what they had once been: possessors of the White House and America's majority party.

REPUBLICAN AWARENESS of the opportunity and eagerness to seize it was evident at the first meeting in 1956 between the party's congressional leaders and President Eisenhower, held at the White House on January 10. The President was sending Congress a legislation to finance construction of new schools. Harlem's Adam Clayton Powell, a Democrat, was planning to attach to the measure an amendment saying that none of that money could be spent in any state whose schools were still segregated. Similar "Powell Amendments" had failed to attract much Republican support in the past, but the minutes of the January 10 meeting show that key House Republican Charles Halleck, adamant conservative though he was, said that this time "Republicans would have to vote for it." At the year's second meeting, on January 24, "It was reaffirmed that there should be no opposition to any anti-segregation amendment that may be offered in connection with this legislation."

As for the President himself, he was to say in his memoirs that while he was committed to the cause of civil rights, "I did not agree with those who believed that legislation alone could institute instant morality [or that] coercion could cure all civil rights problems." His record on the single most pressing civil rights issue—the efforts to implement the *Brown* decision—is a reminder that since Dwight Eisenhower had left the military before Harry Truman's 1948 order to desegregate it, he had spent all his adult life in a Jim Crow army; that, as his biographer Stephen Ambrose puts it, "he had many southern friends and he shared most of their prejudices against Negroes," laughingly repeating their jokes about "darkies"; that he felt education was a local matter, in which the federal government should not intervene—and that before the Court ruled on

Brown, he had tried to get Chief Justice Warren to see things his way: once, after a White House stag dinner, Eisenhower took Warren by the arm as the guests were leaving the dining room and said about the southerners, "These are not bad people. All they are concerned about is to see that their sweet little girls are not required to sit in school alongside some big overgrown Negroes." Six years of his presidency remained after the Court's ruling (which he felt had set back racial progress; "I personally believe that if you try to go too fast in laws in this delicate field . . . you are making a mistake"). Not once during those six years would Eisenhower publicly support the ruling; not once would he say that *Brown* was morally right, or that segregation was morally wrong.

"The Supreme Court has spoken, and I am sworn to uphold the constitutional processes in this country; and I will obey," he said, but, in Ambrose's words, the President refused "to associate himself and his prestige in any way with *Brown,*" dodging every attempt to pin him down. "I think it makes no difference whether or not I endorse it," he said at one press conference. "The Constitution is as the Supreme Court interprets it, and I must conform to that and do my very best to see that it is carried out in this country."

Eisenhower's refusal to publicly support the Court's decision *did* make a difference, of course, for the crucial question was whether or not the President would use the military to enforce the decision if there was a showdown—and in his confusing statements white southerners heard sympathy for them and a deep reluctance to use force; as Ambrose says, "The President's moderation, the Southerners felt, gave them license to defy the Court." "To stand above this battle," Richard Kluger has written, "was to side with the legions of resistance, and Dwight Eisenhower, either by design or by obtuseness, comforted and dignified those who were ranged against the Court." Asked in 1956 by reporters if he would dip into his "tremendous reservoir of good will among young people" and give them some guidance on how they should act at this crucial moment, he replied: "Well, I can say what I have said so often. It is difficult through law and through force to change a man's heart. . . ." He then attacked "the people . . . so filled with prejudice that they even resort to violence; and the same way on the other side of the thing, the people who want to have the whole matter settled today"—a comparison that equated violent southern mobs with men and women whose only crime was to be active in the cause of civil rights. There was no explicit criticism from Eisenhower even for Emmett Till's murderers. The murder occurred a month after Frederic Morrow became the first Negro on the White House staff, and thereafter he attempted repeatedly to persuade the President to speak out on the incident—with no success whatsoever. When Emmett's mother, Mrs. Bradley, sent the President a telegram asking him to intervene in Mississippi to halt the violence against blacks, Eisenhower did not even respond. The Autherine Lucy case certainly seemed like a clear-cut instance of defiance, by the University of Alabama trustees, of a federal court order he was sworn to enforce, but he would do nothing about it. As for the

Montgomery Bus Boycott, when a reporter at an Eisenhower press conference asked the President for a comment on the jailing and trial of Martin Luther King, he replied: "Well, you are asking me, I think, to be more of a lawyer than I certainly am. . . . But, as I understand it, there is a state law about boycotts, and it is under this kind of thing that people are being brought to trial." Even Roy Wilkins, normally so temperate, said that "Eisenhower was a fine general and a good, decent man; but if he had fought World War II the way he fought for civil rights, we would all be speaking German today."

There were, however, other areas, outside the field of education, in which Dwight Eisenhower felt that the responsibility was his, and the issue more clear-cut (his aide Bryce Harlow had been surprised by how "*strong*" the President was for voting rights; "he felt very strongly that nothing good would happen until Negroes got the vote"), and in these areas it was "the compulsion of duty" that won, together with what Ambrose calls "one of his core beliefs—that he was President of all the people." He, not some governor, was Commander-in-Chief of the Armed Forces, and in the District of Columbia it was not a state that had jurisdiction but the federal government. In his first State of the Union address, Eisenhower had promised to carry out Truman's edict and end segregation in the military and in the District, and he had kept that promise. By the end of 1953, all public facilities in the capital had been desegregated, and he could boast that in the Navy and the Air Force, segregated units were "a thing of the past"; that would soon be the case in the Army, too.

Furthermore, Dwight Eisenhower, behind his sunny smile, was a canny political strategist—only now, four decades after he left office, is the true extent of that canniness beginning to be grasped—and a man whose desire to win, to win *everything,* is also inadequately understood. On the evening of his 1956 election victory, he would give his speechwriter Emmet John Hughes a glimpse behind his supposed indifference to the outcome, telling him, when Hughes started to congratulate him on his landslide, that he wasn't yet satisfied: "There's Michigan and Minnesota still to see. You remember the story of Nelson—dying, he looked around and asked 'Are there any of them still left?' I guess that's *me*. When I get in a battle, I just want to win the whole thing. . . . Six or seven states we can't help. But I don't want to lose any more. Don't want any of them 'left.' " Ever since the 1952 election, Eisenhower had seen a chance that he could do for the GOP what Roosevelt had done for the Democrats: make his party the majority party. A delicate balancing act would be required if he was to increase the GOP's appeal to the African-Americans who held the key to the Democratic strongholds of the North while not losing the beachhead he had already established among whites in the once solidly Democratic South, but in his 1956 State of the Union address, he took a first step, making a request—his first request after four years in office—for civil rights legislation, focusing on the right to vote.

Somewhat sparse though it was in civil rights proponents, the Eisenhower

Administration did have Attorney General Herbert Brownell, for whom the President, in Ambrose's words, "had developed unbounded admiration." Not only the keenest of political strategists himself, Brownell was also a longtime civil rights advocate; as a member of the New York State Legislature, he had, he was to recall, first begun fighting "the scourge of segregation" during the 1930s by advocating a compulsory Fair Employment Act with enforcement powers strong enough to ensure compliance; he had left instructions as to the songs to be played at his memorial service at Christ Church on Park Avenue in New York; and when he died at the age of ninety-two in 1996, two hymns were added to the traditional Methodist program: the Negro spiritual "Amazing Grace" and the marching song of Lincoln's armies, "The Battle Hymn of the Republic." And he had been frustrated "quite deeply" by the fact that "our hands were tied" by the lack of federal jurisdiction in the Emmett Till case, and over so many other areas in which black Americans had supposedly been guaranteed "the equal protection of the law." He was anxious to draft a new civil rights law, and Eisenhower gave him permission to do so.

"I initially concentrated almost exclusively on voting rights," Brownell was to recall, but the memory of his frustration in the Till case was too fresh, and "I decided that a more ambitious bill was necessary. So I created . . . a set of proposals that would give the Attorney General unprecedented power to enforce civil rights" in housing, in parks, in theaters, in restaurants, in hotels and motels—in many aspects of daily life—as well as the power to do so without being forced to wait for individuals to sue first, since individuals might be too poor, or too afraid, to sue. Under the Brownell Bill, an Attorney General could institute suits himself, in the name of the United States—suits not only to redress past injustices but to prevent new ones by obtaining judicial injunctions against them.

When Brownell's draft legislation was completed in early 1956, the President called a Cabinet meeting for a full debate on the issue. Sentiment seemed to be moving against introduction of the bill, but Eisenhower interrupted, saying, "Where do you think that the Attorney General's suggestions are moving too rapidly? They look to me like amelioration"—and, of course, sentiment promptly turned the other way.

"After the meeting," Brownell was to write—in a sentence whose ambiguity was later to prove significant—"I was told by the secretary of the cabinet that the President had decided not to support the general civil rights section of the proposed bill" but only the other sections, and "to submit the bill to Congress . . . only as a Justice Department," not as an Administration, proposal. (Cautioning Brownell not to act like "another Charles Sumner" when he testified, Eisenhower illustrated the dangers in stirring up racial emotions with a jocular remark: a southern Negro had recently remarked: "If someone doesn't shut up around here, particularly those Negroes from the North, they're going to get a lot of us niggers killed.") But liberals wanted a broad bill, and in hearings before the House Judiciary Committee, New York's Kenneth Keating, an old ally of Brownell's, elicited from Brownell—probably by prearrangement— the fact that another section had been drafted, asked Brownell to send it over, and then amended the bill so that section was included.

AMONG MEN of good will at both ends of the Capitol there was not only determination but a new unity of purpose. Many Democratic House liberals, including Judiciary Committee Chairman Emanuel Celler of New York, had handed proposed civil rights bills up to the desk in the first days of the 1956 congressional session, but pride of authorship was to be subordinated to a cause. Since Republicans would be more inclined to support a Republican bill, giving it the bipartisan backing it would need for passage, key civil rights strategists Joe Rauh, Clarence Mitchell, Andrew Biemiller, and Richard Bolling, the young representative from Missouri who had become a Rayburn favorite, asked Celler to subordinate his bill to Brownell's—and Celler agreed, and agreed further to delay reporting *any* bill until Brownell's arrived. In the Senate, Paul Douglas helped draft a new civil rights bill, "a model bill," similar to Brownell's in "encompassing a whole battery" of provisions empowering the federal government to move against rights violations in many areas besides voting—"a dream bill from the civil rights movement's point of view," Joe Rauh was to call it. "A perfect bill."

At one end of the Capitol, liberal determination seemed likely to produce results. When, still early in the session, southern vote-counters began polling House members, the results surprised and disturbed them. Conservative Republicans who had stood shoulder to shoulder with them for years were standing there no longer. And neither, in their own party, were more than a few congressmen who had never been particularly liberal on civil rights: solid, dependable, "safe" men who in a crunch had also always come down on the side of the South, partly because of the power of the southern committee (and subcommittee) chairmen over these legislators' own bills, partly because they felt that their party could not afford to lose the South, that the Old Confederacy was the bedrock of Democratic strength. But the burgeoning northern Negro vote had injected into their calculations a new factor—which, the southerners realized with growing astonishment and dismay, was beginning to equal in weight, or to exceed, the old factors.

In the House, of course, the Speaker was a weighty factor in himself, and his reaction was surprising, too. When, after a Board of Education meeting one evening in January, Bolling walked Sam Rayburn upstairs to his office so that he could have a private word with him about civil rights, the brief (as always) discussion was, as was so often the case with Rayburn, not about strategy but about principle, the very simple principle that mattered to Rayburn. "He wanted to find out what was right and fair, and then do it." And to Bolling's surprise, ardent southerner though Rayburn was, with those pictures of Robert E. Lee on his wall, Rayburn felt it was *right,* that it was "only fair," that "black people have the right to vote." Interrupting the eloquent young congressman in full flight, the Speaker said: "I'm not against the right to vote. Every citizen should have that." Though he said no more, "I walked from his office in relief and delight," Bolling was to recall. "I was certain that . . . the Speaker would step in at the critical time in order to give the push that only he could effectively give." Recalling his discussions with Rauh and Biemiller and Mitchell during the early days of 1956, Bolling would say that "We didn't really care what was in the bill as long as there was *something* in it. We felt that as long as we could get the first bill passed, we could get others passed." And these men felt that now, at last, with representatives from both parties behind it, they *could* get a bill passed. "Rayburn was for it. We got the idea that at last we could pass a civil rights bill!" The Supreme Court had, of course, already proven itself a friend of civil rights. Now, in 1956, the executive branch had, however tentatively, at last entered the fight—and it appeared that the House would come along, too.

THAT LEFT ONLY THE SENATE. And its Majority Leader.

If one listened to Democratic liberals in the early days of January, 1956, one would have thought that in the Senate, too, the barriers were crumbling. "I am sick of seeing our party bullied and intimidated . . . in order to accommodate itself to Southern prejudices," one midwestern Democratic senator said. "If the Southern conservatives want to split off, I for one am for letting them do it. I believe it has got to happen sooner or later anyway, and 1956 might be as good a year for it as any." There were the usual liberal prognostications that this was the year that the Senate would pass a civil rights bill.

Hardly had the Senate convened, indeed, when Hennings of Missouri introduced four separate civil rights bills that were referred to the Judiciary Committee's Subcommittee on Constitutional Rights, which he chaired, and which quickly reported out the bills, with a favorable recommendation, to the full Judiciary Committee. The same subcommittee—and committee—would also handle Douglas' bill. Judiciary was one of the three Senate committees chaired by liberals. There was a good chance that under Harley Kilgore's gavel, the full committee would also report these bills out favorably, which would mean that while the South would still be able to kill them, it would not be able to kill them quietly but only after a highly public floor fight it was anxious to avoid.

In reality, however, the Senate was still the Senate. While some—*most*—of the political barriers blocking civil rights legislation were, in 1956, less solid than in the past, the walls of the South's citadel were higher and stronger than ever. On January 3, the first day of its 1956 session—in the very midst of the rosy civil rights prognostications—a meeting of liberal senators was held in Herbert Lehman's office. For a similar meeting in 1953, nineteen senators had shown up, and had decided to try to reform the cloture rule, an attempt that had mustered a total of a meagre twenty-one votes. Now, at the 1956 meeting, exactly twelve senators showed up—and in a discussion among the twelve it was concluded that a similar attempt at reforming cloture would not muster even twenty-one votes. Since the attempt would therefore reveal that they were even weaker than before, they decided not to make it.

And not long after the 1956 session began, the walls were made even higher—with Lyndon Johnson lending a helping hand.

On February 28, the sixty-three-year-old Kilgore died of a stroke, and the ranking Democratic member of the Judiciary Committee, the senator who would, under the seniority rule, succeed to Judiciary's chairmanship, was James O. Eastland of Mississippi.

Surely, said the ADA and the NAACP and the great liberal journals, surely the seniority system would not be allowed to prevail in *this* case. Judiciary (which was referred to as the "powerful Judiciary Committee" so often that its title sometimes seemed to have three words) had jurisdiction over all civil rights legislation. Making Eastland Judiciary's chairman would place at the committee's head the senator most outspokenly committed to killing all civil rights legislation, the senator who openly boasted that he had killed such legislation before when he had been only chairman of one of Judiciary's subcommittees ("I had special pockets put in my pants, and for three years I carried those bills around in my pockets . . ."). Judiciary, what's more, had jurisdiction over all legislation "relating to federal courts and judges." Elevating Eastland to Judiciary's chairmanship would place at the head of the committee in charge of the courts a senator who had openly advocated defiance of the highest court after its *Brown* ruling ("You are not required to obey any court which passed out such a ruling. In fact, you are obligated to defy it"), who had proposed a constitutional amendment to overturn the Supreme Court decisions that had helped "slimy, juicy" African-Americans. The chairmanship of the Senate Judiciary Committee, said *The New Republic,* "is the one seat of power in Washington where a dedicated opponent of civil rights can do his greatest damage." For Eastland to be given that seat "is unthinkable," the ADA said, joining the NAACP in telegrams appealing to Lyndon Johnson to see that Eastland was not given the post. "Maybe there is no easy substitute for seniority," the *New York Times* editorialized. "There is no substitute for wisdom, either. There is no substitute for faith in the American system of democracy. If something has to give way, it had better be seniority."

Which showed only that the ADA and the NAACP and the *Times* didn't fully grasp how the Senate felt about the seniority system—or what Lyndon Johnson's first priority was.

To all such appeals, the Leader replied that it was not he but the Democratic Steering Committee that made committee assignments, and that he was only one member of that committee, and as such had only limited influence. Eastland, however, was in later years to give him more credit than that. "I had Lyndon's support all the way," he was to recall. And, he said, Lyndon had also gone out of his way to spare him the embarrassment of a floor fight on his nomination, or even of a roll-call vote—which might have resulted in an unseemly high number of votes against him. "He [Lyndon] worked it out so that two fellows would make speeches against me, but would not ask for a roll call vote," Eastland was to say. On March 2, the Senate, following a unanimous recommendation of the Democratic Steering Committee—based, the committee said, on seniority—named Eastland to the chairmanship. It did so, on the motion of Majority Leader Johnson, in an unrecorded voice vote so that senators' views would not go on record; the voices of only a very few senators—journalists in the Press Gallery estimated no more than four or five—could be heard shouting *"No."* "A mad dog is loose in the streets of justice," the NAACP's Clarence Mitchell said. Since Jim Eastland was only fifty-one years old, he might be loose a long time.

34

Finesses

EVEN WHILE THE EASTLAND MATTER was being pushed through, another threat to Lyndon Johnson's hopes of winning the 1956 Democratic presidential nomination—another threat born out of the escalating civil rights conflict—was boiling up on Capitol Hill. Feeling itself under attack on a dozen fronts, the South now rallied its forces—with a rallying cry that came from its Capitol citadel.

Infuriated by the *Brown* ruling, southern senators had been working since the beginning of the year on a proclamation that would guide the region's future response to that ruling. "A Declaration of Constitutional Principles" was its formal title, but the press quickly coined a shorter name: the "Southern Manifesto." Drafted by South Carolina's Strom Thurmond, with assistance from Virginia's Harry Byrd, it had been edited by Richard Russell, and its more intemperate phrases had therefore been deleted and its arguments decked out in legalisms that seemed reasonable and logical—as long as one ignored the fact that it had been the Supreme Court, not Congress, that had, in *Plessy v. Ferguson,* interpreted the Fourteenth Amendment to mean that separate but equal facilities were perfectly legal, and that therefore the Supreme Court had the right to reinterpret the Amendment. The southern "Declaration" said that since "there has been no amendment [to the Constitution] or Act of Congress" to override the *Plessy* decision, the Warren Court had had no "legal basis for its action" in overriding it in *Brown*. In a "clear abuse of judicial power," the Manifesto declared, the Court had simply "substituted their personal and social ideas for the law of the land," encroaching on "the reserved rights of the states."

Some of the Manifesto's arguments demonstrated Russell's gift for cloaking injustice in words of reason. The separate but equal doctrine "is founded on elemental humanity and common sense, for parents should not be deprived by government of the right to direct the lives and education of their own children," it said. The *Brown* decision, it said, "is destroying the amicable relations between white and Negro races that had been created through ninety years of patient effort by the good people of both races. It has planted hatred and suspicion where there had been heretofore friendship and understanding." And the Manifesto called on the South to resist the *Brown* decision. Commending "those States which have declared the intention to resist forced integration by any lawful means," it said that "We pledge ourselves to use all lawful means to bring about a reversal of this decision which is contrary to the Constitution and to prevent the use of force in its implementation." Its signatories were nineteen senators and eighty-one representatives from the eleven states of the Old Confederacy, and it was read in full on the Senate floor on March 11—just nine days after the shouted "ayes" that had put Eastland in Judiciary's chair—by the South's greatest orator (in the House it was simply inserted in the record). And it made headlines across the nation—as it should have, for the Southern Manifesto was nothing less than an outright call by one hundred elected legislators in the national government for massive, unified, defiance of an order from the nation's highest court. Hardly had Walter George's organ-like tones stopped rolling across a hushed and solemn Senate when Wayne Morse rose to his feet. "One would think that Calhoun was walking across the floor of the Senate today," he said.

THE SOUTHERN MANIFESTO and Herbert Brownell's civil rights bill menaced—from opposite sides—Lyndon Johnson's master plan. Manifesto and bill both threatened to add kindling to the civil rights issue on Capitol Hill. Johnson's strategy for winning his party's presidential nomination—to hold his southern support while antagonizing northern liberals as little as possible, or at least not antagonizing them any more than he already had—was feasible only if the issue did not blaze up on the Hill, since if it did, he would have to take his position prominently on the southern side. For his strategy to work, the civil rights issue had to be tamped down in Congress, his involvement with it minimized.

And it was. Nineteen of the twenty-two southern senators signed the "Declaration of Constitutional Principles." The three who didn't were the two senators from Tennessee, both of whom had national political aspirations in 1956—Estes Kefauver for President and Albert Gore for Vice President (and Tennessee, of course, was the only southern state in which Negro voters had become a political force to be reckoned with)—and Lyndon Johnson. His explanation for not signing, however, was different from that given by the two Tennesseans. They declared that they hadn't signed the Manifesto because they didn't agree with it, Gore calling it "a dangerous, deceptive propaganda move which encouraged southerners to defy the government and to disobey its laws." Johnson declared that he hadn't signed it because he hadn't been asked to sign it—that, in fact, he had never even *seen* it, that, as William S. White wrote, "he had not been shown the document because" the Southern Caucus "did not want to appear to be trying to 'formulate Democratic or Senate policy.' "

Johnson's statement that he had never seen the Manifesto may have been disingenuous, since he had been present during at least one Southern Caucus—on February 8, in Walter George's office—when the Manifesto was being revised sentence by sentence. And his explanation was to evolve over time, his portrayal of himself—to journalists and to some of the more friendly liberal senators—to become increasingly heroic. The southerners had not asked him to sign, he said, because they knew he wouldn't, as a matter of principle. It evolved further—into an implication that he had *refused* to sign despite intense southern pressure. "You liberals—you have all got your big heroes," Johnson told Hubert Humphrey. "I want you to notice who signed and who didn't. Now all your bomb-throwers over there think I am the worst thing that came down here. . . . But I didn't [sign]."

His explanations were accepted uncritically by those journalists he could count on to be uncritical. His refusal to sign, White was later to write in his biography of Johnson, "was, indeed, an act of courage," although "it was other things as well. [Johnson] believed his responsibilities as leader of *all* the Senate Democrats would have prohibited him from adopting the sectional view of the Manifesto, even if he had not considered it wrong in principle." They were accepted by some liberal senators: Richard Neuberger took the floor of the Senate to call Johnson's refusal to sign "one of the most courageous acts of political valor I have seen take place in my adult life."

Actually, however, it was easy for him to avoid signing the Manifesto because of what Richard Russell wanted for him—and had persuaded the Southern Caucus to want for him. By this time, George Reedy says, "Russell was very determined to elect Johnson President of the United States." And, Reedy says, "There was no question whatsoever that anybody that signed" such an inflammatory, anti–civil rights document "could never become President of the United States." As Russell's biographer, Gilbert C. Fite, wrote, "Russell was much more interested in pushing Johnson for President, which he was then doing, than in having another name on the Manifesto."

By 1956, of course, the other southern senators understood the importance of Russell's plan, and, except for two or three of them, agreed with it. Since it was recognized that "he had to work with all sides" in the Senate, John Stennis says, "it wasn't held against him by the southerners, I'll put it that way, that he didn't sign it." Carried away by his eloquence, Johnson had gone too far, however. Growing worried that his statements might raise doubts among southern senators about his true feelings, he issued other statements—designed to reassure them that while his hand may not have written his name under theirs, his heart was with them. One of his statements dovetailed with the Manifesto's argument that the *Brown* decision had usurped the sacred constitutional rights of the individual states. "In my opinion, the solution of the problem cannot be found on the federal level, for it involves basic values reflected in the sovereignty of our States," Lyndon Johnson said. "It's my hope that wise leaders on the local levels will work to resolve these differences." A reporter who asked him to clarify that statement wrote that "He [Johnson] believed the integration problem was one best left to individual states to handle." And indeed, on the very day, March 12, 1956, on which the front page of the *New York Times* reported the issuance of the Southern Manifesto, there was, also on the front page, another article, which provides more than a hint that Johnson's non-signing of the Manifesto had caused no strain between him and the other southern senators—that it had actually been a strategic maneuver arranged among them. "A JOHNSON BOOM STARTS IN SOUTH," the headline on this article stated, and the article quoted several southern senators as supporting Johnson's possible candidacy for the Democratic nomination—and among the southerners quoted were the Manifesto's two principal architects, Strom Thurmond, the former presidential candidate of the States Rights Party, who said Johnson would be an "attractive candidate," and the South's general, Richard Russell, who said that if Johnson decided to make the race, "I will support him one hundred per cent." In a later statement, Russell said, "There is no question in my mind that Johnson is the best qualified man and more sympathetic with the Southern point of view on civil rights than any other candidate."

The percentage Russell named turned out to be a popular one among Johnson's southern senatorial colleagues—Louisiana's Ellender, for example, said that if he ran, "I'd be one hundred per cent for Johnson"—except when that figure was not large enough to fully express their enthusiasm for his candidacy: "I'm for him not one hundred percent but one thousand per cent," Florida's Smathers said. Within weeks, almost every signer of the Southern Manifesto had endorsed the colleague who didn't sign.*

FINESSING THE SOUTHERN MANIFESTO was easy for Lyndon Johnson, and so was the finessing of Hennings' four civil rights bills, now that Eastland was chairman of the committee under whose jurisdiction they fell. No sooner had Eastland taken Judiciary's gavel than he made clear that in his view filibusters need not be confined to the Senate floor; they could be staged in his committee as well—with one difference: while ending a filibuster on the floor was difficult, in his committee it was impossible. A committee that has no written rules is governed by the general Senate rules, he explained, and "the Senate rules provide that a cloture petition must be signed by sixteen senators." Judiciary,

---

*Johnson loyalists would also argue that Johnson's non-signing was an act of political courage because of the political risk it put him under in Texas, but a better idea of the sentiment in Texas is the fact that of Texas' twenty-one congressmen, seventeen (including Sam Rayburn) did not sign. The other Texas senator, Price Daniel, did sign.

he pointed out, had only fifteen members. "There wasn't any way anyone could file a cloture petition" in the committee. "So we had unlimited debate." A committee member could speak on any subject as long as he wished—and once he began speaking, there was no way on earth to stop him. When Hennings raised his hand to make a motion to bring up one of his civil rights bills for consideration by the committee, the senator sitting next to him, South Carolina's Olin Johnston, quickly raised his, and it was Johnston whom Eastland recognized. "Olin the Solon" asked for permission to read a legal brief that dealt with some other—non–civil rights—matter. The brief was a lengthy one, and Olin was a notoriously deliberate reader. And the committee met—once a week—for only ninety minutes. It was to take Johnston five committee sessions to finish reading the brief. During those five weeks, Hennings or some other liberal member of the committee would sometimes raise a hand and try to make a motion to schedule meetings more frequently, but Eastland would explain that the Senator from South Carolina was speaking, and a senator could not be interrupted. An interruption could be accomplished only by the filing within the committee of a cloture petition, he explained—and he was sorry to have to remind the committee that there were not enough members on it for a petition to be filed. A committee member could, of course, make a motion to establish a rule to permit the filing of a cloture petition with less than sixteen signatures. But of course that motion would be subject to Senate rules—which meant that debate on it would be unlimited. "Stepin Fetchit, in his prime, had nothing on the slow-motion paces through which Eastland is dragging the Senate Judiciary Committee," Louis Lautier of the *Baltimore Afro-American* wrote.

The Brownell Bill now before the House Judiciary Committee was a very different story. Dodging the Manifesto had been easy for Johnson; it was only a symbol, a rallying cry. The bill was substance, hard substance. Broad in scope and skillfully drawn, its passage would revolutionize the treatment of Negroes in America. It had to be stopped.

It had to be stopped, furthermore, before it reached the Senate floor. The South could feel confident that it could stop any civil rights bill on the floor by filibustering, but for Johnson, the South's use of that tactic, guaranteed to antagonize northern liberals, would be damaging. Imbued as it was with drama, the tactic invariably turned a national spotlight on the Senate, and on the Senate's Majority Leader, and liberals would be reminded of Johnson's previous efforts to preserve Rule 22 and thereby preserve the filibuster and thwart civil rights. Johnson could not afford a floor fight of any type, in fact: any public battle would turn that spotlight on the Senate stage—and reveal him standing with the South.

The bill had to be stopped, in fact, before it reached the Senate Calendar, the place from which it could be sent to the floor. Once it was on the Calendar, any liberal senator could then make a motion to bring it off the Calendar to the floor. The southerners would then have three options: to move to table that motion, to defeat the bill outright, or to filibuster it. But in the heated civil rights atmosphere of 1956, any of these options would precipitate an attention-getting floor fight. Once a senator moved to "proceed" to the "consideration" of a House-passed civil rights bill, there was no way, really, to keep the measure from receiving the attention that Johnson didn't want it to have. The very arrival of the House civil rights bill on the Senate Calendar would deal a body blow to his presidential ambitions. And unlike bills introduced by senators—Hennings' bills, for example—a bill that had originated in, and been passed by, the House could not be kept from the Calendar simply by referring it *pro forma* to a committee. Senate rules allowed a House-passed bill to be referred to a committee only by unanimous consent; a single liberal objection would send H.R. 627 not to Judiciary but directly to the Calendar. It had to be kept from getting there.

And it was—because Johnson had Rayburn on his side, and because the Senate was still the Senate.

Eisenhower's insistence on getting input from all Cabinet members delayed the arrival of Brownell's bill at the House of Representatives until April 9, late in a congressional session for a controversial measure to arrive on the Hill. Emanuel Celler's selfless willingness to subordinate his bill to the Brownell version allowed the combined measure, H.R. 627, to be reported out of Celler's Judiciary Committee quickly—on April 25—but scheduling the measure for floor action was the province of the House Rules Committee, a conservative bastion headed by Representative Howard Smith of Virginia. And the bill would only be scheduled for early action if a strong effort was made to push it through—and although Rayburn had let Bolling know he was sympathetic to at least some of the bill's aims, the Speaker did not give it such a push.

Asked years later for an explanation of Rayburn's procrastination, Bolling said it involved the hopes he and other liberals had for civil rights legislation and Rayburn's hopes for a Democratic victory in November—and Johnson's hopes for the presidency.

Bolling—Rayburn's young protégé and "point man" on civil rights—was getting a close-up view of Lyndon Johnson at the Board of Education and at several dinners in a private dining room at Martin's at which he was the only person present with Mr. Sam and Lyndon. And, observing Johnson behind closed doors, he was struck by the depth of Johnson's affection for the Speaker ("I had seen him kiss Rayburn on the head many times, of course, but the first time I saw him do that and say, 'How are you tonight, my beloved?' I just couldn't believe it," Bolling says); by the nakedness of Johnson's desire for the Democratic nomination ("He was just desperate for it, he was slavering for it," he says); and by the extent to which Johnson felt his chances for the nomination depended on H.R. 627 not reaching the Senate in 1956. "He [Johnson] would say he'd be 'destroyed' if it got there—that was his word: 'destroyed.' " In addition, watching Johnson evening after evening behind closed doors, the young liberal got an impression of Johnson's attitude on civil rights. "Johnson said he didn't want to face it [a civil rights bill] in 1956," Bolling says. "He didn't want to confront it. And more. He said he didn't *want* it. I began to have a very funny feeling about Johnson. The more I saw of him, the more suspicious I got. [He was] really quite negative on civil rights." Whatever his reasons, Bolling says, Johnson was "just desperate" for H.R. 627 to be delayed in the House long enough so that the Senate would not have to take it up in 1956. "He didn't want it pushed in the House."

Rayburn, Bolling says, went along with Johnson's wishes. He did so partly because those wishes made political sense. With the congressional session already so far advanced, no matter how hard the bill was pushed through the Rules Committee and the full House, it couldn't possibly be passed by the House in time for there to be any chance of Senate passage. The only result of a Senate floor fight would be to spotlight to the electorate, on the very eve of the Democratic National Convention, the party's deep divisions—and the fact that the committee chairman who was keeping the bill bottled up was a Democrat. There was no point in rushing. Partly, Bolling says, Rayburn was responding with his usual paternal sympathy to Johnson's desperation. While the Speaker knew that Adlai Stevenson had the nomination sewn up and that Johnson had no chance to get it, "Lyndon was asking him for help, and he loved Lyndon, and he didn't want to hurt him."

"To my shame," Bolling admits, he, too, went along and did not try to persuade the Speaker to push the bill. For a civil rights bill to pass the Senate, Johnson's support was essential, he felt; without it there was not even a remote possibility of breaking a southern filibuster. "It was what Lyndon wanted to do that counted over there." There was no chance that Johnson would give a civil rights bill his support in 1956—and therefore there was no point in trying to rush the bill through the House that year; there would be a better chance for the bill to pass the following year, when it might be possible to get it over to the Senate earlier in the session. So, Bolling says, "I didn't press in the Rules Committee, and since I was known as Mr. Rayburn's man on the Rules Committee, and it was generally understood that I was speaking for [him], since I didn't press, no one pressed." It was not until some weeks after Judiciary reported out the bill that Rayburn threw his weight behind it, summoning Rules Committee members to his office. When he did that, Rules Committee Chairman Smith said, "The jig's up. I know it." But, because of Rayburn's delay, H.R. 627 was not reported out by Rules until June 27, and debate on the measure did not begin until July 16. Trying to catch the liberals unprepared, southerners suddenly called for a vote at an unexpected moment on July 23. But "Speaker Rayburn senses the mood of the House better than any living man"; stepping down from the dais, he caught Bolling in the corridor. "You'd better get your boys in here," he said. Bolling started to reply with a joke, but then he saw Rayburn's face. "I started running," he says—"just as fast as I could run." As the members Bolling rounded up came pouring into the Chamber, the House's overwhelming sentiment, out of conscience or calculation or both, for civil rights legislation became clear: the vote by which the bill passed was 279 to 126. July 23 was the Tuesday of the last week that Congress would be in session, however, so that there was obviously no time for it to be passed by the Senate, and Johnson expected no objections to sending it to Judiciary. He had not wanted to confront it in 1956—and, it seemed, he would not have to.

SMOOTHLY THOUGH THE GEARS of Johnson's strategy were running, however, a bit of sand was now to be thrown into them—by the men who were always trying to throw sand into his gears: the "red-hots" and "crazies" he despised, the little group of Senate liberals.

Under the procedure customary at the time, after a bill was passed by the House of Representatives it would be "engrossed"—typed, with any amendments inserted, in the precise form in which it had been passed—in the office of the House Enrolling Clerk, and then printed, by the nearby Government Printing Office; the printed copy would then be brought to the House dais and signed by the Clerk of the House, Ralph R. Roberts, as a guarantee that the copy was correct. Then, one of the "Reading Clerks" at the dais would carry it by hand to the Senate, walking the length of that long corridor that runs between the two Chambers. Opening the swinging doors at the rear of the Senate Chamber, he would wait until one of the Senate clerks on the dais noticed him and walked up the center aisle to stand beside him. When the presiding officer nodded to the Senate clerk to give him permission to speak, he would announce: "Mr. President, a message from the House." Then, making an "obeisance"—a deep bow—to the presiding officer, the House clerk would say: "Mr. President, I am directed by the House to deliver to the Senate H.R. 627, a Bill to provide means of further securing and protecting the civil rights of persons within the jurisdiction of the United States, in which the concurrence of the Senate is requested." Handing the bill to the Senate clerk, he would bow again, and leave. The Senate clerk would bring the bill to the dais, the presiding officer would enact the customary *pro forma* ritual, asking for unanimous consent to have the bill read a first and second time and referred to the "appropriate committee," in this case Judiciary. July 23 was a Tuesday; the Senate was planning to adjourn for the year by Saturday of that week; Judiciary met on Mondays—there wouldn't be another meeting of Judiciary at which the bill could be brought up (not that Eastland would allow it to be brought up anyway). The civil rights bill would be dead on arrival at the committee—quietly dead: no debate, no floor fight, no spotlight on Lyndon Johnson's position on civil rights.

A handful of Senate liberals, notably Paul Douglas, Herbert Lehman and Tom Hennings, were, however, determined, that, in the case of this bill, that would not happen—that the bill would not be buried in Judiciary but brought to the floor. They had decided to try to accomplish this by refusing to give the unanimous consent required in the presiding officer's ritual; when he asked if there were any objections, one of them, probably Douglas, would object. The bill would therefore not be referred to a committee, but instead, as a House-passed measure, would be placed directly on the Senate Calendar.

Other senators could try to stop Douglas from objecting by demanding the floor themselves so he couldn't be recognized; Johnson could use the Leader's first recognition prerogative for the same purpose. But this tactic would work only briefly, not for the four days remaining in the session: for a senator not to be recognized for four days would be virtually, if not totally, unprecedented. "I don't know of any instance in history where that has happened," says the Senate historian Richard A. Baker. "Not recognizing only works for a limited time. Eventually anyone who wants to speak will be recognized. Every other senator knows it could be him someday."

These liberals were fully aware of the arguments against the maneuver they were planning: that, in Douglas' own words, "The session was nearing its end," that there was therefore no possibility of passing the bill, that their fight was a hopeless gesture foredoomed to failure. They understood that, as he would later write, "the Democratic Party would [be] revealed as badly divided on the eve of the national convention," that African-American voters would be reminded that Eastland and other southern committee chairmen were Democrats, that the maneuver would rouse journalists to ridicule and the party's hierarchy—including the party's powerful and vengeful Senate Leader—to fury. But Paul Douglas believed in the Senate's "informing function," believed, as he was also to write, that "even if every battle was unsuccessful, constant but peaceful struggle would hasten the ultimate coming of needed reforms." He believed that justice would prevail if only men would not stop fighting for justice. He and Lehman and other liberal senators believed also that there was an informing function not only of the Senate but *about* the Senate—"that the southerners' power had to function behind the scenes" to be effective, that turning "the searchlight on" that power would eventually erode it—and that there was no better time to turn on the searchlight than a national election year. He felt keenly, as well, that while a lot of public sentiment had been mobilized that year for civil rights, not nearly as much had been mobilized as *could* be mobilized—that while the leaders of the liberal battalions, the officers of labor unions and Jewish organizations and big church groups, were strong for civil rights, the battalions themselves had not been mobilized, their members had not been sufficiently educated; that the support for civil rights, while vocal, was still not the mass movement that was needed—and that there was no better instrument for education and mobilization than a Senate debate. And besides, these liberals felt, why did the session have to be nearing its end anyway? Why couldn't the Senate adjourn instead while the conventions were being held, and then return to work in the Fall? Even Reedy, in his memoir, was to write, in a statement that conflicts rather strongly with the memos he was writing to Johnson in 1956, that while "the prospect of any legislative action [still] seemed more remote than a landing on the moon," and "their [the liberals'] only power was to make noise," nonetheless "it was an uncomfortable noise that grated upon the ears, and, in time, the national conscience. . . ."

Moreover, Douglas and Lehman and their colleagues felt that even if their fight on behalf of black Americans was only a gesture, didn't those women in Montgomery who for months had been trudging long miles every day—who were still trudging that July—didn't those women deserve a gesture? Might not a gesture be meaningful to Emmett Till's mother, to Autherine Lucy, to the millions of black citizens whose children were still not being allowed to attend school with white children—despite an order from the country's highest court more than a year before? Surely they deserved a gesture, *needed* a gesture—a gesture from Capitol Hill, a sign that someone there was making a fight, futile though it might be, on their behalf? Douglas and Lehman had no doubts about the answer to that question. One of Lehman's aides, William Welsh, who loved the old man, tried to dissuade him from making the hopeless fight that year. He might find that only a very few senators were willing to make it with him, Welsh warned. What if it was only a *very* few? Welsh asked. "Even if it's only me, I'll make it," Lehman said.

And there was, to these liberals, yet another consideration. America's black citizens needed to feel that they had a political party; the Democratic Party must stand for their rights, must not supinely surrender to its southern wing. "Paul felt that in a way he was fighting for the soul of the Democratic Party," says Douglas' aide Frank McCulloch. And that fight had implications beyond the party. What would be the reaction of black Americans if they came to feel that even in that party no one was lifting a finger in their behalf, that there was no hope for them within the system? Wouldn't they begin to think more seriously about redressing their wrongs by means outside the system, even by desperate means: by civil unrest, by riots? Paul Douglas was not the only liberal who felt that, as he said, "If we don't fight, someday there will be a revolution."

And finally, to the arguments against what they were planning, there was a further answer that was rooted in the very pragmatism that Johnson and the Democratic Party hierarchy cherished. For, these liberals felt, the party's tough old pols might be wrong in their belief that making this hopeless fight would be disastrous in a presidential election year. They might be very wrong. After all, in 1948, one of their number, a young mayor from Minneapolis, had told the party that it must "get out of the shadow of states' rights" and into the "sunshine of human rights," and had inspired its national convention to defy the South and all it stood for. The result of that defiance had been a southern walkout and a States Rights party—but, for Harry Truman, the result had been victory, a victory in which a crucial factor was much larger than usual pluralities in liberal precincts, pluralities given him in part *because* the Democrats had not surrendered to the South but had, by letting the South leave the party, saved its soul.

Wary of Johnson, the handful of Senate liberals devised a strategy that they felt would ensure against the Leader sneaking the bill past them and into Judiciary. Instead of waiting for H.R. 627 to arrive in the Senate, Paul Douglas would, upon its passage by the House, go immediately to the House Chamber and wait for the bill to be engrossed and then printed by the Government Printing Office, even if that took several hours. He wouldn't leave the House Chamber until the printed document had been brought to the Speaker's dais, and then he would accompany the clerk who carried it to the Senate, so that the liberals would know its exact whereabouts at all times. And as a further safeguard, from the moment Douglas left for the House, another liberal would be stationed on the Senate floor at all times, just in case the bill was somehow sneaked past Douglas, so that if it arrived in the Senate, and the Senate's presiding officer asked if there were any objections to referring it to Judiciary, there would indeed be an objection. But Johnson, with Rayburn's help, was able to keep the gears running smoothly. Notified that the House had passed the bill, he put in the presiding officer's chair Lister Hill, not because the Alabaman was an astute parliamentarian—although he was—but because he possessed another qualification more important for the task Johnson had in mind for him: while most of the southern senators talked in a deliberate drawl, Hill didn't; he was the southerners' fastest talker. And Johnson told Hill not to leave the chair until H.R. 627 arrived—which Johnson knew was not going to take very long. Normally, the engrossing and printing of a House bill took several hours; in the case of H.R. 627, that routine was speeded up—radically. In a seldom-used procedure known as "hand engrossing," the marked-up bill was rushed from the dais down to the House Enrolling Clerk's office on the Capitol's Ground Floor, the floor beneath the Principal Floor on which the House and Senate Chambers are located, and there it was quickly retyped, in clean form. And then its route was changed. Instead of being sent to the Government Printing Office, as was usual, or back to the House dais for signing, the retyped bill was carried directly to the Senate, not from the House but from that Ground Floor office.

The Enrolling Office was not in the House wing but in the Capitol's central portion, so when Joe Bartlett, the House clerk carrying H.R. 627, ran up the nearest staircase to the Principal Floor, he was already near the Rotunda, almost halfway to the Senate wing. Douglas may already have passed that point on his way to the House, or perhaps he simply passed Bartlett without being aware of who he was—or what he was carrying. Whatever the explanation, however, the bill, on its way to the Senate, somehow passed Douglas as he was heading for the House to ascertain its whereabouts. Arriving in the House, Douglas began asking clerks on the dais when H.R. 627 would be sent to the Senate—but H.R. 627 was already in the Senate.

Douglas had stationed Lehman as the liberal sentry back on the Senate floor, but Lehman naturally felt he had time to spare before the House bill could possibly arrive, and "allowed himself," as one account puts it, "to be briefly decoyed off the floor"—no one now remembers how. He was therefore not in the Chamber when Bartlett walked in, to be greeted by the Senate employee Johnson had stationed at the door to meet him: Bobby Baker. Mike Mansfield was delivering a speech on foreign relations, but Baker quickly nodded to Hill, Hill quickly asked Mansfield to yield, and as soon as the bill was delivered to the dais, the Southern Caucus's fastest talker read, very fast, the bill's title, then said, very fast, "Without objection, the bill will be read the second time and referred to the appropriate committee. The Chair hears no objection," and referred it to Judiciary.

Someone on the House dais finally informed Douglas that the bill had already been sent to the Senate. Rushing back along the corridor, banging into tourists, he burst into the Chamber, where Mansfield was speaking again. When Hill saw him, Douglas was to recall, "a half-suppressed smile swept over his face. Then I knew the worst." When he went up to the dais, Hill told him the bill had already had its first and second readings, and had been referred to Judiciary. "Paul, my dear boy, we move in accordance with the time-honored rules and procedure of the Senate," Hill said. Douglas noticed that "the Southern parliamentarian and the clerk looked up with the air of grave and impassive disapproval they always presented to civil-rights liberals," that impassivity which so imperfectly masked the fact that, as the liberals were aware, they were being laughed at.

THE LIBERALS were to make one last effort to bring civil rights to the Senate floor in 1956. Noting that not one of the year's other fourteen civil rights bills had been reported out by the Judiciary Committee, Douglas introduced a motion—actually a petition—to discharge the committee from further consideration of the fifteenth, H.R. 627, a petition that would, the liberals believed, trigger a discussion on the issue.

Leading Democratic pols—the practical politicians—were furious. "As you know, I am an old civil rights man myself," Jim Rowe wrote Johnson. "However, on this one you are so clearly right that I myself should like to shoot Douglas." They needn't have worried, however. Once again, Johnson outmaneuvered the crazies—with a tactic given him by Russell. When they learned what Douglas was about to do, there was a huddle at Russell's desk, with Russell, Johnson, and Walter George whispering and planning, hard and fast. And then Johnson put George in the chair, because what was needed now on the dais was not fast-talking but the figure who best embodied the full dignity and authority of the Senate rules. When Douglas, standing at his desk, made his motion, George told him it was out of order, reminding him that petitions could be filed only during the morning hour, except, of course, by unanimous consent. When Douglas asked for such consent, Russell said curtly, "I object." Douglas thereupon announced that he would file his petition during the morning hour the next day, Wednesday, July 24, but Johnson had a surprise for him. As the Senate was concluding its work on Tuesday evening, instead of making his customary motion that the Senate adjourn until the next day, Johnson moved instead that it *recess* until the next day.

None of the liberal senators or their staff members appear to have realized the significance of the word Johnson used, but they were to learn it the next morning, when Douglas made his motion. Walter George, back on the dais, told him it was out of order because petitions could be filed only during the morning hour. Douglas said this *was* the morning hour. George recognized the Majority Leader. While the southerners and many Republicans, in the words of one reporter, "sat there grinning like so many happy owls," Johnson said that of course it wasn't: the "morning hour," Johnson reminded Douglas, was the first hour of each new legislative day. A legislative day begins after each adjournment, not after a recess, so there would be no morning hour until the Senate adjourned, except, of course by unanimous consent. Douglas asked for such consent. Russell said, "I object."

"So we are stopped from even considering a bill that has already been passed by the House," Senator Lehman said. Not at all, Lyndon Johnson said, with an expression of great earnestness on his face. It was only that civil rights always engendered a long discussion, and a long discussion in the very last days of a session would keep the Senate from considering other legislation, and there was important other legislation to consider, such as the foreign aid bill and a bill to raise executive department salaries which President Eisenhower said was indispensable. It was clear to the liberals that Johnson intended to prolong the current legislative "day" until the session ended.

Douglas made a motion that the Senate adjourn for five minutes so that a new day could begin, but Johnson was ready for that, too. It was the party leadership, not individual senators, who had the right to adjourn the Senate, he said. "There will not be an adjournment based on what one senator says or two senators say!" he shouted. And when the Majority Leader finished, the Minority Leader took the floor to support him. Johnson had told Knowland that if a discussion on civil rights began, the bills considered indispensable by the President—*his* President—would never pass before adjournment. And he had also persuaded Knowland that Douglas, by moving to adjourn the Senate, was usurping the prerogative of party leaders—not only the Democratic Leader but the Republican Leader—and was deliberately insulting them. "It is only kidding the minority groups and the American people" to propose a bill in the last days of a session "which everyone knows as a practical matter cannot be accomplished," Knowland said.

If the southerners were laughing at the liberals, so was the Washington press corps—for the liberals' failure to grasp the implications of the "recess" move. "Let us consider a couple of idealists [Douglas and Lehman], who were so busy thinking good thoughts that they forgot to do their homework on such mundane matters as senatorial procedure. . . . The two students . . . failed their study course in Senate rules," Frederick Othman wrote. There was little discussion in the press about the civil rights issue—from some articles the reader would hardly know there *was* an issue. Journalistic analysis concentrated on the "recess" maneuver, on tactics rather than substance. And the analysis seemed always to accept as a given the Johnson-Knowland argument that bringing up civil rights legislation in the last days of the session would result in the death of other needed legislation; the author has been unable to find a single article pointing out that that possibility could have been avoided by simply changing the session's closing date.

Once Johnson and Knowland had made the discharge petition a "leadership matter," with all the implications of that phrase, it would have taken a foolhardy senator, Democratic or Republican, to support Douglas. His motion to briefly adjourn the Senate was beaten, and he knew it. More important to him, the cause of civil rights was beaten again. Standing at his desk, the picture of defeat, his white head bowed, his blue seersucker suit, which he had worn for two days, rumpled with wear, he said, "I say this with great sadness. The Senate has a very heavy burden on its conscience." Because of the Senate rules, moreover, he could see no hope of the cause winning—ever. "We know as men," he said to his colleagues, in a low, sad voice, "that the rules . . . have been skillfully devised to prevent any action on civil rights which is obnoxious to members from the South. I think it is now clear that it will be impossible under the rules . . . with the present temper of the Southern senators . . . and of the leadership on both sides . . . ever to bring a civil rights measure to a vote in this body." And when Douglas finished, Richard Russell rose to tell him that the rules would not be changed—ever. Russell stood erect, his head tilted back with his nose in the air, his well-tailored suit newly pressed, his white shirt starched, the embodiment of victory ("I can still see him standing there, so calm, just gloating," Frank McCulloch, the mildest-spoken of men, would say years later, hatred in his voice). "All men differ on [this] proposed legislation," Russell said. "Some may believe it is good and salutary. Others . . . believe it is largely political in its inspiration . . . totally and completely in violation of . . . the Constitution, destructive of the rights of the states." Whenever "such nefarious schemes are presented in the future," Russell promised, "there will be members of the Senate who will . . . resort to every weapon at their command to prevent their being imposed upon the people of this country."

LYNDON JOHNSON'S TACTICS to this point can be explained by the imperatives of his presidential strategy: his need to keep civil rights legislation bottled up with as little publicity as possible. Now, however, he made a motion for which strategy alone is not an adequate explanation. Calling for a vote on Douglas' adjournment motion, Walter George, still in the chair, started to ask for a voice vote, which would have been a chorus of a few ayes and many nays, decisive but mercifully brief. Then, however, right in front of him, Johnson stood up at his desk. And when George recognized him, Johnson asked for a roll-call vote.

"This was the dirtiest trick Johnson ever played," Joe Rauh would say forty years later. "It was just Johnson putting his foot on Douglas' face." "It was an effort to humiliate," Frank McCulloch says. "That was its only purpose. A quick voice vote would have defeated it [the motion]. Douglas had made it knowing he was going to lose."

The effort succeeded in its purpose. For a while, Douglas stood at his desk, and then he sat down, as, one by one, his colleagues, the men he had to work with every day, voted against him—almost every one of them. Even men he had thought he could count on did not stand by him in the face of Lyndon Johnson's power. Wayne Morse did not stand by him, or Estes Kefauver, or Richard Neuberger, or Clifford Case, or Pat McNamara or Thomas Kuchel. "Even my friend and ally Humphrey voted 'No,' " Douglas was to say. In the end, only five senators voted for his motion: two members of his own party, Herbert Lehman and Tom Hennings, and three Republicans: Langer, George Bender and Irving Ives. Seventy-six senators voted against him.

Years later, Paul Douglas would remember that after that 76–6 vote, "I tried to walk out of the Chamber with my head high." Muriel Humphrey, who knew she had just seen a man crushed before her eyes, was standing outside the door; Douglas would never forget the "concerned look in her eyes." He paused for a moment to kiss her cheek. Walking on, he came to the elevators, and stood there for a moment—the hero who had charged up a beach when he was too old to charge up a beach, the brilliant economist who had dared to rally economists behind the New Deal—stood there in a kind of daze. By this time, his young assistant Howard Shuman had come running after him, and after a moment, Douglas spoke to him, bitterness in his voice. "Push the button three times," he said. "Let's pretend I'm a senator." When he reached his suite, he went into his inner office, shut the door behind him, and cried, cried "for the first time in years," he was to recall—cried less for himself than for his cause, the great cause, and for the strategic mistakes he felt he had made in fighting for it. "How many senators really care about civil rights? I asked myself. How could we ever reverse the tide? And what an imperfect and erring instrument I was to fail in so crucial a moment."

THE SENATE HAD WON AGAIN. The citadel of the South, the dam against which so many liberal tides had broken in vain, was still standing, as impenetrable as ever. And it was standing thanks in substantial part to its Majority Leader. For years, the South had had a formidable general in Richard Russell. In 1956, as in 1955 and 1954 and 1953, it had had another formidable general in Lyndon Johnson. Lyndon "organized the Southern Democrats against civil rights this year so successfully that it was crushed," Willis Robertson of Virginia wrote a friend.

Johnson's maneuver had paid off not only for the South but for himself. As the *New York Times* reported: "With a series of parliamentary delaying tactics he blocked attempts by Northern liberal Democrats such as Paul H. Douglas of Illinois and Herbert H. Lehman of New York to bring up the bill. He thus retained the friendship of the Southern group, which is expected to give him the . . . convention influence that he desires." As for the northern liberals, those who had followed the fight closely were infuriated with Johnson's tactics. In a formal statement, ADA National Chairman Joseph Rauh said: "He has brought the Democratic Party to its lowest point in twenty-five years." But thanks to Johnson's legislative skills, there hadn't been enough of a fight to capture public attention on a larger scale, so his relationship with the party's liberals in general was no worse than it had been before. Despite the dangers inherent in the Southern Manifesto and H.R. 627, he had kept civil rights from damaging his chances for reaching the presidency.

35

Convention

ANOTHER KEY PART of his strategy for winning the Democratic presidential nomination was also in place: he was not only the chairman of the Texas delegation to the party's national convention, but the state's favorite-son candidate; its fifty-six votes at the convention would be his until he released them.

The ultimatum to Stevenson with which he had hoped to trap him—that Adlai prove his vote-getting ability by entering primaries—had backfired, however. Adlai had indeed entered the primaries—and had won almost all of them. As Democrats headed for Chicago on the weekend before the convention's opening on Monday, August 13, various estimates gave him between 400 and 600 of the 687½ votes needed for nomination. Estes Kefauver had 202, and the third announced candidate, Governor Averell Harriman of New York, trailed far behind. Seven states besides Texas were supporting "favorite son" candidates—a switch of only one or two of the big delegations would give Stevenson victory, and two (Michigan and Ohio) were poised to switch; the *New York Times* reported that "The professional prognosis was that the last ballot might come early"; Stevenson himself was so confident that he was writing his acceptance speech.

One aspect of Lyndon Johnson's strategy had been sound. The wisdom of his decision to pose as merely a favorite-son candidate to avoid mobilizing Democratic liberals against him had been vividly demonstrated by liberal alarm at every journalistic suggestion that he might become a serious contender. Despite the last-minute passage of the Social Security bill, liberal antipathy to Johnson was as strong as ever—stronger, in fact: 1956 had, after all, been the year of the natural gas fight and the exemption of highway workers from the David-Bacon Act, and new revelations about Johnson's relationship with Brown & Root. Under a headline that was an echo from the turn of the century—"THE IRRESPONSIBILITY OF THE SENATE"—the *St. Louis Post-Dispatch* ran a long article by the liberal journalist William V. Shannon filled

with phrases that recalled that gilded and corrupt age: under Johnson's leadership, Shannon wrote, the Senate "has had a rising curve of power and a declining arc of moral prestige. . . . Several forces conspire to intensify the rigidity
and unrepresentative character of the Senate. One is the increasingly important
role of big money. . . . Political power must be purified." Most of all, of course,
1956 had been the year of the civil rights bill, whose denouement had also been
directed by Johnson. Civil rights, ADA National Chairman Joseph Rauh said,
would be the "great issue" of the 1956 campaign. On the eve of the convention,
the ADA issued a report on Johnson's leadership. His constant cloakroom dealing, it said, had turned the Senate into "a legislative brokerage house." Asked in
a subsequent press conference if the liberal organization might consider supporting Johnson, Rauh replied by saying that it would consider supporting any
of three candidates—the three other candidates. Even the admiring Stewart
Alsop had to conclude that "Johnson is no ardent advocate of Negro equality,
and as a Southerner he would probably alienate a big slice of the Negro vote,
increasingly vital in the Northern industrial states. For such reasons, the Northern liberals could be expected to combine to veto a Johnson nomination. . . .
Most political realists doubt that Johnson could ever get a convention
majority." Johnson's strategy and persuasiveness had had an unintended drawback. So convincingly had he told southern leaders he was not a candidate that
some of them had believed him, and had consequently turned to Stevenson as
the least liberal of the three announced candidates—and now had become
rather comfortable with Adlai, not only because they liked him personally but
because, despite occasional lapses into support of the *Brown* decision, he had
in general moved, as his biographer John Bartlow Martin puts it, "toward
gradualism in desegregation."

Rayburn, loyal as ever despite his desire not to split the party with a divisive convention fight, said firmly that he was supporting Johnson, but he tried
to let the younger man of whom he was so fond know that, while he would certainly get the nomination in 1960, there was no realistic possibility of his getting it this year. At a luncheon in the Capitol for business leaders, attended by
several senators and representatives, including Johnson, the old man sat dourly
silent as the others speculated on the possibility of a convention deadlock that
might enable a dark-horse candidate to win. But when one Pennsylvania indus-
trialist opined that "if the convention deadlocks," there might be a "stampede"
to a dark horse like Stuart Symington, Rayburn finally spoke. "I'll agree with
you on a stampede," he said. "But it won't be to Symington." The room fell
silent. Finally the businessman asked, "Why not?" "Because there will be no
deadlock," Rayburn said. "Stevenson will be nominated on the first ballot, or
by the second ballot at the most." The favorite sons will start to jump on the
Stevenson bandwagon, Rayburn said. "He won't need many shifts . . . to put
him over very quickly. Once that rush starts, no one can stop him." Lyndon
Johnson was sitting beside Rayburn. All during lunch, he had been voluble,

telling one anecdote after another, but after Rayburn spoke, Johnson said not a word. Later, when the "dramatic incident," as Robert Allen put it, was "reverberating through inner party circles," reporters asked the Speaker if he was saying that he had swung to Stevenson. "I've never said I'm for anybody but Lyndon Johnson, dammit," he replied, and he never wavered in that stand. But Johnson knew he had heard Rayburn's assessment of the convention—that Stevenson had already won.

And for a while Lyndon Johnson appeared to recognize this reality, and to accept it. The rooms at the Chicago Hilton had been paid for, the special phone lines—and phone booth—installed, the banners ordered; the trappings of a candidacy went forward, and his staff began, in twos and threes, to head for Chicago. Behind the brave front, however, Johnson had all but stopped running. For him to line up the South solidly behind him despite its growing acceptance of Stevenson, he would need Russell, but Russell was reluctant to attend the convention. "Nineteen fifty-two had left a deep scar with him; in 1956—well, he didn't want to participate," John Connally recalls. And when Russell told Johnson that he would not attend—"I'm going somewhere [a fishing camp near Winder] where there are no telephones"—Johnson made no attempt to dissuade him. Seeing the spectre of the "humiliation" he always dreaded if he were to be portrayed as an active candidate and then didn't win— "He didn't want to run and suffer a defeat for personal ego reasons," Connally says—it was important to him that his denials be believed. Over and over again, he told reporters he wasn't a "serious" candidate but only a favorite son; that he had never sought, and would not seek, any delegates outside Texas. To convince skeptical journalists, he even reminded them of his heart attack— which he never would have done had he still thought there was an opportunity for victory—and did so, this man who could teach it either way, as convincingly as he had, for months, been saying that he felt no effects from the attack at all; at one press conference, reporters kept asking if there was any possibility that he would accept the nomination, and he ended the discussion by saying, "Eisenhower may have forgotten he had a heart attack. I have not. Mine still hurts." Another reporter who began a long one-on-one interview with Johnson skeptical of his denials was convinced by the end of the conversation that "he is sincere and would not accept the nomination if it were offered to him. . . . He talked freely and without any of those guarded utterances which betray a man talking for effect rather than in truth." With southern politicians he was just as convincing; it was particularly important to him that he not be portrayed as a "sectional"—southern—candidate, since such a candidacy would look as quixotic as Richard Russell's had in 1952. More than one key southern politician urged him to run, and offered him his state's votes. Harry Byrd had pleaded with him to declare his candidacy; all he had to do was say yes, the Virginian had said, and he would never have to think about Virginia again: its delegates would be solid for him until the end. Johnson thanked them but declined the offers. His actions were those of a man who understood that he had no chance to win.

AND THEN, suddenly, he thought he did.

It had been taken for granted that former President Truman would support Adlai Stevenson for the Democratic nomination in 1956. It was Truman, after all, who in 1952 had suggested to a "flabbergasted" first-term Governor largely unknown outside Illinois that he run for President and that he, Truman, "could get him nominated"—and who had, indeed, sent word to Democratic king-pins shortly after his arrival in Chicago in 1952 to release their delegates to Stevenson.

But things had changed in the intervening four years. For one thing, as Richard Rovere was to write, there was the wholly understandable human reaction. "It has happened time after time in American politics that former Presidents . . . have resented and fought against their rightful heirs." But in addition, Stevenson, his friend George Ball would say, "was affronted by the indifferent morality and untidiness of the Truman Administration," and after the 1952 campaign, showed, in Rovere's words, "his eagerness to have it thoroughly understood that he had never been part of it." He particularly did not want to be associated with Truman's characterization of the Eisenhower Administration as "this bunch of racketeers," and, as Rovere puts it, he simply "does not share Truman's view of Truman as the greatest living expert on everything." Stevenson gave vent to these views only in private, "never in public," but of course "they got back to Mr. Truman, who took it hard." Several months before the 1956 convention, the ex-President growled to a friend, "Why, if Stevenson is ever elected, he won't let us inside the White House."

When Truman's train pulled into Chicago's grimy old Dearborn Street Station at 8 a.m., Friday, August 10, the former President, as jaunty as ever, found a mob of delegates, reporters, and cameramen pushing and shoving to get a glimpse of him, and then grabbed the headlines when he pointedly did not endorse Stevenson but instead said he would announce his choice the next day. All day Friday, Truman held meetings with party leaders in his suite at the Blackstone Hotel, giving them broad hints ("I am not a bandwagon fellow"; "I'm going to stir up a little trouble tomorrow"), and by that evening, while journalists were still writing that the ex-President was keeping the candidates in a state of suspense, party insiders knew—and Lyndon Johnson still down on his ranch was told—that the next day the former President would endorse Harriman.

In a few days, it would be clear that Truman, and the press, had drastically overestimated his influence, but at the time it was almost universally assumed that his choice of Harriman would stop the Stevenson bandwagon, preventing Adlai from getting the necessary 687½ votes on the first, or any early, ballot, and thus throwing the convention open so that some other candidate could win.

Among those making that assumption was Lyndon Johnson. Under the scenario he had devised a year earlier on the Pedernales, the convention would, after a series of deadlocks and bargains, be forced to turn to a compromise candidate—and as a candidate who came to the bargaining table with a solid bloc of almost three hundred southern and southwestern delegates, he would be a logical choice. It suddenly seemed possible again that he might yet be able to win the nomination—and he grabbed for it with an urgency that revealed how desperately he wanted it.

Telephoning eleven Texas congressmen that Friday evening, he told them he wanted them up in Chicago the next day so they could use their acquaintance with congressmen in other state delegations to keep their delegations from switching to Stevenson. "Get up to the ranch early," he told Representative Joe M. Kilgore of McAllen. "We're going up in Wesley West's plane." In the plane Johnson was "thoughtful, but upbeat." "We have a chance to win this thing," he told Kilgore. And soon after driving into the Chicago Loop from the airport and pushing through the crowd in the Hilton lobby and then through the crowd jamming the twenty-third-floor corridor, many wearing scarlet-and-gold "Love That Lyndon" buttons, Johnson emerged from his suite and went down to a press conference in the hotel's Boulevard Room, striding out on the stage with a big smile, to try to convince three hundred reporters of the same thing. For months, he had been insisting that he was only a favorite-son candidate. Now a reporter asked him, "Are you just a favorite son, or are you a serious candidate?" "I'm serious about everything I do," Lyndon Johnson said—and all over the room, pencils started scribbling.

Time and again, the correspondents, some of whom had heard him denying for months what he was now affirming, pressed the issue, and with each answer Johnson made his stand stronger; when he was asked if he would drop out of the race after one or two ballots, he said, "That is very unlikely," and, as one reporter wrote, "that reply erased Johnson from the status of a mere favorite son candidate from Texas, planning only to get a token vote before throwing his state's fifty-six votes to someone else." Asked whether he considered Stevenson or Harriman the best-qualified candidate, he said: "The best qualified now is Lyndon B. Johnson." He was the Democrat behind whom Democrats from all over the nation could unite, he said, and if he received the nomination, he would run "an effective campaign and a winning campaign" against President Eisenhower. There was no more talk about his heart still hurting. "I have been putting in 15- and 16-hour days every day, including Saturday, during the last weeks of Congress," he said. But he had not sought any delegates outside his own state, one reporter pointed out. "In your experience in politics, do you recall any serious contender for a nomination who did not seek delegates from outside his own state?" Johnson answered firmly, "You don't always have to seek something in order to get it."

Soon after he left his press conference, with word "rolling out across Chicago" that Johnson was running in earnest, he received a call from Harry

Truman's suite in the Blackstone across the street. The former President told him what he already knew. He was going down to his own press conference in a minute, Truman said; "I'm opening this thing up so anybody can get it—including you."

Truman told reporters that the "mounting crises" in foreign affairs required the nomination of a man with experience in foreign affairs—Averell Harriman. Johnson, in his suite, was watching the press conference on television. As soon as it ended, he emerged with John Connally, turned left and strode down the corridor, past the closed doors of Adlai Stevenson's suite, to Sam Rayburn's at the end of the hall. "It's wide open now," Connally shouted to a reporter. On Johnson's face was a broad smile. Recalls Tommy Corcoran: "He thought he had a chance. He really believed it."

HE BELIEVED IT in part because there were reasons to believe it. His hope that Stevenson would not win on the first ballot was bolstered by precedent: no contested Democratic presidential nomination in history had been decided on the first ballot. In addition, there existed, as at every Democratic convention, the possibility that civil rights—specifically, the wording of the platform plank dealing with the issue—would ignite an explosion, as it had after Hubert Humphrey's speech in 1948, and upset all calculations. Indeed, Stevenson, after months of tiptoeing around the issue, had already—a few days before the convention—made a slip. When a television reporter unexpectedly caught him on a street, Stevenson said, in what his biographer Martin calls "an ill-considered moment," that the platform "should express unequivocal approval of the Court's decision, although it seems odd that you should have to express your approval of the Constitution and its institutions." At once, "big blocks of southern delegates shifted to the doubtful column," the *New York Times* reported. Only a quick public reversal—Stevenson assured an Alabama supporter, in a telegram released to the press, that he would not use force to uphold the Court's decision—combined with similar private assurances by his aides, enabled Adlai to mend his southern fences. There was always the possibility of another misstep.

But Johnson also believed it for reasons that had no basis in reality—for reasons that were to astonish those who had come to regard him as a consummately practical politician.

He told aides and allies that he had a chance because influential figures in the Democratic Party were on his side, but when he named these figures, almost all of them were senators, or former senators.

His belief in these men—Bob Kerr in Oklahoma, Carl Hayden and Bob McFarland in Arizona, McClellan and Fulbright in Arkansas, Ed Johnson in Colorado, Mike Mansfield in Montana—was in a way understandable. To a man whose life in Washington was spent in the closed, insulated world of the

Senate, a world in which these men had immense authority, it was perhaps only natural to assume that they had authority in their own states. But the belief revealed that Lyndon Johnson, knowledgeable though he was about power in Washington, had a woefully inadequate comprehension of power outside the capital. Anyone who held that belief, as Richard Rovere was to explain in *The New Yorker,* "forgot the wisdom of history, which is that members of the United States Senate almost invariably come to grief when they try to win Presidential nominations for themselves or to manipulate national conventions for any purpose whatsoever. For many reasons—patronage is one, and control of delegations is another—the big men at conventions are governors and municipal leaders." And among these "big men"—the Democratic Party's powerful traditional "bosses" since the onset of the age of Roosevelt: Mayor Daley and Jacob M. Arvey of Chicago, Mayor David L. Lawrence of Pittsburgh, Governors like George Leader of Pennsylvania and Robert B. Meyner of New Jersey, and leaders of the party's major constituencies such as labor's George Meany and Walter Reuther—Lyndon Johnson had very little support.

Moreover, as now became apparent, this most pragmatic of men—capable, in Washington, of looking into others and seeing the fundamental realities behind their behavior—was, in Chicago, incapable of seeing a crucial reality: the true depth of the antipathy toward him of northern liberals.

This, too, was understandable. Lyndon Johnson's world, in Washington, was a world in which deals could always be made, bargains could always be arranged, in which men were reasonable in compromising their principles, except for a few crazies like Lehman and Douglas, who had so little power that they could safely be ignored. It was perhaps only natural that he believed that at least some northern liberals—enough, combined with southern and southwestern votes, to give him the nomination—could be brought under his standard if the right inducements were found, particularly since, in his view, he had already done so much for them by giving Meany and Reuther the Social Security and housing bills they wanted. But this belief demonstrated only that Lyndon Johnson simply had not grasped that there was another world, a world in which Douglas and Lehman were not crazies but heroes, in which principles mattered far more than they did in the Senate. In addition, Lyndon Johnson had not fully appreciated that it didn't matter what he did for the liberals in Social Security and housing so long as he was not on their side on the "great issue."

He should have appreciated this. When the ADA had issued that report accusing Johnson of "bringing the Democratic Party to its lowest point in twenty-five years," it had been civil rights that the report emphasized. It was not two months since United Auto Workers President Walter Reuther had said that the party had "no right to preach morality to the world unless we are fighting equally hard against injustices at home"; even here in Chicago there had already been reminders: labor leaders were supporting the NAACP's demand for a civil rights plank not only endorsing the *Brown* decision but advocating

the use of force to uphold it if necessary. Johnson had exchanged friendly letters with George Meany after the passage of the Social Security bill, but when
Meany appeared before the Platform Committee, it was not Social Security he
emphasized, saying grimly, staring down the southerners facing him, "The
Democratic Party must declare that it is not in favor of thwarting a decision by
the Supreme Court." In Washington, the conservative coalition that ran the Senate could ignore Walter Reuther with impunity, but more than a hundred delegates to the Democratic convention were members of Reuther's UAW, and fifty
of them were members of the Michigan delegation, which had been supporting
favorite-son Governor G. Mennen (Soapy) Williams, but which Johnson was
confidently asserting would swing over to him. And there were other labor
leaders with substantial numbers of delegates: Emil Rieve of the Textile Workers, Joseph A. Bierne of the Communications Workers, Alex Rose of the Hat,
Cap and Millinery Workers, Dave Dubinsky of the Garment Workers, James B.
Carey of the Electrical Workers. Their views may not have mattered much on
the floor of the Senate; they mattered a great deal in Chicago. "I was knocked
for a loop," Tommy Corcoran recalls. "He [Johnson] really thought these guys
were going to come around [to support him]. Hell, as long as he wasn't with
them on civil rights, they were *never* going to support him!"

He believed it, as well, because of the euphoria to which he was prone
when he thought he was winning, a euphoria fed by the trappings of a convention: the excitement in the air in the hotel corridors through which he pushed,
the cheers of the Texas caucus, all those "Love That Lyndon" buttons in his
suite. Truman's announcement was the break he had hoped for; he thought the
nomination was within his grasp, the nomination that would make him the
odds-on favorite to get the party's nod again in 1960, when Eisenhower would
not be running. And, of course, Eisenhower was old, and had already had two
major illnesses; what if there was another before Election Day? As that week's
Newsweek story on the convention put it, "Another new factor . . . is the issue of
Mr. Eisenhower's health. No man can be certain what that will be three months
hence. This dominant political question is, alone and unaided, wiping out the
prospect of a cut-and-dried election this year." In hindsight, it is clear that, barring some new major illness, there was never any possibility that the President
might be defeated; that was not the way it seemed in Chicago in August, 1956.
Most of all, Lyndon Johnson believed it because of the intensity of his desire
that it be true. Sometimes, talking to men like Tommy Corcoran and Jim Rowe,
he was the old, realistic Lyndon Johnson of Washington. Once, during the convention, Rowe says, "he just made a flat statement"—which Rowe had heard
him make many times before—"that he better recognize that for Texans, and
also the South, their base for power was in the Senate, that was all they were
going to have." But, Rowe and Corcoran say, Johnson's feelings veered wildly
between realism and optimism—unrealistic optimism. "He was ambivalent,"
Rowe says. "On one side, I think, deep down, he understood the realities. But

he wanted to be President *so much. . . .*" "On most things, you could talk sense to Lyndon," Tommy Corcoran says. "But there was no talking to him about this." On the morning after Truman's dramatic announcement, the Sunday newspapers delivered to the delegates' rooms were filled with speculation about imminent breaks in the Stevenson ranks from New Jersey, Michigan, and Pennsylvania. But by noon that Sunday, the party's insiders already knew the truth. Counting delegates the evening before, they had found that if Adlai didn't have the necessary 687½, he was close to that number—and needed only another state or two to win, and by noon there was a growing awareness in the press that Truman's coup had failed. But Lyndon Johnson wasn't counting, he was hoping; this man who prided himself on never deluding himself, on always looking unblinkingly at the hard facts, was deluding himself now because he wanted, needed, the prize so badly that, plain though the truth was, he couldn't see it. "He wanted to be President *so much*"—and after Truman's announcement he had persuaded himself that he really might be.

MOST OF ALL, perhaps, Lyndon Johnson believed he had a chance because of Rayburn and Russell.

Although both men had publicly announced that they were supporting him, neither was working actively for his candidacy, since they knew it was hopeless. Russell had not even come to Chicago; Rayburn, the convention's chairman, told delegates privately as well as publicly that he was supporting Johnson, but he had not *demanded* their support for Johnson, had not thrown his immense power behind him because he knew "no one can stop Stevenson." On the day after Truman's announcement, however, Johnson had been presented, as it happened, with an opportunity to work on his *R*s. The crisis in the Mideast that had been precipitated two weeks earlier by Egypt's nationalization of the Suez Canal was worsening. British and French warships were steaming toward Egypt, and Britain was dispatching troops to the Mediterranean in preparation for an attack to regain control of the waterway. John Foster Dulles was about to leave for London to try to resolve the crisis without armed conflict, and Eisenhower had summoned congressional leaders to the White House for a briefing by Dulles before he left, sending an Air Force plane to Chicago to pick up Democratic leaders, and another one to Winder to pick up Russell. As soon as the plane lifted off from Chicago at 7:45 Sunday morning, Johnson's delusions—and desperation—spilled out. Taking the seat beside Rayburn, he began talking the moment the plane took off, and didn't stop until it landed at Washington's National Airport. Truman had halted the Stevenson bandwagon, he said. The convention was deadlocked now, and in a deadlocked convention, who was in a better position to get the nomination than him? Nobody! he said. And he would get the nomination, he told Rayburn, if only you would take the lead, really get in there and fight for me. Some of the other congressional leaders who overheard the conversation had never before seen Lyndon Johnson "working" Mr. Sam, and they were astonished at his pleading and whining. Rayburn, grumpy anyway because he hated flying, didn't say much in reply, aside from an occasional, noncommittal grunt; he sat silent, his broad bald head lowered between his shoulders, puffing on a cigarette. When Rayburn didn't agree to do what Johnson wanted, Johnson escalated his pleas. "Johnson gave him a real sales job," says House Democratic Whip Carl Albert of Oklahoma, who sat across the aisle from the two Texans. "He told Mr. Rayburn, 'I have supported you all these years, and I need your help. I have a chance here. . . .' " Rayburn sat silent, a block of granite in his seat. "It was an embarrassing ride for everyone on the plane," listening to Johnson's acting "like a spoiled child," one of Rayburn's biographers was to write. "But there was silent applause for Rayburn," who during the two-hour flight said hardly a word.

Russell had been keeping himself inaccessible at his place "with no telephones," but his attendance at the White House briefing (at which Johnson told Eisenhower that the proper response was "to tell [the British and French] they have our moral support and go on in; Eisenhower demurred) put him within Johnson's reach, and Johnson had more success "working" him than he had with Rayburn. Determined not to go to Chicago, Russell tried to explain that he could not help Johnson get the nomination, that it was too late, that even the Georgia delegation, under Governor Marvin Griffin's direction, was now so firmly committed to Stevenson that its vote could not be changed. As Evans and Novak were to recount: "Johnson persisted. All right, he said, Griffin is hopeless. But please, *please,* come out with me anyway. Come with me and sit with me in my headquarters and talk to me and eat with me and be with me. The tone was beseeching, pleading." And Russell finally agreed, leaving for the airport with Johnson without even packing a suitcase. "Robert E. Lee could not have dragged Dick Russell to the Democratic National Convention in . . . 1956," Evans and Novak wrote. "But Lyndon Johnson did."

When the plane arrived back at Chicago's Midway Airport at four o'clock Sunday afternoon, Rayburn and Johnson began walking toward their waiting limousines, accompanied by Booth Mooney. When newspaper and television reporters and cameramen ran toward them, the Speaker pushed through them, scowling, but Johnson stayed to talk.

"I don't see why Lyndon lets those buzzards trap him like that," Rayburn said to Mooney. Looking around to make sure that no reporter could hear him, he muttered, "I hate to see Lyndon get bit so hard by the presidential bug at this stage of the game. Stevenson's got it sewed up." When the reporters caught up to him, he "stayed hitched," repeating that "I haven't said I was for anybody but Lyndon, dammit." Asked if Johnson's candidacy was truly a "serious" one, he said, "It's a serious one." He even said that Johnson would get "a good many votes" besides the ones from Texas. But, as Mooney was to say, "he had no illu-

sions." And as soon as Russell started telephoning the leaders of southern delegations, he lost any *he* may have had. Rayburn and Russell were realists; both
saw there was no hope. Rayburn told Johnson privately that he felt he was making a big mistake in actively pushing a hopeless candidacy. "I told Lyndon I
thought he had lost his head," he was to tell a friend later. "I told him that it was
a mistake to become a sectional candidate. He should be thinking of 1960.
Look what happened to Dick Russell." Johnson was getting the same warning
from the only member of his staff besides Connally who dared to give him
warnings. When Johnson had awakened Sunday morning, he had found a
memo slipped under his door. It was from Jim Rowe, who had written it during
the night. In it, Rowe recalls, "I said you must be careful [that] you don't get
yourself where Dick Russell got himself in 1952. . . . Don't get yourself in that
position, don't get out front, you can't make it. . . ." After he returned from
Washington, Johnson came into Rowe's room and said, "I agree with everything you said." Perhaps he did agree—intellectually. But he didn't take the
advice. He couldn't. He was beyond listening to warnings, as was demonstrated the next day, when the convention opened.

ON THAT DAY, Monday, August 13, "one man who thought Lyndon Johnson's
chances were excellent was Lyndon Johnson," Richard Rovere wrote in his
New Yorker analysis. "For somewhere between twelve and eighteen hours on
Monday, he waged a perfectly serious and purposeful campaign for the nomination, and he . . . thought it more likely than not that he and Senator Russell,
of Georgia, could gain control of the Democratic Party and make it a medium
for the expression of their views."

In the International Amphitheatre, party orators were droning away to a
nearly empty auditorium; the real negotiations were going on in the big Loop
hotels, not in the lobbies jammed with boisterous badge-wearing, placard-
waving delegates, but upstairs in the traditional "smoke-filled rooms" of party
leaders, and in the hotel conference rooms where state delegations were cau-
cusing. At the Texas caucus early Monday morning, Johnson sat listening as
one speaker after another predicted he would win the nomination; "Let us tell
the nation and the world that we have here the next President of the United
States," John Lyle proclaimed in that ringing voice that would have been familiar to anyone who had attended the Leland Olds hearings. Emerging from the
caucus, Johnson told reporters that he had no plans to release his delegates;
"My name will stay as long as the American people are interested."

His method of making the race was somewhat unconventional. All that
Monday, Stevenson and Harriman (and Kefauver, who was trying to persuade
his two hundred delegates to switch to Stevenson) rushed from caucus to caucus behind police motorcycle escorts with wailing sirens. The Texas caucus
was the only one Johnson attended. He spent the rest of the day—the entire

day—on the Hilton's twenty-third floor, in his suite, behind closed doors. He had received four formal invitations from delegations to address them that day; he declined all four. Party leaders who wanted to talk to him were told he would be glad to meet with them—in his suite. "He wouldn't go out to seek delegations or to meet with them," Jim Rowe recalls. "It was a very odd performance"—odd unless one takes into account what Rowe calls Johnson's "ambivalence": the conflict between a desire to run and a dread of being *seen* to be running, lest he lose, since losing would then be "humiliation" (that word was on his lips constantly during the convention, particularly when he was asked why he wasn't out appealing for votes; "I didn't come here to be humiliated," he told Marshall McNeil when McNeil asked him that question); the conflict between his emotions and his intellect, which told him how long the odds were against his winning. His emotions veered constantly between extremes: between the despair and depression when he thought he wasn't winning and the overconfidence or euphoria that made him so overbearing when he thought he was winning (when, at a press conference, reporters pointed out that "serious" candidates usually address delegations, he replied, "Different people have different methods. Sometimes they come to you"). His performance is difficult to understand, furthermore, unless one also takes into account two other considerations. One was the self-knowledge that had made him say, when he first got to the Senate, that it was "the right size"—the awareness that he was most effective when he dealt with men in private, behind closed doors, and least effective when he had to speak to them in large groups. The other was not a personal but a political calculation. If he tried openly to rally support for himself, the first states that would announce their support would be southern states. Not wanting to be labeled a southern, regional candidate, he wanted at least one or two states from other regions to announce first.

And, indeed, on that Monday, the leaders *did* come to him. "While the other candidates rushed through the city in cavalcades heralded by sirens, to swoop down on wavering and uncommitted delegates, Lyndon Johnson sat in his white-walled suite overlooking Lake Michigan and received the mighty of his party," Mary McGrory wrote. The Hilton's twenty-third floor, on which Rayburn, Daley, and Stevenson also had suites, was the most crowded spot in Chicago, its long hallways crammed with the heavy, clumsy television cameras and cables of that era, with TV cameramen and newspaper and magazine photographers and reporters and delegates, and most of the delegates in the halls were wearing the "Love That Lyndon" buttons, and most of the visitors turned left after getting off the elevators, toward the wing that he had commandeered, not toward the suites of the other big names.

In the hallway that had in effect become his private corridor, the crush intensified, television cameramen and newspaper photographers shoving each other for vantage points, the TV cameras and cables so thick that when a waiter tried to push through them with a table containing Johnson's lunch, the scene, one reporter wrote, was "not unlike the ship cabin scene" of the Marx Brothers farce *A Night at the Opera*. And down the corridor that day, pushing past the photographers and reporters to the door at the end numbered 2306-A, Stevenson, Harriman, and Kefauver made their way, as did the favorite-son candidates Symington and Magnuson, vice presidential possibilities Humphrey and Kennedy, as well as Ernest McFarland, "flown in," as one reporter wrote, "to deliver his state," Richard Russell, in town to deliver several states, and twenty-one other men. They would knock on the door and sometimes be admitted at once, and sometimes have to wait outside in the corridor, either because someone else was inside or because, alone in the suite or with only Rowe or John Connally present, Johnson was working the phones; so many telephones had been installed in 2306-A and the adjoining small sitting room that wires seemed to stretch everywhere, and Johnson spent hours that day pacing back and forth with a big hand wrapped around a receiver, talking, persuading, selling. Lyndon Johnson's suite, Bill White wrote, "was the most crowded in Chicago"—the epicenter that day of convention maneuvering. Reporters clocked the visits, and attached significance to the length of time Lyndon Johnson deigned to spend with each man—Stevenson, it was noted, was allowed thirty minutes, Kefauver a mere five—before they emerged, to be backed against a corridor wall by the press while they gave carefully noncommittal comments about what had taken place inside. Johnson would emerge and pose for a minute for photographers with a favored few—Stevenson and Harriman, for example—joking and smiling, a bronzed, confident figure towering over shorter men, obviously enjoying himself. Occasionally he would drop a tidbit for the reporters. Harriman had invited Johnson to his suite in the Blackstone Hotel, but Johnson had had one of his secretaries say he would rather have Harriman do the visiting, and Harriman had done so—Johnson made sure the reporters knew that he had made Harriman come to him. All that day, he was the center of attention, and he was reveling in it.

Many of the reporters were from Washington, and they assumed that the closed-door conferences meant what they meant in the Senate: that, as Mary McGrory wrote, "what Lyndon wants Lyndon gets," "that Senator Johnson, whose success in persuading senators to go along with him is nothing less than spectacular, suddenly saw in the delegates some 2,000 twin-brothers of his colleagues, that in this crowded arena he saw a reasonable facsimile of the Senate floor which he so indisputably dominates." That assumption was incorrect, however. The famous political figures beating a path to his door were not offering support for his candidacy but asking for his support for *their* candidacies, and for the support of the southern delegates they thought he controlled. Not one of his visitors from the North was even considering supporting him. And there was another resemblance between suite and Senate, and it was not one that boded well for Johnson's chances. Both locales were filled with senators—almost exclusively with senators. Among the visitors to 2306-A that Monday were no fewer than fifteen senators—and exactly two governors (Harriman and Luther Hodges of North Carolina) and one labor leader. The men with whom Lyndon Johnson was meeting did not have the power to give him what he wanted.

Furthermore, with the exception of Richard Russell, who came by twice that day, few of the visitors were from the South. Since he didn't want journalists' attention on the southerners, he dealt with them that day mostly over the telephone. Once, Lyndon Johnson *could* have had the southern states, could have had them easily. But he had declined their offers—and the South, determined to exercise enough power at the convention to block an unacceptable platform plank or candidate, couldn't wait for him to make a firm commitment to run. The only way for the South to be powerful was for the South to be solid, which meant lining up behind a single candidate. So the South had gone looking for a candidate, and, in Stevenson, had found one. In addition, the senators had stepped out of the picture, leaving the selection of convention delegates to the governors, most of whom were only casually acquainted with Johnson and some of whom were more than a little offended by his rejection of their offers. Most of the eleven southern states had arrived at the convention with the intention either of supporting Stevenson from the opening ballot or of casting that first-ballot vote for a favorite son, so as to keep their leverage over Stevenson and the platform, with the expectation that they would switch to Stevenson later. Nonetheless, that Monday, with Johnson at last—suddenly—a declared candidate, and with pleas from Richard Russell, offers of support for him had been renewed by several of the Old Confederate states in telephone calls to Johnson's suite.

Most of these offers, however, came with a request: that he promise to stay in the race until the end, or close to the end; that he not drop out on an early ballot. For many of the southern states, this pledge was the *sine qua non* for their support; they couldn't take the chance of lining up behind a candidate who might drop out too early in the convention, leaving them without a rallying point in the fight over the civil rights platform plank. The *Dallas Morning News,* well attuned to the southern viewpoint, reported that as soon as Johnson said he was "serious," "Southern states . . . asked him what they could do to help along a fellow southerner," but they also asked, "Would he ride hard to the finish, as Sen. Dick Russell had done in 1952? . . . Southern states wanted that ironclad guarantee." But Johnson still believed he could pick up the southern states whenever he wanted, and was still afraid of the "humiliation" a losing fight to the finish would entail, and, the *Morning News* reported, "That firm assurance never came."

In some cases, Johnson's declaration came too late. The illness of Harry Byrd's wife had prevented him from coming to Chicago, but early Monday morning Johnson telephoned Byrd at his Winchester estate, and for more than two hours, Byrd was on the telephone to Chicago, trying to swing the Virginia delegation to Johnson. But, with Byrd having bowed out of the picture months before, the delegation had been selected by former Governor John Battle, and Battle and the delegation wouldn't switch. Monday evening, there was a meeting of leaders from the eleven southern states. Texas was for Johnson, of course. Two states decided to stay with the candidate who would stay in until the end, who appeared likely to win—and who was so much more acceptable to them than Harriman: Adlai Stevenson. The other eight decided to support favorite sons "until an agreement was reached on a civil rights plank." Some of these delegations were planning at that point to announce for Johnson, but their failure to announce immediately meant that no southern barricade had been thrown up in front of the Stevenson bandwagon.

Lyndon Johnson's failure to acknowledge these realities ran counter to the previous pattern of his political life. A political convention is at bottom an exercise in counting, and if he had been counting delegates as he counted senators—coldly, unemotionally, looking unflinchingly at reality, no matter how unpleasant that reality might be—he would have seen that he had no chance for the nomination. But in Chicago, he was hearing what he wanted to hear, believing what he wanted to believe. At one point late Monday afternoon, Harry Byrd Jr., hastily dispatched to Chicago by his father, gave Johnson an overly optimistic report on the Virginia delegation. Instead of checking it, Johnson simply believed it. Inviting reporters into his suite that evening, Johnson was brimming over with self-confidence. He had had "a very fruitful day," he said—the same type of day that he was accustomed to having in Washington: a day of talks with "many members of the Senate, leaders of the party, for whom I have respect and to whom I have obligations," talks "about the problems which confront us," "the same kind of talks which happen on the third floor of the Capitol when I'm there." And, he said, he expected the results in Chicago to be just as satisfactory as they were in Washington. He had had many pledges of support, he said. Texas would not be the only state in his column; "There will be other states that will vote for me." In particular, he said, one big northern state had been won over. "The biggest bloc of votes that I expect I'll have was a complete surprise to me."

Standing at the back of the room listening to the press conference, Corcoran and Rowe could not even imagine what big state Johnson might be referring to; they knew that nothing that had happened that day offered any hope that Johnson would receive the votes of *any* big state other than Texas. John Connally recalls that "for one day"—that Monday—"there was the feeling that there was hope." But in truth there was no hope, and that day should have made Johnson understand that. The man who had always looked facts in the face wasn't doing so this time. Years later, at their Washington law firm, Corcoran and Rowe would be talking to the author of this book about the 1956 convention. Rowe, thoughtful and analytical, was using terms like "ambivalence" to analyze Johnson's behavior when the blunt Corcoran interrupted with a blunter explanation. "Listen," he said. "He just wanted it [the nomination] so much. He wanted it so much he wasn't thinking straight." There was a pause, and then Rowe nodded agreement. Trying to run for President from behind the closed door of his Hilton suite, Johnson was insulated from reality by his hopes and dreams.

OUTSIDE THE SUITE, however, there was reality just the same.

Truman himself was finding out on Monday, to his chagrin, that his announcement had had little effect on Stevenson's firmly committed delegates. Invitations to his Blackstone suite were accepted far more eagerly—delegates were thrilled to meet a former President—than was his advice. By evening, Murray Kempton wrote, "the old man was down to haggling for the votes of single delegates from Montana and one such came, and came out saying it was an honor to meet one of the great men of American history, but, no, he guessed he hadn't quite made up his mind." And, Kempton wrote, "all afternoon the word rolled in from the Kennedys, the ADAers and the Monroneys—all the names of the future in the Democratic Party—and every one said that he was still for Stevenson." In fact, Truman's statement had boomeranged against Johnson. Worried that Truman's move might improve the chances of the hated Harriman, many southerners felt they could not wait any longer for a Johnson commitment to stay in the race and climbed back off the fence—into Stevenson's camp. Byrd was still making telephone calls, but the growing sentiment in the Virginia delegation was expressed by Thomas Broyhill, who told a reporter that it was time for Virginia to stop "fooling around with dark horses. It's Stevenson or Harriman, and we had better get Stevenson in there as quick as possible." Almost every poll of delegates taken Monday evening, the evening of Johnson's "very fruitful day," showed that in fact Stevenson's delegate count was either close to or over six hundred.

And, unlike Johnson, Stevenson and his canny campaign manager, James Aloysius Finnegan, a tough Irish politician from Philadelphia, were talking to the right people: all that Monday, while Johnson, in his room at the end of one wing of the Hilton, was conferring with senators, Stevenson and Finnegan, in their room at the end of the next wing (when Johnson looked out the window, he could have seen into Stevenson's suite across a fifty-foot courtyard had the blinds in Stevenson's suite not been kept closed), were conferring with the men who really ran the delegations.

Finnegan was using some very strong arguments. To southern leaders still supporting favorite sons, he was saying that Adlai had the nomination all but sewn up and needed only a few votes to win. If southern states supplied those votes, those states would have Stevenson's gratitude, and sympathetic treatment from a Stevenson Administration. On the other hand, if they didn't supply those votes, the North might do so—several northern states were about to throw their votes to Stevenson, he said. If they didn't get aboard the train quickly, he told the southerners, they might find that it had left without them, and that there was no longer a seat for them on it.

To northern leaders, Finnegan was using the same argument in reverse; several southern states were about to throw the decisive votes to Adlai, he said; if northern states didn't board the train quickly, they might find that it had left without *them*. And to northern liberals, Finnegan added another argument: If Stevenson didn't get his majority, and the convention therefore was thrown into deadlock, who would benefit? he asked. Lyndon Johnson. Johnson would be in a position to demand concessions from Stevenson in exchange for the South's support, he said. Do you really want to take a chance on that happening? A prolonged deadlock might even result in Lyndon Johnson eventually winning the nomination, Finnegan warned. Do you really want to take a chance that Lyndon Johnson will be the nominee?

These were chances that northern liberals indeed didn't want to take. As W. H. Lawrence reported that night in the *New York Times:* "Some of the northern liberals [are] restive about the possibilities that the pressure on Mr. Stevenson might force him to make an accommodation with Senator Johnson." Even liberals from Harriman's own state were restive. The *New York Post* reported "uncertainty as to how long Harriman could hold New York's delegation back from Stevenson if it looked like a coup by Johnson was in the making."

One northern leader who didn't want to take such chances was Walter Reuther. Lyndon Johnson had been confident that the big Michigan delegation would hold fast behind favorite-son Williams or would go for Harriman; he kept mentioning that Reuther was his friend, that he used to sleep on the spare bed in Johnson's home when he came to Washington in the 1940s, that Reuther had helped swing labor support to him in his 1948 Senate race. He appears not to have grasped that for Walter Reuther, friendship was not as significant as Emmett Till, and that, in addition, since 1948 there had been Leland Olds and the natural gas bill and the destruction of Paul Douglas. And the Michigan delegation, as Murray Kempton wrote, "is the great fruit of the social revolution of the thirties; there are people in it who were arrested on sitdown strikes twenty years ago. The old CIO is stronger there than anywhere else at this convention."

Monday evening, Michigan held a closed-door meeting, and Stevenson came to it, with a smile, a few jokes—and Mrs. Eleanor Roosevelt.

Entering the room, she saw a photographer, Sammy Schulman of International News Service, who had been her husband's favorite photographer. "Hello, Sammy," she laughed. "Still going around?" Yes, he was, Sammy replied. And you, Mrs. Roosevelt, he asked, are you still going around? Yes, she was, Eleanor Roosevelt replied—and then she told Michigan why she was going around: that there are some things more important than winning—that principles are more important—and that therefore Michigan should be for

Adlai Stevenson. The delegation stood up and cheered, and then Walter Reuther spoke, and said he was for Stevenson. And Soapy Williams had understood Finnegan's warning. The convention was drifting dangerously, the Governor told a reporter; if the liberal forces didn't unite, he said, there was a danger that "a minority power bloc" might name the nominee. By the time the meeting broke up well after midnight, it was clear that when Michigan caucused the next day, Adlai would receive the delegation's vote.

Jim Rowe got the bad news at five o'clock Tuesday morning from one of his "spies" in the Michigan delegation, and he put on a bathrobe and hurried down the hall to relay it to Lyndon Johnson.

Rowe would never forget how Johnson looked when he opened the door. All of him looked asleep—he was in pajamas and his rumpled hair was standing on end—all of him except his eyes. Piercing and intent, they were very wide awake, and when Rowe gave him the news, they narrowed in that calculating look that Rowe had seen so often. But then Johnson responded, and his response was not the usual Johnson response to bad news. "I don't believe it," he said.

Rowe tried to convince him it was true. He knew it was important that Johnson understand what was happening, that Stevenson was about to win, and that if Johnson did not support him, give him Texas' fifty-six votes and bring in other southern states as well, he would lose all his power in the convention. He recalls saying, "It is absolutely true. It is going to happen. Reuther has given his pledge." Michigan was going to caucus at 11 a.m., he said, and once it did, it would be too late for Johnson to do anything. He said, "You have approximately six hours to deliver Texas and to control the convention." But Lyndon refused to believe it.

BELIEVE IT OR NOT, however, it was true, and with the Michigan decision, the bandwagon was rolling. On Tuesday morning, the Arizona delegation also caucused, and, ignoring a last-minute plea by Bob McFarland, voted to cast its sixteen votes for Stevenson. Lyndon Johnson had been pinning a lot of his hopes not only on Michigan but on New Jersey, which had come to the convention with its thirty-six votes ostensibly behind its favorite son, Governor Robert B. Meyner, but Meyner had come to the same conclusion as Soapy Williams: that Harriman couldn't win, and that the South could not be allowed to dominate the convention. On Tuesday morning, he flatly refused to allow his name to be placed in nomination, and New Jersey voted unanimously for Stevenson. Hearing the news, a Harriman aide silently drew his finger across his throat.

Finnegan's gambit was working with southerners as well, as they saw the northern states clambering aboard the Stevenson bandwagon and realized that it was, indeed, leaving without them. Moreover, some of them were by this time quite annoyed at Lyndon Johnson. If they had declined to back Stevenson, it was on Johnson's behalf that they had done so—had remained committed to their favorite sons—and yet he was still refusing to give them a firm commitment to stay in the race to the end. By Tuesday evening, it was apparent that Virginia would go for Stevenson. And since it was also becoming apparent Tuesday that "moderates" would control the Platform Committee, even Russell's Georgia had less reason to hold out. Predicting a civil rights plank that "may not be all that we want but [that] we hope . . . will be one that we could live with," Governor Griffin added—in a jibe at Johnson's indecision—"Of all the candidates here that we know about, I would say that the Georgia delegation holds Mr. Stevenson in the highest esteem."

Truman launched a second, more intemperate, attack on the man he had once persuaded to run for the presidency, calling him "too defeatist to win," but while for the former President's first press conference, the Blackstone's Crystal Ballroom had hardly been big enough to hold all the reporters and cameramen, this time it was half empty—and his attack, as Lawrence wrote, served only "to confirm reports that his backing of Governor Harriman had not shaken" Stevenson's support. Indeed, by Tuesday night, the former President's actions had so "greatly minimized his own stature," James Reston wrote, "that he was in danger of becoming" an ex-President "who no longer has the consolation of being powerful within his own party."

All that Tuesday, Lyndon Johnson stayed in his suite, but in the corridor outside there were signs of the change in his status. During the morning, the cables and cameras were as thickly clustered as they had been on Monday, the callers were still lined up in the hall waiting for an audience, but, as one reporter wrote, "All through the day the Stevenson bandwagon kept on rolling. State after state, delegation after delegation, decided that instead of being on the fence, the place to be was on the side of the winner," and by that afternoon, the television cameras had disappeared, and the number of visitors to Johnson's suite was noticeably fewer. And two of the visitors were Stevenson and Finnegan, keeping an appointment that had been scheduled the previous day. Johnson tried to bargain with them, saying that in order for him to support Stevenson, he needed assurance that the civil rights plank would be acceptable to the South. Jim Rowe, the only Johnson aide present during the meeting, recalls Johnson saying, "I have got to have something that will not hurt my people too much." Stevenson, ever courteous, said, "Well, I would like to think about it," but Finnegan simply said: "No."

"What did you say?" Johnson asked him. "I said no," Finnegan replied. "We are not going to give you anything."

When Johnson asked, "Why not?" Finnegan vouchsafed a further explanation, saying, "Look, all we are asking for [in the platform] is a shotgun. If we don't give this crowd in the North that, they are going to use machine guns, [so] you'd better take it [the proposed plank]. But the answer to you is no." If Lyndon Johnson needed proof that he no longer possessed meaningful power at the

Democratic National Convention of 1956, that one-word reply gave it to him. Finnegan and Stevenson no longer had to bargain with him; he no longer had anything substantial to bargain with. Johnson said simply, "All right." And then, Rowe says, "they left."

Rowe was later to hear Johnson recounting the conversation to Richard Russell. "He said, 'Well, you know, Dick, I was really making some progress with Adlai. I took my knife and held it right against him. All of a sudden I felt some steel in my ribs and I looked around and Finnegan had a knife in *my* ribs.' He laughed, and Russell said, 'Finnegan is a pro,' and that was it."

By Tuesday evening, a reporter who ventured into 2306-A found the outer rooms empty except for Johnson's secretaries. In the living room, Johnson was chatting with Hubert Humphrey, who had thought that Johnson would have only a brief moment or two to spare him. Instead, Johnson had time for a long talk. There was no one else waiting to see him. After a while, he left for a leisurely dinner. When he returned about midnight, he was greeted by an aide who said one wire service was reporting that he was about to withdraw as a candidate. Calling a press conference, he said the report was "a baseless, fantastical rumor. I'm still in. You will always find a lot of panicky folks trying to blitz things in the hours just before the balloting." He talked with his usual bravado—asked if Stevenson had used "any pressure" to get the nomination, Johnson said that pressure wouldn't work on him: "I'm used to pressure, and I know how to handle it"—but the reporters weren't fooled. "The fire was out" on Lyndon Johnson's candidacy, one wrote.

FOR THE NEXT TWO DAYS, however, Lyndon Johnson remained a candidate. Rowe's repeated attempts to persuade him to withdraw and announce that Texas would vote for Stevenson, as so many other states were doing, met with no success.

This obduracy brought Johnson a measure of satisfaction—and a measure of what he was always saying he feared.

The satisfaction came on Wednesday, when, before a huge audience that packed the great stockyard arena to the rafters, the candidates' names were placed in nomination, Johnson's by John Connally. The speech nominating Adlai Stevenson, delivered by John F. Kennedy, and written by Kennedy and his aide Theodore Sorensen, was graceful, urbane and witty. The speech nominating Lyndon Johnson was quintessentially Texan: loud, filled with hyperbole, but delivered by a tall, handsome man with the presence of a movie star.

Connally emphasized the key point Johnson wanted—needed—to have made: "Let there be no mistake about it. He is not the candidate of a state or a section," and his speech was filled with the usual stock phrases—"a dedicated American," "a forceful and persuasive leader of men"—but John Connally had known Lyndon Johnson a long time, and his speech also contained some phrases very particularly suited to the man he was describing. "This man has known poverty," John Connally said. "He is a son of the Hill Country of Texas, where the sun is hot and the soil is meager and life itself is a never-easy challenge." And Connally also said: "Call off the roll of great Democrats of this day. By the name of each, there may be entered many fine qualities and many splendid attainments. But alongside of this man there will surely be written the summation: 'This man works hardest of all.' "

Even before the peroration—"Fellow Americans, fellow Democrats, I offer you for the Presidency of the United States, that son of the Texas hills, that tested and effective servant of the people: Lyndon B. Johnson"—the big Texas delegation had begun to roar, and now they leapt up in their tall red-white-and-blue "Love That Lyndon" hats, and grabbed their "Love That Lyndon" banners and moved into line behind a twenty-piece band playing "The Eyes of Texas Are upon You," and started to march through the aisles. Delegates from other states—many other states—grabbed their state banners and followed, so many that, as Booth Mooney wrote, "television commentators noted with some surprise—*had they missed something?*—that participants were by no means confined to the whooping Texans and their southern neighbors"; was support for Johnson broader than they had thought? But most of the non-southern states were parading because of the short, stocky man, his visage stern and impassive, who was standing on the podium above them, looking as if he was bored by all the noise. Knowing how much demonstrations of affection meant to Lyndon, Sam Rayburn had called in the Texas congressmen attending the convention, and told them to pass the word among their House colleagues from other states that he would appreciate their states' participation in the Johnson parade. He did not threaten, of course; Sam Rayburn never threatened. But, as Mooney wrote, the congressmen "reminded" their colleagues "that Sam Rayburn would go right on being Speaker. No doubt he would be watching with interest, and would remember, which states helped to add to the . . . demonstration for his friend." Because of television constraints, a twenty-minute time limit had been placed on parades, and Rayburn had enforced it strictly for every other candidate. Now, "without a flicker of expression," as one reporter wrote, he stood watching as the river of "Love That Lyndon" signs flowed past him and then wound around the convention hall two more times. An officious convention official went up to the old man and told him that the time limit had been exceeded. Rayburn turned and stared at him. The official went away and sat down. The old man stood unmoving, looking down on the signs bearing the slogan that expressed his feelings, too.

Johnson himself, observing the tradition that candidates do not attend the convention as long as their names are before it, was watching on television, upstairs in Wesley West's Imperial Suite at the Hilton with Richard Russell, but seated in a box on the side of the big hall was not only Lady Bird but his family: his mother, his brother, and his three sisters, who had gone through that terrible childhood with him; who had lived, as he had lived, "at the bottom of the heap"; who had watched their father lose the ranch; who had lived in dread of losing their house in Johnson City, too. As the parade reached their box, Connally, its leader, halted for a moment and raised his banner in tribute to them. Who knows what was in their minds at that moment? Who knows what was in the mind of Lyndon Johnson watching in the Imperial Suite? But how far from that childhood he had come.

But the next day was Thursday, when the convention voted on the candidates.

While Johnson had been watching his parade in the Imperial Suite Wednesday night, Russell had given him a warning. "Lyndon," he said, "don't ever let yourself become a sectional candidate for the presidency. That was what happened to me." If you are labeled as a sectional—southern—candidate, Russell said, "You can't win."

Although Johnson certainly understood, at least intellectually, the wisdom of that advice, that the southern label would be hard to shake off and that it would hurt his chances of winning the nomination not only in 1956 but in 1960, and although day by day he was being given the same advice with increasing urgency by Rowe and others and was always assuring them that he understood that advice and agreed with it, he hadn't followed it on Wednesday. When, that evening, the dimensions of the Stevenson landslide were clear, a reporter asked him skeptically, "Senator, are you really going to keep your name in front of the convention to the end?" Johnson wheeled on him angrily and said, "I've told you forty times since I've been here what Johnson's position is. I'll tell you again." His position, he said, was that his name was going to go before the convention, and stay there.

And he didn't follow the advice on Thursday. During the balloting that evening, most of the favorite sons withdrew in favor of Stevenson. Only seven states did not do so, and five of them were southern states: Texas, Mississippi (the only state besides his own which voted for Johnson), and Georgia, Virginia, and South Carolina, who stayed with their favorite sons. So at the end of the first and only roll call, the figures on the big screen behind the rostrum were stark: Stevenson—905½; Harriman—210; Johnson—80. (Symington received 45 votes, most from his native Missouri.) So of the 466½ votes that Stevenson did not receive, 160 were southern votes. As one of the Texas delegates, Jerry Holleman, was to recall, "It became obvious before the first roll call was over that Adlai Stevenson was going to be the nominee, the Texas delegation wanted to switch over from Lyndon and change its vote, cast its final vote for Stevenson and be on the bandwagon. They were after John Connally, and John was on the phone talking to Lyndon, desperately trying to get Lyndon's permission to let them ask for the floor to switch their vote." But the permission was not given. After Rayburn announced that Adlai Stevenson "is declared the nominee of this convention," Connally attempted to offer the traditional motion that the nomination be made unanimous, but Rayburn recognized Oklahoma instead.

. . .

MEN CLOSE TO JOHNSON would puzzle for years over his actions at the 1956 convention, offering different explanations. Rowe would say that "I never could understand why he didn't [withdraw]. It [his reason] was obviously wrapped up in Texas and his base of power, and the Eisenhower feeling down there. And it may have been just a dislike for Adlai." Others note that during the fight for the Texas delegation earlier that year, the conservative Shivers had charged that if Johnson was a candidate, he would be merely a stalking-horse for Stevenson, secretly pledged to turn over his delegates to him, and speculated that Johnson was afraid to release his delegates lest that action prove Shivers correct. But during the intervening months Johnson had been a leading figure—second only to Truman, *the* leading figure—in the "Stop Stevenson" campaign. Releasing his delegates after Stevenson had already been declared the nominee would not make even Texas conservatives believe he had been plotting for Stevenson all along. And in fact Connally, the representative of the anti-Stevenson, pro-Eisenhower conservative powers in Texas, was among those pleading for Johnson to withdraw. Connally himself was to say years later that Johnson's actions at the convention "made no sense to anyone, myself included."

Men who, like Connally, knew Johnson very well, in the end fall back on considerations that are not political but personal, considerations that revolve around the single-mindedness with which Lyndon Johnson held to his great dream. Connally kept returning to the fact that in politics "you can always have a dream," that even when all seems lost, in the hurly-burly of a convention "you always have hope." He was also to note that 1956 was still in the era (although in fact near the end of that era) "when politicians believed in spontaneous forces, that delegates could be stampeded, in the eleventh-hour draft, in a dead-locked convention turning to a compromise candidate." His statement is a reminder that in 1956 a reporter whose articles often reflected Connally's views wrote that until the very end, Johnson was waiting for some "explosion" that would reverse the Stevenson tide, "the explosion that might send him into presidential contention." George Brown, who sixteen years before had watched Lyndon Johnson turn down a small fortune because it might just possibly, at some long-distant future date, interfere with his pursuit of the presidency, and at whose Falfurrias hunting lodge Johnson rested up after the convention, says that "he hadn't thought he would be so close [to the nomination] in '56, and then when all of a sudden [after Truman's endorsement of Harriman], he felt he was close, he got carried away with the thought that he might get it, and he simply couldn't bear to just admit he didn't have a chance." A key word in Brown's analysis is repeated by Tommy Corcoran. Asked why Johnson hadn't withdrawn, Corcoran said flatly: "Because he couldn't bear to." That vast prize that Lyndon Johnson sought, the prize that had always seemed so far off, had suddenly seemed so close, almost within his reach. It was too hard for him to consign it again to the future, to admit that, under the best of circumstances, four years would have to pass before he could try for it again; he "couldn't bear" to do that.

And this emphasis on the personal is given weight by what happened after the convention chose its presidential nominee—and turned to choosing the vice presidential nominee.

AT LYNDON JOHNSON'S TUESDAY MIDNIGHT PRESS CONFERENCE, one reporter had asked him if he would accept the nomination for vice president. "I have not the slightest interest in such an assignment," he said. When, however, another reporter pressed him to make his reply definitive, to say that he would not accept the vice presidential nomination if it was offered to him, Johnson did not do so. He said something very different. "I am not saying that under *NO* circumstances would I refuse to serve," he said.

Little attention was paid to the reply at the time; only one or two reporters even bothered to include it in their articles on the press conference. But attention should have been paid. Felix McKnight of the *Dallas Morning News,* who was close to Connally and got much of his information from him, was shortly to write that Johnson is "reported ready to accept the vice presidency if he is asked."

In fact, he wasn't waiting to be asked. Early Thursday evening a number of Johnson partisans, Tommy Corcoran prominent among them, "told Johnson that he ought to be Vice President," and Johnson told Rowe: "Go in and talk to Adlai. Tell him I want it." Rowe says that "I went in to where everyone was churning around at Adlai, and I said to Finnegan, 'I have got to talk with you and Adlai right away.' So they came out of the room and I said, 'I have got a candidate for the vice presidency and he says he wants it.' " Stevenson reacted graciously, if noncommittedly, with "a very flowery, attractive speech . . . right off the top of his head, saying 'I am a great admirer of Lyndon Johnson. I don't know what I am going to do. I want you to go back and tell Johnson he is one of the great men,' and so forth." Finnegan was simply flabbergasted. He "just sort of sat there and said something like you can knock me [over with a feather]. I said, 'That's my message, gentlemen,' and left."

It was only after Rayburn had offered a little fatherly advice to Johnson on the subject that he dropped the idea. When Corcoran told Rayburn what Johnson was doing, the Speaker reacted with his unique version of disapproval. "I saw that red [flush] coming up over his neck and head, and I just said to myself, 'Uh-oh,' " Corcoran recalls. The whole subject of the vice presidency had already proved irritating to Rayburn; reporters were constantly asking him if he himself would accept the job, a question Rayburn regarded as insulting; "I have never been a candidate for vice president of anything," he growled to one. The advice he gave to Johnson was blunt, and profane—and within a very short time, Rowe was entrusted with a new message for Stevenson. "Johnson said,

'Go back and tell Stevenson that *NO* Texan wants to be vice president. . . . The only thing I want is to be in the meeting where the vice president is selected.' I don't want to be humiliated by not being called into the meeting." Returning to Stevenson and Finnegan, an embarrassed Rowe said, "I don't understand what I am doing, gentlemen, but I now have a new message."

SEVERAL HOURS BEFORE Rowe delivered his two messages, Stevenson and Finnegan had already privately decided on a startling move: instead of announcing his choice of vice presidential candidate as presidential nominees traditionally do, Stevenson would throw the convention open to make its own choice. An hour or two after Rowe had delivered the messages, at about the time Rayburn was announcing that Stevenson had won the nomination, Stevenson sent word to the Speaker on the podium—and to Johnson in the Imperial Suite at the Hilton—to please join him in a private room at the Stockyards Inn restaurant across a parking lot from the International Amphitheatre, and there gave them, and other party leaders, advance notice of his decision.

Rayburn denounced it, in John Bartlow Martin's words, "profanely and contemptuously," and Johnson was only slightly less violent. After all his work to keep the party united, Rayburn saw, Stevenson was about to divide it and throw the convention into turmoil. And the two Texans feared that in an open convention, the despised Kefauver would win: there were less than twenty-four hours before the balloting for vice president began, and the Tennessean, with his forces already organized, would have a long head start. Moreover, Johnson and Rayburn said, the decision would contribute to the impression, already far too prevalent, that Stevenson was indecisive. His face again red with rage, Rayburn stood there refusing to agree to what Stevenson was suggesting until Johnson took him by his arm and said, "Mr. Sam, it's his decision, he has to live with it, not us," and pulled him away. "All right," Rayburn said, "if your mind's made up, give me your arm and I'll take you out there and introduce you to the convention." Watching them leave the room, Democratic Deputy Chairman Hy Raskin warned a friend: "Stay out of the old man's way—he's madder'n hell." Stevenson's announcement ignited a mad scramble. "Within minutes," *Time* said, "no delegate could buy his own drink and no elderly lady could cross a Chicago street without help from an eager vice-presidential candidate."

Making clear that he himself was no longer interested in the vice presidential nomination ("Under no circumstances that I visualize will my name ever go before the convention," he said now), Lyndon Johnson also made it clear that he intended to determine who did get it, but he had as little success— and adroitness—in the maneuvering for this nomination as he had had for the presidential nomination.

The South's Number One priority was to stop Kefauver, and Johnson kept huddling with the leaders of the southern delegations to determine which of the other candidates—Kennedy, Humphrey, Gore, Wagner—would be most likely to do that, so that the South could unite behind him. The South was looking for leadership from him, but he seemed unable to decide. "I talked to Lyndon, too," John Kennedy was later to recall, "but he gave me a noncommittal answer. Maybe Hubert thought Lyndon was for him and maybe Symington thought the same thing and maybe Gore thought that too and maybe Lyndon wanted them all to think that. We never knew how that one [Johnson] would turn out." In fact, Johnson's indecisiveness was making it difficult for him to keep even his own delegation in line, and he repeatedly had to be rescued by Rayburn.

His first choice to stop Kefauver was Humphrey, but Johnson was afraid of antagonizing his conservative Texas financial backers with that liberal choice and doubtful that the other southern states would rally behind a senator so strong for civil rights. When the Texans held their first caucus of the day at 10:30 a.m. Friday, he suggested Texas vote for Tennessee Governor Frank Clement on the first ballot as a holding action, with the idea of switching later to Humphrey. This idea appealed to almost no one—the delegation's conservatives preferred practically anyone to Humphrey, the liberals preferred Kefauver—and Johnson was losing control of a hectic meeting when Rayburn, who had been sitting silently, stood up and said bluntly that "Kefauver can't win in Texas," and that Kennedy was unacceptable because of anti-Catholic prejudice in America. "You fellows are too young to remember the Al Smith thing," Rayburn was to say later. "I've been through it." (Rayburn had another reason, which he didn't divulge, for opposing Kennedy; he had watched the young man's performance in the House and considered him, as his biographers note, "a wealthy dilettante.") The caucus agreed to vote for Clement on the first ballot.

But when Rayburn, high above the jammed, swirling floor on the podium, gaveled the convention to order that afternoon, Johnson got a rude shock: Clement wasn't going to be on the ballot. The Tennessee Governor came over and informed him that he had withdrawn, and that Tennessee was going to nominate Senator Gore. One of the Texas delegates, Kathleen Voight, standing near Johnson, said sarcastically: "We're gonna vote for a man who's not even running." Johnson then repeated to Clement that Texas intended to vote for him; Clement said politely that he "was very grateful," but didn't want the votes. Johnson hurried up to the podium, where Rayburn told him what to do: vote for Gore. When Johnson told the Speaker that he doubted he could persuade the delegation to do that, Rayburn said, "Use my name"—and it was only when Johnson did so that some order was restored. As Johnson cast Texas's fifty-six votes for Gore, "the delegates sat stone-faced," one account noted.

At the end of the first ballot, Kefauver had 483½ votes, Kennedy 304, the other candidates trailed far behind; it was clear that the race was between two men—neither of whom was Humphrey or Gore, the two men Johnson had suggested.

"As Rayburn surveyed the field," his biographer notes, "Kennedy began to look better—anybody but Kefauver." Johnson felt the same way. He told the delegation that he knew all the senatorial candidates, and that Kennedy was the best man. The delegates were not persuaded, and the Gore backers in the delegation kept fighting for their man. Then, as *Time* reported, "the delegation was faced down by grim old Sam Rayburn." "We've got a choice of two men—Kennedy and Kefauver," he said bluntly. "Gentlemen, you can vote as you please—but Sam Rayburn is voting for Kennedy." Texas decided to vote for Kennedy.

On the second ballot, Kennedy surged ahead of Kefauver, with Gore far behind. When the roll call reached Texas, Johnson grabbed the floor microphone and shouted: "Texas proudly casts its fifty-six votes for the fighting sailor who wears the scars of battle. . . ." With his announcement, it looked for a moment as if Kennedy would win, and Johnson shouted exultantly, "All right, it's over!" But that was just another of his mistakes; at the very moment that he was shouting, the standards of half a dozen states were waving wildly in the air, in signals to Rayburn that they wanted to change their vote—and one of the standards was Tennessee's. Grabbing a microphone himself, Gore announced that he was withdrawing—in favor of Kefauver.

Gore's switch turned the tide. State after state switched to Kefauver. One state that did not switch, however, was Texas. Johnson sat at the foot of the Texas standard, holding the microphone in his lap, chewing his lip and looking more and more uncomfortable. As it became obvious that Kefauver would win, many Texans wanted the state to join him. Pushing his way angrily down the crowded aisle toward Johnson, one delegate shouted, "If we can't drive the bandwagon, at least let's ride on it!" Responding lamely, "We don't want to be changing from one to the other," Johnson was still sitting there, glumly holding the silent microphone, refusing to help nominate Kefauver, when suddenly Kennedy was striding out on the platform above him to move that Kefauver be nominated by acclamation. Over Johnson's face came a grimace, in the words of one man who saw it, "of real, deep pain."

HE HAD REASONS to grimace. His party's nominees were two men he disliked and despised. (While he and his mother were being driven back to the Hilton from the International Amphitheatre after Stevenson's acceptance speech that evening, she asked him what he thought of Stevenson's chances to win the election. "He's a nice fellow, Mother, but he won't make it 'cause he's got too much lace on his drawers," Lyndon Johnson said.) He had done his best during the convention to "stop" both Stevenson and Kefauver—without success.

And there were other, larger, reasons. Before the convention, Lyndon Johnson had been almost universally portrayed as an enormously powerful and influential figure in the Democratic Party. By the end of the convention, it had become obvious that that portrait was overdrawn. His image as a brilliant political strategist had also been smudged. "Lyndon Johnson's reputation as an uncommonly astute Senate leader remains unimpaired, but the fact has been established—as it was not before—that in the jungle of a national convention he cannot employ the gifts he uses in the Senate," Richard Rovere wrote in *The New Yorker.* He had, in fact, looked almost foolish. Before the convention opened, summarized the *Washington Post and Times-Herald,* it had been expected that Stevenson "would have to make bargains if he hoped to win the nomination. He would have to 'deal with' the kingmaker, Sen. Lyndon Johnson of Texas, who was expected to corral a huge bloc of Southern delegates and tie them up until he got what he wanted. Adlai would have to be a supplicant and give Johnson his way with respect to a civil-rights plank and a vice presidential nomination. . . . Of course, it didn't turn out that way. . . . Sen. Johnson, so his friends say, was carried away for a while with a vision of himself in the White House. At any rate, he waited too long to play his cards as a king maker. . . . The idea that [Adlai] would have to make concessions to Sen. Johnson . . . seemed a fantastic one in the storm of ballots and acclaim tonight." "This great maneuverer from Texas has been outmaneuvered," the *Wall Street Journal* said.

Even friendly Texas journalists agreed. "The Johnson bloopers on both candidates cannot be ignored for they were surprising at the hands of such a skilled political technician," Leslie Carpenter wrote. Johnson's tactics at the convention were a "mystery," Sarah McClendon wrote. "Here is a man who wanted to be sought but would not seek. He wanted to be President, but he did not tell some states and would not go to ask for votes, even when invited and urged by those states." Marshall McNeil used the same word. "What's Sen. Lyndon Johnson actually been up to this week? Some regard this as the major mystery of the Democratic convention," he said. "State after state, delegate after delegate," had decided, "instead of being on the fence, to be on the side of the probable winner . . . but not Lyndon Johnson." McNeil said that delegates were asking "a question": "What had happened to a man who had always seemed one of the smartest operators around—never a man to get left out on the end of the issue." "One of his [Johnson's] aides" had assured McNeil early in the week, "He's too smart to stay stuck all the way through. He's too quick on his feet"—but in fact, McNeil noted, Johnson had "stayed stuck all the way through. . . . He is a skillful cloak-room and Senate floor operator, [but] a national convention is not the Senate; the same techniques don't apply." And those were the assessments of *friendly* journalists. Drew Pearson gloated that "Lyndon ended up looking like a cellophane bag with a hole in it." Dreading humiliation though he did, Lyndon Johnson had brought a form of humiliation—ridicule—on himself.

There were also less subjective, more rational reasons for Lyndon Johnson to grimace, considerations that were much more serious than a failure to stop other candidates. Johnson's foremost priority before the convention had been to avoid being labeled as the "southern candidate." So overriding was this objective that his tactics had revolved around it: to achieve it, he had refused to seek southern delegates, had, in fact, declined the southern states' offers of delegates. And yet that label had been pinned on him—quite firmly. Arthur Krock had flatly called him "a sectional candidate," and James Reston had ridiculed his attempts to pretend that he wasn't one. Describing Chicago as "a place . . . full of fantasy," in which "normally serious, intelligent, experienced men, sweating under the Presidential fever . . . can convince themselves of anything," Reston said that one of these "illusions" was that "Lyndon can persuade himself that he is really a national and not a regional figure." In a sentence that must have been particularly hurtful to Johnson, Reston said he "is playing in this convention the role played by Richard Russell of Georgia in the last." And the label fit, as the actual balloting had proved. The only state besides his own which had voted for him was the most segregationist state in the entire country.

Not only had he been tagged at Chicago with the label he didn't want, Lyndon Johnson had also been given dramatic, devastating proof of how damaging that label was to his chances for national office, not only in 1956 but in any future year. He had learned for himself, the hard way, what before he had known only by observing the fate of others: you could not win a presidential nomination as the "southern candidate." Even had he kept the South solid in Chicago—as he could so easily have done, simply by early and openly avowing his candidacy—the South would still not have been able to play a decisive role in the convention. It had, after all, been while the South was still holding aloof from Stevenson that Stevenson had wrapped up the nomination with northern votes. Influential, even decisive, as the South was in the Senate, with its chairmanships and its filibuster, in a national convention, it had only 262 of 1,373 votes, and that wasn't enough. It was those huge non-southern blocs of delegates that a candidate needed—Michigan's 44, Ohio's 58, Illinois's 64, California's 68, Pennsylvania's 74, New York's 98. If you wanted the presidential nomination of the Democratic Party, you had to get votes from the North.

And, Lyndon Johnson had learned the hard way in Chicago, there had never been any realistic possibility that he would get those votes. He had entered the convention believing—and had, after Truman's intervention, believed even more firmly on the Monday and Tuesday of that frantic week in Chicago—that he had a chance of getting at least some significant liberal support, and he had learned, learned beyond possibility of misunderstanding, that there was no chance of that, and never had been. He had thought he could split the North, but the North wouldn't split—in large part because its antipathy toward him was so strong it didn't want to give him an opening. One of the arguments most effective in persuading northern delegates to unite behind Adlai Stevenson, in fact, had been the argument that if they didn't, Lyndon Johnson might exert significant influence at the convention, might even become the nominee. New York might not even have held firm behind its own Governor "if it looked like a coup by Johnson was in the making." Johnson may have been aware before the convention of the depth of northern antipathy to him, of the implacability of liberal resolve to deny power to him, or to any other southern candidate. He could hardly have been unaware of this reality, having watched from a ringside seat as it crushed Richard Russell in 1952. But just as Russell had not understood the reality—understood it emotionally as well as intellectually—until it struck him personally, so Johnson had not understood it fully. When Jim Rowe had awakened him at 5 a.m. to tell him that Michigan was going for Stevenson, his reaction had been: "I don't believe it."

But he had to believe it now.

36

Choices

TWO INTERNATIONAL CRISES in the Fall of 1956—the brutal Russian suppression of the Hungarian uprising and the escalating Mideast conflict over the Suez Canal—rallied Americans behind their President, whose smile was as fatherly reassuring as ever. Dwight Eisenhower's landslide popular plurality in his rematch with Adlai Stevenson approached ten million; Adlai won only seven states (all in the South). The Democrats hung on to Capitol Hill, however, overcoming Earle Clements' medical discharge from the Senate to hold their 49–47 margin there. When Congress reconvened in January, 1957, Lyndon Johnson would still be Majority Leader.

Down in Texas, furthermore, with Sam Rayburn and the state's conservative establishment behind him, Johnson had solidified his power in the state's Democratic Party by ruthlessly putting down a liberal uprising. Freed from the restraints of civility imposed on him in the Senate, his tactics had been very blunt: he ordered Texas congressmen and their aides to determine which delegates to the party's state convention were flirting with the liberals, and these delegates, one congressional aide said, were confronted by their "banker, preacher, lawyer, congressman, brother, and threatened unless they got back in the fold." Some were confronted by Johnson himself, in his most aggressive, lapel-grabbing, chest-poking mode. Holders of federal or state jobs were asked, in a tone described as "ferocious," how they liked their jobs; to others, hoping for jobs, Johnson made the price clear: "If you don't help me, you ain't never gonna get to be a judge!" he said to one. Johnson had supported County Judge Woodrow Bean in an intra-party convention fight in return for Bean's promise of support from his El Paso delegation on other issues; when Bean was unable to deliver, Johnson called him in, and, glaring at him and jabbing his forefinger into his chest, demanded, "You with me or against me?" When Bean tried to explain his dilemma, Johnson cut him off. "Woodrow Bean," he said, "I'm going to give you a three-minute lesson in integrity. And then I'm going to ruin you." And he had the convention's credentials committee decertify Bean's entire delegation.

Nonetheless, during the post-election weeks of November and December, 1956, Lyndon was in one of his black depressions. Not getting the Democratic presidential nomination that year had proven to be something of a blessing: the election results had convincingly reaffirmed that no one could have beaten Eisenhower. But the lesson he had had pounded into him in Chicago—that you couldn't win the nomination as the "southern candidate," that you had to have substantial northern support, and that northern antipathy to him ran very deep—had devastating implications for his chances to win the nomination in 1960. He understood now that there was only one way to change his image in liberals' eyes: to support the cause that mattered to them above all others; that so long as he didn't change his position on civil rights, it didn't matter what he did for them on other issues. That hard fact of Democratic political life was being reiterated that December in a letter written to Paul Douglas by Herbert Lehman. "In all fairness," Lehman wrote, "it must be said that the Democrat-controlled 84th Congress did pass some fairly good legislation in fields like social security and health research. But . . . the civil rights issue was buried alive." This could not be allowed to continue, the New York liberal said. "We must put principle above so-called party unity." Lyndon Johnson will not learn this, Lehman said—"cannot or will not learn it." Therefore, he said, Johnson must be removed as Leader. "I want to run the Senate," Lyndon Johnson told allies in private conversation. "I want to pass the bills that need to be passed. I want my party to do right. But all I ever hear from the liberals is Nigra, Nigra, Nigra." He knew now that the only way to realize his great ambition was to fight—*really* fight, fight aggressively and effectively—for civil rights; in fact, it was probably necessary for him not only to fight but to fight and *win:* given their conviction that he controlled the Senate, the only way the liberals would be satisfied of his good intentions would be if that body passed a civil rights bill. But therein lay a seemingly insoluble dilemma: that way—the only way— did not seem a possible way. Because while he couldn't win his party's presidential nomination with only southern support, he couldn't win it with only northern support, either. Scrubbing off the southern taint thoroughly enough within the next four years to become so overwhelmingly a liberal favorite that he could win the nomination with northern votes alone was obviously out of the question, so dispensing with southern support was not feasible: he had to keep the states of the Old Confederacy on his side. And yet a public official who fought for civil rights invariably lost those states.

The problem seemed one without a solution. Lyndon Johnson's path to power had always been a hard, treacherous, twisting path. Had it now become too twisting, too tortuous, for even him to negotiate?

DURING THE MONTHS following the 1956 election, Lyndon Johnson tried to make himself more appealing to liberal northerners—tried, in the words of one, John Kenneth Galbraith, "to cultivate us, to some degree."

He asked for their pity. Delivering a memorandum from Paul Douglas to Johnson's office in the Capitol one day that December, Douglas' administrative aide Frank McCulloch, accustomed to being treated by Johnson with disdain as the representative of the despised "Professor," was surprised to find that Johnson was making an effort to be friendly. Inviting him into his private office, the Leader had him sit down for a chat, and after a few minutes, asked, in an earnest, sincere tone, "Frank, why do the liberals hate me?" McCulloch responded, "Senator, they don't hate you but they certainly are displeased by your positions and your conduct on some of the key issues on which the Democratic Party has taken a position," but Johnson said that no, it was personal, that liberals just didn't like him, he didn't know why—"He was appealing to me for sympathy as an object of hatred. I tried to explain that they really cared about civil rights, about justice, and that he kept opposing, but I can't recall that it [that argument] fazed him in any way; he just kept on about the personal stuff . . . about people's attitude toward him, about how they just *hated* Lyndon Johnson, speaking in a gloomy, mournful tone. 'No, Frank, they just hate me, and Ah can't understand why.' "

He tried to charm them, and to impress them: to convince them of his selflessness and altruism—of his utter selflessness, total altruism; of his complete lack of interest in political advancement, of the absolute absence in his makeup of any personal ambition whatsoever—and to make them appreciate the difficulties he had to face as Democratic Senate Leader, and the brilliance with which he overcame them; and he tried to convince them as well that he was on their side, that he had always been on their side, that he was more liberal than they thought, particularly on civil rights.

Jim Rowe and George Reedy had made him understand the growing importance in liberal intellectual circles of thirty-nine-year-old Arthur M. Schlesinger Jr., a noted Harvard historian with a gift for incisive phrasemaking, and he wrote Schlesinger inviting him to call on him the next time he was in Washington. And when Schlesinger did so, coming to his office on a Saturday, Johnson pulled out all the stops.

It was a memorable conversation—or, to be more precise, monologue; it lasted for an hour and a half, and although Schlesinger, "never known," as a friend says, "for his shyness," had prepared a long list of questions, Johnson talked the whole time almost without interruption.

First came the disclaimer of ambition. According to an *aide-mémoire* which Schlesinger wrote after the conversation, Johnson reminded him that he had had a heart attack; he was a sick man, he said. He had no political future, and he didn't want one. "His main desire, he said, was to live a few more years. He had no interest in the presidential nomination"; he wasn't cut out for the presidency anyway; he knew that. In fact, he said, he wasn't even going to run for the Senate again. All he wanted to do was "to serve out his present term. Being entirely disinterested, he wanted only to do the best he could for his party and his nation in the three, or two, or one year remaining to him." Then he could go back to Texas, where he belonged, and live out whatever few years the Good Lord gave him in peace.

Then he turned to the Senate—as only Lyndon Johnson could. That morning, Reedy had given Johnson a memorandum on how to handle Schlesinger: "He is a man of genuine intellect and eye [*sic*] think all you really have to do is leave him with the feeling that Senate leadership may be much more complicated than he has realized."

That was indeed the feeling that Johnson left him with. In what Schlesinger's memo calls a "stream-of-consciousness on the problems of leadership in the Senate," Johnson "described the problems of keeping the conservative southerners (he called them 'the Confederates') and the liberal northerners in the same harness; he analyzed a number of insoluble parliamentary situations which he had mastered through his own brilliance and perseverance; he gave a generally fascinating account of the role which timing, persuasion, parliamentary knowledge, etc., have in getting bills through."

Then he turned to the individual senators, the other forty-eight Democratic senators. "I want you to know the kind of material I have to work with," he said. Schlesinger was to recall that "he didn't do all of them, but he did most of them"—in a performance the historian was never to forget. Senator by senator Johnson ran down the list: each man's strengths and weaknesses, who liked liquor too much, and who liked women, and how he had to know when to reach a senator at his own home and when at his mistress's, who was controlled by the big power company in his state, and who listened to the REA cooperatives, who responded to the union pleas and who to the Grange instead, and which senator responded to one argument and which senator to the opposite argument. He did brief, but brilliant, imitations; "When he came to Chavez, whose trouble is alcoholism, Johnson imitated Chavez drunk—very funny."

And who, Lyndon Johnson demanded, had to make all these diverse temperaments and philosophies work together? Who had to unite them into a workable majority? The Leader. He had to do everything, he said. It was as if his senators were a football team. He had to be the coach. He had to be the quarterback and call the signals. He had to be the center who snapped the ball, and the running back who ran the ball, and the blocker who blocked for the running back. To demonstrate, he lunged out of his chair. I'm the center, he said, bending over and snapping an imaginary ball. I'm the quarterback, he said, taking the ball and throwing an imaginary pass. I'm the end, he said, holding out his arms to catch the pass. I'm the runner, he said, tucking the ball under his arm and taking a charging step or two across the office. And I have to be the blocker, too, he said, and he threw a block.

And finally Lyndon Johnson came to the crucial point that he wanted Schlesinger to understand. "He seemed quite annoyed," Schlesinger wrote in his *aide-mémoire,* "that the organized liberals do not regard him as one of their [own]." "Look at Americans for Democratic Action," Johnson said. "They regard me as a southern reactionary, but they love Cliff Case. Have you ever compared my voting record with Cliff Case's? I said, 'No, I hadn't,' whereupon he opened his drawer and pulled out a comparison of his voting record . . . on fifteen issues. On each one he had voted for the liberal side and Case for the conservative side. 'And yet they look on me as some kind of southern bigot.' He added that maybe he was showing undue sensitivity to liberal criticism. 'But what a sad day it will be for the Democratic Party when its Senate leader is not sensitive to liberal criticism.' " In particular, Lyndon Johnson said, there was the civil rights issue. On that issue, he said, the liberal feeling toward him was particularly unjust. "I've never said or done anything in my life to aggravate sectional feeling," he said. Why, he said, every time he ran in Texas, he had the support of Negroes, because he had treated them fairly during his term as NYA director. "Maybe, he said sadly, the northerners won't be satisfied until they split off and try to form a party of their own." But all that would do is destroy the Democratic Party. And the northerners would not get very far on their own, "for several reasons—among them the fact that the southerners were better politicians."

(There was a postscript to this conversation. During it, Schlesinger got to say very few words. "I had carefully thought out in advance the arguments to make when asked to justify my doubts about his leadership," he was to recall, "but in the course of this picturesque and lavish discourse Johnson met in advance almost all the points I had in mind. When he finally paused, I found I had little to say. . . . After nearly two hours under hypnosis, I staggered away in a condition of exhaustion." But evidently even a few words were more than was required. When, some months later, Galbraith, Schlesinger's friend and fellow Harvard professor, was visiting Johnson in Texas, Johnson said: "I had a good meeting with Schlesinger. I found him quite easy to get along with. The only trouble was that he talked too much.")

Another liberal object of his attentions were the Grahams of the *Washington Post,* and Johnson's courtship of them was at its most effective, for it took place on his native heath. In December, 1956, Phil and Kay finally accepted his open, insistent, invitation to the Johnson Ranch. From the moment Lyndon loaded them into his car at the little Fredericksburg airstrip, it was a typical Johnson Ranch weekend: the ritual visits to the "birthplace," to the little family graveyard on the riverbank, and to the stone barn in Johnson City; the stories about the Johnson forebears who had fought the Indians from that barn, about the Johnson brothers who had driven the great herds north to Abilene, about his grandmother Eliza Bunton who had ridden out ahead of the herd to scout and who had, during a Comanche raid, hidden under her log cabin and tied a diaper over her baby's mouth so it wouldn't make a sound. And the rituals and stories made vivid and believable one of the points he had been trying to make to northeastern liberals: that while Texas was certainly below the Mason-Dixon Line, he was, because of the part of Texas from which he came, not really a southerner but more a southwesterner. "The idea was that they were fighting Indians and they were pioneers—this southwestern kind of pioneering," Katharine Graham recalls. "And it was 'my animals' and 'my ranch'—you see him ride over those acres; it was like he was saying, 'This is my background, and my roots.' After that visit, I understood him more."

(A glowing profile of Johnson that appeared in the *Washington Post* shortly after the Grahams' return to Washington showed how well Phil had grasped the point:

> On the civil rights issue, Johnson has always taken the traditional Southern view. But it may be well to remember that Johnson is from the highly individualistic "hill country" of Texas, which seldom echoes the prejudices of other sections of the Deep South. Where did Johnson acquire those unusual persuasive qualities which enabled him to walk into the middle of a party split on almost any issue and come out with an agreement? The story is that he inherited his talent from his father, Sam Ealy Johnson, Jr. . . . Others say it traces from old Grandfather Sam Ealy Johnson, Sr., who predicted that his grandson would be a senator the moment he laid eyes on him. In any event, Johnson's antecedents root deep in the country around Johnson City, which his forebears settled in the 1840s and battled the Comanches to keep.

The article was written by Robert Albright, but Johnson knew whom to thank for it. "I know how much I owe to you," he wrote Phil, "and any time I can donate an arm, a leg or anything else to the Graham cause, you can count on it.")

On his home ground, Lyndon Johnson was, in Mrs. Graham's words, "sort of overwhelming—he sort of smothered you with hospitality and with charm." There was the invariable insistence that the guest shoot a deer—whether the guest wanted to or not. "Phil—who loved hunting birds, in part because they are hard to shoot, which meant he mostly missed them, couldn't stand the idea of killing a deer," Mrs. Graham recalls. When they came upon a small group of deer standing on a hill and Johnson told Phil to shoot, "he couldn't bear the thought," and, with the gun on his shoulder, hesitated until the deer turned away from them and started to leave the scene. Then, when Johnson shouted, "Shoot, Phil!" Graham said, "I can't shoot him in the ass, Lyndon," as the deer bounded away. Spotting another group of deer a few minutes later, Johnson stopped the car again, and again ordered Graham to shoot. "I can't, Lyndon," Graham said this time, "He looks like Little Beagle Johnson." But, Mrs. Graham says, "instead of laughing" and accepting Graham's reluctance, Johnson grew angry. "Phil realized he had no choice but to comply, and he shot his deer"; later, Phil and Lyndon laughed over the episode.

And there was the time spent cementing his bonds with the visitor. After dinner, "he and Phil would sit for hours and drink" and talk in the big living room with the frontier-size fireplace. As she and Lady Bird sat mostly silent, Mrs. Graham says, "Lyndon slouched down, Phil bending his elbow—political talk, political gossip, people talk." (One after-dinner session didn't add much cement to the bonds between Lyndon and Mrs. Graham. "Lyndon started complaining" about journalists, she says. This was par for the course for any politician, of course, but "in the middle of his diatribe," Johnson made a remark that she felt went beyond the usual limits, saying: "You can buy any one of them with a bottle of whiskey." "I was much too reticent to enter into the conversation or to object," Mrs. Graham says, "but when Phil and I went upstairs I denounced Lyndon for saying what he said, and Phil for letting it go unchallenged." "How could you sit there and listen to that?" she demanded. "How could you?")

Johnson's parting gifts did not improve the situation. Phil's present was a ten-gallon Stetson, hers a charm bracelet with charms attached, including one in the shape of Texas, and another of a microphone. "When it hit my hand, it was so heavy I realized it was gold," she recalls, and, in the context of Johnson's remark about the press being purchasable, "it rankled." She asked her husband, "Should I give it back—it's just what he was talking about," but he said not to—that they would return a gift of equal value, which they did, sending Johnson a water purifier that he had mentioned needing.

In addition to the customary rituals, during the Grahams' visit there was an added note, a concentration not only on the publisher but on the publisher's wife—to make another point that Johnson wanted liberals to understand: that it was not through idealism and speeches that civil rights would be attained. Philip Graham had for some years been trying to persuade Johnson to "take the lead" on civil rights. "Phil always wanted Johnson to be President," Joe Rauh was to say. "Maybe that [was] because of . . . his [Graham's] feeling for the South. [Graham had grown up in Florida.] That he wanted a southerner [to be President]. . . . He wants to make Johnson President. Well, you got to clean him up on civil rights." Graham had been "pushing Lyndon on its importance from the beginning of their relationship," Mrs. Graham was to say. Since the publisher was himself pragmatic and realistic, "Phil and Lyndon were completely comfortable with each other" on the issue, but, as she puts it, "Lyndon regarded me quite differently [from Phil]"—as one of the flag-waving "red-hots" who couldn't understand that their methods were not improving the chances for social justice. And during this visit, "looking straight at me, separating me from him and Phil," he kept making that argument, prefacing each supporting point by saying, "You northern liberals . . ." hammering "points home, as though trying to explain to me how the world really worked."

Illustrating the message was an anecdote, which Mrs. Graham would always think of as "The Story of How Civil Rights Came to Johnson City."

"You liberals," Lyndon Johnson said. "You think that you fight for civil rights in the North. Well, I want to tell you how civil rights came to Johnson City." And he launched into a story about an incident he said had occurred during his boyhood, when a road was being built through the town, and the road gang included "some Negras" (which, according to Mrs. Graham's oral history, was how Johnson pronounced the word).

"At that time," Lyndon Johnson said, "niggers weren't allowed to stay in Johnson City" after sundown, but the road was coming "nearer and nearer," and obviously the foreman of the road gang was planning to have the gang sleep in town.

"The town bully found" the foreman in the barbershop, and said, "Get them niggers out of town," Johnson said. And then he said, the foreman "got off the chair, took the towel off his neck, put it aside, and they wrestled up and down Main Street." And finally, Johnson said, the foreman "got on top" and took the bully's head in both hands and started banging it against the pavement, asking, with each bang, "Can I keep my niggers? Can I keep my niggers? Can I keep my niggers"—until finally the bully agreed that he could.

"And that's how civil rights came to Johnson City," Lyndon Johnson concluded.

The story was of course told with the customary Johnson vividness. "It was rather a marvelous example—I think he's the best storyteller in the world," Mrs. Graham would recall years later, and, showing Johnson pounding an imaginary head down with both hands and shouting, "Can I keep my niggers? Can I keep my niggers?" she would break into a fond smile of reminiscence. And it had a very clear theme: that, in Mrs. Graham's words, "that was how civil rights could be accomplished, not by idealism but by rough stuff"; that he, not the speechmaking northern red-hots, knew how to get things accomplished for civil rights. He was, Mrs. Graham recalls, saying that "I was an idealist, this theoretical northern liberal," and he, Lyndon Johnson, "was a practical fellow," and that it was through "practical" means—"rough stuff"—that "things got accomplished."

With Schlesinger and the Grahams, this cultivation bore fruit. Shortly after their return from Washington, the Grahams told Jim Rowe about their visit to the ranch, and Rowe informed Johnson, "You certainly did a remarkable selling job there. They wasted at least an hour of my time telling me what a remarkable man you are." Schlesinger's impression of Johnson was recorded in his memoir to himself: "I found him both more attractive, more subtle and more formidable than I expected." And, the historian said, "One got the sense of a man . . . with a nostalgic identification of himself as a liberal and a desire, other things being equal, to be on the liberal side."

In other liberal fields, however, the seeds Johnson tried to plant after the 1956 elections fell on stonier ground. When Schlesinger told Joe Rauh of Johnson's contention "that he was not running for the presidency or for the Senate in 1960," Rauh just laughed heartily. He "said anybody who will believe that will believe anything." Among most liberals, in fact, no planting was even possible; their antipathy toward the Majority Leader was far too strong to permit informal or social attempts at conversion to the Johnson cause. And overtures he had others make on his behalf to liberal journalists like Doris Fleeson or Thomas Stokes, to liberal labor leaders like Walter Reuther or Alex Rose, or to members of the New Deal–Fair Deal pantheon like Eleanor Roosevelt and Harry Truman were notably unsuccessful. He could not, during these months just before the opening of the 1957 Congress, effect any significant change at all in prevailing liberal opinion about him, in part because to so many liberals the memory of earlier battles was still fresh ("What did he think—that we would forget what he did to Leland Olds?" says Alexander Radin of the American Public Power Association. "Well, I never would, I can tell you that"), but largely because of his more recent record on civil rights. Stokes described the "anguish and guilt" of Democratic northern leaders who "are scouring themselves for compromising with the southern wing of the party and permitting the southern leaders to shove civil rights legislation under the rug at the last session of Congress and, at the national convention, to put over a mealy-mouthed civil rights plank without even making a real fight against it." To other northern leaders, it was the recent cruelty to Paul Douglas that left the bad taste in their mouths when they thought of Lyndon Johnson.

The first weeks after the election brought, as well, fresh signs that in 1957 the liberals were going to take the field again for social justice, and that in their view Lyndon Johnson was still very much the enemy. Declaring that "the Democrats are digging their own grave by inaction in the field of civil rights," Hubert Humphrey announced that on the first day of the new session, he and five other liberal senators would jointly introduce a sixteen-point "Democratic Declaration," a liberal legislative program highlighted by strong civil rights laws—and would also attempt to remove the main barrier to the program's enactment by introducing a motion to repeal Rule 22. Fleeson predicted that Johnson would, as usual, oppose the motion because "Johnson is a southerner, deeply obligated for support and counsel to southerners." Clarence Diggs, the African-American congressman, said that if Johnson was unable to support the motion, he should resign as the party's Senate Leader.

Schlesinger's growing admiration for the Texan was most decidedly not shared by most of the historian's fellow members of the ADA's executive committee, who, while not going as far as Diggs in demanding Johnson's outright resignation, passed a resolution asking him to recuse himself during the Rule 22 fight, and not "use his post to betray the Democratic platform." ADA Chairman Rauh "regards the pivotal position of Lyndon Johnson as a major block to effective liberal legislation," Irwin Ross reported in the *New York Post*. Before the sixteen-point Declaration had even been announced, Rauh said, its six senatorial sponsors, afraid of Johnson's power, had watered it down so that it would "be harder for Lyndon to complain." Another coalition of liberal leaders, the National Committee for an Effective Congress, accused Johnson of wanting "to be the Democratic spokesman nationally—in a position tandem to that of the President," and said that because of his views on civil rights he must not be allowed to have that role. One after another, leading liberals made the same point, none more eloquently than the New Yorker who in the Senate may have been almost an object of ridicule but who outside it, among liberals everywhere, was an object of reverence. In a valedictory interview he gave over the Christmas holidays of 1956, just before his retirement, Herbert Lehman told Irwin Ross that while he might be leaving the Senate, he was not leaving the fight—and that no matter how hopeless the fight seemed, it should be continued. "A fight is worthwhile even if you know you're going to lose it," he told Ross. "It's the only way to crystallize attitudes, educate people. And in the end I've seen many hopeless causes win out." Looking back at the 1920s, when it had seemed impossible to win social advances that were now an accepted part of American life, he said: "We were called radicals and dreamers, but we were willing to wage seemingly hopeless fights. In the same way, we will get complete school desegregation, and Negroes will get the right to vote in the South. These things are coming—quicker than people realize."

Liberal dislike and distrust of Lyndon Johnson was not confined to idealists and intellectuals. At one Democratic conference, a speaker referred to the "great victory" the party had achieved in retaining control of Congress despite Eisenhower's huge plurality. The next speaker was that most practical of politicians, Colonel Jacob M. Arvey of Illinois, who commented caustically: "All this talk about a great victory is fine. I think we scored a great victory. I also think we got hit by a truck." And, the Colonel said, "if 1958 is to be a Democratic year, it may be necessary to get a few new pass catchers on the Democratic team." An attempt was made to institutionalize the opposition. In a secret meeting near the end of November, Arvey and other seasoned professionals— liberal professionals—on the Democratic executive committee instructed National Chairman Paul Butler to formalize the challenge to the southern leadership in Congress by establishing a high-level "Democratic Advisory Council" to shape a party legislative program that would not coincide with, but challenge Eisenhower's policies. Galbraith, one of its members, said that the purpose of the twenty-member council was to take "some of the Texas image off the party." In the *New York Times,* Russell Baker said bluntly that "It is a challenge to Senator Lyndon B. Johnson of Texas."

Butler publicly invited Johnson and Rayburn to join the council—a tactical mistake on two counts. First, by including Rayburn, he infuriated scores of Democratic congressmen who took the formation of an "Advisory Council" as a personal insult to their beloved "Mr. Sam," particularly because of his accomplishments in liberal causes. "I don't think any outside committee can undertake to advise Rayburn," said veteran Ohio congressman Michael Kirwan. "As

Interstate Commerce Committee Chairman, as Majority Leader, and as Speaker, he pushed through the House all the important laws of the New Deal and Fair Deal. Certainly I can't advise him. Who are they to advise him?" Second, by issuing a public invitation—without ascertaining beforehand whether it would be accepted—Butler allowed Johnson and Rayburn to decline publicly (and to make sure that other congressional invitees followed suit) in a statement that emphasized the council's powerlessness by saying that a legislative program could only be promulgated by legislative leaders. "The first blood has gone to the congressional leadership of the party," Gould Lincoln wrote. But with liberal icons like Lehman, Stevenson, Harry Truman and Eleanor Roosevelt as members, the Democratic Advisory Council could hardly be ignored. "Our fight has just started," Butler said, and his efforts were supported by liberal editorial writers, columnists, and cartoonists. They made it clear that the civil rights issue was not going to go away. Supporting the move to repeal Rule 22, the *New York Times* said that "Though similar efforts have failed before this . . . the interests of Democratic government require that it be made again, and again, and again, until at least it succeeds as it eventually will. . . . It is a travesty to wrap the mantle of 'free speech' around the filibuster. That is exactly what the filibuster is not." And in words and pictures they also made clear what side of the issue they felt Lyndon Johnson was on. In the months since the Democratic convention the label he had worn there had been pasted on him more firmly than ever. Even his supporter Arthur Krock had to note that the criticism of his tactics at the convention had now been revived: "that he used his influence, with calamitous consequences, to induce the convention to 'appease' the South in the party platform plank on civil rights." Conceding that the senatorial signers of the "Democratic Declaration" had little power within the Senate, *The Nation* told its readers that that was not the point. "The Declaration," it said, "is an important document" because it is "the first major move in a campaign to reconstruct and rehabilitate the Democratic Party," and because it was also "a vote of 'no confidence' in the leadership of Senator Johnson." A Herblock cartoon on November 28 showed a "Senate Liberal" handing Johnson a paper labeled "Proposals for Cloture and Civil Rights Legislation." In one hand, Johnson is holding a wastepaper basket in which he is going to deposit the paper; his other hand, hidden behind his back, is holding an outsize gavel with which he is preparing to knock the liberal on the head.

WHEN, FURTHERMORE, hard-eyed men in both parties—the poll-takers and strategists to whom politics is percentages—began analyzing the 1956 election results, certain percentages leapt out at them: those in the columns headed *Negro*.

The trend among African-American voters which in 1952 had so disturbed Democrats—and so encouraged Republicans—had intensified in 1956, they realized. In 1952, the 68 percent of the black vote that Adlai Stevenson had polled had been far below the percentages that Democratic strategists had come to expect. In 1956, Stevenson's percentage was 61 percent. "Of all the major groups in the nation's population," pollster George Gallup reported, "the one that shifted most to the Eisenhower-Nixon ticket was the Negro voter." And at the same time that the Democratic share of the Negro vote had declined, the size of that vote had grown—not in the South, of course, where a mere 15 percent of eligible Negroes had voted—but in the North, for between 1952 and 1956 the Negro exodus to northern cities had continued.

The concatenation of these two trends—an increase in the black vote and in the percentage of that vote going Republican—intensified the hopes tantalizing the GOP. It was in the big cities of California and the North's eight big industrial states that the Negro vote—perhaps three million black voters—had been concentrated in 1956, and, "from every available evidence," as the Democratic pollster Richard Scammon told his clients, during the next four years that vote "will continue to increase." This possibility provided the GOP with a great opportunity: to take the big states and thereby to be able to hold the White House even without an Ike at the head of the ticket.

The more closely that these trends were analyzed—congressional district by congressional district, ward by ward—the more attainable that prospect appeared. The larger the Negro population in a particular district or ward, the larger had been Eisenhower's margin of gain between his two elections. The heart of New York's Negro population, for example, was the city's Sixteenth Congressional District: Harlem. And in Harlem, where once a Republican presidential candidate counted himself lucky if he received 10 percent of the vote, Eisenhower had received 17 percent in 1952 and 34 percent in 1956. In Illinois's First Congressional District—Chicago's South Side—his share had increased from 25 percent to 36 percent. And "even a 50-50 break in the up-to-now heavily Democratic Negro vote might well push key doubtful states into the Republican column," Scammon concluded. The Democrats might then be denied the White House until some new major adjustment of American political forces shifted the balance their way."

And, strategists saw, a key reason for the Republican trend among African-American voters remained: the Democrats' control of Capitol Hill. "The Negro voter by and large appears convinced that it is the Democrats who prevent any legislative help in his race's striving for a better share in American democracy," the *Atlantic Monthly* reported. "The Negro voter, and the white voter, too, who feels strongly on the subject, sees only Mississippi Senator Eastland blocking the door of his powerful Judiciary Committee and backed by Southern Democrats determined to filibuster any civil rights legislation." NAACP lobbyist Clarence Mitchell, speaking to NAACP branches across the country during the 1956 campaign, had said that a heavy Negro vote for Republicans "would automatically eliminate twenty-one Southern chairmen from the key committee posts they now hold." Campaigning in Harlem, Vice President Richard Nixon had told audiences that civil rights legislation "cannot pass . . . as long as the filibuster exists in the Senate." (He also said that if Eisenhower was elected, "we are going to have performance on civil rights, not just promises," because Eisenhower "is going to have a vice president who opposes the filibuster.") The effectiveness of such pleas had been documented in the upsurge in the GOP vote in Harlem. Said Mitchell after the campaign: "Seldom in the long political history of our country has a man been so helpful in defeating members of his own party as Eastland." Democrats knew Mitchell was right. Returning to Washington from Oregon, where he and his wife, Maurine, had made more than 350 speeches urging the re-election of Wayne Morse, Richard Neuberger said that although "less than two percent of Oregon's population is colored," "we are continually confronted with the charge that a vote for Senator Morse . . . was a vote to continue Senator Eastland as chairman of the Senate Judiciary Committee. . . ."

There was a further disturbing note for Democrats. The concentration of northern Negro voters in the cities' ghetto wards, together with gerrymandering that kept the Negro vote confined to those wards, meant that the shift in that vote toward the GOP had not yet been heavily felt in elections below the presidential level. But, as *U.S. News & World Report* said, if the shift continues, "it could affect the choice" of aldermen, city councilmen, and scores of House members. "This kind of political fallout in Negro precincts is causing major recalculations of party strength all over America."

The recalculations were going on in both parties. Once a basic Democratic belief had been that the party could not afford to alienate the South. Now there was a new calculation. The eleven southern states had a total of 128 electoral votes, and that figure included Texas, which Eisenhower had carried twice and whose twenty-four electoral votes could no longer be considered safe for a Democratic presidential candidate. Without Texas, the South's electoral vote was 104. The nine key northern states had 223 electoral votes. Accustomed though Capitol Hill had become to discounting Hubert Humphrey's extravagant rhetoric, his remark that the Democrats were "digging their own grave" brought many nods in Democratic offices. "The civil rights dilemma loads down the Democrats in the North, as the Old Man of the Sea sat athwart the shoulders of Sinbad the Sailor," said Senator Neuberger; unless the party's stance on that issue was changed, "the result could be banishment for the Democrats for many decades from the executive branch of government." Long indispensable, the South might, suddenly, now be expendable.

And while Democrats were constrained from taking full advantage of these new calculations by another reality—a change in the party's stance might alienate the committee chairmen who were so important a source of its strength—no such constraint operated on the GOP. Republicans had little to lose, and a great deal to gain. Give us a civil rights bill, one Republican leader told James Reston, "and by 1960 we will break the Roosevelt coalition of the large cities and the South, even without Eisenhower." No sooner had the 1956 election results been analyzed than Republican leaders began laying plans to exploit the situation, and among these leaders were the party's two leading candidates to succeed Eisenhower, both of whom, as it happened, were from California, with its 194,000 Negro voters, which meant that both men had been sensitized to the potentials of black voting power (and both of whom, as it happened, were there in the Senate Chamber with Lyndon Johnson, one of them, William Knowland, seated just across the aisle from him, the other, Richard Nixon, on the low dais just a few feet away, his eyes almost level with those of the tall Majority Leader). Knowland, the Taft acolyte whose passion for civil rights had heretofore been extremely well concealed, now unequivocally promised the NAACP's Mitchell that he would lead the fight to pass a civil rights bill in 1957. As for Knowland's rival, as Marquis Childs said, "One thing even Nixon's bitterest enemies have never denied him. That is a sure understanding of the main chance." And, Childs wrote, Nixon was "working with all the intensity of a very intense nature, to try to shape . . . for his party" a strategy to position it on the right side of "the issue that contributed, more than any other, to the Republican landslide of last November." Nixon's ally, of course, was Brownell, and the Republican Attorney General had lost none of his enthusiasm for his proposed bill that would give the Justice Department "unprecedented power" to enforce a "broad array" of civil rights—the bill in whose inherent aims, and political possibilities, he deeply believed. Within a few days after the election, it was known that the Brownell Bill would be reintroduced in 1957. In 1956, it had been introduced late in the session, late enough for the Senate to avoid confronting it, but the Senate would not be able to avoid confronting it again.

SINCE THE 1956 ELECTION, there had been a further escalation of white hostility in the South. When the new school year had begun in September, before the election, there had been only minor progress in the seventeen states which, before the *Brown* decision, had required school segregation. Of the 2,731,750 Negro schoolchildren who were in school that September in the seventeen states, some 115,000—4 percent—were in schools also attended by whites. And even that small figure was misleading, for almost all of those 115,000 were in border states. In the eleven former Confederate states, 3,400 of Texas' 248,000 Negroes were in integrated schools; a total of 1,200 more were in integrated schools in Arkansas or Tennessee; three years after *Brown,* that was the extent of southern compliance with the Court's decree. And as. John Bartlow Martin found on his tour through the South that Fall, "in recent months resistance [to school desegregation] has been hardening"; in most of the Deep South, he reported, "there is no prospect of school integration in the foreseeable future." State legislatures would be convening in January, and scores of bills had been introduced that would have the effect of nullifying the educational integration decree. In Virginia, they were introduced by legislative members of the Byrd Machine. There was no time to lose, Harry Byrd said; a federal judge had issued a ruling designed to force integration in Virginia. "We face the gravest crisis since the War Between the States." If laws were not passed to circumvent the ruling, he said, six-year-old children of both races would be "assembled in little huts before the bus comes, and the bus will then be packed like sardines. . . . What our people most fear is that by this close intimate social contact future generations will intermarry." The chairman of the Senate Finance Committee called for "massive resistance" to all such court rulings; law enforcement, he said, should be "by the white people of this country."

Other bills dealt with voting, intending to make it more difficult for African-Americans to register—not that such legislation seemed particularly urgent, for while black voting had been rising sharply in the North, in the South voting statistics were little more encouraging than those on schools. Among the more than six million Negroes in the eleven southern states who were twenty-one years of age in 1956, only 1,238,000 had been registered—still only one in five. There were entire counties in these states—counties in which thousands of Negroes lived—in which not a single Negro was registered to vote. In Mississippi, the number of registered Negroes may actually have declined during those four years. Further increases seemed likely to come even more slowly. Five states still had a poll tax, and in all the southern states the use of literacy tests and of outright intimidation, economic and/or physical, was increasing. A new tactic—wholesale "challenges" by Citizens Councils representatives of Negro voters on a county's registration lists—had been instituted in 1956, and it had proven effective: in one Louisiana parish, more than three thousand of the four thousand registered Negroes had been purged from the registration books shortly before the 1956 election—and its use was expected to increase. The number of Negroes who actually voted in the South may actually have been smaller in 1956 than in 1952.

Nor was it only in schools and voting that the South was strengthening its defenses. "The [legislative] hoppers of the South are spilling over with legislation aimed at keeping the Negro 'in his place,' " Stan Opotowsky of the *New York Post* found on a tour of the South in December, 1956. One bill that was about to be introduced—and passed—in Louisiana specifically prohibited the performance of George Gershwin's musical *Porgy and Bess* since it raised the possibility of blacks and whites appearing on the same stage; it also prohibited the annual meeting of the state Red Cross, since a previous annual meeting had been attended by Negroes and whites.

Anger was escalating everywhere in the South. In the White Citizens Councils, the South had found, in John Bartlow Martin's phrase, "a flag to rally round," and in 1956 as in 1955 tens of thousands of white southerners joined their rolls. One huge rally followed another. The Councils' vigilance extended into areas previously not thought of: incensed that some of Southern Bell's party lines were used by both black and white subscribers, Mississippi's Monroe County Council demanded that the company segregate its telephones.

The Councils' targets included not only Negroes but white southerners whose racial views, while perhaps not pro-integration, were unacceptably moderate. They, too, Opotowsky found, "are subjected to the same terror if they dare stray from the most rigid segregation line." "There is a consistent and insistent attempt to force all white southerners into a rigid pattern of defiance of the courts and to a position of rigidity on every aspect of the race question," said Morris B. Abram, president of the American Jewish Committee. And these "enormous pressures," Abram said, were succeeding. "The field is being preempted by the extremists." The White Citizens Councils had the South—the white South as well as the black—firmly in its grip. "The domination is total," Opotowsky wrote. "There is no middle ground, no shade of gray. Only black and white. And woe betide the black." Reported Martin: "The Deep South is solid once more."

Even more ominously, a growing number of southern whites were not satisfied with the Councils' actions. There was, the *New York Times* reported that December, "an upsurge by the frustrated elements that want more boldness and action." The Ku Klux Klan, in disrepute for more than a decade because of its violent redneck tactics, was again on the rise: that Fall, Martin reported, it "has burned crosses in the fields and paraded openly through many a small town." And the Klan, as Opotowsky pointed out, "does not claim the niceties which the Councils wear as their mantle. They're back to flogging again." In one incident, in Camden, South Carolina, a white fifty-two-year-old high school music teacher was taken from his car, tied to a tree, and beaten with tree limbs and with a wooden plank by a group of men in white hoods because it was thought that he had advocated school integration. Only later was it learned that the beating had been given to the wrong man; the music teacher had, in fact, opposed integration.

Everywhere in the South, violence was rising. That November and December, 1956, in the wake of the victory in Montgomery (it had been a week after the November election that the Supreme Court ruled Alabama's bus segregation ordinances unconstitutional), Negroes had begun bus boycotts in other southern cities, and were trying to integrate schools and parks as well. Martin Luther King's Southern Christian Leadership Conference, the organization created to launch civil rights protests all across the South, was organizing for its first meeting, which would be held in Atlanta on January 10. Southern whites were reacting to this new black determination with new fury. The bombings of Negro homes and churches increased; more snipers fired on integrated buses; in one incident, in Montgomery, a Negro woman was wounded in the leg, and when more shots were fired at the bus, it headed for a police station with its passengers lying on the floor. There were new attempts on King's life and family, including a shotgun blast fired into their home while they were sleeping. In Birmingham, Fred Shuttlesworth had announced that he and other Negroes would sit in the front rows of city buses on the day after Christmas. On Christmas night, a bundle of fifteen sticks of dynamite exploded beneath Shuttlesworth's parsonage. The next day, he and a score of other Negroes were arrested on the buses. Police in other Alabama cities also ignored the Supreme Court ruling, arresting Negroes who sat in front. On the eve of the 1957 session of Congress, southern bombings, beatings, sniper fire, and cross-burnings were not stopping but increasing.

The perpetrators evidently felt they could act with impunity—and again and again they were proven correct. Every time black leaders asked Brownell to take action to stop the violence, the Attorney General had to reply that under existing law, the authority for maintaining intra-state law and order rested with the states, not the federal government. Two white men had actually been arrested for one of the bombings of Martin Luther King's home, and had given, and signed, confessions. A Montgomery jury, all white naturally, had acquitted them nonetheless. "Deep Southern resistance," John Bartlow Martin wrote, is "righteous, determined and sure of success. At the outset [it] probably was buying time. Not today. And they believe they have desegregation stopped. This is not a few loudmouth, rabble-rousing politicians. . . . This is all but unanimous white opposition." He had taken a tour of the South to determine when the South might integrate its schools, and he gave his conclusion in the title of the book he wrote: *The Deep South Says "Never."* The region's attitude was personified in the Georgian who in 1956 drove gentlemanly old Walter George out of the Senate. Georgia's new senator was Herman Talmadge—son of Gene Talmadge, hero of the woolhats, the Georgia Governor who during the 1930s and '40s had been the incarnation of the suspender-snapping, tobacco-chewing, southern race baiter; while he had not actually been a member of the Klan, Gene once said, "I used to do a little whippin' myself." Herman was smoother, but just as unabashed a segregationist. As Governor he sponsored a state constitutional amendment allowing Georgia to close her public schools rather than desegregate them, and to send white and Negro children to separate, private, schools. Sitting contentedly in his stately home, filled with echoes of the Civil War ("When we remodeled we dug a few old Minié balls out of the house. . . . The only reason it was not burned was that Sherman occupied it"), he told Martin, "They couldn't send enough bayonets down here to compel the people to send their children to school with Nigras." Talmadge's election to the United States Senate in November, 1956, was by the biggest majority in Georgia's history. To Clarence Mitchell, says Mitchell's biographer, "the supplanting of George by Talmadge" was "a tragedy that reaffirmed the South's intention to stick to its unconstitutional way of life."

The South was determined that its position on segregation would in fact be hardened, that this new civil rights agitation would be defeated. And when southern strategists surveyed the situation, they were confident that it *would* be defeated, for after all, if all else failed, they still had their Senate citadel, where they still held their chairmanships and their subcommittees. When Congress reconvened in January, it would be faced again by the Brownell Bill, but although that bill had been passed by the House in 1956, it had been blocked in the Senate, and, if necessary, it would be blocked there again. And back in the states of the southern senators, the rising Rebel yell was not for compromise but for victory.

LYNDON JOHNSON was in residence at the Johnson Ranch over Christmas vacation in December, 1956, so early each morning Mary Rather would walk down to the Pedernales, passing the family cemetery with its big live oak, and then across the river on the low-water bridge to collect the mail from the large, slightly tilted mailbox.

That December, late in the month, among the missives that Ms. Rather found in the mail and left on the dining room table for her boss to open over breakfast were three communications that were definitely not Christmas greetings. They were warnings—warnings, in the form of memoranda, that Lyndon Johnson took very seriously because of the identity of the men who had written them. Each of the three memoranda warned him that he must act on civil rights, and act soon. And each memo told him also what might never happen if he failed to act.

One of the memoranda, mailed from Washington on December 20, was from the man with whom he could not "afford to argue," and it demonstrated that among people committed to the cause of social justice, not even personal affection could blunt the issue. Philip Graham had discussed the memo with his wife before sending it; in her memoirs, she would describe it as "arguing that the senator needed to counteract the reputation he had as a conservative, sectional . . . politician." The memorandum itself said that Johnson's past response to this "false stereotype . . . has been largely negative. He complains about 'phony liberals,' he criticizes columnists and some other parts of the press, etc." And, Philip Graham told Johnson bluntly, that reaction hadn't worked—and it was never going to. The only way for Johnson to change his stereotype, Graham wrote, was for him to announce a legislative program that would make possible a congressional session "marked by a high order of accomplishment." The program, Graham wrote, would have several "principal themes," of which an "essential" one (Katharine Graham would call it "perhaps the most important") was civil rights. "Civil rights to be strengthened, not by phony speechmaking but by consequential action," Graham wrote. "It is essential for LBJ to create and articulate a realistic philosophy on civil rights . . . a new Civil Rights program which can be embraced by people" of all persuasions, and which "can bring reality to this general field."

Bluntly, Philip Graham warned Lyndon Johnson of the consequences of not acting on civil rights. "Fate's decree may be that LBJ is destined only to be a Jimmy Byrnes or a more energetic Dick Russell," he said. "On the other hand, he may be permitted to play a truly consequential role in the mainstream of history."

"The only way to test the possibilities is to test them," he said. "At the moment LBJ is not doing so."

The other two memos were both from the man who Johnson thought was the person who "might make him Pope or God knows what." Four months earlier, at the Chicago convention, Jim Rowe had warned him, in writing, not to become "another Dick Russell," had told him that if he presented an image of a "Southern candidate . . . it will make it almost impossible for Lyndon Johnson" to be nominated "in 1960," had said that he knew that such an image "is Lyndon Johnson's private nightmare." Now, in December, Rowe warned Johnson, in writing—in two memoranda, dated December 13 and 21—that the nightmare was coming true. There is, Rowe said, a "growing public impression that you are the leader of the Southern Conservatives."

"This has long worried me and I know it worries you, too," Rowe said. Nonetheless, he said, "it is clear to me that enough has not been done to change or stop or turn this impression. All you and I have done essentially is to point out to each other that this picture is utterly untrue. . . . We are inclined to dismiss it." And, he told Johnson, you "cannot afford to" dismiss it if you want to win the presidential nomination. "It is time that we accept the obvious truth that a public impression is just as much a fact as anything else." That impression must be changed—quickly.

To accomplish this, Rowe had a number of suggestions. Some were social—Harry Truman and Adlai Stevenson will be in Washington immediately after the first of the year, he told Johnson, and you should invite them over for a drink and "conciliate" them; think of what they can do to you if they are hostile!: "If these two men would wish to wrap the [southern candidate] tag . . . around your neck, you would have a terrible time trying to get rid of it." And some were strategic, of which the key one was that he immediately put the newly elected Democratic senator from Colorado, former Representative John Carroll, a liberal and ardent civil libertarian, on the Judiciary Committee.

"Your problem in the Senate in 1957 will be twofold," Rowe wrote. The first is "To avoid becoming the symbol of the South," and the second was linked with the first: "To cut the ground out from the northern liberals" by at least appearing to cooperate with them. "So on civil rights," Rowe said, "you should be ready to give the civil libertarians something *which they already have.*" Carroll's appointment to Judiciary would accomplish this, because it would be meaningless, Rowe said: "The appointment of a civil liberty senator to the Judiciary is nothing special, because they already have a large majority [on the committee]." Johnson had Reedy write Rowe a letter temporizing on the appointment, and Rowe didn't press the subject, but in subsequent telephone calls he did press the larger point: that to win the 1960 nomination, Johnson must make himself more acceptable to the North, and the only way to do that was by passing civil rights legislation. "Otherwise," as Rowe was to say in an interview years later, "the northern bosses were just not going to take him. The Negro problem just wouldn't allow it."

The memoranda were not the only warnings from Washington delivered, on the same subject, to the Johnson Ranch that December. At least one other came in a telephone call from the capital, from another man whose advice Lyndon Johnson took very seriously. Tommy Corcoran was, as always, much blunter and less diplomatic than his partner, Rowe, and told Johnson flatly, he was to recall, "If he didn't pass a civil rights bill, he could just forget [the] 1960 [nomination]."

These were warnings to a man who didn't need warnings. "Johnson already knew" what he had to do in 1957, Rowe says. As Doris Kearns Goodwin was to write, "The issue of civil rights had created a crisis of legitimacy for both the Senate and the Democratic Party." And therefore the issue was a crisis for Lyndon Johnson. In a sense—in the journalistic view, the public view— Lyndon Johnson *was* the Senate, its Majority Leader, the senator who would be held responsible for its actions. If the Senate appeared ineffectual, incapable of dealing with the issue, *he* would appear ineffectual, incapable. If it appeared sectional, southern, racist, *he* would appear sectional, southern, racist. Furthermore, as far as the Senate was concerned, he *was* the Democratic Party. If the party looked ineffectual or racist, the blame would fall on his head. If the party split, the chasm between southern and northern senators becoming unbridgeable, the responsibility for that would fall on his head, also. And the issue was, in addition, a crisis for him in terms of his personal ambition. As Goodwin wrote: "As a man with presidential dreams, Johnson recognized that it would be almost impossible for him to escape all responsibility for the Senate to act, that failure on this issue at this time would brand him forever as sectional and therefore unpresidential."

Lyndon Johnson had no choice, and he knew it. Recalling the situation years later, he would say: "One thing had become absolutely certain: the Senate simply had to act, the Democratic Party simply had to act, and I simply had to act; the issue could wait no longer."

"Something had to be done," he said.

He understood as well the consequence of failure on this issue. "I knew," he said, "that if I failed to produce on this one, my leadership would be broken into a hundred pieces; everything I had built up over the years would be completely undone."

"PRODUCING" on civil rights seemed almost impossibly difficult, however. To win the Democratic presidential nomination, Lyndon Johnson had to keep the support of the South. And the key to keeping that support was not passing civil rights legislation but rather stopping it from being passed.

Moreover, despite his success in chipping away some of the South's power in the Senate and concentrating it in his hands, the South's senatorial power was still immense; in 1957, southerners would be the chairmen of no fewer than five of the Senate's eight most powerful Standing Committees, and their ally Hayden would be chairman of a sixth, Appropriations. On the key committees and subcommittees, they were stacked, in fact, more deeply than ever; on Appropriations, for example, there would be in 1957, in addition to Chairman Hayden, eleven other Democratic members. Eight were southerners, two were senators who voted with the South on appropriation bills—exactly one, the most junior member, was a vote of which the southerners could not be confident. Even if he decided to pass a bill, *could* he pass it? In a confrontation with the Majority Leader, the chairmen might still win.

And it was not winning that was the most crucial point, for if there was a confrontation between Johnson and the South, Johnson might no longer *be* Majority Leader. The Leader was elected by the Democratic Caucus. In 1957, there would be forty-nine Democratic senators, so only twenty-five votes, a majority of the forty-nine, would be necessary to remove him and pick a new Leader. Even without his own vote, and that of the other Texas senator, Price Daniel, and, possibly, Gore of Tennessee, the South would still have nineteen or twenty of the necessary twenty-five votes, and it could always muster the few necessary additional votes from its allies. And where would *he* get votes? From the liberals, whose every meeting was an exercise in denouncing him? From the liberals, like Paul Douglas, whom he had repeatedly humiliated? Even if Johnson changed his stance on civil rights, could he really count on liberal support? And how many liberal votes were there in the Democratic Caucus anyway? Nine or ten for certain—that was all. If the South turned against him, he could be voted out of the leadership very easily.

Nor would voting him out even be necessary. The South had not found it necessary to remove Scott Lucas or Ernest McFarland as Majority Leader. The South had simply refused to cooperate with them—and without the South's cooperation, those two men had been ineffectual, objects of ridicule. The South could do the same to Lyndon Johnson.

Even if Johnson was to decide to confront the South, and try to pass legislation over its opposition—was such a course feasible? Even if all the other defenses that the South could erect against civil rights legislation were somehow breached, there would remain still that last defense, the strongest of all, the defense that, decade after decade, had proven impregnable. Even if Lyndon Johnson decided to try to break a filibuster, could it be broken?

With more senators than ever before sympathetic to the plight of black Americans, and with more Republican support due to both conscience and calculation, a civil rights bill might well command a majority of votes in the Senate. But would the bill be allowed to come to a vote? There might be a majority for passage; would there be the necessary two-thirds for cloture? Western senators, of both parties, were supportive (sometimes only lukewarmly) of civil rights but were adamantly opposed to cloture, since the right of unlimited debate was their states' ultimate protection. "Some conservative Republicans (from the Midwest) believe . . . that even the mildest civil rights legislation is wrong," George Reedy notes. They might nonetheless be pressured by the White House into voting for such legislation, he says, but that did not mean they could also be pressured into voting for cloture. "Unlimited debate is regarded as an absolute principle by many senators," Reedy wrote. "It is *NOT* [italics in original] just a dodge to keep civil rights legislation from passage." On the eve of the Eighty-fifth Congress, some liberals were saying, as they had on the eve of the Eighty-fourth Congress, and the Eighty-third, and on the eve of Congresses going back for years before that, that there was a real chance that this time there would be enough votes to impose cloture, but among more realistic Capitol Hill observers there was considerable doubt about that. Only thirty-three votes or absences were necessary to defeat cloture; when to the nineteen or twenty southern votes were added the votes of conservative northeastern Republicans like Styles Bridges and John Marshall Butler and others, and conservative midwestern Republicans like Hickenlooper and Bricker and Jenner and Thye and Capehart and Curtis and Schoeppel and Hruska and Young and others, and western senators like Hayden and Goldwater and Alan Bible and Malone and Henry Dworshak and others, "you got up to thirty-three real fast," as one vote-counter was to explain, even without including those senators who mouthed a support for civil rights that they did not feel in their hearts. Years later, putting down his thoughts in a definitive way, George Reedy was to write, "They [the southerners] unquestionably had the power to defeat—through filibuster—any or all Civil Rights proposals and there was no prospect whatsoever of shutting off their filibuster through a cloture move." The last civil rights law had passed in 1875. During the eighty-two intervening years—eight decades; four generations—some civil rights bills had passed the House (five since the end of the war alone); not one had passed the Senate. And passing a civil rights bill in the Senate in 1957 seemed as difficult—almost impossible—as ever.

There was yet another consideration, the most daunting of all. A successful southern filibuster would wreck Johnson's chances of winning the nomination—but so would an unsuccessful filibuster. The very launching of a filibuster would not only emphasize the split in his party, it would force him, as the Senate's procedural leader, to take a stand on one side or the other, to take steps either to support it or to end it. From the moment one began, there was no way to avoid taking a stand: if he did nothing—took no action to stop the filibuster and simply let it go on—he would be supporting it, standing with the South, and he would never get the northern support he needed for the nomination. Moving to cut the filibuster off—moving for cloture—would cost him the support of the South. To "produce" on civil rights, therefore he would have to pass civil rights legislation—legislation that had invariably provoked the start of a filibuster whenever there was a chance of its passage—without allowing a filibuster to start. He had to persuade the members of the Southern Caucus, not only somewhat open-minded southerners like Hill and Sparkman and Fulbright but also Jim Eastland, to whom black Americans were "unbearably stinking" and who was chairman of Judiciary, and Olin Johnston, who had refused a dinner invitation because his wife might have to sit next to a black person, and who was chairman of Post Office, and Harry Byrd, chairman of Finance, who had called for "massive resistance" to civil rights laws lest there be "close intimate" contact between white and black children, and Allen Ellender, chairman of Agriculture, who studded his speeches with the word "nigger," and Spessard Holland, the "true racist," and John Stennis, a racist "smarter" than but "equally rabid" as his predecessor Bilbo—he had to persuade them all, not to mention the newcomers Talmadge ("They couldn't send enough bayonets down here to compel the people to send their children to school with Nigras") and Thurmond ("I will never favor mixing the races")—Lyndon Johnson had to persuade these senators of the Old South, with all their power and all their hate, to allow a civil rights bill to become law without using their most effective weapon.

HE HAD ONE THING GOING FOR HIM: the southerners' desire to make him President. New fuel had been added to Richard Russell's determination to put Lyndon Johnson in the White House by the injustice he had seen perpetrated on Johnson at the Democratic Convention—the same injustice that had been perpetrated on *him* at the 1952 convention, and for the same reason: northern prejudice against his beloved Southland. And Chicago had also given Russell fresh proof that his plans for Johnson required the erasure from the Texan's image of at least some of the southern tint—and that there was only one possible way to erase it. This was made clear to George Reedy one evening in mid-November in a very unlikely locale: a small bistro in Paris. Aware that his presidential hopes required him to show more interest in foreign affairs, Johnson had reluctantly added his name to a senatorial delegation to a NATO conference in Paris. Russell was a member of the delegation, and Johnson brought Reedy along. Russell and Reedy were having a companionable dinner by themselves at the bistro when suddenly, "out of nowhere," Russell said, "George, we're going to get that man elected President yet." Then, Reedy recalls, there was a long pause, which was broken at last by Russell. "But we can never make him President unless the Senate first disposes of civil rights," Richard Russell said.

The Grahams were not the only important visitors to the Johnson Ranch that December: Russell, accompanied by his favorite nephew, Bobby, came too (not at the same time as the Grahams, of course). Russell's itinerary during his five days in Texas included the trips to St. Joseph Island and the Brown & Root ranch at Falfurrias that he had come to enjoy, but it included as well several long walks alone with Johnson. What the two senators discussed during those walks no one knows ("When they went off down there, they went off by themselves," says Posh Oltorf, who had now become a full-time Brown & Root lobbyist), but it was to become apparent from their aftermath that the conservative southerner Richard Russell was as fully aware as the liberal southerner Philip Graham that for Lyndon Johnson to have a chance to become President he would first have to be "cleaned up on civil rights"—and it was to become apparent as well that to accomplish that objective, Russell had decided to give Johnson some leeway, to cut some slack in the ties that had bound him to the South.

How little leeway was to become apparent even before the session, however, because in December it became known that the key issue at the start of Congress would be again, as it was at the start of each new Congress, Rule 22—"the gravedigger in the Senate graveyard for civil rights bills"— which required sixty-four votes to limit debate, and which also provided that there could be no limit at all on a motion to proceed to a change in the rules.

Russell's reaction to Humphrey's declaration that a new attempt would be made to change Rule 22 was cold anger at this liberal to whom he had been so tolerant. He told Johnson he wanted Humphrey cut off completely from access to "the Senate leadership"—and the "leadership" acquiesced. Humphrey quickly realized that word had been passed that "he was to get the cold shoulder," and he got it not only from the southerners but from his "friend" from Texas. With his usual warmth, Humphrey walked up to Johnson but was met with a chilliness that stopped just short of being an outright snub. Saying, "You broke faith with me," Johnson turned and walked away. Humphrey's reaction was instant grovel. "Now, Lyndon, you know I wouldn't do that," he said in an abject phone call. "You can get more votes out of this body than anybody can. You are a great, great leader, Lyndon. I was simply trying to make you an even better leader." When this personal obeisance proved insufficient, Humphrey had an aide approach Bobby Baker to ascertain the price of peace, and it was promptly paid. The surrender was reported in an Associated Press dispatch about a speech Humphrey delivered in New York City, in which "Senator Humphrey took a decidedly different tack from that of other liberal democrats who recently have urged greater militancy in seeking liberal legislation." The difference was indeed decided. More progress would be made, Humphrey said, if liberals became less militant. The question, he said, is, "Do you want to make progress or do you want to fight?" Sometimes, he said, "You have to be willing to inch along." And he made it clear that on one issue he was certainly not willing to fight. "I'm not going to spend all my time fighting the Senate rules." The dispute with Lyndon Johnson? As one of Humphrey's biographers puts it, "In a few days it was patched up." During the dispute, furthermore, a *Washington Post* reporter asked Johnson "if he himself favors any change in the filibuster rule," and Johnson, the reporter wrote, "replied with a flat 'No.' " Before the 1957 congressional session had begun, Johnson had lined up in support of the measure that was the highest barrier to civil rights legislation.

He had also, before leaving for Paris, tried to take another step to solidify the South's Senate defenses. Earle Clements' loss had left vacant the post of majority whip. There were both liberal and southern candidates for the job, and Johnson's choice was a southerner: George Smathers. Telephoning Smathers at his Miami home, Johnson said, "I want to meet you up here tomorrow at eleven o'clock." "I can't get there by then," Smathers said. "Goddammit, you *can* get there," Johnson replied.

Smathers did, checking into the Mayflower Hotel. But on the flight north he decided not to take the job, partly because his chairmanship of the Democratic Senatorial Campaign Committee had already given him a taste of Johnson's demands on subordinates, and he simply did not want to continue working that hard—but also because if he accepted the post, the South would hold both top Democratic senatorial leadership positions and this, he felt, "might invite trouble." The next morning, a Mayflower desk clerk telephoned up to Smathers' room to tell him that Mr. Johnson and Mr. Baker were on the way up. "There's a knock, and there they are," Smathers was to recall. "Johnson's there in a raincoat, it was cold. He had a big cowboy Texas hat on. And Bobby was with him. Bobby usually was." Taking it for granted that Smathers would accept the Assistant Leader's job, Johnson began issuing instructions. Smathers said, "I don't want to be your assistant," and he was never to forget what followed. "It was just as though you had unleashed an awful smell of something. His nostrils flared, his eyes sort of looked funny. He said, 'What are you saying?' I said, 'I don't know that I want to be the whip.' He said, 'Do you really mean that?' He hadn't sat down the whole time, neither did Bobby, we were all standing. I said, 'Yeah, Johnson, I don't know that I want to do it.' So he said, 'Come on, Bobby, let's go.' " Despite this setback (Johnson gave the post to Mike Mansfield of Montana, a highly respected but unassertive westerner who Johnson was sure would follow his instructions and who, *Time* noted, had been "a special protégé" of Walter George), on the eve of the 1957 session, Johnson appeared to be standing shoulder to shoulder with the enemies of civil rights—as he had been standing with them for more than twenty years.

THE SESSION'S OPENING DAYS did nothing to modify that impression. Johnson's actions during those days furnished new evidence that while he may have been cut a little slack by the South, he hadn't been cut much—that he was still going to be operating at the end of a very tight rope. During those days he moved effectively not for a civil rights bill, but against it.

At a January 2 meeting in Paul Douglas' office on the ground floor of the Senate Office Building, the liberals had decided that Clinton Anderson would offer the same motion he had introduced in 1953, and would have reintroduced in 1955 had not Johnson tricked the liberals out of doing so: that deceptively simple motion to have the Senate adopt rules for the current session. And this year the liberals had a new ally, a very shrewd one. So high had the stakes become in the civil rights game that Richard Milhous Nixon had decided to take a hand himself—at the game's big table, the Senate: to sit in on the game literally, by taking the presiding officer's chair on the Senate dais at crucial moments, including the game's opening hand. Aware of the Republican aim—of Nixon's aim—of winning the African-American vote, Senate liberals had privately sounded out the Vice President, and he had privately let them know he would be on their side. It had therefore been agreed that as soon as Anderson made his motion, Douglas and other liberal senators would ask Nixon to rule on whether it was in order—on whether, in other words, the adoption of new Senate rules was permissible. And Douglas would also ask Nixon, "Under what rules is the Senate presently proceeding?" Nixon would then rule that the motion was in order, because it would be in order under normal parliamentary rules—and he would rule further that the Senate was at that moment proceeding under standard parliamentary rules because it was not a continuing body but a new Senate which had not yet adopted any rules of its own.

Anderson's motion—coupled with Nixon's ruling—would carry in it the seeds of death for the filibuster. Under standard parliamentary rules, all votes are decided by a simple majority. If Nixon held that the Senate was operating under those rules, not only could Anderson's motion be passed by a simple majority, but if the South tried to filibuster against it, a liberal cloture motion to cut off that filibuster could also be passed by a simple majority. And then, approval having thereby been given to adopt new rules, a motion to adopt a new Rule 22—stating that cloture could be imposed by a simple majority—could be introduced. And if a filibuster against that motion was begun, a simple majority would suffice to defeat *it*.

Russell, well aware of the threat, was aware also that the GOP, all too willing to pander to the NAACP, might well make the vote on Anderson's motion a party issue for its forty-seven senators—and that even Republican senators unenthusiastic about civil rights, and even less enthusiastic about making cloture easier, might support their Vice President on an issue that might make them the majority party and give them the chairmen's gavels. Under Nixon's ruling, not sixty-four but only forty-nine votes would be needed for passage of Anderson's motion—and there might well be forty-nine votes to pass it.

Russell reacted by convening the Southern Caucus. Behind the closed doors of his office (on the second floor of the SOB, almost directly over Douglas' office), resentment over "Judge Nixon's" tactics spilled over, but Russell, emerging to meet a hallful of reporters, was urbane and confident, giving, one reporter wrote, "a classic performance of a southern politician uttering hard words in a soft manner." His only hint of criticism was directed at Nixon. "Vice Presidents have always been trying to change the rules of the Senate, over which they have no control," he said. Otherwise, stated another reporter, Russell was "calm and easy-going." He managed nonetheless to make it clear that if Anderson's motion for new rules carried, there would be a filibuster— a king-size one. If the Senate decided it could change rules, he said, then Rule 22 would not be the only rule changed. "We would then have to start with Rule 1, and write a completely new set of rules of the Senate. We would start from scratch." Changes in every one of the Senate's other thirty-nine rules would be introduced. And, as the *New York Times* reported, "Senator Russell suggested" that in this process "legislative business of the Senate might be halted." "Extended debate" would be held on every proposed change, he said, forcing a separate cloture proceeding on every one. Even if votes could be obtained for the passage of thirty-nine cloture motions, the process would tie up the Senate completely for months. In fact, Russell said, if this "Pandora's box" was opened, "there would be no way as I see it to bring the debate to a close." He didn't employ the word "ever," but the word was implicit.

But even as Russell was describing the "Pandora" card, he knew that playing it was not going to be required. He had another, even better, ace up his sleeve, one that he knew would take the opening hand, because he had played it before, in the opening hand of 1953, and it had taken the hand then. It was an ace that could not be played by him, but only by the Majority Leader. In 1953 the then Majority Leader Taft had played it. Now, in 1957, the Majority Leader was Lyndon Johnson—and Johnson played it, too.

He played it the next day. Anderson introduced his motion. The liberals were expecting to make the next move as well: the moment Anderson finished speaking, Douglas and Humphrey were on their feet, waving their arms, requesting recognition from Nixon so that they could ask for the preplanned ruling. But the two liberals' desks were in the far bend of the Democratic arc. Even as Douglas and Humphrey jumped up, a commanding figure rose in front of them, in the center of the floor. Lyndon Johnson was on his feet directly in front of the dais, almost eye to eye with the Vice President, demanding the prior recognition that was the Majority Leader's prerogative. Nixon had no choice but to recognize him first—and when the Vice President did so, Johnson made his own motion: to table Anderson's motion.

Russell's ace took the pot in 1957 as it had in 1953. Since Anderson's motion was no longer the pending business before the Senate—Johnson's motion took precedence over it—Humphrey and Douglas could not ask for a ruling on it as they had planned to do, but could make only a "parliamentary inquiry" as to what would happen if it became the pending business, and Nixon could not give a ruling but only an "advisory opinion." In his opinion, the Vice President came down strongly on the side of civil rights. The Constitution, he said, stated that each House could determine its own rules, "and this constitutional right . . . may be exercised by a majority of the Senate at any time. When the membership of the Senate changes, as it does upon the election of each Congress, it is the Chair's opinion that there can be no question that the majority of the new existing membership" can "determine the rules." Therefore, he said, any "Senate rule adopted in a previous Congress" which denies the right of a majority of a new Senate to adopt rules "is, in the opinion of the Chair, unconstitutional," and, he added, "in the opinion of the Chair," specifically Rule 22 is unconstitutional. But Johnson's motion made Nixon's opinion irrelevant. Had the Vice President been allowed to rule that Anderson's motion was in order, a vote on that motion not only would have been a vote with clear-cut, even dramatic, civil rights implications because it struck at the hated filibuster, but would also have been in effect a vote on Nixon's ruling, and would therefore have attracted heavy Republican support. "He was *their* Vice President, and he was going to be their candidate [for President in 1960], and a substantial number of Republicans would vote to support him because of that," Howard Shuman explains. Their votes, added to the votes of liberal Democrats, might have added up to the necessary forty-nine, the necessary majority, and for the first time in decades, there would have been a realistic possibility of obtaining a civil rights bill. "That [a vote on Anderson's motion] was our big chance," Shuman says.

Johnson's maneuver, however, meant that not Anderson's motion but his own tabling motion would be voted on first. And that vote would not be on Nixon's decision—and not directly on civil rights—but only on "tabling," a procedural matter difficult to explain to voters.

Johnson's work for the South during those first days of January, 1957, was not confined to parliamentary maneuvers. He threw onto the Senate table not only the ace that Richard Russell had placed in his hand, but some cards of his own—cards on which the face was the naked face of senatorial power. The cards were played against liberal members of his own party, to reduce Democratic support for civil rights to a minimum—and the cards were played with a ruthlessness that was striking in the rawness of its violation of what remained of the Senate's seniority system.

The meeting of Johnson's rubber-stamp Democratic Steering Committee, which made committee assignments, had been abruptly postponed until January 7, so that it would come after the vote on the tabling motion. And in more than one instance assignments were made on the basis not of seniority but of a senator's vote on that motion. In the case of senators whose vote had been in doubt, a vote for Johnson's motion—in effect a vote against civil rights—earned a reward, as was shown by the fate of Tennessee's two senators. One of them, Albert Gore, whose sympathy for civil rights had been worrisome to the South, voted for Johnson's motion (and against civil rights), and was rewarded with the Finance Committee seat he had been seeking. Tennessee's other senator, Estes Kefauver, voted against Johnson's motion—and was punished. Having asked repeatedly for a seat on Foreign Relations since the day he arrived in the Senate, Kefauver was confident that he would inherit the seat made vacant by Walter George's retirement, since, with eight years' seniority, he had more than any other applicant. The press, and everyone else familiar with the situation, was treating his appointment as a *fait accompli*. But when the Steering Committee's press release on Democratic committee assignments was dropped on the table in the Capitol pressroom, reporters were startled to see that the new name on Foreign Relations was not "Estes Kefauver" but "John F. Kennedy," who had only four years' seniority but who was a northerner and whose vote against tabling had therefore been anticipated and was excusable. Kefauver's reaction was restrained. "I am disappointed," he said. "Of course, I do not blame Senator Kennedy for trying to better his position, but I am interested to learn that seniority is a rule that may or may not be applied by the Senate leadership in deciding the rights of senators."

Other assignments made by the Steering Committee met the same criteria. Johnson had been seriously considering following Jim Rowe's advice to appoint John Carroll to Judiciary, but Carroll, loyal to civil rights, had voted against his motion. He got neither Judiciary nor his second choice, Finance, for which he was considered well qualified because he had been an active member of the House's counterpart committee, Ways and Means. Instead, he was appointed to Interior, "which he resented," according to his administrative assistant, Harry Schnibbe.

And the loss of a committee assignment was, in some cases, only part of the punishment that Johnson inflicted for the wrong vote—as one of the newly elected senators, thirty-two-year-old Frank Church of Idaho, was to find out.

Having just taken his oath in the well of the Senate on January 3, Church was starting to walk back up the center aisle when, as he was passing the first desk, "I encountered this long arm of Lyndon Johnson reaching out and grabbing me." Pulling him close, Johnson said: "Now Frank, you are the youngest member of this Senate, and you have a great future. There's lots going for you. But the first thing you ought to learn is that in Congress you get along by going along.

"We've got a motion here that Clint Anderson is going to offer and it relates to a matter that is not important to your state," Johnson said. "The people of your state don't care how you vote on this one way or the other, but the leadership cares. It means a lot to me. So I just point this out to you. Your first vote is coming up, and I hope you'll keep it in mind, because I like you, and I see big things in your future, and I want for you to get off on the right foot in the Senate."

Church recalls giving only a noncommittal answer, saying something like,

"I would study it further"—but, he says, "Apparently I left Senator Johnson with the impression that I would vote with him, and he never came back to me for a second time before the vote." Since the new senator didn't understand the importance of the vote—or the significance of Johnson's combined threat and promise—his "studying" consisted only of a casual inquiry to one or two fellow senators as to how they were voting, and when they said they were voting against tabling, Church decided to do the same. When, on Friday, his name was called, he shouted "No."

That was when Frank Church knew he had made a big mistake. From his desk in the back row, he could see Lyndon Johnson sitting below him at his front-row center desk, keeping tabs on the vote on a tally sheet. "When . . . I didn't vote with him, he threw his pen down on the desk, and I didn't see him pick it up again. I knew then that I was in deep trouble."

Just how deep the youthful freshman was soon to find out. "For the next six months," he was to recall, Lyndon Johnson "never spoke to me. He said nothing to me that was insulting, he just simply ignored me. When I was present with other senators, he talked to the other senators."

And one thing Johnson did not talk to him about mattered a great deal to Frank Church. Young as he was to have begun a senatorial career—he was six years younger than any other senator—he had already known for a long time the senatorial footsteps he wanted to walk in: the footsteps of his legendary predecessor, the Lion of Idaho.

Even as a boy, Frank Church had idolized William Borah; in the eighth grade, he had written a letter to a newspaper applauding Borah's warning to avoid foreign "entanglements"; one of his most vivid memories was of Borah's funeral in Boise in 1940, when the fifteen-year-old youth had walked past the open casket; he wanted to be a senator, Church would say, "because *he* was a senator." There was a point of resemblance between Church and Borah, the former Shakespearean actor whose Senate Chamber funeral was held without a eulogy because no one could match his eloquence. Church was also a spellbinding orator who, as a high school junior, had won first prize in a national oratorical contest. Church wanted not only to walk in Borah's footprints but to step beyond them: "He arrived here [in the Senate] very determined to run for President," recalls his legislative aide, Ward Hower. He knew the Senate post that would best help him achieve both goals: the chairmanship of the Foreign Relations Committee that Borah had held for nine years. "He was aiming not just at a seat but at the chairmanship, because that gives a senator from a small state a chance to make a name for himself," Hower says. And Church was aware that if a senator wanted to eventually become chairman of a committee, it was important that he go on that committee early. Talking to Church a day or two before the Senate convened, Johnson had made it clear that he understood that ambition, and might well be willing to help it along, not immediately, of course, but at some early opportunity. Now suddenly any chance of going on

Foreign Relations seemed extremely remote. When Church attempted to make a peace overture through Bobby Baker, Baker was not encouraging. "The Leader's got a long memory," he said.

Johnson's tactics and methods were effective. His tabling motion had cut the ground out from under the liberal attempt to enlist Republican senators on the side of civil rights. When his motion had been voted on—on January 4— only seventeen Republicans had voted against it and for civil rights. Twenty-eight had voted against civil rights. (Two Republicans had been absent.) And his use of raw power on his own side of the aisle had given the southern senators additional proof of his loyalty—that he would, in fact, move on their behalf with all the determination they could desire. Only twenty-one Democrats had defied the Leader's power by voting for civil rights. Twenty-seven Democrats had voted against civil rights. There had therefore been a total of only thirty-eight votes for civil rights, fifty-five against. He had done precisely what the Southern Caucus—and in particular, its general—wanted.

Despite the effectiveness of his tactics and methods, in the light of his longer-term goal, the overall weakness of his position had become very clear during that first week in January—because during that fight Richard Russell's position had become very clear. However much affection Russell might feel for Lyndon Johnson, the overriding reason that Russell wanted him to become President was to protect the interests of the South; when Johnson's interests collided with those interests, it was the South's, not Johnson's, that would be protected. In fact, in the final analysis, it would be only the South's interests that mattered. Aware though Russell might be that Johnson could never become President "unless the Senate first disposes of civil rights," if "disposing" of civil rights entailed Senate actions that hurt the South, and the rigid racial segregation that Russell felt was vital to the South, then the disposing would be dispensed with. Use of the filibuster would put an end to Lyndon Johnson's dreams, but the filibuster was the South's ultimate defense, and Russell's firm determination to fight Clint Anderson's motion to the death had demonstrated that he would never agree to any weakening of that defense, no matter how damaging the consequences of such a fight for Johnson's presidential ambitions. Johnson had stood solidly with the South in that fight, but if he hadn't, and if the South had been losing, what would have been the result? "Extended debate" on forty separate rules—the most massive filibuster of them all. To advance along his path, Lyndon Johnson had to persuade the southerners to allow him to distance himself from them on civil rights, and from the filibuster that defended civil rights, and in the first test of 1957, the southerners had shown not the slightest inclination to allow him any real distance at all.

WITH THE SUCCESS of Lyndon Johnson's tabling motion, voices across the entire spectrum of liberal opinion were raised against him. "Once again, democracy has taken a beating in the halls of the United States Senate," the *New York Post* editorialized. "It was a bad day for the cause of freedom. The unholy alliance [of southern Democrats and midwestern Republicans] still holds sway." And, the *Post* said, it holds sway largely because of the Majority Leader. "How can the Democrats explain the continued eminence of Lyndon Johnson, who is justly taking bows for the grand maneuvers of the filibuster legion?" The *Post*'s was always one of the shrillest voices in the liberal chorus, but that January there was, in liberal discussions of Lyndon Johnson, a harsh note even in voices that were generally calm and reasonable. In a long, thoughtful analysis of the Senate, Richard Rovere wrote in *The New Yorker* that one of the institution's most striking aspects is its *esprit de corps,* which "unites senators of differing political views . . . against the world outside the Senate." And proof of this, Rovere said, is "the support that [Senate] Democrats of left, right and center have given" to Johnson, while outside the Senate, "among liberal northern Democrats as a group, it has become an article of faith that Senator Johnson plays a generally destructive role, and that no good can come of his continuing as spokesman for the party."

This liberal anger certainly appeared justified. In fighting for the filibuster, Lyndon Johnson had seemingly only been doing in early January, 1957, what he had done so many times before. It was only natural for liberals who for twenty years had seen Lyndon Johnson standing squarely on the side of the South and against civil rights to assume that during the rest of 1957 he would be standing on the same side again.

But he wouldn't. During Lyndon Johnson's previous political life, compassion had constantly been in conflict with ambition, and invariably ambition had won. Given the imperatives of his nature, in such a conflict, it had been inevitable that the ambition would win. For the compassion to be released, to express itself in concrete accomplishments, it would have to be compatible with the ambition, pointing in the same direction. And now, at last, in 1957, it was.

So Lyndon Johnson changed—and changed the course of American history. For at last this leader of men would be leading, fighting, not only for himself but for a great cause. This man who in the pursuit of his aims could be so utterly ruthless—who would let nothing stand in his way; who, in the pursuit, deceived, and betrayed and cheated—would be deceiving and betraying and cheating on behalf of something other than himself: specifically, on behalf of the sixteen million Americans whose skins were dark. All through Lyndon Johnson's political life—as congressman and senator, as congressman's secretary and NYA director—there had been striking evidence not only of compassion but of something that could make compassion meaningful: signs of a most unusual capacity, a very rare gift, for using the powers of government to help the downtrodden and the dispossessed. This capacity had always been held in check by his quest for power. Now he had the power. *Power reveals.* The compassion that had been hidden was to be revealed now—in full. Did those sixteen million Americans need a mighty champion in the halls of government? They were about to get one.

HIS FIRST JOB was to persuade southern senators that they should allow a civil rights bill to pass—that even though they had preserved the filibuster, they shouldn't use it.

To persuade them, he employed, in individual conversations with these senators and in meetings of the Southern Caucus in Richard Russell's office, several arguments that his actions on Rule 22 made them more disposed to accept.

Some of these arguments were valid. The times were changing, he told them, and we (he always used "we" in talking with the southerners; he had been using that pronoun since his "We of the South" speech in 1949) had better wake up to that. Demand for civil rights legislation was rising. Civil rights was a big issue, and it was going to get bigger—and we look bad on that issue. The Republicans had decided to do anything they had to do to win the nigger vote. (He usually used that noun in talking with southerners, varying its pronunciation to fit the senator; it was "Nigras" with some senators from the Middle South, "Negras" with Eastland or Olin Johnston.) The Republicans were making civil rights a party issue—their issue. It's a tough issue for the Democrats. It's hurting us. Look what happened in the last election; look at that vote in Harlem! And it's hurting us because of what we're doing here in the Senate. The perception is that the Senate is the roadblock, the reason that no civil rights bill has passed in eighty-two years. And it's easy for Negroes to put the blame on the Senate, because we're exposed here. Did you hear what the voters out in Oregon were saying to Dick Neuberger about ol' Jim? And we're not only weak in the Senate because our Republican friends seem to have suddenly forgotten everything we've done for them, and not only because Bill Knowland is going to run for Governor of California, and he needs the Negro vote. Don't forget who the presiding officer is. Nixon is going to try to out-nigger Knowland. He's conniving with the NAACP right now to put us on the spot so we'll look bad. If we don't do something, that issue is going to hurt the whole Democratic Party even worse in '58 and '60. Look what can happen to us in the Senate. All the Republicans have to do is take one seat. *One seat!* Then it'll be a tie, and Nixon will break it, and we won't even get to organize the Senate again. They will. And the only way to defuse that issue is to let a token bill go through so the Republicans can't say we've stopped all civil rights legislation again.

The validity of some of the other arguments he was making to the southern senators is more difficult to assess. One argument that Johnson made a centerpiece of his case to the southerners was that we might not even win a filibuster this time, that cloture might be imposed—first, because we've got fewer votes: Kefauver isn't going to vote with us, all he can think about is being

President, and maybe Gore won't be with us, either; that brings us down to twenty votes. And there were other arguments. For a long time we didn't have to worry about cloture, because we could count on the support of the Republicans in the Senate. Now, he said, that support was gone, and we'd better realize that. The whole Republican Party, from the top down, was going to pander to the Negroes; the President will put pressure on the Republican senators, the Vice President will, Bill Knowland will—and the Republican senators themselves will see the opportunity not only for the Republican presidential candidate but for *themselves*. What are we going to do, Lyndon Johnson asked the southerners, if one day we go to the Republicans for the rest of the thirty-three votes we need to sustain a filibuster and the votes aren't there? And the problem wasn't only with the Republicans. The times were changing, he told them, agitation for civil rights legislation was rising, and therefore pressure on *all* their Senate colleagues, Democrat as well as Republican, was rising. It was going to be steadily more difficult for non-southern Democrats to vote with the South.

And even if we *do* stave off cloture this year, he told the southerners, filibustering this year will hurt us in years to come. There was just too much sentiment out there in the country against filibustering. It's too easy a target. You heard what Nixon said in Harlem: "If you support Ike and elect a Republican Senate, you'll get action, not filibusters." Thurmond aide Harry Dent, who had been assigned by Thurmond, more suspicious of Johnson than the other southern senators, to "hang out in the Democratic cloakroom" and listen to "what LBJ was up to," says that Johnson was arguing that, "Yes, the southern leaders had power, but these powers would erode." And, Johnson said, if enough Republicans go along with those goddamned bomb-throwers in our own party, how can we be sure that cloture won't be imposed, if not in 1958, then in 1959? What if we lose the next vote to table? If Nixon then firms that opinion up into a ruling, and the Republicans have the votes to sustain it—what're we going to do then? We might win a filibuster this year, but if we use one this year, then next year or the year after we might lose the whole right to filibuster—might lose it forever. And without a filibuster, the South is defenseless. They can pass any goddamn thing they want. Johnson, Reedy says, was telling the southerners, "*Don't filibuster!* You have to let a civil rights bill pass this year! If you don't, God knows what is going to happen!"

Another argument he was using was that they shouldn't filibuster because there was no need to filibuster. The Brownell Bill might be objectionable, he said, but, he said, it could be amended. Some of our friends on the other side of the aisle don't like Brownell, or his bill, any more than we do, he said. There are some people on our side of the aisle who feel the same way, even if they can't say so. These senators, he said, might need to vote for a civil rights bill to satisfy their constituents, but it didn't have to be a strong bill. All these senators were his friends, he said. He could work with them. They would negotiate together. The bill might be a strong bill now, but by the time it came to a vote it would be a very different bill. It would be amended down until it was so weak that it was only a token bill.

They could count on him, he told the southerners. He would get the bill amended down to something so weak that we have no real objection to it, to something we can live with. And then we won't have to filibuster it. We can let it come to a vote. We'll still vote against it, and if it passes, it won't really matter. "We're up against the wall," he told the southerners. "We have to get the best that we can get—*and we can get it!* The future of the South is at stake here. We have to save the South as much as we can. If we don't do this [let a token bill go through], all the southern principles will go down the tubes. We can't have everything the way we want it, but we can have most of it. *We're up against the wall!*" And the way to forestall all these unpleasant possibilities— of the passage of a law that would transform the southern way of life; of a defeat of a filibuster this year; of the outlawing of the filibuster in some year to come—was to allow a civil rights bill to go through this year; a weak bill but a *bill,* so that the Republicans could not say that the Democrats were standing in the way of any civil rights legislation at all.

The validity of these arguments is impossible to evaluate from this distance, for what is involved is the predicting of the votes of individual senators, and so many factors might have influenced the senators that after so many years the votes can't be predicted with any confidence. Even by the most generous estimate, however, those arguments appear to be doubtful. *You got up to thirty-three real fast,* Bryce Harlow says, and not only southern aides but many observers on the liberal side and the Republican side also agree. A typical comment is that of Sam Zagoria, administrative assistant to the liberal Republican Clifford Case. The liberals, he said, "felt they could win a straight vote, but they felt they couldn't beat a filibuster." Murray Zweben, secretary to the Senate Parliamentarian, says, "Down deep, if push came to shove, the liberals wouldn't have had the votes they thought they had." But some of the southerners didn't count, had never counted—Byrd, for example. *"Johnson counted for him."*

And this helped Johnson frighten the southerners. When he told them that a filibuster might lose, many of them believed him. And some of them were frightened: the southern way of life was precious to them; how could they gamble it on an uncertainty?

ANOTHER ARGUMENT BEING MADE to the southern senators was being made much less explicitly—generally only by implication, only in hints. And it was only occasionally made by Lyndon Johnson; usually it was made by Richard Russell—for since the argument concerned Lyndon Johnson, at times it was better that it come from someone else. It was a very persuasive argument. The South should let a civil rights bill pass, this argument said, because if it passed, Lyndon Johnson would have a better chance of becoming President.

Was Johnson, as Reedy puts it, "in private conversations, taking advantage of a growing belief that he might be a presidential candidate"? When he told Eastland or Olin Johnston or Harry Byrd, "I've just got to give those bomb-throwers something to get them off my back," did they understand him to be *really* saying that, as Reedy puts it, he "had to have some leeway to get national recognition"?—that if there was a no-holds-barred fight in the Senate, and he lined up on the side of the South, he would never get to be President?

When this argument was employed on a southern senator, implicit in it, of course, was the assumption that a Johnson presidency would be a desirable thing for the South.

Johnson—and Russell—were, in 1957, reassuring southern senators that this would indeed be the case. With the more senior southerners, those who had been working with Johnson and Russell for years and who understood the implications of the argument, it wasn't necessary to spell them out or in some cases even to mention them. In 1957, however, there were three new southern senators, and to them things were made more explicit. Having won a special election in March, 1957, to replace Price Daniel, Texas liberal Ralph Yarborough would, on his arrival on Capitol Hill that month, pay the obligatory visit to Richard Russell about his committee assignments, and would be asked by Russell to sign the Southern Manifesto, which had been passed the year before. Yarborough declined, and tried to excuse himself by saying that his fellow Texan Johnson hadn't signed. Russell, Yarborough recalls, replied that "he [Johnson] was running for President, and this [signing] would ruin him"—and that it was important that Johnson not be "ruined." Thereafter, listening in the Democratic cloakroom and on the Senate floor to Johnson talk to the other southern senators, Yarborough understood the reason for Russell's feelings. "He [Johnson] made them think he was with them, and that he'd be with them forever," Yarborough says. The two other new members of the Southern Caucus, Herman Talmadge and Strom Thurmond, had both been sworn in on January 3, 1957. As soon as Talmadge arrived in Washington, the facts of Senate life were explained to him: thereafter he would support Johnson for the presidency, explaining his stand by saying, as a story in the *Atlanta Constitution* put it, that as President, "Johnson would be more favorable to the South's position on States' Rights, and therefore his choice . . . would be Johnson." Thurmond, the former presidential candidate of Dixieland's States Right Party and an ardent racist (after listening one day in 1957 to the South Carolinian deliver, in a dispassionate tone, a long, dogmatic discourse on the irremediable inferiority of the Negro race, Olin Johnston, ardent racist himself, was moved to comment: "Strom really *believes* that stuff!"), was astonished to find that Russell was not adamantly opposed to any civil rights bill at all. He felt he understood Russell's reasoning. "I think Russell didn't fight it [the bill] as hard as he ordinarily would have" if he hadn't wanted Johnson to be President, Thurmond was to tell an interviewer. "He was trying to help Lyndon get elected President . . ."

What did this argument mean to the southern senators? What was Johnson saying to make them feel "he would be with them forever"? Did it mean merely, as George Reedy says, that he would use the presidency as a means to heal century-old scars and make the South truly a part of the Union again, that he would "end the Civil War," that he would be "a bridge" for the reconciliation between North and South? Certainly, some of Johnson's aides believe this is the basic meaning. Harry McPherson was to write that "Johnson felt about the race question much as I did, namely that it obsessed the South and diverted it from attending to its economic and educational problems; that it produced among white southerners angry defensiveness and parochialism." And most, if not all, Johnson biographers have believed it, too. "Johnson argued, and he probably believed, that the South was on the verge of new possibilities for rapid expansion," but that those possibilities would not be exploited if the racial issue was not defused by civil rights legislation, Doris Kearns Goodwin wrote. And with some of the more tolerant, less racist southern senators such as Lister Hill or John Sparkman, that was probably what the argument meant. But did Johnson's persuasion of other southern senators rest also on other grounds? Probably there is not one answer; almost certainly there were different emphases, depending on which senator he was talking to—arguments tailored to specific individuals by someone supremely gifted at telling each man what he wanted to hear. "We're talking about twenty different individuals, you know," Harry Dent says. But persuasion is in part a matter of tone, and the tone of the words and phrases that Lyndon Johnson was heard using to the southern senators—"the nigger bill," "Negras," "uppity"—was not that of a man interested primarily in healing wounds or building bridges or facilitating economic progress. What's more, the Southern Caucus included not only southern moderates like Hill and Sparkman but southern racists like Byrd and Talmadge and Eastland and Olin Johnston to whom economic progress was not the predominant concern. And these racists were without exception among Johnson's most enthusiastic supporters for the presidency. Johnson was to joke about the depth of Eastland's racial beliefs, and about the Mississippian's other obsession—Communist subversion—and Johnson's aides and biographers repeat these jokes as if they are evidence of Johnson's true feelings. Writing that "Johnson deplored Eastland's militant racism" as well as his Communist obsession, Booth Mooney quotes him as saying, "Jim Eastland could be standing right in the middle of the worst Mississippi flood ever known, and he'd say the niggers caused it, helped out by the Communists." But until Johnson became President, Eastland did not deplore what he felt were Johnson's beliefs on the issue. There was nothing about Johnson that Eastland deplored. Indeed, this archetypal racist constantly praised Lyndon Johnson in the most laudatory terms. "You have certainly made the best Majority Leader we have ever had," he wrote him in 1956, adding, "I am leaving tomorrow for the Convention and will vote for you for President." And he actively promoted him for the 1960 presidential nomination as well.

And Talmadge's statement that the reason he was supporting Johnson was that "Johnson would be more favorable to the South's position on States'

Rights" was not a statement about wound-healing or bridge-building, as became clear when the author, after ten years of trying to obtain an interview with Talmadge, was finally granted one, which took place on January 10, 2000, at Talmadge's home on Lake Talmadge in Georgia's Henry County (reached by driving south from Atlanta on Herman Talmadge Highway and turning off at the exit marked "Herman Talmadge Road").

Asked about his relationship with Lyndon Johnson in the Senate, Talmadge said, "At first, for years, I liked him. He spent a lot of time cultivating me—hours and hours." They would talk about "everything," Talmadge said. "Girls, hunting." And, Talmadge said, they would talk about civil rights, and the relationships between whites and Negroes. How did Lyndon Johnson view the relationship between whites and Negroes? "Master and servant," Talmadge replied. Well, didn't he have any sympathy for their situation? "None indicated," Talmadge replied.

Talmadge said that during the 1950s, Johnson would assure the southerners that they could count on him to weaken a civil rights bill as much as possible, that he was on their side on civil rights, that he had to pretend that he wasn't, to meet the Southern Caucus as infrequently as possible, but that he really was their ally. "He would tell us, I'm one of you, but I can help you more if I don't meet with you." And, Talmadge said, the southerners believed him, believed that while changes in the civil rights laws were inevitable, Johnson would keep them as minor as possible, that "he was with us in his heart."

"I believed him," Talmadge said, but "I changed my opinion." When? "When he was President," Talmadge said. How did you feel then? "Disappointed," Talmadge said. "Angry." There was a long pause, and then he added, "Sick." When asked, How did you feel when he said, "*We* shall overcome?," Talmadge repeated, "Sick."

The author then asked, "Did you feel that Lyndon Johnson betrayed you?" There was a longer pause. It could not have been easy for a politician as wily as Herman Talmadge to admit he had been fooled so completely. "Yes," he finally said.

Of all the top aides to the southerners, the one with the best view of Johnson's arguments was probably Dent, because of the time he spent "keeping an eye on Johnson" in the Democratic cloakroom. Dent says, "LBJ's whole gambit was, 'You guys can put me in the White House,' and that will give you more authority and power. . . . And that would keep the South where the South wanted to be, which was a certain amount of segregation, at least. He was telling them, If LBJ was in the White House, the South would not get everything it wanted, but it would be far better off than if a Hubert Humphrey was President."

When Dent's assessment was repeated to John A. Goldsmith, head of the United Press Senate staff in the 1950s, Goldsmith said, "I think it's much more ambivalent [than what Dent said]. Whether he [Johnson] or Russell would have said it in words that blunt I doubt." And, Goldsmith said, that argument was just one of "a whole flock of the considerations" that southern senators were taking into account. "I think it was one of the things that the southerners would understand. I have no doubt that Russell conveyed something along these lines to the Southern Caucus." And when Goldsmith was asked, "Was Lyndon Johnson, in 1957, making them believe that if he became President he would do as much as possible to protect segregation?" Goldsmith replied, "These guys would have taken that as a given." What Lyndon Johnson was saying, or hinting, about racial segregation during his private conversations with the members of the Southern Caucus we don't know; we only know the final outcome. Strom Thurmond was suspicious of, and unconvinced by, Johnson, but the other members of the Southern Caucus were not.

Most important, Richard Russell was not. As John Goldsmith has written, Russell's motives "have been debated over the years. . . . Russell himself may not have known" in 1957 "how much his long-standing, reasoned opposition to all civil rights initiatives was being tempered by his hope that Johnson might succeed in national politics and even become a President attuned to the southern culture." And, Goldsmith adds, "Those considerations were not at odds with one another. . . ." Russell validated Johnson's arguments by assuring the Southern Caucus that they were true, and he reminded its members of his grand design; it wasn't necessary for Lyndon Johnson to hint to the southern senators that the South's first priority should be to put him in the White House, because Russell did the hinting. These senators had been following where Russell led for many years now, and they would follow him still. At the end of one Southern Caucus in 1957, Harry Byrd summed up the feeling around the huge mahogany table by saying simply, "Dick, it's up to you." Inconceivable as it might seem that these men would allow a civil rights bill—even a very weak bill—to pass, they would allow one to pass if Russell told them to. That same January of 1957, a strange rumor began circulating on Capitol Hill. Clint Anderson was telling friends that Lyndon Johnson had told him that a civil rights bill was going to be passed in 1957—and that he, Lyndon Johnson, was going to support it. Anderson didn't believe either part of that prediction, but it was being heard elsewhere. "REPORT BEING CIRCULATED IN WASHINGTON THAT MAJORITY LEADER LYNDON JOHNSON HAS PROMISED THAT A CIVIL RIGHTS BILL WILL BE PASSED," Roy Wilkins wired to NAACP headquarters in New York. Then the rumor was put in print; the *Herald Tribune* reported that "The Senate's Democratic leadership had reached an understanding to bring the civil rights issue to a head early in the present session. . . . The leadership is hopeful . . . that if it gets the matter to the Senate floor within the next two months any southern attempt to thwart the decision by 'extended debate' can be beaten down. . . ." And there was an even stranger rumor: that among the senators to whom Johnson had told this were the southern senators. In mid-January, reports began to circulate that Russell had convened a secret meeting of the Southern Caucus, and that at that meeting Johnson had laid down a timetable for action on a civil rights bill. And then that timetable was in print: Johnson,

Newsweek reported, had told southerners that "Floor debate will open in early Spring. . . . By the end of April, the bill will be passed." Lyndon Johnson, who as President just a few years later would do so much to end the racial discrimination that was a keystone of the South's way of life, who would do more to end racial discrimination than any other President of the twentieth century, was being given a crucial boost toward the presidency by the South's own senators, fervent believers, most of them, in racial discrimination. And at least some of them were helping Johnson at least partly because they believed that while, if he were to become President, he might have no choice but to do something about racial discrimination, they could count on him to do as little as possible.

Whether or not Lyndon Johnson was already planning in 1957 to take giant steps toward racial justice if he ever became President, we do not know, and perhaps no one will ever know. But whether or not in 1957 he was misleading the southern senators deliberately, misled they certainly were. Did he intend to mislead them?—we don't know. But if we take him at his word—his word that at Cotulla, "I swore then and there that if I ever had a chance to help those underprivileged kids I was going to do it"—then Lyndon Johnson was misleading the southern senators deliberately. To whatever extent Johnson in 1957 was already planning, at least in outline, the things he would do if he ever became President, he was planning to betray, and to betray on a very large scale, the men, some of them very clever men, who were, for years, not only his most loyal but his most important supporters. "Civil rights didn't get accomplished by idealism but by rough stuff"—that was the lesson that Katharine Graham had taken away from her visit to Lyndon Johnson's ranch. What Johnson was doing now with the Southern Caucus, in the service of both his great ambition and his great purpose, was "rough stuff" indeed.

But a civil rights bill had to be passed. And a civil rights bill was going to be passed.

HIS NEXT JOB, now that he had persuaded the South to let a weak, token, bill pass, was to reduce the bill to a point at which it was so weak that it *was* only a token—and yet was still strong enough to satisfy northern liberals that something genuine had been accomplished for civil rights.

That proved to be very difficult. For more than four months, in fact, it seemed impossible.

The heart of the bill—the part on which both sides were focusing almost exclusively—was its third part (or "title"), the part covering the "broad array" of civil rights, that would make segregation illegal in schools and in public places such as parks, swimming pools, hotels, motels, theaters, and restaurants. For a while, in mid-January, Johnson seemed to be having some success in persuading the southerners that the measure would be sufficiently weakened if an amendment was added to provide that anyone indicted for a violation of any of the bill's provisions be entitled to a trial by jury. With a "jury trial amendment" added, he told them, what would the other provisions matter? They could forgo filibustering against the bill because they could be sure—and could excuse themselves to their constituents by explaining—that the other provisions were now meaningless: what white man had to fear a southern jury? But the bill was simply potentially too destructive to southern mores for that argument to be convincing. The broadness of its attack on the southern way of life—the way in which the bill aimed at reducing it to nothing but a memory by mandating an intermingling of the races in so many "social" settings—infuriated the southern senators. Part III was not only a threat but an insult to their gentle Southland, with its friendly, harmonious relations between the races. And Part III raised, of course, the spectre of that worst of all possibilities: the mongrelization of the noble white race. Adding a jury trial amendment wouldn't be enough. The southern senators couldn't take a chance that the amendment would vitiate the bill sufficiently: what if federal judges found ways to circumvent that provision? Part III was totally unacceptable. It had to go—all of it. None of the senators were angrier than Richard Russell. Among the methods by which Johnson was attempting to influence the Southern Caucus was the planting of newspaper articles "reporting" the understanding among "responsible southerners" of the need for passage of civil rights legislation, and of their increased—and highly responsible—willingness to let the legislation pass if it included the jury trial amendment, but Russell was having none of it. On March 25, William S. White floated just such a Johnson trial balloon, suggesting the likelihood that a civil rights bill would pass with Part III largely intact but with a provision requiring a jury trial for all violations. Tearing White's article out of the paper, Russell scribbled across it a note to himself: "This story embraces LBJ's ideas and I believe was inspired by him—He talked to me as if this amendment was all we could expect—I don't agree if he will go all out."

"All out" meant removing Part III—entirely. To the Senate's true civil rights believers, however—northern liberals of both parties—Part III was the most essential part of the bill, the part that made it their "dream bill." The most hurtful racial injustices occurred in the very areas in which Part III would at last allow the federal government to intervene. Without it, even after Supreme Court decisions, African-Americans were still being forced to ride in the back of buses, and black schoolchildren still couldn't go to school with white children. The liberals flatly refused to consider the elimination of Part III or, indeed, any substantial alteration in its wording. They refused also to consider any form of a jury trial amendment which would make a mockery of a civil rights bill, whatever its other provisions might be. And joining the liberals in refusal were moderate and even some conservative Republicans who were supporting the unamended bill out of loyalty to the Republican Administration which had proposed it, or out of desire for personal political gain.

In attempting to reconcile southern and northern demands, Johnson was engaging in the search for compromise—for some common ground—that is the essence of the legislative process, but on this issue no common ground seemed to exist. For the sake of Johnson's presidential ambitions, for the sake of "cleaning him up" on civil rights, the South—at Richard Russell's command— might allow civil rights legislation to pass, but only legislation so weak as to be meaningless. Nor was there any reason for it to allow any more; it had in the filibuster an unbreakable defense. "In the course of their many private conversations that Spring," Merle Miller says, "Russell . . . advised Lyndon that the South would not under any circumstances accept Part III; they would filibuster first, he personally would lead the filibuster, and not only would Lyndon find it very difficult to pass a bill, he would find himself in an extremely ticklish position." Yet when Johnson approached liberals about eliminating Part III, or substantially modifying it, they refused to consider the suggestion. Nor, they felt, was there any reason for them to consider it. At last, after so many years of frustration, they had Republicans on their side, and therefore had the votes to pass a civil rights bill. They were determined to pass one that was truly meaningful, which meant passing one that included Part III. And there was an additional, less altruistic, motive: revenge. "Frustration had . . . done peculiar things to the psychology of the northern civil rights advocates," George Reedy was to say. "The feeling of impotence was preying on their mind. . . . There was a distinct note of retribution in their voices, and it was apparent that they wanted something more than a civil rights bill that would help blacks. They wanted a bill that would include every civil rights concept that had been concocted in over a half a century and they wanted to rub southern noses in it." Watching Johnson search vainly for a compromise, Reedy felt that "everything had been said that could possibly be said, with the only result a hardening of positions and increasing polarization of attitudes," and that "Movement in any direction was impossible because the question was not being treated as a legislative matter. Instead, it was a clash between the mores of two cultures—deep-seated moral beliefs that could not be compromised."

AT THE START of the four-month period beginning in mid-January, 1957, optimistic predictions had been the order of the day. The fact that the margin for Lyndon Johnson's tabling motion had been only seventeen votes "was hailed by civil rights advocates," the *New York Times* reported, "as 'historic' and a 'landmark' that . . . would strengthen liberal chances 'tremendously' at the opening of future Congresses." "We got thirty-eight votes for it!" Howard Shuman exulted. "In 1953, we only got twenty-one." If Nixon turned his opinion into a ruling in 1959, only forty-nine votes would be necessary to defeat tabling—and to rewrite Rule 22—and suddenly that figure seemed within reach. Declaring that "we made very real gains," an elated Paul Douglas said, "We'll win either next time or the time after."

This view was shared by the press, which, like Douglas, ignored Russell's threat that a ruling to allow the rewriting of Senate rules would be followed by the rewriting of not one rule but forty. Nixon's opinion, *Time* said, "raised an emotional floodgate for a piece of vital legislation that had been dammed too long by Senate rules." *Newsweek*'s Sam Shaffer agreed. The "generation-old coalition of Southern Democrats and certain Northern Republicans in Congress lies in ruins," he said, and with "their former allies defecting from the ranks . . . the final vote in the Senate revealed the southerners in a position hopelessly untenable." Their victory on the tabling motion had been Pyrrhic, Shaffer said. "As they surveyed the field of victory, they saw that, in truth, they had lost."

On January 21, the Brownell Bill, essentially the same bill guaranteeing a broad range of civil rights that had been submitted in 1956, was returned to Capitol Hill. Liberal senators, liberal strategists, columnists of all persuasions, and most of the Washington press corps agreed that this year the bill would pass. The southerners will try their old tactics, *Time* predicted, but this time, with liberals and Republicans united against the South, those tactics will fail. "There should be enough sympathetic votes to force the bill out of the Judiciary Committee lorded over by Chairman [Eastland]. Before Congress adjourns, everyone agreed, there will be a sizzling Senate filibuster," but this time the filibuster will be "broken. When some 20 diehard Southern Senators attempt to talk the bill to death on the floor, there should be enough votes even under present cloture rules to cut off the filibuster and bring the measure to a vote." And then at last, *Time* said, "a tiny band of Southerners who over the years have combined seniority and archaic rules to strangle legislation that displeased them will have suffered momentous defeat."

The optimism was shared by the Republican leaders in Congress, as is shown by the typed summary of their weekly meeting with President Eisenhower on January 8. According to the summary, an unidentified participant said, "Civil rights—has to go early if to get it," but the President was assured by House GOP Leader Joseph Martin that there would be "no trouble" getting "early" action on the Brownell Bill. "Republicans and Democrats want to get that bill out," Martin said. If it came up first in the Senate, he said, there would be fast action. "If Knowland calls it up—pass quick—only 25 votes against." And, as Martin indicated to reporters, if it came up first in the House, action would be even faster. There was "no question," he said, that the House would approve the bill in "about two days." Joining in the assurances, Knowland stated that this year there would not be the usual delays in the Senate—in part because of the cooperation of the Democratic Leader. "I talked with Johnson," he had told Eisenhower during the meeting. "I told him if they [the Democrats] do not take it up, I intend to. He was agreeable, and he's served notice on [the] Southerners." Back at the Capitol, he was equally sanguine. Inviting Clarence Mitchell to his office, he "unequivocally promised" the NAACP lobbyist that if the South tried to filibuster, he would personally lead—and win—the fight for cloture. A filibuster could delay a civil rights bill, he told a reporter for the *Congressional Quarterly;* it couldn't stop it.

The customary route to the Senate floor, of course, was through a Senate committee, and the liberals set out along this route, and at first felt they were making good progress. Tom Hennings was brimming with confidence. His bill, similar to Brownell's, had already been reintroduced and referred to the Senate Judiciary Committee. He himself was chairman of Judiciary's three-man sub-committee that had jurisdiction over civil rights bills, but, he explained to reporters, hearings in that subcommittee would be unnecessary, since it had already favorably reported the same bill to the full committee last year. There-fore, Hennings said, the full committee—eight of whose fifteen members were, after all, strong civil rights supporters—could start holding hearings so early that Eastland's delaying tactics would not work. Knowland agreed. The com-mittee can "have hearings while the House is working, and get it reported by the time the House acts," the Republican Leader said. "I'd like to start by mid-Feb or late Feb on civil rights." And once the bill got to the Senate floor, the delaying tactics of the past would not be successful—not only Hennings but other senators assured reporters of that: there is a "belief that a filibuster now could be broken despite past failures," John D. Morris reported in the *New York Times.* And, the *Times* said, in part this belief was based on the cooperation of the Majority Leader. "The Senate's Democratic leadership has reached an understanding to bring the civil rights issue to a head early in the present ses-sion. . . . The leadership is hopeful . . . that if it gets the matter to the Senate floor within the next two months any southern attempt to thwart the decision by 'extended debate' can be beaten down. . . ."

And then the reality of the Senate took hold, the reality of Henry Cabot Lodge Sr. and the Foreign Relations Committee when Woodrow Wilson had been trying to win approval of the League of Nations, the reality of the Judi-ciary Committee when Franklin D. Roosevelt had been trying to win approval of his court reorganization bill—the reality that was still the reality.

Hennings' confidence about quick subcommittee and committee action lasted only until Judiciary's first meeting, on January 22, at which there were some developments he had not anticipated. It was a chairman's prerogative to appoint the members of his committee's subcommittees, and Chairman East-land now read off the names of the members of Hennings' subcommittee, and there were no longer three names but seven. The chairman had added to it four new members: southerners Olin Johnston and Sam Ervin and conservative Republicans Roman Hruska and Arthur Watkins. Olin the Solon said that of course there would have to be extensive subcommittee hearings on the civil rights bill for the benefit of the new members, and the other new members agreed with that.

At the subcommittee's first meeting, on January 30, Hennings tried to per-suade its members to agree to a two-week limit on hearings. The two holdover members voted with him, making three votes in favor of the proposal. The four new members voted against it. Emerging from the subcommittee room after the meeting, Hennings told reporters he was "very disappointed," but that he would still press for early action, holding long hearings if necessary. Long hearings? Hennings was asked. Was he saying that the subcommittee would meet while the Senate was in session? Did he have the Senate's permission to do that? Senate permission was required for subcommittees as well as committees, he was reminded. Hennings then applied on the Senate floor for unanimous consent for the necessary permission. Do I hear any objection? the presiding officer asked. It turned out he heard several objections—all in southern accents. And the subcommittee's favorable report would not be reported to the full committee until March 19.

And of course that report was not to the Senate, but only to the parent committee: Judiciary—Jim Eastland's Judiciary. After interviewing Eastland, a young reporter, twenty-eight-year-old Tom Wicker of the *Winston-Salem Journal,* wrote that "the soft-spoken man propping his gouty foot on the big cluttered desk doesn't seem to mind" that he had become a "byword for prejudice." And when he asked Eastland about the liberals' plans to hurry the bill through Judiciary, the chairman said, "It's not going to be as easy as they thought, old scout."

The chairman was correct. Every time Hennings attempted to bring up his report for committee action, Eastland recognized another committee member instead, usually one of its three other southerners. Judiciary's once-a-week meetings began every Monday at 10:30 a.m., and at twelve noon the Senate bells rang to signal the beginning of the day's session—the time at which Senate rules required the adjournment of committee meetings. Eastland enforced the rule to the minute, and one of the southerners was almost always still holding the floor, with Hennings still unheard, when the bell rang. Once, Hennings actually got to start reading his resolution, but the bell rang before he finished; before its echo had died away, Eastland had rapped his gavel for adjournment.

And of course, should the bill ever emerge from Judiciary, it would still have to face the Senate itself. Judiciary might, of course, be bypassed if the Senate took up a House-passed version of the bill instead, but unanimous consent was required for the Senate to do that. A *Washington Star* reporter asked Russell whether, in the light of public, and Republican, support for civil rights, there was "any prospect" that the South might be willing to compromise its stand against the passage of any civil rights legislation whatsoever and allow a House bill to be taken up. Compromise? Russell said. "I will not compromise in the slightest degree where the constitutional rights of my state and her people are involved.

"I am well aware of the fact that there is great political pressure for the passage of these misnamed civil rights bills," he said, but "If they reach the floor in their present form, they will be vigorously resisted by a resolute group

of senators." And those senators, he promised, would insist that the Senate follow "orderly procedure." Orderly procedure, of course, included "extended
debate." Writing his story, the reporter put on it a lead that summed it up:
"Senator Russell, Democrat of Georgia, yesterday threw down the gauntlet to
advocates of civil rights legislation who contend this is their victory year." The
North wanted the legislation in essentially its present form. Russell was saying
that if the legislation reached the floor in its present form, there would be a filibuster. And whatever its result, a filibuster would wreck Lyndon Johnson's
chance for the Democratic presidential nomination.

Observers who felt that Russell was short on allies, moreover, were overlooking one—one they seemed to overlook every year. Russell was indeed on
the defensive on Capitol Hill now, seemingly beaten, as Lee had been on the
defensive in 1865, with Grant pressing him back and back; even as Lee devised
one stratagem after another, he had been aware that they were only delaying
actions that could postpone, but not avert, defeat. There was, however, a crucial
difference between the strategic situations facing the two great southern generals, for in war there is no time limit: no deadline at which, if neither side has
won, a final armistice is declared. Robert E. Lee had not had time on his side.

Time was on Richard Brevard Russell's side, though. For him, delay
would not necessarily end in defeat; delay could, in fact, be the means of victory: victory at least for another year, or for another two-year Congress—and
perhaps for many Congresses to come. For there was a time limit on Capitol
Hill: each Congress is only two years long, and a bill that has not been passed
at the end of two years dies, and must start over, from scratch, in the next Congress; must be reintroduced, must renegotiate all the preliminary committee
procedures in both houses, must be passed by both houses.

During the 1950s, in addition, the actual time available to pass a bill was
far less than two years because it was only in wartime that Congress met for a
full year each year. Usually its sessions were considerably shorter. Of the
twenty-three peacetime annual sessions since 1933, when Congress had begun
convening in January, exactly one had lasted as long as the end of August—
eight months. Many had ended in June or July. And because of the holiday
recesses Congress awarded itself—a traditional week in February for Lincoln's
Birthday; another few days in February for Washington's Birthday; ten or
eleven days for Easter; additional vacations for Memorial Day and the Fourth
of July; numerous *pro forma* Monday and Friday sessions at which most congressmen were traveling back and forth from their districts—even eight months
actually meant far less. If a controversial bill, one entailing lengthy hearings
and intra-committee fights and perhaps floor battles as well, was to be passed,
it had to begin moving through the congressional committee processes rather
early.

In the case of a bill controversial enough to possibly provoke a filibuster,
an early start was indispensable for another reason as well. If such a bill was

brought to the Senate floor late in the session, too close to the time when the Senate was rushing toward adjournment and senators were anxious to go home, the prospect of fighting a filibuster out to the end, no matter how many weeks or months it takes, was particularly unappealing. Pressure to end the matter— to simply drop the bill—was intensified. "If you wait too long," George Reedy explains, "then what [happens] is that the looming end of the session becomes a weapon to be used by the filibusterers." So delay was a potent weapon. On a legislative battlefield, delay could mean victory.

This was understood on Capitol Hill in 1957. "Has to go early if to get it," the White House had been told. There was even an understanding of *how* early it had to go—that unless the civil rights bill reached the Senate floor by the Easter vacation in mid-April, or at the very latest, by the early part of May, there would be almost no hope of passing it over a southern filibuster. But there had been confidence among Republican leaders that this year it *would* "go early": the Senate Majority Leader "was agreeable, and he's served notice on the southerners." Knowland had spoken of getting the civil rights bill to the floor by "mid-Feb or late Feb." But that had been in January, when Russell and Johnson had optimistically felt the bill might be made sufficiently meaningless so that the South could let it pass. Now, in February and March and April, Russell was using delay as a weapon. Years later, when he was President, Johnson would explain to Katharine Graham how civil rights bills had invariably been defeated, by delay, on Capitol Hill: "They'd come back about the 18th of January and then they'll have hearings in the [House] Rules Committee till about the middle of March and then they'll pass the bill and it will get over and Dick Russell will say, 'It's Easter and Lincoln's Birthday.' And by the time you get him, he will *screw them to death* because he's so much smarter than they are." Now, in 1957, Russell was screwing them to death in the way that Johnson described to Mrs. Graham—screwing them again, as he had in the past, by delay. And, in February and March and April of 1957, it was beginning to become apparent that in the use of this weapon, the South and Russell were being assisted by the Senate Majority Leader.

IN JANUARY, Lyndon Johnson had assured the southerners that he would be able to make the civil rights bill meaningless enough so that they could live with it, but he had been unable to deliver. Russell's price for forgoing a filibuster—the excision of the "broad array" of civil rights guarantees, and the emasculation of the remaining provisions by the right of jury trial—was payable only in non-southern votes for those southern demands, Johnson had been unable to meet that price: had been unable to find those votes. The irresistible force of civil rights demands was indeed colliding with an immovable object—and Johnson had seemingly decided simply to step out of the way. During those months, he was no less "agreeable" to Knowland than he had been in January, he just wasn't as active. No more was heard of the January "understanding" "to bring the civil rights issue to a head early," to get it "to the Senate floor within the next two months."

And those actions that Lyndon Johnson did take spoke louder than words.

To delay the attack on a stronghold—a citadel—the defenders try to fight first on its outskirts. During those days of Lyndon Johnson's "agreeability," there had been discussion, even optimism, among Republican leaders that he might in effect forgo that delaying action by allowing the battle to begin in the citadel itself—by allowing the civil rights bill to be taken up in the Senate first. Now, however, Johnson repeated what he had said in 1956: that the Senate would not take up the bill until after the House had passed it.

To ensure that flanking movements against the citadel itself were not launched against his wishes, he was employing another tactic. This was a traditional southern tactic—one whose repeated use over the years had not dulled its effectiveness. It was simply to delay consideration of other major bills while waiting to take up the civil rights bill. If all the other major bills *had* been taken up, then by the time the civil rights measure arrived on the floor, precipitating a filibuster, it would be the only major piece of unfinished Senate business. But if other major bills remained to be disposed of at the time a filibuster brought Senate activity to a halt, these bills would become weapons in the southerners' hands. Other senators would realize that if the civil rights bill was not dropped—if the southerners were not allowed to win; if instead the Senate decided to fight it out on the filibuster front as long as it took and not move on to other business—that other necessary legislation might not be taken up. "Therefore," as Reedy explains, "if you know you've got an issue coming up that is going to start a filibuster, you try to get those [other important] bills out of the way. . . ." Otherwise senators will say, "My God, we're holding up this [other] bill." A Leader who wants a filibuster to lose "always tries to get the desks cleared before the filibuster comes up." A Leader tries to clear the decks early in the year, in fact—before "the looming end of the session" made the many senators who didn't particularly care about civil rights say, as the civil rights bill approached, "Don't bring it up. Otherwise, we'll never get to the other important bills."

Lyndon Johnson was not doing this. The Eisenhower Administration had a list of legislation it considered essential: not only its big school construction program but a law to provide federal aid to chronically depressed communities; authorization for United States participation in the Organization for Trade Cooperation; and a badly needed increase in postal rates to cover a rapidly worsening deficit in the Post Office Department. In addition, with Egypt's President Nasser stalling on reopening the Suez Canal, Israel stalling on withdrawing its troops from the Gaza Strip, and the threat of Russian intervention escalating, Eisenhower had asked for a congressional resolution giving him advance authorization to intervene economically or militarily in the Middle

East, authorization Eisenhower considered vitally necessary to deter Russia, since, with "modern war" perhaps "a matter of hours only," there might not be time to go to Congress if an attack occurred. At an extraordinary meeting of thirty congressional leaders of both parties at the White House on New Year's Day, Eisenhower had stressed the need for rapid approval, as he did in a special message he delivered in person on Capitol Hill five days later. Although there were differences within the Senate on the resolution's wording, general agreement existed that some form of authorization was desirable: the situation was precisely the kind on which Lyndon Johnson had, so many times, worked out a unanimous consent agreement.

No such agreement was brought forward now, however. Week after week, the "debate" on the Middle East Resolution dragged on, tying up the Senate before a notably empty Chamber in a scene out of the Senate's pre-Johnsonian foot-dragging past, complete with legalistic nitpicking—"I am waiting for the opposition point of view to provide some answers before I proceed to rebuttal and surrebuttal and rebuttal of the surrebuttal," Wayne Morse announced at one point (he was not kidding)—and senatorial frustration. "Why cannot we vote?" Dennis Chavez shouted one day. "I am ready to vote now." Eisenhower's other "essential" legislation also remained stalled behind the resolution; until that resolution was out of the way, the Senate would not be able to turn to the other Administration priority bills and get *them* out of the way. Slow as is the first year of most Congresses, this was slowness indeed. And the foot-dragging had a special significance this year. "The 85th Congress has been in session now for six weeks," the *New York Herald Tribune* noted on February 14, "and the civil rights issue, which was to have been the burning question at hand, has been pushed into the background . . . by the Senate debate over President Eisenhower's Mideast policy." When the Senate finally voted, it adopted the original resolution, 72 to 19, but that vote was not taken until March 5.

JOHNSON HAD SAID THE SENATE would not act on the civil rights bill until the House acted, and House action was not, in fact, coming in "about two days." The tone of the Republicans' weekly White House legislative conference began to change. At the January 8 meeting, Knowland had predicted that the Judiciary Committee would report the bill to the Senate floor by "mid-Feb or late Feb." In the summary of Knowland's report to the next meeting, held on January 22, a new month is being mentioned: "Hope to get it out by late February or early March." A week later, on January 29, the minutes start mentioning Easter, a holiday which falls not in March but in April: "Every effort will be made to secure action on the legislation prior to any Easter recess. Speaker Martin noted the appearance of some sign of a Democratic desire to delay action." (Eisenhower was moved to muse: "Strange. Years ago, we talked [about] the same things. . . .") The minutes of the March 12 meeting show that reality was beginning to penetrate even the densest material: "Sen. Knowland said that if the President's moderate proposal is to be achieved, then there was a need to get it moving soon. He had to report, however, that the Opposition had told him that if Republicans insisted on moving on Civil Rights, there would be some other legislation that would automatically be lost." And the minutes of the March 26 meeting summarize an exchange between Knowland and Halleck which shows further penetration.

> KNOWLAND.   If we are to get it, must get before last stages.
> HALLECK.   Think you're too late already.
> KNOWLAND.   Not yet, but close.

On April 2, "Senator Knowland thought the Democrats seemed to be dragging hard on this. They did not even want a Committee report to come out until after the Easter recess." Senator Dirksen chimed in that there was a "problem in Committee."

There was a problem, all right. The report of Hennings' subcommittee had finally reached the full Judiciary Committee. The morning of April 1, in fact, Chairman Eastland would actually recognize Hennings, and allow him to make a motion: that the committee take a final vote on the measure by April 15. The reason for Eastland's generosity then became apparent. While he had allowed Hennings to make the motion, he would not allow the committee to vote on it. It "would be patently unfair," he said, for the committee to vote before it had studied the transcript of the subcommittee's hearing. He had inquired of the Senate Printing Office, the chairman said, as to when that transcript would be available, and it would not be ready for two weeks. And, the chairman added, subcommittee member Ervin had notified him that he wanted to write a minority dissent to its report—and that he would not be able to begin writing until he had studied the transcript. Hennings' motion, Eastland said, would therefore not be in order.

At the White House, on April 9, a new month was mentioned in the discussion on civil rights. "Sen. Knowland again pointed to Democratic foot-dragging and their apparent determination to keep this subject off the floor until mid-May . . . so that other legislation may then take priority." That long a delay would probably kill the bill, Knowland said. "He thought the Republicans would have to put on a drive to get earlier action than that if any bill is to be forthcoming this year. If [the Republicans are] to get [a bill], they must make major drive to get [action] pre-Easter."

That warning—that a civil rights bill could pass only if it reached the Senate floor by the Easter recess—had, of course, first been made months before. Now, on April 12, the Easter recess arrived. The bill was not on the floor. It was nowhere near the floor. Furthermore, should it ever get there, other urgent legislation was now piled up behind it, including the thirteen appropriation bills necessary to keep the government running. The House had passed six of those bills. The Senate had passed none. "It is always true that Congress begins slowly and ends in a whirlwind," the *New York Times* said. "But the beginnings this year have seemed even slower than usual."

The tone of press coverage had changed, too. The civil rights bill "is in serious trouble," the *Washington Post* said on April 28. It has "a fair chance of enactment in the House, but the once-bright prospect of Senate enactment this session appears increasingly dim." When Clifford Case said that the tactics fatal to past civil rights bills were being repeated in 1957, and would have the same effect, Roscoe Drummond understood. "Sen. Case is quite right in warning that it is happening all over again this spring," the columnist wrote. "Senator Johnson and Republican leader Sen. William Knowland have both said that they hoped to expedite action on the Civil Rights program so that the Senate would not have to debate it during the closing days of the session. That expediting is not yet visible."

Some civil rights advocates still had hopes, although they were fading. "There is need for a dramatic rescue if the civil rights bill is not to be smothered to death," Philip Graham's *Washington Post* editorialized. For others, hope was all but gone. "Everything is waiting on something else," Senator Norris Cotton of New Hampshire said on April 27. "The Senate is waiting for the House. . . . Aid for school construction is waiting on civil rights. Civil rights seems to be waiting for the millennium."

And among those who had, seemingly, all but lost hope was Lyndon Johnson. In early January, he had predicted that a civil rights bill would pass—but shortly afterwards he had begun pulling back from the fight. Those early optimistic predictions were not repeated, were replaced by silence. From January 19 to May 29, Lyndon Johnson made not a single public statement on civil rights. And if, during these four months, his lack of words spoke loudly, so did his lack of actions. Not only was he not clearing the Senate decks for a filibuster fight, his behind-the-scenes efforts to find a compromise acceptable to both sides had become perfunctory. For a surprisingly large portion of this period, in fact, he *wasn't* behind the scenes—or even in Washington. During this four-month period, he took a nine-day vacation in Florida and a nineteen-day vacation, over Easter, at his ranch. If one includes short trips— one to New York, one to Miami, several to Huntlands—he was away from Washington for some forty-two days out of the 130 days in this period. During these trips he was, as always, constantly on the telephone with his staff in Washington about Senate matters, but civil rights was not uppermost among them. "There was a time, there . . . when you would have thought he had all but given up [on civil rights]," Reedy says. "You could understand that. It looked hopeless."

. . .

CONGRESS'S RETURN from the Easter recess on April 30 brought only more of the same. The minutes of the first post-recess Republican Legislative Leaders' Meeting at the White House report that "It is expected that this legislation [civil rights] will reach the House floor in about two weeks." But somehow that happy event did not occur. (May 14—"The importance of early action on this legislation was again stressed." May 21—"It is expected that this measure will be reported by the House Rules Committee and that the House will begin to discuss it within the next few days.") At the first post-recess meeting of the Senate Judiciary Committee, Senator Hennings raised his hand, intending to introduce a motion setting a firm, early, date for a vote on the civil rights bill. But at the foot of the Democratic side of the committee table, another hand shot up, that of Senator Ervin, and it was Ervin whom Chairman Eastland recognized. Ervin launched into what was evidently going to be a long speech, and every time Hennings attempted to break in, Eastland would ask him not to interrupt another senator.

In the halls of government, there was still no real leadership for the cause of social justice. The President was again ducking every chance to show any, resolutely avoiding every opportunity to press for action on his Attorney General's civil rights bill. Asked if he was "satisfied with the progress" on the bill, Eisenhower replied, "Progress in Congress is a very spotty thing." His party's congressional leaders, he said, had assured him that they were "making their best effort to bring these bills up and get them passed." The House Rules Committee did indeed report the bill—H.R. 6127—out on May 22, so that a date to begin debate on the measure in the House could be set, but that action only began to increase attention on the Senate, and the *Washington Post* reported that "Senate leaders weren't too optimistic"; Knowland forecast a "lengthy debate which some might call a filibuster." "The South is still in control," Senator Alexander Wiley said.

Attention was also beginning to focus on Lyndon Johnson. After his return from the ranch on April 28, he tried to avoid public statements on the issue, as an exchange on the Senate floor on May 13 showed. Responding to White House criticism of senatorial inaction on Eisenhower's program, he listed the various bills that were shortly going to be brought to the floor, without mentioning the civil rights bill. Knowland, standing across the aisle from him, twitted him on the omission: "I notice—perhaps by inadvertence—that my distinguished friend, the Majority Leader, had not mentioned the proposed civil-right legislation. . . . We are now in the month of May. I was very hopeful that the distinguished Majority Leader might throw some light on the question as to when we could expect that proposed legislation on the floor." Johnson's angry reply ("Mr. President, my friend from California has asked me a question. I am not sure that he is really soliciting information . . .") seemed to show a sympathy for the southern view that the Supreme Court had already pushed civil rights as far as could be expected, and that the country should now be allowed a respite from further action. "It is the view of the Senator from Texas," the Senator from Texas said, "that the Supreme Court has acted in connection with the education and transportation problem, and that all over the land the American people are doing their best to adjust themselves to the situation created by the Court's decision and are attempting to evolve a workable solution in the light of that decision." His reply also showed irritation with those who were "nevertheless" still agitating for civil rights. "The Majority Leader," said the Majority Leader, "although he does not agree with all the proposals made—and, indeed, does not agree with many of them—realizes that a substantial number of members of both the House and Senate wish to vote on some so-called civil-rights legislation, because to fail to do so would permit those who have no hesitancy in exploiting this political issue to continue to do so in the months ahead." His reply showed no sympathy for aggressive senatorial action on civil rights. To Knowland's request for a date "when we could expect that proposed legislation on the floor," Johnson's only response was that he would "take no offense if . . . after the [Judiciary] Committee had acted or failed to act," Hennings or Knowland himself "should make a motion to discharge the committee." If they did, Johnson said, "I believe this question will be acted upon. . . . Some action will come by the early part of next month." *Some* action. Not favorable action. And the action he was talking about was not action on a civil rights bill, but only action on a motion to put that bill on the Senate Calendar, a motion that could be filibustered—as the bill, should it ever get to the floor, would be filibustered. When Johnson finished, Hennings rose at his desk and characterized his Leader's statement. "The same old hocus-pocus, and the same old claptrap, and the same old backing and filling," he said. In the *New York Times,* reporter C. P. Trussell was gently sarcastic. "Senator Lyndon B. Johnson, of Texas, the Majority Leader, while letting everybody know that he was against the program, said that he would not be 'offended' if Mr. Knowland, or Senator Hennings . . . should force it to floor action." Trussell concluded that "it does not appear that it will be passed by Congress at this session."

And if dreams of social justice seemed, once more, all but dead, so too did Lyndon Johnson's dreams for himself.

He knew that the realization of that goal at which he had been aiming all his life required him to "produce" on civil rights—knew that "if I failed to produce on this one . . . everything I had built up over the years would be completely undone." And yet producing on civil rights seemed as hopeless a task as ever. A strong, meaningful, civil rights bill was moving, slowly but moving, through the House, but then it would come to the Senate—where, if there was any chance of its passing, it would be filibustered to death. There would be no Civil Rights Act—and no removal from Lyndon Johnson's image of the "scent of magnolias" fatal to his presidential hopes. It seemed that spring of 1957 as if there was scarcely a newspaper or magazine that didn't remind him of that harsh reality. In April, for example, there was an article in the *Progressive.* Entitled "The Legend of Lyndon Johnson," it said that his contention that he stood midway between "Thurmond and Douglas, between the Southerners and

the liberals," is "far from being the whole truth," for while "Johnson himself is
not the type of Southerner whose opposition to civil rights stems from the sincere depths of bigotry," while "early in his life, he taught classes of Mexican-
Americans," and while "his opposition to civil rights springs not from passion
but from political calculation," that fact does not make him any less dangerous
a foe of civil rights. "Johnson never strays far from his real power base in the
Senate—his fellow-Southerners," the article said. "In fact, many observers still
consider him little more than a pliant instrument of Senator Russell." And its
evaluation of Johnson as a Majority Leader was devastating: "He knows everyone's value—and knows even better his price, if he has one. He is not the leader
of great causes, but the broker of little ones."

That article was written by David C. Williams, editor of *ADA World,* the
official publication of that body of "crazies" and "red-hots." But on May 25,
newspapers around the country carried an Associated Press interview with
Colonel Jake Arvey, not a "crazy" (or indeed a particularly ardent civil libertarian) but one of the most pragmatic and most powerful northern political
leaders, about possible 1960 Democratic presidential nominees, and he said
party leaders throughout the North were "very high" on two candidates:
Kennedy and Symington. He didn't mention Lyndon Johnson, but the reporter
asked about him. Senator Johnson, Arvey replied, would be hampered by "the
question mark concerning his health"—and by his "Texas origins": "Northerners," Arvey said, "would be fearful of his position on the segregation issue."

Though Lyndon Johnson realized the situation, however, there seemed to
be nothing he could do about it. Looking back on the situation years later,
George Reedy would be struck by the seeming "impossibility" of negotiating
any type of compromise. The "prospect of any legislative action," he said,
"seemed more remote than a landing on the moon."

BUT THERE HAD BEEN EARLIER EPISODES in Lyndon Johnson's career in
which his chances appeared hopeless—that first campaign for the House, that
campaign for the Senate against the invincible Coke Stevenson, other episodes,
too—and always Lyndon Johnson had reacted, after spells of depression and
despair, in the same way: with a refusal to give up hope, with a willingness to
fight on, and to make in the fight an effort so intense that "days meant nothing,
nights meant nothing, weekdays, weekends, they meant nothing," with that
implacable determination to triumph no matter what the cost that had made Ava
Johnson Cox and Estelle Harbin say about Lyndon Johnson when he was
young that "he could not stand to lose, just could not *stand* it," that "he had to
win, *had to.*"

And that was how Lyndon Johnson reacted now.

What crystallized his feelings is not known, but it occurred on the ranch.
Not long after he had returned to Washington from that three-week Easter vaca-

tion on the Pedernales—even while he was still making public statements that "let everybody know that he was against" a civil rights bill—a difference in his attitude was becoming apparent to those who saw him behind closed doors. Richard Bolling, who had come to hate Johnson, in part because he had felt he was "really quite negative on civil rights," and who had watched Johnson "grow very quiet" during the early months of 1957 as he had grown very quiet during 1956 "whenever civil rights came up" behind the closed doors of Sam Rayburn's late-afternoon Board of Education, now began to see "a change in Lyndon Johnson," a change that began almost imperceptibly, but that, afternoon by afternoon, became more marked.

That was on the House side of the Capitol. On the Senate side there were indications, too. "Something changed," Gerald Siegel would say. And after it did, "he never had any hesitation at all."

37

The "Working Up"

FOR LYNDON JOHNSON, determination had to include belief.

He understood that all his life—as is shown by the fact that as a boy "he was always repeating" the salesman's remark that "You've got to believe in what you're selling," and that decades later, in his retirement, he would say: "What convinces is conviction. You simply *have* to believe in the argument you are advancing: if you don't, you're as good as dead. The other person will sense that something isn't there . . ." And Lyndon Johnson could *make* himself believe in an argument even if he had never believed in it before, even if he had believed in an opposite argument—and even if the argument did not accord with the facts. A devotee like Joseph Califano would write that Johnson "would quickly come to believe what he was saying even if it was clearly not true."

When Lyndon Johnson came to believe in something, moreover, he came to believe in it totally, with absolute conviction, regardless of previous beliefs, or of the facts in the matter, came to believe in it so absolutely that, George Reedy says, "I believe that he acted out of pure motives regardless of their origins. He had a remarkable capacity to convince himself that he held the principles he should hold at any given time, and there was something charming about the air of injured innocence with which he would treat anyone who brought forth evidence that he had held other views in the past. It was not an act. . . . He had a fantastic capacity to persuade himself that the 'truth' which was convenient for the present was *the truth* and anything that conflicted with it was the prevarication of enemies. He literally willed what was in his mind to become reality." Califano, listening to Johnson tell a story which Califano knew was not true, and which Califano knew that Johnson himself knew, or at least had known at one time, was not true, writes of "the authentic increase in the President's conviction each time he recited it." The phrase used to describe the process by longtime Texas associates like Ed Clark—the "revving up" or the "working up"—was homier, but it was the same process: "He could start talking about something and convince himself it was right, and get all worked up, all worked up and emotional, and work all day and all night, and sacrifice, and say, 'Follow me for the cause!'—'Let's do this because it's *right!*' " And, Clark says, Johnson would believe it *was* right—no matter what he had believed before.

To pass civil rights legislation, to convince senators of the need for such legislation, Lyndon Johnson therefore had to believe—to believe totally, with absolute conviction—that there was an urgent need for that legislation. He had to know that it was *right* to fight for it. And knowing it coldly, intellectually, was not enough. He had to feel it—to feel it wholeheartedly, to feel what the color of their skin meant to those Americans whose skin was darker than his. To fight wholeheartedly for justice for those people, he had to *feel* the injustice that had been visited upon them, and that was still being visited upon them. He had to make himself feel their fears and their doubts, had to make himself feel all the injustices and indignities that America had inflicted on them, from the lash and the leg irons all the way down through the decades, the generations, to the word "Colored" above the drinking fountains.

So now began the "working up."

Sometimes, the working up was couched in terms of pragmatism. In the homes of longtime conservative, somewhat racist, friends, the phone would ring now, often long after midnight, and on the phone would be Lyndon Johnson. "I can't sleep," he would say, and he would begin talking—to convince himself as well as them. One of the friends was his protégé Joe M. Kilgore. When Johnson told the young Texas congressman one night in 1957 that a civil rights bill should be passed, Kilgore resisted the suggestion. "The problem with you is that you don't understand that the world is trying to turn to the left," Lyndon Johnson said vehemently. "You can either get out in front and try to give some guidance, or you can continue to fight upstream, and be overwhelmed or be miserable." The congressman had known Lyndon Johnson for a long time, had "traveled the Valley with him" in 1941 and 1948, and, he says, he understood the purpose of the phone call, and of Johnson's words: "He was talking like he was giving me advice, but it was really himself he was giving the advice to. He wasn't talking to convince me; he was talking to convince himself."

And sometimes the working up was couched in very different terms.

At dinner parties in the homes of liberal friends, Lyndon Johnson began to tell again the stories with which, during his early years in Washington, he had won Alice Glass' heart and the hearts of the young New Dealers close to FDR, but which he had been telling less frequently in the years since he had come to the Senate. In the summer of 1957, there was a small dinner party in the Georgetown house of Daz and Richard Harkness, and one of the eight people at the table was Frank Church's wife, Bethine. "I remember at this dinner party, Johnson talking about teaching the Mexican-American kids in Cotulla, and his frustration that they had no books," Bethine Church recalls. "I remember it as one of the most passionate evenings I've ever spent."

He had a new story, too—about a talk he had had some years before, probably about 1951, with Gene Williams, the husband of the Johnsons' maid, Helen Williams.

At the end of each congressional session, the Johnsons' car was driven back to Austin from Washington by Gene and Helen and the Johnsons' third African-American employee, their cook, Zephyr Wright, while the Johnsons flew back in the Brown & Root plane. Then, when Congress reconvened in January, Ms. Wright and the Williamses drove the car back to Washington. During Johnson's talk with Gene Williams, Johnson asked him to take along the Johnsons' dog, Little Beagle Johnson.

Williams hesitated, and then asked, "Senator, do we have to take Beagle?" Johnson asked, "Tell me what's the matter. Why don't you want to take Beagle? What aren't you telling me?" When Williams still hesitated, Johnson said, "Gene, I want an answer."

"Well, Senator," Gene finally replied, "it's tough enough to get all the way from Washington to Texas. We drive for hours and hours. We get hungry. But there's no place on the road we can stop and go in and eat. We drive some more. It gets pretty hot. We want to wash up. But the only bathroom we're allowed in is usually miles off the main highway. We keep goin' 'til night comes—'til we get so tired we can't stay awake anymore. We're ready to pull in. But it takes another hour or so to find a place to sleep. You see, what I'm saying is that a colored man's got enough trouble getting across the South on his own, without having a dog along."

In the memoirs he published during his retirement, Lyndon Johnson was to write that that discussion had been an awakening for him, because he realized "there was absolutely nothing I could say to Gene Williams, or to any black man, or to myself"; that while "of course" he had known "that such discrimination existed throughout the South . . . somehow we had deluded ourselves into believing that black people around us were happy and satisfied; into thinking that the bad and ugly things were going on somewhere else, happening to other people," that the day of the discussion had been "the day I first realized the sad truth: that to the extent Negroes were imprisoned, so was I." If Johnson actually experienced such an epiphany on that day, however, it was an experience he kept to himself, for quite some time. His three employees were excused from taking the dog—Little Beagle continued to fly back and forth to Texas with the Johnsons—but not from taking the car, year after year, twice a year, on that three-day drive across thirteen hundred miles of the South. In 1953, Zephyr simply refused to keep making the trip ("I just wouldn't go," she recalls), but Gene and Helen Williams went on making it every year. And while many associates and acquaintances of Lyndon Johnson interviewed by the author recall Johnson recounting the story of his talk with Gene Williams, if he told the story for some years after the conversation occurred, he didn't tell it often. When the author asked these people when Johnson began telling it, none of them could give a precise answer. But, asked to make an estimate, every one of them who was willing to do so replied with some version of the phrase: "About the time he began fighting for civil rights."

Now, however, in 1957, the story became a staple of his conversation at Georgetown dinner tables—and in other venues as well. He told it over and over—with his customary vividness. Harry McPherson, who overheard the story in 1963, when Johnson was telling it to John Stennis, describes the occasion, in doing so showing Johnson's storytelling gift at work.

"You know, John," Lyndon Johnson said, "the other day [sic] a sad thing happened. My cook, Zephyr Wright, who has been working for me for many years—she's a college graduate—and her husband drove my official car from Washington down to Texas, the Cadillac limousine of the Vice President of the United States. They drove through your state and when they got hungry, they stopped at grocery stores on the edge of town in colored areas and bought Vienna sausages and beans and ate them with a plastic spoon. And when they had to go to the bathroom, they would stop, pull off on a side road, and Zephyr Wright, the cook of the Vice President of the United States, would squat in the road to pee. And you know, John, that's just bad. That's wrong."

And as Lyndon Johnson told it, he felt it.

He may not have been moved by the story—at least not moved enough to tell it, and not moved enough to excuse his three employees from the car-transport assignment—during the intervening years since he had first heard it, but he was certainly moved by it in 1957. He not only had the gift of "reading" men and women, of seeing into their hearts, he also had the gift of putting himself in their place, of not just seeing what they felt but of feeling what they felt, almost as if what had happened to them had happened to him, too. He may not have understood the feelings of Ms. Wright and the Williamses before, but he understood—had made himself understand, had *willed* himself to understand—those feelings now. The hurt Gene Williams felt when a hotel clerk turned him away wasn't only Gene Williams' hurt now; it was Lyndon Johnson's, too. He felt the hurt, and he felt for the people who had been hurt—felt the injustice and humiliation that had been visited upon them—grew angry for them, with an anger that was passionate and real. *John, that's just bad. That's wrong.* And when Stennis tried to say, "Well, Lyndon, I'm sure there are nice places where your cook and . . . ," Johnson, according to McPherson, "just said, 'Uh-huh, Uh-huh,' and just sort of looked away vacantly and said, 'Well, thank you, John,' " and after the Mississippi senator walked away, "Johnson turned around to me and winked," as if to say, "What can you expect?" and McPherson felt that "That was straight from real feelings. That made him angry . . . the simple indignity of discrimination was deep in Johnson." "The indignities" that Ms. Wright and the Williamses had suffered "made him angry, sometimes just about to tears," Califano says. Lyndon Johnson had, at last, put himself in their place as much as any white person could do so—which meant he had, as much as any white person could do so, put himself in the place of all the people of America on whom indignities and injustice were visited because their skins were not white. The empathy and compassion for black Americans had always been there inside Lyndon Johnson, but it had always been held in check. Now it was unleashed. Lyndon Johnson believed in the need for a civil rights bill now, believed with that intensity which, in other crises in his career, had led him to take the "all or nothing" gamble, to "shove in his whole stack," to determine, no matter how long the odds, to *win*. When Lyndon Johnson was this "worked up," when he was as determined as he was upon returning to Washington from the ranch after Easter—beside that determination all other considerations paled. A civil rights bill had to be passed. And a civil rights bill was *going* to be passed.

And shortly after his return to Washington, he said so—to the surprise of a friendly journalist, Tris Coffin, with whom he was having an off-the-record breakfast in the Senate Dining Room. "A civil rights bill is going to be passed by this Congress," Lyndon Johnson said. His tone was thoughtful, but suddenly he raised his big hand and smacked it down on his thigh to punctuate the words. "I'd like to see a bill the country can live with and not get torn apart," he said. "I don't know the answer, but I'm going to do a lot of listening."

"DURING THE LATE SPRING and early summer months of 1957," Booth Mooney would write, Lyndon Johnson began to go "tirelessly from faction to faction," working "quietly, almost in secret," refraining "from making any public statement of his intentions." He was asking, probing, buttonholing senators and staff, lobbyists and lawyers, in the corridors of the Capitol and the SOB, sitting down beside a senator on one of the cloakroom couches and chatting in a relaxed manner, and then, suddenly, his eyes narrowing at some words that had caught his attention (words that had been spoken or words that hadn't been spoken), taking the senator's arm and asking him to step outside into the corridor for a moment for a more private conversation, dropping in on senators in their inner offices, closing the door behind him—listening, listening to what they were saying, and listening to what they *weren't* saying. And out of the buttonholing, and the asking, and the listening, Lyndon Johnson was beginning to form a strategy. For as he listened, he heard something.

The most important thing a man tells you is what he's not telling you. Talking to the southern senators, Lyndon Johnson was listening to a lot of furious tirades about the Brownell Bill. If one didn't listen closely, all of the bill's provisions appeared equally abhorrent to them. But Johnson, listening very closely, realized that one provision was not being mentioned nearly so much as the others. Sometimes, in fact, it was not mentioned at all. And when it was mentioned, while it was assailed just as harshly as the other provisions, Johnson was hearing, beneath the words, a somewhat different undertone.

The provision was not in Part III, the section of the bill that had been occupying most of both sides' attention (and most of Lyndon Johnson's attention) since January, and on which both sides held positions so intractable that compromise seemed impossible. The provision was Part IV, which dealt not with ending segregation on many fronts but instead with a single right: the right to vote.

When southern senators talked about the clauses in Part III that would force employers to hire blacks or that would allow blacks to sit next to whites in classrooms or movie theaters, they poured out their anger harshly, uncompromisingly. But when the right to vote came up, the tone of voice was different: less defiant—sometimes, in fact, almost ashamed.

"It was fascinating for me, a Yankee who might be able to comprehend but could not share, southern feelings, to hear him talk," Reedy recalls. "Most southerners, he said, were not very concerned about depriving blacks of decent jobs. They had hypnotized themselves into a belief that Negroes were inherently unwilling to accept heavy responsibilities and were much more at ease doing menial tasks which did not require them to make decisions. . . . As for segregation, Dixie theoreticians had created a whole mythology about people being 'happier with their own kind.' None of those attitudes were going to change in the near future, in LBJ's estimate, and it was futile to anticipate any 'give' on these points. There was one area, however, in which he contended that southern consciences were hurting. This was in the field of voting rights. Here, he claimed, even the most outspoken of white supremacists had a sense of doing something wrong."

Partly this was because many of the southern senators believed if not always in the spirit but in the literal words of the Constitution, which was explicit on the question of suffrage, saying as it did that "The right of citizens of the United States to vote shall not be denied or abridged" on account of race or color. "They *were* constitutionalists, even though they were quite willing to concoct some peculiar interpretations of the document," Reedy was to say. "The amended Constitution—however much they despised the amendments—*did* guarantee blacks the right to vote. [It] did not say anything about the right to a job or the right to social equality or even the right to decent treatment by society. On voting, however, it was unequivocal." Even Harry Byrd sometimes murmured something about "a basic constitutional right" when the subject of voting came up. Even Thurmond, who had said, "I will never favor mixing of the races," didn't use the word "never" when that subject came up. The southern senators insisted that they were opposed to every aspect of the civil rights bill, but, listening to them closely, Johnson had come to feel that to one aspect of it they might be less opposed than to the others. While the South would not accept a Part III with or without a jury trial amendment, he realized, they might accept Part IV with a jury trial amendment. This price still seemed impossibly high. Liberals would never agree to a jury trial amendment for any part of the bill. But, Lyndon Johnson realized, there was a southern price—where there had never been a price before.

The southerners' feelings were not new. They had almost certainly been expressed to Lyndon Johnson before, during the previous months of discussion of the bill. But they had been obscured during these months by the emphasis on Part III. And they had become obscured as well by the southerners' insistence that *any* provisions in the bill be covered by a jury trial amendment. No one had focused on the voting right because of the overwhelming belief among liberals that no matter *what* rights were covered by the bill, that coverage would be meaningless if southern violators were tried by southern juries. But now Lyndon Johnson was focusing on Part IV, and he saw the potential in the southern attitude toward that part. The South was not insisting, as it had invariably insisted in the past, that it would not accept *any* civil rights bill, that it would, by filibustering, prevent any civil rights bill from coming to the Senate floor, and to a Senate vote. If he was somehow able to get Part III out of the bill, to get the 1957 Civil Rights Act limited to a single right—voting—and to guarantee jury trials to defendants in voting rights cases, the Act would be very weak, but it was possible that the South, while not of course actually voting for it, would not filibuster it: that the South would allow a civil rights bill to come to the Senate floor for the first time in eighty-two years, and then to be voted on there.

THIS VULNERABLE SPOT in the South's position was, furthermore, in the very place he had hoped to find it—for Lyndon Johnson's talents as a legislator went far beyond those of mere listening. He had the great lawmaker's gift of identifying, amid a panorama of many proposed laws, the one that would best accomplish a larger purpose, and he saw now that if he could get only one provision of the civil rights bill enacted, voting was the one it should be. Of all the rights that black Americans had so long been denied, the right to vote was the one which, if he could get it for them, would be most valuable, for the granting of that right would, he knew, lead—perhaps slowly, but inevitably—to all the others. His reasoning sprang from his understanding of, and belief in, power. The way to end the indignities Negroes had to suffer was to give them the power to end them, and in a democracy, power comes from the ballot box. Give Negroes the vote—give them power—and they could start doing the rest for themselves. The liberals wanted to change so many laws: housing laws, transportation laws, public accommodations laws, private accommodations laws, school desegregation laws—all those laws that were covered in Part III of the Brownell Bill. The southern senators would never agree that these laws should be changed, and the southern senators had enough power to ensure that they would not be changed. Therefore, Lyndon Johnson saw, don't try to change the laws; just change the officials who *wrote* the laws. Then *they* would change the laws. And the way to change the officials was to give southern Negroes the right to vote, so that officials who wanted to be elected would have to be solicitous of Negroes' other rights. Those who weren't sufficiently solicitous could be voted out of office: Negro voters could vote them out. Giving black Americans the vote would, moreover, change not only the laws but the administration of laws. The urgency for laws to restrain the brutality of small-town southern sheriffs would be alleviated, for example, since in many a southern small town, blacks had enough votes to elect the sheriff they wanted.

Lyndon Johnson started trying to explain this to liberals. "Just give Negroes the vote and many of these problems will get better," he told James Reston. "Give them [the Negroes] the vote and in a few years, they [the southern senators] will be kissing their ass," he told Hubert Humphrey. If out of all the civil rights that would be guaranteed by the Brownell Bill, only one could pass, he knew which right it should be—and it was the very one that the southerners, not seeing what he saw, were willing to let pass. Lyndon Johnson's purpose was no longer merely to help himself. Now he was trying to lift up a whole people, a nation within a nation. And he knew what to do for these people. He had made himself one of them.

HE KNEW SOMETHING ELSE, too—that the most important thing wasn't what was in the bill. The most important thing was that there *be* a bill.

One of the reasons for this was psychological. The South had won in the Senate so many times that there existed in the Senate a conviction that the South could not be beaten, particularly on the cause that meant the most to it. A number of senators—not the most ardent liberals, but a few others— intimidated already by the southerners' power over their bills and their committee assignments, were further intimidated by this conviction: what was the point of challenging the South, risking so much, when in the end the South was bound to win? "You felt this around the Senate," Jim Rowe was to say. "There was a mystique about them [the southern senators]. 'God, don't get the South mad!' And why get them mad, when you weren't going to win anyway? With westerners or midwesterners who didn't care too much about civil rights anyway, this was a big consideration." A victory over the South would begin destroying this mystique. Demonstrate that the South could be beaten and more attempts would be made to beat it.

Johnson saw this, as Rowe and Corcoran and Reedy and others close to him in 1957 attest. He used a typically earthy phrase to explain it. "Once you break the virginity," he said, "it'll be easier next time." Pass one civil rights bill, no matter how weak, and others would follow.

And there was a further reason, Lyndon Johnson saw, why the passage of *any* civil rights bill, no matter how weak, would be a crucial gain for civil rights. Once a bill was passed, it could later be amended: altering something was a lot easier than creating it. Aware though he became after his return to Washington following the 1957 Easter recess that his only slim hope of passing a civil rights bill would be to amend it down into a very weak bill, Johnson nonetheless realized that however insignificant the bill's provisions, passage of the measure would be deeply significant—not only for his personal dreams but for the dreams of the sixteen million American citizens whose skins were black.

38

Hells Canyon

THE PRICE THAT LYNDON JOHNSON now realized the South would accept to allow a civil rights bill to pass—that the bill be restricted to voting, and include a jury trial amendment—seemed a price simply too high for him to meet. Most of the twenty-seven non-southern Democratic senators, and the overwhelming majority of the forty-six Republicans,* were opposed to both these conditions. "The South," with its twenty-two Senate votes, "is completely without allies," George Reedy wrote in a memo to Johnson in the Spring of 1957, and he was exaggerating only slightly; when, in late Spring, Johnson embarked on his quest for a civil rights bill, there was available, should the South's two conditions come to a showdown, no place to find enough votes to meet them. And since the South would lose on a vote, it would simply not allow one. It would filibuster. And though they had no allies on civil rights, on a filibuster the situation would be far different. On a cloture vote, *you got up to thirty-three real fast.* There could be filibusters at any one—or all—of several points. Since killing the bill was so important to the South, Richard Russell would not want to risk everything on a single cloture vote, and would begin filibustering at the earliest point: the vote to put the bill on the Calendar. The measure would be kept bottled up in the Judiciary Committee as long as possible, and if a motion was finally made on the Senate floor to discharge it from Judiciary and place it on the Calendar, the South would filibuster that motion, beginning debate on it, and then extending the debate, and continuing to extend it—for as long as was necessary to block the motion from coming to a vote. And if that filibuster was cut off by cloture, the South could filibuster again to prevent the bill from being called off the Calendar and brought to the floor for debate and vote, and if that filibuster failed, too, could filibuster yet again to prevent that final floor vote. (The South would also, of course, filibuster a motion to place a House-passed

---

*Joe McCarthy died on May 2, leaving his seat vacant until a special election was held on August 28.

civil rights bill directly on the Calendar without it being sent to Judiciary.) For Lyndon Johnson to pass the bill, he had to find allies for the South: votes for its positions on Part III and jury trials, as well as the assurance of votes against cloture in case it lost on those points. And, with the session already deep in May, he had to find those votes almost immediately. Only if the South felt confident that the votes would be there if they were needed would it allow the bill to reach the Calendar. Johnson had to let the South know that it was not alone, that it had allies in the Senate.

He had, in addition, to let the South know that it had *enough* allies. The bill was too important for Russell to risk everything on a vote in which the margin would be so narrow that it might be changed at the last moment. A handful, or two handfuls, of promised votes would not make the South feel confident that an unacceptable bill could not pass, confident enough so that it could allow the measure to reach the Calendar. Lyndon Johnson had to find not merely a few votes but a whole group of votes: a large, solid Senate bloc.

In May, 1957, with Republicans and liberal Democrats lined up solidly behind a civil rights bill, with the necessity for a bill dramatized by the struggles in the South, and with the press and public demand for a bill rising, the formation of such a bloc seemed outside the realm of possibility. Determined though Johnson might be, determination couldn't create that bloc. Listening couldn't create it. This problem was so dramatically intractable that something more was needed—not only legislative leadership, but legislative genius.

Recruiting an entire bloc of allies for the South would require an ability to conceive and then create not merely individual deals, simple *quid pro quos,* and not merely a series of interrelated deals (complicated though that in itself could be), but a single, much broader, deal—a deal broad enough to bring an entire group of senators to the side of the South in one stroke: a *quid pro quo* of a magnitude so sweeping as to be truly national in scope. Lyndon Johnson found that deal—found a bloc—and found a means of bringing it to the South's side.

The means was a mountain canyon, a canyon not in the South but more than two thousand miles away: beyond the Appalachians, beyond the Mississippi Basin, beyond the Great Plains, beyond the Rocky Mountains—in the rugged Sawtooth Mountains that rose beyond the Rockies in America's far Northwest.

Hells Canyon (it had been given its name by pioneering mountain men whose boats had been capsized by its foaming white rapids) was an astonishing work of nature. Carved into one of the most inaccessible parts of the Sawtooth Range by the Snake River, its rock walls rose from the Snake's turbulent waters in a widening V that was almost eight thousand feet high—a thousand feet higher than the Grand Canyon; it was the deepest river gorge on the continent of North America. And it had been the subject for some years of a debate over who would harness the enormous power generated by its turbulent waters: the public, through a dam built by the federal government, or a private power company.

That question had become in some ways the hottest political issue in Oregon and Idaho, the two states separated by the Snake. For ten years, public power advocates, including both of Oregon's current senators, Wayne Morse and Richard Neuberger, had been trying to obtain authorization to build a federal dam, and for ten years these attempts had been blocked by private power advocates in Congress. And then hardly had the Eisenhower Administration taken office in 1953 when its Secretary of the Interior, Douglas McKay, a former Governor of Oregon, announced that legislation would be introduced to allow the Idaho Power Company to build three hydroelectric dams in Hells Canyon and sell the electricity they generated. The full extent of this "giveaway" of national resources became known when it was revealed that the Administration had granted Idaho Power an accelerated tax write-off that would generate $239 million in additional profits. But to Republicans, including President Eisenhower, the idea of using taxpayers' money to build a project that private capital was willing to finance was a perfect example of New Deal profligacy. Assailing the Administration's "shocking abandonment" of the public power concept, Morse reintroduced his proposed authorization of a federal dam, but when the showdown over his bill came in 1956, "Republican senators reported," as Marquis Childs wrote, "that they had never before [during the Eisenhower Administration] been under such pressure," and the bill had been defeated.

That defeat, however, made the issue hotter than ever. The governors of Oregon and Idaho, supporters of Idaho Power, ran for re-election in 1956, and both lost. In that year, furthermore, McKay returned to Oregon to run against Morse, calling the issue "American free enterprise" against "the left-wing Socialist idea." McKay was routed. Across the Snake, in Idaho, there was another Senate campaign, with Herman Welker, private power advocate, running for re-election against Frank Church. "The campaign was Frank Church versus Idaho Power," one of Church's aides says. "They fought him tooth and nail." Welker lost, too.

Since Morse and Neuberger and Church had made Hells Canyon their central campaign issue, their constituents would be watching to see if they produced on it. And the senators *wanted* to produce on it—all three believed deeply in the concept of public power.

The Hells Canyon fight had reverberations in other states—in the Far Northwest and southward down the long line of the Rockies—for these states were tied together physically by the transmission lines from huge federal dams already built (the lines from the Bonneville Dam on the Oregon-Washington border, for example, ran not only across these states but into Idaho and Montana as well) and philosophically by the concept symbolized by these lines: that America's rivers belonged to the people, and the electricity they generated should be provided to the people at the lowest possible cost. Hydroelectric power generated in these states by the fall of the waters of their rivers down through their tall mountains was the region's greatest natural resource, and in nine states—the seven so-called "Mountain States" (Idaho, Montana, Wyoming, Colorado, Utah, New Mexico, and Nevada) and the Far Northwest states of Washington and Oregon, whose mountains were not the Rockies but the Cascades—the question of how to get water, scarce in those states, and the power that water can generate, out of the rugged mountain ranges to irrigate millions of acres, mechanize tens of thousands of farms, and furnish inexpensive electricity to attract new industry was a fiercely contentious issue. The debate between those who wanted the rivers developed by the federal government in order to keep rates down, preserve natural resources and beauty, and encourage the comprehensive development of river basins, and those who hated the concept of public power because they believed it led to socialism, bureaucracy, and a planned economy (and to lower profits for private utilities) was a continuing focal point of politics in these states—and in the Senate: Morse's speeches on behalf of a Hells Canyon Dam had been notable, but no more notable than those of Washington State's Scoop Jackson; and that state's other senator, Warren Magnuson, while no great speechmaker, had used his Commerce Committee gavel effectively in the dam's behalf. Morse, Neuberger, Jackson, Magnuson, New Mexico's Anderson, Montana's Murray—all were members of a western "public power bloc" in the Senate. In all, there were, from these nine western states, a total of twelve Democratic senators who wanted the dam in Hells Canyon to be a federal dam.

Despite years of effort, however, the public power bloc had not been able to get that dam authorized. The private power forces in the Senate were, as Leland Olds had learned years earlier, very strong. (Olds had the lesson taught to him again in 1955 after he had testified for two days on behalf of the Hells Canyon Dam: a Federal Power Commission examiner called his testimony "irrelevant," and had every word of it stricken from the record except for two items: his name and address.) During the 1956 battle over Morse's Hells Canyon Dam Bill, Republicans had made the necessary arrangements. Welker had secretly approached Louisiana's Russell Long, for example, and pledged to support the Tidelands oil legislation Long wanted if Long would vote against Hells Canyon in the Interior Committee. Long had agreed, and Morse's bill had died in Interior. Now, in 1957, Morse and Neuberger were again trying—with assistance from Church—to persuade Interior to report the bill out, but they weren't succeeding. The western senators simply didn't have enough allies on public power.

As the South didn't have enough allies on civil rights.

LYNDON JOHNSON saw a potential connection between those two realities. No one else had seen it. During the ten years that Hells Canyon had been before Congress, there had never been the slightest link between the dam and civil rights. The civil rights issue had never aroused much interest in these western states—in part because so few of their residents would be directly affected by it. More than half a million people lived in Montana in 1956; about one thousand of them were Negroes. Another half million lived in Idaho; about one thousand of *them* were Negroes. The total Negro population of the nine states was about 79,000—fewer Negroes than lived in some *counties* in Georgia or Mississippi, fewer than lived in the single congressional district that was New York's Harlem. But now Lyndon Johnson saw that not only could the dam authorization bill be brought into a relationship with a civil rights bill, but that that relationship could be the key to passing a civil rights bill.

The very paucity of Negroes in the western states was a key to his reasoning. Although many of the twelve Democratic senators from these states were liberals, civil rights was not a high-priority issue to their constituents, so these senators had flexibility on a civil rights bill: they could support it or not, with impunity. Hells Canyon, on the other hand, *was* a high-priority issue. Years later, talking with Doris Kearns Goodwin, Johnson would explain his reasoning, with his customary hyperbole—and his customary brilliance. "I began with the assumption that most of the senators from the Mountain States had never seen a Negro and simply couldn't care all that much about the whole civil rights issue," he told her. "I knew what they *did* care about, and that was the Hells Canyon issue. So I went to a few key southerners and persuaded them to back the western liberals on Hells Canyon."

Tidelands wasn't the most important issue this year, he told Russell Long; there was more at stake now. Long understood the oblique phrase—and besides, the Louisiana senator was to recall years later, "With Herman Welker out . . . it was a whole new . . . ball game"; with the deal he had made with Welker now void, "it was not a matter of great consequence to me whether you built a high (federal) dam at Hells Canyon or a low (private) dam at Hells Canyon." What mattered was that civil rights bill—the jury trial amendment, for example—and Lyndon managed to "work it out in such a fashion that some of the western senators would go along with us on the jury trial problem if we'd go along with them on the Hells Canyon issue." Long was happy to go along.

With southern gentlemen like Long, the matter was handled in a gentlemanly fashion; putting his arm around one of these southerners in the cloakroom, Johnson would say, "Look, if you don't help them [the western senators], you can't expect them to help you when it's your ox that's getting gored." In other cases, the transaction was more straightforward. Montana's Jim Murray approached Jim Eastland to solicit his vote for the dam. "I need help on Hells Canyon," he said. Eastland's reply was blunt: "I need help on civil rights," he said. He told Murray to "see Dick Russell," and Russell told the elderly Montana liberal—in a statement seconded by Johnson—that southern votes would be available for Hells Canyon if the westerners were prepared to be "reasonable" on civil rights. And with other southerners, the transaction was blunter still. Some of the southern conservatives felt so strongly about the "socialism" symbolized by the proposed dam that they responded to Johnson's overtures by saying they couldn't vote for it. Johnson spelled out for these senators a reality they had overlooked. Senate authorization of a federal dam wouldn't *really* mean that a dam would be built, he said; House authorization and presidential signature would still be required—and neither requirement was likely to be met. Johnson may even have *guaranteed* some southerners that those requirements would not be met; at least one administrative assistant says that Johnson let it be known that the House Interior Committee was not going to let the Hells Canyon bill come to the House floor.

One way or another, Johnson persuaded the southern senators to place at his disposal as many votes as would be needed to pass the Senate bill authorizing a federal dam in Hells Canyon; in a particularly shrewd gesture, Richard Russell agreed that he would be one of those senators, although in previous years he had opposed such authorization. That gesture would be so plain that even the densest westerner would be able to understand it: Russell *was* the South; the westerners would know that if he was with them, the South would be with them—with as many votes as were necessary. Then Johnson let the westerners know what he had done—and why, assuring them that they would have the backing of the South. And "in return," he was to tell Doris Kearns Goodwin, "I got the western liberals to back the southerners" on civil rights.

SINCE THE WESTERNERS *WERE* LIBERALS, and proud of their liberal image, they were not eager to have it known that they had traded away their support for a strong civil rights bill. They let the final arrangement be confirmed through an aide, Morse's trusted assistant Merton C. Bernstein, a young labor lawyer. Shortly before Morse's bill authorizing the high dam was to come to the floor, the confirmation had not yet taken place and the western senators were unsure if they would really have the southern votes. A luncheon was therefore arranged in Bobby Baker's office one flight up in the Capitol at which Johnson would be present along with a group of western senators and Bernstein. During the lunch, Bernstein recalls, "Lyndon Johnson didn't put a bite of food in his mouth. He never stopped talking." But not about Hells Canyon—not a word. After the senators had finished dessert, Morse said, "Well, Mert, you know where everybody stands," and walked out—as did the other senators. "I was left there with Lyndon Johnson," Bernstein recalls. And then, with the westerners not there to hear the sordid details, "Johnson went down the whole list of senators who could be persuaded to do something helpful. He undertook to get those who he could"—and he made clear he could get enough. "Now, Smathers is a private utility man," Bernstein recalls Johnson saying. "But I think I can bring him along." The westerners could stop worrying about Russell Long: "Leave him to me," Johnson said; "I can get Russell Long." They could stop worrying about Alan Bible, he said. "Bible will do whatever I tell him to do." As for Harry Byrd, Johnson said, "Now Harry Byrd is a man of principle. I can't ask Harry Byrd to do anything against his principles. But I *can* ask Harry Byrd—and he *might* oblige me—to stay away [during the vote on the Hells Canyon Dam, and not vote against it]." Bernstein understood what Johnson was doing. The Majority Leader was letting him know—and through him, Morse and the other western senators—that "he was working hard to get the votes for us because he wanted" western votes in return. Johnson was sealing the deal. Bernstein reported the conversation to Morse, and, at Morse's instructions, to the other western senators, and they also understood what Johnson was doing—and the price he wanted in return. "We knew that Johnson was not being a Boy Scout. We knew that he was trying to build a coalition" against the parts of the civil rights bill "to which the southerners were objecting."

The westerners agreed to pay that price. Lyndon Johnson, Russell Long was to say, "put together sort of a gentleman's agreement where about four of us would vote for the high dam at Hells Canyon and about four of the fellows on the other side would vote with us. . . . Four votes shifted in favor of that high dam at Hells Canyon and then four votes shifted, or at least came down on . . . a completely unrelated subject: civil rights."

Long's memory is a little blurry as to the precise figure: the number of votes that actually shifted on that first ballot was not four but five. And the number of western liberal Democratic votes that, as a result of the Hells Canyon deal, would shift to the side of the South on later civil rights ballots would vary from ballot to ballot. Nor is the exact number of votes that shifted an accurate indication of the dimensions of the deal. Since the southerners would not want to be seen voting for the Hells Canyon Dam, Johnson would use as few of them as possible on the Hells Canyon vote. Since the liberal westerners would not want to be seen voting against civil rights, Johnson would use as few of them as possible on the civil rights vote. On each civil rights vote, he would use the minimum number of westerners necessary to accomplish his purposes, not requiring the others to vote with the South. But the fundamental nature of the deal is what Johnson said it was—in return for southern votes for Hells Canyon, "I got the western liberals to back the southerners" on civil rights. While, from vote to vote, the number of westerners would vary, whatever the number needed, the number would be there. It would be there on Part III, and on the jury trial amendment. And the South could be confident that, if it was needed, it would be there on cloture as well. And the total number of these westerners—the number that might, if necessary, be available to the South—was twelve. In a single stroke—by linking Hells Canyon and civil rights—Lyndon Johnson had brought to the side of the South not just a few senators but a substantial bloc.

And the South therefore was now willing to allow a civil rights bill to be placed on the Calendar. Its senators would still vote against the motion to put it on the Calendar, of course, so that they could tell their constituents they had opposed the motion, but they would forgo the filibuster that would, by preventing the motion from coming to a vote, have made their opposition effective. The South had previously been adamant in its opposition to allowing the bill to go on the Calendar; isolated—without allies—it had felt itself defenseless against a strong civil rights bill except for the filibuster, and therefore had not been willing to forgo any of the opportunities to use that tactic. Thanks to Lyndon Johnson, that fear had now been somewhat alleviated; the South had allies now. And the South was therefore somewhat more willing to let the bill proceed, in the hope that as it proceeded it could be watered down; it could allow the bill onto the Calendar because, should the bill thereafter still remain too strong to be tolerated, it would still have two opportunities left to filibuster: on the motion to bring the bill off the Calendar to the Senate floor; and, if that filibuster was defeated, on the motion to vote on the bill. The South had also now been assured that, should it have to make its stand in those last two trenches, it would no longer be standing alone. If, despite its new alliance with the West, it was still unable to muster enough votes to water down Part III and jury trials and it was forced to filibuster, it would have, added to the anti-cloture votes of the Republican reactionaries, some anti-cloture votes from the western liberals—so there would almost certainly be no vote on the bill itself.

SINCE LYNDON JOHNSON was making his Hells Canyon–civil rights deal in secret, the progress he was making was invisible. Working out the deal took time, too, and for some weeks in May the keystone in the South's defense—Jim Eastland's Judiciary Committee—remained solid.

Liberal frustrations kept spilling over on the Senate floor. Once, in late May, with Eastland slouched comfortably at his desk near the center, near the front, Hubert Humphrey, from his desk further to the side, further to the rear, noted that although Judiciary's distinguished chairman had only three southern colleagues on his committee, few as they were, the four southerners "are like the Spartans at the Pass of Thermopylae. They certainly 'mow 'em down.' " Humphrey made his remark with a wry smile, but Douglas, two desks further to the side, could not conceal his bitterness when he rose, and said, "This bill has been before the committee since January. Hearings were started in February. The hearings were concluded in March. It is now very nearly the end of May. If we do not get a bill on the floor very soon, we know exactly what will happen."

It took Eastland a while to rise to respond to Douglas; one might even have thought his deliberateness verged on discourtesy. When he was on his feet at last and had turned to look up at the two liberals, he made it clear that he, too, knew exactly what was going to happen—and that that knowledge was not displeasing. Certainly, he said, he couldn't do anything to increase the pace of the committee's deliberations; that was in the hands of his distinguished fellow committee members. "Ah'm just the errand boy of the committee," he said, but he doubted that any of its members would seriously want to interfere with the right of a fellow member to be heard in committee at whatever length he felt necessary.

Liberal discouragement was echoed in the Republican Legislative Leaders' Meeting in the White House, where reality had finally sunk in fully. The civil rights bill was going to pass in the House, President Eisenhower was told at the June 4 conference. But Knowland, reporting on the Senate, was forced to warn Eisenhower that efforts to push the bill through Judiciary had better stop, for there were other things that could be done in Judiciary—to other Administration programs: What if the liberals on the committee succeeded in their demand that the committee hold uninterrupted civil rights hearings? he asked. Eastland could then simply extend these hearings, which would mean that no other measures could be taken up. "Among the measures that could" then "be tied up" in Judiciary "are changes in immigration laws, which you are anxious to get through, Mr. President." Knowland said he would continue to do his best, "but, to be realistic, the outlook for civil rights in the Senate is not encouraging. I am afraid the bill [will] either die in the Judiciary Committee or be reported too late for favorable action on the floor, even if we could overcome a filibuster."

Discouragement was echoed in the liberal press. "The prospects [for civil rights] in the Senate are, to put it mildly, gloomy; and they are not helped by the fact that the Majority Leader, Mr. Johnson of Texas, is also against it," the *New York Times* said in a May 23 editorial.

There was as little leadership from Dwight Eisenhower as ever. On June 4, Frederic Morrow, the only black executive in the White House, sent a memo to presidential chief of staff Sherman Adams almost begging the President to grant the leaders of his race the courtesy of at least meeting with them. Noting that A. Philip Randolph and Martin Luther King had been asking "for an audience with the President" for more than a year with no response from the White House, Morrow wrote, "I can state categorically that the rank and file of Negroes in the country feel that the President has deserted them. . . . I feel the time is ripe for the President to see two or three outstanding Negro leaders, and to let them get off their chests the things that seem to be giving them great concern. . . . Their present feeling is that their acknowledged leadership is being ignored, snubbed, and belittled by the President and his staff. Even though we may be aware of what these men will say when they meet the President, it is important that they be able to meet him and say it face to face." There was no response from the President. As late as the end of May, as late as the beginning of June, the 1957 civil rights bill seemed destined for the same fate as the 1956 civil rights bill—and of so many previous civil rights bills. Even while Lyndon Johnson was finalizing the Hells Canyon arrangement that would make it possible for the civil rights bill to come to the floor, it was almost universally assumed that the bill was dead.

No connection with civil rights was immediately drawn, therefore, when, suddenly, on June 6, Johnson began, as one article put it, "to turn up the heat" to bring to the Senate floor "the bill authorizing construction of a federal dam in Hells Canyon." But there was a connection: movement was simultaneously beginning on civil rights as well. Five months earlier, Johnson had decreed that the Senate would not take up Brownell's civil rights bill until after the House had passed it, and for months that bill, labelled H.R. 6127, had been blocked by the House Rules Committee. Johnson's ally Rayburn could have intervened, but he had not done so. Now, suddenly, he did—with an unexpected series of parliamentary rulings. On June 6, the same day the "heat" was turned up to bring the Hells Canyon bill to the Senate floor, H.R. 6127 was released by the House Rules Committee and brought to the House floor.

In mid-June, with the bill nearing passage by the House, there was movement—significant movement—in the Senate. It was initiated by Republicans. Knowland announced that he would introduce a motion to bypass the Judiciary Committee by sending the House-passed bill, the Administration bill, directly to the Senate Calendar, Nixon let it be known that he was ready to help get the motion passed—and the Republicans may have thought, as most journalists thought, that they were providing the impetus. Reporting that Nixon and Knowland are "teaming up in a drive to get Senate action," the *Washington Post* said on June 16 that "Both appear to believe the [Republican presidential] nomination will be worth more to the man who gets it if they can get the Republicans credited with passing a civil rights bill." But what was significant was that although the southerners were denouncing the measure, they did not use their most effective weapon against it. On June 18, the House, by a 286–126 vote, passed H.R. 6127, sending it to the Senate. Since Knowland's motion was expected to touch off at least a major Senate floor fight if not a filibuster, the actual denouement came as a considerable surprise. Although the southern senators attacked the motion and their anger against it was genuine— Richard Russell actually shouted as he said, "Don't give me that holier-than-thou talk about voting! What they are thinking about is schools!" and warned of "setting a precedent that will haunt the Senate for many years to come"—their actual resistance was not; its *pro forma* nature became clear when, on June 20, the South, declining to filibuster, allowed Knowland's motion to come to a vote after only nine hours of debate. The motion passed, 45 to 39. (Johnson voted with the South, but took no part in the debate.) And the reason that the opposition was only *pro forma* became apparent immediately after the vote. The very next item of business that the Majority Leader introduced was a motion to call off the Calendar and bring to a vote the bill authorizing construction of a federal dam in Hells Canyon. "Mr. President," Johnson said, "I desire to serve notice on all senators that we expect to have a vote on this bill tomorrow . . . early in the day tomorrow." That schedule was met, and the next day, June 21, in what the *New York Times* called "a surprise vote," the Hells Canyon bill was passed, 45 to 38. And the reason became even more apparent when the votes on these two seemingly unrelated issues were analyzed.

Among the thirty-nine votes against the motion putting a civil rights bill on the Calendar were five cast by senators whose appearance on the anti–civil rights side was startling: Morse of Oregon, Magnuson of Washington, Murray and Mansfield of Montana, and O'Mahoney of Wyoming. (Morse's vote against the motion was particularly startling, since less than a week earlier he had enthusiastically supported it.) Those five western senators, normally liberal stalwarts, had voted with the South this time. Their five votes did not change the outcome: the South did not want the outcome changed. To protect Rule 22 and clean up Lyndon Johnson on civil rights, Richard Russell had decided that the civil rights bill should be allowed to go on the Senate Calendar. Those five votes were the signal Russell wanted that the West would stand with the South on future civil rights votes. Of the forty-five votes in favor of the Hells Canyon bill, five were cast by southerners who had voted against the identical bill in 1956. The bill had been defeated in 1956. It passed in 1957 because those five southerners switched, and voted for it. They were Russell Long, George Smathers, Sam Ervin, Jim Eastland—and Richard Russell, whose vote, since he was the leader of the South, was a signal: that since the westerners would stand with the South on its great issue, the South would stand with the West on *its* great issue.

TWO DAYS BEFORE the Hells Canyon vote, the freshman senator from Idaho had delivered his maiden speech—on the dam that he had made the big issue in his campaign. He had been polishing the speech for weeks, and it showed the Senate why Frank Church had been national oratorical champion. A searing attack on Idaho Power's proposed three small dams—"small plans for small tomorrows"—he asked the Senate to declare instead for big dreams, like the public power dreams of George Norris and his idol, Borah. Assailing the concept that private interests ought to be able to monopolize and reap profit from America's natural resources, he said the Hells Canyon bill "serves no interest, save the people's interest." When he finished, the older public power liberals like Morse and Douglas who had been fighting for Hells Canyon for years crowded around his desk to congratulate him. "Magnificent!" Paul Douglas said. "Truly magnificent!" An Idaho journalist dubbed him "the boy orator of the Snake."

Following their victory two days later, the older western senators knew whom they wanted to get the credit. When a photographer summoned them out to the Vice President's Room for a photograph, they pushed Church to the front. Douglas took one of Church's arms and Hubert Humphrey the other, and raised them high in a victory sign. Church's cheeks were naturally rosy, and he was blushing, so they were even redder than usual, and he gave a loud shout of triumph. His elation over the vote was understandable. "It made him," explains his legislative assistant Ward Hower. Young and untested though he was, by "delivering" on an issue so important to his state, "he was able to convey to the people of Idaho that they had elected a winner, that he *already* had some clout in the Senate."

The elation of all the twelve Hells Canyon Democrats was understandable, at least in political terms. They had been fighting for a federal dam for a long time, and they had never before had a victory in the fight. This Senate vote would not, as it turned out, be a true victory but only a temporary win in a losing battle, because Lyndon Johnson's cynical prediction would prove correct: neither the favorable House vote nor the presidential signature needed to make the dam a reality were realistic possibilities. In the event, some years later, three smaller dams—only slightly improved versions of the ones Idaho Power had proposed—would eventually be built. But at the moment of the Senate vote, these senators saw at least a first step toward the federal dam. And in political terms, the victory truly *was* a victory. They had delivered on their promises to their constituents: the body of which they were members had passed the bill they had promised. How could they be blamed if the bill didn't pass in the House? A great favor had been done for them, and they knew whom to thank for it. Church, still learning the ropes in the Senate, and perhaps understandably a bit overimpressed with the power of his oratory, had had to have the facts of Senate life explained to him. As he had been heading back to his office after his speech, still filled with emotion, he had heard footsteps behind him and, turning, saw Clinton Anderson, who had not merely congratulations but a question: had Church been consulting Lyndon Johnson on the issue? And when Church had replied in the negative, Anderson had said, "If this bill gets passed, it will be his doing, not yours." "I understood that it was true," the young senator would say later. "But until he said it to me, it hadn't gelled." Now, after the victory, as he thought about the southern senators' switch, it gelled further— "All credit is due to your leadership," he wrote Johnson. The older westerners understood the realities without being told. "If it hadn't been for his [Johnson's] leadership, we never would have passed the bill for the high dam in Hells Canyon," Richard Neuberger was to say. "During those days, he worked 'til eleven or midnight buttonholing senators for us. I feared for his health. . . ."

HARDLY HAD THE FIVE WESTERNERS VOTED against putting civil rights on the Calendar when they had to begin defending themselves—against charges that their votes had been a *quid pro quo* for five southern votes on the dam authorization. However ringingly unequivocal their denials—calling the charges "a vicious falsehood," Morse said he had "never in my life made a trade" on a Senate vote; Montana's Mansfield said, "There was no deal of any kind, sort or nature, and there were no trades on the part of any Democrat with any other Democrat for votes"—they nonetheless rang false in some ears. The skeptics included Republicans. "Civil rights yesterday had a lot do with the [dam] vote today, more than most people realize," Arthur Watkins of Utah said.

Republican National Chairman Meade Alcorn charged more flatly that the five Democrats had betrayed the cause of social justice for a dam, making "a deal to swap off civil rights for Hells Canyon," and Charles Potter of Michigan, a fervent Republican supporter of civil rights, expressed misgivings about the deal's future consequences. He noted that "fellows supposed to be great advocates of civil rights" had lined up with the southerners. "These Southerners are pretty shrewd," Potter said. "I hope it doesn't include a sellout of future civil rights votes." And the skeptics also included Democrats—including the Democratic leader in the Senate civil rights fight.

It did not take long for Paul Douglas to grasp the reality beneath the Hells Canyon vote: that, because the House almost certainly would not authorize a federal dam, the Senate vote would prove meaningless. It was only a few hours after he had raised Frank Church's arm that he told the young senator, "Frank, I'm afraid you Hells Canyon people have been given some counterfeit money." On the morning after the civil rights vote, newspapers were filled with Republican cries of triumph—"Look, we did it," a White House aide said, predicting that the Administration's civil rights bill would pass substantially as written— and with journalistic analyses of the "victory" of bipartisan civil rights forces in bypassing the long-impregnable Judiciary Committee. The vote "beat down" the southerners "for the first time in this generation," Robert Albright wrote in the *Washington Post*. Advancing the bill to the Calendar put it "within easy reach of a Senate majority vote to call it up [and] thus opened up a possible route to early passage of the bill." The papers were filled with what journalists saw as proof that, as Albright put it, "the once-powerful Republican-Southern Democratic coalition . . . was knocked into bits and may never get completely together again." William S. White wrote that "The action greatly improves the prospect for the first major Senate action on civil rights since the Reconstruction era." But Douglas, a better judge of the reality, saw in the southern-western alliance ominous implications for future civil rights votes—when the votes would be more crucial to hopes for social justice, when the votes would not be merely about putting a bill on the Calendar but on bringing the bill to the floor, and, on the floor, *passing* the bill. Morse's vote was particularly distressing. The other four defecting westerners were not members of Douglas' civil rights cadre, but Morse had been one of its leaders. Douglas saw Morse's vote as a hint that there would be further cracks in the liberal core essential for victory. And he was incensed that Morse, who had publicly pledged only three days before to vote against the South on the Calendar proposal, had not informed him in advance that he would not in fact be voting with him. Arriving at the SOB that morning, Douglas hurried up the broad steps and called a caucus of his liberal group for three o'clock in the District of Columbia Committee Room, and the meeting turned into a scene of extreme rancor among men who were supposedly celebrating a victory.

Anger made Douglas' face almost as white as his hair when, opening the meeting, he turned to Morse. "The first thing I want to take up is the conduct of the senior senator from Oregon," he said. "If this were a military group he would be court-martialed. He has betrayed our cause. Furthermore, he did it on the Senate floor." At the last caucus, he said, Morse had committed himself to vote with the rest of them—Carroll and Humphrey and Pastore and Neuberger and Clark and the rest—to wrest the bill from Jim Eastland's hands; then he had voted to keep the bill there, and "He did not take the trouble to come back to this group first and discuss it with his colleagues." "We can't court-martial him," but something must be done about this "betrayal." "I won't embarrass his colleague [from Oregon], Dick Neuberger," Douglas said, "but I will call on Joe Clark for advice as to what we should do."

Erupting in return, Morse told Douglas, "That's what you think you're going to do." Instead, he said, "You're going to listen to me and then I'm going to excuse myself. I shan't sit here and listen to myself being abused." His stand had changed, he said, out of conviction, not expediency—the conviction that bypassing Senate rules just to get action on a specific issue was wrong. "What I did was not easy," he said. "I was not lacking in courage. . . . The Senator has said I did not come back to this group. But what good would it have done? It would just create a row." Then, standing up, he said, "I now excuse myself," and stalked out of the room.

There followed what Drew Pearson's handwritten notes (one of the persons in the room evidently gave the columnist an extremely detailed account of the proceedings) referred to as a "hell of a row"—one so bitter that at its end, one of the senators, not identified in the notes, said, "There are so few of us that I feel very sad" that they were disagreeing among themselves. During the argument, Douglas voiced his forebodings, saying that he wondered if Morse's change of heart had resulted from a larger *quid pro quo* with the South for Hells Canyon that would have future repercussions for the civil rights bill. Neuberger tried to reassure Douglas—"I'm sure no such thing happened. I'm sure I would know about it if he had made any such commitments"—and other senators assured him they would hold fast. "Civil rights is not a major issue in my state," John Carroll said. "It isn't popular in Colorado. But I'm sticking to the agreement. I consider this civil rights bill to be important and very much needed."

Douglas' forebodings were justified, however. Even while the westerners were firmly denying the existence of a western-southern alliance, the southerners were not reluctant to spell out for a reporter they trusted, Tom Wicker, the precise details of that alliance. After talking with several of them about their votes for Hells Canyon, Wicker wrote that "authoritative sources indicate that the Southern action was a *quid* for which they expect to receive a *quo* [on] the civil rights bill." The *quo,* Wicker reported, was "that Western senators, who had unsuccessfully sought passage of a Hells Canyon bill for years, would now deliver enough votes for jury trial to attach it to the civil rights bill by about five votes." That, Wicker reported, was the explanation for the five western votes against bypassing Judiciary. On that vote, "Western Democrats handed Southerners five votes—not enough to sustain their position but enough, as one observer put it today, 'to let 'em know where the votes are.' "

Indignant though the western Democrats might be—or at least act—about charges that a deal had been struck,* their subsequent actions during 1957 would provide ammunition for those who believed the charges—as will be seen. Over and over again, during the succeeding weeks, the West would provide votes for the South.

JOHNSON'S DEAL was indeed one of profound cynicism. It wouldn't give the westerners victory on Hells Canyon, it would give them only the opportunity to *claim* victory on Hells Canyon. It was indeed based, as Paul Douglas charged, on "counterfeit money." In that sense, the deal was only one more in the long line of cynical maneuvers that had marked Johnson's political career.

There were, however, differences this time. The deal had created a new reality in the Senate of the United States. For two decades, the dominant reality in the Senate had been its control by a coalition of southerners and conservative Republicans. In January, 1957, that coalition had been "knocked into bits." The South had found itself isolated, without allies. But then Lyndon Johnson had brought new allies to the South's side. In place of the southern-Republican coalition there was a southern-western coalition now.

And the deal had had a further result. Thanks to the arrangement that Johnson had conceived ("I went to a few key southerners and persuaded them to back the western liberals on Hells Canyon. And then, in return, I got the western liberals to back the southerners") and that, against long odds, he had brought to completion, a civil rights bill was on the Senate Calendar, only one step removed from being on the floor, for the first time since Reconstruction. The result of Johnson's cynicism this time was not merely a step forward for himself but a step forward for a great cause.

---

*Their explanation for their votes was the same as Morse's: they were concerned that bypassing a committee would set a bad precedent for the Senate.

39

"*You Do It*"

ANOTHER LEGISLATIVE TALENT would be necessary if a civil rights bill was to become law in 1957, and it was a talent very different from the strategic, conceptual ability on a national scale that could conceive a relationship between Hells Canyon and jury trials—very different, and of a much less elevated order. It was an ability that was needed in the hurly-burly of the legislative battlefield itself: the floor of the Senate during a violent struggle there. But though it was only a tactical ability, not grand strategy but battlefield maneuver, given the inherent nature of the legislative process—the fact that there *was,* on that Senate floor, an actual battlefield—it was no less vital. And because of the unique complexity of the civil rights issue, and the unique intractability of the problems surrounding it, this talent, too, would have to be exercised at a very high level. Passing a civil rights bill would require an ability to suddenly recognize, amid the turmoil, the cut and thrust and parry, of a legislative body in furious contention—amid the barrage of motions and amendments, amid the rapid-fire parliamentary maneuvers and countermaneuvers, the quick back-and-forth ripostes of debate and the magisterial drum roll of long, formal speeches—to suddenly recognize, amid the great mass of cutting words, witty words, brilliant words, empty words, those words that mattered, the phrase that could change the mood, the amendment that could turn the tide, that could swing votes if put to proper use (a use that might not be at all the use the speaker of the words or the author of the amendment had intended); to recognize the opportunity when suddenly, without warning, it came.

The talent required had, moreover, to consist not alone of insight but also of decisiveness, of an ability not only to recognize a crucial moment but to seize it, to see the opening—and to strike; to move fast enough so that the opportunity did not vanish, perhaps never to come again. It was the ability to recognize the key that might suddenly unlock votes that had seemed locked forever away—and to turn the key, and turn it fast. This combination of rare insight, rare decisiveness, rare willingness to act produced, when it was added to unbending determination and a gift for grand strategy, a rare form of political leadership: legislative leadership.

BY THE TIME THE OPENING CAME, Lyndon Johnson had all but given up hoping for it. But when it came, he saw it—and seized it.

It came at a moment when it was desperately needed. He had, through his Hells Canyon deal, been able to persuade the South to allow one step toward passage of a civil rights bill: the placement of H.R. 6127 on the Senate Calendar. But three steps still remained: the bill now had to be called off the Calendar—brought to the floor for debate, in other words; then it had to be brought to a vote; then it had to pass. And those steps were going to be even harder than the first had been. Persuading the South to allow them required him to meet the South's price: amendments that eliminated the Part III provisions protecting a broad array of civil rights; and that added to Part IV a new provision guaranteeing the right of jury trial. That price seemed as difficult to meet as it had ever been.

The allies he had procured for the South through Hells Canyon were enough to reassure the South about cloture. They weren't enough to pass amendments. If every one of the twelve western Democratic votes were available to the South—and every one wouldn't be available on every amendment—those twelve votes, added to a possible twenty-two from the South, would still give the South, at a maximum, a total of thirty-four votes, enough to prevent cloture but not the majority required to pass amendments. To amend—weaken—the civil rights bill, Johnson needed more votes: Democratic liberal votes and Republican votes. And while to western senators a civil rights bill didn't mean much, to liberals and Republicans that bill meant a lot.

The focus came first on Part III. Believing that the most important part of the bill was the voting rights part, Part IV, Johnson had been trying for weeks—utterly without success—to persuade the "Douglas Group" to accept a drastically weakened Part III in the interests of "getting the first one": breaking the Senate's "virginity" on civil rights. But to these liberals it was Part III that made the bill the "dream bill." It was the powers that section would confer on the Attorney General that would strike at injustice most directly. "It was Part III that was the big thing," recalls the ADA's Rauh. Weakening it would cut the very heart out of what those liberals were fighting for. Without Part III, the South could still say "never" to school desegregation. There had been no legal recourse against the men who killed Emmett Till; was there to be no recourse the next time a black body was pulled out of a river? The South was continuing to deny black Americans their rights even in spheres in which courts had ruled. Although blacks could now sit in the front of buses in Montgomery, Alabama, when, in June of 1957, a black minister had tried to do that in Georgia, he had been arrested and jailed. Justice had been denied to black Americans for centuries, these senators felt—were they, by agreeing to amend Part III, to consent to the indefinite continuation of this denial? The Douglas Group refused even to consider amendments that would substantially weaken, much less eliminate, that section. Often, a declaration against compromise is merely a negotiating position; not to these senators, not on this cause.

Some Republican liberals felt this way, too. Since "racial integration in the schools is of the same character as the right to vote," Part III must not be weakened, explained newly elected Jacob Javits of New York, whose heart as well as head was for civil rights. As for the rest of the forty-six GOP senators, almost all of them, from Knowland down, were against compromise from considerations of, in varying degrees, conscience or calculation. Even the densest midwestern Neanderthals could grasp the tremendous benefits that could accrue to their party, and to them—*the gavels!*—through either passage of their Administration's civil rights bill or a Democratic filibuster against it; from the political standpoint, a filibuster, which would dramatize that it was the Democratic Party, through its senators, that was standing in the way of civil rights, might be even better for the GOP than passage.

It is difficult, much as one admires them, to avoid the conclusion that liberals—because they couldn't see more than a few moves down the Senate chessboard and weren't very good at counting votes—also believed that since the Republicans were on their side at last, there was no need to compromise. And the Republicans believed that, too. White House strategists agreed with Knowland's contention that "at least" forty Republicans would be solidly for the bill that had been drawn by a Republican Attorney General and endorsed by a Republican President. With such a solid, possibly overwhelming, majority behind the civil rights bill, its supporters determined to press for passage: to insist on calling the bill off the Senate Calendar and bringing it to the floor before any amendments had been added. But the reality was that despite their optimism and their majority, their insistence did not mean that the bill would pass. It meant that the bill would *not* pass, that in fact it would not even reach the floor: when the motion was introduced to make the bill the Senate's "pending business," the South would begin an outwardly reasonable and logical "extended debate" on that motion, and would simply keep extending the debate as long as necessary so that the motion could not be voted on. Attempts to impose cloture on this filibuster would fail because there would be fewer votes for cloture than for passage. Therefore there would never be a vote on the bill itself. But that was a reality the liberals and Republicans do not appear to have grasped. They felt, almost certainly incorrectly, that because they had the votes to beat the South on the bill, they had the votes to beat the South on cloture, too.

Knowland refused to compromise, saying there was no need to, and he meant it. As the Senate prepared to recess for a long Fourth of July holiday weekend, the Republican Leader pledged that when the Senate reconvened on July 8, he would immediately move to bring an unamended bill, including an unaltered Part III, to the floor. The Douglas Group applauded the move. Lyndon Johnson had been attempting for six months to arrange some sort of compromise on Part III with absolutely no success, and now, with the bill on the Calendar and the crucial debate—or filibuster—on the measure looming close ahead, the chasm separating the two sides seemed more unbridgeable than ever. Getting the votes for compromise seemed impossible.

AND THEN, in an hour, with the delivery of a single Senate speech, the chasm became even wider.

"Surprise," von Clausewitz said, "is half the battle." A great general strikes when his enemy is not expecting the blow. The Senate, winding down to the Fourth of July recess, was in the midst of a desultory discussion on defense appropriations when, on Tuesday, July 2, at the second desk from the front on the Democratic side of the center aisle, an arm was raised, and the chair recognized the senior senator from Georgia. The only sign that something momentous was about to occur was that frugal Richard Russell had purchased a new dark blue suit for the occasion.

The first blow should be a telling one. Russell's first words ensured that this blow would be. "Mr. President," he said, "for the first time since I have been a member of the Senate, I respectfully request that I not be interrupted in the course of my prepared discussion." Senators who had been chatting with their colleagues stopped talking, and went to their desks to listen. Two staff members had been standing in the rear of the Chamber. One said to the other: "I bet this is really going to be something."

It was. Part III of Herbert Brownell's proposal was not a wholly new clause but rather an amendment to another law—to one of those three leftover "fragments" of the civil rights laws that had been on the statute books for almost a century: Section 1985 of Title 42 of the United States Code. The proposed amendment added to Section 1985 a new paragraph authorizing the Attorney General to apply on behalf of the government for a civil injunction by a judge whenever "any persons have engaged or are about to engage in any acts or practices" which would be crimes under the leftover section. But there were discrepancies between the amendment and the section it was amending, among which was the fact that Section 1985 dealt with suits against individuals by individuals, not suits by the government.

These discrepancies, and their possible implications, had been raised by, among others, a youthful attorney on the staff of the Senate Judiciary Committee, Robert Barnes Young—but they had gone largely unnoticed, in part because Brownell had managed, in his testimony before Hennings' Judiciary Subcommittee on February 16, to avoid discussing the questions Young started asking him about them. It is unclear to this day whether Brownell and his assistants had deliberately avoided discussing the discrepancies in the hope that the

Senate would pass the bill without understanding their implications. Later, when he was asked to explain them, Brownell would deny any such strategy. "No intrigue or design was involved," he said; the writing of Part III as an amendment to an existing section rather than as a wholly new section, he said, had been "an accident"—because "so many hands were engaged in the drafting," it was "impossible" to determine even who had done it. This explanantion did not convince some of Brownell's allies. Paul Douglas, talking later about the "mysterious Part III," would recall that "Brownell, who deserves credit for the substance of this provision, although his method of operation was lamentable, had never explained it, nor had others. . . . The Democratic advocates of civil rights had not been taken into Brownell's confidence, and I do not think Knowland had been either. . . . We had been dealt with unfairly." And, they felt, given the caliber of Brownell's opponent, that had been extremely foolish. The senior senator from Georgia had lost some of his energy; he had lost none of his intellect. "On the surface," Part III "seemed innocent enough," Douglas was to say, "but Dick Russell knew what it meant." At night and on weekends, when other senators were socializing or with their families, Russell often sat alone in his apartment and read, and, reading the transcript of the February 16 subcommittee hearings, he had noticed Robert Young's questions—and how Brownell had evaded answering them. One Saturday, June 15, he had asked Young to come to his office in the weekend-quiet Senate Office Building to discuss them, and after that discussion, as Russell was to recall, he had given the discrepancies "a great deal of study." And, now, standing at his desk, he said that "I understand" them "completely." His colleagues had been filing into the Chamber ever since word had spread that "Russell's up," and they now sat, rank on rank in the long arcs, attentive and still. He told them what the discrepancies were and what he felt was the true motive behind them.

He had, Richard Russell said, gone back to that original Section 1985 to learn what "acts or practices" would be covered by the new legislation. "I now read the pertinent part of the already existing law which the [Brownell] bill seeks to amend," he said. "This is the existing law." One part of Section 1985, he said, defined such "acts or practices" as any attempt to deprive anyone "of the equal protection of the laws or of equal privileges and immunities under the law"—*any* law, such as, for example, the law requiring desegregation of the schools.

Nor, Richard Russell said, was that the only significant discovery he had made. He had found that Section 1985 was referred to in another of the leftover civil rights fragments: Section 1993 of Title 42. Nowhere in Brownell's bill was Section 1993 even mentioned, Russell said, but it should have been because Section 1985 automatically invokes Section 1993. And 1993 is the section, passed during Reconstruction, which authorized the President of the United States, "or such person as he may empower for that purpose," to employ the military forces of the United States to enforce judicial edicts in the conquered South. Since the *Brown* decision *was* a judicial edict, Part III of the Brownell Bill would authorize the use of military troops to enforce that decision.

And, Russell said, military power was not the only power that would be conferred on the Attorney General by the passage of Brownell's bill. He understood now, Russell said, other reasons why Part III had not been drafted fresh, but had been made an amendment to an existing section—a section which made violations not criminal but civil offenses, and which said that actions had to be instituted by individuals. In studying the bill, Russell said, "I was greatly puzzled by the fact that this proposed new law" would give the Attorney General power to sue in cases involving individuals—civil cases—and could sue "whether the aggrieved party wished him to sue or not." But he understood it now, he said. "Mr. President, the Attorney General of the United States does not ordinarily participate in civil suits for damages between individual citizens" of the United States. "His primary duty is to enforce the penal or criminal law." Part III would give him the right to enter civil cases with the full power he usually exercises only in criminal cases—including the power to seek injunctions from a federal judge.

Nor were schools the only area in which Part III would confer new powers on the federal government, Russell said, for schools were not the only areas of daily life in which judicial edicts were possible, and even probable. "Mr. President, if the Supreme Court so determines—and who can doubt their intent—that the separate hotels, eating places, and places of amusement for the two races in the South constitute a denial of equal privileges and immunities under the old law [Section 1985]," Part III of the new law would mean that "this great power can be applied throughout the South. . . . Under this bill, if the Attorney General should contend that separate eating places, places of amusement and the like in the South . . . constituted a denial of equal privileges and immunities, he could move in with all the vast powers of this bill," and anyone who refused to conform to an injunction could be held in jail at the judge's order, without benefit of trial by jury. "Under this bill, if the Attorney General should contend that separate places of amusement . . . constituted a denial of equal privileges and immunities, he could move in . . . even if the person denied admission did not request him to do so and was opposed to his taking that action. The white people who operated the place of amusement could be jailed without benefit of jury trial and kept in jail until they either rotted or until they conformed to the edict to integrate their place of business." And, Russell said, "Who can doubt for a moment" that some Attorney General—perhaps not the present Attorney General but some future Attorney General—would do just that, "yielding to the demands of the NAACP and the ADA, who have been most zealous in pushing this proposal?"

The Senate floor was absolutely still now, and the faces of those listening—not only senators but staff members—were sober and intent as the

tall, patrician figure continued reading from the pages on the lectern on his center aisle desk.

The true purposes of the legislation had been concealed from the Senate,
Richard Russell said, and they had been concealed deliberately. An effort is
being made "to sail this bill through the Senate under the false colors of a moderate bill . . . while obscuring the larger purposes of the bill," which is "cunningly designed to . . . bring to bear the whole might of the Federal
Government, including the Armed Forces if necessary, to force a commingling
of white and Negro children in . . . the South, and, indeed, Mr. President, the
unusual powers of this bill could be utilized to force the white people of
the South at the point of a federal bayonet to conform to . . . a commingling of
the races throughout the social order of the South." The bill would, he said,
give an "unlimited grant of powers . . . to govern by injunction and federal
bayonet."

Russell's analysis of the bill's references and cross-references had been
couched in dry, precise legal phraseology, but other portions of his speech were
more emotional, for in studying the proposed legislation, he had found that the
powers given to the President to enforce Part III included powers that the Senate had not been informed about, and he had come to believe that Brownell's
underlying intention was nothing less than to resurrect the spectre that had
haunted his entire life, as it haunted the history of the Southland he loved—
Reconstruction.

Brownell's bill, Russell said, has the same aim "as the measures proposed
by Sumner and Stevens in Reconstruction days in their avowed drive 'to put
black heels on white necks.' " Section 1985 was one of the old Reconstruction
laws, he said, and Reconstruction was what the bill was trying to bring back, in
more subtle, and more pernicious, form. "If this bill is used to the utmost, neither Sumner nor Stevens, in the persecution of the South in the twelve tragic
years of Reconstruction, ever cooked up any such devil's broth as is proposed
in this misnamed civil rights bill."

The South had courage, he said; it would not submit tamely to the proposed persecution. "What I say now is in no sense a threat. I speak in a spirit of
great sadness. If Congress is driven to pass this bill in its present form, it will
cause unspeakable confusion, bitterness, and bloodshed in a great section of
our common country. If it is proposed to move into the South in this fashion,
the concentration camps may as well be prepared now, because there will not
be enough jails to hold the people of the South who will oppose the use of raw
Federal power forcibly to commingle white and Negro children in the same
schools and places of public entertainment." The South would not submit
tamely in the Senate, he said. It would fight there by whatever means were necessary. A filibuster, he said, is "a lengthy educational campaign," and "we shall
require a long time to get the facts across to the country." Turning to his right,
Russell looked across the center aisle at the Republicans who had long been the

South's allies but had now deserted the South. They sat listening as the senator they so deeply respected spoke directly to them. He assumed that they would also use all their rights if they were ever faced with such a terrible threat to the people of their states; he assumed they would use every means at their command to fight it. "If they did not fight it to the very death, they would be unworthy of the people who sent them here." If they were to fight, he said, he would support them. "If it is ever proposed to use the military forces of this Nation to compel the people represented by other senators to conform their lives and social order to the rest of the country, those senators need not be afraid of the word 'filibuster' or of attempting to exercise all their rights under the rules." If they did so, "I hope Providence will give me the strength and the courage to stand by their side." And he hoped they would support him now. "I hope that our colleagues will not be intolerant of us as we seek to discharge our duty to the American people of our states who have honored us by sending us here."

When Russell had finished his speech, Stennis rose to congratulate him on it, saying it "will be a landmark, a turning point." It was. In succeeding days, the Washington press corps portrayed Russell as a towering, tragic figure. Under the headline "CHAMPION OF A LOST CAUSE," William S. White wrote that "Every supreme moment in [his] career . . . every one of those rare times when his power is at its peak, is a moment not of elation and triumph but of melancholy and the inner knowledge of ultimate defeat. For the irony of Senator Russell's life as a public man lies in the fact that he can be a primary leader only in a cause that he knows already to be lost in the unfolding movement of history." White assailed those who would classify the Georgian "erroneously and with great over-simplification, as all but in the company of the 'peckerwoods'—the ill-born, ill-educated and bloody-minded kind of Southerner who uses a word—the word is 'nigger'—that could not pass the lips of Richard Brevard Russell." To Clarence Mitchell, seated in the gallery above, the Georgian was also a towering figure—a very dangerous one. The NAACP's perceptive lobbyist saw a "subtle dramatist" (who had "riveted" the Senate's attention on him with his dramatic opening line) standing with "baronial elegance" as he vented "with volcanic fury the sectional bitterness that had been bottled up inside him for so long—feelings that the South was victim of 'conscious hate.' " But the speech also reminded Mitchell, as his biographer says, "why this normally urbane gentleman was such a highly respected master strategist." By his accusation that the bill's supporters, who had called it a "moderate" measure, had been engaged in a "campaign of deception," he had, with "astounding effectiveness," thrown the "Knowland-Douglas forces on the defensive"; his masterful invocation of the names of Sumner and Stevens had awakened ghosts that stalked the Senate halls.

Russell's speech had another strategic effect. Its charge that the bill was "cunningly designed" to deceive Congress into passing legislation giving the federal government "sweeping" new powers was aimed at the weakest links in the civil rights alliance: the midwestern Republican conservatives who were philosophically opposed to any expansion of federal power. Russell's aim was true. While the Senate was still sitting all but transfixed by his oratory, Olin Johnston jumped up and shouted, "Senators, do you want to be responsible for a second Reconstruction?" Some of the midwestern conservatives did not want that responsibility, as became clear when several of them spoke at the next Republican caucus. One of them, Bourke Hickenlooper of Iowa, said that passage of Brownell's bill would be "a violation of the civil rights of the white race." More votes had been needed to support the southern position on Part III, and Russell had gotten some with his monumental speech.

HE WAS TO GET MORE. A great general has the ability to find a weak spot in his foe's defenses that no one else has found, and Richard Russell was a great general in the civil rights war. There was indeed a weakness related to the Administration's civil rights bill: the head of the Administration didn't know what was in it. And Russell had guessed that. His speech contained the following sentence: "I would be less than frank if I did not say that I doubt very much whether the full implications of the bill have ever been explained to President Eisenhower."

Astonishing as was that statement—that the President was not familiar with a major point (perhaps *the* major point) in his Administration's most highly publicized bill, one that had been a subject of controversy for more than a year—it became apparent the next day that there was, at the least, a considerable amount of truth in it. Russell had said that his statement was based "on my analysis of his [Eisenhower's] answers to questions at press conferences." Eisenhower's next press conference was on the morning after Russell's speech, and at it James Reston of the *New York Times* asked about Russell's charge that the Administration's bill "was a cunning device to enforce [wholesale] integration of the races in the South." Perhaps some of the journalists present had expected the President to reply with a defense of the bill, and of his Attorney General. If so, they were to be disappointed. "Well," Dwight Eisenhower replied, "naturally I am not a lawyer, and I don't participate in drawing up the exact language of the proposals."

The President went on to say that he had thought the bill was primarily a voting rights bill. "I know what the objective was that I was seeking, which was to prevent anybody illegally from interfering with any individual's right to vote. . . ." In light of that, Reston asked, would the President be willing to see the bill rewritten so that it would deal specifically only with the right to vote—in other words, to strike out Part III? "Well," the President replied, "I would not want to answer this in detail, because I was reading part of that bill this morning, and I—there were certain phrases I didn't completely understand. So, before I made any more remarks on that, I would want to talk to the Attorney General and see exactly what they do mean."

Eisenhower's initial ignorance is understandable. The President had, of course, authorized Brownell in April, 1956, to submit only the voting rights portion of the bill; Part III had been put back in the bill through the stratagem worked out by Brownell and Representative Keating. And apparently the fact that it was back in the bill had never—during the intervening fifteen months—been conveyed to Eisenhower. That afternoon, he spoke to Brownell over the telephone. Eisenhower's secretary Ann Whitman heard only the President's side of the conversation, but her notes indicate that Eisenhower may have felt he had not been sufficiently informed about the bill's contents: "He said that some two years ago when they had discussed civil rights legislation, he had understood verbally from the Attorney General that the right of the Attorney General to go into the south was to be concerned with interference of right to vote. Now he understands that the bill . . . is in general terms. . . . He wondered whether this bill was not somewhat more inclusive in that particular factor than had been intended. The President said that when he and the Attorney General had talked, they had mentioned criminal proceedings only in cases where Negroes not give[n] right to vote. . . . If the bill has been expanded to a form so general that it scares people to death, that is something else again. . . ." More than one Republican senator, reading the transcript of the President's press conference, stopped worrying about what the White House reaction would be if the senator voted with the South.

Later that month, the President would write a friend that some of the bill's language "has probably been too broad." And he would also, that July, privately write the friend about his distress about the *Brown* decision ("I think that no other single event has so disturbed the domestic scene in many years"), his lack of distress with the pace of the South's compliance with that decision (it is, he wrote the friend, "impossible to expect complete and instant reversal of conduct by mere decision of the Supreme Court"), and added sentences that hardly evidence a burning desire for sweeping new civil rights legislation, saying that "Laws are rarely effective unless they represent the will of the majority," and "when emotions are deeply stirred," "human feelings" should be given emphasis and progress should be gradual. Eisenhower "had waged two successful campaigns to become the nation's leader, but he did not want to lead on the issue of civil rights," his biographer Ambrose has written.

WHILE RICHARD RUSSELL'S SPEECH had given Lyndon Johnson more of the votes he needed to amend Part III and thereby pay part of the South's price, it hadn't given him enough. Even with four or five midwestern Republicans now joining the southern and western Democrats, there were still not nearly the forty-eight votes necessary to pass an amendment. Liberals were shocked by the speech's revelations. As Russell was linking the Brownell Bill to Sections 1985 and 1993, Paul Douglas whispered to Frank McCulloch, "Why wasn't I told this?" but Douglas' aides hadn't told him because they hadn't known.

"When Russell brought this out, we were all surprised," McCulloch recalls. But their determination was undiminished: to them the cause of social justice was more important than what they considered mere legalisms. Most of the liberal Democrats were still planning to vote for the unamended, strong bill. And despite the midwestern defections, most of the forty-six Republicans were still sticking with Knowland. A comfortable majority was still available to pass it.

Russell had wounded the civil rights cause in another way, however. His speech had shrewdly appealed not only to Republican conservatives' belief in the limitation of governmental powers but also to their belief in a senator's right to unlimited debate. The appeal he had made to them across the center aisle—"I hope that our colleagues will not be intolerant of us as we seek to discharge our duty to the people of our states"—had touched a chord. In the list of conservative priorities, civil rights did not necessarily rank above senatorial rights. Some of these GOP conservatives had never been particularly enthusiastic about civil rights. Considerations of party harmony, of party power and (because of the chairmanships at stake) of personal power had brought them into line behind Knowland to support the Administration's civil rights bill, and despite Russell's speech, those considerations would probably still hold them in line to vote for the measure; the bill itself would still command an overwhelming Senate majority. After Richard Russell's speech, however, many conservatives were no longer willing to vote for limiting debate on the bill—as was shown by another midwestern comment made after that GOP caucus. While not going so far as Hickenlooper in disavowing the aims of the bill, Karl Mundt of South Dakota pledged that the measure is not "going to be rammed down the throats of southerners by relentless or roughshod methods." Russell's speech had won to his side a few votes against Part III—but many more votes against limiting debate. All the pressure that Knowland, Nixon and the White House could apply couldn't hold the GOP midwesterners in line on that issue any longer. There were enough votes to pass the bill. There weren't enough votes for cloture.

Returning to his office after his speech, Russell had made some telephone calls to check on its effect, and then had called a meeting of the southern senators for the following morning, and beginning at 9:45 a.m., they filed in and took seats around the huge table: Byrd of Finance, Eastland of Judiciary, Ellender of Agriculture, Hill of Labor, Fulbright of Banking, McClellan of Government Operations, Johnston of Post Office and Civil Service—the mighty chairmen—all sitting with the chairman of Armed Services (and with the strong young recruits Talmadge, Ervin, Thurmond) around the mahogany oval, in front of the wall with the pictures of Russell's twelve brothers and sisters, and of the old judge with the walrus mustache administering the oath—"Dick Russell's Dixieland Band," the fearsome Southern Caucus. And there, at the very same time that the President, at the other end of Pennsylvania Avenue, was refusing to defend the civil rights bill, the South's general laid out his strategy for attacking it, a surprising strategy, except in light of Russell's larger objectives, both for the South and, in the interests of the South, for Lyndon Johnson.

Hearing Russell's speech as a call to battle, many of the southerners had expected him to announce at the meeting that the South would deploy against Knowland's threatened motion to bring the civil rights bill to the floor the South's most potent weapon—an all-out filibuster in the traditional style that would hold the floor until the bill's proponents gave up and allowed the motion to die. They were more than ready to enlist in the fight: Olin Johnston, for one, had prepared a forty-hour speech, and others had begun making notes for extended presentations.

Instead, Russell, after announcing in that calm southern drawl, "Well, fellows, I think there are some things we ought to talk about," said that in his opinion, although they should hold the floor, they should do so, at least at first, not by reading the telephone book or recipes for pot likker but by arguments to the point, attempting, during the debate on Knowland's motion, to amend the bill drastically by eliminating Part III and inserting a jury trial amendment. "We've got a good case on the merits," he urged. "Let's keep the arguments germane. Let's see if we can keep our speeches restrained and not inflammatory."

Not all of the men around the table agreed with the strategy. Johnston wanted to deliver his *magnum opus* immediately, and Strom Thurmond suggested that they all march in a body down Pennsylvania Avenue to the White House and let Eisenhower know in person that they intended to filibuster. Russell responded that he was not ruling out a no-holds-barred, plainly declared, traditional filibuster, but merely saying that they should hold that weapon in reserve. After arguing Thurmond out of his proposal, he told Johnston to keep his speech handy, that it might well be needed later on. Explaining his reasoning, he used Lyndon Johnson's arguments, the ones Johnson had been using— and had had George Reedy put in writing—in Johnson's own attempt to head off an open filibuster: that this time a filibuster might not win, and that, even if it did, it would inflame northern passions and make more likely a future change in Rule 22. Skeptical of that assessment, several of the southerners weren't sure that Russell himself really believed in it, but no one wanted to argue with him; it was in summing up the feeling around the oval table that Harry Byrd said simply: "Dick, it's up to you." One of the other senators would later describe the strategy agreed on at the meeting: "Instead of rantin' and ravin', we'd talk about the merits of the bill—at least for a while."

The strategy was flawless. Thanks to the new allies Russell's speech had won for the South, there was now little danger that the bill would come to a vote if the southerners didn't want it to. Since an old-style filibuster, an adamant, defiant, blatantly obvious attempt to cripple the Senate, might hurt the South in future years, if possible that type of filibuster should be avoided, held off to the last possible minute and used then only if it was absolutely necessary. And after Russell's speech, a filibuster *could* be held off to the last possible minute. It was no longer necessary at the beginning of the fight over the civil rights bill; the southerners could wait until the end, until just before the votes either on the motion to bring the bill to a vote or on the bill itself, and see if the bill had been hammered into a shape acceptable to them. And if it hadn't—if they still hadn't gotten what they wanted—they could always filibuster then. They could keep that weapon in reserve—holding it for the last stand—because, thanks to the speech and Hells Canyon, they could be sure that, in that last stand, the filibuster would win.

These facts had the most ominous implications both for the cause of civil rights and for Lyndon Johnson. For both the cause and himself, he needed to pass a bill, needed to persuade the South to compromise. His strongest argument to persuade the South to do that had been that it was "isolated," "utterly without allies"—that a filibuster might be defeated. That argument had now been destroyed; the South no longer had to compromise. For months, the South—Russell—had been insisting on the addition of amendments that would eliminate Part III and add jury trials to the bill. Now those amendments *had* to be added, or there would be no bill; the South would have to be given what it wanted. But to add those amendments, Johnson would have to find liberal and Republican votes—votes it seemed impossible for him to find. As the Senate recessed for the Fourth of July holiday, it seemed inevitable that the end of the 1957 civil rights fight would be simply another filibuster.

LYNDON JOHNSON WASN'T IN WASHINGTON that Fourth of July weekend. On June 23, shortly after Russell told him he had decided to give his speech, Johnson had abruptly left Washington for the Pedernales Valley. At least some of his key—and worried—Washington advisers believed that he knew the impact that Russell's speech would have, and felt it would destroy his last hopes of getting a compromise, and that he had, in Tommy Corcoran's phrase, "given up," and wanted to be identified as little as possible with another civil rights defeat. He stayed on his ranch for two weeks, continuing his monthslong public silence on the issue but removing himself as far from the Washington spotlight as possible.

On the ranch, the days were filled with lolling around and occasionally floating in the pool, with business meetings with KTBC salesmen and executives, drives around the ranch to inspect the cattle and into Austin for dinner at El Matamoros and El Toro with his young staff members Bill and Nadine Brammer and Mary Margaret Wiley, and long domino games; one, with Wesley West, A.W. Moursund, and Gene Chambers, began in the morning, resumed after lunch, and then, after dinner at the West Ranch, went on there for several more hours. What was noticeable was the absence, to any substantial degree, of telephone calls back to Washington on Senate business. Mary Rather's log of telephone calls showed that very few were being made to senators.

Near the end of the two weeks, however, George Reedy telephoned Johnson to read him a memo that had been received that day in the Washington office. The memo told him that, hopeless though the fight for a civil rights bill might seem, he could not avoid it and should stop trying to do so, and the memo was from the man who Johnson felt *knew*—had *proven* he knew—how to become President.

The memo's first line was a little sarcastic—"I hope you are finding the Perdenales [*sic*] River peaceful before the coming storm," Jim Rowe wrote— and the rest of it told Johnson, in notably candid terms, that if he wanted to become President, he had no choice as to what he had to do in the civil rights fight. "As you probably know," the memo said, "both your friends and your enemies are saying that this is Lyndon Johnson's Waterloo. They are saying that you are trapped between your southern background and your desire to be a national leader and that you cannot escape. I personally think this is Armageddon for Lyndon Johnson. To put it bluntly, if you vote against a civil rights bill you can forget your presidential ambitions in 1960."

To keep those ambitions alive, Rowe's memorandum said, it was necessary for Johnson not merely to vote for a civil rights bill but to fight for one. "Lyndon Johnson would have to be active in bringing about cloture" if that was necessary. It was necessary not merely that he fight but that he win. "The important thing about civil rights in 1957 is to pass a civil rights bill . . . solely for the purpose of getting this absurd issue off the Hill for a few years. . . ." And, Rowe said, it was necessary that the bill that was passed not be identified as a Republican bill but as a Lyndon Johnson bill. "The public relations . . . are most important. It would be most important that Johnson get all the credit for getting a compromise bill through."

Following this course "is imperative," Rowe said. "It may not be imperative to Johnson, but it is imperative to Rowe! I would not like to see the 1960 nomination go down the drain because of one vote in 1957. . . ."

Rowe's memo was read to Lyndon Johnson on July 3. And the next day there was only one guest for dinner at the Johnson Ranch—and the identity of that guest was interesting in light of the lasting hold on Johnson's emotions that was exerted by anything that had to do with his family.

The guest was his twenty-eight-year-old cousin William (Corky) Cox— and Corky's life had intersected with Johnson's twenty years earlier, when Johnson, then twenty-eight himself, had been in another situation that appeared hopeless. Despite his weeks of desperate effort, newspaper polls published on March 25, 1937, two weeks before Election Day, showed him further behind than ever in his first campaign for Congress. The custom in the Hill Country's little towns was for a candidate to be introduced at rallies by the towns' most prominent citizens; by now these leaders had almost all endorsed one or another of his opponents, and that day Johnson had learned that not a single prominent person could be found to introduce him at any of the next day's rallies.

Lyndon was very dejected as he sat in his parents' home in Johnson City that evening, talking to his parents, his brother, his uncle Tom, his cousin Ava Johnson Cox, and Ava's eight-year-old son, Corky, but as had happened before in times of political crisis for Lyndon, his father had a suggestion for him. The leaders' opposition could be made to work for him, Sam Ealy Johnson said; instead of trying to conceal their opposition, Lyndon should emphasize it by being introduced by the antithesis of a veteran leader—by a young child who would recite a particularly appropriate poem ("You know the poem," Sam told Rebekah—"the one about the thousands"). The child Sam had in mind was Corky, who, in an area in which horsemanship was esteemed, was being called the best young cowboy in the Hill Country because of his riding and calf-roping feats in children's events in recent rodeos. "Corky can do it," Sam said. And Corky did do it. The next day, a vicious Texas norther had hit the Hill Country, but all that day Lyndon and Corky had driven from town to town through freezing rain that rolled across the hills in blinding sheets—and in each town Lyndon would tell the audience, "They say I'm a young candidate. Well, I've got a young campaign manager, too," and then Corky would recite a stanza of Edgar A. Guest's "It Couldn't Be Done" ("There are thousands to tell you it cannot be done, / There are thousands to prophesy failure, / There are thousands to point out to you one by one, / The dangers that wait to assail you. / But just buckle in with a bit of a grin, / Just take off your coat and go to it; / Just start in to sing as you tackle the thing / That 'cannot be done,' and you'll do it"), and when the boy finished, Lyndon would take off his coat and give his version of a bit of a grin, and attack the "thousands" who said that just because he was behind, he couldn't win. That corny poem and the fresh-faced boy who delivered it had touched a chord with the audiences of farmers and their wives and had ignited Lyndon Johnson's campaign, and "hard as he had run before, now, with the race seemingly lost, he ran harder," ran to victory.* No one, of course, can know for certain the role memories may have played down on the Johnson Ranch during those two weeks in 1957, and it may have been only coincidence that on July 4, 1957, the day after he heard Jim Rowe's memo, Ava Cox received a telephone call from her cousin Lyndon asking where Corky was living these days. Ava said that her son was a schoolteacher down in Ingram, near Kerrville, a town about sixty miles south of Johnson City, and Johnson telephoned him and said he'd like to drive down and see him. That evening, he brought Corky back to the Johnson Ranch for dinner. No one knows what they talked about—Corky Cox died in 1993—but when, on July 6, Lyndon Johnson

---

*This scene is adapted from Volume I, *The Path to Power*, pp. 428–30. For another suggestion of his father's during this campaign, see p. 399.

returned to Washington, hard as he had fought before for the civil rights bill, now, with the fight seemingly lost, he fought harder.

TRUE TO HIS WORD, Knowland introduced, shortly after the Senate reconvened on Monday, July 8, his motion to "proceed to the consideration" of the civil rights bill—to bring the bill to the floor for debate. Carrying out Russell's strategy, southern senators began to discuss the motion—not by reading recipes or the phone book but in germane, if lengthy, arguments. The South knew that if the bill came to a vote in its present form, with Part III in it, it would pass. Despite the votes of some Far Northwest and Mountain States senators—and of the five or six reactionary midwestern Republicans whose support for the measure had been stripped away by Russell's speech and Eisenhower's admission—a solid majority of the Senate was still for it. Lyndon Johnson knew, as the historian Robert Mann writes, "the price for southern acquiescence—to render the bill a toothless voting rights measure." Most immediately, the price was the removal of Part III. But Johnson also knew that he "did not have the votes to pay this price." To persuade the South to stop talking and allow the civil rights bill to come to the floor, he would have to get more votes from Republicans, and he would have to get some from liberals, too.

In an attempt to do so, he deployed, upon his return from Texas, his most powerful weapons—against the largest targets.

The intellect and eloquence of Richard Russell were now deployed in the privacy of the Oval Office. During his July 3 press conference after Russell's speech, Eisenhower had said he would be glad to talk to Russell personally about his Administration's bill, but Russell had done nothing about the invitation. Immediately upon his return to Washington on July 6, Johnson, "aware," as Rowland Evans was to put it, of Russell's "rare ability to articulate his point," urged him to accept, urged him so forcefully that, on July 10, Russell met with the President for almost an hour.

That must have been quite a meeting. No one knows exactly what was said in it. Writing to a friend about it, Eisenhower described an exchange that cast him in a favorable light. After Russell had "delivered an impassioned talk on the sanctity of the 1896 decision [*Plessy*] by the Supreme Court," Eisenhower wrote, "I merely asked, 'Then why is the 1954 decision not equally sacrosanct?' Russell 'stuttered,' and finally said, 'There were wise men on the Court. Now we have politicians.' " Then, according to Eisenhower, he asked Russell to name a single member of the 1896 Court, and "He just looked at me in consternation and the subject was dropped." The President's description may not, however, have reflected with total faithfulness the overall tenor of his remarks. Recalling the meeting years later, Russell said: "He [Eisenhower] just sat there and poured out his soul about that bill and the Supreme Court and several other things. I was amazed, and then I realized that he had known me for a long time." Emerging from the White House, Russell, in answering the questions of a small knot of reporters, gave his customary modest disclaimer of influence. "I couldn't say we had a meeting of the minds," he said. "The President and I don't agree on the basic philosophy of the legislation." Asked if he felt better than he had before he saw Eisenhower, Russell replied, "I can't say that I do." But, adding that "I think in the course of the discussion there were some features I emphasized that the President had not considered," he said that the President's "mind is not closed" to possible amendments to "clarify the bill," and privately, reporting on the meeting to his southern colleagues, he went a little further. "The President indicated, in effect, to Senator Russell that he would not be averse to considering some changes," Willis Robertson was to write a friend the next day. And Ann Whitman spoke to the President immediately after Russell left ("While emotional about the matter, he [Russell] conducted himself very well," she wrote in her diary) and while the meeting may or may not have made Russell feel better, it definitely made Whitman, a fervent believer in civil rights, feel worse. Despite her almost invariably unquestioning loyalty to Eisenhower's policies, she wrote in her diary on this occasion that the President "is not at all unsympathetic to the position people like Senator Russell take," and was "far more ready than I am, for instance, to entertain their views." Whitman may even have offered a rare face-to-face rebuke to her boss for doing so, for, she wrote, he reminded her that "I have lived in the South, remember."

RUSSELL'S VISIT TO THE OVAL OFFICE was followed, probably that same day, by one from Lyndon Johnson. The Majority Leader came secretly. No reporters were waiting for him when he emerged from the White House, because no reporters knew he was there—his limousine didn't stop where reporters could see it—and so far as can be determined, neither Eisenhower nor Johnson ever wrote a word about the meeting. "He sneaked down to see us," Bryce Harlow would tell the author. "He called me, and said he wanted to see Ike, and that he couldn't afford to have anyone know he was asking. It was *very* important. I laid it on. *Very* confidential. No one was to know he was there. Just the three of us. In the Oval Office. His limousine drove past the main entrance and stopped by the Oval Office entrance, and I brought him in the side door to the Oval Office."

That must have been quite a meeting, too, if of a tone quite different from the other. "This wasn't fun and games," says Harlow, who sat in on the meeting although "I never wrote a memo for the record about it"—and said he could not recall any details about it. "These were big boys."

In discussing, years later, the fate of Part III, Brownell would link it to that meeting, which Eisenhower had described to him. Eisenhower had indeed, Brownell said, "become worried" that Part III would involve his Administration "in a myriad of school-desegregation cases," but "I had tried to assure the

President otherwise." But, Brownell would say, "Lyndon Johnson went directly to the Oval Office. . . . A shrewd political operator, [he] had unprecedented power over the Senate," and in this meeting he let the President know how he was prepared to use that power—let him know, Brownell says, in very blunt terms, what would happen to the bill if Part III was not removed. "Johnson told Ike that the entire bill would be defeated on the Senate floor if section three . . . was included. He said he had the votes to do this," and he made Eisenhower understand that he *would* do this. "The President was convinced." Beyond this, he let the President know not only what would happen to the civil rights bill but what would happen to other bills the President wanted passed. "Eisenhower was dealing with a hostile Democratic majority in the Senate . . . and the fate of much of the Administration's legislative program in the Senate hung in the balance. Majority Leader Johnson made that clear to the President." And, Brownell says, Eisenhower therefore made "a highly practical decision. . . . It was a political decision. [Eisenhower] concluded that this political compromise was a necessary price to pay . . . to get other badly needed Administration bills through Congress before the end of the session. . . ." At his next press conference, the President made his position on Part III clear. First, he reiterated his belief that the most important part of the bill was not the one that would foster faster school desegregation but the one furthering the right to vote. And when Rowland Evans asked whether, in that case, he was "convinced that it would be a wise extension of federal power at this stage to permit the Attorney General to bring suits on his motion, to enforce school segregation in the South," Eisenhower replied: "Well, no," and later said, "I personally believe if you try to go too far too fast in laws in this delicate field that has involved the emotions of so many million Americans, you are making a mistake."

Eisenhower's statement gave Johnson new Republican votes for the elimination of Part III, but only a few. Having learned that Eisenhower could be flouted with impunity, Republican senators were more susceptible to the arguments, of either conscience or calculation, made to them by Knowland and Nixon, particularly by the latter; they felt that Nixon was likely to become the next President, and that he would be a very different kind of President from Eisenhower, more likely to remember who had not gone along with him. The arguments and pressure of their Senate Leader and the Vice President held a majority of the Republican senators in line behind Part III.

If there was a single key target on the Democratic liberal side, a single liberal who could, more than any other, perform the almost impossible task of persuading other liberals to change their views and accept a civil rights bill limited to voting rights—a bill without Part III, in other words—it was Joe Rauh, chairman of both the ADA and the Civil Rights Leadership Conference.

Rauh was also, however, perhaps the liberal leader whose feelings about

Lyndon Johnson came closest to outright hatred. He hated him because of what Johnson had done eight years before to Leland Olds ("a great American, a hero of mine") and because of that 76–6 vote against Paul Douglas ("It was just Johnson putting his foot on Douglas' face") and because of a score of other anti-liberal and, in Rauh's view, unnecessarily cruel actions by Lyndon Johnson in the years between the Olds and Douglas episodes. Rauh's very acceptance speech, when he had been elected ADA chairman in 1955, had been largely an attack on Johnson. Johnson had been able to go to Eisenhower. There was no point in his going to Rauh.

Rauh's closest friends, however, included the man who was Johnson's most powerful liberal weapon, Philip Graham, and another potent liberal, Supreme Court Justice Felix Frankfurter, for whom Rauh had, in his youth, been a clerk. And now Rauh received a call from Phil Graham inviting him and his wife, Ollie, down to the Grahams' farm, Glen Welby, for the day, and asking him to "bring the Justice" along.

Rauh was to recall that at first he didn't suspect any ulterior motive in the invitation, not even when "all the way out" on the hour-plus drive to Glen Welby, there was "this business from Felix about the only thing that counts is the right to vote. . . . I never even thought there was anything more to it than a nice friendly afternoon" of playing tennis and swimming in the Grahams' pool.

"Then came cocktails," Rauh was to say, "and Phil and Felix and I are starting to talk some more. By God, if Phil doesn't sound just like Felix on the right to vote. . . . Both of them hammered at me: 'The only thing that matters is the right to vote.' We had the goddamnedest argument." At dinner the topic remained the same. "Phil was saying [that] we shouldn't be so obstinate in demanding everything at once. That we'd get the right to vote first. And that was the most important. Both of them hammered at me. And even then I could hardly recognize that this was not just a dinner party," that "I was being worked on." It took a long time, Rauh says, for him to realize that "Felix and Phil and Johnson had had a very thorough talk," and that the afternoon in the country was "a cute way for Lyndon to exercise his will."

The exercise failed, however. The day at Glen Welby left Rauh unconvinced. Black Americans had waited so long for the rights embodied in Part III. Now, at last, there was a solid majority in the Senate behind those rights. Were black Americans to be told they would have to wait still longer? Rauh remained adamant in his determination to keep Part III intact.

Which meant that Lyndon Johnson still couldn't pay the southern price. And there seemed no way for him to get more of the Republican and liberal votes he needed to pay it.

OFFERING HIS MOTION on Monday, July 8, Knowland emphasized that he was asking merely that the bill be brought off the Calendar to the floor and debated there. The motion, he said, was simply "to enable the Senate of the United States to perform its legislative function." From the other side of the aisle, the Democratic civil rights leader reiterated the point. Knowland's motion "is merely that the Senate proceed to consider the civil rights bill," Paul Douglas said. "He is not, at this time, moving its passage." Both senators said that therefore they would refuse to consider any amendments until that motion was passed. "Then, and only then, will it be germane for us to discuss the merits of the bill itself," Knowland said. Until the bill is on the floor, "I shall resist any amendment," Douglas said.

Should the South attempt to filibuster Knowland's motion, the two senators said, they would invoke cloture, and, they said, they had the votes to do so. Republican leaders agreed. A civil rights bill "will pass at this session . . . without compromise," Richard Nixon said flatly. "We'll win on Part III," Sherman Adams said. "We have our finger on the Senate pulse. We know what's going on."

Behind Knowland's bluster was, apparently, belief. He told a GOP Legislative Leaders' Meeting that "he expected the vote" on his motion "to be successful." With the bill then on the floor, there might, perhaps, have to be some "clarifying amendments," he said, but if the southerners continued trying to block it, he would simply put the Senate on a "round-the-clock basis" and secure passage that way. Attempting to inject a note of reality, some of the other leaders had, the conference minutes show, an utter lack of success. "Congressman Halleck asked whether Senator Knowland would interrupt consideration of this bill in order to take up other bills. Senator Knowland said he . . . was inclined to think it best to drive through on the Civil Rights Bill. Mr. Halleck recalled that, for a number of departments, money will run out on August 1st. Senator Knowland said that it is a calculated risk that must be taken. . . ." Behind Nixon's bluster was, apparently, a cold calculation: if attempts to drive the bill through caused a southern Democratic filibuster, that filibuster would be a political boon to the GOP.

Neither Knowland nor the Douglas Group seemed to understand—and if Nixon understood, he did not disclose what he understood—that the existence of sufficient votes to pass the bill simply meant that no vote would be allowed on the bill, not even on the motion to bring it to the floor. Knowland, anxious to be prominently identified with the civil rights bill he was sure would pass, was keeping his name in the newspapers with a stream of communiqués, and his pronouncements were as patronizing as if he were dealing with an already defeated foe. If the southerners permitted a quick vote on his motion, he said, they would find that civil rights supporters "will not be unreasonable" (although, he made clear, that reasonableness would not extend to any substantive weakening of Part III).

The press accepted both Knowland's view of his own role (he was now being identified by journalists as "the leader of the bipartisan civil rights forces in the Senate") and his optimism. With the southerners, during the first day or two of debate, generally obeying Russell's injunction to sound "restrained and not inflammatory," journalists applauded this stance as if good manners were as important as social justice, and interpreted the restraint to mean that the bill would indeed be allowed to come to the floor. Knowland's motion "is likely to be adopted by a decisive majority vote without resort to cloture," said the *Herald Tribune*'s Rowland Evans. "[An] expected Southern filibuster . . . will not materialize until after Sen. Knowland's motion has been adopted and the second stage of the battle is under way." White of the *New York Times* was only slightly more cautious. "There was," he wrote, "at least an even possibility that [the southerners] would reserve their truly implacable resistance until the time to deal with the substance of the bill." And the optimism involved not only the motion but the bill's ultimate fate. With both sides so reasonable, "Speculation concerning ultimate compromise is dominating the atmosphere," readers of the *Times* were told.

Knowland's predictions in July, however, were not only as confident as those he had made in January, February, March, April, May, and June, but as accurate. His July predictions, too, began to slip—faster and faster—almost as soon as they were out of his mouth. On Monday, he predicted passage of his motion "within the week"; on Tuesday, he said flatly that his motion would be brought to a vote "within *a* week" (italics added); on Wednesday, he told a reporter that the debate might run into September. So wildly optimistic were his vote counts and those of his Democratic liberal allies that they appear to have been based on the belief that since the cause was just, the need for a civil rights bill obvious, and press and public support for it widespread, certainly the motion to consider the bill would pass, and the bill was certain to pass, too. Journalistic analyses showed little understanding that Russell was privately insisting not only that Part III be eliminated but that the amendment to eliminate it be agreed upon before he would allow the bill to come to the floor. Most of the journalists somehow managed to ignore a statement Russell had made on the Senate floor that Monday, not long after Knowland and Douglas had finished speaking. There seemed to be some misunderstanding on the part of his distinguished colleagues, Russell had said. "We are . . . told that it is highly inappropriate" to discuss the merits of the bill "in connection with the pending motion to proceed to its consideration." That, he said, was incorrect. "We are justified in discussing it on its merits, at every opportunity we get to discuss it. . . . If that be an unreasonable position for us to take, the Senate must make the most of it. Senators may call it a filibuster if they wish." But whatever it is called, he said, "Mr. President, we will resist. We will resist." Resist, he said, not merely during a debate on the bill itself. "We will explain and discuss the issues which are embraced in the bill *on the motion to take up the bill* [italics added] until we are convinced that each and every Member of the Senate fully understands them in all their implications." The South had two opportunities remaining to filibuster; it was not forgoing one of them. And, indeed, while the southern senators' discussion of the motion remained germane, it continued on Tuesday and Wednesday. If an "extended discussion" is extended long enough, it becomes a filibuster whether it is called by that name or not, and whether or not its tone is, at least at the moment, restrained. *(Instead of rantin' and ravin', we'd talk about the merits of the bill—at least for a while.)* On Wednesday, readers of most newspapers were still being told that this was not a filibuster yet, and that compromise was still the probable outcome. But Philip Graham, in daily touch with Johnson, had a better understanding of the situation, and on Wednesday his *Washington Post* said simply, "The Senate has begun what may become its most momentous filibuster." The southerners intended to keep extending their discussion until they got what they were insisting on. "It became apparent after a few days that the southerners absolutely wouldn't take ... even [a] cleaned-up Title III," George Reedy was to recall. "That if you want Title III, you're going to have to break a filibuster." Asked by a reporter on Wednesday for a response to Knowland's prediction of a September conclusion, Russell said, "If the bill is not modified, we may be here until the snow flies."

During the first three days of debate, one amendment after another to substantially weaken Part III was either suggested or formally introduced by midwestern conservatives or southerners. Determined that their "dream bill" pass unaltered, the liberals whom William White called "the most ardent civil righters"—the Douglas Group—were refusing even to consider proposed modifications. Other, more moderate, liberals in both parties were more willing to consider amendments, but not from such sources. These moderates wanted a civil rights bill but were willing to settle for a more modest one, and were coming to realize that an unaltered bill would result in a filibuster, and no bill at all. Some of them, furthermore, had other legislation they wanted enacted— legislation that might not be enacted if there was a filibuster. More amenable to amendments though they were, however, these moderates were predisposed to distrust any submitted by southerners who they knew were trying to preserve the South's infamous Jim Crow system or by Republican reactionaries who gave lip service to civil rights but whose hearts, they knew, were on the side of the South. The moderates saw amendments from such sources as simply the latest attempts to gut a civil rights bill by senators who had been gutting civil rights bills for years—saw them as attacks on racial justice by senators whose motives on racial justice were indefensible. And even if these moderates could come around to voting for an amendment introduced by a southerner or southern sympathizer, what excuse for doing so could they give to those of their constituents who were knowledgeable about civil rights? There was little support in the Senate for any substantial modification of Part III, and without such modification, the bill was going to encounter a southern filibuster—and the filibuster was going to win. Says Reedy: "I don't think a filibuster could have been broken because the southerners . . . would have enough allies in the western states to keep it going indefinitely. You just weren't going to get a civil rights bill with Title III."

The Civil Rights Bill of 1957 was going to suffer the same fate as the civil rights bills of 1950, and 1948, and 1946, and 1944, and 1938, and 1936. There was not going to be a vote on it on the floor. It was going to die, in a filibuster, on the motion to bring it to the floor. The dam that for so long had held back the tide of social justice was going to hold it back again. Civil rights was going to lose. Lyndon Johnson was going to lose.

JIM ROWE HAD TOLD HIM that it was "most important" that he "get all the credit" for a bill, but what if at the end of the day there was no credit to be gotten, but only, as in every civil rights fight of recent decades, blame? Desperately as he was attempting to find a compromise, therefore, his attempts were cloaked in secrecy. Unavailable to reporters for almost two weeks down on the ranch, the Majority Leader was hardly more available after his return to Washington; there was no leaking to journalists—indeed, almost no contact with them. His decision to allow Knowland to introduce the motion calling up the bill was evidence of his fears that it wouldn't pass, and in other ways too he kept a low profile. Rising at the beginning of the July 8 session to announce the "Order of Business," he did so not by laying out the order, as was his prerogative—a prerogative, of course, which he was customarily adamant in exercising—but by announcing that the Minority Leader would do so instead. The Senate's pending business, Johnson said, was an emergency measure to authorize construction by Robert Moses and New York State of a huge power dam on the Niagara River to replace one washed away by a flood, but, Johnson said, "I am informed that the distinguished Minority Leader" is about to make a motion to bring up the civil rights bill, and, he said, "I should like to inform all my colleagues that the Minority Leader, in his usual gracious and courteous manner, has told me" that after he makes the motion "he and those who support him will resist any motion to proceed to other business" until the civil rights bill is finally disposed of. As he was speaking, standing at his front-row center desk, Knowland rose to stand at *his* front-row center desk, almost at Johnson's elbow, and confirmed that what Johnson was saying was correct. Three senators—New York's Javits and Ives and Robert Kerr, whose Public Works Committee had considered the Niagara situation—jumped to their feet to protest that that situation was, in Kerr's words, an "extreme emergency" which must be acted upon immediately. "This measure must have the right of way," Ives said. Johnson said he certainly agreed. "The Senator from New York understands, I am sure, that I heartily favor the [Niagara] bill." But, he said, it was not his decision to make. "Mr. President, the Minority Leader has pointed out that he does not intend to have other proposed legislation brought before the Senate." He was washing his hands of the situation, Lyndon Johnson said. "That is the decision of the Minority Leader, and, I assume, of this administration. They will have to accept the responsibility for it." Since the day he had assumed the majority leadership, Lyndon Johnson had insisted on keeping strict control of the Senate's schedule. Now he was abdicating that control. The most accurate indication of the true chances for passage of a civil rights bill was the fact that, in William S. White's words, "Mr. Johnson, normally in control of Senate procedure, now in effect folded his arms." Another indication came every afternoon, when newspaper photographers sent in messages to senators asking them to come to the Senate Reception Room to be photographed. Knowland, "the untitled leader of the civil rights coalition," as White described him, invariably came out to be photographed studying the civil rights bill. Russell and Ervin posed together, intently studying it. Lyndon Johnson declined to be photographed. He was trying to distance himself as much as possible from what was likely to happen.

HARDLY HAD THE FOURTH DAY of debate—Thursday, July 11—begun when two statements made it apparent that the gulf separating the two sides on Part III was as wide as ever. Stennis of Mississippi said Part III "should be stricken"—all of it. McNamara of Michigan demanded that none of it be stricken—that the bill be passed with its "basic provisions" intact. When McNamara sat down, furthermore, Javits stood up to express his concern over the failure by the Senate to take action on New York's "vital" Niagara bill—and Knowland's reply showed how adamant he was about any action that might weaken the position of the civil rights forces. The Niagara bill would not be brought up, Knowland said, until the civil rights legislation was disposed of.

As the day dragged on, the debate became, in the *New York Post*'s phrase, "increasingly bitter." From the far right side of the Chamber, Javits shouted across the arcs of desks as he interrupted Olin Johnston of South Carolina, and Spessard Holland of Florida shouted back, literally jumping up and down in rage, with a hostility that leaks through even the carefully sanitized version in the *Congressional Record:* "I hope the distinguished senator from South Carolina will not allow himself to be cozened from his very proper and very correct position by the importunities of the distinguished senator from New York, aggressive though they may be." One by one, the members of the Southern Caucus—Johnston, Ervin, Eastland, Thurmond, Robertson—rose, to denounce the bill in terms that grew less and less restrained. "A rape upon the constitutional and legal systems of the United States," Ervin called it. The proposed new Civil Rights Division would be a "new Gestapo," Olin the Solon said, pounding his desk. "If this monster bill passes, we can all say, 'It *has* happened here.' " Eastland's ponderous drawl seemed inappropriate to the sharpness of his words, and to the glare with which he surveyed, across the aisle, that unfortunate row of desks at which sat not only Douglas and Hennings but Pastore and Humphrey. The Judiciary Committee chairman assailed the measure as "a cunningly devised scheme," "a devious scheme," and a "travesty of justice," and then asked, looking hard at that row of liberals, "We are entitled to know the answer to this question, which I ask the proponents: Do you intend to surround our schools with tanks, troops, guns and bayonets? . . . Is that the object of the bill, the hidden intent?" Liberals had hoped that Lister Hill, more moderate on some non–civil rights issues than his southern colleagues, might this time be a voice of reason from the South on civil rights as well. Then Hill spoke. "Let us all, men of good will everywhere, join hands and send this measure down to the tongueless silence of dreamless dust," he said.

Even more discouraging to Lyndon Johnson, aware that the bill would not be allowed to reach the floor until agreement had been reached on some major compromise on Part III, civil rights supporters remained insistent that the bill be on the floor before compromise was even discussed. Clifford Case of New Jersey, a Republican and a staunch member of the Douglas Group, rose to deplore any talk of amending the bill before the motion was passed to bring it to the floor. "The immediate matter before the Senate is a procedural one— whether to make this bill the pending business of the Senate," Case said. That was the only matter that should be discussed at the present time. "There will be ample time once [Knowland's] motion is agreed to, to debate the substance of the bill and . . . various amendments. . . . Mr. President, as a sponsor of the civil rights bill, I am certainly not willing to consider changes now." Talking to reporters outside the Chamber, Knowland was equally rigid. "There are going to be no amendments agreed to, nor any negotiations or agreements looking toward amendments, until after the bill becomes the pending business in the Senate," he said. The scene in the long, cavernous Senate Chamber— southerners drawling defiance, liberals scorning compromise, the galleries emptying hour by hour as the day went on, as if even the public knew that the civil rights fight had degenerated into a meaningless farce, very few black faces in the gallery now as if America's Negroes, whose hopes had died so often on the Senate floor, had come to feel that they were going to die there again, and couldn't bear to watch—the scene was depressingly similar to the scenes in the last stages of debates in previous years over whether to bring other civil rights bills to the floor, bills that had, every last one of them, died. It seemed that this bill was going to die, too. Time to save it was growing very short. With every moment, the mood of sullenness and hostility on the floor was worsening, hardening. It hardly seemed likely that any amendment from these southerners who were shouting "rape" and "Gestapo" at the liberals—or from the southerners' allies—would be considered by the liberals, much less accepted by them.

Time might, in fact, run out, without warning, at any moment. The seeming impossibility of compromise and the bitterness in the air might have their effect on the impulsive, easily angered, overconfident Knowland. Lyndon

Johnson kept glancing uneasily at the Minority Leader, sitting at his desk right in front of the presiding officer. At any moment—without having consulted with anyone—Knowland might suddenly rise to his feet, ask for recognition, and announce that he would begin rounding up votes for cloture. The moment that word was out of his mouth, it would be in headlines, and so would the companion word—"filibuster"—that would spell the end of the bill, and of all Lyndon Johnson's plans. To save the bill, to avert a filibuster, Johnson needed moderate liberal votes from both parties for a compromise amendment to Part III. And as the day dragged on, his hopes of getting such votes were steadily fading.

And then, sometime that afternoon, Lyndon Johnson, his gaze roving around the Chamber, noticed, beyond the angrily gesticulating men in debate, a tall, lanky figure sitting quietly at his desk in the far corner of the Democratic side, in the front row of the last section before the lobby door. It was Clinton Anderson—and Johnson suddenly realized that all week Anderson had been spending much more time at his desk than he usually did. He walked over to find out why.

Anderson was sitting there only partly because of his interest in civil rights. Proud though he was of his longtime identification with that cause, he was nonetheless less fervent about the cause itself than about the device that was being used, once again, to frustrate it. "I'm afraid I'm one of those senators who, coming from a state in which there were few Negroes, never quite acquired a passionate feeling about racial injustice," he was to say. "My principal outrage" was rather against the filibuster, "which permitted a small body of men to obstruct the business of the Senate." A man who, as Lyndon Johnson often commented, "didn't like to lose," his defeat by a southern filibuster during his term as Secretary of Agriculture had left him with a bad taste in his mouth, and his principal role as a member of the Douglas Group had been to lead three fights against Rule 22—all of which had ended in defeat. He had become somewhat obsessive about "extended debate" ("I took it as a personal challenge to break the challenge of the filibuster"), and he hated to think it was going to win again in 1957—and he saw it was going to, unless something was done. In addition, he had become, since his heart attack, somewhat obsessive about his health, and the two subjects had become linked in his mind: he felt that "I wouldn't get a bit of rest that summer if we had to remain in Washington listening to an endless filibuster." The Douglas Group's most pragmatic and realistic member, one less ideological and more amenable to compromise than its other members, he was also a highly partisan one. Other liberals might discuss the civil rights bill in terms of social reform; Anderson talked also in the language of a tough, practical politician passionately loyal to his party—and he saw clearly the danger to the party from a filibuster, and felt the Republican maneuvers were at least in part designed to provoke one. "Knowland seemed thoroughly willing to let the southerners filibuster the bill to death—an event which would permit him to blame the Democrats for its defeat and permit the Republicans, in future elections, to pose as defenders of the American Negro," he was to recall. "I had no intention of letting" that happen.

Breaking a filibuster once it had started would be as "hopeless" in 1957 as it had been in previous years, Anderson says. Feeling the pressure more than in the past, the southerners "seemed to sense that this time they had to yield a little, if they were not ultimately to lose everything." But they weren't going to yield to the extent of allowing a strong bill to pass. "The [Administration] bill would never pass . . . in its present form," he says. "The southerners were determined, and the northerners didn't have enough votes and they couldn't break the filibuster." So, unlike the other liberals who had ruled out any talk of compromise, Anderson "just sat myself down on the floor and glued myself there . . . to listen to the reason the southerners couldn't do it." And that Thursday afternoon, shortly before Lyndon Johnson noticed him, Anderson felt he had finally found what he was looking for.

"Hints kept emanating from [the southerners] that a compromise bill was possible," he felt, but there could be no compromise on Part III largely because of the fear, enunciated by Russell, that that section could be used to authorize the use of military force against the South. "They seemed to accept" voting, but "it seemed clear to me that as long as [Part III] remained, they would filibuster to defeat the entire measure. . . . They were afraid they were going to have another march through Georgia." Sitting there at his front-row desk near the lobby, turned slightly around and listening carefully as the southerners to his right and behind him spoke, Anderson understood that their anxiety, justified or not, was genuine, and "I thought if you could just remove the southern fears that we would march an army into the South . . . they'd probably yield thereafter. I finally decided one day that we could stop this thing [the impending filibuster] by removing that one threat." Opening the printed draft of H.R. 6127 on his desk, he pulled out a pencil.

At first, he tried to tinker with Part III, rewording it, as other senators had been trying to do. At one point, for example, trying to defuse another southern concern—that Brownell or some other politically motivated Attorney General would be able to institute suits without clearing the action with the President— he crossed out, on page 9 of H.R. 6127, the word "may" in the sentence "The Attorney General may institute for the United States," and substituted, in blunt pencil, the words "upon order of the President shall." But that Thursday afternoon, Anderson had come to feel that no amount of tinkering would be enough to reassure the South about Part III. That section, he concluded, would have to be not merely reworded but removed. Bending over his desk, he turned back to page 9, on which the first fourteen lines of Part III were printed, and drew a large X across all of them. Turning to page 10, on which the rest of the part was printed, he drew an X across the first eight lines on that page. All that was left of Part III was an innocuous last paragraph. All the rest of it was gone.

It was not long after Anderson drew those two *X*s that Lyndon Johnson walked over to his desk and began to chat. "He was curious what I was doing sitting there on the floor for about two or three days," Anderson was to recall. Anderson showed him his work and said Johnson should arrange to have it introduced as an amendment by some southerner or conservative who opposed Part III. And almost without a pause, almost in the instant that Clint Anderson made his suggestion, Lyndon Johnson saw what was wrong with it—and also saw what was right with it, saw what it could mean, if only it was used correctly. And he saw in that instant *how* it could be used correctly. "Okay," he said, approving the amendment. But then he added: "*You* do it."

The introduction of the amendment by a southerner or a conservative would accomplish nothing, Johnson saw. It would then seem like merely one more attempt by civil rights opponents to gut the civil rights bill; it wouldn't get him any of the Democratic votes he needed to meet the South's price. Opponents had already suggested dozens of amendments to weaken Part III; every one had been rejected out of hand by Democratic liberals and moderates because it came from an enemy. But there was a difference—a crucial difference—between this amendment and the others. This one was being suggested not by an enemy of civil rights but by a friend, by a prominent liberal, by a member of the Douglas Group. Johnson felt at that moment, as we know from George Reedy, that moderate Democrats, anxious to find a way out of the civil rights impasse but not willing to accept an enemy's suggestion, might accept an amendment that came from one of their own. He saw in an instant that this amendment should be not merely suggested by but also introduced by a friend: in fact, by the man who had written it. Put the amendment in, Johnson was telling Anderson, but don't have it put in by a southerner. "*You* do it."

And Johnson saw more—in the same instant. When, standing there looking down at Anderson, he said, "*You* do it," Anderson replied, "How can I? I'm a civil rights man." Anderson was saying that he didn't want to be identified with the foes of civil rights, didn't want to be called a betrayer of the cause. Johnson saw the answer to Anderson's question in the very instant the question was asked. And he also saw in that instant that the answer was also the answer to another aspect of the problem that he had not been able to solve: how to get votes to pay the South's price not only from Democratic moderates but from Republican moderates as well. When Anderson asked, "How can I?" Lyndon Johnson told him how he could. Without even a pause, he said: "Get a Republican to go in with you. Get a *good* Republican."

Johnson meant that Anderson should obtain as a co-sponsor for his amendment a Republican with impeccable civil rights credentials. Anderson's name would then be linked on the amendment with a friend of civil rights; he would not appear to be participating in an anti–civil rights move. That end could be accomplished by obtaining a Democratic liberal as a co-sponsor, of course, but Johnson's purpose, the purpose he grasped so quickly, went beyond that. If Anderson could obtain a Republican co-sponsor, a Republican civil rights advocate, a Republican whose opinion carried weight with his colleagues—"a *good* Republican"—Johnson might be able to get some GOP moderates to go along with the amendment; he might at last, despite Nixon and Knowland, be able to crack that solid Republican front.

Clint Anderson took Johnson's meaning. And he picked the right Republican—George Aiken of Vermont, whose liberal credentials were impeccable—approached him, "and," Anderson recalls, "asked him if he would join" him. After thinking it over for a while, Aiken said, in his laconic New England way, "Well, I believe I will." When Aiken gave the news to friends on the Republican side of the aisle, several immediately said not only that they would vote for the amendment, but that they would join Aiken as co-sponsors.

Aiken reported this response to Anderson, Anderson reported it to Johnson, and Johnson reported it to Russell—who understood immediately not only that this amendment would give him what he wanted, by narrowing the scope of the civil rights bill to voting rights—but also that this amendment, unlike the others, would *pass.** The change the South wanted would now be proposed by liberals, by respected liberals of both parties. Moderate liberals in both parties would be happy to support an amendment with so impeccable a liberal provenance. With their votes added to those of the South and the Hells Canyon bloc (and the six or seven Republican conservatives already enlisted), the amendment would command a solid majority. For the first time since the bill had been introduced in January, Russell could be confident that if he allowed it to reach the floor, there would be, on the floor, the necessary votes to eliminate Part III. Johnson had met the first half of the South's price. He still couldn't pay the other half—the addition of a jury trial amendment to Part IV—but if that section remained in a form unsatisfactory to the South, Russell would still have another opportunity to use the filibuster: on the motion to bring the bill to a final vote. He would not be foreclosing the use of that weapon. A big step had been taken toward meeting his demands, and he could therefore allow the bill to take a big step—could allow it to come to the floor. And by so doing, he would avoid using the filibuster now and thereby keep alive his hopes of avoiding the damage to the South, and to Johnson's presidential hopes, that its use would entail. Russell asked for a quorum call, so that he would have time to check with moderate senators, both Democratic and Republican, to make certain that his assessment of the new situation was correct. He found that it was.

The days of Lyndon Johnson's low profile ended abruptly. Late that Thursday afternoon, there was a dramatic announcement. It concerned the Minority Leader's motion, but this time it wasn't made by the Minority Leader.

---

*"The Senate" would now, as Evans and Novak wrote, be "considering not the Russell-Eastland amendment but the Anderson-Aiken amendment, sponsored not by segregationists but by moderate liberals."

"I hope tomorrow we can work out a [unanimous consent] agreement on a time to vote" on Knowland's motion to bring the bill to the floor, Lyndon Johnson said, and, he said, he hoped the time would be during the very next week. Reporters rushed to learn Russell's reaction and were surprised to learn that his feelings had changed—that the southern leader was now, suddenly, amenable to that timetable. Suddenly the name in the headlines about the Senate fight wasn't "Knowland" or "Douglas" but a new name: "JOHNSON SEEKING VOTE ON CIVIL RIGHTS."

The next morning, the southern senators caucused again in Russell's office. Although some of them could hardly bear to go along with his suggestion that they neither filibuster Knowland's motion nor object to a unanimous consent agreement, thereby allowing a civil rights bill to reach the floor, they agreed at last because it was Russell who was making the suggestion. (He reminded them that should the bill later come to a vote, they would of course be able to cast their own, individual votes against it, so they would be able to tell their constituents they had opposed it.) Johnson thereupon introduced the agreement, which did indeed set the vote on Knowland's motion for the next week—for Tuesday, July 16 ("Mr. President, I have at the desk a proposed unanimous consent agreement. . . ." "Is there objection? . . . Without objection, the proposed agreement is approved")—and then delivered a speech. "I believe the Senate . . . is proving that it can meet any issue with dignity and thoroughness," Johnson said. "This may disappoint those who were looking for a bitter and bloody brawl, but it will not disappoint the American people. I think we all realize that in a very real sense the Senate is on trial, and the American people want us to win." And when, immediately after the speech, photographers sent a request to the floor to have Johnson step into the lobby to have his picture taken, they found him newly agreeable, and the Associated Press photograph reproduced the next day in newspapers across the country showed him sitting between Russell and Knowland, as the architect of the agreement that would at last bring a civil rights bill to the Senate floor.

ON TUESDAY, JULY 16, Anderson sent his amendment to the desk, saying, "I do this jointly with the able senior Senator from Vermont . . . a man of outstanding integrity and a man of the highest character, with whom I delight to associate myself," and Aiken told the Senate why he was co-sponsoring the amendment: "We who support the cause of civil rights know that Part III is unacceptable to a sizable segment of the Senate. Its retention in the bill could result in no legislation at all during this session or any other session in the near future." After a last outburst from Harry Byrd, who could barely restrain his rage at what was happening (charging that Earl Warren, the ADA, and the NAACP were the evil geniuses behind the bill, he called Warren a "modern Thaddeus Stevens," and, shaking his fist at Mitchell and Wilkins, who were sit-

ting together in the gallery, he insulted them by likening them to Goldy and
Dusty, the fictitious African-American twins whose ignorance and laziness had
enlivened a 1940s radio comedy. "There they are," he said—"the Gold Dust
twins"), the Senate voted, 71 to 18, to make H.R. 6127 its pending business.
The eighteen votes against the motion were all from southerners; Gore and
Kefauver of Tennessee did not vote with the South, and neither did Yarborough
and Johnson. Johnson announced that his support for the motion to bring the
bill to the floor was "not to be construed" as support for the bill in its present
form. "Some of us to whom this bill is unacceptable in its present form are
ready to allow it to be debated out of a decent respect for the convictions of
others."

At the conclusion of the vote, Lyndon Johnson and William Knowland,
each seated at their front-row desks, leaned across the center aisle and shook
hands. Both had broad smiles on their faces, Johnson because he had won,
Knowland because he didn't realize he had lost.

That realization may not have dawned fully on the Minority Leader for
four days. It was just a few minutes after the vote that allowed the bill to come
to the floor that Anderson stood up at his desk near the far end of the Democratic arc and said, "Mr. President, I call up my amendment" (the amendment
that, by striking from the bill its key provision, made it in effect a different,
much weaker, bill than the one Knowland had been supporting), and no sooner
had the clerk read out the amendment's title than Johnson made a "parliamentary inquiry" of the chair to emphasize that the amendment was now the "pending question" and the chair confirmed that it was. Knowland had been
outsmarted again. He had not wanted to accept amendments, but Johnson's
inquiry meant that the bill could not be voted on until after the amendment had
been voted on. The vote on the Anderson-Aiken Amendment was not held for
four more days, to give senators a chance to get their views on the record. During those days, Knowland apparently grasped what was going to happen in the
vote, and just before the clerk called the roll, he made an emotional last-ditch
plea to his Republicans to stand fast and defeat the amendment. Ten days earlier, however, Johnson had seen in a moment—the moment in which Anderson
handed him the draft with the two *X*s penciled across it—that if Anderson got a
"*good* Republican" to co-sponsor the bill, the near-solid Republican front on
Part III would be broken, and when the roll was called now, it was broken wide
open. No fewer than eighteen of the forty-six Republicans—not only every
midwestern conservative but Aiken's fellow northeastern moderate liberals
Saltonstall (Knowland's own Assistant Leader), Cotton, Flanders, John J.
Williams, and H. Alexander Smith—went against their leader and voted to
eliminate Part III from the Administration's bill. Johnson had seen in a moment
that if Anderson introduced the amendment himself instead of letting a southerner or a conservative introduce it, Democratic moderates and some liberals
would accept it, and they accepted it with open arms. Kerr and Monroney of

Oklahoma, Chavez, Theodore Green, Bible, Frear—they all joined the southerners in voting for the amendment. Johnson had so many votes lined up behind it that he didn't need them all, and "at the last minute," as *Time* reported, "he was able to release" several Hells Canyon westerners from their commitment to vote with the South, and allow them "to vote against the bill to strengthen their civil rights reputations back home"; only four Hells Canyon Democrats—Church, Mansfield, Murray, and O'Mahoney—were recorded for the amendment. The Democratic "coalition" Johnson had put together was a very unusual one. As the *Baltimore Sun* commented, "It was . . . strange to see so-called 'liberals' voting on an issue such as this with Senators Eastland and Johnston." But it was an overwhelming coalition. Thirty-four Democrats— every Democrat but the thirteen most ardent liberals—voted for the Anderson-Aiken Amendment. It was adopted by a vote of 52 to 38. Part III was gone.

"I BELIEVE THE BILL WAS STRENGTHENED" by the amendment, Lyndon Johnson told reporters after the vote. It had not been strengthened, of course, but weakened, weakened quite drastically. No longer would it provide legal recourse for black Americans who were forced to attend segregated schools, to sit in segregated sections of movie theaters, or to take their meals at the back door of restaurants (nor, for that matter, would it provide recourse for a black woman who was forced to "squat in the road to pee"). The two Negro leaders who had roamed the Capitol's corridors for years lobbying for civil rights understood the import of what had happened. Roy Wilkins and Clarence Mitchell had sat in the Senate gallery a week earlier as Virginia's apple-cheeked racist had shaken his fist at them and insulted them, and now Harry Byrd and his allies had won again. Before the vote, Wilkins had telegraphed senators whom he considered "on the fence" on Part III that a vote to remove it would be "impossible to forget and difficult to forgive," but many of those senators nonetheless had voted to remove it. Now, from the Washington headquarters of the NAACP, Wilkins issued a statement: "The adoption of this motion [amendment] says plainly to Negro Americans that, so far as the Senate is concerned, they can expect little, if any, assistance from the federal government in attempts to win the enjoyment of their constitutional rights."

White men who had fought for civil rights in the Capitol understood, too. "This is not a compromise," said Senator Joseph S. Clark of Pennsylvania. "It is an abandonment by the Senate of the United States of all effort to assist in the enforcement of the equal protection of the laws clause of the Fourteenth Amendment."

Liberals knew whom to blame for the removal of Part III. Roy Wilkins said simply: "He won. We didn't." The "he" was Lyndon Johnson. Joe Rauh was enraged every time Johnson told him that Part III had to go because "otherwise you'll have a filibuster." "The filibuster rule gave him a defense against the liberals," Rauh says. "He [Johnson] would say, 'I got you all I could.' " But, Rauh says, if Johnson had helped at the beginning of the session, they could have changed Rule 22. It was his tabling maneuver that had prevented the change—and preserved the filibuster—in January. "So he beats us down on the filibuster rule, and then he says, 'You can't have Part III because you can't beat a filibuster.' Pretty shabby stuff."

Gerald Siegel absorbed some of their anger: Johnson's aide was to remember Paul Douglas, after the vote, "almost literally grabbing me by the arms and shaking me, and saying, 'Gerry, you've gutted the civil rights bill. I hope you're happy.' That's how high the feelings were—'*I* had done it'—that's how angry people were when Title III came out of the bill, which had to come out or the bill wouldn't pass."

One of the journalists in the Senate Press Gallery during the civil rights debate had been Murray Kempton, and what he watched on the floor below him filled him with disgust. "No single body in the Western Hemisphere has done more to abuse human liberty than the United States Senate in the last 10 years; and no member of that body is entitled to discuss the rights of man without apology," he wrote. "The sight of the Senate immunizes one against the feeling that there is any blood in any issue which comes before it. Collectively if not individually, the Senate of the United States is beneath the contempt of men of taste." Not one senator "bothered to protest that 'Gold Dust twins' crack," Kempton wrote. Not one senator suggested defending the NAACP. But, he wrote, "the NAACP is the agency of Willie Mays, limping and hitting a triple in the All-Star game, of Ella Fitzgerald singing the Cole Porter songs, of Autherine Lucy walking through the rocks into class at the University of Alabama. Name me not three, but just one senator in their class." No one was going to remember the name of any of those men on the Senate floor, he wrote. "I will read to our children the names of every child born in Georgia in the last 40 years, and I will tell you now that they will recognize only the names of Ralph Ellison and Willie Mays and Hank Aaron. They will not know Harry Byrd. . . . Who did Mississippi put out lately that William Faulkner could talk to, except Richard Wright. It is people like these who are the legislators of mankind; they are more to the point than any senator can be." And the Senate's Majority Leader, whose allegiance to civil rights Kempton described as being as lukewarm as Karl Mundt's, was not exempt from Kempton's contempt—far from it. Our "children's children's children" will remember poets, he wrote; "they are unlikely to remember Lyndon Johnson."

In their fury, however, the liberals were ignoring an essential fact. Although the civil rights bill had indeed been weakened, even gutted, nonetheless it was still a bill. It had not been killed by a filibuster. It was on the floor of the Senate.

And the bill was still alive because of Lyndon Johnson. At the moment when he had walked over to Clint Anderson's desk, the bill was stalled dead in its tracks, seemingly beyond hope of rescue, about to die, as so many civil rights bills had died before it. The full-fledged filibuster that would spell its death might begin at any minute, thanks to the importunate Knowland and his constant threats to demand a vote. Southern anger, held in check for weeks by Russell, was on the verge of boiling over. Compromise seemed impossible. Seeing, in Anderson's amendment, the weapon that could break the impasse, Lyndon Johnson had seized that weapon, and wielded it. Equally important, he had wielded it decisively, in the instant it came to his hand. He had had to wield it at that instant—at any moment, the opening it gave him might have disappeared; the focus might shift to some other amendment that would divide the Senate even more irreparably than it was already divided. The mood on the floor, already growing more bitter by the minute, might grow so bitter that *no* compromise would be accepted. By seeing the opportunity, seizing it, and making the most of it, Lyndon Johnson had turned the tide. He had gotten the South the support it needed to remove an important element of the bill, but because he had done so, the South had not killed the bill. Thanks to him, it was still alive.

40

Yeas and Nays

IF ONE ASPECT of legislative leadership is a talent for compromise, for determining the essence of different points of view (what Lyndon Johnson called "listening"), and then for composing those differences—locating a common ground, and then, through negotiating, bringing both sides to that place—there is another aspect of legislative leadership that is also a form of compromise, but on another, higher level, for there are cases in which listening and reconciliation cannot help, cases in which the differences between the two sides are so deep that no meeting place can be located, for no such place exists. For legislation to be enacted in such cases, it is necessary for a legislative leader to *create* a common ground. It was this rare creative ability that Lyndon Johnson was going to have to demonstrate if, after eighty-two years, a civil rights bill was finally to be passed, for, with the month of July, 1957, drawing to a close, it was becoming increasingly obvious that all the compromises and deals that had been hammered out in seven months of negotiations had only brought the two sides to an impasse at which no compromise seemed possible. What he had done on Part III had been very hard. What he had to do on Part IV was harder.

From the moment Brownell's bill had been introduced, southern outrage had focused not only on the broad, sweeping powers it conferred on the Attorney General—the powers embodied in Part III—but on a single specific phrase used not only in Part III but in Part IV, which dealt solely with voting rights: in both parts, the Attorney General was empowered to initiate actions, including applications to judges for injunctions, "in the name of the United States." Under existing federal law, a person who violated a judicial injunction and was cited by the judge for criminal contempt was entitled to trial by jury except "in any suit or action brought or prosecuted in the name of the United States," and the South therefore contended, as Senator Sam Ervin of North Carolina put it, that "the only reason this bill provides that these actions shall be brought in the name of the United States is so that those involved in civil-rights cases can be robbed of their right to trial by jury." The South had insisted that the act be amended to guarantee that right to defendants in civil rights cases. In its original form—when it included Part III—the bill would have allowed the Attorney General to ask for injunctions against violators of many types of civil rights. Now, with Part III gone, the bill covered only one civil right, voting, but the southern senators still insisted that the bill include a jury trial amendment—an amendment providing that any person who, in the Attorney General's opinion, "shall intimidate, threaten or coerce . . . any other person for the purpose of interfering" with his right to vote, and against whom the Attorney General moved in either a criminal or a civil injunction proceeding, should be entitled to trial by a jury of his peers. There were political reasons for such insistence, as George Reedy notes. If the bill included that amendment, "Southern senators could tell their constituents that . . . they had added jury trials so that no southerner could be jailed as a 'criminal' at the whim of a federal judge" (and those constituents could, of course, be confident also that there was little chance of a southerner—a white southerner—being jailed by a southern jury). But constitutional and moral considerations also militated for its inclusion: so integral to the American concept of freedom was the right of the accused to trial by jury that it had been incorporated in the Bill of Rights; it was as sacred to Americans as the right to vote.

In one area of the country—the West, where judges had broken the great railroad strikes at the turn of the century by the arbitrary use of injunctions and jail terms against strikers—the right to jury trial had special resonance, and a jury trial amendment to the civil rights bill had been drafted by a western senator, a senior senator who as a junior senator two decades earlier had demonstrated a particular susceptibility to constitutional and moral considerations.

Seventy-two-year-old Joseph C. O'Mahoney of Wyoming was in a way the embodiment of senatorial resistance to unwarranted expansion of executive authority. A small man with large, bushy eyebrows and a large, "crowd-challenging" voice, the Wall Street–hating Populist had been an eloquent, even impassioned, supporter of the New Deal after he arrived in the Senate in 1934. When Franklin Roosevelt's 1937 court-packing proposal came before the Judiciary Committee, however, O'Mahoney had been noticeably silent. The White House, noting that he would shortly need Administration help on a bill vital to Wyoming, was confident that, in the end, he would come around, but after a while an Administration representative had had an intermediary telephone O'Mahoney in his rooms at Washington's Wardman Park Hotel to make sure he was in line. O'Mahoney thereupon telephoned the Administration's man directly. He was sorry that there seemed to be some doubt about his views on the President's court bill, he said; he was calling to remove those doubts. The bill, he said, was "undemocratic," "obnoxious," and an "insult to the Senate." It would violate the constitutional separation of powers. He would never vote for it. And when some Democratic colleagues on Judiciary suggested killing the bill by simply not reporting it to the floor—thereby saving as much Administration face as possible—O'Mahoney demanded that it *be* reported, together with a recommendation that it be defeated. He wrote the recommendation himself. Roosevelt's bill, it said, "is a measure which should be so emphatically rejected that its parallel will never again be presented to the representatives of the free people of America."

Now, in 1957, O'Mahoney felt that Brownell's bill violated the constitutional guarantee to jury trial. While the fight on Part III had still been raging, he had drafted and on July 8 had sent to the desk a brief amendment adding to Part IV a guarantee of a jury trial for defendants in civil rights cases, and had announced that he was going to fight for that amendment. The bushy brows were white now, the challenging voice a little gravelly with age, the name of his hotel had been changed to the Sheraton-Park, but O'Mahoney still lived in the same suite there, and while the voice was hoarse, the words it spoke were still eloquent, and, with his seniority and his passionate independence, this "spirit out of the Senate past" was to some extent the spiritual leader of the younger Democratic liberals from the West. Even while attention had still been focused on Part III, the jury issue was bubbling up below the surface, and it reinforced the alliance with the South that had already been forged among the western senators by Hells Canyon. A jury trial amendment was part of the South's price—its rock-bottom, non-negotiable price—for not filibustering. And in its fight on this issue, the South would not have to stand alone.

But if the South would not, could not, compromise on a jury trial amendment, compromise was not an option for its opponents, either. The acquittal of Emmett Till's murderers was only one of hundreds of verdicts that documented the prejudice of southern juries; not two months earlier, two white men who had confessed to bombing Negro churches and ministers' homes in Montgomery had nonetheless been given a trial. The defense attorney had waved the banner not of innocence but of segregation—"Every white man, every white woman and every white child in the South is looking to you to preserve our sacred traditions," he told the jury. The two men had been acquitted. "It is this kind of justice, dispensed by these kinds of juries, that the opponents of the civil rights bills in Congress are trying to tack onto that bill," Roy Wilkins said. The amendment "can only be intended to cripple the enforcement of the law by introducing into the proceedings the very local prejudice against which protection is sought," declared a committee of southern liberal educators and churchmen. Senate liberals agreed. How could any senator who truly cared about civil rights vote for this amendment? asked Charles Potter of Michigan, standing beside his desk on crutches because he had lost both legs in World War II. "I fought beside Negroes in the war," he said. "I saw them die for us. For the Senate of the United States to repay these valiant men . . . by a watered-down version of this legislation would make a mockery of the democratic concept we hold so dear." The elimination of Part III had removed everything but voting rights from the bill, Paul Douglas said. Now the South was trying to make voting rights meaningless, too. The Douglas Group vowed "to resist [any jury trial amendment] to the end."

With the raising of the jury issue, the civil rights battle at once became even more complicated—a tangle now not only of legal and parliamentary complications but of moral complications as well. No longer was all the right clearly on the side of the liberals. Even Hubert Humphrey, who was to stand fast against the amendment because "you could not really rely on southern juries to be fair," was to confess that his emotions were "mixed, really"—"This was a terribly difficult issue for me because my Populist background had always emphasized the importance of jury trial. My father talked to me about things like that." With the raising of the jury issue, both sides held some moral high ground—and since granting one right, the right to a jury trial, would nullify the other right, the right to vote, there seemed to be no basis for compromise between them. And if the South, with the West on its side, would not have to stand alone in the fight to come, neither would the liberals: the GOP was standing by *their* side. On Part IV, unlike on Part III, Brownell had his boss's support. The elimination of Part III narrowed the scope of the Administration's bill to the one area, voting, for which Dwight Eisenhower's support was unequivocal, and the President understood that the amendment would, as Brownell put it, "practically nullify" any voting rights provision. Placing "a jury trial between a court order and the enforcement of that order" would mean that "we are really welcoming anarchy," Eisenhower told a press conference. With the President behind him, Knowland was taking the step, rare with Republicans, of making the vote on O'Mahoney's amendment a "party policy" position, and Knowland's efforts were being supplemented now by a politician much more wily, and far tougher, than he. Recognizing the magnitude of the stakes involved in the struggle for civil rights legislation, and recognizing as well the caliber of his main adversary, Richard Nixon had decided to engage him hand to hand. He had begun spending long hours in the Vice President's office off the Senate lobby. Visiting him there, Stewart Alsop found him, as he reported to Johnson through George Reedy, "full of admiration for the job you have done." (On Nixon's desk, Alsop told Reedy, was "a list of nine Republicans that are going to be worked on. One of them is [Gordon] Allott but Alsop did not see the other names.") "It is Nixon, maneuvering quietly and deftly in the background, who is spearheading the bipartisan 'no compromise' bloc that is adamantly against writing a jury trial amendment into the bill," Robert S. Allen reported. "[He] is working closely" not only with Knowland but with "such Democratic militants as Douglas, Humphrey, and McNamara. . . ."

Knowland may not have been able to count votes, but Nixon could, and he was counting more than enough. After talking with the Vice President, Allen told his readers that "Defeat is in store" for the amendment. Conservative columnists agreed. Many Republican senators had "been willing to support amendments against Section III, [but] they are not expected to go along with the jury trial amendment," Gould Lincoln reported. As soon as Part III was removed on July 24, Knowland announced that he would press for an early vote—during the very next week, in fact—on Part IV, and predicted that "an overwhelming majority" of the GOP senators would vote against the amendment. Defeat did indeed appear to be "in store" for the South on the vote—which, of course, meant that the South would not allow a vote: that it would launch a filibuster that would mean defeat for civil rights, and for Lyndon Johnson.

The chasm between the two sides seemed unbridgeable. "Every so often the play of history turns up an issue so full of personal and regional conflict, so grounded in moral philosophy, and so subject to the clash of ancient but contending principles, that it stands apart from all the normal preoccupations of political life," James Reston wrote. "Such an issue is now before the Senate. . . ."

"At this point," George Reedy writes, "Johnson rose to what I will always regard as his greatest height. . . . He was absolutely determined that there would be a bill. . . . Against all reason, Johnson kept insisting that a compromise must exist somewhere. . . . Most observers thought that [the] two poles were too far apart to find a middle ground. But using the same set of facts, LBJ insisted that the reality was the other way around—that if two opposing sides had a degree of validity in their contentions, there simply had to be a legitimate way of meeting them both."

IF THERE WAS A WAY, Lyndon Johnson was going to find it. "He pleaded and threatened and stormed and cajoled," Reedy recalls. "He prowled the corridors of the Senate grabbing senators and staff members indiscriminately, probing them for some sign of amenability to compromise."

He had begun while the Part III fight had still been going on. Trying to find a middle ground—some form of jury trial amendment acceptable to both liberals and the South—he had "spent hours on the phone in nonstop conversations with the most ingenious legal minds he knew," pleading with Corcoran, Rowe, Clifford, Fortas, Acheson, and a dozen other lawyers "for something to break the logjam." He had had Tommy Corcoran assemble a group of lawyers—a dozen leading legal minds of the New and Fair Deals—in the conference room at Corcoran & Rowe, and Corcoran had told them how important it was that a solution be found: "You know, we're all pros here, and we can talk to each other. We know we're here to elect Lyndon Johnson President. Who's kidding whom, and *let's get going!*" Dean Acheson put several bright associates at his law firm, Covington & Burling, to work on the problem. Senators were flooding the Democratic Policy Committee with amendments and suggestions for amendments (O'Mahoney edited and reedited the version he had introduced), where they were run by the committee's lawyers, Siegel and the brilliant Solis Horwitz. "We drafted twenty-five or thirty different versions," Horwitz was to recall. "We were constantly trying to satisfy both sides." The search grew desperate. "O'Mahoney kept introducing these various amendments one right after the other. It got ridiculous. . . ." Each suggestion proved to have a fatal weakness; some foundered on conflicts with other statutes already on the books, others on either the rock or the hard place: every amendment that would add to the civil rights bill a provision that required jury trials—in no matter what form—was totally unacceptable to liberals; every amendment that did not include an absolute guarantee of jury trials was totally unacceptable to Russell and the South. For some time, Reedy says, "every effort turned out to be a false start." And time was running out—and now, with Part III disposed of, it was running out fast, thanks to Knowland's stubbornness. Confident that he would win a vote on Part IV, the "leader of the bipartisan civil rights coalition" was pushing for one more and more insistently, repeatedly announcing that he was prepared to move for an immediate vote. If that motion came to the floor without a compromise already in place, the civil rights bill, bipartisan coalition or not, would be dead.

At the close of a Senate session one evening in July, however—while the fight, and the focus, were still on Part III—Lyndon Johnson had returned to his office and reached for Walter Jenkins' yellow legal pad with the list of persons who had telephoned during the day, and Jenkins had silently pointed to a name on the pad, and Johnson, before he turned to the rest of his messages, told Jenkins, "Get me Ben Cohen."

By the 1950s, the name of Benjamin V. Cohen had faded in Washington's memory, in part because it had been a long time since he and another young bill-drafter, Tommy Corcoran, working closely with Sam Rayburn, had drafted the Securities Exchange Act and the Public Utilities Act, and other keystones of the great New Deal arch; in part because while the accordion-playing, story-telling, relentlessly self-promoting Corcoran had made himself a flamboyant figure in the Capitol, head of one of Washington's most influential political law firms, the shy and dreamy Cohen, who looked and talked, as a friend wrote, "like a Dickens portrait of an absent-minded professor," had withdrawn from the Washington social scene to spend more and more time alone in his book-cluttered Dupont Circle apartment. In the days since they had been part of the same little group of New Dealers,* Lyndon Johnson had seen less and less of Ben Cohen—"You had to be very patient with him," Gerald Siegel was to explain, and Johnson was "an impatient man"—but decades before, men who knew Corcoran and Cohen well had learned that despite his charm and gift for the blarney, Corcoran's mind, canny and politically astute though it was, was not the equal of his silent partner's. A remark of Sam Rayburn's still circulated

*See Volume I, *The Path to Power*, pp. 450–53.

among men on Capitol Hill who had been there during the early days of the
New Deal: after one meeting at which Corcoran did almost all the talking, Rayburn confided to a friend, "Cohen's the brains." Cohen had been among the
lawyers whom Johnson had telephoned to ask for suggestions about the jury
trial amendment, and now, on that July evening when Johnson returned his call,
Cohen said he had a suggestion to make, and Johnson asked him to come to
lunch, and, as Gerald Siegel said, reminiscing years later, "Everyone came up
with a different plan. And all of them were worth nothing, except one man, Ben
Cohen."

Cohen was to recall, after the author, during an interview in 1976, had
finally persuaded him to talk about the 1957 episode, that he had been "working on the problem" of reconciling the right to trial by jury with enforceable
civil rights legislation when his attention had been caught by an article that had
appeared in the April 29 issue of a journal of liberal opinion, *The New Leader.*

The article, by a University of Wisconsin law professor, Carl A. Auerbach,
addressed that problem—and had a solution for it. It was not necessary to rely
only on jury trials to enforce civil rights, Professor Auerbach had written,
because jury trials are required only in criminal contempt proceedings. They
are not required in civil contempt proceedings—and civil contempt proceedings could also be employed to enforce civil rights.

In criminal contempt, Auerbach said, the judge is punishing a defendant
for violating—disobeying—a judge's specific injunction, or order. In civil contempt, Auerbach said, the aim is different—not to punish a defendant for having violated a court order, but to force the defendant to obey the order in the
future. "If the court's order is disobeyed, the judge will hold the violator of his
injunction in contempt of court and have him imprisoned until he does obey."
As soon as he does, he will be freed. "He can open his prison door and walk out
anytime he pleases by obeying the court's order"—and therefore jury trials
were not required.

The impasse over the 1957 civil rights bill, Auerbach wrote, had come
about because the bill contemplated only criminal contempt proceedings. If a
provision for civil contempt was added, the impasse would be broken. "If the
United States proceeds against an alleged violator of a civil-rights injunction in
order to punish him for criminal contempt, all the protections accorded the
accused in a criminal trial should be extended," including a jury trial, he said.
But "the United States should" also "be authorized to bring civil-contempt
actions against alleged violators of civil-rights injunctions. . . . Its objective
would be purely remedial—not to punish the violators for their past disobedi-
ence but to coerce future obedience to the court decree. If the decree, for example, ordered the registration of Negro voters, the local officials refusing to do so
could be imprisoned until they obeyed the order." If they did so, they would be
released. There would therefore be no need for a jury trial.

Auerbach's solution would require merely the addition to O'Mahoney's amendment of a new paragraph, one authorizing the use of civil as well as criminal contempt, Cohen explained. But, he explained, that new paragraph might help create the necessary new ground, the new ground that could become the middle ground, the common ground, for a compromise that would enable the civil rights bill to pass. While southern senators would still be able to tell their constituents that the bill, by including a jury trial amendment, guaranteed southerners trials by southern juries and was therefore so weak as to be meaningless, northern senators, on the other hand, would now know that, despite that guarantee, the bill contained strong enforcement provisions unvitiated by any provision for trial by southern juries.

Twenty years before, Cohen told the author, he had considered young Representative Johnson "promising material." Subsequently, he said, he had been somewhat put off by the "intensity" of Johnson's ambition. But now, in 1957, talking to Johnson over lunch, he felt that the promise had been fulfilled: "He was a man with a mission"—to pass a civil rights bill—who grasped with impressive speed the significance of the Auerbach article. "He asked Senator O'Mahoney to see me," Cohen recalled, and together—along with Siegel—by July 17, they had worked out the wording of the necessary new paragraph. ("Ben was simply my closest adviser," Siegel says. There were seemingly insuperable problems to arriving at a wording that would be accepted by all sides, but every time there was a problem, "Ben solved it.") O'Mahoney's amendment guaranteed jury trials in civil rights criminal contempt proceedings; the new paragraph said that that guarantee shall not "be construed to deprive courts of their power, by civil contempt proceedings, without a jury, to secure compliance with . . . any lawful writ, process, order, rule, decree or command of the court . . . including the power of detention." On that date, while the fight over Part III was still being waged, O'Mahoney had sent the revised amendment to the desk, and now, on July 24, as soon as the 52–38 vote on Part III was announced, it became the Senate's pending business.

The new version of the O'Mahoney Amendment allowed Lyndon Johnson to add additional numbers, representing new votes for the amendment, on the left or "yea" side of the names on his long tally sheet, but only a few more numbers; they were next to the names of Hells Canyon westerners who had wanted to help the South but had been shying from doing so because the amendment would have made the whole civil rights bill too blatantly meaningless. Their tentative commitment was now solidified. Even if every one of the twenty-two southerners and twelve Hells Canyon Democrats voted for the amendment, however, that would be a total of only thirty-four votes, whereas forty-eight were required for passage. There were still no numbers, or almost none, in that left-hand "yea" column next to the names of the forty-six Republicans and about fifteen non-southern and non–Hells Canyon Democrats who made up the bulk of the "civil rights coalition"—a solid majority against the amendment. The odds against passage of the civil rights bill were still very long. The South was willing—to avoid being forced to filibuster, and also to help Lyndon Johnson become President—to accept a weak bill, and since the amendment's new version still contained a jury trial guarantee, it was still weak enough for the South to accept it. Republicans and liberals, however, still would not accept it. While the new version gave them part of what they wanted—a means of allowing judges to jail civil rights violators without a jury trial—it still ensured that southerners would not be jailed for criminal contempt, and it was therefore still too weak to be acceptable. Since, with a solid majority, they could pass the bill unweakened—without any jury trial amendment at all—they felt they had no reason to accept one. They would vote against, and defeat, the amendment; the South would then filibuster, and thereby defeat, the bill. To pass the amendment, and thus the bill, Lyndon Johnson still needed perhaps fourteen Republican and liberal votes. The main advantage of the O'Mahoney Amendment was not that it in itself got Johnson the votes he needed—it didn't—but that it provided a base from which to fight for those votes. While before the new version, no ground for a compromise had existed, there was new ground now, ground too narrow but nonetheless more than had existed before.

HE SET OUT to broaden that ground. With the Senate's attention now focused on Part IV, the hailstorm of proposed changes in the jury trial amendment pouring into G-14 increased in intensity, and Johnson read every one that Siegel or Horwitz thought might be a possibility, and as he read each proposed change, he asked the same question: "If I take this one, how many votes will it get me?" And suddenly, out of that storm of proposals, there was one—no one remembers who made it—that he felt might get him quite a few votes.

This proposal would create more new ground. Since the civil rights bill was going to deal with jury trials, the proposal went, maybe this bill was the place to remedy an injustice that had been perpetrated against labor unions in 1948 when the Taft-Hartley Act had limited strikers' right to jury trials in contempt cases arising out of labor disputes. Unions had attempted repeatedly to have the right restored but without success. Perhaps, the proposal went, it could be restored in the civil rights act.

This suggestion—about labor disputes, not civil rights—was new ground indeed. But Johnson saw how it could win him some new votes for the amendment from liberal senators—not the most ardent civil righters, but liberals with more moderate civil rights views. The opposition of these senators to any jury trial amendment was intensified by their fear of the reaction of their pro–civil rights constituencies if they supported an amendment that weakened the civil rights bill. But a key element of their constituencies was organized labor: big unions such as Walter Reuther's UAW and Jim Carey's Electrical Workers and the dominant national labor organization, the AFL-CIO, were ardent supporters of civil rights, and therefore adamant opponents of jury trials. If labor could be persuaded, through the inclusion of this new provision, to look more kindly on the jury trial amendment, it would be much easier for liberal senators to vote for it. New additions to the O'Mahoney Amendment were hurriedly drafted by Johnson's young bill-drafters, and on Friday, July 26, O'Mahoney introduced them. The key provision extended the guarantee of jury trial for criminal contempt beyond civil rights cases: "In *any* [italics added] proceeding for criminal contempt . . . of any court of the United States, the accused, upon demand therefor, shall be entitled to trial by jury." When O'Mahoney rose at his desk in the far corner of the third row and announced that "I desire to have laid before the Senate [a] modification of my amendment," Douglas, in the third row three desks closer to the center, rose to attack this constant rewriting. "Is there to be another edition tomorrow?" he asked. Sitting right in front of Douglas, however, was the more moderate Kefauver. Turning around, he told Douglas that the modification "represents a great advance of civil liberties because . . . it will again assure labor unions of their day in court before a jury of their peers." "Labor," Kefauver said, "should be anxious for the passage of this act with this amendment [included]."

JOHNSON HAD SOME GROUND to fight on now—and he fought.

To keep the two sides negotiating—to keep the 1957 civil rights fight from degenerating into the open hostility and bitterness on the Senate floor in which so many previous civil rights bills had died—he had to persuade them to conduct the debate in an atmosphere of outward friendliness and respect, or at least civility, so for some days after Part III had been disposed of, the opening scene of the Senate each noon hour featured the Majority Leader as Emily Post. In statements written by Reedy and delivered during his opening remarks each day, Johnson encouraged the Senate to mind its manners, saying on one day that the Senate was on trial, that the world was watching it, and that he was confident that the Senate would do itself proud, that his colleagues would "continue the debate as reasonable men." On another day, he said he was happy to see that his confidence was justified. "Never before have I seen in the Senate a debate which has contributed so much to understanding. In that sense, I think the debate has been one of the finest the Senate has ever had." Day after day, he reminded his colleagues that they were taking part in an historic debate, repeated his plea that they be fair and open-minded, open to reason and compromise, and praised them for being so reasonable and open-minded thus far—which of course made it harder for them to act otherwise, and kept them, as much as possible, on their best behavior.

Often, on Friday of that week, and during the next week, those statements were read to long arcs of almost empty desks—desks that stayed empty all day. In the days following the hectic floor fight on the Anderson-Aiken Amendment, the Senate Chamber was a scene, as the *New York Times* put it, "of such calm that at times hardly half a dozen senators were on the floor." Johnson's opening homilies, moreover, were almost his only public utterances on the subject of civil rights. He had again assumed a low profile, and was not often on the Senate floor, spending his time in the Democratic cloakroom or huddling behind the closed doors of G-18 with George and Solis and Gerry, or with senators in his offices in the Capitol or back in the SOB. But there, in the cloakroom or behind closed doors, he was fighting, too, using the gifts he had demonstrated so vividly during his entire life.

All his life, he had had what George Brown called a "knack" for simultaneously convincing people on opposite sides of an issue that he was on their side, and that knack was desperately needed now. He was the only bridge between the two sides, and if he was to keep them negotiating through him, he had to convince each side that it was in its best interest to negotiate through him, that he was trying to obtain for it the best deal that could be obtained; that while it was necessary for him to maintain a veneer of neutrality for the benefit of the outside world, in reality he was on their side, that he believed what they believed, that he was their friend, that he wanted them to win. And never had this knack been more vividly displayed. He did it with the tone of his voice: with northerners, his Texas twang became harder, more clipped; when he talked to southerners the twang softened into a full-fledged southern drawl. He did it with words. "If we're going to have any civil rights bill at all, we've got to be reasonable about this jury trial amendment," he said to Paul Douglas in the cloakroom one day. Five minutes later, he was at the opposite end of the cloakroom, telling Ervin to "be ready to take up the Nigra bill again." "Let's face it, our ass is in a crack—we're gonna have to let this nigger bill pass," he told Stennis.

With the southern senators, the key words—in addition to "nigger" and "Nigra"—were *we* and *us,* to emphasize that he was one of them. Keeping the South in line—persuading Thurmond not to march on the White House and Eastland not to give the Judiciary Committee a monthlong vacation and Olin Johnston not to deliver his forty-page speech—was, despite all that Richard Russell could do, becoming increasingly difficult. He had to persuade the southerners to allow some sort of civil rights bill to pass, not to employ the filibuster to kill it, even though their constituents were expecting them to use the filibuster if necessary. To do so, he made things personal. Over and over again, he told the southerners, "We have to give them *something*"—and, he told them, as long as they trusted him, the something would be as little as possible. "I'm on your side, not theirs. Be practical. We have to give them something. But we don't have to put teeth in it." He made it political. "You always thought you wouldn't have to worry about Republican opponents. Well, look around you. I look around and I see the Republicans shaking bushes all over the South. Well, one day, they'll shake the right bush and flush out an opponent for you. . . . My ass is on the line, and your ass is on the line, and the Democratic Party's ass is on the line. . . ." He tried to make them understand that as long as the bill contained a jury trial amendment, its passage would have minimal political repercussions for them. "You can go back [home] and say, 'Listen, we couldn't stop them entirely. They just had too many votes, so they rolled over us. But look what we got. We fought and fixed it up so that those damned Yankee carpetbaggers couldn't come back, and also they couldn't brand you a criminal without a jury trial.' " He played on their pride as southerners. We've got a chance to show the Yankees that we're not all ignorant redneck racists down here like they'd like to think, he said. He played on their hopes: their hope that he might become President, and that if he did, that would be a victory for the South, a victory so great that its possibility should overrule all other considerations. "He used this feeling, he played on it—this was a deliberate tactic of his," Reedy says. He played on their fears for the South. For the first time, he said, Negroes have a real leader. "A religious leader. A nonviolent man of the cloth. You all know what that means, don't you? A colored Baptist preacher? That's one man who controls the colored community. . . . The colored are not going to give up. They're determined. . . . We can't continue to push these things down their throats. They won't sit still any longer. We have to give them *something*." He told them, "If we don't allow progress on this issue, we're going to lose everything. There's going to be cloture. Rule 22 is going to go. And our opportunity to delay, or to slow down, and to bring some kind of an order to change, will be gone." Or: "These Negroes, they're getting pretty uppity these days and that's a problem for us since they've got something now they've never had before, the political pull to back up their uppityness. Now we've got to do something about this, we've got to give them a little something, just enough to quiet them down, not enough to make a difference. For if we don't move at all, then their allies will line up against us and there'll be no way of stopping them, we'll lose the filibuster and there'll be no way of putting a brake on all kinds of wild legislation. It'll be Reconstruction all over again."

And he played on their fears for themselves—an effective tactic, because Matt Neely's death, expected daily, would reduce the number of Democrats in the Senate to forty-eight. There were currently only forty-six Republicans, but the Republican Governor of West Virginia was expected to name a Republican to Neely's seat, so there would be forty-seven. Joe McCarthy had died in May, and a special election to fill his seat would be held on August 28, between a Democrat, William Proxmire, and a Republican, Walter J. Kohler, a popular former governor. Since no Democrat had won a Senate seat from Wisconsin in twenty-five years, it was expected that after the special election, the Republicans would have forty-eight seats. The party count would be tied, a tie would be broken by the Vice President—the Republicans were planning to reorganize the Senate as soon as Kohler was sworn in. A confidential memo sent to Lehman in Switzerland by Julius Edelstein reported that "Lyndon Johnson [has] been warning all the southerners that unless they relaxed a little and let some kind of a civil rights bill go through, they were in danger of losing their chairmanships. He urged them not to filibuster because to filibuster the civil rights bill would ensure a victory for Kohler. . . ."

With the liberals—not with the most ardent "red-hots," for with them there was no hope, but with the rest of the Democratic liberals—the key words were also *we* and *us*. He made them feel that they were in a battle, and that in that battle he was on their side. Warning one liberal senator that there must be a liberal "sentry" on the floor at all times to guard against a sudden southern legislative maneuver, he told him, "They'll get us on the floor if we're not manned on the floor at all times, so we always have to have a man there." He told him, "They'll pick our moment of least resistance and move in." He played on their fears—the fear of what southern power in the committees could do to their vital projects. Once, when Wayne Morse was threatening, in order to bring the South to heel, to block a unanimous consent agreement some southerners wanted, Johnson told him, "Look, you're going to be in the position of wanting [their] support in the future. This [the jury trial amendment] isn't that hurtful to your state's interest or to your own convictions. Don't build it up into a blockage."

He had to persuade the northerners to allow some sort of jury trial amendment in the bill, even though such an amendment stripped the bill of its teeth. He tried to make them understand that the important thing was to get *some* bill, *any* bill, passed "to show them we can do it"—"Once we've got the first one passed, we can go back and improve it"—and that the only way to get it passed was to vote for the amendment. "Jim Eastland knows we have to have a civil rights bill," he said to them. "But he has to have a jury trial amendment. We've got to give him a jury trial amendment." He tried to make them understand that so long as the bill contained provisions for voting rights, it was still worth passing: "Give them the vote, that's what matters. Then things'll change, you'll see," he said. When Humphrey tried to argue with him, he said, "Yes, yes, Hubert, I want all those other things—buses, restaurants, all of that—but the right to vote with no ifs, ands or buts, that's the key. When the Negroes get that, they'll have every politician, north and south, east and west, kissing their ass, begging for their support."

Keeping the liberals from forcing the issue to a vote was becoming more and more difficult, for, knowing that they had a majority of the Senate on their side, they thought only about the vote, not about the maneuvers that would precede it, and he tried to make them understand. Because of their distrust of him, he often relayed his word through others. In one liberal caucus, Clint Anderson interrupted a barrage of red-hot bravado about their chances of carrying some amendment to tell them their vote count was wrong ("Let me give you some advice," Anderson said. He named five Democratic senators whom the liberals were counting on their side. You're right in thinking that "you're going to need their help," he told them. "But you haven't got it now") and to advise them to stick with a man whose counts were more accurate (particularly since that man was of their party): "I remember that for many years whenever we tried to do something on civil rights, Bob Taft would go over and whisper to Dick Russell and we'd be licked. So let's follow our own leader and not these recent Republican converts." Once, John Carroll told his administrative assistant, Harry Schnibbe, "Goddammit, we'll go on the floor with this. McNamara will do this, and Paul will do that, and we'll make an issue of this." Having learned of the liberals' plans, Johnson sent Bobby Baker to intercept Schnibbe on the floor: "Harry, this is a grave mistake. If you do this, Russell will do this, and Ellender will do this. . . . The Majority Leader has got to cool this down before we can go forward." And sometimes he delivered the warning himself. "Look, if you press too hard, if you insist on perfection, you'll get it, but it won't be passed."

Day after day, he was arguing one side of a point with the southerners and the other side with the liberals—and arguing both sides with equal persuasiveness. At the same time that he was telling the South that he had counted votes and had found that a filibuster couldn't win, he was telling liberals that he had counted votes and had found that they couldn't beat a filibuster. "He was playing it out of both sides," Harry McPherson was to recall. "He was down in the trenches with guys who were determined not to let the bill pass, and he was doing his damnedest by every conceivable device to bring them around. He warned them [the southerners] that much worse would come unless they would pass this modest bill." They believed him. *"He made them think . . . he'd be with them forever."* At the same time, McPherson says, "he would tell some of the northerners that if they would only let this modest bill go through, they would get a better bill later." And *they* believed him. He told Joe Rauh, "You can't beat a filibuster," and Rauh says he was correct: "We had the majority, but we didn't have two-thirds."

HIS VOTE-COUNTING ABILITY was needed, too, for if the jury trial amendment came to a vote without the necessary number of yeas and was therefore defeated, the South would not then permit a vote on the overall bill. Lying before him on the desk in his office was a long Senate tally sheet; when he left the office, the sheet was in his breast pocket. In contrast to most of his tally sheets, this one was notably untidy, for so intense was the pressure from both sides that senators were changing their votes, and then changing back again— some of them several times; the long, narrow paper was smudged with erasures and covered not only with numbers but with notes he had jotted down to remind him of what might be the best time to approach a particular senator again, or of some new argument that might work with him. In the cloakroom, he would, over and over again, pull the tally sheet out of his pocket, put on his eyeglasses and study it intently, his thumb moving very slowly down the sheet, seeming to pause at every line, making sure that he was certain of every vote, that he wasn't just thinking, that he *knew*. And what he knew, counting the votes, was that he didn't have enough. Knowland, as Doris Fleeson was to write, "twice daily assured his Democratic allies he would lose at most five or six GOP votes," and Johnson knew that for once Knowland's error was not on the side of optimism. Johnson needed forty-eight absolutely "sure" votes to make passage of the amendment certain. The exact number of votes he was counting at this stage cannot be determined, but it appears to have been no more than forty-two.

To try to get more votes, he used all the weapons at his command—used them with his customary ruthlessness. The ruthlessness was usually cloaked under senatorial courtesy; it took the form of hints rather than threats. But with these men, threats were not needed. Senators understood the nuances of power; they were well aware that the man asking for their help on the civil rights bill had the power to help them—or not help them—on other bills, bills that were vital to them; to help them with committee assignments or campaign cash or office space.

The Niagara situation was becoming desperate because frost comes early in autumn on the Niagara Frontier, and time was running out. The bill authorizing New York State to begin construction of the huge power dam had been passed through Public Works, but it was still stalled on the floor behind the civil rights bill, and Johnson let New York's senators know that it was going to stay stalled until a civil rights bill was passed. Addressing the Majority Leader, New York's Irving Ives said that the "Niagara Frontier is without adequate power. Business will have to cease there. Unemployment will increase. There will be a dire situation there in a very short time unless this redevelopment is begun this year. . . . This measure must have the right-of-way. . . ." But the Majority Leader, standing at his desk looking across the aisle at Ives and Javits, said that while "I shall do what I can to have it brought to a vote in this body as soon as possible," it might not be possible in the immediate future. Thanks to a decision by the Republican Leader and the Republican White House, the pending business, he said, was still civil rights. The next voice came from a desk behind him—in the back row of the Democratic side of the aisle. "The bill authorizing the Tennessee Valley Authority to issue . . . revenue bonds . . . is of an emergency nature equal to that of the Niagara Bill," Albert Gore said; "It is urgent that it be considered." "I thank the Senator from Tennessee," Lyndon Johnson said. "I assure him that I shall urge the Senate at the appropriate time to give consideration to the Tennessee Valley Bill, in which he is so deeply interested." But, he said, the appropriate time would be when "a majority of the Senate" want to proceed to business other than the civil rights bill. "So far as the Majority Leader is concerned, he is prepared to proceed to the consideration" of these bills "and get the earliest possible decision. . . ." But it wasn't up to him, he said, but to "the majority of the Senate." Couched though it was in soft senatorial courtesy, the message was hard and clear. If the South was pushed too hard on the civil rights bill, it would filibuster. And if there were not sufficient votes to get the bill off the floor by imposing cloture on the filibuster, the only way to get it off the floor, so that the Senate could move on to other business, such as Niagara and the TVA, would be to withdraw the bill. So the South had better not be pushed too hard.

And if the South was insisting on a jury trial amendment, maybe it would be a good idea to give it one.

HE WAS WORKING the cloakroom and the corridors now, working them with everything he had.

He used his health. He had had his heart attack, he said, he was a sick man and he knew it, he had no interest in a presidential nomination or even for another term in the Senate, all he wanted to do was what was best for the country. The strain was too much for him, he said, when he went home at night, he couldn't sleep, the doctors kept giving him new pills, they didn't work, he was starting to get chest pains again. "Ah don't want to die right here," he said. "Ah don't want to fall on my face, drop dead right on the floor of the Senate." He couldn't take much more strain; "He made you feel that if you wouldn't go along with what he was asking, you might be *murdering* this man," one senator recalls.

He used the liberals' fear of Russell to explain why he couldn't give them more; when a liberal senator had a suggestion, he would reply that *he* thought it was a good idea, but of course there was no sense pushing it unless Russell approved. "I'll have to run that by Dick," he said. He used the southerners' fear of the wild men to explain why he couldn't give *them* more. "Well, you do that, you're gonna lose Wayne Morse and them," he said.

He used their pride in the Senate: "We've got the *world* looking at us here! We've got to make the world see that this body *works*!" He used their pride in their party: "You're the party of Lincoln," he reminded one Republican. "That's something to be proud of. You're the image of Lincoln." To Democrats, he said, "Our party's always been the place that you can come to whenever there's injustice. That's what the Democratic Party's *for*. That's why it was born. That's why it survives. So the poor and the downtrodden and the bended [*sic*] can have a place to turn. And they're turning to us now. We can't let them down. We're down to the nut-cutting now, *and we can't let them down*." He used his power and his charm. "I can see him now," Bobby Baker says, "grasping hands and poking chests and grabbing lapels, saying to the southern politicians something like, 'We got a chance to show the way. We got a chance to get the racial monkey off the South's back. We got a chance to show the Yankees that we're good and decent and civilized down here, not a bunch of barefoot, tobacco-chewin' crazies.'" When he had finished presenting his arguments to a senator, Harry McPherson was to say, "he would sink back into the chair, his eyes wide with the injustice of his burdens, the corners of his mouth inviting pity and support." Then he "would come back face to face, perhaps sensing that the other wanted to help and in that event should hear the whole story, all the demands, the pressures and the threats, as well as the glory and the achievement that awaited reasonable men if they would only compromise, not on the main thing, but just on this part that the other side would never accept as it was; unless there could be some accommodation, there would be nothing, the haters would take over, the Negroes would lose it all, I need your help." He used his stories, and he used his jokes, he used his promises, used his threats, backing senators up against walls or trapping them in their chairs, wrapping an arm around their shoulders and thrusting a finger in their chests, grasping lapels, watching their hands, watching their eyes, listening to what they said, or to what they didn't say: "The greatest salesman one on one who ever lived"—trying to make his biggest sale. Never had he tried harder. In the intensity of his effort, he even instituted a new variation on one of his old devices. Lapels had long been for grabbing, but now he used them—or rather the buttonhole in them—for another purpose. Trying to persuade a senator who was resisting persuasion, Lyndon Johnson would stick his long forefinger through the hole in the senator's lapel to prevent him from moving away. "The other day," George Dixon wrote, "I spied Majority Leader Lyndon Johnson holding Senator Estes Kefauver in captive conference. Kefauver couldn't have gotten away without leaving his lapel behind."

To every crisis in his life, he had risen with that effort that made men say, "I never knew it was *possible* for anyone to work that hard," that effort in which "days meant nothing, nights meant nothing." Now, in this greatest crisis, Lyndon Johnson, heart attack or no, rose again to that kind of effort. In the early-morning hours the residential districts of Washington and its suburbs were dark and silent, but now, in the night, the silence of a darkened street would be broken by the faint ringing of a telephone in a senator's house. The senator, picking it up, would hear, "This is Lyndon Johnson." The persuasion would begin, and it might go on for quite some time. Finally, the call would be over. The senator would go back to bed, to sleep if he could. And on another street, in another senator's home, the phone would ring. The streets of the Kalorama section of the District were, in the early-morning hours, row after row of darkened houses—and of one house, on Thirtieth Place, in which, night after night during these climactic last weeks of July, every night, lights would be on.

TRY THOUGH HE DID, however, it appeared, as July drew to a close, that he wasn't going to win. On Friday, July 26, the lines had stiffened dramatically. That morning, there had been another meeting of the Southern Caucus in Richard Russell's office, Ellender and Byrd in ice cream suits, most of the others in senatorial dark blue despite the heat, and around the huge mahogany table that morning there weren't many smiles. Emerging from the meeting,

Russell was accosted by Bill White of the *Times*. Russell told him that the Caucus had decided to support the jury trial amendment "to the end." If the amendment was defeated, Russell said, the southerners would then fight the complete bill "with every resource open to us." In his article the next day, White explained the meaning of Russell's phrases. "He meant that [if the amendment was defeated] the southerners would put in the most implacable filibuster of which they were capable."

At the other end of Pennsylvania Avenue that Friday morning, Knowland and Saltonstall were breakfasting with Dwight Eisenhower. Encircled by reporters as he was leaving the White House, Knowland held up a copy of the President's July 17 statement and pointed to a sentence that someone had underlined at that breakfast table: "A jury trial should not be interposed in contempt of court cases growing out of violations of [court] orders." Knowland told the reporters that he was authorized to say that that sentence still represented the President's views.

Arriving back at the Senate Office Building, Knowland took the statement into a waiting Republican caucus in the Senate Caucus Room, and emerged to say that most of the eighteen Republicans who had deserted the Administration on Part III had returned on Part IV, and had pledged to stand against any jury trial amendment. Pressed for the number of Republican votes that were certain against the amendment, Knowland said, "Thirty-nine or forty." Saltonstall said, "More than forty." Checking with individual senators, reporters felt that these estimates were correct. If the fifteen "ardently civil rights" Democrats stick together, the *New York Post* observed, "their votes plus this GOP strength would be ample to insure the amendment's defeat."

Johnson flew to Texas late that Friday, but during his weekend on the ranch, he received another blow: proof that he had underestimated the depth of organized labor's commitment to civil rights. He had been hoping that labor would be enticed into support of the amendment by the extension of its jury trial guarantee to unions, but on Saturday, July 27, labor began to be heard from, in the form of a letter to Johnson from James B. Carey, president of the International Union of Electrical, Radio and Machine Workers. The amendment, Carey wrote, in a letter read to Johnson by Reedy over the telephone, "would prevent effective enforcement of the right to vote."

"The issue must be faced squarely," Carey said. "With respect to voting rights we can have either the right to vote or trial by jury for contempt. We cannot have both." And he said, "Labor will not barter away effective protection of the right of a Negro to register and vote" just to obtain gains for itself. Reedy also told Johnson that when the AFL-CIO issued its statement, it would echo Carey's. (Reedy's information was to prove reliable. Assailing the "iron determination of the Southern bloc in the Senate to resist any civil rights legislation," the labor federation would say that it "cannot and will not permit itself" to support a "crippling amendment" just because it offers "advantages to organized labor." Hubert Humphrey said he had checked with many union leaders, and had not "found a soul who was buying this stuff."

That weekend was filled with the boasts of Johnson's liberal and Republican opponents. Beaming out of the television screens on CBS's Sunday *Face the Nation* show, Humphrey said that the amendment's supporters "haven't got the votes." Announcing that he was going to demand a ballot that very week, Knowland said he had the votes—enough to defeat the amendment and pass the bill intact, not only enough votes but votes to spare. Journalists agreed. "The Republicans have an extraordinary unity" on Part IV, Doris Fleeson wrote. "Not more than five will join the Southern demand for jury trial." There was also a significant statement that weekend from Richard Russell. Catching him in the Senate Dining Room on Saturday, the AP's John Chadwick asked him if he would be willing to vote on the amendment during the next week. "I can't say that I am," Russell replied. Having come to the same conclusion as Knowland—that the South did not have enough allies to pass the amendment, and would lose the vote—the South was going to "extend debate" so that there would be no vote. The only news Johnson received that weekend was bad news. He had waged a spectacular fight, but he was going to lose. All his work, it seemed, had been for nothing.

ON MONDAY AND TUESDAY, or at least most of Tuesday, developments on the Senate floor appeared to confirm that appraisal. Monday, when Johnson returned from Texas, was bad, with Carey's letter being read into the record by Joe Clark, who used the occasion to jeer at Johnson's attempt to get labor support ("I hope that in due course the Majority Leader . . . will feel free to reveal to the Senate who are the labor leaders who favor a jury trial amendment"), with Javits holding the floor for hours, further antagonizing southerners by his manner, and with increasingly bitter squabbling between liberals and southerners. Knowland could not contain his gloating. In Robert Mann's words, "He taunted the southerners to begin their filibuster. 'Let's have it now and fight it out,' he said."

Tuesday—for most of the day at least—was worse. The day began for Johnson when, still in bed that morning, he was leafing through the *Washington Post* and came upon a large advertisement. It was "An Open Letter" to "the Senate of the United States," but it might have been addressed to him personally, so directly did it attack what he had been doing: "It would be better not to pass any civil rights legislation at all than to pass [this] bill. . . . We are in a better position to get justice in civil rights cases under existing laws than we would be if you pass the proposed 'jury trial' amendment." The letter was signed by eighty-one southern liberal leaders—including Aubrey Williams, Johnson's onetime boss at the National Youth Administration and for two decades one of his staunchest supporters. When he reached his office in the

Capitol, the day got even worse, for Reedy handed him the AFL-CIO statement, and just as he walked down the stairs and out onto the Senate floor, his
attempt to tamp down the outright antagonism between the South and the liberals that would destroy any hopes of compromise appeared to explode.

The explosion may have occurred partly because that morning two officers of the Tuskegee Civic Association appeared in the Senate Office Building
to describe the ongoing voting dispute in Alabama's Macon County. They did it
at a news conference called by "the all-out civil rights forces." The conference
had been designed to attract publicity, and in that aim it failed: coverage the
next day would be scant; the *New York Times* didn't carry a word. But while
reporters didn't come to the conference, senators did—eleven of them, including Paul Douglas and ten members of the Douglas Group, Republicans as well
as Democrats—and they heard for themselves as the two Alabamans, W. P.
Mitchell and Linwood T. Dorsey, told not only about the voucher system and
other devices employed to discourage Negro voting, but also about brutal
police raids on the offices of organizations that encouraged Negro registration.
As the senators listened, the gravity that some of them had assumed for the
benefit of the one or two photographers present seemed to deepen into a feeling
more genuine, and several picked up the printed text of the two Alabamans'
statements and began reading intently, with expressions of shock on their faces.
If these liberal senators had forgotten what they were really fighting for, they
were reminded that morning. The news conference ended shortly after the Senate's noon bell rang, and they walked out on the Senate floor full of indignation, and as they came through the double doors, Richard Brevard Russell was
speaking, at his center-aisle desk, as courteous and urbane as ever, and he was
denying that Negroes were excluded from voting or jury service in the South,
illustrating his point with homey anecdotes ("Mr. President, I well remember
the first time I ever went into a federal court as an attorney. . . . I think it was in
the year 1920. . . . It so happened that I was representing a man by the name of
Polk Manders, who had been caught at a still where illicit whiskey was being
made. . . . A great deal of that kind of activity has occurred in my section of the
country in times past. . . . On the panel which tried him were two of our Negro
citizens . . .")—and their indignation boiled over. As soon as Russell finished,
Javits said, "Mr. President, I do not think it is fair to let the record stand as it
is. . . . I know, and every other senator knows, that there are Negroes who serve
on juries in the South. We also know that there are Negroes who vote in the
South. . . . I invite the attention of senators to the facts on the merits, Mr. President. One fact is that in case after case after case, including cases in Georgia,
the Supreme Court has had to void verdicts of juries in cases involving crimes
as serious as murder because there was a systematic exclusion of Negroes from
juries." Then Douglas was recognized. Russell had referred to the recent race
riots in Chicago and Detroit, and Douglas admitted that such riots had
occurred. "But I can say that in the city of Chicago, Negroes vote," he went on.

"They are not compelled to ride on segregated cars. They are not segregated in the schools. They have access to the parks and other public facilities. In these respects and many others their dignity is not offended. They are treated as human beings." He pointed a long arm at Russell, sitting among his massed southerners in the center section. "We are not trying to cover up abuses," Douglas shouted. "We are trying to remedy them; and I only wish my good friends from the South would adopt a similar attitude, instead of trying to sprinkle rose water on what we know to be great abuses."

And Johnson's long attempt to avoid outright antagonism on the Senate floor may also have exploded because Russell was losing on the jury trial amendment—and because losing was something that, despite his urbanity, Russell could not bear. At one point during Douglas' outburst, the Illinois Senator, still pointing across the floor at Russell, said that "the Senator from Georgia has evidently been counting noses," and knows he is losing. And when Douglas said that, Russell jumped to his feet, and, as William V. Shannon wrote, "stood upon the Senate floor and tore the mask of civility from the face of the civil rights debate"—and in the process also allowed the mask to fall from his own face, as it had fallen before on the rare occasions when he had been losing. The high patrician brow and the arched patrician nose were flushed with anger, and in his eyes as he stared across the desks at Paul Douglas was fury. "The Senator from Illinois points his admonitory finger," Russell shouted. "He says, 'You gentlemen are too sensitive.' Then he proceeds against our social order."

"Hypocrisy!" Richard Brevard Russell shouted. "Sanctimony! Holier-than-thou!" Then, as Shannon reported, "he defended segregation in all its aspects."

"You've failed in the North," Russell said. "Your method does not work. You have race riots. But you come down and say, 'We know better. We are going to force you to do things our way.' I say, keep your race riots in Chicago. Don't export them to Georgia."

Suddenly the scene among the four long arcs of desks was a scene unpleasantly reminiscent of Senate civil rights debates of previous years. Hoisting himself upright and holding on to his desk for support because in his emotion he had forgotten to pick up his crutches, Potter of Michigan shouted to the dais, "Mr. President, will the Senator yield?" Russell had no choice because, by mentioning Detroit, he had referred to Potter's state, and if there was anything almost as sacred to Richard Russell as the untainted blood of a pure white race, it was the Senate rules. "I yield," he said grudgingly.

"None of us from the North are proud of the fact that race riots took place," Potter began. "But Negro citizens in our state have every opportunity to vote."

Russell interrupted him. "Oh, they vote in my state, too," he said. "They vote as freely in Georgia as they do in Michigan. I am becoming tired of hearing that kind of statement." Russell had no right to interrupt him, Potter said. "The Senator referred to Michigan." "Yes, I did," Russell admitted. "I should like to have him listen to my reply for a moment," Potter said. His reply was that despite the riots, "great progress has been made in Michigan. . . . Because there are tensions we do not stick our heads in the sand."

Russell's face was a very deep red now. "I am delighted to hear the Senator say that progress is being made," he said. Then he said, "The system which the senator from Michigan wants to impose on Georgia brought about race riots in Michigan. . . . If the Senator from Michigan would simply not seek to invade our state to fasten the race riot–generating system upon us, we would appreciate it. Let him keep it in Michigan." All over the Chamber, on both sides of the aisle, senators were on their feet shouting for the floor. At first Russell refused to yield it, but one of the senators was Pat McNamara, also of Michigan. "Yes; I yield to the Senator from Michigan," Russell said at last. "I mentioned his state." McNamara said Michigan needed no defense, that his state could handle its affairs without outside interference. "Then why does not the Senator let us do the same?" Russell asked. There was applause from the southern senators seated around him, but he had asked a question, and he was to receive an answer to it. "McNamara," Doris Fleeson wrote, "roared in the bull voice trained in a thousand union meeting halls: 'Because you've had ninety years and haven't done it!' "

The galleries above burst into applause; appalled ushers rushed to still it. The two senators stood there shouting at each other, in their contrasting accents. "I do not know what all the smog is about," McNamara said. "I agree with the Senator from Michigan that he doesn't know what it is all about," Russell said. The southerners laughed. "I agree that one of us does not know what it is all about, but I am not sure that I am the one," McNamara said. The galleries applauded. Russell's rhetoric escalated into the rhetoric of martyrdom: when Florida's Spessard Holland tried to change the subject, Russell said, "Here we have a senator who wants to take time out from being crucified." *He* didn't want any time-outs; for more than three hours, he stood there, lashing out at the North—while the North lashed back.

Almost as dramatic to the journalists as the shouts of the debaters was the demeanor of the Majority Leader. "As Russell raged on," Shannon wrote, "Lyndon Johnson slumped further and further down in his seat. Misery and nervous irritability distorted his features." Then, as the man standing at the desk immediately behind him continued to rage, Johnson turned his chair all the way around, either to look right up at Russell—or, as Doris Fleeson suggested, for another reason: so that his face would be concealed from the Press Gallery, "so that the reporters could not judge his reaction to the damage being done" to his plans.

For seven months he had managed to maintain a layer of civility between the liberals and the South—against long odds. But now, "in three hours," as

Mary McGrory wrote, "the veneer of senatorial courtesy which has given a high gloss to . . . weeks of debate" had cracked wide open. "The attempt to make the whole question a constitutional problem rather than a human one abruptly collided, as Senator Russell . . . shouted . . . at the opposition."

Contained in the angry exchanges that had rumbled back and forth just over Lyndon Johnson's head, moreover, almost lost in the general invective but picked up quite clearly by his keen ears, had been some particularly disturbing sentences. At one point, Douglas, taunting Russell because he didn't have the votes, had demanded that the ballot on the jury trial amendment come soon— and had made the demand not only of Russell but of him: "I think the Majority Leader could do very well" by scheduling the vote "not later than Saturday," Douglas had said. "I wonder if the Majority Leader would consider that as a possible proviso." And when Johnson had replied that he had "not given any thought to the matter," Douglas had been insistent: "How about Monday? How about voting on the O'Mahoney Amendment on Monday?" The civil rights forces, knowing they had the majority, were pressing for a vote—as they had pressed for a vote in past years. Russell, lashing back at McNamara, had suddenly said, apropos of nothing in his previous remarks, "So, Mr. President, we have tried to act like reasonable men. We have tried to act with restraint in the face of great provocation. . . . But, Mr. President, we reserve the right to defend ourselves. . . . As responsible men, we shall insist on our right to be heard fully on all amendments to the pending bill." And there had been another development, peripheral but also an ominous straw in the wind. With funds for the Small Business Administration due to run out on Wednesday, July 31—the very next day—Johnson, attempting to avoid the closing of the agency, had requested a unanimous consent agreement to take up its appropriation bill, and then return immediately to the civil rights debate. His request, however, had not been granted: Wayne Morse had objected; and there had been other hands raised on the floor when the presiding officer had recognized Morse; other senators were prepared to object. The Senate had not been able to take up urgent public business. That Tuesday afternoon, the body had, as Fleeson wrote, "suddenly reverted to type." It was beginning, more and more, to resemble Senates of the past, in which the position of the Majority Leader had not been an enviable one. Scott Lucas and Boob McFarland had been in the same position that Lyndon Johnson was very close to being in now, unable to muster either the votes to end a filibuster or the votes to pass the amendment that alone could persuade the South *not* to filibuster. He was coming closer and closer to losing control of the Senate—as Lucas had lost control, as McFarland had lost control just before becoming objects of ridicule. A column by Murray Kempton published that Tuesday showed how perilously close Lyndon Johnson was to the same fate that had befallen his two hapless predecessors. Johnson, Kempton wrote, was "almost the prisoner of the South," and "with the 20-year dominant coalition between Southern Democrats and Midwestern Republicans in ruins,

Lyndon Johnson's cupboard is bare. The politicians who count in the Senate today are William F. Knowland and Richard M. Nixon; and Lyndon Johnson is a state of things whose time is past." Kempton wrote about "the desperation with which Lyndon Johnson wriggled for delay," and about the fact that his wriggling was hopeless. "The Democrats wondered yesterday, with Johnson in the shadows, how they could meet Nixon's triumphant kind of calculation." There was a phrase in Kempton's column that the leader was not used to seeing written about himself; the phrase was "poor Lyndon Johnson." And the most hurtful aspect of the column by this bellwether of liberal opinion may have been its implications for Johnson's hope that he could use the civil rights fight to get closer to the Democratic Party's liberal wing. Kempton's column showed how very far he was from achieving that end.

LATE TUESDAY AFTERNOON, however, things began to improve. There had, during those last days in July, been two developments that Lyndon Johnson had hoped would get him some of the votes he needed, and they both began to come to fruition not long after he had dejectedly returned, at about four o'clock, to his office from those three hours of "misery" on the Senate floor.

The first development could be called a lucky break—unless one believes that man in part makes his own luck, and that if he pushes against a wall long enough and hard enough, refusing to stop, a crack will eventually appear somewhere in the wall; and unless one believes also that the "crack" wouldn't have produced Senate votes for civil rights had not Lyndon Johnson known, as apparently no one else knew, how to widen it.

While Lyndon Johnson had been in Texas the previous weekend, the telephone calls from Reedy had told him that his attempt to woo leaders of organized labor like Reuther and Carey and Meany with a jury trial amendment had apparently failed. That Sunday, however, a dissenting if informal, even offhand, remark had been made by a less important labor figure, Cyrus Tyree (Cy) Anderson, the rough-spoken, incisive chief Washington lobbyist for the Railway Labor Association, a loose central committee representing twelve railroad unions, or "brotherhoods." The remark was made in the unlikely setting of the Glen Echo Amusement Park in Maryland, where Anderson had taken his children for a Sunday outing, and it was made in the course of a rambling, desultory conversation with another man—a casual Capitol Hill acquaintance of Anderson's—who had taken his children there, too. But this casual acquaintance to whom Anderson made the remark—"Any labor guy who is against jury trials ought to have his head examined"—happened to repeat it to George Reedy Monday morning. Reedy didn't consider it especially significant, but he quoted it in a memorandum he gave to Johnson sometime after Johnson arrived back on Capitol Hill on Monday afternoon.

And Johnson acted on it.

No one had thought of the railroad brotherhoods as potential allies in the civil rights fight—for a very obvious reason: for almost a century they had been fighting *against* equal rights for black Americans. Ever since they had been formed, shortly after the Civil War, the brotherhoods had, in fact, been among the most rigid bastions of racial segregation in the entire labor movement. Most of them—including the four largest: the Brotherhood of Railroad Trainmen, the Brotherhood of Locomotive Firemen and Enginemen, the Brotherhood of Locomotive Engineers, and the Order of Railway Conductors and Brakemen—had outright "whites only" clauses in their constitutions which barred Negroes from membership. When, in 1955, some of the brotherhoods had sought affiliation with the AFL-CIO, they had employed subterfuges to evade the Federation's anti-discrimination requirement; the Trainmen, for example, had amended its constitution—not to remove the "whites only" clauses but rather to say that these clauses would not apply in states in which they conflicted with state law. In 1957, fewer than 2,000 of the Trainmen's 217,000 members—fewer than one out of a hundred—were not Caucasian. And some of the brotherhoods were even more rigidly racist than the Trainmen: the Firemen's Brotherhood, which had never had a Negro member, was that year determinedly contesting a lawsuit brought by Negro firemen to force that brotherhood to admit them. Few unions seemed less likely to be active supporters of a civil rights bill.

But Johnson saw why the brotherhoods might be turned into supporters. He understood what Cy Anderson had meant by his remark: the brotherhoods had suffered greatly from judges' use of criminal contempt proceedings without jury trials during the railroad labor wars of the 1880s and 1890s; and with the Taft-Hartley Act, which had revoked provisions of Norris–La Guardia, the spectre of such proceedings hung over the brotherhoods again. He understood, as well, that while the brotherhoods' once-immense political power had been declining because of the decline of the railroads, in one area of the country that power was still substantial—the immense flat plains of the Midwest. The Midwest, across which ran the great transcontinental rail lines, the Union Pacific and the Central Pacific and the Southern Pacific; the Midwest, which contained so many of the railroads' switchyards and stockyards and roundhouses, as well as the great hubs (Chicago, St. Louis, Topeka) from which lines ran out like spokes of a wheel; the Midwest, where so many small towns numbered railroad employees, well paid by the area's standards, among their leading, and politically influential, citizens; where so many of the leading law firms were on retainer to the railroads; where railroads, and their unions, had always been a particularly potent political force; where the support of railroad brotherhoods was still a key factor in deciding which senators were sent to, and kept in, Washington—the Midwest, whose senators were Republicans, conservative Republicans, the conservative Republicans whom he had, despite months of effort, been unable to break off from Knowland and Nixon.

On Tuesday morning, Lyndon Johnson telephoned Cy Anderson and asked for support for the jury trial amendment from the twelve brotherhoods—including a formal statement he could use to counter Carey's.

With his eyes focused on organized labor as a source of support for a jury trial amendment, suddenly Johnson saw more. There was one union to whom the memory of the power of federal court injunctions was especially fresh and bitter: the United Mine Workers. It had been as recently as 1946 that Harry Truman had seized the coal mines, and a federal judge had enjoined the UMW from striking, had then held the UMW's glowering, bushy-eyebrowed John L. Lewis in contempt of court for refusing to obey the injunction, and had forced him to order his miners back to work by imposing a potentially ruinous fine on the union.

The center of the UMW's power was West Virginia. It was a one-industry state, and the industry was coal. No fewer than 117,000 miners, every one of whom belonged to the UMW, lived there. And West Virginia's two senators were the Republican Chapman Revercomb and the Democratic liberal Matthew Neely, both of whom had refused—Revercomb loudly on the Senate floor, Neely through aides from his hospital bed—to support the jury trial amendment. The UMW's chief counsel, and a man Lewis trusted as much as he trusted anyone, was none other than Johnson's friend Welly Hopkins; it had been Hopkins who had dragged the raging Lewis back into his seat in the courtroom in 1946 before Lewis could compound the contempt offense; and then Hopkins, beside himself with anger, had shouted defiantly at the judge, "This day will live in infamy, sir!" Now, on Tuesday morning, Johnson telephoned Welly, and asked him for a formal statement of support from John L. Lewis.

Anderson had to go through channels, with twelve separate brotherhoods. Hopkins had to make only one telephone call. At 2:48 that same day—Tuesday, July 30—while Johnson had been slumped down in his seat on the Senate floor listening to Richard Russell rant, John L. Lewis sent him a telegram. The United Mine Workers, the telegram said, "HAVE TRADITIONALLY, AND DO NOW, SUPPORT APPROPRIATE LEGISLATION LOOKING TO THE FULL ENJOYMENT BY ALL CITIZENS OF ALL CIVIL RIGHTS." And, the telegram said, the UMW also supported the jury trial amendment—"A WISE, PRUDENT AND PROPER AMENDMENT. . . . THE STRONG POWER OF INJUNCTION HAS BEEN IN THE PAST SO OFTEN ABUSED. . . ."

Sometime after Johnson had returned to his office from the Senate floor about four o'clock, the telegram was shown to him. He returned to the floor. The time was about 5:40. Olin Johnston was droning on. Asking the South Carolinian to yield, Johnson read the telegram, maximizing the impact by implying that it was an unsolicited bolt from the blue. "John L. Lewis had never communicated with me directly or indirectly until 2:48 p.m. today, when he sent me the following telegram," he said. And even before he came to the floor, Johnson had used the telegram; he "saw to it," as James Reston commented drily, that it "was brought to Revercomb's attention." On Lyndon Johnson's smudged tally sheet, a number was erased from the right side of Revercomb's name, and a number was written on the left side.

And Neely's staff had been contacted, and a message had been sent to Bethesda. The dying liberal had promised Douglas and Knowland that he would leave the hospital and come to the Chamber in a wheelchair to cast his vote against the amendment if it was needed. Now, through his aides, that promise was withdrawn. Neely could not bring himself to vote for the amendment, but he said he would not leave the hospital to cast a vote at all. Although only one West Virginia vote would be added to the votes for the amendment, therefore, two were subtracted from the votes against it. The count had been perhaps 53–42 against Johnson before, but it was 51–43 now. He was only eight behind.

WITH THE OTHER DEVELOPMENT that came to fruition that Tuesday, luck had no connection at all. It was the result of another talent Lyndon Johnson had been displaying during the civil rights fight. Although it was not a new talent, it had previously been used mainly with his own staff. It had never before been used with senators—because never before had Lyndon Johnson been fighting for a great cause.

It was a talent not merely for persuading men, but for inspiring them.

Frank Church had had six months now to learn the cost of crossing Lyndon Johnson. Young as he was, the tall, slender senator looked even younger with his big, toothy grin, shiny black hair, and cheeks so pink that he seemed to be perpetually blushing; once, while he was waiting for an elevator in the Capitol, a woman tourist said to him, "I understand that one of you page boys gets mistaken for Senator Frank Church"; "Yes, ma'am," Church replied, "one of us often does." And sometimes during his first months in the Senate, he acted younger, too, and not only because he was, as his biographer wrote, "bursting with energy and ambition"; in some ways, in those days, he displayed an idealism reminiscent of Jimmy Stewart as the young senator in the movie *Mr. Smith Goes to Washington*—right down to the fact that both of them had been amateurs in politics (a lawyer by profession, Church's only political venture before his victorious Senate campaign had been an unsuccessful try for the State Legislature), and for both of them their first major Senate issue was the same: opposition to a private power company dam. Wags in the Press Gallery, amused by Church's naïveté as much as by his youthfulness, mockingly called him "Senator Sunday School." But he was already making a mark in Washington, with the help of his vivacious wife, Bethine.

Bethine Clark Church did not fit that era's mold of the docile Washington political wife, for while Frank was new to politics, she had been born into it, into Idaho's Democratic dynasty, the "Clark Party." She had been raised in the

Governor's Mansion; during her girlhood her father was Idaho's Governor, one of her uncles, D. Worth Clark, was Idaho's United States Senator; another uncle had been the state's Governor some years before. She and the young man who had fallen in love with each other in high school were an exceptionally close couple; years later, one of Church's staffers would call their marriage "the longest-running high school romance in history." She loved to watch the Senate. "I had one child when we came here, and then two, but somehow I always managed to go," she would say. "It was the best show in town. . . . I was so fascinated. The Senate . . . made you think of the letters of Jefferson and Adams." And she understood the Senate, and explained its mores to her husband ("It was through his wife mainly that he understood the senatorial tradition," says his administrative aide, John Carver), giving him advice with a canniness that would later lead political insiders to call her "Idaho's third senator."

In early July, Johnson's iciness—his refusal even to speak to Church which had begun in January after Church cast the vote that made Johnson throw his pen down on his desk—had not begun to melt. After Clint Anderson had made him understand that it was Johnson's "doing, not yours," that had gotten the Hells Canyon bill passed, he had tried to mend fences in writing ("All credit is due to your leadership"), but while Reedy wrote a warm response for Johnson's signature, the Leader was as cold as ever in person, and Bobby Baker's warning that "The Leader's got a long memory" was proven correct. After six months, her husband was still "a pariah," Bethine recalls; "I was in a deep freeze," Church would say. And he very much wanted to thaw it.

Although Church was in favor of civil rights legislation, his interest in the subject was, according to his legislative aide, Ward Hower, "only intellectual," not "a visceral thing." The plight of black Americans "was not a big issue to Frank Church," perhaps because out of the six hundred thousand persons who lived in Idaho in 1957, only about one thousand were black. Bethine recalls that "one night Frank came home, and I asked are you going to get into this thing deeply, and he said, 'I've got a lot on my platter. It's not something I'm going to get involved over my head in.' " He would vote for the civil rights bill but not become an active participant in the struggle to pass it, he told her. Furthermore, in 1957, Idaho had only two representatives in the House, "so," Hower explains, "the Senate was the key for Idaho, like it was for the southerners. In the Senate, Idaho is equal to New York. For all the western senators, the Senate is their states' protection. The right to filibuster is important to them." He felt—as did many western senators from sparsely populated states—an identity with the southern senators' need to preserve the Senate's rules. But, Hower says, Church also knew that a reconciliation with Johnson was essential for his career, and "He was looking for a way to do something major for Johnson"—and "he understood that the civil rights bill was a key to Johnson's strong ambition to be President." And it was this understanding that, in mid-July, first got Church involved more deeply in the civil rights fight. In January, on the vote that had angered Johnson, Church had voted against the South; on July 24, on the vote to eliminate Part III from the bill, Church voted with it. Johnson's attitude toward him became noticeably warmer. On July 26, when O'Mahoney was introducing the jury trial amendment that the South wanted, Church rose from his back-row desk as O'Mahoney was speaking, walked down one row and over along the desks to O'Mahoney's, and whispered in his ear, whereupon O'Mahoney announced, "Mr. President, since I began the presentation of this matter, the distinguished junior senator from Idaho has asked to be recognized as a co-sponsor of the amendment. . . . We shall be happy to welcome the Senator from Idaho as a co-sponsor."

Johnson had appealed to Frank Church on civil rights partly on pragmatic grounds; Hower, for one, believes that the Foreign Relations seat was the key: "I don't think anything explicit was ever said—you didn't deal with Lyndon Johnson that way. But you knew that if you did him a favor, when the time came, if he could do you a favor. . . . This was the way Lyndon Johnson operated. There was a tacit *quid pro quo*." But Johnson had also appealed to elements in the young senator's character that were not pragmatic at all, as Bethine Church came to understand when, late each July evening now, her husband "replayed" for her the day's events. The Leader had appealed to her husband's sense of duty. "You're a senator *of the United States,*" he told Church. "You have to function as a senator of the United States. This is your national duty." He appealed to his sense of history—and to his desire to be part of it. "Frank always had a sense of history," Bethine says, "and he made Frank feel like he would be a *big* piece of history if he got involved in this." He appealed to his love of a challenge. "Lyndon knew he [Lyndon] needed something [to get the civil rights bill passed], and [he knew] he didn't have it," Bethine says. "They weren't going to beat a filibuster. They just wouldn't get the votes. And unless they got something more, there was going to be a filibuster. The South had said the blood was going to flow if there wasn't a jury trial amendment. And yet the other people felt the blood would flow if there *was* a jury trial amendment. Lyndon had to have something more." And, she says, he made her husband want to find that something. "He made Frank realize that they needed him. Lyndon said: If you don't help with this, there's not going to be a civil rights bill. It was a tremendous challenge, and Frank never loved anything as much as a challenge."

And Lyndon Johnson appealed to elements in Frank Church's character that were even less pragmatic than that.

Her husband's sense of justice, his wife says, was one of the things that had made her love him. Although she understood that the nickname "Senator Sunday School" was a sneer at his idealism, she "loved" that nickname, she would say. "That's how I saw him." Johnson made Church understand that the important thing was to get a bill passed, even if it wasn't a perfect bill ("that you could go on later and make it better," in Bethine's words), and that even if the bill protected only voting rights, it was worth passing, for voting rights were the key to equality for Negroes. And Johnson also made Church understand why equality for Negroes was important. Although her husband had never said it, Bethine says, "I knew that down deep underneath he cared terribly about equality. He just had never thought about it. And Lyndon brought it out. He appealed to this feeling in Frank. Lyndon made him realize that he cared very much about a civil rights bill. And that they needed him to get one passed. He would come home: 'This is *my* fight, too. I'm a *United States Senator,* and this is the only right way for the country.' Lyndon brought that out. It's almost a disservice to Frank to say this, but in the Senate, you have so much to do—you have too much to do. You really *do* have to pick your fights. And then suddenly Frank found out this was his fight, that this was something he deeply believed in." *Why did Frank come to feel this way?*—"Lyndon. Lyndon brought this out. It was a crusade for Lyndon. He was not going to be stuck with this southern image. And he believed in it—he talked about Cotulla. Lyndon brought this out in Frank."

Astute politically, Bethine Church understood that her husband was far from the only senator with whom Johnson was employing such appeals—that "when he said something like, We need you, if you don't help, there's not going to be a civil rights bill—well, I think Lyndon said that to everyone he could, to get them enlisted in this crusade." But she saw how effective such appeals were with her husband. Frank had said he wasn't going to get deeply involved. "And the next thing I knew, he was staying late, and at night, he was dead tired, but he just couldn't unwind. He was in all the way. Lyndon had gotten him in."

Knowing that Johnson needed "something more"—something that would attract new liberal and Republican votes for the jury trial amendment while not making it totally unacceptable to the South—Church, "being a lawyer," tried to "think about the amendment" as a lawyer, Bethine says, trying to imagine the details of a voting rights trial. He drafted—often in the evening, at home, on a yellow legal pad—more than a few proposed changes, but discarded them himself either after rereading them or after conferring on the telephone with O'Mahoney. And then one afternoon—probably on the Monday or Tuesday of that climactic week of July 29—while sitting with Bethine in his inner office in the Senate Office Building, "he started to think about the juries themselves and . . . it was like a light bulb going off!" Liberal antipathy to the amendment centered on the impossibility of getting a just verdict from the South's all-white juries. "All right," Bethine recalls Frank saying, "how about this?"—what if the juries weren't all-white? "If the juries couldn't be segregated, we could get the jury trial amendment through."

Church telephoned O'Mahoney, who, Bethine says, "refined the language—he was a wonderful lawyer," and then it was further refined, by Ward

Hower and Siegel and Horwitz, and when they had all finished, the proposed new paragraph in the jury trial amendment—the technical name for this amendment to an amendment is *addendum*—repealed the section of the United States Code that barred from federal jury duty citizens who did not meet their state's qualifications for jury duty. Since in southern states, one of the qualifications for proposed jurors was that they be registered to vote in the state, and since in southern states most Negroes were not registered to vote, it was primarily this section that allowed southern states to bar Negroes from jury duty. Church's addendum said that with the exception of illiterates, mental incompetents, and convicted criminals, "any citizen" twenty-one years old "is competent to serve as a juror." No one recalls who came up with the phrase that summed up the addendum's purpose in persuasive terms: with the addition of the new paragraph, the phrase went, the civil rights bill would not only reinforce an existing civil right, the right to vote, but would also confer on southern Negroes *"a new civil right"*: the right to sit on juries.

Church's addendum would appeal to northern liberals of both parties—Republicans like Case of New Jersey and Smith of Maine, Democrats like Frank Lausche, Green, Pastore, and Kennedy—who had been unwilling to vote for a civil rights bill that included a jury trial amendment that weakened the bill's primary purpose of strengthening the civil rights of Negroes to vote. That weakness would now be at least partially offset because the bill would give Negroes a *new* civil right. And for those liberals who were worried about the reaction of their constituencies ("They didn't want to be seen as participating in too much vitiating of the bill," Hower explains), the addendum would furnish them with a response to constituent anger. They could say that the addendum ensured that juries in voting cases would no longer be all white. While this statement was true, it ignored a significant point: although the addendum would allow Negroes to serve as jurors, there would still be whites on the juries, in the southern states probably a majority of whites, and even if there was only one white on a jury, one vote on a jury would be enough to prevent conviction, so that southern juries would probably still not convict whites in racial cases. Church saw the addendum as "symbolic," less a means of ensuring justice than "the means to pass the bill," says his administrative assistant, Carver; Church's legislative assistant, Hower, says, "In practice it would have meant very little in the Deep South, and I think he realized [this]. I'm tempted to use the word 'gimmick'—okay, I'm *using* the word 'gimmick.'" At first glance, however, the addendum appeared to make the bill significantly stronger, and that gave these civil rights–conscious senators an argument—a catchphrase, "a new civil right," which might be as effective with their constituents as the southern senators' catchphrase ("You can't be tried as a criminal without a jury") was with *their* constituents. The addendum "enabled a number of senators who could not have otherwise supported [the civil rights bill] to do so," Hower says. "All this going on in the context of the very delicate balance of changing one, or two, or three votes without losing someone on the other side," and the new paragraph accomplished that. What had been needed to attract new votes for the bill was an excuse, an excuse that would allow liberals to vote for it without provoking the South to vote against it. Now Church had thought of one. The "gimmick" might give the civil rights bill the last few votes it needed to pass—and the important thing was that it pass.

CHURCH WANTED to introduce his addendum immediately, but Johnson told him to wait. Every previously proposed alteration designed to make the jury trial amendment more acceptable to liberal senators had been scrutinized for flaws by liberal lawyers, and then those flaws had been criticized by liberal newspapers and by civil rights organizations until it was difficult for these senators to accept it. To minimize scrutiny of this proposed change, Johnson wanted it introduced only at the last possible moment, so that, as Reedy explains, "there would be no chance for opposition to be mobilized." He wanted it introduced at exactly the right moment—at the moment when the addition of a new, unexpected, element to the civil rights debate had the best chance of tipping the balance. And he didn't want the addendum simply to be introduced, he wanted its introduction staged for maximum effect. Lyndon Johnson, master of so many aspects of the legislative art, was about to demonstrate his mastery of one final aspect: the floor debate. While debates seldom change votes, there are rare issues on which they can do so, and this jury trial amendment with its tangle of compelling and conflicting arguments on both sides which had left many senators torn, might be one of them. If Frank Church's addendum was introduced at the right moment, and if the debate on the addendum was properly orchestrated for maximum effect, it might change a few votes—and a few was all Lyndon Johnson needed.

ON THE MORNING of Wednesday, July 31, Johnson still had only about forty-three votes. Knowland still had about fifty-one. That morning, the Republican Leader repeated his earlier flat refusals to compromise—to accept a jury trial amendment in any form whatsoever. With the amendment included, he said, the bill simply "would not be a workable piece of legislation." And he sent to the desk three unanimous consent agreements to set a definite hour for a vote on the complete bill. Under the first, the vote would be held on Thursday; under the second, on Friday; under the third, on Saturday. Each would allow six hours for debate prior to the vote. It quickly became apparent, however, that to the South the details of such agreements were irrelevant; no agreement was going to pass. When the clerk finished reading each agreement, Richard Russell said, "Mr. President, I object." After the third objection, Knowland, calling it "obvious that there are in prospect a considerable number of speeches on this issue," announced that he would insist on longer sessions "with a view to forcing a vote." But the South was not going to be forced. Russell rose to speak, and senators waited to hear what the South was going to do. "I have no desire to unduly prolong the debate but I shall insist that it be carried on so long as the representative of a single sovereign state . . . desires to address himself to it," he said. The escalation of debate into open filibuster was very near.

That morning, however, at eleven o'clock, Cy Anderson had been ushered into Johnson's private office in G-14 by George Reedy. Although the railroad brotherhoods had begun lobbying some senators on behalf of the jury trial amendment on Tuesday, their efforts had been desultory, and the brotherhoods themselves had not issued a statement publicly backing the amendment, as John L. Lewis had done. Lewis' support had brought West Virginia's two senators around, but in the midwestern states where the brotherhoods were strong, not a single senator's vote had been changed.

Behind the closed door of his office, Johnson explained to Reedy and Anderson why some of these midwestern Republican conservatives *should* change their votes, and the following day, Reedy, at Johnson's direction, embodied these arguments in a memorandum. Typed on plain white paper, the memo bore neither signature nor attribution. Its authorship and purpose, however, are clear from an attached cover note from Reedy to Johnson calling it "Some arguments tailored for Jenner, Goldwater, [Frank] Barrett, et al." It had been written by Reedy—at Johnson's close suggestion, if not dictation—to be handed to Republican conservatives to sum up, and lend the force of the printed word to, Johnson's attempts to persuade them to change their votes.

The memo struck at the heart of the argument that Nixon, Knowland, and the White House liaison men had been making, thus far with success, to hold these senators in line: that it was to the senators' political advantage to array themselves on the side of black Americans by opposing the jury trial amendment.

Despite the "glib talk" about "political advantages," the Johnson-Reedy memo said, "there are senators who had better stop, look, listen and think about the politics." Certainly "there *is* some political advantage for a man who is running for the Presidency in opposing the jury trial section," the memo said, but, it pointed out, these senators weren't running for the presidency. "A senator must run within his state," and therefore a senator "should think about those groups *within his state* that feel strongly." Among the groups opposing the jury trial amendment, the memo said, are the NAACP, "the Walter Reuther–Jim Carey–CIO–social reform section of labor," and "possibly some unorganized negroes," and a senator primarily interested in the support of such groups the next time he runs for re-election should therefore vote against the amendment. But, "on the other hand," the memo said, there are also groups supporting the amendment: "a) the railroad brotherhoods; b) Americans who feel strongly about the jury trial issue." And "some senators may feel that they would rather have the good will of the railroad brotherhoods and of [these] Americans." Senators should weigh this support against the other—"they should weigh carefully."

For senators more interested in the support of the brotherhoods than of the NAACP, for senators from states in which the right of jury trial was at least as prized as civil rights for Negroes—for midwestern senators, in other words— these were compelling reasons to reverse their position and support the jury trial amendment. And the memo gave other reasons, too, and while the political analysis had been couched in conventional, if incisive, terms, and cushioned with civility and ostensible sympathy, in the memo's discussion of these other reasons, the cushioning grew very thin, as if, with time almost run out, the velvet glove of senatorial courtesy was being stripped off the iron fist of senatorial power. In giving the other reasons, this memo, written by Reedy but embodying the thinking of Lyndon Johnson, comes close, in these last desperate days of a great battle, to putting in writing some realities of life in the Senate, where projects vital to a senator's future are at the mercy of leaders and chairmen with long memories.

"Another factor which must be considered," the memo said, "is the future relationships which Senators will have with their fellow Senators. *This frequently affects the type of legislation they can pass in the Senate* [italics in text]. Those who feel they are better off legislatively cooperating with Douglas, McNamara, Javits and Clifford Case will naturally have a tendency to vote against the jury trial amendment. Those who feel they are better off cooperating with Russell, Mansfield, Pastore, Young, etc. . . . . may have a tendency to vote" for the amendment.

WERE THE GLOVES almost off in the memo? In the face-to-face discussions that Johnson held with Anderson and lobbyists for the other brotherhoods, the gloves may have been removed completely, as not merely "future relationships" but present realities were laid bare. That 15 percent increase in retirement benefits that the brotherhoods wanted so badly? That bill was before the Senate Labor Committee, Lister Hill chairman—and southerner. Another bill giving the brotherhoods a generous tax exemption on retirement contributions was before the House Ways and Means Committee, Jere Cooper chairman— and southerner. And there were other unions with bills they wanted passed— and with their lobbyists, too, with time almost run out now, the gloves were off. There was a bill that would grant a pay raise to postal workers. The senatorial facts of life about that bill were laid out to representatives of the postal workers—not by Lyndon Johnson but by others, possibly by the chairman of the Senate's Post Office and Civil Service Committee, Olin Johnston. The facts were evidently laid out clearly enough so that they were understood. Suddenly, that Wednesday, outside the east door to the Senate Chamber, in that ornate, chandeliered reception room, there was a crowd of lobbyists, "the swarming representatives," as *Newsweek* put it, "of a dozen railroad brotherhoods and fifteen different postal workers unions. . . ."

"These lobbyists felt that if they urged the jury-trial amendment upon doubtful Republicans, they could reasonably expect a certain amount of gratitude on the part of Southern legislators," *Newsweek* reported. "And so they went to work, buttonholing one Republican after another" as the senators emerged from the Chamber to go to the dining room or the bathroom, sending notes in to senators who tried to avoid them by not emerging, and then, when in response to the notes these senators emerged, circling them in packs. That Wednesday afternoon, Knowland telephoned President Eisenhower to tell him, Ann Whitman's notes state, that "the lines were holding and that the Senate was in pretty good shape—that they had all the votes necessary." Actually, however, the lines were not holding, and late that afternoon there began to be word of "dramatic shifts" in Republican votes. It seems impossible, after the passage of so many decades, to determine exactly what factors motivated various Republican senators to change their stance on the jury trial amendment that day. In most cases, it was probably a combination of factors, and their relative weight can't be determined. In the case of one midwestern Republican, Schoeppel of Kansas, a key reason, according to contemporary news accounts, was a promise that Eastland's Judiciary Committee would at last report out the bill authorizing an additional federal judgeship for Kansas. But among the senators of whom Nixon and Knowland had been confident but who, according to news reports, changed their stance that day were not only Schoeppel but two other midwestern conservatives, Capehart and Curtis. And Republicans were not the only senators highly sensitive to union feelings. Thanks to John L. Lewis' telegram, as Evans and Novak were to write, "Wobbly Democratic liberals who, until then, had refused to join Johnson and the jury trial amendment, out of fear of alienating their liberal constituencies, now had a soft cushion to fall back on: support from an important segment of organized labor." At least one Democratic liberal, John Pastore, was swayed to the amendment's side that Wednesday. Under intense pressure from Nixon and Knowland, one or perhaps two Republicans who had been leaning toward the amendment leaned back that day, and the exact count shown on that smudged tally sheet in Lyndon Johnson's hands is not known, but if he had started the day with forty-three votes, he had more now, and if Knowland had started the day with fifty-one, he had fewer now.

The margin was down to two or three—or less.

IT WAS ALMOST TIME for the curtain to rise—for the drama that Lyndon Johnson was staging for the Church Addendum to begin—and Johnson had it all arranged. He had assembled an all-star cast of orators—fiery old O'Mahoney, fiery young Church, fiery little Pastore—and even the minor roles had been filled with care: a slow-talking, fast-thinking southerner with great presence, Herman Talmadge, was playing "the presiding officer." Johnson had given all of them their cues, and Church could hardly wait for his moment, but it was dinnertime, and many senators had left the floor to eat. Johnson told him to wait a little longer. He wanted a full house, and at about eight o'clock, when most senators had finished dinner, he asked for a quorum call. And when the floor was again full of senators—almost every desk occupied—the curtain went up.

O'Mahoney had the opening lines—two or three eloquent minutes: "Mr. President, it is my purpose tonight . . . to explain to the Senate, and to those who may be listening in the galleries, the reasons why I believe, from the depth of my soul, that the trial-by-jury amendment" should pass. Defeating it won't help Negroes to vote, O'Mahoney said. "Denial of trial by jury will not hasten a wise and permanent solution of the grave social problem of racial discrimination that is before us. . . . It will only make matters worse than they are, for trial by jury for criminal offenses is itself a civil right guaranteed to every citizen." And then, recalls Bethine Church, who was seated in the gallery, "Frank looked up at me, and I knew it was going to come."

Standing up at his desk in the back row, Church shouted, "Mr. President, will the Senator yield?" and O'Mahoney acted surprised at the interruption, and pretended reluctance. "I yield only with the understanding that I shall not lose the right to the floor," he said. Johnson, playing himself as Majority Leader, delivered his line in the charade. "Mr. President," he said, "I ask unanimous consent that the Senator from Wyoming may yield for not to exceed two minutes, with the understanding that he shall not lose the floor." Presiding Officer Talmadge intoned, "Without objection, so ordered," and Church introduced his amendment, saying it "is designed to eliminate whatever basis there may be for the charge that the efficacy of trial by jury in the Federal courts is weakened by the fact that, in some areas, colored citizens, because of the operation of State laws, are prevented from serving as jurors." Standing tall and straight among the freshmen in the back row, he said, "We believe the amendment constitutes a great step forward in the field of civil rights. We believe also that it can contribute significantly in forwarding the cause to which most of us are dedicated—the cause of enacting a civil rights bill in this session of the Congress." Then, as if he was unsure of the answer, he asked if O'Mahoney "would be agreeable to modifying [his] amendment to include the addendum I have before me." It turned out that O'Mahoney was indeed agreeable. "It was perfectly appropriate for the Senator from Idaho to offer this amendment, which I [am] so happy to accept," O'Mahoney assured him with a straight face. Ardent Johnson supporter that he was, Richard Neuberger could barely contain himself. In a reference to a hokey stage melodrama of the nineteenth century, he muttered: "What's next week? *East Lynne?*"

Stilted though it may have been, the opening scene captured the critics. Daughter of a governor, niece of a senator, born to politics, Bethine Clark Church glanced automatically over at the Press Gallery when O'Mahoney agreed to accept the amendment, and what she saw was rows of reporters jumping up "like a wave" and running up the stairs to the telephones in the Press Room.

Then the rest of Johnson's scenario unfolded. The Rhode Island bantam with the nimble mind asked for recognition from the chair. No one—not even Johnson's staff—knew "what John Pastore was going to do," says Solis Horwitz, who had been invited to sit, on a folding chair, next to Johnson to watch the show. "[Lyndon] did, because he said, 'Now you just watch the little Italian dancing master and see what happens here.' "

Johnson had cast Pastore in a demanding role: that of a skeptic and doubter who, by giving voice to his doubts, convinces himself that they are groundless and is converted into a true believer. The subject of his doubts, of course, was the jury trial amendment; Johnson had arranged with Pastore to, in Mann's words, "feign skepticism" of the amendment, to raise the questions about it that many senators were asking, and then to think through the answers to the questions out loud—and finally, seeing the validity of the answers, to be convinced by them, to "almost imperceptibly dissolve his skepticism into outright support" for the amendment. The Rhode Islander began to ask questions of O'Mahoney—the questions that many senators, uncertain about the amendment, were asking themselves: Would the amendment, for example, permit a southern registrar who had been jailed by a judge for civil contempt and then freed when he promised to register Negroes then be able to violate his promise and be in effect immune from punishment because that violation would be criminal contempt, and he would therefore be eligible for trial before a sympathetic jury that would not convict him? When O'Mahoney replied that there was no danger of this, because the judge would have ordered the registrar to register Negroes, and any violation of this order would still be civil, not criminal, contempt, Pastore said, "I think the Senator from Wyoming is moving a little too quickly. I think I know what he means, but I do not believe the *Record* is abundantly clear"—and led O'Mahoney through the reasoning again step by step until the densest senator could grasp it. And with each question that he asked, Pastore reiterated that he was asking it only to try to resolve his own doubts, that he still had "an open mind. . . . I have not as yet definitely resolved the matter in my own mind." As he assured himself on point after point—after saying, on point after point, "I have not been able to make up my mind"—his "misgivings" about the amendment faded, to be replaced by support.

"All of this had been preplanned," Horwitz was to realize, "and [Pastore] did one of the most effective jobs that was ever done." His colloquy with O'Mahoney riveted the attention of both sides of the aisle. There were senators—Republican conservatives from the Midwest, most of them—who still had sincere questions about the amendment. From far across the floor, Thye of Minnesota, hater of Democrats, interrupted to ask a question of a Democrat. "The Senator from Rhode Island was making a very impressive statement," Thye said. "He asked a question. I am as vitally concerned with the answer to that question as [he] is. . . . If he [O'Mahoney] has the answer, I hope he will give it." And while O'Mahoney was giving it—during the entire long colloquy, in fact—the Chamber was so still that although the two Democrats' desks, both in the third row, were somewhat far to the side of the Chamber, and only three desks apart, no one in the Chamber had any difficulty hearing them. By the time Pastore finished "resolving" his doubts—in favor of the jury trial amendment—and said earnestly, "I cannot subscribe to the argument" that the amendment "would be emasculating the bill . . . I cannot go along with that argument," he had convinced others. The show Johnson had staged produced the result he wanted. "The impact of Pastore's performance was profound," Mann writes. "He played the role of an earnest, undecided senator. But he had actually led his colleagues through a crafty, subtle argument for the amendment." All through Senate history, there had been speeches that made senators rethink their views. This was one of them. It "actually changed some votes," George Reedy says. And the next morning—Thursday, August 1—brought to Lyndon Johnson's office the telegram he had been waiting for: a statement signed by the presidents of the twelve railroad brotherhoods. It was much shorter than John L. Lewis' and quite straightforward: "WE FAVOR THE ENACTMENT OF AN AMENDMENT TO THE CIVIL-RIGHTS BILL THAT WOULD PRESERVE OR EXTEND THE RIGHT TO TRIAL BY JURY." Now Johnson had all the ammunition he needed. That morning, Welly Hopkins telephoned him to ask how things were going. They were going just fine, Johnson said. Hopkins recalls that Johnson mentioned "certain senators. . . . He said, 'I've got them. I'm just going to pick my time to call them. That's when I'm going to put it to a vote.'" And that day, August 1, Lyndon Johnson sprang his trap.

WILLIAM KNOWLAND WALKED straight into it—blind till the last. That very Thursday morning, at about the same time that Johnson was telling Hopkins that everything was going fine, Knowland was telling reporters—and the White House and Vice President Nixon—that everything was going fine, and reiterating his confidence that "at least thirty-nine or forty" Republican senators would join at least a dozen Democratic liberals in voting against the jury trial amendment. Asked by a reporter whether Church's addendum would strip away any of the Republican votes, the Republican Leader said he thought not. That morning, copies of the brotherhoods' telegram were delivered to the offices of individual senators, to be followed by visits from Cy Anderson and other union lobbyists. Pastore's logic had had time to sink in. And that morning, Lyndon Johnson made his calls—and after several of them, erased the number that he had placed next to senators' names in one column on his tally sheet and wrote a number in the other column. Richard Russell was also keeping his own very careful tally sheet, and early that afternoon he told Johnson, "I'm ready to vote. I've got fifty votes."

Knowland, however, still believed his own vote count. At any time he might realize the truth, and if he did, he would naturally change tactics: stop pressing for an early vote, and instead try to delay one. Votes had been changing back and forth for days and White House pressure might well change some back again; a delay would afford time for that pressure to do its work. So Johnson made it very difficult for Knowland to change tactics. In a private talk now, he said he assumed that Knowland still wanted to vote as soon as possible. Knowland said he did, and Johnson quickly made those feelings public. Interrupting an exchange about the bill, he said, "I have conferred with the Minority Leader. I know how anxious he is for an early vote. I . . . am equally anxious to vote [and] I express the hope that we may be able to call the roll before the evening is over." Turning to Knowland, who was standing next to him, he said, "I would assume that meets with the pleasure of my friend from California." His friend from California said, "Yes . . . I wish to say that I am encouraged by the remarks of my good friend, the Senator from Texas, that he feels we may be approaching a time when we can get a vote."

Later that afternoon, the GOP had yet another encounter with reality. While Knowland couldn't count, Nixon could, and coming to the Capitol, he did so—and promptly launched a frantic Republican lobbying campaign. One after another, GOP senators were summoned to the Vice President's Room, "for," in Douglas Cater's words, "the kind of subtle persuasion an administration in office can exert." General Persons hurried over from the White House, and so did Postmaster General Arthur E. Summerfield, who, as Cater puts it, "suddenly found it a matter of convenience to discuss postmaster appointments." Deputy Attorney General William P. Rogers arrived to answer senators' technical questions. But at 5:40 p.m., Lyndon Johnson asked for recognition from the chair to propose a unanimous consent agreement to set a time for the vote on the jury trial amendment. And the Majority Leader didn't propose his own agreement, but rather the very same agreement that had been proposed on Wednesday—had been proposed three times on Wednesday—by the Minority Leader. "Mr. President," Lyndon Johnson said, "yesterday the distinguished Minority Leader offered a unanimous consent agreement. I wish to offer the same agreement today with two modifications." The modifications would bring on the vote even faster than the distinguished Minority Leader had wanted; Knowland had, for example, allowed six hours for debate on the amendment. "In view of the fact that we have spent a good deal of time today on the bill, I am reducing the . . . hours from six to four," Johnson said. Knowland, aware now that the vote would be, at the least, very close, said he still preferred six, and Johnson suavely said that that was fine with him. Knowland could offer no other objection—he could hardly object to an agreement he himself had proposed over and over, telling the Senate each time how vital its passage was. As they realized the significance of Johnson's proposal, and the reason why he had made it, liberal senators from both sides of the aisle gathered in little groups on the floor, trying to think what they could do about it. But they could do no more than Knowland had. If Knowland had proposed the agreement yesterday, they had supported it, with equal vehemence; they were hardly in a position to object to it now. Spessard Holland, in the chair, asked, "Is there objection to the unanimous consent request?" There was only silence. "The Chair hears none, and it is so ordered," Holland said.

Johnson then addressed the chair again. The vote on the jury trial amendment would probably take place that very evening, he said. "It is the intention of the leadership to remain here until a vote is had."

Irving Ives asked: "When does the debate start? Does it start right now?"

"Right now," Lyndon Johnson said.

Checkmate.

THE REST was anticlimax. Offstage, off the floor, the Republican efforts intensified now that the Vice President was directing them in person. Aware now that every vote was needed, the GOP managed to contact Maine's Senator Frederick G. Payne, who had been recuperating from a heart attack and was at his fishing camp in the Maine woods, and persuaded him to fly to Washington for the vote.

Other attempts were less successful, however. Schoeppel and Butler had been two votes of which Knowland had been confident, but now it was suddenly realized that that confidence had not been justified. General Persons telephoned the White House to have Eisenhower speak to the two senators in person. Ann Whitman had to tell the General that the President was out on the golf course, at Burning Tree. Whitman managed to get in touch with him there, and he agreed to see Schoeppel, but when Persons attempted to contact the Senator to arrange a time for the appointment, it proved so difficult that it became obvious that Schoeppel was "avoiding" Persons. "Senator Butler also would not come to see the President," Whitman wrote in her diary.

That evening, Joe Rauh and Paul Sifton, chief lobbyist for Reuther's UAW, bumped into Nixon and Rogers right outside the Chamber. "They stopped us and we compared notes on how the votes were going to go, and it was clear it was going to go very badly," Rauh was to recall. "It was clear that Johnson had the votes." Nixon could barely contain his anger. Encountering Johnson in the Senate Reception Room, he said, smiling tightly, "You've really got your bullwhip on your boys tonight, Lyndon." As he started to walk by, Johnson replied angrily, "Yes, Dick, and from the way you've been trying to drive your fellows, you must have a thirty-thirty strapped to your hip, but it's not doing you any good." "Just wait," Nixon said grimly (and incorrectly). "You'll find out."

The setting was the Senate Chamber, of course.

The word had gone out through official Washington that the big vote would be that evening, and the galleries in the Chamber had begun to fill up early in the evening, not with visitors to the city but with its own people, men and women connected with, or fascinated by, government, who wanted to see one of government's big shows. Evening became night, a hot, muggy Washington summer night, and more spectators came in from dinner parties, some of which had been formal parties at foreign embassies, and in the galleries were jewels and bare shoulders and white shirtfronts and dark suits. The Capitol dome was lit. It gleamed over Washington, high above the men and women walking toward the long, shadowy eastern façade, or driving down Pennsylvania Avenue. The visitors came in out of the dark evening, up the broad marble stairs and between the tall columns, through the bronze doors into corridors sparkling with the crystal and cut glass of chandeliers, and they walked along those corridors past the busts of statesmen and the paintings of heroes, under the richly hued frescoes, into the galleries rimming the long, high-ceilinged room with its pale walls and its four glowing mahogany arcs, until finally even the aisles in the galleries were filled to overflowing, spectators sitting on each step. "There are times—they are very rare—when a scene worth remembering, a moment of real drama and meaning, occurs on the Senate floor," Stewart Alsop was to write. "[This] was such a moment. . . . It was a scene of a sort that occurs only once or twice in a decade—every fit Senator on the floor, and the galleries choked with spectators. All present, spectators and senators alike, were caught up in the excitement of the great Senate game. A man's pulse can be quickened, after all, by a close contest at chess, or on the golf course. But there is nothing quite like the Senate game. . . ."

Below the spectators, among the arcs of desks, senators were making speeches as senators had been making speeches among the desks since the birth of the Republic. There were speeches by liberals assailing the amendment. "Somehow this debate got off on the wrong foot," Hubert Humphrey said. "Somehow or other we have been more concerned about those who have abused the law, who have denied people the equal protection of the law, than we have been with those who have been victimized." Paul Douglas said, "All that the pending bill seeks to do is to permit the government of the United States to come into the lists in defense of the poor, the weak, the disinherited, and the disenfranchised. The proposal to inject a jury trial will, if adopted, nullify the law in most cases." Liberals had become furious as there sunk in on them the realization that they had been outgeneraled, and that their victory was about to be snatched away from them, in that vote that was suddenly so close upon them. "I hope some of my colleagues . . . will give real and serious thought to whether the Church Amendment which was offered so recently is really understood by the members of this august body who are being called upon to pass it at this time," Joe Clark said. Some of the liberals cited past cases—such as the one in Alabama's Bullock County—to prove that southern justice could not be trusted; Cliff Case asked that the judge's opinion in *Sellers et al. v. S. B. Wilson et al.* be read into the record, and said the outcome of this "travesty of justice" proved the need for a stronger bill. "What happened, Mr. President?" Case cried. "All members of the Board resigned. The court found, of course, that it was unable to grant the relief, because there was no one on whom its order could operate. . . . Mr. President, I suggest that the opponents of the pending legislation from those states do not come before the Senate with clean hands." There were speeches by liberals emphasizing that it was only the addition of the Church Addendum that made it possible for them to vote for the jury trial amendment. "A vote against this amendment is not only a vote against the jury trial," old Jim Murray said. "It is also a vote against the rights of Negroes to serve on our federal juries. I cannot cast a vote against two elementary civil rights."

There was also a speech by Frank Church. Many speeches in great Senate debates since the birth of the Republic were bombast for the record, but there were some in this debate that were more than that, and Church's was one of them. "I can still see him standing there in that back row, so tall and straight," his wife was to say more than forty years later. "Senator Sunday School." And she was not the only one in the Senate Chamber who was moved, particularly by the part of the speech in which the young senator was echoing the argument of his Leader that the most important consideration was to take a first step, even if it was not a perfect step.

"Civil rights legislation is long overdue," Frank Church said. "But in no field of legislative endeavor must we build more carefully or more thoughtfully than here. This field bears the same relationship to other legislative fields as the building of a cathedral bears to the building of a factory. In the field of civil rights, we give voice to the finest impulses of our humanity. . . . Our workaday structures, as our workaday laws, may be built with ordinary materials. But we must build our places of worship and our laws of liberty with the finest of materials and the greatest of care. These we build for the ages. . . . Mr. President, I submit that our work in safeguarding civil rights cannot be accomplished in a single stroke. This law is but a single step. It is a law confined to voting rights. It may well be . . . that in the future this bill may need to be enlarged. . . . If we provide proper procedures in this bill that accord with the timeless principles of our ancient law, then we will find it possible in years to come to enlarge the scope of this . . . bill. But if we depart from our traditional procedures in this bill, our departure will haunt us as a recurring barrier to enlarging the scope of . . . civil rights in future years. That is why I am persuaded that this amendment is indispensable to the long-term interest of civil rights."

And there was a speech by another young senator, forty-year-old John Fitzgerald Kennedy, who also sat in the back row, a speech explaining why he had now—at last—decided to support the amendment. His explanation was based in part on pragmatism—one reason to give the southerners what they want, he said, is to avoid a filibuster. "After observing the course of debate during the past days, I am persuaded that if the O'Mahoney Amendment is not accepted, the passage of the bill will be delayed for weeks and perhaps indefinitely," he said. It was buttressed with expert opinion—"from outstanding liberal attorneys whom I have consulted. . . . I ask unanimous consent to have printed at this point in the *Record* a memorandum which is the result of a telephone conversation with Prof. Mark De Wolfe Howe, professor of law, Harvard Law School. . . ." And it displayed concern not to offend the South, whose votes might be crucial at the 1960 convention. "I am confident that southern juries, presented with convincing evidence and ever mindful of the watching eyes of the nation—and indeed the world—will convict those who dare to interfere with orderly legal processes," Kennedy said. But in its peroration, Kennedy's speech rose to an eloquence that gave a hint of things to come. "Finally, Mr. President, this debate . . . represents . . . a turning point in American social and political thought. It represents a confrontation of problems which have plagued us too long. . . . It represents an almost universal acknowledgment that we cannot continue to command the respect of peoples everywhere, not to mention our own self-respect, while we ignore the fact that many of our citizens do not possess basic constitutional rights. However late, we have at last come to the point of a great decision. It is this fact which overshadows our deliberations. To this overarching achievement, history will bear witness."

All during the hours consumed by speeches, however, the focus of the galleries' attention was on Lyndon Johnson, who wasn't speaking.

Johnson wanted it there, and he made sure it stayed there. This evening session of the Senate was his moment, and he made the most of it, and to any spectator who had arrived wondering who was going to be the victor in "the great Senate game," or who was in charge on the Senate floor, his actions made the answers clear. Dressed in a dark blue suit and gleaming white shirt, with a bright bow tie and, in his breast pocket, a bright handkerchief, he sauntered up and down the aisles with long, loping strides, stopping by one desk to put an arm around a colleague's shoulders, grinning widely at another, gesturing across the floor at another, bending close to still others to whisper in their ears, sometimes with a hand ostentatiously up to his mouth to make the spectators realize that something secret and important was being said, so that, even though other senators were speaking, he constantly caught the galleries' eye. When he sat down at his desk, of course, he was sitting down front and center on the Senate stage, and at the adjoining desk, on the other side of the center aisle, was the perfect foil.

"There were many speakers, but the floor was wholly dominated by two big men, stationed cheek by jowl on the center aisle—big, chunky, earnest Minority Leader William Knowland, and lanky Majority Leader Lyndon Johnson," Stewart Alsop wrote. "They made a fascinating contrast. Knowland sat stolidly, like a great cornered bull, his enormous forehead furrowed in parallel wrinkles, foretasting defeat. Johnson sat back easily, his long legs negligently crossed, when he was not moving restlessly about. Once, when Everett Dirksen of Illinois rose to support Knowland with his special brand of empty grandiloquence ('I have been thinking much of Runnymede'), Johnson half-yawned and lazily scratched his chest, in a magnificent gesture of casual confidence." The speeches didn't matter; Johnson's every gesture made that clear. What mattered was the votes—and he had the votes.

Finally, after Dirksen had finished, Knowland rose to make a last appeal, poignant because by this time even he knew what its result would be. "This will be a historic roll call. Let it come. Our successors and history will be able to judge the issues, even if for the moment there is confusion here tonight." He ended by bellowing out a line that must have been difficult for him to say, but which he may have felt represented the only hope left for him. "Support our President, Dwight D. Eisenhower!" he shouted.

Then, as the hands on the clock neared midnight, and Nixon came in to take the presiding officer's chair, a page placed a lectern on the Majority Leader's desk, and Johnson himself rose to give the last speech. "Mr. President, sometimes in the course of debate we use loose language. But it is not speaking loosely to say that the Senate is approaching a truly historic vote. By adopting this amendment, we can strengthen and preserve two important rights. One is the right to a trial by jury. The other is the right of all Americans to serve on juries, regardless of race, creed or color." And his last line was the perfect climax, the most fitting last line, the *only* last line, really, for a legislative drama.

"Mr. President," Lyndon Johnson said, "I ask for the yeas and nays."

For a time, to those in the galleries, the vote may have seemed to be going against the Leader. The first two senators called—Aiken and Allott— responded "Nay," and at the end of twenty-five names, with the roll just finishing the *D*s, the tally was 16 to 9 against the amendment. But Johnson, sitting at his desk with the smudged tally sheet in front of him, wasn't worried. He knew what was coming—and, with the start of the *E*s, it came. "Eastland?" *Aye.* "Ellender?" *Aye.* "Ervin?" *Aye.* By the time the clerk reached the *M*s, the *ayes* were ahead—and so many of the *M*s were from the Mountain States and the Northwest. "Magnuson?" *Aye.* "Malone?" *Aye.* "Mansfield?" *Aye.* "Murray?" *Aye.* Shortly after midnight—at 12:19 a.m. on August 2—Nixon announced that the amendment was approved, by 51 votes to 42.

Before the last words were out of Nixon's mouth, a senator jumped up at his desk on the far left-hand side of the Democratic arc and started not for the cloakroom but for the lobby, because that was where the closest telephone was.

He was a senator who no longer moved very fast, because he was old, but he was moving as fast as he could. It was Joseph O'Mahoney. His wife, Agnes, was in a wheelchair, and hadn't been able to come. He was hurrying to call her to give her the news.

IN THE WAKE OF THE VOTE, emotions spilled over. Richard Nixon could not contain his frustration and rage. When, as he was leaving the Chamber, reporters asked his reaction, the Vice President said, "This is one of the saddest days in the history of the Senate. It was a vote against the right to vote." Clarence Mitchell went to Knowland's office to discuss what to do now, and could hardly believe what he saw there. "That big, strong, brusque Knowland actually broke down and cried," Mitchell was to recall.

What overflowed in Bethine Church was pride. She had been sitting in the Family Gallery all evening, and when the vote began, she did not know how it was going to go. "You couldn't take notes in the gallery, so I was tallying the vote on my hands and feet," she was to recall. The vote went, of course, the way her husband wanted it to go, "and when I left the gallery I was so excited." She hoped there was awareness of Frank's importance in the civil rights fight, and as she was leaving the Capitol that night, she found out there was. "I got to the bottom floor, and I started through the swinging doors, and Jack Kennedy caught my arm as I was going through the door and he said, 'Your man pulled it off! He did a great job!' "

Kennedy wasn't alone in that assessment. "After my role in the passage of that civil rights legislation, Lyndon Johnson was warmly and massively grateful, so much so that I was almost stifled in his embrace," Frank Church said. "He would pick you up and wrap his arms around you and just squeeze the air out." The gratitude of the Leader took tangible forms. At a cocktail party early in the year, Bethine, talking with a group of people, had remarked that she had always wanted to visit South America. Johnson had heard her, and two weeks after the jury trial vote, she was in South America. After the vote, Johnson named her husband the Senate's representative to a ten-day conference, in Buenos Aires, of the Organization of American States. The assignment was "a kind of indication of his new friendship and embrace," Church realized.

There were other indications. "Nothing was too good for me," Church was to say. "First [in March, 1958] he put me on the McClellan [Labor] Rackets Committee," which was about to begin its publicity-rich hearings into the Teamsters Union and Jimmy Hoffa, and told Church why he was doing so: "I've got a vacancy there to fill, and it will give you some good exposure. . . . I think it will be good for you." And then there was the committee appointment for which Church had longed. "After a decent interval [after the jury trial addendum], Johnson put him on Foreign Relations, in what was a tacit *quid pro quo,* which was never expressed, but which I think was understood," Ward Hower says.

Actually, the interval was barely decent. The very next vacancy on Foreign Relations occurred in January, 1959, and Church was appointed to it. In making the appointment Johnson simply bypassed not only Estes Kefauver but Scoop Jackson and a half dozen other senators with greater seniority than Church who had requested the post. Church had wanted "not only to go on" the committee, but "to go on early," so that he could be chairman, like Borah, someday. Now he had gone on early; calling on its staff director, Carl Marcy, not long after his appointment, he looked at the portraits of the committee chairmen hanging on the wall, and said, "Maybe someday I'll be there."

And there was a note—undated, but it was probably written in 1958—scribbled by Lyndon Johnson one day when he was sitting in on a meeting of the Interior Committee of which Church was a member, a note that indicates how accurately Johnson had read the easy-to-follow text that was Frank Church. "Frank," the note said, "I told Drew Pearson yesterday I wanted him to help me give you a build up over the years that would give you the recognition your ability deserve[s]. Someday you can, may & should be our President."

41

Omens

THE PASSAGE OF THE JURY TRIAL AMENDMENT, coming on top of the elimination of Part III, infuriated Republicans—those who had been fighting for Brownell's unamended bill out of a sincere belief in civil rights because they felt that those two changes rendered the original bill meaningless, those who had been fighting for political advantage for the GOP because they felt the advantage had been lost. They sought to regain it. Fuming from his long and fruitless day trying to win back GOP senators, Vice President Nixon, flanked by Deputy Attorney General Rogers, was heading out for dinner on the evening of the jury trial vote when he encountered Joe Rauh and Paul Sifton in a Senate corridor. They had a brief conversation—the conversation in which all four agreed that they were about to lose that vote—and then Nixon said, "Boys, I think we ought to consider whether the best strategy wouldn't be to just let the civil rights bill die in conference this year, and then make an all-out fight for a stronger bill next year." President Eisenhower, informed of the result when he awoke the next morning, could not have been angrier if he had missed an easy putt. He opened that day's Cabinet meeting by calling the Senate action "one of the most serious political defeats of the past four years, primarily because of a denial of a basic principle of the United States," the right to vote, and his formal statement at that day's press conference, read with a grim expression on his face, was one of the angriest he had ever made publicly about Congress. "Rarely in our entire legislative history have so many extraneous issues been introduced into the debate," he said, adding how "bitterly disappointing" the vote had been to "millions of Americans who . . . will continue . . . to be disenfranchised." "The blackest of black days," Ann Whitman wrote in her diary.

The gutting of the bill—even with Church's addendum to the jury trial amendment—infuriated some African-American leaders. Among those who urged Eisenhower not to sign it were some from a new generation, like Jackie Robinson, who telegraphed, "HAVE WAITED THIS LONG FOR BILL WITH MEANING—CAN WAIT A LITTLE LONGER," and some from the old, like

A. Philip Randolph, who said, "It is worse than no bill at all." And some black Americans blamed Lyndon Johnson for the gutting. Ethel Payne, who was covering the Senate for the *Chicago Defender,* was to recall how "We all sat watching while Lyndon Johnson, the most astute maneuverer on the Hill, cracked his whip and marshalled his forces to cut the guts and the heart out of the bill." And the changes infuriated liberals, who saw the addendum as a cynical device to give the appearance of meaningfulness to something that had no meaning since southern juries would almost certainly include at least one white. "Can one then picture a jury from the Deep South unanimously finding a white election official guilty for depriving a Negro of the right to vote?" Paul Douglas asked. "A hung jury is almost as good as an acquittal." Church's idealistic young staff members Ward and Phyllis Hower felt their senator had been wrong to introduce it; so "emotional" was Phyllis about it that for weeks she could barely bring herself to talk to her boss.

What good was the bill as a whole? liberals asked. The jury trial amendment rendered toothless the provisions about voting—and voting was now the only right covered by the bill. "The Federal government is still prevented from coming to the aid of hard-pressed citizens whose civil rights to unsegregated schooling, transportation, and other public facilities are denied," Paul Douglas said. "These people, who are almost universally poor and weak [must still] fight their costly and protracted legal battles alone. . . . It has been the advocates of segregation and white domination who have won the major triumph." An old man who for years had stood shoulder to shoulder with Douglas, and who had left the Senate battlefield because he was afraid he could no longer be effective on it, had been anxiously following the debate in a *Congressional Record* that he had arranged to have flown every day to his hotel in Switzerland, and he wrote to console his longtime ally. "I know how deeply you have felt on this subject, and of your inevitable sense of disappointment and frustration," Herbert Lehman wrote. "I want you to know, however, how much I have admired your leadership. . . . What you have done has been one of the few bright spots in an otherwise very gloomy and frightening situation." But Lehman had to confess that he himself was "sorely disappointed. . . . The bill in its present form will be merely a gesture and quite ineffective." The anger of such liberals focused on Lyndon Johnson—"I was so mad at Johnson I was speechless, for gutting the bill so much," recalls Joe Rauh—and was given voice by liberal columnists. On August 5, for example, Thomas Stokes denounced "the sham perpetrated upon the Senate and the American people" which "intrudes upon the human dignity of millions of persons who for a long time have suffered denial of guaranteed rights which the rest of us take for granted."

"The civil rights fiasco in the Senate . . . was admittedly a triumph for the southern wing," Stokes wrote. "It was, too, a compliment, if of dubious character, for the ingenious and slick leadership of Senator Lyndon Johnson of Texas.

In this case, he virtually compromised the civil rights bill out of existence in the zeal of exercising his talents of maneuver and behind-the-scenes negotiations of which he is so proud. . . . Looking back on it all, we might say that never was strategy so brilliant to bring about so evil a result." The *New York Post,* which had been denouncing Richard Nixon for years, said that in this fight Lyndon Johnson had made even Nixon look good.

FRUSTRATION AND ANGER LED some Republican senators at first to favor the course that Nixon had suggested in the Senate corridor. Somehow the civil rights issue, which was *their* issue, had been captured by the Democrats. "The Republicans are understandably quite furious that Senator Lyndon B. Johnson, the Senate Democratic Leader, is now getting the credit of sorts for having navigated a civil rights bill through the Senate without . . . a filibuster," Rowland Evans wrote. And if the Democrats got credit, the Republicans might well get blame. The bill had been stripped of its enforcement provisions—and the burden of enforcement would fall on a Republican Justice Department. When enforcement efforts failed, as, thanks to the jury trial amendment, they would inevitably fail, "the Republicans, not the Democrats, will have to make the explanations to disillusioned Negro voters," Evans wrote. The solution for the GOP might lie in the next stage of the bill's legislative journey: the House had passed a bill—Brownell's original bill, a bill that included Part III and did not include any provision for jury trials—very different from the bill the Senate had passed. The two bills had to be reconciled, and unless some unusual step was taken, they would go for reconciliation to a joint House-Senate conference committee. Southern representatives and senators were generally heavily represented on these committees, which also included key members of the committees into whose jurisdiction the bill fell—so not only Judiciary's Olin Johnston but Judiciary's Chairman Jim Eastland might well be members of the Senate delegation. If a compromise could not be agreed on, the bill would die in conference. That prospect was not at all displeasing to some Republicans: Since the bill could only hurt their party, why not just let it die? Since the conference committee would be dominated by Democrats, Democrats would be blamed for the death, and civil rights would then be a potent issue for the GOP in the 1958 election year. "It would be infinitely better to let the bill die and wait three months [until January, 1958, when the next session of Congress would begin] and get a real bill," House GOP Leader Joseph Martin said.

In the first flush of resentment over the jury trial amendment, those senators who were derided as "the all-out civil rights forces" felt the same way. Nixon's suggestion had struck a responsive chord in the deeply disappointed Rauh, and after the yeas and nays had confirmed their gloomy prediction and Rauh was leaving the gallery, he told Paul Sifton angrily, "This bill is worth less than nothing." Leaving Sifton, he walked out of the Capitol, into the night, and felt himself seized with anger. "Well, let's kill the bill, maybe Nixon's right," he muttered to himself. Other members of the Douglas Group felt the same way. Wayne Morse said he hoped the Senate would reject "this bad bill" when the vote on the entire bill was taken on August 7. And of course the South agreed. What, from Richard Russell's standpoint, had been the most desirable result all along but the death of the bill? What difference did it make, ultimately, where it was killed? If it hadn't been done on the Senate floor, then the Conference Committee would do just fine.

While that was liberals' first reaction, however, it didn't last. Liberals and black leaders—the veteran, battered crusaders for civil rights—had been fighting for so long in vain that, on more sober consideration, they realized how hard it had been to pass *any* civil rights bill, and how essential it was that that accomplishment, no matter how meagre it was, be recognized. The morning after the 51–42 vote, Joe Rauh was just getting out of bed when his telephone rang, and it was Clarence Mitchell saying, as Mitchell's biographer recounts, "that the civil rights forces had to support what was left of the bill before people got the idea that the legislative process could not work in the field of civil rights." This bill, no matter how weak it was, was proof that the process could work, Mitchell said. Congress hadn't passed a civil rights law in eighty-two years, but it was on the very verge of passing one now. Mitchell recognized, his biographer says, "the psychological and historical importance" if it was actually passed.

Dealing with these leaders was made easier also by their hope that if the accomplishment was finalized—if the House and Senate versions were reconciled into one bill, and the bill was signed into law—future accomplishments would become easier; Johnson's argument was being accepted, right down to its wording. Recalls Richard Bolling: "All of a sudden you started hearing it all over the place: 'We've got to break the virginity.' You heard guys saying that thing about 'Once they do it the first time, it won't be so hard to get them to do it the next time.' " And it was made easier by their understanding—since they for so long had gotten, for all their efforts, nothing—that this bill, no matter how weak it was, was *not* nothing. It may not have been much, but it was *something*.

In addition, Johnson had on his side, in Philip Graham, a very potent weapon. Johnson needed that weapon. It was difficult for him to talk directly to some of these leaders—including the one who was probably the single most influential, ADA National Chairman Rauh—so great was their distrust of him. So the weapon had to be deployed, no matter what the cost.

"By the summer of 1957, Phil was clearly exhausted and in need of rest," Katharine Graham would say. She did not know then how ill her husband was, but it was, she would write, "obvious . . . that he was high-strung and had overextended himself." They had decided, in her words, to "retreat to Glen Welby," and had spent the summer "playing with the children and just doing nothing," except for occasional interludes like the luncheon for Rauh and Frankfurter. And then, right after the passage of the jury trial amendment, Lyndon Johnson telephoned Phil at the farm and asked him "to come back to Washington to help him win passage" of the civil rights bill. Mrs. Graham tried to persuade him not to go. "I knew that he was very frail," she would say. "I knew that he shouldn't go up and do that." She was, however, unsuccessful. "So Phil returned to Washington, somewhat to my concern, and stayed with Lyndon almost constantly for several days, working day and night," telephoning Rauh and other civil rights leaders to urge them to support the bill even in its weakened form, making one call after another, far into the evening. On several nights, he slept on a couch in Johnson's office. Graham would, of course, have been a wonderful advocate even had he not brought with him the power of the *Post,* so deeply did he believe in what he was fighting for. "From the point of view of many political observers, what LBJ did was to take everything out of the bill except the right to vote," Mrs. Graham was to write. "Phil's argument was that the only thing that really counted about the bill was the right to vote." He spent a great deal of time on the telephone with Rauh, George Reedy recalls. "You could see he was very tired, nervous, but more than anyone else, I think you have to say it was he who persuaded Rauh."

Graham persuaded Rauh, and Rauh helped persuade Roy Wilkins, who in 1957 was another civil rights leader whose feelings about Lyndon Johnson were, at best, ambivalent. "In those days, Johnson was just beginning to get religion on civil rights," Wilkins was to write in his autobiography. "He dreamed of becoming President himself, and knew that so long as he had Jim Crow wrapped around him, the rest of the country would see him only as a Southerner, a corn-pone Southerner at that, rather than a man of national stature. So around 1957 he began to change his course on civil rights."

"With Johnson, you never quite knew if he was out to lift your heart or your wallet," Wilkins was to write. He and other black leaders had had "a number of meetings with Johnson during the spring and early summer" of 1957, at which "he told us frankly that all he cared about was voting rights, that the bill couldn't pass with Title III." Wilkins could understand that—"That was too much for Dixie," he was to say. But it was much harder to swallow the jury trial amendment. That, he was to say, "was simply a device to defend segregation, not to defend the sanctity of the jury system." But Rauh and other liberals worked on Wilkins—"Roy," Hubert Humphrey said to him one day, "if there's one thing I've learned in politics, it's never to turn your back on a crumb"—and Wilkins finally agreed to call a meeting of the Leadership Conference on Civil Rights: the leaders of sixteen organizations—the NAACP, the ADA, three Jewish organizations including the American Jewish Congress, the American Council on Human Rights, the international Elks organization, a Quaker organization, the National Community Relations Advisory Board, and seven major labor unions—to "thrash the problem out."

The Senate vote on the overall civil rights bill was scheduled for Wednesday evening, August 7, and the meeting, held in the library of Rauh's law firm on K Street, began on Wednesday morning. At the beginning of the day, the prevailing sentiment was to decline to support the bill, but the prevailing sentiment hadn't had Phil Graham talking to it. "Joe [Rauh] argued that . . . once Congress had lost its virginity on civil rights, it would go on to make up for what had been lost," Wilkins wrote.

Johnson, on the Senate floor, was waiting anxiously for news, and that morning Reedy handed him a note giving him some, which Reedy had received from one of the participants in the meeting, Ken Birkhead: "NAACP, ADA, and other civil rights organizations are going to put out a statement about noon damning the Senate bill . . . but saying in effect they prefer it to no bill at all," the note said. That seemed like good news—but it turned out to be premature; "All day long we argued and struggled," Rauh was to recall.

The most prominent African-American in that room was Wilkins. "If I had gone against the bill, I think it would have collapsed," he was to say, and he was probably correct. "The Republicans . . . were for letting it die. The liberals would not have gone on against me."

"I had never felt quite so much on the spot," Wilkins was to recall. He was torn between the two sides. "I had wanted something much stronger [than the bill]. I had opposed the jury trial amendment. I had winced at the arguments of old friends who said that since the South had not filibustered to kill the bill it had to be too weak to be worth anything." On the other hand, "from a dry-eyed point of view, I thought it was impossible to argue that the bill was worth less than nothing." And "in the end," he says, "I concluded that at the very least the measure would expand Negro registration. . . . I also hoped that if the bill passed we would be able to demonstrate its weaknesses by the 1960 election and get much stronger legislation. With the bill passed we were in a better position to campaign than we would have been without it. . . . At the end of that long afternoon, I decided to buck the prevailing sentiment against the bill and support it." That decision, Wilkins was to say, "was one of the hardest I have ever made." But it was crucial. Johnson had persuaded Graham, and Graham had persuaded Rauh, and Rauh had persuaded Wilkins—and now, in that law library on K Street, Wilkins persuaded the Leadership Conference. In the late afternoon, at the end of a long day, the conference issued a statement saying that "Disappointing as the Senate version is, it does contain some potential good," and therefore should be passed. The *Washington Post* found the statement good. "The 16 national organizations . . . have taken a realistic view," said its editorial the next day. "All of them recognize that an amended bill is vastly preferable to no bill at all. It is noteworthy that among the signers is Roy Wilkins. . . ."

. . .

THE SENATE VOTE on the overall bill began at about eight o'clock that Wednesday night, by which time the Leadership Conference statement supporting the measure had been circulated on Capitol Hill. Its passage had already been assured, but it had been expected that some Republicans and liberals would join the South in voting against it. The statement changed that, even for Knowland. "With the pending bill we have made some advances in civil rights," the Republican Leader said in his closing statement. And the bill, he said, "will be further improved in the [conference] committee. It will be greatly improved over the Senate version." Not a single Republican, and only one liberal—Wayne Morse—voted against it. Only seventeen of the twenty-two southern senators joined Morse in voting against the bill. Florida's Smathers voted for it, as did Tennessee's Gore and Kefauver, and the two senators from Texas: Ralph Yarborough and Lyndon Johnson. Five senators didn't vote, and the vote for passage—the decisive vote in the 1957 civil rights fight: the first time in eighty-two years, the first time since Reconstruction, that the Senate had passed a civil rights bill—was 72 to 18.

The next morning, at about six o'clock, Rauh received another telephone call, this time from Phil Graham. "I just had the strangest call," Graham said. "I had the strangest call from Lyndon. He said, 'Phil, of all the strange things, who the hell do you think is saving that bill for me? That crazy, goddamned friend of yours, Joe Rauh, is saving that bill for me.' "

"I wasn't saving it for him, because I hated his guts for what he was doing to school desegregation," Rauh was to say. "That was a crime against the Negroes when Lyndon Johnson knocked out Part III. . . . But Johnson was right. We had to have a breakthrough." Thirty-five years later, when Joe Rauh died, Katharine Graham summed it up in the eulogy she delivered at his memorial service. "Joe understood that you had to show you could pass something, even something small, to go forward and pass something big."

Whether or not Joe Rauh "saved" the civil rights bill, he certainly smoothed the way for the next steps needed if it was to become law. For more than two weeks following that Senate vote, Republicans sincerely committed to civil rights (notably New Yorkers Brownell, Rogers, and congressmen Emanuel Celler and Kenneth Keating) insisted—as did Knowland and Joe Martin, both of them still unable to grasp the strategic situation—that the House reject the Senate version and repass its original, stronger version of the bill. Unless "major steps" were taken to "put more teeth" back into the measure, Martin said on August 10, the bill would be sent to a joint House-Senate conference committee—where, of course, it would die. But the Civil Rights Leadership Conference issued another statement—reiterating that the Senate version should be accepted as the best that was realistically possible. With that statement, the opposition to the bill crumbled. How could anyone contend that a civil rights bill should not be passed when the pre-eminent civil rights organization said it should? Knowland and Martin continued to bluster to reporters,

Martin saying that it would be "infinitely better" to have no bill than to pass one as "bitterly disappointing" to America's Negroes as the one the Senate had passed, and threatening to withhold Republican support from the bill and have the Republicans on the Conference Committee hold the bill there indefinitely unless it was strengthened. But there was one question—asked by reporters virtually every time Knowland or Martin made such statements—which punctured their bravado, a question to which every possible response was lame. As the *New York Times* put it: "Asked how he reconciled this [statement] with the fact that the NAACP was seeking approval of the Senate bill as the best available, Martin replied that the NAACP leaders did not speak for all Negroes."

There was bluster, too, in the weekly meetings of GOP legislative leaders at the White House. Brownell's deputy Rogers called the bill "a monstrosity— the most irresponsible act he had seen during his time in Washington. . . . [the] revised Section IV limited to voting rights and providing for jury trials would be like giving a policeman a gun without bullets." The President, apparently firmly convinced by Brownell and Rogers of the unwisdom of a jury trial amendment, supported them. At one meeting, the minutes reported, "the President spoke at length in favor of fighting it out to the end to prevent the pseudo-liberals from getting away with their sudden alliance with the southerners on a sham bill. . . . The President thought it ironic that the Democrats had succeeded in making it appear that any civil rights legislation that might be enacted would be their proposal." But there was a master of *realpolitik* in the room. "The Vice President summarized that the Republicans would be blamed for any failure to enact Civil Rights legislation in the event that Republicans voted to send the bill to Conference [a conference committee] and it died there."

Eventually Nixon's pragmatism carried the day in Republican councils. On the Democratic side of the House there were no councils; Sam Rayburn made his wishes known. On August 27, by a vote of 279 to 97, the House accepted the Senate bill with only one minor change—a face-saving compromise Johnson had worked out that slightly diluted the jury trial amendment and therefore slightly strengthened the bill. (It allowed judges to try minor voting rights offenses without a jury.) That crucial vote, unexpected in its one-sidedness, meant the measure could go back to the Senate, and if the Senate accepted that change, repassing the bill with that one change written into it, the bill would not go to conference.

More than a few of the southern senators, most notably Thurmond, Talmadge, and Harry Byrd, did not want to accept that change, and they felt they didn't have to: that the year was by now so far advanced—and senators so eager to get out of Washington—that the will and the votes to close off a filibuster did not exist, if indeed they ever had. "When, however, Thurmond attempted to persuade the Southern Caucus to filibuster, Dick Russell countered with the same reasoning he had been using all year to deflect one. The southerners could use that reasoning to deflect the anger of constituents over their failure to filibuster—and they did. As Willis Robertson wrote one constituent, "I can assure you that a careful appraisal of the situation confronting us convinces the Southern Senators that if we attempt a filibuster, cloture would promptly be imposed, in which event, not only would we lose our present fight but would invite the establishment of a precedent to plague us next year should an effort be made" to amend Rule 22. And in the end, all of the southerners but one agreed, as usual, to accept their general's decision. When the bill returned to the Senate, Strom Thurmond held the floor for twenty-four hours and eighteen minutes—the longest one-man filibuster in the Senate's history—drawling out the Declaration of Independence, the Bill of Rights, and George Washington's Farewell Address—but that scene from the Senate's past was a solo performance; none of his fellow southerners would join him, and they were furious at him because they felt he was showing them up for not filibustering themselves; "They felt," as one article said, "that Mr. Thurmond was leaving in the South a public image of a single southern senator standing at barricades that had been deserted by the others." "Oh, God, the venomous hatred of his southern colleagues," George Reedy was to recall. "I'll never forget Herman Talmadge's eyes when he walked in on the floor of the Senate that day and saw Strom carrying on that performance." Even Russell, faced with what the *Atlanta Constitution* called "rumblings of criticism [that] are being heard" in Georgia, felt a need to justify his strategy, telling the *Constitution* that the South had "nothing to gain and everything to lose" by filibustering, and declaring, "Under the circumstances we faced, if I had undertaken a filibuster for personal aggrandizement, I would forever have reproached myself for being guilty of a form of treason against the South." Thirty-five years later, Thurmond himself, his biographer Nadine Cohodas wrote, "was [still] adamant" that a full-scale filibuster would have been successful "if Russell had gone along. He refused to concede that the Georgian's tactical compromises were necessary and remained convinced that Russell was motivated more by a desire to help Lyndon Johnson pass a civil rights bill—and thereby boost the Texan's presidential hopes—than by a wish to protect the South or the filibuster rule." When Thurmond finished talking, the Senate, on August 29, passed the revised bill by a 60–15 vote, and on September 9, President Eisenhower signed it into law.

AUGUST 27, the day of the crucial House of Representatives vote to approve the Senate's version of the 1957 Civil Rights Act, was Lyndon Johnson's forty-ninth birthday.

His fortieth birthday had been a very bad day in his life, a day on which it had seemed likely that he would never sit in the United States Senate. August 27, 1948, had been the eve of Election Day in his senatorial contest with Coke Stevenson, and polls taken that election eve showed that Stevenson was still solidly ahead. Johnson was intending to leave politics forever if he lost that election—and on his birthday, it had seemed likely that he would lose. He was convinced that a man's fortieth birthday was a milestone in his life: that if he hadn't accomplished anything by forty, he was unlikely ever to accomplish anything. On his fortieth birthday, Horace Busby recalls, he felt "he had done very little in his life"—and he felt that he never would.

August 27, 1957, was a very different day. He had come a long way in the nine years since 1948, and on this day, the day on which the House vote made his great achievement a certainty, he seemed to know it. He spent much of the day in the Senate Democratic cloakroom that he had made his domain, telephoning the twenty Texas representatives in the House to try to persuade them to vote for the bill, and in the end twelve of the twenty voted for it, a small exclamation point accentuating his triumph. During the day, Mary Rather came to the door of the cloakroom with a message that meant a lot to him. That morning's *Baltimore Sun* had contained a favorable cartoon by Richard Yardley, whose drawings were a barometer of liberal opinion. He had told Willie Day Taylor to ask Yardley for the original. Willie Day had done so, and when Yardley agreed, had invited him to see the cartoon collection in Johnson's office. Yardley said he would like to, "but I'd like to come see them hanging in the White House." Ms. Rather relayed the message to Johnson, and when she returned to the Senate Office Building, told Willie Day his reaction: "This message made our tired boss smile."

And there would be, that day, broader smiles.

The team that had won the Little League Baseball world championship was brought to the Capitol steps to meet the Majority Leader, and the team was from Monterrey, Mexico. As the little Mexican boys clustered around him, one of them, Angel Macias, handed him his baseball cap, and Lyndon Johnson suddenly bent down and scooped Angel up, holding him in one arm while he tried on the cap with the other. Thirty years before, he had made it possible for the Mexican boys in Cotulla to play baseball, and it had hurt him when, in the early mornings, he had heard trucks taking them away instead. He had wanted to do something for them, and had promised himself that if ever he had the power, he would. And now, on Lyndon Johnson's face, as he held the little Mexican boy in his arms, posing for a photographer, was an expression that photographers almost never caught, an expression that was almost never on Johnson's face when a camera was pointing at it because he always wanted to look statesmanlike or shrewd, so that when a camera was pointing at him, he looked either solemn and pompous, or calculating. On his face this time, as Angel Macias hugged him, and Lyndon Johnson tilted the baseball cap back as the photographer asked, was a wide, carefree smile, a smile that lit up his whole face, a smile as big and lighthearted—as *happy*—as the smile of the little boy grinning up at him.

That evening, at about six o'clock, there was a little party in Skeeter's office to cut his birthday cake. Only a few senators had been invited, and all of them who were still in Washington came, and their names reveal the scope of his triumph: Russell, Byrd, Ervin, Smathers, Kerr, Fulbright—he had managed, despite passing a civil rights bill, to hold the South; Humphrey, Pastore, Kennedy—he had held some liberals, too.

And then there was the big party. It was a Texas party, so of course it was in Dale and Scooter Miller's Mayflower suite. Before he went, Lyndon Johnson changed into a blue suit. Did he remember how, just two years before, he had told Bird to keep the blue one, that he would be able to wear it however things worked out? Now he knotted a tie, bright yellow because it was a Texas party, and tucked a bright yellow handkerchief into his breast pocket, and Bird, radiant in a lacy lemon-colored dress, a smile all over her face, too, pinned a yellow rose on his lapel, and walked behind him, carrying the remnants of the cake— there was no sense in wasting it—as he strode out to the long limousine with the chauffeur holding open the door, and was driven down to the Mayflower, where Scooter was arranging and rearranging the big bouquet of yellow roses that the Nixons had sent, and where Dale had been nervously telling the band for an hour that he wanted "The Yellow Rose of Texas" to be struck up the instant Senator Johnson appeared.

The party was perfect, too. Everyone was there: a dozen ambassadors (there was a brief ceremony when the Korean Ambassador made him an honorary citizen of that nation); Washington royalty—the Cafritzes and Perle Mesta; Texas royalty; as well as the man who mattered most to Lyndon Johnson. Sam Rayburn had a rare smile on *his* face, and a present that said a lot about this gruffly sentimental man's feeling toward Johnson; it was a set of gold cuff links and shirt studs that he had, years before, given as a very special gift to his friend Alben Barkley. Barkley's widow, Jane, had given them back to Rayburn when Barkley died, and Rayburn said he wanted Lyndon to have them now. Accepting the gift, Johnson told Rayburn, "I don't know of anyone for whom I have had more affection in my forty-nine years than for you. But the greatest thing you have ever done is what you and twelve other Texans did today when you voted as you did on this civil rights bill." And then there was the moment that was the perfect ending to the perfect day. All that evening, back in the Senate Office Building, Walter Jenkins had been on the telephone to Wisconsin, where the special election to fill Joe McCarthy's seat had been held that day. All evening, the news had been getting better and better, and just before midnight, it was confirmed, and Jenkins telephoned Johnson at the Mayflower, just moments before William Proxmire did so himself. "Senator Johnson," Proxmire said, "I've got the biggest birthday present of them all for you: me." Proxmire had indeed pulled off the upset victory, and would be the fiftieth Democratic senator. Even if Matthew Neely died (as, indeed, he would, four months later), Johnson would still be *Majority* Leader.

When Proxmire gave him the news, Lyndon Johnson said, "Well, the people of Texas have been awfully good to me for a long time. But I must say I never expected this much kindness from the people of Wisconsin." He was almost beside himself with joy. The next evening, while he was in the Senate cloakroom waiting for Thurmond to finish his filibuster, he sent an aide to find out when Proxmire was planning to come to Washington, and was told he was already on his way, that he was flying in that night and was expected to arrive shortly. He hustled the nearest five senators out to his limousine and off to National Airport, where they were waiting on the tarmac to welcome the Proxmires when they came down the stairs from the plane. Seeing Proxmire there in the flesh—the living proof that he would still be Majority Leader when Congress reconvened in 1958—Johnson couldn't do enough for him. He announced that he would give the newest senator a luncheon to celebrate his swearing-in the next day—a lunch for one hundred people in the grandest setting he could provide: the Old Supreme Court Chamber. And he gave him the committee he wanted: Banking and Currency. As soon as he took his desk, after the swearing-in, Proxmire asked for recognition from the chair and said that he knew it was tradition for a new senator to remain silent for a while, but that he felt it was his duty to thank Johnson "for the fine things that the Majority Leader has done for us." Johnson jumped up to reply. Was Proxmire thanking him for the things he had done? He would do more! He announced on the spot that he was giving the newest senator the most prized junket he had available: a trip to West Germany at the invitation of the West German Bundestag. Reporters watching Lyndon Johnson saw a man transfused with happiness; as Mary McGrory wrote in the *Washington Star:* "Leadership of a Senate majority is not among the usual remedies prescribed for victims of a heart attack. In this case it seems to have been good medicine." Johnson works very hard, McGrory wrote, but "he works hard because he enjoys it. One gets the impression that no matter what the future may hold, Senator Johnson right now would rather be Senate Majority Leader than anything else in the world."

LYNDON JOHNSON'S EXULTATION was justified for many reasons, but one of them was not the effectiveness of the bill he had gotten passed. To excuse its inadequacies, his partisans in later years would argue what Joe Rauh argued at the time: that little as it was, it was better than nothing. There was a phrase that summed up that argument—"Half a loaf is better than none"—and the phrase could be employed to evoke poignant overtones: "It seems to me," George Reedy said, "that people who sneer at half a loaf of bread have never been hungry." The validity of this metaphor to describe the Civil Rights Act of 1957 was undercut, however, by the Act's results, for in terms of what was needed to bring justice to black Americans, the Act was not half a loaf of bread, or even a slice. Hubert Humphrey had described it more accurately when he called it a "crumb."

Even before it was signed, events overtook it. On September 3, five days after the final Senate vote had sent the measure to the White House for signature but before Eisenhower had signed it, Governor Orval Faubus of Arkansas had, as Stephen Ambrose writes, "presented Eisenhower with exactly the problem he had most wished to avoid, outright defiance of a court order by a governor," and after three weeks of further defiance, all the controversy that had surrounded Part III became moot. Richard Russell had said that if Part III was passed, it would give the President power to enforce school desegregation with federal bayonets; Part III had been removed. But on September 24 the President nonetheless enforced school desegregation with bayonets, sending a thousand paratroopers of the 101st Airborne Division, bayonets fixed, into Little Rock to ensure the safety of nine Negro schoolchildren who wanted to attend Central High School. At least part of the blame for the crisis has to be laid at the President's doorstep: as Ambrose was to write, "By allowing events to run their course, by attempting to negotiate with Faubus, by failing to ever speak out forcefully on integration, or to provide real leadership on the moral issue, he found himself in precisely the situation he had most wanted to avoid. His options had run out. [He had] no choice but to use force." But when he decided to use it, there was no legal impediment; as Brownell had contended all along, the President clearly had the power to use force to compel obedience to a court order—with or without Part III.

Equally important, with Part III gone, the Civil Rights Act of 1957 dealt only with voting rights. The Act did not even pretend to deal with such manifestations of injustice as segregation in housing, in restaurants, in schools. "When Johnson took Part III out of the House bill, he set back integration in the South for seven years," Joe Rauh was to say. "Part III passed in 1964—the Part III that was taken out in '57 in essence became a part of the '64 Act. But for seven years there was no federal power to bring injunction suits."

As for Part IV—the amended Part IV—it proved to be all but useless, not only because local election officials, certain that they would still be tried by friendly juries, were emboldened to continue discriminatory election practices, but because of what would be called a "lack of will within the administration to enforce" that Part. During its remaining three years in office, the Eisenhower Justice Department filed only ten suits against southern registrars for "arbitrary refusals to register" qualified Negroes. These suits were stalled by state judges; one Georgia judge ordered officials in Terrell County to withhold voter records from federal agents even if a special police force had to be enlisted—and presumably armed—to enforce that order. At the end of 1958, in the eight southern states in which the Southern Regional Council was able to obtain official figures, not only had the number of registered black voters not risen, it had actually fallen—and those states did not include Mississippi or Alabama, probably the two most recalcitrant states, where no official registration figures were kept; at the end of 1960, the net gain in black registration in the Old Confederacy appears to have been a flat zero.

There were other reasons, however, to justify Johnson's sense of accomplishment.

The Act was, after all, the first civil rights legislation that had been passed in eighty-two years—and that fact had tremendous significance. For decades, for more than three-quarters of a century, men and women, black and white, who fought for social justice had watched as civil rights bills died in the Senate—every bill, without exception. Many supporters of civil rights no longer believed that a civil rights bill would *ever* be passed by the Senate.

The Civil Rights Act of 1957 changed that, as Lyndon Johnson tried to explain to journalists and liberals who criticized its inadequacies. "It's just a beginning," he told them. "We've shown that we can do it. We'll do it again, in a couple of years." Critics of the Act "were right in claiming that it contained only limited substance . . . but they failed to recognize the irrelevancy of the point," George Reedy was to write. "The crucial significance of the civil rights bill was that it opened a major branch of American government to a tenth of the population for which all legislative doors had been slammed shut since 1875"—and once the doors were opened, it would be impossible to close them again. Johnson believed "that if he got one civil rights act through, he could get more. . . . He felt if you could get something through, it would be no longer a question of yes or no, but how much." Lyndon Johnson tried to explain this, over and over again, to the journalists and liberals who criticized the bill at the dinner parties he attended. "We've started something now," he would say. "Don't worry, it's only the first. We know we can do it now. We know the ropes." He was right. After decades, generations, in which the great dam had been impenetrable, the sharp point of a wedge had now been hammered into it. The point could hardly have been tinier. But once the point of a wedge is hammered in, the rest of the wedge will, sooner or later, follow.

GETTING THE FIRST ACT THROUGH—"starting something"—was important for another reason. If "half a loaf" is an invalid metaphor with which to justify the Civil Rights Act of 1957, there is another metaphor which, though even more amorphous, is more justifiable, when there is taken into account the effect of the bill's passage on men and women who for so long had watched every other bill die in the Senate.

The opening of "legislative doors" that "had been slammed shut since 1875" meant, Reedy says, that perhaps other laws, stronger laws, "could be passed someday," and the "impact of this upon people who had previously been denied participation in the institutions that ruled over them was extraordinary." On the afternoon of the day on which the Senate was passing the civil rights bill, Robert Graetz, a white minister whose Montgomery home had twice been dynamited because of his support of the bus boycott, was talking to Murray Kempton. Kempton, having observed the Senate in action, was pessimistic about the prospects of future legislation, but Graetz said that now that one bill was being passed, soon "There will be a [strong] voting rights bill, and then sooner than you think, there will be Negro representatives in the Legislature." Kempton said that this seemed like a wild dream. "Perhaps it is," Graetz said, "but if we did not believe it, we could not live here, and we would be wrong to be as happy as we are."

The Civil Rights Act of 1957 was more than half a loaf, a lot more. It was hope.

AND THERE WERE STILL OTHER REASONS for Lyndon Johnson to be exultant.

In 1957, great historical forces—a rising demand for social justice, a new militancy among blacks, new political equations that endowed the black vote with new significance—had come together in a tide sweeping toward the enactment of new civil rights legislation. But great forces had swept forward before and always, if they reached the Senate, they had been blocked by the Senate. Had it not been for Lyndon Johnson, they would have been blocked by the Senate again. At the moment that he stepped wholeheartedly into the civil rights fight, these forces *had* seemingly been blocked by the Senate again. That they had in some measure been victorious in that body, and therefore in government as a whole, had been due to him; he had understood the forces ("The world is moving to the left; you can either move with it or be crushed"), and had ridden them, and at the same time had directed them into channels that made it possible for them to flow forward and win for social justice a beachhead staging area from which, the next time the forces came together, they could advance still further.

The direction that he had given these forces, and the maneuvers he had made on their behalf, had all been legislative in nature. During the civil rights fight of 1957, Lyndon Johnson had displayed, in discovering underneath the seemingly impenetrable southern defiance a weak spot (voting) on which southerners might yield; in locating underneath the impassioned northern rhetoric an area (loss of the right of jury trial) in which some northerners felt themselves on weak moral ground; and in using these two points of vulnerability to carve out, amendment by amendment, an area of reconciliation that could attract a majority—in doing all this he had displayed a remarkable ability in that most vital of legislative arts: the art of compromise. In seeing the need to bring together the South and the West, and in recognizing, in the Hells Canyon Dam, the means of bringing them together, he had displayed a mastery of legislative strategy on a grand, nationwide, scale. By grasping in a moment, on the Senate floor, the possibilities in Clint Anderson's amendment; by seizing that moment before it could vanish from the floor; by delicately adding jury trial amendment after jury trial amendment until he finally had the amendment that would attract enough votes to let the bill pass, he had displayed a mastery of small-scale, intricate legislative maneuver. In a republic which had, during the past century of its existence, grown accustomed to thinking of governmental leadership almost solely in terms of executive leadership, he had provided a vivid demonstration of the potentialities in legislative leadership. A master of a profession cannot but know he is a master, cannot but feel joy and pride in exercising that mastery. Lyndon Johnson knew what he had done, and gloried in what he had done. *So I went to a few key southerners and persuaded them. . . . And then, in return, I got the western liberals . . . and then I was able to show that as long as they trusted me . . .*

His triumph was a triumph of something even larger than legislative expertise and leadership. The common ground on which he had at last brought both sides together was not ground he had discovered, but ground he had created. The bill he had gotten passed might still bear the number— H.R. 6127—that it had been given in the House of Representatives when it was still the Eisenhower Administration's bill, but it bore little resemblance to the bill drawn up by Attorney General Brownell. The excisions in and amendments to it that Lyndon Johnson had fashioned had been so substantial that the bill was in effect a new bill, in whose creation he had had the major hand. The Civil Rights Act of 1957 was therefore a demonstration not only of legislative expertise and leadership, but of legislative creativity—of creativity on a very high order.

And this was a demonstration that was badly needed. As C. Vann Woodward, perhaps the nation's pre-eminent historian of southern history, wrote in the October, 1957, issue of *Commentary,* "The trouble was not in the House of Representatives, which frequently yielded to the pressure, but in that formidable institution," the United States Senate. "Moving between the incorrigible right and the immovable left, Senator Johnson worked mainly in the shifting center to shape and mold a . . . workable compromise to replace a futile stalemate. The air of compromise is rarely appreciated fully by men of principle," and working out this compromise was very difficult. Its success "called for political astuteness on Johnson's part amounting to genius . . . The senator, it proved, had what it took."

ON THE SUNDAY after the Act's passage the great media organs that set the liberal tune pulled out all the stops. There was so much praise in the *New York Times* and the Washington papers that it couldn't be confined to one section. The *Post,* that Sunday, carried not only an editorial that reflected Philip Graham's opinions ("Mr. Johnson came out of the debate a national rather than a regional figure"), but, under the headline "JOHNSON'S MASTERPIECE," a political analysis by Robert Albright ("The Senate last week did an incredible thing. . . . Famed for his legislative miracles, this beyond any doubt was Johnson's masterpiece"), and, in the Society section, a long profile by Mary Van

Rensselaer Thayer that began "This, but definitely, is LBJ Week." In the *Washington Star* there was an editorial, as well as an analysis of his tactics by David Koonce ("Some of the veteran observers in the Senate Press Gallery . . . confidently expected to be writing about a civil rights filibuster for weeks and months. . . . *Everybody* knew there would be a filibuster. Everybody, that is, except Lyndon Baines Johnson . . ."), and a long profile in the Society section by Liz and Leslie Carpenter. A few days later, *The New Republic* weighed in: "Moderates of both parties share [a] feeling of triumph. . . . [T]he leaders were thoroughly reasonable men. . . . Here was bipartisanship at its best. . . ." Douglas Cater of the *Reporter,* so critical of Johnson in the past, now extended himself to make amends. Reedy had written a long memorandum and given it to Cater "for background," and Cater asked permission to use sentences from Reedy's memo as if Johnson himself had spoken them to him, Cater, in an interview. Reedy edited the quotes ("Eye think it is all right providing the words I have bracketed in the first paragraph are eliminated," he told Johnson), and Cater used them as edited, no matter how they distorted reality. His article said, "Johnson remarked to me recently: 'It was realized that there could be no "compromise" in the sense of an empty and evasive deal.' . . . 'Everything that happened, short of technical drafting work, took place right on the Senate floor in plain sight of the press and public.' " The article as a whole substantially revised Cater's earlier view of Johnson. And there was praise for Lyndon Johnson in publications that had very seldom bestowed praise on him in the past—the publications that he needed. "Senator Lyndon Johnson's performance in driving the 'right-to-vote' bill through the Senate . . . is the most remarkable feat of political generalship in years. . . . Johnson is a spectacular operator." Those sentences came from the *AFL-CIO News.* The AFL-CIO! Meany! Labor! Labor, which always liked liberals—and which had never liked him. That Sunday he sat at home watching the morning television shows on which he was invariably praised, and on Monday morning there was a memorandum from Willie Day Taylor on shows he hadn't been able to watch: "Sen. Bible was also complimentary of your leadership on WTOP's *City Side.*" Columnists compared him favorably to America's great legislative leaders of the past. "Majority Leader Lyndon B. Johnson is now recognized as a modern Henry Clay, the great compromiser on the issue of slavery," said Ray Tucker. No wonder he was exultant, euphoric. Just before he left for Texas, Joseph C. Duke, the Senate Sergeant-at-Arms, presented him with a large American flag, together with a letter "to certify that the enclosed flag was flown over the Senate wing of the United States Capitol from the First to the Thirtieth of August, Nineteen Hundred and Fifty-seven, during which period was adopted by the United States Congress the Civil Rights Bill." Lyndon Johnson took the flag back to the ranch with him, and on his first morning home, Lady Bird had it raised to the top of the tall flagpole on the front lawn. It fluttered there against the sky— that brilliant blue "sapphire" Hill Country sky, so often cloudless in summer, that had spelled doom for his father and his father's father. When he had been a boy, Lyndon had watched his father and mother look up at that sky, hoping in vain for a sign of the rain that could save their land. He had looked up at it himself then, in vain. When he looked up now, the blue in the flag was deeper than the sky's blue, and across the sky's pitiless brightness, broad red and white stripes waved triumphantly, sapphire blue no longer doom but only background.

Liberal suspicion of Lyndon Johnson had not been completely dissipated, though—far from it. Even during the first chorus of praise there were dissenting voices. Some of the liberal senators who had fought to the end for a stronger bill were unable to reconcile themselves to the one that had passed, feeling the public had been led to believe it would achieve at least small advances in civil rights, while they felt that in fact there was no chance of that. Wayne Morse, urging Eisenhower to veto it, called it a "hoax and sham bill." And they were bitter about Lyndon Johnson. "Johnson," Paul Douglas was to write, somehow "emerged from the shadows of opposition as the great apostle of civil rights. . . . [The bill] was a triumph, so he said, for his policy of moderation over the extremists, who would have prevented action by their wild talk. Some of his favorite columnists, including William S. White, burst into a chorus of antiphonal praise. Somehow I now became the man who had impeded progress. Johnson, our opponent, became, in their version, the great hero." Not all liberal newspapers saw good in the bill—or in the man who had masterminded its passage. "The moderate Texas leadership . . . seems willing to sacrifice anything except party unity," the *Detroit News* editorialized. Liberals at their dinner parties still argued among themselves about the bill, and about Lyndon Johnson. Bethine Church would never forget the explosion of pent-up anger with which Clayton Fritchey, director of the Democratic National Committee's Public Affairs Division, greeted her husband when, at a Georgetown party, Frank walked through the front door, or how Fritchey continued, "for hours, it seemed," to assail Frank in a "brutal, brutal argument" for helping to pass the jury trial amendment. "Some of his [Church's] liberal friends thought it was the damnedest sellout in history," his aide John Carver would recall. Paul Douglas used a memorable phrase: the bill, he said, reminded him of Lincoln's old saying that "it was like a soup made from the shadow of a crow which had starved to death." Within a day, it seemed, that saying was being repeated over dinner tables in Georgetown and Cleveland Park. And as time passed, and the ineffectiveness of the Act became increasingly evident, liberal criticism was to grow louder.

Nonetheless, while after the 1957 Civil Rights Act there remained substantial liberal suspicion and criticism of Lyndon Johnson, there was not nearly so much as there had been before. At least some of the southern stigma—the fatal "smell of magnolias"—had scrubbed off. Philip Graham had felt that for Johnson to become President, he had to be "cleaned up on civil rights," and that cleaning up had gotten off to a good start. Among the signatures at the bottom of the letters to the editor that appeared in newspapers during and just after the 1957 civil rights fight were names with real significance to liberals. One letter argued that "The Senate bill may not go as far as many think it should, but [its] significance should not be minimized. . . . If progress is to be achieved, differences as to what should be done must yield to a consensus as to what can be done." The letter assured "friends and supporters of civil rights" that they could support the bill with "clear consciences." And the arguments and assurances were given weight by the signature at the end of the letter: Benjamin V. Cohen. Another letter was from Dean Acheson. "I don't think it is an exaggeration to say that the bill is among the great achievements since the war and, in the field of Civil Rights, the greatest since the Thirteenth Amendment. . . . Can't we for once be proud of ourselves when we do the right thing?" (Richard Rovere was to note in *The New Yorker* that "If Mr. Eisenhower decides to sign the bill, he will have in common with Franklin Roosevelt and Harry Truman the experience of approving a piece of legislation whose vital and operative sections have come largely from the hands of Benjamin V. Cohen and Dean Acheson.") That was a telling point for liberals: how could any true liberal ignore the opinions of men like Cohen and Acheson? When the American Civil Liberties Union denounced the bill, *The New Republic* denounced the American Civil Liberties Union. "It took the U.S. Senate nearly 90 years to approve a civil rights bill, and it took the ACLU lawyers several hours to decide (and notify the press) that the bill was worse than nothing," a *New Republic* editorial said. "Unprecedented progress has already been made," and the progress, *The New Republic* said, had been made because of Lyndon Johnson, who called "on two of the New Deal's best draftsmen, Ben Cohen and Dean Acheson, for aid."

And finally there was, under the dateline "Hyde Park," a word from the liberal whose word meant the most of all. She had been torn as to whether or not to support the amended bill, Eleanor Roosevelt wrote in "My Day." "It is one of those difficult decisions in which you know that the way you are voting may possibly injure the objective you are trying to attain," but, she said, she had finally decided that "the civil rights bill with the amendment would be a small step forward and I hope it will become law." And, of course, the NAACP and the Leadership Conference on Civil Rights had supported the measure. By passing the Civil Rights Act of 1957, Lyndon Johnson had obtained the political gain that his political ambition demanded. A moderate columnist, Roscoe Drummond, may have summed up the situation most definitively when he wrote, "If you think the Senate did wrong in cutting back the civil rights bill, much of the blame goes to Johnson. If you think the Senate acted responsibly and usefully in passing a compromise bill, much of the credit goes to Johnson. . . . He proved himself the ascendant leader of the whole Democratic party in Congress, Northern and Western liberals as well as Southern conservatives. . . . Because he voted for and is an architect of the right-to-vote law, he is the first Southern Democratic leader since the Civil War to be a serious candidate for the presidential nomination."

AND THERE WAS YET ANOTHER REASON—the most important reason of all—that the Civil Rights Act of 1957 meant hope. There may have been only meagre significance in the Act itself, but there was massive significance in what the fight for the Act's passage had revealed about the potentialities of the man who led that fight, about the possibilities that lay within that man for the advancement of social justice in America.

In the great "struggle for America's soul" that was the civil rights movement, extraordinary black leaders had already emerged—Randolph, Wilkins, Thurgood Marshall—and during the 1950s, of course, another figure, who would eclipse them all, was coming to the forefront among blacks. But as that leader, Martin Luther King, was to say, the evil of racial discrimination in America was "so great that the Negro cannot fight it alone." Help was needed not only from among men whose skins were dark but from among men whose skins were white; leadership was needed—effective leadership: leadership that not only enunciated ideals but that made progress, limited though it might be, toward achieving them. It was needed particularly in the halls of government, because it could only be from those halls that laws, the only permanent remedy for injustice, could issue. And until 1957 governmental leadership was particularly lacking, its absence particularly glaring and destructive. Dwight D. Eisenhower declined to provide moral leadership on the fundamental moral problem of the time, and on Capitol Hill the leadership of the fight for civil rights laws provided not laws but only words. In 1957, however, effective leadership in the fight for civil rights laws had been provided—by Lyndon Johnson. If he was not able to do more, if the leadership he had provided had been only on behalf of a weak bill, he had nonetheless done all he could, the most he could do in the position—Majority Leader of one of the two houses of Congress—in which he was situated.

But what if he were to rise, one day, to another position?

Lyndon Johnson was eventually to attain the post to which he had aspired all his life. And when he did, he would as President of the United States ram to passage the great Civil Rights Acts of 1964 and 1965, legislation that would do much to correct the deficiencies of the 1957 legislation. He would give black Americans a Voting Rights Act that was truly meaningful, would make them, at last and forever, a true part of American political life. It was Lyndon Johnson, among all the white government officials in twentieth-century America, who did the most to help America's black men and women in their fight for equality and justice. It was he who was, among all those officials, their greatest champion. And it was in 1957—in that fight for the Civil Rights Act of 1957—that Lyndon Johnson's capacity to one day be that champion was first foreshadowed.

The foreshadowing came not only in his drafting of the Act, and in his dealing and maneuvering, but, perhaps most significantly, in a speech he gave.

The speech was delivered on the Senate floor. It came near the end of the 1957 fight, on the evening of August 7. Sitting at his desk just before the 72–18 final vote, he made a small gesture with his hand, and a blue-suited page carried over a portable lectern and placed it on the desk. Johnson laid the speech on the lectern, put on his thick-lensed glasses, and rose to read.

Jim Rowe had told Lyndon Johnson that if he wanted to become President, he had to vote for a civil rights bill, to pass a civil rights bill, and to get the credit for that bill, and Johnson had done all those things. But Rowe had also told Johnson something else. "I know also that Lyndon Johnson is intellectually not a southerner but a national leader," he had said. The need for such a leader was terribly urgent, he said. There would be "a very good chance to bury this plague of civil rights" if only a national leader would step forward. And with this speech, Lyndon Johnson showed that, if he was still not yet such a leader, he had the potential to become one.

In the speech—his first formal announcement that he would vote for the bill—he portrayed the measure in terms that would make it acceptable to his Texas constituency: it repeals a "bayonet-type Reconstruction statute," he said, and under its provisions, "basic rights"—such as the jury trial—"are reemphasized and broadened." Such sentences were typical Lyndon Johnson sentences, the careful, cliché formulas of a cautious politician.

But there were other sentences in that speech.

Some set forth the pragmatic philosophy that was part of Lyndon Johnson's most fundamental belief: a belief in the possible. "In the past few days there has been considerable discussion about the things which the bill does not do," he said. "I am aware" of those things. "But," he said, "I cannot follow the logic of those who say that because we cannot solve all the problems we should not try to solve any of them. . . . I can understand the disappointment of those who are not receiving all they believe they should out of this bill. I can understand but not sympathize with their position." The bill doesn't have to be perfect, Lyndon Johnson said. "The possible necessity for change is no bar to action. The Senate will not disappear after the vote tonight. We shall be present throughout the years to come."

And there were sentences that rose above pragmatism to something higher. Lyndon Johnson had, all his life, expressed a deep distrust of ringing phrases. But there were phrases in this speech that seemed to verge on what he had always said he distrusted.

"Out of [this] debate has come something even more important than legislation," Lyndon Johnson said. "This has been a debate which has opened closed minds. . . . This has been a debate which has made people everywhere examine hard and fast positions. For the first time in my memory, this issue has been lifted from the field of partisan politics. It has been considered in terms of human beings and the effect of our laws upon them."

Then he turned to politics. "There are," he said, "people who are still more interested in securing votes than in securing the right to vote. There are . . . people who are still more interested in the issue than in a solution to the issue. But I state—out of whatever experience I have had—that there is no political capital in this issue. Nothing lasting, nothing enduring, has ever been born from hatred and prejudice—except more hatred and more prejudice." Look at the legislation passed during Reconstruction, Lyndon Johnson said. That legislation was born out of hatred. But, he said, "We do not have to reconstruct Reconstruction in order to have a bill. We do not have to reopen the wounds." He wanted to remove politics from the civil rights issue, he said. "There is no compelling need for a campaign issue." But, he said, "there is a compelling need for a solution that will enable all America's people to live in dignity and in unity."

And finally Lyndon Johnson turned again to his own vote on the Civil Rights Act of 1957, and to his own feelings about that vote. He knew, he said, that his vote "will be treated cynically in some quarters, and it will be misunderstood in others. . . . But the Senate has dealt fairly and justly with this measure. This is legislation which I believe will be good for every state of the Union—and so far as I am concerned, Texas has been a part of the Union since Appomattox."

A part of the Union since Appomattox. That was a phrase that could rally men to a cause. "When at last Johnson revealed his own feelings about the bill, and said, 'So far as I am concerned, Texas has been a part of the Union since Appomattox,' I was ready to commit myself to him, his ambitions and purposes, for the duration," his young aide Harry McPherson was to recall. The man who distrusted ringing phrases, who despised men who used such phrases, was using some himself now. In that moment it was even possible, seeing that tall man standing at that desk on the floor of one of the houses of the Congress of the United States and uttering such phrases, to picture that man standing one day on the dais of one of the houses of Congress—and speaking not merely to his colleagues but to an entire nation in ringing phrases.

Phrases like *"We* shall overcome!"

YEARS LATER, years after the passage of the great civil rights acts of Lyndon Johnson's presidency, Harry McPherson, who had served in Johnson's White House, would be riding in a parade in his native East Texas. There were floats in the parade, and high school bands, and, McPherson realized, "the bands— were mixed!" There was "a Negro trombonist, next to a white cornetist; three black drummers, and a white cymbal player! And at the front of it all, black and white majorettes, in perfect unison." There was a big sign on the side of the car in which McPherson was riding. It said: "Counsel to President Lyndon B. Johnson," and as the car passed, spectators pointed to the sign and quietly applauded. And then the car entered a Negro neighborhood. Suddenly there was more than applause. Men and women were cheering. They were waving at the car. And many of them were holding up their arms, and with their fingers making the sign of "V"—"V" for Victory. McPherson's eyes met those of an elderly black man. The man grinned at McPherson, and nodded his head. "That's right," he said. "That's right."

"So there had been change," McPherson would write, "so much that one could scarcely remember . . . the careful apprehensive steps which the Senate had taken in 1957, the struggle over Title III and the jury trials, the different words for Douglas and Ervin, the praise and resentment." But, McPherson says, "it had all started there." The great civil rights acts of 1964 and 1965 had all started there, in 1957.

That's right. That's right.

Part VI

AFTER THE BATTLE

42

Three More Years

DURING LYNDON JOHNSON'S next three years in the Senate—his final three years in the Senate—there would be a challenge to his style of leadership. In the 1958 elections, recession, growing unemployment, anger among farmers at President Eisenhower's veto of a bill to increase farm price supports (and at his Secretary of Agriculture, Ezra Taft Benson), and the revelation of influence-peddling by the President's top aide, Sherman Adams, cost the Republican Party forty-eight seats in the House of Representatives and twelve in the Senate (including, improbably, even the Ohio seat that had been held by John W. Bricker; William Knowland, having resigned, lost his race for the governorship of California). In 1959 and 1960, Democrats outnumbered Republicans by almost two to one in both houses of Congress, in the Senate by 64 to 34.

Of the new Democratic senators elected, none were conservatives and five were liberals, "eager," as Evans and Novak wrote, "to make common cause with the tiny, beleaguered faction of liberals" who had been challenging Johnson's leadership. "You know there has been this undercurrent of emotion against your leadership in the last six years," Jim Rowe wrote Johnson shortly after the election. "It is much stronger today than it has ever been in the past."

Within weeks of the election, this undercurrent had risen to the surface: a letter to Johnson from Joe Clark of Pennsylvania, demanding increased representation for liberals on the Democratic Policy and Steering Committees, found its way into the press. Pat McNamara demanded more frequent caucuses. And several of the newly elected liberals, notably Edmund Muskie, who had broken the Republican hold in Maine by twice winning election as governor and then had defeated Republican incumbent Payne to win a Senate seat, and, surprisingly, William Proxmire, were unwilling to be relegated to the spear-carrier roles that Johnson's method of operation required. Offering Muskie advice on his Senate career, Johnson told him not to make up his mind on issues too early—to wait, in fact, "until they get to the *M*s in the roll call." But when, a few weeks later, Johnson said he assumed Muskie would be supporting him in the first big Senate fight of January, 1959—the attempt, once again, to amend Rule 22—Muskie responded by saying, "Well, Senator, I think I'll follow your advice, and just wait until they get to the *M*s." And when he voted with the liberals, Johnson, while not throwing down his pencil, responded otherwise as angrily as he had with Frank Church; Bobby Baker was dispatched to tell other senators that Johnson considered Muskie a "chickenshit." As for Proxmire, who had once called himself Johnson's "biggest birthday present," he turned out to be a somewhat unwelcome gift. During his early days in the Senate, in 1958, Proxmire had seemed willing to pay, in both silence and obsequiousness, the price for admission to the Senate "club," entering debates only upon an invitation from a senior senator, scheduling his first major speech for the day before Easter recess, when most senators would already have left Washington and wouldn't have to listen to him, and tendering a strikingly full measure of deference to the Majority Leader at every opportunity. But he soon decided that the price was too high. Talking one day to an acquaintance about a freshman colleague who also spoke seldom, he exclaimed, "He might as well not be a senator!"

Proxmire decided, he was to say, to "be a senator like Wayne and Paul," and became outspoken on the floor. In 1959, after Johnson refused his request for appointment to the Finance Committee—Proxmire felt the refusal was due to his opposition to the oil depletion allowance—Proxmire went further, in a full-dress Senate speech attacking Johnson's leadership. "There has never been a time when power has been as sharply concentrated as it is today in the Senate," he said. At the first caucus he had attended, in January, 1958, he said, "senators assembled and listened to the Majority Leader read a speech which he had previously released to the press in full. There was not a single matter of party business discussed. There wasn't even a mention of a party program, not a whisper concerning any legislation." And the next meeting of the Democratic caucus wasn't until "a full year later. . . . Senators had to surrender for another year their right and duty to determine the Democratic Party's policies and programs." Proxmire then gave a series of talks attacking "one-man rule" in Congress, in the Senate by Johnson, in the House by Rayburn ("When you get these two men together with the power of making committee assignments, you see the obsequious bowing, scraping senators and congressmen around them"), and demanding more frequent caucuses and larger, more democratic party committees.

All during 1958, 1959, and 1960, the liberal attacks on Johnson continued; in January, 1960, the liberals embodied in a formal resolution demands for more frequent caucuses, for selection of the Policy Committee membership by a vote of all Democratic senators instead of by the Leader alone, and for the drawing up by the Policy Committee of a Democratic legislative agenda. And these attacks were treated by the Washington press corps as significant revolts against Johnson's leadership, with headlines and cutting cartoons; one, by

Herblock, showed "King Johnson" on a throne with a spear knocking off his crown as he said, "Methinks, milord, that the peasantry is getting restless."

Johnson's grip on the reins of senatorial power, however, was far too firm for the attacks to have any real significance. He was stung by Proxmire's attacks into answering him on the floor, saying the Wisconsin freshman needed a "fairy godmother" or a "wet nurse." "This one-man rule is a myth," he said. "I do not know how anyone can force a senator to do anything. I have never tried to do so. I have read in the newspapers that I have been unusually persuasive with senators. I have never thought these were accurate reports. Usually when a senator wants something done and does not get his way, he puts the blame on the leadership. It does not take much courage, I must say, to make the leadership a punching bag." As for Clark, Johnson didn't deign to reply to him himself; he delegated that task to Majority Whip Mike Mansfield, who said that instead of restructuring the Senate, the Democratic senators should rely on "the leadership and parliamentary skill of Lyndon Johnson."

Johnson refused to meet any of the liberal demands. They had asked for more frequent caucuses. That first Democratic Caucus of 1958—the one at which, in Proxmire's phrase, "not a single matter of party business" was discussed—was the only caucus held in 1958. In 1959, there was also only one caucus. Then, during the first days of January, 1960, the Senate liberals "determined to speak out" and to make an all-out attempt at reform. At the Democrats' January 7 caucus, Clark introduced a resolution stating that if at least fifteen senators requested a meeting of the Democratic Party Caucus, one would be held every two weeks. A debate ensued, "the more senior members generally speaking in opposition," as Clark recalls, until Johnson ended it by saying he would be happy to call a caucus anytime at the request of even a single senator. Johnson was as good as his word—but he added some other words. During that January, he scheduled no fewer than four additional caucuses—but also let it be known that he would not be displeased if senators found they had better things to do. Attendance steadily declined. Sixty of the sixty-four Democratic senators had come to that first, January 7, caucus. By the January 20 caucus, attendance was down to twenty-four.* And, Clark was to say, "that was the end." The liberals did not even request another caucus "largely because those of us who wanted regular meetings became convinced that without leadership support, which was not forthcoming, we could not turn out enough members to make the conferences worthwhile." The liberals had proposed another resolution: that the Policy Committee be selected not by the Leader but by an election. The vote on that resolution was 51 to 12—against it. Proxmire had to concede that despite two years of attacks, he had failed to make "any real dent" in Johnson's power. The *Star*'s "Washington Window" column

---

*Another January caucus was attended by thirty-eight senators but, Clark was to say, only because it was an unusual case; it met to discuss a bill "close to floor action."

summed up the denouement of Proxmire's revolt against Lyndon Johnson: it
had been a "David and Goliath drama," but with a non-traditional ending:
"Instead of Goliath being slain, it was David who was slain." Talking with
Proxmire, Richard Russell told him that his "position reminded him of a bull
who had charged a locomotive train. . . . That was the bravest bull I ever saw,
but I can't say a lot for his judgment."

THROUGHOUT LYNDON JOHNSON'S LIFE, in every institution of which
he had been a part, a similar pattern had emerged: as he rose to power within
the institution, and then, as he consolidated that power, he was humble—
deferential, obsequious, in fact. And then, when the power was consolidated,
solid, when he was in power and confident of staying there, he became, with
dramatic speed and contrast, autocratic, overbearing, domineering.

Now, during his final three years in the Senate, this pattern was repeated.
"The success of his leadership affected the Lyndon Johnson lifestyle visibly,"
George Reedy was to say. "During his early years as leader, he put on a
humble-pie act that would have done credit to Ella Cinders. This faded
overnight and a major task of his staff was to keep the hubris from showing—
too much." This task was difficult. He already had an unprecedented amount of
office space. Now he took over more—a lot more—not in the Senate Office
Building but in the Capitol itself. He already occupied most of the western end
of the Capitol's Gallery Floor in the Senate wing, with his two-room Majority
Leader's suite in G-14 and his three-room Policy Committee suite in G-17, 18,
and 19. But between these two suites was a third, the only space on that end of
the floor that he didn't occupy—a two-room suite, G-15 and G-16, filled with
the staff of the Commerce Committee. Now he commandeered that as well, so
that, as one reporter wrote, "He will have a seven-room spread of offices
replete with crystal chandeliers and rich furniture, occupying the entire northwest Senate wing on the third floor of the Capitol." Sometimes, for a new visitor, he would sweep aside the heavy drapery behind his desk there, and
suddenly the window would be filled, as one reporter wrote, with the "marbled
city below with its great avenues running toward the White House." Grand as
this suite was, it was still too far from the Chamber floor for his liking, but on
the same level as the Chamber floor, and conveniently near it, was a suite of
two huge rooms that had been the staff and meeting rooms of the Senate's District of Columbia Committee. He commandeered that, too. On its high ceilings,
above its big crystal chandelier, were frescoes (as soon as he chose the office,
painters began touching them up) of boys carrying baskets of flowers and
young maidens reclining on couches: a Roman emperor's banquet. Reporters
began referring to it as "the Emperor's Room" before coining another name,
which stuck: "the Taj Mahal." Lady Bird imported an interior decorator from
New York to redo the suite in green and gold. "On entering the office," Sam

Shaffer wrote, "one was immediately confronted" by an extremely well-lit, fully life-size portrait of its occupant, hung above its marble fireplace. The artist had portrayed Johnson leaning against a bookcase, but he had captured at least some of the piercing quality in Johnson's eyes; "That huge picture of Lyndon looking squarely in the visitor's eye first thing on entering Lyndon's office is a sure irritant," John Steele reported in a memo to his editors at *Time*. And it was not only Lyndon Johnson's portrait that was well lit. High above the desk, concealed in the chandelier, two spotlights had been placed, focused so that as the man himself sat at the desk, they cast on him what one reporter called "an impressive nimbus of golden light." In a corner of the immense room he had ordered high walls of polished mahogany built, and behind them was a bathroom—a Johnsonian bathroom (a "monument of a toilet," James Reston called it) used as Johnson used bathrooms: soon secretaries, assistants, and senators were having to take dictation from him or discuss issues with him as he sat before them on the toilet.

Johnson made other changes, too, in that Capitol wing that was his world. When he came to the deserted Capitol on a Sunday, he sometimes had to wait a minute or two for an elevator since only one elevator operator was on duty. Now the waiting time was eliminated: three operators were on duty all Sunday. And the operators of the subway between the Capitol and the Senate Office Building no longer stopped working at six o'clock; they remained on duty until Johnson had left the Capitol.

The pattern was discernible not only in the office but in the way visitors to it were treated—not the committee chairmen, of course, but almost all his other colleagues. Often, they were kept waiting; sometimes there would be three or four senators of the United States cooling their heels in the Majority Leader's antechamber. Even the placid Mansfield once lost his temper over the length of time he was kept waiting for an audience and left, saying to Ashton Gonella, "Well, I'm not going to wait this long for anybody." (Mansfield's attitude displeased Ms. Gonella; in recounting this incident, she told the author, "I did not like people who did not respect Mr. Johnson.") While the time senators spent in the suite's outer office was sometimes uncomfortably long, the time they spent in the inner office was sometimes uncomfortably short; a request might be made of the Leader, and it might be denied, quickly and curtly, after which, it was clear, the applicant was expected to get up and leave.

Lyndon Johnson's attitude toward his colleagues was increasingly proprietary and paternalistic. "They were his children; it was his Senate," Ms. Gonella explains. Some of them were wayward children; that was all right, that was why he was there—the firm, fair father, to see that they didn't get into trouble. In November, 1958, he would tell John Steele, in an off-the-record interview, "You know, I feel sort of like a father to these boys. A father loves his sons, though one son may drink a little too much, another may neck with the girls a little too much. A good father uses a gentle but firm rein, checks his sons, guides them, and above all understands them." He knew what each of them needed. In 1958, he selected his new favorite, Frank Church, for the honor of reading George Washington's Farewell Address in the Senate on Washington's Birthday; telling a reporter why he had selected Church, he explained that he "needed a bit of bringing forward—just like my daughter does at school." More and more, he was unguarded in his estimates of his colleagues' abilities, and in his description of their relationship with him—after all, why should he watch his words; what could they do about it if they didn't like them? "Now, Alan," he said about Bible—said to a journalist—"Alan is a good, mediocre senator. He'll do what I tell him."

He let reporters know how cleverly he manipulated them.

His attitude was also apparent in the terms in which he described his own activities. In January, 1958, two days before the President's State of the Union address to Congress, Johnson delivered a speech to the Senate Democratic Caucus, instructing George Reedy to tell reporters it was Johnson's "State of the Union address." Did a President have a Cabinet? During the course of his speech, Johnson, as *Time* put it in a March, 1958, cover story on him, "hoisted himself to political heights without precedent by referring to himself, in effect, as President of the U.S. (South Pennsylvania Avenue Division). 'As majority leader of the Senate,' said he, 'I am aided by a cabinet made up of committee chairmen.' " Doris Fleeson might poke fun at his pronouncements, asking if he had worked out a disability agreement with his second-in-command, Mansfield, but most of the Washington press corps, which had overplayed each attack on Johnson's leadership (and then, after each one had failed, had conceded that his power was greater than ever), agreed with *Time*'s assessment that Johnson is "without rival the dominant face of the Democratic 85th Congress. . . . As such . . . he does indeed stand second in power only to the President of the U.S." Asking, "Who is the most powerful man in the United States today?" Stewart Alsop, in January, 1959, answered his own question: "The President." But, he added, "Sen. Lyndon Baines Johnson . . . certainly runs the President a close second, especially now that voters have given him a huge majority to lead. There are those who argue that Johnson is, in fact, if not in theory, the country's most powerful man, because he loves . . . to exercise power, and President Eisenhower does not."

BUT ALTHOUGH DURING THE FINAL THREE YEARS of his Senate career, Lyndon Johnson's power over the Senate was as great as ever, the legislative achievements of this last stage of his Senate career were in many ways no more than a reprise of his early years in the Senate.

This late period opened with a repeat of the theme—"preparedness"—that had been so prominent during the early period, more full-throated but in most aspects remarkably similar to its earlier form. On October 4, 1957, during the

Senate recess before the opening of the Senate's 1958 session, Russia launched *Sputnik* ("traveling companion"), the first man-made satellite to orbit the earth. Americans were shocked, having been confident of their nation's technological and scientific superiority over the Soviet Union. A new age—the Space Age—had been launched, and it wasn't America that had launched it but America's most feared enemy. Despite the Eisenhower Administration's attempts to minimize the Soviet Union's achievement (Sherman Adams said that America was not about to play the Russians in "an outer-space basketball game"), in the first excitement its implications seemed ominous. The Russians had beaten America in the race to develop a missile capable of placing a satellite in orbit; might they not also win in the race to develop a missile capable of delivering nuclear warheads? Lyndon Johnson was down on his ranch when the news came over the television late that afternoon. He was to recall that when, after dinner, he, Lady Bird, and their guests, Dale and Scooter Miller, took the evening walk on the dirt road next to the Pedernales, they peered up at the dark Hill Country sky, unsuccessfully "straining to catch a glimpse of that alien object" among the skyful of stars. He felt, he was to recall, "uneasy and apprehensive"—as did much of America that night and in the weeks to come. The country's first reaction was an alarm that approached panic; in the excitement it seemed that the Administration had squandered America's lead in missilery, and that the nation had been caught unprepared, as unprepared as it had been seven years earlier, when Communist troops in Korea had attacked without warning across the 38th parallel.

With the nation possibly in danger, Richard Russell was again not the bigot but the patriot—a patriot who, in love of his country, was pure of heart. On October 4, Russell was back in the big white frame house in Winder, and all that evening, telegrams and telephone calls arrived there from his colleagues, for, apprehensive over the news, they knew, as they had known during the MacArthur crisis, who was the best senator to handle the necessary investigation, the senator who was, moreover, chairman of the Senate committee—Armed Services—into whose jurisdiction the investigation fell. "This is so vital a matter that nothing short of your own guidance will give it the necessary prestige and force," John Stennis said. Stuart Symington was particularly insistent, urging "complete hearings" before the full committee so that "the American people can learn the truth"; in such hearings, he, as former Secretary of the Air Force and a longtime critic of Eisenhower's defense policies (and as a Democratic presidential candidate planning to base his campaign on the defense issue), envisioned himself playing a substantial role. But Russell, more and more aware of his loss of "energy," felt there was someone better suited for the work than himself: the senator who had done such yeoman work during that earlier time of unpreparedness. Having returned from his walk to the Pedernales, Johnson was about to put in a call to Winder when the phone rang in his living room. It was a call *from* Winder, and Russell told Johnson that the investigation should be carried out not by the full Armed Services Committee but by its Preparedness Subcommittee. Symington, he was to tell Johnson, "has a lot of information and would raise a lot of hell, but it would not be in the national interest." Soon, in a time of possible peril to the Republic, the telephone calls were again going back and forth between the big frame house in sleepy Winder and the ranch in the isolated Hill Country. Russell's tone was again avuncular. "You're so thorough you've got to have the answers before you ask the questions," he told Johnson. "Maybe this time you should ask the questions first." To Stennis and Symington and any other senator who asked him to conduct the investigation, Russell said, as he was to put it, that he "had more or less turned this whole matter over to Senator Johnson."

PREPAREDNESS HAD BEEN THE ISSUE THAT HAD, in 1950, catapulted Lyndon Johnson to Senate prominence, of course, and what he did now with that issue—and with that subcommittee (which, George Reedy was to say, "he had kept alive" during the intervening years "through the same instinct that causes people to store obsolete furniture in an attic rather than throw it in the trash")—duplicated in many ways what he had done with the issue and the subcommittee in 1950.

There was the same instant creation of an extremely able staff from outside the Senate world. Johnson's first choice for general counsel, in fact, was the subcommittee's earlier general counsel, Donald Cook. But Cook, now president of American Electric Power and determined never to work for Lyndon Johnson again, declined, and Johnson persuaded the man who had engineered Cook's move to American Electric, the New York attorney Edwin Weisl Sr., to accept the job in his place, and Weisl brought with him the brightest of the young lawyers at his big New York law firm, Cyrus R. Vance (who quickly caught Johnson's eye, would be boosted by him up through government ranks, and, during Johnson's presidency, would become Secretary of the Army), as well as Edwin Weisl Jr., a young attorney. Scientific expertise of the same quality came with the recruitment for the subcommittee's staff of scientists from Harvard and Rice Institute. These lawyers and scientists were added to the nucleus of the subcommittee's staff, headed by Daniel McGillicuddy, that was already in place, since Johnson had kept that nucleus intact over the years. Reedy was informally seconded to the subcommittee to be, again, its publicity director. There were the same assurances to a President—now not Harry Truman but Dwight Eisenhower—that the subcommittee would not attempt to lay blame on the Administration; after one Johnson visit to the Oval Office, Eisenhower would tell Ann Whitman that Johnson had "said all the right things. I think today he is being honest"—the same eloquent assurances of nonpartisanship to Senate Republicans, particularly to Styles Bridges, who was still the subcommittee's ranking Republican member; there would be "no 'guilty party' in this inquiry except Joe Stalin and Nikita Khrushchev," Johnson said; the material being assembled by the committee's staff was so "deeply disturbing" that even "the most hardened ward-heeler would forget politics if he knew the facts." He therefore pledged not to embarrass the "one man who can give the orders that will produce the missiles. That man is the President of the United States." "We very much appreciate the way you are approaching this," Secretary of Defense Neil McElroy replied. ". . . If through your efforts it is kept out of partisan politics, it will be for the good of the public and we want to work with you." To Republicans, he held up Symington as a spectre, the way he had held up Joe McCarthy to Democrats in 1950. "If he did not initiate it [an inquiry], it would be done by Symington, and that would be much worse," he told John Foster Dulles. There was the same journalistic praise over the nonpartisanship. The investigation "will serve a useful purpose," *Time*'s editors were told in a memo from the magazine's Washington bureau. ". . . It is not, repeat not, being conceived as a witch hunt. Johnson knows that a good investigation is the only kind that will satisfy anyone, and in the end bring credit to everyone. . . . Here, as downtown, there is a sense of urgency, of consideration of the national interest." There was the same understanding that nonpartisanship was, in this instance, the best politics, for the facts that would undoubtedly be brought out could hardly reflect other than unfavorably on the Administration. As a memo to Johnson from Reedy put it: "This may be one of those moments in history when good politics and statesmanship are as close to each other as a hand in a glove."

There was the same emphasis on publicity, the same squeezing out of every possible drop of that mother's milk of politics. "Johnson's running things . . . hit the extreme this week," John Steele was to report to his editors. "He was running the photographers and they were, for once, not objecting. He'd usher them [to closed committee sessions] for pictures, then usher them out and turn his attention to newsmen. Speaking so fast that no one could take a word-by-word account, he would rip through a briefing on a committee session, pant that he was ten minutes late for a luncheon speech he had to make. 'The statements will be up in a minute anyway,' burst out of the room to give the television interviewers time for 'just three' questions, then flaring up when a fourth was asked—'I told you, just three.' "

There was the same cultivation of the press, the same leaking of news to the most influential newsmen, the same long background sessions with columnists, a cultivation that extended into evenings, when he would invite them home to dinner, or weekends, when especially favored newsmen would be invited down to Huntlands, or even to Texas, with the most favored newsmen of all, Bill White and Stewart Alsop and Rowland Evans, coming to the ranch. (White, the most favored newsman of them all, secured the prize invitation: a visit to the ranch for Christmas.)

And there was the same skill in the obtaining of publicity, the same sure touch for public relations: for the right witnesses, the nation's most renowned nuclear scientists, like Edward Teller, Vannevar Bush, and Wernher von Braun,

and the nation's most bemedaled generals and admirals of the nuclear age—
Curtis LeMay, Hyman Rickover, James Gavin—called in the right order:
the scientists first—"To elevate the hearings into the realm of space and away
from interservice battles in the Pentagon," Reedy explains—and, first of all
the scientists, the one whose reputation as "the father of the hydrogen bomb"
assured maximum press interest. Teller didn't disappoint: in Reedy's words, he
"painted a verbal picture of a universe in which mastery of outer space meant
mastery of the world. The message he sent was clear. The Soviet Union had
taken the first step into the heavens and unless we hurried to catch up, the later
steps would find us under Communist domination." Then came the generals, to
paint a disturbing picture of how an overly economy-conscious Administration
had allowed its emphasis on a balanced budget to interfere with the nation's
security.

During the Korean War, the Senate Preparedness Subcommittee had been
a source of vivid, apt, headline-making phrases. One phrase that Reedy now
tried to suggest to Johnson, in fact, would have repeated a key word from the
subcommittee's earlier heyday: Reedy suggested that Johnson say that *Sputnik*
presented the American people with a challenge, a challenge that would require
"a call to action instead of a summons to a siesta." Johnson rejected the suggestion out of hand: why would a great phrasemaker need to repeat himself?
New phrases evolved in his press relations, press conferences, and letters to
constituents. Some linked this moment of unpreparedness to another—one
worse even than Korea. *Sputnik* was "a disaster . . . comparable to Pearl Harbor," Lyndon Johnson said. The Space Age is "an even greater challenge than
Pearl Harbor," he said on another. Pledging nonpartisanship, he said, "There
were no Republicans or Democrats in this country the day after Pearl Harbor."
Some evoked—not all that subtly—the speeches of a man whose speeches he
wanted to imitate. By pulling together, Americans could make the Space Age
"our finest hour," he said. (To Texans he likened *Sputnik* not to Pearl Harbor but
to the Alamo. Texans had lost that battle, he said, but had won the war against
Mexico: "History does not reward the people who win the battles, but the people who win the war.")

His very demeanor made newsmen feel, as they had felt in 1950, that the
nation was in trouble, that there was not a moment to lose, that news of the subcommittee was *big* news. A memo from Rowe reminded Johnson of the necessity of creating "a sense of urgency to counteract the complacency of the
administration," and it would be hard to imagine a more superfluous piece of
advice. Yet Johnson did not, in fact, seem to feel all that much urgency himself.
News of *Sputnik* had come on October 4, and Russell had in the next day or so
turned over the investigation to Johnson, but Johnson did not come to Washington until October 16, and he returned to Texas two days later—and, except for
a day he spent sightseeing in Monterrey, Mexico, he stayed in Texas until, on
November 2, the Russians launched a second, much larger, satellite that carried
a live dog (and was therefore named *"Muttnik"*); only then, on November 3,

did he return to Washington for the subcommittee's organizational meetings and a seven-and-a-half-hour briefing for himself, Russell, and Bridges at the Pentagon. He stayed in Washington for four days, and then went back to Texas for twelve days, returning to the capital on November 20 to prepare for the subcommittee's hearings, so that during the more than six weeks following the launching of *Sputnik,* he was in Washington for six days. But during those six days—and when, in January, he returned to the capital full time—he put on quite a show. (A memo from Steele told his editors: "This was the pace Johnson was traveling at as he breakfasted one day at the Pentagon with McElroy, another day at the Pentagon with [Wilber] Brucker, as he whisked the Senate through its opening session. . . . Johnson was moving through days of seven hours of committee sessions, hours of planning future sessions with his staff, the long party conferences, innumerable confabs with fellow senators and other party officials, speeches . . . television films for a Texas network, innumerable telephone conversations with government officials, a mountain of mail—all with a lopping [*sic*] speed but with a deadly purpose. Johnson was working this week as though the orbiting of an American *Sputnik* was his own responsibility and that it should have been done yesterday. His speed, intensity, and energy was contagious. An Army Brigadier General grabbed a sheaf of news releases to hurry the distribution to reporters at a Johnson committee session. . . .") Leaving Capitol Hill in the evening after filing their stories for the next day's papers, reporters would glance back at the darkened Capitol and see lights still blazing in that corner office on the third floor. "There seems to be a terrible sense of urgency about all this, doesn't there?" one reporter said to another, as he snatched up his notepad and ran down the hall to cover still another Johnson press conference. Watching Lyndon Johnson hurry through the corridors, coattails flapping, journalists coined jokes about his intensity. "Light a match behind Lyndon and he'd orbit," was one.

There was new proof that, in 1958 as in 1950, no matter how skilled Reedy might be, Lyndon Johnson was his own best public relations man. One day in January, the Preparedness Subcommittee, which had met in open session that morning, was scheduled to meet behind closed doors to hear sensitive testimony from Major General John B. Medaris, commander-in-chief of the Army Ballistic Missile Agency. During the noon break, however, while Johnson was, in John Steele's phrase, "lapping up a creamed chicken dish in his ornate green and gold Senate office," the phone rang. Defense Secretary McElroy wanted to tell him that he was about to make an important announcement: that the Army was being authorized to proceed on a "top-priority basis" with the development of a solid-fuel missile instead of relying on liquid-fueled missiles as in the past. Johnson didn't hesitate. Without so much as a pause, he asked McElroy not to make the announcement himself, but instead to let General Medaris make it—during his testimony before the subcommittee.

The headline-making news would therefore come not from the Pentagon, but from the Johnson Subcommittee, and Johnson made sure that the headlines would be big. The time was already about 2:22 p.m. The closed-door session was scheduled to begin in eight minutes. Johnson sent aides and secretaries scurrying to the Press Room and to the Senate cafeteria where some journalists ate lunch, to announce that at 2:30 sharp the subcommittee's doors would be thrown open—very briefly—for an important announcement. Reporters and photographers came running, some still chewing, and as they entered the room, Johnson, pounding his gavel for order, shouted, with the air of someone delivering a communiqué from a war zone, "General Medaris has a brief announcement to make. Copies of his statement will be ready in a few minutes." Two senators—Saltonstall and Flanders—were entering the committee room at a leisurely postprandial senatorial pace, and then, as soon as Flanders sat down, he got up again and started to leave the room. "Senator, Senator—where are you going?" Johnson asked. "Oh, I'll be back in fifteen seconds," Flanders replied. "But you can't leave us—this isn't going to take fifteen seconds," Johnson said curtly. Flanders sat back down, and Medaris made his announcement. And although there had been very little time to prepare a quotable phrase, one was ready on Lyndon Johnson's lips. As soon as Medaris had finished reading, Johnson told the General, as reporters' pens scribbled, "I hope this is not just a directive but that it is backed up with cold, hard cash. If you will convey that message to him [McElroy] maybe it will persuade him to make some more decisions." In case anyone had missed them, Johnson repeated the key words— twice. "Cold, hard cash," he said. "Cold, hard cash."

There was still television to be accommodated. This was a problem, because the TV camera crews, anticipating a closed session to which their bulky cameras would not be admitted, had left them down by the Caucus Room while they had lunch and had not been able to lug them downstairs in time for the announcement. Even as Medaris was speaking, Johnson aides were telling the cameramen to set up their cameras in the corridor outside the committee room, and as soon as the General had finished, Johnson stepped around the committee table, grabbed his arm, pulled him bodily out of his chair, and propelled him into the hall. "Now fellas, let's roll it!" Johnson said, standing so close to Medaris that it would have been difficult to show the General without showing him, too. One of the cameramen, still panting from his race upstairs, managed to say that one of their number had not yet arrived. "Well, you take it and give it to him," Johnson said angrily, and when the cameramen said that was impossible, he replied, "Now, listen, I told you to be ready." ("No one dared to mention that he had given them eight minutes to do so," Evans and Novak said.)

THERE WERE OTHER SIMILARITIES between 1958 and 1950, the same tendency toward hyperbole and oversimplification, for example. Dramatic though the *Sputnik* launchings may have been, their military significance—their significance, in other words, for America's safety—was minimal. The launchings showed that the Russians had indeed developed rockets with more thrust than America's, but it was not thrust but rather the rockets' accuracy and the destructive power of the nuclear warheads they carried that would count in war, and in both accuracy and explosive power the United States was still far ahead. In addition, America's bomber fleet of huge B-52s, constantly on alert or in the air, was vastly superior to Russia's bomber fleet, and had the added advantage of access to airfields virtually on Russia's borders. A Soviet attack on the United States would, for all Nikita Khrushchev's blustering, have been suicidal: America had enough nuclear capacity and missile technology—many times more than enough—to reduce the Soviet Union's cities and factories to ruins should the USSR launch an attack. Moreover, during the Eisenhower Administration the American margin of superiority had not narrowed but widened.

Quite sure of these facts—in part because of amazingly detailed photographic evidence from U-2s, supersonic reconnaissance aircraft that overflew the USSR at heights of up to 15,000 feet—Dwight Eisenhower attempted, in the weeks after *Sputnik,* to reassure a jittery America (although believing, incorrectly, that Russia was unaware of the U-2 flights, he shied away from revealing any facts that might have given the Russians a hint of their existence). In an October 9 news conference, in which journalists' questions, reflecting the mood of the moment, were more suspicious than at any other conference during his presidency, Eisenhower said that the satellite "does not raise my apprehensions, not one iota"; he would "rather have one good Redstone nuclear-armed missile than a rocket that could hit the moon," he said. "We have no enemies on the moon." Repeatedly during this period, the President sought to explain that we had more than enough nuclear capacity already so that massive emergency spending to develop more bombs was "unjustifiable"; "What is going to be done with this tremendous number of enormous weapons?" he asked on one occasion; how many times "could [you] kill the same man?" he asked on another. Furthermore, he said, the greatly accelerated spending would have "unfortunate effects" which his critics did not seem to have considered. As Ambrose puts it: "He deplored the Pearl Harbor atmosphere, the readiness to forget economics and spend whatever had to be spent to win the war. 'We face,' the President said, 'not a temporary emergency but a long-term responsibility. . . . Hasty and extraordinary effort under the impetus of sudden fear . . . cannot provide for an adequate answer.' He said he knew he could get whatever he asked for from Congress in the way of defense spending . . . but the suggested expenditures were at the expense of needed civilian expenditures and were 'unjustifiable.' . . . We must remember that we are defending a way of life." Turning America into a "garrison state" would mean taking the risk that "all we are striving to defend . . . could disappear."

Lyndon Johnson, briefed repeatedly by the Pentagon, must have been aware of these reassuring facts, but his statements continued to be short on facts and long on "Pearl Harbor atmosphere." His subcommittee's first report, filed on January 23, 1958, said: "We have reached a state of history where defense involves the total effort of a nation." Total effort meant in 1958 what it had meant in 1950; once again, the Senate Preparedness Subcommittee called for America to place itself—immediately—on an all-out war footing. In a prepared speech Johnson delivered on October 17, he said that the forty-hour workweek "will not produce intercontinental ballistic missiles," and therefore the entire nation "must go on a full, wartime mobilization schedule." His rhetoric escalated. America's first attempt to orbit a satellite, the *Vanguard 1*, failed on December 6, when the missile exploded as it was leaving the Cape Canaveral launching pad. The news was delivered to Johnson as he was chairing a subcommittee hearing before a large crowd in the Senate Caucus Room. "How long, how long, oh, God, how long will it take us to catch up with the Russians' two satellites?" he asked. His speeches, the author Alfred Steinberg says, "painted a frightening picture of the horror that would overtake the United States if it did not treat Soviet leadership in missilery as a war." "Control of space means control of the world," Johnson said. "From space, the masters of infinity would have the power to control the earth's weather, to cause drought and flood, to change the tides and raise the levels of the sea, to divert the Gulf Stream and change temperate climates to frigid." The subcommittee hearings were to generate headlines day after day, but even Reedy was to admit that "in retrospect some of the material should have been examined more carefully before being spread on the record in *ex parte* proceedings. One of the results was the public creation of a 'missile gap'—a concept that we were hopelessly behind the Soviets in the possession of ICBMs."

And in 1958 as in 1950, the Preparedness Subcommittee produced a publicity bonanza—hearings in the Senate Caucus Room jammed with radio and television cameras and microphones; cover articles in national magazines ("In a week of shot and shell in Washington . . . Lyndon Johnson went a far piece toward seizing, on behalf of the legislative branch, the leadership in reshaping U.S. defense policy," *Life* asserted)—and there were again, in '58 as in '50, indications that it was less preparedness than publicity that was the subcommittee chairman's primary concern. Eisenhower's calm assurances began to be understood, and they were bolstered by the successful launching of America's first satellite, *Explorer,* on January 31, 1958—and the resultant slackening of media interest in the missile crisis was mirrored by a corresponding slackening in the chairman's interest.

As usual the shift followed a Jim Rowe memo, this one typed on February 5. "I believe you have gained all you can on space and missiles," it said. "You have received a tremendous press, increased your national stature and gotten away scot-free without a scratch." A major recession was under way and, Rowe wrote, "I think you should turn now to the obvious new issue, which is unemployment." Johnson turned. "In the early spring," George Reedy was to say, he "just plain lost interest in the space issue. The public had begun to calm down and the Buck Rogers serials had played themselves out. He had never been comfortable with the subject matter and welcomed the rise of a new issue that he really understood—unemployment. . . . Unfortunately, Johnson . . . could see the [missile] issue only in terms of newspaper space and public attention. It did not involve poverty, education, or economic opportunity—problems which really held his attention. Therefore, as column inches devoted to outer space dwindled and as polls registered a diminution of popular interest, he virtually abandoned the entire project." "Abandoned" was not an overstatement: Lyndon Johnson's loss of interest in the space and missile investigation was complete—as became clear when aides approached him to ask for guidelines for the final subcommittee report. To their astonishment, Johnson didn't want a report; he "would actually have preferred that the subcommittee issue nothing at all," Evans and Novak would later report.

Johnson did not see a problem in this. "It did not bother him to abandon a program once he had concluded that it had lost its popular appeal," Reedy was to say. Reedy, however, saw a big problem: danger that the 1958 investigation would come to resemble the 1950 investigation in another respect, and that journalists who had been around in 1950 might recognize—and call attention to—the similarity. "Some of the staff members . . . recognized that leaving it [the subcommittee report] in limbo would ultimately work against Johnson," he says. "He had something of a reputation of exploiting issues without bringing them to a head, and to forget outer space after all the drama would have been deadly." A final report, including seventeen tersely worded, extremely general recommendations (sample: "Start work at once on the development of a rocket motor with a million pounds of thrust"), was drafted by Weisl and Vance and approved by the six other subcommittee members (in yet another example of bipartisan unanimity). And, Reedy says, Johnson's "worried assistants, who realized that his language [during the hearings] had been too strong to close the books with nothing accomplished, pushed him" into introducing a bill to create a new Senate committee, a Special Committee on Space and Astronautics, whose chairmanship Johnson took, to draft legislation for a national space program. "We'd shove the bills into Johnson's hands and get him to introduce them and that's the way the act emerged," Reedy was to say, in a recollection confirmed by other aides. What Reedy calls the "bills" were actually amendments—to legislation that had been drafted not by the committee but by the Eisenhower Administration, which sent to Congress a bill creating a National Aeronautics and Space Agency (NASA).

Identifying the bill's principal weakness—its lack of provision for a central policy-making body—Weisl, Vance, and Solis Horwitz recommended an amendment creating within NASA a small nine-member Space Council. Although during "the ensuing legislative process" Johnson, in Robert

Divine's words, "let his staff do most of the work," he insisted that the recommendation be incorporated in the Act. Eisenhower wanted only a purely advisory body, "not one which makes decisions," but in a meeting on Sunday, July 7, he and Johnson worked out a compromise, keeping the Policy Council but appointing the President as its head, and on July 29, 1958, Eisenhower signed the NASA Act into law. "Ike knew," as Divine writes, "that he had outmaneuvered Johnson. Over the next three years, the Space Council met on only rare occasions," without Eisenhower in attendance, and during that time had relatively little influence on national space or defense policies. But Johnson, in introducing the bill, said, reading from a memo drafted by Reedy, that he wanted to be a major figure in "the greatest of mankind's adventures," and Reedy's maneuvers successfully concealed from journalists his boss's lack of interest; their reaction is summarized in Evans and Novak's judgment that the Preparedness Subcommittee's space investigation was "a textbook example of what a Senate investigation ought to be."

Despite such statements, in 1958 as in 1950 the actual results of a much-publicized Lyndon Johnson "preparedness" investigation were virtually nonexistent. Johnson "made it clear that he was going through the motions" of introducing and supporting the bill "only to quiet the insistent demands of his staff," Reedy says. The creation of a space agency was significant in its institutionalization of the drive to explore space, but its form in practice was little different from the form it would have taken had Johnson not held his preparedness investigation. It would not be until 1961, when President Kennedy put Vice President Johnson in charge of the space program, that Johnson became genuinely active in a field with which he would become prominently identified. ("In later years, when he was reaping the public-image benefits of NASA achievements, he persuaded himself that they had taken place because of *his* prodding of *his* colleagues and *his* staff," Reedy would comment.)

THE SPACE INVESTIGATION'S lack of accomplishment, and its other similarities to episodes in Lyndon Johnson's early Senate career, was typical of the overall pattern of Lyndon Johnson's last three years in the Senate. "The last two years of the congressional decade"—1959 and 1960—"can only be described as dreary," Reedy was to write, and, with the exception of the space investigation, that adjective can be applied to the 1958 session as well.

There was, again, as in the Bricker Amendment battle of 1954, a fight against right-wing attempts to cripple another branch of the federal government, this time not the presidency but the Supreme Court. The South, of course, had been eager to punish the Court and limit its power ever since the *Brown* decision that year. In 1956 and '57, in a series of civil liberties rulings, the Court overturned or narrowed anti-Communist or anti-subversive legislation passed by individual states and reaffirmed the supremacy of federal over state law. The southern ranks were therefore swelled by the Jenners and Butlers and Curtises—by northern right-wingers of both parties. In August, 1958, shortly before adjournment, the conservatives had enough votes in both House and Senate to pass three anti-Court bills.

Having rolled through the House, the bills were reported favorably to the Senate by Jim Eastland's Judiciary Committee. As ill-drafted as they were ill-considered—they would be called a "legal monstrosity"—they were the kind of bills that gave the Senate a bad name (they would, for example, force interstate business to comply with forty-eight different, and not infrequently conflicting, state laws). It was too much even for Russell, who also realized that passage of such legislation would be a severe blow to Lyndon Johnson's efforts to woo liberal support for his presidential bid; Georgia's senior senator had spoken for the bills publicly, of course, but behind the closed doors of the Policy Committee had not disagreed with Johnson's decision to delay bringing them to the floor until August, when they could be buried in end-of-the-session confusion. Johnson had put Humphrey and Hennings in charge of counting votes, and when they assured him the bills would be defeated, he told the Policy Committee, "Well, I'm going to have to let them [conservatives] have their day on this stuff."

When he called the Court-ripper bills up on Tuesday, August 19, and the first two were defeated, Humphrey's count appeared correct. But when the third bill was brought up late Wednesday evening, with the Senate tired and querulous, the Court's civil rights record suddenly was brought into a dialogue on the Senate floor, and in a moment all the old passions were aroused, angry exchanges broke out, positions hardened, and when the roll was called on a motion to table and thus kill the third bill, the motion lost, 39 to 46. A second vote lost, 40 to 47. Richard Russell saw what was coming. As the Senate floor erupted in shouting matches, he leaned forward and whispered to the man at the desk in front of him, "Lyndon, you'd better adjourn this place. They're going to pass this goddam bill." Jumping to his feet, Johnson said, "Mr. President, I move that the Senate adjourn," but so infuriated were the conservatives by his action that, although adjournment was the Majority Leader's prerogative, several senators insisted on a roll call on his motion. As it began, Lyndon Johnson stood up at his desk. There was a clipboard in his hand, and on it a long sheet of paper. When a vote was cast against him, the Majority Leader wrote down the name of the senator who had done so, making sure that what he was doing was obvious. This act of less than subtle intimidation had its desired effect: at the end of the vote, there were only eighteen names on the paper.

Walking over to Humphrey, who was shaking his head in bewilderment, Johnson let him know that he had failed—again—at vote-counting. "You boys screwed up," he said. "I don't know what you did, but you screwed up. You told me wrong." Then he said, "If you want to beat this thing, there's still a way." Starting to explain the strategy that would have to be used, he suddenly realized that there were reporters listening. "I don't know these people," he said. "Let's get out of here." He started to lead Humphrey to his office. As he was crossing the Senate Reception Room, he saw Anthony Lewis, the *New York Times* Supreme Court reporter, coming down the stairs. Grabbing Lewis' arm, Johnson brought him along, and Reedy as well, and the four men settled down for a talk, the Majority Leader behind the big desk, the three men facing him. Every twenty minutes or so, a secretary would come in and hand Johnson a fresh Cutty Sark and soda, which he would gulp down.

They settled down, to be more precise, for a monologue. "In the course of two hours, Humphrey may have gotten out about three sentences," recalls Lewis, who, familiar with Humphrey's customary garrulousness, was astonished. As for himself and Reedy, "I don't think we said a word."

Lewis would never forget that monologue. An acute political observer, he understood its purpose. It was, he would say, "a display of his being on the right side of issues." (McPherson would explain Johnson's thinking: "What an opportunity: to defeat a bad bill, save the Court, and win the embarrassed thanks of Senate liberals! It was worth doing.") But nonetheless the monologue was awesome: not only a step-by-step exegesis of the complicated parliamentary maneuvers that alone could stop the bill from passing, but an exposition of why it should be stopped, an exposition so passionate that from that day forward, Anthony Lewis would believe in Lyndon Johnson's commitment to liberal causes. "Johnson always wanted to be seen by people like me as a defender of civil liberties," he would say decades later. "On the other hand, I think he actually believed in it—at least that's my opinion. It's my opinion because of things like the passionate lecture I saw him give Hubert Humphrey that night."

Lewis would remember with particular vividness one incident that occurred during the monologue while Johnson was explaining that he would need time to carry out his maneuvers, and that therefore Humphrey would have to filibuster to give him that time. And if the maneuvers failed, Johnson said, Humphrey would still have to filibuster—because if the maneuvers failed, a filibuster would be the only way to defeat the bill. Humphrey, who, of course, as Lewis knew, "had been fighting filibusters all his life," was reluctant to agree to do that, and Johnson said he understood Humphrey's feelings. But then Lyndon Johnson said, "Hubert, they're really gonna lambaste you for filibustering because you've always been against the filibuster. But if they hit you on one cheek, Hubert, you gotta turn the other cheek." And as Lyndon Johnson said that, he took one of his huge hands and slapped one of his own cheeks with the flat of that hand—slapped it hard. And then he took his other hand and slapped his other cheek—hard. "So hard!" Anthony Lewis would recall decades later. "He took his hand, which was a very large hand, and hit himself on the cheek— so *hard*! I thought, That must have *hurt*! And then he took the other hand. . . . I felt he believed in what he was saying. Definitely."

As it turned out, a filibuster would not be necessary. When the Senate convened the next day, Johnson put into motion the tactics he had outlined during the monologue: first, he had a motion introduced to return the bill to the Judiciary Committee, so that the vote would not be on the bill but only on the procedural motion, and therefore senators Johnson wanted to switch their vote "could," as Mann says, "truthfully claim that they had voted not to kill the bill but only to return it to committee." Then, using pressure and persuasion, he got enough senators to switch so that the vote on the motion was a tie, 40 to 40. And finally he got the forty-first vote, by persuading the GOP conservative Wallace Bennett of Utah to switch. An ardent supporter of Richard Nixon, Bennett very much wanted Nixon to be President. Johnson pointed out to him that a tie vote would have to be broken by Nixon, and no matter how Nixon voted, Johnson told Bennett, the vote would hurt Nixon's chances to become President: he would have to antagonize either liberals or conservatives. The way to save Nixon from this dilemma, Johnson said, was to make sure the vote wasn't a tie. So, as startled exclamations came from the gallery, Bennett voted aye—to send the anti-Court bill back to Judiciary, and death there.

DURING THESE LAST THREE YEARS, Lyndon Johnson would again, as in his early years, have to placate Herman Brown and the Texas right-wingers (which he did by steering to passage, in behind-the-scenes maneuvers, the harshly anti-labor Landrum-Griffin Act) and the great Senate bulls (he paid off a lot of debts to Clinton Anderson by cooperating in Anderson's efforts to defeat President Eisenhower's nomination of Lewis Strauss to be Secretary of Commerce, the first defeat of a presidential nominee for a Cabinet office since 1925). To try to placate liberals, he produced in each of the three years—1958, 1959, and 1960—a legislative package of progressive proposals that he said should be passed. The 1958 package had one fewer proposal than the thirteen-point Program with a Heart of 1956, but was otherwise quite similar—and the fate of all three packages was similar to that of the 1956 program, too: the few proposals that were passed had been watered down to inconsequentiality.

His interest in the 1960 Democratic presidential nomination made it impossible for him to avoid the civil rights issue, but his civil rights enthusiasm of 1957 had noticeably faded, possibly because, much as he needed liberal support to obtain the nomination, southern support was still the *sine qua non,* and in 1957 he had pushed southern senators, and Richard Russell, as far as they would go.

The net result of the 1959 and 1960 Senate civil rights battles was, at best, the smallest of steps forward—and it may even have been a step back. In 1959 (as in 1953, 1955, and 1957), Johnson first cut the ground out from under a liberal attempt to revise Rule 22 by engineering a compromise which, although technically a very modest weakening of that rule, might very well have proved in practice to strengthen it—John Stennis praised Johnson's "matchless leadership" in obtaining the compromise. Forced into introducing a civil rights bill of his own when both the liberals and the White House introduced their bills, he devised a measure so tame that Roy Wilkins called it a "sugar-coated pacifier." And then he allowed even that bill to die within the Judiciary Committee.

In 1960, the southerners staged a filibuster—the filibuster they had forsworn in 1957—against another liberal attempt to pass a civil rights bill. Lining up on the side of the South, Johnson opposed a liberal attempt to impose cloture. The vote on cloture, after two months of southern speeches, was 42 for, 53 against, figures that may be the clearest indication as to whether cloture could have been imposed in 1957; liberals had taken the 38 votes they obtained in the 1957 Rule 22 fight as a hopeful sign that they were in sight of the two-thirds vote needed to change the rule and make cloture possible; now, two years later, a vote had been taken on the cloture issue itself, and not only had they not obtained the necessary two-thirds, they had not even obtained a majority. As Robert Mann was to write: "Gone was their argument that an outmoded cloture rule was preventing the Senate from voting." The civil rights bill that eventually passed in 1960, with the tacit acquiescence of Russell and the South, was a bill that Johnson, working with Eisenhower's new Attorney General, William P. Rogers, had weakened to the point of meaninglessness. Liberals could only be thankful that, as Joe Clark put it, Russell, "the southern generalissimo," was a gracious victor who threw the liberals "a few crumbs." When the bill passed, Clark approached Russell and said, "Dick, here is my sword. I hope you will give it back to me so that I can beat it into a plowshare for spring planting."

43

The Last Caucus

THE STORY OF LYNDON JOHNSON'S CAMPAIGN for his party's 1960 presidential nomination, of his failure to win the nomination, and of his decision to accept second place on the ticket instead, will be told in the next volume of *The Years of Lyndon Johnson.* One aspect of the aftermath of the 1960 election, however, belongs in this volume, because it is part of the story of Lyndon Johnson and the Senate.

On November 5, 1960, Lyndon Johnson won election for both the vice presidency of the United States, on the Kennedy-Johnson ticket, and for a third term as Senator (he had had Texas law changed to allow him to run for both offices). When he won the vice presidency, he made arrangements to resign from the Senate, as he was required to do under federal law, as soon as it convened on January 3, 1961.

Johnson was sure he would still be a figure of power in Washington, no matter how powerless a job the vice presidency had been in the past. He would break the mold. "Power is where power goes," he told journalists. Furthermore, although he was giving up his seat in the Senate, he did not plan to give up his power there. During the weeks between November 5 and January 3, he devised an unprecedented plan: to continue, although he would no longer be a senator, to exercise power over the Senate's Democratic majority. Under his plan, he would do this not as Majority Leader but as Chairman of the Senate's Democratic caucus.

The new Majority Leader was going to be his whip, Mike Mansfield. In the past, the Leader had routinely been elected chairman of the caucus—as Johnson himself had of course been elected. Sometime in December, however, the Vice President–elect asked a few key senators—Russell, Kerr, Smathers and Humphrey—to have lunch with him, not on Capitol Hill but in a private dining room at the Sheraton-Carlton Hotel, "probably hoping," Hubert Humphrey was to say, "to keep it a secret." And at this lunch, he revealed his plan: that at the caucus, he, not Mansfield, would be elected chairman—that he would remain in the post that he had held for the past eight years.

It was apparent to the men in the dining room that Johnson intended to use the chairmanship to do more than merely preside over the caucus—that, in Humphrey's words, he wanted to use the post to "hang on to [the] power" he had had as Majority Leader as a "*de facto* Majority Leader"; Johnson, Humphrey was to say, "had the illusion that he could be in a sense, as vice president, the Majority Leader." Although the men in the room were all friends of Johnson's, doubts were immediately expressed. Humphrey, worried always about inflicting pain, said the plan "would offend Mike Mansfield and other leaders," and when Johnson said he was sure Mansfield would go along, the fact that the plan would violate the constitutional separation of powers between the Executive and Legislative Branches was raised. But, Humphrey was to say, "he's not an easy man to tell that you can't do something." Johnson may have said—he was to use these arguments later—that the Constitution already assigned the Vice President functions in the Senate: to preside over it, and to vote in it in case of a tie; he was later to say that chairing a party caucus would be only another, similar, function.

Whatever he said, he apparently believed he had persuaded the others to go along. He certainly persuaded Mansfield to go along—by telling him the caucus chairmanship was only a symbolic honor. He persuaded Mansfield, in fact, not only to let him be chairman, but to nominate him for the job. Johnson, Mansfield was to say, "asked if I would propose that he be permitted to attend future caucuses as Vice President and also to preside. In my view, this would constitute only an honorary position, and I had no objection." While he was at it, Johnson also persuaded Mansfield to allow him to retain not only the chairmanship but another symbol of his power: the Taj Majal. It had formerly been designated the Majority Leader's Office; now it would become the Vice President's Office, so Johnson would still be operating out of it when he was in the Capitol. Mansfield said he would be happy to use a much smaller suite—about half the size of the Taj Majal—on the other side of the Senate Chamber. And Johnson also persuaded Mansfield that he should retain Bobby Baker as Secretary for the Majority. When Baker received a call to come to the Taj Majal, he found Lyndon Johnson exultant. "There was a buoyancy about him that lately had been missing," Baker was to say. Johnson seemed, in fact, almost "manic." Waving Baker to a chair, he paced around the room. "Bobby," he said, "I've been thinking about where I can do Jack Kennedy the most good. And it's right here on this Hill, the place I know best." Jack Kennedy, he said, "never learned how things operate around here," and "all those Bostons and Harvards" with whom Jack was surrounding himself "don't know any more about Capitol Hill than an old maid does about fuckin'." His eyes shining with triumph, he gave Baker a piece of good news. "I'm gonna keep this office," he said, waving his arm in an expansive arc to emphasize its grandeur. He gave him another piece of good news—good news for Baker as well as for himself. "You can keep on helpin' me like you've always done," he said. "It's gonna be just the way it was!"

Then, coming over to Baker and standing close to him, Lyndon Johnson lowered his voice dramatically as he gave him the best news of all. "Just between me and you and the gatepost, Bobby," he said, "I'm workin' it out with Mike and Hubert to attend meetings of the Senate Democratic Caucus. Maybe even preside over 'em. That way I can keep my hand in. I can help Jack Kennedy's program, and be his eyes and ears. Whatta you think of that?"

Baker knew what he thought of it. "To tell the truth, I was both astonished and horrified," he was to say. "If anyone knew the United States Senate, its proud members and its proud traditions, it was Lyndon B. Johnson. Surely he knew that the prerogatives of membership were jealously guarded, that no member of the Executive Branch—even a Lyndon Johnson—would be welcomed in from the cold. Indeed, it seemed apparent that senators who long had chafed under LBJ's iron rule would have conniptions at the very idea of his continuing to exercise control over its affairs." Johnson certainly understood all this, Baker felt. "I originally couldn't believe that LBJ believed" he could successfully carry off his plan. But as Johnson "continued to expound on his new scheme," Baker "realized he was serious. I saw a disaster in the making." But when, after a while, Baker worked up the nerve to voice a few reservations, Johnson, "blinded by his plans, his ego, and his past Senate successes . . . overrode them," and just kept talking. The most he would agree to do was to allow Baker to "do a little pulse-taking."

Taking the pulse, Baker found that his fears were justified. News had already seeped out about the proposed retention of the Taj Majal and of Baker, raising what he called "apprehensions" among Senate liberals that Bobby would be in the future as in the past less the Democrats' agent than Johnson's. The Democratic liberals were, Evans and Novak explain, "brooding that Johnson would try to run the Senate from the Vice President's chair, with Mansfield, the self-effacing, introspective former professor who was uncomfortable with power, deferring to him." And, although Baker kept his hints about a retention of a caucus role by Johnson carefully vague, these hints heightened senatorial fears. "Having watched him [Johnson] operate for eight years, Democratic senators were fearful of what he might do now if he got a toe in the door," Evans and Novak were to explain. "An unspoken sentiment among many senators was the fear that if Johnson became *de facto* chairman of the conference, he would use that position as a lever to become *de facto* Majority Leader, with tentacles of power into both the Steering and Policy Committees, newly headed but not controlled by Mansfield." Wary of Baker's closeness to Johnson, senators were, Baker was to say, "reserved in their responses," but he had been taught to "listen to what they weren't saying," and his findings were "not comforting."

Refusing to take Baker's findings seriously, Johnson put his plan into operation. When the Democratic caucus was held at 9:45 a.m. on January 3, he had not yet resigned as senator—he would do so after the Senate convened at noon—so he was still a senator, and still Majority Leader, and he strode into the caucus with a broad, easy smile, the faithful Baker at his side, went up to the table that had been set up in front, sat down in the seat he had held for eight years, and called the conference to order. Mansfield was then elected Majority Leader by acclamation—but Johnson did not hand him the gavel and vacate his chair. Mansfield took a chair that had been set up next to Johnson's at the table, and made a motion, the minutes report, that "the Vice President–elect preside over future conferences."

As one of the senators in the room, Robert C. Byrd of West Virginia, was to write, "Can you imagine that? This action by the new Majority Leader reflected the quiet and unassuming nature of Mike Mansfield, but it was a mistake." As Evans and Novak were to write, "Mansfield was proposing that the Senate of the 87th Congress do what no other Senate had done: breach the constitutional separation of powers by making the Vice President the presiding officer of all the Senate Democrats whenever they met in a formal conference."

Several senators jumped to their feet to object. Johnson, as chairman, had to recognize them. Among the first were Joe Clark and Albert Gore. Looking directly at Johnson, Gore said angrily, "We might as well ask Jack [Kennedy] to come back up to the Senate and take his turn at presiding. I don't know of any right for a Vice President to preside or even be here with senators. This Caucus is not open to former senators." As Gore defied him, standing only a few feet away from him and staring him in the eye, an angry flush spread over Johnson's face, but Gore and Clark were liberals; their opposition had been anticipated, and it could be disregarded; for eight years, Johnson had been disregarding liberal objections with the support of the Old Senate Bulls.

But then other hands went up, and among them were the hands of three Bulls: Olin Johnston, Willis Robertson, and Clint Anderson. One after another, Johnson recognized them, expecting them to support Mansfield's motion; one after another, they attacked it. "Unbelievably" to Baker, even Anderson attacked it. He was a friend of Lyndon's, Anderson said, he had supported him in the Senate, and, he said, all Democratic senators owed Lyndon a great debt for his leadership. But, Anderson said, the Vice President was an official of the Executive Branch. Selection of a member of that branch to preside over a senatorial body would not only shatter the principle of separation of powers but would also make the Senate "look ridiculous." Bobby Baker sneaked another look at Johnson. The Leader's face, red a moment before, had "gone completely ashen." He recognized Mike Monroney, for so long the most loyal of allies. If we support Mansfield's motion, Monroney said, "We are creating a precedent of concrete and steel. The Senate will lose its powers by having a representative of the Executive Branch watching our private caucuses." All of the Old Bulls included praise of Johnson in their remarks, Bobby Baker was to say, "but there was no getting around that they were inviting him out of their Senate inner circle."

It was obvious that sentiment in the room was heavily against the motion, but Mansfield spoke in favor of it. He had no intention of "sharing either his responsibility or authority," he said; he intended the motion only as recognition for Johnson's achievements. And the new Majority Leader made it personal, threatening to resign from the post to which the senators had just elected him if they did not support his proposals.

"Under Mansfield's threat to resign, the Caucus did uphold his motion"—the vote was 46 to 17—"but everyone in the room knew that Johnson had been rebuffed," Bobby Baker was to say. "Even though we lost, we won," Gore said, "because the size of the vote didn't reflect the true sentiment. You could feel the heavy animosity in the room, even from many who voted for Lyndon—and Lyndon does possess a long antenna." As John Goldsmith of the United Press was to report, "With senators—*no* and *aye* alike—filing out of the conference room with grim expressions and angry whispers, it was clear . . . that it wasn't going to work." Word soon was circulating along the corridors of the Senate Office Building that, if necessary, there could be another vote—one that would have a different result.

THAT WOULD NOT PROVE NECESSARY. Several friendly senators tried to make Johnson grasp the reality of the situation. "I was one of those who told him that it was no good, and no good for him," Hubert Humphrey was to say. "It was just building up animosities. . . ." They also saw how difficult it was for him to accept the reality. "It was too much for him to leave that center of power," Humphrey says. "He was just very reluctant to give up those reins. . . ." Realizing that the situation had to be made clear to Johnson by someone who could make him understand, and realizing that there was only one senator capable of doing that, they delegated the task to him. "It fell to Richard Russell, his old friend, to bring him the obvious news that he could not hang on to the power he once had," Humphrey says.

After Russell spoke to him, he did understand. When the Democratic senators caucused again the next day, Lyndon Johnson was not present. Nor was he present at the next two caucuses. He did attend one on February 27, perhaps so that a statement from his new boss, relayed through Mansfield, would not sound like a rebuke of him. Mansfield told the caucus that he had been meeting with President Kennedy about a legislative program. He said, "The President has made suggestions, but he wanted the conference to know that the President and Vice President know the line of demarcation between the legislative and executive branches of government."

After that, Lyndon Johnson did not attend another caucus for almost two years; by the time he did appear at a Democratic conference again—at two caucuses in January, 1963—his attendance was no longer a threat to anyone, since by that time Washington understood that he had lost all his power, so completely that he had become almost a figure of ridicule in the capital. He called those two caucuses to order, and, when their business was completed, said they were adjourned. Aside from those functions, he did not, in the memory of senators who were present, participate in the caucuses at all, sitting through them saying little or nothing, staring gloomily down at the top of the table in front of him.

DURING HIS EARLY WEEKS AS VICE PRESIDENT, when he was presiding over the Senate while a senator was delivering a lengthy speech to an almost-empty chamber, he would sometimes step down from the dais, walk over to one of the few senators on the floor and begin to chat. The senators he approached were always courteous to him, but often they had to break off the conversation. They had other things to do. When he had had power, they had been anxious to talk to him, eager for a few moments of his time. They weren't anxious now. After a little while, he stopped coming down from the dais.

Once he came into the Democratic cloakroom which had been his domain, the cloakroom where he had stood holding fistfuls of telephone receivers, the wires stretching out from his hands, the cloakroom in which he had kicked the telephone booths, the cloakroom in whose center he had stood, Bobby Baker running up to him for whispered conferences, senators clustered around him waiting for instructions, trying to get a minute to plead with him for a favor, the cloakroom in which, for eight years, he had been the center of attention. When he came in now, several senators were there, sitting in the armchairs or on the sofas. He said hello to them. They said hello to him. He stood there for several minutes, apparently waiting for someone to stand up and talk to him, or to invite him to sit down. No one did. Says one of the men who were present, "I don't think he ever came into the cloakroom again."

IN LATER YEARS, when Lady Bird Johnson would talk about the time that her husband had been a senator, she would sometimes say, "Those were the happiest twelve years of our lives."

Those years *had* been happy—and now they were over. The Senate had been Lyndon Johnson's home. Now he had left it.

DEBTS
SOURCES
NOTES
INDEX

Debts

DURING THE TWELVE YEARS since the previous volume of *The Years of Lyndon Johnson* was published, the research team that works with me on the project has published its own book, and is well under way on a second, yet it has found time—*made* time, really—to continue doing research on the current volume.

The team—Ina Caro, that's the whole team, the only person besides myself who has done research on the three volumes, or on the biography of Robert Moses that preceded them, the only person I would ever trust to do so—has, during these twelve years, ranged all across the United States in search of information about Lyndon Johnson and the years he spent in the Senate. She has traversed mountains of files in presidential libraries: the Franklin D. Roosevelt Library in Hyde Park, New York; the Harry S Truman Library in Independence, Missouri; the Dwight D. Eisenhower Library in Abilene, Kansas—archivists in each of these libraries have taken occasion to tell me how deeply, watching her at work, they came to admire her tirelessness and diligence. And of course she has searched painstakingly and perceptively through the red and gray document boxes at the Lyndon Baines Johnson Library in Austin, Texas. That's just presidential libraries. Archival collections from Athens, Georgia (the Richard B. Russell Library) to Williamsburg, Virginia (the A. Willis Robertson Papers at the College of William and Mary), to Norman, Oklahoma (the Robert Kerr and Elmer Thomas Papers at the University of Oklahoma) have been subject to her incisive historian's eye, as have collections at a place to which she didn't have to take a plane but only a subway: Columbia University, where she has gone through, among many archives, the papers of Herbert H. Lehman.

Among the more memorable pieces of original research she accomplished is her work at the Russell Library, and she may also have read through more letters, memoranda, drafts of legislation and other documents from the members of the Senate's Southern Caucus of the 1950s than any human being on the face of the earth. For the previous volumes, the libraries in which Ina worked included the tiny libraries of isolated towns all across the Texas Hill Country, where she found early histories of the towns, and copies of ancient weekly newspapers that the librarians had thought no longer existed, and for those books, also, she accomplished other notable feats of research—transforming herself into an expert on rural electrification and soil conservation, for example—that I tried to acknowledge at the time. But I don't think that even for those books, Ina Caro achieved more in the way of pioneering archival research than she did for this one.

Ina was meant for libraries. She doesn't like to do interviews, but is always happy when she knows that the next week—or month—will be spent among books and papers, and there is still the same lilting joyfulness in her voice when she telephones me about some new discovery as I remember in her voice thirty years ago. This book, like the others before it, is improved in a hundred—or a thousand, who can count?—ways by the discoveries she has made in the files of vanished statesmen and bigots. The more I learn about history and historians, the more I realize what an exceptional historian she is: a researcher of remarkable tenacity and unshakable integrity—my beloved idealist, always.

THIRTY YEARS AGO, Bob Gottlieb and I began working together, over the 3,300-page manuscript of the Robert Moses book, *The Power Broker.* We are still working together, so all four of my books have benefited from the unique literary gifts of this talented and energetic editor. I am very grateful for that, as the dedication of this book attests.

Thirty years ago, another person was often in the room with her "two Bobs." Katherine Hourigan, Knopf's managing editor, has also been an integral part of both the editorial and production process on all four of my books. After the last one, I wrote that "Her editorial judgments are characterized not only by perceptivity but by an unflinching integrity that has only grown stronger over the years." Now more years have passed. The statement is still true. I also wrote, after that book, that it "presented daunting production problems. I have seen the ingenuity and tireless effort she put into solving them—and I have appreciated it." I *would* have to amend that. The production problems for *Master of the Senate,* a book by an author who can't seem to stop rewriting at every stage, were even more daunting. And I have appreciated even more deeply her efforts to solve them.

In a literary world of which so many aspects seem increasingly transitory, it seems marvelous to me that I have somehow managed to have been working with the same people for such a long time. And I don't mean just Bob and Kathy. As I walk around the halls of my publishing house, Alfred A. Knopf, they seem filled with friends of three decades. The ads for every one of my four books have been designed by the same person: Nina Bourne. When I came to Knopf in 1970, while I was still writing *The Power Broker,* Nina was Knopf's advertising manager, and when the book was published in 1974, she designed the ads for it, and I can still remember how thrilled I was by them. She designed the ads for the first two volumes of the Johnson project, and she is still Knopf's advertising manager.

Nina offers editorial criticism of my books, too. She never presses it on me, but I have learned that when this uniquely gifted woman says something, I'd better listen. When I came to Knopf, Bill Loverd and his enthusiastic love of books were part of the house, and they are a part still. Every one of my Johnson books has been designed by the same person: Virginia Tan.

Other people at Knopf have not been there quite as long, but they have been there long enough for me to appreciate them. The president and editor-in-chief, Sonny Mehta, published my last book as perfectly as a book could be published, in my opinion, and in the years since, he has always been there when I needed him. The guidance that Paul Bogaards, now Knopf's executive director of promotion and publicity, gave me on my last book made me understand and appreciate his energy and intelligence.

I have, luckily for me, had the same legal adviser for three decades—for longer than three decades, in fact, for when, during the 1960s, I was a young and totally inexperienced investigative reporter for *Newsday,* Andrew L. Hughes was its calm, deliberate—and ever wise—attorney. On *Master of the Senate,* as on my first three books, he has given me not only valuable legal guidance, but valuable literary guidance, too. It seems only a fitting part of the wonderful continuity of my writing life that his son Andrew W. Hughes is also a big part of my work. Andy, Knopf's vice president of production and design, supervised the production of my first two Johnson volumes, and is of course supervising it on this volume, too. I want to say a special word about Andy. I am aware of all the problems that my possibly excessive attention to detail has caused, and I want to say thanks to him for solving them—and for the way my books look when, finally, they actually appear.

Thanks also to these people at Knopf: Pat Johnson, Karen Mugler, Carol Carson, Kathy Zuckerman, Nicholas Latimer, and Gabrielle Brooks. For the past year and a half, Nathan Chaney has been Kathy Hourigan's assistant. His unfailing cheerfulness has meant a lot to me in rushed times.

As for Carol Shookhoff, also a longtime compatriot, she has been of help to me in so many ways that I hardly know how to thank her.

My literary agent—she has, of course, always been my agent—is Lynn Nesbit. She was one of the first people to read the manuscript of this book, and I waited anxiously for her opinion, for I have learned that she has a literary sensibility I can always trust.

Lynn has always been there when I needed her. Thanks.

IN 1975, the Senate created a Senate Historical Office, and within a remarkably short time thereafter the institution possessed, for the first time, an institutional memory, and, for journalists and historians, a storehouse—a treasure house, really—of information about it.

This occurred because of the two historians who were appointed—and to this day have been its only—Senate Historian and Associate Historian, respectively: Richard A. Baker and Donald A. Ritchie. It would have been easy for the Historical Office to become simply another bureaucratic backwater lodged in a few rooms in the Senate's Hart Office Building. But Drs. Baker and Ritchie are historians in the highest sense of the word. They made it their business to learn their subject, previously a real *terra incognita* on the American political landscape—to learn it, and to *know* it, inside and out, in all its ramifications, and to make that knowledge available to anyone who wanted to write about it.

A principal beneficiary of their largesse has been me. Since I began trying to learn about the Senate twelve years ago, I have badgered Dick Baker and Don Ritchie incessantly for information about the institution's history, its rules and precedents, its procedures, and the men who have served it.

I have been impressed times beyond counting with the extent to which these two men have had the most arcane facts at their fingertips—and impressed even more by their willingness, which so far as I can tell has no limits, to spare no effort to find out facts they didn't know. A single example—it involves Dr. Ritchie but plenty of other examples would involve Dr. Baker—will show what I mean. To illustrate how early in his Senate years Lyndon Johnson's quest for extra office space had begun, members of his staff laughingly told me about his attempt, during 1950, his second year in the Senate, to do something—it is not clear exactly what—to commandeer a tiny passageway (four square feet in size) that had once existed in the thick wall between his office—SOB 231 in what is now the Senate's Russell Building—and the Senate Cafeteria next door; the passageway had at some time in the past been boarded up and plastered over on the side leading to Johnson's office and used as a closet for cafeteria workers. Johnson's staffers couldn't tell me exactly how the attempt had been resolved, and I couldn't find out, so I asked Don Ritchie to help. He ran down architectural drawings, and correspondence, but, as it happened, he couldn't find out. On May 2, 1994, after a final effort, he wrote me, "Dear Bob: I've spent this morning in search of four square feet. . . . How I wish I could report that I know exactly the answer to your question, but honestly I don't." In a sense, then, he had not been able to help me in that instance (which is the reason the incident is not in the body of my book), but in a more important sense, what mattered was his willingness to make so earnest an effort to help. And the closet inquiry was one of the few inquiries I made during the twelve years I was working on this book to which Don—or Dick Baker—didn't find the answer, often after painstaking effort. I have abused shamefully the helpfulness of these two distinguished historians—each of them is the author of several books of his own—interviewing and telephoning them constantly, at their homes and in the evenings and on weekends, to fill in the vast blanks in my knowledge about the Senate. They never complained, were always helpful—and I will be forever grateful for that help. Any mistakes about the Senate in this book are there in spite of them; the responsibility is all mine. But to whatever extent the book is an accurate depiction of the Senate, it is accurate because of them.

. . .

FOR ME, during the past twelve years, the Lyndon Baines Johnson Library has meant a single person: Claudia Wilson Anderson.

Claudia came to work on Johnson's papers before there *was* a library. It opened in 1971; she had already been working on Johnson's papers since March, 1969, when the archives of the newly departed President were still stored at the Federal Building in downtown Austin.

During the intervening years, she has become the Library's great expert on the domestic presidential papers of the Johnson Administration, and on what the Library calls "Pre-Presidential Material"—which includes, of course, the Senate archives which form so large a part of the foundation for this volume.

Claudia is a Senior Archivist at the Library—a title which does not adequately do justice to her abilities, or to her significance in the study of American history. Like Dick Baker and Don Ritchie, she is an historian in the highest sense of the word. She knows—she has made it her business to know—the archival material in her charge as thoroughly as it is possible for a single human being to know those thousands of boxes of documents. And she wants historians—and through them history and the world—to know that material. And in addition to this motivation—the motivation of the true historian—there is about her work a rare integrity and generosity of spirit. I can't even imagine how many questions I have asked of Claudia (Where would I find material on this senator or that issue? Didn't I once, years ago, see a piece of paper somewhere in which George Reedy was advising Johnson not to keep ignoring Hubert Humphrey? What file might that be in?). No matter how many questions I asked her, however, I cannot remember one on which she didn't make as much of an effort as possible to answer it. And beyond such help on individual inquiries, her overall expertise—her guidance through the Lyndon Johnson Archives—has been the guidance of a perceptive and discriminating expert. I notice that every biographer of Lyndon Johnson has thanked Claudia for her help. They should have. History's knowledge of Johnson will be richer for her help. I can't imagine any biographer who owes her more than I do.

AT THE JOHNSON LIBRARY ALSO, Linda Seelke, E. Philip Scott, Ted Gittinger, and Kyla Wilson have been of help with this volume, and I thank them.

INA AND I are deeply indebted to a number of librarians at archival collections around the United States. We are especially indebted to the Russell Library's Sheryl Vogt. Her knowledge of the Russell papers was invaluable in steering Ina through the manuscript collection, as was her assistance in reading Russell's handwriting. Not only did she make Ina's trips to Athens productive, she was always available, even years later, to answer any questions we might have. The Eisenhower Library's Dwight Strandberg was also invaluable to Ina, both with his archival expertise and in making the library a pleasant and efficient research facility. The archivists at the Truman Library were so helpful and efficient that they had every file relating to Lyndon Johnson available and waiting every time Ina arrived in Independence. And Robert Parks at the Roosevelt Library, who remembers Ina from the time she first came to that library twenty-nine years ago as the researcher for *The Power Broker,* has for all that time been unstintedly generous in his assistance. Our gratitude also goes to Norman Chase at the Library of Congress, to Michael Gillette at the National Archives, and to Matthew Gilmore and Roxanna Deane at the Martin Luther King Library in Washington. The morgue of the defunct *Washington Star,* now in residence at that library, has been an invaluable resource for *Master of the Senate,* and Mr. Gilmore and Ms. Deane were very helpful in making it available.

I first met Greg Harness, the Senate Librarian, twelve years ago, when I was starting on this book, and for twelve years he has, with great expertise and unfailing graciousness, been providing me with information that I needed.

WILLIAM H. JORDAN JR. went to work for Richard Russell in 1955, and worked for him until Russell died in 1971, staying in the Senator's office every night until Russell went home. Bill revered the Senator, whom he considers one of the greatest of American statesmen, and during the three decades since his death has worked faithfully to ensure that he received his proper place in history. To try to ensure that I understood Russell and portrayed him accurately, Bill spent many hours talking to me, as well as driving me to Winder and arranging for me to spend time in Russell's home, and in the family graveyard behind it, as well as to talk with the Senator's grandnephew, Richard Brevard Russell III. I thank him for that, and for the hospitality that he and his wife, Gwen (who was also a member of Russell's staff and whose comments on him were also perceptive) extended to me. I thank Bill the more especially because he did all this although I think he understood that my view of Russell would coincide with his only in some respects. There was an honorableness about that that I admire.

Howard E. Shuman brought to the Senate the keen eye of a political scientist and economist, and he observed the Senate close-up for twenty-seven years, as an administrative assistant first to Senator Paul Douglas and then to Senator William Proxmire. His perceptive observations have been embodied in books and in many articles, and they were embodied also in the many hours of his time which he spent educating me about the Senate. I thank him for them.

Many journalists who covered the Senate during the 1950s and Lyndon Johnson during his senatorial and presidential years generously gave me the benefit of their observations and insights in hundreds of hours of interviews. These included Bonnie Angelo, John Chadwick, Benjamin Cole, Allen Drury,

Tex Easley, John Finney, Alan Emory, Rowland Evans, John A. Goldsmith, Seth Kantor, Murray Kempton, William Lambert, Anthony Lewis, Sarah McClendon, Karl Meyer, John Oakes, Irwin Ross, Hugh Sidey, Alfred Steinberg, J. William Theis, Theodore H. White, and Frank Van der Linden.

To a number of journalists, I am more than usually indebted. The word pictures of Lyndon Johnson briefing the press on the Senate floor just before noon each day that were given to me by Robert A. Barr were especially helpful, as was the research on the Senate which Bob volunteered to do for me.

In Neil MacNeil, who came to Washington with the United Press in 1949, and was immediately assigned to the Senate, and who later was the congressional correspondent for many years for *Time* magazine, I found a journalist with a remarkable knowledge of the institution, its history, its mores, and its men. Neil shared all this with me most generously, in many hours of interviews, and in rereading my notes on these talks, I was struck over and over with the depth of his insights. I could use almost the same words in thanking John L. Steele. Over and over again, when I needed a detail to fill out a scene, or a piece of Senate history or custom to augment my knowledge, I had only to pick up a telephone and call Mr. Steele, and my problem was solved. I thank him for both the keenness of his perceptions and his willingness to share them with me.

I had long admired the photographs of George Tames, and after I began talking with him, I learned that his eye was sharp even when it was not behind a camera. On several days—long days—George took me from room to room in the Capitol and the SOB, recounting to me scenes he had observed in each one, and helping me immeasurably in my attempts to grasp what the Senate was like decades ago.

Katharine Graham provided me with many hours of insights into Washington, into Lyndon Johnson, and into the relationship between Philip Graham and Johnson, so crucial in this volume, and crucial also in the volume to come. Moreover, she graciously provided me with transcripts of a few of her own interviews with people who figure in this book. I list Mrs. Graham here, among the journalists, because I believe this is where she would want to be listed. And I thank also her researcher, Evelyn Small.

In Margaret Mayer, I found a remarkable journalist. Her interviews with Johnson, and the vivid portraits her words painted of him, helped me in my attempts to see him as he was. Ms. Mayer covered him for the *Dallas Times-Herald* for many years, and worked for a short time on his staff. She has a very keen eye, and a real gift for words, and she put both at my disposal.

During our many visits to Austin, Greg Curtis and his wife, Tracy, made things very pleasant for Ina and me, generously driving Texas-length distances to introduce us to various versions of barbecue. My conversations with Greg, who during his many years as editor of *Texas Monthly* elevated that magazine to the first rank of American journalism, were an education to me about Texas' changing culture. I am grateful for those conversations.

Sources

IN TRYING TO RE-CREATE the world of the Senate of the 1950s, and Lyndon Johnson's place in it, a basic source is of course the written materials found in the Senate Historical Office, the Senate Library, and the National Archives and Records Administration in Washington; in the collections of the papers of individual senators in various libraries around the United States—the papers of Richard B. Russell at the Russell Library in Athens, Georgia, were especially helpful for this work, but so were the papers of senators like A. Willis Robertson at the College of William and Mary in Williamsburg, Virginia; Robert Kerr and Elmer Thomas at the Carl Albert Center at the University of Oklahoma in Norman, Oklahoma; and Herbert H. Lehman at Columbia University in New York City—and in collections such as the NAACP Papers at the Library of Congress. And of course there are the papers in the Johnson Library in Austin, Texas. As I have explained in previous volumes of *The Years of Lyndon Johnson*, the papers in the Johnson Library are stored in document cases, some plain red or gray cardboard, most covered in red buckram (and stamped with a gold replica of the presidential seal). There are 2,082 boxes that deal with the Senate, and they contain, by the Library's estimate, about 1,665,000 pages of documents. Some of them are only newspaper clippings or form letters to constituents, but there are hundreds of thousands of pages of significant letters, inter- and intra-office memoranda, scribbled notes, transcripts of telephone conversations, and speech texts in various edited versions. I don't know how many of those pages I've read during the twelve years I've been working on this volume, but I've read a lot of them.

In some areas, these papers are illuminating. The series in the Johnson Senate Papers labeled "Papers Relating to the Armed Services Preparedness Investigating Subcommittee," for example, are valuable because in order for freshman Senator Lyndon Johnson to obtain the staffing and funding he wanted for this subcommittee, he had to submit to senior senators detailed requests, and not only these requests but the work papers that went into the final requests provide significant insight into his thinking and maneuvers. The Senate Papers (which are described at the end of this Note) contain the office files and memoranda of various Johnson assistants, most notably Walter Jenkins, George Reedy, Solis Horwitz, and Gerald Siegel, and their reports to Johnson are detailed and informative.

I have found the Johnson papers rather unrevealing, however, about an area that is a major concern of this book: the nature of senatorial (or, in a larger sense, legislative) power, and how Johnson acquired and employed that power; how the Senate works, in other words, and how Lyndon Johnson *made* it work.

Primary written sources for the Senate itself, in the National Archives and the Senate Library and in other collections in Washington, are also not as helpful as they might be. For one thing, the source that should be the most basic and complete record for events on the Senate floor—the *Congressional Record*—cannot always be relied on as an accurate reflection of what occurred there. Senators and their assistants routinely "corrected"—meaning "edited," and, not infrequently, meaning expunged, or made more politic—the words they actually spoke on the floor. Lyndon Johnson made extensive use of this opportunity to alter the historical record, which during his later years in the Senate took place, as his assistant Colonel Kenneth E. BeLieu, staff director of Johnson's Preparedness Subcommittee from 1957 to 1961, states, in a room behind the Senate floor that "we called Dino's room, only because it was supervised by a man named Dino. This was ... where staffs corrected the Senators' floor statements for spelling, grammar and content."

"Often," BeLieu says, after Senator Stuart Symington and Johnson "had engaged in a spirited floor argument, Ed Welch and I went to Dino's to do our duties, Ed for Symington and I for the Leader. We both had written their respective and suggested remarks. I announced to Ed, 'What Lyndon said bears no resemblance to what I wrote for him.' Ed countered, 'What Symington said will bear no resemblance to what I'm now writing.' "* During Johnson's earlier years in the Senate, the editing was often done by Donald Cook and George Reedy, sometimes by other members of his staff, and sometimes by Johnson himself. His staff member Solis Horwitz, who worked for him from 1957 to 1959, was to recall that one morning in 1957, when a number of Johnson staffers were meeting in the office of Secretary of the Senate Felton (Skeeter) Johnston, "the Senator came in, and he had made a long speech on the floor that morning and had gotten into a great deal of dialogue. He had the transcript with him, and ... he was correcting the transcript while sitting there." (Horwitz says he "never saw him do that again in all the years that I was with him. Because after that, we always corrected the transcript.")† Other members of the staff said that while

---

*BeLieu, *The Captains and the Kings*, p. 196.
†Horwitz OH, p. 5.

Johnson did the editing himself infrequently during the years after he became Democratic Leader, he did it more frequently during the years before that. One area in which this altering of the *Record* is particularly damaging to historical accuracy is that of civil rights; during interviews, journalists and Senate staff members would vividly recall for me venomous racist remarks that some southern senator or other had made during a debate, but time and again when I went to the *Record* for the relevant date, no such remark (or any approximate version of it) was there.

Primary written sources are also not particularly helpful because of the nature of Senate life in the 1950s, in which so much crucial business—negotiating, persuading, the fashioning of compromises—was conducted not in writing but orally, face to face, or over the telephone, between the people involved, so that the only way to try to re-create the world of the Senate, and of Johnson's role in it, was to talk to these people.

I began my work on this volume in time for it to be possible for me to do this—but only just in time, as I was reminded, poignantly, by a letter written to the Caros (actually to my wife, Ina), on April 16, 2000, by Johnson's longtime assistant Horace W. Busby. Buzz, as Ina and I had come to call him, had been rushed to a hospital in Santa Monica, California, the previous weekend. "Quite a time," he wrote. "In and out of it for two nights—remember thinking it will be hard on Robert, nobody else can tell him about the Vice Presidency."

In the letter, Buzz said he was recovering. I was not sure he meant that; he closed the letter with a word he had never used before: "Farewell." He never really recovered, and he died, on May 31, 2000, at the age of seventy-six, without talking to me again.

Buzz's memory had failed him a bit in the hospital on one point: he *had* talked to me about "the Vice Presidency"—Lyndon Johnson's vice presidency—and about the presidency, as he had, of course, about Lyndon Johnson's years in the Senate. I had begun interviewing Buzz in 1976 in Austin. During the 1980s and 1990s, the interviews continued in Washington, some in his office, some in his apartment, some in a coffee shop, the Cozy Corner on Twentieth Street NW, that he liked to frequent, some in restaurants of a higher caliber. Some went on all day. In 1999, in failing health, he moved to Santa Monica, where his children could care for him, and the interviews continued by telephone. And he would write letters to clarify points he felt he had not made clear enough—or that I had stubbornly refused to accept because of conflicting information from other sources—during the conversations. Sometime after he moved, he lost his eyesight. He could still touch-type, however, and the letters continued. The occasional line which ran off the page, and the large, scrawled, very shaky *B* with which he signed the letters in hand, was the only sign of his disability. ("This *B* is not an affectation—best I can do since stroke," he typed once.)

It is difficult to calculate how many interviews I had with Horace Busby. I formally transcribed only seventeen of them; for scores of other lengthy interviews I made only handwritten notes (sometimes these, too, ran many pages); and is it correct to dignify with the title "interview" a brief telephone call he made to me in order to add a detail to a story he had previously told me, or to tell me a new anecdote about Lyndon Johnson that he had just remembered? I only know that when Buzz died, I still had so many more questions I wanted to ask him.

I had received previous reminders that among the problems involved in the writing of this volume was that of the human life span. Horace Busby was not the only member of Lyndon Johnson's staff who made an extensive effort to help me understand the extraordinary individual for whom they had worked, and to understand the years Johnson spent in the Senate of the United States. And he was not the only member of Johnson's staff whose help was cut off abruptly. George Reedy, whom I began interviewing in 1985 over gargantuan platters of choucroute in Milwaukee's German-American rathskellers, was in later years talking to me by telephone from his room in a nursing home in that city, with the same eagerness as Busby for me to get it right. My notes for a call I made to him on January 14, 1999, show that his first sentence was "I was hoping you would call me back. One point I didn't make clear . . ." One day in March, 1999, when I telephoned his room, there was no answer. I didn't attach any significance to that; there had been other occasions when I hadn't been able to get in touch with him for a few days. But this time, a day or two after my call, I picked up the *New York Times* and found myself reading his obituary. Ken BeLieu, John Connally, Walter Jenkins, Gene Latimer, Dan McGillicuddy, Mary Rather, Jim Rowe, Slug Tyler, Mary Louise Glass Young—all these people worked in Lyndon Johnson's various offices during his Senate years, all talked to me at length, and the assistance and insights of each of them were cut off while I still had questions to ask—as has also been the case, I must add, with an unfortunately large number of other men and women who were, in one capacity or another, involved in Johnson's life, and who have also died. Over and over again during the course of researching these books, I was abruptly reminded of the opportunity I was being given by the cooperation of these men and women—and of how that opportunity wasn't going to last indefinitely.

I feel it would be gratuitous to say that some of them—perhaps all of them—would not agree with everything I have written. But whatever success I may have had in re-creating the Senate of Lyndon Johnson is due beyond measure to the effort of these people to help me understand him, and the world of the Senate (and it is also due, of course, to the help of members of Johnson's staff who thankfully are still with us; particularly valuable insights and descriptions have been given me by Roland Bibolet, Yolanda Boozer, Nadine Brammer Eckhardt, Ashton Gonella, Gerald Siegel, and Warren Woodward). Some other members of Johnson's staff refused my requests for interviews, but they have given extensive oral history interviews to the Johnson Library, so that at least some of their views are on record. And the help of those who did talk to me has, I hope, reduced the significance of those refusals.

In addition to Johnson's staff, there were other interviews. Eleven were with senators: Bill Bradley of New Jersey, Robert Byrd of West Virginia, Carl T. Curtis of Nebraska, William J. Fulbright of Arkansas, Eugene J. McCarthy of Minnesota, Edmund S. Muskie of Maine, William Proxmire of Wisconsin, Abraham A. Ribicoff of Connecticut, Stuart Symington of Missouri, Herman Talmadge of Georgia, and Ralph W. Yarborough of Texas. Some of these interviews—with Fulbright, Muskie, and Symington—were extensive and valuable. And about others a particular word might be said. Ralph Yarborough was interviewed, after his retirement from the Senate, in a one-man law firm in Austin that seemed out of a daguerreotype of the Old West, with the mounted horns of a Texas longhorn over the receptionist's desk and, in his inner office, a long, long old-fashioned conference table covered, from one end to the other, in deep stacks of legal papers. He lavished time on me, in five intensive discussions, in an attempt to make me understand the Senate as he found it when he arrived there in 1957, and Lyndon Johnson as he had known him since he began encountering him in Texas politics during the 1930s. The interview with Herman Talmadge at his home in Henry County, Georgia, was painful—literally, since he was suffering badly from congestive heart failure, and every answer he made to my questions required an effort that was hard to watch. But the answers were given, and they provided me with new insight into Lyndon Johnson's relationship with the southern senators. Bill Bradley had thought quite deeply about the workings of the Senate, and about the nature of power in it. A series of interviews with him in 1996 both in Washington and in New York were more like lectures from a very thoughtful and perceptive scholar. In addition, Senator Bradley provided one bit of assistance that he was unusually (almost uniquely, in fact) qualified to give. Many of the men who had been present on the Senate floor during the 1950s had told me how Lyndon Johnson was so tall that he "towered" over senators in the well as he stood at his Majority Leader's front-row desk one step above it, and how his eyes were almost at the level of the clerks and the presiding officer on the dais across the well. Bill Bradley, as I realized from perusing an old program I had kept from a Princeton University basketball game, was six feet four and a half inches tall, just slightly taller than Johnson. When, near the end of the wonderful day on the floor that he arranged for me, he asked if there was anything further he could do to be of assistance, I said there was. The then Majority Leader, Bob Dole, wasn't at his desk. I asked Senator Bradley if he would mind going over and standing at it, so I could get a picture of precisely to what degree Johnson had in fact "towered" as he stood there. Bill was gracious enough to comply. Since this was an opportunity I was not likely to have again, I was determined to get the picture fixed firmly in my mind no matter how long that took. After a while, I realized that Bill had been standing there for quite some time, and that he was in fact looking at me as if to inquire if he had been there long enough. I said I would appreciate it if he would stand there a while longer, and he did, uncomplainingly—for as long as I needed.

It seems to have become a custom for biographers to total up the number of interviews they conducted for a book. I see by my notes that the number of people I interviewed is 263, but of course not just Busby and Reedy and Yarborough but many of these people were interviewed many times. With some of the key sources for this book—Bob Barr, Dick Bolling, Herbert Brownell, Ed Clark, Ava Johnson Cox, Tex Easley, Bryce Harlow, L. E. Jones, Bill Jordan, Margaret Mayer, Neil MacNeil, Posh Oltorf, Joe Rauh, Jim Rowe, Howard Shuman, John Steele, Arthur Stehling, many others, too—our relationship became so friendly that whenever I had a question, I was able to simply pick up a telephone and call them, informally. And of course those names do not include Dick Baker and Don Ritchie, who during these twelve years have spoken to me, formally, informally, in person, over the telephone, from their office, from their homes, so many times that I am sure they never want to hear from me again. Adding up the interviews I conducted is difficult, but by the most conservative estimate the number is more than a thousand.

Here is a description of the papers in the Johnson Library that form part of the foundation for this third volume—and an explanation of how they are identified in the Notes that follow.

Senate Papers, 1949–1961 (JSP): The papers kept in files in Johnson's various offices, including the one he maintained in Austin, Texas; his "Texas Office" in the Senate Office Building; his Democratic Majority Leader's Office in the Capitol; and from files of the Democratic Policy Committee, from 1949 through January, 1961. These include memoranda (both intra-office and with others), correspondence from and to constituents, correspondence relating to presidential nominees to federal and diplomatic positions for which Senate confirmation was required; correspondence, drafts of bills, reports and drafts of reports as well as memoranda and work papers and press relating to his work on the various Senate committees and subcommittees of which he was a member; transcripts of committee and subcommittee executive sessions and hearings. These papers include *Congressional Record* tear sheets. They also include the "Papers of the Democratic Leader," which are made up of the files of individual members of his staff, including Policy Committee staff members George Reedy, Solis Horwitz, and Gerald W. Siegel. They include meeting agenda, analyses of proposed legislation, intra-office and inter-office memoranda, correspondence with other senators, and with members of the House of Representatives, and with lobbyists, officials of federal agencies; speech drafts and final versions, and drafts and final versions of press releases. "George Reedy's Confidential Memo File," part of these Senate Papers, contains memos on many topics. Many have no date recorded, but some are filed in folders by month. Some are from Reedy to Johnson, giving him information; some were written by Reedy at Johnson's instructions, or dictation, to be shown to other senators as if they were Reedy's own thoughts, to reinforce arguments Johnson wanted to make to them.

Senate Political Files (SPF): These files cover a time period from 1949 to 1960. They concern the consolidation of Johnson's position in Texas following the 1948 campaign; the 1954 Senate campaign; his 1956 bid for the presidency; and his bid in 1960 for the presidential nomination. They also contain numerous Texas county files. They were made into a separate file by the Library staff.

Lyndon Baines Johnson Archives (LBJA): These files were created about 1958, and consist of material taken both from the House of Representatives Papers and from Johnson's Senate Papers. It consists of material considered historically valuable or of correspondence with persons with whom he was closely associated, such as Sam Rayburn, Abe Fortas, James Rowe, George and Herman Brown, Edward Clark, and Alvin Wirtz; or of correspondence with national figures of that era. These files are divided into four main categories:

1. Selected Names (LBJA SN): Correspondence with close associates.
2. Famous Names (LBJA FN): Correspondence with national figures.

3. Congressional File (LBJA CF): Correspondence with fellow congressmen and senators.

4. Subject File (LBJA SF): This contains a Biographic Information File, with material relating to Johnson's year as a schoolteacher in Cotulla and Houston; to his work as a secretary to Congressman Richard M. Kleberg; to his activities with the Little Congress; and to his naval service during World War II.

Pre-Presidential Confidential File (PPCF): This contains material taken from other files because it dealt with potentially sensitive areas.

Pre-Presidential Memo File (PPMF): This file consists of memos taken from the House of Representatives Papers, the Johnson Senate Papers, and the Vice Presidential Papers. While these memos begin in 1939 and continue through 1963, there are relatively few prior to 1946. While most are from the staff, some are from Johnson to the staff. The subject matter of the memos falls in numerous categories, ranging from specific issues, the 1948 Senate campaign, and liberal versus conservative factions in Texas to phone messages and constituent relations.

Family Correspondence (LBJ FC): Correspondence between the President and his mother and brother, Sam Houston Johnson.

Personal Papers of Rebekah Baines Johnson (RBJ PP): This is material found in her garage after she died. It includes correspondence with her children (including Lyndon) and other members of her family, and material collected by her during her research into the genealogy of the Johnson family. It also includes scrapbooks.

Personal Papers of Alvin Wirtz (AWPP): Twenty-five boxes.

White House Central File (WHCF): The only files in this category used to a substantial extent in this volume were the Subject Files labeled "President (Personal)" (WHCF PP). They contain material about the President or his family, mainly articles written after he became President about episodes in his early life.

White House Famous Names File (WHFN): This includes correspondence with former presidents and their families, including Johnson correspondence when he was a congressman with Franklin D. Roosevelt.

Documents Concerning Lyndon B. Johnson from the Papers of Franklin D. Roosevelt, Eleanor Roosevelt, John M. Carmody, Harry L. Hopkins, and Aubrey Williams (FDR-LBJ MF): This microfilm reel was compiled at the Franklin D. Roosevelt Library in Hyde Park and consists of correspondence to and from Johnson found in various PPF and OF files at the Roosevelt Library. Whenever possible, the author has included the file number, by which the original documents can be located at the Roosevelt Library.

A WORD OF EXPLANATION is necessary about the citations in the Notes that read "Georgia Giant."

These citations refer to a three-hour television documentary, "Richard Russell: Georgia Giant," which aired in 1970 on Cox Broadcasting's WSB-TV in Atlanta, Georgia. When the citations read "unedited transcript," they refer to the typed transcript of twenty-five hours of interviews conducted with Russell by the journalist Harold Suit that were filmed for the documentary, mostly on the front porch of the Russell home in Winder. Quotations from this transcript are identified by the number of the reel of film to which the transcript refers. The citations that read "edited transcript" refer to the typed transcript of the three-hour documentary which actually aired. In two instances, Russell is seen on the first hour of the documentary (actually on the first of three videotapes of the program) talking about his father, and the edited transcript does not contain those quotes, so in those two instances the source is cited as " 'Georgia Giant,' Tape, Part I." All transcripts are in the Richard B. Russell Library.

When a citation refers to an "interview conducted by Katharine Graham," it means one of the interviews that Mrs. Graham conducted for her own book, *Per-*

sonal History, sometimes in conjunction with her researcher, Evelyn Small. Transcripts of these interviews were given to the author by Mrs. Graham.

AUTHOR'S INTERVIEWS

Lola Aiken • Bonnie Angelo • James Anton • Rodney Baines • Richard A. Baker • Ross K. Baker • Inspector Leonard H. Ballard • Jean Douglas Bandler • Robert Barr • Alan Barth • Joseph Bartlett • Robert T. Bartley • Melinda Baskin • Kenneth E. BeLieu • Merton Bernstein • James Bethke • Roland H. Bibolet • Andrew Biemiller • Rebekah Johnson Bobbitt • Richard Bolling • Paul Bolton • Yolanda Boozer • Bill Bradley • Jim Brady • T. Edward Braswell • Howard Bray • George R. Brown • Herbert Brownell • Marcus Burg • Horace W. Busby • Robert Byrd • John Carlton • John Carver • James Casey • Emanuel Celler • John Chadwick • Brady Chapin • Zara Olds Chapin • Evelyn Chavoor • Bethine Church • Blair Clark • Edward A. Clark • Ramsey Clark • Benjamin V. Cohen • Benjamin Cole • W. Sterling Cole • James P. Coleman • John B. Connally • Nellie Connally • John Sherman Cooper • Thomas J. Corcoran • Ava Johnson Cox • Anne Fears Crawford • William E. Cresswell • Margaret Tucker Culhane • Carl T. Curtis • Lloyd Cutler • Patrick Dahl • William H. Darden • Hadassah Davis • Phil Davis • Willard Deason • Earl Deathe • Harry Dent • Oliver J. Dompierre • Helen Gahagan Douglas • Allen Drury • H. G. Dulaney • Lewis T. (Tex) Easley • Nadine Brammer Eckhardt • Julius G. C. Edelstein • Albert Eisele • Gerry Eller • Alan S. Emory • Grover Ensley • Rowland Evans • Creekmore Fath • Bernard J. Fensterwald • Thomas C. Ferguson • John Finney • O. C. Fisher • Gilbert C. Fite • Abe Fortas • William J. Fulbright • Barbara Gamarekian • David Garth • Sim Gideon • Michael L. Gillette • Tom Glazer • Stella Gliddon • Arthur J. Goldberg • Reuben Goldberg • Arthur (Tex) Goldschmidt • John Goldsmith • Glee Gomien • Ashton Gonella • William Goode • Katharine Graham • Ralph Graves • Kenneth Gray • Bailey Guard • John Gunther • Jack Gwyn • D. B. Hardeman • Bryce Harlow • Lou Harris • Richard Helms • Charles Herring • Pat Holt • John Holton • Alice Hopkins • Welly K. Hopkins • Barbara Howar • Phyllis Hower • Ward Hower • Thomas Hughes • Dr. J. Willis Hurst • Patrick B. Hynes • Edouard V. M. Izac • Eliot Janeway • Elizabeth Janeway • Beth Jenkins • Walter Jenkins • Lady Bird Johnson • Sam Houston Johnson • Herman Jones • James Jones • Luther E. Jones • Gwen Jordan • William H. Jordan Jr. • Seth Kantor • Carroll Keach • Chapman Kelly • Murray Kempton • Mylton (Babe) Kennedy • Vann M. Kennedy • Eugene J. Keogh • Theodore W. Kheel • Joe M. Kilgore • Robert (Barney) Knispel • Fritz Koeniger • Louis Kohlmeier • Henry Kyle • Joseph Laitin • William Lambert • Joseph P. Lash • Trude Lash • Gene Latimer • Anthony Lewis • Oliver Lindig •

R. J. (Bob) Long • Kathleen Louchheim • Wingate Lucas • Diana MacArthur • Neil MacNeil • George H. Mahon • Frank Mankiewicz • Gerald C. Mann • Caryl Marsh • Maury Maverick Jr. • Margaret Mayer • Edward A. McCabe • Eugene J. McCarthy • Sarah McClendon • Richard T. McCulley • Frank C. McCulloch • Daniel J. McGillicuddy • Bill McPike • Dale Miller • Powell Moore • Ernest Morgan • Edmund S. Muskie • Roger Newman • John Oakes • John Olds • Dr. Marianne Olds • Frank C. (Posh) Oltorf • Donald Oresman • J. J. (Jake) Pickle • William Proxmire • Edward Puls • Julie Leininger Pycior • Carolina Longoria Quintanilla • Alexander Radin • Richard Rashke • Mary Rather • Joseph L. Rauh Jr. • Elwyn Rayden • Benjamin H. Read • Emmette Redford • George Reedy • Abraham A. Ribicoff • Horace Richards • Floyd Riddick • Donald A. Ritchie • William P. Rogers • Irwin Ross • Elizabeth Rowe • James H. Rowe Jr. • Richard B. Russell III • Darrell St. Claire • Ray Scherer • Arthur M. Schlesinger Jr. • Harry Schnibbe • Budd Schulberg • John Sharnick • Emmet Shelton • Howard E. Shuman • Hugh Sidey • Gerald L. Siegel • E. Babe Smith • Lon Smith • Carl Solberg • Bernard V. Somers • Theodore Sorenson • Natalie Springarn • Jerome Springarn • John L. Steele • Arthur Stehling • Alfred Steinberg • Philip M. Stern • Walter J. Stewart • Steve Stibbens • Elizabeth Stranigan • Marsha Suisse • James L. Sundquist • Mimi Swartz • Stuart Symington • Herman Talmadge • George Tames • J. William Theis • Bernard R. Toon • Dr. Janet G. Travell • Marietta Tree • J. Mark Trice • Margaret Truman • Lyon L. Tyler • Cyrus Vance • Frank Van der Linden • Melwood W. Van Scoyoc • James Van Zandt • William Walton • Delbert C. Ward • Gerald Weatherly • Robert C. Weaver • O. J. Weber • Edwin Weisl Jr. • William Welsh • John Wheeler • Theodore H. White • Vernon Whiteside • Elizabeth Wickenden • Tom Wicker • Claude C. Wild Jr. • Wendy Wolff • Claude E. Wood • Wilton Woods • Warren Woodward • Ralph W. Yarborough • Harold H. Young • Mary Louise Glass Young • Sam Zagoria • Murray Zweben

ORAL HISTORIES

Lyndon B. Johnson Library, Austin, Texas

George D. Aiken, Carl B. Albert, Robert S. Allen, Stewart J. Alsop, Clinton P. Anderson, Eugenie M. Anderson, James Anton, Robert G. (Bobby) Baker, Malcolm Bardwell, Charles E. Bohlen, Richard Bolling, Paul Bolton, Kenneth E. BeLieu, Levette J. (Joe) Berry, Roland Bibolet, Sherman Birdwell, James H. Blundell, Charles K. Boatner, T. Edward Braswell, George R. Brown, Richard Brown, Russell M. Brown, Raymond E. Buck, Cecil E. Burney, Horace W. Busby, Bo Byers, James Cain, Clifton C. Carter, Clifford P. Case, S. Douglass Cater, Emanuel Celler, Oscar L. Chapman, James E. Chudars, Frank Church, Ramsey Clark, Tom C. Clark, Earle C. Clements, Clark Clifford, W. Sterling Cole, James P. Coleman, Donald C. Cook, John Sherman Cooper, John J. Corson, Ben Crider, Ernest Cuneo, Carl T. Curtis, Price Daniel, William H. Darden, Willard Deason, Marjorie Delafield, Helen Gahagan Douglas, Paul H. Douglas, David Dubinsky, Clifford and Virginia Durr, L. T. (Tex) Easley, James O. Eastland, Allen J. Ellender, Virginia Wilke English, Truman and Wilma G. Fawcett, Thomas K. Finletter, Elaine Fischesser, O. C. Fisher, Sam Fore Jr., Abe Fortas, Gordon Fulcher, Hector T. Garcia, Reynaldo G. Garza, Eugene B. Germany, W. Sim Gideon, Irving L.Goldberg, Arthur and Elizabeth Goldschmidt, Ashton Gonella, Callan Graham, Katharine Graham, Walter G. Hall, Bourke B. Hickenlooper, Estelle Harbin, D. B. Hardeman, Robert Hardesty, Bryce Harlow, Mrs. Jessie Hatcher, Carl Hayden, Richard M. Helms, Charles Herring, Welly K. Hopkins, Welly K. and Alice Hopkins, Ardis C. Hopper, Walter Hornaday, Solis Horwitz, Hubert Humphrey, Henry M. Jackson, Robert M. Jackson, Jake Jacobsen, W. Ervin (Red) James, Leon Jaworski, Walter Jenkins, Alfred T. (Boody) Johnson, Sam Houston Johnson, Luther E. Jones Jr., Marvin Jones, Edward Joseph, Carroll Keach, Jesse Kellam, Mylton L. Kennedy, Sam Kinch Sr., William Knowland, John Fritz Koeniger, Eugenia Boehringer Lasseter, Gene Latimer, Ray Lee, Erich Leinsdorf, Kittie Clyde Leonard, Gould Lincoln, Otto Lindig, C. P. Little, R. J. (Bob) Long, Russell Long, Stuart M. Long, J. C. Looney, Kathleen C. Louchheim, John E. Lyle Jr., Warren Magnuson, George Mahon, Gerald C. Mann, Leonard Marks, Joe Mashman, Margaret Mayer, Sarah McClendon, Frank McCulloch, Ernest W. McFarland, Vicky and Simon McHugh, Marshall McNeil, Harry McPherson, George Meany, Dale and Virginia (Scooter) Miller, Clarence Mitchell, A. S. (Mike) Monroney, Booth Mooney, Powell Moore, Robert W. Murphey, Dorothy J. Nichols, Frank C. (Posh) Oltorf, Wright Patman, Harvey O. Payne, Drew Pearson, Arthur C. Perry, J. J. (Jake) Pickle, W. Robert Poage, Ella SoRelle Porter, Paul A. Porter, Harry Provence, William Proxmire, Graham Purcell, Daniel J. Quill, Mary Rather, Joseph L. Rauh Jr., Benjamin H. Read, Cecil Redford, Emmette S. Redford, George E. Reedy Jr., Horace E. Richards, Chalmers M. Roberts, A. Willis Robertson, Fenner Roth, Payne Rountree, Leverett Saltonstall, Harold Barefoot Sanders, Josefa Baines Saunders, Norbert A. Schlei, Arthur Schlesinger, Emmett Shelton, Polk and Nell Shelton, Hugh Sidey, Gerald W. Siegel, Margaret Chase Smith, Anthony M. Solomon, John Sparkman, Max and Evelyn Starcke, John C. Stennis, Sam V. Stone, O. B. Summy, James L. Sundquist, Stuart Symington, Herman E. Talmadge, Willie Day Taylor, J. William Theis, Strom Thurmond, Bascom N. Timmons, Grace Tully, Mary Margaret Wiley Valenti, Carl Vinson, H. Jerry Voorhis, Harfield Weedin, Edwin L. Weisl Jr., Edwin L. Weisl Sr., June White (Mrs. William S. White), William S. White, R. Vernon Whiteside, Tom G. Wicker, James Russell Wiggins, Claude C. Wild Sr., Roy Wilkins, Glen and Marie Wilson, Wilton Woods, Warren G. Woodward, James C. Wright Jr., Zephyr Wright, Milton R. Young.

United States Senate Oral History Program, Senate Historical Office

Leonard H. Ballard, Roy L. Elson, Grover W. Ensley, Pat M. Holt, Carl M. Marcy, Stewart E. McClure, Jesse R. Nichols, Scott I. Peek, Warren Featherstone Reid, Floyd M. Riddick, Darrell St. Claire, Dorothye G. Scott, Howard E. Shuman, George A. Smathers, George Tames, J. William Theis, Rein J. Vanderzee.

Dwight D. Eisenhower Library, Abilene, Kansas

George Aiken, Jack Z. Anderson, John Bricker, Herbert Brownell, Prescott Bush, Ralph Flanders, Barry Goldwater, Andrew J. Goodpaster, Homer Gruenther, Bryce Harlow, Robert C. Hill, Jacob Javits, Kenneth B. Keating, William F. Knowland, Edward A. McCabe, L. Arthur Minnich, Gerald Morgan, E. Frederick Morrow, Maxwell Rabb.

Sam Rayburn Library, Bonham, Texas

Carl Albert, Robert S. Allen, Robert T. Bartley, John Brademas, Cecil Dickson, H. G. Dulaney, John Holton, Walter K. Jenkins, Lady Bird Johnson.

Richard Brevard Russell Memorial Library
University of Georgia, Athens, Georgia

Harry F. Byrd Jr., Robert Byrd, Lawton Miller Calhoun, John Thomas Carlton, Earl Cocke Jr., George W. Darden, William H. Darden, Robert Mark Dunahoo, James O. Eastland, Allen Ellender, Sam J. Ervin Jr., Luck Coleman Flanders Gambrell, Spenser M. Grayson, Mary Willie Russell

Green, Roy Vincent Harris, Roman Lee Hruska, Hubert H. Humphrey, Lady Bird Johnson, Felton Johnston, Wayne P. Kelly Jr., Earl T. Leonard, Russell B. Long, Mike Mansfield, Powell Moore, Richard Nixon, Patience Russell Peterson, William Proxmire, Barboura Raesly, Dean Rusk, Fielding B. Russell, Reverend Henry Edward Russell, Leverett Saltonstall, Carl Sanders, George Smathers, Clara Smith, Jack Spain, Ina Russell Stacy, Betty Talmadge, Strom Thurmond, Robert Troutman Jr., Samuel E. Vandiver Jr., Cash Williams.

BOOKS CITED IN TEXT

Adams, Henry. *Democracy.* New York: Meridian, 1994.

———. *History of the United States of America During the Administrations of Jefferson and Madison.* New York: Library of America, 1986.

Alsop, Joseph, and Turner Catledge. *The 168 Days.* Garden City, N.Y.: Doubleday, 1937.

Alsop, Joseph, with Adam Platt. *"I've Seen the Best of It": The Memoirs of Joseph W. Alsop.* New York: W. W. Norton, 1991.

Alsop, Stewart. *The Center: People and Power in Political Washington.* New York: Harper & Row, 1968.

Ambrose, Stephen E. *Eisenhower,* Vol. II, *The President.* New York: Simon & Schuster, 1984.

Anderson, Clinton P., with Milton Viorst. *Outsider in the Senate: Senator Clinton Anderson's Memoirs.* New York: World Publishing, 1970.

Anderson, J. W. *Eisenhower, Brownell, and the Congress: The Tangled Origins of the Civil Rights Bill of 1956–1957.* University, Ala.: University of Alabama Press, 1964.

Ashby, LeRoy, and Rod Gramer. *Fighting the Odds: The Life of Senator Frank Church.* Pullman: Washington State University Press, 1994.

Baker, Bobby, with Larry L. King. *Wheeling and Dealing: Confessions of a Capitol Hill Operator.* New York: W. W. Norton, 1978.

Baker, Leonard. *Back to Back: The Duel Between FDR and the Supreme Court.* New York: Macmillan, 1957.

Baker, Richard A. *The Senate of the United States: A Bicentennial History.* Malabar, Fla.: Krieger, 1988.

Baker, Richard A., and Roger A. Davidson, eds. *First Among Equals: Outstanding Senate Leaders of the Twentieth Century.* Washington, D.C.: Congressional Quarterly, 1991.

Baker, Ross K. *Friend and Foe in the U.S. Senate.* New York: Free Press, 1980.

Baker, Russell. *An American in Washington.* New York: Knopf, 1961.

———. *The Good Times.* New York: Signet, 1992.

Barkley, Alben W. *That Reminds Me.* Garden City, N.Y.: Doubleday, 1954.

Bass, Jack, and Marilyn W. Thompson. *Ol' Strom: An Unauthorized Biography of Strom Thurmond.* Atlanta: Longstreet, 1998.

Bearss, Edwin C. *Historic Resource Study . . . Lyndon B. Johnson National Historic Site, Blanco and Gillespie Counties, Texas.* Denver: U.S. Dept. of Interior, National Park Service, 1971.

BeLieu, Kenneth E. *The Captains and the Kings.* Baltimore: Gateway Press, 1999.

Berry, Margaret C. *The University of Texas: A Pictorial Account of Its First Century.* Austin: University of Texas Press, 1980.

Beschloss, Michael R., ed. *Reaching for Glory: Lyndon Johnson's Secret White House Tapes, 1964–1965.* New York: Simon & Schuster, 2001.

———. *Taking Charge: The Johnson White House Tapes, 1963–1964.* New York: Simon & Schuster, 1997.

Bohlen, Charles E. *Witness to History: 1959–1969.* New York: W. W. Norton, 1973.

Bolling, Richard. *Power in the House.* New York: Dutton, 1968.

Bone, Hugh A. *Party Committees and National Politics.* Seattle: University of Washington Press, 1960.

Branch, Taylor. *Parting the Waters: America in the King Years, 1954–1963.* New York: Simon & Schuster, 1988.

Brownell, Herbert, with John P. Burke. *Advising Ike: The Memoirs of Attorney General Herbert Brownell.* Lawrence: University Press of Kansas, 1993.

Burdette, Franklin L. *Filibustering in the Senate.* Princeton, N.J.: Princeton University Press, 1940.

Burns, James MacGregor. *The Crosswinds of Freedom.* New York: Knopf, 1989.

———. *Roosevelt: The Lion and the Fox, 1882–1940.* New York: Harcourt Brace and Co., 1962.

———. *Roosevelt: The Soldier of Freedom, 1940–1945.* San Diego: Harcourt Brace Jovanovich, 1970.

———. *The Vineyard of Liberty.* New York: Knopf, 1982.

———. *The Workshop of Democracy.* New York: Knopf, 1985.

Burns, Vincent G. *Out of These Chains.* Los Angeles: New World Books, 1942.

Byrd, Robert C. *The Senate, 1789–1989: Addresses on the History of the U.S. Senate,* Vols. I and II; *Historical Statistics, 1789–1792,* Vol. III. Washington, D.C.: Government Printing Office, 1988–93.

Califano, Joseph A., Jr. *The Triumph and Tragedy of Lyndon Johnson: The White House Years.* New York: Simon & Schuster, 1991.

Caro, Robert A. *Means of Ascent: The Years of Lyndon Johnson,* Vol. II. New York: Knopf, 1990.

———. *The Path to Power: The Years of Lyndon Johnson,* Vol. I. New York: Knopf, 1982.

Carrey, Johnny, Cort Conlay, and Ace Barton. *Snake River of Hells Canyon.* Cambridge, Idaho: Backeddy, 1978.

Chandler, David Leon. *The Natural Superiority of Southern Politicians: A Revisionist History.* Garden City, N.Y.: Doubleday, 1977.

Church, F. Forrester. *Father and Son: A Personal Biography of Senator Frank Church of Idaho by His Son.* New York: Harper-Collins, 1985.

Civil Rights Education Project. *Free at Last: A History of the Civil Rights Movement and Those Who Died in the Struggle.* Montgomery, Ala.: Southern Poverty Law Center, n.d.

Clark, Joseph S. *Congress: The Sapless Branch.* New York: Harper & Row, 1964.

Cohodas, Nadine. *Strom Thurmond and the Politics of Southern Change.* New York: Simon & Schuster, 1993.

Connally, John, with Mickey Herskowitz. *In History's Shadow: An American Odyssey.* New York: Hyperion, 1993.

Crawford, Ann Fears, and Jack Keever. *John B. Connally: Portrait in Power.* Austin: Jenkins Publishing Co., 1973.

Dallek, Robert. *Lone Star Rising: Lyndon Johnson and His Times, 1908–1960.* New York: Oxford University Press, 1991.

Davie, Michael. *LBJ: A Foreign Observer's Viewpoint.* New York: Duell, Sloan, and Pearce, 1966.

Dickerson, Nancy. *Among Those Present.* New York: Random House, 1976.

Divine, Robert A., ed. *The Johnson Years,* Volume 2: *Vietnam, the Environment and Science.* Lawrence: University Press of Kansas, 1987.

Donald, David Herbert. *Charles Sumner and the Coming of the Civil War.* New York: Knopf, 1960.

Donovan, Robert J. *Conflict and Crisis: The Presidency of Harry S. Truman, 1945–1948.* New York: W. W. Norton, 1977.

———. *Tumultuous Years: The Presidency of Harry S. Truman, 1949–1953.* New York: W. W. Norton, 1982.

Douglas, Helen Gahagan. *A Full Life.* Garden City, N.Y.: Doubleday, 1982.

Douglas, Paul H. *In the Fullness of Time: The Memoirs of Paul H. Douglas.* New York: Harcourt Brace Jovanovich, 1972.

Drukman, Mason. *Wayne Morse: A Political Biography.* Portland: Oregon Historical Society Press, 1997.

Drury, Allen. *A Senate Journal, 1943–1955.* New York: Da Capo Press, 1972.

Dugger, Ronnie. *The Politician: The Life and Times of Lyndon Johnson.* New York: W. W. Norton, 1982.

Dulles, Foster Rhea. *The Civil Rights Commission: 1957–1965.* East Lansing: Michigan State University Press, 1968.

Egerton, John. *Speak Now Against the Day: The Generation Before the Civil Rights Movement in the South.* New York: Knopf, 1994.

Eisele, Albert. *Almost to the Presidency: A Biography of Two American Politicians.* Los Alamitos, Calif.: Piper Publishing, 1972.

Eisenhower, Dwight D. *Public Papers of the Presidents, 1953–1961.* Washington, D.C.: Government Printing Office, 1954–1962.

———. *The White House Years: Waging Peace, 1956–1961.* Garden City, N.Y.: Doubleday, 1965.

Elsmere, Jane Schaffer. *Justice Samuel Chase.* Muncie, Ind.: Janevar Publishing Co., 1980.

Evans, Rowland, and Robert Novak. *Lyndon B. Johnson: The Exercise of Power.* New York: New American Library, 1966.

Fairclough, Adam. *Race and Democracy: The Civil Rights Struggle in Louisiana, 1915–1972.* Athens: University of Georgia Press, 1995.

Federal Writers' Project. *Washington: City and Capital.* Washington, D.C.: Works Progress Administration, 1937.

Fisher, O. C. *Cactus Jack*. Waco, Tex.: Texian Press, 1978.

Fite, Gilbert C. *Richard B. Russell, Jr., Senator from Georgia*. Chapel Hill: University of North Carolina Press, 1991.

Foner, Philip S., and Ronald L. Lewis, eds. *The Black Worker: A Documentary History from Colonial Times to the Present*. Philadelphia: Temple University Press, 1978.

Fox, Harrison W., Jr., and Susan Webb Hammond. *Congressional Staffs: An Invisible Force in American Lawmaking*. New York: Free Press, 1977.

Galloway, George B. *Congress at the Crossroads*. New York: Crowell, 1946.

———. *The Legislative Process in Congress*. New York: Crowell, 1953.

Garraty, John A., and Mark C. Carnes. *The American Nation*. Boston: Addison-Wesley, 1999.

———. *Henry Cabot Lodge: A Biography*. New York: Knopf, 1953.

Gilfry, Henry H. *Precedents—Decisions on Points of Order in the United States Senate, for the Sixty-third Congress, March 4, 1914, to March 3, 1915*, Vol. II. Washington, D.C.: Government Printing Office.

Goldsmith, John A. *Colleagues: Richard B. Russell and His Apprentice, Lyndon B. Johnson*. Washington, D.C.: Seven Locks Press, 1993.

Goodwin, Doris Kearns. *The Fitzgeralds and the Kennedys: An American Saga*. New York: Simon & Schuster, 1987.

———. *Lyndon Johnson and the American Dream*. New York: Harper & Row, 1976.

Goodwin, Richard N. *Remembering America: A Voice from the Sixties*. Boston: Little, Brown, 1988.

Goodwyn, Frank. *Lone-Star Land: Twentieth-Century Texas in Perspective*. New York: Knopf, 1955.

Goulden, Joseph C. *The Best Years, 1945–1950*. New York: Atheneum, 1976.

Graham, Katharine. *Personal History*. New York: Knopf, 1997.

Griffith, Winthrop. *Humphrey: A Candid Biography*. New York: William Morrow, 1965.

Gunther, John. *Inside U.S.A.* New York: Harper & Bros, 1947.

Hagerty, James C. *The Diary of James C. Hagerty: Eisenhower in Mid-Course, 1954–55*, ed. Robert H. Ferrell. Bloomington: Indiana University Press, 1983.

Halberstam, David. *The Fifties*. New York: Villard Books, 1993.

Hamilton, Alexander, James Madison, and John Jay. *The Federalist Papers*. New York: Mentor, 1961.

Hamilton, Charles V. *Adam Clayton Powell, Jr.: The Political Biography of an American Dilemma*. New York: Simon & Schuster, 1991.

Hardeman, D. B., and Donald C. Bacon. *Rayburn: A Biography*. Austin: Texas Monthly Press, 1987.

Harwood, Richard, and Haynes Johnson. *Lyndon*. New York: Praeger, 1973.

Haynes, George H. *The Senate of the United States: Its History and Practice*. New York: Russell & Russell, 1960.

Heinemann, Ronald. *Harry Byrd of Virginia*. Charlottesville: University Press of Virginia, 1996.

Horn, Stephen. *Unused Power: The Work of the Senate Committee on Appropriations*. Washington, D.C.: Brookings Institute, 1970.

Humphrey, Hubert. *The Education of a Public Man: My Life and Politics*. Garden City, N.Y.: Doubleday, 1976.

Humphrey, William. *Farther Off from Heaven*. New York: Knopf, 1977.

Javits, Jacob, and Rafael Steinberg. *Javits: The Autobiography of a Public Man*. Boston: Houghton Mifflin, 1981.

Jewell, Malcolm E. *Senatorial Politics and Foreign Policy*. Lexington: University of Kentucky Press, 1962.

Johnson, Lyndon. *The Vantage Point: Perspectives of the President, 1963–1969*. New York: Holt, Rinehart and Winston, 1971.

Johnson, Rebekah Baines. *A Family Album*, ed. John S. Moursund. New York: McGraw-Hill, 1965.

Johnson, Sam Houston. *My Brother Lyndon*. New York: Cowles, 1970.

Josephson, Matthew. *The Politicos, 1865–1896*. New York: Harcourt, Brace and Co., 1938.

———. *The President Makers: The Culture of Politics and Leadership in an Age of Enlightenment, 1896–1919*. New York: Harcourt Brace, 1940.

Josephy, Alvin M., Jr. *The American Heritage History of the Congress of the United States, 1975*. New York: American Heritage, 1975.

Kennedy, John F. *Profiles in Courage*. New York: Harper & Row, 1961.

Kiley, James M. *The Leland Olds Manual on Long-Range Rate Making*. Denver, Colo.: Mid-West Electric Consumers Assoc., 1961.

Kluger, Richard. *Simple Justice: The History of* Brown v. Board of Education *and Black America's Struggle for Equality*. New York: Knopf, 1976.

Lash, Joseph P. *Eleanor and Franklin.* New York: W. W. Norton, 1971.

Lawson, Steven F. *Black Ballots: Voting Rights in the South, 1944–1969.* New York: Columbia University Press, 1976.

Lemann, Nicholas. *The Promised Land: The Great Black Migration and How It Changed America.* New York: Knopf, 1991.

Leuchtenberg, William. *Franklin D. Roosevelt and the New Deal, 1932–1940.* New York: Harper & Row, 1963.

Lindley, Betty Grimes. *A New Deal for Youth.* New York: Viking, 1938.

Link, Arthur S. *Wilson: The New Freedom.* Princeton, N.J.: Princeton University Press, 1956.

Link, Arthur S., and William Bruce Catton. *American Epoch: A History of the United States Since 1900—An Era of Economic Change, Reform, and World Wars, 1900–1945,* Vol. 1. New York: Knopf, 1963.

Lippman, Walter. *U.S. Foreign Policy: Shield of the Republic.* Boston: Little, Brown, 1943.

MacNeil, Neil. *Dirksen: Portrait of a Public Man.* New York: World, 1970.

Maddox, Robert F. *The Senatorial Career of Harley Martin Kilgore.* New York: Garland Press, 1981.

Madison, James. *Notes of Debates in the Federal Convention of 1787.* New York: Norton, 1987.

Malone, Dumas. *Thomas Jefferson and His Time,* Vol. IV: *The President, First Term: 1801–1805.* Boston: Little, Brown, 1970.

Manchester, William. *American Caesar: Douglas MacArthur, 1880–1964.* Boston: Little, Brown, 1978.

———. *The Glory and the Dream: A Narrative History of America, 1932–1972.* Boston: Little, Brown, 1974.

Mann, Robert. *The Walls of Jericho: Lyndon Johnson, Hubert Humphrey, Richard Russell, and the Struggle for Civil Rights.* New York: Harcourt Brace, 1996.

Martin, John Bartlow. *Adlai Stevenson and the World.* Garden City, N.Y.: Doubleday, 1977.

———. *Adlai Stevenson of Illinois.* Garden City, N.Y.: Doubleday, 1976.

———. *The Deep South Says "Never."* New York: Ballantine, 1957.

Martin, Ralph G. *Ballots and Bandwagons.* New York: Rand McNally, 1964.

Matthews, Donald R. *U.S. Senators and Their World.* Chapel Hill: University of North Carolina Press, 1960.

Matthews, William. *Oratory and Orators.* Chicago: S. C. Griggs, 1879.

McCullough, David G. *Truman.* New York: Simon & Schuster, 1992.

McKeever, Porter. *Adlai Stevenson: His Life and Legacy.* New York: William Morrow, 1989.

McPherson, Harry. *A Political Education.* Boston: Little, Brown, 1972.

Mendelson, Wallace. *Discrimination: Based on the Report of the United States Commission on Civil Rights.* Englewood Cliffs, N.J.: Prentice-Hall, 1962.

Miller, Merle. *Lyndon: An Oral Biography.* New York: Putnam, 1980.

Montgomery, Ruth. *Mrs. LBJ.* New York: Holt, Rinehart and Winston, 1964.

Moody, Anne. *Coming of Age in Mississippi: An Autobiography.* New York: Dial Press, 1968.

Mooney, Booth. *LBJ: An Irreverent Chronicle.* New York: Crowell, 1976.

———. *The Politicians: 1945–1960.* Philadelphia: Lippincott, 1970.

Morison, Samuel Eliot, Henry Steele Commager, and William Edward Leuchtenberg. *The Growth of the American Republic,* Vol. II. New York: Oxford University Press, 1969.

Newlon, Clarke. *L.B.J.: The Man from Johnson City.* New York: Dodd, Mead, 1966.

Oates, Stephen B. *Let the Trumpet Sound: A Life of Martin Luther King, Jr.* New York: Harper & Row, 1982.

O'Brien, Lawrence F. *No Final Victories: A Life in Politics from John F. Kennedy to Watergate.* Garden City, N.Y.: Doubleday, 1974.

Orum, Anthony. *Power, Money, and the People: The Making of Modern Austin.* Austin: Texas Monthly Press, 1987.

Oshinsky, David M. *A Conspiracy So Immense.* New York: Free Press, 1983.

Parker, Robert, with Richard Rashke. *Capitol Hill in Black and White.* New York: Dodd, Mead, 1986.

Patterson, James T. *Mr. Republican: A Biography of Robert A. Taft.* Boston: Houghton Mifflin, 1972.

Pearson, Drew. *Diaries, 1949–1959,* ed. Tyler Abell. New York: Holt Rinehart, 1974.

Pearson, Drew, and Jack Anderson. *The Case Against Congress: A Compelling Indictment of Corruption on Capitol Hill.* New York: Simon & Schuster, 1968.

Peterson, Merrill D. *The Great Triumvirate: Webster, Clay, and Calhoun.* New York: Oxford University Press, 1987.

Phillips, Cabell B. *The 1940s: Decade of Triumph and Trouble.* New York: Macmillan, 1975.

———. *The Truman Presidency.* New York: Macmillan, 1966.

Preston, Nathaniel Stone. *The Senate Institution.* New York: Van Nostrand, 1969.

Price, Margaret. *The Negro Voter in the South.* Atlanta: Southern Regional Council, 1957.

Pycior, Julie Leininger. *LBJ and Mexican Americans: The Paradox of Power.* Austin: University of Texas Press, 1997.

Quezada, J. Gilberto. *Border Boss: Manuel B. Bravo and Zapata County.* College Station: Texas A&M University Press, 1999.

Raines, Howell. *My Soul Is Rested: Movement Days in the Deep South Remembered.* New York: Putnam, 1977.

Reedy, George. *Lyndon B. Johnson: A Memoir.* New York: Andrews & McMeel, 1982.

———. *The U.S. Senate: Paralysis or a Search for Consensus?* New York: Crown, 1986.

Reeves, Thomas C. *The Life and Times of Joe McCarthy.* New York: Stein and Day, 1982.

Reston, James. *Deadline: A Memoir.* New York: Random House, 1991.

Reston, James, Jr. *The Lone Star: The Life of John Connally.* New York: Harper & Row, 1989.

Riddick, Floyd M. *Majority and Minority Leaders of the Senate—History and Development of the Offices of Floor Leaders.* Washington, D.C.: Government Printing Office, 1979.

———. *The United States Congress: Organization and Procedure.* Manassas, Va.: National Capitol Publishers, 1949.

———. *Riddick's Senate Procedure: Precedents and Practices,* rev. and ed. Alan S. Frumin. Washington, D.C.: Government Printing Office, 1992.

Rosenman, Samuel I. *Working with Roosevelt.* New York: Harper & Bros., 1952.

Ross, Irwin. *The Loneliest Campaign: The Truman Victory of 1948.* New York: New American Library, 1968.

Rovere, Richard H., and Arthur M. Schlesinger, Jr. *The General and the President, and the Future of American Foreign Policy.* New York: Farrar, Straus and Young, 1951.

Rowan, Carl T. *Go South to Sorrow.* New York: Random House, 1957.

Rowe, Robert. *The Bobby Baker Story.* New York: Parallax, 1967.

Russell, Jan Jarboe. *Lady Bird: A Biography of Mrs. Johnson.* New York: Scribners, 1999.

Russell, Francis. *The Shadow of Blooming Grove: Warren G. Harding in His Times.* New York: McGraw-Hill, 1968.

Sanders, Elizabeth. *Regulation of Natural Gas: Policy and Politics, 1938–1978.* Philadelphia: Temple University Press, 1981.

Schlesinger, Arthur M., Jr. *The Age of Jackson.* Boston: Little, Brown, 1945.

———. *The Coming of the New Deal.* Vol. 2 of *The Age of Roosevelt.* Boston: Houghton Mifflin, 1959.

———. *The Crisis of the Old Order, 1919–1933.* Vol. 1 of *The Age of Roosevelt.* Boston: Houghton Mifflin, 1957.

———. *The Imperial Presidency.* Boston: Houghton Mifflin, 1973.

———. *The Politics of Upheaval.* Vol. 3 of *The Age of Roosevelt:* Boston: Houghton Mifflin, 1960.

———. *A Thousand Days: John F. Kennedy in the White House.* Boston: Houghton Mifflin, 1965.

Scobie, Ingrid Winther. *Center Stage: Helen Gahagan Douglas.* New York: Oxford University Press, 1992.

Seidman, Joel. *Brotherhood of Railroad Trainmen: The Internal Political Life of a National Union.* New York: John Wiley, 1962.

Shaffer, Samuel. *On and Off the Floor: Thirty Years as a Correspondent on Capitol Hill.* New York: Newsweek Books, 1980.

Sherrill, Robert. *The Accidental President.* New York: Grossman, 1967.

Shuman, Howard E. *Politics and the Budget: The Struggle Between the President and the Congress.* Englewood Cliffs, N.J.: Prentice Hall, 1988.

Sidey, Hugh. *A Very Personal Presidency: Lyndon Johnson in the White House.* New York: Atheneum, 1968.

Sinclair, Barbara. *The Transformation of the U.S. Senate.* Baltimore: Johns Hopkins University Press, 1989.

Smith, A. Robert. *The Tiger in the Senate: The Biography of Wayne Morse.* Garden City, N.Y.: Doubleday, 1962.

Smith, Gene. *When the Cheering Stopped: The Last Years of Woodrow Wilson.* New York: William Morrow, 1964.

Smith, Marie. *The President's Lady: An Intimate Biography of Mrs. Lyndon B. Johnson.* New York: Random House, 1964.

Solberg, Carl. *Hubert Humphrey: A Biography.* New York: W. W. Norton, 1984.

Southern Regional Council. *Black Elected Officials in the Southern States.* SRC Report. Atlanta: Southern Regional Council, 1966.

———. *The Negro and the Ballot in the South.* SRC Report. Atlanta: Southern Regional Council, 1959.

———. *School Desegregation.* SRC Report. Atlanta: Southern Regional Council, 1966.

Standard & Poor's Corp. *Standard Corporate Descriptions, 1949–1956.* New York: Standard & Poor's Corp., Quarterly.

Stehling, Arthur. "A Country Lawyer," unnumbered pp., unpublished memoir (in author's possession).

Steinberg, Alfred. *Sam Johnson's Boy: A Close-Up of the President from Texas.* New York: Macmillan, 1968.

———. *Sam Rayburn.* New York: Hawthorn Books, 1975.

Stone, I. F. *The Haunted Fifties.* New York: Random House, 1963.

Strong, Donald. *Registration of Voters in Alabama.* Birmingham: University of Alabama Press, 1956.

Swanstrom, Roy. *The United States Senate, 1787–1801, a Dissertation: The First Fourteen Years of the Upper Legislative Body.* Washington, D.C.: Government Printing Office, 1986.

Talmadge, Herman E., with Mark Royden Winchell. *Talmadge: A Political Legacy, a Politician's Life, a Memoir.* Atlanta: Peachtree Publishers, 1987.

Tananbaum, Duane. *The Bricker Amendment Controversy: A Test of Eisenhower's Political Leadership.* Ithaca, N.Y.: Cornell University Press, 1988.

Thomas, Evans. *The Man to See: Edward Bennett Williams, Ultimate Insider, Legendary Trial Lawyer.* New York: Simon & Schuster, 1991.

Tocqueville, Alexis de. *Democracy in America,* Vol. I. New York: Knopf, 1945.

Tuskegee Institute. *Annual Reports.* Tuskegee Institute, Ala.: 1954–63.

U.S. Commission on Civil Rights. *Civil Rights Commission Hearings in Alabama.* Washington, D.C.: Government Printing Office, 1959.

———. *Commission Report of North Carolina.* Washington, D.C.: Government Printing Office, 1961.

———. *Employment: 1961; Education: 1961* (two volumes). Washington, D.C.: Government Printing Office, 1961.

———. *Freedom to the Free, Century of Emancipation, 1863–1963.* A Report to the President. Washington, D.C.: Government Printing Office, 1963.

———. *Report of the Florida Advisory Committee: A Survey of the Gap in Florida.* Washington, D.C.: Government Printing Office, 1963.

———. *1963: A Report of the Mississippi Advisory Committee.* Washington, D.C.: Government Printing Office, 1963.

———. *Voting in Mississippi.* Washington, D.C.: Government Printing Office, 1965.

———. *With Liberty and Justice for All.* Civil Rights Commission Report. Washington, D.C.: Government Printing Office, 1959.

U.S. Senate. *Creation of the Senate: From the Proceedings of the Federal Convention, Philadelphia, May–September 1787.* Washington, D.C.: Government Printing Office, 1987.

U.S. Senate, Committee on the Armed Services. *Reports of the Preparedness Investigating Subcommittee, 81st and 82nd Congress, 1950, 51, 52.* Washington, D.C.: Government Printing Office.

U.S. Senate, Committee on the Judiciary. *Hearings Before the Subcommittee on Constitutional Rights of the Committee on the Judiciary,* Civil Rights, 1957: 85/1, Vol. 71.

U.S. Senate, Democratic Conference. *Minutes of the U.S. Senate Democratic Conference, 1903–1964,* ed. Donald A. Ritchie. Washington, D.C.: Government Printing Office, 1998.

U.S. Senate, Preparedness Investigating Subcommittee of the Committee on Armed Services and Committee on Aeronautical Space Services. *Reports and Hearings re Missile and Space Activities for 85th and 86th Congress, from April 1957 to June 1959.* Washington, D.C.: Government Printing Office.

Van Deusen, Glyndon Garlock. *The Life of Henry Clay.* Boston: Little, Brown, 1937.

Warren, Earl. *The Memoirs of Chief Justice Earl Warren.* Garden City, N.Y.: Doubleday, 1977.

Watson, Denton L. *Lion in the Lobby: Clarence Mitchell Jr.'s Struggle for the Passage of Civil Rights Laws.* New York: William Morrow, 1990.

Weisenberger, Carol A. *Dollars and Dreams: The National Youth Administration in Texas.* New York: Peter Lang Publishing, 1994.

White, Theodore H. *The Making of the President, 1960.* New York: Atheneum, 1961.

White, William S. *Citadel: The Story of the U.S. Senate.* New York: Harper & Bros., 1957.

———. *The Professional: Lyndon B. Johnson.* Boston: Houghton Mifflin, 1964.

———. *The Taft Story.* New York: Harper & Bros., 1954.

Whitfield, Stephen J. *A Death in the Delta: The Story of Emmett Till.* New York: Free Press, 1988.

Wicker, Tom. *JFK and LBJ: The Influence of Personality upon Politics.* New York: Morrow, 1968.

——. *On Press.* New York: Viking, 1978.

——. *One of Us: Richard Nixon and the American Dream.* New York: Random House, 1991.

Wilkins, Roy, with Tom Mathews. *Standing Fast: The Autobiography of Roy Wilkins.* New York: Viking Penguin, 1982.

Wilkinson, J. Harvie III. *Harry Byrd and the Changing Face of Virginia Politics, 1945–1966.* Charlottesville: University Press of Virginia, 1968.

Williams, Juan. *Eyes on the Prize: America's Civil Rights Years, 1954–1965.* New York: Viking, 1987.

Williams, Nancy, ed. *Arkansas Biography: A Collection of Notable Lives.* Fayetteville: University of Arkansas Press, 2000.

Wilson, Woodrow. *Congressional Government: A Study in American Politics.* Boston: Houghton Mifflin, 1885.

Wiltse, Charles M. *John C. Calhoun.* 3 vols. Indianapolis: Bobbs-Merrill Company, 1944–1951.

Wiltse, Charles M., ed. *The Papers of Daniel Webster, Vol. I, 1800–1833.* Hanover, N.H.: University Press of New England, 1986.

Wright, Richard. *12 Million Black Voices: A Folk History of the Negro in the United States.* New York: Viking, 1941.

Young, Roland. *This Is Congress.* New York: Knopf, 1943.

Zangrando, Robert L. *The NAACP Crusade Against Lynching, 1909–1950.* Philadelphia: Temple University Press, 1980.

Notes

ABBREVIATIONS

AA-S	*Austin American-Statesman*
AC	*Atlanta Constitution*
ACWD	Ann C. Whitman Diary
APSR	*American Political Science Review*
AWNS	Ann Whitman Name Series
AWPP	Alvin Wirtz Personal Papers
AWRP	A. Willis Robertson Papers
CCC-T	*Corpus Christi Caller-Times*
CR	*Congressional Record*
DDEL	Dwight D. Eisenhower Library
DDEPP	Dwight D. Eisenhower *Public Papers of the Presidents*
DMN	*Dallas Morning News*
DT-H	*Dallas Times-Herald*
FDRL	Franklin Delano Roosevelt Library
FWS-T	*Fort Worth Star-Telegram*
HC	*Houston Chronicle*
HHLP	Herbert H. Lehman Papers, Columbia University
HP	*Houston Post*
HSTL	Harry S Truman Library
JNYA	Johnson National Youth Administration Papers
JSP	Johnson Senate Papers
KGP	Katharine Graham Papers
LAT	*Los Angeles Times*
LBJA	Lyndon Baines Johnson Archives
LBJA CF	LBJA Congressional File
LBJA FN	LBJA Famous Names File
LBJA SF	LBJA Subject File
LBJA SN	LBJA Selected Names File
LBJL	Lyndon Baines Johnson Library
LC	Library of Congress
LLM	Legislative Leaders Meetings
LMS	Legislative Meetings Series
LOP	Leland Olds Papers
MP	MacNeil Papers
NA	National Archives
NAACPP	NAACP Papers
NARA	National Archives and Records Administration
NYHT	*New York Herald Tribune*
NYP	*New York Post*
NYT	*New York Times*
NYWT	*New York World Telegram*
OH	Oral History
PPCF	Pre-Presidential Confidential File

PPMF   Pre-Presidential Memo File
RBRL   Richard B. Russell Library
RP   Rauh Papers
SAE   *San Antonio Express*
SEP   *Saturday Evening Post*
SHO   Senate Historical Office
SLP-D   *St. Louis Post-Dispatch*
SP   Steele Papers
SPF   Senate Political Files
SRL   Sam Rayburn Library
USN&WR   *U.S. News & World Report*
UVaL   University of Virginia Library
WHFN   White House Famous Names File
WN   *Washington News*
WP   *Washington Post and Times Herald*
WS   *Washington Star*
WSJ   *Wall Street Journal*
W-SJ   *Winston-Salem Journal*
WT   *Washington Times*

Introduction: The Presence of Fire

Barbour County episode: "Testimony of Margaret Frost, Eufaula, Barbour, Ala.," U.S. Commission on Civil Rights, *Hearing Held in Montgomery, Alabama, Dec. 8, 1958,* pp. 262–67; Ina Caro and Robert Caro interviews with David Frost and Margaret Frost; see also Testimony of George R. Morris and Andrew Jones, pp. 248–262. **"There is":** U.S. Senate, *Hearings Before the Subcommittee on Constitutional Rights of the Committee on the Judiciary, Eighty-fifth Congress, First Session, on S. 83, And Amendment 2.S.83, S. 427,* p. 239. See also Strong, *Registration of Voters in Alabama;* U.S. Commission on Civil Rights, *With Liberty and Justice for All,* pp. 59–75, 84–95.
"Back then": Hugh Sidey, "The Presidency," *Time,* Dec. 15, 1985.
240: Hurst interview.
"If you're": Humphrey, quoted in Miller, *Lyndon,* p. 166. For Humphrey describing Johnson's gesture in slightly different words, see his OH II, pp. 10, 11, and OH III, pp. 9, 10.
"For all": Steele to Williamson, June 9, 1955; March 4, 1958; SP; Steele interview. **"It was":** Sidey, *Personal Presidency,* p. 45. **"He signaled":** Sidey interview.
"I do understand": Johnson, quoted in McPherson, *Political Education,* p. 450. **"Would explain":** Jackson, quoted in Reston, *Deadline,* pp. 304, 305. **"I'm just":** Johnson, quoted in Dickerson, *Among Those Present,* pp. 154–55.
"The South's unending": White, *Citadel,* p. 68.

1. The Desks of the Senate

Webster's reply to Hayne: Wiltse, ed., *Papers of Daniel Webster,* pp. 349–93 (Reported Version); Byrd, *The Senate,* Vol. I, pp. 109–15; Vol. III, pp. 3, 4.
"Coarse homespun"; "White, triumphant": Byrd, Vol. I, p. 111. **"Could shake"; "great cannon":** Emerson, quoted in Schlesinger, *Age of Jackson,* p. 84. **Smile faded:** Byrd, Vol. I, p. 113. **Tears; "even Calhoun":** Byrd, Vol. I, p. 114. **"Thrilled":** Josephy, *The Congress,* p. 178.
"Embellished": Wiltse, ed., *Papers of Daniel Webster,* p. 286. **Edition followed:** Wiltse, ed., p. 286. **"Has probably"; "No speech"; "raised"; "part":** Peterson, *The Great Triumvirate,* pp. 179–80.
"The Founding": Schlesinger, *Imperial Presidency,* p. 79. **"The turbulence":** Madison, *Notes of Debates* (1920 ed.), p. 34. **"Real":** Madison, *Debates,* (1987 ed.), pp. 193–94; Hamilton, *Federalist Papers,* p. 387. **"A necessary":** Madison, *Debates* (1987 ed.), p. 194. **"To be guarded"; "first":** Madison, pp. 194–95, 193.
"The use": Madison, *Debates* (1920 ed.), p. 34, quoted in Haynes, *The Senate of the United States,* Vol. I, p. 14. **"An anchor":** Hamilton, p. 385. **"Why":** Josephy, p. 46.
"Numerous": Hamilton, pp. 379, 380. **When Wilson:** Haynes, Vol. I, p. 11. **"The people"; "the evils":** Madison, *Debates* (1920 ed.), p. 71, quoted in Haynes, Vol. I, p. 11.
"Filtration"; "refinement": Madison, *Debates* (1920 ed.), p. 69, quoted in Haynes, Vol. I, p. 13. **"Change of men"; what good:** Hamilton, pp. 380, 381. **"The object"; "hold":** Madison, p. 34, quoted in Haynes,

Vol. I, p. 16. **"It was so"**: White, *Citadel,* pp. 33–34. **"Where else"**: Hamilton, No. 65, p. 441.

"The senatorial trust": Hamilton, p. 376. **"As"**: Haynes, Vol. I, p. 15.

Judiciary Act: Byrd, Vol. I, pp. 14, 17; Josephy, pp. 10, 67–69. **"Almost an appendage"**: Josephy, p. 67.

The desks: Description of Senate Chamber from Adams, *History,* pp. 454–55.

"Better calculated"; "such success": Adams, pp. 437, 438. **"To impeachment"**: Schlesinger, *Imperial Presidency,* p. 30. **Republicans succeeded**: Josephy, p. 134; Malone, *Jefferson: First Term,* pp. 148, 460–64.

"Outrageously": Garraty, *American Nation,* p. 220. **"Towered"**: Malone, p. 464.

"Nothing more": John Quincy Adams, *Memoirs,* Vol. I, pp. 321–22, quoted in Schlesinger, *Imperial Presidency,* p. 30. **Endangered**: Garraty, p. 220.

"Aged patriot": Harper, quoted in Elsmere, *Justice Samuel Chase,* pp. 285–86. **Description of the voting**: Adams, pp. 462, 463; Elsmere, pp. 293–306. **White House pressure**: Elsmere, p. 295, says, "The President had attempted discreetly throughout the trial to aid the prosecution. Guests at several dinners included Aaron Burr, some of the managers, and the more important senators or those whose votes were in doubt."

"Crooked gun"; offered two: Elsmere, p. 217; Adams, p. 450. **"Almost"**: Samuel Taggert, quoted in Elsmere, p. 269. **"Fresh"; "a stillness"**: Josephy, p. 135. **Burr's speech**: Baker, *The Senate,* "Reading No. 16: Aaron Burr's Farewell to the Senate, March 2, 1805," pp. 148–49. **"The Senate"**: Byrd, Vol. I, p. 48.

"Ideal": Josephy, p. 176. And see Baker, *The Senate,* p. 33. **Ridiculous; "within"**: Byrd, Vol. I, p. 86. **Houston's clothing**: Josephy, p. 203. **Bluntly**: Byrd, Vol. I, p. 177.

Buzzing: Byrd, Vol. I, p. 122; Josephy, p. 179. **"Disunion"; "within"**: Peterson, pp. 216, 221. **On the day**: Peterson, pp. 222–23. **The most difficult**: Peterson, p. 409. **"Commanding"**: Schlesinger, *Age of Jackson,* pp. 242–43. **"His voice"**: Matthews, *Oratory and Orators,* p. 312, quoted in Peterson, pp. 408, 409. **How much; "the arch"**: Byrd, Vol. I, p. 123. **"A caged"; "the impious"**: Peterson, p. 222.

"Hypnotize"; "depopulate"; "white gloves"; "No lover"; "Stepping": Peterson, pp. 167, 379; Matthews, *Oratory and Orators,* Van Deusen, *Life of Henry Clay, passim;* Josephy, p. 200. **"So penetrating"**: Matthews, p. 38. **"Made"**: Schlesinger, *Age of Jackson,* p. 83. **Clay's speech**: Peterson, pp. 227–30.

"Such was": William T. Hammett to F. W. White, Feb. 12, 1833, quoted in Peterson, p. 227. **"Day and night"; "Would generally"; "ornaments"**: Peterson, pp. 232–34.

"He spoke": Peterson, p. 457. **"If any"**: Byrd, Vol. I, p. 188. **Visiting Webster**: Kennedy, *Profiles in Courage,* pp. 61–62, 65–67. **"Rose"**: Van Deusen, p. 399. **"I implore"**: Byrd, Vol. I, p. 189. **"When"**: *National Era,* July 18, 1850, quoted in Peterson, p. 472. **"Seized"**: Peterson, p. 459. **"What"**: *New York Herald,* Jan. 31, Feb. 8, 1850, quoted in Peterson, p. 458. **"Emaciated"**: Charles Wiltse, ed., *John C. Calhoun,* Vol. III, quoted in Byrd, Vol. I, p. 190. **Sitting at his desk**: Richard M. Ketchum, "Faces from the Past—XXII," *American Heritage,* Oct. 1967. **"The greatest"**: Byrd, Vol. I, p. 190. **"Not since"**: Peterson, p. 462. **Webster's speech**: Byrd, Vol. I, pp. 191–92. **Their last exchange**: Byrd, Vol. I, pp. 193, 194; *Congressional Globe,* 31/1, Appendix, pp. 271, 273. **"If I"**: Wiltse, *John C. Calhoun,* Vol. III, p. 475, quoted in Byrd, Vol. I, p. 194; *Congressional Globe,* 31/1, p. 520.

"A higher": Garraty, p. 386. **"Let him fire!"**: Baker, *The Senate,* p. 48. **"A truly"; "the mighty"**: Peterson, p. 495.

The fuse: Josephy, p. 210. **Sumner's caning**: Burns, *Vineyard of Liberty,* p. 552.

Bought the time: Baker, *The Senate,* p. 33. **"Perhaps"**: Byrd, Vol. I, p. 200. **"Beginning"**: Peterson, p. 234. **"The Senate contains"**: Tocqueville, *Democracy in America,* Vol. I, pp. 204, 205. **"The only"; "the most"**: Lindsay Rogers, "The Gentlemen and Their Club," *NYT Book Review,* Jan. 13, 1957.

"It only": Byrd, Vol. I, p. 227. **"If people"**: Josephy, p. 233.

"Andrew Johnson"; "Johnson's opponents": Schlesinger, *Age of Jackson,* p. 73. **"The condition"**: Kennedy, pp. 134–35. **"Let me"; "the question"; "fearful"**: Kennedy, pp. 131, 148, 135. **"His level"; "he has"**: Byrd, Vol. I, pp. 241, 283. **"The country"**: Kennedy, p. 145. **Grimes' vote: "We have"; "I shall"**: Kennedy, p. 150. **The removal**: Schlesinger, *Age of Jackson,* p. 74.

"One of": Garraty, quoted in Josephy, p. 249. **"After"; "agreed"; "unspoken"**: Josephy, pp. 247–50. **Numbered men**: Byrd, Vol. I, pp. 336–37; Garraty, p. 684. **"Fount"; "more"; "unequaled"**: Josephy, pp. 247, 250. **"Senate Supreme"**: Josephy, Chapter 6. **"A government"**: Adams, *Democracy,* p. 28.

"A social": Josephson, *The Politicos,* p. 327. **"The members"**: Josephy, p. 269; Josephson, p. 445. **"The best"; "to keep"**: Josephy, p. 267. **"Behind"; "but to whisper"**: Josephson, p. 446.

Great care; "dissidents": Byrd, Vol. I, pp. 365–66. **"Operated":** Josephy, p. 206.

"Was not": Josephy, p. 269. **"Does not"; "singularly":** Garraty, p. 683. **"Not a single":** Garraty, p. 696.

"The Bosses": Keppler's cartoon is reproduced in Josephy, pp. 254–55. **"The Senate":** Ostrogorski, *Democracy and the Organization of Political Parties,* quoted in Baker, *The Senate,* p. 207.

"With relish": Schlesinger, *Imperial Presidency,* p. 80. **"As a servant":** Wilson, *Congressional Government,* pp. 49, 59, 233–34. **Most secretaries:** Twenty of the twenty-four secretaries of state between 1811 and 1892 had previously been senators (Schlesinger, *Imperial Presidency,* p. 80).

"I have": Garraty, p. 722. **Beveridge, Hoar speeches:** Byrd, pp. 360–62.

"The international": The discussion of the rise of the executive agreement is based on Schlesinger, *Imperial Presidency,* pp. 79–92. The quotations are from these pages.

Leaving New York harbor: Burns, *Workshop,* p. 448. **"To found":** Burns, *Workshop,* p. 450. **"Tended":** Garraty, p. 790. **In favor:** Burns, *Workshop,* p. 458; Garraty, p. 792. **Had been known:** Smith, *When the Cheering Stopped,* p. 55; Thomas A. Bailey, "Woodrow Wilson Wouldn't Yield," *American Heritage,* June 1957. **"I never"; "sinister":** Burns, *Workshop,* p. 459. **"Shifty":** Smith, p. 55. **"Pygmy-minded":** Thomas A. Bailey, "Woodrow Wilson Wouldn't Yield," *American Heritage,* June 1957. **Wilson refused:** Smith, p. 55.

"The thing": Josephy, p. 329. **"(It) has never"; "war can":** Lodge, quoted in Widenor, "Henry Cabot Lodge: The Astute Parliamentarian," in Baker and Davidson, eds., *First Among Equals,* p. 43. **"At weakening":** Lodge, *The Senate of the United States,* quoted in Widenor, in *First Among Equals,* p. 42. **"At the core"; "faith":** Burns, *Workshop,* pp. 459, 468. **"Who":** Josephy, p. 329. **"Round Robin"; "The Senate":** Thomas A. Bailey, "Woodrow Wilson Wouldn't Yield," *American Heritage,* June 1957. **"Anyone":** Garraty, p. 792. **"The gentlemen":** Byrd, Vol. I, p. 424.

"No one": W. Stull Holt, quoted in Baker and Davidson, eds., *First Among Equals,* p. 44. **"The only":** Burns, *Workshop,* p. 458. **"Reverberated":** Burns, *Workshop,* p. 457. **Hearings:** Byrd, Vol. I, pp. 424–26; Thomas A. Bailey, "Woodrow Wilson Wouldn't Yield," *American Heritage,* June 1957. **"You may call me"; if Lodge:** Byrd, Vol. I, pp. 425–26. **"Mustering":** Burns, *Workshop,* pp. 461–62. **"Where am I":** Smith, *When the*

Cheering Stopped, p. 59. **"Appeal to Caesar":** Smith, p. 58. **"I have it":** Burns, p. 465. **An epic:** Burns, pp. 463–65. **"By crusading":** Burns, p. 465. **"For decades"; "ultimately":** Burns, pp. 466–67.

The "Senate Four": Byrd, Vol. I, pp. 371–87. **Sitting:** A picture of them on the porch is in Byrd, Vol. I, p. 372. **"The four bosses":** Byrd, Vol. I, p. 372. **Across Long Island Sound:** Josephson, *President Makers,* pp. 123–24. **"I want to be sure":** Josephson, p. 150. **While:** Josephy, pp. 302–04. **"Sound and wise":** Josephson, p. 125. **"The current":** Josephson, p. 168. **"Paramount"; "we'll get you":** Josephy, p. 305. **Did not require:** Garraty, pp. 750–52.

Since he was; "drawn": Josephy, pp. 314–15; Morison, Commager, and Leuchtenburg, *Growth of the American Republic,* Vol. II, p. 322. **"Prairie fire":** Josephson, *President Makers,* p. 299. **Summoned:** Garraty, p. 756. **"Dictator":** Byrd, Vol. I, p. 381. **"Where":** Byrd, p. 383. **Progressives' fight:** Byrd, pp. 382–87; Josephy, pp. 315–16; Garraty, p. 757. **"Consummation":** Josephy, p. 316.

2. "Great Things Are Underway"

Inaugural Address: Burns, *Workshop,* p. 384; Morison et al., *Growth of the American Republic,* Vol. II, pp. 425–28. **For a century:** Byrd, *The Senate,* Vol. I, pp. 409–10; Josephson, *President Makers,* p. 476. **As was the Leader:** Walter J. Oleszek, "John Worth Kern: Portrait of a Floor Leader," in Baker and Davidson, eds., *First Among Equals,* pp. 20, 23–25, 27–33. **Kept attacking:** Morison et al., pp. 431–38; Josephson, pp. 478–79. **Dramatic appeal:** Burns, *Workshop,* p. 385; Link, *The New Freedom,* p. 187. **"Think of it":** Burns, *Workshop,* p. 386–87. **Sitting:** Josephson, p. 479. **During it transformed:** Garraty, *American Nation,* pp. 761–63; Josephson, pp. 489–94; Josephy, *The Congress,* pp. 320–22.

"Like a deck": Russell, *Shadow of Blooming Grove,* p. 380. **"Will not try":** William C. Widenor, "Henry Cabot Lodge: The Astute Parliamentarian," in Baker and Davidson, eds., *First Among Equals,* p. 51. **"Sign"; "Bouncing":** Josephy, pp. 338, 389.

"Frankly": Josephy, p. 338.

Raised duties: Schlesinger, *Crisis of the Old Order,* p. 164. **"The product":** Byrd, Vol. I, p. 447. **"No doubt":** Burns, *Workshop,* p. 499.

Mail sacks: Caro, *Path,* pp. 240–46. **Little help:** Caro, pp. 246–52.

"COME": Garraty, p. 839. **"They know":**

Schlesinger, *Coming of the New Deal,* p. 13. **"Roosevelt had":** Josephy, pp. 347–48. **"This should":** Burns, *Crosswinds,* p. 26. **Norris had fought:** Byrd, Vol. I, pp. 435–36. The discussion of Norris and the TVA is also from Schlesinger, *Coming of the New Deal,* pp. 320–34. **"Magna":** Josephy, p. 350. **"Never lifted":** Byrd, Vol. I, p. 474. **Are actually monuments:** As Schlesinger writes (*Coming of the New Deal,* pp. 554–55), "The contemporary cliché about 'rubberstamp' Congresses should not conceal the fact that the national legislature at this time . . . on crucial occasions itself assumed the legislative initiative. . . . It played a vital and consistently underestimated role in shaping the New Deal. A number of important measures . . . were entirely of congressional origination."

"An all but"; "The smiling": Alsop and Catledge, *168 Days,* pp. 48, 22. **Meeting at the White House; "Boys":** Alsop and Catledge, pp. 65–67; Baker, *Back to Back,* pp. 3–8, 17; Josephy, p. 351.

Holding his nose; "the people": Alsop and Catledge, pp. 69, 184. **"Because":** Baker, *Back to Back,* p. 65. **Sumners refused:** Baker, *Back to Back,* pp. 19, 65. **"The shabby":** Alsop and Catledge, p. 10. **"Here is":** *NYT,* March 5, 1937. **"You who":** *NYT,* March 10, 1937.

"Was also": Alsop and Catledge, p. 87. **"On board":** Corcoran interview. **"Kentucky's":** Baker, *Back to Back,* p. 63. **"Prelude":** Alsop and Catledge, p. 65. **"I replied"; "Received":** Baker, *Back to Back,* p. 68. **Judiciary hearings:** Josephy, p. 352. **"It is easy"; "The great":** Alsop and Catledge, pp. 107, 177.

"You were": Alsop and Catledge, p. 257. **"May not"; "rather"; O'Mahoney unexpectedly:** Alsop and Catledge, pp. 155, 195. **Wheeler's refusal; "I'm going"; "Save"; Norris' question:** Baker, *Back to Back,* pp. 237–39; Alsop and Catledge, pp. 100–01, 95. **"The high, wide"; "Robinson and"; "All":** Alsop and Catledge, pp. 254–55, 258–59, 262. **Freshmen:** Baker, *Back to Back,* pp. 255–56.

"Like a": Alsop and Catledge, p. 277. **"Do you":** Fisher, *Cactus Jack,* pp. 133–34. **"The Supreme Court"; let:** Alsop and Catledge, pp. 293–95; Baker, *Back to Back,* pp. 272–73. **"In a way":** Byrd, Vol. I, p. 477. **Headlines:** Garraty, p. 851. **"The sense"; "Marked":** Garraty, p. 849.

"Congressional procedure": *Life,* June 18, 1945. **Three hundred:** Henry F. Pringle, "Can Congress Save Itself?" *SEP,* Oct. 6, 1945. **Six persons:** Sen. 81A-F15, "Rules &

Administration (402), Various Subjects & Correspondence," NA. **Smallness of staffs; lack of expertise:** Galloway, *Congress at the Crossroads;* Byrd, Vol. I, pp. 537–47; Henry F. Pringle, "Can Congress Save Itself?" *SEP,* Oct. 6, 1945. **Four of seventy-six:** William Hard, "Congress' Biggest Job," *Reader's Digest,* Oct. 1942. **Still three:** Byrd, Vol. I, p. 552. **"There could be":** Wilcox OH, SHO, p. 35. **"With occasional":** Floyd M. Riddick, "Third Session of the Seventy-Sixth Congress, Jan. 3, 1940 to Jan. 3, 1941," *APSR,* April 1941." **Unable to create it:** From the turn of the century through 1946, 19 of the most significant pieces of legislation that became law were substantially created by the executive branch, 29 were joint products of the executive and Congress, and 35 were essentially congressional in origin. (Seven had non-governmental origins.) But, as Raymond Moley wrote in 1946, "if we consider only those laws among the 90 which were passed after 1932, . . . 70 per cent have been executive products," only 30 percent were created in Congress. "Congress," he wrote, "has lost most of its effective power over the content of legislation" (Raymond Moley, "Can a Location Run Congress?" *Newsweek,* May 6, 1946). **"Technical equipment":** Corcoran, quoted in Baker and Davidson, eds., *First Among Equals,* p. 137. **600, eight employees:** Byrd, Vol. I, p. 543.

Barkley's lectern: Donald A. Ritchie, "Alben W. Barkley: The President's Man," in Baker and Davidson, eds., *First Among Equals,* pp. 127–62. **"The damned":** MacNeil interview. **MacLeish's proposal:** Byrd, Vol. I, p. 438.

Pragmatic considerations: Interviews with Richard Baker, MacNeil, Ritchie, Steele. And see Byrd, Vol. I, p. 544. **"A cadre"; A "suspicion":** Byrd, Vol I, p. 544. **"A deep, vested":** Strout, *New Republic,* March 18, 1946.

"Senator Borah": Coolidge, quoted in Byrd, Vol. I, p. 483. **"It seemed"; Coolidge proposed:** Byrd, Vol. I, p. 483. **World Court:** Garraty, p. 859. "I do not think the Senate would take favorable action on any such proposal, and unless the requirements of the Senate resolution are met, I can see no prospect of this country adhering to the Court," Coolidge said. **Japan invaded Manchuria:** Leuchtenberg, *FDR and the New Deal,* p. 212. **Shadowed:** Josephy, pp. 348–49. **In 1933:** Schlesinger, *Imperial Presidency,* p. 96. **In 1935:** Garraty, p. 865; Josephy, pp. 359–60. **The President urged:** Leuchtenberg, pp. 215–16. **"Señor Ab Jap"; "To hell":** Leuchtenberg, p. 216. **"Thank God!"; that same**

year: Schlesinger, *The Politics,* pp. 5, 270. **1936:** Byrd, Vol. I, p. 489; Garraty, p. 866. **So Congress passed:** Josephy, p. 360. **"While German":** Garraty, p. 866.

"With every": Leuchtenberg, p. 224. **"No"; "quarantine":** Byrd, Vol. I, p. 490. **Nye and Borah:** Borah said that "this running around all over the world trying to placate every situation and adjust every controversy" was "not the business of democracy." A number of isolationist congressmen called for Roosevelt's impeachment. "It's a terrible thing to look over your shoulder when you're trying to lead, and find no one there," Roosevelt said privately (Byrd, Vol. I, pp. 490, 491). **"The Atlantic":** Byrd, Vol. I, p. 491.

"We are not going": Schlesinger, *Imperial Presidency,* p. 100. **"Gad":** Leuchtenberg, p. 287.

"I've fired"; "Well, Captain": Leuchtenberg, p. 292. **Not until:** Byrd, Vol. I, pp. 491, 492. **84 percent:** Leuchtenberg, p. 293.

Planes could: Leuchtenberg, p. 299. **"A step"; Senate amended:** Schlesinger, *Imperial Presidency,* pp. 105, 106. **Roosevelt, fearing:** Schlesinger, pp. 105–09; Garraty, p. 868.

"The new Triple A": Burns, *Soldier of Freedom,* p. 44. **"I had":** Josephy, p. 362.

Nye was speaking; "Twenty years"; for once: Byrd, Vol. I, p. 495. **"The emasculation":** Lippman, *U.S. Foreign Policy,* p. 42. **"A bunch":** Bohlen, *Witness to History,* p. 210. **"To saving":** Wilkie, quoted in Schlesinger, *Imperial Presidency,* pp. 127. **Mary:** Schlesinger, p. 99.

"Congress quickly": Josephy, pp. 364–68. **"All":** Byrd, Vol. I, p. 539. **An irrelevancy:** Baker, *The Senate,* pp. 86–87; Josephy, p. 364. **"In the event":** Byrd, Vol. I, p. 540.

Bitterness: Josephy, p. 364. **"A real":** Drury, *A Senate Journal,* p. 87 [Feb. 22, 1944].

Drury's *A Senate Journal:* The quotations are on pp. 156–57, 144, 125, 228, 34, 33, 78–80. **Pensions, Bundles:** Byrd, Vol. I, p. 539. **"I never":** *NYT* magazine, May 25, 1947.

3. Seniority and the South

Not even mentioned: Haynes, *Senate of the United States,* Vol. I, pp. 294–300; George Goodwin Jr., "The Seniority System in Congress," *APSR,* June 1959, pp. 413–29. **A child:** Josephy, *Congress,* pp. 205–06.

In December: Baker, *Senate,* p. 45; Byrd, *Senate,* Vol. IV, p. 514; Chandler, *The Natural Superiority of Southern Politicians,* p. 178; Josephy, p. 206. **"Once appointed":** Gal-

loway, *Congress at the Crossroads,* p. 188; Matthews, *U.S. Senators,* pp. 160–75. **"Are not awarded"; "once"; "Perquisite"; "ineluctable":** White, *Citadel,* pp. 183–84. **"Assignments":** Byrd, *Senate,* Vol. I, p. 365.

Governed every: Baker, Barr, MacNeil, Muskie, Proxmire, Riddick, Ritchie, St. Claire, Shuman, Steele, Yarborough interviews. **Where senators sat:** Galloway, *Legislative Process,* p. 368. **"Proceeds":** White, *Citadel,* pp. 196–97. **When a subcommittee:** Matthews, pp. 162–63. **"What chance":** Haynes, Vol. I, p. 334. **Almost invariably; "tremendous powers":** Haynes, Vol. I, p. 333. **"Too often":** Humphrey interview.

Assignment of office suites: "Memorandum—Confidential," St. Claire to Jenner, Jan. 13, 1957; Hayden to Chapman, Hayden to Flanders, both Nov. 29, 1948; Martin to Seidel, Dec. 27, 1948—all from Sen. 81A-F15, "Rules & Administration (402), Various Subjects & Correspondence," NA; Galloway, *Legislative Process,* pp. 367–68. **At dinners:** Galloway, p. 367.

Formulas: Byrd, Vol. IV, p. 189; Goodwin, *Lyndon Johnson,* p. 413. **"One may":** White, *Citadel,* p. 183. **"Passage":** White, p. 82.

"Did not rise": Matthews, p. 93. **"Any fledgling":** Albright, *WP,* Feb. 25, 1951. **"Freshmen":** Matthews, p. 94. **"That son":** Matthews, p. 93. **"Skeptical"; "back home":** Matthews, p. 103; Muskie interview. (Matthews does not identify the "former Governor," but it appears to be John Pastore of Rhode Island.) **"Reached national fame":** White, *Citadel,* p. 82.

In 1949: *Congressional Directory,* 81/1, March 1949. **Average age; Hiram Johnson shuffling in:** Drury, *Senate Journal,* p. 357. **"The ghost":** Drury, p. 381.

The real powers: Galloway, *Legislative Process,* p. 289; White, *Citadel,* pp. 179–80, 189–97; Byrd, Vol. I, pp. 295, 649. **Could not even:** Senate Rule XXVI, Riddick, *Senate Procedure,* p. 315; White, *Citadel,* pp. 189–90. **No chairman:** Three chairmen, Robert M. La Follette (R-Wis.), Edwin F. Ladd (R-N.D.), and Albert B. Cummins (R-Iowa), had been removed from committee chairmanships in 1924 by the Republican caucus, the first two because of their support for the Progressive Party, Cummins because he had been responsible for controversial railroad legislation that the GOP wanted repealed. Prior to 1924, no committee chairman had been removed since 1871, when Charles Sumner was removed because of GOP anger over his opposition to President Grant's proposed annexation of the Dominican Republic (Byrd, Vol. IV, pp. 612–13). **"Old Bulls'":** Barr interview. **"A living":** Drury, p. 36. **"He

could neither": George Goodwin Jr., "The Seniority System in Congress," *APSR*, June 1959, p. 420. "From the guarded": Drury, p. 364. "In his day": Drury, p. 3. Would pound: Steinberg, *Sam Johnson's Boy*, p. 286. "In reply: Baker, *American in Washington*, pp. 143–44. Five other: The five, and their committees and ages were: Tom Connally, Foreign Relations, age 72; Walter George, Finance, 71; Pat McCarran, Judiciary, 73; Carl Hayden, Rules, 72; Elmer Thomas, Agriculture, 73.
"It has": Lindley, "Washington Tides," *Newsweek*, Nov. 29, 1948. "The utilization"; "flaunts": Young, *This Is Congress*, pp. 108–09. "Gerontocracy"; "adherence": *WP*, Nov. 8, 1948. "The accident": Galloway, *Congress at the Crossroads*, p. 190. "The seniority line"; "if either": Oliver, quoted in Galloway, p. 191. "A protection": Reedy OH VIII, p. 8. "A new": George Goodwin Jr., "The Seniority System in Congress," *APSR*, June 1959, p. 420.
"Nobody"; "would no more": White, *Citadel*, p. 184. "The longer": George Goodwin Jr., "The Seniority System in Congress," *APSR*, June 1959, p. 420 fn. A part: *WP*, n.d.
"If you": "A History of the Russell Senate Office Building," SHO, pp. 7, 8. "Never"; "a thousand": *NYT*, March 14, 1909. The man: Elliott Woods to Charles Moore, June 22, 1903, quoted in Curtis Blake, "The Architecture of Carrere and Hastings," unpublished Ph.D. thesis, Columbia University, 1976, p. 287. Descriptions of building and architects' philosophy: Curtis Blake, "The Architecture of Carrere and Hastings," unpublished Ph.D. thesis, Columbia University, 1976, *passim;* Mechlen, "New Public Buildings," *The Architectural Review*, July 1908, pp. 180–89. Senate Historical Office: "A History of the Russell Senate Office Building," SHO; Jean-Pierre Isbouts, "Carrere and Hastings," unpublished Ph.D. thesis, Kunsthistorisch Institut, Rijksuniversiteit Leiden, 1980; "Cornerstone Laid for Senate's New Building," *WP*, Aug. 1, 1906; "The Senate's Office—Cost Five Millions," *NYT*, March 14, 1909; Senate Historical Office, "The Russell Office Building," S. Pub 105–57; Federal Writers' Project, *Washington: City and Capital*, pp. 282–85.
"Detract from the effect": *WP*, Aug. 1, 1906. "More": Curtis Blake, "The Architecture of Carrere and Hastings," unpublished Ph.D. thesis, Columbia University, 1976, p. 288. "Elegance": Jean-Pierre Isbouts, "Carrere and Hastings," unpublished Ph.D. thesis, Kunsthistorisch Institut, Rijksuniversiteit Leiden, 1980, p. 184. "Color would": Carrere to Woods, May 7, 1906, quoted in Blake, p. 293.
"It was": MacNeil interview.
McClellan's boast: Baker, *Friend and Foe*,

p. 93. "You can tread": Robert Albright, "Glimpses," *WP*, April 8, 1951. "Dropping in": Stranigan interview. "When he got": Ballard interview. "If you saw": Trice interview. "He just": BeLieu interview. "Where else": Blair Moody, "The United States Senate," *Holiday*, Feb. 1954.
Talked in private: This specific dialogue from Rules Committee meetings is found in U.S. Senate, Report of Proceedings: *Hearings Held Before the Committee on Rules and Administration, S. Res. 17, Executive Session*, Jan. 24, 1951, Ward & Paul, official reporters, pp. 4, 22.
"You just didn't barge in": Dompierre interview.
"Of every single": Josephy, p. 206. "Human institutions": Baker, *American in Washington*, p. 46. 7 of the 9; "on the other": White, *Citadel*, p. 70.
The three most powerful: Matthews rates these three first for the period his book covers, 1947 through 1956 (pp. 149–50). Horn, covering the period from 1957 to 1966, notes the "agreement in both periods on the most prestigious, although in his ranking, Appropriations and Foreign Relations are the most prestigious, Finance was tied by Armed Services" (*Unused Power*, p. 10). "Not especially relevant": White, *Citadel*, p. 180. In 1949, southerners were chairmen not only of Appropriations (Kenneth McKellar of Tennessee), Foreign Relations (Tom Connally of Texas), and Finance (Walter George of Georgia), but of Banking (Burnet Maybank of South Carolina), Expenditures in the Executive Departments (John McClellan of Arkansas), and Post Office and Civil Service (Olin Johnston of South Carolina). The committees chaired in 1949 by firm southern allies were Agriculture (Elmer Thomas of Oklahoma), Armed Services (Millard Tydings of Maryland), Commerce (Ed Johnson of Colorado), Judiciary (Pat McCarran of Nevada), Labor (Elbert Thomas of Utah), and Public Works (Dennis Chavez of New Mexico). Joseph O'Mahoney of Wyoming, the chairman of Interior, was not a southern ally.
"No matter"; "latitude"; "unchallenged": Horn, *Unused Power*, pp. 16, 10, 37. "Interlocking": An unidentified senator quoted in Horn, p. 100.
"A modest": Donald A. Ritchie, "Watkins, Charles Lee," in Williams, ed., *Arkansas Biography*, p. 303.
"Because of": White, *Citadel*, p. 74. "I recommend": Ritchie interview.
In 1604: Galloway, *The Legislative Process in Congress*, p. 560. For many years: Burdette, *Filibustering in the Senate, passim;* Galloway, p. 560. In 1872: Galloway, p. 569. "A

little group": Byrd, *The Senate*, Vol. II, p. 122. **"Whose stated purpose"; a loophole:** Galloway, p. 561; White, p. 61; Riddick, Zweben interviews. **"The reading"**: Rule III, *Standing Rules of the Senate*, para. 1; Riddick, *Senate Procedure*, p. 713; Riddick, Zweben interviews. **Harrison sauntered:** Haynes, *Senate of the United States*, p. 411; Galloway, p. 561; Riddick, Zweben interviews. "The cloture rule was safe, because it was its own defense; you could not get to it to change it, without using it" (McPherson, *A Political Education*, p. 136).

"To most peculiar": All following quotes are from White, *Citadel*, pp. 68–72.

All remarks: Riddick, *Senate Procedure*, p. 623. **"A safeguard"; "There is"**: *CR*, 61/1, pp. 2431–32, quoted in Haynes, *Senate of the United States*, Vol. I, p. 387. **"If you think"**: Barkley, *That Reminds Me*, p. 255. **"No Senator"; "offensively"**: Rule XIX, *Standing Rules of the Senate*, paras. 2, 3. **"When such matter"**: Riddick, pp. 503–04, 591. **"When a senator"**: Rule XIX, *Standing Rules*, paras. 4, 5; Riddick, pp. 588–89. **"To be called"**: Ritchie interview. **"Gracefully"**: White, *Citadel*, p. 76. **"As elaborately"**: Baker, *American in Washington*, p. 144.

"Archaically": White, *Citadel*, pp. 72, 73. **"Was peculiar"; "chat"**: White, pp. 68–70.

"A oneness"; "for all": White, *Citadel*, pp. 74, 78. **"Walk as a body:** A vivid picture of the southerners marching into the Chamber is in Drury, *A Senate Journal*, p. 162. **"The South"**: Steele interview. **Had allies:** Baker, *American in Washington*, pp. 154–56; Shuman OH, interview.

"We seldom": Drury, p. 196. **"Hell"**: Drury, p. 169. **Leaving"; "warning"**: Drury, p. 167. **"Regardless"**: Drury, pp. 138–41.

"Happily": McCullough, *Truman*, p. 468. **Homebuilding:** Phillips, *The 1940s*, p. 347. In Chicago alone, McCullough says, "there were reportedly 100,000 homeless veterans" (*Truman*, p. 470). **Other Truman programs:** Phillips, pp. 347–49.

Went further on race: Phillips, *The 1940s*, pp. 346–47; McCullough, p. 586. **Thirty-one:** Phillips, p. 347. **"Congressmen"**: *Time*, Dec. 24, 1945.

"Rewriting": *USN&WR*, March 15, 1946. **The Senate stood:** Baker, *American in Washington*, pp. 151–52; Byrd, Vol. I, p. 586; Josephy, p. 366. **"My very"; "when the mob"**: McCullough, pp. 588, 589. **Special message:** Phillips, *The 1940s*, pp. 349–51. **"The crime"**: McCullough, p. 587. **"A lynching"**: Donovan, *Conflict and Crisis*, p. 354. **Jefferson-Jackson Dinner:** McCullough, p. 588.

"The inefficiency": Strout, *New Republic*, March 18, 1946. **"The life"; "the people"**: Henry F. Pringle, "Can Congress Save Itself?" *SEP*, Oct. 6, 1945. **"The Senate's"**: Baker, *American in Washington*, p. 142. **"For generations"; "breaking down"**: *Fortune*, Feb. 1952. **"For years the House diligently"**: Baker, *American in Washington*, p. 153. **"Never"**: Matthews, p. 6. **"I've never"**: Barkley, quoted in *Pathfinder*, Feb. 11, 1948.

"Run by": McCullough, p. 661. **"No, we're"**: Manchester, *Glory*, p. 459. **"A mob"; "Majority to hades!"; "we are"; "Dear Dago"; "It was cloture"**: I. F. Stone, "Swastika over the Senate," *The Nation*, Feb. 9, 1946. **"I don't like you"**: *NYT*, Sept. 5, 1977. **"Ten thousand"; "Typically"; "There is"**: I. F. Stone, "Swastika over the Senate," *The Nation*, Feb. 9, 1946. **"This is"**: I. F. Stone, *The Nation*, 1948.

"Communistic"; "un-American": McCullough, *Truman*, p. 667. **"There's not"**: Bass and Thompson, *Ol' Strom*, p. 188.

4. A Hard Path

The material in this chapter is drawn from Volumes I and II of *The Years of Lyndon Johnson*.

5. The Path Ahead

The description of Johnson and the circle of young New Dealers is based on the author's interviews with the following members of that circle: Benjamin V. Cohen, Thomas G. Corcoran, Abe Fortas, Arthur (Tex) Goldschmidt, Elizabeth and James H. Rowe, and Elizabeth Wickenden.

The description of Johnson's relationship with his office staff is based on the author's interviews with the following members of that staff: Roland Bibolet, Yolanda Boozer, Horace W. Busby, John Connally, Nadine Brammer Eckhardt, Ashton Gonella, Jack Gwyn, Charles Herring, Walter Jenkins, Sam Houston Johnson, Eugene Latimer, Margaret Mayer (the same Margaret Mayer who was also, at different times, a journalist), J. J. (Jake) Pickle, Mary Rather, George Reedy, James H. Rowe, Gerald W. Siegel, O. J. Weber, Warren Woodward, and Mary-Louise Glass Young.

It is also based on the author's interviews with the following persons who observed Johnson's relationship with his staff: Richard Bolling, Thomas G. Corcoran, Helen Gahagan Douglas, Bryce Harlow, Welly Hopkins, Joe M. Kilgore, Frank McCulloch, Daniel

McGillicuddy, Dale Miller, Edward Puls, Benjamin H. Read, Harry Schnibbe, Howard Shuman, Stuart Symington, George Tames, and Harold Young. And with journalists Rowland Evans, Neil MacNeil, Sarah McClendon, Hugh Sidey, John Steele, and Alfred Steinberg.

It is based as well on oral history interviews, many of them with the same persons, conducted by the Lyndon B. Johnson Library, the Senate Historical Office, and other institutions; on the intraoffice memoranda found in many different files in the Lyndon B. Johnson Library; and on books and magazine articles cited individually below when they are quoted directly.

Bunton clan: Caro, *Path,* Chapters 1 and 3. **"Commanding":** Caro, p. 4. **"If you":** Cox, quoted in Caro, p. 3. **"Afterward":** Davie, *Foreign Observer's Viewpoint,* p. 8. **"Exceptional":** Davie, *The Observer,* July 18, 1965. **Santa Claus incident:** Busby interview.

"He just": John Skuce, quoted in Miller, *Lyndon,* p. 213. **"A mountain":** Benjamin Read interview. **Weight:** Dr. Willis Hurst interview. **"You could":** Tames interview. **"Fun":** Elizabeth Rowe, in Caro, *Path,* p. 453. **"Never a dull":** Fortas, in Caro, pp. 454–55. **Take his ball:** Edwards, SHJ, in Caro, p. 71. **Sleeping at table:** Eliot Janeway, Elizabeth Rowe interviews. **"If he'd":** Redford, in Caro, p. 76.

"Always repeating": SHJ interview. **"What convinces":** Goodwin, *Lyndon Johnson,* p. 124. **"Revving up":** Clark interview. **"Got bigger":** Donald Oresman interview. **"Let it fly":** Goodwin, *Remembering America,* p. 258. **"I want to":** Sidey, "Way Out There in Vietnam, He Can't See 'Em or Hear 'Em," *Life,* June 3, 1966.

Pissing: Lucas interview. **Urinating:** Bolling, Busby, Reedy interviews. **"Jumbo":** Caro, *Path,* p. 155; SHJ interview. **"And shaking":** Walton interview. **"Have you"; "crude":** Bolling interview; Bolling, quoted in Miller, p. 541.

Relationship with Latimer, Jones: Caro, *Path,* pp. 229–40. **"Apparently":** Goodwin, *Remembering America,* pp. 256–58. **"Lubriderm"; inhaler:** For example, Busby, Gonella, Mary-Louise Young interviews.

Harsh lesson: Caro, *Means,* p. 128. **Trying for Appropriations:** Caro, *Path,* p. 541. **"The only":** Garner, quoted in Caro, *Path,* p. 317.

"No Democrat": Douglas, *Fullness of Time,* p. 205. **The plaque:** Steinberg, *Sam Rayburn,* p. 236.

Johnson and his staff: Interviews listed above; also Mooney, *LBJ,* Chapter 5 and *passim;* Miller, pp. 533–57; Steinberg, *Sam*

Johnson's Boy, pp. 277–81. **Roosevelt imitation:** Busby, Jenkins interviews. **"Johnson created":** Connally interview. **Day Roosevelt died:** Busby interview. **Johnson had not:** Steinberg, *Sam Rayburn,* p. 226. **"You felt":** L. E. Jones interview. **"That":** Pickle interview.

Gonella's strategy: Gonella interview. **"That's forty-five":** Busby interview. **"His rages":** Bolling interview; Bolling quoted in Miller, p. 214. **Latimer's map:** Latimer interview. **"You've poisoned":** Mooney, *LBJ,* p. 85; Busby interview. **"I didn't get":** Nellie Connally, quoted in Russell, *Lady Bird,* p. 135. **"Had to be":** Gonella interview. **Ordering women's lives:** Boozer, Gonella interviews. **"Well, I see"; "A little windy"; "he was":** Boozer, quoted in Miller, p. 536. **"Why don't":** Steinberg, *San Johnson's Boy,* p. 280. **"I don't":** Busby interview. **"Everybody":** Gonella interview. **"There wasn't":** Jones interview. **"Like a slave":** Sidey interview. **Asleep in the bathtub:** Puls, quoted in Caro, *Path,* p. 496. **"Loyalty":** Halberstam, "Lyndon," *Esquire,* Aug. 1972. Another version was given by Hubert Humphrey to Merle Miller: "Mr. Johnson always said, 'I want a guy to be 150 percent loyal, kiss my ass in Macy's window and stand up and say, "Boy, wasn't that sweet" ' " (Miller, p. 542).

Connally had: Connally, Busby, Jenkins interviews. **Pleading with Harlow:** Harlow interview. **"I can't":** Gwyn, in Caro, *Path,* p. 118. **"It was":** James Rowe interview.

"Well, I"; Inaugural Ball tickets: Woodward interview. **Forcing Connally to return:** Connally, Busby, Jenkins interviews.

6. "The Right Size"

Marlin meeting: Oltorf interview. A somewhat different version, in which Johnson is asking only for the Finance Committee, was given by Oltorf in his OH, but the version he gave in the interview was confirmed by an interview with John Connally.

Telephoning Hayden; Hayden's reply; "Tendered": Hayden to Johnson, Nov. 18, 1948, Box 45, LBJA CF; Connally, Jenkins interviews. And see Woodward to Jenkins, Dec. 3, Box 61, LBJA CF. **Asked the Speaker:** Johnson to Rayburn, Dec. 2, 1948. **And Rayburn did:** Rayburn to Barkley, Dec. 8, 1948, Papers of Tom C. Clark, Box 48, LBJ(1), HSTL; Jenkins interview. **"Put in":** Johnson to Corcoran, Dec. 15, 1948; Corcoran interview. **"I want very much"; "since Texas":** Johnson to McKellar, Johnson to Barkley, both Nov. 13, 1948; Johnson to Corcoran, undated, with attached Johnson to McKellar, Dec. 22, 1948—all Box 48, LBJ(1), Papers of Tom C. Clark, HSTL. Also, Johnson to McKellar, Nov. 19, 1948, Box 49, LBJA SN. Trying to enlist Tom Connally's support for Appropriations, Johnson wrote him expressing "my intense interest in being assigned to Appropriations," and then including Agriculture and Armed Services among "other committees for which I would like to be kept in mind," but Johnson's staffers explain that that letter—and a similar one to Barkley (a copy of which Johnson sent to Connally)— were really intended only as "a sop" to make Connally think he was taking his advice seriously (Johnson to Connally, Dec. 12, Box 49, LBJA SF; Johnson to Barkley, Box 49, LBJ(1), Papers of Tom C. Clark, HSTL; Busby, Connally, Corcoran, Jenkins interviews). **Parking encounter:** Steinberg, *Sam Johnson's Boy*, pp. 276–77; Carpenter, "The Whip from Texas," *Collier's*, Feb. 17, 1951. **Senate's response:** Busby, Connally, Corcoran, Jenkins, Rather interviews. **Pro forma:** For example, McKellar to Johnson, Dec. 23, McMahon to Johnson, Dec. 24, Box 49, LBJA SF. As late as Dec. 27, Tydings replied to Johnson's request with a polite note (Tydings to Johnson, Dec. 27, 1948, Box 116, LBJA SF). In an interview thereafter—apparently that same day—Johnson realized that Tydings was not really intending to help (Busby, Connally, Corcoran, Jenkins interviews). **Barkley's letter:** Barkley to Johnson, Nov. 27, 1948, Box 52, LBJA SN. **"Of course":** Rayburn to Johnson, Dec. 8, 1948, Box 48, LBJ(1), Papers of Tom C. Clark, HSTL. **Showed him:** Busby, Connally interviews. **"Your letter":** E. Chance to Johnson, Dec. 29, 1948, Box 116, LBJA SF. **"The trouble":** Busby, Jenkins interviews. **"I am pleased":** Hayden to Johnson, Dec. 18, 1948, Sen. 81A-F15, Rules and Administration (402), NA. **Extra room:** Busby, Jenkins interviews; Hayden to Gillette, Jan. 3, 1949, Sen. 81A-F15, Rules and Administration (402), NA. From other senators, Johnson received, in answer to his committee-assignment requests, *pro forma* replies to "do everything I can to help you." For example, O'Mahoney to Johnson, Dec. 23, 1948; Tydings to Johnson, Dec. 27, 1948, Box 116, LBJA SF. **Johnson in doorway:** Jenkins interview; Jenkins, quoted in Miller, p. 141. Jenkins repeated Johnson's remarks to Busby at the time (Busby interview). **"Watch":** Busby interview. **"Seemed to *sense*":** Baker, *Wheeling and Dealing*, p. 87. **"One on one":** Latimer interview. **People had been saying this since col-**

lege: Caro, *Path*, p. 177. **"The knack":** Brown, quoted in Caro, p. 552. **"Operated best":** Reedy interview.
   "Could be": Theis OH.
   "Most interactions": Goodwin, *Lyndon Johnson*, p. 126.
   Being sworn in: *CR*, 81/1, pp. 3–5; *AA-S, DMN, HP, HC,* Jan. 4, 1949. **his own desk:** The desk is Desk No. 18.
   Winked and grinned: Mayer, "Your Capital City," *AA-S*, Jan. 12, 1949.
   Tirades during campaign: Caro, *Means*, pp. 239–42. **"I had":** Busby, quoted in Caro, *Path*, p. 422.
   Graciousness during campaign; "Here, Buzz": Caro, *Means*, p. 269; Busby interview.
   Driving to work: Paul F. Healy, "The Frantic Gentleman from Texas," *SEP*, May 19, 1951; Steinberg, *Sam Johnson's Boy*, p. 318; Rather interview. **Shouting:** Miller, p. 182. **Glass affair:** Caro, *Path*, Chapter 25.
   Douglas' career: Douglas, *Full Life;* Scobie, *Center Stage.* **"Ten of":** Broun, quoted in Scobie, p. 24. **"Has made":** *NYHT*, Oct. 25, 1936. **"Had prepared":** *Louisville Courier-Journal*, quoted in Scobie, p. 170. **"Surrounded":** *Baltimore Sun*, Jan. 28, 1945, quoted in Scobie, p. 171. **"She stood":** Bethune, quoted in Scobie, p. 270. **"Her waistline":** *NYP*, July [date unclear], 1949. **"Number One":** *New York Daily News*, June 4, 1950.
   "Draped": Douglas, *Full Life*, p. 204. **"He never":** Douglas interview. **"In a hurry":** Douglas OH. **"Willing":** Douglas, p. 260. **"Was it":** Douglas OH. **"One of"; "he cared":** Douglas OH. **"He knew":** Douglas, *Full Life*, p. 205. **FDR's funeral; "He looked":** Douglas OH, Douglas interview. **Rankin episode:** Douglas, *Full Life*, pp. 226–31; Douglas OH.
   Arriving together: Davidson, "Texas Political Powerhouse," *Look*, Aug. 4, 1959. **Holding hands:** Busby, Mary-Louise Young interviews. **Dinner, parties together:** Evelyn Chavoor, Charles A. Hogan OHs. **"Over the":** Scobie, *Center Stage*, p. 181. **"Strikingly handsome":** Hogan OH.
   "Affair with Lyndon": Mary-Louise Young interview. **"It started":** Busby, quoted in Russell, *Lady Bird*, p. 196. **"For quite":** Busby interview. **"Lyndon would":** Fath, quoted in Scobie, p. 172.
   Helped her: Scobie, pp. 244, 283; Busby interview. **Swimming pool scene:** Busby, quoted in Russell, *Lady Bird*, p. 212.
   "Blow open": Skuce, quoted in Miller, p. 213. **"Tell Jake"; "What does":** Mary-Louise Young interview. **Necktie-tying:** Califano, *The Triumph*, p. 27; Connally interview.

"What that woman needs"; "LBJ made": Califano, pp. 169–70. "Lyndon's idea": Woods, quoted in Caro, *Path*, p. 182. "Let nature": Sidey, *Time*, May 13, 1974. "When he barks": Healy, "Frantic Gentleman," *SEP*, May 19, 1951. "The other"; "He wouldn't": Woodward interview. **Sending in note**: Goodwin, *Lyndon Johnson*, p. 104. "Hi, Jake": Carlton interview. **Walter George scene**: Busby interview; Steinberg, *Sam Johnson's Boy*, p. 345. "He took": Woodward interview.

Joking with Vandenberg: AA-S, DMN, HP, Jan. 4, 1949. **Drawing for desk**: Pearson, WP, Feb. 12, 1949. "Howdy": Steinberg, *Sam Johnson's Boy*, p. 276. **Photograph**: FWS-T, Jan. 1, 1949. **At Graham party**: Gooch to Johnson, March 12, 1951, Box 483, JSP. **Unceasingly**: For Johnson's credit-grabbing in the House, see Caro, *Path*, pp. 523–33. "Avoid": Busby to John Connally and Walter Jenkins, Jan. 7, 1949, Box 863, JSP. **Let his aides**: Busby, Connally, Jenkins interviews.

Johnson on the floor: Busby interview. "A general feeling": Woodward interview. "Gentlemen": Busby interview.

"Time and again": Connally interview.

"Mild-mannered": Willard Shelton, "The New 'Truman Committee," *The Nation*, Oct. 21, 1950. "His manner": "The Watchdog Committee and How It Watches," *Newsweek*, Dec. 3, 1951. "I found": Lucas, quoted in Evans and Novak, *LBJ: Exercise*, p. 33.

"I always": Johnson, quoted in Goodwin, *Lyndon Johnson*, pp. 120–21. **Flattery at college; contemporaries' contempt**: Caro, *Path*, Chapters 8, 11, 16. "Uriah Heep": Caro, p. 489. "Smiling and": Corcoran, quoted in Caro, p. 449. "I never": Clark, quoted in Caro, p. 363.

Johnson and Rayburn: Caro, *Path*, Chapter 18. **Betraying Rayburn**: Caro, Chapter 30. **Heart melting**: Caro, Chapter 36.

"Don't forget": Vinson to Johnson, Dec. 22, 1949, Box 57, LBJA.

"He could": Goodwin, *Lyndon Johnson*, p. 103. "Now they": Johnson, quoted in Goodwin, p. 120.

"A classic prototype"; "as nearly pro-labor"; "To hear Senator Murray's response": William S. White, "Democrats' 'Board of Directors,' " *NYT Magazine*, July 10, 1955. **Murray aging**: McClure OH; Reed, Tames interviews. **Sometimes**: McClure OH. **Lit up**: Tames interview.

"Real sweet": Busby, Latimer interviews. "I certainly": Johnson to Ed Johnson, April 23, 1956, Box 381, JSP. "Boy, whenever": Reedy interview. "During": Shuman to Caro, Jan. 13, 1984, p. 2 (in author's possession).

"The very": Baker, *Friend and Foe*, p. 22. "Christ": Connally interview. "Johnson thought": Mooney OH. **Hayden found**: Hayden to Wever, Jan. 27, Box 116, LBJA SF. "When he": Busby interview. "After": Connally interview. "Mr. Johnson": Jenkins, quoted in Miller, p. 141.

Baker conversation: Baker, *Wheeling and Dealing*, pp. 40, 41; Parker, *Capitol Hill*, p. 73. "Mr. Baker, I understand": Johnson, quoted in Baker, *Wheeling and Dealing*, p. 34. "Just another": Baker, *Wheeling and Dealing*, p. 40. **Waiter saw**: The waiter was Parker, who described the scene in *Capitol Hill*, p. 73. "The power": Baker, quoted in Miller, p. 142.

Johnson and Evans: Caro, *Path*, pp. 149, 152, 192. **And Wirtz**: Caro, pp. 392–93. **With Roosevelt**: Caro, pp. 448–49 and *passim*.

7. A Russell of the Russells of Georgia

The boy's game: Fite, *Richard B. Russell*, p. 9; Harold H. Martin, "The Man Behind the Brass," *SEP*, June 2, 1951; Reedy recalls Russell telling him about "Fort Lee" and reenacting the southern charges (Reedy interview).

"From the oldest": Robert Paul Turbeville, *Eminent Georgians*, quoted in Fite, p. 1. **Father's legislative, judicial career**: Marion H. Allen, "Memorial to Chief Justice Richard Brevard Russell," Georgia Bar Association, *Report of Proceedings*, 56th Annual Session, May 25–27, 1939, pp. 171–77. "Always looking": Fite, p. 3. "The Senate post": Russell speaking in "Richard Russell, Georgia Giant," three-hour documentary, Atlanta, Ga.: WSB-TV, Cox Enterprises, broadcast 1970, Tape, Part 1. (Referred to hereafter as "Georgia Giant.") "Speaking": Martin, "The Man Behind the Brass," *SEP*, June 2, 1957. "Radical" or: "Georgia Giant," Tape, Part 1. "The poorest": Leonard, "The Russells of Our Flock," University of Georgia *Alumni Record*, May 1967, quoted in Fite, p. 3. "Got in": And Ina Russell Stacy says in her OH, "He was never defeated for a judicial position, and never elected to any of the others."

Moving to Winder; "would be"; "distraught": Fite, pp. 4, 5.

"I was": "Georgia Giant," edited transcript, Part I, p. 10. "Round the curve!": Author's visit to Winder; "Georgia Giant," edited transcript, Part I, p. 4; Richard B. Russell III interview; Fielding Russell OH. "He might": Fite, p. 6. "Thought that": *WS*, March 9, 1969.

"My mother": "Georgia Giant," edited transcript, Part I, p. 3.

"With a sense": *WS,* March 9, 1969. Family close: Fite, pp. 12–15. A gang: Harold H. Martin, "The Man Behind the Brass," *SEP,* June 2, 1951; Griggs to Williamson, Aug. 1, 1957, SP. "Those funny songs": Stacy OH. "Although": Peterson OH.

"My own": Ina Russell Stacy, quoted in Fite, p. 14.

"Where"; "I read": Fite, p. 12. Listening to the veterans: Karen K. Kelly, "Richard B. Russell: Democrat from Georgia," unpublished Ph.D. dissertation, University of North Carolina, 1979, p. 22.

Father's letters: Fite, pp. 24, 22, 29. Mother's letters: Fite, p. 22. "She wrote": "Georgia Giant," edited transcript, Part I, p. 9.

"Becomingly": Fite, p. 17.

"Oh"; "you bear": Fite, pp. 20, 18.

"The finest"; "I expect": "Georgia Giant," edited transcript, Part I, pp. 12–13, 18.

"Almost": Fite, p. 37.

"His tribute": *Winder News,* April 27, 1922. "Was careful": Fite, p. 41. "Young Turks": Robert Byrd, *CR,* 87/2, p. S 349; Roy Harris OH. Father's 1926 campaign: Fite, p. 49; Mann, *Walls of Jericho,* p. 32. "A great bit": Rev. Henry E. Russell OH.

"Though young": Fite, p. 50.

"These are": Fite, p. 51. "The closest thing": Griggs to Williamson, Aug. 1, 1957, SP. "Leader who": Isaac S. Peoples, quoted in Fite, p. 58.

Race for Governor: Harold H. Martin, "The Man Behind the Brass," *SEP,* June 2, 1951; Griggs to Williamson, Aug. 1, 1957; Fite, Chapter 4. Borrowing a thousand dollars: "The Southern General," *Time,* Aug. 12, 1957. "Nothing save": Fite, p. 66. "No man": "Georgia Giant," edited transcript, Part I, p. 21. "Never used"; "Ananias"; "farmers seemed": Fite, pp. 65, 63.

"He considered": Fite, p. 96. Who realized: Fite, p. 361. Dated women: Griggs to Williamson, Aug. 1, 1957.

"So many": Jordan interview. "Lights glow": *Atlanta Georgian,* Dec. 26, 1931, quoted in Fite, p. 96. Governorship: Fite, Chapter 5; *Life,* March 24, 1952. Agricultural research: *WS,* March 9, 1969. "Flatter, cajole": Fite, p. 87. "A new day": Fite, p. 83.

"The worst": Fite, p. 102. Without canceling: Harold H. Martin, "The Man Behind the Brass," *SEP,* June 2, 1951. "Kilowatt Charlie": Griggs to Williamson, Aug. 1, 1957.

"If I can't": "Footnotes on Russell," Robert Allen and John Goldsmith, *Macon Telegraph,*

Jan. 30, 1971. Ultimatum to Robinson: "Georgia Giant," edited transcript, Part I, p. 28. "A wild-spoken": "Georgia Giant," edited transcript, Part I, p. 28. "Buy his peace"; "Old Ed"; "I got to be": "Georgia Giant," edited transcript, Part I, p. 29.

"To a minimum": Fite, p. 125. Memorizing the rules; He borrowed: Harold H. Martin, "The Man Behind the Brass," *SEP,* June 2, 1951; McConaughy to Williamson, July 31, 1957, SP. Discussing with Watkins: Riddick interview. A legend: Fite, p. 125.

Not a single: "The Rearguard Commander," *Time,* Aug. 12, 1957. "Sis": Fite, p. 502. Lunch: Reedy, Tames interviews. "You're lucky": Fite, p. 473. "Well": Shaffer, *On and Off,* pp. 202–03; *Time,* Aug. 12, 1957. "In addition": Ervin OH, RBRL.

"I would attribute": Ervin OH.

"Very unobtrusive": Krock, *NYT,* March 17, 1935. "When he spoke": Fite, p. 126.

"With the blood": *CR,* 78/1, pp. 8859–66. "Let us": Russell to Truman, Aug. 7, 1945, White House Central Files, OF 197, HSTL. Truman's reply is revealing of the difference between the two men. The President wrote "Dear Dick" that while Japan was "a terribly cruel and uncivilized nation in warfare," he could not agree that "because they are beasts, we should ourselves act in the same manner." He was unwilling, he said, to decimate an entire people because of their leaders' "pigheadedness" unless "it is absolutely necessary" (Truman to Russell, Aug. 9, 1945, White House Central Files, OF 197, HSTL).

"No more ardent": Robert Byrd, "Richard Brevard Russell," *CR,* 100/2, p. S 353. "If Sherman": Milton Young OH; Fite, p. 353. "I want": Fite, p. 353. "In the field": Jack Bell, "Dick Russell, King of the Filibusterers," advance for AMs of Sunday, July 28, 1963, III Speech, Box 78, folder "Russell Material (Biog. and articles)," RBRL. "He is considered": Manatos to Johnson, May 20, 1968, WHCF, Box 344, LBJL.

"Every great": Fite, pp. 466–67. Agreeing with Humphrey: Meg Greenfield, "The Man Who Leads the Southern Senators," *The Reporter,* May 21, 1964. For thirty-eight years: Russell's long fight for farmers is based on Fite, pp. 149–60, 212–16, and Robert Byrd, "Richard Brevard Russell," *CR,* 100/2, pp. 350–51. "He kept": Harold H. Martin, "The Man Behind the Brass," *SEP,* June 2, 1951. "Essentially": Fite, p. 187. "Throughout": Robert Byrd, "Richard Brevard Russell," *CR,* 100/2, pp. 350, 351.

"He considered": Fite, p. 145. "There are no": Fite, p. 167; *CR,* 75/3, p. 1101. "I was": *WS,* Feb. 29, 1960. "The rights": Meg Greenfield, "The Man Who Leads the Southern Senators," *The Reporter*, May 21, 1964. Challenged in his bid for a full Senate term by Georgia's most politically powerful racist, Governor Eugene Talmadge, he replied to Talmadge's charge that he was unreliable on segregation by calling the Governor "despicable" for "doing what every candidate who is about to be beaten does. He comes in crying nigger." But Russell vigorously defended white supremacy and segregation, and said in one speech that "this is a white man's country, yes, and we are going to keep it that way." In another speech, he said that it was an insult to the people of Georgia "to even insinuate that I stand for political and social equality with the Negro." As Fite puts it (p. 149), "He used legal arguments in contrast to Talmadge's bombastic accusations of dictatorship, but the difference between the Russells and the Talmadges in the South was mainly one of degree rather than substance." **Full-dress speeches:** *CR*, 75/3, pp. 374–75, 1098–1115; *CR*, 77/2, pp. 8804–05; *CR*, 78/2, pp. 8859–66; *CR*, 80/2, pp. 7355–64; *Current Biography*, 1949. **"More"; "strike vital":** Fite, p. 167.

"Been evolved": *CR*, 75/3, p. 1101. **"We believe"; "promotes":** *CR*, 79/2, pp. 10259–61. **"In a short":** *CR*, 75/3, p. 1101. **"I challenge":** *CR*, 77/2, p. 8904. **"Whites and blacks alike":** *CR*, 75/3, p. 1101. **"We have worked":** *CR*, 77/2, p. 8904.

"Unnecessary": *CR*, 75/3, pp. 374–75, 1098–1115. **"As interested":** "The Rearguard Commander," *Time*, Aug. 12, 1957. **"If it":** *CR*, 75/3, p. 1101.

"Let the": *CR*, 77/2, p. 8904.

"I don't know": *Time*, Aug. 12, 1957. **"We've had":** Fite, p. 184. **"Russell did not":** Fite, pp. 184, 168.

Borah, Norris: Fite, pp. 167–68.

"At opposite": "Senator Russell of Georgia: Does He Speak for the South," *Newsweek*, Aug. 19, 1963. **"Not a racist"; "must be respected":** Shaffer, pp. 202, 206. **"Honest":** Harold H. Martin, "The Man Behind the Brass," *SEP*, June 2, 1951. **"Roots":** *Time*, Aug. 12, 1957.

"Knightly": Ervin OH. **1908 lynching:** *Winder Weekly News*, Dec. 10, 1908. **1922 lynching:** *Winder Weekly News*, Sept. 7, 1922.

Dorsey attempting; He "avoided": Fite, p. 43.

"Georgia exceeds": Burns, *Out of These Chains*, p. 369. A vivid description of the chain gangs is in T. H. Watkins, "A Fugitive's Epic," *Constitution*, Fall 1993. **"I used to":** Martin, *Deep South*, p. 176. **"I suppose"; "had never":** "Georgia Giant," edited transcript, Part I, pp. 25, 26. **"So hungry":**

NYWT, undated, but obviously 1932. **Promise broken:** Burns, *Out of These Chains*, p. 387; T. H. Watkins, "A Fugitive's Epic," *Constitution*, Fall 1993. **"Real importance":** *NYT*, Jan. 31, 1932. **"One would":** *NYHT*, Jan. 18, 1932.

Georgia's Governor demanded; affidavits: Burns, *Out of These Chains*, pp. 382–83. **Russell's statements:** *AC*, Dec. 23, 1932. **"A slander":** Russell, quoted in Burns, *Out of These Chains*, pp. 396–97. Russell added, in what Watkins calls "a nasty aside," that "the decision makes it easy to understand how the most horrible crime of modern times—the kidnapping of the Lindberg baby—could occur and go unpunished in a State whose Governor has such ideas of law. . . ." (T. H. Watkins, "A Fugitive's Epic," *Constitution*, Fall 1993). **"Telling the world":** *NY Sunday News*, Dec. 25, 1932.

Russell saw it: David B. Potenziani, "Look to the Past: Richard Russell and the Defense of White Supremacy," unpublished Ph.D. dissertation, University of Georgia, 1981, pp. 15 ff. Potenziani's thesis is a perceptive analysis of Russell's racial views. **"To force":** *CR*, 77/2, p. 9065. **Blocked:** *NYT*, Nov. 24, 1942.

"I am afraid": Russell to Cobb C. Torrance, May 31, 1944, X. Civil Rights Series, FEPC, 1944–1949, RBRL. **"Any southern":** Russell to Alan Reid, Feb. 4, 1936, IV, Early Office Series, RBRL. **"A terrible":** Russell to Storey, Feb. 13, 1942, Series X, Box 158, RBRL. **Not necessary; "Fully aware":** Marion Young to Russell, Aug. 15, 1942; Russell to Mrs. Young, Aug. 18, 1942, X. Civil Rights Series, Negro File, Box 139, RBRL.

"In the last": Russell to R. F. Hardy, July 4, 1942, Series X, Box 158, RBRL. **"Fading away":** Russell in *CR*, 80/2, p. 7360. **Marines:** When S. D. Mandeville of Tennille, Ga., wrote Russell that the Marine Corps "have achieved a brilliant record and a great fighting spirit without the aid of the Negro. Don't let them ruin the morale of the boys by letting the Negro in the Marine Corps," Russell wrote back, "I feel just as you do about the enlistment of Negroes in the Marine Corps, and I have vigorously protested any such policy." (Mandeville to Russell, Feb. 5, 1942; Russell to Mandeville, Feb. 13, 1942, both from X. Civil Rights Series Negro File (subject) Correspondence, Box 139, RBRL. **"These people":** Patience Russell Patterson OH. **"In spite":** David B. Potenziani, "Look to the Past: Richard Russell and the Defense of White Supremacy," unpublished Ph.D. dissertation, University of Georgia, 1981, p. 41. **"Health and morals":** *CR*, 80/2, p. 5666. **"No more intimate":** *CR*, 80/2, pp. 7356,

7361. Special camps: Russell to George Reynolds and to Theodore Cowart, Jan. 25, 1943, X. Civil Rights Series, Negro File, 1942–43, Box 157, RBRL.

"All of the men": III A. Speech, Box 32, Folder, "Dragon Speech," pp. 18, 19, RBRL. This is a typed, 22-page text, evidently transcribed from notes taken by a secretary to whom Russell dictated it. On the typed text are changes made in Russell's handwriting. Archivists at the RBRL say that Russell dictated the text after rushing from the Senate floor in a rage after he had suffered a setback during the 1957 civil rights debate, and that the speech was never delivered. The purpose of the speech would have been "to ask unanimous consent that" an article, dated July 20th, from the *Portland Oregonian* describing the rape "be printed in the Record." The precise date that Russell dictated it is unknown. It was filed in his office files on Sept. 28, 1957. An unknown individual in Russell's office named it the "Dragon Speech" because its theme is that in order to slay an imaginary "Southern dragon," northerners had given themselves illegal powers. As a result, says the text Russell dictated, "the N.A.A.C.P. had achieved such power"—"controlling the policies of [America's] only two political parties" that "the rights of ordinary white people, the most numerous group in the country, are enjoyable contingent upon the possibility that they may collide with any right, real or imaginary, claimed by a Negro citizen" (p. 20).

"No such thing": Russell to Hansell, Sept. 30, 1957, Civil Rights, Little Rock, Box 345, RBRL. **"They are determined":** Undated newspaper clipping, Mrs. Ina Russell's scrapbook, 1947–48, RBRL, cited in Fite, p. 233.

"Scathingly": Drury, *A Senate Journal,* p. 122.

"I am sick": Fite, p. 183.

Even "baseball [and] football": Fite, p. 184. **"Almost entirely":** Russell to John M. Slaton, Aug. 17, 1944, Series X, RBRL. **"A wild-eyed":** Fite, p. 229.

Transit plot: Drury, p. 238.

1948 FEPC speech: *CR,* 80/2, pp. A-1863–64. **"The agitation":** *CR,* 76/3, p. 1102. **"This bill":** *CR,* 79/2, p. 179. **"Any white man":** *CR,* 79/2, p. 380.

Lynching in Monroe: *NYHT, NYT,* July 27, 1946. **"We can't cope"; "persons unknown":** *NYT, NYHT,* July 28, 1946. **"Mr. President":** *CR,* 79/2, pp. 10258–60; *NYT,* July 28, 1946. **Other 1946 lynchings:** Zangrando, *NAACP Crusade,* p. 174; Egerton, *Speak Now Against the Day,* p. 362. **"I mean":** Donovan, *Conflict and Crisis,* p. 334.

"South haters"; "hellhack"; "obloquy": Meg Greenfield, "The Man Who Leads the

Southern Senators," *The Reporter,* May 21, 1964. **"To alienate":** Fite, p. 226. **"Cannot":** Russell to Lemuel S. J. Smith, Feb. 20, 1948, RBRL. **"Gestapo":** Fite, p. 231. **"hordes":** *CR,* 80/2, p. A-1864.

Facing Connally down: Margaret Shannon, *Atlanta Journal and Constitution,* Nov. 24, 1963. **"A good case":** "The Rearguard Commander," *Time,* Aug. 12, 1957.

"Whether": *CR,* 79/2, p. 161. **"We've had":** Fite, p. 184.

"The Negro"; "Under Russell": Harold H. Martin, "The Man Behind the Brass," *SEP,* June 2, 1951.

"Almost Roman"; "Olympian": Frederic W. Collins, *NYT Magazine,* Oct. 20, 1963. **"No one laughed":** Wicker, *On Press,* p. 40.

"A monumental": Douglas Kiker, "The Old Guard at Its Shrewdest," *Harper's,* Sept. 1966. **"dishonorable":** *WS,* March 15, 1964; BeLieu interview. **"His colleagues":** Fite, p. 200. **"A thousand":** Harold Davis, quoted by Fite, p. 200. **"His bond":** Fite, p. 289. **"Incomparably":** White, *Citadel,* p. 87.

"Remember so well": Humphrey OH. **"A wink":** Mann, *Walls of Jericho,* p. 75. **"Check it":** Jack Bell, "Dick Russell, King of the Filibusters," advance for AMs of Sunday, July 28, 1963. **"No major":** Don Oberdorfer, "The Filibuster's Best Friend," *SEP,* March 15, 1965. **"Well, I want":** Gale McGee, quoted in Fite, p. 323. **"Scores":** Fite, p. 317. **"Favorite uncle":** Fite, pp. 323, 199.

"It has not": Meg Greenfield, "The Man Who Leads the Southern Senators," *The Reporter,* May 21, 1964.

"Of their own": *CR,* 80/2, pp. 7355–64. **"I could not":** *CR,* 80/2, p. 5666. **Not one got through:** Mann, p. 43. **"As such":** *CR,* 77/2, pp. 8904–05.

"Thin gray line": *NYT,* March 2, 1960. **"Words of war":** Meg Greenfield, "The Man Who Leads the Southern Senators," *The Reporter,* May 21, 1964. Don Oberdorfer, "Richard Russell, Senator of Influence," *WP,* Jan. 22, 1971. **"The last ditch":** Ervin OH. **"Our position":** Russell to Ervin, July 29, 1948, Dictation Series, Civil Rights, RBRL.

8. "We of the South"

"That persuasive"; "The greatest": Fite, *Russell,* pp. 43, 203. **"That's a":** Russell, replying to a question by Harry Reasoner on "Portraits," CBS News, July 17, 1963.

Collins relationship: Fite, pp. 171–72, 201.

"About as close": Fite, p. 326. **Puttering around:** Richard Russell III interview (the

Senator's nephew). **Could think best:** Griggs to Williamson, Aug. 1, 1957, SP. **"We could run":** Rev. Henry E. Russell OH.

"He just": Harry O. Smith, quoted in *WP,* May 11, 1952. He often walked around the town barefoot. **"Warm feelings"; "A host"; "somewhat":** Fite, p. 208. **"I had always"; six months:** McConaughy to Williamson, July 31, 1957, SP. **Stopped; "frankly":** Fite, pp. 201–02.

With his staff, and the pattern of his life: Fite, *passim;* interviews with BeLieu, Braswell, Darden, Gwen Jordan, William H. Jordan, Moore, Reedy; and the OHs of BeLieu, John T. Carlton, Darden, Robert M. Dunahoo, Felton M. (Skeeter) Johnston, Gwen Jordan, William Jordan, Barboura Raesly, Dorothye Scott. **" 'Miss' ":** Fite, p. 207.

Going to Opening Day: Felton Johnston OH. **Eating at O'Donnell's:** Jordan, BeLieu interviews. BeLieu saw him there; Fite, p. 468. **"My life and work":** Cecil Holland, *WS,* March 15, 1964.

"I knew": Goodwin, *Lyndon Johnson,* p. 103. Actually, Johnson had included Armed Services—as his third choice—on his list of desired committee assignments in some of his earlier letters requesting a seat on Appropriations. John Connally and Walter Jenkins say this was done as what Connally calls a "sop" to Tom Connally, to make the senior senator feel Johnson was following the suggestion Connally had made to him in Marlin. The Bobby Baker discussion apparently took place during the week after Christmas, 1948. **Dropping by:** Busby, Connally, Jordan interviews. **Invitations to dinner:** Lady Bird Johnson OH. **"An entirely":** Oltorf interview.

"The best of *us*": Caro, *Path,* p. 759. And see also *Path,* pp. 762–63.

"I early knew": Lady Bird Johnson OH. **Were encouraged:** Baker, *Wheeling and Dealing,* p. 42; Dugger, *The Politician,* p. 344. **"We both like":** "Georgia Giant," unedited transcript, Reel 19, p. 30, Atlanta, WSB-TV, Cox Enterprises, 1970. **"Hot dogs":** Lady Bird Johnson OH. **"I doubt":** Connally with Herskowitz, *In History's Shadow,* p. 122. **Now began:** Busby, Connally, Jenkins interviews. **"With no one":** Goodwin, *Lyndon Johnson,* p. 105. **"You never":** Oltorf interview. **"I shall take you":** Caro, *Path,* Chapter 17. **"My mentor":** Goodwin, p. 105. **"Snickered":** Baker, *Wheeling and Dealing,* p. 42. **"He flattered":** Baker, quoted in Miller, *Lyndon,* p. 142. **"Had he":** Baker, on *The American Experience: LBJ,* PBS Home Video, 1997. **"Well, I suppose":** "Georgia Giant," unedited transcript, Reel 21, p. 30.

"Bosom friend": Stennis interview, April 21, 1971, quoted in Stephen B. Farrow,

"Richard Russell and Lyndon Johnson: Principle and Pragmatism in Senatorial Politics, 1949–52," unpublished senior thesis, University of Tennessee, 1979, p. 34. Stennis also said, "Personal things didn't mean anything to Russell where constitutional principles were concerned" (Stennis OH, RBRL). **Maiden speech:** *CR,* 81/1, pp. 2042–49. **A "novel":** *CCC-T,* March 9, 1949. **"No quarrel":** Dallek, *Lone Star,* p. 367. **Russell telling reporters:** Dugger, p. 344; Steinberg, *Sam Johnson's Boy,* p. 291. **"Worth a story":** "Sense and Sensitivity," *Time,* March 17, 1948. **"Long line":** *Lubbock Journal,* March 10, 1949. **Russell the first:** *San Angelo Standard-Times,* March 10, 1949. **"One of the ablest":** Goodwin, *Lyndon Johnson,* p. 106. And the conservative columnist Holmes Alexander reported that "Russell pronounced it to be the best speech on the subject ever made before this body" (*Berkeley* [Calif.] *Gazette,* April 28, 1956). **"The President":** Stokes, quoted in Donovan, *Tumultuous Years,* p. 22. **"It seems":** Krock, *NYT,* Jan. 30, 1949.

"Gird our loins": *NYT,* Feb. 1, 1949. **"Know if":** Russell to Anderson, Dec. 13, 1949, Civil Rights, FEPC, Correspondence, Box 127, folder FEPC Dictation, 1944–49, RBRL. **"Made it"; Russell told:** Fite, p. 246; *NYT,* Feb. 27, 28, 1949. **"A number"; "Will forecast"; "Taft's help":** Thomas Sancton, *The Nation,* April 9, 1949. **Vandenberg's ruling:** *NYT,* March 11, 12; *WP,* March 12, 1949. "In the final analysis," Vandenberg also said, "the Senate has no effective cloture rule at all. . . . The existing rules . . . still leave the Senate, rightly or wrongly, at the mercy of unlimited debate *ad infinitum*" (*NYT,* Jan. 30, 1949). **Strategy worked:** For example, Krock, *NYT,* Feb. 22, 1949. **"Working":** *New Republic,* March 14, 1949. **"Has virtually":** NAACP, Box 61, "Press Releases, 1949," LC. **Lucas confessing:** *NYT,* March 15, 1949. **Barkley's ruling; Russell's appeal:** *Newsweek,* March 21, 1949; *NYT, WP,* March 11, 12, 1949. See also *NYT,* March 5, 11, 1949. **"Not simply":** *Newsweek,* March 21, 1949. **"Sinking heart":** *Time,* March 21, 1949. **"Mr. Vandenberg has":** *The Nation,* March 19, 1949. **"An aura":** *NYT,* March 12, 1949. **The vote:** *NYT, WP,* March 15, 1949. Agreeing after the vote to drop attempts at cloture, Lucas said, in a definitive statement on the southerners' strength: "We realize that the filibuster can go on for weeks. They [the southerners] have the manpower to do it. Meanwhile, rent control would go out the window." The *Times* said: "Senator Lucas noted also that other major bills . . . were lagging in the legislative process. There was thus, he declared, a log jam that could not be allowed to continue." **"With less":** Byrd to Chapman, March 16, 1949, Box 118, Personal Miscellaneous, RBRL. A sample of the feeling of other members of the Southern Caucus toward their general is in Stennis to Russell, and Johnston to Russell, March 18, 1949 (same file as Byrd letter).

"To his cohorts": Stephen B. Farrow, "Richard Russell and Lyndon Johnson: Principle and Pragmatism in Senatorial Politics, 1949–52," unpublished senior thesis, University of Tennessee, 1979, p. 44. **"compromise":** *NYT, WP,* March 18, 1949.

An accepted part: Goodwin, p. 106; Evans and Novak, *LBJ: Exercise,* p. 32; Mann, *Walls of Jericho,* p. 82. Dallek, who seems to feel that the Caucus was formed in 1949 (it had actually been a major fact of Senate life for at least a decade before that), writes (p. 367): "To defeat Truman's cloture proposal and his whole civil rights program, senators from the former eleven Confederate states organized themselves into a southern caucus and met to map strategy. . . . Johnson stayed away from the southern strategy meeting." **"Senator Johnson":** Darden OH. **"I was":** Darden interview.

"No, no": Busby, Connally, Young interviews. When the author interviewed Busby in 1985, Busby related this incident, and said he wasn't sure whether Johnson had or had not been at the Caucus (he also said he didn't know which Caucus it was), but in 1988, when he was interviewed by an oral history interviewer for the Lyndon Johnson Library, he said Johnson had not been at the Caucus, and related an elaborate explanation that Johnson had given him to explain he had been elsewhere. When, also in 1985, the author asked John Connally about the incident, Connally at first didn't recall it, but after the author told him about Busby's account, did remember it, and said, smilingly, "We didn't know whether he didn't want to comment because he wasn't there, or because he *was* there." Mary-Louise Young was not in the office at the time of the incident but was told about it later by other members of the staff. She says that Johnson didn't want to comment because he had been at the Caucus. In his book, *The Walls of Jericho,* Mann, relying on Dallek's account, says that Johnson was holding the door closed to keep the Associated Press reporter from asking "why he was not at the meeting" (Mann, p. 82). More importantly, both Mann and Dallek write as if there was only one meeting of the Southern Caucus or bloc in 1949; in fact, there were many.

"Yes, he did": "Georgia Giant," unedited transcript, Reel 19, pp. 34, 35; Reel 24, pp. 11–12.

"At another": *NYT,* Jan. 13, 1949.

"Twenty-one met": *NYT,* Feb. 15, 1949. Coverage of this Caucus shows the discrepancies between newspapers on the total number of attendees. The *New York Herald Tribune* put the number of attendees at fifteen, the *Washington Post* at eighteen. (The *Post* also said that that number included some "Border State senators" but longtime observers of the Caucus say that only senators from the eleven southern states were invited to the Caucuses.) **"The caucus counted":** *NYT, WP,* Feb. 25, 1949. **Rather entries:** Johnson's "Desk Diary" for the appropriate dates, Desk Diary, Box 1, LBJL; Rather interview. **"During his first":** "Sense and Sensitivity," *Time,* March 17, 1958. **"Russell knew little":** McConaughy to Beshoar, June 10, 1953, SP. **"At the first":** *Atlanta Journal and Constitution,* Nov. 24, 1963. **"Senator Lyndon":** Stennis to Ina Smith, March 7, 1949, Box 55, LBJA CF.

"In view": Russell to Byrd, June 7, 1949. (At the bottom is a note: "This letter sent to attached list of 19 southern senators." The two senators to whom the letter was not sent were Pepper and Kefauver. Johnson is one of the nineteen.) **"Relative to":** Johnson to Russell, June 9, 1949. Both from Dictation, Civil Rights, March–Sept. 1949, RBRL. **Vote for Eastland bill:** The bill, "District of Columbia Home Rule Act of 1949 (S.1527), would have required a referendum of qualified voters on any change in segregation policy in the District of Columbia. ("Entire Senate Voting Record of Senator Lyndon Johnson, by Subject, from January 3, 1949, to October 13, 1962," Senate Democratic Policy Committee, p. 147.)

"Stood right with us": "Georgia Giant," unedited transcript, Reel 22, p. 3. **"Our political"; "In a way":** "Georgia Giant," unedited transcript, Reel 19, p. 30.

"Impressed"; "well-organized": Darden OH.

"Can-do": "Georgia Giant," unedited transcript, Reel 4, p. 2. **"Made more":** Meg Greenfield, "The Man Who Leads the Southern Senators," *The Reporter,* May 21, 1964.

9. Thirtieth Place

"Turkey hash": Mayer interview. **"Makes me feel":** Quoted in *WP,* Dec. 17, 1950. **"By God":** Bartley interview.

Lady Bird's life: See the "Lady Bird" chapters in Caro, *Path* and *Means.* Unless otherwise indicated, all quotes are from those chapters.

Glass affair: See "Longlea" chapter in Caro, *Path,* and, in *Means,* pp. 25–27, 34,

58–60, 70, 237; Connally, *In History's Shadow*, pp. 69–71. **"I can write":** Glass to Oltorf, Sept. 16, 1967 (in author's possession). **"Disgusted"; "sexual side":** Young interview.
"Changed": Caro, *Means*, p. 69.
"Nigger maid": Caro, *Means*, p. 70.
KTBC: See "Buying and Selling" chapter in Caro, *Means*.
"Who's in town"; "Goddammit": Rather, Jenkins interviews. **"Look":** Young interview. **"Contempt":** Fisher interview. **"Beatendown":** Lucas interview. **" 'Bird!' ":** Mahon interview. **"The women":** Nellie Connally interview.
Scenes with Symington: Symington interview. **"Heavens, no":** Lady Bird, quoted in Russell, *Lady Bird*, p. 116.
"Every inch": Elizabeth Rowe interview. **"Texas friends":** *Time*, June 22, 1953. **Signing at home:** Steinberg, *Sam Johnson's Boy*, p. 405.
"You may be": Johnson to Jones, Nov. 22, 1943, Box 21, LBJA SN. **"I do assure":** Rowe to Johnson, March 4, 1944, Box 32, LBJA SN. **"Here's hoping"; "I hope":** Jones to Johnson, March 13, 1944, Box 21, LBJA SN; Johnson to Jones, March 17, 1944, Box 21, LBJA SN.
Doctors advised: Miller, *Lyndon*, p. 113. **Miscarriage:** Virginia Wile English OH. **"We're waiting":** Stehling interview. **"Never thought":** Russell, *Lady Bird*, p. 153. And see Steinberg, *Sam Johnson's Boy*, pp. 209–10, 229. **"You know":** Gonella interview. **"I've always wished":** LBJ, quoted in Alsop, "Lyndon Johnson: How Does He Do It?" *SEP*, Jan. 24, 1959.
"Daddy was": *WP*, July 9, 1989. **"I never":** Mayer, quoted in Russell, *Lady Bird*, p. 155. **"A second mother":** Lady Bird, quoted in Steinberg, *Sam Johnson's Boy*, p. 283. **"Raised by":** Steinberg, p. 283. **"I felt deprived":** Lucy, quoted in Russell, *Lady Bird*, p. 155. **"Why":** Lynda Bird, quoted in Mooney, *LBJ*, p. 250. **"Cut the pattern":** Lady Bird, quoted in *Washington Sunday Star*, Aug. 15, 1954. **"So subservient":** Quoted in Harrington, "A Woman Between Two Worlds," *WP*, July 9, 1989. **"Just so sad":** Bentsen, quoted in Harrington, "A Woman Between Two Worlds," *WP*, July 9, 1989.

10. Lyndon Johnson and the Liberal

All dates are 1949 unless otherwise indicated.

Leland Olds' life: From interviews with members of his family—his daughter Zara (now Mrs. Wallace Chapin); his son John; his grandson, Brady Chapin; and his daughter-in-law Marianne Egier Olds. With the Oldses' neighbors on McKinley Street—Philip Davis, Caryl Marsh, Jerome and Natalie Springarn. With members of his staff at the FPC—Reuben Goldberg and Melwood Van Scoyoc. With Alex Radin, general manager of the American Public Power Association. With members of Washington's liberal community: Alan Barth, Benjamin V. Cohen, Thomas G. Corcoran, John Gunther (then a lobbyist for the ADA), Joseph L. Rauh, James H. Rowe, Jr. With Paul Douglas' administrative assistant Frank McCulloch. From the oral histories of Rauh and Rowe.
From Delos W. Lovelace, "What's News Today," *NY Sun*, May 23, 1944; Oliver Pilat, "Head Man in the Nation's Powerhouse," *NYP*, Sept. 23, 1944; Sherrill, *Accidental President*, pp. 155–66; Douglas, *Fullness of Time*, pp. 463–65.
From the transcript of Olds' own testimony at the hearings on his renomination: "Reappointment of Leland Olds to Federal Power Commission," *Hearings Before a Subcommittee of the Committee on Interstate and Foreign Commerce, United States Senate, Eighty-first Congress, First Session, Sept. 27, 28, 29, and Oct. 3, 1949*, Washington: Government Printing Office, 1949 (hereafter identified as *Hearings*). And from material in the Leland Olds Papers (LOP) at the Franklin D. Roosevelt Library, Boxes 73–161.
"The central": "The Enemies of Leland Olds," *New Republic*, Oct. 17.
"Jolly": Van Scoyoc interview. **Olds at work:** Goldberg, Van Scoyoc interviews.
"Liked fun": Delos W. Lovelace, *NY Sun*, May 23, 1944. **Beloved:** Sherrill, p. 156.
"I learned": Olds, *Hearings*, p. 108. **"I searched"; "a great deal"; "people really":** *Hearings*, p. 109. **"Were not":** *Hearings*, p. 115. **"That the church":** Douglas R. Chapin, "The Persecution and Assassination of Federal Power Commissioner Leland Olds, as Performed by the Honorable Lyndon B. Johnson Under the Direction of the National Gas and Oil Industries of these United States" (unpublished paper, Jan. 16, 1973, p. 1). **"My experience":** *Hearings*, p. 109.
Shock: *Hearings*, p. 116. **"Inspiring":** *Hearings*, p. 114. **"Railroad workers":** *Hearings*, p. 120.
"Labor angle"; Federated Press: *Hearings*, pp. 131–32. **Baldwin persuaded:** *Hearings*, p. 132.
"A genuine"; "along socialistic": Schlesinger, *Crisis of the Old Order*, pp. 40, 41.
"Hardships": Olds, *Industrial Solidarity*, July 1, 1925, quoted in *Hearings*, p. 50.

Saw the power: Olds, *The Daily Worker,* July 26, 1925, quoted in *Hearings,* p. 37.
Bishop: Olds, *Federated Press Labor's News,* July 20, 1929, quoted in *Hearings,* p. 340.
"Give": *The Daily Worker,* July 16, 1925, quoted in *Hearings,* p. 36.
"Hollow"; "a political": *Federated Press Labor Letter* (hereafter abbreviated as *FPLL*), June 14, 1928, quoted in *Hearings,* p. 45.
"The complete": Olds, *The Daily Worker,* July 5, 1928, quoted in *Hearings,* p. 43.
Transformation had: Olds, *FPLL,* April 27, July 28, 1927, quoted in *Hearings,* pp. 61, 65.
"In my opinion": "Supplemental Statement of Leland Olds," *Hearings,* p. 291. **"I rejected":** Olds, *Hearings,* p. 108. **New party:** "Statement of Leland Olds— Resumed," *Hearings,* p. 136. **"Leads the world":** Olds, *FPLL,* April 27, 1927, quoted in *Hearings,* p. 344. **"The attempt":** Olds, *FPLL,* Nov. 11, 1925, quoted in *Hearings,* p. 343. **"Theories developed":** Olds, *Hearings,* p. 136.
"Two alternatives": *FPLL,* April 6, 1927, quoted in *Hearings,* p. 40. **"Socialistic, if you like":** Franklin D. Roosevelt, quoted in Schlesinger, *Crisis of the Old Order,* p. 124.
"Giant": *FPLL,* May 4, 1927, quoted in *Hearings,* p. 41.
"Even men": Oliver Pilat, "Head Man in the Nation's Powerhouse," *NYP,* Sept. 23, 1944.
At Crerar Library: Oliver Pilat, "Head Man in the Nation's Powerhouse," *NYP,* Sept. 23, 1944; *Hearings,* p. 140. **"Who and what":** Gunther, *Inside U.S.A.,* p. 183. **When:** Schlesinger, *Crisis of the Old Order,* p. 120. **"All his life":** James M. Kiley, *Leland Olds Manual,* p. v.
"I haven't; Walsh call: Olds to Jerome Walsh, Sept. 16, 1949, Box 74, LOP, FDRL; Oliver Pilat, "Head Man in the Nation's Powerhouse," *NYP,* Sept. 23, 1944. **Executive Mansion discussion:** Samuel I. Rosenman, *Working with Roosevelt,* pp. 34–35; Burns, *Lion and the Fox,* p. 113.
Camping: Zara Chapin interview.
Olds at NYS Power Authority: Adolf Berle, *Hearings,* pp. 18–21; Julius H. Barnes to Ed Johnson, Sept. 26, 1949, in *Hearings,* p. 336. **"Just one day":** *Hearings,* pp. 148, 9.
Views changed: *Hearings,* p. 134; Douglas, *Fullness of Time,* p. 463; McCulloch, Rauh, Van Scoyoc interviews; *NYT,* April 12, 1944. **"Great reforms":** *Hearings,* p. 134. **"The greatest":** *NYT,* Aug. 16, 1942. **Impassioned attack:** *NYT,* March 2, 1937. **Formation of ALP:** Burns, *Lion and the Fox,* pp. 287, 377–78; Schlesinger, *Crisis of the Old*

Order, p. 593. **Joined because; "invites all":** *NYT,* Oct. 4, 1938. **He resigned:** See Chapter 11.
Olds at the FPC: C. Herman Pritchett, "Staff Report on the Federal Power Commission," Committee on Independent Regulatory Commissions, Sept. 1, 1948, pp. II, 5–6; Goldberg, Radin, Van Scoyoc interviews. **"In Butte":** Goldberg interview. **"Like Einstein":** Kiley, p. 5. The Einstein comparison was made by others, including William C. Wise, then deputy administrator of the Rural Electrification Agency, who said: "There was only *one* Lee Olds. . . . Just as there has only been one Albert Einstein in mathematics— only one George Norris in the United States Senate—there has been only one who, having been blessed . . . with a fertile and imaginative brain, force[d] himself to work as much as fourteen and sixteen hours, six and seven days, week in and week out, in an attempt to bring to fruition . . . dreams" of low-cost electric energy (Wise, quoted in Kiley, p. iv). **"Many of you":** *NYT,* April 12, 1944.
Moore quoted: *Hearings Before a Subcommittee of the Committee on Interstate Commerce, United States Senate, Seventy-eighth Congress, Second Session, on Leland Olds' Reappointment as Commissioner to the Federal Power Commission, July 6, 7 and 8, 1944.* Washington: Government Printing Office: 1944 (hereafter referred to as *1944 Hearings*), pp. 176–77. **Without a job:** *NYHT,* June 20, July 9, 1944; *NYT,* July 9, 1944. **"I think":** *1944 Hearings,* pp. 166–67. **"I do not":** Tunnell, *CR,* 78/2, pp. 7692, 7693. **Not a single:** *NYT,* Sept. 14, 1944; McCulloch interview.
Brown & Root purchasing: Dugger, *The Politician,* pp. 282–83; *Time* Feb. 24, 1947; *Newsweek,* Nov. 24, 1947; "Natural Gas— Whoosh!" *Fortune,* Dec. 1949; *Time,* July 1, 1957. **Johnson's intervention:** Clark, Connally, Corcoran, Harold Young interviews. **Natural gas and FPC:** *The New Leader,* Oct. 15; *NYP,* Oct. 30. **Phillips:** Stokes, *WS,* June 18, 1955; Joseph P. Harris, "The Senatorial Rejection of Leland Olds: A Case Study," *American Political Science Review,* Sept. 1951, p. 680. **"Courageously":** Joseph P. Harris, "The Senatorial Rejection of Leland Olds: A Case Study," *APSR,* Sept. 1951, p. 679. **Truman's veto:** Box 156, LOP, FDRL; *Newsweek,* April 29, 1950; *NYHT,* April 16, 1950. **A single figure:** Among many statements on this point is one by one of the country's most respected experts in the public utility field, Professor James C. Bonbright of Columbia University, who said in 1949, "In my opinion, millions of people in this country

today are presently paying lower utility rates than they would be paying but for the presence of Leland Olds on the Federal Power Commission" (Joseph P. Harris, "The Senatorial Rejection of Leland Olds: A Case Study," *APSR,* Sept. 1951, p. 676). **"Would establish":** Dugger, p. 351. **"Nothing":** Francis to Johnson, June 28, 1949, attached to Francis to Tom Connally, June 28, Box 18, LBJA SN. **"Olds was":** Oltorf interview. **"Transcended":** Connally interview.

Lyndon knew: The description of Johnson's strategy and tactics is from interviews with Horace Busby, Ed Clark, John Connally, Walter Jenkins, Mary Rather, and Mary Louise Glass Young, and from Dugger, pp. 351–55, and Sherrill, pp. 155–66. **Persuaded Ed Johnson:** "Clifford—Tel. to LO—Talk w Frank Myers," undated, Box 73, LOP, FDRL; Dugger, p. 351.

"He suggested": Lyle OH, p. 38. "We did an awful lot of research on Olds," Walter Jenkins recalls (Jenkins OH IX, p. 25). **HUAC memorandum:** "Information from the files of the Committee on Un-American Activities, United States House of Representatives; date, July 14, 1949; subject, Leland Olds," quoted in *Hearings,* pp. 255–56. And Johnson's staff was also in communication with HUAC: Busby, Young interviews; Young to Johnson, Oct. 10, Box 216, JSP.

Coordinating research in Austin: Clark, Jenkins, Yarborough interviews. **Wirtz description:** Caro, *Path,* pp. 373–76.

Johnson decided: Lyle OH, Busby interview and OH. **Forty thousand shares;** **" 'Communists!' ":** Clark interview. **"I don't care":** Rather to Johnson, Sept. 20, 1949, Box 216, JSP. **Wirtz hated:** Clark, Hopkins, L. E. Jones, Rather, Harold H. Young interviews. **Sent lists:** Clark to Johnson, Sept. 8, 1949, Box 216, JSP. **Suggestions:** Francis to Johnson, Aug. 8, Sept. 16, Box 336, JSP. **Culled:** Johnson to Francis, Aug. 28; to Nixon, Sept. 24, Box 336, JSP. He also asked HUAC for information on William Berle (Glass to Johnson, Oct. 10, Box 863, JSP).

"A hero of mine": Rauh interview.

They believed: Cohen, Corcoran, McCulloch, Rauh, Rowe interviews. **The link:** Caro, *Path,* pp. 450–51, 469, 518–19. **Brief disagreement:** Olds to Ellis, Feb. 17, 1960, Box 6, WHCF, OF, HSTL. **"In fact":** Olds to James Lee, June 15, LOP, FDRL. **"What can I do":** William A. Roberts to Olds, June 15, Box 75, LOP, FDRL. **The assumption:** For example, Cooke to Johnson, June 18, Box 75, LOP, FDRL. Cooke noted that eight of the thirteen members of the Commerce Committee were Democrats, and said, "We who sup-

ported you in the past urge you to press for favorable action Olds."

"Good deal": "Kefauver," "Miscellaneous Notes," Box 73, LOP, FDRL. **"Afraid":** Olds' note to himself, undated but August from surrounding materials, following a conversation with Clark Clifford, "Miscellaneous Notes: Phone Conversations re Nom.," Box 73, LOP, FDRL. **Believed . . . Kerr:** For example, *SLP-D,* June 19; *NYP,* July 1, 13. **"Rather agreed":** "Kefauver, 8/18," "Miscellaneous Notes," Box 73, LOP, FDRL. **"Serious danger":** Stokes, *WS,* Aug. 25.

"Open hostility": Olds to Fred Freestone, Sept. 16, Box 74; Olds' "Desk Diary," Sept. 22, Box 73, LOP, FDRL. **Five members:** *WS,* Aug. 25. **Now seven:** Ed Johnson to Lyndon Johnson, Aug. 24, in *Hearings,* p. 1. **"Unalterably"; "unsatisfactory":** Olds, "Clifford—Tel to LO," undated, Box 73, LOP, FDRL. And McGrath's report to Clifford, who relayed the report to Olds, shows how totally Olds' fate was linked to his abandoning his attempts to make natural gas companies adhere to the law. After talking to Clifford, Olds made the following note to himself: "Reed—will not be opposed if before my nomination amendments to natural gas act are passed." **Johnson's reason for increase:** *The New Leader,* Oct. 15; Busby interview. **Truman had:** MW to Clifford, Aug. 8, Box 12, Papers of Clark Clifford, HSTL.

"Stacked": "Clifford—Tel to LO," undated, Box 73, LOP, FDRL. **"I am":** Olds to Berle, Sept. 15, 1949, Box 74, LOP, FDRL. **"Seldom":** Childs, *NYP,* July 1, 1949. **"We thought":** McCulloch interview. **Olds had no idea:** MuCulloch, Rauh, Van Scoyoc interviews.

11. The Hearing

All dates are 1949 unless otherwise indicated.

Room 312: That room has been renumbered, and is now Room 318 in the Senate's Russell Building.

Olds didn't know: Busby, Rauh, Van Scoyoc interviews. **Lyle's testimony:** "Reappointment of Leland Olds to Federal Power Commission," *Hearings Before a Subcommittee of the Committee on Interstate and Foreign Commerce, United States Senate, Eighty-first Congress, First Session, Sept. 27, 28, 29, and Oct. 3, 1949,* Washington: Government Printing Office, 1949 (hereafter identified as *Hearings*), pp. 28–101.

Tobey sympathetic: Othman, *El Paso Herald Post,* Sept. 28. **Had given proxy:** Tobey to

Johnson, Sept. 29, Box 216, JSP. **"A man has"**: Tobey, *Hearings*, p. 30. **"The Congressman"**: Lyndon Johnson, *Hearings*, p. 31.

"Without objection": Lyndon Johnson, *Hearings*, p. 44. **"Shocked"**: McFarland, *Hearings*, p. 101. **Tobey left**: That evening, he took back the proxy he had given Lyndon Johnson and gave it to Ed Johnson instead, writing Lyndon, "I will explain more fully when we meet again" (Tobey to Johnson, Sept. 29, Box 216, JSP).

"Mr. Olds": Lyndon Johnson, *Hearings*, p. 106. **"Rejected"**: Olds, *Hearings*, p. 108. **Never . . . for *Daily Worker***: *Hearings*, pp. 132–33. **"An open book"**: *Hearings*, p. 154.

Capehart began: *Hearings*, p. 107. **"Mr. Chairman"**: McFarland, *Hearings*, p. 101. **"Let us"**: Johnson, *Hearings*, p. 108.

"Had he not"; **"it may be**: Johnson, Olds, *Hearings*, p. 110. **"When you accepted"**: Johnson, *Hearings*, p. 111. **Brandishing it**: Johnson's demeanor at the hearings is described by Busby and Van Scoyoc. Sherrill (*Accidental President*, p. 159) speaks of the "cold sarcasm" with which Johnson questioned Olds, and of his "mocking" Olds. **"It was my"**: *Hearings*, p. 111. **"Did you ever"**: Capehart, *Hearings*, p. 110. **Olds' exchange with McFarland**: *Hearings*, pp. 111–22. **"I am telling"**: Olds, *Hearings*, p. 114. **"Wirtz picked up"**: Yarborough, quoted in Steinberg, *Sam Johnson's Boy*, p. 295.

"Is it correct"; **" 'yes' or 'no' "**: Johnson, *Hearings*, p. 120. **"No, sir"**: Olds, *Hearings*, p. 120. His exchanges with Johnson, Capehart, and Reed are on pp. 120–25.

"The important thing": Johnson, *Hearings*, p. 126. **"Let me make"**: Reed, *Hearings*, p. 126. **"A full-fledged . . . Communist"**: Reed, *WP*, Sept. 29.

"Rocked": *HP*, Sept. 29. **"Tic"**: Busby interview. **"He kept"**: Van Scoyoc interview.

Stokes, Othman columns: *WS, WDN,* Sept. 28. **Johnson felt**: Busby, Jenkins interviews. Johnson began the afternoon session by saying, "During the lunch hour I was informed, and, I might say, somewhat entertained by today's press reports on our hearings. . . . While we are waiting for some of the members, I would like to put in the record . . ." And he proceeded to read the two columns into the record verbatim. **"So far"**: Johnson, *Hearings*, p. 133. **"Frequently"**: Olds, Johnson, *Hearings*, pp. 134, 135. **"I thought"**: *Hearings*, p. 145.

"Make it clear": Olds, *Hearings*, p. 136. **"What date"**: Johnson, *Hearings*, p. 136. **Found**: His letter—Olds to William Barlo, Sept. 18, 1939—was inserted in *Hearings*, p. 138, after the hearings were over.

"I gather you";**"I do not think"**: Johnson, Olds, *Hearings*, p. 142. **"You are aware"**; **"I did not know"**: Johnson, Olds, *Hearings*, p. 143.

The impression; Johnson's demeanor: Busby interview. **"You do not"**; **"unless I can answer"**: Johnson, Olds, *Hearings*, pp. 155, 156. **Unleashed Capehart**: *Hearings*, pp. 151–52.

"Olds' FPC record": "Reward for Service," *New Republic*, Oct. 10. **"Do you really believe"**: *Hearings*, p. 197. **Johnson's response**: *Hearings*, p. 198. **"Single-minded"**: Reed, *Hearings*, p. 174.

"A full-fledged": Reed, *WP*, Sept. 29. **"SENATOR REED"**; **"SENATOR SAYS"**: *NYT, WP,* Sept. 29.

"The money": Gunther interview. **"Despicable"**: *WP*, Sept. 30. **"I found"**: Mellett, *WS,* Oct. 1. **"And then"**: Van Scoyoc interview. **Johnson making calls**: Busby, Jenkins interviews. **Stopwatch**: Pearson, *WP*, Oct. 4; Busby interview.

"Witnesses": Joseph P. Harris, "The Senatorial Rejection of Leland Olds: A Case Study," *APSR*, Sept. 1951, p. 681. **"You have"**: Alpern, *Hearings*, p. 213. **"If we"**; **"Well, I"**: Johnson, Alpern, *Hearings*, p. 214. **"The courageous"**: Alpern, *Hearings*, p. 215. **Exchange over time**: *Hearings*, p. 215.

"Human memory": Proctor, *Hearings*, p. 219. **"A man"**: Houston, *Hearings*, p. 205. **"Any"**: Sanders, *Hearings*, p. 207. **"Numerous"**: Van Scoyoc to Caro, Dec. 7, 1992 (in author's possession).

"The man"; **"We never"**: *CCC-T*, April 6, 1980. **"Am sure"**: Johnson to Nixon, Sept. 3. Nixon had, in fact, volunteered Head's services to Johnson for the Olds fight, writing Johnson that "His head is really in the task assigned him. Here is hoping for success." Both from "Appts—Olds, Leland," Box 336, JSP.

"Is Mr. Bonner"; **"a traitor"**: Johnson, Bonner, *Hearings*, pp. 255, 259–60. **"All the more"**: Head, *Hearings*, pp. 280–85.

Told callers: Busby interview. **"Now, Mr. Bonner"**: Johnson, *Hearings*, p. 257. **"Dear Lyndon"**: Bonner to Johnson, Oct. 31, Box 216, JSP. **Reading the Photostat**: *Hearings*, pp. 255–56. **Bricker**: *Hearings*, pp. 258, 285.

Headlines: *HP, Philadelphia Inquirer, Chicago Tribune,* Sept. 30.

"The rumor": *Hearings*, p. 252. **"I think"**: *Hearings*, p. 173. **"Not be available"**; **"the material"**: Olds to Johnson, Sept. 29, Box 74, FDRL. **Cooper's call**: Olds' Desk Diary, Sept. 29, Box 11, LOP, FDRL.

"I had asked": "Conversation with Leland Olds" (verbatim typed transcript), Sept. 30,

Box 336, JSP. **"Very kind":** "Later Conversation with Leland Olds," Sept. 30; Olds' Desk Diary, Sept. 30, Box 73, LOP, FDRL. **"At the outset"; "Do you repudiate":** *Hearings,* pp. 291–94, 305–06, 313–20. **"The committee has not":** Johnson, *Hearings,* p. 316.

"I am not asking": *Hearings,* p. 313. **"The question":** *Hearings,* p. 315.

"Mr. Olds himself": Lincoln, "The Political Mill," *WS,* Oct. 15. **"Chameleon-minded":** *DMN,* Oct. 5. **"He is":** McNaughton to Bermingham, Oct. 7, McNaughton Papers, HSTL.

"I am aware": Truman to Ed Johnson, Oct. 3, in *NYT,* Oct. 5. **"Beside the point":** Ed Johnson to Truman, Oct. 4, in *NYT,* Oct. 5. **7–0 vote:** Lyndon Johnson to Ed Johnson, Oct. 4, Box 316, JSP; *NYHT, NYT,* Oct. 5. **"President Truman's":** *NYT,* Oct. 6.

Rebel yells: Danciger to Johnson, Oct. 5, Box 321, JSP. **"What a subcommittee!":** "Washington Wire," *New Republic,* Oct. 10. **"Olds, shouts":** "The Enemies of Leland Olds," *New Republic,* Oct. 17. **"I know of":** Lerner, Childs, *NYP,* Oct. 6. **"Vendetta":** *The Nation,* Oct. 15. **"This is the reason":** Stone, *Baltimore Sun,* Oct. 7. **"Hardly":** Joseph C. Harsch, "State of the Nation," *Christian Science Monitor,* Oct. 12. **Editorial:** *WP,* Sept. 30.

"So hostile": *New Republic,* Oct. 10. **"Against Olds is":** *New Republic,* Oct. 17.

Fortune **article:** "Men of the Gold Coast," Oct. 1949. **"This may explain":** Mellett, *WS,* Oct. 4. The headline over his column was "Big Inch and Little Inch Pipelines, Senator Lyndon Johnson and Mr. Olds."

"Because he": Rowe interview. Similar feelings surfaced in his Oral History. **"I told":** Corcoran, quoted in Joe B. Frantz, "Opening a Curtain: The Metamorphosis of Lyndon B. Johnson," *The Journal of Southern History,* Feb. 1979, p. 17. **"Shameful":** Cohen interview. **"Disgusted"; "There were":** Rauh interview. **"Really":** Rauh, quoted in Frantz, "Opening a Curtain," *The Journal of Southern History,* Feb. 1979, p. 15. **"I sort of":** Rowe interview.

"My, I wish": Rowe OH. **"Enthusiastic":** "Clifford," Olds' "Miscellaneous Notes: Phone Conversations," Box 73, LOP, FDRL. **"The main":** Olds to Eleanor Roosevelt, Oct. 1, Box 75, LOP, FDRL. **"I knew Mr. Olds":** Eleanor Roosevelt, "My Day," *NYP,* Oct. 2. **Other friends attempting:** Box 73, LOP, FDRL; McCulloch interview. **"Certain":** *CR,* 81/1, p. 14371. **Voorhiis statement:** Voorhiis to Douglas, Oct. 7, Box 74, LOP, FDRL. **Too late:** Campbell to Douglas, Oct. 7, Box 74, LOP, FDRL.

"No place": "Clifford," undated, Box 73, LOP, FDRL. **"Importance":** "Notes for Talk with Clifford," undated, Box 73, LOP, FDRL.

Only twenty-nine: *Newsweek,* Oct. 17. **Truman orders Boyle:** *WS,* Oct. 6; *NYT,* Oct. 7. **"Brazen":** *WS,* Oct. 7. **"Deliberate":** *WP,* Oct. 8. **"Deliberately"; to twenty-four:** *Newsweek, Time,* Oct. 17. **"Most important":** *FWS-T,* Oct. 17.

12. The Debate

All dates are 1949 unless otherwise noted.

"Because of": McCulloch interview. **"In the afternoon":** Douglas, *Fullness of Time,* p. 464.

Speeches for Olds: *CR,* 81/1, pp. 14362–375.

Lyndon Johnson's speech: *CR,* 81/1, pp. 14379–385.

"Did change": McNaughton to Bermingham, Oct. 14, p. 2, McNaughton Papers, HSTL. He also reported that "several senators said they knew of 'four or five' votes changed. . . . Ed Johnson confirms this." **"It took":** Sherrill, *Accidental President,* p. 163. **"Most":** Michael Gillette, "The Leland Olds Controversy," unpublished paper cited in Miller, *Lyndon,* p. 145. **"Stunned":** McNaughton to Bermingham, p. 4. **"About":** *WS,* Oct. 14.

"It's not"; "I've never": *FWS-T,* Oct. 17. **"Almost alone":** Rauh, quoted in Miller, p. 146. **During:** Gunther interview. **"In the minds":** Mellett, *WS,* Oct. 18.

"The outstanding": *DT-H,* Oct. 16. **"A whopping":** *DMN,* Oct. 14. **"PRINCIPLE":** *HP,* Oct. 15. **Carpenter article:** *FWS-T,* Oct. 17. **"The junior":** *DMN,* Oct. 16.

"People all over": Caro, *Path,* p. 767. **Doubts had lingered:** Among other interviews, those with Busby, Clark, Connally, Jenkins. **"I hope":** Busby to Johnson, undated, but with Dec. 1949 letters, Box 863, JSP.

REA speech: *HP,* Oct. 20. **At 8-F and hunting camp:** Clark, Oltorf interviews. **Busby careful:** Johnson even got mail in 8-F (Busby to Rather, Lamar Hotel, c/o Suite 8-F, Dec. 19, Box 863, JSP). **"Senator cannot":** Jenkins to Johnson, Nov. 9, Box 863, JSP. **"Shinnery":** Glass to Busby, Nov. 4. **Even the:** Glass to Jenkins, Nov. 7—all Box 863, JSP.

"Even after": Oltorf interview. **"Listen, you":** Brown interview. **"It is":** Woodward to Busby, undated but attached to Woodward to

Busby, Oct. 31, Box 863, JSP. **"One of"**: Johnson to Douglas, Dec. 23, Box 3, LBJA.

Almost exhausted: Zara Olds Chapin interview.

"Of course": Truman to Olds, Nov. 10. President's Personal File, 5124, HSTL. **"Would still"**: *NYT, WS,* Oct. 20. And see *NYT,* Oct. 21. **Boyle told**: Blumenthal to Pearson, undated, Box F165 (3 of 3), Drew Pearson Papers. **Water Policy Committee**: *WS,* Jan. 4, 1950; *NYT,* Aug. 5, 1960. **Interagency**: *NYT,* Aug. 5, 1960.

On the advice: Radin, Van Scoyoc interviews. Kiley says the firm was "created for the purpose of giving him a modest living. . . ."; Kiley, *Leland Olds Manual,* p. v. **"Yes"**: Author's interview with Radin. **"A poor man"**: Davis interview.

"My mother": Zara Olds Chapin interview. **"Very upset"**: Zara Chapin, Marsh, Marianne Olds interviews. **"Never once"**: Radin, Davis interviews. **"Quite possibly"**: *Fortune,* May 1952. **"Olds was crushed"**: Douglas, *Fullness of Time,* p. 464. **"Killed"**: Rauh, quoted in Joe B. Frantz, "Opening a Curtain: The Metamorphosis of Lyndon B. Johnson," *The Journal of Southern History,* Feb. 1979.

"Lee": Van Scoyoc, Zara Olds Chapin interviews. (Olds recounted this incident to Ms. Chapin.)

"A great": Murray, *CR,* 86/2, p. 15010. **"In a sense"**: Kennedy, *WP,* Aug. 5, 1960.

13. "No Time for a Siesta"

All dates are 1950 unless otherwise noted.

"I'm young": Johnson to Russell, Oct. 17, 1949, V., Intra-Office Communications, Personal Miscellaneous, Jan. 1950, RBRL.

Hunting trip: Connally, Oltorf interviews. **"Dear Lyndon"**: Russell to Johnson, Nov. 25, 1949, V., Personal Miscellaneous, Jan. 1950, RBRL.

Only once: "Contacts with President Truman," Box 8, WHFN. **Starting to brood**: Busby, Corcoran, Rowe interviews.

Call to Rusk: Alsop with Platt, *I've Seen the Best of It,* p. 308. **"He called me"**: Busby interview.

"Usurped": Phillips, *Truman Presidency,* p. 299.

Johnson's letter: Johnson to Truman, June 28; Truman to Johnson, June 30, Box 471B, "Tender of Services – J," Official File, HSTL. **"I remember"**: Busby interview. **"Never quite"**: Margaret Truman interview.

"Truman Committee": McCullough, *Truman,* Chapter 7. **"The most"**: McCullough, p. 287.

Had McClellan: For Johnson's concern about the Committee on Expenditures, see *Report of Proceedings, Hearing Held Before Committee on Armed Services, Executive Session,* July 17, Box 345, JSP, p. 8; and memo, "Congressional scrutiny of . . . ," undated, unsigned, Box 345, JSP. **Had Symington**: Busby interview. A summary of these arguments is in an article by Bascom Timmons on July 31, newspaper not identified. **Truman took**: Busby interview.

Tydings' dilemma: Goldsmith, *Colleagues,* p. 20; Steinberg, *Sam Johnson's Boy,* p. 305. **Tried to keep**: *NYHT,* July 18. **Pursuant to**: *Report of Proceedings,* pp. 9–15. **"Millard"; "I believed"**: Johnson to Tydings, July 19. **Sought to reassure**: "Memorandum to Senator Tydings," July 25, "Preliminary Organizations: Preparedness Subcommittee," Box 345, JSP.

Reassuring Truman: "Memorandum: Visit at White House," Aug. 8; Library of Congress Legislative Reference Service, W. C. Gilbert to Johnson, Aug. 25, Box 8, WHFN; Steinberg, *Sam Johnson's Boy,* pp. 306–07. **"Talked it over . . . with Russell"**: Steinberg, p. 304; Goldsmith, p. 20. **"No other factors"**: Symington interview. **"No rancor"**: Goldsmith, p. 20. **Saying privately**: Busby interview. **Tydings' announcement**: *NYHT,* July 28.

"Today faces": *FWS-T,* July 31. **"With the outbreak"**: *The Nation,* Oct. 21.

Assembling staff: "Memorandum for the Record of the Preparedness Subcommittee—Staff Meeting with Senator Johnson," Aug. 1, 2, 3, Box 346, JSP; interviews with staff members Anton, Busby, McGillicuddy, Siegel, and Tyler. **Codifying regulation**: Legislative Reorganization Act of 1946, Section 202(f), Senate Resolutions 319 of the 78th Congress and 77 of the 79th Congress, cited in Smith to Thompson, Sept. 23, 1948, p. 2, Box 345, JSP. **"Nearly all"; "highest-ranking"**: Smith to Thompson, Sept. 23, 1948, pp. 4, 5.

Cook's reluctance; he was told: Steinberg, *Sam Johnson's Boy,* p. 307; Busby, Rowe interviews. **Circumventing; "temporary"; violated**: "Minutes," Aug. 23, "The Preparedness Subcommittee met . . . ," Box 346, JSP; "Executive Session, Transcripts," *The U.S. Senate Report of Proceedings: Hearing Held Before the Committee on Rules and Administration, Pursuant to Senate Resolution 17, Executive Session, Jan. 24, 1951,* Ward & Paul, official reporters, pp. 18, 21, 22, 26–29; Ritchie, Tyler interviews; Cook to

Johnson, Jan. 24, 1951, Box 116, LBJA SF; Committee on Rules & Administration, SEN 82A-E16, pages attached to printed transcript, Executive Session, Jan. 24, 1951, NA.

Hiring Siegel; Making it clear: Siegel OH, interview. **Rent-free rooms:** McGillicuddy, Tyler interviews.

Tyler's hiring: Tyler interview. **twenty-five:** *CR*, 81/2, p. 8624; 82/1, p. 474.

First report: *Investigation of the Preparedness Program, First Report of the Preparedness Subcommittee of the Committee on Armed Services, United States Senate Under the Authority of S.Res.93 (81st Congress)— Interim Report On: Surplus Property, Rubber,* letter of transmittal, Johnson to Tydings, Sept. 5. (Hereafter the subcommittee's reports will be cited as *Subcommittee Reports.*) **Simply a recycling:** Busby, McGillicuddy, Tyler interviews; Donald Cook, "Work of the Preparedness Subcommittee," *The Federal Bar Journal,* March 1951, p. 232. After boasting about the speed with which the subcommittee had gotten under way, Cook wrote: "I must qualify this statement to a degree. In fact the Subcommittee's work began before it was created. Senator Lyndon Johnson had for some time been blowing the bellows hard under our synthetic rubber and surplus disposal programs. Hence, the Subcommittee, when it brought the hammer down, found the iron already hot."

"A number"; Symington told Johnson: *Investigation . . . First Report,* p. 3; Busby, McGillicuddy interviews. **Johnson wrote Hise:** Johnson to Hise, July 29, *Investigation . . . First Report,* p. 27. **Symington had informed:** Symington to Hise, July 28; Symington to Johnson, Aug. 3; Hise to Johnson, Aug. 17; *Investigation . . . First Report,* pp. 29, 30; "Surplus Property Generally," handwritten Johnson memo, undated, "Preliminary Organization," Box 345, JSP; Donald Cook, "Investigations in Operation: Senate Preparedness Subcommittee," *University of Chicago Law Review,* Spring 1951. **Body of opinion:** "Akron Rubber Plant," Box 350, JSP; Howard to Johnson, *Investigation . . . First Report,* pp. 114–15. **"Truman appears:** *SLP-D,* Oct. 8; *NYT,* Sept. 7; Symington interview. **"Because of this":** *Investigation . . . First Report,* p. 4.

Drafting the report: Busby interview. **Newspaper reaction:** *NYHT, NYT,* Sept. 7; *WS,* Sept. 8, 10; *WP,* Sept. 17. **"A model":** Krock, *NYT,* Sept. 19.

As a Schenley: *NYHT,* Nov. 22. **"Lagging seriously":** *NYT,* Dec. 31. **Actually larger:** *NYT,* Dec. 31.

"Government agencies"; "paper pre-

paredness"; "Compulsory"; " 'Pearl Harbor' ":** Newspaper clippings, Boxes 354, 2012, 2013, JSP. **$6.89:** *NYT,* Nov. 10. **Busby's determination:** Busby interview. **"A joking":** Reedy OH I, p. 2. **"Inevitable":** *WP,* June 12, 1951. **"It's all right":** Alexander, "Some Hot Reading," *LAT,* June 17.

Drawing up agenda; Truman's reaction: "Subjects to be Covered at Meeting on Friday, Aug. 4," attached to Johnson to Secretary of Defense Louis Johnson, Aug. 2; Truman to Louis Johnson, Aug. 4, which includes: "I am returning the letter from Lyndon Johnson, together with the subjects he desires to cover. Apparently he has never read about the conduct of the war in the 1860s." President's Secretary's Files—General File, PSF Box 124, HSTL. **Masterstroke:** "General Survey of the Truman Committee (Requested by Senator Johnson Aug 2) . . . (The following are direct quotes from the Final Report of the Truman Committee), Box 116, LBJA SF, "Statement of Senator Lyndon B. Johnson, Statement of Policies and Procedures of Subcommittee" (with Johnson's markings in margins). This statement is dated July 31, but it is based on the Aug. 2 "General Survey" and Busby says it was drafted in response to Truman's displeasure; Official File 419, OF Box 1239, HSTL. Johnson sent him: "Dear Matt, I want you to see a copy of a statement. . . . Some paragraphs in which you might be especially interested are marked. . . . I hope, whenever you can, you will have the President look this over, too . . . ," Johnson to Matt Connelly, Aug. 3; "I . . . have passed it on to the President," Matt Connelly to Johnson, Aug. 7, Official File 419, OF Box 1239, HSTL. In furtherance of this strategy, Johnson also sent Truman a list of "Excerpts from Truman Committee Reports," with the covering note: "Reverting again to the President's own experiences serving in a similar capacity, we have attempted on the subcommittee to follow the President's example in vigorously criticizing those situations where it appeared that criticisms would forward the national defense. As a matter of interest, we are attaching some precedents in that respect, set for this subcommittee by the Truman Committee" (Box 124, General File, HSTL). **Phrases that echoed:** McCullough, pp. 255–91. **"Approved them"; "MEMORANDUM: Visit at White House":** Aug. 8, unsigned, Box 116, LBJA SF.

"A NEW": Albright, "Gallery Glimpses," *WP,* Aug. 6. In talking to Albright, Johnson noted another similarity to the original Truman Committee. After talking to him, Albright wrote that the Johnson Subcommittee "will get down to 'cases' and try to correct them. The old Truman Committee used the 'case system,' scouting out bottlenecks in the preparedness effort and trying to break them." **"Like father":** *WS,* Sept. 19.

Work of one man; involving other: McCullough, Chapter 7. **"They would":** McCullough, p. 263. **Johnson discouraging participation:** Busby, McGillicuddy, Reedy interviews. **Kefauver's proxy:** Transcript of Johnson telephone conversation with Allen, March 30, 1951, "Notes and Transcripts of Johnson Conversations—1951," Box 1; Kefauver to Johnson, Aug. 28, Box 345, JSP. **Chapman's drunkenness:** Busby, Jenkins interviews. **Receptivity:** Goldsmith, p. 21. **"An apparatus":** MacNeil interview. **Would value:** Anton interview. **Get his** *quid:* Anton, McGillicuddy interviews. **"Work will take":** AP story, paper unidentified, Aug. 1.

Truman Committee's openness: *Preliminary Inventory of the Records of the Special Committee of the Senate to Investigate National Defense Program, 1941–1948,* compiled by Harold E. Hufford, assisted by Toussaint L. Prince; General Services Administration; 1952, 8E-2, 5/15/5, Boxes 14, 27, NA; National Archives Preliminary Inventory No. 48: Records of the Special Committee, 1952; NA, Washington, D.C.; Gillette, McCulley interviews. (Truman was chairman from April 15, 1941, to June 19, 1944.) **"Memorable Days":** McCullough, pp. 272 ff. The contrast between the Truman and Johnson committees came through in a memo from Cook to Johnson "Re: Work of the Truman Committee." The memo covers the earlier committee's work even after Truman, having become vice president, was no longer chairman. The memo says that "during the seven years of its existence, the Committee issued fifty-one reports (including two minority reports) and held 432 public hearings. . . . In the first year of its existence, the Committee issued only six reports. During the remainder of 1942, it issued eight more reports . . . On the other hand, the Committee held a large number of public hearings . . . Hearings were in progress during almost every month of the Committee's existence during the first year, and the record indicates that this procedure continued practically throughout the Committee's entire existence." As for the Johnson Subcommittee, Cook was to write—in an article published in 1951—that "in practice, the subcommittee had not found it necessary to conduct elaborate hearings where witnesses are interrogated at great length" because the information it needed was available in documents or was given to the subcommittee's staff "informally." "Occasionally," he wrote,

"the explanations are made at a formal hearing before the subcommittee in executive session. Since it is a policy announced by Senator Johnson . . . to develop the substantial rather than to exploit the sensational, very rarely are the hearings public." (Donald Cook to Johnson, July 11, 1951, Box 116, LBJA SF; Cook, "Investigations in Operation: Senate Preparedness Subcommittee," *University of Chicago Law Review,* Spring 1951). See also unsigned, "General Survey of the Truman Committee (Requested by Senator Johnson, Aug. 2); "Excerpts from Truman Committee Reports"; "Memorandum to the Senator," unsigned, undated, all Box 116, LBJA SF.

Few Johnson hearings: S. Res. 18, U.S. Congress, Senate, *Committee on Armed Services, Legislative Calendar,* 81st Cong., 1949–1950; 82nd Cong., 1952; "Senate Armed Services Committee Calendar," *CR,* 82/2; 83/1 and 2. **Bulk closed:** *Ibid.,* 82/2; 83/1 and 2; BeLieu; Busby, McGillicuddy, Reedy interviews. **"On S. 1"; "to facilitate"; not even funded:** Richard T. McCulley, *Memo Concerning Preparedness Investigating Subcommittee on Armed Service and the Universal Military Service and Training Act of 1951 (82nd Congress, 1951–1952),* Oct. 19, 2001, Finding Aid for the Senate Committee on Armed Services, Center for Legislative Archives, NA. **Nineteen open hearings:** Even this figure may be misleading. Nine of the nineteen were on alleged scandals in the construction of overseas bases, and they followed a series of articles by Homer Bigart in the *NYHT.* Johnson had no choice but to open these hearings to the press, Daniel McGillicuddy says. "After all the press had broken the story. We *couldn't* keep them closed." **Staffers involved:** Busby interview. **"Unusual":** Darden OH. Stennis became a member of the Presidential Preparedness Subcommittee on March 13, 1951, after the hearing on S.1 had been concluded. **"Skillfully guided":** Fite, p. 253. **"The UMT thing":** Busby interview. **Task forces; "Chairman Johnson":** Richard T. McCulley, *Memo Concerning Task Forces of the Preparedness Investigating Subcommittee of the Senate Armed Services Committee,* Oct. 4, 2001, Reference Reports, 7/1999, Center for Legislative Archives, NA, Busby, McCulley, Reedy interviews.

Several simply rewritings; drafting procedure: Busby, McGillicuddy, Reedy interviews. **"If you get":** McGillicuddy interview. **"He looked"; "fifteen":** McGillicuddy interview. **"We just"; "Johnson wanted":** Busby interview. "He got every report unanimous.

Sounds great. You're talking statesman" (MacNeil interview). **Infused:** MacNeil, Steele interviews; McNeil OH. **"PACKETING":** Levison to Beshoar, Aug. 31, 1951. **"NOT FOR USE":** "Johnson—Acheson—McNaughton," undated. **"Trouble is":** McConaughy to Beshoar, undated. **"Had a long"; "I think":** Beal to Elson, Sept. 16, all SP. **"He worked":** McNeil OH. **"TEXAS WATCHDOG":** *Time,* Sept. 18. **"Mild-mannered but determined":** *The Nation,* Oct. 21. **"Prominence":** Leslie Carpenter, "The Whip from Texas," *Collier's,* Feb. 17, 1951. **"It was"; "when Tydings":** Busby interview. **McCarthy defeating Tydings:** Reeves, *Joe McCarthy,* Chapters 13, 14. **Big money from Texas:** Theodore H. White, "Texas: Land of Wealth and Fear," *The Reporter,* May 25, 1954. **Ten thousand dollars:** Reeves, p. 337.

14. Out of the Crowd

All dates are 1951 unless otherwise noted.

"The whole": McGillicuddy interview. **"No":** BeLieu interview. **Complaints about Lackland:** *NYT, WP, WS,* Jan. 27. **Rumors were all they were:** *NYT, WP,* Jan. 30; *WS,* Feb. 4. **"We are all":** Finletter to Johnson, Feb. 6, Appendix 2, *Investigation of the Preparedness Program: Fifth Report . . . Interim Report on Lackland Air Force Base,* Feb. 26 (referred to hereafter as *Fifth Report*). **Johnson emerged:** *WP,* Jan. 28. **"To make":** Johnson quoted, *NYT, WP,* Feb. 1. **"We've got":** Johnson, quoted by Busby, Tyler. **"He points":** Johnson quoted in Tyler interview. **Busby's feelings; "Listen":** Busby interview. **"INVESTIGATORS SLEEP":** *DMN,* Feb. 1. **"No undue"; no suicides; no pneumonia epidemic, etc.:** *Fifth Report,* pp. 2–4. **Johnson was informed:** Busby interview. **"Many parents":** *FWS-T,* Feb. 19. **Johnson touch:** *Fifth Report,* pp. 1–13.

McNeil's prediction: *NYWT,* Feb. 19. **"Sizzling":** For example, *AA-S,* Feb. 18. **"It was":** *FWS-T,* Feb. 19. **"GREED"; "MESS"; "HOARD":** *WS, WT-H, WP,* Feb. 19. **"Completely":** *FWS-T,* Feb. 19.

"I want": Johnson, quoted in *FWS-T,* Feb. 19. **"All branches":** *Investigation of the Preparedness Program . . . Ninth Report: Military Indoctrination Centers,* April 16. **McGillicuddy at Breckenridge:** McGilli-

cuddy interview. **"We hit":** McGillicuddy, Tyler interviews. **Housing conditions at Breckenridge:** *Investigation of the Preparedness Program . . . Twenty-eighth Report . . . Interim Report on Substandard Housing and Rent Gouging of Military Personnel,* July 19, and *Thirtieth Report: Second Report on Substandard Housing and Gouging. . . ,* Sept. 24. **"This will":** Reedy, quoted by McGillicuddy in interview. Reedy confirmed McGillicuddy's account. **"When you go"; Johnson's rage:** McGillicuddy interview.

"A thousand signs": Smathers OH. **"He had to win":** Emmette Redford interview. **"Any kind":** Siegel OH. **"A real challenge":** Goldsmith, *Colleagues,* p. 21. Kefauver had, in fact, given Johnson his proxy to use in subcommittee meetings, Kefauver to Johnson, Aug. 28, Box 345, JSP. **"Drinking makes you"; "Bobby, you tryin' "** Baker, *Wheeling and Dealing,* pp. 75–77. **His drinks weaker:** Gonella interview. **Drinking with Chapman:** Busby interview.

"As trustworthy": McPherson, *Political Education,* p. 79. **"Why, you":** Mooney, *LBJ,* p. 47. **Tactics with Saltonstall:** Reedy interview. Saltonstall once said of Johnson: "He knew how to go after people, so to speak. He never put the whips on men, to use that expression, in any sense of the word. He would say, 'Help me' " (Saltonstall OH, quoted in Mooney, p. 54).

Helping Bridges on wool: Cook to Bridges, March 30, Box 353, JSP. **Help against constituents:** *Report of Proceedings, Hearing Held Before Preparedness Subcommittee of the Committee on Armed Services—Executive Session, July 9, 1951.* **"Some investigator":** Bridges, *ibid.,* pp. 33, 4. **"Whenever":** Cook, *ibid.,* p. 34. **Rapport:** Busby, Reedy interviews.

"Wake him up!": Busby interview. **Chapman's death:** *WS,* March 8. **Obtaining unanimity:** BeLieu, Busby, McGillicuddy interviews. **"Sometimes":** McGillicuddy interview. **"He'd tell":** BeLieu interview.

Aides would hear: Busby, Jenkins interviews. **"A detailed":** Goodwin, *Lyndon Johnson,* p. 123. **"Most chairmen":** BeLieu interview. **"Especially remarkable":** "The Watchdog Committee and How It Watches," *Newsweek,* Dec. 3.

"Chiselers": *NYT,* Sept. 30. **Biloxi:** *WP,* Oct. 20. **"Inexcusable":** *NYHT, NYT,* Nov. 11. **Warm clothing:** *NYHT,* Nov. 1.

"Congress has": Alexander, *Boston Herald,* Nov. 22. **Long articles:** Leslie Carpenter,

"The Whip from Texas," *Collier's*, Feb. 17; Eliot Janeway, "Johnson of the Watchdog Committee," *NYT Magazine*, June 17; Paul Healy, "The Frantic Gentleman from Texas," *SEP*, May 19.

Leaking to *Newsweek*; "not very substantive": Reedy OH IV, p. 21; Reedy interview. **"We didn't":** *Investigation of the Preparedness Program . . . Thirty-fifth Report: Interim Report on Defense Mobilization*, p. 15. **"This report":** *FWS-T*, Nov. 29; *Newsweek*, Dec. 3. **Foster's letter:** *NYHT*, Nov. 28, 29; *NYT*, *FWS-T*, Nov. 29.

Waiting for the cover: Jenkins interview. **"Walter says":** Rather to Johnson, Nov. 28. **"TOO MUCH BUTTER":** *Newsweek*, Dec. 3. **Getting Reedy out of town:** Reedy OH IV, pp. 21–24. **"Unfair":** Jenkins, quoted in *NYHT*, Nov. 29. **"Doubletalk":** *NYT*, *NYHT*, Nov. 20. **"Just didn't know"; "people":** *NYHT*, Dec. 2. Also see *NYT*, Dec. 3, *NYHT*, Dec. 7. **Friendly's study:** *WP*, May 12–17, 1952.

"Often criticized": McConaughy to Beshoar, June 19, 1953. **"Much ado":** Blair to Beshoar, June 13, 1953, both SP.

15. No Choice

Development of leadership: Primarily Baker and Davidson, eds., *First Among Equals*, Vol. II, pp. 167–268, and Vols. I and II, *passim;* Galloway, *Legislative Process*, pp. 542–90; Matthews, *U.S. Senators*, pp. 118–46; Floyd M. Riddick, *Majority and Minority Leaders;* Alsop and Kintner, "Sly and Able: The Real Leader of the Senate, Jimmy Byrnes," *SEP*, July 20, 1940.

Interviews particularly with Richard A. Baker, Neil MacNeil, Floyd M. Riddick, Donald A. Ritchie and Howard E. Shuman.

"Were generally": Byrd, *The Senate*, Vol. II, p. 187. **"No one":** Wilson, *Congressional Government*, p. 147. **"No single":** Walter J. Oleszek, "John Worth Kern: Portrait of a Floor Leader," in Baker and Davidson, eds., *First Among Equals*, p. 8. **"Baronial":** Baker and Davidson, eds., *First Among Equals*, p. 1. **Lacked; "Priority":** Riddick, *Senate Procedure*, p. 883.

Primarily: Oleszek, "John Worth Kern," in Baker and Davidson, eds., *First Among Equals*, p. 24. One study states: "Never before had the president's party in the Senate intentionally elected a floor leader for the primary purpose of implementing an executive-initiated legislative program" (Margaret Munk, "Origin and Development of the Party Floor Leadership in the United States Senate," *Capitol Studies*, Winter 1974).

"He roars": Alsop and Catledge, "Joe Robinson: The New Deal's Old Reliable," *SEP*, Sept. 26, 1936. **Ran it on behalf:** Donald Bacon, "Joseph Taylor Robinson: The Good Soldier," in Baker and Davidson, eds., *First Among Equals*, pp. 74, 75. George Norris was to accuse Robinson of voting "contrary to his party's policies" during the Coolidge Administration. During the Depression, Al Smith was to say, "He has given more aid to Herbert Hoover than any other Democrat." **"A socialistic dole"; "the most humiliating"; "I know":** Bacon, "Joseph Taylor Robinson," in Baker and Davidson, eds., *First Among Equals*, pp. 77–78. H. L. Mencken was to write that although Robinson "was still" the New Deal's "spokesman on the floor of the Senate, and he roared and sweated for it every day, everyone knew that he was in the forefront of the opposition to it behind the arras, and the only question in doubt was whether he would ever summon up courage enough to denounce it in the open" (Mencken, "Hero or Hack," *The American Mercury*, Dec. 1937).

"Congress doesn't": Will Rogers, quoted in Bacon, "Joseph Taylor Robinson," in Baker and Davidson, eds., *First Among Equals*, p. 82. **"Not interested"; "his loyalty":** Bacon, "Joseph Taylor Robinson," in Baker and Davidson, eds., *First Among Equals*, pp. 86, 83. **"Joe's job"; Huey Long "drove":** Alsop and Catledge, "Joe Robinson: The New Deal's Old Reliable," *SEP*, Sept. 26, 1936. **"He did"; of which:** Bacon, "Joseph Taylor Robinson," in Baker and Davidson, eds., *First Among Equals*," pp. 93, 83–84.

"Woe"; "no one"; "there remains"; "a large": William S. White, "Rugged Days for the Majority Leader," *NYT Magazine*, July 3, 1949.

Forced; "Dear Alben"; "public humiliation": Ritchie, "Alben W. Barkley: The President's Man," in Baker and Davidson, eds., *First Among Equals*, pp. 127–34. **"Real leader":** Alsop and Kintner, "Sly and Able," *SEP*, July 20, 1940. *Life* **poll:** "Washington Correspondents Name Ablest Congressmen," *Life*, March 20, 1939. **"Bumbling Barkley":** Ritchie, "Alben Barkley," in Baker and Davidson, eds., *First Among Equals*, p. 129. Barkley was to admit that that label stuck to him "like tar did to Br'er Rabbit."

Salted; "as the unhappy": Alsop and Kintner, "Sly and Able," *SEP*, July 20, 1940. **McKellar incident:** Ritchie, "Alben Barkley," in Baker and Davidson, eds., *First Among Equals*, pp. 142–43. **"Now he":** Sen. Elbert Thomas of Utah, quoted in Ritchie, "Alben Barkley," in Baker and Davidson, eds., *First Among Equals*, p. 148. **"I have noth-**

ing": Drury, Reedy interviews. A different version ("I didn't have anything to threaten them with, and it wouldn't have worked even if I had tried") is given in Matthews, p. 126, quoting Truman, *Congressional Government,* p. 136.
"Taft is": White, Wallace, quoted in "Old Guard Supreme," *New Republic,* Jan. 13, 1947. **Looked back; "Rearview":** White, *The Taft Story,* p. 58; Drury interview. **"Boss":** *Time,* Jan. 1947, quoted in Robert Merry, "Robert A. Taft: A Study in the Accumulation of Legislative Power," in Baker and Davidson, eds., *First Among Equals,* p. 177. **"No desire":** Merry, "Robert Taft," in Baker and Davidson, eds., *First Among Equals,* p. 174.
"Barrymore": Sidney Shallett, "The Senator Almost Got an Ulcer," *Collier's,* Jan. 14, 1950; Robert Albright, *WP,* Feb. 20, 1949. **"Formidable"; "worn"; "hostile":** William S. White, "Rugged Days for the Majority Leader," *NYT Magazine,* July 3, 1949. **Russell approved:** Evans and Novak, *LBJ: Exercise,* p. 40. **Caught between:** Krock, *NYT,* March 20, 1949. **"Ever more"; "rumors":** "The Perennial Filibuster," *New Republic,* April 18, 1949. **"It now"; little poems:** Shallett, "Senator Almost Got an Ulcer," *Collier's,* Jan. 14, 1950. **Without even:** Willard Shelton, "Battle in a Paper Bag," *The Nation,* May 20, 1950. **Displaced-persons bill; "snake":** "Everything but Liars," *Newsweek,* March 20, 1950. **"Out of control":** "Taft Holds the Key," *New Republic,* May 22, 1950.
"Debating" empty chair: MacNeil, *Dirksen,* p. 90. **In "a serious":** Shallett, "Senator Almost Got an Ulcer," *Collier's,* Jan. 14, 1950. **The most unhappy:** Evans and Novak, p. 41.
One item: Reedy, *U.S. Senate,* pp. 41–42. Other than that: Reedy interview.
Johnson's feelings; staff would hear: Goodwin, *Lyndon Johnson,* pp. 106–11; Busby, Jenkins, Rowe interviews. **"Restlessness":** Johnson, quoted in Goodwin, p. 106. **To wait:** Rowe interview. **"He told Russell":** Goodwin, p. 107.
"With him": Darden interview. **Russell felt:** Fite, *Russell,* p. 266; Goldsmith, *Colleagues,* p. 23; Darden, Jordan interviews. **"And there":** Darden interview. **"You could":** Sparkman to Russell, Nov. 28, 1950; Russell to Sparkman, Dec. 1, 1950, VI A— Dictation Series, Personal Political Files, "Majority Leader," Box 31, RBRL.
Solid on cloture: Robert Albright, "Gallery Glimpses," *WP,* Dec. 3, 1950. **"Perhaps yearning":** Evans and Novak, p. 43. **"Amiable":** Mellett, *WS,* Jan. 2, 1951. **Liberals behind O'Mahoney:** Steinberg, *Sam Johnson's Boy,* p. 317; *WS,* Dec. 12, 1950.

"Johnson had": Robert Byrd, "Addresses on the History," *CR,* Feb. 1, 1988, p. S 354. **"Once"; "eyebrows went":** MacNeil interview. **"Simply":** Evans and Novak, p. 39. **"Lyndon, you":** Stennis OH. **"The world outside":** Evans and Novak, p. 39. **Walking:** Goldsmith, p. 24. **Sparkman withdrawing:** *AA-S,* Jan. 3, 1951.

16. The General and the Senator

"It is doubtful": Rovere and Schlesinger, *The General,* p. 5.
"The homecoming": *Life,* April 30, 1951. **"The largest":** Nixon, quoted in *Life,* April 23, 1951. **First seventy thousand:** Manchester, *American Caesar,* p. 648. **"A gesture":** *Life,* April 30, 1951.
"Most Americans": *Life,* April 30, 1951. **"Stepped down"; "we heard God"; sobbing"; "reincarnation":** Manchester, *American Caesar,* p. 661. **"A senior":** White, *Citadel,* pp. 243–44. **"The only":** Reedy OH IV, p. 7. **"[T]he adoring":** Reedy, *U.S. Senate,* p. 58. **"One of":** White, *Citadel,* p. 244. **"The greatest":** *Time,* April 30, 1951.
"Almost runaway": White, *Citadel,* p. 250. **"What was bad":** *Life,* April 9. **"Perhaps":** White, *Citadel,* pp. 241–42. **"Popular":** Reedy, *U.S. Senate,* p. 14.
"Absolutely"; "Boy": Reedy OH IV, p. 8.
"When the U.S.": Hugh Sidey, "Playing the Middle Octaves," *Time,* Dec. 15, 1986. **"Rather amusing":** Reedy, *U.S. Senate,* pp. 13, 14; Reedy OH IV, p. 4.
"Deep sense": Reedy, *U.S. Senate,* p. 15. **"Russell believed":** Reedy OH IV, p. 5. **"He believed":** Fite, *Russell,* p. 256.
"Anxious": *Time,* May 14, 1951. **"We are entering":** *Time,* May 21, 1951. **"Whether closed":** Fite, p. 257. **"I have been":** *Time,* May 14, 1951.
"Down from the Cross": Richard Rovere, *The New Yorker,* April 21, 1951. **"On the permanent":** Rovere and Schlesinger, p. 184. **"For three":** *Time,* May 14, 1951. **"No man":** *Life,* May 14, 1951. **"I was operating"; "no policy":** Rovere and Schlesinger, pp. 187, 188. **"It isn't":** Manchester, *American Caesar,* p. 667. **"I am not"; "quite a difference":** *Time,* May 14, 1951.
Johnson loaning Reedy, Cook, and Siegel: Reedy, Cook, Siegel OHs; Reedy interview. **"I do not":** Manchester, *American Caesar,* p. 669. **Lodge brought up:** *Time,* May 14, 1951. **What if Mao:** Rovere and Schlesinger, pp. 238–40. **"If we":** Manchester, p. 671. **"That doesn't":** *Time,* May 14, 1951. **"Senator, I have asked you":** Rovere and Schlesinger, p. 241; Manchester, p. 671.

"When General": *Time,* May 14, 1951. "Among themselves": Manchester, p. 670.

A compliment: Fite, p. 259. "The civilian"; "flat": *Time,* May 14, 1951. Marshall's testimony: *Life,* May 21, 1951.

"Quiet, unruffled": White, *Citadel,* p. 246. "It is possible": Rovere, "Letter from Washington," *The New Yorker,* May 19, 1951. "I am asking"; "compliment"; "Private": *Time,* May 28, 1951. "Private"; "Frantic"; "iron": Fite, pp. 260–61. "Every half": Rovere, "Letter from Washington," *The New Yorker,* May 19, 1951. "A careless": Fite, p. 260; Reedy interview. "In doing so"; "Russell put": *Time,* June 4, 1951.

"One by one": Manchester, *American Caesar,* p. 673. "The glamour": *Time,* May 21, 1951.

"Capitol corridors": *Time,* June 11, 1951. "The dramatic": *Time,* June 4, 1951. "Hey, Mac": Manchester, *American Caesar,* p. 683. Only twenty thousand: *Time,* June 25, 1951.

"Can only": Goldsmith, *Colleagues,* p. 26. Essentially: Fite, pp. 262–64; Galloway, *Legislative Process,* pp. 156–57. "Without"; "at its best": White, *Citadel,* pp. 251, 246. "Power and prestige": Shaffer, *On and Off the Floor,* p. 208. "Firmness, fairness": *Life,* March 24, 1952. Johnson had suggested: Reedy, *U.S Senate,* p. 14; Reedy interview. "Preeminent": Reedy, p. 15. "George, please": Reedy OH IV, p. 7. "By 1951": Reedy OH IV, pp. 1, 2. "Russell has soberly": "Washington Report—Staff," "Politics," p. 5, undated, signed Levison, MP.

17. The "Nothing Job"

"Without reference"; "Never before," "unless I want to": "simply"; Schlesinger, *Imperial Presidency,* pp. 135–38. "I don't ask": Donovan, *Tumultuous Years,* p. 323. "Great debate:" Donovan, pp. 321–25; Josephy, *Congress,* pp. 379–80; Manchester, *Glory and the Dream,* pp. 556–58; Schlesinger, pp. 137–40. Eisenhower's testimony: Manchester, p. 557. "What this foggy": Galloway, *Legislative Process,* p. 173. "The effect": "Has Congress Broken Down?" *Fortune,* Feb. 1952.

Years of investigation: Robert Albright, *WP,* Oct. 21, 1951. "Scarcely got discussed": *Fortune,* Feb. 1952. "Completed less": *WS,* July 6, 1952. "Almost as many": "Gallery Glimpses," *WP,* May 18, 1952. "Congress is": *Fortune,* Feb. 1952. "Many"; "Now that": Galloway, *Legislative Process,* pp. 583, 581. Absenteeism worse: *WP,* June 1, 1952. Senators were remarking on it on the floor. On May 15, 1952, for example, Hubert

Humphrey said, "This place looks like an apartment house which has just been vacated" (*CR,* 82/2, p. 5240). Medical facilities bill: *WP,* Oct. 21, 1950. "Never say die": Pearson, *WP,* March 27, 1952.

"Lies in"; "have delayed": Galloway, *Legislative Process,* p. 583. "Would be cutting": Monroney, quoted in *Fortune,* Feb. 1952. "The Senate": Morse, *CR,* 82/2, p. 9080.

"Blind rush": Cordon, *CR,* 82/2, pp. 9253–54. A "relic": Galloway, *Legislative Process,* p. 584. "The decay"; "Twenty-nine countries"; "obsolescence": Galloway, pp. 584, 581.

McFarland's first press conference: Darby to Bermingham, Jan. 6, 1951, MP. "I just try": *WP,* Dec. 3, 1950. "That's all right": Blair Moody, "A Reporter-Senator Reports on the Senate," *NYT Magazine,* Aug. 5, 1951. "There are not": White, *Citadel,* p. 106. "A nigra mayor": "Has Congress Broken Down?" *Fortune,* Feb. 1952. "Simply ineffectual"; "no leader at all": For example, *Time,* July 9, 1951. "We'll be here": *WS,* Aug. 22, 1951. First voice: Reedy interview. "Congress is taking": *WP,* Sept. 30, 1951.

" 'Lying Down Johnson' ": Pearson, *WP,* July 23, 1951.

McFarland often: Bibolet, Cole, Easley, Reedy interviews.

"Most people"; "Bobby didn't": McPherson OH II, pp. 14, 15. "True believers": McPherson, *Political Education,* p. 25. "A great counter": Rowe, Fortas, quoted in Caro, *Path,* p. 455. "What the fuck"; McCarran: Busby interview. And see Baker, *Wheeling and Dealing,* p. 45. White House learned: Jenkins, Reedy interviews. Maybank's appointment: Ben Bagdikian and Don Oberdorfer, "Bobby Was the Boy to See," *SEP,* Dec. 3, 1963. In the drugstore; "homesick": Baker, *Wheeling and Dealing,* p. 22. "So": "The Silent Witness," *Time,* March 9, 1964. "Brought"; [learned]: Baker, pp. 29, 30. The other quotes from Baker are from pp. 32, 55, 34, 37. "Made the Senate": *SEP,* Dec. 7, 1963. "Made it": Evans Thomas, *The Man to See,* p. 182. "Fascinating": Baker, p. 45. "Unabashed": *Time,* March 9, 1964. "A bootlicker": Thomas, p. 182. "He would": Rowe, *Bobby Baker Story,* p. 19. "His voice": Rowe, p. 19. "A son": Evans and Novak, p. 68.

"The men": Evans and Novak, *LBJ: Exercise,* p. 69. Truman had no confidence in Lucas' counts: Steinberg, *Sam Johnson's Boy,* p. 314. "No prying"; "where": Baker, *Wheeling and Dealing,* pp. 38–39, 34. "Whenever": Bibolet interview.

Scheduling: Steinberg, *Sam Johnson's Boy,* p. 318. "He wanted": Bibolet interview.

Persuaded Bridges; May 1 Calendar Call: *CR,* 82/2, pp. 4647–649. Word got around: Bibolet interview.

Pairing: Henry H. Gilfry, *Precedents-Decisions,* Vol. II, pp. 188–89; Floyd M. Riddick, rev. and ed. Alan S. Frumin, *Senate Procedure,* pp. 968–70; Floyd M. Riddick, *United States Congress,* pp. 298–301; Alfred Steinberg, "Shepherds of Capitol Hill," *Nation's Business,* Jan. 1952, who wrote: "In a general pairing, both members are absent. But in a live pair, which is a gentleman's agreement between whips, a member of one party promises not to vote on a bill even though he will be present, but to permit himself to be paired off with an absent member of the other party who would have voted the opposite to him"; Baker, Ritchie interviews. "A voluntary": Riddick, *Senate Procedure,* pp. 777–78. "When accused": Baker, *Wheeling and Dealing,* p. 55. Not "strategic": Bibolet interview. Skeeter might forget: Bibolet, Reedy interviews.

Maneuvering over foreign aid: "Slicing the Bundle," *Newsweek,* June 9, 1952; Bibolet interview. "We've already": *NYHT,* May 29, 1952. "Unless": *NYT,* June 1, 1952. "Heavy absenteeism": *NYHT,* May 28, 1952. "Sensing": *Newsweek,* June 9, 1952. "Nothing less": *NYT,* May 29, 1952. "Then you": *NYT,* May 27, 1952. Russell's efforts: *WP,* Oct. 21, 1952. Johnson's maneuvering; "If Magnuson": Bibolet interview. Statements before the vote: *CR,* 82/2, p. 6098. "I am": *NYHT,* May 29. Welker-McCarthy exchange: *Newsweek,* June 9, 1952. "By adroit": *WP,* June 1, 1952.

"I do understand": McPherson, p. 450.

Betrayal of Rayburn: Caro, *Path,* Chapter 30. Exclusion: Caro, pp. 754–57. On his first day back: Caro, pp. 757–63. Calling twenty: Steinberg, *Sam Johnson's Boy,* p. 409. "I don't": Bolling interview. "The Chair": Hardeman and Bacon, *Rayburn,* p. 342.

Jenkins' assignment: Jenkins, Reedy interviews. "Tell Lyndon": Steinberg, *Sam Johnson's Boy,* p. 281. "I've got": Rowe interview. "Every time"; "Beloved": Bolling interview. "In that room"; descriptions of Johnson-Rayburn relationship, Harding and of the Board of Education: Caro, *Path,* Chapters 18, 30, 36; Bolling, Connally, Corcoran, Helen Gahagan Douglas, Dulaney, Hardeman, Holton, Izac, Mahon, McFarlane, Miller, Oltorf, Rayden, Elizabeth Rowe, James H. Rowe interviews. "It was never": Oltorf interview. "Deferential": Hardeman interview.

"Lyndon couldn't"; "that was"; "vaulting": Bolling interview. "He understood": Ramsey Clark interview.

"Our . . . problem": Anderson to Johnson, June 12; Johnson to Anderson, June 16, 1958, "Papers of the Democratic Leader," Box 365, JSP. "You put": Nichols to Johnson, April 30, 1956, Masters, Box 56, JSP. "I want": Johnson to Ellender, March 28, 1958, Box 366, JSP.

"These $200 droplets": Johnson to Rayburn, Oct. 10, 1942, Box 52, LBJA CF. "We didn't know": Brown interview.

Wild's testimony: "In the United States District Court for the District of Columbia," Securities and Exchange Commission vs. Gulf Oil Corporation, Claude C. Wild Jr., Civil Action No. 75-0324, April 26, 1978, pp. 8, 9, 28. "Hundreds"; "envelopes": Wild interview.

Not the largest: Clark, Connally, Corcoran interviews. Also Herring, Hopkins, Jenkins, Herman Jones, Kilgore, Lucas, Miller, Oltorf, Rowe, Stehling, Woods, Woodward, Young interviews. "I handled": Connally interview. "I knew": Clark interview.

"I have": "Resumé of telephone conversations—George Brown," Jan. 5, 1960, SPF, "WJ Special," Box 262, JSP. "Ed Clark tells me": Jenkins to Woodward, Jan. 11, 1960, SPF, "WJ Special," Box 262, JSP. "How could": Clark interview. "All we knew": Corcoran interview. "I'd go get it": Connally interview. Unions' cash: Corcoran, Hopkins, Rowe, Young interviews. "Because"; neither . . . trusted"; other Clark, Wild quotes: Clark, Wild interviews. And in his own book, Baker says that Wild "once told" Senator Kerr "that I had a bad reputation and was a crook." (Baker recounts that he protested to Kerr that "I've never had a nickel's worth of dealings with the man," and Kerr then said, "Well, maybe you and Claude ought to get to know each other a little better. He's got $5,000 that Gulf Oil wants to deliver to [a senator], and I want you to go with him to make the delivery." Baker says, "I did so," and he and Wild "walked together to the Old Senate Office Building, where he surrendered the cash" to the senator.) (Baker, with King, *Wheeling and Dealing,* p. 113) When Connally was asked to whom the money was handed, he refused to reply. "Official bagman": Baker, *Wheeling and Dealing,* p. 51. Baker's conviction: *NYT, WP,* Jan. 30, 1967. An account of Baker's trial is in Thomas, *The Man to See,* pp. 182, 184, 214–224. "He has $500": Roberts to Connally, Aug. 14, Box 59, JSP.

"Asked me": Kilgore interview. "I personally carried": Mooney, *LBJ,* pp. 127–28.

"Never enough"; "How much": Clark, Wild interviews. The Davis contributions: Clark interview. "We called them": Connally interview. He said he would make up different lists for different amounts that Johnson wanted to raise: "If he needed fifty thousand, I'd give him ten people who would give him five thousand each, if he reminded them what he had done for them. If he needed a hundred (thousand) . . ." The only list the author could find in the Johnson Library, however, dealt with smaller amounts, ranging from $2,500 down to $500. ("Dear Lyndon, Enclosed is the list. . . . Regards, John. p.s. Keep my comments on these people confidential"; Connally to Johnson, undated but found in Box 63, Senate Political Files for 1956.) The quotations are all from that list. **"Let me see":** "Telephone conversation between Lyndon Johnson and Dudley Doughty, Beeville, Jan. 25, 1960," SPF, "WJ Special," Box 262, JSP.

Two Convention incidents: Mooney, *LBJ* p. 134; Baker, *Wheeling and Dealing*, pp. 85–86.

$5,000 to Bridges: Baker, *Wheeling and Dealing*, p. 86. **Blakeley contribution:** Kilgore interview.

Clements contribution: Clark interview. **"We can't":** D. W. Gilmore to Johnson, undated, SPF, Box 173. **"I gave him":** Brown, quoted in Selig Harrison, "Lyndon Johnson's World," *New Republic*, June 13, 1960. **"Well, I remember":** Symington interview. **Ten thousand;** " 'Well, I've got' ": Stehling interview. **"Roosevelt would":** Clark interview.

Byrd funeral: Busby interview.

"You know"; "made it": Steinberg, *Sam Johnson's Boy*, p. 347. **With Taft:** Steinberg, pp. 347–48. Steinberg says Johnson used this tactic after Taft became Majority Leader in January 1953, but others say it started in 1951 and 1952. Wherry died in November, 1951. **Johnson had Baker:** Reedy interview. **"Sometimes":** Symington interview. **"He frequently":** Smathers OH. **"Schoolteacher habit":** Busby interview. **"People like":** Woodward interview.

"I like to": "The Humor of LBJ—25th Anniversary" audiocassette, LBJL. **"genius for":** Evans and Novak, p. 104.

18. The Johnson Ranch

General description of the ranch, its history, and the Johnsons' life on it: from Newlon, *LBJ;* Reedy, *LBJ;* Smith, *President's Lady;* Montgomery, *Mrs. LBJ;* Russell, *Lady Bird;* Steinberg, *Sam Johnson's Boy;* Bearss, *Historic Resource Study;* Dugger, *Politician;* Bill Davidson, "Texas Political Powerhouse," *Look,* Aug. 4, 1959; Flora Rheta Schreiber, "Lady Bird from Texas," *Family Weekly,* Sept. 10, 1961; Robert B. Semple, Jr., "The White

House on the Pedernales," *NYT,* Oct. 3, 1965; Tom Wicker, "LBJ—Down on the Farm," *Esquire,* Oct. 1964.

Also from Kowert, "Johnson Finds Escape from Senate Worries," *SAE,* Sept. 12, 1954; unidentified clipping, "Lyndon Johnsons Improve Farm on Pedernales River," December 1951, LBJA Sen F, Box 2016; "The LBJ Ranch," "Interpretive Training" (post-Pres), LBJ National Historic Site, LN-1; *The Home Place,* LBJ Ranch, "Reference File," LBJL; *The Hill Country: Lyndon Johnson's Texas* transcript, NBC-TV, May 9, 1966, "Reference File," LBJL. "A President's Legacy," *Southern Accents Magazine,* Summer 1983.

Also from oral histories of Reedy, Evie Symington, and Stuart Symington, and interviews with Busby, Burg, Ed Clark, Cox, Jenkins, SHJ, Lindig, Mayer, Rather, Reedy, Stehling, Tiff.

The original Johnson Ranch and original Johnson brothers: Caro, *Path,* Chapter 1. **Sam paying too much, going broke:** Caro, Chapter 6.

Martin's relationship with Sam Ealy Jr.: Dugger, pp. 68–69; SHJ, Cox interviews. **Feeling that:** Dugger, p. 81; SHJ interview. **"The *big* house":** Cox interview. **Looking for a buyer:** Dugger, p. 356; Russell, *Lady Bird,* p. 161.

"A haunted house": "Addams Cartoon," *Southern Accents,* Summer 1983; *WS,* July 19, 1960. **"Oh, my Lord"; "appalled":** Evie Symington, quoted in Montgomery, p. 44. **Visit with Symington:** Symington interview, OH. **"To my horror":** *AA-S,* Jan. 20, 1965. **"How could you":** Lady Bird Johnson, quoted in Russell, *Lady Bird,* p. 161. **"You're not":** *WS,* July 19, 1960. **Purchased the ranch:** Russell, p. 161; Montgomery, p. 207; *NYT,* Dec. 26, 1966.

Sam Johnson as legislator: Caro, *Path,* Chapters 3, 5, 6. **Lyndon Johnson's selling of airtime for influence:** Caro, *Means,* Chapter 6. **$3,000 per week:** In 1951, KTBC had revenues of $345,115 and expenses of $212,400, leaving a profit for the year of $132,715. That did not include $13,210 written off for depreciation. Mrs. Johnson took a salary for that year of $23,000 and interest of $4,800 on $80,000 in KTBC debentures that she held. At the end of 1951, the station had assets of $439,310, of which $133,465 was in cash (1951, "Financial Reports—FCC General Correspondence [KTBC], FCC Records, RG 173, NA). **Television profits:** This topic will be dealt with in detail in Volume IV.

"Used to run dry": Johnson, quoted in Dugger, p. 86. **Building the dam:** Burg, Lindig, Tiff interviews; *DT-H,* Aug. 26, 1953.

"The first thing": Lady Bird, quoted in Steinberg, *Sam Johnson's Boy*, p. 419.

Building up the soil: Lindig, Tiff interviews. "Spiritual home": Lady Bird Johnson, quoted in Smith, *President's Lady*, pp. 45–46. "Horror turned": Lady Bird Johnson, quoted in *AA-S*, Jan. 1, 1965.

"Only one picture": Lady Bird Johnson interview; she said it in writing, in tour, p. 2, "There is only one picture in the room—our dear friend, Speaker Rayburn." **Scratching "Welcome":** Burg interview. "When it wasn't much": Symington OH.

1952 storm: Russell, *Lady Bird*, pp. 161–63; Lady Bird Johnson interview. "Lucy and I": Russell, p. 162; Burg, Cox interviews. **Contacted Stehling:** Stehling interview. When Lady Bird came to the door, she said to Stehling: "Dr. Livingston, I presume." "Just where": Burg, Stehling interviews. "The only time": Lucy, quoted in Russell, pp. 161–62.

"Every man": *DT-H*, Aug. 26, 1953. "All my life"; "lonesome": "The Hill Country: Lyndon Johnson's Tapes," NBC-TV, May 1966, transcript.

"Haven't thought": *DT-H*, Aug. 26, 1953. "Best people": *SAE*, Sept. 12, 1954. **Wicker portrait:** Wicker, "LBJ—Down on the Farm," *Esquire*, Oct. 1964.

The gully: Caro, *Path*, pp. 87–88. **Filling it in:** Cox, SHJ, Lindig interviews; Robert B. Semple Jr., "The White House on the Pedernales," *NYT*, Oct. 3, 1965. "Fixation": Lindig interview.

Portrayed her life: Rebekah Johnson, *A Family Album*, pp. 25–26, 28–32. Her life is described in Caro, *Path*, Chapters 4, 5, 6, and 7. **Sam's funeral:** Caro, pp. 542–43. **What she did:** RJB, SHJ interviews. **Had been rented:** Lyndon Johnson to Rebekah Baines Johnson, Jan. 15, 1938. "There is": LBJ to J. Frank Kendall, March 30, 1938—both from "Family Correspondence, Johnson, Mrs. Sam E., Dec. 1929–Dec. 1939," Box 1, *Family Correspondence*. **She never did:** RJB, SHJ interviews. The author has not been able to determine if that is literally true, but the first lease she gave on the house, to Ross B. Jenkins and his family, was from Jan. 1, 1938, to Dec. 31, 1940. Mrs. Betty Prehn lived in the house "from 1943 until 1947," according to the *Historic Resource Study* made for the Department of the Interior. "Oscar Foss rented" the house from Mrs. Johnson "in 1949–1951." And it was in 1951 that Aunt Frank took possession of the house. The author has not been able to determine who lived in the house during the years not covered by these leases; during at least part of them, Lyndon's sister Josefa lived there. Blanco

County Deed Book, 53, pp. 326–27; Book 55, pp. 407–08, cited in Bearss, pp. 136–37. During those years, Mrs. Johnson rented various apartments in Austin. **Died intestate:** Bearss, p. 137. **Relinquished; Lyndon bought:** Blanco County Deed Book, 53, pp. 326, 327; Deed Book, 55, pp. 407–408, quoted in Bearss, p. 137.

"I have been": RBJ to LBJ, July 24, 1951. "Courage": RBJ to LBJ, May 29, 1952, "Family Correspondence, Johnson, Mrs. Sam E., March, 1950–August, 1958," Box 1, *Family Correspondence*. **Written by staff:** Busby, Jenkins, Latimer interviews. "He used": Latimer interview. "Next Sunday": Henderson to LBJ, May 12, 1939. "She was"; "would case"; "I liked": "The First Lady Talks About Her Mother-in-Law," *McCalls*, Dec. 1965. "If I had": Lady Bird Johnson, quoted in Miller, *Lyndon*, pp. 13, 14. **Visitors:** Among those who noticed this were Corcoran and Rowe.

Rebekah's ulcer; "highly precarious": RBJ to Lyndon Johnson, March 7, 1950; July 24, 1951. **Stories about Josefa:** Busby, Knispel, Kyle, Smith, Stehling interviews. **Called on:** Stehling interview. "If there": Mayer interview.

"Josefa situation": Busby interview. **If she wasn't:** Lyndon Johnson to RBJ, Jan. 6, 1940, Box 1, *Family Correspondence*. "These wonderful": Caro, *Path*, p. 183. "He worships": RBJ to Lyndon Johnson, undated but among 1937 letters, "Family Correspondence, Dec. 1929–Dec. 1939," Box 1. "Smarter": Deason interview. "More than": Mooney, *LBJ*, p. 195. "He didn't": Brown OH. **New York trip:** SHJ interview; Johnson, *My Brother Lyndon*, pp. 50–51. "Alcoholic haze": Lloyd Shearer, *Texas Parade*, March 9, 1975. **NYA:** SHJ interview. **Wirtz trying:** Wirtz to Johnson, July 3, 1940, Box 5, AWPP, LBJL. "When": Brown OH. **Seeing Sam on TV:** *Sunday Hereford* (Tex.) *Brand*, Sept. 28, 1958. "Just a flunky": SHJ interview. **Would disappear:** Koeniger interview.

Rodney, Sam's son: Rodney Baines interview. "The 1948": Baines interview. **Died of AIDS:** William M. Adler, "A Death in the Family," *Texas Monthly*, April 1989.

120: SHJ OH. "A shrunken": Mooney, *LBJ*, p. 192. "Shattered nerves": RBJ to LBJ, Feb. 4, 1953, "Family Correspondence, Johnson, Mrs. Sam E., March, 1950–August, 1958," Box 1, *Family Correspondence*. **Hardshell; "Sneaking"; "almost":** Caro, *Path*, pp. 91–93. "I don't": Caro, p. 163.

"Didn't sleep": Rather interview. **Picture of Johnson on ranch:** Busby, Cox, SHJ, Rather, Reedy, Stehling interviews. "A wild drinking bout": Reedy, *LBJ*, p.

53. **More often on the ranch:** Jenkins, Rather interviews.
"Her constant pacification": Sidey, *Time,* Jan. 14, 1985. **Incident in car:** Busby, quoted in Russell, *Lady Bird,* p. 205. **"Slapped":** Busby, quoted in *Texas Monthly,* Aug. 1999; interview with author. **"Harem":** Janeway, quoted in Dallek, *Lone Star,* p. 189.

19. The Orator of the Dawn

"Johnson fixed": White, *Professional,* p. 201.
"His native strength": Hawthorne, quoted in Schlesinger, *Age of Jackson,* p. 42.
Convention scene, Humphrey speech: Eisele, *Almost to the Presidency;* Griffith, *Humphrey;* McCullough, *Truman;* Ross, *The Loneliest Campaign;* Solberg, *Hubert Humphrey.* **"The very air":** McCullough, p. 636. **"Interpret":** Ross, p. 117. **Their first look; "dazzled":** Solberg, pp. 12–13. **"Lead":** Humphrey, *The Progressive,* April 1946. **"Who does"; "sellout":** Solberg, p. 14. **Only his:** Griffith, p. 153. **"Joe, you":** Niles, quoted in Solberg, p. 16. **"ADA bastards"; "not at all":** Griffith, pp. 152, 153. **"Sacrificing":** Ross, pp. 119–20.
"It was sobering": Humphrey, *Education,* pp. 112, 113. **Freeman:** Goulden, *Best Years,* p. 385.
"Shining": McCullough, p. 639. **"I can see"; "hard-boiled":** Douglas, *Fullness of Time,* p. 133. **"The audience":** Solberg, p. 17. **Not in text:** Solberg, p. 18. **"Parade":** Douglas, *Fullness of Time,* pp. 133–34. **"The latter":** Ross, p. 122. **"In part":** Humphrey, *Education,* p. 115. **"Can you":** Anderson, quoted in Solberg, p. 119.
"At the"; "the fact": McCullough, p. 640. **"The only":** Solberg, pp. 18, 19. **"It was"; "on fire":** Douglas, quoted in Eisele, p. 68. **"The orator":** Douglas, *Fullness of Time,* p. 133.
"Glib, jaunty": "Education of a Senator," *Time,* Jan. 17, 1949. **"Well-knit":** *New Republic,* Oct. 18, 1948. **"I had":** Humphrey, pp. 115–16.
Press conference; "I'll knock"; Howard speech: Solberg, pp. 135–39. **"My God":** Rowe interview. **Taking King to lunch:** Humphrey, p. 121. **"I would be":** Humphrey, p. 147.
"Sometimes": Solberg, p. 137; Eisele, p. 89. **"unprepared":** Humphrey, *Education,* p. 124. **"Anathema":** Solberg, p. 129. **"Still":** Humphrey, p. 157. **Committee assignments:** Solberg, p. 136. **"The most sacred":** Eisele, p. 89. **Small Business Committee:**

Humphrey, p. 158. **"Of course":** Humphrey OH I, p.12.
The snubbing: Humphrey, pp. 123–25; Solberg, pp. 136–38. **"Too early":** Jenner, quoted in Eisele, p. 89. **"Can you imagine' ":** Russell, quoted in Humphrey, p. 124.
Byrd Committee: Eisele, pp. 90–93; Solberg, pp. 143–45. **"Ominously"; "The senator":** Solberg, p. 144; "Paddling a Freshman," *Newsweek,* March 13, 1950; "The Elephant Hunt," *Time,* March 13, 1950; Anderson and Blumenthal, "The Washington Merry-Go-Round," *WP,* Aug. 2, 1950. **Capehart incident:** Eisele, p. 94; Solberg, p. 161.
"I just": Humphrey OH I, p. 11. **"Dark days:"** Humphrey, *Education,* p. 147. **"Just couldn't believe"; "I always worked":** Humphrey OH I, p. 11. **"I was prepared"; "I hated":** Humphrey, pp. 124–25. **"I didn't feel":** Eisele, p. 93. **Crying:** Solberg, p. 136; McCulloch interview.
"Johnson and I": Humphrey, *Education,* p. 161. **Conversation on subway:** Reedy, *U.S. Senate,* p. 34. **"He started":** Humphrey OH I, p. 4. **"To invite":** Humphrey, *Education,* p. 162. **"Fascinating":** Humphrey OH I, pp. 15, 16. **"I am learning":** Humphrey to Johnson, Dec. 9, 1955, Box 2, WHFN. Humphrey told an oral history interviewer: "In some ways I suppose he was a kind of teacher." (OH I, p. 18). **"Johnson said":** Humphrey OH II, p. 5. **"Very beginning":** Humphrey, quoted in Miller, *Lyndon,* p. 149. **"Knew Washington":** Humphrey, *Education,* p. 162. **"At the feet":** Humphrey, on *The American Experience: LBJ.* PBS Home Video, 1997.
"You have just"; "a lion": Humphrey OH III, p. 7. **"Like a plant":** Humphrey, quoted in Miller, p. 420. **"Those great big"; "muscular":** Humphrey, quoted in Miller, pp. 166, 346. **"A very strong":** Humphrey OH III, p. 27. **"Political lover":** Humphrey OH III, p. 8. **"Like a tidal wave":** Humphrey, quoted in Miller, p. 175.
"Always able": Humphrey OH III, p. 8. "Johnson was like a psychiatrist," he said on another occasion. "Unbelievable man in terms of sizing up people, what they would do, how they would stand up under pressure, what their temperament was" (Humphrey OH I, p. 26). **"What's so":** Eisele, p. 59. **"From the moment":** Rauh interview. **Hyde Park visit:** Solberg, p. 125.
Why Johnson befriended: Reedy to Johnson, undated but attached to GER to Senator, Jan. 2, 1957, Box 5, PPMF; Reedy, Solberg interviews.
"Nobody can": "London Dispatch 5434, from Robert Manning" to NA, Nov. 13, 1958

(in author's possession), p. 3. **Humphrey repeated:** Manning, Rauh, Rowe, Solberg interviews; Rowe to Johnson, April 8, 1957, Box 32, LBJA SN. In interviews with Solberg, Thomas Hughes said, "Johnson was . . . opening vistas to him." Rowe said, "For Johnson Humphrey was a bridge to the liberals. For Humphrey Johnson was a bridge to power" (Hughes interview with Solberg, March 3, 1981; Rowe interview with Solberg, Nov. 3, 1980; both in author's possession).

"Our little": Humphrey, quoted in Solberg, p. 161; Humphrey OH I, p. 8.

"A Roosevelt man": Humphrey OH III, p. 11; OH I, p. 6. **"I knew":** Humphrey OH III, p. 11. **"Never was":** Humphrey OH I, pp. 6, 7. **"We were":** Solberg, p. 163. **"I really":** Humphrey OH I, p. 36. **"Johnson had":** Humphrey, quoted in Goodwin, *Lyndon Johnson*, p. 132. **"The same old":** Steele to Williamson, March 4, 1958, SP.

Letters from Texas: Johnson to Humphrey, Dec. 15, 1953; Sept. 18, 1956; Feb. 27, Sept. 9, 1957, all Box 2, WHFN; Aug. 27, 1954, "1954 Austin Office General Files," Box 533, JSP. **"The privilege":** Humphrey to Johnson, Jan 26, 1957, Box 2, WHFN.

"You know": Califano, *Triumph*, p. 66.

The 7:30 conversations: Solberg, p. 163. **"Compromise":** Humphrey, pp. 136, 137. **"It doesn't bother me":** Humphrey OH I, p. 17.

"Senator, Hubert": White, *Professional*, pp. 201, 202; Reedy interview. **Humphrey and George in cloakroom:** Steinberg, *Sam Johnson's Boy*, p. 345. **Working on Russell:** Reedy interview. **"The South and"; Russell present:** Humphrey, p. 162. **"Humphrey utilized":** Steinberg, p. 345. **"Came to":** Goldsmith, *Colleagues*, p. 23.

"Actually becoming": Humphrey OH I, p. 5. **"Since there":** Humphrey, p. 161. **"My apprenticeship":** Humphrey, p. 161. **Brought Russell around:** Humphrey OH II, p. 8.

"Seemed to foresee": Goodwin, *Lyndon Johnson*, p. 132.

20. Gettysburg

All dates are 1952 unless otherwise noted.

Steinberg interview: Steinberg, *Sam Johnson's Boy*, pp. 320–21. **"Despite":** "Who will run with Truman?" undated, Feb. 1952, from internal evidence, SP.

"The only way": Reedy interview. **"Russell has":** *Time*, March 10. **"The chances":** Russell to Ayres, March 2, 1951, Dictation Series, Political, RBRL. **"I'm under":** *NYT*, Dec. 12, 1951.

More for: Fite, *Russell*, pp. 271–77. **"Has to all":** *NYT*, April 16. **"Destroy a fable":** *Atlanta Journal*, May 29.

Big Ed; McCarran: Fite, p. 287. **"Assuming":** Van Linden interview. **"Those":** Young, quoted in *NYT*, March 2. **"I am the only":** *AC*, April 26. For another version of this thought, see Roscoe Drummond, "State of the Nation," *Christian Science Monitor*, June 26. **"Dick: I hope":** "March, 1945, from President Truman," in XV, General EE, Redline File, 1941–67, RBRL.

Johnson had persuaded: Unidentified to Russell, Feb. 4, Box 24, II, Intra-Office Communications A., Memoranda: 1952, RBRL. **"We felt":** Connally interview. **"Richardson regarded":** Connally with Herskowitz, *In History's Shadow*, p. 142.

"A new league": Russell to Cocke, March 14, Political, Presidential Campaign, 1952, RBRL. **Arranging:** Clark, Connally interviews.

Lined up Texas: Dugger, *Politician*, pp. 374ff. **"Let's Hussle":** Johnson to Russell, March 18; Russell to Johnson, March 21, LBJ Congressional File, RBRL. **Russell's optimism:** Fite, p. 289. **"I told":** RBR, "Truman, Harry Memo," June 10, VI Political, G., Pres. Cmpn., "Winder" Folder, RBRL. And see Fite, p. 290.

"When he started": Darden interview. **"He had":** Connally interview. **"A fixation":** *WS*, April 25.

"Enumerated"; "He could not"; "Morally bound"; ignore: Fite, pp. 285–89.

"Of all of them": Muskie interview. " 'My God, Senator' ":** Reedy OH IV, p. 34; Shaffer, *On and Off*, p. 207. **Bad news:** *Atlanta Journal*, July 13.

"They thought": Connally interview. **"Surprise":** Roy V. Harris OH, RBRL. **"Senator Lyndon":** *AC*, July 25. **"In one day":** Anne O'Hara McCormick, *NYT*, July 22, quoted in Manchester, *Glory*, p. 622.

"Things began": Vandiver OH.

A **"visceral":** Goldsmith, *Colleagues*, p. 30. **"It's one":** Reedy OH IV, p. 34. **Began to complain; "excellent":** Goldsmith, p. 30. **From this time on:** Darden interview. **"Energy":** Lady Bird Johnson OH, RBRL, pp. 11, 14. **"Something":** Shaffer, p. 207. **"Bitterness":** Reedy OH IV, p. 35. **"Querulous":** Reedy interview.

"He worked": Russell, "Georgia Giant," 1970 unedited version, Reel No. 19, p. 25. **"Soberly predicted":** "Washington Report—Staff," p. 5, undated but with 1952 memos, MP. **"Became aware"; "as an**

instrument": Reedy interview. **"Made no bones":** Reedy OH V, p. I I. **"Hope that":** Goldsmith, p. 65. **Because "Johnson":** Talmadge, *AC,* Feb. 20, 1959. **"Gave me"; "Master and Servant"; "None":** Talmadge interview. **"Bosom friend":** Stennis interview, April 21, 1971, quoted in Stephen B. Farrow, "Richard Russell and Lyndon Johnson," unpublished senior thesis, University of Tennessee, 1979, p. 34. **"You're just fighting"; "I know":** "The Rearguard Commander," *Time,* Aug. 12, 1957; *NYT,* Jan. 22, 1971. **"Was very determined":** Reedy OH VIII, p. 100.

Including, notably: For a discussion of Johnson's role in the 1952 presidential campaign, see Dugger, pp. 376–77, 471; Martin, *Adlai Stevenson of Illinois,* pp. 652, 682, 734; Miller, *Lyndon,* p. 153; Steinberg, *Sam Johnson's Boy,* pp. 328–31.

"When McFarland lost": Ralph Huitt, quoted in Miller, p. 154. **"Well, thank you":** O'Brien, *No Final Victories,* pp. 36–37. **"I'll do"; "must have"; set one:** Evans and Novak, *LBJ: Exercise,* p. 51. **"All you've":** Baker, *Wheeling and Dealing,* pp. 60–61; Dugger, p. 379. **"I very frankly":** Stennis OH. **"I was strong":** Hoey to Russell, Nov. 14, VI, Personal Political 1951–1954, RBRL.

To every: McConaughy to Beshoar, June 10, 1953, SP; MacNeil, Steele interviews. **Russell replied:** "I have no desire to serve as leader of either the majority or the minority in the Senate. I think Lyndon is entitled to a promotion, and he will do a good job" (Russell to Hoey, Nov. 12, VI. Personal Political 1951–1954, RBRL). **"Saw L. Johnson":** Nov. 10, "Winder Materials—Calendars, 1952," RBRL. **"A number":** *NYT,* Nov. 11. **"Practically":** McConaughy to Beshoar, Nov. 12, MP. **By November 10:** Evans and Novak, p. 54. **A majority:** McConaughy to Beshoar, June 10, 1953, SP.

He had in mind: Johnson's thinking is explained in Baker, *Wheeling and Dealing,* p. 61; Evans and Novak, p. 54; and in Reedy and Rowe interviews. **To Hayden:** Bibolet, Reedy, Rowe interviews. Bibolet's boss, McFarland, wired Johnson, "Talked to Carl. All OK and he will call you . . . ," McFarland to Johnson, Nov. 8, Box 117, LBJA SF. **"A good":** Rowe to Johnson, Jan. 12, 1953. On the same date, he wrote Joe Kennedy, "I think Lyndon did very well for Jack on the committee assignments, and I hope you do" (Rowe to Kennedy and Landis, Nov. 12, 1953, Box 32, LBJA SN). **"I want":** Kennedy to Johnson, Nov. 13, Box 117, LBJA SF.

McCarran's problem, possible solution: Murray Marder, "Modern Marbury," *WP,* Jan.

I, 1953; Chalmers Roberts, "Political David," *WP,* Jan. 4, 1953; "(McCarran)," wire service bulletin, Dec. 29, in Pearson Papers, Box F 162. **McCarran asked; Johnson said; McCarran agreed:** Truman to Johnson, Jan. 13, 1953, Box 8, WHFN; Jenkins, Reedy, Rowe interviews.

Lists; Winder: VI, political E, Special Name Lyndon Johnson, RBRL; Boxes 116, 117, LBJA SF. **Explanation of lists:** Jenkins, Reedy, Rowe interviews.

Jenkins snatched: Jenkins interview. **"Happy":** "Statement of United States Senator Theodore Francis Green, Nov. 12, 1952," Box 117, LBJA SF. **"At the direction"; "THANKS":** Higgins to Johnson, Nov. 12; Johnson to Green, Nov. 13, Box 117, LBJA SF. **"Identified":** *NYT,* Nov. 13. **"Senator Clements":** Jenkins to Johnson, Nov. 12, Box 117, LBJA SF.

"Suggests": *NYT,* Nov. 16. **"Upset":** Humphrey, *Education,* p. 163. **"Worried":** McConaughey to Beshoar, June 10, 1953, SP. **"Knife you":** Jenkins to Johnson, Nov. 13, Box 117, LBJA SN.

"Humphrey wanted": Baker, quoted in Miller, p. 154. **"Their only":** Goodwin, *Lyndon Johnson,* pp. 107–08. She says that Hill had agreed to support Johnson "only a few minutes earlier," but actually Hill had agreed several days before this, because the meeting was some time after Nov. 13.

Settling on Murray: Humphrey, quoted in Miller, p. 154. **"He had":** Stewart McClure OH. **Stevenson telephone call:** "Adlai—Stevenson—LBJ," Nov. 20, "Notes and Transcripts of Johnson Conversations," Box I; Johnson to Stevenson (and attached telegram), Jan. 22, 1953, Box 118, LBJA SF.

"Although": Excerpt from Humphrey on "Reporters Roundup," Dec. 15, JSP. **"More calls":** Reedy interview.

"Hubert can't win": Johnson, quoted in Baker, *Wheeling and Dealing,* p. 61. **Promised "candy":** Baker, *Wheeling and Dealing,* pp. 61, 62. **Telephoning; "exhilarating"; "prepared":** Humphrey, p. 163.

Meeting with Hunt, Lehman, Douglas: Humphrey, p. 163; Humphrey OH I, pp. 19, 20. **Coming back alone:** Humphrey, pp. 163–64; Humphrey, quoted in Miller, p. 154.

Democratic caucus: "Minutes of Democratic Conference, Friday, Jan. 2, 1953," *Minutes of the U.S. Senate Democratic Conference, 1903–1640,* Donald A. Ritchie, ed., Washington, USGPO, 1998, pp. 487–93. **"Very wonderful":** "Attached are Senator Russell's notes which he wrote in preparation for the speech. Senator Johnson wants you to put them away safely . . . ," Rather to Lady

Bird Johnson, Jan. 8, 1953, LBJA Subject Files, "Senate, U.S.," Box 118, "Minority—Russell Remarks." **"Senator Murray":** Humphrey, p. 155. **"I'll never forget":** Humphrey, quoted in Miller, p. 155. **"Number One"; "don't come"; "I would be":** Humphrey OH and *Education*, pp. 164, 165.
   The youngest: Richard A. Baker to Caro, Dec. 2, 1994 (in author's possession). **"He had just":** Pearson, *Diaries*, p. 246. **"Almost":** Evans and Novak, p. 50.

21. The Whole Stack

All dates are 1953 unless otherwise noted.

"I shoved in": McConaughy to Beshoar, June 10, MP; John Steele, "A Kingmaker or a Dark Horse?" *Life*, June 25, 1956. **"The Senate would":** White, *Citadel*, p. 184.
   Grasped quickly; "was a personal": Reedy to Johnson, Nov. 12, Box 7, SPF; Reedy interview. **"Total decay":** Joseph and Stewart Alsop, "The Democrats Rally," *NYHT*, Feb. 1.
   Foreign Relations going; should be shored; "Mansfield": *NYT*, Jan 13; *NYT Magazine*, Feb. 1; Fleeson, *WS*, Jan. 14; McConaughy to Laybourne, Jan. 14, SP. **Only one example:** McConaughy to Berger, Jan. 16, MP; Evans and Novak, *LBJ: Exercise*, pp. 63, 64; *HP*, Jan. 19.
   The description of Johnson's changing the committee-assignment system and the Policy Committee's significance is drawn from memoranda written to Johnson by Reedy between November 21, 1953, and June 18, 1954, Boxes 116 and 118, LBJA SF, and "Papers of George Reedy," Box 413, JSP; from the intraoffice memoranda and "Confidential Worksheets" cited below; from the Drew Pearson Papers at the LBJL; from Baker, *Wheeling and Dealing*, pp. 63–65; Evans and Novak, pp. 61–65, Goldsmith, *Colleagues*, pp. 33–35; Goodwin, *Lyndon Johnson*, pp. 110–17; Steinberg, *Sam Johnson's Boy*, pp. 344–48; from McConaughy to Laybourne, Jan. 14, SP, and to Berger, Jan. 16, MP. It is also drawn from the oral history interviews of Humphrey, McClure, Reedy, and Siegel, and from the author's interviews with Bibolet, Corcoran, Goldsmith, Jenkins, MacNeil, Reedy, Ritchie, Rowe, Siegel, and Steele. Baker says that changing the seniority system was his idea, but Reedy says that it was *his* idea.
   Sold with humor: Various versions of the story are in Miller, *Lyndon*, p. 157; Steinberg, *Sam Johnson's Boy*, p. 344; Reedy OH. I have used the version from "The Humor of LBJ—

25th Anniversary" audiocassette. **The South's last; "I've just"; No one was being forced:** Reedy, Steele interviews. **"LBJ very early":** Reedy OH V, pp. 10, 11. **"The foundation"; "Johnson dissembled":** Goodwin, *Lyndon Johnson*, p. 112.
   "We'll be making": Steele interview. **Proved:** Goodwin, *Lyndon Johnson*, p. 113. Also see Goldsmith, p. 33. **"A leg up":** Goldsmith, p. 33. **"When Johnson broached":** Evans and Novak, p. 64. **"You're dealing":** Steinberg, *Sam Johnson's Boy*, p. 344. **"Playing with"; While he:** Evans and Novak, p. 64; Reedy interview.
   Byrd said: Childs, *SLP-D*, Jan. 17, 21; Reedy interview. **Magnuson unmoved:** "Confidential Work Sheet No. 1, Present Democratic Membership of Standing Committees of the Senate (Requests for Assignments)," pp. 2, 3, and "Confidential Work Sheet No. 2"; Jenkins to Johnson, "Requests of Senators with Reference to Committee Assignments, Nov. 14"; "Requests of Senators. . . ," Jan. 5, Box 116, LBJA, SF; Jenkins interview. **Johnson scrawled:** "list of committees and committee assignments. . . ," Nov. 6, 1952, Box 116, LBJA SF.
   Morse problem: *CR*, 83/1, pp. 143–44; Bibolet to Johnson, Jan. 12, Box 116, JSP; "one of," Reedy to Johnson, undated, Box 116, JSP; McConaughy to Laybourne, Jan. 14; Ralph K. Huitt, "The Morse Committee Assignment Controversy: A Study in Senate Norms," *APSR*, June 1957, pp. 315–18; *Newsweek*, Jan. 12; *Time*, Jan. 12, 19; *NYT*, Jan. 8, 14; *WP*, Jan. 14; Ritchie interview. **At four a.m.:** McConaughy to Berger, Jan. 16, MP.
   Outmaneuvering Taft: Case, Taft, Butler (Nebr.), Jenner, Cooper, "Proposed Report for Special Committee on Size and Number of Committees," Jan. 2, Box 116, JSP. (On which Johnson shows that he was thinking of the Appropriations increase, writing on it by hand, evidently at a later date, "Russell, McCarran, Murray—acceptable to them for one each to be added to Appropriations"); "S. Res [blank]," undated, "Resolved that section (1)," Box 116, JSP; Simms to Johnson, "Memorandum for Senator Lyndon Johnson," Jan. 9, Box 116, JSP; *CR*, 83/1, pp. 232–33, 279–81; McConaughy to Berger, Jan. 16, McConaughy to Beshoar, June 10, MP. **"So far":** Taft to C. Wayland Brooks, Jan. 17, quoted in Patterson, *Mr. Republican*, p. 589. **No plans:** "Freshmen Republican Senators. . . ," *Merry-Go-Round Release*, Feb. 5, 1957, Box 116, JSP; Ritchie interview; Steinberg, *Sam Johnson's Boy*, p. 343. **Appears; both senators agreed:** "Senators Receiving

New Committee Assignments," undated, Box I I6; *WP,* Jan. I3; Reedy interview.

Humphrey-Johnson conversation: Humphrey OH II. **"A forum":** Baker, *Wheeling and Dealing,* p. 65. **Clements-Johnson arrangement:** Reedy interview. **Persuading Russell Long:** *NYT,* Jan. I3; Baker, *Wheeling and Dealing,* p. 64; Connally, Reedy interviews.

McCarthy was going: Evans and Novak, p. 64. **"McCarran requests":** "Memorandum to Senator Johnson," Jan. 5, p. 2, Box I I6, LBJA SF. **Hinting:** "Political David Girding Against Nevada Goliath," *WP,* Jan. 4. **McCarran forced:** "(McCarran)," AP Dispatch, Dec. 29, I952, Drew Pearson Papers, F I62, 2 of 3, LBJL. **"Is not":** *WP,* Jan. I. **"All right":** Drew Pearson, *WP,* Feb. 6. **"As you know":** Truman to Johnson, Jan. I3, Box 8, WHFN; Jenkins interview. **Drew a line:** On "Requests of Senators," Jan. 5; Reedy interview. And see *NYT* and *WP,* Jan I3. **"None":** Evans and Novak, p. 64. **When he filled:** *WP,* Jan. I3. **"I disapprove":** Kennedy, quoted in *WP,* Jan. I3.

McClellan suggested: McConaughy to Berger, Jan. I6; Reedy interview. **"Desirable":** Johnson to Johnston, Jan. I3, Box 43, LBJA CF.

Through wall: Jenkins, Rather interviews. **"It was like":** Carroll Keach, quoted in Caro, *Path,* pp. 425–27. **Appealing to them; "Bob Taft is"; "McCarthy's going":** This description of Johnson's arguments is based on recollections of the phraseology he used by members of his staff who heard him, and by friends in Washington and Texas to whom he repeated his arguments in describing how he persuaded various senators. Their names are in the fifth paragraph of the notes to this chapter. And see McConaughy to Laybourne, Jan. I4; *NYT, WP,* Jan. I3; White, "The Foreign Relations Committee," *NYT Magazine,* Feb. I. **Russell nodded:** Reedy interview. **"Now":** McConaughy to Berger, Jan I6, MP.

Dropped: "For Immediate Release—Chairman Lyndon B. Johnson announced today," Jan. I2, Box I6, LBJA SF. **"I still remember":** Goldsmith interview. **"Dared":** *Time,* Jan. 26. **"Remarkable":** Fleeson, *WS,* Jan. I4. **"Rather miraculously":** Alsop and Alsop, *NYHT,* Feb. I. **"FRESHMAN DEMOCRATS":** *WP,* Jan. I3. **"Extraordinary":** *NYT,* Jan. I3. **"In barely two weeks":** McConaughy to Berger, Jan. I6, MP. **"Was greeted":** Childs, *SLP-D,* Jan. I7.

"Dear Lyndon": Rowe to Johnson, Jan. I3, Box 32, LBJA SN. **"We've got"; "more control":** Baker, *Wheeling and Dealing,* pp. 65, 64.

Had not fulfilled: Reedy, *U.S. Senate,* pp.

I I, I2; Galloway, *Legislative Process,* p. 604. **Memoranda:** "Dr. Galloway's views. . . ," Reedy to Johnson, undated, and "The material available on the policy committees. . . ," Nov. I9, I952, Box I I6, LBJA SF; Bone, *Party Committees,* pp. I66–96; "An Introduction to the Senate Policy Committees," *APSR,* June I956. The Legislative Reorganization Act of I946 had charged the two Policy Committees with "the formulation of over-all legislative policy of the respective parties"; Robert C. Byrd, "Mr. President, as to the Democratic Policy Committee," *CR,* 96/2, pp. I06I2–6I6; Galloway to Reedy, Nov. 2I, I952, Box I I6, LBJA SF; Jewell, "The Policy Committees," Chapter 5, *Senatorial Politics;* Reedy, Siegel OHs; Bibolet, Reedy, Siegel interviews.

"Would emerge": McPherson, *Political Education,* p. I5. **"All we got":** Evans and Novak, p. 6I.

Cook wouldn't: Evans and Novak, pp. 6I, 62; Siegel OH; Weisl interview. **Harlow unwilling:** Harlow interview. **Rowe turned down:** Rowe interview.

"We'd call"; "make the changes": Siegel OH. **Membership of Policy Committee:** Bone, p. I73; William S. White, "Democrats' 'Board of Directors,' " *NYT Magazine,* July I0, I955. **Murray's dotage:** McClure OH. **"An echo"; "solidify":** Baker, *Wheeling and Dealing,* p. 64. **"One hundred percent":** Baker, *Wheeling and Dealing,* p. 65. **"Unless":** Siegel OH. **"Was really it":** Smathers OH. **Hawaiian bill:** "Minutes of Meeting—Democratic Policy Committee, Monday, Feb. 3, I953, Room G-I8, U.S. Capitol, I2:45 p.m.," Box 364, JSP.

"Usually late": White, *Citadel,* p. 2I0; Bibolet to Caro, March 4, I995 (in author's possession); Bibolet, Reedy interviews. **"Nowhere":** Bone, p. I75. **"No leaks":** Steele interview. **Liberals "saw"; "Private":** Baker, *Wheeling and Dealing,* p. 65.

Few caucuses: *CR,* 96/2, pp. SI06I I–6I3. **$25:** "Minutes—Feb. 3," p. I. **"Senator Johnson . . . explained":** "Minutes . . . Feb. 3," p. 2, Box 364, JSP. **"Replies furnishing":** "Minutes of Meeting—Democratic Policy Committee, Tuesday, Feb. I7, I953, I2:45 p.m., Room G-I8, U.S. Capitol," p. I, Box 364, JSP. **"The Senate":** Johnson to (each committee chairman), Feb. 6, Box I I6, LBJA SF. **Staff would be better:** Bibolet, Reedy, Siegel interviews.

"He came in": McClure OH. **"Of course":** Bibolet interview.

"He accomplished this": Goodwin, *Lyndon Johnson,* p. I I4.

22. Masterstrokes

All dates are 1953 unless otherwise noted.

"**For three**": Ambrose, *Eisenhower,* p. 31. "**Statesmanlike**": Richard Rovere, *The New Yorker,* Jan. 31. **Shot his arms**: Ambrose, p. 42.
"**Privately**"; "**The great**": Alsop and Alsop, *NYHT,* Feb. 1. "**Looking for an excuse**"; "**The General Manager**": *Time,* June 22.
Mooney "interview": Mooney, *LBJ,* p. 13. **Would be easy**: Reedy, *U.S. Senate,* pp. 104, 105. "**Had actually**": Reedy OH V, p. 5; OH VI, p. 6.
"**A wonderful**": Hardeman and Bacon, *Rayburn,* p. 377. "**I told**": Rayburn to Hall, April 2, quoted in Hardeman and Bacon, p. 378. "**Any jackass**": *DMN,* Jan. 3.
"**Old-fashioned**": Evans and Novak, *LBJ: Exercise,* p. 170.
Hour after hour; "cheap and partisan": Reedy, *U.S. Senate,* p. 104. "**To announce**": Reedy OH V, p. 4. "**I have**": *FWS-T,* Jan. 3.
"**Americans everywhere**": "Minutes of Meeting—Democratic Policy Committee, Feb. 3, 1953," Box 364, JSP.
"**Resurgent**": Richard Rovere, *The New Yorker,* Feb. 14. "**The form**": Ambrose, p. 66. "**It should**": Shaffer, *On and Off,* p. 63. "**Republican senators**": DDE Diary, Feb. 7, Box 3; April 1, Box 4, DDEL. "**The adoption**": Shaffer, p. 67. "**Would not**": Ambrose, pp. 65–67.
Allies were planning: Ambrose, p. 67; *NYT,* Feb. 24. "**President Eisenhower's**": *NYT,* Feb. 24. "**It would**": LLM, Supplementary Notes, March 2, Box 1, DDEL. "**How can we**": "Memorandum of Telephone Conversation—Secretary Dulles calling Senator Johnson," March 3, Notes and Transcripts of Johnson Conversations—1953." "**I really**"; "**forget**": Ambrose, p. 67. "**The picture**": Reedy, *U.S. Senate,* p. 79.
"**I reject**": MacNeil, *Dirksen,* p. 114. "**Nominations passed over**": "Executive Calendar," *CR,* 83/1, various dates. **McCarran, McCarthy attacks**: Ambrose, pp. 59–61; MacNeil, pp. 113–14; Patterson, *Mr. Republican,* pp. 595–96. "**I have known**"; "**Confident**": Eisenhower, quoted in Ambrose, p. 60. "**There was**": Taft, quoted in White, *Taft Story,* p. 237.
"**High-water**": Reedy, *U.S. Senate,* p. 80. "**As if**": This remark is generally attributed to the *NYHT*'s television critic John Crosby. **Introduction of S.J. Res. 1**: *CR,* 83/1, pp. 156, 160–61.
Conservatives' fear: Ambrose, p. 68;

Brownell, *Advising Ike,* pp. 264–65. "**A complex**": Ambrose, p. 154; Tananbaum, *Bricker Amendment,* p. 91. "**Making it**": Minnich, LMS, Jan. 11, 1954, DDEL. "**Stupid**": Hagerty, *Diary,* p. 7 (Jan. 14, 1954). **Touched**: Ambrose, p. 68. "**Many**": *NYT,* Feb. 6, 17, 1954.
"**An incredible**"; "**no hope**": Reedy, *U.S. Senate,* p. 82. Neil MacNeil says, "It was plain that there were enough votes in the Senate to approve the Bricker amendment" (MacNeil, *Dirksen,* p. 117). "**In all**": Reedy, quoted in Miller, *Lyndon,* p. 158. "**The worst**": Baker, *Wheeling and Dealing,* p. 90. "**A slap**": Evans and Novak, p. 76. "**Probably**": DDE Diary, Phone Calls, Jan. 28, 1954, Box 5, DDEL.
"**Bricker seems**": Hagerty, p. 8 (Feb. 8, 1954). "**People *for* it**": DDE Diary, Phone Calls, Box 5, DDEL. "**There was**": Ambrose, p. 69. "**A secret**": Manchester, *Glory,* p. 674. **Reported it out**: Steinberg, *Sam Johnson's Boy,* p. 359. "**Lyndon Johnson**": Dulles to Eisenhower, DDE Diary, June 25, Box 5, DDEL. "**Unalterable**": *NYT,* Jan. 31, 1954. "**Insured that**": MacNeil, p. 118.
Johnson's broadcast: "Address by Senator Lyndon B. Johnson . . . For Release to Monday AM's, Sept. 14, 1953," Statements, Box 13, JSP. **Down on the ranch**: Rather, Reedy interviews. **Johnson's thinking**: Reedy interview and OH; Steele interview; Siegel OH; Baker, *Wheeling and Dealing,* pp. 90–91; Steinberg, *Sam Johnson's Boy,* pp. 358–60; Tananbaum, pp. 145–46; "Senator Johnson Discusses Bricker Amendment," Sept. 14, Statements, Box 13, JSP; Reedy to Johnson, Jan. 21, 1954; Siegel to Johnson, Jan. 23, 26, 28, 29, 30, 1954, Box 374, JSP.
"**We've got**": Baker, *Wheeling and Dealing,* p. 91. "**To get**": Humphrey OH II, p. 16. **Two memoranda**: Siegel to Johnson, both Jan. 23, 26, 1954, Box 374, JSP. "**Just a quick**": Siegel OH. **George amendment**: *NYT,* Jan. 28, 1954. "**Sounded**": Reedy, *U.S. Senate,* p. 83. Johnson further flattered George by making it appear as if he was the leader of the fight. When he and Russell met reporters during the fight, he said, "We're standing with Walter" (*NYT,* Jan. 30, 1954), "**Within**": *NYT,* Jan. 28, 1954.
"**DDE Diary,**" **Phone calls**: Eisenhower to Smith, Jan. 27, 1954, Box 5, DDEL. "**Broadly**"; **Bricker's speech**: *NYT, WP,* Jan. 29. "**Republicans**": Telephone call from Smith, Jan. 28, 1954. "**Were reluctant**": Tananbaum, p. 150. "**Pretty soon**": DDE Diary, Phone Calls, Eisenhower to Brownell, Jan. 29, Box 5, DDEL. "**Couldn't:**" DDE Diary, Phone Calls, "Conversation with Atty. Gen. Brownell," Feb. 3, 1954, Box 5, DDEL.

"So tired": Hagerty, pp. 13, 14 (Feb. 1, 2, 1954). "The fight was"; "Different philosophies"; "the headlines": *NYT*, Jan. 31, 1954.

GOP liaison men: DDEP, OF 116-H-4, DDEL; Harlow, Holt interviews; Tananbaum, p. 174. 42 to 50: *NYT, WP*, Feb. 26, 1954. And see DDE Diary, Jan. 18, 1954, Box 4.

"Passed the word": *Newsweek*, Feb. 15, 1954. Tried to prepare: Baker, *Wheeling and Dealing*, pp. 90, 91; Tananbaum, pp. 179, 188–89; Steinberg, *Sam Johnson's Boy*, p. 359; Harlow, Reedy, Rogers interviews. William S. White would later report that Jackson and Magnuson first voted for the George Amendment as a substitute and then, "out of respect" for George, switched and voted against it (*NYT*, Feb. 27, 1954). "Continued": Tananbaum, p. 174. "Mr. President": Knowland, *CR*, 83/2, pp. 2371–372. "If we are not": "Vote! Vote! Vote!": *CR*, 83/2, pp. 2373–375; *Time*, March 8, 1954. "Mark"; saluted: George, quoted in *Time*, March 8; *CR*, 83/2, pp. 2373–374.

Switching: *NYHT, NYT, WP, WS*, Feb. 27. Kilgore's vote: Maddox, *Kilgore*, p. 317; *Time, Newsweek*, March 8, 1954. Baker, *Wheeling and Dealing* (p. 91), says he was ill. *Time* says he "had been resting on a couch in his office all afternoon." Others, including Tananbaum (pp. 179–80) and Holt (interview), say the reason he was resting was alcohol. "Stall"; "How am I": *Time*, March 8, 1954. The *CR* (83/2, p. 2373) has a different version of Magnuson's statement.

"Wanted major": Ambrose, pp. 65, 66.

Told Brown, Richardson: Clark interview. "We had": Johnson to Clark, March 3, 1954, Box 15, LBJA SN (folder 4 of 4).

23. Tail-Gunner Joe

"The most": Robert Sherrill, "The Trajectory of a Bumbler," *NYT Book Review*, p. 11, June 5, 1983. "A fraud": Byrd, *The Senate*, p. 571. "From the": Byrd, p. 573. Johnson was asked: White, quoted in Miller, *Lyndon*, p. 163; McCulloch, Rauh, Rowe interviews. "Something": Rowe interview. In his OH, White says he told Johnson, "You really must do something about this damned fellow."

"I'm for": Malone, quoted in Sidey, "The Presidency," *Life*, April 29, 1966. Asset; "Keep talking": Patterson, *Mr. Republican*, p. 446. "There was": *NYT*, Jan. 7, 1951. Lehman episode: Alsop, *The Center*, pp. 8, 9. "At that": Reedy, quoted in Miller, p. 166. "For what he says": White, *Citadel*, p. 123. "Would be forced": Evans and Novak, *LBJ: Exercise*, p. 81.

"Joe will go": Evans and Novak, p. 81. "About how": Arthur Stehling, "A Country Lawyer," unnumbered page, unpublished memoir (in author's possession). "He said": Stehling interview. "Well, I met": Oltorf interview (Oltorf was present during this exchange). "it seems": Evans and Novak, p. 81. "Loudmouthed": Baker, *Wheeling and Dealing*, p. 94.

Largest: Oshinsky, *Conspiracy*, pp. 319, 419; Gary Cartwright, "Hugh Roy Cullen's Last Hurrah," *Texas Monthly*, Jan. 1986; Theodore H. White, "Texas: Land of Wealth and Fear," *The Reporter*, May 25, June 8, 1954; Edward T. Folliard, "Texas Big Dealers," *WP*, Feb. 14–19, 1954. "A nut": Clark interview. "A screwball": Reedy interview; Reedy, quoted in Miller, p. 162. "Old witch": Fath, quoted in Miller, p. 161.

"Bill, that's": Miller, p. 163. "to kill a snake"; "He kept": Miller, p. 166. "He just": Humphrey OH I, p. 24. "To realize": Reedy, *LBJ*, p. 106. "Has been dragged"; "Joe has made": Miller, p. 166. "God": Reedy OH III, p. 12. "The Hayden episode": Reedy, p. 107; St. Claire interview. Also see Reedy, *U.S. Senate*, p. 143.

Russell's signal: Fite, *Russell*, p. 284. "Come on": Humphrey, quoted in Miller, p. 170, and OH. "Give names: Miller, p. 170. "Tarnished"; "hurt": Oshinsky, p. 321. "The fact": Symington interview. "You wait": Oshinsky, p. 293. "Behind"; "I would not": Patterson, pp. 594, 595.

Liberals pleaded: Byrd, p. 573; Cohen, McCulloch, Rowe, Symington interviews; Humphrey, quoted in Miller, p. 171. Lehman asked: Steinberg, *Sam Johnson's Boy*, p. 362. "Everybody": Maverick to Johnson, April 2, 1954; Johnson to Maverick, April 27, May 12, 1954, LBJA CF, Box 50. "If I were": Johnson told: Evans and Novak, pp. 81, 82. Popularity began; "Ike wants": Oshinsky, pp. 464, 438. "He knew": SHJ, quoted in Miller, p. 168. 30 percent; "that weapon": Oshinsky, p. 465. "That Maine": Shaffer, *On and Off*, p. 23.

On July 29: "Minutes of Democratic Policy Committee, Room G-18, July 29, 1954," Box 364, JSP. He had lined up: Baker, *Wheeling and Dealing*, p. 94.

Selecting the committee: Evans and Novak, pp. 83–84; White, *Citadel*, pp. 127–31. "Knowland theoretically": White OH. "It had never": Reedy, quoted in Miller, p. 172. Ed Johnson hated; "Essential": Evans and Novak, p. 84.

"Left": Oshinsky, p. 481. "Contrary": White, *Citadel*, p. 132. Lined up behind it: Oshinsky, pp. 484–85, 491; Humphrey, quoted in Miller, p. 171. **"Squiggly"**: Reedy, *Johnson,* p. 108.

"The size"; "on rather"; "We have": Oshinsky, p. 492. **"Whatever"**: McCulloch interview. **"Splendid"**: Douglas OH.

"Could have been": Oshinsky, p. 507. **"Johnson's role"**: Dallek, *Lone Star,* p. 458.

24. The "Johnson Rule"

All dates are 1955 unless otherwise noted.

Morse deal: Drukman, *Wayne Morse,* pp. 224–25; Smith, *Tiger in the Senate,* Steinberg, *Sam Johnson's Boy,* p. 392; White, *Citadel,* pp. 187–88; Fleeson, *WS,* Jan. 11; Pearson, *WP,* Jan. 2; Steele to Williamson, Jan. 13, SP. **"Morse never"; "I don't know"**: Steinberg, p. 392. **"He would"**: *NYT,* Jan. 11.

"I respectfully"; "I would": Quoted in Goodwin, *Lyndon Johnson,* p. 115. **"Four measures"**: O'Mahoney to Johnson, Aug. 15, 1958, "Papers of the Democratic Leader," Box 367, JSP.

Using Siegel, Reedy, Bibolet: Siegel, Reedy, Bibolet interviews and OHs. **Starting to manage the bills**: Riddick, Shuman, Zagoria, Zweben interviews. **"In the past"**: Riddick interview. **"A spring"**: Johnson, quoted in Goodwin, *Lyndon Johnson,* p. 121. **"Assurance that"**: Robertson to Johnson, March 15, 1956, "Legis—B&C Com., Bank Holding Co. Bill, Sen. Res. S. 2577," Robertson Papers, College of William and Mary. **"Now"**: Riddick interview.

"Save": Stokes, *WS,* Jan. 6. **"We have"**: *NYHT,* May 6. **"Have been"**: Stewart Alsop, *WP,* May 21. **"He didn't"**: Smathers OH.

"Lyndon, I want": "Conversations with Senator Kefauver, 11 a.m., Jan. 11, 1955," Box 47, LBJA.

Badly wanted: Lehman to Johnson, Nov. 4, 1954; Dec. 2, 1954; Jan. 13, 1955; Johnson to Lehman, Nov. 8, Dec. 21, 1954, Jan. 13, 1955, HHLP. **"Was more concerned"**: Pearson, *WP,* Jan. 2. **No Senate rule**: Edelstein to Kilgore, Dec. 10, 1954; Edelstein interview. **Johnson gave**: Pearson, *WP,* Jan. 2.

"The finance": Evans and Novak, *LBJ: Exercise,* p. 101. **"It had been"**: Stokes, *WS,* Jan. 11. **"I'm gonna"**: Baker, *Wheeling and Dealing,* p. 66.

"At his best": Fleeson, *WS,* Jan. 11. **"Just not"**: St. Claire interview; Maybank to Skeeter, Nov. 7; Kefauver to Johnson, Sept. 9, Oct. 22, 1953, Dec. 18, 1954; Johnson to Kefauver, Dec. 27, 1954; Gore to Johnson, Aug. 31, Box 506, JSP.

Master keys: Jenkins interview. **The startled Ensley**: Ensley to Caro, Dec. 11, 1981 (in author's possession); Ensley interview, OH. **"After"**: Goodwin, *Lyndon Johnson,* p. 103.

A silence: Busby, Jenkins interviews. **"He wouldn't"**: Edelstein interview. **Incident**: "Lehman, Telephoned . . . ," Nov. 26, "Immigration Bill re: hearings" folder, HHLP; Edelstein interview.

"You'd walk": Edelstein interview. **Chat with assistant**: McCulloch, Shuman interviews. **"Skeeter would"**: Shuman interview. **"Longshoremen's"**: MacNeil interview. **"Cutting"**: Edelstein interview. **"What the"**: Schnibbee interview.

"My God": Evans and Novak, p. 102. **Aides gossiped**: Interviews with aides, including BeLieu, Bernstein, Fensterwald, McCulloch, McGillicuddy, Schnibbe, Shuman, Zweben.

Symington's feelings: Symington interview, OH. **Johnson resented**: BeLieu, Busby interviews.

"Not a team player": Baker, *Wheeling and Dealing,* p. 65. Baker says that "this was another way of saying that Symington was an independent loner who refused to let LBJ get a grip on him." Johnson felt that Symington was an "ingrate" because of the "campaign money" Johnson had raised for his campaigns. Sam Houston Johnson says that "Johnson didn't like" Symington because Symington was a rival for the presidential nomination (SHJ interview); Symington interview.

"Senators mutually": MacNeil, *Dirksen,* p. 137. **"Hell"**: Lucas, quoted in Reedy interview. **If President Kennedy**: Jackson, quoted in Reston, *Deadline,* pp. 304–05.

"As for": Long, quoted in Steinberg, *Sam Johnson's Boy,* p. 456. **"When somebody"**: Van den Linden interview.

"Unanimous Consent Agreements": In 1955, Rule XII, paragraph 3 read: "No request by a senator for unanimous consent for the taking of a final vote on a specified date upon the passage of a bill or joint resolution shall be submitted to the Senate for agreement thereto until, upon a roll call ordered for the purpose by the presiding officer, it shall be disclosed that a quorum of the Senate is present; and when unanimous consent is thus given the same shall operate as the order of the Senate, but any unanimous consent may be revoked by a unanimous consent granted in the manner prescribed above, upon one day's notice" (*Senate Manual,* 83/1, pp. 18–19).

Prior to World War II: Galloway, *Legislative Process,* pp. 555–56.

"It was": Riddick interviews; OH. **"After Mr. Johnson came"**: Riddick OH, p. 253. Riddick says that with these innovations "Mr. Johnson . . . introduced a new procedure in the

Senate or at least expanded it, or made it more common than it had ever been before in modern times." This discussion of his unanimous consent agreement innovations and their impact on the Senate is drawn from Riddick, *Senate Procedure,* principally pp. 1064–1102; Evans and Novak, pp. 114–15; Galloway, *Legislative Process,* pp. 552–57; from interviews with Riddick, who was assistant parliamentarian of the Senate from 1951 to 1964, and parliamentarian from 1964 to 1974; with Murray Zweben, assistant parliamentarian from 1964 to 1974 and parliamentarian from 1974 to 1980; with Bernard V. Somers, assistant journal clerk during the 1950s; with Senate Historian Richard A. Baker and Associate Historian Donald A. Ritchie; and with many senatorial staff members, of whom Frank McCulloch, Darrell St. Claire, and Howard Shuman were especially helpful.

"**Johnson would come up**": Riddick interview.

"**There is . . . no rule**": Riddick, *Senate Procedures,* p. 1066. "**Can be set aside**" only: Riddick, p. 1066. **Rules very different**: Riddick, pp. 1065–1102. "**Must be presented . . . without debate**": Riddick, p. 1069. "**Where an amendment**": Riddick, p. 1073. **Had to be subtracted**: Riddick, pp. 52–56, 1073, 1083–85.

"**Russell held**": Riddick interview. "**Not germane . . . out of order**": Riddick, p. 51.

"**A senator cannot be recognized**": Riddick, p. 1083. And see pp. 886–87. "**Because of**"; "**if a senator offered**": Zweben interview.

"**Of course**": Evans and Novak, p. 115.

"**As long as**": Reedy, *U.S. Senate,* p. 3. "**diversionary**": Reedy, *LBJ,* pp. 82, 86. "**Hubert prepares**": Johnson, quoted in Moody, *LBJ,* p. 52. "**Whenever**": Reedy, *U.S. Senate,* p. 4. "**Relic**"; "**interlude**": McPherson, *Political Education,* p. 76. "**Keep it**"; "**We've got**": Edelsten, Shuman interviews. "**Greek tragedy**": Douglas, quoted in Goodwin, *Lyndon Johnson,* p. 136. "**It is**": Johnson, quoted in Goodwin, p. 141.

"**He regarded**"; "**absolutely**"; "**merely exercises**": Reedy, *Johnson,* pp. 6, 7, 68. "**Attitude left no room**": Reedy, p. 82. "**The role of public debate**": Reedy, p. 7. "**A natural**": Goodwin, p. 130. "**Abhorred**": Reedy, p. 6. "**His constant**": McPherson, p. 169. **Did not believe:** Edelstein interview. "**If**": Shuman interview.

25. The Leader

"**He would stand**": The description of Johnson briefing the journalists, and of Johnson running the Senate, is based on interviews with journalists Robert Barr, Jim Brady, John Chadwick, Benjamin Cole, Allen Drury, Lewis T. (Tex) Easley, Alan S. Emory, Rowland Evans, John Finney, John Goldsmith, Neil MacNeil, Sarah McClendon, Hugh Sidey, John L. Steele, Alfred Steinberg, George Tames, J. William Theis, Tom Wicker, Frank Van Der Linden, and Sam Zagoria; with the following Senate staff members (who would often have been on the podium): Parliamentarian Floyd Riddick, Secretary to the Parliamentarian Murray Zweben, and Assistant Journal Clerk Bernard V. Somers; as well as the senators, assistants to senators, and members of the Senate's staff and Lyndon Johnson's staff listed in the "Note on Sources." "**He would**": Steele interview. "**Somebody**"; "**if you**"; "**he knew**": Barr interview. "**There would**": Mooney, *LBJ,* p. 162. "**He would answer**": MacNeil interview. "**You didn't**": Barr interview. "**The buildup**": Drury interview. "**Power just**": Barr interview. "*In command*"*:* Cole interview.

"**C'mon, c'mon**": Riddick, Zweben interviews.

Potter exchange: *CR,* 83/1, May 26, 1955. "**And even**": Barr interview. "**Lister**"; "**if you**"; "**he would**": Patrick J. Hynes interview. "**Viciously**": Reedy interview. "**Good places**": Hynes interview. "**Don't quit**": McCulloch interview. **Sending Baker:** Riddick interview. "**Don't talk**"; "**I'd go**": Edelstein interview.

"**Make it short**": McCulloch interview. "**Like a coon dog**"; "**The Senate was**": Steele to Williamson, March 4, 1958, SP. "**Get the lead**": Fensterwald interview. "**Why don't**": Davidson, quoted in Miller, *Lyndon,* p. 220.

"**Seeing how**": Read interview. "**You ready**": Schnibbe interview. "**Jiggling**": Shuman interview. "**Going from**"; "**baggy-cut**": MacNeil to Williamson, March 4, 1958, MP.

"*By God!*"*:* Fensterwald interview. "**Fucking senator**": Schnibbe interview. **Grabbed Baker's:** Fensterwald, Steele interviews. "**Look**": Robert S. Allen, quoted in Miller, p. 175; Allen OH, SRL.

Lifting up Pastore: Mooney, p. 31; Reedy interview. **Mutter along;** "*CALL THE QUESTION!*"*:* Riddick, Steele, Zweben interviews.

"**Revving up**": Reedy, *U.S. Senate,* p. 177;

Reedy interview. **"Orchestra conductor":** Steele interview and Steele to Williamson, March 4, 1958, SP. **Johnson directing Senate voting:** Interviews with Barr, Fensterwald, MacNeil, Shuman, Steele, and Evans and Novak, *LBJ: Exercise,* p. 114; Goodwin, *Lyndon Johnson,* p. 130; Steinberg, *Sam Johnson's Boy,* p. 412. **"You would see":** Wicker interview. **"In front":** MacNeil interview. **"Change your vote":** Evans and Novak, p. 96; Steinberg, p. 497. **"His mind attuned":** Sidey, *Personal Presidency,* p. 45. **"Signal, and":** Sidey interview.

"Often": Baker, *Wheeling and Dealing,* p. 90. **"Played Leader":** Sidey interview. **"Master":** Dugger, *Politician.* The subtitle of Ronnie Dugger's biography of Johnson, *The Politician,* is *The Life and Times of Lyndon Johnson, the Drive for Power, from the Frontier to Master of the Senate.*

26. "Zip, Zip"

All dates are 1955 unless otherwise noted.

Reciprocal trade bill: Fleeson, *WS,* June 3; McClendon, *Sherman Democrat,* May 17, *HP,* June 12; *NYT,* April 5, May 21; *WP,* April 5; Steele to Williamson, May 5, SP. **"Could have":** Stewart Alsop, "A Real Pro at Work in the Senate," *WP,* May 21.

Kilgore report: *CR,* 84/1, May 25. **In a single:** *Newsweek,* June 27. **"Certainly":** Alsop, *CR,* 84/1, May 25.

"Engage"; "elbow room": Reedy, *U.S. Senate,* pp. 93, 107; interview. **"Southern dons":** Mooney, *LBJ,* p. 48. "Lyndon": Mooney, p. 31. **Not invited:** Reedy interview.

"Just as": Dent interview.

"We had": Douglas, *Fullness of Time,* p. 280. **"Shrewd":** "FROM: Walter White . . . For release . . . Jan. 13, 1955" attached to Humphrey to Johnson, Jan. 13, Box 2, WHFN. **Using Hubert:** Douglas, p. 280; Solberg (*Hubert Humphrey,* pp. 169–71) says dryly: "It is hard to see what Humphrey was getting in legislation in return for his cooperation with Johnson. Not a single one of his measures went through in those years." **"Abandon":** Steele to Williamson, Jan. 6, quoted in Dallek, *Lone Star,* p. 478. **"Should give"; "bad mistake"; "sealed":** Douglas, p. 280.

Powell's amendment: Hamilton, *Adam Clayton Powell, Jr.,* pp. 225–35. **"The issue":** *WS,* June 6. **Eisenhower spoke:** *NYT,* June 9.

"The informal . . . footrace": Cormier, AP story, newspaper unidentified, Jan. 9, clippings file, LBJL. **"Millions":** Ambrose, *Eisenhower,* p. 249. **Shunted; "It is diffi-**

cult": Donahue, "The Prosecution Rests," *The New Republic,* May 23. Same point made by Fleeson, *WS,* April 21.

Democratic dinner: *HP, WP,* April 17. **"Moderation":** *WN,* April 18. **Truman interview:** *NYT,* April 18. **"I have got":** *CCC-T,* April 19. **"My heart":** *WP,* April 19. **"Many Democrats":** *WN,* April 18. **"Some Democrats":** Fleeson, *WS,* May 11. **"Southern":** Fleeson, *WS,* June 3. **"Malleable":** Drummond, *DT-H,* May 6. **"Lyin' Down":** Pearson, *WP,* quoted in Dugger, *Politician,* p. 377.

70,000: *CR,* 84/1, p. 7723.

Anathema: Goldsmith, *Colleagues,* p. 48. **Capehart's amendment:** *CR,* 84/1 pp. 7726–727.

"Taken for granted": Reedy, *U.S. Senate,* p. 108. **"Exercises":** Shaffer, *On and Off,* p. 113. **Counts the same; "the housing bill":** Reedy memo, June 8, Box 412, JSP; Steele to Williamson, June 9, SP. **With an air:** Evans and Novak, *LBJ: Exercise,* p. 150. **"Affably":** *Baltimore Sun,* June 8; Steele to Williamson, June 9, SP. **A mask:** Reedy interview. **It was true:** Johnson's arguments to the southerners are in Matthews, *U.S. Senators,* pp. 128–29; in Miller, *Lyndon,* pp. 177–78; in Reedy memo, June 8; Reedy, *U.S. Senate,* pp. 107–10, and *LBJ,* pp. 83–84; Humphrey, Sparkman OHs; Reedy, Steele interviews. **"Only a little":** Reedy, quoted in Miller, p. 178. **"One":** Reedy, *U.S. Senate,* p. 178. **"Lyndon":** Steele to Williamson, June 9, SP. **For an expurgated version:** Reedy, quoted in Miller, p. 178.

"Anyone": Douglas, in *CR,* 84/1, pp. 7734–735.

Getting Humphrey to Chamber: *CR,* 84/1, p. 7759; Humphrey OH II; Reedy interview. **"Damn it"; "as the"; had Johnson needed:** Steele to Williamson, June 9, SP. **"Capehart's head":** Reedy, *U.S. Senate,* p. 109. **Vote:** *CR,* 84/1, p. 7753. Later, when it was certain that their votes would make no difference in the outcome, Russell and Eastland voted aye, and were so recorded. **60 to 25:** *CR,* 84/1, p. 7754. **"As soon":** Reedy, pp. 109–10. And see Goldsmith, p. 49. **"A genius"; "I am frank":** *CR,* 84/1, p. 7759. **Scene in G-14:** Evans and Novak, p. 151; Shuman interview.

Eisenhower had proposed; working on subcommittee: Evans and Novak, p. 149. **One-dollar minimum:** Lincoln, *WS,* June 5.

"The cloakroom": McCulloch interview. **"I think":** Humphrey OH III, p. 27. **"Mr. President":** *CR,* 84/1, p. 7873. **"Zip, zip"; "boy, oh":** Humphrey OH III, p. 27. **Hill didn't know; Lehman "speechless":** Evans and Novak, p. 150.

"Obviously": Reedy, *U.S. Senate,* p. 13.

Neely's agreement; "some of": *CR*, 84/1, p. 7874. "I was wrong": McCulloch interview. The last time: *Entire Senate Voting Record*, p. 301; Dugger, p. 293. Laughing among themselves: Fleeson, *WS*, June 9. "The talk": Carpenter, *HP*, June 12. "LYNDON MOVES": Lincoln, *WS*, June 11. "The Texas-sized": *WSJ*, June 10. "On several": *WP*, June 30. "Snatched": Fleeson, *WS*, June 9. "The deftness": Pearson, *WP*, June 13. "THE TEXAN": *Newsweek*, June 27.

Lack of enthusiasm: For example, Fleeson, *WS*, June 3. Russell's withdrawal; "Will inherit": Timmons, *DMN*, May 28. Byrd himself: *CR*, 84/1, p. 9559. Smathers had; editorial: *Abilene Reporter-News, Orlando Sentinel*, July 3; Jenkins interview. "Exuberant": *The New Republic*, July 4. "Gallery Glimpses": *WP*, July 3. "Be on": Evans and Novak, p. 89.

27. "Go Ahead with the Blue"

All dates are 1955 unless otherwise noted.

Krock luncheon: *NYT*, July 7. "More than": Gonella interview; Mooney, *LBJ*, p. 58. "It has": *WP*, July 3. So ashen: Leslie Carpenter, *HP*, June 12. Hardly one: Jenkins interview. "Chain-smoking": Baker, *Good Times*, pp. 335–37. "A starving": Baker, *Wheeling and Dealing*, p. 70.

Illness during first campaign: Caro, *Path*, pp. 433–36. "I never": Caro, *Path*, p 425. During second campaign: Caro, *Means*, Chapter 10.

Suddenly clutched: *WP*, Aug. 14; Mooney OH; Busby interview. "He ate": Smathers, quoted in Steinberg, *Sam Johnson's Boy*, p. 413. Cursory: Steinberg, p. 298. "A flutter": Chadwick interview. "Near the edge": Steele, *WS*, July 6. Dinner: Symington OH I, pp. 14, 15.

During the morning: Steinberg, *Sam Johnson's Boy*, p. 414. Chadwick episode: Chadwick, Theis interviews; Theis OH; Chadwick, "When a Lieutenant Outranked a Commander," *AP Cleartime*, Nov. 1998, pp. 1, 2. Lunch: Evans and Novak, *LBJ: Exercise*, p. 91. "I remember": Lyndon B. Johnson, "My Heart Attack Taught Me How to Live," *American Magazine*, July 1956; Johnson, quoted in Miller, *Lyndon*, p. 101. At Huntlands: Brown, Oltorf interviews, OHs; Anderson OH. "Lyndon, I think": Anderson OH; Anderson, quoted in Evans and Novak, p. 91, and in Miller, p. 181. "An absolute": Caro, *Path*, p. 156; also see p. 174. Coolness in Pacific:

Caro, *Means*, Chapter 3. Ambulance ride: Oltorf interview.

At Bethesda: Dr. J. Willis Hurst, Lady Bird Johnson interviews; Jenkins, Reedy interviews and OHs; Montgomery, *Mrs. LBJ*, p. 53; Russell, *Lady Bird*, pp. 175–76; Steinberg, *Sam Johnson's Boy*, p. 416. "A real": *Newsweek*, Nov. 7; Reedy interview. "Where his will": Jenkins OH. "Tell him": Mrs. Johnson, quoted in Miller, p. 181. "Sensuous": Mrs. Johnson, quoted in Dallek, *Lone Star*, p. 486. Doctors said: Dr. Hurst interview; Jenkins OH.

28. Memories

All dates are 1955 unless otherwise noted.

"Fifty-fifty": Lyndon B. Johnson, "My Heart Attack Taught Me How to Live," *American Magazine*, July 1956; *Los Angeles Inquirer*, Dec. 2; Reedy OH VIII.

Details of heart attack: Interviews with Dr. Willis Hurst, M.D.; Cain OH; Lady Bird Johnson, "Can You Prevent a Heart Attack?" *This Week*, Feb. 12, 1956. "A myocardial": *NYT*, *WP*, July 6. "The immediate": Fleeson, *WP*, July 5. "HEART ATTACK": *Nashua Telegraph*, July 6. "Six months": *NYT*, July 10.

"He felt": Jenkins OH. "White": Culhane interview. "For almost": Baker, *Wheeling and Dealing*, pp. 151, 152. "For the": Reedy OH VIII. "Project Impossible": Mooney, *LBJ*, pp. 60, 61.

"His nurses": Cain, quoted in Miller, *Lyndon*, p. 182. "Simultaneously": *NYP*, May 28, 1956. "He really": Reedy OH VIII. "Demanding": Baker, *Wheeling and Dealing*, pp. 151, 152. "We": Jenkins to Johnson, July 18, Box 96, Masters, JSP. "Oh, now": *Boston Globe*, Sept. 15. "Why": Lyndon B. Johnson, "My Heart Attack Taught Me How to Live," *American Magazine*, July 1956. "If he": Cain OH. "To cut": Reedy OH, interviews. "Mary": Jenkins to Rather, July 23, Chronology, "Chronologies," 1955, LBJL.

"Over and over": Reedy OH VIII. Illness had deepened: Reedy OH VIII; Busby, Jenkins, Rather, Reedy interviews. "Give Lyndon"; "I miss": Smith, *President's Lady*, pp. 64, 65. "Everybody": McGrory, *WS*, Aug. 21.

"Stay with me"; "at first"; Worley dinner: Montgomery, *Mrs. LBJ*, p. 53. "Lyndon wanted": Steinberg, *Sam Johnson's Boy*, p. 418. "Did fear": Jenkins OH.

Put the pack: Lyndon B. Johnson, "My Heart Attack Taught Me How to Live," *American Magazine*, July 1956; *Newsweek*, Nov. 7; Mooney, p. 62; Steinberg, *Sam Johnson's Boy*,

p. 419; Jenkins, SHJ interviews. **"Every":** Gonella interview. **Did not smoke; Cigarettes and coffee:** Jenkins, SHJ interviews; Jenkins OH. **"He became"; "incautiously":** Reedy OH VIII. **"A fatty":** WP, Sept. 14. **"A cantaloupe":** Jenkins OH. **"I believe":** Mrs. Johnson to Terrell Maverick, July 28, LBJA SN, Box 27. **"I've thrown":** Steinberg, *Sam Johnson's Boy*, p. 419.

"Stories began": Mooney, p. 62. **"There are":** McGrory, WS, Aug. 21. **"Sprawled":** *Newsweek*, Nov. 7. **"Innumerable":** *Beaumont Journal*, Aug. 29. **"Easy-going":** McClendon, AA-S, Aug. 21. **"A man":** McGrory, WS, Aug. 21.

"Representatives": AA-S, Aug. 26. **"Thinnest":** Rather, quoted in Miller, p. 182. **Drew an** *X:* SHJ interviews. **Nightmares:** Goodwin, *Lyndon Johnson*, p. 125.

Responses to Little Beagle: Montgomery, p. 56; SHJ, Rather interviews. **"Some days"; "He's going"; Sam Houston knew:** SHJ, Rather interviews. **"Many things":** *SAE*, Sept. 11. And see Jenkins to Johnson, Aug. 26, Box 3, PPCF.

"The only deal": Califano, *Triumph*, pp. 29, 30.

Life at the ranch: SHJ interviews; Jenkins, Rather, Reedy interviews and OHs. **"Oh":** Jenkins OH. **"Every":** Reedy OH. **"Outlets":** Stewart Alsop, "Lyndon Johnson: How Does He Do It?" *SEP*, Jan. 24, 1959. **"His finger":** Califano, pp. 51, 52. **"Hog call":** Corcoran interview. **"When this":** Steinberg, *Sam Johnson's Boy*, p. 420. **"Get along":** Lady Bird to Nellie Connally, July 16, Box 39, JSP.

"On new": Johnson to Reedy, Sept. 21, Box 566, JSP. **"Dear John":** Johnson to Bricker, Sept. 16, Box 557, JSP. **"Never seemed"; "going":** Palmie OH. **Subcommittee reports, leaks:** *Newsweek*, Sept. 26; *NYT*, Sept. 13, Oct. 9; WS, Oct. 13; Reedy to Siegel, Sept. 5, Box 555, JSP. **To persuade** *Time:* Jenkins to Carter, Aug. 25, Box 30, "Master Files," JSP; Carpenter to Johnson, undated, Box 557, JSP.

"Johnson's Manso": Rather to Moursund, Dec. 20, Box 566, JSP. **"I don't":** Jenkins OH. **KANG negotiations:** Steinberg, *Sam Johnson's Boy*, p. 335–36; for example, Jenkins to Johnson, Aug. 31, Box 96, "Masters File," JSP; *Life*, Aug. 21, 1964; WSJ, Nov. 23, 1964; WS, June 9, 1964; Jenkins interview and OH; Stehling interview. **"It speeded":** Reedy OH VIII.

Johnson's strategy: *Newsweek*, Oct. 31; CSM, Oct. 18, Nov. 7; HP, Nov. 13. See notes for Chapter 35 ("Convention"). **"If his":** Corcoran ms., Corcoran Papers, quoted in Dallek, *Lone Star*, p. 491.

Johnson's reaction: Reedy OH VIII, and see notes for Chapter 33. **Instead:** Rather OH. **Press conference:** "A Social Visit," *Time*, Oct. 10; AA-S, NYHT, NYT, Sept. 30; HP, Oct. 2; Reedy OH VIII. **"Pointedly":** NYT, Oct. 18. **"I'm not":** Martin, *Adlai Stevenson*, p. 211. **Johnson and Rayburn:** Corcoran, Rowe interviews. **"He spoke":** Rowe to Johnson, Oct. 26, LBJA SN. **"Lyndon will be":** Steinberg, *Sam Johnson's Boy*, p. 426.

"Political capital": Reedy to Johnson, Oct. 19, Box 3, PPMF. **Polls:** SA News, Dec. 9. **"Backing":** Fleeson, WS, Oct. 31. **"Outside of":** HC, Oct. 2. **"Reasonable":** HP, Nov. 13, attached to Johnson to Rowe, Oct. 28, LBJA SN. **"Here":** *New Republic*, Oct. 18. **"Some of":** NYT, Oct. 18.

"Unjustified": Reedy interview. After a visit to Rayburn, Corcoran wrote that "Sam was disturbed by the way he thought the William White story might upset the calculations of convenience on which the State Chairman—favorite son—plans had been built" (Corcoran to Mrs. Johnson and Johnson, Nov. 10, Corcoran Papers). **Joseph Kennedy episode:** Dallek, pp. 490, 491; Goodwin, *The Fitzgeralds*, pp. 780–81; Johnson, *Vantage Point*, p. 3. **"He never"; "malaria-ridden":** Goodwin, *The Fitzgeralds*, p. 780.

"I am sure": Cain to Corcoran, Nov. 14, Corcoran Papers. **"Lyndon":** Cain to Johnson, Nov. 19, Corcoran Papers. **"Back":** Reedy to Johnson, Box 3, PPMF. **"A Program with a heart":** AA-S, NYT, Nov. 22; *Baltimore Sun*, Nov. 23; WP, Nov. 25; WS, Nov. 27. A glowing description of the Whitney event is in Rather to Corcoran, Nov. 27, Corcoran Papers. **"It looks":** Nichols to Johnson, Nov. 23, Box 566, JSP.

"Is talking": Albright, WP, Nov. 27. **"The Democrats":** FWS-T, Aug. 24. **Met:** Hughes' representative was Noah Dietrich, one of his top aides. Reedy OH VIII; "Chronology," 1955, LBJL; Clark, Connally interviews. **Kefauver visit:** *Abilene Reporter News*, DT-H, Nov. 24. **Taking steps:** Pearson, WP, Oct. 19. **"I'd like":** Johnson to Stevenson, Nov. 22, Box 566, JSP.

"Lyndon Johnson Day": *San Marcos Record*, Nov. 25; Whiteside interview. **Who had cut out:** Caro, *Path*, pp. 197, 198. **"I knew":** Carol Davis and Lyndon Johnson are discussed in Caro, pp. 161, 172–73, 205, 294.

"With his feet": *Providence Bulletin*, Dec. 13. **Doctors' report:** NYT, Dec. 15.

"Every time": Johnson, quoted in Flora Schreiber, "Lyndon B. Johnson: Courageous Man of Action," *Family Weekly*, Feb. 2, 1964. **"Could scarcely"; "whatever"; "sensed":** Montgomery, pp. 54, 55. **"Of course"; "I**

never": Reedy OH VIII. **"They weren't:** Rather OH. **"Some of":** Flora Schreiber, "Lyndon B. Johnson: Courageous Man of Action," *Family Weekly,* Feb. 2, 1964.

Laugh: Montgomery, pp. 58–61.

"Let's each": Flora Schreiber, "Lyndon B. Johnson: Courageous Man of Action," *Family Weekly,* Feb. 2, 1964. **"Lyndon has":** Rowe to Lady Bird, Nov. 8; Lady Bird to Rowe, Nov. 26, LBJA SN. **Changing her excuse; "rediscovering":** Lady Bird Johnson, "Can You Prevent a Heart Attack?" *This Week,* Feb. 12, 1956. **"I firmly":** Irwin Ross, *NYP,* March 28, 1957.

"Her greatest achievement": Sidey, "The Second Toughest Job," *Time,* Jan. 14, 1985. **"Politics was":** Lady Bird OH, RBRL. **"Somebody":** Steele interview. **"Deliver":** Ross, *NYP,* March 28, 1957. **"If ever":** Mooney, p. 236. **"That's enough"; coattail; Scotch:** Mooney, pp. 236, 241, 244. **"Right behind you":** Tames interview. **"Don't let":** Steele, Feb. 22, 1965, SP.

"Next to us": Rowe, Corcoran interviews. **"He enjoyed":** Reedy, *Johnson,* p. 52; Reedy interview. **"Loved *people*":** Lady Bird Johnson, quoted in *People,* Feb. 2, 1987.

"I felt"; "He became": Jenkins OH. **"Never seen":** BeLieu interview. **"Now he *had*":** Connally interview.

29. The Program with a Heart

All dates are 1956 unless otherwise noted.

Opening day: *Baltimore Sun, NYHT, NYT, WP,* Jan. 4. **"Everlasting":** "Minutes of Meeting—Democratic Policy Committee," Jan. 5, Box 364, JSP, Reedy interview. **Press Club:** *NYT, WS,* Jan. 4.

Rowe's memorandum: McCullough, *Truman,* pp. 590–92; Reedy OH IX, p. 71; Reedy, Rowe interviews.

"I wish": Rowe interview.

"Napping": Scott OH.

"Very, very": Smathers OH.

"All know": Paul Douglas, "The Case for the Consumer of Natural Gas," *Georgetown Law Review,* June 1956, p. 573. **Taken the stance:** Elizabeth Sanders, *Regulation of Natural Gas,* pp. 83 ff; Walter Goodman, "Piping Hot Air to the Consumer," *New Republic,* June 27. **During those:** Edgar Kemler, "Democratic Giveaway: The Natural Gas Bill," *The Nation,* Feb. 4. **FPC reversal:** Richard Smith, "The Unnatural Problems of Natural Gas," *Fortune,* Sept. 1959. Each one-cent increase for the price of a thousand cubic feet of natural gas would, *Fortune* estimated, "pour some $70 million a year into the producers' pockets." **Superior oil:** *W-SJ,* Dec. 22,

1955; *NYT,* Feb. 22. **Texas Eastern:** Standard & Poor's Corp., *Standard Corporate Descriptions, 1949–1956;* Clark interview.

Michigan and Wisconsin vs. FPC: Richard Smith, "The Unnatural Problems of Natural Gas," *Fortune,* Sept. 1959. **Two committees:** *WP,* Aug. 8. **Funds collected by Maston Nixon:** "The Oil Lobby," *New Republic,* Sept. 24. **Distributed by:** Clark, Connally, Herring, Wild interviews. **"Once the lines"; "to eliminate":** Walter Goodman, "Piping Hot Air to the Consumer," *New Republic,* June 27. **Southerners split; had been intending:** Joseph and Stewart Alsop, *WP,* Dec. 12; McPherson, *Political Education,* p. 89. **"Lyndon was"; "transcended":** Oltorf interview. **Estimates:** Walter Goodman, "Piping Hot Air to the Consumer," *New Republic,* June 27, 1955.

Stakes: Paul Douglas, "The Case for the Consumer of Natural Gas," *Georgetown Law Reviews,* June 1956, p. 585. **"Very frankly":** "Minutes—Democratic Policy Committee," July 26, 28, 1955," Box 364, JSP. **"I wanted":** "Minutes," Jan. 5, 1956, Box 364, JSP.

"They sent": Oltorf interview. **Mayflower scene:** Connally, Dale Miller, Wild interviews. **Humble paying Clark:** Clark interview. **Patman was informed:** "The question has been raised. . . ,"undated statement but obviously 1961, G 242, I of 3, Drew Pearson Papers; Wild interview. **"I remember":** Miller interview. **"For twenty years":** Caro, *Path,* pp. 269–73. **"You know":** Wild interview.

"At whoever's": Brammer interview. **Allowed them to use:** Crawford and Keever, *Connally,* p. 62; Brammer, Clark, Connally, Jenkins, Miller, Wild interviews. **"He would call":** Clark interview. **"Harder"; Bridges at Huntlands:** Oltorf interview. **"I was asked":** Baker, *Wheeling and Dealing,* p. 86. **Patman's in New Hampshire:** *NYT,* March 8. **"The reason":** Connally interview. **Rubbed together:** Clark interview. **Patman sent Neff:** *NYT,* Feb. 12. **"I was":** Wild interview. **"He got":** Oltorf interview. **Enough to win:** Wild interview.

Outrage: *NYT,* Jan. 27; *Nation,* Feb. 4; *New Republic,* June 27, 1955; Fleeson, *WS,* Jan. 27. **Proclaiming:** Johnson, quoted in Stokes, *WS,* Jan. 26; *NYT,* Jan. 8.

Johnson had told: "Bob has gotten word to all our folks not to question the opponents in debate" (Jenkins to Johnson, Jan. 19, Box 268, JSP). **"That left":** Othman, *WDN,* Jan. 25. **"For the":** Stokes, *WS,* Jan. 26. **"The concentrated":** *Congressional Quarterly,* Feb. 7. **"In droves":** *WP,* Jan. 27. **"Never":** Pearson, *WP,* Jan. 25. "Douglas gave a (long) speech against the gas bill," Howard Shuman recalls. "No one came. Johnson wouldn't let them come" (Shuman interview).

Case's speech: *CR*, 84/2, Feb. 3. **"SENATOR TELLS":** *WP*, Feb. 4. **"You are":** Clark interview. **Vacant rooms; Connally knew:** Clark, Wild interviews. **"White-faced":** Pearson and Anderson, *Case*, p. 142. **"Sat paralyzed":** Reston Jr., *Lone Star*, p. 170. **"No attempt":** Connally with Herskowitz, *In History's Shadow*, p. 147.

"I think": Steinberg, *Sam Johnson's Boy*, p. 433. **"A vague":** AP wire, PA121PM, Feb. 4. **"Thus far":** *NYT*, Feb. 5. **A deliberate; "a complete"; no delay; "just":** *NYT, WP*, Feb. 5, 6, 7. **"Can ill afford":** *NYT*, Feb. 7. **"Casting aside":** *NYT*, Feb. 7. An indication of how anger at Case crossed party lines is given in a memo from Jack Anderson to Drew Pearson (Feb. 15, Pearson Papers): "Postmaster General Summerfield was commenting at a cocktail party the other day. . . . He said that Case was like the little boy at the Sunday School picnic who spit in the lemonade. (Except he used a stronger word than spit.)"

Hennings said: *NYT*, Feb. 7. **"The whisper":** *NYT*, Feb. 19. **"On reflection":** Russell Baker, *NYT*, March 11. **"If there":** James Reston, *NYT*, Feb. 20. **Johnson pulled:** Reston Jr., *Lone Star*, p. 170; White, *NYT*, Feb. 19. **Digitalis:** Childs, *WP*, Feb. 15; Pearson, *WP*, Feb. 14. **"I felt":** Reston Jr., *Lone Star*, p. 170.

Johnson-Knowland resolution: "S. Res. 205, In the Senate of the United States," in Report No. 1724, *Select Committee for Contribution Investigation*, March 29, 1956, pp. 1, 2, Box 117, LBJA SF. Krock, *NYT*, Feb. 9, 15; Pearson, *WP*, Feb. 16. **"Without known":** *NYT*, Feb. 15. **Letter:** George to Case, Feb. 7, Box 400, JSP. **"Mr. George just":** *NYT*, Feb. 9. **Johnson's meeting with Hennings, Gore:** *WP*, Feb. 16. **"Let's go":** *WP*, Feb. 16. Also see Pearson, *Diaries*, p. 356. **Attempt to gag:** Stokes, *WS*, Feb. 9. **"IT DOESN'T PAY":** *NYT*, Feb. 9.

"Bored in": *NYT*, Feb. 11. **Neff, Patman testimony:** Report No. 1724, pp. 3, 4; *NYT*, Feb. 12. **Ross declared:** Report No. 1724, p. 4; *NYT*, Feb. 18, 21; *Congressional Quarterly Almanac*, 1956, p. 474. **"This handful":** *Time*, Feb. 27. **"To get in contact":** *NYT*, Feb. 21, 29; *Congressional Quarterly Almanac*, 1956, p. 474. **"Had $2,500":** *NYT, WP*, March 1, 6. **"Inadvertently":** Report No. 1724, p. 6. **The list:** Report No. 1724; *NYT, WP*, March 1. **"Substantial":** *Congressional Quarterly Almanac*, 1956, p. 473. **"He was worried":** Mooney, *LBJ*, p. 97.

At one point; "He was not asked"; "scratching": *NYT*, Feb. 14. **"Only":** *NYT*, Feb. 22. **"Or was":** Krock, *NYT*, Feb. 14. **"Per-**

sonally": Richard Rovere, "Letter from Washington," *The New Yorker*, Feb. 25; *NYT*, Feb. 16. **It "was limited":** Report No. 1724, p. 2. **Suspended sentences:** *NYT*, Dec. 15, 1956.

Its "strangest": *WP*, April 9. **"Carefully circumscribed":** Childs, *WP*, April 4.

"A great stench": Ambrose, *Eisenhower*, pp. 302, 303. **"Doubt":** *NYT*, Feb. 18. **Ike's veto:** Ambrose, p. 302. Ambrose notes that "Eisenhower wrote private letters to a number of his oil-industry friends, including Sid Richardson, explaining his motives and assuring that he felt the 'questionable aura that surrounded its passing' had been created 'by an irresponsible and small segment of the industry.' " **"Since":** *NYT*, Feb. 18.

"Slippery": *Denver Post*, Feb. 16. **"The honor":** *WP*, Feb. 20. **"every reason":** *NYT*, Feb. 15. **"This city":** Reston, *NYT*, Feb. 20.

"Unfairly": *NYT*, Feb. 22. **"Saddle your horse":** *Time*, March 5. **"Has been":** *NYT*, Feb. 21. **"Liveliest":** *Time*, Feb. 27.

Bridges' maneuvers: *Congressional Quarterly Almanac*, 1956, pp. 743, 744; *NYT, WP, WS*, March 1–10. **"Boiling":** *Newsweek*, March 12. **"Bipartisanship":** *New Republic*, March 12. **McClellan's law firm:** "Memo to DP from Donovan," March 8, Pearson Papers. **"Evinced":** *NYT*, March 1.

"Which might": *NYT*, March 12. **"File clerk":** *WDN*, April 13. **Never asked:** A discussion of the committee's work is in *Congressional Quarterly Almanac*, 1956, pp. 743–48.

"The big to-do": Wild interview. **"As his first assignment":** "Report of the Special Review Committee of the Board of Directors of Gulf Oil Corporation, In the United States District Court for the District of Columbia, Civil Action No. 75–0325: Securities and Exchange Commission v. Gulf Oil Corporation and Claude C. Wild, Jr., Defendants," p. 64.

"Shirks"; "Insufficient": Richard A. Smith, "The Unnatural Problems of Natural Gas," *Fortune*, Sept. 1959. **$10.7 billion:** *Ibid.* **Value of Kecks' stock:** *NYT*, June 20, 1959. **Had Texas Eastern:** Richard A. Smith, "The Unnatural Problems of Natural Gas," *Fortune*, Sept. 1959; Standard & Poor, 1959–1960, p. 9051. **A billion:** Actually $1,045,943,000; *ibid.*, p. 1286.

"I don't": Smathers OH. **"I have had":** Cain to Corcoran, Feb. 8, "Lyndon Johnson," Thomas Corcoran Papers, LC. **Johnson's examination:** *NYT, WP*, Feb. 20. **"He could be":** Brammer interview. **Rowe told Johnson:** Jenkins, Rowe interviews.

Brown could not: Clark, Oltorf interviews. **"Quite sincere":** Evans and Novak, *LBJ: Exercise*, pp. 154, 155.

"Over a year": Evans and Novak, p. 157. "Clearly": Reedy interview. "I happen": Johnson to Meany, July 19, LBJA FN. "The Administration": Reedy, quoted in Miller, p. 189. **Malone vote:** Evans and Novak, pp. 158, 159; Miller, p. 189; Oliver OH. "Dog loyal": Mooney, p. 50. "Serious": Smathers OH. "Bob": Oliver OH. "Johnson fully": Evans and Novak, p. 159. **Refused:** Clark interview. "Was seated": Baker OH. "He arranged"; "infuriated": Mooney, pp. 50, 51. "I remember": Mooney OH. "No doubt": Evans and Novak, p. 159. "Put a lot": Baker OH. **Johnson's reaction:** Mooney, p. 51. "Senator Clements"; "Johnson tried": Baker OH. **Does not jibe:** Busby, Clark, Wild interviews. "Pointed out": Mooney, p. 51.

30. The Rising Tide

Six works are the basic sources for the general background on black voter registration and on the legal situation of black Americans and the civil rights movement up to 1960. They are Taylor Branch's *Parting the Waters,* John Egerton's *Speak Now Against the Day,* Richard Kluger's *Simple Justice,* Steven F. Lawson, *Black Ballots: Voting Rights in the South, 1944–1969,* Margaret Price, *The Negro Voter in the South,* and United States Commission on Civil Rights, *With Liberty and Justice for All,* 1959.
Bullock County incident: *Aaron Sellers et al. versus S. B. Wilson et al.*—United States District Court, Middle District, Alabama, Sept. 10, 1954, 123 F. Supp. 917, in *CR,* 85/1, pp. 13320–322; United States Commission on Civil Rights, Dec. 8, 1958, "Hearing Held in Montgomery, Alabama," pp. 267–81, 313–14, 321 (referred to as "1958 Hearing"); United States Commission on Civil Rights, *With Liberty and Justice for All: The Report of the U.S. Commission on Civil Rights,"* 1959; Price, *Negro Voter,* p. 11; Strong, *Registration of Voters in Alabama;* and author's interviews with John Holt, Aaron Sellers, and Gladys Sellers Washington.
"Voucher System": 1958 Hearing, pp. 176–77, 313–14.
Out of eleven thousand, five: *With Liberty and Justice for All, An Abridgement of the Report of the U.S. Commission on Civil Rights, 1959,* p. 73; *Birmingham News,* Sept. 18, 1960. "Was not connected": Kennamer, district judge, in *CR,* 85/1, p. 13321. "What's your trouble": Sellers, in 1958 Hearing, pp. 270–71; Sellers interview. "The white people": Sellers interview. **Only Wilson appeared:** *CR,* 85/1, p. 13321. "Told us":

Sellers, 1958 Hearing, p. 272. "I just": Sellers interview. "Whenever the plaintiffs": Kennamer ruling, in *CR,* 85/1, p. 13321. "We couldn't": Sellers, 1958 Hearing, p. 275.
"Fragments": William P. Rogers, in U.S. Senate, *Hearings Before the Subcommittee on Constitutional Rights of the Committee on the Judiciary,* p. 225. "Flashed": Kluger, p. 88. "The Jim Crow era": Kluger, p. 72. "Officially": Kluger, p. 9. "Blotted out": Bilbo, quoted in Egerton, pp. 402–03.
"Serious consideration"; **Only about 2 percent:** Henry W. Grady, quoted in Kluger, pp. 62, 233. *Smith v. Allwright:* Egerton, p. 380; Kluger, pp. 234–36. **15 percent, "the warning siren"; "success":** Egerton, p. 397.
"Things *would* be different": Egerton, p. 329. "A lot of": Hastie, quoted in Kluger, p. 294. *Life* covers: Egerton, p. 513. "Spreading sense": Egerton, p. 324.
"Stomach turned": William E. Leuchtenburg, "The Conversion of Harry Truman," *American Heritage,* Nov. 1991.
Brown v. Board of Education: General situation from Kluger. "I have": Kluger, p. 667. **Reed looking at Marshall:** Marshall, quoted in Egerton, p. 608. And see Kluger, pp. 7, 8, 9. **Knelt:** A vivid scene of two black preachers—the Revs. Wyatt T. Walker and Vernon Johns—kneeling by the side of a Virginia highway when they heard the news over the car radio is in Branch, p. 285.
Confederacy rose in rage: Egerton, pp. 615–18. Martin, *Deep South, passim;* Stan Opotowsky, "Dixie Dynamite: The Inside Story of the White Citizens Councils," series in *NYP,* Jan. 7–17, 1957. "Refuses to recognize": Brady, quoted in Martin, *Deep South,* p. 16. "A separate suit": Martin, p. 73.
"These laws": Egerton, p. 615; Kluger, pp. 702, 720, 723–24, 752–53, 778; Martin, pp. 72–73, 79–103. **Fifty-three Negroes:** Martin, *Deep South,* pp. 20–30; Halberstam, *The Fifties,* p. 430. **Jackson petition:** Martin, *Deep South,* p. 29. **1955 situation:** Martin, *Deep South,* p. 163.
Attempts to liberalize Rule 22 in 1947, 1949, 1951, 1953: See notes for Chapters 3, 7, 8, 19, 20. Also Douglas, *Fullness of Time,* p. 277. **Sixty-one separate bills:** *Congressional Record Index,* 1953, 1954, 1955.
"In view": Douglas, *Fullness of Time,* p. 281.
Rev. George Lee murder: Civil Rights Education Project, *Free at Last,* pp. 36, 37. "A real": Halberstam, p. 430. "Get the niggers"; "When I saw": Ruby Hurley, quoted in Howell Raines, *My Soul Is Rested,* p. 132. **Could "have been fillings":** Wilkins, *Stand-*

ing Fast, p. 222; Civil Rights Education Project, *Free at Last,* p. 37.

Lamar Smith murder: Civil Rights Education Project, *Free at Last,* pp. 38–39.

Gus Courts wounding: Price, *Negro Voter,* pp. 21–22. Senate Committee on Judiciary, "Hearings Before the Subcommittee on Constitutional Rights," 1957, pp. 532–63; *WP,* March 1, 1957. **Brownell said:** Brownell, *Advising Ike,* p. 204; *NYT,* Dec. 7, 1955. **"The nation's press":** Halberstam, p. 431.

Emmett Till murder: Basic sources are Halberstam, pp. 430–40; Whitfield, *A Death in the Delta;* Williams, *Eyes on the Prize;* William Bradford Huie, "Approved Killing in Mississippi," *Look,* Jan. 24, 1956; I. F. Stone's columns, collected in *The Haunted Fifties;* and Murray Kempton's columns in *NYP,* Sept. 19–26, 1955.

Talking "fresh": Whitfield, p. 16; Williams, pp. 41–42.

Taking Till away: Whitfield, pp. 20, 38. **"Mama, Lord have mercy":** Reed, a witness at the trial, quoted in Whitfield, p. 40.

"Went by custom": Smith, quoted in Whitfield, p. 21. **Identified by ring:** Williams, p. 43. **"Have you ever":** Mamie Till Bradley, quoted in Williams, p. 44. **"Is aroused":** Whitfield, p. 22. **"Jungle fury"; For many reasons; "Here":** Halberstam, p. 436.

"The boy who"; "How old": Williams, p. 42. **If he testified:** Whitfield, p. 38.

Unusual public officials: *The Nation's* correspondent singled out Swango and Chatham as "native Mississippians whose devotion throughout this occasion was to justice above states' rights and local customs"; Wakefield, quoted in Whitfield, p. 44.

Not a single Negro: Whitfield, pp. 44–45. **"There ain't":** Strider, quoted in Halberstam, p. 49. **Diggs incident:** Halberstam, p. 440; Whitfield, p. 37. **"Like a circus":** Hurley, in Raines, p. 132. **Wright at the trial:** Vivid descriptions of the trial are in Whitfield and Halberstam, among others, but best is Kempton in *NYP,* Sept. 19–25, 1955.

"An expression"; "humble": Whitfield, pp. 40–43; Stone, p. 107; Williams, p. 41.

"Sexy whopper": Stone, *Haunted Fifties,* Oct. 3, 1955. **"Your ancestors":** Carlton, quoted in Halberstam, p. 441. **Bottle of pop:** Whitfield, p. 42. **"If she tried":** Jury foreman J. A. Shaw Jr., quoted in Stone, Oct. 3, 1955. **"For the first time"; "We've got":** Whitfield, p. 333. **"The fear":** Moody, *Coming of Age,* pp. 121, 127. **"Shook the foundations":** Myrlie Evers, quoted in Whitfield, p. 60. **"Cried"; "Everyone":** Williams, pp. 43, 47. **"Covered":** Hicks, quoted in Williams, p. 51.

"The fact remains": *NYT,* Sept. 7, 1955;

Whitfield, p. 24. **"Both the wolf whistle":** Whitfield, p. 46. **"Scandalous"; "the life":** Quoted in Whitfield, p. 46.

"The other"; "needs a Gandhi": Stone, pp. 107–09. **"The same disease":** Whitfield, pp. 45–46. **"Evil, bigoted":** *NYT,* Sept. 25, 1955. **"A critical junction":** Halberstam, pp. 436–47. **"Emmett Till's River":** Quoted in Martin, p. 8. **"That river's":** Whitfield, p. 34. **"Controlled hostility":** *NYT,* Sept. 20, 1955. **"You lie":** Dan Wakefield, "Justice in Sumner," *The Nation,* Oct. 1, 1955. **"Historic":** Diggs, quoted in Williams, p. 49.

Start of Montgomery Bus Boycott: Branch, pp. 131–35.

31. The Compassion of Lyndon Johnson

"I'm not": Johnson, quoted in Goodwin, *Lyndon Johnson,* pp. 232, 230. **"The man":** Reedy OH III, p. 27. **"I'm telling":** Douglas, *Full Life,* p. 363.

"You're dead": Clifford and Virginia Durr OH.

In 8-F: Brown, Clark, Oltorf interviews. "He went *out of his way* to let them know he felt the way they did," Oltorf says. "He didn't wait to be asked." **Clark's "joke":** Clark interview.

"We were": Stibbens interview. **"Natives very much":** "LBJ World War II Diary," p. 3, Box 73, LBJA SF. **Reinforced:** Connally interview. **"Negro problem":** "LBJ World War II Diary," p. 8. **"I don't think":** Stibbens tape. **"I know":** Wicker, *JFK and LBJ,* p. 196. **"If we":** Sidey to NYK, Jan. 29, 1968, p. 4, SP. **Eurasian references:** Dugger, *Politician,* p. 312; *AA-S, DMN, HP,* May 23, 1948; Busby, Clark, Vann Kennedy, Lawson interviews. **"I talk":** Caro, *Path,* p. 70.

"He said": Hopkins OH. **"My God":** Hopkins interview. **Snake joke:** Dan White to Caro, April 2, 1986 (in author's possession); Bethke, Lon Smith, Stehling interviews. **"Boy, you":** Clark interview. **"I'll make you":** Bethke interview.

"We shall overcome": Caro, *Means,* pp. xiii–xix.

"No 'darkies' ": Johnson, *Vantage Point,* p. 155.

"Yet for years": Parker, *Capitol Hill,* pp. v, vi, 16, 23. When Parker's book was published in 1986, Jack Valenti and Horace Busby attacked his veracity. Busby said that although he was on Johnson's staff in 1949 and 1950, Parker was "no one I knew. I never saw him." Valenti called the book a "hoax." But Johnson aide Lloyd Hand, who was on his Senate staff from 1957 until 1960, "confirmed" to Lois Romano of the *Washington Post,* as she reported on June 14, 1986, "that Johnson had known Parker, and said he remembered Parker serving at Johnson's parties." John Connally confirmed to the author that Parker had indeed served as Johnson's part-time chauffeur and as a bartender and waiter at his parties. Walter Jenkins, during a discussion with the author—some years before Parker's book was published—about Johnson's use of "patronage" employees to supplement his own staff, mentioned Parker as an example.

"There wasn't": Crider, quoted in Dugger, p. 71. Description of picking cotton: Caro, *Path,* pp. 115–16. "A man-killing": Humphrey, *Farther Off,* p. 55. "Boy": Ava Johnson Cox, quoted in Caro, *Path,* p. 121. Working on the road gang: Caro, pp. 121, 132–33. "Did not": McPherson, *Political Education,* p. 138.

Lyndon Johnson in Cotulla: Caro, *Path,* Chapter 10 ("Cotulla"). "I saw": Goodwin, *Lyndon Johnson,* p. 66. "I could never": Dugger, p. 115.

"I'm gonna": Johnson–Walker Stone telephone tape, Jan. 6, 1964, citation 1196, White House Tapes. "No teacher": Caro, *Path,* p. 168.

Saving from foreclosure: Caro, *Path,* pp. 256–58. Brought electricity: Caro, Chapter 27 ("The Sad Irons") and Chapter 28 (" 'I'll Get It for You' ").

"The best": Corcoran interview.

"Hustle"; "It sorta": Dugger, pp. 187–88. "You have any": Elliott, quoted in Miller, *Lyndon,* p. 56; Monroe Billington, "Lyndon B. Johnson and Blacks: The Early Years," *The Journal of Negro History,* Jan. 1975, p. 29.

Choreographed: Interviews with Deason, Morgan, and one NYA staff member who asked not to be quoted by name.

"Easily": Akridge, "Brief Report by Mr. Akridge on the States in His Region," Feb. 2, 1937, Box 10, JNYA. "He always"; "I think"; " 'You can't' ": Brown OH. "Kept talking": Weaver, quoted in Miller, p. 56. "One who has proven": Bethune to Johnson, May 3, 1937, "Box 1, Correspondence B, 1937 Campaign," JHP, cited in Christie Bourgeois, "Lyndon Johnson's Years with the National Youth Administration," unpublished M.A. thesis, University of Texas, May, 1986, p. 73. "Whenever": Brown OH.

"He never asked": Deason, quoted in Miller, p. 56. "Johnson did": Goodwin, *Lyndon Johnson,* p. 231. "Mules": Durr OH.

"Daily": Jones interview. Wirtz accompanying Johnson: Deason, Jones, Rather interviews.

Told by NYA administrators: Johnson was to note that he had "discussed this matter thoroughly" with Corson on the telephone and "at some length" when he came to Washington to attend a conference of the NYA's state directors in August. On Sept. 17, Corson pressed him further. (See below.) "Outstanding": "Special Report of Negro Activities of the NYA of Texas . . . ," March 5, 1936, Submitted by Lyndon B. Johnson, Box 9, JNYA. "Large number": Corson to Johnson, Sept. 17, 1935, Box 8, JNYA. Johnson's letter: Johnson to Corson, Sept. 22, 1935, Box 8, JNYA. "Under": Corson to Williams, Sept. 25, 1935, "Copies of Internal Memoranda, 1935–1940," Box 10, JNYA.

Seven of the ten: McKelvey to Linville, Dec. 2, 1935, "Directors—File of Reports of State Directors of Negro Affairs," RG 119, E 120, NA, gives the names of the Negro Board members for Alabama, Arkansas, Florida, Louisiana, South Carolina, North Carolina, and Virginia. Tennessee's African-American Board member, Dr. Charles Johnson, was appointed March 9, 1936. Georgia's, Alva Tabor, was appointed Jan. 28, 1937 ("Reports of the State Advisory Commissions and Membership Data, 1937–1942," Box 2, RG 119, NA). Mississippi's two black Board members, William H. Bell and Laurence Jones, were appointed Feb. 11, 1937, and Nov. 10, 1939, respectively ("Report on Mississippi," April 1, 1941, Box 7, RG 119, NA). Alabama also had two black Board members (Bryan to Williams, April 10, 1941, Box 3, RG 119, NA).

"It does not": Bethune, quoted in Weisenberger, *Dollars and Dreams,* p. 130. "In those states": "Summary of Program—NYA," Feb. 26, 1936, Box 2, RG 119, NA. Ten of eleven: "Negro Representatives on State Staffs," "Director's File of Reports of State Directors of Negro Affairs," RG 119, NA. Did not appoint: No administrator for Negro Affairs was hired by the Texas NYA until Mr. J. W. Rice was hired in 1940 (Weisenberger, p. 135). Used as liaison: "Special Report of Negro Activities of NYA in Texas," March 16, 1936, Box 9, JNYA.

Not given adequate; "feels . . . that": Saddler to Brown, March 28, 1936, Records of the NYA, Records of the Director, Division of Negro Affairs "Inactive Files" Correspondence, 1935–38, Box 4, NA; B. Joyce Ross, "Mary McLeod Bethune and the National Youth Administration," *The Journal of Negro History,* Jan. 1975, p. 14; Stanford P. Dyer, "Lyndon B. Johnson and the Politics of Civil Rights, 1936–1960," unpublished Ph.D. thesis, Texas A&M University, 1978, pp. 37, 38; Deason, Jones interviews. "I was": Saddler to Johnson, April 9, 1936, Box 2, JNYA.

"We feel": Brown to Johnson, Aug. 3, 1936; Johnson to Brown, Aug. 12, 1936, Box 9, JNYA. **"What was said"; "Apparently":** Weisenberger, p. 135. Billington agrees with this conclusion. "He operated a segregated administration," he wrote, adding that "that was to be expected in view of the . . . times." And he wrote that Johnson "did not appoint blacks to paid supervisory capacities" (Monroe Billington, "Lyndon B. Johnson and Blacks: The Early Years," *The Journal of Negro History*, Jan. 1975, p. 31).

Further down: One of Johnson's white administrators, Joseph Skiles, says, "I don't think . . . that we had any black staff members of great stature" (Skiles OH). **Two top supervisors; every counselor:** Saddler to Johnson, March 28, 1936; Deason interview. And see Stanford P. Dyer, "Lyndon Johnson and the Politics of Civil Rights, 1936–1960," unpublished Ph.D. thesis, Texas A&M University, 1978, pp. 39, 48–50.

Mrs. Roosevelt insistent; Williams sought: Lash, *Eleanor and Franklin,* pp. 537–54; Weisenberger, p. 127; Lash interview. **"Certainly"; "while":** NYA Division of Negro Affairs, "Problems and Suggestions in Regard to the Operation of the Program Among Negro Youth," Nov. 1936, Records of the National Youth Administration, Box 118, RG 119, NA.

"In going over": Brown to Johnson, Jan. 22, 1936, NYA RG 119, Box 49, NA. Monthly racial breakdowns of the Texas NYA's overall programs can be found for only two months, March 1936, when the percentage of the Texas NYA's total aid distributions that went to black youths was 11.3 percent, and February 1937, the last month of Johnson's tenure, when the figure was 13.7 percent (U.S. Govt. Records, NYA, 1935–1938, Box 9, LBJL). "Special Report of Negro Activities of the NYA of Texas, in response to letter from Richard R. Brown . . . March 16, 1936," Box 9; L. B. Griffith to Johnson, April 27, 1936, Box 10, U.S. Govt. Records, NYA, 1935–1938, LBJL. (Administrative Reports: Jan.–June 1937, NYA 1935–38, Box 6, LBJL. Appendix to NYA Monthly Narrative and Statistical Report, ESTIMATED REPORT ON EMPLOYMENT . . . for Month Ending Feb. 28, 1937, attached to Kellam to Brown, March 10, 1937, Administrative Reports: Jan.–June 1937, NYA 1936–38, Box 6, LBJL.) **Scattered and incomplete:** NYA Administrative Reports, Boxes 5, 6, LBJL. **"Considerable difference":** McKelvey to Morrow, Jan. [29?], NYA Box 3, LBJL. Another possible criterion of fairness is noted by Stanford P. Dyer: "Under Johnson's leadership, Texas's NYA helped 18,000 high school

and college students stay in school. He also found employment on work relief projects for 11,000 out-of-school youths. Included in these numbers were about 3,600 blacks or about twelve percent of the total. At that time blacks made up a little more than fourteen percent of Texas's population; thus their participation was a little less than their actual numerical proportion. However, in 1937 black youths constituted over forty percent of those who qualified for NYA assistance. On the basis of need, then, blacks received far less than their proper proportion" (Stanford P. Dyer, "Lyndon B. Johnson and the Politics of Civil Rights, 1936–1960," unpublished Ph.D. thesis, Texas A&M University, 1978). A more detailed analysis of these figures casts more light on Dyer's "far less" phrase. When Lyndon Johnson became Texas NYA Director, there were 123,890 men and women between the ages of sixteen and twenty-five (the age group, characterized as "youth," that the NYA was authorized to help) on relief in the state (*AA-S*, Sept. 3, 1935). The best estimate available says that 40 percent—or about 50,000 — of this number were black (Weisenberger, p. 134; "Youth Population by States," Box 10, JNYA). Since the number of blacks receiving NYA assistance during Johnson's tenure seldom (if ever; for many months, the figures are unavailable) rose above 4,000, the NYA was helping, at the most, about 8 percent of the eligible blacks. There were, by this estimate, about 74,000 white youths on relief, and the monthly NYA roll included assistance to about 23,000 of them—or about 30 percent.

Treatment of Mexican Americans: Pycior, *LBJ and Mexican Americans,* pp. 30–35. **Not a single:** Johnson to Brown, June 15, 1936, Box 1, JNYA; and see Weisenberger, p. 142. **Classifying them:** Pycior, p. 31. **"Know how":** "Suggested Labor Supervisory Requests for Johnson City NYA-REA Building, n.d., Box 191, JHP. **"Categorized":** Pycior, p. 35.

"It was": Birdwell OH. **"Thus":** Pycior, pp. 31–33. **"Did not":** Pycior, p. 33; Deason interview.

"Real, though expendable": Dugger, p. 14. **Saw headline:** Caro, *Path*, pp. 389–95.

Austin housing problems: Orum, *Power.* **Cash payments:** Caro, *Path*, p. 407. **"It might"; "I think"; "I'll never":** E. H. Elliot, F. R. Rice, B. E. Conner, respectively, all quoted in Dugger, p. 197. **"Now look":** Dugger, p. 209.

"Tarnish" speech: *CR*, 75/3, Feb. 3, 1938; Pycior, pp. 37, 38. **"Because":** Keyserling, quoted in Miller, p. 72.

Story after story: Summed up in Orum, p. 133. **Every one:** *AA-S*, Jan. 25, 1938.

Strong opposition; Johnson named: Orum, pp. 133–35, 170; Clark, Gideon, Herring interviews. **"Lyndon was":** Brown, quoted in Caro, *Path,* p. 471. **"Serious flaw":** Dugger, p. 211. **Number of apartments:** Housing and Home Finance Agency, Public Housing Administration, "State of Texas—Congressional District No. 10—as of March 31, 1948," Box 70, LBJA SF. "War Projects, Vets Housing, Austin, Jan. 1946," Box 221, *Annual Report, Housing Authority of the City of Austin for 1950,* Housing Authority; Berry, *University of Texas,* pp. 52–53; Boxes 221, 273, JHP.

Assured: Johnson to Johnny Clark, March 4, 1948, JHP. **Voting record:** "Complete House Voting Record of Congressman Lyndon Johnson, by Subject, from May 13, 1937, to December 31, 1948," Box 75, LBJA SF. **"A farce":** *AA-S,* May 23, 1948. **"He just":** Izac, quoted in Caro, *Path,* p. 549.

"Hardly mentioned": Billington, "Lyndon B. Johnson and Blacks: The Early Years," *The Journal of Negro History,* Jan. 1975, p. 34. **"For U.S.":** *Houston Informer,* July 24, 1948, quoted in Dyer, p. 69. **"They had":** Clark interview. **"DO NOT RELEASE":** Statements File, Box 6, LBJL.

32. "Proud to Be of Assistance"

All dates are 1949 unless otherwise indicated.

Longoria's death: Si Dunn, "The Legacy of Private Longoria," *Scene Magazine, DMN,* April 6, 1975.
"The whites won't like it": "Statement," Mrs. Beatrice Longoria before notary public Hector de Pena, Feb. 9, Box 2, PPCF.
"The white people": Kennedy, quoted in *CCC-T,* Jan. 11. **"But in this case":** "Conversation on the telephone," Gladys Blucher before de Pena, Feb. 9, Box 2, PPCF. **Garcia's telegram:** Garcia to Johnson, Jan. 10, Box 2, PPCF.
"By God": Connally interview. **Arlington burials:** "Procedure on Joint Funerals Held in Arlington National Cemetery," Box 2, PPCF.
Johnson's "*immediate* reaction": Connally interview; Jenkins OH. **Checking Garcia's account:** Connally, "Memo for the Files, Re: Felix Longoria," Jan. 11; Connally, "Re: Felix Longoria File," Jan. 14, both Box 2, PPCF. **Johnson's telegram:** Johnson to Garcia, Jan. 11, Box 2, PPCF.
G.I. Forum rally: *CCC-T,* Jan. 12; Busby interview. **"HUMBLY GRATEFUL":** Beatrice Longoria to Johnson, Jan. 12, Box 2, PPCF.
Johnson dissatisfied with Jenkins' draft: His rewriting of the last sentence is on John-

son to Beatrice Longoria, Jan. 12, Box 2, PPCF.
Called in White; telephoned Winchell: Connally, Busby interviews. **"The State of Texas":** Winchell, quoted in Pycior, *LBJ and Mexican Americans,* p. 69. **"U.S. TO BURY":** *NYHT,* Jan. 14. **"G.I. DENIED":** *WS,* Jan. 13. **"A ringing blow":** *Sherman Democrat,* Jan. 16. **"A WRONG IS RIGHTED":** *Denison Press,* Jan. 24. **VFW wire:** Peter J. White, Cmdr., NYC Post 505, VFW, to Johnson, Jan. 13, Box 2, PPCF. **"It was impossible":** Johnson to Beatrice Longoria, Jan. 13, Box 2, PPCF. **"His reaction":** Connally interview.
"We began": Connally interview. **"I think":** Jenkins OH. **"Inspired":** Pycior, p. 71. **"The phones":** Connally, quoted in Pycior, p. 71.
First sign; "any answer": "Buzz," "Memo to Mr. Johnson," Jan. 14, Box 2, PPCF. **Kennedy and Ramsey statements:** *CCC-T,* Jan. 13, 14; *Valley Morning Star,* Jan. 13. **"It's too bad":** Buzz to Connally, undated, Box 2, PPCF. **Johnson understood:** Connally interview. **"No wild-eyed":** Caro, *Path,* p. 273. **"Realized":** Oltorf interview.
Voting practices in South Texas: Caro, *Path,* pp. 720–23, 732–33; Caro, *Means,* pp. 182–83, 321. **"You get":** Clark interview.
"WE DEPLORE": Three Rivers C of C to Johnson, Jan. 15 (two telegrams), Box 2, PPCF.
Brought him: "Statement," Carolina Longoria, March 7, before notary public J. Guadalupe Trevino, and statement, "On this 20th day of February . . . ," Guadalupe Longoria Sr., Feb. 20, both Box 3, PPCF. **Statement he wouldn't sign:** "The following is a statement made . . . ," Box 2, PPCF. **"His grief":** Stanford Dyer and Merrell Knighten, "Discrimination After Death: Lyndon Johnson and Felix Longoria," *Southern Studies,* Winter 1978, p. 421.
"They gave it": *CCC-T,* Jan. 15. **"There were reasons":** Kennedy, quoted in *Three Rivers News,* Jan. 20. **Blucher on extension:** Stanford Dyer and Merrell Knighten, "Discrimination After Death: Lyndon Johnson and Felix Longoria," *Southern Studies,* Winter 1978, p. 415. **"Latin people get drunk":** "Sworn Statement," signed Gladys Blucher, Feb. 9.
"The stigma"; "Gray was"; Connally interview and quoted in Pycior, p. 71. **"Dear Lyndon":** Chesnut to Johnson, Jan. 14, Box 2, PPCF. **Kennedy issued:** "Statement by T. W. Kennedy," *CCC-T,* Jan. 12.
Bexar resolution: "The Bexar County Central Council of the American Legion . . . passed the following resolutions," Jan. 27,

Box 2, PPCF; *CCC-T,* Jan. 28. **"Many who":** *DMN,* Jan. 30. **"Became"; "there were":** Connally interview. **He and Clark:** Clark, Connally interviews. **"They were":** Oltorf interview.

"Previous": Cunningham and Goebel to Johnson, *Three Rivers News,* Jan. 20. **Implored:** Smith to Garcia, Jan. 17, Box 3, PPCF. **"Honored"; "proud":** For typical letters, see Johnson to Chapter 76, Disabled American Veterans, Jan. 12, or Johnson to Sergi, Jan. 13, both Box 2, PPCF.

"According to": *CCC-T,* Jan. 16; Connally interview. **Successive drafts:** Johnson to Ramsey, Jan. 21; Johnson to "My dear Friend," undated, Box 2, PPCF. **"I did not":** Johnson to Rabe, Jan. 26, Box 2, PPCF. **"MY ONLY":** Johnson to Montgomery, Jan. 28. By February 3rd, Johnson would be putting it this way: "I am not, nor have I ever been, personally interested in where the body of Felix Longoria is laid to rest. I received a telegram from a constituent setting out certain facts which I investigated before I replied to that telegram. I told the widow of Felix Longoria his body could be reburied in the Arlington National Cemetery or the National Cemetery at Fort Sam. I did not recommend what Mrs. Longoria should do, and I have consistently maintained that it was none of my business where the boy was reburied, but it was a matter for the next of kin, Mrs. Beatrice Longoria, to decide" (Johnson to Floore, Feb. 3, Box 3, PPCF). By March 15, Johnson would be writing that all he had done was to arrange "for the burial of an American soldier killed in action in the National Arlington Cemetery upon the request of his widow. This is, as you know, the privilege of every soldier. All that I did was to comply with the widow's request by making this information available to her" (Johnson to Farley, March 15, Box 2, PPCF).

Johnson's actions during Longorias' visit: Busby, Connally, Jenkins, Woodward interviews. Johnson's Desk Diary, which lists his appointments, has no mention of the Longorias on February 15th or 16th, or indeed at any time during that entire week ("Johnson's Desk Diaries," Box 1). **"I don't":** Connally interview. Johnson's aides attempted to put the best face possible on his actions. For example, Busby says that Johnson didn't stand with the Longoria family and the other dignitaries because "he didn't want to detract from the family." Connally said, "He didn't go because his presence would have been interpreted as he was trying to make political capital out of the incident." Given the closeness between Johnson and William S. White, and the extent to which the *New York Times*

accepted White's evaluation of the newsworthiness of Johnson's activities, the contrast between the paper's coverage of the original story about Longoria and of the funeral may be significant. The original story was on page 1. The paper apparently did not send White, or any other reporter, to the funeral. Its story on the funeral—a small story on page 18—was a UP dispatch. Articles in other newspapers may indicate that Johnson attempted—successfully—to stay out of the public eye at the funeral. The story in the *New York Herald* said that General Vaughan "stood at the head of the two long rows of coffins." It does not mention Johnson. The Associated Press dispatch on the funeral—the article used by most newspapers—lists persons who attended, and includes Vaughan, Sierra, and the members of the Longoria family. The dispatch does not mention Johnson. (See, for example, the dispatch as carried in the *CCC-T,* Feb. 18.) Exactly where he stood during the service is unclear. The *Washington Post* said that Johnson "was joined at the graveside" by Vaughan, but the *Dallas Morning News* said Johnson "stood not far away as the family gathered at the graveside." Johnson does not appear to have given a statement to reporters. Many newspapers carried this quote from Vaughan: "I came here because of the stupidity of that undertaker" (see, for example, *WP,* Feb. 18). No newspaper, so far as the author could determine, carried a quote from Johnson. **"Because of":** Vaughan, quoted in Richard Zalade, "Last Rites, First Rights," *Texas Monthly,* Jan. 1986.

"Impressive ceremony": Johnson to Hector Garcia, Feb. 16, Box 2, PPCF. **Texas House resolution:** *CCC-T, DMN, AA-S,* Feb. 18. **"Truth or":** *DMN,* Feb. 17.

Clark's role: Clark, Oltof interviews. **"Without Clark":** Oltorf interview. **Oltorf understood:** Oltorf interview, confirmed by Clark, Connally interviews. **"He would ask":** Oltorf interview. **Hearings:** Pycior, pp. 72–73; *DMN, HP, AA-S, CCC-T,* March 10–12. **"We don't serve":** Sworn statement of Juventino Ponce, before notary public Hector de Pena, March 12, Box 3, PPCF. **"Every time"; "no one ever":** Oltorf interview.

"Your name": Gus Garcia to Johnson, March 16, Box 2, PPCF, confirmed by Oltorf interview. **"John":** Nichols to Connally, undated; **"I trust":** Johnson to Gus Garcia, March 18, Box 2, PPCF.

Majority, minority drafts: "Reports of the Committee Pursuant to H.S.R. No. 68, April 7, House Journal, pp. 1510–15. **"A slap":** *CCC-T,* April 8. **"I could not":** "Reports of the Committee, Minority Report," p. 1514.

"The two dissensions"; "a catalyst"; "into": Richard Zalade, "Last Rites, First Rights," *Texas Monthly,* Jan. 1986.; *CCC-T,* April 9. **Before that:** Hector Garcia, quoted in *AA-S,* Dec. 15, 1985. **"He never":** Connally interview.

"He hated": Connally interview.

Recounted: Pycior, *LBJ and Mexican Americans,* p. 80. **"Olé":** Pycior, p. 92; Reedy interview.

"He addressed"; **Corpus Christi boy; "I'm the helpful"; "He (Johnson)":** Hector Garcia OH. **Adroit:** Pycior interview. **"Garcia thought":** Pycior, p. 76. **"He answers":** Pycior interview.

Garza's judgeship: Garza OH. **Bravo's job:** Quezada, *Border Boss,* pp. 194–95, 201–05. **"Johnson had":** Reedy OH VIII, p. 104.

"Bracero" program: Goodwyn, *Lone Star Land,* pp. 35–38. **"Exiled":** Goodwyn, p. 35. **"Something must be done":** Torres to Johnson, Mar. 10, 1952, Box 233, JSP. **"Delighted"; "The people":** Johnson to growers, May 29, 1951; Looney to Johnson, July 13, 1951, Box 233, JSP. Looney was to recall that Johnson "abided by what you told him pretty much" (Pycior, p. 76).

In 1951 and 1952: Ronnie Dugger, "Johnson's Record—I," *The Texas Observer,* June 3, 1960.

"Flooded"; "Whereas": Ed Idar Jr., "To Whom It May Concern," July 6, 1952, Box 20, LBJA SN. **"I am sorry":** Johnson to Idar, Nov. 14, 1952, Box 20, LBJA SN. **"Opposed":** Brownell interview.

"Where else": Clark, Connally interviews. **"Johnson was aware":** Dyer, pp. 87, 88. **"Disappointed":** Pycior, p. 93. **"Believe me":** Johnson to Garcia, July 31, 1954, Box 66, JSP.

33. Footsteps

Bryant and Milam's story: William Bradford Huie, "Approved Killing in Mississippi," *Look,* Jan. 24, 1956. **Pride of their lawyers:** J. J. Breland, quoted in Whitfield, *Death in the Delta,* p. 54; Halberstam, *The Fifties,* p. 434.

"Day": Autherine Lucy, quoted in "Alabama's Scandal," *Time,* Feb. 20, 1956. **"Chased"; "murder"; Folsom's orders:** "Where Responsibility Lies," *New Republic,* Feb. 20, 1956. **"I could still":** Lucy, quoted in "Alabama's Scandal," *Time,* Feb. 20, 1956. **Trustees' action:** "Miss Lucy of Alabama," *Commonweal,* Feb. 24, 1956. **"God knows":** *Time,* Feb. 20, 1956. **At Moore's home; "All I could do":** "South Worries over Miss Lucy," *Life,* Feb. 20, 1956. **At La Guardia:** "Round

Two in Alabama," *Time,* March 12, 1956; "Segregation Victory," *Newsweek,* March 12, 1956. **Riot "worked":** Dennis Holt, quoted in *Time,* March 12, 1956; Branch, *Parting the Waters,* p. 181. **"Woke"; "They filed":** Quoted in Martin, *Deep South,* p. 39. **"Solid once more":** Martin, p. 41. Also see "Where Responsibility Lies," *New Republic,* Feb. 20, 1956.

"Come": Gayle, quoted in Halberstam, p. 556. **"To a largely":** Branch, p. 145. **"I'm not walking":** Quoted in Oates, *Let the Trumpet Sound,* p. 76. **"Every member":** King, quoted in Branch, p. 116. **"That's where":** King, quoted in Halberstam, p. 554. **"Just happened":** King, quoted in Halberstam, p. 561. **"Never given":** King, quoted in Oates, p. 78. **"Hate begets":** King, quoted in Oates, p. 79. **King's arrest:** Branch, p. 160; Oates, p. 86. **"Get up"; Johns dropping his dime:** Halberstam, pp. 544, 545.

"In every stage": Eastland, quoted in Oates, pp. 91–92.

Grand jury and indictments: Branch, pp. 168, 176–78. **"We have walked":** Abernathy, quoted in Branch, p. 173. **King in Atlanta:** Oates, pp. 92–94. **With a number:** Branch, p. 178.

Bombing of King's home: Branch, pp. 164–66. **"The remote calm":** Branch, p. 165. **"I owe":** Oates, p. 90. **A Gandhi:** "Many of the Negroes would liken the sight of King with his hand raised to the famous poses of Gandhi or to Jesus calming the waters of the troubled sea" (Branch, p. 166).

Press coverage of bus boycott: Halberstam, pp. 555 ff.; Oates, pp. 97 ff.; Branch, pp. 185 ff. **"The more coverage":** Halberstam, p. 560. **"Are you afraid"; "the kind of welcome":** *New York Amsterdam News,* March 31, 1956, quoted in Branch, p. 185. **"I went directly":** Edita Morris to King, Aug. 10, 1956, quoted in Lamont H. Yeakey, "The Montgomery Alabama Bus Boycott, 1955–56," unpublished Ph.D. dissertation, Columbia University, 1979, Vol. II, p. 606.

Injunction and King's trial: Oates, p. 102; Branch, pp. 192–94. **"I'm afraid"; "clock said":** King, quoted in Oates, p. 102. **"Yes, I am":** Halberstam, p. 562.

Heightened fury: Oates, pp. 108–09. **"Lord":** King, quoted in Oates, p. 110.

Dawson's political power: Lemann, *Promised Land,* pp. 74–75. **"Just one step":** Dawson, quoted in White, *Making of the President, 1960,* p. 232.

Train and bus stations: Lemann, pp. 15, 43. **Black migration to North:** Lemann, *passim;* Halberstam, pp. 442–55; White, *Making of the President, 1960,* pp. 203, 230–37. **"They went north":** Halberstam, p. 443.

"Money and dignity": Lemann, p. 65.
Twenty thousand, etc.: Lemann, p. 70.
Ninety percent: White, p. 231. A better job:
Reston, quoted in Halberstam, p. 442.
Kennelly and Dawson: Lemann, pp.
76–77.
"A new kind"; "these men": White, *Making of the President, 1960*, pp. 232–36; Carl Rowan, "Who Gets the Negro Vote?" *Look*, Nov. 13, 1956.
Democratic strategists: Branch, p. 192; White, *Making of the President, 1960*, pp. 232–34; Watson, *Lion in the Lobby*, pp. 355–56; Richard L. Neuberger, "Democrats' Dilemma: Civil Rights," *NYT Magazine*, July 7, 1957; Cabell Phillips, "Civil Rights Pose Hard Choice for Democrats," *NYT*, Sec. IV, April 18, 1956. Also such 1956 newspaper articles as *Amarillo Globe-Times*, Nov. 1; *WSJ*, April 6; *WP*, April 1; Stokes, *WS*, April 3. Thirty-five districts: Reston, *NYT*, July 24, 1957. "We Negroes": Rowan, "Who Gets the Negro Vote?" *Look*, Nov. 13, 1956. Republican strategy: *NYT*, Dec. 2, 1956; *WP*, May 14, 1955; *USN&WR*, July 26, 1957; Brownell interview.
"Republicans would": Minnich, LLM, Jan. 16, 1956, Box 12, DDEL. "Reaffirmed": Minnich, LLM, Jan. 24, 1956, Box 12, DDEL. "I did not agree": Eisenhower, *White House Years*, p. 149. "He had many"; "darkies": Ambrose, *Eisenhower*, p. 125. Stag dinner: Warren, *Memoirs*, p. 291–92. "I personally": DDEPP (1957), pp. 546–57, 555, quoted in Ambrose, p. 410. Not once: Kluger, *Simple Justice*, p. 753. Kluger, pp. 726–28, 753–54, has a summary of Eisenhower's attitude on Brown. In Ambrose, it's pp. 190–92, 304–06, 408. "to associate himself": Ambrose, p. 143. "I think": DDEPP (1956), pp. 736–37, DDEL; Williams, *Eyes on the Prize*, p. 38. "The President's": Ambrose, p. 409. "To stand": Kluger, p. 753. "Tremendous": Kluger, p. 753. "The people": Ambrose, p. 337.
Eisenhower and Till case: Ambrose, p. 305; Whitfield, pp. 70–75. Did not even respond: Whitfield, pp. 74–75. Lucy case: Ambrose, p. 306. On King case: DDEPP (1956), p. 335, DDEL. "A fine general": Wilkins, *Standing Fast*, p. 222.
"Strong": Harlow interview. "Compulsion"; "core beliefs": Ambrose, pp. 327, 125. Nelson story: Ambrose, p. 369. Had seen a chance: Lawson, *Black Ballots*, pp. 150–52; Manchester, *Glory*, pp. 769–70; *New Republic*, Aug. 12, 1957; *Amarillo Globe-Times*, Nov. 1, 1956; *NYT*, Jan. 8, 1956, July 21, 1957; Reston, *NYT*, July 24, 1957.
Brownell's attitude and strategy: Anderson, *Eisenhower*, pp. 14–27; Brownell, pp.

190–218; Brownell, Harlow, Rogers interviews. "Unbounded": Ambrose, p. 124. "Scourge": Brownell, p. 199. Had left instructions; "quite deeply": Brownell interview. "Our hands": Brownell, p. 219. Gave him permission: Ambrose, p. 304; Brownell, p. 199. "I initially": Brownell, p. 218. "Where": Cabinet Series, March 9, 1956, Box 6, DDEL. "After": Brownell, p. 219. "Another Charles Sumner": Brownell, *Advising Ike*, p. 219. "If someone": Eisenhower, quoted in Ambrose, p. 327. Keating maneuver: Anderson, pp. 40–41, 43.
Celler subordinating: Edelsberg and Brody, "Civil Rights in the 84th Congress," p. 5; Washington, D.C., Office, Anti-Defamation League of B'nai B'rith, Welsh Collection, File No. 4, "Civil Rights," Oct. 29, 1956; Bolling, Celler, Rauh interviews. "A model bill": Douglas, *Fullness of Time*, p. 281. "A dream bill": Rauh interview. Situation in the House: Hardeman and Bacon, *Rayburn*, pp. 418–21; Bolling, Brownell, Celler interviews. "He wanted": "only fair": Bolling interview. "Rayburn was for it.": Bolling, Rauh interviews. Anderson (*Eisenhower*, p. 47) says, "By things left unsaid and undone, rather than by any affirmative commitment, the Speaker had given his party's liberals a clear impression that he would not block the bill if it could be brought to the floor."
"I am sick": Unidentified senator, in *NYT*, April 8, 1956. Hennings' bills: *Congressional Quarterly Almanac*, 1956, pp. 463–64; Watson, p. 335; *NYT*, March 4, April 1, 10, 1955; Jan. 1, 12, 1956. And then: "Telephone call from Tom Hennings," March 19, 1956, Box 45, LBJA SN; *NYT*, March 4, April 1, 10, 1956. Exactly twelve: Edelsberg and Brody, "Civil Rights in the 84th Congress," Washington, D.C.: Anti-Defamation League of B'nai B'rith, Oct. 29, 1956, p. 1.
"I had special": Eastland, quoted in Lawson, *Black Ballots*, pp. 156–57; in Sherrill, *Accidental President*, p. 210; "Eastland Speech Excerpts," Aug. 13, 1956, NAACP, WB-134, LC, quoted in Watson, p. 338. "You are not required": Eastland, quoted in Whitfield, p. 35. "The one seat": *New Republic*, March 12, 1956. "Unthinkable": *NYT*, Feb. 24, 1956. "Maybe": *NYT*, March 4, 1956. Johnson's reply: Reedy, Steele interviews. "I had": Eastland OH; Watson, p. 338. Out of his way: Eastland OH. Unrecorded vote: *NYT*, March 3, 1956; *Time*, March 12, 1956. "A mad dog": *NYT*, March 5, 1956.

34. Finesses

All dates are 1956 unless otherwise noted.

"Southern Manifesto": *NYT*, March 12, 13. **Drafted by Thurmond, Byrd; edited by Russell:** Cohodas, *Strom Thurmond*, pp. 283–84; Fite, *Russell*, p. 333; Goldsmith, *Colleagues*, p. 51; *NYT*, March 13. **"One would":** Morse, quoted in Cohodas, p. 286.

"A dangerous, deceptive": Gore, quoted in Miller, *Lyndon*, p. 187. "Kefauver said, 'I just don't agree with it.' The Supreme Court decision is now the law of the land and must be followed, Mr. Kefauver said" (*NYT*, March 12). **"He had not been shown":** *NYT*, March 12. Johnson's formal statement said: "I have neither seen this document, nor have I been asked to sign it." "STATEMENT BY SENATOR LYNDON B. JOHNSON (D-TEX), MARCH 10, 1956," Box 423, JSP.

He had been present: *LBJ Chronologies*, 1956, p. 3. In his oral history interview with George Reedy, Mike Gillette, then Director of Oral History for the Johnson Library, said, "LBJ did attend a meeting for southern senators in Senator George's office in early February, I guess, and they did discuss the issues of segregation and interposition." Reedy replied, "Yes. I don't remember it at all" (Reedy OH VIII, p. 102). When the author asked Reedy if Johnson had attended any of the Southern Caucus meetings about the Southern Manifesto, Reedy said, "Well, I remember one where there was one heck of a fight, but I wasn't there." Asked how he knew about it, he said he had been told about it by both Johnson and Russell.

"You liberals": Humphrey OH III, p. 13. **Humphrey also said:** "He was very proud of the fact that he didn't sign it. Also, he used it" (Humphrey, quoted in Dallek, p. 496). **"Was, indeed":** White, *Professional*, p. 211. **"One of the":** Neuberger, quoted in Miller, p. 188. Reedy said: "I suspect that what he [Russell] sold them on was 'Hey, look, we might get a southerner in the White House, don't queer it.' He wouldn't use that kind of language, but I believe that's what he probably told them privately. But the public rationale was you would not ask the leadership to sign something like this" (OH VIII, p. 100). **"Russell was very":** Reedy OH VIII, p. 100. **"Anybody that signed":** Reedy OH VIII, p. 99. In his 1996 book, Robert Mann wrote, "An unabashed Johnson fan, Neuberger perhaps exaggerated the extent of his leader's valor" (Mann, p. 164). **"The real reason":** Fite, p. 336. **"He had to":** Stennis OH. **"In my opinion":** "STATEMENT BY SENATOR LYNDON B. JOHNSON (D-TEX), MARCH 10, 1956,"

Box 423, JSP. **"He believed":** *NYT*, April 22. **"No question":** Russell, quoted in *AC*, June 29.

"One hundred percent": Ellender, quoted in *San Antonio News*, March 23. **"One thousand percent":** Smathers, quoted in *Mexia Daily News*, March 12. **Almost every:** For Holland's endorsement, see *Richmond Times-Dispatch*, May 8; for Byrd's, *Williamson Star*, April 26; for Robertson's, Robertson to Symington, April 12, Drawer 115, Folder 11, Robertson Papers; for Price Daniel's, *NYT*, March 12; for Russell's official endorsement, *WP*, July 1; for a general roundup of the support for Johnson from southern senators, *Baltimore News-Post*, March 20; *WS*, March 25.

Hennings' bills: Hennings to Johnson, March 19, Box 45, LBJA SN. **"The Senate rules":** Eastland OH. **Eastland's tactics in committee:** Eastland, quoted in Watson, *Lion in the Lobby*, p. 347.

Rayburn let Bolling know: Bolling, quoted in Hardeman and Bacon, *Rayburn*, p. 419. And see Rayburn statements on pp. 420, 421.

Rayburn's tactics: Steinberg, *Sam Rayburn*, pp. 313–316. Hardeman and Bacon, pp. 410–20; Watson, *Lion in the Lobby*, pp. 344–45; Edelsberg and Brody, "Civil Rights in the 84th Congress," Washington, D.C., Anti-Defamation League of B'nai B'rith, Oct. 29, p. 5. **LBJ at Board of Education:** Bolling interview. **Rayburn's feelings, "Lyndon was asking"; "To my shame," etc.:** Bolling interview; Hardeman and Bacon, p. 419, say that not only did he not "press" in the Rules Committee, but that he "decided that his best course was to impede the bill's progress even more" to ensure that it didn't reach the Senate too early. **Stepin Fetchit:** Quoted in Watson, p. 342. **"The jig's up":** *NYT*, June 28. **"Rayburn senses"; "You'd better get":** Harry R. Sheppard (D-Calif), quoted in Hardeman and Bacon, p. 420. **"I started":** Bolling interview.

Tricking Douglas: Douglas, *Fullness of Time*, pp. 281–82; interviews with Richard A. Baker, Bartlett, McCulloch, Shuman, Reedy, Welsh. **"I don't know":** Richard Baker interview. **"Nearing its end"; "Badly divided"; "Even if":** Douglas, p. 283. **"Behind the scenes"; "searchlight":** Shuman interview. **"More remote"; "Only power":** Reedy, *LBJ*, pp. 109–10. **"Even if":** Welsh interview. **"Paul felt":** McCulloch interview. **"If":** Rauh interview. **"Might be wrong":** Edelstein, McCulloch, Shuman, Rauh, Welsh interviews. **"Allowed himself":** Miller, p. 191. Douglas says (p. 281) that Lehman was "overworked and ill." **Hill asking Mansfield to yield;**

"without objection": *CR*, 84/2, July 23, p. 13937. "My dear boy": Douglas, p. 282.

Humiliating Douglas: Douglas, *Fullness of Time*, pp. 282–83; Watson, p. 346; Othman, "Senators Stop the Calendar," *Abilene Reporter-News*, July 26; "Why Those Poor Senators," *HP*, July 27; Alsop, "Johnson Civil Rights Strategy," *DT-H*, Aug. 1. "As you know": Rowe to Johnson, July 24, Box 32, LBJA SN. Russell's tactic: McCulloch, Shuman interviews. "Sat there": *Abilene Reporter-News*, July 26. Of course it wasn't: *CR*, 84/2, p. 14161. "I object": *CR*, 84/2, pp. 14163, 14171. "So we are"; not at all: *CR*, 84/2, pp. 14161–62; *Abilene Reporter-News*, July 26. "There will not be": "In the Nation," *NYT*, Aug. 3. Johnson persuading Knowland: Alsops, *DT-H*, Aug. 1. "It is only kidding": "In the Nation," *NYT*, July 26. "Let us consider"; "I say": *HP*, July 27. "I can still": McCulloch interview. "All men differ": Russell, quoted in "In the Nation," *NYT*, Aug. 3. Watson wrote (p. 346) that "The defeat was a glaring example of how practical politics could overwhelm principles."

"The dirtiest trick": Rauh interview. "An effort": McCulloch interview. "Even my friend": Douglas, *Fullness of Time*, p. 283. "Push": Shuman OH, p. 142; Shuman interview. Douglas, *Fullness of Time*, on p. 283, gives a slightly different wording. Cried: Douglas, *Fullness of Time*, p. 283.

"Organized": Robertson to John L. Whitehead, Sept. 20, Drawer 114, Folder 14, Robertson Papers. For further documentation of Johnson's role in bottling up the 1956 civil rights bill, see Robertson to Ralph Widener and to Lindsay Almond, July 24, Drawer 113, Folder 58, and Drawer 40, Folder 14, Robertson Papers. Robertson wrote Widener: "The Policy Committee, headed by Majority Leader Johnson, has the privilege of scheduling what is to be taken up for floor actions and Johnson, of course, is against the civil rights bill."

"With a series": *NYT*, July 30. "He has brought": Rauh, quoted in *AA-S*, March 24.

35. Convention

All dates are 1956 unless otherwise noted.

"Professional prognosis": *NYT*, Aug. 2. Stevenson writing speech: *Newsweek*, Aug. 20.

"THE IRRESPONSIBILITY": Shannon, *SLP-D*, June 7. "Brokerage house": Rauh, quoted in *Waco Tribune*, Aug. 10. "No ardent advocate": Alsop, *WP*, May 9.

Southerners believed him: For example, *Richmond (Va.) Times-Dispatch*, May 8; *WP*,

Aug. 12. On the eve of the convention, John Sparkman told journalist Ronnie Dugger, "Lyndon has told me repeatedly that he does not regard himself as a serious candidate" (*Texas Observer*, Aug. 15). Southerners comfortable: Luther Hodges of North Carolina, for example, said, "Mr. Stevenson is a great person" (*WP*, Aug. 12). "Toward gradualism": Martin, *Adlai Stevenson and the World*, p. 248.

"Dramatic incident": Allen, *Abilene Reporter-News*, June 24. "I've never said": Rayburn, quoted in *Abilene Reporter-News*, Aug. 16. When another reporter asked him whom he was for, Rayburn said: "Johnson. I don't play them two ways" (*WP*, Aug. 12). Rayburn's assessment: Connally, Corcoran, Rowe interviews.

"A deep scar": Connally interview. "I'm going": Russell, quoted in *NYP*, Aug. 13. Spectre of "humiliation": Explaining just prior to the convention that he was not a serious, but only a favorite son, candidate, Johnson said that he didn't intend to leave his name before the convention too long. "I don't invite humiliation, and I don't intend to have my name up there without cause and purpose," he told Ronnie Dugger (*Texas Observer*, Aug. 15). "Ego reasons": Connally interview.

"Mine still hurts": *NYP*, Aug. 2. "He is sincere": James Saxon Childers, *Atlanta Journal*, June 21.

Byrd's pleading: *Texas Observer*, Aug. 15. And as late as May 8, asked if Johnson would be a candidate, Byrd could say only, "I think we'll have to wait and see" (*Richmond [Va.] Times-Dispatch*).

"It has happened"; "does not share": Rovere, "Letter from Chicago," *The New Yorker*, Aug. 25. "Was affronted": Ball, quoted in McKeever, *Adlai Stevenson*, p. 198. "Why, if": *Time*, Aug. 20.

"I am not"; "I'm going": Truman, quoted in *Time*, Aug. 20. Party insiders knew: *Newsweek*, Aug. 20.

"Get up": Kilgore interview. "Serious about everything": Johnson, quoted in *DMN*, Aug. 12, 19. "Very unlikely": *FWS-T*, Aug. 12. "Erased": Allen Duckworth, *DMN*, Aug. 12. "The best qualified now": *DMN*, Aug. 12. "15- and 16-hour": *Time*, Aug. 20; *DMN*, Aug. 12. "You don't always": "I'm opening": Truman, quoted in *Time*, Aug. 20. See also *DMN*, Aug. 19; *Newsweek*, Aug. 20. "Wide open": Connally, quoted in *DMN*, Aug. 12. "He thought": Corcoran interview.

Adlai's slip: Martin, *Adlai Stevenson and the World*, p. 348. "Big blocks": *NYT*, Aug. 11, 1956. *Newsweek* (Aug. 20) said it more strongly: "If the favorite sons failed to come to Stevenson's rescue, hundreds of southern del-

egates were planning to switch to Johnson."
Quick reversal: *Time,* Aug. 20. **Telegram:**
NYT, Aug. 11.

Johnson's belief: Evans and Novak, *LBJ:
Exercise,* pp. 234–39; Connally, Corcoran,
Jenkins, Reedy, Rowe interviews and OHs;
Mooney, *LBJ,* pp. 118–21; Oliver OH. **"For-
got":** Richard Rovere, "Letter from Chicago,"
The New Yorker, Aug. 25.

"Knocked"; "no talking": Corcoran inter-
view. **"Another new":** *Newsweek,* Aug. 10.
"He just": Rowe interview. **"Ambivalent":**
Rowe OH.

Johnson, Rayburn on plane ride: Albert
OH, SRL; Mooney, p. 119; Steinberg, *Rayburn,* p. 306; Evans and Novak, p. 235.
"Embarrassing": Steinberg, p. 306. **White
House briefing:** *Time,* Aug. 20; Johnson,
quoted in Ambrose, *Eisenhower,* p. 333. **"Persisted":** Evans and Novak, pp. 235–36. **"I
don't see"; "I haven't said":** Mooney, p.
119. **"It's a serious"; "a good many":** Rayburn, quoted in *NYT,* Aug. 13. **"No illusions":**
Mooney OH. **"I told":** Rayburn, quoted in
NYP, Aug. 13. **"I said you"; "I agree":** Rowe
interview, OH.

"One man": Rovere, "Letter from
Chicago," *The New Yorker,* Aug. 25. **"Let us
tell":** Lyle, quoted in *NYT,* Aug. 14. **"My
name":** *NYP,* Aug. 13.

Declining invitations: Steinberg, *Sam
Johnson's Boy,* p. 437; *Houston Press,* Aug.
14; *Wichita Falls Record-News,* Aug. 15. **"A
very odd":** Rowe interview. **"I didn't":** *HP,*
Aug. 17. **"Different":** *Wichita Falls Record-
News,* Aug. 15. **"While":** McGrory, *WS,* Aug.
15. **"Not unlike":** *DMN,* Aug. 14; *WF R-N,*
Aug. 15. **"Flown in":** *HP,* Aug. 14. **"Most
crowded":** *NYT,* Aug. 14. **Stevenson thirty,
Kefauver five; Johnson made sure:** *DMN,*
Aug. 14; *Amarillo Daily News, DMN, NYP,
WS,* Aug. 15.

Southern states maneuvering: *DMN,*
Aug. 19; Kempton, "The Last Hurrah," *NYP,*
Aug. 13; *Baltimore Sun,* Aug. 13; *WS,* Aug.
13; Connally interview. **"Asked him"; "that
firm":** *DMN,* Aug. 19. **Byrd, Battle maneuvering:** *WS,* Aug. 13; Kempton, "Last Hurrah," *NYP,* Aug. 13; *WP,* Aug. 14. **Georgia
maneuvering:** *NYT, Amarillo Daily News,*
Aug. 15. **"Until an":** *NYT,* Aug. 14, 18.

Believing Harry, Jr.: *WP,* Aug. 13; Kempton, *NYP; Wichita Falls Record-News,* Aug.
15. **"A very fruitful"; "Lyndon Leaves 'Em
Guessing":** *Houston Press,* Aug. 14.
"Biggest block": *Wichita Falls Record-News,*
Aug. 15. **Could not imagine; "Listen":** Corcoran, Rowe interviews. **"For one day":** Connally interview.

Reality: *DMN,* Aug. 15, 19.

"The old man": Kempton, "Last Hurrah,"
NYP, Aug. 13. **"Fooling around":** Breyhill,
quoted in *WS,* Aug. 13.

Finnegan's arguments: Evans and Novak,
p. 236; Martin, *Adlai Stevenson of Illinois,* pp.
348–49; Miller, *Lyndon,* pp. 197–98; *Time,*
Aug. 27; Rowe OH. **"Some of":** *NYT,* Aug.
15. **"Uncertainty":** *NYP,* Aug. 15. **Johnson's
confidence about Reuther:** Rowe OH, interview. **"The great fruit":** Kempton, "Last
Hurrah," *NYP,* Aug. 13.

"Hello, Sammy": Kempton, "Last Hurrah," *NYP,* Aug. 13. And see *Time,* Aug. 27. **"A
minority":** Williams, quoted in *WP,* Aug. 15.
Bringing the news to Johnson: Rowe OH,
interview.

Meyner's refusal; finger across throat:
Time, Aug. 27. **Southerners annoyed; "may
not":** *WS,* Aug. 13; *NYT,* Aug. 14, 15.

"Too defeatist": Truman, quoted in *NYT,*
Aug. 15. **"To confirm":** *NYT,* Aug. 15. **Bar-
gaining with Finnegan:** Miller, p. 198; Rowe
OH, interview.

"Fire": *DMN,* Aug. 19. **"Let there be":**
Waco News-Tribune, SAE, Aug. 17. **"*Had they
missed"*:** Mooney, p. 120. Mooney quoted in
Miller, p. 198; Connally interview. **"Without
a flicker":** *Waco News-Tribune,* Aug. 17. In
his autobiography, Connally wrote: "The
show was Sam Rayburn's doing. . . . Whether
Johnson won or lost, Sam Rayburn would still
be Speaker of the House and no one wanted to
offend Mr. Sam" (Connally with Herskowitz,
In History's Shadow, p. 133). For descriptions
of the demonstration, see also *Amarillo Daily
News,* Aug. 16, *SAE, San Angelo Times,* Aug.
17; Connally, Jenkins interviews.

"Lyndon, don't ever": Russell, quoted in
Oliver OH.

"Senator, are you": *Houston Press,* Aug.
16. **"It became":** Holleman, quoted in Miller,
p. 199. **Rayburn recognized:** *Waco News-
Tribune,* Aug. 17; *Texas Observer,* Aug. 22.

Puzzling over his actions: Rowe, Connally, Corcoran, Jenkins, Reedy interviews.
Because of Shivers: McGrory, *WS,* Aug. 15.
"I never could": Rowe OH. **"Made no
sense":** Connally interview. **"Explosion":**
Felix McKnight of the *DMN,* quoted in Crawford and Keever, *Connally,* p. 68. **"He hadn't:**
Brown interview. **"He couldn't bear":** Corcoran interview.

"I have not"; "I am not": *DMN,* Aug. 15.
"Reported ready": McKnight, quoted in
Crawford and Keever, p. 69. And Mike Monroney told the Associated Press that "he
understood Senator Johnson might now be
receptive to the (vice presidential) nomination. 'Don't count Johnson out,' he said" (*WP,*
Aug. 17).

"Go in": Rowe OH, interview. **Rayburn advising Johnson:** *Texas Observer*, Aug. 22. **"I saw":** Corcoran interview. **"I have never":** Rayburn, quoted in *Abilene Reporter-News*, Aug. 17. **" 'Go back' ":** Rowe OH, interview.

"Profanely": Martin, *Adlai Stevenson of Illinois*, p. 350. **"Mr. Sam"; "All right"; "Stay out":** Martin, *Ballots and Bandwagons*, pp. 400–02. **"Within minutes":** *Time,* Aug. 27. **"Under no":** *San Antonio News*, Aug. 17. **"I talked":** Kennedy, quoted in Evans and Novak, p. 238. **Humphrey first choice:** Reedy, quoted in Miller, pp. 199–200. **"Kefauver can't":** Rayburn, quoted in *Abilene Reporter-News,* Aug. 18.

"Al Smith"; "a wealthy": Hardeman and Bacon, *Rayburn*, pp. 404–05. Texas caucus is described there, and p. 104, and in *Texas Observer,* Aug. 22.

Clements withdrawing; "We're gonna"; "very grateful": *Texas Observer,* Aug. 22. **Rayburn told him; "use my name"; "stone-faced":** *Texas Observer,* Aug. 22; *Time,* Aug. 27.

"As Rayburn": Hardeman and Bacon, p. 405. **Johnson's talk:** *Texas Observer,* Aug. 22. **"We've got":** Pearson, *Texas Observer,* Aug. 29; *Time,* Aug. 27.

"Texas proudly"; "All right": *Texas Observer,* Aug. 22. **Scene in Texas delegation; "if we can't"; "We don't":** *Abilene Reporter-News,* Aug. 18; *Texas Observer,* Aug. 22.

"Lace": Ian Campbell to author, Dec. 27, 1989.

"Lyndon Johnson's": Rovere, "The Last Hurrah," *The New Yorker,* Aug. 25. **"Would have to":** *WP,* Aug. 17.

"Bloopers": Leslie Carpenter, *Abilene Reporter-News,* Aug. 18. **"Mystery":** McClendon, *Waco Tribune-Herald,* Aug. 19. **"What's?":** *Houston Press,* Aug. 17. **"Cellophane bag":** Pearson, *WP,* Aug. 22.

"A sectional": Krock, *NYT,* Aug. 14. **"Fantasy":** Reston, *NYT,* Aug. 14.

36. Choices

All dates are 1957 unless otherwise noted.

General background for this chapter is found in the following magazine articles: Douglass Cater, "How the Senate Passed the Civil-Rights Bill," *The Reporter*, Sept. 5; Tris Coffin, "How Lyndon Johnson Engineered Compromise on Civil Rights Bill," *The New Leader,* Aug. 5; Richard L. Neuberger, "Democrats' Dilemma: Civil Rights," *NYT Magazine,* July 7; Reinhold Neibuhr, "The

Civil Rights Bill," *The New Leader,* Sept. 16; Richard Rovere, "Letter from Washington," *The New Yorker,* Aug. 31; William S. White, "Battle Lines on Civil Rights," *NYT Magazine,* July 7; C. Vann Woodward, "The Great Civil Rights Debate," *Commentary*, October; "Washington," *The Atlantic Monthly*, March; "Purists and Progress," *The New Republic,* Aug. 12.

"Banker, preacher": Larry L. King, quoted in Steinberg, *Sam Johnson's Boy,* p. 443. **"Ferocious"; "if"; "Woodrow Bean":** Steinberg, pp. 443–45.

Depression: Mooney, *LBJ,* p. 122. **"In all fairness":** Lehman to Douglas, Aug. 10, Special File 224b, HHLP. **"I want":** Johnson quoted in Evans and Novak, *LBJ: Exercise of Power,* p. 119. **Johnson's post-convention thinking:** Clark, Connally, Corcoran, Jenkins, Reedy, Rowe interviews and OHs.

"To cultivate": Galbraith, quoted in Miller, *Lyndon*, p. 202. **"Frank, why":** McCulloch interview. **Rowe and Reedy:** Reedy to Johnson, March 30 (with attached memo, "The Liberal Line"); Rowe to Johnson, March 22 (attached to Reedy to Johnson, March 29), Box 420, JSP. **"Never known":** Evans and Novak, p. 104. **Schlesinger conversation:** Schlesinger, *Aide-Mémoire,* "Washington, March 30–31, 1957: Conversations with Lyndon Johnson, Joe Clark, David Bruce," pp. 1–2; Schlesinger interviews; Schlesinger, *A Thousand Days,* pp. 10–11. See also Evans and Novak, pp. 104–05. **"He is a man":** Reedy to Johnson, March 30, Box 420, JSP. **"I had carefully":** Schlesinger, *A Thousand Days,* p. 11. **"A good meeting":** Galbraith, quoted in Miller, p. 202.

Graham visit: Katharine Graham interview; Graham, *Personal History,* pp. 236–38. **Profile of Johnson:** Robert Albright, " 'Johnson Formula' Heals His Party," *WP,* Jan. 13. **"I know":** Johnson to Philip Graham, Jan. 14, KGP. **"Sort of"; Shooting the deer:** Graham interview; Graham, p. 237. **"Phil always":** Rauh interview. **"Pushing Lyndon":** Graham, p. 241. **"Completely"; "Looking":** Graham, p. 237. **"How Civil Rights Came to Johnson City":** Katharine Graham OH, pp. 36–37; Graham, p. 237; Graham interview. **Water purifier:** Johnson to Philip Graham, May 21, Box 101, LBJA SN.

"You certainly did": Rowe to Johnson, Dec. 21, 1956, Box 32, LBJA SN. **"I found":** Schlesinger, *Aide-Mémoire.* **"Will believe anything":** Rowe to Johnson, April 8, Box 423, JSP.

"What did?": Radin interview. **"Anguish":** Stokes, *San Angelo Standard-Times,* Dec. 8. **"Digging":** *NYT,* Nov. 10, 23,

1956; *WP,* Nov. 23, 1956; Eisele, *Almost to the Presidency,* p. 104; Solberg, *Hubert Humphrey,* p. 178. **"Johnson is a southerner":** Fleeson, *AA-S,* Nov. 12, 1956. **Diggs:** *AA-S,* Nov. 30, 1956. **ADA resolution:** Rauh, in Irwin Ross, *NYP,* Dec. 19. **National Committee:** *WS,* Feb. 27. **"A fight":** Lehman, in Ross, *NYP,* Dec. 22, 1956. **"All this talk":** Arvey, in *NYT,* Dec. 27, 1956. **"Some of":** Galbraith, quoted in Miller, pp. 201–2. **"A challenge":** *NYT,* Nov. 28, 1956.

"I don't think": Kirwan, in *WP,* Dec. 19, 1956. **"First blood":** Lincoln in *WS,* Dec. 12, 1956. **"Our fight":** Butler in *WP,* Dec. 14, 1956. **"Though similar":** *NYT,* Dec. 27, 1956. **"That he":** Krock, in *NYT,* Nov. 13, 1956. Not the point: *The Nation,* Dec. 8, 1956. **Herblock cartoon:** *WP,* Nov. 28, 1956.

African-American voting trend: Branch, *Parting the Waters,* p. 192; Henry Lee Moon, "The Negro Vote in the Presidential Election of 1956," *Journal of Negro Education,* Summer 1957. **"Of all":** Watson, *Lion in the Lobby,* p. 355. **"Not in the South":** Moon, *ibid.,* p. 227; Carol A. Cassel, "Change in Electoral Participation in the South," *The Journal of Politics,* Aug. 1979, p. 910.

"From every": Scammon in *New Republic,* Sept. 16. **The larger; Harlem and Chicago South Side trends:** Reston, "Politics and Civil Rights," *NYT,* July 24. **Boston trend; "even a 50-50":** Scammon in *New Republic,* Sept. 16. **"The Negro voter"; "Washington":** *Atlantic Monthly,* March 1957. **"Would automatically":** Mitchell, Sept. 9, 1956, Mitchell Papers, cited in Watson, p. 352. **Nixon in Harlem:** Mitchell, pp. 354, 355; Wicker, *One of Us,* p. 184. **"Seldom":** Mitchell, Nov. 11, 1956, Mitchell Papers, cited in Watson, p. 355. **Eastland as liability:** Neuberger, "Democrats' Dilemma: Civil Rights," *NYT Magazine,* July 7.

"It could": *USN&WR,* Aug. 16. **"the . . . dilemma":** Neuberger, "Democrats' Dilemma: Civil Rights," *NYT Magazine,* July 7. **Give us:** Reston, "Politics and Civil Rights," *NYT,* July 24.

"One thing": Childs, *NYP,* Aug. 1. **Brownell's enthusiasm:** Brownell, Rogers interviews.

Southern situation: Martin, *Deep South Says Never,* pp. 163–67. **"In recent"; "no prospect":** Martin, p. 167. **"We face"; "assembled":** Heinemann, *Harry Byrd of Virginia,* p. 345. **"Massive":** Heinemann, pp. 334–37. An overall account of Byrd's policy is in Heinemann, pp. 325–49, and Wilkinson, *Harry Byrd and the Changing Face of Virginia Politics, 1945–1966,* pp. 113–46.

Voting in the South: Price, *Negro Voter in the South*; Mendelson, *Discrimination;* South-

ern Regional Council, *The Negro and the Ballot in the South;* Fairclough, *Race and Democracy;* Lawson, *Black Ballots.* **Klan on the rise:** Martin, p. 157. **"Legislative hoppers":** Stan Opotowsky, "Dixie Dynamite: The Inside Story of the White Citizens Councils," *NYP,* Jan. 7–18. **Porgy, Red Cross:** Opotowsky, *NYP,* Jan. 7.

"A flag": Martin, p. 41. **"Are subjected":** Optowsky, "Dixie Dynamite," *NYP,* Jan. 7. **"Consistent and insistent":** Abram, quoted in *NYT,* Dec. 1, 1956. **"Solid once more":** Martin, p. 41. **"An upsurge":** *NYT,* Dec. 2–27, 1956. **Klan:** Martin, pp. 157–59; Optowsky, "Dixie Dynamite," *NYP,* Jan. 7, 1956. **Camden incident:** *NYT,* Dec. 29, 1956. **Violence rising; Brownell's attitude:** Branch, pp. 197–203. **"Resistance":** Martin, p. 169. "Most southerners agree," he concluded. "One, a liberal editor, said regretfully, 'It's gone now. The segregationists moved too fast.' Never? Never is a long time. But for so long that I can't see when." **Talmadge interview:** Martin, pp. 176–81. **"The supplanting":** Watson, p. 382.

Philip Graham memo: Undated, but attached to note, "This memo is very rough . . . ," Graham to Johnson, Dec. 20, 1956, Box 101, LBJA SF. Johnson's reply, on Dec. 22, is *pro forma*: "I have read and reread your memorandum a number of times and I am greatly impressed. . . . I don't know that I agree with every part of it, but it has a direction and an impact with which I am greatly intrigued and I am going to ponder it thoroughly." Johnson to Graham, Dec. 22, 1956, Box 101, LBJA SF. **Arguing; "perhaps":** Graham, *Personal History,* p. 238.

"Pope or God": Reedy OH IX, p. 71. **Rowe memos; temporizing:** Rowe to Johnson, Dec. 13, 21, 1956; Johnson to Rowe, Dec. 17, 1956, Box 32, LBJA SN. At the bottom of the typed letter, Johnson wrote in hand what he considered an important question about Carroll: "How does he feel about Johnson?" **"If he didn't":** Corcoran interview. **"Already knew":** Rowe interview. **"The issue"; "as a man"; "One thing"; "I knew":** Goodwin, *Lyndon Johnson,* pp. 147–48.

Almost impossibly: Description of Johnson's thinking relies on Reedy memos and on interviews and OHs with Clark, Connally, Corcoran, Jenkins, Reedy, Rowe. **"Some conservative":** Reedy OH. **"Unlimited":** Reedy to Gillette, June 2, 1982, p. 5, attached to Reedy OH XI. **Some liberals:** For example, Stokes, *WS,* June 20, Box 2045, JSP. **Among more realistic:** Including Corcoran, Harlow, Rowe interviews; *WP,* June 22. **"You got up":** Harlow interview. **"They unquestionably":** Reedy to Gillette, June 2, 1982, p. 4, attached to Reedy OH I. **Five since:** The House passed bills to outlaw the poll tax in 1945, 1947, and 1949; a bill to make the FEPC permanent and expand its powers in 1950, and, of course, the Brownell civil rights bill in 1956 (SHO). **"They couldn't send":** Talmadge, quoted in Martin, p. 180. **"I will never":** Thurmond, quoted in Cohodas, *Strom Thurmond*, p. 90.

"Out of nowhere": Reedy interview. Reedy remembered Russell's words slightly differently on other occasions. In an oral history interview for the Lyndon Johnson Library, he said that in Paris Russell had said, "George, maybe we can get this man elected President yet" (Reedy OH V, p. 12). He told John Goldsmith that Russell had said, "George, we'll make this man President yet!" (*Colleagues*, p. 52). In a letter, Reedy wrote that "During one memorable (to me) evening . . . in Paris, he confided to me that 'we can never make him President unless the Senate first disposes of civil rights.' " In this letter Reedy added that "Russell never went so far as to say to me that if he had to choose between accepting a civil rights bill or leaving the gap unbridged that he would accept the bill. But I had the clear impression that such a thought was somewhere in his mind" (Reedy to Gillette, June 2, 1982, p. 6, attached to Reedy OH XI). **"When they":** Oltorf interview.

Russell's reaction, Johnson's acquiescence: Solberg, p. 178. **"You broke":** Pearson, *WP*, Jan. 13; Solberg, p. 178. **"Now, Lyndon":** Eisele, p. 104. **"Senator Humphrey":** AP 11, 12, 15—"Humphrey," undated. **"In a few":** Solberg, p. 178. **"A flat 'No' ":** *WP*, Nov. 27, 1956. **Smathers scene:** Smathers OH.

Liberal meeting: Shannon, *NYP*, Jan. 2; *NYT*, Jan. 3. **Nixon's decision:** Childs, *SLP-D*, Aug. 1. **Nixon's maneuver:** Anderson with Viorst, *Outsider in the Senate*, pp. 144–45; *NYT, NYHT, WP, WS*, Jan. 5. "MEMORANDUM: It has been suggested," attached to Rauh to Wilkins and Aronson, Jan. 7, Box 44, Rauh Papers, LC; Rauh, Rogers, Schnibbe interviews. And see Mann, p. 183.

"A classic performance"; "calm": Shannon, *NYP*, Jan. 3. **"Vice Presidents":** *NYHT*, Jan. 5. **"We would then":** *NYT*, Jan. 3. **"Senator Russell suggested":** Howard Shuman, "Senate Rules and the Civil Rights Bill: A Case Study," *APSR*, Dec. 1957, p. 958; *NYT*, Jan. 3. **Johnson demanding recognition; Nixon's opinion:** CR, 85/1, pp. 9–11, 178–79; Howard Shuman, "Lyndon B. Johnson: The Senate's Powerful Persuader," in Baker and Davidson, eds., *First Among Equals*, p. 225; Krock, *NYT*, Jan. 4; *NYT*,

NYHT, WP, Jan. 5; Howard Shuman, "Senate Rules," *APSR*, Dec. 1957, p. 960; Watson, p. 359; Rauh, Zweben interviews. **"Their vice president"; "our big chance":** Shuman interview. **"Fait accompli":** Fleeson, *NYP*, Dec. 6, 1956. And see Robertson to Johnson, Dec. 1, 7, 1956, Box 53, LBJA SN. **"Disappointed":** *Amarillo News*, Jan. 9. **"He resented":** Schnibbe interview. **"I encountered":** Church, quoted in Miller, pp. 209–10.

Church wanted to follow Borah: Ashby and Gramer, *Fighting the Odds*, pp. 11–12; Carver interview. **"He arrived"; "was aiming"; Johnson had:** Ward Hower interview. **"The Leader's":** Carver interview. **Vote on Johnson's motion:** *NYT*, Jan. 5.

"Once again": *NYP*, Jan. 6. **Rovere:** In *The New Yorker*, Jan. 26.

Persuading the southerners: This description of Johnson's conversations with the southern senators is based on the author's interviews with BeLieu, Cresswell, Dent, Easley, Fulbright, Goldsmith, Guard, Harlow, Reedy, Steele, Talmadge, Van der Linden, Yarborough, and Zweben; on the oral history interviews of, among many others, Ellender, Ervin, Harlow, Hill, Rowe, Siegel, Smathers, Sparkman, Stennis, Talmadge, and Thurmond. With Reedy, Steele, and Yarborough, in particular, the author had them try to re-create, at length, the arguments they heard Johnson using to the southerners. William Jordan's perceptive analysis of the southerners' thinking was also helpful. **"Hang out"; "would erode":** Dent interview. **"Don't filibuster!":** Reedy interview. Doris Kearns Goodwin (*Lyndon Johnson*, p. 148) deals with this point this way: Johnson, she says, influenced "the action of others by persuading them to share in his apprehension of dangerous possibilities. Johnson determined that his first task must be to persuade the 'reasonable' southerners to abandon their support for a filibuster, by demonstrating that even if it was successful the only result would be a Pyrrhic victory for the South. Northern passions were rising . . . and would no longer accept defeat by filibuster; instead the attack would focus on the filibuster rule itself." Siegel told Miller (*Lyndon*, p. 209): "His approach to the southern senators was, 'Well, if you don't allow progress on this issue, you're going to lose everything. There's going to be cloture; and your opportunity to delay or to slow down and to bring some kind of order or change will be gone.' They recognized this was a possibility, and it had an effect."

Validity difficult: Reedy, in his books, *Lyndon B. Johnson: A Memoir* and *The U.S. Senate*, in his oral histories and in his interviews with the author, sometimes seems to feel that a filibuster could be beaten, and, at other times, that it couldn't. On p. 144 of *LBJ*, for example, he writes: "There was sufficient Southern strength in the Senate to kill this measure by filibuster. Legislative victory for civil rights was possible only if they were persuaded that the cost of successful obstruction would be too high." In his OH III, p. 15, he says, "I don't think a filibuster could have been broken because the southerners all by themselves couldn't sustain one, but they would have enough allies in the western states to have kept it going indefinitely." On June 2, 1982, he wrote an eleven-page letter to Michael L. Gillette, then Chief of Acquisitions and Oral History Programs at the LBJ Library, to clarify his views. In it (p. 4) he states that the senators "from the former Confederate states ... unquestionably had the power to defeat—through any fillibuster—any or all Civil Rights proposals and there was no prospect whatsoever of shutting off their fillibuster through a cloture move." And Reedy was also to write (in *Lyndon B. Johnson*, p. 84) that "His capacity to exaggerate liberal strength in talking to conservatives and conservative strength in talking to liberals was little short of outrageous."

No need to filibuster: Goodwin, *Lyndon Johnson*, p. 149. **"We're up against":** Dent interview. **"Felt":** Zagoria interview. **"Down deep":** Zweben interview.

"In private conversations"; "some leeway"; "he deliberately": Reedy OH V, pp. 10, 11. And during one interview with the author, Reedy said, "He now [by 1957] had the southerners under sufficient control that they understood that he had to do something on civil rights if he was ever going to become President. And if they had gone this far, they might as well go the rest of the way." In his oral history interviews with the Johnson Library, Reedy said, "I *know* that he was deliberately using the fact that he might be President as one of the ways of buying elbow room from the southern Democrats. That I know. Because I wrote too many memos that he used and too many speeches and everything else based on that assumption" (OH V, p. 13—italics in original). "He used this feeling; he played on it; this was a deliberate tactic of his," Reedy said.

"He was running"; "he made them think": Yarborough interview. **"Johnson would be":** Talmadge, quoted in *AC*, Feb. 20, 1959. **"Strom really":** Barr interview. **"I think":** Thurmond OH.

"Johnson felt": McPherson, *A Political Education*, p. 153. **"Johnson argued":** Goodwin, *Lyndon Johnson*, p. 148. **"We're talk-**

ing": Dent interview. **"Johnson deplored":** Mooney, *LBJ*, pp. 49, 50. **"You have":** Eastland to Johnson, Aug. 11, 1956, Box 43, LBJA CF. **Actively:** "Sen. Eastland ... yesterday put Senate Majority Leader Lyndon Johnson at the top of his list for the Democratic presidential nomination": *WS*, July 10, 1959. **Supported for presidency:** Wilkinson, p. 250. **Stennis:** *Face the Nation*, transcript, Jan. 6, 1959. **Robertson:** Robertson to Johnson, Aug. 29, 1958, Box 53, LBJA CF.

"At first": Talmadge interview. In his memoir, *Talmadge: A Political Legacy, A Politician's Life*, Talmadge wrote (pp. 192, 193) that when Johnson became President, "It came as quite a surprise to me that he would become a crusader for civil rights." Although Johnson "shifted his loyalties from the Southern bloc to the national party" after he became Majority Leader, "still, Lyndon seemed more of a follower than a leader on this issue. . . . *We thought that in his heart Lyndon was still one of us*" (italics added).

"LBJ's whole gambit": Dent interview. **"I think"; "these guys":** Goldsmith interview. **"Have been debated":** Goldsmith, *Colleagues*, p. 65. **"We'll do":** Byrd, quoted in McConaughy to Williamson, July 31, SP. **Anderson telling:** Evans and Novak, p. 24. **REPORT BEING:** *NYP*, Jan. 12. **"The Senate's":** *NYHT*, Jan. 12. **Even stranger:** *Newsweek*, Jan. 21; Douglass Cater, "How the Senate Passed," *The Reporter*, Sept. 5; "Washington," *Atlantic Monthly*, March 1957. **"Floor debate":** *Newsweek*, Jan. 21.

"This story": Russell's handwritten note on White's article in *NYT*, March 25, "Winder Materials 10, Civil Rights," RBRL. **"Dream bill":** Rauh, in interview conducted by Katharine Graham, p. 26. **Most hurtful:** Rauh interview with author; McCulloch interview. **"In the course":** Miller, *Lyndon*, p. 208. **"Frustration":** Reedy, *LBJ*, p. 111.

"Was hailed": *NYT*, Jan. 5. **"We got":** Shuman OH. **"In 1953":** Shuman interview. **"We made":** Douglas, quoted in *NYT*, Jan. 6. **"Raised":** *Time*, Jan. 21. **"Generation-old"; "As they":** *Newsweek*, Jan. 21, Jan. 14. **"There should":** *Time*, Jan. 21.

"Civil Rights": LLM, Box 2, Jan. 8, DDEL. **"No trouble":** Minnich, LMS, Box 4 (handwritten notes), Jan. 8, DDEL. **"No question"; "Unequivocably":** *CR*, Jan. 9, p. 312; *Congressional Quarterly*, Jan. 11, p. 61; Watson, p. 361. **Couldn't stop it:** *Congressional Quarterly*, March 1.

Hennings and Judiciary: Javits with Steinberg, *Javits*, pp. 324–26; Howard E. Shuman, "Senate Rules and the Civil Rights Bill: A Case Study," *APSR*, Dec. 1957, pp. 955–75, particularly pp. 961–65; *CR*, 85/1, pp. 6191–94; Mitchell to Wilkins, Jan. 22; Jackson, M. D., "Telephoned messages from Clarence Mitchell—Apr. 29," NAACP III A73 (Civil Rights Legislation), NAACPP, LC; McCulloch, Reedy, Shuman interviews; *WP*, Jan. 23. **"Have hearings":** Knowland, in Minnich, LMS, Box 4 (handwritten notes), Jan. 8, DDEL. **Eastland now:** *NYT, WP*, Jan. 23; *WS*, Jan. 22, 24. **"Very":** *WP*, Jan. 31. **"The soft-spoken":** Wicker, *W-SJ*, March 15. **"I will not":** *WS*, Jan. 13.

Length of sessions: Joint Committee on Printing, *Congressional Directory*, 106th Cong., S. Pub. 106–21, Washington, GPO, pp. 530–31. **"If you wait":** Reedy OH VII, p. 16. **"They'd come back":** Johnson, in Beschloss, *Taking Charge*, p. 85.

Senate would not: Johnson, quoted in *NYT*, May 1. **"Therefore":** Reedy OH VII, pp. 15, 16. **Administration's list:** *NYT, NYHT*, July 14. **"I am waiting": "Why can't?":** Morse, Chavez, quoted in *Time*, March 11. **"The 85th":** *NYHT*, Feb. 14.

Tone changing: Minutes, "Supplementary Notes," and Minnich's handwritten notes of Legislative Leadership Meetings, Jan. 23, 29, Feb. 5, March 5, 12, 26, April 2, Bi-Partisan Legislative Meeting, Feb. 20, "Pre-Press Conference Notes," March 7, Box 5, DDEL. And see *WP*, Feb. 15, *NYT, WP*, Feb. 19, *NYT*, Feb. 22, 27, 28.

Eastland's generosity: Best is Wicker, *W-SJ*, April 2, April 16; Pearson in *WP*, April 28. **"Sen. Knowland again":** Minnich, LMS, Box 4, April 9, DDEL. **"It is always":** *NYT*, April 11. See also *NYT*, April 23. **"In serious":** *WP*, April 28. **"Quite right":** Drummond, in *NYHT*, April 29. **"There is need":** *WP*, May 5. **"Everything":** Cotton in *WP*, April 28.

Johnson losing hope: Corcoran, Reedy, Rowe interviews. **"There was":** Reedy OH, interview.

"It is expected": "Legislative Leadership Meetings," May 1, 14, 21. **Hennings raised:** *WP*, May 5; Wicker, *W-SJ*, May 14. **Eisenhower's leadership:** *NYT*, May 23. **"Senate leaders":** *WP*, May 22. **"Still in control":** Wiley in *NYHT*, May 14. **May 13th exchange:** *CR*, 85/1, pp. 6782–84; *NYT*, May 14. **"Far from":** Williams, "The Legend of Lyndon Johnson," *The Progressive*, April. **Arvey interview:** For example, in *FWS-T*, May 26. **"Impossibility":** Reedy interview. **"More remote":** Reedy, *LBJ*, p. 109.

"A change": Bolling interview. **"Something changed":** Siegel interview.

37. The "Working Up"

Lyndon Johnson's need to believe in arguments he was making was explained to the author by, among many others, George R. Brown, Edward A. Clark, John Connally, Thomas G. Corcoran, Ava Johnson Cox, Sam Houston Johnson, Joe Kilgore, Frank C. (Posh) Oltorf, and James H. Rowe Jr.

"He was": SHJ. **"What convinces":** Johnson interview with Doris Kearns Goodwin, quoted in Goodwin, *Lyndon Johnson*, p. 124. **"Would quickly":** Talking about Johnson's "credibility problem" as President, Joseph Califano writes that it "was exacerbated because LBJ became the most gullible victim of his own revisionist claims." Citing an example of Johnson's coming "to believe" a certain story even though "what he was saying . . . was clearly not true," Califano writes that he "had witnessed the authentic increase in the President's conviction each time he recited it" (*Triumph*, pp. 174–75, and see pp. 99–100). **"I believe":** Reedy, *LBJ*, pp. 2, 3. **"He was an emotional man":** Clark interview.

" 'The problem' ": Kilgore interview. **"I remember":** Bethine Church interview.

A new story: There are many versions of Johnson telling it. This one is the version Johnson himself gave in his memoir, *Vantage Point*, pp. 154–55, 160. Eugene Williams, in his oral history interview, recalls Johnson demanding, "Gene, I want an answer." **Probably about 1951:** In his OH, p. 7, Williams says, "Then in '51, I would make the drive twice a year. . . . At this time, he asked me to take Beagle with us." But, Williams makes clear, although he explained to Johnson why he was reluctant to do so, and was excused from taking the dog, they still had to make the drive twice a year: "From here to [Texas] and back twice a year. . . . I would go from here [Washington] to the ranch and from the ranch back here. . . . I remember one night . . . I won't forget. I believe Zephyr was with us. We got into Knoxville, Tennessee, I guess, around ten o'clock. I guess it was one o'clock that night before we could find a place to sleep. You know, things like that. So that's most of the experience I had, from here to Texas and back on those kind of deals." Saying that Johnson's three black employees began making the drive to Texas "about 1950 or '51, I guess," Jenkins said that after they expressed reluctance to take Beagle, they no longer had to do so, but that they continued to drive the Johnsons' car back and forth each year. Asked how long they did so, he said he couldn't recall exactly but that they did so "all through the Senate period, so far as I can recall. And thereafter." **"I just wouldn't go"**: Wright OH, p. 7. She says, "I wouldn't go to Texas for ten years; I just wouldn't go." It is impossible to date her refusal exactly, but Jenkins says it came "quite early on, as I remember." **McPherson's description**: McPherson OH. **"Made him angry"**: Califano, p. 53.

A civil rights: Coffin, "How Lyndon Johnson Engineered Compromise on Civil Rights Bills," *The New Leader*, Aug. 5, 1957. **"Tirelessly"**: Mooney, *LBJ*, p. 99. **"Quietly"**: Mooney, *The Politicians*, pp. 268–69. **"Areas"; "They *were*"**: Reedy, *Lyndon B. Johnson*, pp. 112–14; Reedy interviews. **"A basic"**: Byrd, quoted in Miller, *Lyndon*, p. 434. **Lyndon Johnson realized**: This description of Johnson's feelings is from interviews with Connally, Corcoran, Reedy, Rowe, and from Cater, "How the Senate," *The Reporter*, Sept. 5, 1957.

"Just give": Johnson, quoted in Reston, *Deadline*, p. 307. **"Kissing their ass"**: Johnson, quoted in Humphrey OH. **"You felt this"**: Rowe interview. **"Break the virginity"**: Rauh interview.

38. Hells Canyon

All dates are 1957 unless otherwise noted.

Price too high: Reedy, *LBJ*, p. 114. **"Now completely"**: Reedy to Johnson, undated, Box 420, JSP. **Had to find allies**: Evans and Novak, *LBJ: Exercise*, pp. 141–42; Shuman OH.

The Hells Canyon issue: Drukman, *Wayne Morse*, particularly pp. 230–31, 267–68, 285, 302; Gunther, *Inside U.S.A.*, pp. 127–29; Smith, *Wayne Morse*, pp. 304–07, 343–47; "The Hells Canyon Controversy," *Congress and the Nation, 1945–1964* (Washington: Congressional Quarterly, Inc., 1965). **"Last year the governors . . ."**: undated, pp. 23–25, "Interior—Hells Canyon" folder, Box 288, JSP; Carver, Ward Hower, McCulloch, Shuman interviews.

McKay's "giveaway"; "shocking": Drukman, p. 230; Smith, *Wayne Morse*, p. 343; *WP*, June 9; *NYP*, June 21. **"Republican"**: Smith, p. 305. **"Tooth and nail"**: Carver interview. For an example of Senate speeches on the subject, see Mansfield's in *CR*, 85/1, pp. 9775–76.

"Irrelevant": Fite, *Russell*, p. 340; Wicker, *W-SJ*, June 22.

Secret deal: Merton Bernstein interview. **Long**: "I had voted against the high dam in Hells Canyon because Herman Welker had

supported my position in the Tidelands," Long OH II, p. 4.

Negro population of Mountain States: *The World Almanac and Book of Facts for 1956*, p. 259. **"I began"**: Johnson, quoted in Goodwin, *Lyndon Johnson*, p. 150. **Arranging the deal**: Fite, p. 340. **"With Herman"**: Long OH II, p. 6. **"Look"**: Siegel OH IV, p. 3. **"I need"**: Pearson, *WP*, June 20; Shuman, quoted in *NYP*, June 27. Pearson wrote in this column that "although Murray was tempted, . . . no deal was made." But Murray did, in the event, vote with the South despite his earlier support for civil rights. See, for example, Rowe interview, and *WP*, June 21. Steinberg, among others, says, "Russell now proposed a swap. . . . Five northern liberal senators agreed," and names Murray as one (Steinberg, *Sam Johnson's Boy*, p. 469). **Southern votes available**: Steinberg, *Sam Johnson's Boy*, p. 469; Rowe interview. **Johnson spelled out**: Smith, *Wayne Morse*, p. 344.

Russell agreed: Steinberg, *Sam Johnson's Boy*, p. 469. **"In return"**: Johnson, in Goodwin, *Lyndon Johnson*, p. 150. **Luncheon conversation**: Bernstein interview. **"Put together"**: Long OH III, p. 4. **As few as possible**: Ward Hower, McCulloch interviews.

Humphrey, Douglas, Eastland encounter: Javits, *Autobiography*, pp. 325–26.

Discouragement in White House: Pearson in *WP*, June 9. **"Prospects"**: *NYT*, May 23. **Morrow's memo**: Morrow Papers, Records Box 10, DDEL. **"Turn up the heat"**: clipping, June 6, Box 2030, JSP. **Rayburn's rulings, Republican moves**: *NYT, WP, NYHT*, June 14–22. **"Teaming up"**: *WP*, June 16. **"Don't"**: Russell, in *WP*, June 20. **45 to 39 vote; the very next item**: *CR*, 85/1, p. 9827. **Johnson voted with**: *NYT*, June 21. **"I desire"**: Johnson, *CR*, 85/1, p. 9832. **"A surprise"**: *WP*, June 22, 1957. **Analysis of votes**: "UNITED STATES SENATE VOTE ON PASSAGE OF S. 555. . . . June 21, 1957"; Lyndon Johnson's tally sheet, undated but with "Hells Canyon," written in his handwriting on top, both Box 1299, JSP; *WP*, June 22. Senator Arthur V. Watkins (R-Utah) said, "Civil rights yesterday had a lot to do with the vote today—more than most people realize." Wicker wrote in the *W-SJ* (June 22), "Southern Democrats apparently assured themselves of a trial by jury amendment" by their Hells Canyon vote. "Authoritative sources indicate that the Southern action was a *quid* for which they expect to receive a *quo* composed of a trial-by-jury amendment to the civil rights bill.

"Western Democrats handed southerners five votes—not enough to sustain their position but enough, as one observer put it, 'to let 'em know where the votes are.' A source within liberal ranks reported his belief that western senators would now deliver enough votes for a jury trial amendment."

Church's maiden speech: *NYT, WP,* other papers, June 22. **"Magnificent":** Ashby and Gramer, *Fighting the Odds,* p. 80. **"Boy orator":** *WS,* Jan. 11; quoted in Ashby and Gramer, p. 81. **Photograph:** *NYT,* June 22. **"It made him":** Ward Hower interview. **Only a temporary:** Church OH; Mann, *Walls of Jericho,* p. 188. **"If this bill":** Church OH. **"All credit":** Church to Johnson, June 22, Box 41, LBJA CF. **"If it":** Neuberger, *AA-S,* June 28.

"A vicious": AP story in *W-SJ,* June 22. **"No deal":** Mansfield, in UP story, in *W-SJ,* June 24. He also said he hoped "the author (Sen. Potter) will reconsider his position and retract a statement which is untrue on the face of it" (AP in *W-SJ,* June 22). **"Civil rights yesterday":** Watkins, *WP,* June 22. **"A deal":** Alcorn in *WP,* June 24. **"Fellows supposed":** *NYT,* June 22.

"Frank, I'm afraid": Douglas, *Fullness of Time,* p. 287; *Newsweek* (July 1) said: "In any event, the bill was not expected to be taken up by the House this session, and even if it passed there, President Eisenhower would certainly veto it." **"Look":** Childs, in *NYP,* June 26. **"Beat down":** *WP,* June 22. **"The action":** *NYT,* June 23. **Liberal caucus:** Drew Pearson described it in his *WP* column of June 22. His description is apparently based on his handwritten notes, which are found in Pearson Papers, Box G201 LBJL. The senator who gave him the information was apparently Morse, for a handwritten note (not in Pearson's handwriting) in the upper-right-hand corner of the first page says, "file—Morse." Douglas, describing the caucus himself, wrote: "I told Morse to his face that his action was unpardonable. If he had experienced an honest conversion from his earlier position, he should have informed me before taking the floor. Morse left the room in anger. The break was complete. . . ." (Douglas, *Fullness of Time,* p. 286). **"Authoritative":** Wicker, *W-SJ,* June 22.

39. *"You Do It"*

All dates are 1957 unless otherwise noted.

"It was Part III": Rauh OH. **Feelings of liberals and Republicans:** For example, *NYP* editorial, June 23; Stokes, *WS,* June 27. Brownell, Harlow, McCulloch, Rauh, Reedy, Rogers, Rowe, Shuman, Yarborough inter-

views. **"Racial integration":** *NYHT,* July 15. **As the Senate:** *WS,* July 4; Childs, *WP,* June 26; Stokes, *NYP,* June 27; *WP,* June 23, July 4; *NYT,* June 28, July 1; Alsop, *WP,* July 3; *Time,* July 1; Minnich, LLM (handwritten notes), July 9; June 27; July 2, Box 4, DDEL; Brownell, Harlow, McCulloch, Rauh, Reedy, Steele interviews.

Russell speech: *CR,* 85/1, pp. 10771–78. **Atmosphere on Senate floor as he spoke:** Mann, *Walls of Jericho,* pp. 192–94. Although Mann says that Russell spoke "in his usual low voice," this was not the case after he got to the Reconstruction portion of his speech, according to several persons who heard it, including McCulloch, Rauh, and Zweben, and others recall Russell's statement about putting "black heels on white necks," for example, as being delivered in a hoarse, shouting tone. **Two staff members:** Zweben interview.

Raising of discrepancies: "Hearings Before the Subcommittee on Constitutional Rights of the Committee on the Judiciary," "U.S. Senate, 85th Cong., 1 Sess, on S. 83. . . ," Feb. 16, pp. 210–20. Perhaps the most complete analysis of the Brownell-Young exchanges is by Senator Ervin in *CR,* 85/1, pp. 11333–35. Ervin sums up his view of them by saying: "The Attorney General did not want to be asked whether the President of the United States would be empowered to call out the Army, the Navy, and the militia, under section 1993 of title 42, to enforce the decrees the Attorney General was asking the Congress to authorize him to obtain without trials by jury, under section 1985 of title 42. . . . Mr. Young was merely asking the Attorney General a question of law. . . . But I [Ervin] was never able to get an answer to that question. . . . Attorney General Brownell, who was asked that question, but did not answer it, is the gentleman who asks for the vast power which would be conferred on him by the bill . . ."

"No intrigue"; "an accident"; "so many hands": "A spokesman for the drafting group," quoted in Krock, "The Part III Issue Made Clearer," *NYT,* July 12. Rogers told the author the "spokesman" was actually Brownell, and Brownell, in an interview, repeated the gist of the contention Krock quotes. **"Mysterious"; "on the surface":** Douglas, *Fullness of Time,* p. 288. **Russell and Young:** Young to Russell, June 17, Series III, A. Speech, Box 32, RBRL; *CR,* 85/1, pp. 10771–78; "Hearings," pp. 214–15, 224–25.

"A landmark": *CR,* 85/1, p. 10775. **"CHAMPION":** *NYT,* July 3. **"Subtle dramatist":** Watson, *Lion in the Lobby,* pp. 383–86.

"Senators": Woodward, "The Great Civil Rights Debate," *Commentary*, Oct. 1957. "A violation": Coffin, "How Lyndon Johnson Engineered Compromise on Civil Rights Bill," *The New Leader*, Aug. 5.

Eisenhower's press conference: Reston, *NYT*, July 4; *USN&WR*, July 12, Telephone conversation: Telephone conversation, July 3, AWNS, DDEL. "He said": ACWD, Telephone Calls, July 3, Box 25, DDEL. Supporting Brownell's contention are pp. 16–20 in Anderson, *Eisenhower*, which state that the first draft of the bill "said . . . explicitly" that Part III "could be used to initiate school desegregation suits" and that "the draftsmen wrote them as separate bills" and that it was at this point that "the Department's lawyers began constructing the intricate chains of double and triple reference that were to give their final drafts an extraordinary technical complexity." Support for Eisenhower's contention that he had not understood the bill's content is found, among other places, in his pre–press conference briefing of June 19. Summary notes state: "*Civil Rights*—President will say he is delighted it passed; very moderate bill, intended to persecute nobody. It was designed in the hope that all thinking Americans would see that it is the least that can be done" (DDEPP [1957], p. 357). Republican senators' reaction: Harlow, Rogers interviews. "I think": DDE to Swede Hazlett, July 22, AWNS, DDEL. "Had waged": Ambrose, *Eisenhower*, p. 410.

"Why": McCulloch interview. "So I could": Shuman recalls Douglas saying he should have been told "so I could [have been] prepared when Senator Russell brought all this out" (Shuman interview). "When": McCulloch interview. Not "going": Mundt, quoted in Lincoln, "The Political Mill," *WS*, July 25. Southern Caucus: Fite, *Russell*, p. 339; "The Rearguard Commander," *Time*, Aug. 12; McConaughy to Williamson, July 31; "A Round for the South," *Newsweek*, July 22; *NYT*, July 4. "Instead of: McConaughy to Williamson, July 31, SP.

"Given up": Corcoran interview. Life on the ranch: Rather, Stehling interviews. "I hope": "Lyndon Johnson, Civil Rights and 1960," Rowe to Johnson, July 3, Box 32, LBJA SN. Only one guest: July 4–5 page, *Appointment Book and Daily Memoranda*, 1957, Box 2, Desk Diaries of LBJ. Corky in 1937: Caro, *Path*, pp. 428–30. Telephone call to Ava: Ava Johnson Cox interview.

"Proceed": *CR*, 85/1, pp. 10983, 10988. "The price"; "did not": Mann, p. 199. "Eisenhower's invitation": *NYT*, July 4. "Aware": Evans and Novak, *LBJ: Exercise*, p.

132. "Impassioned, emotional, poured out"; Eisenhower-Russell meeting: Ambrose, p. 408. "Poured out": "Georgia Giant," quoted in Goldsmith, *Colleagues*, p. 61. "Couldn't say": Russell, quoted in *WS*, July 10. "Indicated": Robertson to Jones, July 11, Dr. 45, File 2, Legislative Files, AWRP, College of William and Mary. "Not at all": ACWD, 7/10, DDEL.

Johnson's visit: Harlow interview. "Become worried": Brownell interview. "I had tried"; "Lyndon Johnson went"; He had the votes": Brownell, *Advising Ike*, pp. 223–25; confirmed by Rogers interview. Brownell, in his memoir, goes so far as to concede that "Eisenhower may also have had some reservations (unexpressed to me) about granting power in such broad terms to the attorney general." If, however, Brownell genuinely felt that the President's reservations were "unexpressed," he hadn't been listening carefully to presidential statements such as the one of July 3 reported by Whitman above. Brownell says he "had tried to assure the President otherwise, but Senators Richard Russell and Lyndon Johnson undoubtedly pressed this point in their conversations with him during this period" (*Advising Ike*, p. 225). President made his position: Evans and Novak, p. 133. "Well, no": DDEPP (1957), pp. 546–47, 555.

Could be flouted: For example, *Time*, July 29. And see *Time*, July 22; Harlow interview. "It was just": Rauh interview. The day at Glen Welby: Graham, *Personal History*, p. 241; Rauh OH, Graham OH and her OH with Rauh, Rauh interview.

"To enable": Knowland, in *CR*, 85/1, p. 10986. "Merely": Douglas, *CR*, 85/1, p. 10988. "Will pass": Nixon, in *NYP*, July 9. "We'll win": Adams, quoted in Mann, p. 198. "He expected": Legislative Leaders Meeting, July 16, pp. 4–7, DDEPP. A cold calculation: Harlow, Rauh interviews. "Will not be": *NYT*, July 9.

"The leader of": For example, *NYT*, July 11, 14, 17, 25. Journalists applauded: For example, *NYHT*, July 18; Drummond, *NYHT*, July 15; *Philadelphia Inquirer*, July 16; *WP*, July 14; *WS*, July 14. "Is likely": Evans in *NYHT*, July 9. "At least": *NYT*, July 9. "Speculation": *NYT*, July 11.

Knowland's predictions: *NYT*, July 10. "Justified": Russell, *CR*, 85/1, p. 10989. The *CR* does not show the second "We will resist," but Albright (*WP*, July 9) quotes him as likening the South "to a chained bear being poked with a pole and ordered to dance" and saying: "we will resist—we will resist. We will explain and discuss the issues involved in this bill until each and every Senator fully understands them in all their implications . . . You may call it a filibuster if you wish." **"Became apparent"; "I don't":** Reedy OH III. **"Until the snow":** Russell, quoted in *WS*, July 10.

Johnson's fears: Reedy, Rowe interviews; Reedy OH. **Rising:** *CR*, 85/1, pp. 10983, 10985; William White, *NYT*, July 9. **Niagara Dam pending business:** Johnson, *CR*, 85/1, pp. 10963, 10964. **"I should like":** Johnson, *CR*, 85/1, p. 10983. **Protest:** Javits, Ives, and Kerr, *CR*, 85/1, pp. 10983–85, July 9, 10. **"Folded his arms":** *NYT*, July 9. **Declined:** Tames interview.

The gulf: Stennis, McNamara, Javits, Knowland in *CR*, 85/1, pp. 11311–313. **"Increasingly":** *NYP*, July 12. **"A rape":** Ervin, in *CR*, 85/1, p. 11333. **A "new gestapo":** Johnston, *CR*, 85/1, p. 11335. **"Cunningly devised":** Eastland, *CR*, 85/1, pp. 11347–53. **"Let us all":** Hill, *CR*, 85/1, p. 11365. **Case:** *CR*, 85/1, p. 11346. **"No amendments":** Knowland, in *NYP*, July 12.

Noticed a figure, realized: Mann, p. 202; Anderson OH; Reedy interview. **"I'm afraid"; "My principal":** Anderson with Viorst, *Outsider in the Senate*, p. 129. **"Didn't like":** Busby interview. **Defeat as Agriculture Secretary:** Howard E. Shuman, "Lyndon B. Johnson, The Senate's Powerful Persuader," in Baker and Davidson, eds., *First Among Equals*, pp. 211, 234; Shuman, Wood interviews. **"I took it":** Anderson with Viorst, p. 129. **It was going:** Anderson OH. **"I wouldn't get"; "Knowland seemed":** Anderson with Viorst, pp. 147, 146. **"Hopeless"; "Determined"; "Just sat":** Anderson OH. **"Hints"; "They seemed"; "It seemed clear":** Anderson with Viorst, pp. 146, 147. **"They were"; "I thought":** Anderson OH.

His tinkering: Anderson's handwritten changes are on his copies of H.R. 6127 as it was printed and placed on his desk—National Archives Record Group 46, Sen. 54-A-C2, Bill Files, Calendar No. 485, H.R. 6127, NA. **"Curious":** Anderson OH. **"You do it"; "How can I?":** Evans and Novak, p. 131. Goldsmith, p. 62, says: "Anderson, as a supporter of the bill, was reluctant to take the lead." **"Get a Republican":** Anderson OH; Reedy, Steele, Wood interviews. Although some accounts, such as Mann, p. 202, say that "Anderson found two respected Republican moderates," Aiken and Francis Case of South Dakota, in fact, Aiken was the key, as Anderson himself said ("I went to George Aiken, whom I admire greatly, and asked him if he would join in such a plan") and Case came along later (Anderson and Viorst, *Outsider in the Senate*, p. 147); Anderson OH. The role of

Case, not nearly as respected a figure in the Senate as Aiken, was not, in fact, particularly significant. When Anderson introduced his amendment, he said he was doing so jointly with Aiken; he never even mentioned Case's name (*CR*, 85/1, p. 11826). **Johnson meant:** Evans and Novak, pp. 131–32. Anderson, in his memoir, says that he himself thought of going to Aiken, and only thereafter "went to see Lyndon Johnson" to tell him "my plan" (Anderson and Viorst, p. 147). But Anderson appears to be giving himself too much credit. His version is not accepted by others familiar with the sequence. And in his oral history, Anderson himself said, "He thought I should get a really good Republican to join with me." Also see Steinberg, *Sam Johnson's Boy*, p. 471. **"Well, I believe":** Aiken, quoted in Anderson and Viorst, p. 147.

Russell's confidence: He called Anderson's amendment "highly encouraging" because "Senator Anderson is an acknowledged leader of the civil rights forces" (*Baltimore Sun*, July 15). **Johnson's announcement:** *NYT*, July 12. **"I hope":** Evans, *NYHT*, July 12. **Russell amenable:** *NYT*, July 12.

Southerners agree to UCA: " 'We have endeavored and shall continue to endeavor to comport ourselves as responsible men,' Mr. Russell told the Senate in accepting the" UCA, *NYT*, July 13. The southerners' agreement "was a measure of the changed atmosphere in the Senate today," *NYHT*, July 13. **Johnson introduces UCA:** *NYT*, July 13.

"I do this": Anderson, *CR*, 85/1, p. 11826. **"We who support":** Aiken, *CR*, 85/1, p. 11827. **A "modern":** Byrd, *NYT*, July 17. **"Gold Dust Twins":** Watson, p. 398, Rauh interview. **71 to 18:** Kempton, *NYP*, July 17. **"Not to be":** *NYT*, *Baltimore Sun*, July 17. **Leaning across:** *Newsweek*, July 29.

"Parliamentary": *CR*, 85/1, p. 11838. **Knowland outsmarted:** Rauh, Riddick interviews. **"At the last":** *Time*, Aug. 5. Roy Wilkins was to estimate that between 57 and 60 votes were available to support the amendment had they been needed. Wilkins to Morsell, July 23, NAACP III B-55, LC, quoted in Watson, p. 388. **"Strange":** *Baltimore Sun*, July 25.

"I believe": *CR*, 85/1, p. 12714, quoted in Mann, p. 204. **"The adoption":** *NYT*, July 25. **"This is not":** *CR*, 85/1, p. 12549. **"He won; we didn't":** Wilkins, quoted in Miller, *Lyndon*, p. 209. Clarence Mitchell called the passage of the Anderson-Aiken Amendment "a direct hit amidships" (Watson, p. 389). **"The filibuster":** Rauh interview. **"Almost literally":** Siegel OH. **"No single":** Kempton, *NYP*, July 17.

40. Yeas and Nays

All dates are 1957 unless otherwise noted.

Analysis of Part IV: Ambrose, *Eisenhower*, pp. 407–10; Dulles, *Civil Rights Commission;* Goldsmith, *Colleagues*, pp. 62–66; Lawson, *Black Ballots*, Chapter 7; Mann, *Walls of Jericho*, pp. 200–24; U.S. Congress, Senate, Committee on the Judiciary, "Hearings Before the Subcommittee on Constitutional Rights of the Committee on the Judiciary," Civil Rights, 1957: 85/1, Vol. 71, particularly pp. 55–67; Paul Douglas, "Politics and the Passage of the Civil Rights Act of 1957," *CR*, 85/1, p. 100; *Congressional Digest*, April 1957; Eisenhower, Papers as President, LMS, 1957, Box 2; Press Conference Series, Box 6; Cabinet Series, Boxes 4, 9; Ann Whitman Diary Series, Box 9, DDEL; Carl Auerbach, "Jury Trials and Civil Rights," *The New Leader*, April 29. **"The only reason":** Ervin, *CR*, 85/1, p. 10995. **"Southern senators":** Reedy interview. In his memoir, *Lyndon B. Johnson*, Reedy wrote (p. 118) that the southerners "could go home and say to their constituents: 'They can't brand you a criminal now without a trial before a jury of your fellow citizens.'" **"Sacred":** See, for example, Ernest K. Lindley, "Another to Ponder," *Newsweek*, July 29.

O'Mahoney in 1937: Alsop and Catledge, *168 Days*, pp. 87, 192, 229–233. **"Crowd-challenging"; "gravelly"; "spirit":** McPherson, *Political Education*, p. 48. **His amendment:** *CR*, 85/1, pp. 11005–06.

"Every white man": "Trial by Jury," *New Republic*, June 10. **"It is":** Wilkins, in *NYT*, June 1. **"Can only be":** Southern Conference Educational Fund, Inc., "An Open Letter to the U.S. Senate," *WP*, July 30. **"I fought":** Potter, in *NYP*, June 19. **"To resist":** *NYT*, July 25. And Martin Luther King said that addition of a jury trial amendment would make the bill "almost meaningless" (*NYP*, July 28). **"Mixed, really":** Humphrey OH I, pp. 27, 29.

"Practically": *NYT*, June 4. **"Anarchy":** *NYT*, June 6. **"Full of admiration":** Reedy to Johnson, July 26, Box 418, JSP. **"It is Nixon":** Allen, "Inside Washington," *NYP*, July 25. **"Been willing":** Lincoln, "The Political Mill," *WS*, July 25. **"An overwhelming":** Knowland, *NYT*, July 27. **"Every so often":** Reston, "Trial by Jury vs. The Right to Vote," *NYT*, July 14.

"At this point"; "he pleaded": Reedy, *LBJ*, pp. 116, 117. **"You know":** Corcoran, quoted by Reedy, in interview with author. **Acheson put:** Reedy, p. 118. **"We drafted":** Horwitz OH. **"Every effort":** Reedy, *LBJ*, p. 117. **Knowland constantly announcing:** For example, on July 8, he said, "I hope that within this week the Senate of the United States will be allowed to vote" (*CR*, 85/1, p. 10988). On July 13, he said, "I move that the Senate now proceed to consideration of the Civil Rights Bill" (*NYT*, July 14). On July 28, the *WP* said that "Knowland, predicting victory, said he was prepared." And in a Legislative Leaders Meeting at the White House on July 30, he said, "As of now we can beat jury trial [amendment]." Minnich, LMS, Box 4, handwritten notes, DDEL.

"Get me Ben Cohen": Jenkins interview.

Cohen's career: Caro, *Path*, pp. 450–51. **"You had"; "Everyone":** Katharine Graham interview with Siegel, Jan. 16, 1991. **"Cohen's the brains":** Caro, p. 450. **"Working":** Cohen interview with author. **Attention caught by Auerbach article:** Cater, "How the Senate Passed the Civil-Rights Bill," *The Reporter*, Sept. 5; Cohen, Jenkins, Siegel interviews. Not surprisingly, several other people try to claim credit for bringing the article to Johnson's attention, including George Reedy, but Siegel and Jenkins interviews are conclusive. Richard Rovere was to write that the "vital and operative sections" of the proposed legislation "come largely from the hands of Benjamin V. Cohen and Dean Acheson. . . . Cohen and Acheson supplied the effective language of compromise" (Rovere, *The New Yorker*, Aug. 31). **Auerbach's article:** Auerbach, *The New Leader*, April 29. **Cohen's reasoning:** Interview with author. **"Ben was simply":** Siegel told Katharine Graham, "I have never, never found a public servant who I thought was as important to this country as Ben Cohen—going way back to the Roosevelt times." **The new paragraph:** *CR*, 85/1, p. 12819.

Adding new names: The shifting of votes during the negotiations over Part IV is based on articles in "general background" note for Chapter 36; on Evans and Novak, *LBJ: Exercise*, pp. 133–39; Mann, pp. 206–17; Miller, *Lyndon*, pp. 209–10; on Cooper, Horwitz, Reedy, Rauh, Shuman, Siegel OHs; and on the author's interviews with Carver, Fensterwald, Ward Hower, Jenkins, McCulloch, Rauh, Reedy, Schnibbe, Shuman, and Steele. **Tally sheets:** Evans and Novak, *LBJ: Exercise*, p. 138.

"If I take": Reedy interview.

Remedy an injustice: A good summary is Kefauver, *CR*, 85/1, p. 12820. **Drafting:** Horwitz, Siegel OHs. **Johnson says:** Reedy interview. **"Is there":** Douglas, *CR*, 85/1, p. 12818.

"In *any*": "PART V. AMENDMENT TO THE FEDERAL CRIMINAL CODE. . . . Sec. 391," *CR*, 85/1, p. 12819.

As Emily Post: For example, Johnson said, "This issue will . . . require the careful analysis of thoughtful, reasoning men. Never before have I seen in the Senate a debate which has contributed so much to the understanding . . . the finest the Senate has ever had" (*CR*, 85/1, 12651). And see *CR*, 85/1, pp. 11623, 13165; and Drummond, *NYHT*, July 15; *NYHT*, July 14, 17, 18; *NYT*, July 13, 14, 23; *WP*, *WS*, July 14; *Philadelphia Inquirer*, July 16. And see Mann, p. 204.

"If we're going to"; "Be ready": McPherson, p. 145. **"We have to"; "I'm on":** Parker, *Capitol Hill*, p. 81. **"You always"; "my ass":** Baker, *Wheeling and Dealing*, p. 92. **"You can":** Reedy OH XI; Reedy interview. **"We've got":** Baker, p. 145. **"A religious leader":** Parker, p. 79. **"If we don't allow":** Siegel, quoted in Miller, *Lyndon*, p. 209; Reedy interview. **"These Negroes":** Goodwin, *Lyndon Johnson*, p. 148. **Playing on Wisconsin fears:** Edelstein to Lehman, Aug. 28, Lehman Special File 727, Lehman Papers, HHLP, CU. **"They'll get us":** Bethine Church interview. **"Look":** Siegel OH IV. **"Jim Eastland knows":** Pearson, *WP*, undated. **"Yes, yes, Hubert":** Humphrey, quoted in Miller, p. 371.

"Let me"; "I remember": Pearson, *WP*, July 19. **"Goddamnit":** Schnibbe interview. **"A grave mistake":** Schnibbe interview. **"Look":** Siegel OH. **"Out of both"; "he would tell":** McPherson OH. **"He made them":** Yarborough interview. **"You can't":** Rauh OH; Rauh interview.

Tally sheet: Evans and Novak, p. 138. **"Twice daily":** Fleeson, *WS*, Aug. 5. **Johnson knew:** Reston, *NYT*, Aug. 3.

Niagara bill: Miller, *Lyndon*, p. 206. **"Without adequate," etc.:** *CR*, 85/1, pp. 10985, 10986. Also see pp. 12979–980.

Using his health: "Johnson has privately told at least two other senators that he will not run for re-election in 1960 because of his health. He becomes so tense and excited after a week of maneuvering that he is unable to sleep more than three or four hours a night. This, after his serious heart attack a year ago, has forced his decision." Tris Coffin, "How Lyndon Johnson Engineered Compromise on Civil Rights Bill," *New Leader*, Aug. 5. **"Ah don't":** Johnson's wording on this page is recreated from recollections by people who heard him speak at the time, particularly Reedy, Schnibbe and Steele, and from the wording he used in conversations on the same subjects over the telephone during his presidency, as transcribed by Michael Beschloss in *Taking Charge*. **"He made you":** Fensterwald interview. **"I'll have to":** John Sherman

Cooper OH. **"Well, you":** Ward Hower interview. **"I can see him":** Baker, *Wheeling and Dealing*, p. 145. **"He would":** McPherson, p. 146. **Holding Kefauver:** Dixon, Aug. 1, Box 2042, JSP.

July 26 Southern Caucus; White House meeting: LMS, Box 2, DDEL; *Time*, July 29; *Baltimore Sun*, *NYHT*, *NYP*, *WP*, July 27. **"To the end"; "he meant":** *NYT*, July 27. **"A jury trial":** Knowland, *NYT*, July 27.

"Would prevent": Carey to Johnson, Kefauver, O'Mahoney, July 27, *CR*, 85/1, pp. 12874–875. **Reedy told; "Here is the situation":** Reedy to Johnson, July 29, Box 418, JSP. **"Iron determination":** "Statement by the AFL-CIO Executive Committee on Civil Rights Legislation," July 30, *CR*, 85/1, pp. 12998–999. **Not "found a soul":** Humphrey, quoted in *NYP*, July 28.

"Might be difficult": Evans, *NYHT*, July 28; in the *NYT*, July 28, John D. Morris wrote "Stiffening opposition to any jury-trial provision in the Administration's civil rights bill threatened today to delay *indefinitely* [italics added] a decision on the provision. Earlier prospects of a vote Tuesday on that phase of the civil rights controversy appeared to have all but vanished. . . ." The *Washington Star* reported (July 29) that "The possibility of a filibuster was increased today." **"Haven't got":** Humphrey, qouted in *NYT*, July 29. **Knowland said:** *NYT*, July 28. **"Extraordinary":** Fleeson, *WS*, July 30. **"I can't say":** Russell, quoted in *WP*, July 28.

"I hope": Clark, *CR*, 85/1, p. 13294. **Javits:** *CR*, 85/1, pp. 12892–899. **Murray:** *CR*, 85/1, p. 13298. **"He taunted":** Mann, p. 211.

"Open Letter": *WP*, July 30.

Tuskegee hearing: Described in *NYP*, *WP*, July 31. **Effect of hearing on senators:** *WP*, July 31; McCulloch interviews. **Polk Manders:** Russell, *CR*, 85/1, p. 12980. **Javits, Douglas, Russell exchanges:** *CR*, 85/1, pp. 12983–986. **"Tore the mask":** Shannon, *NYP*, July 31. **"The Senator . . . points":** Russell, *CR*, 85/1, p. 12986. **Angry scene on Senate floor:** *CR*, 85/1, pp. 12993–994. **Described in three vivid columns:** Fleeson, McGrory, *WS*; Shannon, *NYP*, all July 31.

Small Business Administration request: *WP*, *NYT*, July 31. **"Suddenly":** Fleeson, "Senate Debate Back to Normal," *WS*, July 31. **"The prisoner":** Kempton, "Changing of the Guard," *NYP*, July 30.

"Any labor guy": Reedy to Johnson, July 29, Box 418, JSP; Mann, pp. 211–12; Evans and Novak, p. 137; Cater, "How the Senate Passed the Civil-Rights Bill," *The Reporter*, Sept. 5; Reedy interview. **Brotherhoods' prejudice:** Foner, *Black Worker*, p. 166; Ferguson to Fleete, Sept. 29, "Switchmen's Union of North America Records, 1894–1971," Collection No. 5034, Box 254, Kheel Center, Cornell University School of Industrial and Labor Relations; *Cleveland News,* Sept. 27; *Cleveland Plain Dealer,* Sept. 28. This does not apply, needless to say, to A. Philip Randolph's Brotherhood of Sleeping Car Porters. **Railroad lobbyists:** *Newsweek,* Aug. 12. **Johnson understood:** Reedy interview; Mann, p. 212, notes that "The railroad lobbyists were particularly effective with midwestern Republicans." **Brotherhoods' political power:** Curtis, Hradko, Kennedy, Mahoney interviews; Catton and Link, *American Epoch,* p. 58; Seidman, *Brotherhood,* pp. 2–4. **Telephoned Anderson:** Pearson, *WP,* Aug. 8.

UMW bitterness: Mann, p. 212; *WS,* Aug. 1; Hopkins interview. **Telephoned Hopkins:** LBJ Desk Diary; Pearson, *WP,* Aug. 8; Hopkins interview. **UMW telegram:** *CR,* 85/1, p. 13015. **"Had never":** *CR,* 85/1, p. 13015. Evans and Novak accepted Johnson's contention, calling Lewis' telegram "unsolicited" (p. 137). **"Saw to it":** Reston, *NYT,* Aug. 3. And see Pearson, *WP,* Aug. 8. **Neely's change:** Roy Wilkins to Elmer A. Carter (chairman, N.Y. State Commission Against Discrimination), Sept. 5, 1957, NAACPP III A 71, CR, LC. **"Labor":** *Fortune,* June 1957.

Church and Johnson: Interviews with Bethine Church, and Church aides John A. Carver, Ward and Phyllis Hower.

"I understand"; "Senator Sunday School": Ashby and Gramer, *Fighting the Odds,* p. 73. "Journalists in the press gallery made up a little ditty: 'His name is Church, but if age was the rule, we'd call him Senator Sunday School.' " **"Bursting":** Ashby and Gramer, p. 32. **"Longest-running":** Wetherall, quoted by Ashby and Gramer, p. 101.

Bethine in Washington; "deep freeze": Bethine Church interview. **"It was"; "Long memory":** Carver interview. **"Pariah":** Bethine Church, quoted in Ashby and Gramer, p.78. "For the next six months," Church himself said, "he [Johnson] never spoke to me. He said nothing to me that was insulting. He just simply ignored me. When I was present with other senators, he talked to the other senators. It was clear to me that I was *persona non grata* with Lyndon Johnson" (Miller, p. 210). **"Only":** Ward Hower interview. **"One night":** Bethine Church interview. **Vote . . . but:** Ashby and Gramer, p. 87. **Church's attitude on filibusters:** Bethine Church, Phyllis Hower, Ward Hower interviews. **"Looking"; "I don't think":** Ward Hower interview, and quoted in Ashby and Gramer, p. 96. **Whispering to O'Mahoney:** *CR,* 85/1, p. 12819.

"You're a senator": Bethine Church interview. **Church's idea:** Mann, p. 213; Bethine Church interview.

Drafting, discarding, refining amendment: Bethine Church, Ward Hower, Siegel interviews; Horwitz, Siegel OHs. **Appealed to northern liberals:** *Newsweek, Time,* Aug. 12; Roy Wilkins to William Walker, Aug. 19; Wilkins to C. B. Powell of *Amsterdam News,* Aug. 20, NAACP III, Box A 73, NAACPP, LC; *WP,* Aug. 1, 2. **"They didn't"; "symbolic":** Carver, Ward Hower interviews.

Told him to wait: Church OH. **"No chance":** Reedy interview; *Newsweek, Time,* Aug. 12. **Knowland's refusal:** *CR,* 85/1, July 31, pp. 13111, 13112. **Three agreements; Russell objecting:** *CR,* 85/1, pp. 13128–132.

Anderson in Johnson's office: Reedy interview. **Embodied:** "One of the most unusual aspects . . . ," Reedy to Johnson, Aug. 1, Box 420, JSP.

Retirement benefits; suddenly: *Newsweek,* Aug. 12; Shannon, *NYP,* Aug. 2. **"The lines":** July 31, ACWD, Telephone Calls, Box 25, DDEL. **"Dramatic switches":** *WP,* Aug. 2. **Schoeppel's judgeship:** Cater, *The Reporter,* Sept. 5; Pearson, *WP,* Aug. 17. **"Wobbly":** Evans and Novak, p. 137. **Pastore swayed:** Reston, *NYT,* Aug. 3.

The drama: Descriptions of it are in Mann, pp. 213–14; *Time* and *Newsweek,* Aug. 12; Stewart Alsop, "Who Really Won," *NYHT,* Aug. 5; Shannon, *NYP,* Aug. 2. And in Frank Church, Horwitz OHs; and in interviews with Bethine Church, Rauh, Reedy, Rogers. It is in *CR,* 85/1, pp. 13137–53, 13234–96, 13306–56. **A full house:** Ashby and Gramer, p. 89. **"Frank looked":** Bethine Church interview. **"East Lynne?":** Neuberger, quoted in *Newsweek,* Aug. 12. **"Like a wave":** Bethine Church interview. **"What John Pastore":** Horwitz OH. **"Feign"; "the impact":** Mann, p. 214. **"All of this":** Horwitz OH. **"Actually changed":** Reedy, *LBJ,* p. 119. **Lewis' telegram:** *CR,* 85/1, p. 13015. **"I've got them":** Hopkins OH.

"At least thirty-nine": Knowland, quoted in *Time,* Aug. 12; Cater, *The Reporter,* Sept. 5. Nixon, who was still getting his information from Knowland, gave the same figures to Marquis Childs, and Childs reported that "Nixon is confident that 39 or 40 of the 47 Republicans will vote against the amendment" (*SLP-D,* Aug. 1). And see *NYP,* Aug. 2.

Knowland's blindness: Cater was to write that Knowland told him later that he had been prepared later that week "to force a vote by moving to table the O'Mahoney amendment even though he knew he would lose a few votes by staging such a showdown. But the votes had already left him." **"I'm ready":** Pearson, *WP*, Aug. 7.

"I have conferred"; "I am encouraged": Johnson, Knowland, *CR*, 85/1, pp. 13272–273. **Nixon's counting:** Rogers interview. **"Subtle persuasion":** Cater, *The Reporter; Time*, Aug. 12. **"Yesterday":** Johnson, *CR*, 85/1, p. 13296. **Liberal senators gathering:** *NYP*, Aug. 2. **"Is there objection"; "Right now":** *CR*, 85/1, p. 13296. **Persuading Payne:** *NYHT*, *WP*, Aug. 2. **Ike, Butler and Schoeppel:** Telephone calls, July 31, 1957, DDE Diary Series, July 1957, Box 25, DDEL; ACW Diary Series, Aug. 1, Box 9, DDEL. **"They stopped":** Rauh OH, interview with author; Katharine Graham interview with Rauh; Cater, "How the Senate," *The Reporter*, Sept. 5. **"Bullwhip":** Evans and Novak, pp. 138, 139. **"Just wait":** Mann, p. 216; Fleeson, *WS*, Aug. 6. **"There are times":** Stewart Alsop, *NYHT*, Aug. 5.

"Somehow": Humphrey, *CR*, 85/1, p. 13330. **"All that":** Douglas, *CR*, 85/1, pp. 13333–34. **"I hope":** Clark, *CR*, 85/1, p. 13294. **"Travesty":** Case, *CR*, 85/1, pp. 13321–22. **"A vote":** Murray, *CR*, 85/1, p.13298. **Church's speech:** *CR*, 85/1, pp. 13353–54. **Bethine's reaction:** Bethine Church interview. **Kennedy's speech:** *CR*, 85/1, pp. 13305–307.

Johnson on the floor: Descriptions of the final debate and vote in Alsop, *NYHT*, Aug. 5; *NYP*, Aug. 1, 2.

"There were": Alsop, *NYHT*, Aug. 5. **"This will be":** Knowland, *CR*, 85/1, p. 13354. **"Support our President":** Knowland, quoted in *NYT*, Aug. 2. **"I ask for the yeas and nays":** Lyndon B. Johnson, *CR*, 85/1, p. 13356. **O'Mahoney hurrying:** Bethine Church interview.

"One of the saddest": Nixon, quoted in Cater, *The Reporter*, Sept. 5. **Knowland crying:** Watson, *Lion in the Lobby*, p. 394. **" 'Your man' ":** Church, *Father and Son*, p. 50; Bethine Church interview. **"After my role":** Miller, p. 210. **"Pick you up"; "A kind":** Ashby and Gramer, pp. 95, 96. **McClellan Committee:** Baker, *Friend and Foe*, p. 157. The senator is not identified in the book, but Prof. Baker identified him to me as Church. **"After":** Ward Hower interview. **"Maybe someday":** Marcy OH. **Johnson's note:** A photocopy of the handwritten note was given to the author by Bethine Church.

41. Omens

All dates are 1957 unless otherwise noted.

"Boys": Rauh interview. Slightly different wording in Wilkins, *Standing Fast*, p. 245; Rauh OH I, p. 25; Katharine Graham interview with Rauh, p. 29, and Cater, "How the Senate Passed the Civil Rights Bill," *The Reporter*, Sept. 5. **When he awoke:** Ambrose, *Eisenhower: The President*, p. 411, describes the President as "furious." **"One of":** "Minutes of Cabinet Meeting," Aug. 2, Cabinet Series, Box 9, DDEL. **"Rarely":** "Statement by the President," Aug. 2, Cabinet Series, Box 9, DDEL. **"Blackest":** ACWD, Aug. 2. Box 9, DDEL.

Jackie Robinson and Randolph: Eisenhower, *White House Years: Waging Peace*, p. 160. **"We all sat watching":** Rauh, *Chicago Defender*, May 31, 1958," quoted in Watson, *Lion in the Lobby*, p. 397. **"Can one":** Douglas, *CR*, 85/1, p. 13841. **"Emotional":** Phyllis Hower interview. **"I know":** Lehman to Douglas, Aug. 6, "General Personal Correspondence, Box 224B, Lehman Papers, HHLP, CU. **"So mad":** Rauh OH, quoted in Mann, *Walls of Jericho*, p. 220. **"The sham":** Stokes, *WS*, Aug. 5. **Had made Nixon look good:** *NYP*, Aug. 7.

"Quite furious": Evans, *NYHT*, Aug. 22. **Conflict between two bills:** Mann, p. 220; Evans and Novak, *LBJ: Exercise*, pp. 139–40; *HP*, *NYHT*, *NYP*, *NYT*, *WP*, *WS*, Aug. 6–14; Bolling, Brownell, Rauh, Rogers interviews; Rauh OH. **"Infinitely":** *NYT*, Aug. 14.

"Less than nothing": Rauh interview. **"This bad bill":** Reprint of Morse speech in NAACP III B-55, NAACPP, LC, quoted in Watson, p. 395. **Mitchell's call; "psychological":** Watson, p. 395; Rauh interview. **"All of a sudden":** Bolling interview. That expression caught on: Roy Wilkins quotes Joe Rauh as saying, "Once Congress has lost its virginity on civil rights, it would go on to make up for what had been lost" (*Standing Fast*, p. 245).

"By the summer": Graham, *Personal History*, p. 240. **"I knew":** Graham interview. **"So Phil":** Graham, p. 241. **Sleeping on couch:** Graham, Reedy interviews. **"From the point":** Graham, p. 241. **"You could see":** Reedy interview. Confirmed by Rauh interview.

"In those days": Wilkins, pp. 243–44. **"If":** Humphrey, quoted in Wilkins, p. 246. **Leadership conference meeting:** Wilkins, pp. 245–46. **"Reedy's note":** Reedy to Johnson, Aug. 7, Box 420, JSP. **"All day long":** Rauh OH. **"If I had":** Wilkins, p. 246. **"Disappointing as": *CR*, 85/1, pp. 13852–853. See also "To: Executive Staff, From: Secretary," Aug. 7, NAACP Papers, Box III, A 71, LC. **"The 16"; "Give it a try"**: *WP*, Aug. 8. Lyndon Johnson wrote Philip Graham on that date: "You stepped into the breach at the critical hour. That is something that I will never forget, and I wish there was some way of telling the country that your contribution to an effective, enforceable bill was decisive." **"The strangest call"**: Philip Graham, quoted by Rauh, OH and interview. **"Joe understood"**: "Katharine Graham—Joe Rauh memorial—September 27, 1992." A few other sentences from that eulogy: "Joe never changed from the time Phil and I first knew him and Olie over fifty years ago, to the moment of his death. . . . Joe always lived his beliefs more than anyone in our whole generation, or anyone I know. . . . He never lost his faith in the ultimate victory of liberal values. He never gave up the fight." **Unless**: *NYHT, NYT*, Aug. 11. **"Infinitely better"**: *NYT*, Aug. 14. **"Asked how"**: *NYT*, Aug. 13. **"A monstrosity"**: Minnich, "Supplementary Notes," Aug. 6, LMS, Box 4, DDEL. **"Spoke at length"; "The Vice President"**: Minnich, "Supplementary Notes," Aug. 13, LMS, Box 4, DDEL. **Rayburn's wishes; House compromise**: *Baltimore Sun,* Aug. 10; *NYT*, Aug. 23; Bolling, Rogers interviews; Ambrose, pp. 412, 413.

More than a few: Byrd said, "I can't conceive that the Senate would agree to that [compromise]. I stand on the principle that where there is a criminal action involved, the federal judge should not have the right to deny a jury trial" (*WP*, Aug. 23). Talmadge said, without a jury trial, "a judge would have to prejudge a case without evidence" (*WP*, Sept. 23). Olin Johnston said, "The cornerstone of human liberty is being shattered" by "the House measure" (*HP*, Aug. 29). Sam Ervin said, "The compromise leaves the question of whether a defendant shall have a jury trial dependent on 'the discretion and caprice' of man rather than on law" (*HP*, Aug. 29). **Russell countering Thurmond**: Cohodas, *Strom Thurmond*, p. 294. **"I can assure"**: Robertson to Davis, Aug. 28, Drawer 45, AWRP, College of William and Mary.

Thurmond's filibuster: *CR*, 85/1, pp. 16263–456; Cohodas, pp. 294–97. **"They felt"**: White, *NYT,* Aug. 30. **"Oh, God"**: Reedy OH III, p. 20. **"Rumblings"**: Bates, "Political Notebook," *AC*, Aug. 30, X. Civil Rights Material, Winder, RBRL. **"Nothing to gain**: *AC*, Aug. 31, quoted in Cohodas, p. 298. **"Adamant"**: Cohodas, p. 299.

"I'd like to come"; "this message": Tay-

lor to Johnson, with Mary Rather's note to Taylor written on it, Aug. 27, Box 420, JSP. **Lyndon Johnson and Angel Macias**: The photograph appeared in the *Philadelphia Inquirer*, Aug. 28. **The little party**: *WP*, Aug. 29. **The big party**: Rowan, "Eyes of Texas Turn on Lyndon," *WP*, Aug. 28; Walsh, "Majority Leader Has a Birthday," *WS*, Aug. 28; *HP*, Aug. 29; Dale Miller interview. **"The biggest birthday present"**: *HP*, Aug. 29; *Time*, March 2; Jenkins interview. Neely's weight on this day was less than ninety pounds.

"Well, the people"; Welcoming Proxmire: *HP, NYT, WP*, Aug. 29. **"For the fine things"**: Proxmire, *CR*, 85/1, p. 16684. **Junket**: *WP*, Aug. 31. **"Good medicine"**: McGrory, *WS*, Sept. 3.

"It seems": Reedy interview. Reedy was given to frequently repeating some version of this phrase. In his *The U.S. Senate* (p. 13), for example, he wrote, "Obviously, we were proceeding on the 'half a loaf' theory at which many people scoff. But it seems to me that the scoffers must be men and women who have never been hungry." **A "crumb"**: Humphrey, quoted in Wilkins, p. 246. **"Presented"; "by allowing"**: Ambrose, pp. 414, 419. **As Brownell had contended**: Brownell, *Advising Ike*, pp. 365–84. **"When Johnson took"**: Rauh, quoted in Miller, pp 208, 209; Rauh interview. **"Lack of will"**: Watson, p. 401; Burns, *Crosswinds*, p. 322; United States Commission on Civil Rights, *With Liberty and Justice for All: An Abridgement of the Report of the United States Commission;* Lawson, *Black Ballots*, pp. 231–32, 249. **A flat zero**: Dallek, *Lone Star*, p. 526.

"Just a beginning": Johnson, quoted in McPherson, *Political Education*, p. 148. **"Failed to recognize"**: Reedy, *LBJ*, p. 120. **"Crucial"**: Reedy, *U.S. Senate*, p. 179. **"If he got one"**: Reedy interview. **"We've started"**: Johnson, quoted in Goodwin, *Lyndon Johnson*, p. 152. **"Impact"**: Reedy, *U.S. Senate*, p. 179. **"Perhaps it is"**: Kempton, "The Happiest Man in Town," *NYP*, Aug. 8. **"It was Congress"**: Woodward, "The Great Civil Rights Debate," *Commentary*, Oct. 1957.

Praise: *NYT, WP, WS*, Aug. 11; "Purists and Progress," *New Republic*, Aug. 12. **"Background" memo**: "In analyzing the so-called 'victories,' " Aug. 8, Box 420, JSP. **Used them as edited; Cater asked; "Eye think"**: For example, Reedy wrote, supposedly for Cater's "background" information: "From the beginning, it was realized that there could be no 'compromise' in the sense of an empty and evasive deal." Cater wrote: "Johnson remarked to me recently, 'It was realized that there could be no "compromise" in the sense of an empty and evasive deal.' " "George— Sen. Johnson said OK," Mary Rather reported. Undated, but attached to Reedy to Johnson, Aug. 24, Box 420, JSP; Cater, "How the Senate Bill Was Passed," *The Reporter*, Sept. 5. **"Most remarkable":** *AFL-CIO News,* Aug. 12. **"Sen. Bible was":** Taylor to Johnson, Aug. 12.

"A modern Henry Clay": Tucker, *Tucson* (Ariz.) *Daily Citizen,* Aug. 9. **"To certify":** Duke to Johnson, Sept. 4, "Legislative Files," Box 291, JSP.

"Hoax and sham": Morse, quoted in Drukman, *Wayne Morse,* p. 307. **"Emerged":** Douglas, *Fullness of Time,* pp. 290, 291. **"The Moderate Texas":** *Detroit News,* Aug. 5. **Fritchey's anger; "some of":** Carver, Bethine Church, quoted in Ashby and Gramer, *Fighting the Odds,* p. 91. **"A soup":** Shuman OH.

"The Senate bill": Cohen to Johnson, Aug. 13, Box 290, JSP. **"I don't think":** Acheson to Johnson, Aug. 13, Box 408, JSP; Rovere, "Letter from Washington," *The New Yorker,* Aug. 31. **"It took":** "Purists and Progress," *New Republic,* Aug. 12. **"It is one":** Eleanor Roosevelt, "My Day," *NYP,* Aug. 6. **"If you think":** Drummond, *NYHT,* Aug. 30

"Struggle": Roger Wilkins, *NYT,* July 4, 1990. **"So great":** King, quoted in *NYT,* Sec. IV, Jan. 17, 1988. **"Led them into voting booths":** Caro, *Means,* p. xxi.

Johnson's speech: *CR,* 85/1, pp. 13897, 13898. **"When at last":** McPherson, *Political Education,* p. 147. **Description of East Texas parade; McPherson's reaction:** McPherson, *Political Education,* pp. 154–55.

42. Three More Years

"Eager": Evans and Novak, *LBJ: Exercise,* p. 196. **"You know":** Rowe to Johnson, Dec. 4, 1958, Box 32, LBJA SN.

Clark letter: Steinberg, *Sam Johnson's Boy,* p. 494. **McNamara demanded:** *NYT,* April 9, 1949. **Proxmire and Muskie attitude; "until":** Proxmire, Muskie interviews. **A "chickenshit":** Baker, quoted in Steinberg, p. 495. **"Might as well":** Ralph K. Huitt, "The Morse Committee Assignment Controversy: A Study on Senate Norms," *APSR,* June 1957, pp. 313–29. **"Like Wayne and Paul":** Ralph K. Huitt, "The Outsider in the Senate: An Alternative Role," *APSR,* Sept. 1961, p. 569; Shuman interview. **"Never been":** *WS,* Feb. 23; *NYT,* Feb. 24, 1959; Steinberg, p. 496. **Proxmire's attacks:** *NYT, WP,* Feb. 24,

March 1, 10, April 13, May 29, 30, 1959; Byrd, *Senate,* Vol. I, pp. 620–21.

"Fairy godmother": Johnson, quoted in Steinberg, *Sam Johnson's Boy,* p. 496. **Delegated to Mansfield:** Evans and Novak, p. 199.

Democratic caucuses: "Minutes of the Senate Democratic Conference, Tuesday, Jan. 7, 1958, Room 201, Senate Office Building," *Minutes of the U.S. Senate Democratic Conference, 1903–1964,* ed. Donald A. Ritchie, Washington: GPO, 1998, pp. 505–72 (cited hereafter as "Conference Minutes"). **"Determined":** Clark, *Sapless Branch,* p. 12. **Clark resolution:** Conference Minutes, p. 515. **"The more senior":** Clark, p. 12. **Would be happy:** Conference Minutes, p. 518. **"The end":** Clark, p. 12. **51 to 12 vote:** Conference Minutes, p. 535. **"Any":** Proxmire, quoted in Steinberg, *Sam Johnson's Boy,* p. 497. **"David and Goliath":** Public Affairs Institute, "Washington Window," March 13, 1959. **"Bravest bull":** Fite, *Russell,* p. 405.

"The success": Reedy, *U.S. Senate,* p. 178. **"Seven-room spread":** *Chicago Tribune,* Dec. 21, 1958. **Taj Mahal descriptions:** Office of Senate Curator, Lyndon Baines Johnson Room, S. Pub. 105–60; "The Lyndon Baines Johnson Room, Remarks for the Secretary of the Senate," Senate Historical Office; Miller, *Lyndon,* p. 217; Steinberg, *Sam Johnson's Boy,* pp. 505–06; Fleeson, *WS,* Jan. 7, 1959; Busby, Gonella, Reedy, Shuman, Sidey, Steele, Tames interviews. **"Marbled city":** Hugh Sidey, "Eye on the Oval Office," *Time,* Aug. 26, 1985. **"On entering":** Shaffer, *On and Off,* p. 214. **"That huge"; "monument":** Steele to Williamson, Jan. 30, 1959, SP. **"Nimbus":** Dallek, *Lone Star,* p. 540. **Elevators:** Tames interview.

"Well": Mansfield, quoted in Gonella interview. **"His children":** Gonella interview. **"You know":** Johnson, quoted in Steele to Williamson, Nov. 12, 1958, SP. **"Needed":** Steele to Williamson-III, March 4, 1958, SP. **"Alan":** Bernstein interview. **Stennis:** Evans and Novak, p. 102.

Instructing Reedy: Steele to Williamson-XIV, March 4, 1958, SP; Reedy interview. **"Hoisted"; "Without rival":** "Sense and Sensitivity," *Time,* March 17, 1958. **Disability:** Steinberg, *Sam Johnson's Boy,* pp. 483–84. **"Who is":** Stewart Alsop, "Lyndon Johnson: How Does He Do It?" *SEP,* Jan. 24, 1959.

"Straining"; "uneasy": Johnson, *Vantage Point,* p. 272. **"This is":** Stennis to Russell, Oct. 17, 1957. **Symington's insistence:** Symington to Russell, Oct. 5, 1957, J. General, Missile File, Box 403, RBRL. **Russell**

calling Johnson; "so thorough": Steele to Williamson, March 4, 1958, SP. **"Has a lot"**: "Nov. 5, 1957—LD conversation with Senator Bridges in Concord, New Hampshire," Box 40, LBJA CF. **"More or less"**: Russell to Marcy, Jan. 9, 1958, J. General, Missile File, Box 9, RBRL.

"Kept alive": Reedy, *U.S. Senate,* p. 182. **Weisl, Vance involvement:** McGillicuddy, Edwin Weisl Jr., Vance interviews.

"All the right": ACWD, Nov. 6, 1957, quoted in Ambrose, *Eisenhower,* p. 430. **"No 'guilty' "**: Minutes of Preparedness Subcommittee meeting, Nov. 22, 1957, SP, Box 405, quoted in Divine, ed., *Johnson Years,* Vol. II, p. 222. **"Very much"**: "Oct. 21, 1957—LD conversation between Secy. Neil McElroy . . . and Sen. Johnson in Corpus Christi," Box 433, JSP. **"If he"**: LBJ-Dulles telephone conversations, Oct. 31, Nov. 5, 1957, Dulles Papers, quoted in Dallek, p. 530. **"Will serve"; "hit the extreme"**: McConaughy to Williamson, Feb. 15, 1958, SP. **"This may"**: Reedy to Johnson, Oct. 17, 1957, Reedy: Memos, SP, Box 420, quoted in Divine, p. 219. **Leaking:** Busby, Reedy interviews. **"To elevate"**: Evans and Novak, p. 192. **"Painted"**: Reedy, *U.S. Senate,* p. 183.

Reedy's suggestion: Reedy to Johnson, Nov. 23, 1957, Box 421, JSP. **Johnson's rejection:** Busby, Reedy interviews. And Busby, at Johnson's suggestion, then used the Pearl Harbor comparison in Johnson's speeches. **"Comparable to Pearl Harbor"**: Press releases, undated, Preparedness Subcommittee, SP, Box 355. **"An even greater challenge"**: "Inquiry into Satellite and Missile Programs," Hearings Before the Preparedness Investigating Subcommittee of the Committee on the Armed Forces, U.S. *Senate,* 85 Cong, 1st and 2nd Session (Washington, D.C.: GPO, 1958), pp. 1–3. **"Our finest hour"; Alamo:** Divine, pp. 223, 224.

"A sense": Rowe to Johnson, Nov. 21, 1957, Box 421, JSP. **"This was"; "light"; Medaris announcement:** Steinberg, *Sam Johnson's Boy,* p. 482; *Time,* Jan. 20, Feb. 17, 1958; *Newsweek,* Feb. 17, 1958; *USN&WR,* Jan. 17, 1958; Steele to Williamson, Jan. 10, Feb. 15, March 4-VIII; to Lunsden, Jan. 9, 1958, SP; BeLieu, McGillicuddy, Reedy, Steele interviews.

Eisenhower's reassurances: Ambrose, pp. 427–35. **Johnson's statements:** Johnson, pp. 273–75. **"We have reached"**: Johnson, p. 275. **"Full mobilization"**: Johnson, quoted in Steinberg, p. 480. **"How long"; "Painted"**: Johnson, quoted in Steinberg, pp. 481, 480. **"Control"**: "Johnson speech to Democratic caucus, Jan. 7, 1958," Statements file, JSP. **"In retrospect"**: Reedy, *U.S. Senate,* p. 184.

"In a week": "Lyndon Johnson Has the Ball," *Life,* Jan. 20, 1958. **"I believe"**: Rowe to Johnson, Feb. 5, 1958, Box 32, LBJA SN. **"Just plain"**: Reedy, *U.S. Senate,* p. 185; *LBJ,* p. 13; Reedy OH, interview. **"Would actually"**: Evans and Novak, p. 193. **"Did not bother"**: Reedy, *LBJ,* pp. 12, 13. **"Some of the staff"**: Reedy, *U.S. Senate,* p. 186. **"Worried"**: Reedy, *LBJ,* p. 13.

NASA bills: Divine, pp. 226–28. **"A textbook"**: Evans and Novak, p. 191.

"Made it clear"; "in later": Reedy, *LBJ,* p. 13. **Little different:** Divine (pp. 227–28) notes that "over the next three years, the Space Council met on only rare occasions. . . . Johnson could not force the president to use the Space Council to give central guidance to the nation's space program." Also BeLieu, Reedy interviews.

"Dreary": Reedy, *U.S. Senate,* p. 187. **"Monstrosity"**: Rauh, "The Truth About Congress and the Court," *The Progressive,* Nov. 1958. **"Well"**: Johnson, quoted in Mann, p. 232. **"Lyndon"; jumping to his feet:** McPherson, p. 133. **"Mr. President"; writing the names:** Mann, p. 233. **"You boys"**: McPherson, quoted in Mann, p. 233. **"If you want"**: Johnson, quoted in Evans and Novak, p. 166. **"I don't know"; bringing Lewis, Reedy along:** Evans and Novak, p. 166; Lewis, Reedy interviews. **"In the course"**: Lewis interview. **"A display"**: Lewis, quoted in Mann, p. 234. **"Johnson always"; slapping his own cheeks:** Lewis interview. **Tactics the next day:** Evans and Novak, pp. 166–67; Mann, pp. 234–35; McPherson, p. 134. **"Could truthfully"**: Mann, p. 234.

1959 and 1960 civil rights bills: Clark, pp. 13–14; Douglas, pp. 291–92; Evans and Novak, pp. 22–222; Fite, pp. 374, 375; Mann, pp. 239–61; Watson, pp. 415–26. **Rule 22 compromise:** Mann, pp. 239–41. **"Sugarcoated"**: "News from NAACP," Jan. 22, 1959, Box 408, JSP. **"Gone was"**: Mann, p. 258. **Johnson working with Rogers:** Rogers interview. **"Crumbs"; "Here is"**: Clark, *Sapless Branch,* p. 14.

43. The Last Caucus

"Power is": Evans and Novak, *LBJ: Exercise,* p. 280.

"Probably hoping"; his plan: Humphrey, *Education,* p. 243. **"Hang on to"; "The illusion"; "Would offend"; "He's not"**: Humphrey OH. **"Asked if I"**: Mansfield, quoted in Steinberg, *Sam Johnson's Boy,* p. 547. **Retaining the Taj:** Evans and Novak, p.

306. **Retaining Baker:** "Mansfield put up no argument . . . when Johnson suggested he retain Bobby Baker as the secretary for the majority. Senators expected Bobby to carry out Lyndon's orders in the next Congress, just as he had in the past (Steinberg, p. 547); Evans and Novak, p. 306.

"**A buoyancy**": Baker, *Wheeling and Dealing*, pp. 133–34. "**Apprehensions**"; "**Brooding**": Evans and Novak, p. 306. "**Having watched**": Evans and Novak, pp. 308, 307. "**Reserved**": Baker, p. 134.

Mansfield's motion: "Minutes of the Democratic Conference," Jan. 3, 1961, *Minutes, 1903–1964*, p. 578. "**Can you imagine**": Byrd, *Senate*, Vol. 1, p. 624. "**Mansfield**": Evans and Novak, p. 306. **Description of caucus:** *Minutes, 1903–1964*, pp. 577–81; Baker, *Wheeling and Dealing*, pp. 135–36; Byrd, p. 624; Evans and Novak, pp. 306–08; Goldsmith, *Colleagues*, pp. 83–84; Humphrey, p. 243; Miller, *Lyndon*, pp. 275–76; Steinberg, pp. 547–48. "**Might as well**": Gore, quoted in Miller, p. 276. **Other hands:** "The depth of the revolt against Mansfield's motion . . . was discernible only in the" opposition of Ander-

son, Robertson and Johnston, Evans and Novak write on p. 307. "**Unbelievably**": Baker, *Wheeling and Dealing*, p. 136. "**Look ridiculous**": Evans and Novak, p. 307. "**Ashen**"; "**no getting around**": Baker, p. 135. "**We are creating**": Monroney, quoted in Steinberg, p. 547.

Mansfield in favor: *Minutes*, p. 578. **Resignation threat; "under":** Baker, *Wheeling and Dealing*, p. 135. "**Even though**": Gore, quoted in Steinberg, p. 548. "**Wasn't going to work**": Goldsmith, p. 84.

"**I was one**": Humphrey OH. "**It fell**": Humphrey, p. 243.

Not present at next three caucuses: "Minutes of the Democratic Conference," Jan. 4, 5, 10, 1961, pp. 581–88. "**The President has**": Mansfield, "Minutes," February 27, p. 588. **1963 caucuses:** "Minutes," Jan. 9, Feb. 7, 1963; Muskie, Proxmire, Yarborough interviews.

Stepping down from dais: Muskie interview. **Coming into cloakroom:** McPherson, *Political Education*, p. 184; Muskie, Hynes interviews. "**Those were**": Lady Bird Johnson interview.

Index

PHOTOGRAPHIC CREDITS